THE OXFORD HANDBOOK OF

POLITICAL EXECUTIVES

THE OXFORD HANDBOOK OF

POLITICAL

EXECUTIVES

Edited by

RUDY B. ANDEWEG, ROBERT ELGIE,
LUDGER HELMS, JULIET KAARBO,

and

FERDINAND MÜLLER-ROMMEL

OXFORD

UNIVERSITY PRESS

OXFORD
UNIVERSITY PRESS

Great Clarendon Street, Oxford, OX2 6DP,
United Kingdom

Oxford University Press is a department of the University of Oxford.
It furthers the University's objective of excellence in research, scholarship,
and education by publishing worldwide. Oxford is a registered trade mark of
Oxford University Press in the UK and in certain other countries

Published in the United States of America by Oxford University Press
198 Madison Avenue, New York, NY 10016, United States of America

British Library Cataloguing in Publication Data
Data available

Library of Congress Control Number: 2020937387

ISBN 978-0-19-880929-6

Printed and bound by
CPI Group (UK) Ltd, Croydon, CR0 4YY

This Handbook is dedicated to the memory of Robert Elgie *(1965–2019):*
A dear friend and leading political scientist

PREFACE

As most Oxford Handbooks, this volume has a history spanning several years. Still, the present volume could claim to be a special case of co-edited volumes. It emerged from two different and independent proposals that arrived at Dominic Byatt's desk at OUP at about the same time: one from Robert Elgie and Ludger Helms and the other from Rudy Andeweg and Ferdinand Müller-Rommel. Initiated by Dominic, the four of us met in London in May 2016 to explore whether there was sufficient common ground to join forces. We immediately agreed on the content of a joined volume and felt that an expert on political executives in the field of International Relations was still missing. Robert suggested to add Juliet Kaarbo to the editorial team. What followed could be considered a case study on how close scholarly collaboration can possibly get. Apart from countless email exchanges between the co-editors and our contributors, the volume took shape and was advanced step by step through a series of personal meetings in Lüneburg, Germany, which were generously funded by Leuphana University's Centre for the Study of Democracy, and its former director, Ferdinand Müller-Rommel.

This volume is dedicated to our fellow co-editor and dear friend Robert Elgie who sadly passed away tragically just a few weeks before completing our joint work on the volume. Robert will be deeply missed by all of us. His special role within the editorial team can be captured from the fact alone that he is the only scholar who contributed more than one original chapter to this Handbook. While not being planned originally, Robert volunteered to invest his talent, time, and energy to close suddenly occurring gaps that we felt should not be part of a volume designed to serve a whole generation of scholars of executive politics. The three original chapters authored or co-authored by Robert bear witness to a scholar at the very peak of his time. They are a testimony to how much Robert would have had to give over the years to come.

The four editorial meetings, held in Lüneburg between late 2016 and early 2019, provided us with the unique opportunity to develop also a personal relationship with each other that reaches well beyond collegial professionalism. Those meetings proved a rare privilege of spending some time together. During these meetings we got to know Robert even better as he talked about his other interests, such as music and cricket. His trademark ironic smile and good-natured humour, but also his loyalty and reliability made him a wonderful colleague and co-editor. With hindsight, the time we spent with Robert gains a deeper meaning if looked at in the awareness of his tragic loss. Robert was in many ways the backbone of the whole project, until he was torn out of life from the very heart of our community. We will miss him and his seminal contributions to political science.

Rudy Andeweg (Leiden), Ludger Helms (Innsbruck), Juliet Kaarbo (Edinburgh), and Ferdinand Müller-Rommel (Lüneburg)

January 2020

Contents

PART I THEORIZING AND RESEARCHING POLITICAL EXECUTIVES

PART IV DYNAMICS AND DEVELOPMENTS BETWEEN POLITICAL EXECUTIVES AND THE BROADER POLITICAL CONTEXT

PART V   POLITICAL EXECUTIVES BEYOND THE DEMOCRATIC NATION-STATE

LIST OF CONTRIBUTORS

Rudy B. Andeweg is Professor of Political Science at Leiden University. His work has focused on legitimacy, political representation, personalization in voting behaviour, as well as the formation of, and the decision-making within, coalition government.

Tobias Bach is Professor of Public Policy and Administration at the University of Oslo (Norway). He is a political scientist specializing in executive politics and comparative public administration. His research interests include the selection and de-selection of senior public officials, the politics of public sector reform, organizational decision-making, and the interplay of political control and bureaucratic autonomy. His research has been published in leading journals of the field, such as the *Journal of Public Administration Research and Theory*, *Governance*, *Public Administration*, and *Public Management Review*.

Hanna Bäck is Professor of Political Science at Lund University, and has previously held a position as Junior Professor at University of Mannheim. She obtained her PhD from Uppsala University in 2003. Her research focuses mainly on political parties, parliamentary legislatures, and governments, and she has published extensively on portfolio allocation in coalition governments, and on the selection and de-selection of cabinet members. Bäck's work on governments and portfolio allocation has, for example, been published in *European Journal of Political Research*, *European Union Politics, Party Politics, Political Science and Research Methods, and Public Choice*.

Alexander Baturo is Associate Professor at Dublin City University. His research is centred on various aspects of comparative democratization, dictatorships, and leadership, particularly presidentialism and personalism. He was Visiting Professor in Leiden University and the Essex University International Fellow. He has published in journals such as *Journal of Politics, Comparative Political Studies, British Journal of Political Science*, and *Political Research Quarterly*. His book, *Democracy, Dictatorship, and Term Limits*, was published by University of Michigan Press in 2014 and won the Political Science Association of Ireland's Brian Farrell book prize in 2015. He is also a co-editor of the *Politics of Presidential Term Limits* with the Oxford University Press.

Karen Beckwith is the Flora Stone Mather Professor and Chair of the Department of Political Science at Case Western Reserve University. Teaching primarily in the areas of political parties, political movements, and women, gender, and politics, she has special interests in the United States and West Europe. Her research has been published in the *European Journal of Political Research*, the *Journal of Politics, Perspectives on Politics*, and *West European Politics*, among others; and she is author of *Cabinets, Ministers, and Gender*, with Claire Annesley and Susan Franceschet (Oxford University Press, 2019).

Donatella Campus is Associate Professor of Political Science at the University of Bologna. Her research focuses on political communication and political leadership. Her recent publications include *Women Political Leaders and the Media* (2013) and *Lo stile del leader. Decidere e comunicare nelle democrazie contemporanee* (2016).

Royce Carroll is Professor in Comparative Politics at the University of Essex, where he teaches graduate and undergraduate courses on comparative politics and American politics. He received his PhD in Political Science at the University of California, San Diego, in 2007. His research focuses on comparative politics of political parties, legislatures, and coalitions, as well as the measurement of ideology. Carroll's publications have appeared in a number of academic journals, including *American Journal of Political Science, Comparative Political Studies, Electoral Studies, Political Analysis*, and *Legislative Studies Quarterly*. Carroll is also Co-Director of the Essex Summer School in Social Science Data Analysis.

Paul Chaisty is Professor of Russian and East European Politics at the University of Oxford. His publications include *Legislative Politics and Economic Power in Russia* (2006) and (co-author) *Coalitional Presidentialism in Comparative Perspective: Minority Executives in Multiparty Systems* (2018), as well as articles in journals such as *Electoral Studies, Europe-Asia Studies, European Journal of Political Research, Government and Opposition, Legislative Studies Quarterly, Party Politics, Political Studies, Political Research Quarterly, Post-Soviet Affairs*.

Nic Cheeseman is Professor of Democracy and International Development at Birmingham University. He is co-editor of the collections *Our Turn to Eat* (2010), *The Handbook of African Politics* (2013), and *African Politics: Major Works* (2016); the author of *Democracy in Africa: Successes, Failures, and the Struggle for Political Reform* (2015); and the co-author of *Coalitional Presidentialism in Comparative Perspective: Minority Executives in Multiparty Systems* (2018) and *How to Rig an Election* (2018).

Jack Corbett is Professor in Politics at the University of Southampton. He is the author of *Being Political: Leadership and Democracy in the Pacific Islands* (University of Hawaii Press, 2015); *Australia's Foreign Aid Dilemma: Humanitarian Aspirations Confront Democratic Legitimacy* (Routledge, 2017); and co-author of *Democracy in Small States: Persisting against All Odds* (Oxford University Press, 2018); and *The Art and Craft of Comparison* (Cambridge University Press, 2019). He has also co-edited two volumes, and sixty articles and book chapters.

David Doyle is Associate Professor of Politics at the Department of Politics and International Relations at the University of Oxford. He is Fellow of the Latin American Centre at Oxford and Fellow of St Hugh's College. He works on issues related to political economy and political institutions. His work has been published in the *American*

Political Science Review, the *Journal or Politics*, the *British Journal of Political Science*, and *Comparative Political Studies*, among others.

Robert Elgie (1965–2019) was Paddy Moriarty Professor of Government and International Studies at Dublin City University since 2001, and a member of the Royal Irish Academy since 2017. After receiving his PhD from the London School of Economics in 1992 he held university positions in Loughborough, Limerick, and Nottingham. He was a founding editor of the journal *French Politics* and review editor of *Government and Opposition*. Robert has published numerous books and articles on semi-presidentialism and political leadership from a comparative perspective, and on French politics.

Maria C. Escobar-Lemmon is Professor of Political Science at Texas A&M University. She received her PhD from the University of Arizona in 2000. She is currently working on a project examining women's representation in high courts around the world which builds on her prior work examining the representation of women in presidential cabinets. Her work also examines the role of local governments in federal and decentralized systems. She is the co-author of *Women in Presidential Cabinets* and editor of *Representation: The Case of Women* (both with Oxford University Press), and has published articles in a wide range of journals including the *American Journal of Political Science*, *Journal of Politics*, *Political Research Quarterly*, *Politics and Gender*, *Politics, Groups, and Identities*, and *Publius: the Journal of Federalism*.

Klaus H. Goetz holds the Chair in Political Systems and European Integration at the Department of Political Science, University of Munich, Germany. He previously taught at the London School of Economics and the University of Potsdam. His most recent book is *Managing Money and Discord in the UN: Budgeting and Bureaucracy* (with R. Patz; Oxford University Press, 2019). He has been co-editor of *West European Politics* since 2000.

Dennis C. Grube is Lecturer in Public Policy at the University of Cambridge, and a Fellow of Girton College. He has previously held faculty posts at the University of Tasmania and Griffith University, and remains an adjunct at both. His research interests focus on political and administrative leadership, and the role of political rhetoric in public policy in both contemporary and historical contexts. He is the author of *Megaphone Bureaucracy: Speaking Truth to Power in the Age of the New Normal* (Princeton University Press 2019), *Prime Ministers and Rhetorical Governance* (Palgrave Macmillan 2013), and *At the Margins of Victorian Britain: Politics, Immorality and Britishness in the Nineteenth Century* (I.B. Tauris 2013).

Ludger Helms is Professor of Political Science and Chair of Comparative Politics at the University of Innsbruck. He has previously been Senior Research Professor in the Department of International Relations at Webster University and held visiting fellowships around the globe, including Harvard, Barnard, UC Berkeley, CEU, LSE,

LUISS, and the University of Tokyo. He serves on the editorial board of several major journals, such as *European Political Science, Government and Opposition,* and *The Asian Journal of Comparative Politics.* His research interests focus on comparative political institutions, political elites, and executive politics and leadership. He is the author of some 150 scholarly publications in those fields.

Margaret G. Hermann is Gerald B. and Daphna Cramer Professor of Global Affairs and Director of the Daniel Patrick Moynihan Institute of Global Affairs at the Maxwell School at Syracuse University. Hermann has been President of the International Society of Political Psychology and the International Studies Association as well as editor of *Political Psychology* and the *International Studies Review.* Among her books are *Describing Foreign Policy Behavior; Political Psychology: Issues and Problems;* and *Leaders, Groups, and Coalitions: Understanding the People and Processes in Foreign Policymaking.* Her journal articles and book chapters include 'Using Content Analysis to Study Public Figures'; 'Transboundary Crises through the Eyes of Policymakers'; and 'Leadership and Behavior in Humanitarian and Development Transnational Non-Governmental Organizations'.

Magna Inácio is Associate Professor in the Department of the Political Science at the Universidade Federal de Minas Gerais, in Brazil. She is currently carrying out research on presidents and presidencies with focus on the dynamic of multi-party cabinets, executive–legislative relations, and internal organization of the executive branch. Her research interests include coalition governments, the institutional presidency, and parliamentary elites in Brazil and Latin America. She has co-edited the books *Legislativo Brasileiro em Perspectiva comparada* (with Lucio Rennó); *Elites Parlamentares na América Latina* (with Anastasia, Mateos, and Mendes); and published articles in several journals such as *Presidential Studies Quarterly, Journal of Politics in Latin America, Brazilian Political Science Review,* and *America Latina Hoy.*

Indriði H. Indriðason is Professor of Political Science at the University of California—Riverside. He received his doctorate from the University of Rochester in 2001. His research focuses on coalition politics, cabinets, campaign strategies, and elections. It has appeared (among others) in the *American Journal of Political Science, Journal of Politics, British Journal of Political Science, Political Science Research and Methods,* and *Comparative Political Studies.*

Juliet Kaarbo is Professor of International Relations and Chair in Foreign Policy at the University of Edinburgh. She is founding co-director of Edinburgh's Centre for Security Research. Her research focuses on political psychology, leadership and decision-making, group dynamics, parliamentary political systems, and national roles, and has appeared in journals such as *International Studies Quarterly, European Journal of International Relations, International Studies Review, Political Psychology, West European Politics, Cooperation and Conflict, Foreign Policy Analysis, Journal of International Relations and Development,* and *Leadership Quarterly.* In 2012, Professor Kaarbo published *Coalition Politics and Cabinet Decision Making: A Comparative*

Analysis of Foreign Policy Choices (University of Michigan Press) and in 2016 she co-edited *Domestic Role Contestation, Foreign Policy, and International Relations* (Routledge). She is Associate Editor of the journal *Foreign Policy Analysis*, since 2013 and the 2018 *Distinguished Scholar of Foreign Policy Analysis* in the International Studies Association.

Christopher Kam is Associate Professor in the Department of Political Science at the University of British Columbia. He received his doctorate from the University of Rochester in 2002. He writes on the historical development and internal dynamics of parliamentary government. He is the author of *Party Discipline and Parliamentary Government* (Cambridge, 2009) and a past co-editor of the *Legislative Studies Quarterly*.

Direnç Kanol is Associate Professor of Political Science at Near East University, Cyprus. He teaches courses in comparative public policy, comparative governance, research methods, institutions and policy-making in the EU, and interest groups and lobbying. His primary research interest is the comparative study of interest groups and lobbying. He has published many articles on this topic in journals such as *Business and Politics*, *European Journal of Government and Economics*, *Interest Groups and Advocacy*, *Journal of Contemporary European Research*, *Journal of Public Affairs*, and *Public Integrity*.

Jonathan W. Keller is Professor and Chair of the Political Science Department at James Madison University. He received his PhD in Political Science from The Ohio State University in 2002. His research focuses on foreign policy decision-making, political psychology, international security, and US foreign policy. His work has appeared in the *Journal of Politics, International Studies Quarterly*, the *Journal of Conflict Resolution, Political Psychology, Foreign Policy Analysis, Journal of Peace Research, Conflict Management and Peace Science*, and elsewhere.

Corinna Kroeber is Assistant Professor in the Department of Political and Communication Sciences at the University of Greifswald (Germany). Her research focuses on political careers and parliamentary representation, and addresses barriers for the inclusion of women and immigrants into politics. She has published on these and related topics in several peer-reviewed journals including the *Journal of European Public Policy*, the *European Journal of Political Research, Government and Opposition*, and *Representation*.

Matthew Laing is Lecturer and Research Fellow in Politics and Leadership at the School of Social Sciences, Monash University, Australia. He received his doctorate from the Australian National University. His work focuses on leadership, policy and political development, with a particular interest in the interactions between time, history and political leadership. His current project is the forthcoming textbook Political Leadership: An Introduction (Palgrave Macmillan 2020).

Jody LaPorte is Tutorial Fellow at Lincoln College, University of Oxford, where she holds the Gonticas Fellowship in Politics and International Relations. She received her PhD in Political Science at the University of California, Berkeley. Her research centres on the dynamics of politics and policy-making in non-democratic regimes, with a regional focus on post-Soviet Eurasia. Her work has appeared in *Comparative Politics*, *Post-Soviet Affairs*, *Political Research Quarterly*, *Slavic Review*, *PS: Political Science and Politics*, and the *Oxford Handbook of Political Methodology*.

Natasha Lindstaedt is Professor of Government at the University of Essex, where she also serves as the Deputy Dean of Education for Social Sciences. She holds a PhD in Political Science from the University of California at Santa Barbara (2002). She specializes in authoritarian regimes, corruption, and failed states, and has written several books on these topics including *Dictators and Dictatorships*, *The Politics of Dictatorships*, *Failed States and Institutional Decay*, and a forthcoming book titled *Democracies and Authoritarian Regimes*. Professor Lindstaedt has consulted for the United Nations Economic and Social Commission of Western Asia, the European Union External Action Service and IDEA International. Because of her work on dictatorships she has been featured as an analyst on *CNN*, *BBC World*, *BBC News*, the *BBC Breakfast show*, *Al Jazeera*, *Sky News*, and *France 24 News*. Professor Lindstaedt enjoys teaching modules in the areas of International Development and Comparative Politics.

Mariana Llanos is Lead Research Fellow at the GIGA German Institute of Global and Area Studies, Institute of Latin American Studies, in Hamburg, Germany, and the head of the Accountability and Participation research programme at the same institution. She has been conducting comparative research on the political institutions of Latin America, with a special focus on Argentina and Brazil for many years, and has published several books and numerous peer-reviewed articles and book chapters. Her most recent research interests include the institutional presidency, presidential term limits, impeachments and impeachment threats, and the relationship between courts and the elected branches. Her newest projects examine the impact of presidential term limit reforms on political regime developments in Latin America and sub-Saharan Africa and institutional innovations for social participation in the decision-making processes of Latin American courts. These projects are funded by the German Research Foundation.

Pedro C. Magalhães is Research Fellow at the Institute of Social Sciences of the University of Lisbon. He does research on public opinion, voting behaviour, and judicial politics. He has published on those topics in journals such as the *American Journal of Political Science*, the *European Journal of Political Research*, *Experimental Economics*, *Electoral Studies*, *Political Psychology*, and many others; and in volumes published by Oxford University Press, Cambridge University Press, Routledge, and others.

Brendan McCaffrie is Senior Research Fellow at the Institute for Governance and Policy Analysis, University of Canberra. His research focuses on political leadership, political participation and public policy. He recently co-edited *From Turnbull to Morrison: Understanding the Trust Divide*, and is an associate editor of the journal *Policy Studies*.

Ferdinand Müller-Rommel is Professor Emeritus of Comparative Politics at Leuphana University Lüneburg, Germany. He is affiliated Professor at the Center for the Study of Democracy (CSD), University of California, Irvine and held positions at the Free University of Berlin, the University of New South Wales, the University of Miami, the University of Düsseldorf and at the European University Institute (EUI) in Florence. Over the past thirty years, he has published numerous books and peer reviewed journal articles on political executives, party government, and party systems in Western democracies.

Fortunato Musella is Full Professor of Political Science at the University of Naples Federico II. He has served on the Italian National Council and on the Editorial Board of the Italian Political Science Review. He is currently a member of the Executive Board of Federica WebLearning, Center for Innovation and Dissemination of Distance Learning, and Principal Investigator for the research of national interest entitled *Monocratic Government: The Impact of Persononalisation on Contemporary Political Regimes* (Prin 2019–21). His main research interests include the study of government, presidential politics, political parties, and concept analysis. Among his recent publications the volumes *Political Leaders beyond Party Politics* (Palgrave, 2017), *Il Governo in Italia. Profili costituzionali e dinamiche politiche* (ed.; il Mulino, 2019), and seventy book chapters and articles published in journals such as *European Political Science Review, Representation, Contemporary Italian Politics, Zeitschrift für Vergleichende Politikwissenschaft, Rivista Italiana di Scienza Politica, Quaderni di Scienza Politica*.

Yee-Fui Ng is Senior Lecturer in Law at Monash University. She researches in the areas of political integrity and the law, as well as the interaction between public law and politics. Yee-Fui is the author of *The Rise of Political Advisors in the Westminster System* (Routledge, 2018) and *Ministerial Advisers in Australia: The Modern Legal Context* (Federation Press, 2016), which was a finalist for the Holt Prize. She has previously worked as Policy Adviser at the Australian Department of the Prime Minister and Cabinet, Senior Legal Adviser at the Victorian Department of Premier and Cabinet, as well as Manager at the Victorian Department of Justice.

Diana Z. O'Brien is Albert Thomas Associate Professor in the Department of Political Science at Rice University. Her research and teaching focuses on the causes and consequences of women's political representation in established democracies and across the globe. She has published articles on these topics in journals including the *American Political Science Review, American Journal of Political Science, Journal of Politics, Politics & Gender*, and *Comparative Politics*.

Gianluca Passarelli is Associate Professor in Political Science at the Department of Political Sciences, Sapienza University, Rome. He is also member of Italian National Election Studies. His main research interests concern: presidents of the Republic, political parties, electoral systems, elections, and electoral behaviour. His recent publications include *Preferential Voting Systems* (Palgrave 2020); *The Presidentialization* *of Political Parties* (2015). His articles appeared in *Party Politics, Political Geography, Representation, French Politics,* and *Political Studies Review.* He is co-editor of the 'Presidential Politics' book series (Palgrave), and convenor of the ECPR Standing Group on "Presidential Politics".

Timothy J. Power is Professor of Latin American Politics at the University of Oxford. He is the author of *The Political Right in Postauthoritarian Brazil* (2000) and co-author of *Coalitional Presidentialism in Comparative Perspective: Minority Executives in Multiparty Systems* (2018); and his articles have appeared in the *Journal of Politics, Political Research Quarterly, Comparative Political Studies, Legislative Studies Quarterly, Party Politics, Electoral Studies,* and many other journals.

Catherine Reyes-Housholder is Postdoctoral Researcher at the Centre for Social Conflict and Cohesion Studies (COES) and Associate Researcher at the Institute for Social Science Research (ICSO) at the Universidad Diego Portales in Santiago, Chile. She researches presidency and gender primarily in Latin America. Her work has been published or is forthcoming in *Comparative Politics, Politics Groups and Identities, Latin American Politics and Society,* and the *Journal of Politics in Latin America.* She also has written book chapters on women, gender, and executive politics for several edited volumes. She won the 2017 Best Dissertation prize awarded by the American Political Science Association's Women and Politics section.

R. A. W. Rhodes is Professor of Government (Research) and Director of the Centre for Political Ethnography at the University of Southampton, and Adjunct Professor, Centre for Governance and Public Policy, Griffith University, Queensland, Australia. He is the author or editor of forty-two books including, most recently *Networks, Governance and the Differentiated Polity. Selected Essays,* Volume I. (Oxford University Press, 2017), *Interpretive Political Science. Selected Essays,* Volume II (Oxford University Press, 2017), and the *Routledge Handbook of Interpretive Political Science* (with Mark Bevir; Routledge 2015). He is Fellow of the Academy of the Social Sciences in Australia, and Fellow of the Academy of Social Sciences (UK). In 2015, the ECPR awarded him their biennial Lifetime Achievement Award for his 'outstanding contribution to all areas of political science, and the exceptional impact of his work'.

Mark Schafer is Professor of Security Studies at the University of Central Florida. He is a political psychologist working in the field of international relations. Schafer received his PhD from Arizona State University in 1994 and spent seventeen years at LSU before coming to UCF in 2011. His research interests include groupthink, the operational code, and psychological correlates of foreign policy. Schafer has published his research in journals such as *Journal of Politics, International Studies Quarterly, Journal of Conflict Resolution,* and *Political Psychology.* His two most recent book projects are: *Groupthink vs. High Quality Decision Making in International Relations* (Columbia University Press, 2010; co-authored with Scott Crichlow), and *Rethinking Foreign Policy Analysis* (Routledge, 2011; co-edited with Stephen G. Walker and Akan Malici).

Petra Schleiter is Professor of Comparative Politics at University of Oxford (St Hilda's College) and Fellow of the Constitution Unit at University College London. Her research focuses on the comparative effects of political institutions—including constitutions and party systems. She is interested in the implications of these institutions for governments (their formation, duration, and termination) and political outcomes such as the survival of democracies, political corruption, and electoral accountability. She has published in leading academic journals including the *American Political Science Review, Journal of Politics, Comparative Political Studies,* the *British Journal of Political Studies,* the *European Journal of Political Studies, Party Politics, Government and Politics, Parliamentary Affairs, Post-Soviet Affairs, Europe-Asia Studies,* and the *Political Quarterly.*

Gary Smith is an Adjunct Professor and Research Fellow in the University of Central Florida's Department of Political Science, where he received his PhD in 2018. His research interests include: elite decision-making, foreign policy analysis, inter- and intrastate conflicts, and political leadership. His collaborative research is published (or forthcoming) in *African Affairs, PS: Political Science & Politics, Politics, The Oxford Encyclopedia of Foreign Policy Analysis,* and *The Oxford Handbook of Behavioral Political Science.*

Anna Sunik was Associate Research Fellow at the Middle East Institute of the GIGA German Institute for Global and Area Studies (Hamburg). She holds a PhD in political science from the University of Heidelberg. Her dissertation focused on the foreign policy of Middle East monarchies. Her research interests are in the fields of International Relations, the politics of the Middle East, and autocratic regimes.

Michelle M. Taylor-Robinson is Professor of Political Science at Texas A&M University. She received her PhD from Rice University in 1990. She is currently working on a project with funding from the National Science Foundation to study mass public attitudes about women as leaders, and much of her research studies representation of women in executive and legislative branches of government. She is the author or co-author of books published with Oxford University Press, Pennsylvania State University Press, and the University of Pittsburgh Press; and has published articles in a wide range of journals including the *American Journal of Political Science, Journal of Politics, Comparative Political Studies, Political Research Quarterly, Politics and Gender,* and *Journal of Legislative Studies.*

Ingeborg Tömmel is Professor Emeritus in International and European Politics and Jean Monnet Chair at the University of Osnabrück (Germany). She held positions at the Free University of Berlin and the Radboud University of Nijmegen (The Netherlands) and was Visiting Professor in Canada and Egypt. She is holder of the Diefenbaker Award of the Canadian Council for 2005/6. Her research focuses on the political system of the EU, European governance and policy-making, policy implementation in the member states and political leadership in the EU. Recent publications include: *Innovative Governance in the European Union* (with Amy Verdun) (Lynne Rienner,

2009), *The European Union: what it is and how it works* (Palgrave Macmillan 2014), and a Special Issue on Political Leadership (*Journal of European Integration*, 2017) (with Amy Verdun).

John Uhr is Professor of Political Science, Research School of Social Sciences, Australian National University. His publications include the recent book *Performing Political Theory* (Palgrave 2018) and *Prudential Public Leadership* (Palgrave, 2015). Among his co-authored books are *Leadership Performance and Rhetoric* (Palgrave, 2017); and several co-edited books, including *Elections Matter* (Monash University Publishing, 2018), *Eureka: Australia's Greatest Story* (The Federation Press, 2015), *Studies in Australian Political Rhetoric* (ANU Press, 2014), *How Power Changes Hands* (Palgrave, 2011), and *Public Leadership* (ANU Press, 2008). Earlier books include *Deliberative Democracy in Australia* (Cambridge University Press, 1998) and *Terms of Trust: Arguments over Ethics in Australian Government* (UNSW Press, 2005).

Georg Vanberg is Ernestine Friedl Distinguished Professor of Political Science and Law and Chair of the Department of Political Science at Duke University. His research focuses on political institutions, including courts, legislatures, and coalition governance. His work has been published in the *American Political Science Review*, the *American Journal of Political Science*, and the *Journal of Politics*, among others. He is the author of *Parliaments and Coalitions* (with Lanny Martin, Oxford University Press) and *The Politics of Constitutional Review in Germany* (Cambridge University Press).

Michelangelo Vercesi is Research Associate in Comparative Politics at the Center for the Study of Democracy of the Leuphana University of Lüneburg. Previously, he was Adjunct Lecturer at the University of Milan. He studied and held research positions in Austria, Germany, the Uk, and Italy, where he obtained a PhD in Political Science from the University of Pavia. His research focuses on comparative government, political elites, and party politics. On these topics, he has published in journals such as *Regional & Federal Studies, Parliamentary Affairs, Representation, Journal of Modern Italian Studies, European Politics and Society, Government and Opposition*, and in edited books.

Kai Wegrich is Professor of Public Administration and Public Policy at the Hertie School in Berlin (Germany). His research interests are in the comparative study of executive politics, policy innovation, and regulatory reform. Recent publications include *The Governance of Infrastructure* (OUP; co-edited with Genia Kostka and Gerhard Hammerschmid) and *The Blind Spots of Public Bureaucracies and the Politics of Non-Coordination* (Palgrave; co-edited with Tobias Bach).

CHAPTER 1

THE POLITICAL EXECUTIVE RETURNS

re-empowerment and rediscovery

RUDY B. ANDEWEG, †ROBERT ELGIE, LUDGER
HELMS, JULIET KAARBO, AND FERDINAND
MÜLLER-ROMMEL

1.1 INTRODUCTION

RECENT developments across political landscapes have contributed to a re-empowerment of the political executive. The authority of political executives was once largely autonomous and unchecked, but diminished with the development of constitutional and democratic constraints and was further curtailed by more pressures on and more competitors to the state. The drivers behind the re-empowerment of political executives are also diverse, stemming from both domestic and international sources. The study of political executives has also experienced a revival; political executives are being rediscovered by students and scholars of politics. This is partly due to the re-empowerment trend, but it is also connected to developments within the research program on political executives.

The term 'political executive', unlike several other concepts in political science, will be clear to most readers within and beyond academia without lengthy explanations. Any off-the-cuff definition would seem likely to naturally centre on prime ministers, ministers, and cabinets or, in other institutional contexts, presidents and their entourage. To be sure, there is considerable room for different notions of the exact position and functions of political executives in different types of political regime. Some issues have been reflected upon since the early stages in the history of parliamentary government, when, for example, scholars such as John Stuart Mill and Walter Bagehot wondered whether the cabinet should be considered as just a committee designed to faithfully execute the will of the legislative assembly, or the actual driving force using parliamentary party support to materialize its agendas. Similarly, the separation-of-powers doctrine at the heart of the United States (US) government has, since its very inception, left much room, both scholarly and politically, for redefining the exact status of the executive in that wider arrangement of separate institutions sharing power. However, such developments and debates do not seem to stand in the way of identifying the political executive as we see it. In most pre-constitutional or non-democratic regimes lacking such institutional features, the executive would appear to be even easier to identify, if only because there are usually no other institutionally acknowledged power centres around, with party dictatorships being the most obvious exception.

Some terminological ambiguity has been caused by using the terms 'executive' and 'government' as synonyms—which is standard in Western Europe and other strongholds of parliamentary democracy, but which sounds strange to many in the US for whom the presidency is just the executive branch of the government, alongside the legislative and judicial branches, while 'government' as a whole is the closest equivalent to what Europeans would refer to as the 'state'.

Overall, however, the term 'political executive' is immediately understood by scholars and non-scholars alike, and this is why this introduction first sets out to revisit the historical evolution of political executives in real-world politics, and the scientific study thereof, before returning to some of the more sophisticated terminological and conceptual issues relating to our subject, and their implications for this volume. This introductory chapter closes with a note on the organizational framework that underlies this volume's agenda.

1.2 Stepwise Weakening and Re-Empowerment: The Historical Evolution of Political Executives

The existence of a political executive is a key feature of any political system. Unlike other political institutions such as legislatures, executive institutions can be found in political systems of all kinds, from eminently democratic regimes to totalitarian dictatorships, and every shade in between. The position and power of the political executive, however, varies across political systems as well as across time. This is not the place for another *History of Government from the Earliest Times*—the title of S. E. Finer's (1997a, 1997b, 1997c) unique three-volume *opus magnum*—but (at least in Europe, if not more widely) we can discern a historical evolution of political executives since the middle ages in which their powers were stepwise weakened first, until the tide changed relatively recently.

We take as our starting point the era of monarchies and empires in which the political executive enjoyed absolute power. There have been notable exceptions to monarchical rule, such as the city-states in Northern Italy, and at times secular rulers were constrained by ecclesiastic powers, notably during the investiture controversy with famous episodes such as Henry IV's 'Walk to Canossa' (1077) to submit himself to the authority of Pope Gregorius VII. But such episodes stand out because they are exceptional, and apart from such exceptions the powers of the political executive were virtually unchecked. Interestingly, though, even those absolutist monarchies were not always marked by simple hierarchical structures and strict lines of command (see Blondel 1982: 45–46). While the sovereignty of these early power-holders was still undivided, the executive as a decision-making agency often already displayed some features extending beyond a single person.

The first step in the weakening of the powers of political executive involved the imposition of constitutional constraints on the kings and emperors. Finer speaks of 'The Great Political Invention of the Middle Ages' when he describes how

> during the thirteenth and fourteenth centuries when the free cities and the Italian Republics were moving into their heyday, a sea-change was occurring in the kingdoms and principalities. Beginning with Spain, next in England and France, then spreading into Germany, Scandinavia and even Poland and Hungary, there sprang up a multitude of conciliar bodies to give consent to but also—by the same token—to exert some control over their rulers.   (Finer 1997b: 1024)

In exchange for their approval of taxes to finance the monarch's military exploits, these parliaments sometimes also demanded that the monarch accepted the drawing up of constitutional charters outlining limits to their powers. The English Magna Carta (1215) was a forerunner of such charters. Finally, the judicial powers—traditionally also exercised by the king—were vested in an independent judiciary, although in some countries, such as Poland and England, they moved to parliament first before the creation of an independent judiciary. By 1748, the separation of the executive, legislative, and judicial powers had proceeded sufficiently in England to inspire Montesquieu to the formulation of his famous *trias politica* (Montesquieu 1989). The separation of powers limited the monarch's scope of power, but both theoretically and practically that power remained absolute within this narrower scope. However, where the three institutions were given the means to control each other within their own domains—Madisonian checks and balances—the power of the political executive was not only limited, but also constrained, and for good. This is true also for those rare cases which Finer refers to as 'self-limited absolutism' (Finer 1997c: 1589), such as in Germany, where princes in many of the states agreed more or less voluntarily, as an act of grace, to let constitutionalism spread. Notwithstanding this peculiar evolutionary pattern, these devolved powers of the executive could not simply be reclaimed later on.

Following in the steps of constitutionalization, democratization further and significantly reduced the autonomy of the political executive. In many political systems, the hereditary monarchy was replaced with a directly or indirectly elected president, and where the monarchical regime was retained, the political executive moved from the palace to the cabinet room and/or the office of prime minister. These democratically accountable political executives are, by definition, continuously at risk of losing popular support. Thus, compared to their pre-democratic counterparts, political executives in democratic contexts are not just marked by reduced autonomy, but also by a structurally enhanced vulnerability. Other things being equal, this vulnerability is considerably lower in regimes with fixed-term tenures for executive office-holders than in parliamentary regimes. While public unpopularity no doubt limits the authority and room for manoeuvre of elected presidents (or their 'leadership capital', to use the language of Bennister et al. [2015, 2017]), they cannot be ousted for political reasons before the end of their term. By contrast, prime ministers in parliamentary regimes can and often do lose office well before the end of the legislative term. They are living on borrowed time as soon as their party senses that they might become an electoral liability. Further, in 'coalition democracies' even the most unwavering support of a prime minister's party cannot always save his or her premiership; in particular multi-party coalitions tend to face the danger of breaking up well before the end of the legislative term.

It is only in a few countries that the development of constitutional and democratic constraints on the political executive has been gradual and linear. Often there have been discontinuities and reversals as well as unlikely coincidences. Some countries, such as the Netherlands or the United Kingdom (UK), experienced parliamentarization (i.e. the right of parliament to hold the government accountable and oust it from power) well before a full-scale democratization of the suffrage. Others, such as Germany and Austria, were frontrunners in democratizing the suffrage, but their democratically elected parliaments lacked the right to dismiss the government, which continued to operate at the monarch's will. In those latter countries the power-holders' ill-disguised purpose was to provide the regime with some plebiscitary legitimation without having to establish a democratically accountable government (Helms 2007: 31–2). Such differences between countries aside, in most polities the political executive eventually had to accept that other political institutions (parliament and the courts) and actors (including in particular the electorate) shared in its erstwhile powers. Even in matters of national security and foreign policy (long the *domain réservé* of political executives), executive power has become increasingly constrained by the electorate, parliaments, and courts.

In recent times, some have perceived a third phase in which the powers of the political executive have been further curtailed. In a seminal essay, Rhodes (1994) observed a 'hollowing out of the state', and in particular of the political executive: *The Hollow Crown* (Weller et al. 1997). This hollowing out is caused by several different developments that have taken place more or less simultaneously. Some of these developments are internal to the nation-state. The scope of executive politics is reduced, for example, by privatization and by hiving off the delivery of public services to agencies that are not under immediate political control. In many countries a process of devolution or decentralization has also transferred the responsibility for several policy areas to regional and local authorities. At the subnational level these policy areas may still be under control of political executives, but for national political executives it is a reduction of scope.

Other factors contributing to the hollowing out are external: globalization implies that many economic and cultural activities are no longer confined within national borders, limiting the degree to which national political executives are able to exercise control over these activities. National borders do not keep out problems such as environmental pollution, migration, or organized crime, and those affected by national policies escape across those same borders (such as tax exiles and brain drains). Political executives themselves contribute to this external hollowing out through membership of international organizations, in particular when powers are transferred to a supra-national organization with the European Union (EU) as an obvious example.

The hollowing out thesis is not without critics. It is argued that many tasks that have been privatized had been acquired only recently, and that compared to the long-term expansion of state activities (from 'night-watchman state' to 'welfare state') the contraction of recent decades is less than impressive. Others have pointed out that political executives may simply have exchanged one instrument of control (ownership) for another (regulation), or that, even if the contraction is real, this reduced span of control only allows the political executive to better control what remains. Even Europeanization has been interpreted as an antidote to globalization: by pooling resources, the political executives of the member states have secured more control over globalization than they would have had when acting on their own (Moravcsik 1998; Milward 1999).

We need not dwell on the strengths and weaknesses of the hollowing out thesis because the new millennium does seem to witness a new phase in the evolution of the political executive, with the evidence pointing to a combination of developments that together constitute a re-empowerment. First, the era of democratic expansion seems to have come to an end. There is evidence of an autocratic turn, for example through democratic 'backsliding' in several mostly young democracies in which the political executive gradually undermines free and competitive elections by manipulation and intimidation (see Bermeo 2016; Norris and Inglehart 2019). Even where elections are not tampered with, the combination of electoral democracy with civil liberties is no longer automatic. In 1997, Fareed Zakaria first warned of the rise of such 'illiberal democracy' (Zakaria 1997), and two decades on this has indeed become a hallmark of the new century in many parts of the world.

In many countries, the rise of populist parties and politicians has coincided with, and facilitated, this autocratic turn. Populism is not anti-democratic as such, but in order to allow the executive to implement the popular will undiluted, it is critical of checks and balances on the political executive. In 2014, Hungarian Prime Minister Viktor Orbán even openly announced his desire to transform his country into an illiberal democracy. In the US, the Trump presidency has been identified as having a corrosive effect on the constitutional institutions and democratic norms (Lieberman et al. 2019). Some of the most impressive examples come from Latin America, including in particular Venezuela, Bolivia, and Ecuador (see Pérez-Liñán et al. 2019), and more recently Brazil under Bolsonaro. What has been the result of outright repression in some cases, has been driven by an apparent demand for enhanced executive authority elsewhere. Trying to offer a new start after Sarkozy's 'hyper-presidency' (2007–12) by seeking to return to a 'normal presidency', France's François Hollande soon became so hopelessly unpopular that he refrained from seeking re-election (Gaffney 2015).

It is developments such as these that Freedom House summarized as 'Democracy in Retreat' in its 2019 report, a retreat that has been sustained for the last thirteen years and has affected not only new democracies, but also countries such as the US and several EU member states (Freedom House 2019). Just as democratization once constrained political executives, so an autocratic turn re-empowers political executives.

Re-empowerment also occurs as a side-effect of other developments. Here we mention internationalization, securitization, and coordination. Above we noted how membership of international organizations has been listed as contributing to the hollowing out of the state, but it has also been argued that EU membership in particular has affected the domestic balance between the national political executive and other powers, most notably parliament. As more and more policies are decided in international organizations, the main beneficiaries are those who have privileged access to these negotiations: political executives. Parliaments are weakened because they are presented with the outcome of these negotiations as a *fait-accompli* (e.g. Johansson and Tallberg 2010) and in the case of the expansion of the North Atlantic Treaty Organization, new member states were, in some cases, obliged to weaken parliamentary control over multilateral security operations (Peters and Wagner 2011).

The rise of international 'summit politics' marks perhaps the most visible feature of deeply internationalized governance. People have become used to equating whole countries with their respective political chief executives, that is, presidents and prime ministers. Many contemporary leaders have shown a remarkable willingness and capacity to transform their international prominence into a powerful resource at the domestic level—both in relation to their own parties and to political would-be challengers from other parties. There are now many formats of international summitry, some of which have firmly institutionalized decision-making rules. Established transnational regimes, such as the EU, mark only the most advanced format of internationalized governance, which does not imply that the EU is immune to unforeseen dynamics. The recent episode of electing a new president of the European Commission in the summer of 2019— when the EU's heads of government and heads of state conspicuously ignored the *Spitzenkandidaten* model introduced in 2014 (see Hobolt 2014), and autonomously nominated a different candidate—suggests that nation state-based executive power may bounce back even in contexts where it seemed to have been constrained permanently.

Second, the rise of international terrorism has prompted an accumulation of powers in the hands of political executives and their intelligence services to monitor the movements and choices of citizens and social organizations, and to take swift action whenever a crisis is perceived. National security has long been a *chasse réservée* of political executives, but after 9/11 in particular, counterterrorist measures have significantly added to the powers of the political executive, and not only in the US. Both the nature of intelligence work, and the immediateness that is required of any response to a terrorist attack remove many of the parliamentary and judicial constraints that customarily apply to other actions by the executive. This development has led some observers to suggest the emergence of a 'security state' contributing to the autocratic turn discussed above (e.g. Minzner and Yuhua 2015). The impact of the 2020 coronavirus pandemic may very well include a global strengthening of national political executives similar to that caused by international terrorism.

A third development contributing to the re-empowerment of the political executive is the growing complexity of policymaking. This has been said to call for more coordin-ation of the state apparatus, and it falls to the political executive to provide this coordin-ation, strengthening its role (Peters et al. 2000: 9–10). This line of reasoning has an element of wishful thinking to it (coordination is needed, thus it is provided), but there is some supportive evidence. It is hard, for example, to find a country where the legisla-ture has not increasingly delegated the power to fill in the details of legislation to the executive. Such delegated or secondary legislation takes the form of executive orders or ministerial decrees. For the UK, for example, Page (2001: 24) shows a growth in the number of Statutory Instruments—one form of delegated legislation—from about 1000 per year in 1895 to 3500 per year in 2000, but with a particularly rapid increase from 2000 to 3500 per year in the three most recent decades.

There are other indicators as well, such as the growth of staff of the political executive other than the departmental bureaucracies. Historically, the US was the unchallenged frontrunner in this regard. The 'institutional presidency', that is, the Executive Office of the President with the White House Office at its core, was established only one-and-a half centuries after the creation of the office of president in 1787. What has emerged in the US since the 1930s, with more personnel being added over the decades, has found some (if obviously mostly rather limited) equivalent in many other democratic regimes (see King 1993; Rose 2005: 80–4; Inácio and Llanos 2016). Party politicization of the admin-istrative branch, in addition to increasing staff figures, has been an important topic in many parliamentary democracies for decades, though with changing logics at work. In many countries, the motives for party patronage changed from 'reward' to 'control' more recently (see Peters and Pierre 2004; Kopecký et al. 2012). In the twenty-first century, special advisers to the political chief executive have become a widespread occurrence across different types of regime, including autocracies, and in many parliamentary sys-tems this ongoing transformation has been perceived as a process making political executives in parliamentary regimes more similar to those in presidential democracies.

Despite temporary setbacks, such as the aftermath of Watergate, US presidents have gradually assumed more powers. The overall growth of presidential power over the past century obviously cannot, however, be explained with a steady increase in institutional resources alone. In fact, some observers have considered the enormous growth of the Executive Office of the President over the decades as a source of presidential weakness rather than strength (Neustadt 2001). It was in particular mounting public expectations that caused presidents to accept the role of the unchallenged focal point of the whole political process, and the system's chief agenda setter. While not being fitted by the con-stitution with any particularly powerful resources for creating legislation, no president since Eisenhower, who initially was reluctant to promote his own legislative agenda, has dared, or considered it expedient, to deny the case for a 'legislative presidency'. Presidents' efforts to prevail have not remained confined to the legislative arena, but included a wealth of other activities designed to enhance presidential authority in the public mind. The underlying dynamics of this process are complex and ambivalent: while political leaders, certain to be judged in light of their followers' and opponents' expectations, would have good reason to keep expectations reasonably low (see Helms 2019), it has proven irresistible for most presidents to breed public beliefs in their own potency. And they may have had a point. As Dowding (2017: 9) has observed, 'perceptions of power become actual power as these perceptions become part of the belief set of each person in a power game'.

The more particular theme of an 'Imperial Presidency' (Schlesinger 1973), originally launched by scholars in the 1970s, has been powerfully resumed in the twenty-first century (see, e.g., Rudalevige 2008), and well before the arrival of Donald Trump in the White House. To the extent that 'presidential imperialism' is understood to rest on the president's attempt to make the very most of his unilateral powers, both Bush and Obama also contributed to that trend (Goldgeier and Saunders 2018).

Hegemonic or 'imperial' elements are not, however, confined to presidential or semi-presidential democracies. Indeed, the title of a recent book on the changing role of British prime ministers in foreign policy—*The Imperial Premiership* (Goodman 2016)—offers a frame for a more general narrative of changing patterns of prime-ministerial and executive power in different parts of the world. Even countries notorious for the inherent weakness of their political executive, such as Japan, have more recently taken a turn towards a more power-concentrating, prime-ministerial-centred executive politics (Mulgan 2017). Thus, the developments that contribute to the re-empowerment of the political executive, may also contribute to a shift of power within the political executive to the chief executive (Poguntke and Webb 2005).

1.3 FROM RE-EMPOWERMENT TO REDISCOVERY: THE STUDY OF POLITICAL EXECUTIVES

What is true for the historical evolution of political regimes highlighted in the section above, also applies in some ways to the post-classic study of politics: In the beginning there was the political executive. Machiavelli's *Il principe* (1513) is widely seen as the first major contribution to the 'realist' study of politics, and more generally the beginning of modern political thought, which for the first time considered politics as a particular sphere of its own located beyond the realm of religious or other sources of morality (Machiavelli 2016). While Machiavelli's key concern in *The Prince* related to the conditions for 'mantenere lo stato', his notion of 'stato' was not the state but rather the power status of the incumbent ruler at the apex of the executive branch. His ultimate interest was with uncovering the secrets of crisis-proof statecraft and strong leadership. While Machiavelli's 'ultra-realist' approach set the stage for a new age in political theory and philosophy, he remained a revolutionary leader without many followers as much as his commitment to making a powerful executive prevail at any cost was concerned. Most political thought of the seventeenth, eighteenth, and nineteenth century reflected, or more often foreshadowed, real-world developments by contemplating ways of constraining the political executive by making it part of a more complex checks-and-balances arrangement.

In the more particular world of political science as an academic discipline, which originated in the US at the turn to the twentieth century, political executives have obviously always received *some* attention, but overall considerably less than one would expect. To some extent, differences in the structure of the political executive and its wider institutional context can explain the varying degrees of attention the executive has received in different countries. Taking into account these institutional differences, and the dominant perceptions and ideas within the institutional regime, it is not surprising that scholarly works on the president and the presidency in presidential systems have figured considerably more prominently than work on cabinets and prime ministers in parliamentary systems. More sophisticated conceptualizations of presidentialism apart, presidential systems are, after all, marked by the existence of a political chief executive that is commonly seen as the unchallenged focal point of the political process (see Mezey 2013: 8–9). By contrast, politically, the executive in parliamentary systems cannot really be thought of in the absence of a parliamentary majority supporting it, and prime ministers, while having moved to the forefront of the public political process more recently, are not directly elected and depend on the support of parties and parliamentary groups throughout their term.

But even in the US, which has certainly been the country with the relatively best researched executive branch in the world, the executive long remained conspicuously understudied. Half a century ago, Aaron Wildavsky famously complained about the dearth of studies on the US executive, contending that 'the eminence of the institution [...] is matched only by the extraordinary neglect shown to it by political scientists' (Wildavsky 1969: ix). In the same vein, a study on the US executive branch published shortly afterwards, started from the perception that 'somehow the Executive Branch has been either ignored or mistreated' (Davis 1970: ix). In particular comparative research on political executives from different types of regime (either within the family of democratic regimes or beyond) did not emerge much before the 1980s, and has continued to mark an exception rather than the rule.

That there have been less than a handful of noteworthy attempts at providing an overview of the literature on political executives (e.g. King 1975; Campbell 1993; Andeweg 2003) to date testifies both to the relative dearth of research specifically devoted to the political executive and the exceptionally loose boundaries of the field that may scare off potential reviewers. Indeed, the study of political executives may simply be too broad and too variegated to be recognized as a particular and more or less clear-cut subfield. It encompasses a multitude of definitions, concepts, and intellectual challenges that pertain to institutional, behavioural and psychological aspects and cut widely across political science subfields as well as into other disciplines.

In International Relations (IR), the lack of attention to executives, executive leaders, and executive leadership was primarily due to predominance of systemic, structural theories (e.g. realism, liberalism, constructivism) which sideline domestic political influences on international politics, treating the state as a unitary actor. There has been some attention to political executives within the subfield of foreign policy analysis, however, with its origins in 1950s scholarship that focused on elite decision-makers' subjective definition of the situation. This scholarship continued along psychological lines with work on leaders' beliefs (Schafer and Walker 2006), leader personalities and leadership styles (Hermann 2003), and social dynamics of small leadership groups (Janis 1972). This work, however, was largely focused on single leaders and singular foreign policy decisions, with very little systematic, cross-national research (exceptions include Hermann 1980). And overall, foreign policy analysis research remained disconnected from 'mainstream' IR work, which continued to privilege international structures rather than states and their representatives as agents. This has only changed rather recently as IR theories took a domestic politics and decision-making turn (Kaarbo 2015) and new datasets allowed for more comparative study of political executive leaders (e.g. Horowitz and Stam 2014). Foreign policy research on leaders has been and continues to be detached from the more institutionalist work in comparative politics on political executives, drawing more on individual, social, and organizational psychology.

Given this state of affairs in the two major areas of Comparative Politics and IR it is no wonder that political executive research has experienced protracted problems in creating an institutional home for itself at the level of professional organizations and scholarly publication outlets. While there have long been specialist journals for legislative or electoral studies and even federalism research, there is still no major international journal whose agenda would focus explicitly on executive politics. *Governance* (launched in 1989), which originally started out as a prime resource for studies on the executive branch, successively refocused its agenda to public administration and public policy research after the farewell of the founding co-editors. *Public Administration* remains a journal of special interest to scholars of the political executive, but its key agenda has always been concerned with issues relating to the administrative executive. Thus, *Presidential Studies Quarterly*, initially launched as *Center House Bulletin* in 1971, and renamed in 1974, actually stands out as the only major journal specifically committed to the study of political executives. However, not only are more than 90 per cent of all papers published in that journal devoted to the study of the US presidency, but the remaining 10 per cent or so are also effectively reserved to 'presidential politics' in other countries, thus ignoring large parts of the world.

There have been more positive recent developments at the level of book series, such as *Palgrave Studies in Presidential Politics* (launched in 2015), *Executive Politics and Governance* (Palgrave, launched in 2013), and *Palgrave Studies of Political Leadership* (launched in 2012). The latter is representative of a more general trend towards a significantly greater attention to leadership issues in international political science (see, e.g., Helms 2012; Rhodes and 't Hart 2014; Elgie 2015a). That said, the recent rise of leadership studies is not an unqualified indicator of an upcoming 'golden age' of political executive research. Within the wider field of political leadership, executive leadership continues to be just one subject among many others (as at the level of leadership studies more generally, political leadership still accounts for just a fraction of the whole body of literature as the contents of such journals as *Leadership*, or *The Leadership Quarterly* clearly suggest). Moreover, even where the focus is on political leadership exercised by presidents, prime ministers, and/or other representatives of the executive branch (i.e. executive leadership), the 'leadership turn' has often tended to overemphasize 'agency' at the expense of institutional aspects of executive research. There have been attempts to do justice to the institutions by relating observable leadership patterns to the institutional contexts from which they emerge (see Elgie 2014, 2018; Helms 2014). Yet many recent contributions to political leadership tend to, almost involuntarily, consider the individual leader as the single most important variable, which seems difficult to maintain in many cases (see Brown 2015).

Similar developments can be identified at the level of professional associations, such as the International Political Science Association (IPSA), the American Political Science Association (APSA) or the European Consortium for Political Research (ECPR). There are conspicuously few established research groups in this field, and those in place do not specifically, or at least not exclusively, focus on political executives. While IPSA's 'Structure and Organization of Government' or the UK's Political Studies Association's group on 'Executive Politics and Governance' have a strong emphasis on public administration, rather than on the political aspect of executive institutions, the more recently established standing group on 'Elites and Political Leadership' of the ECPR is deliberately not confined to studying issues of executive leadership. While thus, another recently established ECPR group, 'Presidential Politics', could in some ways claim to be the natural home of executive politics research at the level of European political science, it is marked by obvious limits due to the deliberate focus on presidents and presidencies (mostly in presidential and semi-presidential regimes).

For all that, as the individual chapters gathered in this volume demonstrate, the past two decades have seen an impressive outpouring of research on political executives, including many studies that reach beyond the established boundaries of executive research in terms of conceptualization and content, and with regard to the methodological approaches applied. At the risk of oversimplifying, we can distinguish different sources that have led to the discovery, or rediscovery, of political executives in international political science. Some of this recent research more or less directly reflects real-world changes. For example, the major volumes by Blondel and Müller-Rommel (2001), Dimitrov, Goetz, and Wollmann (2006), or Blondel, Müller-Rommel, and Malová (2007) would have been inconceivable without the world political changes of 1989 and the spread of democracy and cabinet government beyond the former iron curtain. Similarly, the ambitious study by Helmke (2017) on inter-branch conflicts in Latin America refers to real-world developments to launch a novel argument on the emergence and spread of institutional crises, with an assessment that concentrating too much power in the executive branch not only fuels presidential crises under divided government, but also triggers broader constitutional crises.

Other research, while not always being strictly confined to the field of executive politics, is characterized by a combination of capturing real-world developments on the one hand and conceptual and terminological ambition on the other. This is true, for example, of the burgeoning debate about a possible 'presidentialization' of politics, and political executives more specifically, which reached a first peak with the seminal volume by Poguntke and Webb (2005). Still other developments in international research were primarily triggered 'from within' the profession, by the interest of scholars to exploit the methodological tools available better and to provide conceptual innovation when studying established subjects and familiar phenomena. This would appear to be true for recent work on coalition government (Strøm et al. 2008), the performance of prime ministers, including the rating and ranking of different office-holders (Strangio et al. 2013), and the 'Leadership Capital Index' (Bennister et al. 2017), the latter of which not being categorically limited to holders of executive-office. This development also includes an explosion of research on leader personality using automated content analysis profiling (e.g. Schafer and Walker 2006; Foster and Keller 2014).

Intriguingly, much important work appeared just as the discipline experienced its 'governance turn' with its notorious pledges to 'governance without government' and 'governance beyond the state'. This is remarkable in itself, although it would seem difficult to establish how much of it truly reflected the emergence of a new paradigm, and how much was paying lip service to the latest terminological fashion: quite a few scholars of the political executive quietly adapted to the new age by making use of the new term 'governance' even when dealing with issues of intra-executive decision-making (such as 'coalition governance'). There have, however, also been a few determined reminders that 'governance' may not be the end of either governing or government, after all, and that political executives in particular have historically proven a remarkable ability to adapt to even fundamentally new circumstances and governing challenges (see, e.g., Goetz 2008).

It is the ambition of this Handbook to help advance the state-of-the-art in this field further by systematically bringing together the large variety of approaches and traditions in the study of political executives in a single volume. This requires a critical reassessment of some terminological and conceptual issues revolving around the political executive as well as the creation of a suitable structure, which will be at the centre of the two remaining sections of this chapter.

1.4 POLITICAL EXECUTIVES AND THE WIDER EXECUTIVE TERRITORY

While it is true, as we have argued in the beginning of this introductory chapter, that the political executive is not a particularly elusive subject of study, it is not a completely self-explaining term or concept either. The key challenges do not primarily stem from a possible confusion of the executive with other branches of government, though the intense involvement of the executive branch in the law-making process does indeed point to the limits of a strict functional distinction between executives and legislative assemblies. In particular with regard to the executive in parliamentary regimes, the literal meaning of the term 'executive' is somewhat of a misnomer. Both normatively and empirically, executives tend to set the agenda and direct the overall public policy-making process, rather than merely 'execute' any other actors' will. The latter notion is meaningful and tenable only in the context of more complex ideas of representative government, such as principal-agent theory, where the executive is conceived of as an agent of a democratic principal—either the people directly or parliament (see, e.g., Strøm 2000). In contemporary real-world politics, executives in parliamentary democracies tend to dominate parliament and the parliamentary arena, rather than the other way round, although recent comparative research has rightly pointed out that parliaments, even in Westminster-type parliamentary systems, are clearly more than mere sounding-boards and rubber-stamps (see, e.g., Bräuninger and Debus 2009; Russell and Cowley 2016).

A more general challenge relates to the 'political' dimension of what we refer to as political executives. Many notions of 'executive politics' encountered in the discipline of political science explicitly extend to the bureaucracy, and conceive of politicians and civil servants as nearly equally important actors, or elements, in the executive territory. There is in fact good reason for doing so, as no serious scholar would have dared to deny ever since Aberbach, Putnam, and Rockman's seminal *Bureaucrats and Politicians in Western Democracies* (Aberbach et al. 1981). In parliamentary systems, most of the executive's activities in drafting bills and accommodating interest groups, has traditionally rested in the hands of the administrative elite in the different departments. Other things being equal, the independent impact of the administrative elite is particularly strong if ministers are new to their job; this may temporarily transform party government into de facto administrative government (see Rose 1969). In semi-presidential systems, in particular in those in which the president is the dominant player in constitutional practice, the executive coordination between presidents and prime ministers also rests heavily on both sides' civil servants; in this regard, France marks only the internationally best-known example (see Hayward and Wright 2002).

Many scholars agree that, over recent decades, the bureaucracy has experienced major structural change (both driven by novel philosophies of administrative governance and, no less importantly, the rise of special advisers) and expanded its overall role in the executive decision-making process (see, e.g., Kane 2009; Dahlström et al. 2011). In several areas only inquiries that seek to capture the developments in both parts of the executive branch, the political and the administrative one, can hope to produce a realistic and reasonably complete picture of decision-making in the executive branch (see Peters 2013). This includes the identification of important interrelated, if possibly divergent, trends in both realms.

> While the political executive has experienced much centralization over the past decades, with leadership resources increasingly being concentrated with the chief

executive, the 21st-century developments within the bureaucracy of many developed countries have rather been marked by a dispersion of leadership roles.

(Helms 2017: 10)

with wide-ranging implications for issues of legitimacy, efficiency, and control.

The importance of other actors than elected politicians in the executive branch, namely bureaucrats and special advisers, is explicitly acknowledged in this Handbook but, as its title indicates, the key focus of this volume is on political executives, understood as those actors that hold power and make decisions and that claim legitimacy to be in a superior position to do so—mainly, but not only or necessarily, in terms of electoral legitimacy. This definition implies the important distinction between politicians' and bureaucrats' political responsibility. At least in theory, it is for the former to take the heat if things go wrong. However, more importantly in our context, such an understanding of political executives also opens the door to the world of political executives in non-democratic systems, including both pre-democratic and modern authoritarian regimes. While usually not enjoying any (or only very limited) electoral legitimacy, those political executives, or holders of executive office for that matter, still claim to rule legitimately (von Soest and Grauvogel 2017). More often than not, their legitimation strategies include massive attempts to de-legitimatize their opponents, which has been identified as a key feature in particular of single-party regimes (see Dukalskis and Patane 2019).

This leaves us with a third type of executives that can be meaningfully distinguished from political executives as we define them: constitutional executives. By this, we mean formal heads of state that lack the electoral legitimation and the institutional and political resources to make major binding decisions for the polity, and which are therefore not really political executives in the more narrow sense of the term. This applies most obviously to hereditary monarchs in parliamentary monarchies; though elected presidents in parliamentary democracies (and even in some formally semi-presidential regimes) also may lack the necessary authority and legitimation to make wide-ranging political decisions in terms of public policy. The study of both structure and agency at the level of constitutional executives is neither trivial nor unimportant; their perceived status and performance can tell us much about a given regime (for a comparative assessments of such different heads of state in Europe, see Elgie 2015b). Occasionally, some of those constitutional executives have been significant for their country's political fate. This is true of King Juan Carlos during Spain's *transición* (Bernecker 1998) or King Bhumibol of Thailand (Pongsudhirak 2008) as much as for President Napolitano in Italy (Grimaldi 2015). Some scholars have even argued that such representatives with a limited institutional power base might more generally gain in importance as a point of reference, and valuable integrating actors, in ever-more complex and fragmented societies (see Czada 1998). However, these assigned qualities as integrators operating 'above the fray' only underscore the difference between constitutional and political executives. The latter are genuinely political actors, and very often partisan actors, who cannot and sometimes do not even want to avoid divisive decisions and conflicts, which are at the very heart of politics at different levels.

Some of the most difficult questions concerning political and constitutional executives relate to the family of semi-presidential systems. Generally, while being the formal head of state, presidents in semi-presidential regimes clearly tend to be more than mere constitutional executives. Those who take the Fifth French Republic, arguably the world's best-known semi-presidential system, as the archetype of semi-presidentialism will even tend to consider the president in this type of regime as the unchallenged chief executive. However, even in France, the prime minister, while being clearly subordinate to the president with the exception of periods of *cohabitation*, is no *quantité négligeable* (see Elgie 1993; Elgie and Grossman 2016). Both the French president and the prime minister hold a share in France's political executive, and the government's administration is under the control of Hôtel Matignon rather than the Elysée.

More importantly, though, there is a wide variation of different types of semi-presidential regimes, and even sophisticated and meaningful scholarly distinctions, such as that between 'president-parliamentary' and 'premier-president' (see Elgie 2011) tend to have obvious limits in constitutional practice. For example, while being formally located in the group of semi-presidential systems with a powerful president, Austria since 1945 has clearly been a regime dominated by chancellors and their governments rather than by the president (Elgie 2011: 85–6). Although directly elected, Austrian presidents have rarely, if ever, sought to perform the role of a political executive determining government formation and shaping the governing process; they have, overall, been much closer to some formally constrained heads of state in parliamentary democracies.

It is also important to note that while in many parliamentary and semi-presidential systems presidents have operated as a particular check on prime ministers and their government, be it as a 'reserve power' or a more dominant political interface, it would seem difficult to maintain that constitutional executives generally, or necessarily, limit or constrain political executives. The most obvious exceptions relate to presidential systems: The presidency clearly encompasses elements of both the political and the constitutional executive and, under certain circumstances, the latter's particular resources can be used to the former's advantage. As political chief executives, presidents tend to command the support of those who elected them; in their role as heads of state they enjoy a considerably wider authority that, the possession of reasonably rhetorical and performative skills provided, may be exploited to fuel the president's political agenda with additional dignity, legitimacy, and power.

Having discussed the sometimes permeable boundaries between political executives and bureaucratic and constitutional boundaries, it is time to address an alternative conceptualization: the core executive approach. Originally devised by Patrick Dunleavy and R. A. W. Rhodes (1990; see also Rhodes 1995), the core executive paradigm has been a unique success story in European executive politics research (Elgie 2011), if not very much beyond Europe, with the only exception of the major Anglo-Saxon Westminster democracies. More recently, the core executive approach has also proven useful for conceptually integrating new actors on the scene, such as in particular political advisers (see, e.g., Craft 2015). The core executive is defined as including 'all those organizations and structures which primarily serve to pull together and integrate central government policies, or act as final arbiters within the executive of conflicts between different elements of the government machine' (Dunleavy and Rhodes 1990: 4). Although explicitly intended as a means to liberate studies of the UK political executive from the strangle-hold of the debate over prime-ministerial versus cabinet government, the core executive approach derived much of its broader appeal from the governance turn in executive studies that we discussed in the previous section. The core executive approach, with its recognition of several 'organizations and structures' fitted with the shift from govern-ment to governance, and by emphasizing the function of coordination, it offered a solu-tion for the growing complexity that resulted from that shift.

The key message of the 'inventors' of the core executive approach is that power is con-tingent and relational rather than positional. Actors in the executive territory are not powerful because of the offices they hold, but because of the relations they develop with other actors, and the relational resources they possess. Even prime ministers in Westminster systems, notorious for the abundance of resources they command, can be strikingly powerless at times. While we subscribe to the ideas about contingency and the importance of relations and relational resources, we also believe in the power of institu-tions, including institutionally defined positions held by different actors within and beyond the executive. Indeed, ultimately, most of the agenda of this volume flows from an institutionalist logic that acknowledges the crucial importance of different forms of government for the politics of political executives, and the scientific study thereof.

1.5 THE HANDBOOK

This Handbook gathers a truly international team of leading scholars that have shaped recent cross-national research on political executives and will continue to define the field. Despite its ambitious and extensive agenda, the volume follows a clear five-part structure: the study of political executives, the composition of political executives, internal dynamics, external dynamics, and political executives beyond the democratic nation-state.

Part I, 'Theorizing and Researching Political Executives', is devoted to the theoretical, conceptual, and methodological approaches and issues involved in the study of political executives. Eight chapters discuss the contributions to our understanding of political executives that have been made, and are still being made, by historical, neo-institutional, psychological, rational choice, ethnographic, feminist, constructivist, and ethical approaches. Many of these approaches favour a particular quantitative or qualitative methodology while some are more eclectic in this respect. A ninth chapter in this Part I discusses these choices, and the issues inherent to them.

Part II looks at the 'Composition and Life Cycle of Political Executives'. In any polit-ical system there will always be an institution that conforms to the definition of a polit-ical executive offered in the preceding section, but that institution is occupied by successive cabinets or administrations, and each of them is composed of one or more particular political parties and/or political leaders, and as such these political executives have a beginning and an end. Seven chapters are devoted to both the party composition—the formation and termination of governments, and the portfolio allocation—and the personal composition—the career paths of presidents, the career paths of prime ministers and ministers, their post-executive activities, and their characteristics in terms of gender and personality.

The two subsequent Parts deal with the dynamics of political executives, their internal dynamics and the dynamics between political executives and other actors and institutions within the polity. The eight chapters of Part III are devoted to the 'Dynamics and Developments within Political Executives', such as hierarchical relations (presidentialization and prime-ministerialization, measuring presidential and prime-ministerial power, presidents and cabinets, and leadership styles of political executives) and internal political processes (coalition management under minority presidentialism, cabinet decision-making in parliamentary systems, parties and executives in parliamentary systems, and chief executives and political advice). The seven chapters of Part IV focus on the Dynamics and Developments between Political Executives and the Broader Political Context', including relations between politicians and the bureaucracy, executive-legislative relations, judicialization and the political executive, mediatization of politics and political executives, public opinion and approval of political executives, and performance and evaluation of political executives.

As the study of political executives primarily concentrates on political executives in democratic nation-states, inevitably so does this Handbook. But political systems that are not democratic or that are of a supra-national nature do have political executives as well, and therefore Part V ('Political Executives beyond the Democratic Nation-State') offers five chapters that discuss executive politics in the multi-level system of the EU, and in various types of non-democratic regimes, which concludes the Handbook.

We are—of course—aware that any Handbook bringing together international specialists runs the risk of becoming a collection of separate research articles. In order to maximize the overall coherence of the volume, the various chapters have a common three-part structure. First, each chapter states the basic research questions and paradigms at stake in the field covered by the chapter: what are we trying to discover?; why does it matter?; how long have we been asking these questions?; etc. Second, each chapter identifies the state of contemporary responses to these questions, resulting in a comprehensive literature review. And, third, each chapter looks ahead, setting a research agenda for the coming generation of studies in the field. We also added cross-references to help manoeuvre our readers through these expansive fields of scholarship. While even the finest Handbooks are unlikely to be read from cover to cover, we still hope that our most committed readers will find that this volume as a whole amounts to more than the sum of its individual parts and contributes to the return of study of political executives.

ACKNOWLEDGEMENT

Although Robert Elgie passed away before this chapter was completed, we have included him as a co-author because he had taken an active role in our discussions about the contents and structure of the chapter.

REFERENCES

Aberbach, J. D., Putnam, R. D., and Rockman, B. A. (1981). *Bureaucrats and Politicians in Western Democracies*. Cambridge, MA: Harvard University Press.

Andeweg, R. B. (2003). 'On Studying Governments,' in J. Hayward and A. Menon (eds) *Governing Europe*. Oxford: Oxford University Press, 39–60.

Bennister, M., 't Hart, P., and Worthy, B. (2015). 'Assessing the Authority of Political Office-holders: The Leadership Capital Index,' *West European Politics* 38(3): 417–40.

Bennister, M., 't Hart, P., and Worthy, B. (2017) (eds). *The Leadership Capital Index: A New Perspective on Political Leadership*. Oxford: Oxford University Press.

Bermeo, N. (2016). 'On Democratic Backsliding,' *Journal of Democracy* 27(1): 5–19.

Bernecker, W. L. (1998). 'Monarchy and Democracy: The Political Role of King Juan Carlos in the Spanish Transición,' *Journal of Contemporary History* 33(1): 65–84.

Blondel, J. (1982). *The Organization of Government: A Comparative Analysis of Governmental Structures*. London: Sage.

Blondel, J. and Müller-Rommel, F. (2001) (eds). *Cabinets in Eastern Europe*. London: Palgrave Macmillan.

Blondel, J., Müller-Rommel, F., and Malová, D. (2007). *Governing New European Democracies*. London: Palgrave.

Bräuninger, T. and Debus, M. (2009). 'Legislative Agenda-setting in Parliamentary Democracies,' *European Journal of Political Research* 48(6): 804–39.

Brown, A. (2015). *The Myth of the Strong Leader: Political Leadership in the Modern Age*. London: Vintage.

Campbell, C. (1993). 'Political Executives and Their Officials,' in A. W. Finifter (ed.) *Political Science: The State of the Discipline, II*. Washington, DC: American Political Science Association, 383–406.

Craft, J. (2015). 'Revisiting the Gospel: Appointed Political Staffs and Core Executive Policy Coordination,' *International Journal of Public Administration* 38(1): 56–65.

Czada, R. (1998). 'Kommentar. Amt ohne Zukunft? Anmerkungen zum Staatsoberhaupt in parlamentarischen Demokratien,' in E. Jäckel, H. Möller, and H. Rudolph (eds) *Von Heuss bis Herzog. Die Bundespräsidenten im politischen System der Bundesrepublik*. Stuttgart: Deutsche Verlags-Anstalt, 129–42.

Dahlström, C., Peters, B. G., and Pierre, J. (2011) (eds). *Steering from the Centre: Strengthening Political Control in Western Democracies*. Toronto: University of Toronto Press.

Davis, J. W. (1970). *The National Executive Branch*. New York: Free Press.

Dimitrov, V., Goetz, K. H., and Wollmann, H. (2006) (eds). *Governing after Communism: Institutions and Policymaking. With Contributions by Radoslaw Zubek and Martin Brusis*. Lanham: Rowman & Littlefield.

Dowding, K. (2017). 'Social and Political Power,' in W. Thompson (ed.) *Oxford Research Encyclopedia of Politics*. New York: Oxford University Press, doi: 10.1093/acrefore/9780190228637.013.198

Dukalskis, A. and Patane, C. (2019). 'Justifying Power: When Autocracies Talk About Themselves and Their Opponents,' *Contemporary Politics* 25(4): 457–78.

Dunleavy, P. and Rhodes, R. A. W. (1990). 'Core Executive Studies in Britain,' *Public Administration* 68(1): 3–28.

Elgie, R. (1993). *The Role of the Prime Minister in France, 1981–1991*. London: Macmillan.

Elgie, R. (2011). 'Core Executive Studies Two Decades On,' *Public Administration* 89(1): 64–77.

Elgie, R. (2014). 'The Institutional Approach to Political Leadership,' in J. Kane and H. Patapan (eds) *Good Democratic Leadership: On Prudence and Judgment in Modern Democracies*. Oxford: Oxford University Press, 139–57.

Elgie, R. (2015a). *Studying Political Leadership: Foundations and Contending Accounts*. Basingstoke: Palgrave Macmillan.

Elgie, R. (2015b). 'Types of Heads of State in European Politics,' in J. M. Magone (ed.) *Routledge Handbook of European Politics*. London: Routledge, 311–27.

Elgie, R. (2018). *Political Leadership: A Pragmatic Institutionalist Approach*. London: Palgrave.

Elgie, R. and Grossman, E. (2016). 'The Study of Executive Politics,' in R. Elgie, E. Grossman, and A. Mazur (eds) *The Oxford Handbook of French Politics*. Oxford: Oxford University Press, 177–97.

Finer, S. E. (1997a). *The History of Government from the Earliest Times I: Ancient Monarchies and Empires*. Oxford: Oxford University Press.

Finer, S. E. (1997b). *The History of Government from the Earliest Times II: The Intermediate Ages*. Oxford: Oxford University Press.

Finer, S. E. (1997c). *The History of Government from the Earliest Times III: Empires, Monarchies and the Modern State*. Oxford: Oxford University Press.

Foster, D. M. and Keller, J. W. (2014). 'Leaders' Cognitive Complexity, Distrust, and the Diversionary Use of Force,' *Foreign Policy Analysis* 10(3): 205–23.

Freedom House (2019). *Freedom in the World 2019; Democracy in Retreat*, www.freedom-house.org

Gaffney, J. (2015). *France in the Hollande Presidency: The Unhappy Republic*. Basingstoke: Palgrave Macmillan.

Goetz, K. H. (2008). 'Governance as a Path to Government,' *West European Politics* 31(1–2): 258–79.

Goldgeier, J. and Saunders, E. (2018). 'The Unconstrained Presidency: Checks and Balances Eroded Long Before Trump,' *Foreign Affairs* 97(5): 144–56.

Goodman, S. (2016). *The Imperial Premiership: The Role of the Modern Prime Minister in Foreign Policy Making, 1964–2015*. Manchester: Manchester University Press.

Grimaldi, S. (2015). 'The President during the So-called Second Republic: From Veto Player to First in Command?,' *Contemporary Italian Politics* 7(1): 76–92.

Hayward, J. and Wright, V. (2002). *Governing from the Centre: Core Executive Coordination in France. Core Executive Coordination in France*. Oxford: Oxford University Press.

Helmke, G. (2017). *Institutions on the Edge: The Origins and Consequences of Inter-Branch Crises in Latin America*. Cambridge: Cambridge University Press.

Helms, L. (2007). *Die Institutionalisierung der liberalen Demokratie*. Frankfurt a.M./New York: Campus.

Helms, L. (2012) (ed.). *Comparative Political Leadership*. Basingstoke: Palgrave.

Helms, L. (2014). 'Institutional Analysis,' in P. 't Hart and R. A. W. Rhodes (eds) *The Oxford Handbook of Political Leadership*. Oxford: Oxford University Press, 195–209.

Helms, L. (2017). 'Leadership and Public Administration,' in W. Thompson (ed.) *Oxford Research Encyclopedia of Politics*, New York: Oxford University Press, http://politics. oxfordre.com/view/10.1093/acrefore/9780190228637.001.0001/acrefore-9780190228637-e-175, 1–19

Helms, L. (2019). 'When Less Is More: "Negative Resources" and the Performance of Presidents and Prime Ministers,' *Politics* 39(3): 269–83.

Hermann, M. G. (1980). 'Explaining Foreign Policy Behavior Using the Personal Characteristics of Political Leaders,' *International Studies Quarterly* 24(1): 7–46.

Hermann, M. G. (2003). 'Assessing Leadership Style: A Traits Analysis,' in J. M. Post (ed.) *The Psychological Assessment of Political Leaders: With Profiles of Saddam Hussein and Bill Clinton*. Ann Arbor: The University of Michigan Press, 178–215.

Hobolt, S. B. (2014). 'A Vote for the President? The Role of Spitzenkandidaten in the 2014 European Parliament elections,' *Journal of European Public Policy* 21(10): 1528–40.

Horowitz, M. C. and Stam, A. C. (2014). 'How Prior Military Experience Influences the Future Militarized Behaviour of Leaders,' *International Organization* 68(3): 527–59.

Inácio, M. and Llanos, M. (2016). 'The Institutional Presidency in Latin America: A Comparative Analysis,' *Presidential Studies Quarterly* 46(3): 531–49.

Janis, I. (1972). *Victims of Groupthink*. Boston: Houghton Mifflin.

Johansson, K. M. and Tallberg, J. (2010). 'Explaining Chief Executive Empowerment: European Union Summitry and Domestic Institutional Change,' *West European Politics* 33(2): 208–36.

Kaarbo, J. (2015). 'A Foreign Policy Analysis Perspective on the Domestic Politics Turn in IR Theory,' *International Studies Review* 17(2): 189–216.

Kane, J. (2009). 'The Democratic Legitimacy of Bureaucratic Leadership,' in J. Kane, H. Patapan and P. 't Hart (eds) *Dispersed Democratic Political Leadership*. Oxford: Oxford University Press, 119–39.

King, A. (1975) 'Executives,' in N. W. Polsby and F. I. Greenstein (eds) *Handbook of Political Science*. Reading, MA: Addison-Wesley, 173–256.

King, A. (1993). 'Foundations of Power,' in G. C. Edwards III, J. Kessel, and B. A. Rockman (eds) *Researching the Presidency*. Pittsburgh: Pittsburgh University Press, 415–51.

Kopecký, P., Mair, P., and Spirova, M. (2012) (eds). *Party Government and Party Patronage in European Democracies*. Oxford: Oxford University Press.

Lieberman, R. C., Mettler, S., Pepinsky, T. B., Roberts, K. M., and Valelly, R. (2019). 'The Trump Presidency and American Democracy: A Historical and Comparative Analysis,' *Perspectives on Politics* 17: 470–9.

Machiavelli, N. (2016 [1513]). *The Prince and Related Works*. Boston: Bedford/St. Martin's.

Mezey, M. L. (2013). *Presidentialism: Power in Comparative Perspective*. Boulder, CO: Lynne Rienner.

Milward, A. S. (1999). *The European Rescue of the Nation State*. 2nd ed. London: Routledge.

Minzner, C. and Yuhua, W. (2015). 'Rise of the Chinese Security State,' *The China Quarterly* 222: 339–59.

Montesquieu, C. (1989 [1748]). *The Spirit of the Laws*. Cambridge: Cambridge University Press.

Moravcsik, A. (1998). *The Choice for Europe: Social Purpose and State Power from Messina to Maastricht*. London: Routledge.

Mulgan, A. G. (2017). *The Abe Administration and the Rise of the Prime Ministerial Executive*. London: Routledge.

Neustadt, R. (2001). 'The Weakening White House,' *British Journal of Political Science* 31(1): 1–11.

Norris, P. and Inglehart, R. (2019). *Cultural Backlash. Trump, Brexit and Authoritarian Populism*. Cambridge: Cambridge University Press.

Page, E. C. (2001). *Governing by Numbers: Delegated Legislation and Everyday Policy-Making*. Oxford: Portland.

Pérez-Liñán, A., Schmidt, N., and Vairo, D. (2019). 'Presidential Hegemony and Democratic Backsliding in Latin America, 1925–2016,' *Democratization* 26(4): 606–25.

Peters, B. G. (2013). 'The Future of Public Administration,' in J. Bickerton and B. G. Peters (eds) *Governing: Essays in Honour of Donald J. Savoie*. Montreal: McGill University Press, 203–21.

Peters, B. G. and Pierre, J. (2004) (eds). *Politicization of the Civil Service in Comparative Perspective: The Quest for Control*. London: Routledge.

Peters, B. G., Rhodes, R. A. W., and Wright, V. (2000). 'Staffing the Summit—The Administration of the Core Executive: Convergent Trends and National Specifics,' in B. G. Peters, R. A. W. Rhodes, and V. Wright (eds) *Administering the Summit: Administration of the Core Executive in Developed Countries*. London: Macmillan, 3–22.

Peters, D. and Wagner, W. (2011). 'Between Military Efficiency and Democratic Legitimacy: Mapping Parliamentary War Powers in Contemporary Democracies, 1989-2004,' *Parliamentary Affairs* 64(2): 175–92.

Poguntke, T. and Webb, P. (2005) (eds). *The Presidentialization of Politics*. Oxford: Oxford University Press.

Pongsudhirak, T. (2008). 'Thailand since the Coup,' *Journal of Democracy* 19(4): 140–53.

Rhodes, R. A. W. (1994). 'The Hollowing Out of the State: The Changing Nature of Public Service in Britain,' *Political Quarterly* 65(2): 138–51.

Rhodes, R. A. W. (1995). 'From Prime Ministerial Power to Core Executive,' in R. A. W. Rhodes and P. Dunleavy (eds) *Prime Minister, Cabinet and Core Executive*. London: Palgrave Macmillan, 11–37.

Rhodes, R. A. W. and 't Hart, P. (2014) (eds). *The Oxford Handbook of Political Leadership*. Oxford: Oxford University Press.

Rose, R. (1969). 'The Variability of Party Government: A Theoretical and Empirical Critique,' *Political Studies* 17(4): 413–45.

Rose, R. (2005). 'Giving Direction to Government in Comparative Perspective,' in J. D. Aberbach and M. A. Peterson (eds) *The Executive Branch*. New York: Oxford University Press, 72–99.

Rudalevige, A. (2008). *The New Imperial Presidency: Renewing Presidential Power after Watergate*. Ann Arbor: University of Michigan Press.

Russell, M. and Cowley, P. (2016). 'The Policy Power of the Westminster Parliament: The "Parliamentary State" and the Empirical Evidence,' *Governance* 29(1): 121–37.

Schafer, M. and Walker, S. G. (2006) (eds). *Beliefs and Leadership in World Politics: Methods and Applications of Operational Code Analysis*. New York: Palgrave Macmillan.

Schlesinger, A. M. (1973). *The Imperial Presidency*. Boston: Houghton Mifflin.

Strangio P., 't Hart, P., and Walter, J. (2013) (eds). *Understanding Prime-Ministerial Performance: Comparative Perspectives*. Oxford: Oxford University Press.

Strøm, K. (2000). 'Delegation and Accountability in Parliamentary Democracies,' *European Journal of Political Research* 37(3): 261–89.

Strøm, K., Müller, W. C., and Bergman, T. (2008) (eds). *Cabinets and Coalition Bargaining: The Democratic Life Cycle in Western Europe*. Oxford: Oxford University Press.

von Soest, C. and Grauvogel, J. (2017). 'Identity, Procedures and Performance: How Authoritarian Regimes Legitimize Their Rule,' *Contemporary Politics* 23(3): 287–305.

Weller, P., Bakvis, H., and Rhodes, R. A. W. (1997) (eds). *The Hollow Crown: Countervailing Trends in Core Executives*. Houndmills: Macmillan.

Wildavsky, A. (1969). 'Rescuing Policy Analysis from PPBS,' *Public Administration Review* 29(2): 189–202.

Zakaria, F. (1997). 'The Rise of Illiberal Democracy,' *Foreign Affairs* 76(2): 22–43.

PART I

THEORIZING AND RESEARCHING POLITICAL EXECUTIVES

CHAPTER 2

....

HISTORICAL APPROACHES TO THE STUDY OF POLITICAL EXECUTIVES

....

MATTHEW LAING AND
BRENDAN MCCAFFRIE

2.1 INTRODUCTION

....

HISTORICAL approaches are those which seek to understand and explain the present and future by studying and analysing the past. It is a very general term, potentially encompassing everything from narrative-driven political biographies to precise method-driven analyses. However historical approaches are united in arguing that 'history matters' and that no political institution or actor operates within a historical vacuum.

It is also an approach that has a long history of its own, as political scholars and politicians alike have long sought to understand and shape the present by looking to the past. Plato's *Republic* is replete with historical lessons, direct and indirect, which buttress his arguments on the ideal form of executive government. Machiavelli's *The Prince* is a rich catalogue of the successes and failures of executive government derived from European history. This relationship between historical analysis and executive politics is a dialogue, and going back to the earliest histories, such as Plutarch's *Parallel Lives* and *The Histories* of Herodotus, history itself has been told through the recorded lives and times of political executives.

Yet historical approaches also occupy a somewhat awkward place between the fields of history and politics. In recent years the 'political historian' has become progressively harder to find in university departments and what might constitute a 'historical approach' to politics has diversified. Traditional political histories continue to be both popular and essential as catalogues of the political executive through time. But political scholars have developed more sophisticated methods and frameworks with which to employ history in the study of politics. This chapter will map the broad topography of this increasingly heterogeneous area, including some of the most important recent developments and popular variations, and the future of this field.

2.2 USING HISTORY TO UNDERSTAND THE EXECUTIVE

In contemporary political science, a 'historical approach' might entail any number of more specific approaches. One can identify several distinctive agendas in this vein, though they are not mutually exclusive and historically-focused political analysis will readily borrow from multiple traditions:

- **Political History:** Using historical methods as a counterpoint to normative, philosophical, and institutional studies of politics, often doing so to paint rich pictures of how politics and politicians have 'actually' functioned and occasionally in striking contrast to public appearances and institutional norms. Political history is a large area in its own right, and we might further subdivide this approach into two categories:
  - *Descriptive* political history, which is purely historical, and its focus is upon developing narratives of the political past for their own sake. In the case of the political executives such studies may take on the characteristics of a biography also.
  - *Prescriptive* political history, which is interested in drawing out the lessons and rules from history and looking analytically as how the politics of the past might inform our thinking of current or future politics.
- **Historical Patterns:** Looking at history may involve looking for patterns, cycles, consequences, and recurrences that help explain common occurrences in the past and predict their re-emergence in the future. Comparative historical analysis (CHA) is often used to develop theories, establish causality and identify common factors amongst historical cases.
- **Historical Institutionalism:** Often rooted in the concept of path dependence, historical institutionalists seek to describe and explain political systems as the result of long chains of unique historical development, and rules, customs, and cultures that emerge out of tradition and history as major determinants of contemporary actor behaviours.
- **Hermeneutic:** Following on from a rich tradition in philosophy and brought into sociological inquiry, hermeneutics sees acts, statements, and ideas as inextricably linked with their historical context. Thus, the study of a political document, like a constitution, is impossible without intimate knowledge of the historical and social context in which its authors operated and thought.

Political history is the most developed historical approach, in both political studies generally and the study of political executives specifically, as for millennia politicians and scholars have been interested in understanding and describing the political executives of the past. Descriptive political histories date back to the earliest works of political and social philosophy, and often take the form of political biography. Suetonius' *Lives of the Twelves Caesars* (121 CE) is arguably the first example of a historical approach to the political executive, in that he explicitly discusses (amidst gossip, anecdote, and personal histories) the different ways in which the executive office of the emperor had been exercised by emperors of the past.

Descriptive political histories have subsequently become a staple of the study of executive politics and continue to be popular. Indeed, they are essential chronicles of executive politics and foundational to its proper study. Although historically these often took the indirect route of observing the historical practice of executive politics through biography, in the twentieth-century political histories more explicitly focused on executive politics have become common and, indeed, routine. The Australian Commonwealth Public Administration series has, for example, been releasing volumes on the workings and challenges of executive governments that have been formed federally in Australia since 1983. Similar projects exist in many other countries. Historical assessment, and re-assessment, of executive politics is common and has contributed to an evolving set of norms and standards in its practice. US President Andrew Jackson, for example, was generally praised by historians and chroniclers for his forceful use of executive power to advance policy goals, yet his historical reputation has plummeted since World War II as the negative consequences of his leadership style have received greater attention. By the same token, some political leaders long considered ineffective have received historical re-assessments in recent decades that have highlighted how unorthodox or uncommon approaches to executive politics can yield important results. For example, Fred Greenstein's historical analysis of the administration of US President Dwight D. Eisenhower, *The Hidden-Hand Presidency* (1982), shed light on long-obscured but highly effective political strategies deployed by the president. Similarly, Kenneth Harris' biography of UK Prime Minister Clement Attlee (1995), Gao Wenqian's of Chinese premier Zhou Enlai (2007) and Kristina Spohr's of German Chancellor Helmut Schmidt (2016) have each allowed for a re-assessment of the success of these leaders in executive government.

Descriptive political histories need not be stale and academic exercises. Indeed, they are so popular that they have at times, directly or indirectly, exercised great influence over the subsequent practice of executive politics. For example, Doris Kearns Goodwin's *Team of Rivals* (2005) is a political history of the cabinet of Abraham Lincoln that proved a best-seller and was cited by President Barack Obama as an inspiration for the construction of his own executive cabinet.

Many have tried to use the 'lessons of history' to inform the development and understanding of politics in their own time, and in doing so have developed political histories that have been more prescriptive in nature. At the debates at the Constitutional Convention of the newly formed United States in 1787, and in the subsequent influential tracts published by the Federalist and Anti-Federalist camps arguing for and against ratification of the constitution, both sides explicitly justify their arguments through the lessons of history. For example, founding father James Wilson describes the historical examples used to defeat the proposed New Jersey Plan for the new constitution:

> On another great point, the contrast was equally favorable to the plan reported by the Committee of the Whole. It vested the executive powers in a single magistrate. The plan of New Jersey vested them in a plurality. In order to control the legislative authority, you must divide it. In order to control the executive, you must unite it. One man will be more responsible than three. Three will contend among themselves, till one becomes the master of his colleagues. In the triumvirates of Rome, first Caesar, then Augustus, are witnesses of this truth. The kings of Sparta, and the consuls of Rome, prove also the factious consequences of dividing the executive magistracy.   (Elliot 1845: 197)

Indeed, the impact is compounded throughout history, and examples invoked and used to justify constitutional provisions in America in 1787 on the executive were used in subsequent European debates. For example, the apparent success of the American model of the executive and the historical arguments used to justify it are fused with the recent history of France and Napoleon Bonaparte by historians like Alexis de Tocqueville (*Democracy in America*, 1835–40) in crafting the central justifications for the creation a constitutionally-limited and democratically-elected presidency in France after the Revolutions of 1848 (Fortescue 2005: 137–40). Political historians were relatively common fixtures in political discourse and politics departments during the nineteenth and early twentieth centuries, though they have become a much rarer species in contemporary political studies, the tradition's long pedigree notwithstanding.

Political history has frequently been used to form the basis of historical patterns and cycles that might allow looking back to help us look forward. That is, to find historical causal pathways, explore contingencies, and unlock the potentially predictive power of the past. *The Muqaddimah*, written by Arab historian Ibn Khaldun in the fourteenth century, is one of the earliest texts to expound upon a concept of 'cycles' of executive leadership. Khaldun argued that the success and security of a civilization created by a first generation of talented and driven political leadership will inevitably foster a sedentary and arrogant environment in which subsequent leaders will become progressively weaker and idle, and inevitably the dynasty will decline and be replaced. Thus Khaldun elucidated a key principle—political executives do not inherit a blank historical slate—they are shaped by those that came before and by the existing relationships between executives and other political actors and publics. The cycle as a method of explaining politics more broadly is much older—in the first century BCE Polybius in Book IV of *The Histories* describes the 'anacyclosis'—a theory of political evolution in which political society and role of the political executive therein inevitably evolves and decays through seven distinct stages in a cycle from dictatorships to democracies and back again, regardless of the society in question. This singular contention has provoked over two millennia of debate—it has been invoked and discussed in works ranging from

John Adams' *Defence of the Constitutions of the United States* to Niccolò Machiavelli's *Discourses on Livy*.

Historical institutionalism by contrast is a relatively young framework for political analysis and is generally focused on explaining how contemporary actor choices and behaviours in politics are constrained by the historical development of political structures (Blyth 2002: 300–301). As Harvey Mansfield argues in *Taming the Prince*, executive power is generally expressed as a duality of strong and weak forms, and where the true powers of decision-making lie in any given polity or era is usually not where the formal executive powers lie (Mansfield 1989: 13–16). Executive government can easily become a black box of informal realities that belie or even directly contravene formal constitutional dictates or public expectations. It is through historical analysis that we might understand who exercises power and how, and how the historical development of political power and institutions can meaningfully guide our understanding of the modern political executive.

Yet the flowering of historical institutionalist scholarship in recent decades has also produced more precise and more theoretically-driven methods with regards to revealing the mechanisms by which the past can shape modern institutions and their occupants. Whereas once political scholars satisfied themselves with a variety of historical anecdotes to furnish their explanations, modern scholarship has tended towards the development of historical inquiry that is far more comprehensive and focuses on long-chains of development. We can neither appreciate nor be precise about how history informs practice without explaining the specific, general and independently-operating temporal mechanisms by which it does so. The most significant strides in recent scholarship have sought to be more precise in identifying those mechanisms.

At its narrowest, some schools of thought within the growing field of historical institutionalism concentrate very squarely on the evolution of specific institutions, and the story of how legal, administrative or political dynamics have shaped the powers of the executive in more explicit ways. Peri Arnold's *Making the Managerial Presidency* (1986) stands as a landmark early study in this vein, focusing on the evolution of administrative power with the United States executive. But at its broadest, historical approaches have cast a much wider net—long-running societal, economic or intellectual change can also be held up to shape the opportunities and obstacles that political executives face in decision-making within a polity, such that it can be hard to discern whether the talent of leaders or the vagaries of time are the more consequential.

Jurgen Habermas and Zygmunt Bauman are amongst some of the influential political and social philosophers who have used approaches that fall under the hermeneutic tradition to explore discourse and meaning in politics. Yet this approach is the least developed by political scientists, particularly in fields such the study of the political executive, as the hermeneutic focus upon uncovering meaning through appreciation of historical and social context trends has been more commonly been taken up by legal scholars and philosophers. It is a relevant approach for the study of political executive with genuine practical bearing. For executive power in most polities is defined in now long-established constitutional or legal frameworks which are subject to constant revision through legal and public reinterpretation, a discourse in which hermeneutics often plays a central role (Natelson 2007).

2.3 Prevailing Historical Approaches to Studying the Executive

Historical approaches to studying executive politics are diverse, however two principal directions have dominated this space in recent decades. The first has been historical institutionalism, much of which has attempted to elucidate the precise mechanisms by which history can be said to act on the present in executive politics and shape the behaviours of political executives. The second related but distinct approach is American Political Development (APD), a subfield of historical study that has focused upon taking the long-view of political institutions and developing causal narrative histories of politics. However, there are notable cases of original and probing research of executive politics that have employed other historical approaches, some of which will also be included here.

2.3.1 Historical Institutionalism

The most influential mechanism to explain how time or history matters in politics has come about through the influence of the path dependency concept in the social sciences since the 1990s. A cluster of studies focusing on how past developments can directly shape and constrain future developments, many borrowing concepts or work done previously in studies of economic development (Collier and Collier 1991; Arthur 1994; Clemens and Cook 1999; Pierson 2000), has impacted the research agenda in politics and renewed interest in developing more precise historically-informed studies of politics. Initially, much of this work, such as Ertman's *Birth of Leviathan* (1997), took a wide view and explored the role of path dependence and timing from the vantage point of institutions and the entire state. In such studies the role of the political executive and agency within it is easily lost. However, Paul Pierson's *Politics in Time* (2004) provides one of the most systematic explorations of the mechanisms by which history might influence the future, which in turn provided a toolkit by which the role of history might be unpacked within the context of the political executive.

Positive feedback, for one, holds that decisions made in politics and policy tend to be self-reinforcing and increasingly so over time as the costs of changing course continue to increase, creating a tendency towards institutional and policy inertia that become more challenging to break away from with time. *Ordering* can similarly impact upon politics in specific ways—particular events or decisions may have radically different effects depending on where they fall in a longer sequence. Pierson offers other long-term historical mechanisms, such as *cumulative effects, threshold effects* and *causal chains*, all of which may exert an impact over politics and society over a long-term but may have radically difference time horizons of both cause and effect (Pierson 2004). Streeck and Thelen in *Beyond Continuity* (2005) provide a further set of tools for conceptualising the mechanisms by which history plays a role in shaping the political order, though from the perspective of how evolution and change might be created over a long-period. *Displacement*, when an existing order or rules are removed and new ones are introduced; *layering*, when existing institutions or rules are not replaced and new ones are added over the top of them; *drift*, when shifts in the external conditions means that policies, rules or institutions exert different impacts than were originally intended; and *conversion*, where pre-existing institutions or rules are interpreted and implemented in new ways (Streeck and Thelen 2005).

Such tools have added significant heft to the idea that 'history matters' and have been used potently to demonstrate that politics does not operate in a temporal vacuum. Moreover, increasingly precise mechanisms of action have answered some of the earlier critiques that historical approaches to political studies tended to be vague and under-theorized (Gorges 2001; Kay 2005; Howlett and Rayner 2006). Such devices have been used liberally to explain the evolution and behaviour of the political executive and how historical pathways explain their changing powers and roles, in polities and regions like the European Union (Christiansen and Vanhoonacker 2008; Goetz 2014), Japan (Woodall 2014), Latin America (Falleti 2005) and Africa (Awortwi 2010).

Historical institutionalism has provided insight into the evolving place of executive government within a broader landscape of political institutions, but it has proved considerably weaker when examining the political executive as the primary agent of leadership and change within politics. A long-standing criticism of historical institutionalist approaches to explaining politics is that they are much better at explaining stability, inertia and the role of structures in politics, but much worse at allowing for the dynamic nature of political agents and how and why change arises through agential effort (see Hall and Taylor 1996; Hay and Wincott 1998; also Hira and Hira 2000). Indeed, such can be the sweeping explanatory assumptions of historical institutionalism that the approach can be accused of inviting deterministic explanations in which agents, including those within the political executive, are essentially inconsequential to politics. Yet, routinely, political executives break free of established conventions and defy the weight of history. Some have sought to resolve the dilemma through dichotomous models which cast individuals as pivotal actors within periodic bursts of transition and paradigm-change, but minor background players in subsequent periods of paradigm stability where path-dependency and the weight of history create lock-in. More recent studies, including Mahoney and Thelen (2010), have made significant inroads into the problem and have used mechanisms such as layering, drift and conversion to allow for more dynamism and capacity for agent-driven change within periods of stability and institutional constraint, yet critics contend that a great challenge still lies in empirically detecting, validating and measuring such causal mechanisms (Rocco and Thurston 2014).

Such concepts have been joined by theories of the nature of stability and change in politics and historical patterning, such as the work on *punctuated equilibrium* (Baumgartner and Jones 1993), *policy windows* (Kingdon 1984) or *critical junctures* (Katznelson 2003), which observe that for the most part, policy and political agendas tend to remain stable and stagnant for long stretches, punctuated by periods of intense and significant change.

A particular problem when working with the specific mechanisms of historical influence is how to utilise historical processes at a scale that is meaningful at the level of the political executive and individual decision-makers. Studies that have adopted the methods and mechanisms established in this subfield have tended towards long-running chains of political development from the vantage point of structures and institutions. Such structures may include the evolution of the political executive as an institution itself. But to understand events at the level of political executives as individual agents within a system often requires further, more complex, causal mechanisms. Some studies emphasise cultural and structural conventions and expectations around the behaviour of the executive that may develop and induce path-dependent decision-making, or at least create a higher likelihood of it (Greener 2005). Others focus on individual policy-making or decision-making areas, in which learning, memory and past decisions within a body effectively creates heuristics or cognitive biases which affect decision-making in the future (List 2004, Koch et al. 2009). After all, when political executives make decisions, analyse policy and utilise power, they are doing so cognisant of the well-established traditions of their position and some of the historical consequences of prior occupants who have decided or acted similarly (e.g. Hoefer 2011). Yet the precise way in which this historical influence manifests, and its relative weight compared to other rational, institutional and contextual factors is much harder to assess.

Indeed, political executives have a tendency to break free of the supposed constraints of history, ignoring seemingly unshakable orthodoxies and even repeating historical mistakes. For example, healthcare policy is a frequent target for historically-informed analysis, and often path dependency and temporal feedback are used to explain the near impossibility of major reform to Western healthcare policy even in the face of crisis. Such studies typically struggle to explain periods of reform when they do occur, those dogged reformers who managed to defy the gravity of history, and why historical policy successes and failures are not more influential in guiding future policy choices (Wilsford 1994; Hakkinen and Lehto 2005; Haeder 2012).

2.3.2 Political Development

Using history and taking the long-view of the development of executive politics and subsequent impact on those who lead it has come in and out of fashion in political studies, and such analysis has been more commonly undertaken by sociologists and historians. The popularity of large historical studies that transcended mere chronology and storytelling to provide deeper political analysis has its modern origins in the nineteenth century, when a spate of historians-cum-politicians sought to produce new accounts of the relationship between history and politics, and its ramifications for contemporary circumstances. Foremost nineteenth-century examples include Theodor Mommsen's *A History of Rome* and George Grote's *A History of Greece*, both ambitious works of ancient history that put political development and executive politics at the centre, both drawing parallels and conclusions of significance for contemporary politics in Prussia and Great Britain respectively (Carr 1961: 42–4). Other influential contemporaries of the period such as Alexis de Tocqueville, Konstantin Leoniv, and Augustin Thierry produced similar work. They were followed by an even more ambitious series of studies in the early twentieth century which sought to cast the development of politics and the state as a leading actor in the role in the fate of civilizations, such as Oswald Spengler's *Decline of the West*, Arnold Toynbee's *Study of Civilization*, and the various works of Fernand Braudel, the ambitions and themes of which have continued to live on in the works of scholars such as Samuel Huntington, Francis Fukuyama, and Liu Zhongjing in recent decades.

During the 1950s, 1960s, and 1970s political studies and sociology entered the historical fray more explicitly, through figures like Barrington Moore, Seymour Lipset, Reinhard Bendix, Immanuel Wallerstein, Stein Rokkan, and Theda Skocpol. Yet the most significant push came in the US in the 1980s. Stephen Skowronek's *Building a New American State* (1982), Charles Tilly's *Big Structures, Large Processes, Huge Comparisons* (1984), and *Bringing the State Back In* (Evans et al. 1985) began to solidify a new platform for political inquiry through which large, regime-level questions could be posed through historical analysis, with special emphasis on the evolution of political institutions. Although in many ways informed by, and a part of, historical institutionalism, the emphasis on longitudinal historical narratives, causal explanations, and the search for patterns led to a distinct character, now known as APD.

An early key work in this vein was Jeffrey Tulis' *Rhetorical Presidency* (1987), which rejected some of the established literature on the US presidency that tended toward formal and legalistic explanations of the office, instead seeing it as beholden to two diverging traditions rooted in historical change—the first being the original constitutional traditions which sought to diminish and restrain popular rule, and the second being the fundamental socio-political changes of the Progressive Era which led to new expectations of popular rule and democratic leadership (on Tulis, also see Chapter 8 in this volume). The result, argues Tulis, is a 'rhetorical presidency' layered upon the formal constitutional one, and each president strikes a complex balance in attempting to satisfying both, using methods beyond the imagination of the original constitution to supplement the limited powers of the office and to meet public expectations of the executive. Tulis' contention has been highly influential in recasting the nature of executive power and its development far beyond the terms originally prescribed for it. It has in turn inspired significant scholarship on the continuing development of the 'rhetorical presidency' concept, as well as bolstering the historical evidence for it (Medhurst 1996; Ellis 1998), examining its relationship with the evolution of political rhetoric and campaigning in the United States (Doherty 2012; Lim 2012), and documenting the emerging strategies and limits of the approach in contemporary politics (Kernell 1993; Canes-Wrone 2005; Edwards 2006).

In recent years, Julia Azari's *Delivering the People's Message* (2014) has highlighted the potential for quantitative methods to augment traditional APD approaches in studying the evolution of presidential rhetoric and positioning, while still reaching for the 'big questions' of executive power and positioning. Even within the APD canon there are distinct approaches to the study of executive politics, diverging perhaps most importantly on whether the focus of analysis is executive institutions like the presidency, or the state and its administrative capacity and functions. Though the former perhaps has more relevance to those interested in executive politics, the latter approach has equally significant ramifications for executive politics nonetheless.

Theodore Lowi's *The Personal President: Power Invested, Promise Unfulfilled* (1985) foreshadowed Tulis' argument over the dualistic tensions of the president torn between a constitutional order and growing public expectations. The charting historical course of the growth of presidential power, and debating the subsequent implications for national politics and policy, has been a recurring topic periodically revived with new major works (Rudalevige 2006; Posner and Vermeule 2011), though arguably the most influential names in recent historical scholarship on the institutional presidency, such as Richard Ellis, Sidney Milkis, and Michael Nelson have sought dispassionate historical analysis with less emphasis on the normative questions surrounding of the growth of executive power (Milkis and Nelson 2011; Ellis 2015).

Another key achievement of the APD tradition has been to promote a far more comprehensive understanding of executive branch as a whole and the administrative capacity of the office, with great attention to the relationship between the presidency and the bureaucracy, policy-making capacity, and the 'administrative presidency', which casts a smaller net than other studies but has broken significant ground on patterns of development largely unappreciated previously (Nathan 1983; Arnold 1986; Hooton 1997; Burke 2000). The relationship between the office of the presidency and the rest of the executive branch, and particularly the spectre of the 'unitary executive' in which the president has the constitutional power to control the entire executive branch, has been of especial interest to scholars in recent years (Calabresi and Yoo 2008; Barilleaux and Kelley 2010).

A long-held mission of APD has been to 'bring the state back in', and the state more broadly has been a core focus within the tradition. Yet, invariably, analysis of the evolution of the state itself often has more implications for the executive branch of government than any other, particularly as the administrative and policy-making capacities of the state become the primary focus. Stephen Skowronek's *Building a New American State* (1982) is a landmark work in APD which draws upon economic and social history, and the complex interactions between political institutions to explain the growth of the administrative and executive capacities of the state throughout the Progressive Era. Yet the precise place of, and implications for the understanding of, executive politics has varied significantly in subsequent works in which the state is the primary object of analysis. Many subsequent works have focused on specific executive departments and the evolution of administrative capacities, which has heavily fragmented the study of the executive as a whole. Recently, a reaction has seen a return to the state as an administrative, executive, and policy-making whole (Balogh 2015; Orren and Skowronek 2017), though these studies almost suffer from the opposite problem, threatening to drown out the executive as an actor within an increasingly large cast of other political institutions and formidable exogenous forces. Studying politics at the level of the state and casting a wide net over politics, society, and history to explore the 'big questions' requires a delicate balancing act between giving appropriate explanation to the overall institutional landscape and maintaining the central place of executive politics as a primary driver of change within the system.

The study of executive politics within the APD tradition, broadly constituted, has fragmented in many different directions and into increasingly specialized historical analysis around clusters of specific powers, relationships, or themes. Major historically-driven studies can be found in areas as diverse as the relationship between the executive and political parties (Holt 1992; Milkis 1993); the judiciary (Engel 2011); legislative and policy agendas (Rudalevige 2002; Cohen 2012); state governors (Ambar 2012); executive orders (Mayer 2001; Dodds 2013) and appointment powers (Lewis 2008; Alvis et al. 2013). Amongst this too there have been attempted fusions between quantitative methods and the APD tradition, creating important syntheses that may well prove important to the future of the field. Other studies have chosen to emphasise particular presidencies or historical turning points in the development of the office, often with particular interest in the changes in politics of the Progressive Era (Arnold 2009; Milkis 2009; Skowronek et al. 2016) and the New Deal (Rozell and Pederson 1997; Grisinger 2012).

However, growing interest in the 'long view' of executive politics, and more comprehensive analysis of the political development and institutional evolution of the executive, has by no means been confined to the Anglo-Saxon world, and various works adopting similar lenses are to be found elsewhere increasingly in recent decades. Japan, for example, which does not have a tradition of dominant political executives, has increasingly sought to explain its somewhat unique governing institutions through historical and comparative analysis with more emphasis on developmental patterns and long causal chains (Hayao 1993; Gaunder 2007, Woodall 2014).

2.3.3 Political History and Historical Patterns

The dominance of historical institutionalism and APD within the historical approach to executive power has been matched by the decline of traditional political history as a scholarly field. A flourishing area since its founding in the nineteenth century by historian Leopold von Ranke, the number of scholars identifying as 'political historians' has dropped precipitously since the 1970s, as have the number of scholarly publications on the subject (Leuchtenburg 1986; Graham 1993). As highlighted previously, political history, both descriptive and prospective, continue to be popular in their own right, but have increasingly become the exclusive domain of history, rather than political science, departments.

Subsequently, historical approaches to studying the political executive have been increasingly theory and method driven, and more narrowly-cast, than those once conducted by political historians. Moreover, these newly popular analytical approaches have shed some of the normative and discursive character that is found in older political histories. For example, Arthur Schlesinger's *The Imperial Presidency* (1973). Primarily a historian, Schlesinger himself was driven to write the book from a normative perspective, seeing the presidency as having dangerously exceeded its constitutional moorings over the past half-century (Schlesinger 1973). Influential and widely discussed in its time, nonetheless this 'lessons of history' style once favoured by political historians has moved to the fringe of mainstream political science. Some observers have taken particular issue with the relative dearth of serious political histories on twentieth-century executive politics, particularly in Europe where some have observed that the inevitable normative questions about the implications of its exercise have made objective historical analysis challenging (Pasquino 2009; Readman 2009). Others have seen the increasingly strident demands for methodological rigour within political scholarship as effectively demoting traditional narratives of executive politics (like political biography) due to its reliance on descriptive and undertheorized methods, a lack of comparative utility and inherent problems of bias and selectivity (see Walter 2014). This is despite that fact that historical narratives of executive politics, particularly political memoirs and biographies, are often best-sellers and popular with the reading public.

Historical patterning has also declined in salience since its auspicious early beginnings, however some notable theories have emerged in recent decades that have continued to provoke interest and debate, even if somewhat idiosyncratic and isolated within the broader field (Resnick and Thomas 1990). The strongest branch of these cyclical approaches owes much to APD scholarship. While some of these conceptions are spurious, in that they appear to occur at random, others are founded in fluctuations of public opinion, and the rise and fall of coalitions of political actors and groups. Arthur M. Schlesinger Jr (1986) conceived of a series of roughly thirty-year periods, allowing for about ten years of liberal predominance, or national involvement in public purpose, about ten years of conservative predominance, or national interest in private interest, and between these about ten years in which neither was obviously dominant. However, in Schlesinger's system there is little to explain how these periods come about, they are merely empirically observed. Although he frequently uses examples of presidential action to illustrate them, it is unclear to what extent these cycles are driven by the political executive rather than being driven by society or public opinion. Hargrove and Nelson (1984; also Hargrove 1998) defined a cyclical version of American history that was more clearly focused on the presidency, through which certain presidents were defined as presidents of achievement, while others were either presidents of consolidation or of preparation. Like Schlesinger's cycle, this was observed and demonstrated, but it was not entirely clear what caused the pattern to exist.

Stephen Skowronek's *The Politics Presidents Make* (1993) drew from the APD canon he had helped found, to define three historical patterns evident in the history of American executive politics. A *persistent pattern* in which the presidency is caught between competing demands on the office to simultaneously affirm and create but also shatter the existing political order. An *emergent pattern*, in which the institutional powers and nature of the executive can be seen to have changed and evolved in a linear fashion from the eighteenth century. And a *recurrent pattern*, in which executive power and the warrants for presidential action wax and wane depending on the strength of the current political *regime* and the president's affiliation (or opposition) to it. Skowronek's theories effectively stipulate different timelines on which history impacts presidential action—in the emergent pattern, the office and its occupant are shaped by rules, norms, and memory that has evolved since the founding of the republic, whilst in the recurrent pattern history has a more immediate impact, in that the style, successes, and failures of the previous administrations impact the opportunities for the next.

The recurrent pattern is essentially cyclical—political regimes are created, rapidly grow to become the new orthodoxy, slowly decline in efficacy, and eventually become vulnerable and are destroyed to be created anew. It is this recurrent pattern that has received the most attention in the literature, with the vast majority of such scholarship devoted to deepening understanding of how this pattern operates, what causes the regimes to rise and decline, and how presidents have coped with the roles that have been shaped by this pattern.

Skowronek's 'political time' approach provoked significant discussion and criticism. Initially, the most prevalent criticism was that the approach was deterministic (Arnold 1995; Hoekstra 1999), with the presidents exercising little or no agency, while the outcomes of their presidencies were shaped around them. The success of historically 'great' presidents like Abraham Lincoln and Franklin D. Roosevelt became more the result of the situation they inherited, than the actions they undertook. While Skowronek himself denied that this was the case (1995), at the least, there was little doubt that his work gave presidents less agency than then prevailing approaches to understanding presidential outcomes, most of which focused on presidents as individuals, explaining their success or failure through examination of their psychology, skills, and leadership style (see Chapter 24 in this volume). *The Politics Presidents Make* served as a powerful corrective, reminding scholars of political executives, and of the presidency in particular, that the historical situation mattered, and that individual actors were rarely, if ever, the unchallenged masters of their own fate. This task of balancing the influence of history with the agency of political executives has been followed up elsewhere (see Nichols and Myers 2010; Laing and McCaffrie 2017) and is particularly focused on exploring the capacity of agents to act and succeed, even in unfavourable historical or temporal circumstances.

Skowronek's historical patterns also questioned the common trend of the literature to treat the Modern Presidency, from Franklin Roosevelt onwards, as analytically separate from those that preceded him, on the grounds of the institutional differences of the office at this time. The existence of a recurrent pattern of authority built on regimes created a framework for the comparison of executive leaders struggling with similar authority problems from the beginning of the presidency to the present. From this perspective the experiences of chronologically distant executives assumes a greater relevance to explaining contemporary problems.

While there is a tendency to view the US presidency through a lens of American exceptionalism, with America's unique constitutional and historical structures creating unique outcomes in its political executive, the recurrent authority pattern with its series of regime formations of political order has been found to exist in a number of other democracies. Most notably, the pattern has been observed in a number of 'Westminster' democracies, where one of two ideologically distinct parties tend to dominate government, and where prime ministers and their executives are the main drivers of national direction, such as Australia (Laing and McCaffrie 2013, McCaffrie 2013), the UK (Studlar 2007; Byrne et al. 2017), and New Zealand (Johansson 2009). However, Stephen Azzi (2017) argues that the prospects for similar patterns in Canada are limited. The prospect of such historical patterning for greater comparative study between countries has been raised, and the prospect that historical experience might potentially provide comparative analytical opportunities for disparate polities is alluring. However, this potential remains largely unexplored, and the patterns of history remain a relatively minor interest within the historical approach to executive politics.

2.4 FUTURE RESEARCH AGENDA

2.4.1 Reconciling with Political History

As the preceding sections have shown, historical approaches to the study of political executives include several rather disparate areas of study. However, each of these is underpinned by traditional empirical historical work. While many of the works mentioned above include important examples of this method, it is evident that much of the more theoretical work we have referred to leans heavily on the empirical work of others. The currency of this work is not likely to decline, and its capacity to intersect with the approaches discussed at length here, is unlikely to diminish. The relative decline of the political history tradition thus seems problematic in this light. As Harold Lasswell famously commented, 'political science without biography is a form of taxidermy' (1962: 1) and there is perhaps a danger that that the more theory- and method-driven historical institutionalism risks missing something essential about nature and practice of executive politics that traditional political histories provide. Moreover, that political science has vacated the field of political history to such an extent has potentially denuded the field of those with the history background and training, and the decline of such is likely to be to the detriment of historical approaches generally. Ideally, political science and history should go hand-in-hand in this regard, yet the widening gulf between the two and the decreasing number of political historians working across both disciplines should be cause for concern.

2.4.2 Reducing Idiosyncrasy

Perhaps the greatest danger of the field of historical and temporal studies of politics is that it tends to be atomized and idiosyncratic in its approach. Though there has been much greater work in recent decades on developing a consistent analytical tool-kit and vocabulary for *how* and *why* time and history matter, it is far from universal in its use. A great many studies that tell a historically-informed story to explain a phenomenon often do so idiosyncratically, each trying to highlight causal pathways in their own way. Undoubtedly, the field would benefit enormously from a more consistent approach to the methods and vocabulary used.

This is particularly true when approaching the subject of political executives. As highlighted previously, there remain significant doubts and questions over how to resolve the problem of agents within historical and temporal narratives. Overemphasis on the weight of history inevitably leads to accounts which are deterministic and in which individuals had no capacity to change the outcome. Many scholars are wary of this problem, and yet the approach to resolving this issue is often unique and largely unconnected to other studies in the field. Though Mahoney, Thelen, and others have developed a more nuanced set of tools for reconciling what agents can do within a structured landscape, they are not widespread in their use yet. Though there will inevitably be arguments over how to define and apply such tools, working from a common tool-set to begin with would at least make for a better starting point and allow a more sophisticated and precise debate to evolve. As it is, there is still too much temptation to embark on isolated 'grand histories' in which the agents of the moment and the structures of time are meshed together in an idiosyncratic fashion, with each new iteration creating its own set of rules, terms, and conclusions to navigate the sticky pathway between the two. Some of the enduring success of ideas like Skowronek's 'political time' has been the interest of scholars to continue to refine, augment, and debate the theory on its own terms and within its own framework of mechanisms, allowing a much more technical debate to emerge, unlike earlier decades when various 'patterns of history' were developed and tended to stand on their own as self-contained and novel but ultimately stagnant contentions.

2.4.3 Internationalization

The most significant potential for growth in many aspects of historical and temporal studies is in its internationalization. The last decade has seen significant advances in the development of a vocabulary and tool-kit of temporal mechanisms which demonstrate *how* and *why* history and time matter independently of the specific history of the area or polity studied. This gives the entire field great potential to cast off its traditionally single-minded focus on the executive politics of individual nations and look to the consistency with which these mechanisms have operated comparatively. Comparative politics has long looked to explain the evolutionary differences of political systems across nations, particularly executive politics, but now more than ever we have a much more precise set of tools and ideas to test against this backdrop and provide sharper insight into *when* history mattered and *how*.

Moreover, there is increasing evidence that *global* history and timing has a far greater impact on domestic politics, even the operation of executive politics, than was ever previously the case. The US focus of many of its scholars, and even the single-nation focus of most who have applied political time and other historical approaches elsewhere, appears to have obscured the international effects of many of the ideas, and of many actors and institutions. Arguably, regimes based on Keynesian economics in the mid-twentieth century were a feature of most Western democracies, supported by international agreements, laws, and bodies. Similarly, both the monetarist turn of the 1980s, and the rise of populist opposition to globalization in the 2010s have been highly international events. While much is known about these events, and they are closely studied within other academic traditions, greater attention to international institutions and actors may reveal much about how the ideas that have defined eras of our recent political history have spread, and why it is that combating dominant ideas within a polity is so difficult. For example, Harshan Kumarasingham's work on the legacy of the British Empire on the politics of India and Sri Lanka demonstrates just how acutely global historical factors can echo through to the practice on executive politics over half a century later (Kumarasingham 2013).

In the twenty-first century world, political and social trends are increasingly globalized still. The resurgence of populist politics and anti-elite sentiment in the 2010s has left few Western nations untouched and has brought with it new debates and models for the exercise of executive power. A poignant but seemingly isolated act of political defiance in Tunisia in 2010 spiralled into a dramatic re-appraisal of the nature and legitimacy of executive politics right across the Arab world, seemingly riding roughshod over the varied histories and institutions of neighbouring nations, and stunning many domestic and international political observers. New regional and international phenomena are redefining *which* history matters and perhaps drawing many polities closer together in political time. It is time, too, that we started to move away from historical and temporal studies that focus on the initiate of our local past and look instead to how a globalized future may be the new historical overlay that will matter most.

References

Alvis, J. D., Bailey, J. D., and Flagg, F. (2013). *The Contested Removal Power, 1789–2010.* Lawrence, KS: University Press of Kansas.

Ambar, S. (2012). *How Governors Built the Modern American Presidency.* Philadelphia, PA: University of Pennsylvania Press.

Arnold, P. (1986). *Making the Managerial Presidency*. Princeton, NJ: Princeton University Press.

Arnold, P. (1995). 'Determinism and Contingency in Skowronek's Political Time,' *Polity* 27(3): 497–508.

Arnold, P. (2009). *Remaking the Presidency: Roosevelt, Taft, and Wilson, 1901–1916*. Lawrence, KS: University Press of Kansas.

Arthur, W. (1994). *Increasing Returns and Path Dependence in the Economy*. Ann Arbor, MI: University of Michigan Press.

Awortwi, N. (2010). 'The Past, Present, and Future of Decentralisation in Africa: A Comparative Case Study of Local Government Development Trajectories of Ghana and Uganda,' *International Journal of Public Administration* 33(12–13): 620–34.

Azari, J. (2014). *Delivering the People's Message*. Ithaca, NY: Cornell University Press.

Azzi, S. (2017). 'Political Time in a Westminster Democracy: The Canadian Case,' *American Review of Canadian Studies* 47(1): 19–34.

Balogh, B. (2015). *The Associational State*. Philadelphia, PA: University of Pennsylvania Press.

Barilleaux, R. and Kelley, C. (2010). *The Unitary Executive and the Modern Presidency*. College Station, TX: Texas A&M University Press.

Baumgartner, F. R. and Jones, B. D. (1993). *Agendas and Instability in American Politics*. Chicago, IL: University of Chicago Press.

Blyth, M. (2002). 'Institutions and Ideas,' in D. Marsh and G. Stoker (eds) *Theory and Methods in Political Science*. Basingstoke: Palgrave Macmillan.

Burke, J. P. (2000). *The Institutional Presidency*. Baltimore, MD: Johns Hopkins University Press.

Byrne, C., Randall, N., and Theakston, K. (2017). 'Evaluating British Prime Ministerial Performance: David Cameron's Premiership in Political Time,' *The British Journal of Politics and International Relations* 19(1): 202–20.

Calabresi, S. and Yoo, C. (2008). *The Unitary Executive*. New Haven, CT: Yale University Press.

Canes-Wrone, B. (2005). *Who Leads Whom?* Chicago, IL: University of Chicago Press.

Carr, E. H. (1961). *What is History?* Cambridge: University of Cambridge Press.

Christiansen, T. and Vanhoonacker, S. (2008). 'At a Critical Juncture? Change and Continuity in the Institutional Development of the Council Secretariat,' *West European Politics* 31(4): 751–70.

Clemens, E. and Cook, J. (1999). 'Politics and Institutionalism: Explaining Durability and Change,' *Annual Review of Sociology* 25: 441–66.

Cohen, J. (2012). *The President's Legislative Policy Agenda, 1789–2002*. Cambridge: Cambridge University Press.

Collier, R. B. and Collier, D. (1991). *Shaping the Political Arena*. Princeton, NJ: Princeton University Press.

Dodds, G. (2013). *Take Up Your Pen: Unilateral Presidential Directives in American Politics*. Philadelphia, PA: University of Pennsylvania Press.

Doherty, B. (2012). *The Rise of the President's Permanent Campaign*. Lawrence, KS: University Press of Kansas.

Edwards, G. (2006). *On Deaf Ears: The Limits of the Bully Pulpit*. New Haven, CT: Yale University Press.

Elliot, J. (1845). *The Debates in the Several State Conventions on the Adoption of the Federal Constitution 5*. Washington, DC: United States Congress.

Ellis, R. J. (1998). *Speaking to the People: The Rhetorical Presidency in Historical Perspective*. Amherst, MA: University of Massachusetts Press.

Ellis, R. J. (2015). *The Development of the American Presidency*. 2nd ed. New York, NY: Routledge.

Engel, S. (2011). *American Politicians Confront the Court*. Cambridge: Cambridge University Press.

Ertman, T. (1997). *The Birth of the Leviathan*. Cambridge: Cambridge University Press.

Evans, P., Rueschemeyer, D., and Skocpol, T. (1985). *Bringing the State Back In*. Cambridge: Cambridge University Press.

Falleti, T. (2005). 'A Sequential Theory of Decentralization: Latin American Cases in Comparative Perspective,' *American Political Science Review* 99(3): 327–46.

Fortescue, W. (2005). *France and 1848: The End of Monarchy*. Abingdon: Routledge.

Gaunder, A. (2007). *Political Reform in Japan: Leadership Looming Large*. Abingdon: Routledge.

Goetz, K. (2014). 'Time and Power in the European Commission,' *International Review of Administrative Sciences* 80(3): 577–96.

Goodwin, D. K. (2005). *Team of Rivals*. New York: Simon & Schuster.

Gorges, M. J. (2001). 'New Institutionalist Explanations for Institutional Change: A Note of Caution,' *Politics* 21(2): 137–45.

Graham, H. (1993). 'The Stunted Career of Policy History: A Critique and an Agenda,' *The Public Historian* 15(2): 15–37.

Greener, I. (2005). 'The Potential of Path Dependence in Political Studies,' *Politics* 25(1): 62–72.

Greenstein, F. (1982). *The Hidden-Hand Presidency*. New York: Basic Books.

Grisinger, J. (2012). *The Unwieldy American State*. Cambridge: Cambridge University Press.

Haeder, S. (2012). 'Beyond Path Dependence: Explaining Healthcare Reform and Its Consequences,' *Policy Studies Journal* 40(1): 65–86.

Hakkinen, U. and Lehto, J. (2005). 'Reform, Change, and Continuity in Finnish Health Care,' *Journal of Health Politics, Policy and Law* 30(1–2): 79–96.

Hall, P. and Taylor, R. (1996). 'Political Science and the Three New Institutionalisms,' *Political Studies* 44(5): 936–57.

Hargrove, E. (1998). *The President as Leader: Appealing to the Better Angels of our Nature*. Lawrence, KS: University Press of Kansas.

Hargrove, E. and Nelson, M. (1984). *Presidents, Politics and Policy*. New York: Alfred A. Knopf.

Harris, K. (1995). *Attlee*. London: Weidenfeld & Nicholson.

Hay, C. and Wincott, D. (1998). 'Structure, Agency and Historical Institutionalism,' *Political Studies* 46(5): 951–7.

Hayao, K. (1993). *The Japanese Prime Minister and Public Policy*. Pittsburgh, PA: University of Pittsburgh Press.

Hira, A. and Hira, R. (2000). 'The New Institutionalism: Contradictory Notions of Change,' *American Journal of Economics and Sociology* 59(2): 267–82.

Hoefer, R. (2011). 'Using the Historical Approach,' in R. Hoefer (ed) *Policy Creation and Evaluation: Understanding Welfare Reform in the United States*. Oxford: Oxford University Press.

Hoekstra, D. (1999). 'The Politics of *Politics*: Skowronek and Presidential Research,' *Presidential Studies Quarterly* 29(3): 657–71.

Holt, M. (1992). *Political Parties and American Political Development from the Age of Jackson to the Age of Lincoln*. Baton Rouge, LA: Louisiana State University Press.

Hooton, C. G. (1997). *Executive Governance: Presidential Administrations and Policy Change in the Federal Bureaucracy*. Armonk, NY: M. E. Sharpe.

Howlett, M. and Rayner, J. (2006). 'Understanding the Historical Turn in the Policy Sciences,' *Policy Sciences* 39(1): 1–18.

Johansson, J. (2009). *The Politics of Possibility: Leadership in Changing Times*. Wellington, NZ: Dunmore Publishing.

Katznelson, I. (2003). 'Periodisation and Preferences,' in J. Mahoney and D. Rueschemeyer (eds) *Comparative Historical Analysis in the Social Sciences*. Cambridge: Cambridge University Press.

Kay, A. (2005). 'A Critique of the Use of Path Dependency in Policy studies,' *Public Administration* 83(3): 553–71.

Kernell, S. (1993). *Going Public New Strategies of Presidential Leadership*. Washington, DC: CQ Press.

Kingdon, J. W. (1984). *Agendas, Alternatives, and Public Policies*. Boston, MA: Little, Brown.

Koch, J., Eisend, M., and Petermann, A. (2009). 'Path Dependence in Decision-Making Processes: Exploring the Impact of Complexity under Increasing Returns,' *Business Research* 2(1): 67–84.

Kumarasingham, H. (2013). *A Political Legacy of the British Empire: Power and the Parliamentary System in Post-Colonial India and Sri Lanka*. London: I.B. Tauris.

Laing, M. and McCaffrie, B. (2013). 'The Politics Prime Ministers Make: Political Time and Executive Leadership in Westminster Systems,' in P. Strangio, P., 't Hart, and J. Walter (eds) *Understanding Prime-Ministerial Performance: Comparative Perspectives*. Oxford: Oxford University Press.

Laing, M. and McCaffrie, B. (2017). 'The Impossible Leadership Situation? Analyzing Success for Disjunctive Presidents,' *Presidential Studies Quarterly* 47(2): 255–76.

Lasswell, H. (1962). *Psychopathology and Politics*. New York: Viking Press.

Leuchtenburg, W. (1986). 'The Pertinence of Political History: Reflections on the Significance of the State in America,' *The Journal of American History* 73(3): 585–600.

Lewis, D. (2008). *The Politics of Presidential Appointments*. Princeton, NJ: Princeton University Press.

Lim, E. (2012). *The Anti-Intellectual Presidency: The Decline of Presidential Rhetoric from George Washington to George W. Bush*. New York: Oxford University Press.

List, C. (2004). 'A Model of Path-Dependence in Decisions over Multiple Propositions,' *American Political Science Review* 98(3): 495–513.

Lowi, T. J. (1985). *The Personal President*. Ithaca, NY: Cornell University Press.

Mahoney, J. and Thelen, K. (2010). *Explaining Institutional Change: Ambiguity, Agency and Power*. Cambridge: Cambridge University Press.

Mansfield, H. (1989). *Taming the Prince*. New York: The Free Press.

Mayer, K. R. (2001). *With the Stroke of a Pen: Executive Orders and Presidential Power*. Princeton, NJ: Princeton University Press.

McCaffrie, B. (2013). 'A Contextual Framework for Assessing Reconstructive Prime Ministerial Success,' *Policy Studies* 34(5–6): 618–37.

Medhurst, M. (1996). *Beyond the Rhetorical Presidency*. College Station, TX: Texas A&M University Press.

Milkis, S. (1993). *The President and the Parties*. Oxford: Oxford University Press.

Milkis, S. (2009). *Theodore Roosevelt, the Progressive Party, and the Transformation of American Democracy*. Lawrence, KS: University Press of Kansas.

Milkis, S. and Nelson, M. (2011). *The American Presidency: Origins and Development 1776-2011*. Los Angeles, CA: CQ Press.

Natelson, R. (2007). 'The Founders' Hermeneutic: The Real Original Understanding of Original Intent,' *Ohio State Law Journal* 68(5): 1239–305.

Nathan, R. (1983). *The Administrative Presidency*. New York: John Wiley.

Nichols, C. and Myers, A. S. (2010). 'Exploiting the Opportunity for Reconstructive Leadership: Presidential Response to Enervated Political Regimes', *American Politics Research* 38(5): 806–41.

Orren, K. and Skowronek, S. (2017). *The Policy State*. Cambridge, MA: Harvard University Press.

Pasquino, G. (2009). 'Political History in Italy', *Journal of Policy History* 21(3): 282–97.

Pierson, P. (2000). 'Increasing Returns, Path Dependence, and the Study of Politics', *American Political Science Review* 94(2): 251–67.

Pierson, P. (2004). *Politics in Time*. Princeton, NJ: Princeton University Press.

Posner, E. and Vermeule, A. (2011). *The Executive Unbound*. Oxford: Oxford University Press.

Readman, P. (2009). 'The State of Twentieth-Century British Political History', *Journal of Policy History* 21(3): 219–38.

Resnick, D. and Thomas, N. C. (1990). 'Cycling through American Politics', *Polity* 23(1): 1–21.

Rocco, P. and Thurston, C. (2014). 'From Metaphors to Measures: Observable Indicators of Gradual Institutional Change', *Journal of Public Policy* 34(1): 35–62.

Rozell, M. and Pederson, W. (1997). *FDR and the Modern Presidency*. Westport, CT: Praeger.

Rudalevige, A. (2002). *Managing the President's Program*. Princeton, NJ: Princeton University Press.

Rudalevige, A. (2006). 'The Decline and Resurgence and Decline (and Resurgence?) of Congress: Charting a New Imperial Presidency', *Presidential Studies Quarterly* 36(3): 506–24.

Schlesinger, A., Jr (1973). *The Imperial Presidency*. Boston, MA: Houghton Mifflin.

Schlesinger, A., Jr (1986). *The Cycles of American History*. Boston, MA: Houghton Mifflin.

Spohr, K. (2016) *The Global Chancellor*. Oxford: Oxford University Press.

Skowronek, S. (1982). *Building a New American State*. Cambridge: Cambridge University Press.

Skowronek, S. (1993). *The Politics Presidents Make: Leadership from John Adams to George Bush*. Cambridge, MA: Harvard University Press.

Skowronek, S. (1995). 'Response', *Polity* 27(3): 517–34.

Skowronek, S., Engel, S. M., and Ackerman, B. A. (2016). *The Progressives' Century*. New Haven, CT: Yale University Press.

Streeck, W. and Thelen, K. (2005). *Beyond Continuity: Institutional Change in Advanced Political Economies*. Oxford: Oxford University Press.

Studlar, D. T. (2007). 'From Collectivist Consensus to 21st Century Neoliberalism: Orders and Eras in Postwar Britain', *The Forum* 5(3).

Tilly, C. (1984). *Big Structures, Large Processes, Huge Comparisons*. New York: Russell Sage Foundation.

Tulis, J. (1987). *The Rhetorical Presidency*. Princeton, NJ: Princeton University Press.

Walter, J. (2014). 'Biographical Analysis', in R. A. W. Rhodes and P. 't Hart (eds) *The Oxford Handbook of Political Leadership*. Oxford: Oxford University Press.

Wenqian, G. (2007). *Zhou Enlai: The Last Perfect Revolutionary*. New York: Public Affairs.

Wilsford, D. (1994). 'Path Dependency, or Why History Makes It Difficult but Not Impossible to Reform Health Care Systems in a Big Way', *Journal of Public Policy* 14(3): 251–83.

Woodall, B. (2014). *Growing Democracy in Japan: The Parliamentary Cabinet System since 1868*. Lexington, KY: University Press of Kentucky.

....

CHAPTER 3

NEW INSTITUTIONAL APPROACHES TO THE STUDY OF POLITICAL EXECUTIVES

....

KLAUS H. GOETZ

3.1 INTRODUCTION

....

THE New Institutionalism—NI—sometimes also referred to as neo-institutionalism—has become the widely accepted summary term for a set of theoretical propositions that guide the academic analysis of politics, government, and public policy. Recent texts on the NI in political science (Lowndes and Roberts 2013; Peters 2019) stress its internal theoretical diversity, which raises the question of whether there is one NI 'or many' (Peters 2019). Most scholars who identify themselves with NI would, however, agree that political life is fundamentally shaped by institutions; that institutions can be understood as the more or less stable and more or less formal rules shaping politics, government, and public policy; that these rules require organizations to bring them to life and to give them effect, which implies that institutions and organizations are not the same; and that the behaviour of political actors—whether individuals or groups—is deeply affected, albeit not fully determined, by the institutional and organizational settings in which they find themselves.

Why has NI had such a pervasive influence on the study of political executives over the past three decades? Four qualities of NI help to explain its attraction to students of political executives. First, NI has a common theoretical core. It is centred on the interactions between institutions, organizations, actors, interests, preferences, ideas, resources, and decisions. As such, NI selects and structures empirical observations related to formal and informal rules; organizational properties; individual and collective actors and what motivates them; the importance of ideas; the dependence of political executives on resources, be they finance, personnel, information, trust, or legitimacy; and the linkage between rules, routines, resources, and substantive policy choices made by, and within, executives.

Beyond these common core concerns, there is, as already noted, a great deal of variation in NI scholarship in relation to definitional, conceptual, and explanatory issues. These differences concern, in particular: (i) the specific definitions of institutions and organizations; (ii) assumptions about the origins of the motivations of actors, notably the question of whether actors' interests and preferences are understood as exogenous or endogenous, that is, external or internal to a given institutional-organizational setting; (iii) the question of whether ideas and discourses possess explanatory power in their own right; and (iv) the attention that is paid to organizational resources and the type of resources that are seen to matter.

As a consequence, different versions of NI have evolved, including, in particular, sociological-constructivist NI (see also Chapter 8 in this volume); rationalist NI (see also Chapter 5 in this volume); historical NI (Fioretos et al. 2016); and ideational-discursive NI (Schmidt 2008; Carstensen and Schmidt 2015). It is this diversity and the capacity of NI to accommodate and, to some extent, absorb important definitional, conceptual, and explanatory differences that help to account for its influence. NI, as a theory, is inclusive rather than exclusive. Like other theories, it guides the selection of observations and privileges certain empirical insights over others; but its internal pluralism opens up a wide and deep horizon of concerns in the study of political executives.

Second, it is important to recognize at the outset that NI is something of a misnomer. NI did not 'rediscover' the centrality of institutions—in our case: executive institutions. Rather what was novel was the stress on the importance of the linkage between institutions and organizations. This emphasis on the organizational foundations of politics and the interweaving of institutional and organizational dimensions is well-captured in the titles of the foundational text by James March and Johan Olsen *The New Institutionalism: Organisational Factors in Political Life* of 1989; and of Paul J. DiMaggio and Walter W. Powell's highly influential edited volume *The New Institutionalism in Organisational Analysis* of 1991. Thus, NI has been, at heart, an organizational institutionalism (for an excellent recent survey, see Greenwood et al. 2017b). As Sverdrup and Trondal put it in a volume dedicated to the analysis of the 'organisational dimension to politics':

> Organizational variables regulate, constitute and construct the decision-making processes that emerge within political institutions, ultimately affecting the decisions being made. By focusing on dimensions like formal organizational structures, role, routines, and standard operating procedures, physical structures, demography and recruitment, organizational theory has succeeded in explaining decision-making processes and human behaviour.   (Sverdrup and Trondal 2008: 9)

As will be explained in the next section, this systematic attention paid to the interaction of institutional and organizational factors makes NI especially well-suited to the study of political executives.

Third, and following on from the previous point, NI manages to capture not just the dual nature of executives as both institutions and organizations, but also their dual nature as both governments and administrations. For example, cabinets are at the heart of government, as are prime minister's offices or ministries; as such they are infused with political power. But cabinet offices, chief executive offices, or ministries are also public administrations in which political and administrative rationalities are often in tension and sometimes clash openly. As a consequence, as Lodge and Wegrich (2012b) under-line, the study of political executives and of executive politics requires paying attention to both 'the administrative factor in political life' and 'the political factor in administra-tive life' (see also Lodge and Wegrich 2012a).

The strong orientation of NI to understanding the administrative factor in politics makes it highly fruitful when it comes to analysing executive settings in which the dis-tinction between politics and administration is ambiguous. The European Commission is a case in point (see also Chapter 33 in this volume). It is not surprising, therefore, that the administrative culture within the Commission (Ban 2013), its role as a corner stone of 'the emergent European executive order' (Trondal 2010) and of a 'common political order' (Trondal 2017), and also its 'normalization' as an executive that balances 'politics and bureaucracy' (Wille 2013) have attracted much NI-oriented scholarly attention.

Fourth, NI is open to empirical approaches that combine the systematic analysis of intra-institutional and intra-organizational perspectives with concerns about the porosity of institutional-organizational boundaries and interinstitutional and interor-ganizational connectedness. Thus, NI is closely identified with the study of institutional-organizational networks and organizational fields rather than understanding individual institutions and organizations as discrete objects of analysis. As a recent review of the development of scholarship on organizational fields (Wooten and Hofman 2017) points out, 'the central construct of neo-institutional theory has been the *organizational field*' (emphasis in the original), defined by the density of exchanges amongst the member organizations and shared meanings. Importantly, '[t]he bfehaviour of organizations within fields was said to be guided by *institutions*: the cultural-cognitive, normative and regulatory structures that provided stability and collective meaning to social behaviour' (p. 57; emphasis in the original).

At least in the European context, this foundational orientation of NI towards under-standing the connectedness of institutions and organizations has proved crucial. Thus, NI has established a theoretical framework that has done much to explain the emergence and operation of European multi-level executive politics (e.g. Egeberg 2006); the impact on European integration on national executives, that is, Europeanization (e.g. Goetz and Meyer-Sahling 2008; Meyer-Sahling and van Stolk 2015); the workings of vertically and horizontally integrated executive-administrative 'spaces' (see, e.g., Heidbreder 2011; Trondal and Peters 2015) and a 'European administrative system' (Bauer and Trondal 2015); or the coordination between national ministries and inter-national organizations (see, e.g., Benz et al. 2016a, 2016b). NI has a basic affinity to the study of multi-level settings characterized by intense exchanges across institutional and organizational boundaries.

In sum, it is not difficult to see why NI proves so attractive to scholars of political executives and executive politics. The following sets out the NI agenda as it relates to political executives in more detail and highlights key NI insights (section 3.2). The discussion then notes developments that pose a challenge to the explanatory core of NI, including 'unruly' actors and systemic 'turbulence' (section 3.3), before concluding (section 3.4).

3.2 STATE OF THE DISCIPLINE: AGENDA AND INSIGHTS

The study of political executives, executive politics, and very closely related topics, such as political leadership (Helms 2012a, 2012b; Rhodes and 't Hart 2014), encompasses a broad range of substantive concerns, as set out in Chapter 1, which introduces this volume. They include, in particular, the developmental trajectories of executives, their composition and inner workings, their interrelationships in national and international political contexts, and the effects of executives, notably on policy, representation, and legitimacy. The following sketch of the NI agenda as it relates specifically to political executives focuses on those substantive concerns that have an especially close affinity to NI, that is, where NI is making distinct contributions to executive scholarship (see also Peters 2008; Helms 2014). These contributions can be grouped under three broad headings: political executives as institutions and organizations; actors in political executives; and institutional-organizational effects.

3.2.1 Political Executives as Institutions and Organizations

Political executives are constituted by, and operate on the basis of, elaborate sets of formal and informal rules that govern their powers, functions, responsibilities, and prerogatives; their membership and internal division of labour; their decision-making procedures; and the relationships between the executive and other political institutions and organizations, notably parliaments, political parties and interest groups. The study of these systems of rules—that is, of institutions—notably those that are based on law (especially public law)—has long been at the heart of comparative executive studies. Even in countries such as the United Kingdom (UK), where, traditionally, there was a great deal of legal discretion in how the executive was organized and how it operated, progressive constitutionalization and judicialization have meant that formal-legal rules, as expressed, for example, in constitutional provisions relating to the government or standing orders of cabinet or individual ministries, matter centrally for executive analysis (Harlow and Rawlings 2009). The long-standing concern with the legal basis of executives at national level has been increasingly complemented by studies that have examined executive power within supra-national settings, as exemplified by Curtin's (2009) important book on the legal underpinnings of the European Union's (EU) executive power.

Executives are, at the same time, sets of organizations that confront political problems; require authority; possess formal and informal hierarchies; function on the basis of standard operating procedures and defining routines; rely on resources, notably professional staff, finance, and information, to prepare and give effect to decisions; and engage in sense-making (Weick 1995). In the context of the study of political executives, organization is, to a large extent, synonymous with the study of administration, to be precise: public administration. Of course, other types of organizations also matter, notably political parties. After all, party organizations often reach deeply into executives, sometimes to the extent of becoming interwoven, as suggested by the notion of 'party government' (Katz 1986; also see Chapter 23). Similarly, interest organizations matter critically for understanding how executives work (see recently, e.g., Dür and Matteo 2016). But NI has drawn special attention to the administrative features of executives (Goetz 2003, 2004).

The duality of executives as institutions and organizations, and the co-existence of politics and administration within executives have provided the empirical focus for much NI-inspired work on the 'core executive' (see also Chapter 1 in this volume). Thus, core executives are defined as

> all those organizations and procedures which coordinate central government policies [...] The core executive is the heart of the machine, covering the complex set of institutions, networks and practices surrounding the prime minister, cabinet, cabinet committees and their official counterparts, less formalized ministerial 'clubs' or meetings, bilateral negotiations and interdepartmental committees.
> (Rhodes 1995: 12; emphasis in the original)

The administration of core executives has, accordingly, been a central concern since the concept first gained currency in the 1990s (see, e.g., Peters et al. 2000; for a review, see Elgie 2011a).

How the relationship between politics and administrations plays out in the institutional-organizational settings of executives is a core theme in executive studies (see also Chapter 26 in this volume). Some scholars focus on policy-making. Edward C. Page's (2012) important comparative study on the policy influence of bureaucrats, building, in part, on earlier work on the British 'policy bureaucracy' (Page and Jenkins 2005), provides an outstanding example of the insights that can be generated through such a focus. Others concentrate on the patterns of interactions (or non-interaction) between 'politicians' and 'bureaucrats' (see recently, e.g., Kopecký et al. 2016). For example, Dahlström and Holmgren (2019) have investigated the determinants of the career paths of Swedish executive agency heads. They find that

> despite serving on fixed terms and under a constitution that explicitly promotes bureaucratic autonomy, impartial implementation and meritocratic recruitment,

> Swedish agency heads leave their posts at considerably greater rates following shifts in government [...] these findings indicate that even in institutional systems designed to insulate bureaucratic expertise from political control, partisan politics can drive bureaucratic turnover.   (p. 2)

A recent study on political appointees in the Norwegian executive government by Askim et al. (2017) suggests that the roles they perform can be understood as a resource exchange between ministers and their appointees, with 'the qualifications and resources appointees bring with them' as 'a significant predictor of the appointees' roles' (p. 354); but formal factors, notably 'the ministry's centrality in the government apparatus' (p. 354) matter most. Finally, a study on bureaucratic tenure by top officials in the German federal ministries found that both partisan factors and professional experience helped in accounting for the likelihood that ministers would use their formal power of forcing senior officials into early retirement (Fleischer 2016). These studies underline that it is useful to make a conceptual distinction between the institutional and organizational dimensions of executives and between their governmental and administrative dimensions; they also underline the importance of focusing on how these dimensions interact.

Attention to the administrative dimension of political executives has grown in recent decades, notably under the influence of internationalization and Europeanization. National executives have been drawn deeply into networks of international cooperation and coordination with both other national governments and international and supranational organizations. To a large extent, these inter-executive relationships are developed and sustained by national executive administrations and the administrations of international organizations. In Europe, the emergence of multi-level executive systems and the profound impact of progressive integration on national administrations have led to a proliferation of work on the 'Europeanization' of national executives over the last twenty years, with important contributions from rationalist, sociological, historical, and discursive NI. The pioneering work at ARENA in Oslo is a case in point. Led initially by Johan P. Olsen, one of the key proponents of NI, scholars closely associated with ARENA, such as Tobias Bach, Morten Egeberg, Asa Gornitzka, and Jarle Trondal, have drawn attention to the emergent European executive system and its implications for national executives.

3.2.2 Actors in Political Executives

A second core NI concern in the study of executives has been the interaction between institutional-organizational settings and individual and group behaviour, irrespective of whether the latter is understood to be motivated by a 'logic of consequentiality', a 'logic of appropriateness', or a combination of the two. The range of questions raised here has naturally been very broad. For example, how does the design of ministerial portfolios affect the behaviour of ministers? Or how do regulations affecting the management of the senior civil service affect the likelihood of corrupt behaviour on the part of senior officials, through the creation of 'danger zones of corruption' (Heywood and Meyer-Sahling 2013, see also Dahlström et al. 2012; Meyer-Sahling et al. 2018)? The specificity of NI in this context is that rules are not considered in isolation from organizational factors, but that the effect of rules is mediated through organizations.

Closely linked to the latter concern has been work that has looked at the longer-term influence of institutional-organizational settings on behaviour through processes of socialization (for a recent review, see Moyson et al. 2018). Again, the European multi-level experience has promoted much of the research on socialization in executive settings, and sociological NI, with its stress on how institutional-organizational settings mould the motivations, orientations, interests, preferences, and priorities of actors has been highly influential in this context (Checkel 2007; see recently, e.g., Meyer-Sahling et al. 2016). Thus, from the early 2000s, the socializing influence of the EU and multi-level executive politics emerged as a major theme both in international relations and in comparative government. One of the key themes in this work has been the implicit or explicit stress on endogeneity, that is, the extent to which individual and group interests, motivations, orientations, preferences, and priorities are moulded and remoulded by the multi-level settings, such as working groups of the Council of the European Union, in which political and administrative actors meet regularly (see recently, e.g., Michalski and Danielson 2018, with further references).

It is consistent with this orientation towards understanding how institutional-organizational settings matter for actors that NI perspectives are open to probing the individual characteristics of actors. There is a rich vein of work that looks into sociodemographic data, such as nationality, education, gender, and other characteristics—such as party membership—of both executive politicians and officials. The common thread in this work is not just to find out who governs, but, perhaps more importantly, who succeeds under which type of institutional-organizational conditions. For example, recent research has examined the impact of gender on prime ministerial careers in the EU, noting that the partisan composition of governments acts an important intermediating variable (Müller-Rommel and Vercesi 2017; also see Chapter 13 in this volume). Other studies inquire, for example, into the mix of both personal and institutional-organizational factors influencing ministerial selection (e.g. Fleischer and Seyfried 2015; Costa Pinto et al. 2018; also see Chapters 12 and 16 in this volume).

By contrast, there is less systematic and comparative work on how individuals seek to shape actively the institutional-organizational context in which they find themselves. To the extent that this question is addressed, attention has largely tended to focus on chief executives—presidents and prime ministers—and their capacity to exploit the often considerable leeway that formal institutions, such as constitutional provisions, leave in adapting the office to individual requirements. In more recent years, much of this work has been tied to questions of 'leadership' (see, e.g., Helms 2012a, 2012b) and associated concepts, such as 'leadership capital' (Bennister et al. 2015), but with few notable exceptions (Helms 2012a; Elgie 2018), genuinely comparative work has been rare.

3.2.3 Institutional-Organizational Effects

It is axiomatic to NI that institutional-organizational settings 'matter'. As Guy Peters (2008: 202) put it: 'The fundamental justification for our [...] interest in institutions is that they help to explain the performance of government, we obviously need to move beyond that (deceptively) simple statement to examine what those consequences are'. Greenwood et al. (2017a) argue in their introductory overview to the state of organizational institutionalism 'into the fourth decade':

> if there is one area that distinguishes research over the last decade from earlier trends and that promises to redirect institutional scholarship, it is the attention given to outcomes and consequences of institutions. Whereas earlier work directly or indirectly regarded the primary consequence of institutional processes rather abstractly as the accomplishment of legitimacy or the associated implications of field-level isomorphism, today concrete and significant societal outcomes [...] are vying for centre stage.   (pp. 1–2)

Whilst the latter statement does not refer specifically to research on executives, it applies with equal force to this field of enquiry.

Two types of effects have attracted particular attention: first, the linkage between institutional-organizational design and political stability; and, second, the effect of institutional-organizational factors on public policy. As regards the first of these foci, there is a long-standing debate on whether presidential executives or parliamentary executives are more likely to lead to democratic stability. The volume on the *Failure of Presidential Democracy*, edited by Juan Linz and Valenzuela (1994), or Stepan and Skach (1993) remain important reference points for those advocating parliamentarism as a superior system of government, whilst others suggest that 'it is not the institution itself but rather the conditions under which it exists that leads to the instability of presidential democracies' (Cheibub 2007: 7). Similarly, the second and third 'wave of semi-presidential studies' (Elgie 2016), focused on newly democratized countries and both recent and consolidated democracies respectively, directed attention to the linkages between different variants of semi-presidentialism and the likelihood of democratic consolidation and longer-term stability (Elgie 2011b; Sedelius and Linde 2018).

Whilst the debate on presidentialism, semi-presidentialism, and parliamentarism has centred on concerns about democratic stability, much policy-oriented work has focused on variation in executive configurations and how it matters for policy outcomes, across a range of policy domains. For example, Hallerberg, Strauch and von Hagen (2009) paid detailed attention to the institutional powers of finance ministries within executives to explain, in particular, the ability of governments to limit budgetary deficits. Adopting a similar approach, Dimitrov et al. (2006), in their work on post-Communist executives, distinguished between three types core executives—'centralized prime ministerial', 'centralized cabinet', and 'decentralized ministerial'—and found that 'centralized executives achieve lower fiscal deficits than do decentralized executives' (p. 247). Importantly, the effects of institutional-organizational variables can rarely be isolated from political conditions. Thus, the study by Hallerberg and Yläoutinen (2010) on executive institutional arrangements and budget outcomes in Central and Eastern Europe found that, 'Institutional differences lead to differences in fiscal outcomes' (p. 58); but 'the effectiveness of a given form of fiscal governance varies according to the underlying form of government in place [...] Institutions should not be examined in isolation from broader political context' (p. 59).

NI has contributed greatly to our understanding of how the subtle interactions between institutions, organizations, and actors shape the effects of political executives. Comparative work has been critical in this regard, as it has allowed research designs that provide sufficient variation in executive arrangements as causal variables. However, at least in the multi-level European context, research that probes the linkages between institutional-organizational factors, system effects (such as stability), and policy effects faces the challenge that the consequences of complex multi-level institutional-organizational fields and networks, which matter ever more in European executive politics, are more difficult to capture than in nationally-bounded settings. It is not least for this reason that the method of process-tracing, which is especially closely aligned with the historical variant of NI (see Chapter 10), is gaining growing attention in executive research, for example, in work on government formation (Andeweg et al. 2011). What Beach and Pedersen (2013) label the 'explaining-outcome' variant of process tracing is particularly relevant in this regard, in that it helps to arrive at valid causal arguments in empirical settings in which variation on independent variables cannot be built into the research design.

By now, the main observational foci in the study of political executives that are strongly associated with NI and the type of questions that NI-inspired approaches are good at tackling should have become apparent. If we take one step back and try to identify key insights that NI has helped to establish firmly in the study political executives, five deserve particular consideration.

First, NI has helped to throw into relief the interdependency between formal and informal executive institutions (see Helmke and Levitsky 2004 for a discussion of the distinction). Both matter and which matters more, or rather: which matters more under what conditions, is a question of empirical observation rather than prior theoretical assumption. The systematic attention that NI pays to informal institutions—rather than relegating them to a secondary or residual status—coupled with a broad understanding of what institutions are—notably that they are more than decision-making rules—has opened up analytical perspectives that are especially valuable in 'emerging' settings, where formal executive institutions are still in the process of taking shape; 'transitional' settings where formal institutions are subject to rapid change; or highly 'contested' settings, where formal institutions are rejected by some actors within or outside the executive and informal arrangements may be required to keep the executive working. This analytical orientation helps to generate insights across the study of executives, including their composition, internal dynamics, or external relations (Andeweg 2003).

Second, because of its organizational focus, NI has been fruitful in advancing research agendas that centre on executive resources and on how different resources may matter differently, depending on the specific institutional and organizational context (Helms 2019). The traditional foci have been on finance and personnel, in particular, but NI inspired work has also drawn attention to resources such as information, legitimacy, or trust. The importance of such an empirical focus is sketched out in an article on 'executive politics in the age of the depleted state' by Martin Lodge (2013), although the extent of depletion may be overstated. Thus, Lodge suggests that

> The notion of the depleted state defines an era in which three essential resources—legitimacy, organization and finance—are no longer capable of steering behaviours and therefore achieving outputs or outcomes. It raises central concerns for the study of executive politics as it points to the conditions affecting political and bureaucratic life.   (p. 388)

The 'depleted state' 'turns attention towards structural resources and constraints that shape the way in which executives are confronted by and address challenges posed by legitimization as well as organizational and financial resources' (pp. 388–9).

Information is amongst the resources that have received growing attention in recent years. That information matters critically for the operation of the executive is, of course, no new insight. But the advent of big data, social media, and digitalization have radically transformed the informational environment in which executives operate (Dunleavy et al. 2006; Margetts 2019) and NI can guide research into the challenges to executive organizational cultures that this entails. One important aspect of the broader question of how executives deal with information concerns practices of executive secrecy. The latter encompasses both secret executive politics—that is, aspects of executive activity intentionally concealed from the public—and the governance of executive secrecy, that is, the political processes and regulatory frameworks governing secret keeping (see Rittberger and Goetz 2018). In work on state and, more specifically, executive secrecy, actor- and interest-centred perspectives that highlight the motivations for secrecy, are complemented by institutional and organizational perspectives that focus on contestation over secrecy norms and the diversity of secrecy cultures, respectively (see Rittberger and Goetz 2018). A recent detailed examination of the relationship between British prime ministers and the UK intelligence services by Aldrich and Cormac (2016) demonstrates the vital contribution that such scholarship can make to understanding how modern political executives work.

Third, NI underlines the importance of the connectedness of executives. Coordination is a classical theme in executive studies, at both political and administrative levels (Bouckaert et al. 2010; Peters 2015). However, both the emergence of a multi-level European executive system and evidence of close interconnectedness between national executives and the administrations of international organizations have opened up new research agendas in the study of political executives to which NI, with its sensitivity to the porousness of institutional and organizational boundaries, contributes vigorously.

Fourth, NI is sensitive to the diversity of motivations of executive actors and their related action repertoires. There is more to this than the distinction between a 'logic of consequentiality' and a 'logic of appropriateness'. Not only is there more and more work that enquires into the complex motivational foundations of individual and collective behaviour, including, for example, the importance of personality traits or emotions (see also Chapter 14 in this volume). The key insight of NI is not that people and groups act for very different, and sometimes 'irrational' reasons. Rather, it draws attention to how specific institutional-organizational settings privilege some reasons over others or allow certain personality types to thrive, whilst frustrating and marginalizing others. To examine these selective effects of institutional-organizational settings, experimental work is becoming increasingly influential, notably as regards the administrative dimension of executives (James et al. 2017).

Fifth, NI draws attention to the importance of path-dependencies and of legacies in explaining both the evolution of executives and executive effects. For example, work on post-Communist executives has stressed the extent to which Communist legacies have shaped the post-1989 development of Central and Eastern European executive systems, despite the profundity of the political, economic, and social transformation (Grotz and Müller-Rommel 2015). And even where path change rather than path dependency prevailed, suppressed legacies may re-assert themselves, as suggested by studies of the development of ministerial civil services in Central and Eastern Europe (Meyer-Sahling 2011; Meyer-Sahling and Yesilkagit 2011).

3.3 CHALLENGES

NI has had a transformative impact on the study of political executives. Yet, it is facing challenges that go to its explanatory core. With a degree of simplification, the challenges to the theoretical assumptions that inform NI can be grouped under two broad headings: 'unruly' actors and 'turbulence', with implications for the qualities of executive power. To be sure: rule-breaking executive actors, external and internal turbulence, power struggles, and fundamental power shifts are nothing new to students of political executives. But there are indications that the legal, political, and ideational foundations on which mature democracies have been built may be less stable and less resilient than many had assumed. As a consequence, the constraining effects of institutional-organizational settings, making for high degrees of routinization, regularity and path dependency (Helms 2014: 198), may decline. Behaviour in executives and institutional-organizational development may become less predictable and, thus, uncertain.

3.3.1 Unruly Actors

NI, in its different variants, is heavily oriented towards rules—be they formal or informal—that interact with motivations, interests, preferences to shape the behaviour of individuals and groups. There is certainly no expectation that actors always follow rules. Students of executive politics know that deliberate rule-breaking, of, say, established procedures for the preparation of cabinet proposals, so as to gain an advantage over political rivals, is a recognized part of the behavioural repertoire of executive politicians. Playing tricks with time, for example, by springing surprises, upending usual sequences, or accelerating processes, is another well-known part of that repertoire (Goetz 2015, 2017). Moreover, multiple and, possibly, conflicting rules and rationalities may have profoundly disorienting effects. For example, under conditions of crisis and emergency, established interministerial coordination procedures may become dysfunctional, but the new rules to be followed may be unclear (or non-existent) (Boin and 't Hart 2012). Yet, if rules are to have central explanatory status, rule-breaking has to be understood as the exception rather than the norm.

But there are conditions under which the linkage between rules and behaviour may be systematically—rather than incidentally or temporarily—weakened. Four such conditions are of growing importance. First, low levels of institutionalization imply that institutions are less capable of guiding behaviour than in more highly institutionalized settings (Zubek and Goetz 2010). Whilst comparative executive studies have done much to demonstrate differences in institutional-organizational configurations, trying to document different degrees of institutionalization has proved more difficult. Second, where institutions are not supported by resources, they remain facades. For example, elaborate codes of conduct for ministers will remain dead letter without behavioural consequences, unless resources are made available to monitor, investigate, and, if necessary, sanction rule-breaking behaviour.

A third condition favouring 'unruly' behaviour exists where executive power becomes highly personalist, as, for example, in sultanistic regimes (Chehabi and Linz 1998). Much has been written about the trend towards personalization in executive politics, coupled with a trend towards the concentration of power in chief executives (see, e.g., Poguntke and Webb 2005; also see Chapter 18). Personalization implies that the institution and organization of the office becomes merged with the person of the office holder, or, in more extreme forms, even submerged. As a consequence, executive behaviour becomes less rule-bound but rather shaped by the personal traits, emotions, and volatile moods of the ruler. It is this personalization (Rahat and Kenig 2018; Cross, Katz, and Pruysers 2018) and its analytical implications that help to explain why behaviourist approaches are making a strong comeback in comparative politics, government, and public policy.

Finally, institutionalist-organizational approaches reach their limits where intentional rule-breaking and the cultivation of irrational and inappropriate behaviour become the norm, where the 'rule books' are thrown aside, and erratic or even bizarre behaviour becomes a governing technique. Where 'anything goes', 'anything can happen', and the explanatory capacity of institutional-organizational approaches is diminished.

3.3.2 Turbulence

Turbulence—whether at national levels (Margetts et al. 2016; Ansell and Trondal 2017) or in the international sphere (Katzenstein and Seybert 2018)—has emerged as a central theme in accounts of the contemporary politics of Western democracies. Turbulence is associated with a range of phenomena, such as variability, volatility, unexpectedness, uncertainty, unpredictability, inconsistency, randomness, or 'chaos'. Scholars who study political turbulence tend to stress its systemic qualities; turbulence is more than the erratic behaviour of individuals or groups. Rosenau (1990), writing about turbulence at a time of fast and far-reaching change in international politics, emphasized that 'When the system's boundaries no longer contain the fluctuations of the variables [...] anomalies arise and irregularities set it [...] regularities disappear when turbulence sets in' (p. 8).

Similarly, Margetts et al. (2016: 203–4) describe turbulence as 'one kind of a chaotic system, a dynamic system with unpredictable behaviour despite the fact that its governing rules are known and deterministic'. Some analyses focus on trying to explain the causes of turbulence. They include, for example, Margetts's et al. (2016) account of the unpredictability, instability, and unruliness of political mobilization via social media, giving rise to a 'chaotic pluralism', or Katzenstein and Seybert's (2018) recent book on 'protean power', which directs attention to the 'uncertain and unexpected' in world politics. Others, such as Ansell et al. (2017; see also Ansell and Trondal 2018) focus on how policy-makers and administrators deal with 'turbulence as interactions of events or demands that are highly variable, inconsistent, unexpected or unpredictable' (Ansell et al. 2017: 2).

At its analytical core, turbulence suggests high levels of both irregularity and variability. If turbulence is understood as an increasingly common exogenous condition under which executives operate—what Ansell and Trondal (2017) call 'environmental turbulence'—then, for students of executives, the key question is to what extent institutional-organizational responses follow detectable patterns. For example, several studies have investigated how European finance ministries have responded organizationally to the financial crisis triggered by events in 2008 (Fleischer and Parrado 2010; Parrado 2012; McCowan 2017). However, where turbulence becomes endogenous—'turbulent organizations' in the terminology of Ansell and Trondal—rules tell us increasingly little about how an executive works. If such institutional-organizational turbulence is combined with personalist, deliberately unpredictable executive leadership, NI approaches may still be able to explain longer-term institutional-organizational developmental trajectories; but they reach their limits in explaining patterns of individual and group behaviour.

Institutional-organizational turbulence, combined with voluntaristic, 'unruly' leaders intent on weakening systematically the formal and informal constraints on their offices, make for executive settings in which the only reliable rule appears to be that traditional rules and norms no longer count. Populist leaders who conceive of the institutional-organizational settings that they inherit from their predecessors primarily as a barrier between them and the 'people', an obstacle to the unfettered exercise of their electoral mandates, will have few inhibitions in attempting to reshape radically the rules under which they operate. Simply put, populism and institutional-organizational stability do not go together.

However, it is important not to treat evidence of external and internal turbulence as necessarily synonymous with an absence of any regularity. With specific reference to the study of executives, at least two NI insights should be heeded in this in this respect: the possibility of decoupling; and the institutionalization of new practices. Decoupling has long been a central concept in NI (for a recent review see Boxenbaum and Jonsson 2017). At its core, 'decoupling means that organizations abide only superficially by institutional pressure and adopt new structures without necessarily implementing the related practices' (Boxenbaum and Jonsson 2017: 80); 'organizations decouple if they experience strong coercive pressure to implement a new practice, and more so if they distrust the actor that exerts the pressure on them' (Boxenbaum and Jonsson 2017: 87). In the context of executives, it is, therefore, not unlikely that the challenge of new leaders intent on refashioning radically the institutional-organizational setting is, at least for some time, met by attempts aimed at decoupling, notably on the part of career officials. Put differently, whilst leaders may be radical and erratic, officials within the executive may seek to preserve institutional-organizational routines, notably where there is an entrenched career civil service.

It is also worth remembering that turbulence may well be followed by the institutionalization of new rules and practices that may become more visible and more authoritative over time, even if there are continuous institutional-organizational 'irritations' originating at the level of the political executive leadership. It may take the administrative parts of the executive and the organizations constituting the immediate environment of the executive some time to understand and adjust to the new rules of the game; and the latter may be less predictable and also less consistent that those they have replaced. But even highly volatile or mercurial chief executives will not be able to operate without routinization and bureaucratization.

3.3.3 What Kind of Power?

Paying attention to the analytical implications of unruly actors and political turbulence leads to the question of how NI conceptualizes political power. After all, no other institutional-organizational setting is as closely identified with the exercise of political power as are executives.

It would be misleading to suggest that NI has been oblivious to the importance of power; but it would be equally misleading to suggest that power has been at the very centre of NI concerns. As Lawrence and Buchanan (2017) note in their recent review, 'Power, Institutions and Organizations',

Even with the close connection between power and institutions, a longstanding critique of organizational institutionalism is that it tends to downplay the role of power [...] the explicit integration of theories of power in organizational institutionalism is still underdeveloped [...] there still has been little formal engagement with existing insights on power.   (pp. 477–8)

Dowding (2009: 45) reached a similar assessment with regard to rational choice theories: 'rational choice theory provides analyses central to discussions of political and social power. Rarely, however, is the relationship between the explanations offered and power analysis made explicit.'

Lawrence and Buchanan's proposal of 'an organizing framework for understanding the multidimensional relationship between power and institutions' (p. 478) can serve to illustrate the insights to be gained from power-centred NI analysis. Thus, they distinguish between two basic institutional dynamics—'institutional control', which 'involves the effects of institutions on actors' beliefs and behaviour'; and 'institutional agency', which 'describes the work of actors to create, transform, maintain and disrupt institutions' (p. 478). Whilst institutional control is associated with 'systemic power' that makes itself felt through 'domination' and 'discipline', institutional agency is 'episodic', characterized by discrete acts, and is exercised through influence and force. Since 'conflict and contestation' are nearly always present when episodic power is exercised, 'resistance' is frequent, especially where episodic power is exercised through force (Lawrence and Buchanan 2017: 495ff.).

What are the implications of such an NI approach to the analysis of power? With specific reference to the study of political executives, two deserve highlighting. First, NI can help to clarify how different institutional-organizational executive settings encourage particular modes and forms of power, whilst making others less likely or impossible. For example, malleable executive settings with few institutional constraints on the chief executive will be associated with different modes and forms of power than those in which there are heavy limitations on chief executive agency. Second, NI has much to offer when it comes to understanding attempts at resistance to executive force, in particular. At a time when we see determined attempts at extending the boundaries of executive power—and the power of individual actors within executives—within many democratic systems, NI can direct executive research not just to charting and explaining phenomena such as power concentration and personalization, but also organizational resistance and 'damage limitation'.

3.4 CONCLUSION

NI has shaped the study of political executives over the past three decades. NI has been apt at capturing the ambiguous duality of political executives as institutions and organizations; as governmental and as administrative settings; and as collections of both impersonal offices, with legally defined powers, prerogatives, and responsibilities, and of sometimes highly idiosyncratic office-holders. In the process, we have learned a great deal about variation in the institutional-organizational characteristics of executives; their functional and dysfunctional features; the growing importance of multi-level executive fields; and the consequences of diverse executive configurations for political outputs and outcomes.

NI-inspired executive research, as it relates to Western democracies, is confronted with empirical developments that challenge expectations and assumptions; more importantly, they point to previously understudied phenomena. Unruly actors and turbulent politics combine to underline the degree to which executive settings even in consolidated democracies can be destabilized and previously broadly accepted 'logics of appropriateness' or 'logics of consequentiality' called into doubt or openly repudiated. They also underline that formal institutions can be quickly eroded if they are not sustained by congruent informal practices (Helmke and Levitsky 2004).

As far as executive research in Europe is concerned, its research agenda over the past two decades was strongly influenced by empirical trends, such as the evolution of post-Communist executives; the rise of executive power above the nation-state, most notably in the shape of the European Commission, and of multi-level executive systems; and the gradual strengthening of core executives and chief executives. In the coming years, executive research is likely to have to pay increasing attention to instances of path change rather than path-dependent development; of disruption rather than gradual adaptation; and of fundamental contestation over the powers of executives. NI provides the conceptual and theoretical tools to guide such research.

REFERENCES

Aldrich, R. and Cormac, R. (2016). *The Black Door: Spies, Secret Intelligence and British Prime Ministers*. London: Collins.

Andeweg, R. (2003). 'On Studying Governments,' in J. Hayward and A. Menon (eds) *Governing Europe*. Oxford: Oxford University Press, 30–60.

Andeweg, R., De Winter, L., and Dumont, P., (2011) (eds). *Puzzles of Government Formation: Coalition Theory and Deviant Cases*. London: Routledge.

Ansell, C. and Trondal, J. (2018). 'Governing Turbulence: An Organizational-Institutional Agenda,' *Perspectives on Public Management and Governance* 1(1): 1–15.

Ansell, C., Trondal, J., and Øgård, M. (2017) (eds). *Governance in Turbulent Times*. Oxford: Oxford University Press.

Askim, J., Karlsen, R., and Kolltveit, K. (2017). 'Political Appointees in Executive Government: Exploring and Explaining Roles Using a Large-N Survey in Norway,' *Public Administration* 95: 342–58.

Ban, C. (2013). *Management and Culture in an Enlarged European Commission: From Diversity to Unity*. Basingstoke: Palgrave Macmillan.

Bauer, M. W. and Trondal, J. (2015) (eds). *The Palgrave Handbook of the European Administrative System*. Basingstoke: Palgrave Macmillan.

Beach, D. and Pedersen, R. B. (2013). *Process-Tracing Methods: Foundations and Guidelines*. Michigan: University of Michigan Press.

Bennister, M. et al. (2015). 'Assessing the Authority of Political Office-Holders: The Leadership Capital Index', *West European Politics* 38(3): 417–40.

Benz, A., Corcaci, A., and Doser, W. J. (2016a). 'Unravelling Multi-Level Administration: Patterns and Dynamics of Administrative Coordination in European Governance', *Journal of European Public Policy* 23(7): 999–1018.

Benz, A., Corcaci, A., and Doser, W. J. (2016b). 'Multilevel Administration in International and National Contexts', in M. W. Bauer, C. Knill, and C. Eckhard (eds) *International Bureaucracy: Challenges and Lessons for Public Administration Research*. Basingstoke: Palgrave Macmillan, 151–78.

Boin, A. and 't Hart, P. (2012). 'Aligning Executive Action of Times of Adversity: The Politics of Crisis Coordination', in M. Lodge and K. Wegrich (eds) *Executive Politics in Times of Crisis*. Basingstoke: Palgrave Macmillan, 179–96.

Bouckaert, G., Peters, B. G., and Verhoest, K. (2010) (eds). *The Coordination of Public Sector Organizations: Shifting Patters of Public Management*. Basingstoke: Palgrave Macmillan.

Boxenbaum, E. and Jonsson, S. (2017). 'Isomorphism, Diffusion and Decoupling: Concept Evolution and Theoretical Challenges', in R. Greenwood, C. Oliver, T. B. Lawrence, and R. E. Meyer (eds) *The SAGE Handbook of Organizational Institutionalism*. 2nd ed. London: SAGE, 77–101.

Carstensen, M. B. and Schmidt, V. A. (2015). 'Power Through, Over and In Ideas: Conceptualizing Ideational Power in Discursive Institutionalism', *Journal of European Public Policy* 23(3): 318–37.

Chehabi, H. E. and Linz, J. (1998) (eds). *Sultanistic Regimes*. Baltimore: The Johns Hopkins University Press.

Checkel, J. T. (2007) (ed.). *International Institutions and Socialization in Europe*. Cambridge: Cambridge University Press.

Cheibub, J. A. (2007). *Presidentialism, Parliamentarism, and Democracy*. Cambridge: Cambridge University Press.

Costa Pinto, A., Cotta, M., and Tavares de Almeida, P. (2018) (eds). *Technocratic Ministers and Political Leadership in European Democracies*. Basingstoke: Palgrave Macmillan.

Cross, W. P., Katz, R., and Pruysers, S. (2018) (eds). *The Personalization of Democratic Politics and the Challenge for Political Parties*. Colchester: ECPR Press.

Curtin, D. (2009). *Executive Power of the European Union: Law, Practices, and the Living Constitution*. Oxford: Oxford University Press.

Dahlström, C. and Holmgren, M. (2019). 'The Political Dynamics of Bureaucratic Turnover', *British Journal of Political Science* 49(3): 823–36.

Dahlström, C., Lapuente, V., and Teorell, J. (2012). 'The Merit of Meritorization: Politics, Bureaucracy, and the Institutional Deterrents of Corruption', *Political Research Quarterly* 65: 656–68.

DiMaggio, P. J. and Powell, W. W. (1991) (eds). *The New Institutionalism in Organisational Analysis*. Chicago: Chicago University Press.

Dimitrov, V., Goetz, K. H., and Wollmann, H. (2006). *Governing after Communism: Institutions and Policy-Making*. Lanham: Rowman & Littlefield.

Dowding, K. (2009). 'Rational Choice Approaches', in S. R. Clegg and M. Haugaard (eds) *The SAGE Handbook of Power*. London: SAGE, 40–53.

Dunleavy, P., Margetts, H., Bastow, S., and Tinkler, J. (2006). *Digital Era Governance: IT Corporations, the State and e-Government*. Oxford: Oxford University Press.

Dür, A. and Matteo, G. (2016). *Insiders versus Outsiders: Interest Group Politics in Multi-Level Europe*. Oxford: Oxford University Press.

Egeberg, M. (2006) (ed.). *Multi-Level Union Administration: The Transformation of Executive Politics in Europe*. Basingstoke: Palgrave Macmillan.

Elgie, R. (2011a). 'Core Executive Studies Two Decades On,' *Public Administration* 89(1): 64–77.

Elgie, R. (2011b). *Semi-Presidentialism: Sub-Types and Democratic Performance*. Oxford: Oxford University Press.

Elgie, R. (2016). 'Three Waves of Semi-Presidential Studies,' *Democratization* 23(1): 49–70.

Elgie, R. (2018). *Political Leadership: A Pragmatic Institutional Approach*. Basingstoke: Palgrave Macmillan.

Fioretos, O., Faletti, T. G., and Sheingate, A. (2016) (eds). *The Oxford Handbook of Historical Institutionalism*. Oxford: Oxford University Press.

Fleischer, J. (2016). 'Partisan and Professional Control: Predictors of Bureaucratic Tenure in Germany,' *Acta Politica* 51(4): 433–50.

Fleischer, J. and Parrado, S. (2010). 'Power Distribution in Ambiguous Times: The Effects of the Financial Crisis on Executive Decision-making in Germany and Spain,' *dms—der modern staat* 3(2): 361–76.

Fleischer, J. and Seyfried, M. (2015). 'Drawing from the Pool: Determinants of Ministerial Selection in Germany,' *Party Politics* 21(5): 503–14.

Goetz, K. H. (2003). 'Executives in Comparative Context,' in J. Hayward and A. Menon (eds) *Governing Europe*. Oxford: Oxford University Press, 74–91.

Goetz, K. H. (2004). 'Regierung und Verwaltung,' in L. Helms and U. Jun (eds) *Politische Theorie und Regierungslehre: Eine Einführung in die politikwissenschaftliche Institutionenlehre*. Frankfurt a.M.: Campus, 74–96.

Goetz, K. H. (2015). 'Synchronisation demokratischen Regierens in der Europäischen Union,' in H. Straßheim and T. Ulrich (eds) *Zeit der Politik: Demokratisches Regieren in einer beschleunigten Welt*. Leviathan Sonderband 30: 132–51.

Goetz, K. H. (2017). 'Political Leadership in the European Union: A Time-Centred View,' *European Political Science* 16(1): 48–59.

Goetz, K. H. and Meyer-Sahling, J.-H. (2008). 'The Europeanisation of National Political Systems: Parliaments and Executives,' *Living Reviews in European Governance*. Bonn: Institute for European Integration Research.

Greenwood, R., Oliver, C., Lawrence, T. B., and Meyer, R. (2017a). 'Introduction: Into the Fourth Decade,' in R. Greenwood, C. Oliver, T. B. Lawrence and R. Meyer (eds) *The SAGE Handbook of Organizational Institutionalism*. 2nd ed. London: SAGE, 1–23.

Greenwood, R., Oliver, C., Lawrence, T. B., and Meyer, R. (2017b) (eds). *The SAGE Handbook of Organizational Institutionalism*. 2nd ed. London: SAGE.

Grotz, F. and Müller-Rommel, F. (2015). 'Schwache Regierungschefs? Politische Erfahrung und Amtsdauer von Premierministern in Mittel- und Osteuropa,' *Zeitschrift für Parlamentsfragen* 46(2): 310–27.

Hallerberg, M. and Yläoutinen, S. (2010). 'Political Power, Fiscal Institutions and Budgetary Outcomes in Central and Eastern Europe,' *Journal of Public Policy* 30(1): 45–62.

Hallerberg, M., Strauch, R. R., and von Hagen, J. (2009). *Fiscal Governance in Europe*. Cambridge: Cambridge University Press.

Harlow, C. and Rawlings, R. (2009). *Law and Administration*. 3rd ed. Cambridge: Cambridge University Press.

Heidbreder, E. (2011). 'Structuring the European Administrative Space: Policy Instruments of Multi-Level Administration,' *Journal of European Public Policy* 18(5): 709–27.

Helmke, G. and Levitsky, S. (2004). 'Informal Instiutions and Comparative Politics: A Research Agenda,' *Perspectives on Politics* 2(4): 725–40.

Helms, L. (2012a) (ed.). *Comparative Political Leadership*. Basingstoke: Macmillan.

Helms, L. (2012b) (ed.). *Poor Leadership and Bad Governance: Reassessing Presidents and Prime Ministers in North America, Europe and Japan*. Cheltenham: Elgar.

Helms, L. (2014). 'Institutional Analysis,' in R.A.W. Rhodes and Paul 't Hart (eds) *The Oxford Handbook of Political Leadership*. Oxford: Oxford University Press, 195–209.

Helms, L. (2019). 'When Less is More: "Negative Resources" and the Performance of Prime Ministers and Presidents,' *Politics* 39(3): 269–83.

Heywood, P. and Meyer-Sahling, J.-H. (2013). 'Danger Zones of Corruption: How Management of the Ministerial Bureaucracy Affects Corruption Risks in Poland,' *Public Administration and Development* 33(3): 191–204.

James, O. et al. (2017) (eds). *Experiments in Public Management Research: Challenges and Contributions*. Cambridge: Cambridge University Press.

Katz, R. S. (1986). 'Party Government: A Rationalistic Conception,' in F. G. Castles and R. Wildenmann (eds) *The Future of Party Government*, Volume 1: *Visions and Realities of Party Government*. Berlin: de Gruyter, 31–71.

Katzenstein, P. J. and Seybert, L. A. (2018) (eds). *Protean Power: Exploring the Uncertain and Unexpected in World Politics*. Cambridge: Cambridge University Press.

Kopecký, P. Meyer-Sahling, J. H., Panizza, F., Scherlis, G., Schuster, C., and Spirova, M. S. (2016). 'Party Patronage in Contemporary Democracies: Results from an Expert Survey in 22 Countries from Five Regions,' *European Journal of Political Research* 55(2): 416–31.

Lawrence, T. B. and Buchanan, S. (2017). 'Power, Institutions and Organizations,' in R. Greenwood, C. Oliver, T. B. Lawrence, and R. Meyer (eds) *The SAGE Handbook of Organizational Institutionalism*. 2nd ed. London: Sage, 477–506.

Linz, J. and Valenzuela, A. (1994) (eds). *The Failure of Presidential Democracy: Comparative Perspectives*, Vol. 1. Baltimore: Johns Hopkins University Press.

Lodge, M. (2013). 'Crisis, Resources and the State: Executive Politics in the Age of the Depleted State,' *Political Studies Review* 11: 378–90.

Lodge, M. and Wegrich, K. (2012a) (eds). *Executive Politics in Times of Crisis*. Basingstoke: Palgrave Macmillan.

Lodge, M. and Wegrich, K. (2012b). 'Public Administration and Executive Politics: Perennial Questions in Changing Contexts,' *Public Policy and Administration* 27(3): 212–29.

Lowndes, V. and Roberst, M. (2013). *Why Institutions Matter: The New Institutionalism in Political Science*. London: Red Globe Press.

March, J. G. and Olsen, J. P. (1989). *Rediscovering Institutions: The Organizational Basis of Politics*. New York: The Free Press.

Margetts, H. (2019). 'Rethinking Democracy with Social Media,' *The Political Quarterly* 90(S1): 107–23.

Margetts, H., John, P. Hale, S., and Yasseri, T. (2016). *Political Turbulence: How Social Media Shape Collective Action*. Princeton: Princeton University Press.

McCowan, M. (2017). 'Turbulent Times for Ministries of Finance,' in C. Ansell, J. Trondal, and M. Øgård (eds) *Governance in Turbulent Times*. Oxford: Oxford University Press, 137–58.

Meyer-Sahling, J.-H. (2011). 'The Durability of EU Civil Service Policy in Central and Eastern Europe,' *Governance* 24(2): 231–60.

Meyer-Sahling, J.-H. and van Stolk, C. (2015). 'A Case of Partial Convergence: The Europeanization of Central Government in Central and Eastern Europe,' *Public Administration* 93(1): 230–47.

Meyer-Sahling, J.-H. and Yesilkagit, K. (2011). 'Differential Legacy Effects: Four Propositions on the Impact of Historical Legacies on Administrative Reform in Europe East and West,' *Journal of European Public Policy* 18(2): 311–22.

Meyer-Sahling, J.-H., Lowe, W., and van Stolk, C. (2016). 'Silent Professionalization: EU Integration and the Professional Socialization of Public Officials in Central and Eastern Europe,' *European Union Politics* 17(1): 162–83.

Meyer-Sahling, J.-H., Mikkelsen, K. S., and Schuster, C. (2018). 'Civil Service Management and Corruption: What We Know and What We Don't,' *Public Administration* 96(2): 276–85.

Michalski, A. and Danielson, A. (2018). 'Conditions for Socialization in International Organizations: Comparing Committees of Permanent Representatives in the EU and NATO,' *Journal of International Relations and Development* 23 July: 1–25.

Moyson, S., Raaphorst, N., Groeneveld, S., and Van de Walle, S. (2018). 'Organizational Socialization in Public Administration Research: A Systematic Review and Directions for Future Research,' *The American Review of Public Administration* 48(6): 610–27.

Müller-Rommel, F. and Vercesi, M. (2017). 'Prime Ministerial Careers in the European Union: Does Gender Make a Difference?,' *European Politics and Society* 18(2): 245–62.

Page, E. C. (2012). *Policy without Politicians: Bureaucratic Influence in Comparative Perspective.* Oxford: Oxford University Press.

Page, E. C. and Jenkins, B. (2005). *Policy Bureaucracy: Government with a Cast of Thousands.* Oxford: Oxford University Press.

Parrado, S. (2012). 'The Executive at Work during Times of Crisis,' in M. Lodge and K. Wegrich (eds) *Executive Politics in Times of Crisis.* Basingstoke: Palgrave Macmillan, 197–216.

Peters, B. G. (2008). 'Institutional Theory and the Study of Political Executives,' in J. Pierre, B. G. Peters, and G. Stoker (eds) *Debating Institutionalism.* Manchester: Manchester University Press, 195–209.

Peters, B. G. (2015). *Pursuing Horizontal Management: The Politics of Public Sector Coordination.* Lawrence, KS: University of Kansas Press.

Peters, B. G. (2019). *Institutional Theory in Political Science: The New Institutionalism.* 4th ed. Cheltenham: Edward Elgar.

Peters, B. G., Rhodes, R. A. W., and Wright, V. (2000) (eds). *Administering the Summit: Administration of the Core Executive in Developed Countries.* Basingstoke: Macmillan.

Poguntke, T. and Webb, P. (2005) (eds). *The Presidentialization of Politics: A Comparative Studiy of Modern Democracies.* Oxford: Oxford University Press.

Rahat, G. and Kenig, O. (2018) (eds). *From Party Politics to Personalized Politics? Party Change and Political Personalization in Democracies.* Oxford: Oxford University Press.

Rhodes, R. A. W. (1995). 'From Prime Ministerial Power to Core Executive,' in R. A. W. Rhodes and P. Dunleavy (eds) *Prime Minister, Cabinet and Core Executive.* Basingstoke: Macmillan, 11–38.

Rhodes, R. A. W. and 't Hart, P. (2014) (eds). *The Oxford Handbook of Political Leadership.* Oxford: Oxford University Press.

Rittberger, B. and Goetz, K. H. (2018) (eds). *Secrecy in Europe*, special issue of *West European Politics* 41(4).

Rosenau, J. (1990). *Turbulence in World Politics: A Theory of Change and Continuity.* Princeton: Princeton University Press.

Schmidt, V. (2008). 'Discursive Institutionalism: The Explanatory Power of Ideas and Discourse,' *Annual Review of Political Science* 11: 303–26.

Sedelius, T. and Linde, J. (2018). 'Unravelling Semi-Presidentialism: Democracy and Government Performance in Four Distinct Regime Types,' *Democratization* 25(1): 136–57.

Stepan, A. and Skach, L. (1993). 'Constitutional Frameworks and Democratic Consolidation: Parliamentarism versus Presidentialism,' *World Politics* 46(1): 1–22.

Sverdrup, U. and Trondal, J. (2008). 'The Organizational Dimensions of Politics,' in U. Sverdrup and J. Trondal (eds) *The Organizational Dimension of Politics*. Bergen: Fagbokverlaget, 9–14.

Trondal, J. (2010). *An Emergent European Executive Order*. Oxford: Oxford University Press.

Trondal, J. (2017) (ed.). *The Rise of Common Political Order: Institutions, Public Administration and Transnational Space*. Cheltenham: Edward Elgar.

Trondal, J. and Peters, B. G. (2015). 'A Conceptual Account of the European Administrative Space,' in M. W. Bauer and J. Trondal (eds) *The Palgrave Handbook of the European Administrative System*. Basingstoke: Palgrave Macmillan, 79–92.

Weick, K. E. (1995). *Sensemaking in Organizations*. London: SAGE.

Wille, A. (2013). *The Normalization of the European Commission: Politics and Bureaucracy in the EU Executive*. Oxford: Oxford University Press.

Wooten, M. and Hoffman, A. J. (2017). 'Organizational Fields: Past, Present and Future,' in R. Greenwood, C. Oliver, T. B. Lawrence and R. Meyer (eds) *The SAGE Handbook of Organizational Institutionalism*. 2nd ed. London: SAGE, 55–74.

Zubek, R. and Goetz, K. H. (2010). 'Performing to Type? How State Institutions Matter in East Central Europe,' *Journal of Public Policy* 30(1): 1–22.

CHAPTER 4

PSYCHOLOGY AND THE STUDY OF POLITICAL EXECUTIVES

MARGARET G. HERMANN
AND JULIET KAARBO

How do the personalities and experiences of political executives shape their decision making? Under what conditions is it critical to know something about political executives to understand the behaviour of the institutions that they lead? How do contexts affect the type of political executive likely to be elected or selected for a leadership position? As these questions suggest, this chapter focuses on the study of political executives as individuals (or individuals in small groups). In contrast to rational institutionalist and sociological perspectives, we focus here on the subjectivity involved in politics and individuals' interpretations of what is happening. We are interested in viewing events through the eyes of the political executive. We explore why having a Jiang Jemin, Hu Jintao, or Xi Jinping as the head of the Communist Party in China, a Sarkozy, Hollande, or Macron as the president of France, or a Bush, Obama, or Trump as the United States (US) president might make a difference in how the government operates and what it does. Psychological approaches help us answer these questions on the importance and effects of individuals as political executives.

Using a psychological approach to study political executives means that we conceptualize institutions as collections of individuals. Such individuals include presidents, prime ministers, cabinet ministers, and authoritarian rulers sitting at the apex of the executive hierarchy as well as advisors, deputies, and members of the senior executive corps. Although most research focuses on national executives (and that is the primary focus in this chapter), political executives can be more broadly conceived to include those holding similar positions in sub-national, international, and non-governmental organizations. These individuals are all *leaders* with authority to set agendas, gather and interpret information, shape policy-making processes, establish the tone of discourse, frame political and policy debates, and contribute to policy decisions and their interpretation.

In effect, a psychological approach to political executives has leaders and leadership as its core concepts.

Also at its core, a psychological approach focuses on how political executives as leaders perceive their political environments. The defining characteristics of political environments, including institutional incentives, role expectations, and political constraints, are rarely unambiguous. They must be recognized, defined, and acted upon by leaders. Indeed, how leaders interpret their political environments often does not match how outside observers view them. The same is the case for policy and political problems which must also be defined, framed, and represented by leaders. Consider, for example, research (Beasley et al. 2001) that has shown around 75 per cent of the time leaders involved in dealing with foreign policy issues disagree about the nature of the problem, the options that are feasible, or what should happen. Note how the same event—11 September 2001 (9/11)—was framed differently by the leaders of Britain and the US. Tony Blair announced at the Labour Party Conference just hours after the Twin Towers collapsed that this was a crime against civilization—police, courts, and the rule of law were the instruments for dealing with it—while at the same time George W. Bush framed the event as an attack on America and pronounced a war on terror, engaging the military and calling forth nationalism.

A psychological approach also involves taking into account what Simon (1985) termed bounded rationality. His experimental studies of decision-making showed that individual's rationality is bounded by how they process information, what they want, the ways in which they represent the problem, their experiences, and their beliefs. In effect, decision-makers 'do not have unlimited time, resources, and information' on which to make choices that maximize their movement toward their goals (Chollet and Goldgeier 2002: 157). They 'satisfice' and settle for the first acceptable option rather than pushing for more information and a more optimal choice. Indeed, leaders, as humans, engage in slow, deliberative, focused, and what might be considered rational, thinking *only* about those aspects of their environments that are salient or important to deal with at the time and they engage in fast, more categorical and stereotypical thinking about the rest. And even when deliberative, leaders' subjective interpretations of their environments, their policy choices, and their political behaviours are influenced by their experiences and their personalities. As Kahneman (2016: 169) has observed, 'positions we favor have no costs and those we oppose no benefits.'

Finally, a psychological approach forces those studying political executives to note when the people in these roles change. New individuals may bring differences in perspectives regarding how institutional incentives, role expectations, political constraints, and problems are perceived and defined and shape action. Such changes are more endemic to politics than one might suppose. We note that a study of twenty-nine Asian countries bordering the Pacific Rim found 133 different governments in these countries during the decade 1998–2008 (Hermann and Sakiev 2017). With each new government came a change in leaders and political executives, and changes in the individual characteristics and interpretations of the political environments. For instance, where the ruling group had been more open to contextual information, it became more closed;

where it had had a more bureaucratic approach to solving problems, its successor evidenced groupthink; and where the ruling group had been a coalition, a coup led to a predominant leader.

In sum, a psychological approach to the study of political executives examines such executives as individuals and leaders, observing their subjective interpretations of their political environments, and exploring how these interpretations are influenced by their personal characteristics and experiences and, in turn, can shape government policy-making and executive action.

4.1 EVOLUTION OF A PSYCHOLOGICAL APPROACH TO POLITICAL LEADERSHIP

President Eisenhower once said: 'leadership is a condition and a concept that has been more argued about than almost any other I know.' Psychologically oriented research on political leadership reflects this and has moved across time from focusing on leaders as having a specific set of traits that made them leaders, to viewing leadership as a set of behaviours that were required for effective leadership, to leadership as interaction between what the leader is like and the nature of the context.

Roughly seventy years ago, those involved in studying political leadership, including political executives, became interested in identifying a set of traits distinct to individuals who became political leaders. These researchers were intrigued by Lasswell's (1948) research that indicated people became involved in political leadership positions to compensate for low self-esteem or low self-confidence. They wondered if we could go further and distinguish one type of executive from another—for example, those in cabinets from those in parliaments or legislatures. Armed with such information, we would be able to identify persons who were born to become political leaders and foster their careers as well as weed out those without appropriate characteristics. This line of research was fueled by Burns' (1978) description of the leadership traits involved in being a transformational leader as opposed to traits for the transactional type, as well as by Barber's (1977) description of the traits that define effective presidents. It was further promoted by wide-ranging studies of the social backgrounds of various types of political elites (e.g. Quandt 1970; Rejai and Phillips 1983).

In general, the results of these studies showed little homogeneity among political leaders and researchers became frustrated by difficulties in finding consistent patterns relating trait and biographical data to accession to positions of political leadership. At this same time, others involved in the study of political leadership thought that an examination of the behavioural characteristics of political leaders would be more fruitful. These scholars shadowed political leaders to see what they did. Could they identify behaviours that were more characteristic of effective leaders? Consider Kotter and Lawrence's (1974) studies of mayors of effective and ineffective cities in the US and

Wriggins's (1969) study of what it takes to be a successful leader of an independence movement in a decolonization period. These studies were consistent with psychologists' examinations of behaviours that were associated with particular leadership roles in business and social service organizations (Bass 1990).

Looking for traits and behaviours that characterized political leaders, researchers began to agree with President Eisenhower, coming to the conclusion that leadership was a more complicated concept than previously thought. In the process, these same researchers were discovering that who becomes a political leader involves interaction between what the leader is like and the context in which leadership is exercised. Consider that there are no leaders without some kinds of followers. So part of the answer to who becomes a political leader rests with learning more about those choosing who should lead. Moreover, leadership involves the relationship between leaders and these constituents (be they special interests, the military, party members, or the voting public) to whom leaders are accountable. And leadership is exercised in a particular context—a point in time, an institutional setting, a culture. The study of the interrelationships among these various leadership ingredients has evolved into a contingency theory of leadership (e.g. Haslam et al. 2010; Hermann 2014). This psychological approach to the study of political leadership emphasizes the importance of the 'match' between what the potential leader is like, what relevant followers or constituents want, and what the setting calls for in understanding who is likely to become a political leader. For example, individuals choose to run for offices that facilitate their particular leadership style (Browning and Jacob 1971); crisis and non-crisis situations seem to catapult different types of leaders into positions of power (Stewart 1977; Hermann and Gerard 2009); and large demographic groups, if they can be mobilized, can not only set political agendas, but can also define who can become a political leader (Winter 1987; Kotkin 2010).

4.2 Methods Used in Applying a Psychological Approach

Since it remains difficult to gain access to prime ministers, presidents, and authoritarian political leaders—to interview them or to give them psychological assessments— researchers using a psychological approach have had to become innovative. These innovations include the development of psychobiographical techniques, assessment-at-a-distance tools, comparative case studies, and the simulation of history via experiments.

4.2.1 Psychobiography

Psychobiography involves 'the systematic application of psychological theory or concepts—usually (but not always) drawn from psychoanalysis or some other variant of personality theory and research—to the explanation of certain biographical "facts"' (Winter 2003: 12–13). While some use psychobiography to describe what their subject is like generally, most employ the technique to help them understand behaviour that is puzzling, that does not fit the subject's own interests, the demands of the situation, or role or normative expectations. Consider the classic psychobiography on Woodrow Wilson by George and George (1964). These researchers sought to understand Wilson's consistent pattern across his career of undoing his accomplishments by not being able to compromise when success was possible if he did. The fight with Senator Lodge over US ratification of the League of Nations is a good example. The Georges argue that Wilson had a compulsive drive for power and domination growing out of a damaged self-esteem forged by a need for approval and respect that resulted in compulsive stubbornness when challenged.

Greenstein (1969) described three tasks that face the psychobiographer. The first is simple description of what is to be explained. What is the unusual or surprising behaviour or pattern of behaviour to be studied? In clinical terms, what are the 'presenting symptoms'? For example, why was Margaret Thatcher called the 'Iron Lady' (Genovese 2013)? The second task is to construct a psychological explanation to account for these symptoms. Post (2009) has described a number of such explanations and applied them to contemporary political leaders, such as Saddam Hussein. The third task is to trace the origins of these psychological dynamics in the leader's early experiences. Examples of this can be found in Kearns' (1976) study of President Lyndon Johnson's strong need for approval and McCullough's (1983) discussion of the 'Mommy factor' and its effect on President Harry Truman and General Douglas MacArthur.

A challenge to doing psychobiography is the number of different psychological explanations applicable to understanding a particular set of presenting symptoms. For example, Runyan (1981) finds thirteen possible extant psychological explanations intended to answer the question of why Van Gogh cut off his ear. He poses some ways of considering which explanations seem more viable than others. Psychobiographies are also susceptible to circular reasoning. Woodrow Wilson's inability to compromise resulted from his obsessive-compulsive personality, which, in turn, led him to be uninterested in compromise. As Winter (2003: 14) proposes, it is important 'to develop independent measures of the postulated psychological dynamics.' Psychobiographies also must balance showing empathy as well as detachment to the subject under study and include a sensitivity to the array of contextual, institutional, and cultural factors that may be operative.

4.2.2 Assessment-at-a-Distance

Assessment-at-a-distance tools were developed to move beyond psychobiographical case studies and to introduce objective standards of scientific measurement into the study of political elites. As noted earlier, it is difficult for researchers to gain access to political executives to give them personality tests, which are the typical way of systematically and objectively studying what people are like. Not only do political leaders not have time or tolerance for such procedures, they are inherently wary that the results, should they become public, might prove politically damaging. Content analysis of what leaders say is one way of assessing their characteristics systematically without direct access. Indeed, in this era of social media, most of what political leaders say is recorded and available online or in print. By analysing leaders' words, we can learn about them in a way that does not require their direct cooperation and we can analyse what they are like in different contexts. Computer-assisted content analysis with programs such as Atlas.ti and Profiler+ reduce the time necessary for content-based analyses and increase the reliability of the results (see, e.g., Hermann 2009; Conway et al. 2014; Schafer 2014).

Content analysis involves developing 'a set of procedures to make inferences from text' (Weber 1990: 19); it is a method 'capable of throwing light on the ways [people...] use or manipulate symbols and invest communication with meaning' (Moyser and Wagstaffe 1987: 20). Generally assessment-at-a-distance tools involve, like personality tests, arriving at scores on characteristics for a particular figure and comparing those scores to the mean and standard deviations of similar groups of leaders to see if they are high or low. For example, is the leader high or low in need for power (e.g. Winter 2003), more or less conceptually complex (e.g. Conway et al. 2014), more or less interested in engaging in cooperation with others (e.g. Schafer and Walker 2006), likely to challenge or respect constraints (see Chapter 24 in this volume), or agenda driven versus process driven in policy-making (e.g. Hermann 2003). An assumption is made that the more frequently leaders use certain words or phrases, the more salient such content is to them and the more representative it is of what they are like.

At-a-distance tools assess the 'public persona'—that person on view in the public arena. These tools, however, do let analysts compare and contrast profiles of leaders using a variety of materials—speeches, interviews, tweets, blogs, emails—to see if there are differences across these types of communication and to check how responsive the person is to the materials used. Analysts can also contextualize the materials analysed to see if leaders' characteristics change across time with experience, in different roles, in crisis as opposed to routine events, with regard to particular topics or audiences, and when directed at different targets. Moreover, one can study groups of leaders from similar or different cultures, with changes in governments, in different types of political structures, and appointed versus elected officials (e.g. Hermann and Sakiev 2017; Chapter 14 in this volume). A number of tests have been conducted to ascertain the validity of these measures of personal characteristics. Studies have shown predictive validity by relating what we know about leadership style to what governments do (e.g. Hermann and Hermann 1989; Winter 2003). Tests have also compared results measured on a set of leaders using assessment-at-a-distance tools with forecasts by people who have worked with them at the national level. Such comparisons have shown, on average, correlations of .84 (Hermann 2009).

4.2.3 Comparative Case Studies

What if we want to compare across a set of case studies in order to systematically assess a hypothesis or theoretical assertion? For example, do political leaders engage in decision-making processes in different ways if they frame a crisis situation as a surprise as opposed to an expected event (e.g. as a 9/11-type event versus an anticipated hurricane)? Structured, focused comparison is a method proposed to explore such questions across a set of cases (George and Bennett 2005). In this method, comparison across cases is focused because it only deals with certain aspects of the cases. In our example, the focus is on cases where the political executive views the crisis as a surprise and cases where the crisis is viewed as expected. Comparison is made by structuring a set of questions that are asked in each case. These questions grow out of research related to hypotheses in the study. In our example, research on crisis management and crisis decision-making would generate the structured questions. To facilitate systematic comparison among cases, researchers can also structure a set of possible answers to these questions. The result is a set of focused in-depth case studies on a particular topic as well as a potential database that facilitates systematic, and even statistical, comparison among a larger set of cases.

An example of structured, focused comparison is Jentleson's (2018) examination of peacemakers. His focus is on political leaders who have won the Nobel Peace Prize and the behaviours for which they won the prize, asking a set of 'who, why, how, and what' questions of each case and comparing various resulting actions exploring what differentiates among those who were more and less successful in establishing the changes they sought. Hermann and Dayton (2009) have explored decision-making behaviours of political executives with differing perceptions of time urgency and surprise in seventy-seven events considered to be crises by journalists, historians, and biographers. In both of these examples, researchers selected a representative sample of cases to study from a known population of cases. In the crisis study, two researchers went through each case, asking the structured set of questions as a reliability check and a check on confirmation bias (the tendency to confirm one's pre-existing views).

4.2.4 Experiments

Because it remains difficult to gain access in real time to policy-makers when they are involved in policy-making processes, the experiment has become a tool for simulating 'history' and for doing so under controlled conditions. Experiments allow us to explore causal relationships in the temporal sequence that occurs during the decision-making process and to study how policy-makers' preferences can shape what happens both in the nature of the process and resulting decisions. Experiments also provide opportunities to investigate what happens when a particular problem, process, or type of leader is absent or present and when decisions not to act are made versus when overt actions are taken. Indeed, early experiments helped us determine that political executives engage in bounded rationality (Simon 1985); that their beliefs are 'like possessions' guiding behaviour and are only reluctantly relinquished (Abelson 1986); that the more complex and important (the more life-like and ill-structured) a problem, the less decision-makers act like Bayesian information processors (Alker and Hermann 1971); and that prior knowledge about problems shapes cognition and focuses decision-making (Sylvan and Voss 1998). Probably the most influential experiments of this nature are those, conducted by Kahneman and Tversky (e.g. 1979), that led to prospect theory. Their findings indicate that how individuals frame a situation shapes how risk-averse or risk-prone they are likely to be. If political leaders perceive themselves in a domain of gains (things are going well), they are likely to be risk-averse; if their frame is in the domain of losses (things are going poorly), they are likely to be more risk-prone or risk-seeking (e.g. McDermott 2001).

These experiments focus on individuals and how they make decisions. But governments are not single individuals nor do they act as a unit. Indeed, consider the wide array of entities responsible for making policy from leaders and advisers to party standing committees, to cabinets, to parliamentary committees, to loosely structured coalitions. Of interest are the effects of aggregation as one moves from decision-making at the individual level—that of the leader—to that of a group or coalition. Here, too, experiments have proven a useful tool in helping us understand policy-making processes. Such experiments have examined the effects of being in the minority or majority in the policy-making process, the nature of the decision rule guiding decision-making (whether majority rule, consensus, or unanimity), and the nature of the advisory structure and advice (for reviews, see Kaarbo 2008; Hermann and Ozkececi-Taner 2011).

As with any methodology, there are problems encountered with experiments. For example, most of the experiments just described have been conducted in a laboratory setting and have focused on ad hoc groups, bringing participants together at one point in time rather than ongoing groups. Another problem is that most experiments have involved college students who are not currently policy-makers. Recent experiments, however, have begun to tackle these deficiencies by replicating their research with older subjects and those actually involved in policy-making, such as military officers. And there have been attempts to bring some flavour of the ongoing group into the laboratory, for instance, by having leader and delegate groups be composed of upper and lower classmen—the lower classmen assigned to represent and be accountable to the upper classmen. There continue to be questions regarding experimental realism given that policy-makers often face multiple problems, are often not responsible for identifying the problem or implementing the decision. Nevertheless, experiments continue to assist researchers in examining questions that are difficult to study in other ways.

4.3 CURRENT RESEARCH AREAS

Currently there are three broad areas of research involving psychological approaches to the study of political executives, revolving around three questions: (1) What is it we should know about political leaders to understand their behaviour? (2) What influences the behaviours of individuals aggregated into groups and coalitions? (3) In what contexts is it critical to know something about presidents, prime ministers, authoritarian leaders or other individuals in the executive? Each of these areas focuses on a different element of the psychological approach to leadership. The first question concentrates directly on leaders and their characteristics. The second is concerned with how political executives interact in political processes—on the relationships among political executives. The third focuses on the context in which political executives act and whether the context makes what they are like critical to understanding government processes and outcomes. We address each of these current research areas separately.

4.3.1 What Personal Characteristics Matter

Research on the psychology of political executives suggests five characteristics of individuals are important in understanding their behaviours: (1) their basic political beliefs and views on politics; (2) their motivations for seeking and maintaining political leadership positions; (3) their leadership styles; (4) their reactions to stress and pressure; and (5) certain background factors (e.g. their previous political experiences). In effect, political executives' rationality is bounded by these characteristics (Simon 1985).

Beliefs. One of the most direct means of understanding the relationship between what political executives are like and what they are likely to urge on their cohorts and constituents involves learning about their basic political beliefs—in other words, how they view political realities. Beliefs indicate how leaders are likely to interpret their political environments and map the political terrains in which they operate (for detailed discussion, see Chapter 24 in this volume). In effect, beliefs have implications for the goals and strategies that executives adopt as well as what aspects of political environments are likely to capture their interest and attention. Moreover, beliefs often become embodied in norms guiding the political institutions the executives are leading, framing what is 'right' and 'wrong' behaviour, and resistant to change (e.g. Hagan 2001; Feng 2006). A psychological approach to executives' beliefs focuses on the content of the beliefs and on the psychological dynamics of belief systems.

For more than a half century research on leaders' beliefs has focused on their 'operational codes'—the particular philosophical and instrumental beliefs that set executives' parameters for action (e.g. Holsti 1962; George 1969; Walker 2004; Schafer and Walker 2006; Renshon 2008). Philosophical beliefs represent leaders' understanding of the political universe (e.g. politics are inherently zero-sum); instrumental beliefs portray leaders' proclivities toward strategies for reaching goals (e.g. punishment is more effective than reward). These beliefs guide executives' perceptions of others, how they process information, and their policy choices. Malici (2006), for example, has found that German participation in the Gulf, Yugoslav, Kosovo, Afghan, and Iraqi conflicts was constrained by executives' belief systems. Recent operational code research has focused on connecting leaders' beliefs with game and role theories (Malici and

Walker 2016), comparing operational codes across cultures (Dirilen-Gumus 2016), and exploring operational code indicators of risk propensity (Macdonald and Schneider 2017). Operational code analysis is just one way that political beliefs of executives have been studied. Other approaches include cognitive mapping and image theory (see Young and Schafer 1998; Herrmann 2013).

Psychologists have found a number of reasons why beliefs are resistant to change. The resulting theories have been used to understand how executives' beliefs affect information processing during political decision-making. For example, leaders often distort information that does not align with their extant beliefs, preferring consistency in their environments to dissonance (Holsti 1962; Jervis 1976; Vertzberger 1990). Leaders are also motivated to make sense of the world in a way that protects their self-esteem or their in-group and, when making attributions, engage in common errors and biases (e.g. Lebow 1984; Johnson 2004; Kahneman 2016). Moreover, belief systems can be thought of as schemas that form cognitive structures for information processing (Larson 1985). Once others or a situation are categorized consistently with one schema, the mind, in a cognitively miserly way, ignores, blocks, or distorts schema-inconsistent information (Duelfer and Dyson 2011). Furthermore, such cognitive efficiency generates heuristics or mental shortcuts for executives, historical analogies being one shortcut used by decision-makers (Khong 1992). Recent research on information processing and the dynamics of executives' belief systems has focused on how leaders interpret signals from others (Yarhi-Milo 2013), the cognitive effects of time horizons (Krebs and Rapport 2012) and emotions (Dolan 2016), and under what conditions political executives' beliefs change or adapt to current circumstances (e.g. Malici and Malici 2005; Renshon 2008).

Motives. Leaders come to political positions with a variety of motives that often shape their interpretations of and interactions with their political environments. They may be driven to solve problems or address a cause, have a sense of obligation to serve, seek approval from others, have a need to compensate for personal shortcomings, or seek status and recognition. Motives are driven by situational awareness and the more situations that arouse a particular motive, the stronger that motive is in driving behaviour. The most developed approach to the study of political leaders' motivations is that by Winter who has adapted McClelland's (1987) research on human motivation and, in particular, the role that power, achievement, and affiliation motives play to the political arena. As Winter (e.g. 2002, 2013) argues, once in office, leaders' motivations often shape their behaviour—their interests, their interactions with others, and how they structure advisory systems. Winter's research indicates that political leaders high in need for power are willing to take risks, are strategic and can be manipulative, see politics as 'fun', are interested in having 'political experts' as advisors, engage in strong, forceful actions, and are often viewed as charismatic by their followers. Those who are high in need for achievement prefer moderate risks, use feedback to modify their behaviour, want personal control over outcomes and if they do not have such control can become frustrated and rigid, focus on reaching their goals, and engage 'technical experts' to help them succeed. Political leaders high in need for affiliation are generally cooperative and friendly but can become prickly and defensive when threatened, tend to be peacemakers and consensus builders, choose friends as advisors—those who will be loyal to them, and, as a result, are prone to scandal.

In addition to influencing political executives' behaviours, their motives can also drive them to seek leadership positions that provide them opportunities for satisfying these needs. Indeed, a number of studies have reported a match between leaders' motivations and the demands of the leadership role they occupy. Studies of Senior Executive Service officials in the US government (O'Leary et al. 2012), chief executive officers (CEOs) of transnational non-governmental organizations (Hermann and Pagé 2016), and national political leaders (Hermann and Sakiev 2017) indicate that it takes certain kinds of motivations for persons to enter into these executive positions. Moreover, those with the strongest motivation tend to seek leadership positions with the greatest likelihood of satisfying their needs (Winter 2010). In effect, there is often a fit between what the leadership position enables a leader to do and what the particular leader wants to do. The needs and interests of important constituents also influence who will be selected as a political leader. Winter (1987) has shown how US presidents were more likely to be elected if their needs matched those of the public's at that point in time, as assessed through the mass media. Others have found leaders are often forced out of their positions when their motives and those demanded by the situation differ (e.g. Hermann and Gerard 2009).

Leadership Style. Leadership style can also influence what prime ministers, presidents, and authoritarian leaders do, although more indirectly than the effects of beliefs and motives. Whereas beliefs and motives can directly impact policy, leadership style sets the tone and pattern of governing: how leaders interact with those they lead and how they act when representing those being led. For example, does the leader emphasize personal diplomacy and face-to-face meetings or does he or she prefer to work through intermediaries? Does the leader tend to work with other people or does he or she prefer to 'go it alone'? Is there an emphasis on political rhetoric and propaganda? Does the leader have a flair for the dramatic? Is the leader interested in studying problems in detail or satisfied with general information? Each of these questions focuses on key elements of leadership style (for a detailed discussion of leadership style, see Chapter 24 in this volume).

The Leadership Trait Analysis software (see https://socialscience.net) was developed to assess leadership style. This assessment-at-a-distance tool helps analysts study ways leaders interact with others by providing a surrogate measure of leadership style (Hermann 2003, 2009; Young and Hermann 2014; Hermann and Sakiev 2017). This leadership style measure has helped researchers investigate leaders' approaches to others around them, their policy-making processes, and their decisions. This area of research is expansive, covering a variety of types of executives, including US presidents; European and Israeli prime ministers; Turkish, Russian, Iranian, and sub-Saharan African leaders; and heads of the EU and the United Nations (e.g. Kaarbo and Hermann 1998; Preston 2001; Taysi and Preston 2001; Keller 2005; Dyson 2009; Kille 2006; Çuhadar et al., 2017a). Recent work using Leadership Trait Analysis has focused on prime ministers and presidents' responses to financial crises (e.g. Foster and Keller 2014;

Van Esch and Swinkels 2015; Brummer 2016; Dyson 2018) and on how changing institutional positions (e.g. from prime minister to president) affects leadership style (Çuhadar et al. 2017b). (For a review of this tool and literature, see Chapter 14 in this book.)

A leader's style can have limiting effects on those working with the leader in at least two ways. First, those around the leaders tend to cater to their stylistic preferences in order to keep open access to them. Second, there is a doppelganger effect, in that political leaders tend to surround themselves with people who are their doubles—people who have similar stylistic preferences and/or complementary styles. They select staff with whom they feel comfortable and compatible (e.g. George and Stern 1998; Preston and Hermann 2004; Mitchell 2005). It may mean that at times they look for a 'team of rivals' while at other times a group that is loyal, depending on their own leadership style (Greenstein 2009).

Reactions to Stress and Pressure. Leadership positions are often stressful because the situations leaders face generally involve uncertainty and high stakes, depend on cooperation of multiple groups and organizations, and force value trade-offs. To achieve such positions, political executives have had to learn to deal with stress. But what happens when stress becomes higher than usual or occurs in situations when executives are particularly vulnerable to stress? A large literature has developed on political leaders' reactions to stress (for reviews, see Hermann 2008; Boin et al. 2017). From this research, we know that as stress increases, leaders tend to reach conclusions more quickly, focus less on the consequences of their actions, see the present in terms of the past, rely only on close associates whose opinions and support can be counted on, and want to take direct control of decision-making processes. These reactions reduce the number of options as well as the amount and kinds of information considered and allow executives to focus more on searching for support than on dealing with the situation, enabling them to deal with stress by avoiding facing the ramifications of the problem.

How political executives are likely to respond to stress becomes particularly relevant in situations where the stress is no longer something threatening to the group, organization, or government but is threatening to them personally—that is, they have internalized the threat and their own self-esteem has become involved. Internalization often occurs in situations that pose a threat to the executives' positions, to a policy in which they have invested time and political capital, and/or to those immediately around them or to issues over which the executives have little control but for which they will be held accountable. The Iranian hostage crisis, 9/11, and the meltdown of Wall Street in 2008 have posed such situations for US presidents, the Arab spring to executives in the Middle East, and the 2011 tsunami for the leadership of Japan. When internalized, these situations and problems can become all consuming for leaders and those they lead. Other issues are forgotten or set aside and attention becomes riveted on dealing with what to the executive is a 'life or death' issue; all resources are directed toward coping with the problem. Leadership becomes focused, drawing attention of all in the political unit to what is now the leader's problem. By studying how leaders have handled this type of stressful situation through psychobiography and structured, focused comparative case studies, researchers have begun to identify which threats are likely to be internalized and how executives deal with stress once the threat is personalized (e.g. Stern 2003; Hermann and Dayton 2009; Boin et al. 2017).

Political executives with different leadership styles also respond to crises differently (Dyson and Preston 2006; Hermann and Gerard 2009; Hermann and Sakiev 2017). Unsurprisingly, those with an opportunist leadership style approach crises on a case-by-case basis—taking into account what is happening here and now. With a strategic leadership style, political executives believe themselves in a zero-sum world and focus on dealing with threats and coming out ahead. Political executives who are advocates or ideologues, though more crisis-prone, perceive that crises can be managed and, if one is vigilant, there are opportunities to be used to one's advantage. As the leader's stress increases, the effects of these leadership styles may become accentuated (Hermann 2008).

Background Factors. Political executives' backgrounds, particularly the nature of their political experiences, can also affect the kind of leadership they exercise. With experience, executives gain a sense of what will work and also which cues in the environment need to be taken into account and which are superfluous in specific situations (e.g. Dyson and Preston 2006; Saunders 2017). Moreover, political leaders are more likely to be active in areas in which they have experience and to assume control over others in these arenas. The nature of the person's first political position also has implications for future behaviour. The means by which executives acquired their first political positions and the ways in which they behaved in it can affect future leadership activities. Because it is the first, this experience is often given added significance in memory and remains especially vivid (e.g. George and George 1964; Genovese 2013; Jentleson 2018).

In addition to their experiences, executives are products of their times. What was going on when the leader was growing up, seeking that first job, and assuming responsibility? What were the problems and issues facing people moving from adolescence through early adulthood, often the time when political socialization is occurring most intensively? Put succinctly, we are all prisoners of our own experiences. Common generational experiences have an effect on those who become executives, helping to shape the norms and beliefs of both leaders and their constituents about the political environment. If not completely imbued themselves with the ideas that have shaped their generation, executives have to deal with these ideas in their constituents to retain their positions of leadership (e.g. Strategic Assessment Group 2003; Jennings 2004).

4.3.2 Factors Affecting Behaviour in Groups

While a psychological approach to the study of political executives focuses on individuals, as we recognized earlier, most political behaviour occurs in groups. Here we review research examining behaviours of executives in groups. What have we learned about how individual executives interact in groups? Research on group dynamics in policy-making, grounded in work in social psychology, has shown that groups are more than the sum of their parts; groups have emergent effects. Some areas that have been explored include: (1) influence in groups; (2) group decision-making; and (3) advisory structures.

Influence in Groups. Early on in research on groups it was learned that groups tend to come to more extreme positions when compared to members' individual inclinations before group interaction (Myers and Lamm 1976). Groups are willing to accept more risk on some occasions and to be more cautious on others than they would be if members acted individually. In effect, groups tend to polarize. This phenomenon has been found across a range of cultures and different political groups including juries and coalition cabinets (Kaarbo 2008). Group polarization stems from a variety of psychological dynamics, including persuasive arguments by leaders or in-group experts, conformity to majorities, cohesion in group identity and desire to remain a part of the group, and diffusion of responsibility (e.g. Vertzberger 1997). Characteristics of individuals comprising the group and the group's norms affect which polarization dynamic is likely to be present ('t Hart et al. 1997).

One area of research on group polarization that has received attention in both psychology and political science is minority influence. Under what conditions can a minority (those with a dissenting opinion) influence what happens in a group? This question is of particular interest in studying political executives given the number of inter-agency groups, parliamentary committees, and cabinets in the political arena. Moscovici (1976) was one of the first psychologists to become interested in this question. An important finding out of his and others' research is that minorities can influence majorities if they are consistent in their opposition, demonstrating resolve and commitment to the position they hold (De Vries and De Dreu 2001). Minority influence is even more likely if they can refute the majority's argument, if the issue is not of great personal relevance to members of the majority, and if the minority uses a shared frame to discuss the problem under review (Kaarbo 2008). When successful, minorities have been known to cognitively change the views of members of the majority, not just gain their acceptance (Brown 2000).

Group Decision-Making. A psychology-informed approach to group decision-making has had considerable impact in research on political executives. This research demonstrates that decision-making processes of groups tend toward two ends of a continuum—from groupthink where groups rush to judgment, often circling the wagons and engaging in path-dependent behaviour to that of bureaucratic politics, or polythink, where decisions are compromises or deadlocks ('t Hart et al. 1997; Hermann et al., 2001). Cohesion and consensus dominate one end of this spectrum, while conflict among members and paralysis dominate the other. In groupthink processes, members engage in excessive concurrence seeking, self-censorship, and mindguarding, which can lead to ineffective decision-making and even policy fiascos (e.g. Janis 1972; 't Hart 1994; Badie 2010; Schafer and Crichlow 2010). With polythink and bureaucratic political processes, group members have many 'ways of perceiving the same decision problem, goals, or solutions' (Mintz and Wayne 2018: 11). This generates considerable disagreement and dissension and can lead to leaks, decision paralysis, narrow consideration of policy options, and a variety of frames and reframes of the issue by those involved (e.g. Marsh 2014; Mintz and Wayne 2018).

Hermann and his colleagues (2001) proposed that loyalty is the key distinction between these two types of group decision-making. Where do the group members' loyalties lie? In groupthink processes, loyalty generally is with the group; in bureaucratic politics and divided groups, loyalty lies in outside groups that members represent. Others have found the new group syndrome, in which new group members, in the process of establishing a comfort level for expressing their opinions, can become overwhelmed by those in the group with expertise on a particular issue or problem, with the direction and control of the assigned leader, and with the search for the rules and norms governing 'appropriate' behaviour. New groups are susceptible to groupthink unless norms are set forth encouraging discussion and debate ('t Hart et al. 1997).

Advisory Structures. The chemistry and relations among individuals in advisory structures can have as much effect on policy as their preferences. Of particular concern is how executives can shape the agenda when problems and issues are being identified and often defined elsewhere and how they can keep control over agendas while delegating implementation authority to others (see Chapter 25 in this volume). Johnson (1974) proposed a typology of presidential management styles resulting in three ways of organizing advisory systems—formalistic, competitive, and collegial. In the formalistic system, authority is hierarchical with the leader at the top, information from below is funnelled through a chief-of-staff, and the focus is on finding best solutions to problems in an orderly and analytic fashion. The competitive system is relatively unstructured with the leader as the hub of the information wheel, advisors are given overlapping assignments, and conflict is encouraged in order to facilitate creative ideas and opposing viewpoints; the president makes the final decision. In the cooperative system, the president emphasizes teamwork and shared responsibility, procedures are informal with an emphasis on building consensus, and the focus is on a 'doable' solution to the problem.

Johnson's framework launched a number of research projects exploring the dimensions underlying the typology (e.g. George and Stern 1998; Preston 2001; Preston and Hermann 2004; Mitchell 2005). What factors lead executives to be organized around one or another of these advisory systems. Research has focused on how willing leaders are to tolerate conflict, their reasons for leading (e.g. a cause, power, popularity), their preferred strategies for managing information (e.g. hub of information wheel, at end of hierarchy), and their preferred strategies for managing conflict (e.g. consensus building, majority rule, leader rules). Preston (2010) further developed the typology to include presidents' interest and involvement in policy-making, their need for power and control, their experience, and how sensitive they are to outside information. Preston's framework yields eight different advisory systems that capture the wider range of advisory structures seen in modern day governments.

4.3.3 When Does Knowledge about Executives Matter?

Although executives are certainly constrained by their roles and the institutions they lead, research has identified a number of conditions when it becomes critical to know something about what executives are like to understand governing processes and outcomes. We highlight three contexts here: (1) the extent of executive experience and involvement; (2) the tendency of authority to contract to those in charge in crises; and (3) the match between what constituents want and the nature of the executive.

Experience. As discussed above, experience is an important differentiator among executives, affecting how leaders interpret and respond to events and how they structure their advisory systems. Experience brings the ability to engage in situations on a case-by-case basis and to assert and actively advocate for one's positions in policy-making processes. Experience also acts as a mediating factor for other personal characteristics of executives. With less experience, or without experience, executives are more affected by their personal predispositions such as their beliefs, motivations, and leadership style and they depend on those around them that do have experience (e.g. Hermann 2014; Saunders 2017).

Experience is even more critical to understand if an executive is highly interested and insists on being involved in policy-making. Executives who are interested in being involved but lack experience are likely to rely on and push forward their own ideas, seek advisors who are implementers not advice-givers, and want to not only frame problems but also influence how problems are resolved (Preston 2010). Without interest, on the other hand, the executive may delegate decision-making and defer to others with experience. And then it is those others' individual characteristics that become important to understand. Experience and level of interest interact to multiply the effects of individual characteristics on policy.

Crisis. Research has generally shown that there is a contraction of authority to those most accountable for policy and decision-making in times of crisis (Boin et al. 2017). Crises involve a serious threat to the values and interests of the political unit being observed, provide little time for making a response, and come with a large degree of uncertainty with regard to what is happening and what to do (Stern 2003). Contraction of authority during crises appears to happen in both decentralized and centralized political executives (Hermann and Kegley 1995; Trumbore and Boyer 2000). When the decision-making body is limited, defining the nature of the situation and reaching an initial decision regarding how to handle what is happening become the responsibility of those in charge or those individuals perceived to be most accountable for what happens.

Executives' interpretations of what is happening become very important in these situations. Indeed, how much time political leaders perceive they have available to them in which to respond and how surprised they are by the situation have been found to lead to different kinds of decision-making processes (Hermann and Dayton 2009). In other words, how executives defined crises shaped both their decision-making and decisions. For example, in seventy-seven crises that were identified as such by journalists, historians, and political scientists, when leaders perceived they had little time to respond and were surprised by the event (e.g. a 9/11-type event), they pushed to frame the event quickly, reach consensus rapidly on what to do, and implement their decision with little interest in, or reaction to, feedback regarding what they were doing. However, when executives perceived less time pressure, even if they were caught by surprise (e.g. the US reaction to the Iraqi invasion of Kuwait), they became more reflective and innovative—searching for information and persons with expertise who could help them ascertain what was happening and work on thinking outside-the-box. These executives became interested in viewing the crises as opportunities as well as threats to the institution. Interestingly, when executives anticipated the event and believed that they had plenty of time to respond, they viewed what was happening as just 'part of their job'; decision-making proceeded as usual and was more deliberative and decentralized.

Effects of Constituents. Leadership involves the relationship between those chosen to lead and their followers. It is an interaction or exchange between leaders and those constituents (be they special interests, the military, party members, fellow bureaucrats, or the voting public) to whom they are accountable. Indeed, there is a correlation of .56 on average across the last three decades between national leaders' scores on responsiveness to the political context and how democratic the government is that they lead (e.g. Hermann and Kegley 1995; Hermann and Gerard 2009; Kotkin 2010). There is a bias in the selection process in more and less democratic societies. The more democratic the society, the greater the push for voters to select leaders who are not only attuned to public opinion but also inclined to empower people and who concentrate their attention on building coalitions through bargaining and compromise. But research also suggest that in less democratic, more autocratic political systems, leaders are more likely to be selected if they espouse and are guided by a set of ideas, a particular cause, a problem to be solved, or an ideology and are good at persuading or coercing others to accept their positions and shape norms and institutions to achieve their goals.

Demographics and the political zeitgeist of the moment can also affect who becomes a political leader. Consider, for example, what will happen as the median age of populations in countries like Japan move above 50? If the older group participates in elections in numbers even roughly proportional to their size, they will increasingly influence not only the nature of issues given priority in party platforms but also the types of candidates who will be viewed as viable. Similarly, what about countries like many in the Middle East and Africa where the median age is 20 or less? Large demographic groups, if they can be mobilized, have the ability not only to set the issue agenda but also to define who can become a political leader (e.g. Kotkin 2010; *The Economist* 2016).

4.4 POTENTIAL FUTURE RESEARCH

We have overviewed what has been done to date in applying a psychological approach to the study of political executives. Where should we go from here? We have four proposals that build on and enhance previous work.

4.4.1 Broadening the Focus

Most of the research literature discussed in this chapter has focused on national political executives. In studying political executives more generally, how relevant is an understanding of executives at the national level to the study of those leading sub-national political institutions as well as managers in bureaucracies? For example, Zoli and her colleagues (2015) examined how the leadership styles of members of the US Senior Executive Corps were related to their behaviour in the formation of public-private partnerships. Differences have been found between the leadership styles of CEOs of humanitarian and development-oriented transnational non-governmental organizations (Hermann and Pagé 2016). In both cases, context affected the types of leaders exercising authority and the nature of that authority. Several researchers have explored if the leadership of international organizations bear a resemblance to that at the national level (e.g. Kille and Scully 2003; Kille 2006). Still others have studied intelligence analysts (McDermott et al. 2016), central bankers (Thies 2006), the leadership of terrorist groups (Smith 2013), and that of independence movements (Hermann and Gerard 2009). As we move outside our current tendency to focus on top national political executives, does context continue to make a difference and, if so, in a similar or different manner? Consider Winter's (2010) finding that achievement motivation is associated with entrepreneurial success for business leaders, but low approval ratings for political leaders. Broadening the focus of study not only widens our empirical scope, but also helps us identify what is distinct about national political executives.

4.4.2 Effect of Social Media

The appearance of social media in its many forms provides those studying political executives a new opportunity to learn about leadership (see Chapter 29 in this volume). The use of social media offers us another source for assessment-at-a-distance techniques, a source that is more timely and perhaps more reflective of leaders and their thoughts at the moment. Moreover, social media, particularly Twitter, has been viewed as a new, faster mode of engaging in diplomacy. Indeed, world leaders have used 'twidiplomacy' to announce a possible coup (Erdogan in Turkey), indicate an upcoming summit (Trump in the US), and say no to paying for a border wall (Pena Nieto in Mexico) (Lufkens 2017). How do the results we find with more typical kinds of materials like speeches and interviews compare with the results based on social media? Moreover, political leaders have often been frustrated by what they call 'mediated' leadership, that is, having their words, thoughts, and policies interpreted by the media and, often in their view, misinterpreted. Social media lets them have more direct access to their constituents. How reliably do social media, indeed, reflect their message and is it interpreted by their constituents as they intended?

4.4.3 Mapping Strategic Interactions

Using a psychological approach to study political executives involves learning how leaders' actions are perceived by others; leaders are involved in multiple levels of strategic interaction. Walker and his colleagues (e.g. Schafer and Walker 2006; Malici and Walker 2016) have explored how mapping the operational code beliefs of adversaries provides clues as to how each may respond to moves made by the other. Tracking such views of self and other provides insights into the overlap or non-overlap of two (or more) leaders' beliefs and their implications for behaviour by both sides in the interaction, be it a negotiation or escalating conflict. Scholars studying two-level games in multilateral and bilateral negotiations have noted that government leaders are central actors and 'gatekeepers' in these processes with some autonomy to blend interests and motivations of their own constituency with those of the leaders with whom they are negotiating (for a review, see Conceicao-Heldt and Mello 2018). How do the various personal characteristics that we have described in this chapter shape the roles that these leaders play in negotiations? Does the nature of the group or constituency the leader represents make a difference? What if we could map the leadership styles, for example, of all the leaders heading up multilateral negotiations, could we forecast if agreement is possible and, if so, the nature of any agreement?

4.4.4 New Unit of Analysis

Given the research reviewed here, the question arises as to whether we need to delve below the government as a unit of analysis and look at administrations—what the leadership is like and the ways in which it is organized. When governments change, new decision units can be activated; these may take the form of predominant leaders, various types of single groups, or coalitions. These different units can affect how domestic opposition and contextual opposition are managed, the likelihood of lasting out a term in office, the degree of control top leaders have over political processes, where attention is focused and the nature of the political agenda, and how cooperative and willing to commit their resources executives are likely to be (Hermann et al. 2001; Hermann and Sakiev 2017). Given the availability of these multiple forms of governing, we would do well to look below the government writ large and focus on the particular administration. It is not difficult to collect information to classify the nature of administrations. In country handbooks, government information services, and research on particular governments, those in the leadership of the new administration are often the topic of conversation as are the results of any election or selection process and any irregular change in who is in charge. By exploring administrations, can we begin to contextualize the government and become aware of the nuances that account for a change in response that we, as outside observers, may not have expected?

4.4.5 In Sum

We encourage others to join us in this future research. As we have argued in this chapter, the psychological approach to the study of political executives has a long and impressive record of examining executives as collections of individuals. This approach focuses on the characteristics of leaders and leadership and on individuals' subjective perceptions of their political environments. While treating contextual effects and the interaction between leaders and their contexts seriously, a psychological approach nevertheless serves as a balance to other more social, historical, rational, and institutional perspectives.

REFERENCES

Abelson, R. P. (1986). 'Beliefs Are Like Possessions,' *Journal for the Theory of Social Behavior* 16(3): 223–50.

Alker, H. A. and Hermann, M. G. (1971). 'Are Bayesian Decisions Artificially Intelligent?,' *Journal of Personality and Social Psychology* 19(1): 31–41.

Badie, D. (2010). 'Groupthink, Iraq, and the War on Terror: Explaining US Policy Shift Toward Iraq,' *Foreign Policy Analysis* 6(4): 277–96.

Barber, J. D. (1977). *The Presidential Character: Predicting Performance in the White House.* Englewood Cliffs, NJ: Prentice Hall.

Bass, B. H. (1990). *Bass and Stogdill's Handbook of Leadership: Theory, Research and Managerial Applications.* New York: Free Press.

Beasley, R., Kaarbo, J., Hermann, C. F., and Hermann, M. G. (2001). 'People and Processes in Foreign Policymaking,' *International Studies Review* 3(2): 217–50.

Boin, A., 't Hart, P., Stern, E. K., and Sundelius, B. (2017). *The Politics of Crisis Management: Public Leadership under Pressure.* 2nd ed. Cambridge: Cambridge University Press.

Brown, R. (2000). *Group Processes.* Oxford: Blackwell.

Browning, R. P. and Jacob, H. (1971). 'The Interaction Between Politicians' Personalities and Attributes of Their Roles and Political Systems,' in F. I. Greenstein and M. Lerner (eds) *A Source Book for the Study of Personality and Politics.* Chicago: Markham.

Brummer, K. (2016). '"Fiasco Prime Ministers": Leaders' Beliefs and Personality Traits as Possible Causes for Policy Fiascos,' *Journal of European Public Policy* 23(5): 702–17.

Burns, J. M. (1978). *Leadership.* New York: Harper & Row.

Chollet, D. H. and Goldgeier, M. M. (2002). 'The Scholarship of Decision Making: Do We Know How We Decide?,' in R.C. Snyder, H. W. Bruck, B. Sapin, V. M. Hudson, D. H. Chollet, and J. M. Goldgeier (eds) *Foreign Policy Decision Making Revisited.* New York: Palgrave Macmillan.

Conceicao-Heldt, E. and Mello, P. A. (2018). 'Two-Level Games in Foreign Policy analysis,' in C. G. Thies (ed.) *The Oxford Encyclopedia of Foreign Policy Analysis.* Oxford: Oxford University Press.

Conway, L. G. III, Conway, K. R., Gornick, L. J., and Houck, S. C. (2014). 'Automated Integrative Complexity,' *Political Psychology* 35(5): 603–24.

Çuhadar, E., Kaarbo, J., Kesgin, B., and Özkeçeci-Taner, B. (2017a). 'Examining Interactions Between Agents and Structures: Turkey's 1991 and 2003 Iraqi War Decisions,' *Journal of International Relations and Development* 20(1): 29–54.

Çuhadar, E., Kaarbo, J., Kesgin, B., and Özkeçeci-Taner, B. (2017b). 'Personality or Role? Comparisons of Turkish Leaders Across Different Institutional Positions,' *Political Psychology* 38(1): 39–54.

De Vries, N. K. and De Dreu, C. K. W. (2001). *Group Consensus and Minority Influence: Implications for Innovation*. Oxford: Blackwell.

Dirilen-Gumus, O. (2016). 'Cross-Cultural Comparison of Political Leaders' Operational Codes,' *International Journal of Psychology* 52(S1): 35–44.

Dolan, Jr, T. M. (2016). 'Go Big or Go Home? Positive Emotions and Responses to Wartime Success,' *International Studies Quarterly* 60(2): 230–42.

Duelfer, C. A. and Dyson, S. B. (2011). 'Chronic Misperception and International Conflict: The U.S.-Iraq Experience,' *International Security* 36(1): 73–100.

Dyson, S. B. (2009). *The Blair Identity: Leadership and Foreign Policy*. Manchester: Manchester University Press.

Dyson, S. B. (2018). 'Gordon Brown, Alistair Darling, and the Great Financial Crisis: Leadership Traits and Policy Responses,' *British Politics* 13(2): 121–45.

Dyson, S. B. and Preston, T. (2006). 'Individual Characteristics of Leaders and the Use of Analogy in Foreign Policy Decision Making,' *Political Psychology* 27(2): 265–88.

Feng, H. (2006). 'Crisis Deferred: An Operational Code analysis of Chinese Leaders across the Strait,' in M. Schafer and S. G. Walker (eds) *Beliefs and Leadership in World Politics: Methods and Applications of Operational Code Analysis*. New York: Palgrave Macmillan.

Foster, D. M. and Keller, J. W. (2014). 'Leaders' Cognitive Complexity, Distrust, and the Diversionary Use of Force,' *Foreign Policy Analysis* 10(3): 205–23.

Genovese, M. A. (2013). 'Margaret Thatcher and the Politics of Conviction Leadership,' in M. A. Genovese and J. S. Steckenrider (eds) *Women as Political Leaders*. New York: Routledge.

George, A. L. (1969). 'The Operational Code: A Neglected Approach to Political Leaders and Decision-Making,' *International Studies Quarterly* 13(2): 190–222.

George, A. L. and Bennett, A. (2005). *Case Studies and Theory Development in the Social Sciences*. Cambridge, MA: MIT Press.

George, A. L. and George, J. L. (1964). *Woodrow Wilson and Colonel House: A Personality Study*. New York: Dover Publications.

George, A. L. and Stern, E. (1998). 'Presidential Management Styles and Models,' in A. L. George and J. L. George (eds) *Presidential Personality and Performance*. Boulder, CO: Westview Press.

Greenstein, F. I. (1969). *Personality and Politics*. New York: Markham.

Greenstein, F. I. (2009). *The Presidential Difference: Leadership Style from FDR to Barack Obama*. 3rd ed. Princeton: Princeton University Press.

Hagan, J. D. (2001). 'Does Decision Making Matter? Systemic Assumptions vs. Historical Reality in International Relations Theory,' *International Studies Review* 3(2): 5–46.

Haslam, S. A., Reicher, S. D., and Platow, M. J. (2010). *The New Psychology of Leadership: Identity, Influence and Power*. Abingdon: Routledge.

Hermann, C. F., Stein, J., Sundelius, B., and Walker, S. G. (2001). 'Resolve, Accept, or Avoid: Effects of Group Conflict on Foreign Policy Decisions,' *International Studies Review* 3(2): 133–68.

Hermann, M. G. (2003). 'Assessing Leadership Style: A Traits Analysis,' in J. M. Post (ed.) *The Psychological Assessment of Political Leaders: With Profiles of Saddam Hussein and Bill Clinton*. Ann Arbor, MI: The University of Michigan Press, 178–215.

Hermann, M. G. (2008). 'Indicators of Stress in Policymakers during Foreign Policy Crises,' in R. A. Boin (ed.) *Crisis Management*, Vol. 2. Beverly Hills, CA: Sage Publications.

Hermann, M. G. (2009). 'Content Analysis,' in A. Klotz and D. Prakash. (eds) *Qualitative Methods in International Relations: A Pluralist Guide*. New York: Palgrave Macmillan, 151–67.

Hermann, M. G. (2014). 'Political Psychology,' in R. A. W. Rhodes and P. 't Hart (eds) *The Oxford Handbook of Political Leadership*. Oxford: Oxford University Press.

Hermann, M. G. and Dayton, B. W. (2009). 'Transboundary Crises through the Eyes of Policymakers: Sense Making and Crisis Management,' *Journal of Contingencies and Crisis Management* 17(4): 233–41.

Hermann, M. G. and Gerard, C. (2009). 'The Effects of Leaders and Leadership,' in B. W. Dayton and L. Kriesberg (eds) *Conflict Transformation and Peacebuilding*. New York: Routledge.

Hermann, M. G. and Hermann, C. F. (1989). 'Who Makes Foreign Policy Decisions and How: An Empirical Inquiry,' *International Studies Quarterly* 33(4): 361–87.

Hermann, M. G. and Kegley Jr, C. W. (1995). 'Rethinking Democracy and International Peace: Perspectives from Political Psychology,' *International Studies Quarterly* 39(4): 511–34.

Hermann, M. G. and Özkececi-Taner, B. (2011). 'The Experiment and Foreign Policy Decision Making,' in J. Druckman, A. Lupia, D. Kinder, and R. Lau (eds) *Handbook of Experimental Political Science*. Cambridge: Cambridge University Press.

Hermann, M. G. and Pagé, C. (2016). 'To Challenge or Respect Constraints? Leadership Style and Leadership in Non-Governmental Organizations,' *Politics and Governance* 4(2): 127–37.

Hermann, M. G. and Sakiev, A. (2017). 'Governance in Context: Understanding the Ingredients of Political Leadership,' in U. Morth, C. Parker, and F. Bynander (eds) *The Bridge Builder: Essays in Honor of Bengt Sundelius*, Vol. 47. Stockholm: Swedish Defense University.

Herrmann, R. K. (2013). 'Perceptions and Image Theory in International Relations,' in L. Huddy, D. O. Sears, and J. S. Levy (eds) *The Oxford Handbook of Political Psychology*. Oxford: Oxford University Press.

Holsti, O. R. (1962). 'The Belief System and National Images: A Case Study,' *Journal of Conflict Resolution* 6(3): 244–52.

Janis, I. (1972). *Victims of Groupthink*. Boston: Houghton Mifflin.

Jennings, M. K. (2004). 'American Political Participation as Viewed Through the Political Socialization Project,' in M. G. Hermann (ed.) *Advances in Political Psychology*. London: Elsevier, 1–15.

Jentleson, B. W. (2018). *The Peace Makers: Leadership Lessons for Twentieth-Century Statesmanship*. New York: W.W. Norton.

Jervis, R. (1976). *Perception and Misperception in International Politics*. Princeton: Princeton University Press.

Johnson, D. D. P. (2004). *Overconfidence and War: The Havoc and Glory of Positive Illusions*. Cambridge, MA: Harvard University Press.

Johnson, R. T. (1974). *Managing the White House: An Intimate Study of the Presidency*. New York: Harper Row.

Kaarbo, J. (2008). 'Coalition Cabinet Decision Making: Institutional and Psychological Factors,' *International Studies Review* 10(1): 57–85.

Kaarbo, J. and Hermann, M. G. (1998). 'Leadership Styles of Prime Ministers: How Individual Differences Affect the Foreign Policymaking Process,' *Leadership Quarterly* September 9(3): 243–63.

Kahneman, D. (2016). *Thinking, Fast and Slow*. New York: Farrar, Straus, and Giroux.

Kahneman, D. and Tversky, A. (1979). 'Prospect Theory: An Analysis of Decision Under Risk,' *Econometrics* 47(2): 263–91.

Kearns, D. (1976). 'Who Was Lyndon Baines Johnson?,' Art I: "The Man Who Would Be Loved,' *The Atlantic* May: 33–55.

Keller, J. W. (2005). 'Leadership Style, Regime Type, and Foreign Policy Crisis Behavior: A Contingent Monadic Peace?,' *International Studies Quarterly* 49(2): 205–31.

Khong, Y. F. (1992). *Analogies at War: Korea, Munich, Dien Bien Phu and the Vietnam Decisions*. Boulder, CO: Westview Press.

Kille, K. J. (2006). *From Manager to Visionary: The Secretary-General of the United Nations*. New York: Palgrave Macmillan.

Kille, K. J. and Scully, R. M. (2003). 'Executive Heads and the Role of Intergovernmental Organizations: Expansionist Leadership in the United Nations and the European Union,' *Political Psychology* 24(1): 175–98.

Kotkin, J. (2010). *The Next Hundred Million: America in 2050*. New York: Penguin.

Kotter, J. P. and Lawrence, P. R. (1974). *Mayors in Action: Five Approaches to Urban Governance*. New York: John Wiley & Sons.

Krebs, R. R. and Rapport, A. (2012). 'International Relations and the Psychology of Time Horizons,' *International Studies Quarterly* 56(3): 530–43.

Larson, D. W. (1985). *Containment: A Psychological Explanation*. Princeton: Princeton University Press.

Lasswell, H. D. (1948). *Power and Personality*. New York: Viking Penguin.

Lebow, R. N. (1984). *Between Peace and War: The Nature of International Crisis* Baltimore: Johns Hopkins University Press.

Lufkens, M. (2017). *Twidiplomacy 2017: How World Leaders Use Social Media*. New York: Burson-Marstellar.

Macdonald, J. and Schneider, J. (2017). 'Presidential Risk Orientation and Force Employment Decisions: The Case of Unmanned Weaponry,' *Journal of Conflict Resolution* 61(3): 511–36.

Malici, A. (2006). 'Germans as Venutians: The Culture of German Foreign Policy Behavior,' *Foreign Policy Analysis* 2(1): 37–62.

Malici, A. and Malici, J. (2005). 'The Operational Cods of Fidel Castro and Kim Il Sung: The Last Cold Warriors?,' *Political Psychology* 26(3): 387–412.

Malici, A. and Walker, S. G. (2016). *Role Theory and Role Conflict in US-Iran Relations*. London: Routledge.

Marsh, K. (2014). 'Obama's Surge: A Bureaucratic Politics Analysis of the Decision to Order a Troop Surge in the Afghanistan War,' *Foreign Policy Analysis* 10(3): 265–88.

McClelland, D. C. (1987). *Human Motivation*. Cambridge: Cambridge University Press.

McCullough, D. (1983). 'Mama's Boys,' *Psychology Today* March: 32–8.

McDermott, R. (2001). *Risk-Taking in International Politics: Prospect Theory in American Foreign Policy*. Ann Arbor: University of Michigan Press.

McDermott, R., Lopez, A. C., and Hatemi, P. K. (2016). 'An Evolutionary Approach to Political Leadership,' *Security Studies* 25(4): 677–98.

Mintz, A. and Wayne, C. (2018). *Polythink Syndrome: US Foreign Policy Decisions on 9.11, Afghanistan, Iraq, Iran, Syria, and ISIS*. Stanford: Stanford University Press.

Mitchell, D. (2005). *Making Foreign Policy: Presidential Management of the Decision-Making Process*. Burlington, VT: Ashgate.

Moscovici, S. (1976). *Social Influence and Social Change*. London: Academic Press.

Moyser, G. and Wagstaffe, M. (1987). *Research Methods for Elite Studies*. London: Allen and Unwin.

Myers, D. G. and Lamm, H. (1976). 'The Group Polarization Phenomenon,' *Psychological Bulletin* 83(4): 602–27.

O'Leary, R., Choi, Y., and Gerard, C. M. (2012). 'The Skill Set of the Successful Collaborator,' *Public Administration Review* 72(S1): S70–S83.

Post, J. M. (2009). 'Political Personality Profiling,' in A. Klotz and D. Prakash (eds) *Qualitative Analysis in International Relations*. New York: Palgrave.

Preston, T. (2001). *The President and His Inner Circle: Leadership Style and the Advisory Process in Foreign Affairs*. New York: Columbia University Press.

Preston, T. (2010). 'Leadership and Foreign Policy Analysis,' in R. A. Denemark (ed.) *International Studies Encyclopedia*. New York: Siley Blackwell Publishing.

Preston, T. and Hermann, M. G. (2004). 'Presidential Leadership Style and the Foreign Policy Process,' in E. R. Wittkopf and J. McCormick (ed.) *The Domestic Sources of American Foreign Policy*. New York: Rowman & Littlefield.

Quandt, W. B. (1970). 'The Comparative Study of Political Elites,' *SAGE Professional Papers in Comparative Politics*, No. 01–004. Beverly Hills, CA: SAGE Publications.

Rejai, M. and Phillips, K. (1983). *World Revolutionary Leaders*. New Brunswick, NJ: Rutgers University Press.

Renshon, J. (2008). 'Stability and Change in Belief Systems: The Operational Code of George W. Bush from Governor to Second-term President,' *Journal of Conflict Resolution* 52(6): 820–49.

Runyan, W. (1981) 'Why Did Van Gogh Cut Off His Ear? The Problems of Alternative Explanations in Psychobiography,' *Journal of Personality and Social Psychology* 40(6): 1070–7.

Saunders, E. N. (2017). 'No Substitute for Experience: Presidents, Advisors, and Information in Group Decision Making,' *International Organization* 71(S1): S219–S247.

Schafer, M. (2014). 'At-A-Distance Analysis,' in R. A. W. Rhodes and P. 't Hart (eds) *The Oxford Handbook of Political Leadership*. Oxford: Oxford University Press.

Schafer, M. and Crichlow, S. (2010). *Groupthink vs. High-Quality Decision Making in International Relations*. Columbia University Press.

Schafer, M. and Walker, S. G. (2006) (eds). *Beliefs and Leadership in World Politics: Methods and Applications of Operational Code Analysis*. New York: Palgrave Macmillan.

Simon, H. A. (1985). 'Human Nature in Politics: The Dialogue of Psychology with Political Science,' *American Political Science Review* 79(2): 293–304.

Smith, A. G. (2013). *The Relationship between Rhetoric and Terrorist Violence*. New York: Routledge.

Stern, E. K. (2003). 'Crisis Studies and Foreign Policy Analysis: Insights, Synergies, and Challenges,' *International Studies Review* 5(2): 183–205.

Stewart, L. H. (1977). 'Birth Order and Political Leadership,' in M. G. Hermann (ed.) *A Psychological Examination of Political Leaders*. New York: Free Press.

Strategic Assessment Group (2003). *The Next Generation of World Leaders*. Washington, DC: Central Intelligence Agency.

Sylvan, D. A. and Voss, J. F. (1998) (eds) *Problem Representation in Foreign Policy Decision Making*. Cambridge: Cambridge University Press.

Taysi, T. and Preston, T. (2001). 'The Personality and Leadership Style of President Khatami: Implications for the Future of Iranian Political Reform,' in O. Feldman and L. O. Valent (eds) *Profiling Political Leaders: A Cross-Cultural Studies of Personality and Behavior*. Westport: Praeger.

't Hart, P. (1994). *Groupthink in Government*. Baltimore: The Johns Hopkins University Press.

't Hart, P., Stern, E., and Sundelius, B. (1997). *Beyond Groupthink: Political Group Dynamics and Foreign Policy Policymaking*. Ann Arbor, MI: University of Michigan Press.

Thies, C. (2006). 'Bankers and Beliefs: The Political Psychology of the Asian Financial Crisis,' in M. Schafer and S. G. Walker (eds) *Beliefs and Leadership in World Politics: Methods and Applications of Operational Code Analysis*. New York: Palgrave Macmillan, 219–36.

Trumbore, P. F. and Boyer, M. A. (2000). 'Two-Level Negotiations in International Crises: Testing the Impact of Regime Type and Issue Area,' *Journal of Peace Research* 37(6): 679–98.

Van Esch, F. and Swinkels, M. (2015). 'How Europe's Political Leaders Made Sense of the Euro Crisis: The Influence of Pressure and Personality,' *West European Politics* 38(6): 1203–25.

Vertzberger, Y. (1990). *The World in Their Minds: Information Processing, Cognition, and Perception in Foreign Policy Decisionmaking*. Stanford: Stanford University Press.

Vertzberger, Y. (1997). 'Collective Risk-taking,' in P. 't Hart, E. Stern, and B. Sundelius (eds) *Beyond Groupthink. Political Group Dynamics and Foreign Policy-Making*. Ann Arbor: University of Michigan Press.

Walker, S. G. (2004). 'Role Identities and the Operational Code of Political Leaders,' in M. G. Hermann (ed.) *Advances in Political Psychology*. London: Elsevier.

Weber, R. (1990). *Basic Content Analysis*. Newbury Park, CA: Sage.

Winter, D. C. (1987). 'Leader Appeal, Leader Performance, and the Motive Profiles of Leaders and Followers: A Study of American Presidents and Elections,' *Journal of Personality and Social Psychology* 52(1): 196–202.

Winter, D. G. (2002). 'Motivation and Political Leadership,' in L. Valenty and O. Feldman (eds) *Political Leadership for the New Century: Personality and Behavior Among American Leaders*. Westport: Praeger, 25–47.

Winter, D. G. (2003). 'Assessing Leaders' Personalities: A Historical Survey of Academic Research Studies,' in J. M. Post (ed.) *The Psychological Assessment of Political Leaders*. Ann Arbor: University of Michigan Press.

Winter, D. G. (2010). 'Why Achievement Motivation Produces Success in Business but Failure in Politics: The Importance of Personal Control,' *Journal of Personality* 78(6): 1637–67.

Winter, D. G. (2013). 'Personality Profiles of Political Elites,' in L. Huddy, D. A. Sears, and J. S. Levy (eds) *The Oxford Handbook of Political Psychology*. Oxford: Oxford University Press.

Wriggins, W. H. (1969). *The Ruler's Imperative: Strategies for Political Survival in Asia and Africa*. New York: Columbia University Press.

Yarhi-Milo, K. (2013). 'In the Eye of the Beholder: How Leaders and Intelligence Communities Assess the Intentions of Adversaries,' *International Security* 38(1): 7–51.

Young, M. D. and Hermann, M. G. (2014). 'Integrative Complexity Has Its Benefits,' *Political Psychology* 35(5): 635–45.

Young, M. D. and Schafer, M. (1998). 'Is There Method in Our Madness? Ways of Assessing Cognition in International Relations,' *Mershon International Studies Review* 42(1): 63–96.

Zoli, C., Hermann, M. G., Gerard, C., Pagé, C., and Wicker, W. (2015). *Understanding Global Opportunity: Exploring the Role of the US State Department's Office of Global Partnerships in the Development of the Global Alliance for Clean Cookstoves*. Washington, DC: US Department of State.

....

CHAPTER 5

A RATIONAL CHOICE PERSPECTIVE ON POLITICAL EXECUTIVES

....

INDRIÐI H. INDRIÐASON AND
CHRISTOPHER KAM

5.1 IMPORTANCE, MAIN QUESTIONS, AND METHODS

....

5.1.1 Introduction

RATIONAL choice analysis has played a significant role in the study of executive politics. Rational choice approaches assume that individuals are rational in the sense that they possess 'well-defined' preferences and, simply put, that they try to achieve the outcome that they like the most. Even so, rational choice approaches do not require individuals to be wholly self-regarding. That is, adopting a rational choice approach does not involve making any particular assumptions about the content of individuals' preferences (although any given application must make some assumption). Rational choice analysis, thus, seeks to explain the strategies that rational actors adopt given their preferences, the preferences of other actors, and the exogenous constraints those actors face.

For the purpose of this chapter, we take 'the executive' to refer to the set of actors who exercise executive political authority. This is how most comparative political scientists would understand the term, and it explains our focus on dictators, presidents, and prime ministers. A more expansive conception of the executive might include the bureaucracy that carries out the executive's policies. This is the conception that one tends to find in public administration. Alternatively, one might cast the executive as the set of key decision-makers in a state, be they political, bureaucratic, or military actors. This is how international relations scholars often use the term, and such a definition can be useful where constitutional detail is irrelevant.[1]

We start our discussion by considering the fundamental challenges faced by a generic executive in a context-free environment, that is, where institutional rules are minimal. Bueno de Mesquita et al.'s (2003) selectorate model is a useful starting point for our discussion because it is predicated on just two assumptions: (1) that the executive—whether a monarch, dictator, or elected leader—wishes to remain in power; and (2) the executive requires the support of others—a support coalition—to remain in power. It follows that the main problems of executive politics revolve around the bargain that the executive must strike with his or her support coalition. In particular, survival requires that all parties expect *the bargain to be honoured* and that it be *implemented faithfully and correctly*. These two requirements give rise to problems of *credible commitment* and *agency-loss*, respectively. Much of the rational choice work on political executives has been done in the context of democratic rather than dictatorial regimes (though see Bueno de Mesquita et al. 2003; Gandhi 2008; Svolik 2012). We thus consider how parliamentary and presidential executives deal with the twin problems of credible commitment and agency-loss.

5.1.2 Historical Origins

The historical origins of the rational choice perspective on executive politics can arguably be traced to Machiavelli's *The Prince*. One can read *The Prince* as a handbook for early executives, one that tells them how to survive in office and to accomplish their ends given a set of commonly encountered challenges. The roots of the more explicit and formal development of rational choice approaches to the study of elites can be traced most directly back Riker's (1962) *The Theory of Political Coalitions*. While Riker did not dwell much on political executives, it laid the groundwork for the rich literature on coalition formation and duration, which are central concerns of parliamentary executives (see Chapter 15 of this volume).

One may also view the ground-breaking work in game theory and its applications to deterrence during the Cold War as having been motivated by a rational choice understanding of executive politics, although the focus was largely on the interactions of states. Allison's (1971) classic study of the Cuban Missile Crisis is an example of work in this tradition precisely because it explicitly presents the 'rational actor' model as the dominant model for analysing the behaviour of national governments. It is also worth noting that the work of some of Riker's contemporaries influenced the study of executive politics indirectly; Niskanen's (1971) work on the bureaucracy undoubtedly later

---

[1] There are, of course, a wealth of examples in the international relations literature where 'the executive' is not merely a synonym for 'the state'. The literature on two-level games (Putnam 1988) and audience costs (Fearon 1994), for example, explicitly focus on, respectively, the executive's need to negotiate with other branches of government or to be concerned with electoral considerations.

motivated the literature on the relationship between executives and their bureaucracies (also see Chapter 26 of this volume).

5.1.3 Fundamental Assumptions

Three ontological assumptions define rational choice analysis. The first assumption is that individuals have preferences. The second is that these preferences are 'well-defined' in the sense that they are complete, reflexive, and transitive. The third is that individuals are rational maximizers. That is, individuals seek to secure the best outcome possible— or alternatively, to achieve their desired goals.[2] It is on the basis of these assumptions that rational choice analyses understand observed behaviour to be rational and purposive (i.e. goal-seeking) as a matter of course. Rational choice analysis is also often associated with methodological individualism; the idea that (political) outcomes must be explained in terms of the motives and actions of individuals rather than groups. While this can be viewed as a desirable quality for theories to have—as group preferences are not necessarily well-defined—it is not unusual for rational choice analysis to focus on collective actors such as parties, cabinets, and interest groups.

The assumption that actors possess well-defined goals relates only to the existence of goals; it does not stipulate the content of those goals. Consequently, any rational choice analyses of executives must make some substantive assumption about what it is that executives want—much like any (non-rational) theory of political executives must.

Two substantive assumptions about executives' goals are common. The first is that executives are driven to maintain power. To do this the executive must build a winning coalition among the 'selectorate' (Bueno de Mesquita et al. 2003). As we note below, the definition of the selectorate and the methods the executive employs to stays in power differ across dictatorial and democratic regimes and across parliamentary and presidential regimes.

A second assumption is that executives want to influence policy. This assumption may appear incidental to the first assumption in that an executive may seek to advance certain policies because those policies help them maintain power; policy is thus valued only in an instrumental sense.[3] However, as we argue below, many of the institutional structures we observe and much of what executives do can only be explained—at least from a rational choice perspective—by assuming that executives seek to implement policies that reflect their preferences.

Rational choice approaches are often identified with formal and especially game theoretic modelling. This is misleading. The distinction between formal and non-formal approaches is a methodological one. That is, formal modelling need not proceed from

---

[2] Implicit in this third assumption is that the individual possesses a set of beliefs about the connection between actions and outcomes. These beliefs must themselves be rational in the sense that they must be based on all available evidence (Elster 1986: 4).

[3] Similarly, maintaining office can be seen as an instrument to influence policy.

rational choice assumptions. Approaches based on bounded rationality or evolutionary behaviour, for example, sometimes rely on formal modelling but are not rational choice approaches as defined above.

A common and longstanding criticism of rational choice theory is that its foundational assumptions about human psychology are manifestly false. The human mind is incapable of evaluating what are often large, complex, and inchoate sets of options to make the utility maximizing choice. Thus, humans rely on heuristics to satisfice (Simon 1947) or fall prey to a variety of psychological illusions (framing effects, status quo bias, etc.) that limit their capacity to optimize (Kahneman and Tversky 1979). A related critique is that rational choice cannot generate defensible empirical claims in part because its foundational assumptions are empirically false (Green and Shapiro 1994).

The merits of rational choice theory in general have been extensively debated elsewhere (e.g. Elster 1986; Green and Shapiro 1994; Shepsle 1995; Cox 1999). More relevant is the contrast that Allison (1971) drew between the rational actor model of executive decision-making on one hand, and organizational process and governmental politics models, on the other hand. The organizational model, inspired by Simon (1947) and March and Simon (1958), stressed the importance of set repertoires and satisficing in the decision-making process. The governmental politics model highlighted the importance of persuasion, personality, charisma, and psychology; it was motivated by Neustadt's work on the US presidency, but elements of Allison's governmental process model recall Lasswell's (1948) psychological perspective on the exercise of power. While dated and increasingly rare in modern political science, one can take these approaches as the main alternatives to a rational choice approach to political executives.

Rational choice approaches typically consider aspects of individuals' personality, for example temperament, personability, charisma, etc., to be irrelevant (for these aspects see Chapters 4 and 14 of this volume). Some aspects of personality may, of course, be modelled. For example, rational choice models routinely make assumptions about individuals' preferences for risk. However, psychological factors that render the individual's preferences ill-defined or incomplete are incompatible with rational choice approaches. Similarly, a rational choice perspective on executive politics is fundamentally incompatible with organizational approaches that cast behaviour as routine- or norm-driven. However, permitting a slight abuse of terminology, rational choice approaches can incorporate certain types of irrationality. For example, while it is typically assumed that individuals update their beliefs in Bayesian fashion when confronted with new information, other forms of updating of beliefs can be modelled (see, e.g., Hafer and Landa 2007).

If executives are driven to stay in power and to implement their preferred policies, then the obvious questions to ask are:

- What challenges do political executives face in remaining in power, and how do they respond to those challenges?
- What challenges do political executives face in implementing their preferred policies and, how do they respond to those challenges?

Selectorate theory offers a context-free answer to the first question: regardless of the nature of the regime, the executive must maintain the loyalty of a support coalition among the wider selectorate to fend off rivals. To do this, the executive must reach a bargain with potential supporters. As we discuss below, the precise nature of this bargain will depend on the regime's institutions. However, we know that if the winning coalition is very small relative to size of the selectorate, this bargain is likely to involve the distribution of private goods to supporters. If, in contrast, the winning coalition comprises a large fraction of a selectorate that is itself large, the bargain is likely to involve the provision of public goods (Bueno de Mesquita et al. 2003). The former conditions obtain in many dictatorships; the latter, in representative democracies.

Striking a bargain with a support coalition is the executive's first order of business. But from a rational choice perspective, the main 'problems' of executive politics are pursuant to this initial bargain. In particular, the bargain must be *honoured* (by both sides) and it must be *implemented*. These two requirements create problems of *credible commitment* and *agency-loss* respectively. The problems of credible commitment and agency-loss are closely related—the difference rests in which actor constitutes the threat; a party to the bargain who has power to deviate (i.e. the executive or supporters) or an 'outside' actor with their own preferences (e.g. bureaucrats or, in some cases, cabinet ministers).

5.2 Executive Politics in Democratic Regimes: Parliamentary and Presidential Executives

In order to make more specific statements about the challenges that executives face, and how they deal with those challenges, we must consider the institutional context or regime type. We limit our attention to democratic regimes as they have been the focus of the bulk of the rational choice literature on executive politics. We then consider how the problems of credible commitment and agency-loss provoke different responses in parliamentary and presidential regimes.

5.2.1 The Problem of Credible Commitment

5.2.1.1 *Parliamentary Responses to the Credible Commitment Problem*

In a parliamentary system, the executive is comprised of a prime minister and ministers, collectively designated the cabinet. The cabinet's support coalition consists of a legislative majority. The bargain between the cabinet and the legislative majority involves a legislative majority delegating control over the legislative agenda to the cabinet subject to the cabinet using this agenda control to advance the interests of the legislative majority. This bargain is threatened by moral hazard on both sides: on one hand, the cabinet may use its agenda power to advance interests other than those of the legislative majority; on the other, the legislative majority may fail to support the cabinet's legislative initiatives. A number of institutions have evolved to mitigate these credible commitment problems.

Constitutional Conventions. Parliamentary government is characterized by a set of constitutional conventions that delineate the executive's and legislature's responsibilities to one another and power over one another. These conventions can be understood as mechanisms that allow the cabinet and legislative majority to resolve their mutual credible commitment problems.

The confidence convention, for example, requires the cabinet to seek legislative support for its policy proposals and to resign should it fail to secure that support. Ostensibly, the confidence convention gives the legislative majority the power to bring down a cabinet that fails to advance the majority's interests. This view is subject to three important caveats. First, in many parliamentary systems the prime minister can subject legislative proposals to a vote of confidence. If the cabinet loses a vote of confidence, it resigns, and it is either replaced by an alternative cabinet or the legislature is dissolved, and new elections take place. To the extent that the legislative majority prefers to avoid an alternative cabinet or new elections, the prime minister can use a vote of confidence to induce legislators to support the cabinet's proposals—even when those proposals do not align with the interests of the legislative majority (Diermeier and Feddersen 1995; Huber 1996). Second, even in parliamentary systems where the prime ministers lack the authority to call a vote of confidence, the cabinet is usually allowed to offer the last amendments. Cabinet ministers can use this last amendment power to give the legislative majority a better deal than the one currently on the floor of the legislature (Heller 2001). Third, there is no requirement that the legislative majority that places the cabinet in power be identical to the legislative majority that supports the cabinet's proposals. Thus, the cabinet can survive by playing off contending legislative coalitions against one another.

Political Parties. Modern parliamentary government is party government (see Chapter 23 of this volume). One can understand political parties as another solution to the credible commitment problem that the cabinet and its legislative support coalition confront. Parliamentary parties accomplish this mainly by exerting monopoly control over the channels of election to the legislature and advancement within it. Party leaders offer their members an implicit contract: If you consistently support our preferred cabinet, we will promote you to more prestigious and influential positions within the legislature; otherwise we won't (Kam 2009). That this contract also works to bind the cabinet to its legislative support coalition is not so obvious. However, as Strøm (2000) has argued, these arrangements also operate as screening devices that prevent unreliable or disloyal party members from being promoted to the cabinet. Indeed, there is evidence to suggest that prime ministers tend to reflect the preferences of their support coalitions (Kam et al. 2010).

Coalition Government. Coalition governments are the norm in most multi-party parliamentary systems. This is of central importance: Even if political parties succeed in resolving commitment problems that exist between leaders and followers, each coalition party must consider the possibility that its partners will use their cabinet positions to advance their own partisan interests. The commitment problem thus re-emerges in a slightly different form.

The rational choice perspective understands many of the institutions and conventions that govern the formation and conduct of coalition governments as efforts to mitigate this credible commitment problem. Laver and Shepsle (1996) argue that coalition partners deal with their credible commitment problem via a convention of ministerial autonomy. Thus, each party gets to dictate policy in the portfolios that it controls. However, creating portfolio dictators results in Pareto-inefficient outcomes, that is, there exist policy compromises preferred by each coalition partners to the coalition policy. The problem with any such compromise is that each party has an incentive to renege on the compromise and impose its preferred policy in its portfolios. Coalition cabinets thus face a choice between an inefficient but self-enforcing policy agreement or an efficient but unstable policy agreement. This paradox has attracted several theoretical responses.

- The first is that coalition partners assign junior ministers in a way that allows the parties to monitor one another's portfolios (Thies 2001). Thus, a minster from party A will be paired with a junior minister from party B. The junior ministers can then report back to their parties as to whether the ministers is honouring the coalition agreement.
- A second strategy involves using legislative committees to keep tabs on one's partners (Martin and Vanberg 2005). Before a minister's bill is put to a final vote in the legislature, it passes through a legislative committee that assesses and amends the bill to ensure its compliance with the coalition agreement. The effectiveness of legislative committees may further be enhanced by pairing of cabinet ministers with committee chairs from a different coalition party (Kim and Loewenberg 2005; Carroll and Cox 2012).
- A third strategy involves writing coalition agreements that detail the polices that the coalition will pursue (Müller and Strøm 2008). These agreements cannot directly resolve the parties' credible commitment problems for the simple reason that coalition agreements are not subject to third-party enforcement—although reneging on the coalition agreement may hurt the parties' reputations as well as have electoral consequences (Eichorst 2014). Moury (2013) finds that coalitions tend to observe coalition agreements, and Indriðason and Kristinsson (2013) find that their length increases with ideological heterogeneity, which is what would be expected if they serve to constrain coalition partners.
- Finally, coalitions reduce ministerial autonomy by adopting dispute resolution mechanisms or cabinet committees charged with dealing with contentious issues.

Bowler et al. (2016) argue that the decision to adopt dispute resolution mechanism is a function of the coalition parties' ideological heterogeneity and the disparity in their legislative representation. In some instances, cabinet committees are established at the outset to address specific issues while in other instances their presence may be a response to uncertainty about the salience of issues.

It is worth observing that all of these coalition-monitoring arrangements are obsolete if cabinet portfolios are purely distributive goods—that is, the portfolio simply provides the holder with a set of perks. If the cabinet is simply a 'pie' to be shared among coalition partners, there is no reason for one partner to concern itself with how the other partners operate their portfolios. Hence, it is difficult to explain the existence of these institutions from a rational choice perspective unless one posits that executives have policy preferences.

5.2.1.2 *Presidential Responses to the Credible Commitment Problem*

Credible commitments take a slightly different form in presidential regimes. This is because presidents—in contrast to prime ministers—are popularly elected, and hence they do not rely on the support of others to retain office. Nevertheless, presidents confront some of the same problems as prime ministers because they may want to build legislative majorities to advance their policy agendas (also see Chapters 21 and 27 of this volume).

Carey and Shugart (1998) note that presidents have two strategies to obtain the policies that they want: (1) they can adopt a *legislative strategy* that involves working with the legislature; or (2) they can adopt a *prerogative strategy* that involves issuing executive decrees. Conditions that make it difficult for a president to build a legislative majority (e.g. undisciplined parties or legislative fragmentation) or to protect themselves from agency-loss (e.g. weak veto powers) make a prerogative strategy more attractive. While Carey and Shugart largely cast the president's choice in terms the attractiveness of using decrees to affect policy change, Amorim Neto (2006) notes that a legislative strategy may involve building a stable legislative coalition via the formation of a multi-party cabinet. Much like the parliamentary coalitions discussed above, such coalitions raise the issue of credible commitment. The allocation of ministerial portfolios to the president's legislative coalition partners can be seen as tool to facilitate a credible commitment to the coalition agreement. The effectiveness with which the coalition's credible commitment problem can be solved has implications for the president's decision to pursue a legislative or prerogative strategy.

The president's constitutional powers play an important role in shaping which strategy the president pursues. The president's most relevant powers in this context are the ability to veto legislation and to issue presidential decrees that have the force of law. The former represents a reactive power, that is, it can only be issued in response to the legislature's action, while the latter is a proactive power that can be wielded without the legislature's prior involvement. Both influence the balance of power between the president and the legislature. Intuitively, retroactive powers have little value to the executive when the legislature favours the status quo, whereas the ability to issue decrees can be useful. In situations where the constitution grants the executive only the power to veto legislation, the legislature is the agenda-setter (Cameron 2000; McCarty 2000). The stronger the president's veto—in terms of the number of votes required to override the president's veto—the more attractive a legislative strategy will be to the president.

Veto-powers also vary in terms of whether the president must veto the legislative bill as a whole (package veto) or can veto parts of the bill (item-veto). Generally, the item-veto, is considered to provide presidents with greater flexibility to shape legislation, for example to trim pork barrel projects from legislation (see, e.g., Carter and Schap 1987). Thus, an item-veto ought to make a legislative strategy more attractive. There are, however, reasons to think that the effects of the item-veto are more complex. As Indriðason (2011) and Palanza and Sin (2014) point out, the anticipated use of the president's item-veto will shape the original legislation. This is because one of the effects of the item-veto is to render the president's commitments non-credible: any bargain struck in the legislature that involves concessions to individual legislators can be unravelled by the president. The set of credible bargains that can be struck thus shrinks as the president's flexibility in wielding his or her veto increases. In this respect, stronger veto-power may reduce the appeal of pursuing a legislative strategy.

Stronger decree powers increase the incentives to act unilaterally. Carey and Shugart (1998) identify two aspects of executive decrees that influence their effectiveness: first, whether a decree becomes a permanent law or expires within after a set period; second, whether the degree comes into effect immediately or after some delay. Decrees are most valuable when they come into effect immediately and do not expire. In this scenario, the president is effectively a legislative agenda setter and, the legislature must respond with its own legislation if it wishes to affect the policy outcome. Thus, while the president cannot simply by-pass the legislature, his or her decree places the onus on the legislature to counter with its own legislation. This in turn requires legislators to solve a collective action problem that can be onerous—especially in fragmented legislatures where legislators depend on a personal vote rather than party labels to secure re-election (Carey and Shugart 1998; Moe and Howell 1999).

A prerogative strategy is clearly less attractive when decrees expire, but this also depends on the executive's ability to re-issue the decree (Carey and Shugart 1998). However, the difficulty or costliness of rolling certain policies back once in effect may exert pressure on the legislature to act and turn the decree into legislation. Others note that presidents may be reluctant to issue decrees that may be overturned by legislative action for a risk of harming their reputation (Neustadt 1960). Finally, there are executive decrees that do not take effect immediately but require the legislature to act within a set period to *prevent* the decree from becoming law as with the *guillotine* in France that effectively attaches, but does not force, a vote of confidence to the executive's proposal (Huber 1996). That is, under normal circumstances, the legislature must take action to turn a bill into law, whereas this form of a decree and the guillotine are similar in that both require the legislature to take an action in order to *prevent* a bill (or decree) from becoming law.

In addition to *constitutional decree authority*, presidents may also have *delegated decree authority*. This occurs when the legislature delegates law-making to the executive. Carey and Shugart (1998) argue that difficult legislative bargaining situations and lack of expertise within the legislature make delegation to presidents more likely. Concerns over agency-loss also affect the decision to delegate law-making to the president. Legislatures are less likely to delegate law-making authority when the president's preferences diverge from those of the legislative majority, for example. Similarly, delegating law-making to the president carries greater risk if the president can veto the legislature's subsequent amendments of the presidential decree, that is, strong veto-powers can obliterate the legislature's ability to exercise oversight over its agent.

5.2.2 Problems of Delegation

The second general challenge that executives face is agency-loss to actors—typically, bureaucrats—on whom the executive relies to implement its favoured policies (also see Chapter 26 of this volume). The essential structure of the problem is the same regardless of constitutional nature of the regime. Bureaucrats not only know more about the state of the world and about the costs and benefits of various policy technologies than do political executives, they sometimes also have divergent interests. Bureaucrats are therefore in a position to exploit their information and expertise to advance their own interests.

Many of the actions that prime ministers and presidents take can be understood from a rational choice perspective as efforts to limit the agency-losses they suffer at the hands of bureaucrats. This argument has a long history, and efforts to characterize the problem formally start with the public choice work of Buchanan and Tullock (1962), Niskanen (1971), Barro (1973), and Becker (1983). The actions that the executive takes to limit agency-loss differ across presidential and parliamentary regimes because the relationship between the executive, the bureaucracy, and the legislature vary across presidential and parliamentary regimes in three crucial ways.

1. Parliamentary systems are characterized by hierarchical chain of delegation, with the legislature delegating control over the policy agenda to the cabinet, and the cabinet in turn delegating policy development and implementation to bureaucratic departments, each of which is overseen by a cabinet minister Strøm (2000). In contrast, presidential systems are characterized by a chain of delegation in which the legislature develops policy and then delegates implementation of that policy to a bureaucracy that is staffed by the executive.

2. It follows that cabinet ministers in parliamentary regimes have policy-making authority that cabinet ministers in presidential systems do not. Cabinet ministers in presidential regimes are appointed and dismissed at the president's pleasure, and their task is primarily to direct bureaucratic actions in a given portfolio.

3. Finally, principle of separation of powers that underpins presidential government means that cabinet minister in presidential regimes cannot, with some exceptions, be members of the legislative branch. In contrast, the fusion of the executive and legislative branches that characterizes parliamentary government typically constrains prime ministers to choose ministers from the legislature. In a coalition government, moreover, the prime minister will likely have to accept ministers advanced by his or her coalition partners.

5.2.2.1 *Parliamentary Responses to the Delegation Problems*

One can understand some of conventions of parliamentary government as operating to limit agency-loss to bureaucrats. Many parliaments, for example, have procedures that allow legislators to put question to ministers on issues relevant to the minister's portfolio. Some parliaments also permit the legislature to censure individual ministers. These institutions ostensibly underscore the executive's on-going accountability to the legislature in parliamentary systems. However, Kam (2000) argues that an indirect effect of these rules is to incentivize ministers to keep tabs on their bureaucratic agents. In a similar vein, Berlinski et al. (2012) argue that prime ministers can use calls for ministerial resignations as signals of their ministers' performance.

Indeed, prime ministers have strong incentives to keep tabs on their ministers because the very structure of cabinet government generates significant agency problems (Andeweg 2000). This is so for two reasons. First, whilst the prime minister depends on ministers to develop and implement policy, the prime minister cannot immediately assess his or her ministers' competence or suitability for a given portfolio. The prime minister thus faces a problem of *adverse selection* (Huber and Martinez-Gallardo 2008). Second, ministers have inherently mixed-motives vis-à-vis the prime minister and government; on one hand, minister's political fortunes are tied to the government's political fortunes; on the other hand, ministers may not share the prime minister's policy preferences and may even see themselves as rivals. In this respect, the prime minister faces a problem of *moral hazard* (Kam and Indriðason 2005).

The prime minister's power to hire and fire ministers is not always sufficient to deal with these agency problems. It is not simply that coalition partners, for example, may veto a prime minister's efforts to hire or fire a given minister. The convention that ministers must be drawn from the legislature can limit the prime minister's ability to control his or her ministers even when prime ministers enjoy the unilateral authority to hire and fire ministers. Dewan and Myatt (2010) formalize this argument in a model in which ministerial effort is connected to the arrival of scandals: when ministers work hard, the rate of scandals decreases and the prime minister's utility increases; when ministers reduce their efforts, the rate of scandals increases and the prime minister's utility decreases.

Some scandals are inevitable, however, and when one strikes, the prime minister can either sack the minister or protect him or her. The direct effect of protection is to retain a talented minister in the cabinet, but its indirect effect is to induce all sitting ministers to reduce their efforts and hence to invite further scandal. Ministers do so because they see that the prime minister is likely to protect them too, and so they reason that it is irrational to continue to exert costly effort. Similarly, the direct effect of sacking a minister incentivizes sitting ministers to increase their efforts—because they appreciate that one scandal will end their careers. The indirect effects of sacking a minister, however, are to undercut ministerial effort and invite further scandals. This is so for two reasons. First, any replacement minister is less capable than his or her predecessor (else the former would have been appointed at the outset) and hence less able to avoid scandal. Second, the finite nature of the parliamentary talent pool means that the prime minister cannot commit to sacking his or her ministers indefinitely; backward induction thus leads sitting ministers to reduce their efforts.[4]

If Dewan and Myatt's work shows that the convention that ministers be drawn from the legislature dilutes prime minister's power to hire and fire ministers, another set of papers establishes that prime ministers can use their power to reshuffle ministers and restructure portfolios to limit ministerial drift. In Indriðason and Kam's (2008) model, ministers have preferences that depart from the prime minister's and can use spending in their portfolio to shift policy toward their ideal points. The authors show that prime ministers can use reshuffles to limit this agency-loss because a minister benefits from spending in his or her portfolio but pays for drift across all portfolios. In the face of a reshuffle, the minister may reduce spending in his or her current portfolio to limit the drift that the minister's successor can impose on him or her, and by extension, on the prime minister.

In Dewan and Hortala-Vallve (2011), ministers hold policy views that are in conflict with those of the prime minister. Once assigned to a portfolio, a minister gains an informational advantage over the prime minister, giving rise to an agency problem. Dewan and Hortala-Vallve show that the prime minister's power to allocate ministers to portfolios and assign tasks across portfolios is nevertheless sufficient to keep policy at the prime minister's ideal point. It is worth observing that this result, like that in Indriðason and Kam (2008), requires some heterogeneity in ministers' preferences. Taken together, then, these papers (see also Dewan and Myatt 2005) provide a rationale as to why prime ministers might prefer diverse cabinets.

There is also a view that that agency-loss to the bureaucracy is less severe in a parliamentary setting than a presidential setting because the cabinet has full control of the bureaucracy and can therefore simply dismiss underperforming or subversive bureaucratic agents or restructure the agency to ensure that it is more responsive (Moe and Caldwell 1994: 178; Horn 1995). However, Huber and Lupia (2001) show that ministerial

---

[4] Dewan and Myatt also consider what happens when the parliamentary talent pool is replenished, by elections for example. On one hand, the replenished talent pool allows the prime minister to reduce the level of protection he or she extends to ministers, and this incentivizes ministers to work hard to avoid scandal; on the other hand, sitting ministers realize that their careers are now more precarious (and hence less valuable); given that, they reduce their efforts. Which effect dominates is an empirical question.

turnover may result in a less responsive bureaucracy. If changing policy requires costly effort at the hand of the bureaucrat and if the sitting minister is likely to be replaced, the bureaucrat may prefer to ignore the sitting minister's directives to avoid having to move policy in one direction and then—possibly—having to move it back again.

5.2.2.2 *Presidential Responses to the Delegation Problems*

The roles of the executive and the legislature in the principal-agent model are flipped around in presidential systems; the legislature plays a more active and an independent role in terms of formulating policies but relies on the executive to implement those policies. Thus, delegation problems in presidential regimes tend to be somewhat more complex. Labelling the presidential executive as an agent of the legislature is not unproblematic, however, because presidential systems are defined in terms of the separation of powers, that is, the legislature neither selects the executive nor has the ability to remove him or her (except through the use of extraordinary measures). Moreover, presidents appoint their own cabinet—although cabinet appointments may require congressional confirmation.

Presidents face similar delegation problems vis-à-vis their cabinet ministers and the bureaucracy as prime ministers in parliamentary systems do. However, as delegation problems are rooted in the coincidence of two factors—diverging preferences and incomplete information—there are reasons to believe that those problems will be less severe in presidential systems. For example, the president's ability to assemble his or her own cabinet should reduce the degree to which the preferences of the president and his or her ministers diverge. Presidents can also appoint non-partisan cabinet ministers whose preferences align closely with their own.

The chief executive's independence from the legislature and its ability to select cabinet ministers has sometimes been taken to suggest that the president has relatively free rein in implementing the policies adopted by the US Congress. However, as, for example, Moreno et al. (2003), Moe and Caldwell (1994), and McCubbins et al. (1987) note, the bureaucracy in presidential systems may be better viewed as serving two principals. Given the legislature's constitutional inability to directly influence how the president conducts her business, it stands to reason that the legislature's efforts to manage the delegation problem will focus on bureaucratic oversight. McCubbins and Schwartz (1984) and McCubbins et al. (1987) argue that the apparent dominance of the executive is due to the legislature's strategic choices about how to exercise oversight. In particular, they distinguish between oversight relying on 'police patrols' (i.e. the active surveillance of the actions of executive agencies) or 'fire alarms'—(i.e. rules and procedures that allow individuals and organized interests to monitor and challenge executive agency actions) and argue that the latter represents a more effective means of oversight while giving the appearance of Congress not exercising oversight over the executive.

Bureaucratic appointments, like cabinet appointments, confront the president with adverse selection problems. In accordance with the ally principle, the president generally has an incentive to appoint top-level bureaucrats and agency heads who share her policy preferences. The delegation problem is somewhat more complicated in dual-principal situations where the decision-making authority within the bureaucracy (the receiver) relies on information held by career bureaucrats (the sender) whose incentives are, in part, shaped by the structure of the agency that was created by Congress. Gailmard and Patty (2012) consider the role that information plays in the decisions of the executive and Congress in making bureaucratic appointments and show that the legislature has an incentive to defer bureaucratic appointments to the executive; if the legislature has a say in appointing 'a sender', its best option is to appoint one whose preferences are similar to the executive's preferences. It might appear that Congress would have a clear incentive to appoint 'a sender' that shares its preferences but doing so would only serve to hinder credible communication; 'the receiver' is less likely to take information from 'a sender' whose preferences are known to be very different from his or her own. Thus, the legislature has an incentive to create or support administrative hierarchical administrative structures in which the power of appointment rests with the executive.

Much of the formal literature on delegation in presidential systems has focused on the United States. But presidential systems are far from homogeneous (see, e.g., Shugart and Carey 1992). In fact, Cox and Morgenstern (2002) consider the modal Latin American presidential system to fall somewhere in between a parliamentary system and a pure, US-style, presidential system. The main reason for this depiction of the modal Latin American presidential system is the fact that the separation between the executive and legislative branch tends to be less clear than in the US case. For example, most Latin American presidents can introduce legislation whereas in the US Congress holds agenda-setting power. In the US, cabinet members cannot also be members of Congress, whereas in some Latin American countries legislators can serve as cabinet ministers. In their review of scholarship on Latin American presidential regimes, Crisp and Botero (2004) argue that these institutional differences beg to be modelled formally.[5]

One expression of these differences is the frequency with which coalition cabinets form in Latin American presidential systems. This is indicative of presidents using their cabinet appointments to build legislative coalitions as an alternative to pursuing their policy goals using their unilateral decree powers (see Chapter 21 of this volume). This is interesting given that most Latin American presidents wield stronger decree powers than US presidents (Cox and Morgenstern 2002), and one would expect greater decree powers to render legislative and coalitional strategies less attractive to the president. Clearly, the electoral system plays an important role in this relationship, with electoral systems that encourage multi-partyism (such as those found in many Latin American countries) setting the stage for the formation of presidential coalitions.

---

[5] Most of the examples here focus on the executive veto, for example Baldez and Carey (1999); Alemán and Tsebelis (2005); and Alemán and Schwartz (2006).

5.3 FUTURE DEVELOPMENTS

We argue that the literature on political executives can in substantial part be viewed through the lens of two basic problems that have been thoroughly analysed in the rational choice approach: credible commitment and agency-loss. Both problems have clear implications for the types of bargaining over policy that takes place both among political executives and between the executive and other actors within the political system; it is difficult to make an agreement if there are reasons to think that the actors involved may renege on it or if they are unable to deliver. That is, while credible commitment and agency-loss is itself often the subject of analysis, we have sought to show that the solutions to these problems are central to executive politics. While there are areas of executive politics that we have not touched much on, such as the formation and survival of coalition cabinets (see Chapter 15 of this volume), credible commitments and agency-loss are also of central concern here. A government coalition only forms if the parties perceive that the two problems can be solved adequately (or at least better than an alternative) and it only lasts as long as that perception can be maintained.

For the most part, the literature on political executives focused on these issues is firmly grounded in rational choice theory. While it is increasingly rare that scholars identify their work as being in the rational choice tradition, its intellectual lineage is often clear through explicit references to concepts such as principals or agents or through the discussion of actors' preferences, institutions, incentives, etc. Criticism of formal modelling approaches to politics are typically criticized for going too far in their level of abstraction and failing to produce empirically verifiable predictions about many of the things that are of interest to scholars. While we do not want to engage these criticisms directly, one of the interesting things that we found in preparing this chapter was how *little* formal work there is on political executives—at least, when compared to the extensive literature that employs 'softer' rational choice approaches. This suggests to us that the value of formal rational choice approaches does not (only) rest in producing empirically verifiable hypotheses but rather in offering us ways to think about politics and political executives in novel and fruitful ways. The formulation of the principal-agent problem, for example, has shaped how we think about the relationship between politicians and bureaucrats and cabinets and ministers. Importantly, work that employs this abstract framework for thinking about delegation has also added to our understanding about politics by adding substantive nuance to the factors that influence preference divergence and information transmission, whether formally or informally. Similarly, Laver and Shepsle's (1996) model of ministers as portfolio dictators has been tremendously influential—not because it is 'correct' (as it clearly rests on some implausible assumptions) but because it highlights the issue of credible commitment in very vivid terms, which spurred a significant literature focused on how else coalitions make credible commitments.

The rational choice approach has become so embedded in the study of executive politics that it is difficult to envision a sharp change in focus—at least as long as it continues to be exploited in a useful manner as it has been over the last few decades. However, in the light of the more recent empirical work in the rational choice vein, it may be time to revisit the formal analysis of executives to incorporate some of the findings in the literature. As Crisp and Botero (2004) pointed out some while ago, formally modelling the empirical variation in institutions remains on the agenda. The literature has identified a number of strategies to circumvent the credible commitment problems, but less attention has been devoted to whether the different strategies are substitutes or complements (Indriðason and Kristinsson 2013) and how they affect coalition bargaining. Formally modelling how the different strategies interact with one another may provide insights into how they complement one another and help explain, for example, cross-national variation in their uses. There are also some gaps in our knowledge where further empirical work may provide important insights that would be valuable in formal applications. The literature on presidential executives is, for example, largely silent on the role of cabinet ministers. The formation of coalitions in presidential systems has been motivated by the need to build legislative majorities but it remains unclear as to what the nature of the bargains being struck is. Is it simply the case that presidents trade office for policy (as the findings of Gaylord and Rennó [2015] suggest) or particularistic benefits, or do such trades involve delegating policy formulation to cabinet ministers (as the findings of Pereira et al. 2016 may suggest)?

References

Alemán, E. and Schwartz, T. (2006). 'Presidential Vetoes in Latin American Constitutions,' *Journal of Theoretical Politics* 18(1): 98–120.

Alemán, E. and Tsebelis, G. (2005). 'The Origins of Presidential Conditional Agenda-Setting Power in Latin America,' *Latin American Research Review* 40(2): 3–26.

Allison, G. T. (1971). *Essence of Decision: Explaining the Cuban Missile Crisis*. Boston: Little, Brown and Company.

Amorim Neto, O. (2006). 'The Presidential Calculus: Executive Policy Making and Cabinet Formation in the Americas,' *Comparative Political Studies* 39(4): 415–40.

Andeweg, R. B. (2000). 'Ministers as Double Agents? The Delegation Process Between Cabinet and Ministers,' *European Journal of Political Research* 37: 377–95.

Baldez, L. and Carey, J. M. (1999). 'Presidential Agenda Control and Spending Policy: Lessons from General Pinochet's Constitution,' *American Journal of Political Science* 43(1): 29–55.

Barro, R. J. (1973). 'The Control of Politicians: An Economic Model,' *Public Choice* 14(1): 19–42.

Becker, G. S. (1983). 'A Theory of Competition Among Pressure Groups for Political Influence,' *Quarterly Journal of Economics* 98(3): 371–400.

Berlinski, S., Dewan, T., and Dowding, K. (2012). *Accounting for Ministers: Scandal and Survival in British Government 1945–2007*. Cambridge: Cambridge University Press.

Bowler, S., Bräuninger, T., Debus, M., and Indriðason, I. H. (2016). 'Let's Just Agree to Disagree: Dispute Resolution Mechanisms in Coalition Agreements,' *Journal of Politics* 78(4): 1264–78.

Buchanan, J. and Gordon Tullock. (1962). *The Calculus of Consent*. Ann Arbor, MI: University of Michigan Press.

Bueno de Mesquita, B., Smith, A., Siverson, R. M., and Morrow, J. D. (2003). *The Logic of Political Survival*. Cambridge, MA: MIT Press.

Cameron, C. M. (2000). *Veto Bargaining: Presidents and the Politics of Negative Power*. Cambridge: Cambridge University Press.

Carey, J. M. and Shugart, M. S. (1998). 'Calling Out the Tanks or Filling Out the Forms?', in J. M. Carey and M. S. Shugart (eds) *Executive Decree Authority*. Cambridge: Cambridge University Press, 1–29.

Carroll, R. and Cox, G. W. (2012). 'Shadowing Ministers: Monitoring Partners in Coalition Governments', *Comparative Political Studies* 45(2): 220–36.

Carter, J. R. and Schap, D. (1987). 'Executive Veto, Legislative Override, and Structure-Induced Equilibrium', *Public Choice* 52(3): 227–44.

Cox, G. W. (1999). 'The Empirical Content of Rational Choice Theory: A Reply to Green and Shapiro', *Journal of Theoretical Politics* 11(2): 147–69.

Cox, G. W. and Morgenstern, S. (2002). 'Epilogue: Latin America's Reactive Assemblies and Proactive Presidents', in S. Morgenstern and B. Nacif (eds) *Legislative Politics in Latin America*. Cambridge: Cambridge University Press, 446–68.

Crisp, B. F. and Botero, F. (2004). 'Multicountry Studies of Latin American Legislatures: A Review Article', *Legislative Studies Quarterly* 29(3): 329–56.

Dewan, T. and Hortala-Vallve, R. (2011). 'The Three As of Government Formation: Appointment, Allocation, and Assignment', *American Journal of Political Science* 55(3): 610–27.

Dewan, T. and Myatt, D. P. (2005). 'Scandal, Protection, and Recovery in the Cabinet', *American Political Science Review* 101(1): 63–77.

Dewan, T. and Myatt, D. P. (2010). 'The Declining Talent Pool of Government', *American Journal of Political Science*, 54(2): 267–86.

Diermeier, D. and Feddersen, T. (1998). 'Cohesion in Legislatures and the Vote of Confidence Procedure', *American Journal of Political Science* 92: 611–21.

Eichorst, J. (2014). 'Explaining Variation in Coalition Agreements: The Electoral and Policy Motivations for Drafting Agreements', *European Journal of Political Research* 53(1): 98–115.

Elster, J. (1986) (ed). *Rational Choice*. New York: NYU Press.

Fearon, J. D. (1994). 'Domestic Political Audiences and the Escalation of International Disputes', *American Political Science Review* 88(3): 577–92.

Gailmard, S. and Patty, J. W. (2012). 'Formal Models of Bureaucracy', *Annual Review of Political Science* 15, 353–77.

Gandhi, J. (2008). *Political Institutions under Dictatorship*. Cambridge: Cambridge University Press.

Gaylord, S. and Rennó, L. (2015). 'Opening the Black Box: Cabinet Authorship of Legislative Proposals in a Multiparty Presidential System', *Presidential Studies Quarterly* 45(2): 247–69.

Green, D. and Shapiro, I. (1995). *Pathologies of Rational Choice Theory: A Critique of Applications in Political Science*. New Haven: Yale University Press.

Hafer, C. and Landa, D. (2007). 'Deliberation as Self-Discovery and Institutions for Political Speech', *Journal of Theoretical Politics* 19(3): 329–60.

Heller, W. B. (2001). 'Making Policy Stick: Why the Government Gets What It Wants in Multiparty Parliaments', *American Journal of Political Science* 45(4): 780–98.

Horn, M. J. (1995). *The Political Economy of Public Administration: Institutional Choice in the Public Sector*. Cambridge: Cambridge University Press.

Huber, J. D. (1996). *Rationalizing Parliament: Legislative Institutions and Party Politics in France*. Cambridge: Cambridge University Press.

Huber, J. D. and Lupia, A. (2001). 'Cabinet Instability and Delegation in Parliamentary Democracies', *American Journal of Political Science* 45: 18–32.

Huber, J. D. and Martinez-Gallardo, C. (2008). 'Replacing Cabinet Ministers: Patterns of Ministerial Stability in Parliamentary Democracies', *American Political Science Review* 102(2): 169–80.

Indriðason, I. H. (2011). 'Executive Veto Power and Credit Claiming: Comparing the Effects of the Line-Item Veto and the Package Veto', *Public Choice* 146(3–4): 375–94.

Indriðason, I. H. and Kam, C. (2008). 'Cabinet Reshuffles and Ministerial Drift', *British Journal of Political Science* 38(4): 621–56.

Indriðason, I. H. and Kristinsson, G. H. (2013). 'Making Words Count: Coalition Agreements and Cabinet Management', *European Journal of Political Research* 52(6): 822–46.

Kahneman, D. and Tversky, A. (1979). 'Prospect Theory: An Analysis of Decision under Risk'. *Econometrica* 47: 263–91.

Kam, C. (2000). 'Not Just Parliamentary "Cowboys and Indians": Ministerial Responsibility and Bureaucratic Drift', *Governance* 13(3): 365–92.

Kam, C. and Indriðason, I. H. (2005). 'The Timing of Cabinet Reshuffles in Five Westminster Parliamentary Systems', *Legislative Studies Quarterly* 30(3): 327–63.

Kam, C., Bianco, W. T., Sened, I., and Smyth, R. (2010). 'Ministerial Selection and Intraparty Organization in the Contemporary British Parliament', *American Political Science Review* 104(2): 289–306.

Kam, C. J. (2009). *Party Discipline and Parliamentary Politics*. Cambridge: Cambridge University Press.

Kim, D.-H. and Loewenberg, G. (2005). 'The Role of Parliamentary Committees in Coalition Governments: Keeping Tabs on Coalition Partners in the German Bundestag', *Comparative Political Studies* 38(9): 1104–29.

Lasswell, H. D. (1948). *Power and Personality*. New York: WW Norton & Co.

Laver, M. J. and Shepsle, K. A. (1996). *Making and Breaking Governments: Cabinets and Legislatures in Parliamentary Democracies*. Cambridge: Cambridge University Press.

March, J. G., and Simon, H. A. (1958). *Organizations*. Oxford: Wiley.

Martin, L. W. and Vanberg, G. (2005). 'Coalition Policymaking and Legislative Review', *American Political Science Review* 99(1): 93–106.

McCarty, N. (2000). 'Proposal Rights, Veto Rights, and Political Bargaining', *American Journal of Political Science* 44(3): 506–22.

McCubbins, M. D. and Schwartz, T. (1984). 'Congressional Oversight Overlooked: Police Patrols versus Fire Alarms', *American Journal of Political Science* 28(1): 165–79.

McCubbins, M. D., Noll, R. G., and Weingast, B. R. (1987). 'Administrative Procedures as Instruments of Political Control', *Journal of Law, Economics, & Organization* 3(2): 243–77.

Moe, T. M. and Caldwell, M. (1994). 'The Institutional Foundations of Democratic Government: A Comparison of Presidential and Parliamentary Systems', *Journal of Institutional and Theoretical Economics* 150(1): 171–95.

Moe, T. M. and Howell, W. G. (1999). 'The Presidential Power of Unilateral Action', *The Journal of Law, Economics, and Organization* 15(1): 132–79.

Moreno, E., Crisp, B., and Shugart, M. S. (2003). 'The Accountability Deficit in Latin America', in S. Mainwaring and C. Welna (eds) *Democratic Accountability in Latin America*. Oxford: Oxford University Press, 79–131.

Moury, C. (2013). *Coalition Government and Party Mandate: How Coalition Agreements Constrain Ministerial Action*. New York: Routledge.

Müller, W. C. and Strøm, K. (2008). 'Coalition Agreements and Cabinet Governance,' in K. Strøm, W. C. Müller, and T. Bergman (eds) *Cabinets and Coalition Bargaining: The Democratic Life Cycle in Western Europe*. Oxford: Oxford University Press, 159–99.

Neustadt, R. E. (1960). *Presidential Power*. New York: John Wiley & Sons.

Niskanen, W. A. (1971). *Bureaucracy and Representative Government*. Chicago, IL: Chicago University Press.

Palanza, V. and Sin, G. (2014). 'Veto Bargaining and the Legislative Process in Multiparty Presidential Systems,' *Comparative Political Studies* 47(5): 766–92.

Pereira, C., Bertholini, F., and Raile, E. D. (2016). 'All the President's Men and Women: Coalition Management Strategies and Governing Costs in a Multiparty Presidency,' *Presidential Studies Quarterly* 46(3): 550–68.

Putnam, R. (1988). 'Diplomacy and Domestic Politics: The Logic of Two-Level Games,' *International Organization* 42(3): 427–60.

Riker, W. H. (1962). *The Theory of Political Coalitions*. New Haven: Yale University Press.

Shepsle, K. A. (1995). 'Statistical Political Philosophy and Positive Political Theory,' *Critical Review* 9(1–2): 213–22.

Shugart, M. S. and Carey, J. M. (1992). *Presidents and Assemblies: Constitutional Design and Electoral Dynamics*. Cambridge: Cambridge University Press.

Simon, H. (1947). *Administrative Behavior*. New York: Free Press.

Strøm, K. (2000). 'Delegation and Accountability in Parliamentary Democracies,' *European Journal of Political Research* 37: 261–89.

Svolik, M. W. (2012). *The Politics of Authoritarian Rule*. Cambridge: Cambridge University Press.

Thies, M. F. (2001). 'Keeping Tabs on Partners: The Logic of Delegation in Coalition Governments,' *American Journal of Political Science* 45(3): 580–98.

CHAPTER 6

....

ETHNOGRAPHIC APPROACHES TO THE STUDY OF POLITICAL EXECUTIVES

....

R. A. W. RHODES AND JACK CORBETT

6.1 INTRODUCTION

....

ANTHROPOLOGY comes in many guises, often referred to as the four pillars of archaeology, physical anthropology, anthropological linguistics, and cultural anthropology. For the study of politics, the most relevant pillar is cultural anthropology. But what is cultural anthropology? The usual answer is a puzzle—'ethnography is what cultural anthropologist do'. However, the practices of ethnography are not confined to anthropology. It is a major approach in sociology. Irrespective of discipline, everyone employing ethnography owes a major debt to the Chicago School and Whyte's (1993 [1943]) famous study of *Street Corner Society*. In both these disciplines, 'ethnography does not have a standard, well-defined meaning' (Hammersley and Atkinson 2007: 2).

Some words and phrases recur. The ethnographer studies people's everyday lives. Such fieldwork is unstructured. The aim is to recover the meaning of their actions. By long association, meaning is captured by participant observation; the defining method of ethnography. So, what is participant observation? The answer will commonly involve reference to fieldwork or deep immersion or thick descriptions, whether looking at a Congressional district, a government department or a tribe in Africa. What is fieldwork? Historically, in cultural anthropology, it meant making the *exotic* familiar by going to another country, learning the language and studying the everyday lives of the inhabitants of a village, tribe, or whatever unit of social organization judged relevant. Latterly, the researcher stayed closer to home, seeking to make the *familiar* exotic. For the novitiate in both disciplines, fieldwork was the only way to become an ethnographer;

'you can't teach fieldwork, you have to do it' (and see Barley 1986 for a humorous account of learning how to do it). For Wood (2007: 123), it is 'research based on personal interaction with research subjects in their own setting', not in the laboratory, the library or one's office. It is deep hanging out or intensive immersion in the everyday lives of other people in their local environment normally for many months if not years.

To consider the application of an ethnographic method to the study of the political executive, this chapter focuses on five questions.

What is ethnography?
Why does ethnography matter?
Who does ethnography?
What are the limits to an ethnographic approach?
What is the research agenda?

We can draw on few ethnographic studies of the political executive to answer these questions. Political anthropology is a minority sport and until recently there was little work by political scientists.[1] Auyero and Joseph (2007: 2) examined 1,000 articles published in the *American Journal of Political Science* and the *American Political Science Review* between 1996 and 2005. They found that 'only one article relies on ethnography as a data-production technique'. Little has changed. In the 2000s, there was more interpretive political ethnography mainly in the fields of comparative politics (see, e.g., Schatz 2009; Wedeen 2010; Aronoff and Kubik 2013), and public policy analysis (Fischer 2003; Wagenaar 2011). There was little change elsewhere in political science. A recent review by Kapiszewski et al. (2015: 234) concluded that 'political science has yet to embrace ethnography and participant observation wholeheartedly'.

All is not well with ethnography in sociology either. Taylor (2014) argues ethnography is 'endangered' because it takes a long time, is ethically sensitive, difficult to fund, and does not fit well with the performance assessment regime in UK universities. The irony is not lost on us that we argue for an approach that is out of favour in one of its traditional heartlands.

To study the executive using an ethnographic approach we treat it as synonymous with 'court politics' and focus on the intentions and actions of the political leadership networks at the heart of government. For us, the main value of an ethnographic approach is the ability to study the *Realpolitik* of the governing elite.[2] This position differs from an institutional approach (see Chapter 3 in this volume), which focuses on the offices of the political executive, namely president, prime minister, cabinet, and central agencies, but not parliaments and the courts. It differs also from a functional approach, which focuses on 'all those organizations and procedures which coordinate central

---

[1] See also: Fenno (1990: 128); Schatz (2009a: 1); Wedeen (2010: 79); Aronoff and Kubik (2013: 19). For a review of 'classical' political anthropology, see Lewellen (2003); and for examples, see Fortes and Evans-Pritchard (1940); Leach (1954); and Bailey (1969).

[2] This chapter draws on the authors' previous work. See: Rhodes (2011, 2014, 2017); Rhodes, 't Hart, and Noordegraaf (2007); Rhodes and Tiernan (2014); Corbett (2015); Boswell et al. (2018, 2019).

government policies, and act as final arbiters between different parts of the government machine' (Rhodes 1995: 12).

6.2 What is Ethnography?

Broadly, the field divides into naturalist and anti-naturalist ethnography. Naturalist ethnography strives to develop predictions and causal explanations as in the natural sciences (Werner and Schoepfle 1987). Anti-naturalist or interpretive ethnography emphasizes the importance of meanings in the study of human life (see Bevir and Rhodes 2003). It shifts analysis away from institutions, functions, and roles to under-standing the beliefs, actions, and practices of actors; to court politics.

The aim of interpretive research is complex specificity in context. Schwartz-Shea and Yanow (2012: 26–34) suggest that the inductive and deductive logics of inquiry so common in political science are not relevant to interpretive ethnography. They suggest that the logic of abduction is better suited. They describe abductive reasoning as a: 'Puzzling out process [in which] the researcher tacks continually, constantly, back and forth in an iterative-recursive fashion between what is puzzling and possible explanations for it' (2012: 46–9).

A surprise or a puzzle occurs when 'there is a misfit between experience and expectations'. The researcher is 'grappling with the process of sensemaking; of coming up with an interpretation that makes sense of the surprise'. The researcher is on an 'interpretive dance' as one discovery leads to another. There are no hypotheses to test. If deduction reasons from its premises, and induction from its data, then from abduction reasons from its puzzles. The researcher does not deduce law-like generalizations but infers the best explanation for the puzzle. So, the ethnographer does not ask if the findings are generalizable but whether 'it works in context' (Geertz [1973] 1993: 23; Wolcott 1995: 174; Schwartz-Shea and Yanow 2012: 46-49).

To puzzle abductively, ethnographers typically employ two core methods—participant observation and open-ended, or ethnographic interviewing.

6.2.1 Participant Observation

The extended case study based on observation and interviews is the historic heart of interpretive political ethnography. The researcher both observes and participates in everyday life. He or she needs to get to know the people being studied. Commonly observations are recorded in a fieldwork notebook. Involvement can vary from being a bystander with little rapport, through a balance between 'insider' and 'outsider' roles; to full involvement and the risk of 'going native' (see DeWalt et al. 1998). 'Data' is captured by participant observers in a document known as the 'fieldwork notebook' (see: Sanjek 1990; Bryman 2001: volume 2, part 7; Emerson et al. [1995] 2011). The notebook is simultaneously invisible and ever present, part of the tacit knowledge of ethnographers. Ethnographers learn about the fieldwork notes in the field. There is no agreed definition of a fieldwork notebook. For some it includes note taking from documents. For others, it is mainly notes about what they have observed. Even then, 'observation' is a broad category, covering everyday activities, conversations, pen portraits of individuals, new ideas about how to do the research, the diary of the ethnographer recording personal impressions and feelings. Jackson (1990: 33–4) suggests field notes are a key symbol of professional identity and they 'represent an individualistic, pioneering, approach to acquiring knowledge, at times even a maverick and rebellious one'. They symbolize the 'ordeal by fire' that is journeying to the field and the 'uncertainty, mystique and [...] ambivalence' of that journey.

6.2.2 Interviewing

The common format for an elite interview is a recorded, one-hour conversation around a semi-structured questionnaire (see, e.g., Dexter [1970] 2006). Of course, it can be revealing in the hands of a skilled interviewer but when studying political elites it can become a confining ritual. All elite interviewers know the politician who can negotiate such an encounter with ease and 'talk for an hour without saying anything too interesting' (Rawnsley 2001: xvii–xviii citing Robin Cooke, former British Foreign Secretary). There is another choice besides this format—intensive repeat interviews. Elites will be more open in a more extended encounter because, as Rawnsley (2001: xi) observes 'they have to tell an outsider because they are so worried about whether it makes sense or, indeed, whether they make sense'. Such interviews are still a negotiation. Their success depends on intangibles like trust and rapport. With trust and rapport comes far more information than can be obtained from working through a semi-structured questionnaire. The conventional elite interview is a poor substitute for the repeat, two-hour long conversation. Such open-ended interviews are an essential complement to observation, enabling the observer to compare what is said with what is done.

The 'data' produced by the combination of participant observation and in-depth interviewing has various pen names, such as 'thick descriptions' (Geertz [1973] 1993: chapter 1) and 'the extended case study' (Aronoff and Kubik 2013: 56–7). There are affinities with the case studies common in political science, which are detailed studies of a single unit or event. The method is often criticized for being idiographic, thereby curtailing generalizations. Latterly, political scientists have devoted much effort to assimilating the case method to naturalism and its language of variables and hypothesis testing (e.g. Gerring 2004). For example, Wood analysed five case studies of peasant support for insurgent groups explicitly 'sacrificing ethnographic depth of analysis for analytical traction through comparison of cases that vary in the extent of mobilization observed'. It was her way of overcoming 'the obstacles to making valid causal inferences based on field data' (Wood 2007: 132, 142). So, case studies can be simple descriptions of specific subjects but political scientists are enjoined to use them to build theory, to test the validity of specific hypotheses, and to test theories by treating them as the equivalent of decisive experiments (see Eckstein 1975: 92–123; see also Yin 2008).

An interpretive approach to fieldwork is markedly different because it goes for ethnographic depth; for deep hanging out. Anthropologists would not refer to their fieldwork site as a 'case study' because it is not a 'case' of anything until they withdraw from the field to analyse and write up their field notes. Indeed, interpretive ethnography is less concerned with generalizations than with raising new questions and 'shaking the bag'. The aim is edification; to find 'new, better, more interesting, more fruitful ways of speaking about' everyday life (Rorty 1980: 360). So, fieldwork provides detailed studies of social and political dramas. As Burawoy (1998: 5) suggests, it 'extracts the general from the unique, to move from the "micro" to the "macro"'. For example, Crewe's (2005: 240) study of the British House of Lords focuses on rituals, rules, symbols, and hierarchies, especially 'the meaning of its rituals and symbols and how people use them to make sense of the past, present and future'. Her 'anthropological perspective' draws on the analysis of political ritual; of 'ritual as the process of politics itself, rather than as a servant to it' (Kertzer 1988). She was a participant observer for two years between 1998 and 2001. She had a staff pass and 'was able to take part actively in House of Lords' working life'. It was deep hanging out. She shows how the everyday rituals of an institution seen only as a dignified part of the constitution 'give the backbenchers the feeling that they are transcending their individual powerlessness to become important components of an influential whole'. As a result, the rituals ensure acquiescence and executive dominance. The important point is that political rituals are not 'trivial and backward looking' but 'key elements in the symbolism of which nations are made' (paraphrased from Crewe 2005: 229–35).

6.3 Why Does Ethnography Matter?

Imagine doing research on one of the intelligence services. Immediately there is a problem because much of their work is secret. There is little or no public documentation. You do not know any of the 'spies'. The only way to get any information is to get inside—to infiltrate—the organization, and observe and talk to the people who work there. That is exactly what Paul 't Hart did with Dutch Intelligence Service (*Binnenlandse Veiligheidsdienst*) ('t Hart 2007). Observation provided data not available elsewhere and identified key individuals and core processes. It is surprising how little we know about many organizations. Ethnography can pioneer the exploration of virgin territory. Even for a government department such as the Department of Industry, you may get to interview the top brass but there will be other people lower down the organization you never see and whose voices are never heard. Rhodes (2011) attended an away day for middle and lower level managers to discover it was the first time they had been consulted about the department's strategic plan. They had 'voice' for the first time and Rhodes now knew there were several dissenting voices in the organization that he had yet to hear from. In other words, observation enabled him to disaggregate organizations into its competing voices and to open 'the black box' of internal processes. Such disaggregation, or decentring of the organization, means focusing on individual agency by recovering the beliefs and practices of actors. In this way, the researchers gets behind the surface of official accounts by providing texture, depth, and nuance, so their stories have richness as well as context. They let interviewees explain the meaning of their actions, providing an authenticity that can only come from the main characters involved in the story.

Ethnography is also an open-ended research strategy. Its proponents do not go into the field with a set of hypotheses derived from a review of the existing literature. Rather, they go where they are led and frame (and reframe, and reframe) questions in a way that recognizes that understandings about how things work around here evolve during the fieldwork. This flexibility admits of surprises—of moments of epiphany, serendipity, and happenstance—that can open new research agendas. Such surprises can be small—the importance of the diary secretary in the daily life of a department. Or big—some ministers avoid making decisions to be actors on a public stage. The researcher has to look behind the public face to see and analyse the symbolic, performative aspects of political action. Ministers perform many roles. They are the magisterial committee chair. They are royalty magnanimously receiving a delegation. They are a parent, hosting an event for school children. They are the party member gossiping scurrilously about party colleagues. They are much else besides, and they move seamlessly between their several parts. By shadowing ministers, the researcher can watch them enact their parts in the political dramas. Ethnography matters because it reaches the parts of government that other research methods do not reach.

6.4 WHO DOES ETHNOGRAPHY?

Political ethnography largely ignores elites. As Shore and Nugent (2002: 11) comment, 'Anthropology, by definition, is the study of powerless "Others"'. It focuses on everyday practices of citizen in villages, factories, schools, and local communities. Nader (1972: 289) was an early voice calling for anthropologists to 'study up', recognizing that 'there is comparatively little field research on the middle class and very little-first hand work on the upper class'. Indeed, most of the studies using ethnography in political science 'study down' with street level bureaucrats a favoured topic (see, e.g., Maynard-Moody and Musheno 2003; Zacka 2017).

We cannot answer the question of who does ethnography solely by reviewing the existing ethnographic literature on political executives. Whenever possible, we discuss ethnographic work that focuses on the political executive but we draw also on studies that could serve as models of ethnographies of executive studies. The latter group encompasses a rich smorgasbord of studies that are not ordinarily part of executive studies but are germane to the more general subject of elite ethnography.

We begin with a brief excursion into naturalist ethnography and consider three pioneering examples in political science: Fenno (1978, 1990); Heclo and Wildavsky ([1974] 1981); and Kaufman ([1981] 2011).

For nearly eight years, Fenno (1978, 1990) shadowed eighteen US members of Congress in their Districts. He made thirty-six separate visits to the districts and, spent 110 working days with them. His visits varied from three to eleven days. In eleven cases, he supplemented the visits with 'a lengthy interview' in Washington. He sought to answer two questions. What does an elected representative see when he or she sees a constituency? What are the consequences of these perceptions for his or her behaviour? What his fieldwork revealed was how each member of Congress developed their own 'home style'—a way of presenting themselves to their constituency—that helped them to achieve the three goals of re-election, power in Congress, and good public policy (Fenno 1990: 137). The presentation of self by members of Congress in their everyday constituency life was the surprise finding.

In his analysis of central bureau chiefs, Kaufman ([1981] 2011) studied six federal bureaux for fourteen months, including thirty-one full days when he observed the bureaux chiefs sitting in their offices and at meetings. The conventional wisdom is that bureaux chiefs have much power and independence. Kaufman ([1981] 2011: chapter 3) highlights the 'confines of leadership'. He compares it to 'stepping into a large fast-flowing river' and contending with 'an array of forces not of his own making that carried him and his organization along—sometimes at an unwanted rate and in an unwanted direction'(Kaufman [1981] 2011: 134). So, 'they make their marks in inches, not miles'. He suggests that, 'for all the power and influence attributed to their office and for all their striving, [bureau chiefs] *could not make a big difference in what their organizations did during the period in which they served*' (Kaufman [1981] 2011: 174, 139; emphasis added). Getting up close and personal changes the angle of vision and leads, as Kaufman freely admits, to surprises, especially about the confines of administrative leadership (see also Kaufman [1960] 2006).

In the UK, there was little political ethnography before the 2000s, and the little that existed was not called ethnography. An important and still cited book on British politics is a *tacit* ethnography: Heclo and Wildavsky's ([1974] 1981) study of budgeting in British central government. They show the value and feasibility of intensive interviews at the top of British government when the operating assumption of most British political scientists was 'there's no point in asking because they'll say no'. Their fieldwork demonstrates the value of getting out there. Unfortunately, they are less than informative about their methods. They conducted two rounds of interviews totalling 'two hundred or so'. They were 'intensive' interviews with ministers and civil servants but they do not say anything about their structured or semi-structured interview schedule. There is no breakdown of interviews by rank. They refer to their interviewees as co-authors, to 'seeing the world through their eyes', and describe themselves as 'observers' [...] 'watching how people work together' (Heclo and Wildavsky [1974] 1981: lvii, lxvii–lxviii, lxxi). Hugh Heclo recollects 'we did nothing *but* observational fieldwork' (personal correspondence 9 May 2012). No matter they fail to report their methods in detail. Their work exemplifies the value of intensive interviews and observation (and see Weller 2014).

There is a great deal more interpretive ethnography but few researchers study the political executive. Notable exceptions include Rhodes' (2011) study of three British government central departments. It is not a classic intensive fieldwork study but a hit-and-run ethnography; that is, repeat visits to multiple sites. He observed the office of two British ministers and three permanent secretaries for two days each, totalling some 120 hours. He also shadowed two ministers and three permanent secretaries for five working days each, totalling some 300 hours. He conducted lengthy repeat interviews with: ten permanent, five secretaries of state, and three ministers; and twenty other officials, totalling some sixty-seven hours of interviews. He also had copies of speeches and public lectures; committee and other papers relevant to the meetings observed; newspaper reports; and published memoirs and diaries. Shadowing produced several surprises; for example, he found that a key task of civil servants and ministers was to steer other actors using storytelling. Storytelling organizes dialogues, and fosters meanings, beliefs, and identities among the relevant actor. It seeks to influence what actors think and do, and fosters shared narratives of continuity and change. It is about 'willed ordinariness' or continuities. It is about preserving the departmental philosophy and its everyday (or folk) theories. It is about shared languages that enable a retelling of yesterday to make sense of today. This portrait of a storytelling political-administrative elite, with beliefs and practices rooted in the nineteenth century Westminster constitution, that uses protocols and rituals to domesticate rude surprises and recurrent dilemmas, overturns the conventional portrait.

In the same vein, Corbett (2015) studied the working life of politicians in the Pacific Islands. He undertook more than a hundred interviews across fourteen countries; read around fifty published auto/biographies; and spent time watching politicians on the campaign trail, in their constituency, in parliament, at international meetings, and in their offices, businesses, and homes. Corbett's account details the depth of concern about the corruption and incompetence of contemporary politicians in this region. Unflattering comparisons were made with the so-called Golden Generation who had led most Pacific states to independence in the 1970s and 1980s. But, contrary to the common perception, Corbett (2015) found marked similarities in the dilemmas that politicians in the Pacific Islands confront—for example, how to appear 'of' and 'apart' from voters; the need to overpromise to win elections in full knowledge that public expectations could not be met; and being powerful and yet feeling powerless. These dilemmas reoccurred across countries, and eras. Also, they bore a family resemblance to the findings of studies like Rhodes (2011) and others across the world. In doing so, Corbett made a context typically characterized as exotic familiar to readers beyond the region.

While not specifically focused on the executives of nation-states, there is a body of work on other types of executives that further demonstrates the potential of this method. Given the popular disaffection with the EU, for example, Shore's (2000) account of the inner workings of the European Commission foreshadows Rhodes' portrayal of a cocooned civil service. Affinities are also clear in studies of the elite of global governance. Weaver's (2008) ethnographic study of the World Bank shows how organized hypocrisy is central to the Bank's work while, similar to Corbett's account of powerless politicians, Ouroussof's (2010) ethnography of Wall Street elites reveals how these supposedly omnipotent kingpins of the global economy remain enthralled to limiting beliefs and entrenched practices.

The other notable exception is biography. Few biographers would call themselves ethnographers but many adopt an ethnographic sensibility and employ similar data collection techniques. For example, Weller's (1989) research on Australian Prime Minister Malcolm Fraser, conducted soon after he lost power in 1983, combined cabinet documents with in-depth interviews to probe how Fraser exercised power. Weller may not have been in the room but by combining the written record and the fresh memoires of key participants he got as close as a researcher is likely to get to describing how these meetings operate. Weller's (2014: chapter 14) biography of Australian Prime Minister Kevin Rudd, included sitting for more than a month in the prime minister's office. His 'a week in the office' account adds depth and richness to the reflections of his interviewees.

All of these examples reveal a side of the executive that other forms of analysis cannot reach. They open up the 'black box' of decision-making, revealing the webs of shared beliefs, but also personal rivalries, conspiracy and intrigue, that dominate life at the top of government. They provide a sentient account of decision-making; one grounded in everyday experience, knowledge, and recurring dilemmas. They humanize executive processes and practices, and in doing allow us to appreciate the fragility and contingency of authority.

6. 5 What Are the Limits of Ethnography?

Every method has limits. In this section, we discuss briefly the most common dilemmas confronting ethnographers, namely: representation, objectivity, explanation, and generalization (Rhodes 2017: chapter 3).

6.5.1 Representation

The claim to ethnographic authority when representing other cultures, whether of a tribe or of an organization, is a prime target for critics. They argue that it produces gendered and racist texts with a specious claim to objectivity that ignores power relations between observers and observed and fails to link the local to the global (see, e.g., Clifford 1986). Ethnographers grapple with the question of for whom are they doing the research. For example, van Willigen (2002: 150 and chapter 10) claims that fieldwork provides information for policy-makers so they can make rational decisions while for Agar (1996: 27), 'no understanding of a world is valid without representation of those members' voices'. For him, 'ethnography is *populist* to the core' and the task is to be 'sceptical of the distant institutions that control local people's lives'. The practices of ethnography have become so diverse that Marcus (2007a) describes them as 'baroque'.

The common response to questions about representation is to call for ethnographers to be reflexive about their position, not only in their field research but also about the field of study in which their findings are situated, and the influence each has on what they saw, heard, and read, and how they have represented it (see, e.g., Corbett 2014). As Hammersley and Atkinson ([1983] 2007: 14–15) point out 'the reflexive character of social research [...] is not a matter of methodological commitment, it is an existential fact'. So, 'rather than engaging in futile attempts to eliminate the effects of the researcher [on the research], we should set about understanding them'. Critical self-awareness is essential but we have much sympathy with Watson's (1987) prayer, 'make me reflexive— but not yet' because the goal of remaining a 'professional stranger' balancing engagement, detachment, and critical self-awareness is equivalent to searching for the Holy Grail—always out of reach. Yet, there is no alternative to trying—it's life as we know it (for discussion, see Boswell and Corbett 2015a, 2015b] and published responses).

6.5.2 Generalization

Ethnographic fieldwork is invariably seen as idiographic by political scientists. Critics claim that, it is not possible to deduce laws and predict outcomes from fieldwork; that is, it is not possible generalize. Of course, researchers can and do make general statements from a case. What they cannot do is make statistical generalizations and propound laws. For Lincoln and Guba (1985: 110), 'the only generalization is: there is no generalization'. However, we can aspire to 'plausible conjectures'; that is, to making general statements which are plausible because they rest on good reasons and the reasons are good because they are inferred from relevant information (paraphrased from Bourdon 1993). We can derive plausible conjectures from intensive fieldwork. As Geertz ([1973] 1993: 23) suggests, 'small facts speak to large issues'. In which case, ethnographic studies should be held to a different set of standards than are commonly accepted by the mainstream of the discipline (see Boswell and Corbett 2015b; Rhodes 2017: 30–3, 50–1, 100–2).

6.5.3 Objectivity

For the naturalist political scientist, ethnographic research fails to meet the standards posed by the logic of refutation. For the interpretive ethnographer, there are only partial truths. For all qualitative researchers, there is the question of how to evaluate the quality of research. We must start by accepting that the knowledge criteria of the naturalist ethnography—the logic of vindication and of refutation—are inappropriate. Such notions as reliability, validity and generalization are not seen as relevant when the aim of research is 'complex specificness' (Geertz [1973] 1993: 23; Wolcott 1995: 174). A way forward can be found in Bevir and Rhodes (2003: 38–40) who argue objectivity arises from criticizing and comparing rival webs of interpretation; from the forensic interrogation of rival stories (cf. Boswell and Corbett 2015b). Such debates are subject to the provisional rules of intellectual honesty such as established standards of evidence and reason. We prefer webs of interpretation that are accurate, comprehensive, and consistent. There is no point in trying to pretend the ethnographic approach and its distinctive research methods are just a 'soft' version of the naturalist approach with its penchant for 'hard' quantitative data. They are simply different in both the aims and the knowledge criteria they employ. But there are criteria. It is not a case of anything goes.

6.5.4 *Explanation*

A common misconception about interpretive ethnography is that it aims only to understand actions and practices, not explain them. A distinction is drawn between the nomothetic search for explanatory laws of the social sciences and idiographic understanding of the interpretive sciences. Interpretive ethnography describes actions and practices, but it does not explain them. It need not be so. The philosophical analysis of meaning in action that informs an interpretive approach suggests a distinctive form of explanation, which Bevir (1999: 304–6) refers to as narrative. For Bevir (1999: chapters 4 and 7), narratives are the form theories take in the human sciences. They explain actions by specifying the beliefs and desires that caused the actions. People act for reasons, conscious and unconscious. A memoir or a story or a life history is a narrative if it explains actions by spelling out beliefs. So, interpretive ethnography is about explanation, not just understanding.

Our brief review does not exhaust the limits to ethnography. For example, with hit-and-run ethnography (see below), the question arises of how short can a fieldwork trip be and still count as ethnography (Hammersley 2006; Marcus 2007b)? If we seek to locate (say) focus groups in their broader traditions or folk theories, how do we identify those traditions? If we employ a broad toolkit, how do we reconcile the different findings that can arise? However, ethnography is not unique in having limits. It is a fact of life for every method (see Chapter 10 in this volume).

6.6 What is the Research Agenda?

What would 'chugging ahead' (Wedeen 2010: 264) to an ethnography of the political executive in the twenty-first century involve? It involves dissolving the distinction between quantitative and qualitative methods; embracing *bricolage* and an 'ethnographic sensibility'; and an analytic focus on court politics.

6.6.1 Quantitative and Qualitative

The distinction between 'qualitative' and 'quantitative' methods is unhelpful (Schwartz-Shea and Yanow 2002). It suggests, for example, that researchers do not interpret their quantitative data (on which, see Stone 2015). Rather, an interpretive approach does not necessarily favour particular methods. It does not prescribe a particular toolkit for producing data but prescribes a particular way of treating data of any type. It should treat data as evidence of the meanings or beliefs embedded in actions. So, it is a mistake to equate an interpretive approach with only certain techniques of data generation such as reading texts and participant observation. It is wrong to exclude survey research and quantitative studies from the reach of interpretive analysis. Shore (2000: 7–11) is a true *bricloeur* because his cultural analysis of the beliefs and practices of European Union elites uses participant observation, historical archives, textual analysis of official documents, biographies, oral histories, recorded interviews, and informal conversations as well as statistical and survey techniques.

6.6.2 *Bricolage*

Ethnographic methods are analogous to *bricolage*. We piece together sets of representations that are fitted to the specifics of a complex situation (Levi-Strauss 1966) using whatever tools are available. Both qualitative and quantitative methods are used as appropriate.

When studying the political executive, the classic practices of the ethnographic craft, participant observation, and ethnographic interviewing, encounter some obvious practical problems in 'being there' (see Rhodes et al. 2007). The most obvious game changer is that 'the research participants are more powerful than the researchers' (Shore and Nugent 2002: 11). They control access and exit. They end interviews, refuse permission to quote interviews, and deny us documents. They can control what we see and hear. The researcher's role varies, at times with bewildering speed. One day you are the professional stranger walking the tightrope between insider and outsider. Next day you are the complete bystander, left behind in the office to twiddle your thumbs. They not only enforce the laws on secrecy but also decide what a secret is. We are playing a game with a stacked deck of cards, and we are the punters. Of course, there are many circumstances in which these difficulties do not arise. For example, Rhodes (2011) was allowed to shadow ministers and their top public servants. But the brute fact is that when problems do arise, the executive wins. In practice, it means the researcher is involved in continuous negotiations over access and who can and cannot be seen. Elites are different (and see Gains 2011 and Rhodes 2017 for a more detailed discussion.) To deal with these problems, the ethnographer needs more tools than just observation and interviewing. We have to find other ways of 'being there'; of sidestepping the problems of access and secrecy (see Rhodes and Tiernan 2014). Table 6.1 identifies several such ways.

Table 6.1 Bricolage

Ethnographic methods	Definition	Potential data sources	Model
Hit-and-run fieldwork	Repeated, short bursts of intensive observation as researchers move in-and-out of the field	Legislatures, constituency offices, campaign events, government departments	Rhodes (2011); Crewe (2015)
Ethnographic interviewing	Extended and where possible repeated, semi-structured and unstructured interviews	Recently retired politicians and public officials	Reeher (2006); Corbett (2015)
Memoirs	First-person reflections on governing	Auto-biographies and authorized biographies; radio and television interviews	Blunkett (2006); Rhodes (2017)
Elite focus groups	Group reflections that encourage elites to flesh out and challenge each other's claims	Recently retired politicians and public officials	Rhodes and Tiernan (2014)
Para-ethnography	Ethnographic interviews with a decision-maker to explain a specific decision or event (see Holmes and Marcus 2005)	Focused on particular legislative documents, departmental files	Novel in political science but see Holmes and Marcus (2005)
Visual ethnography	Using video recordings as a form of remote observation (see Pink 2013)	C-SPAN (and similar footage elsewhere); press conferences, parliament live	Novel in political science, but see Pink (2013)

Source: Boswell et al. (2018).

We do not have the space to expand on every method. So, we limit ourselves to one example. Focus groups are widely used in electoral studies but they are not seen as a tool for political ethnographers. They involve getting a group of people together to discuss their beliefs and practices. The groups are interactive and group members are encouraged by a facilitator to talk to one another. For Morgan (1997: 2), the 'hallmark' of focus groups is 'the explicit use of group interaction to produce data and insights'. Focus groups have some singular advantages. They provide a detailed understanding of the participants' beliefs and experiences, and embrace a diversity of views. The method produces context-specific qualitative data on complex issues. Thus, Rhodes and Tiernan (2014 and 2015) ran two focus groups comprising the former chiefs of staff (CoSs) of Australian prime ministers to discuss such questions as how each CoS approached the task of working with the prime minister. They conclude focus groups are a useful tool for recovering the beliefs and practices of governing elites. However, they are not a stand-alone tool. They are part of a larger toolkit that encompasses intensive interviewing, official documents, biographies, memoirs and diaries, informal conversations, as well as observation. Finally, as Agar and MacDonald (1995: 85) also conclude, focus groups can take the ethnographic researcher into new territory when the conversation is located in broader folk theories, such as in the example given here, the governmental traditions in which the participants work.

This last point applies to the several ways of 'being there'. None are stand-alone methods. Ideally, we would supplement each method with shadowing. Most important, the data generated by focus groups and other methods require an 'ethnographic sensibility' for interpreting the conversations (Agar and MacDonald 1995; Schatz 2009). The various ethnographic methods suggested in Table 6.1 are still about recovering meaning and locating that meaning in its broader context. So, focus groups are considered ethnographic because we have broadened the meaning of ethnography to incorporate a diverse set of practices linked not by a shared method—participant observation—but by a shared focus on the recovery of meaning—the ethnographic sensibility.

We expect 'bricolage' to be an important feature of ethnographic approaches to the study of the political executive in the future. As well as observation and interviews, we will construct research from diverse methods and materials (Denzin and Lincoln 2011: 4 and table 1.3)—and bring an 'ethnographic sensibility' to bear on the data, however collected (and for a more detailed account, see Rhodes 2017: chapters 3–5).

6.6.3 The Network Analysis of Court Politics

It is commonplace to talk of an inner circle surrounding the prime minister or president. Around this core we also talk of circles of influence (Hennessy 2000: 493–500); usage that accords with political folklore. In the more formal language of political science, the core executive is a set of interlocking, interdependent networks. The chief executive, be it prime minister or president, is at the core of these networks supported by courtiers who constitute his or her supporting central capacity (see, e.g., Burch and Holliday 1996, 2004; Savoie 1999, 2008).

The court is a key part of the organizational glue holding the centre together. It coordinates the policy process by filtering and packaging proposals. It contains and manages conflicts between ministerial barons. It acts as the keeper of the government's narrative. It acts as the gatekeeper and broker for internal and external networks. And its power ebbs and flows with that of the prime minister.

Court politics focuses on the games politicians and their support players play in these networks. Tony Blair, Gordon Brown, Kevin Rudd, and Julia Gillard are all familiar with blasts of wild treachery, as were the Manchu Court, Imperial Rome, and the English court during the Wars of the Roses. It is the stock of fiction, whether the faction of *The White Queen* or the fantasy of *The Game of Thrones*. It is our business to report and analyse who does what to whom, when, where, how, and why.

Court politics exists as journalists' reportage and in the auto/biographies, diaries and memoirs of politicians but is rarely at the heart of academic analyses of present-day government. Of course, the study of the court politics poses many challenges around access, secrecy, and publication. The obvious objection is that the secrecy surrounding court politics limits access. The point has force, but we must not succumb to the rule of anticipated reactions and just assume access will be denied. There are examples of outsiders gaining good access, whether biographers (Seldon 2004; Seldon et al. 2007; Seldon and Lodge 2010; Moore 2015; Seldon and Snowden 2015), journalists (Rawnsley 2001, 2010; Peston 2005), or academics (Shore 2000; Rhodes 2011).[3] Biographers probe the reasons. Journalists with their exposé tradition probe actions to show 'all is not as it seems'. Each has their explanations of the changes in the court politics of executive government. Both observe people in action; they are tacit ethnographers. All gained access, observed, interviewed, and published. If we want to know this world, then we must follow their example, tell our stories, and strive to help readers see executive governance afresh. The volume of 'private information' reported in the work of biographers like Anthony Seldon and journalists like Andrew Rawnsley is impressive, and will bear such secondary analysis as mapping the membership of prime ministers' courts. We need to mine all publicly available information, irrespective of discipline or profession. Perhaps we are too concerned to comment on the present-day. We may have to wait for documentary material to become available from families and friends as well as official sources but for most countries some eighty-five years of the twentieth century are available to consult. Perhaps we underestimate just how much is out there. There is much that political scientists could use in exploring the webs of beliefs, practices, and traditions in the shape shifting core executive networks. A political anthropology of the executive's court politics may be a daunting prospect but it behoves us to try because court politics matter for effective and accountable government.

6.7 CONCLUSION

This chapter has defined the ethnographic approach and surveyed the state of the art of the, admittedly scarce, literature on the political executive. We have suggested that the way forward is to abandon any essentially arbitrary distinction between qualitative and quantitative methods and resort to *bricolage*. The analysis of court politics is a prime setting for such hit-and-run ethnography. Like all research methods, ethnography has its limits and we discuss them. We do not consider these problems insurmountable. We would argue that we need to be explicit about the limits to the approach so readers can assess the value of the findings. The limits associated with ethnography are not specific to studying the political executive. They are common problems for anyone practicing

---

[3] In addition to the examples cited in the text, recent examples for Britain include: Beckett and Hencke (2004); Blunkett (2006); Mandelson (2010); Richards (2010); Andrews (2014); and Shipman (2016). Recent examples for Australia include: Blewett (1999); and Watson (2002). Recent examples for Canada include Savoie (2008) and Wells (2013).

the art and such a discussion raises a further problem—it can discourage newcomers. So, our final task is to refer the reader to the key question of whether ethnography brings anything new to the study of executive government. Table 6.1 makes it clear that ethnography is an edifying approach because it enables us to see beyond institutions and functions by opening the daily life of executive courts, replete with drama, conspiracy, prejudice, and intrigue, that are central to any political story worth telling.

References

Agar, M. ([1980] 1996). *The Professional Stranger*. 2nd ed. San Diego: Academic Press.

Agar, M. and MacDonald, J. (1995). 'Focus Groups and Ethnography,' *Human Organization* 54: 78–86.

Andrews, L. (2014). *Ministering to Education*. Cardigan: Parthian.

Aronoff, M. J. and Kubik, J. (2013). *Anthropology and Political Science: A Convergent Approach*. New York: Berghahn Books.

Auyero, J. and Joseph, L. (2007). 'Introduction: Politics under the Ethnographic Microscope,' in J. L. Mahler and J. Auyero (eds) *New Perspectives on Political Ethnography*. New York: Springer, 1–13.

Bailey, Frederick G. (1969). *Stratagems and Spoils: A Social Anthropology of Politics*. Oxford: Blackwell.

Barley, N. (1986). *The Innocent Anthropologist: Notes from a Mud Hut*. Harmondsworth: Penguin Books.

Beckett, F. and Hencke, D. (2004). *The Blairs and their Court*. London: Aurum Press.

Bevir, M. (1999). *The Logic of the History of Ideas*. Cambridge: Cambridge University Press.

Bevir, M. and Rhodes, R. A. W. (2003). *Interpreting British Governance*. London: Routledge.

Blewett, N. (1999). *A Cabinet Diary: A Personal Record of the First Keating Government*. Kent Town: Wakefield Press.

Blunkett, David (2006). *The Blunkett Tapes: My Life in the Bear Pit*. London: Bloomsbury.

Boswell, J. and Corbett, J. (2015a). 'Embracing Impressionism: Revealing the Brush Strokes of Interpretive Research,' *Critical Policy Studies* 9: 216–25.

Boswell, J. and Corbett, J. (2015b). 'Who Are We Trying To Impress? Reflections on Navigating Political Science, Ethnography and Interpretation,' *Journal of Organizational Ethnography* 4: 223–35.

Boswell, J., Corbett, J., Flinders, M., Jennings, W., Rhodes, R. A. W., and Wood, M., (2018). 'What Can Political Ethnography Tell Us About Anti-Politics and Democratic Disaffection?,' *European Journal of Political Research* 58 (1) 2019: 56–71.

Boswell, J., Corbett, J. and Rhodes, R. A. W., (2019).*The Art and Craft of Comparison*. Cambridge: Cambridge University Press.

Bourdon, R. (1993). 'Towards a Synthetic Theory of Rationality,' *International Studies in the Philosophy of Science* 7: 5–19.

Bryman, A. (2001) (ed.). *Ethnography*. Volume 1: *The Nature of Ethnography*; Volume 2: *Ethnographic Fieldwork Practice*; Volume 3: *Issues in Ethnography*; Volume 4: *Analysis and Writing in Ethnography*. London: Sage Benchmarks in Social Research Methods.

Burawoy, A. (1998). 'The Extended Case Method,' *Sociological Theory* 16: 4–33.

Burch, M. and Holliday, I. (1996). *The British Cabinet System*. Englewood/Hemel Hempstead: Prentice Hall/Harvester Wheatsheaf.

Burch, M. and Holliday, I. (2004). 'The Blair Government and the Core Executive', *Government and Opposition* 39: 1–21.

Clifford, J. (1986). 'Introduction: Partial Truths', in J. Clifford and G. E. Marcus (ed.) *Writing Culture: The Poetics and Politics of Ethnography*. Berkeley: University of California Press, 1–26.

Corbett, J. (2014). 'Practising Reflection: Empathy, Emotion and Intuition in Political Life Writing', *Life Writing* 11: 349–65.

Corbett, J. (2015). *Being Political. Leadership and Democracy in the Pacific Islands*. Honolulu: University of Hawai'i Press.

Crewe, E. (2005). *Lords of Parliament. Manners, Rituals and Politics*. Manchester: Manchester University Press.

Crewe, E. (2015). *The House of Commons. An Anthropology of MPs at Work*. London: Bloomsbury.

Denzin, N. K. and Lincoln, Y. S. ([1994] 2011). 'Introduction: The Discipline and Practice of Qualitative Research', in N. K. Denzin and Y. S. Lincoln (eds) *Handbook of Qualitative Research*. 4th ed. London: Sage, 1–19.

Dexter, L. ([1970] 2006). *Elite and Specialized Interviewing*. Colchester, Essex: ECPR Press.

DeWalt, K. M., DeWalt, B. R., and Wayland, C. B. (1998). 'Participant Observation', in H. R. Bernard (ed.) *Handbook of Methods in Cultural Anthropology*. Walnut Creek, CA: Altamira Press, 259–99.

Eckstein, H. (1975). 'Case Study Theory in Political Science', in F. I. Greenstein and N. Polsby (ed.) *Handbook of Political Science*. Volume 7: *Strategies of Inquiry*. Reading, MA: Addison-Wesley, 79–137.

Emerson, Robert M., Fretz, Rachel I., and Shaw, L. L. ([1995] 2011). *Writing Ethnographic Fieldnotes*. 2nd ed. Chicago: University of Chicago Press.

Fenno, R. F. (1978). *Home Style: House Members in their Districts*. Boston, MA: Little, Brown.

Fenno, R. E. (1990). *Watching Politicians: Essays on Participant Observation*. Berkeley, CA: Institute of Governmental Studies, University of California.

Fischer, F. (2003). *Reframing Policy Analysis*. Oxford: Oxford University Press.

Fortes, M. and Evans-Pritchard, E. E. (1940) (eds). *African Political Systems*. Oxford: The Clarendon Press.

Gains, F. (2011). 'Elite Ethnographies: Potential, Pitfalls and Prospects for "Getting Up Close and Personal"', *Public Administration* 89: 156–66.

Geertz, C. ([1973] 1993) 'Thick Description: Toward an Interpretive Theory of Culture', in C. Geertz (ed.) *The Interpretation of Cultures*. London: Fontana, 3–30.

Gerring, J. (2004). 'What Is A Case Study and What Is It Good For?', *American Political Science Review* 98: 341–54.

Hammersley, M. (2006). 'Ethnography: Problems and Prospects', *Ethnography and Education* 1: 3–14.

Hammersley, M. and Atkinson, P. ([1983] 2007). *Ethnography: Principles in Practice*. 3rd ed. London: Routledge.

Heclo, H. and Wildavsky, A. ([1974] 1981). *The Private Government of Public Money*. 2nd ed. London: Macmillan.

Hennessy, P. (2000). *The Prime Ministers*. London: Allen Lane, The Penguin Press.

Holmes, D. R. and Marcus, G. E. (2005). 'Refunctioning Ethnography: The Challenge of an Anthropology of the Contemporary', in N. K. Denzin and Y. S. Lincoln (eds) *Handbook of Qualitative Research*. 3rd ed. London: Sage, 1087–101.

Jackson, J. E. (1990). '"I Am a Fieldnote": Fieldnotes as a Symbol of Professional Identity,' in R. Sanjek (ed.) *Fieldnotes: The Making of Anthropology*. Ithaca, NY: Cornell University Press, 3–33.

Kapiszewski, D., Lauren, M., MacLean, B., and Read, L. (2015). *Field Research in Political Science: Practices and Principles*. Cambridge: Cambridge University Press.

Kaufman, H. ([1960] 2006). *The Forest Ranger: A Study in Administrative Behavior*. Baltimore, MD: Johns Hopkins Press.

Kaufman, H. ([1981] 2011). *The Administrative Behaviour of Federal Bureau Chiefs*. Washington, DC: The Brookings Institution.

Kertzer, D. (1988). *Ritual Politics and Power*. New Haven: Yale University Press.

Leach, E. (1954). *Political Systems of Highland Burma: A Study of Kachin Social Structure*. Cambridge, MA: Harvard University Press.

Lewellen, T. C. (2003). *Political Anthropology: An Introduction*. 3rd ed. Westport, CT: Praeger Publishers.

Levi-Strauss, C. (1966). *The Savage Mind*. London: Weidenfeld and Nicolson.

Lincoln, Y. S. and Guba, E. G. (1985). *Naturalistic Inquiry*. Newbury Park, CA: Sage.

Marcus, G. E. (2007a). 'Ethnography Two Decades after Writing Culture: From the Experimental to the Baroque,' *Anthropological Quarterly* 80: 1127–45.

Marcus, G. E. (2007b). 'How Short Can Field Research Be?,' *Social Anthropology* 15: 353–67.

Maynard-Moody, S. and Musheno, M. (2003). *Cops, Teachers, Counsellors: Stories from the Front Lines of Public Service*. Ann Arbor, MI: The University of Michigan Press.

Morgan, D. (1997). *Focus Groups as Qualitative Research*. 2nd ed. London: Sage Publications.

Moore, C. (2015). *Margaret Thatcher: The Authorized Biography*. Volume 2: *Everything She Wants*. London: Allen Lane.

Nader, L. (1972). 'Up the Anthropologist-Perspectives Gained from Studying Up,' in D. H. Hymes (ed.) *Reinventing Anthropology*. New York: Pantheon Books, 284–311.

Ouroussof, A. (2010). *Wall Street at War: The Secret Struggle for the Global Economy*. Cambridge: Polity Press.

Peston, R. (2005). *Brown's Britain*. London: Short Books.

Pink, S. (2013). *Doing Visual Ethnography*. 3rd ed. London: Sage.

Rawnsley, A. (2001). *Servants of the People: The Inside Story of New Labour*. Revised ed. London: Penguin Books.

Rawnsley, A. (2010). *The End of the Part:. The Rise and Fall of New Labour*. London: Viking.

Reeher, G. (2006). *First Person Political*. New York: New York University Press.

Rhodes, R. A. W. (1995). 'From Prime Ministerial Power to Core Executive,' in R. A. W. Rhodes and P. Dunleavy (eds) *Prime Minister, Cabinet and Core Executive*. (London: Macmillan), 11–37.

Rhodes, R. A. W. (2011). *Everyday Life in British Government*. Oxford: Oxford University Press.

Rhodes, R. A. W. (2014). 'Core Executives, Prime Ministers, Statecraft and Court Politics: Towards Convergence,' in G. Davis and R. A. W. Rhodes (ed.) *The Craft of Governing: Essays in Honour of Professor Patrick Weller*. Crows Nest, NSW: Allen & Unwin, 53–72.

Rhodes, R. A. W. (2017). *Interpretive Political Science*. Oxford: Oxford University Press.

Rhodes, R. A. W. and Tiernan, A. (2014). *Lessons of Governing: A Profile of Prime Ministers' Chiefs Of Staff*. Melbourne: Melbourne University Press.

Rhodes, R. A. W. and Tiernan, A. (2015). 'Focus Groups as Ethnography: The Case of Prime Ministers' Chiefs of Staff,' *Journal of Organizational Ethnography* 4: 208–22.

Rhodes, R. A. W., 't Hart, P., and Noordegraaf, M. (2007) (eds). *Observing Government Elites: Up Close and Personal*. Houndmills: Palgrave-Macmillan.

Richards, S. (2010). *Whatever It Takes: The Real Story of Gordon Brown and New Labour*. London: Fourth Estate.

Rorty, R. (1980). *Philosophy the Mirror of Nature*. Oxford: Blackwell.

Sanjek, R. (1990). *Fieldnotes: The Making of Anthropology*. Ithaca, NY: Cornell University Press.

Savoie, D. (1999). *Governing from the Centre*. Toronto: Toronto University Press.

Savoie, D. (2008). *Court Government and the Collapse of Accountability in Canada and the United Kingdom*. Toronto: University of Toronto Press.

Schatz, E. (2009) (ed.). *Political Ethnography: What Immersion Contributes to the Study of Power*. Chicago: University of Chicago Press.

Schwartz-Shea, P. and Yanow, D. (2002) '"Reading" "Methods" "Texts": How Research Methods Texts Construct Political Science,' *Political Research Quarterly* 55: 457–86.

Schwartz-Shea, P. and Yanow, D. (2012). *Interpretive Research Design: Concepts and Processes*. London: Routledge.

Seldon, A. (2004). *Blair*. London: Free Press.

Seldon, A. with Snowden, P. and Collings, D. (2007). *Blair Unbound*. London: Simon and Schuster.

Seldon, A. and Lodge, G. (2010). *Brown at 10*. London: Biteback Publishing.

Seldon, A. and Snowden, P. (2015). *Cameron at 10: The Inside Story 2010–2015*. London: William Collins.

Shipman, T. (2016). *All Out War: The Full Story of How Brexit Sank Britain's Political Class*. London: William Collins.

Shore, C. (2000). *Building Europe: The Cultural Politics of European Integration*. London: Routledge.

Shore, C. and Nugent, S. (2002). *Elite Cultures: Anthropological Perspectives*. ASA Monographs 38. London: Routledge.

Stone, D. (2015). 'Quantitative Analysis,' in M. Bevir and R. A. W. Rhodes (eds) *The Routledge Handbook of Interpretive Political Science*. London: Routledge, 157–70.

Taylor, L. (2014). 'On the Endangered Art of Ethnography,' *Times Higher Education* 19 June: 1–5.

't Hart, P. (2007). 'Spies at the Crossroads: Observing Change in the Dutch Intelligence Service,' in R. A. W. Rhodes, Paul 't Hart, and M. Noordegraaf (eds) *Observing Government Elites: Up Close and Personal*. Houndmills, Basingstoke: Palgrave-Macmillan, 51–77.

Van Willigen, J. (2002). *Applied Anthropology: An Introduction*. 3rd ed. Westport, CT: Bergin & Garvey.

Wagenaar, H. (2011). *Meaning in Action: Interpretation and Dialogue in Policy Analysis*. New York: M. E. Sharpe.

Watson, D. (2002). *Recollections of a Bleeding Heart: A Portrait of Paul Keating PM*. New York: Knopf.

Watson, G. (1987). 'Make Me Reflexive—But Not Yet: Strategies for Managing Essential Reflexivity in Ethnographic Discourse,' *Journal of Anthropological Research* 43: 29–41.

Weaver, C. (2008). *Hypocrisy Trap: The World Bank and the Poverty of Reform*. Princeton, NJ: Princeton University Press.

Wedeen, L. (2010). 'Reflections on Ethnographic Work in Political Science,' *Annual Review of Political Science* 13: 255–72.

Weller, P. (1989). *Malcolm Fraser, PM: A Study in Prime Ministerial Power*. Harmondsworth: Penguin Books.

Weller, P. (2014). *Kevin Rudd: Twice Prime Minister*. Melbourne: Melbourne University Press.

Weller, P. (2014). 'Anticipating Interpretivism: Heclo and Wildavsky as Pioneers,' *Australian Journal of Public Administration* 73: 331–9.

Wells, P. (2013). *The Longer I'm Prime Minister: Stephen Harper and Canada, 2006-*. Toronto: Random House Canada.

Werner, O. and Schoepfle, G. M. (1987). *Systematic Fieldwork*. Vol. 1; *Foundations of Ethnography and Interviews*, Vol. 2; *Ethnographic Analysis and Data Management*. London: Sage.

Whyte, W. F. (1993) [1943] *Street Corner Society: The Social Structure of an Italian Slum*. 4th revised ed. Chicago: University of Chicago Press.

Wolcott, H. F. (1995). *The Art of Fieldwork*. Walnut Creek, CA: Altamira Press.

Wood, E. J. (2007). 'Field Research,' in C. Boix and S. C. Stokes (eds) *The Oxford Handbook of Comparative Politics*. Oxford: Oxford University Press, 123–46.

Yin, R. K. (2008). *Case Study Research: Design and Methods*.4th ed. London: Sage.

Zacka, B. (2017). *When the State Meets the Street: Public Service and Moral Agency*. Harvard: Harvard University Press.

CHAPTER 7

FEMINIST APPROACHES
TO THE STUDY OF
POLITICAL EXECUTIVES

KAREN BECKWITH

OF all the arenas of political science research, the study of executive politics should find feminist analyses to be most trenchant, appropriate, insightful, and constructive. Positions of executive political power—presidencies, prime ministerships, cabinet posts—have long been highly gendered, insofar as they were exclusively occupied by men until the twentieth century. Only men contended for these positions; only men were thought suitable for executive political office; male networks of class, education, family, friendship, and prestige reinforced male dominance in executive political institutions, shaping those institutions to the experiences and needs of male political elites and gendering those institutions to the masculine, in practice and buttressed by law and judicial decisions. It is worth stating the obvious: scholarship on executive politics and executive political elites has generally been silent on the sex and gender of political executives,[1] and it has taken feminist analysis to focus attention on the sex and gender of presidents and prime ministers, and of the members of the cabinets they form.

Women's access to executive political power has been limited and recent. Although women's executive power came first through their limited inclusion as monarchs, it took until the early 1900s for women to be appointed as cabinet ministers, and until the second half of the twentieth century to be selected as prime ministers or elected as presidents with executive powers; it was not until the twenty-first century that European monarchies ended agnatic primogeniture.[2] The advent of the first female

[1] For modest and limited early mention of sex and political elites, see, for example, Duverger (1955); Putnam (1976: 32–4, 36); Blondel (1985, 1987). These works identify the small numbers of women in positions of executive political power; as Duverger writes (1955: 75), 'the proportion of women playing a real part in political leadership is ridiculously small.'

[2] Sweden (1980), the Netherlands (1983), Norway (1990), Belgium (1991), Denmark (2009), and the United Kingdom (2013) changed their monarchical succession rules to equal primogeniture, detaching

prime minister[3] is still within living memory, as is the date of the first female president.[4] As of May 2019, two women serve as queens regnant;[5] nine women are elected presidents, of whom only one of whom is head of government,[6] and eleven women serve as prime ministers.[7] The numbers of women who hold, and who have held throughout history, positions of executive power are very small, and mark the gendered, patriarchal exclusion of women from executive political power that makes feminist analysis both necessary and fruitful.

This chapter focuses on the theoretical underpinnings of scholarship on women and gender in regard to executive politics, with specific reference to feminist theory. The chapter explicates feminist approaches to the study of executive politics, gender, and power, identifying their key assumptions and their normative commitments, and discusses the range of methods employed by scholars in recent research. The chapter shows how gender as a concept and a process informs executive political analysis,[8] and concludes with reflections on a future research agenda for feminist scholarship on political executives.

7.1 Feminist Theory and the Study of Political Executives

Feminist theory has a wide sweep and has informed scholarship on women, gender, and politics in every realm of the political. Feminist political thought nonetheless is unified by its emphasis on patriarchal constructions of political power and the recognition that 'the secondary status of women [...] is reinforced by the total pattern of men's privileges' (Chowdhury et al. 1994: 3) and that 'apparently universal categories, such as the "individual", the "worker", the "social", or the "political", are sexually particular, constructed on the basis of male attributes, capacities, and modes of activity' (Pateman 1986: 7).

---

succession from the gender of the heir; in these cases, the first-born child is the heir apparent, regardless of sex. Spain has not yet changed to equal primogeniture. Succession to the monarchy in Muslim countries and in Japan is by agnatic primogeniture, reserved for a first-born male child. For the political impact of equal primogeniture and female monarchs, see McDonagh (2009). Thanks to Professor Pete Moore for information on succession in Middle East monarchies.

[3] Sirivamo Bandaranaike, Sri Lanka, 1960.   [4] Isabel Perón, Argentina, 1974.

[5] Margrethe II, Denmark, and Elizabeth II, United Kingdom. Margrethe II was the first female monarch of Denmark (1972) since 1412; Elizabeth II was the first female monarch in the UK (1952) since 1901.

[6] Hilda Heine (Marshall Islands).

[7] Jacinda Ardern (New Zealand); Ana Brnacík (Serbia); Viorica Dăncilă (Romania); Sheihk Hasina (Bangladesh), Kátrin Jakobsdóttir (Iceland); Saara Kuugongelwa-Amadhila (Namibia); Leona Marlin-Romeo (Sint Maarten); Theresa May (UK); Mia Amor Mottley (Barbados); Angela Merkel (Germany); and Erna Solberg (Norway). Thanks to Professors Farida Jalalzai and Aili Mari Tripp for information about women currently in political executive office.

[8] This chapter does not report on findings in regard to how feminist approaches have been employed in political research (see O'Brien and Reyes-Housholder, Chapter 13 in this volume).

Feminist theory recognizes the role of the state in shaping politics as a public sphere, where 'the citizen is a gendered category based on women's exclusion' (Zerilli 2006: 106), and where the state constructs a private sphere within which women are subordinated. Zerilli (2006: 106–7) summarizes the project of feminist theory in regard to the canon of (Western) political thought as (1) exposing the absence of women from the political; (2) revealing the constitution of categories of the 'political' as embedded in and inseparable from women's exclusion; and (3) 'reconstituting the category of politics anew.'

Feminist theory has been clear about the mutually constitutive nature of gender and the political, where formal political positions are imbued with gendered meanings, constructing the exclusion of women as 'outsiders' of the state. Hence, a feminist theory of the state undergirds (or should undergird) our understandings of executive political power. As Brown argues (1992: 14):

> The state can be masculinist without intentionally or overtly pursuing the 'interests' of men precisely because the multiple dimensions of socially constructed masculinity have historically shaped the multiple modes of power circulating through the domain called the state. [...A]lthough all state power is marked with gender, the same aspects of masculinism do not appear in each modality of state power. Thus, a feminist theory of the state requires simultaneously articulating, deconstructing, and relating the multiple strands of power comprising both masculinity and the state.

Feminist theory sees women positioned by political thought as political outsiders of the state and of civic personhood, requiring then that, when women enter the state, under limited terms and few in number, they enter on masculinist terms. 'The "universal" standing that is to be won is that of a being with masculine characteristics engaging in masculine activities' (Pateman 1986: 8).[9] This should be particularly evident when applied to women's political inclusion at the highest level of political power: the political executive.

How then does feminist theory inform and understand executive political power and women's access to it? Feminist political thought recognizes that women interact with the state and are shaped by it. Therefore, insofar as gender and politics are mutually constitutive, transforming politics and the political should be possibilities available to activist feminists and feminist movements. For feminist political scientists, this entails a focus on how gender and political power intersect and reinforce (or undermine) each other at the highest level of governance: cabinet ministers, presidents, and prime ministers, those at the centre of governing power.[10]

---

[9] Escobar-Lemmon and Taylor-Robinson's (2016) findings, comparing women's and men's cabinet credentials, provide empirical support to this claim. See also Jaquette (2017: 37) and Annesley et al. (2019), who find that female presidents and prime ministers are no more likely to appoint more women to cabinet posts than are their male counterparts. See O'Brien et al. (2015); Schwindt-Bayer and Reyes-Housholder (2017b: 94); and Reyes-Housholder and Thomas (2018).

[10] This chapter explicitly excludes presidential advisors (Arana Araya 2018: 1), the judiciary, party leaders and opposition leaders; and diplomats and ambassadors (for the latter, see Towns and Niklasson 2017; Aggestam and Towns 2018).

Midrange Theory and Feminist Approaches. Primarily engaging at the level of midrange theory, feminist approaches engage specific, 'delimited aspects of [political] phenomena' (Merton 1949: 448). Midrange theorizing 'directs us to a set of hypotheses that can be empirically tested' (Merton 1949: 449), but also connects empirical results to the project of theory-building. Although feminist theory has emphasized the gendered nature and construction of masculinist political power at the level of the state, unified theories of patriarchy, masculinism, and gendered political power have yet to be connected in specific pathways to the empirical work of feminist scholars on political executives. Instead, typical of 'a comparatively young subfield' (O'Brien and Housholder, Chapter 13 in this volume), feminist approaches to the empirical side of theory-building have engaged in midrange theorizing, where theoretical abstractions 'are close enough to observed data to be incorporated in propositions that permit empirical testing' (Merton 1949: 448). Midrange theory permits concerted empirical analysis, asking questions of political specificity (i.e. 'under what conditions'), with the purpose of identifying gendered processes and outcomes that are, if loosely, connected with feminist theory and with political science models and midrange theories of the political executive, for the purpose of further theory development.

Employing empirical investigation to establish regularities in women's activism and empowerment, turning on questions concerning male-female differences in executive power, feminist approaches to political executives have involved ground-clearing primary research, asking the necessary questions that provide the basis for more fully developed theorizing. Such research includes, for example, political histories of women's presidencies and prime ministerships (Murray 2010; Jalalzai 2013, 2016), foci on individual credentials that establish access to executive power (Escobar-Lemmon and Taylor-Robinson 2016), examination of gendered categories of ministries (Krook and O'Brien 2012; Barnes and O'Brien 2018), and case-specific studies of appointment rules and processes to identify gendered pathways to executive power (Martin and Borrelli 2016; for additional examples, see also Chapter 13 in this volume). Research questions at the level of midrange theorizing ask about gendered patterns of executive replacement and whether women are more likely to be included in initial, post-election cabinets than in subsequent reshuffled cabinets, ultimately recurring to an electoral competition model for explaining women's cabinet inclusion. Feminist approaches to the executive less frequently rely on research on (or refer to) coalition governments to ask if women's cabinet inclusion varies according to whether the government is constructed as a multi-party coalition government, a minority government, or a single party majority government where the prime minister or president is fully empowered to construct the cabinet.

Midrange feminist theorizing of executive politics, absent a firm connection to high-level feminist theory regarding patriarchal power, reveals how new the feminist approaches to the study of executive politics are, as well as the challenges such research faces. First, for the most part, feminist approaches to executive politics have focused on sex rather than gender. This focus allows us to see and to understand women, and men, in positions of executive power (how many, where, who) but not to understand the patriarchal political forces that are the context for women's access to executive positions and that provide the mechanisms of (some) women's inclusion in power, women's general exclusion from the executive, and how patriarchal power functions within the executive, including gendered power within all-male cabinets.

Second, many studies involve research questions that derive from sexist assertions in actual politics about women's executive power: that female executives are not as 'meritorious' as their male counterparts (see Annesley, Beckwith and Franceschet 2019); that women's underrepresentation in cabinets can be explained by their lack of appropriate credentials (see Escobar-Lemmon and Taylor-Robinson 2016); and that women are insufficiently ambitious for political office (see Kenny and Piscopo 2019). Sexist assertions in popular politics are tautological, in their claim that women are not qualified for executive office, given women's historical absence from presidencies, prime ministerships, and cabinet posts; that is, women's exclusion from executive power is evidence of their lack of qualification for such power.

These two challenges for feminist approaches to the study of political executives have important implications. A primary focus on sex rather than gender, and on category rather than process (Acker 1992; Beckwith 2005), obscures how patriarchal executive power is not limited to cabinets and heads of state and heads of government and how gendered executive power can interact with and support exclusion and disempowerment of women across a range of political venues. A concern with research hypotheses derived from sexist assumptions of female unworthiness and unsuitability for executive office reinforces those assumptions and directs our attention away from feminist theorizing on patriarchy and masculinist power and from more pertinent contemporary questions of gender and executive power.

There are three major approaches that feminist scholars have employed at the mid-range of feminist theorizing in regard to executive political power. These are (1) cultural approaches, (2) the impact of gender norms (Murray 2010; Tremblay and Stockemer 2013; Schwindt-Bayer and Reyes-Housholder 2017a; Yates and Hughes 2017), and (3) feminist institutionalism (Kenny and Mackay 2009; Mackay and Waylen 2009, 2014; Kenny 2014; Lowndes 2014; Thomson 2018; Annesley et al. 2019).[11] Feminist scholars have also returned to debates concerning political power and the relationship of power and gender at the executive level (Weldon 2019; Chapter 13 in this volume).

Cultural Explanations. Cultural and gender norm expectations, performances, and reports (especially via mass media) fit well with understandings of the masculinist nature of political executives, although such explanations are as yet unsatisfying. Cultural explanations are difficult to move across national boundaries; operationalizing culture as an explanatory variable is challenging; and masculinities vary within as well as across cultures, and with reference and applicability of appropriateness to specific executive

---

[11] Note that Escobar-Lemmon and Taylor-Robinson employ a social control model to assess the inclusion of women in cabinet and the extent to which female *ministrables* must match male cabinet credentials in order to be included in cabinets, mitigating against conflict. They argue that women's appointments will be the result of 'intense political pressure' and that 'women will receive the smallest feasible number of appointments' (2016: 4).

political offices. Yates and Hughes (2017: 102) discuss such cultural explanations as encompassing ideology, religious tradition, and 'attitudes, beliefs, and norms [that] shape gender inequalities in politics', recognizing that these factors regularly produce male political executives across a range of political systems, noting as well that 'no religious tradition has proved to be an insurmountable obstacle for women leaders' (2017: 107).

Gender Norms. Political executives are required to engage in some performance of masculinity, and specific presidents and prime ministers employ various masculinities appropriate to their context, in terms of country, ethnicity, party, and time frame. 'Men vying to become (and stay) national leaders must actively construct their masculinity in line with cultural expectations and ideals' (Yates and Hughes 2017: 102). Such expectations may shift in response to real world events. The Year of the Woman Conferences, particularly the 1995 Conference in Beijing, influenced understandings of appropriateness for political executives in many countries, with particular resonance for countries attempting a transition to democracy (Yates and Hughes 2017: 107).[12] Moreover, '[c]ulture is not static' (Yates and Hughes 2017: 116); changes in gender norms are possible as appropriate masculinities at the highest levels of political power are renegotiated, re-instantiated, and re-appropriated by new actors. Feminist movements and activist women outside and inside the state have had an impact on reshaping understandings of masculinities appropriate to executive politics, masculinities performed by women as well as by men.[13] As O'Brien and Reyes-Housholder conclude, however, 'cultural variables [...] do not explain women's inclusion in executive politics [...]. Instead, candidate supply and the existence of political opportunities are more important factors' (Chapter 13 in this volume, p. 252).

Supply and Demand Models. Supply and demand models have been employed for understanding the gendered limitations of candidate pipelines for national legislatures (Norris and Lovenduski 1995); they have subsequently focused on the numbers of women available for inclusion in cabinets as well. In cases where members of a cabinet must be drawn from the legislature, as in parliamentary systems, it is not surprising that supply and demand models find a positive relationship between women's presence in the legislature and women's inclusion in cabinets (Davis 1997; Reynolds 1999; Siaroff 2000; Bauer and Okpotor 2013; Krook and O'Brien 2012; Claveria 2014; Stockemer 2017; Scherpereel, Adams, and Hayes 2019). The relationship is less clear for presidential systems, where cabinet ministers may be selected from outside parliament; moreover, the relationship between women's legislative presence and women in cabinet posts varies in strength across regions and time frame (Annesley et al. 2019).

Because fewer cabinet posts than parliamentary seats are available in any political system, and because the selection routes for cabinet ministers and legislators are so different (see Chapter 16 in this volume), a supply and demand model may be less fruitful

---

[12] Jaquette (2017: 55 n100) notes that 'Fujimori tried to use his pro-women stance to burnish his democratic credentials internationally', as the 'only president to attend the Beijing conference.'

[13] For discussions of executive political masculinities, see Duerst-Lahti and Kelly (1995); Duerst-Lahti (1997); Murray (2010); Borrelli and Goren (2016); Chhabria (2016); Gooding (2016); Schwindt-Bayer and Reyes-Housholder (2017b: 83–4).

for explaining the gendered nature of women's cabinet inclusion than for explaining women's election to parliaments. The actual numbers necessary for staffing a gender parity cabinet are quite small, and hence the supply of female potential ministers, especially for presidential political systems, is likely to be sufficient in most countries. Defining a gender parity cabinet as one where women constitute 50 per cent of cabinet (plus or minus one minister, for cases of odd-numbered cabinets), it would take as few as seven women to construct a gender parity cabinet in the United States (n = 15). Even for a cabinet of relatively large size, such as that of Canada (n = 30), constructing a gender parity cabinet would require a supply of only fifteen women—presumably a simple task in a nation of thirty-seven million persons. Annesley et al. (2019) define gender parity cabinets as those where women constitute 50 per cent + 1 minister. For example, France has had three successive gender parity cabinets, under Presidents Nicolas Sarkozy, François Hollande, and Emmanuel Macron (Beckwith et al. 2017). Supply and demand models for women's inclusion in cabinet need to be further theorized, taking into account the numbers required.

Feminist Institutionalism. Feminist institutionalist approaches address the structural factors that shape opportunities for women's access to the political executive. Feminist institutionalist analysis has followed the rise of 'new institutionalism' generally in political science (e.g. Thelen 1999; Helmke and Levitsky 2004; Chapter 3 in this volume). Feminist institutionalist research has addressed the rules and norms that structure state political power, with reference to gender and political executive power. This is not surprising: 'no other institutional-organizational setting is as closely identified with the exercise of political power as are executives' (Goetz, Chapter 3 in this volume). Moreover, in an area of research where there are few women, emphasis on the institutions themselves—presidencies, prime ministerships, cabinets—is similarly unsurprising. Emphasis on individual female political executives or a regional subset of women in executive posts was characteristic of the early research in this arena (e.g. Murray 2010; Jalalzai 2008, 2013); the shift to an institutional analysis relied on this research but has shifted the focus, asking implicitly (and sometimes explicitly) about masculinist advantage in rules and practices (Murray 2014).

Feminist institutionalist analysis has focused on structural barriers to women's access to state power, underscoring the masculinist construction of such institutions across time and the path dependency of women's political exclusion. Nonetheless, institutions offer gendered opportunities. First, institutions are not seamless sets of formal rules perfectly complied with and enacted throughout a political system; instead, informal rules and practices may accommodate variation within formal rules;[14] institutional components, established for other purposes, can be employed or exploited by marginalized groups to gain access where access appeared to be blocked. Second, subnational institu-

---

[14] As Helmke and Levitsky (2004: 736 n103) observe, 'Many informal institutions emerge endogenously from formal institutional arrangements. Actors create them in an effort to subvert, mitigate the effects of, substitute for, or enhance the efficiency of formal institutions.'

tions, developed locally, can challenge and shift national institutional understandings of appropriate rules and rulers.

Third, institutions change over time. 'If institutions are the products of gendered power struggles and contestation', as feminist theory insists, 'then the creation of new institutions involves changing or creating new gendered rules, norms, and practices that will then shape actor's strategies and preferences' (Mackay and Waylen 2014: 491). Finally, masculinist components of institutions may present the potential for female as well as male actors to access their masculinities and to employ them appropriately for access to political office. 'How things are done' in institutions concerns not only the formal rules of access and inclusion, but the informal means by which politics and political power are constructed (Lowndes 2014).[15]

Feminist institutionalists have thus contributed to understandings of how changes in institutions might advantage or disadvantage women's political inclusion at the highest levels of political power. With the third wave of democracy, political institutions were changing rapidly or being replaced entirely. In the context of new institutions, feminist scholars analysed the impact of 'newness' and opportunities associated with the new (Kenny 2014; Mackay and Waylen 2014).[16] Countries in transitions to democracy have been shown to offer both opportunities for (Schwindt-Bayer and Reyes-Housholder 2017a) and barriers to female political executives. New institutional arrangements, post-conflict, post-war, or post-transition, offer opportunities to women (Hughes 2009; Tripp 2015)—although the extent, scope, and location of such opportunities vary across countries and institutions.[17] Several scholars have found that gendered opportunities for women are greater in parliamentary systems, where women may have relatively easy access to prime ministerships that place them 'first amongst equals', or as a member of a larger party team; others have found that, in post-transition countries, women have better opportunities for presidencies than their sisters in parliamentary systems. Variation in political system and in institutional type appears not to predict women's access to presidencies or prime ministerships (Jalalzai 2017; Jaquette 2017), nor to predict women's appointment as cabinet ministers in terms of their numbers, date of first female minister, or date of last all-male cabinet (Annesley et al. 2019). These competing, or perhaps complementary, findings raise the question, for feminist institutionalists, of 'what is meant by a "new" institution and the extent to which any institution can be described as new' (Mackay and Waylen 2014: 491; see also Thomson 2018: 180).

Bringing Power Back In. Political executives hold serious political power. As Arana Araya (2018: 2) reminds us,

[15] For the range of feminist uses of institutionalist approaches, see Mackay and Waylen (2009: 237).

[16] See, in particular, Mackay (2014) on 'nested newness'; Chappell 2014 on the new International Criminal Court.

[17] See Hughes 2009; Tripp 2015. Much of the work on post-conflict transitions focuses on women's access to legislatures rather than to the political executive. See, however, Montecinos (2017). Htun and Weldon (2018: 242) find that the impact of new institutions is mediated by 'the animating influence of civil society movements.'

Political elites have the capacity to dramatically increase and harm the collective well-being of society. They [...] give life and manage the institutions that shape intrastate, state-society, and civil society relations [...]. In short, like no other group, political elites define the path that a country will follow.

Although not writing specifically to political executives, Weldon (2019: 128) advocates for

an account of power that helps us to understand why change sometimes seems to come from the bottom-up, and why women and men leaders sometimes lead—and sometimes resist—change. [...A] feminist understanding of power points to the importance of civil society and broader social norms as a potential area for resistance and empowerment. [...] The study of gender inequality has required feminist political scientists to develop new ways to understand power, ideas that have implications for understanding important political phenomena such as representation and exclusion.

Weldon (2019: 130) connects power to 'social identity and institutional position', linking gender to power in terms of who the actors are and how they are (and are perceived to be) gendered. Thomson (2018: 181) emphasizes that institutions are 'sites of resistance and obstruction to gender-positive movement' and hence institutional sites, such as the political executive, are locations for the gendered exercise and expression of political power. Feminist political theory ultimately is concerned with 'how power is produced and reproduced through gender' (Kenny and Mackay 2009: 275).

The non-civic personhood of women should mitigate against women's executive political power; nonetheless, women have been prime ministers in arguably two of the most powerful states in West Europe (Britain and Germany), in the Middle East (Israel), and on the Indian subcontinent (India, as well as Bangladesh and Pakistan). Female presidents, with head of government powers, have been few in number, but have recently governed in Brazil, Chile, and South Korea. The challenge for the study of gender and political executives is to theorize gendered executive power.

7.2 FEMINIST METHODOLOGY AND APPROACH IN EXECUTIVE POLITICS

Feminist theorizing in regard to gender, the political, and power, and feminist institutionalism, focuses research on women, gender, and the political executive. Feminist scholars share among them the key assumptions that political power is gendered; that high political office imbued with strong power will be masculinist and gendered to women's disadvantage, and that the gendered political executive, as an institution and peopled with political actors, will construct gendered relations of domination and subordination between men and men, as well as exemplifying that relationship.

These foundational assumptions and the research questions associated with them drive the selection of methods employed by scholars of gender and political executives.

The methodological choices of the feminist scholar depend, as for all social scientists, upon the research question and on the availability of data. 'One general feature of women's direct part in political leadership [is] its extreme smallness' (Duverger 1955: 75). With small numbers of female political executives,[18] cross-sectional large-n statistical analyses are generally precluded (Stauffer and O'Brien 2018), although longitudinal and comparative research serve to establish large- (or larger-) n data bases for quantitative analysis of cabinet appointments, where the numbers are larger than for heads of government and heads of state (see Davis 1997; Escobar-Lemmon and Taylor-Robinson 2016; Barnes and O'Brien 2018). Hence, methodological choices are constrained in part by limitations on methods (see Weldon 2014; Stauffer and O'Brien 2018). Process-tracing for access to political executive office is a fruitful methodological approach for understanding women's access to presidencies and prime ministerships, although it is rarely identified as such in case studies of female political executives.

Feminist institutionalism recognizes the impact of informal institutions on women's access to political power. Discourse analysis is one means of identifying informal institutions—that is, non-codified but known sets of practices and values—and 'chains of equivalence' (Kenny 2014: 680). These, supported by 'a more complex process of *linking* and *differentiation*', may reveal how apparently neutral practices and choices are nonetheless gendered (Kenny 2014: 680; emphasis in original).[19] Kenny (2014: 681) emphasizes the utility of qualitative methods, including 'institutional ethnography [...] and participant observation' to undercover informal rules that support informal institutions, such as candidate selection processes in the Scottish Labour Party. Using an inductive method of identifying rules for qualifying for cabinet positions in seven democracies, Annesley, Beckwith, and Franceschet (2019: chapters 5, 11) conclude that the language of 'merit' is a prevalent strategic and gendered discourse employed at the level of cabinet appointments. Although 'merit' appears on its face to be gender-neutral, claims of 'merit' have been employed primarily to justify exclusion of women as unqualified and hence undeserving of appointment to cabinet, but also on occasion to justify women's inclusion, as highly qualified—despite few actual formal qualifications attached to any cabinet position. Finally, textual analysis, of speeches and performances of 'being the executive', has been applied to individual executives to assess the requirements of gender, as well as the impacts in political executive office (Chhabria 2016; Gooding 2016; Martin and Borrelli 2016; Wood 2016).

A challenge of the methodology for studying gender and the political executive is this very emphasis on methods of discourse analysis, in-depth interviews, and talking to the actors themselves (Kenny 2014: 681). The strategy of these methods is challenged by the

---

[18] Small numbers are typical of political executives, compared to numbers of legislators generally. Hence, a small-numbers problem is endemic to this arena of political research (see Chapter 10 in this volume).

[19] Again, this methodology has been applied primarily to legislative candidacies. See also, for example, Bjarnegård (2013).

difficulties of 'contact[ing] political elite members. [...E]ven if contacted, they may be unwilling to answer researchers' requests or answer them sincerely' (Arana Araya 2018: 4). The necessity of close, detailed work based on personal interviews to identify the ways in which gender works through the political executive confronts the general difficulties of access, including elites' geographical distance from scholars (requiring funds for travel, particularly in comparative political research), and the major pre-existing commitments of even the most potentially willing of political elites (see Chapter 13 in this volume).

7.3 RESEARCH AGENDA: GENDER, FEMINISM, AND EXECUTIVE POLITICS

In *The Gendered Executive*, Martin and Borrelli (2016: 2) assert, 'How we study executive politics in the twenty-first century must undergo a decisive change'. This brief chapter suggests three such changes.

First, the study of executive politics should be detached from research on legislative politics. Feminist institutionalists have focused primarily on women's legislative presence and how the gendered structure of electoral systems functions to facilitate women's access to candidacies (e.g. multi-member proportional representation systems; candidate gender quotas) or to impede them (e.g. single-member plurality systems). It is not clear that the gendered nature of the political executive is similar to the gendered nature of access to legislative power; it may be more useful to start from the scholarship on political executives, with the recognition that such scholarship has not generally focused on gender but yet has much to offer, particularly in regard to formal institutions, institutional path dependencies, and political structures.

Second, and relatedly, the study of executive politics should be institution-specific. Given that '[p]olitical power does not come in only one variety' (Brown 1992: 13), and despite the masculinist nature of the political executive, recognition that political executive offices have multiple forms, including cabinet ministers, heads of state, and heads of government, with political powers varying by political system. The numbers of positions that are available to any aspiring political executive vary across type of office: presidential and prime ministerial positions are limited to an n of 1 in real time for any political system. Cabinet positions, however, are more numerous, although not large, and simultaneous. For the cases examined in *Cabinets, Ministers, and Gender* (Annesley et al. 2019), cabinet size ranged from thirteen (Spain, 2016) to thirty (Canada, 2015). Numbers of available political executive positions determine whether competition for the position is zero-sum, with only one possible victor and where intraparty competitors are pitted against each other, or whether the position is potentially positive-sum, where multiple seats present the opportunity for intraparty inclusion of many office-seekers. This is particularly the case where the head of government has the unfettered capacity to increase the number of cabinet posts (e.g. Canada, Sweden) and hence the ability to construct a positive-sum context for sharing cabinet posts among multiple potential appointees. Under such conditions, or where the size of cabinet is already large, a head of government may be more willing to appoint substantial numbers of women to cabinet, where women's appointment to cabinet may not displace male *ministrables*, potentially protecting the selector from criticism and resistance from party elites.

Specific institutions construct different access routes to political executive positions. Prime ministers come to power through decisions of their political party, which selects them as party leader; success in parliamentary elections elevates the leader to prime minister without a direct vote by the mass public; prime ministers need not present themselves directly to the electorate. Moreover, party leader replacement can occur without a legislative election. Hence, strategic competition among potential party leaders, in contexts of electoral defeat or likely success, produces the party leader and the eventual political executive in the prime minister (see Chapter 23 in this volume). The route to political executive is through the party first. These routes to executive power differ substantially from executive offices that rely on the electorate to choose a president. Scholars have only recently begun to examine the gendered nature of the party leader selection process and its gendered outcomes (Cross and Blais 2012; Pilet and Cross 2014; Beckwith 2015; Thomas 2018).

Presidents who are heads of government, in contrast, must present themselves as potential candidates to their party and as the successful nominee to the general electorate. Although specific formal rules vary by political system, presidential candidates face different sets of veto players, establishing different arenas of competition (see Chapter 11 in this volume). Candidates must first be selected by their party, sometimes by a party primary election involving a relatively large number of voters who are at least nominal 'members' of the party. The successful candidates must then present themselves to the general electorate, who vote to choose the president. These two selection stages are likely to involve men and women differently and to gender the electoral competition differently at each stage. There is some evidence that women are less likely to achieve presidential office, where the president is an elected head of government, than they are to become prime ministers (Jalalzai 2013).

The mechanism for selecting heads of state, whose function is primarily symbolic, varies by country (Alexander and Jalalzai 2016). Presidents who are heads of state, such as the president of Ireland, are elected by majority popular vote; others, such as the president of the Republic of Italy, are elected by the national legislature. The difference in method of selection, and the differences in executive power, produce gendered outcomes. There is some evidence that women are most likely to achieve executive power as heads of state, where power is limited, than as presidents who are heads of government and or as prime ministers (Jalalzai 2013).

Cabinet ministerships are distinct political executive positions. Although specific formal rules vary by political system, in general cabinet ministers are selected by the head of government. Formal and informal rules leave the head of government relatively unrestrained in his or her ability to appoint ministers, and few formal eligibility or qualifying criteria shape the pool of potential ministers. As a result, it is often the simple will of the president or prime minister that determines who will be appointed as a cabinet minister. *Ministrables* need not, in most cases, be approved by a second selector or by an investiture vote. The increase in numbers of women in cabinets has come quickly, although variably, without gender quotas, and it is not unusual for women to be represented in cabinet in higher percentages than they are in a nation's legislature. The relative ease with which women can be included in cabinets is in part responsible for this increase; however, it is likely that selectors are learning from their predecessors that the inclusion of women provides legitimacy benefits to cabinets and to the selector, for whom there appear to be few costs. The recent phenomenon of gender parity cabinets is a strong indication of the distinctive nature of cabinet appointments as political executive positions. Gender parity cabinets also challenge Putnam's 'law of increasing disproportion', where 'within each strategic elite the proportion of women declines as we move from lower to higher strata' (1976: 36).

Because there are different routes to different political executive positions, eligibility requirements differ as well, shaping distinct eligibility pools. The extent to which eligibility criteria, and qualifying criteria, differ may also determine how they are differently gendered, providing easier or more difficult access to such positions for women. Although all political executive positions are gendered, they are likely to be gendered differently. In sum, to apprehend how gender functions in positions of executive power, feminist approaches will need to hypothesize about the specific institutional arrangements of each set of executive positions—presidents, prime ministers, and cabinet members—and to develop midrange theories from the empirical results.

Third, although work on women's access to prime ministerships focuses on accountability (Schwindt-Bayer and Reyes-Housholder 2017b: 94), research on gender, prime ministers, and cabinet ministers should include consideration of the impact of removal power. Presidents cannot be easily removed, although mass demonstrations have been successful in persuading some chief executives to resign. Presidential impeachment is a complicated removal process involving multiple actors, and is generally restricted to a narrow range of removal rationales (e.g. treason, major violations of law). As a result, presidential impeachment is rare. However, two female presidents were recently impeached and removed from office: Dilma Rousseff (Brazil, 31 August 2016) and Park Geun-hye (Korea, 10 March 2017). As more women are elected as heads of government, there will be more scope for assessing the extent to which impeachment becomes a more conventional, less difficult, and gendered means of removal of political executives, and whether increasing ease of impeachment increases the likelihood of electing female presidents.

Prime ministers are more easily removed than are presidents, given that they are leaders of their party first; they can be removed by their party and replaced by the party's preferred alternative, without requiring a general election. In semi-presidential systems, prime ministers serve at the pleasure of the president. Does ease of removal offer an institutional opening to women? That is, confident that a female prime minister can be removed, are (primarily male) party elites more willing to support a female party leader?

And, if so, under what conditions?[20] Does ease of removal present disadvantages to female leaders not faced by their male counterparts (Thomas 2018)? In 2013, Prime Minister Julia Gillard lost her position as Australian Labor Party leader in a party caucus vote. Throughout her tenure as British Prime Minister, Theresa May was repeatedly challenged by her own party elites, withstanding a formal leadership challenge in 2018, but eventually resigning in June 2019, triggering a Conservative Party leadership contest. Again, as more women become prime ministers, there will be more scope for assessing the extent to which means of removal of political executives are gendered, and whether such gendering increases the likelihood of women becoming (and being removed as) prime minister.

7.4 CONCLUSION

If, as quoted earlier, feminist political theory is ultimately concerned with 'how power is produced and reproduced through gender' (Kenny and Mackay 2009: 275), how does that inform understanding of gender and political executives? Although feminist theory, and the study of gender and political executives, views 'power as dispersed and constitutive', how does it recognize 'how powerful actors anchor their privileged institutional positions' when women hold those positions (Kenny and Mackay 2009: 276)? How does feminist political thought address gender and the political executive when 'governance feminism is simply identified with [...] walking the halls of power' (Cruz and Brown 2016: 76)? 'Institutions are not just gendered but also gendering: they produce the very gendered subjects of politics' (Celis et al. 2013: 14–15). What gendered subjects are being produced today by women's inclusion in the political executive—from larger numbers in cabinet posts to fewer than a dozen prime ministerships and a single presidency empowered as head of government—and what gendered subjects are produced by women's exclusion?

In asking these questions, this chapter offers two potential answers. The first recurs to the question of what difference it makes to have women in high political office—and what difference it makes to have all-male political executive leadership. For cabinet appointments, since the 1990s, for many democracies, all-male governing cabinets have become unacceptable and are seen as illegitimate. Although individual political systems and political parties will have different minima for establishing a legitimate gender balance in cabinets—or 'concrete floors' (Annesley et al. 2019), women's inclusion in cabinet is a system legitimacy issue, undergirded by a justice argument. O'Brien and Reyes-Housholder (Chapter 13 in this volume) identify the justice argument as based on women's presence in the population: 'women make up half the population and should thus hold half of all political posts.' Although they are unable to rest a justice argument on representational grounds for the political executive, a justice argument employed for

---

[20] See Beckwith (2010, 2014, 2015).

women's legislative inclusion, a justice argument might better be grounded in the strong political relevance of gender and of women as a politically relevant demographic group, excluded from political power and subordinated by it, across millennia, by law, legislation, and state violence. Women constitute half the population in many countries; in countries where women are less than half the population, state policy has often structured female infanticide, women's malnourishment, and, again, violence against women and femicide (Sen 1999: 189–203; Htun and Weldon 2018: 28–83). Where the state has structured women's subordination, half the state's political executive should be women. This is not to argue that increasing the numbers of women in the political executive would regender political outcomes; that is an empirical question. O'Brien and Reyes-Housholder address this question (Chapter 13 in this volume), considering how women's inclusion might serve to improve governance and have positive impacts on women's mass political participation (see also Reyes-Housholder 2016, 2019).

The second potential consequence of women's inclusion in the political executive is the possible connection with feminist movements outside the state. Feminist approaches to the study of political power identify women's movements, and specifically feminist movements, as key actors in establishing a feminist legislative agenda, supporting the development and implementation of feminist public policy (Mazur 2002; Weldon 2011), and advocating for women in public office.

> Feminist movements are key fighters for new visions of women's rights, while women politicians serve as critical actors or bulwarks against rollbacks in reforms [....] Women's presence in power helps to erode the cultural status hierarchy associating masculinity with power.   (Htun and Weldon 2018: 240)

Women's presence in politics, at the highest levels of the political executives, may provide the 'positional power' (Celis and Lovenduski 2018: 153–5) that provides the possibility of active power. As Celis and Lovenduski state (2018: 150), 'the persistence of gender inequalities cannot simply be attributed to the failure of feminist strategies; rather, they are the consequence of power struggles that need to be more coherently understood', including at the level of political executives.

As Duverger (1955: 76) observed in the past mid-century, 'There are hardly any women in the bodies which take political decisions and direct the state.' This is still the case. Feminist political thought and feminist approaches provide insight into the persistence of male predominance in and masculinist domination of political executives; these insights, while making no promises, offer the opportunity for regendering the political executive for the purpose of the feminist politics that feminist theory envisions.

ACKNOWLEDGEMENTS

I am grateful to Claire Annesley, Susan Franceschet, Diana O'Brien, and Laurel Weldon for critical conversations across several years concerning gender and political executives, much of which informs this chapter. Many thanks as well to those who participated in the Skytte

Manuscript Workshop on 'Cabinets, Ministers, and Gender', September 2016, University of Uppsala, Uppsala, Sweden, with special gratitude to Elin Bjarnegård.

References

Acker, J. (1992). 'From Sex Roles to Gendered Institutions,' *Contemporary Sociology* 21(5): 565–9.

Aggestam, K. and Towns, A. E. (2018) (eds). *Gendering Diplomacy and International Negotiation*. London: Palgrave Macmillan.

Alexander, A. C. and Jalalzai, F. (2016). 'The Symbolic Effects of Female Heads of State,' in J. M. Martin and M. Borrelli (eds) *The Gendered Executive*. Philadelphia: Temple University Press, 25–43.

Annesley, C., Beckwith, K., and Franceschet, S. (2019). *Cabinets, Ministers, and Gender*. Oxford: Oxford University Press.

Arana Araya, I. (2018). 'Comparative Political Elites,' in A. Farazmand (ed.) *Global Encyclopedia of Public Administration, Public Policy, and Governance*. New York: Springer International Publishing.

Barnes, T. D. and O'Brien, D. Z. (2018). 'Defending the Realm: The Appointment of Female Defense Ministers Worldwide,' *American Journal of Political Science* 62(2): 355–68.

Bauer, G. and Okpotor, F. (2013). '"Her Excellency": An Exploratory Overview of Women Cabinet Ministers in Africa,' *Africa Today* 60(1): 77–97.

Beckwith, K. (2005). 'A Common Language of Gender?,' *Politics & Gender* 1(1): 128–37.

Beckwith, K. (2010). 'Someday My Chance Will Come: Women Contesting for Executive Leadership in West Europe,' paper presented at the American Political Science Association meetings, Washington, DC, 1–5 September.

Beckwith, K. (2014). 'From Party Leader to Prime Minister? Gender and Leadership Contests in West Europe,' paper presented at the European Consortium for Political Research Joint Sessions of Workshops, Salamanca, Spain, 10–15 April.

Beckwith, K. (2015). 'Before Prime Minister: Margaret Thatcher, Angela Merkel, and Gendered Leadership Contests,' *Politics & Gender* 11(4): 718–45.

Beckwith, K., Annesley, C. and Franceschet, S. (2017). 'Cabinets and Concrete Floors: The Women in Macron's Cabinet Strengthen the Case for Gender Parity in Government.' LSE Blog on European Politics and Policy, 26 May; http://blogs.lse.ac.uk/europpblog/2017/05/26/cabinets-and-concrete-floors-the-women-in-macrons-cabinet-strengthen-the-case-for-gender-parity-in-government/

Bjarnegård, E. (2013). *Gender, Informal Institutions, and Political Recruitment: Explaining Male Dominance in Parliamentary Representation*. Basingstoke: Palgrave.

Blondel, J. (1985). *Government Ministers in the Contemporary World*. London: SAGE Publishing.

Blondel, J. (1987). *Political Leadership: Towards a General Analysis*. London: SAGE.

Borrelli, M. and Goren, L. J. (2016). 'Sarah Palin's and Paul Ryan's Vice Presidential Acceptance Speeches: Gender and Partisan Appeals to the Republican Party,' in J. M. Martin and M. Borrelli (eds) *The Gendered Executive*. Philadelphia: Temple University Press, 81–99.

Brown, W. (1992). 'Finding the Man in the State,' *Feminist Studies* 18(1): 7–34.

Celis, K., Kantola, J., Waylen, G., and Weldon, S. L. (2013). 'Introduction: Gender and Politics: A Gendered World, a Gendered Discipline,' in K. Celis, J. Kantola, G. Waylen, and

S. L. Weldon (eds) *The Oxford Handbook of Gender and Politics*. Oxford: Oxford University Press, 1–26.

Celis, K. and Lovenduski, J. (2018). 'Power Struggles: Gender Equality in Political Representation,' *European Journal of Politics & Gender* 1(1–2): 149–66.

Chappell, L. (2014). '"New", "Old", and 'Nested' Institutions and Gender Justice Outcomes: A View from the International Criminal Court,' *Politics & Gender* 10(4): 572–94.

Chhabria, S. (2016). 'India's Prime Minister: Narendra Modi, Gender, and Governance,' in J. M. Martin and M. Borrelli (eds) *The Gendered Executive*. Philadelphia: Temple University Press, 64–80.

Chowdhury, N. and Nelson, B. J., with Carver, K. A., Johnson, N. J., and O'Loughlin, P. L. (1994). 'Redefining Politics: Patterns of Women's Political Engagement from a Global Perspective,' in B. J. Nelson and N. Chowdhury (eds) *Women and Politics Worldwide*. New Haven: Yale University Press, 3–24.

Claveria, S. (2014). 'Still a 'Male Business'? Explaining Women's Presence in Executive Office,' *West European Politics* 37(5): 1156–76.

Cross, W. P. and Blais, A. (2012). *Politics at the Centre: The Selection and Removal of Party Leaders in the Anglo Parliamentary Democracies*. Oxford: Oxford University Press.

Cruz, K. and Brown, W. (2016). 'Feminism, Law, and Neoliberalism,' *Feminist Legal Studies* 24(1): 69–89.

Davis, R. H. (1997). *Women and Power in Parliamentary Democracies: Cabinet Appointments in Western Europe, 1968–1992*. Lincoln: University of Nebraska Press.

Duerst-Lahti, G. (1997). 'Reconceiving Theories of Power: Consequences of Masculinism in the Executive Branch,' in M. Borrelli and J. M. Martin (eds) *The Other Elites*. Boulder, CO: Lynne Rienner, 11–32.

Duerst-Lahti, G. and Kelly, R. M. (1995) (eds). *Gender Power, Leadership, and Government*. Ann Arbor, MI: University of Michigan Press.

Duverger, M. (1955). *The Political Role of Women*. Paris: UNESCO.

Escobar-Lemmon, M. and Taylor-Robinson, M. M. (2016). *Women in Presidential Cabinets: Power Players or Abundant Tokens?* New York: Oxford University Press.

Gooding, C. C. (2016). 'President Barack H. Obama and the Rhetoric of Race: Between Responsibility and Respectability,' in J. M. Martin and M. Borrelli (eds) *The Gendered Executive*. Philadelphia: Temple University Press, 44–63.

Helmke, G. and Levitsky, S. (2004). 'Informal Institutions and Comparative Politics: A Research Agenda,' *Perspectives on Politics* 2(4): 725–40.

Htun, M. and Weldon, S. L. (2018). *The Logics of Gender Justice: State Action on Women's Rights around the World*. Cambridge: Cambridge University Press.

Hughes, M. M. (2009). 'Armed Conflict, International Linkages, and Women's Parliamentary Representation in Developing Nations,' *Social Problems* 56(1): 174–204.

Jalalzai, F. (2008). 'Women Rule-Shattering the Executive Glass Ceiling,' *Politics & Gender* 4(2): 1–27.

Jalalzai, F. (2013). *Shattered, Cracked or Firmly Intact? Women and the Executive Glass Ceiling Worldwide*. New York: Oxford University Press.

Jalalzai, F. (2016). *Women Presidents of Latin America: Beyond Family Ties?* New York: Routledge.

Jalalzai, F. (2017). 'Global Trends in Women's Executive Leadership,' in V. Montecinos (ed.) *Women Presidents and Prime Ministers in Post-Transition Democracies*. London: Palgrave MacMillan, 59–79.

aquette, J. S. (2017). 'Women at the Top: Leadership, Institutions, and the Quality of Democracy,' in V. Montecinos (ed.) *Women Presidents and Prime Ministers in Post-Transition Democracies.* London: Palgrave MacMillan, 37–58.

Kenny, M. (2014). 'A Feminist Institutionalist Approach,' *Politics & Gender* 10(4): 679–84.

Kenny, M. and Mackay, F. (2009). 'Already Doin' It for Ourselves? Skeptical Notes on Feminism and Institutionalism,' *Politics & Gender* 5(2): 271–80.

Kenny, M. and Piscopo, J. (2019). 'The Gender 'Ambition Gap' Revisited: Comparative and International Perspectives,' Unpublished ms.

Krook, M. L., and O'Brien, D. Z. (2012). 'All the President's Men? The Appointment of Female Cabinet Ministers Worldwide,' *Journal of Politics* 74(3): 840–55.

Lowndes, V. (2014). 'How Are Things Done Around Here? Uncovering Institutional Rules and Their Gendered Effects,' *Politics & Gender* 10(4): 685–91.

Mackay, F. (2014). 'Nested Newness, Institutional Innovation, and the Gendered Limits of Change,' *Politics & Gender* 10(4): 549–71.

Mackay, F. and Waylen, G. (2009). 'Critical Perspectives on Gender and Politics: Feminist Institutionalism,' *Politics & Gender,* 5(2): 237–80.

Mackay, F., and Waylen, G. (2014). 'Introduction: Gendering "New" Institutions,' *Politics & Gender* 10(4): 489–94.

Martin, J. M. and Borrelli, M. (2016). 'Learning What We Know: The Complexity of Gender in US and Comparative Executive Studies,' in J. M. Martin and M. Borrelli (eds) *The Gendered Executive*. Philadelphia: Temple University Press, 1–21.

Mazur, A. G. (2002). *Theorizing Feminist Policy*. Oxford: Oxford University Press.

McDonagh, E. (2009). *The Motherless State*. Chicago: University of Chicago Press.

Merton, R. K. (1949). 'On Sociological Theories of the Middle Range,' in R. K. Merton, *Social Theory and Social Structure*. New York: Simon & Schuster, 448–59.

Montecinos, V. (2017). 'Introduction,' in V. Montecinos (ed.) *Women Presidents and Prime Ministers in Post-Transition Democracies*. London: Palgrave MacMillan, 1–31.

Murray, R. (2010). 'Introduction: Gender Stereotypes and Media Coverage of Women Candidates,' in R. Murray (ed.) *Cracking the Highest Glass Ceiling: A Global Comparison of Women's Campaigns for Executive Office*. Santa Barbara, CA: Praeger, 3–27.

Murray, R. (2014). 'Quotas for Men: Reframing Gender Quotas as a Means of Increasing Representation for All,' *American Political Science Review*, 108(3): 520–32.

Norris, P., and Lovenduski, J. (1995). *Political Recruitment: Gender, Race, and Class in the British Parliament*. Cambridge: Cambridge University Press.

O'Brien, D. Z., Mendez, M., Peterson, J. C., and Shin, J. (2015). 'Letting Down the Ladder or Shutting the Door: Female Prime Ministers, Party Leaders, and Cabinet Ministers,' *Politics & Gender* 11(4): 689–717.

Pateman, C. (1986). 'Introduction: The Theoretical Subversiveness of Feminism,' in C. Pateman and E. Grosz (eds) *Feminist Challenges: Social and Political Theory*. Routledge, 1–10.

Pilet, J. and Cross, W. P. (2014) (eds). *The Selection of Political Party Leaders in Contemporary Parliamentary Democracies*. London: Routledge.

Putnam, R. D. (1976). *The Comparative Study of Political Elites*. Englewood Cliffs: Prentice Hall.

Reyes-Housholder, C. (2016). 'Presidential Power, Partisan Continuity and Pro-Women Change in Chile: 2000–10,' in J. Martin and M. A. Borrelli (eds) *The Gendered Executive: A Comparative Analysis of Presidents, Prime Ministers and Chief Executives*. New York: Temple University Press.

Reyes-Housholder, C. (2019). 'A Constituency Theory for the Conditional Impact of Female Presidents,' *Comparative Politics* 51(3): 429–49.

Reyes-Housholder, C. and Thomas, G. (2018). 'Latin America's Presidentas: Challenging Old Patterns, Forging New Pathways,' in L. A. Schwindt-Bayer (ed.) *Gender and Representation in Latin America*. New York: Oxford University Press, 19–38.

Reynolds, A. (1999). 'Women in the Legislatures and Executives of the World: Knocking at the Highest Glass Ceiling,' *World Politics* 51(4): 547–72.

Scherpereel, J., Adams, M., and Hayes, K. (2019). 'Gendering Gamson's Law.' Paper presented at the annual meetings of the American Political Science Association, Washington, DC, August 30.

Schwindt-Bayer, L. A. and Reyes-Housholder, C. (2017a). 'Citizen Responses to Female Executives: Is It Sex, Novelty or Both?,' *Politics, Groups and Identities* 5(3): 373–98.

Schwindt-Bayer, L. A. and Reyes-Housholder, C. (2017b). 'Gender and Institutions in Post-Transition Executives,' in V. Montecinos (ed.) *Women Presidents and Prime Ministers in Post-Transition Democracies*. London: Palgrave MacMillan, 81–99.

Sen, A. (1999). *Development as Freedom*. New York: Anchor.

Siaroff, A. (2000). 'Women's Representation in Legislatures and Cabinets in Industrial Democracies,' *International Political Science Review* 21(2): 197–215.

Stauffer, K. E. and O'Brien, D. Z. (2018). 'Quantitative Methods and Feminist Political Science,' in W. R. Thompson (ed.) *Oxford Research Encyclopedia of Politics*. Oxford: Oxford University Press.

Stockemer, D. (2017). 'The Proportion of Women in Legislatures and Cabinets: What is the Empirical Link?,' *Polity* 49(3): 434–60.

Stockemer, D. and Sundström, A. (2017). 'Women in Cabinets: The Role of Party Ideology and Government Turnover,' *Party Politics* 24(6): 1–11.

Thelen, K. (1999). 'Historical Institutionalism in Comparative Politics,' *Annual Review of Political Science* 2: 369–404.

Thomas, M. (2018). 'In Crisis or Decline? Selecting Women to Lead Provincial Parties in Government,' *Canadian Journal of Political Science* 51(2): 379–403.

Thomson, J. (2018). 'Resisting Gendered Change: Feminist Institutionalism and Critical Actors,' *International Political Science Review* 39(2): 178–91.

Towns, A. and Niklasson, B. (2017). 'Gender, International Status, and Ambassador Appointments,' *Foreign Policy Analysis* 13(3): 521–40.

Tremblay, M. and Stockemer, D. (2013). 'Women's Ministerial Careers in Cabinet, 1921–2010: A Look at Socio-Demographic Traits and Career Experiences,' *Canadian Public Administration* 56(4): 523–41.

Tripp, A. M. (2015). *Women and Power in Postconflict Africa*. Cambridge: Cambridge University Press.

Weldon, S. L. (2011). *When Protest Makes Policy: How Social Movements Represent Disadvantaged Groups*. Ann Arbor: University of Michigan Press.

Weldon, S. L. (2014). 'Using Statistical Methods to Study Institutions,' *Politics & Gender* 10(4): 661–72.

Weldon, S. L. (2019). 'Power, Exclusion, and Empowerment: Feminist Innovation in Political Science,' *Women's Studies International Forum* 72: 127–36.

Whitford, A., Wilkins, V. M., and Ball, M. G. (2007). 'Descriptive Representation and Policymaking Authority: Evidence from Women in Cabinets and Bureaucracies,' *Governance* 20(4): 559–80.

Wood, E. A. (2016). 'Hypermasculinity as a Scenario of Power', *International Feminist Journal of Politics* 18(3): 329–50.

Yates, E. A. and Hughes, M. M. (2017). 'Cultural Explanations for Men's Dominance of National Leadership Worldwide', in V. Montecinos (ed.) *Women Presidents and Prime Ministers in Post-Transition Democracies*. London: Palgrave MacMillan, 101–22.

Zerilli, L. (2006). 'Feminist Theory and the Canon of Political Thought', in J. S. Dryzek, B. Honig and A. Phillips (eds) *The Oxford Handbook of Political Theory*. Oxford: Oxford University Press, 106–24.

CHAPTER 8

....

CONSTRUCTIVIST APPROACHES TO THE STUDY OF POLITICAL EXECUTIVES

....

DENNIS C. GRUBE

WHEN it comes down to it, just how 'real' is reality? To the constructivist, this ontological question drives all that follows. To be a constructivist is to live in a 'reality' that is continually being shaped and reshaped not just by the actions of our fellow human beings, but by our *perception* of what that actually means. This belief that reality is a construction has enormous implications for the study of political executives in particular. To begin with it places actors right at the centre of our deliberations. If reality is constructed, who is doing the constructing and how are they doing it? It drives us to look at the words of presidents, ministers, civil servants and monarchs to work out how they are framing the world for their listeners. It leads us to hunt out the ideas that underpin both change and stasis, and theorize their relationship to power. Constructivists strive to analyse the interaction of discourse with culture, behaviour, traditions, ideas, and 'data and evidence' to bring the world into being in a shape that we can recognize. 'Reality' is inherently subjective rather than objective—something to be experienced rather than discovered. For political science, this has profound implications for the very nature of the discipline, and in how we might view what it is that political executives are doing.

This chapter has three goals. First, I seek to outline the core tenets of the constructivist approach through the work of the scholars who gave it life. Second, I analyse how the constructivist approach has been applied to the study of political executives in particular. Third, I make the case for what the constructivist perspective offers in terms of future study. In a modern era sometimes characterized as a 'post-truth' world, I argue that constructivism can potentially help us to explain why a data-driven analysis of interests alone is proving insufficient in clarifying the shape of modern political 'reality'.

8.1 THE CONSTRUCTIVISM STORY

In the past two decades in particular, constructivism has emerged as one of the dominant theoretical approaches to the study of political science. It has provided a very wide umbrella under which poststructuralists, interpretivists, and some versions of new institutionalists have all been able to carve out a space. It is not my intention here to recount every twist and turn of the scholarly debates that have brought this about. There are many excellent discussions available that cover the breadth of this material (Bevir 2008; Hay 2010, 2016; Parsons 2010). For my purposes here, I want to focus on the core strands of constructivism that have driven much of the work on political executives in particular, reflecting the focus of this volume. So I want to focus on the power of ideas, and the influence of discourse.

The constructivist perspective finds its origins, perhaps unsurprisingly, in cultural and sociological explanations of human behaviour. The works of Durkheim ([1893] 2014) and Weber ([1930] 2002) provide the philosophical underpinnings of a theoretical approach that begins with the essential insight that human beings are a social animal. As such, even what we conceive of as the rational calculation of our interests is revealed to be a socially constructed phenomenon. As Mark Bevir puts it, constructivism

> suggests that ideas that might appear to be inherently rational or natural are in fact the artefacts of particular traditions or cultures. Likewise, it implies that our social and political practices are not the result of natural or social laws, but are the product of choices informed by contingent meanings and beliefs.   (Bevir 2008).

In moving from the broader social sciences to political science in particular, constructivism has worked its way relentlessly into all corners of the discipline. This has occurred perhaps most notably within international relations (IR) theory through the work of Alexander Wendt. His book introducing a *Social Theory of International Politics* (1999) suggested that we stop looking at states as rational actors ruthlessly calculating their interests on some kind of abacus of world domination. Wendt emphasized the power of ideas and beliefs about national character and destiny as playing an important role in shaping the norms that govern state interaction. Whilst describing his philosophy as a 'thin constructivism' willing to acknowledge some aspects of the realist perspective, Wendt drew on a range of sociological theory in particular to carve out his seminal argument that ideas matter for state behaviour (for the case in favour of 'thin constructivism', see Marsh 2009). As he explains, the precipitating event that drove much of this new theorizing was the sudden collapse of the Soviet Union and the concomitant end of the cold war.

> Mainstream IR theory simply had difficulty explaining the end of the Cold War, or systemic change more generally. It seemed to many that these difficulties stemmed

from IR's materialist and individualist orientation, such that a more ideational and holistic view of international politics might do better.   (Wendt 1999: 4)

The modern breadth of constructivist scholarship in IR is a testament to the persuasiveness of Wendt's criticism that existing explanations did not do enough to allow for unexpected change. If change does not come from the cold calculation of interests, then from whence does it come? That question provided the lens through which theorists began to challenge not just existing IR theory but also structuralist and behaviouralist accounts of how political institutions work *within* states. Through a cloudburst of so-called 'new institutionalisms' in the 1980s and 1990s, there was a concerted attempt to look anew at the institutional forces which purport to bound the rationality of the actors within them (see Chapter 3 in this volume).

In the last decade in particular, these new institutionalisms—which I discuss below— have in their turn come under challenge from scholars who argue that they still do not do enough to explain the concept of change. All institutionalist accounts, old and new alike, share as their starting point the view that institutions form the centre of political life, and that if we are able to understand and explain how institutions work, we should be able to explain most political phenomena. That starting point is also pretty much the endpoint of agreement amongst political scientists about just what institutions are, and how they interact with actors. Traditional institutionalism took as a given the explanatory power of structural hierarchy. An institutional explanation of government was essentially a constitutional explanation of government (although, see Rhodes 2008). To understand US government and how it worked, you had to map the constitution, the Congress, the president, and the Supreme Court, and explain who was in charge of what. The interactions between these well-structured institutions could be studied to yield explanations for why any particular outcome was reached.

That picture came to be seen by critics as epistemologically deficient compared to the purported ontological certainty that underpinned it. The 'new institutionalisms' sought to inject some dynamism into the study of institutions by letting actors back in through various guises. Whilst the critiques were powerful, they found little upon which to immediately agree. As explained by Hall and Taylor in their much cited 1996 article, the new institutionalisms might all critique the old, but they do so from very different vantage points. Rational-choice institutionalism, sociological institutionalism, and historical institutionalism all agree that institutions are important for understanding political reality, but each privileges a different driving force (see Chapter 3 in this volume). For historical institutionalists, history is the powerful pull on the handbrake, shaping institutional structures over long time periods and putting in place path dependencies that make change less likely and inherently difficult (see Pierson 2000, 2004; Mahoney and Thelen 2010).

For sociological institutionalists, the answers for understanding institutions are to be found in understanding the culture within them (March and Olsen 1989; Mackay et al. 2009). So, in theory, an institution like a government department or a police force might operate differently in Germany than in Italy because of cultural differences.

Equally, different government departments within the same country will also have unique cultural aspects of their own. For rational-choice institutionalists, what drives institutions are the *interests* of those within them (Hardin 1982; Shepsle 2008). Utilizing the language of economics, there are rational trade-offs to be made, and transaction costs to be calculated, to yield predictions about likely behaviour. Collectively, these new theoretical perspectives undoubtedly succeeded in reshaping the inherited picture of institutions as inert structures in which human agency counted for little. In more recent times, that new sense of dynamism has been questioned by a yet newer critique, which suggests that even with the recognition that institutions are shaped by the people who inhabit them, these new institutionalisms are better at explaining stasis than they are at explaining change. History, culture, and interests—the critique runs—are presented as things that constrain actors from freely reshaping institutions, leaving us without a coherent story about how change does actually happen.

By asking once more 'what causes change', constructivist theorists have argued for the embrace of a fourth 'new institutionalism'. Dubbed 'discursive institutionalism' by one of its leading proponents Vivien Schmidt, it looks to the power of discourse in all its permutations as the key thing which gives shape to institutions. Schmidt argues that a discursive approach allows us to access both the 'background ideational abilities that explain the internal processes by which institutions are created' and the ' "*foreground discursive abilities*" through which sentient agents may change (or maintain) their institutions following a logic of communication' (Schmidt 2010: 15; emphasis in original). Ideas are given institutional shape by the way they are communicated.

Other authors have referred to this model as effectively a constructivist institutionalism, with some points of differentiation that make it distinctive. Colin Hay for example stresses that a true constructivist institutionalism needs to do away in its empirical analyses with the concept of 'material self-interest' in favour of studying *perceptions* of material self-interests. To do otherwise is to allow for a creeping in of an ontological acknowledgement that interests are in fact 'real' rather than simply a construction. According to Hay, actors are 'irredeemably ideational' (Hay 2010) in how they perceive their interests, and those ideas will lead to particular destinations based on how they interact with one another and the order in which they occur. Mark Blyth, both in his earlier work and in investigations of the global financial crisis, argues that only a constructivist approach grounded in the explanatory power of ideas is capable of making sense of how and why policy paradigms shift (Blyth 2002, 2013).

Both Blyth and Hay suggest there is a form of 'ideational path dependence' which explains why particular ideas take the shape that they do in political or policy terms. This same logic of *constructed* path dependence, as opposed to a purely historical institutionalist type, can also be applied to the words through which ideas are expressed—that is, through political rhetoric (see Grube 2016). The words that political leaders use when describing a particular policy, for example, can shape the boundaries of the future rhetorical pathways that are available when speaking about that policy. Whilst wholly an ideational construction by political actors, a form of rhetorical path dependency can operate to narrow the opportunities to deviate from the rhetoric laid out to begin with.

Critics of constructivist institutionalism have suggested that it is essentially unnecessary. Stephen Bell for example has argued that an agent-centred form of historical institutionalism is capable of fulsomely explaining change, without making the leap to a more socially and discursively constructed version that doesn't engage sufficiently with the shaping power of institutions. He argues that 'an account of HI that places active and interpretive agents at the centre of its analysis and locates agents dialectically interacting with institutional and wider structural contexts can absorb core elements of constructivism and explain institutional change' (Bell 2011: 884.). He is critical of the work of Hay, Blyth, and Schmidt as rendering institutions too vague—so dependent on the ideas of the actors within them as to leave them shapeless as a unit of analysis (Bell 2011: 890). In rejoinder, Schmidt suggests that Bell is really something of a constructivist institutionalist in historical institutionalist clothing, arguing for theoretical distinctions that he cannot sustain in practice in his own work (Schmidt 2012).

Discursive institutionalism of course draws on a breadth of previous theoretical work, including elements of discourse theory (see Howarth 2000; Howarth, et al. 2000). Whilst generally welcomed by discourse scholars for breaking new theoretical ground, discursive institutionalism continues to draw critiques from those seeking a sharper analytical edge. For example, Francisco Panizza and Romina Miorelli applaud Schmidt's contribution but argue that post-structuralist discourse theory (PSDT) remains better at providing a deeper understanding of the inherently political nature of all discourse. '[B]y arguing that discourses are intrinsically political and that politics involves the discursive construction of antagonisms and political frontiers, PSDT allows for a fuller understanding of discourse as constitutive of power and not just as a complement to it' (Panizza and Miorelli 2013).

8.2 CONSTRUCTIVISM AND POLITICAL EXECUTIVES

Constructivist institutionalism allows for a more dynamic sense of agency. It suggests that the ideas and values of individual actors matter. In the study of political executives, this offers new opportunities for scholarship which was once treated warily by historians and political scientists alike as being too focused on 'high politics' at the expense of more nuanced appreciations of history (Craig 2010; Grube 2017). Constructivism certainly should not be seen as giving undue encouragement to the study of agents in isolation as once personified by the 'great man' school of history. Rather, the sophistication it offers is to interrogate the tensions between the path dependent aspects of historical institutionalism, the systemic force of wider class-based analyses, and the agential power of political executives to drive change.

If political executives are indeed to be successful in creating change based on their own ideas and values, what tools do they have at their disposal? One answer to that question is the power of rhetoric—the ability to persuade (see Chapter 29 in this volume). There has been something of a 'rhetorical revival' within the wider 'argumentative turn' that has examined how political executives seek to frame ideas and beliefs in ways that build a momentum for change. For constructivists, this has seen the embrace of techniques such as 'rhetorical political analysis' (Finlayson 2007), and storytelling as a way for executives to give narrative shape to their policy agenda (see Grube 2012; Stone 2012). It has extended to examining politics through dramaturgy theory, in which actors—consciously or subconsciously—follow a script of their own creation. The work of the Dutch theorist Maarten Hajer has been particularly influential in this regard (2005a, 2005b, 2006).

Seeing politics in this way—as a performance—is a uniquely constructivist contribution to understanding the nature of modern leadership. John Gaffney's extensive work in the area persuasively analyses the recent politics of both France and the UK through a performative framework (see for example: 2014 and 2017). In particular, he focuses on how rhetorical strategies are deployed to build a particular narrative of leadership, and argues that a narrative is something that has to be 'performed' by the leader (2017: 3). The success of a performance of course relies partly on the qualities of the performer, leading scholars to turn to that most elusive of qualities—'charisma'—as a way of understanding why some leaders are better 'performers' than others.

Most studies of charisma start with Weber's three-part categorization of authority as legal, traditional, or charismatic: 'In the case of charismatic authority, it is the charismatically qualified leader as such who is obeyed by virtue of personal trust in his revelation, his heroism or his exemplary qualities' (Weber 2005: 193). In other words, the citizenry follow such a leader because of their belief in the 'extraordinary quality of the specific person' (2005: 217). That being the case, can charisma—by definition a characteristic that attaches specifically to an individual—provide purchase for analysing the political executive as a whole? The answer is a resounding yes. As we have seen frequently in all systems of government, the way a charismatic leader can sway the rest of the political executive matters just as much if not more than how they can sway the wider public. The main point remains that charisma is a construct—a projection—rather than an objective reality capable of duplication or replication (for a discussion, see Grint 2014: 244–6).

One key limitation of the research on charismatic leadership is that it has perhaps tended to focus too much attention on leaders and not enough on the followers. As Duncan McDonnell has noted:

> if we look more closely at how scholars of populism use the term 'charismatic', we find that its application is invariably based on how leaders *present* themselves (as 'saviours' endowed with extraordinary qualities) and how they *perform* in public (as commanding speakers, able to rouse crowds or communicate well on television) rather than on how their purported followers *perceive* them.
>
> (McDonnell 2016; emphasis in the original)

This opens up promising areas for further research, as I return to later.

Much of the recent work on political executives has focused on creating and ana-lysing various categories of leadership, with debate aplenty both on what leadership actually is and how it can be measured (see Elgie 2015; Bennister et al. 2017). Political leaders enjoy a range of structural advantages and material resources. They often have large numbers of staff and the resources to hire more if they wish. Depending on the system of government—presidential, semi-presidential, or parliamentary—they also have a range of institutionalized powers guaranteed either by the constitution or by long-practiced convention. These are not easy to measure, and nor is there consistent comparative agreement about what is actually being measured (see Doyle and Elgie 2014; Chapter 19 in this volume). Leaders seem to have great power; they control budgets, they have command and control over the military and so on. And yet, none of this guarantees success or failure, because we cannot simply equate the provision of more resources with the enjoyment of greater political power (see Helms 2019). Power remains contextual, to be negotiated by individual agents in pluralist democratic systems. Political capital that seems unassailable on one day can quickly appear ephemeral the next. As Kane and Patapan (2012) argue, this combination of perceived power to rule as one wishes and the concomitant need to be seen as a faithful servant of the people is the defining conundrum of democratic leadership. It cannot be changed or escaped from because it sits at the very heart of what it is to be a democratic leader.

But of course political executives encompass not just presidents and prime ministers, but the wider group of cabinet ministers, advisers, parliamentarians, and monarchs who exercise political power. There are two conceptual-level observations that underpin many of the advances in the use of constructivism to examine the interactions of this wider group of political executives. The first is the acknowledgement that leaders are not all-powerful by themselves, and that their hierarchical position no longer guarantees their power status. If we characterize the world as a place where power is constructed, each leader must build for him- or herself the conditions in which he or she can hold power and exercise it effectively. This, for example, explains why Margaret Thatcher in the UK went through different stages of power without any change in her erstwhile hierarchical position. During the mid-1980s she was all-dominant, but this followed a period early on when she was still establishing herself, and was followed in turn by the slow diminution of her power to the point where she was replaced by her own party rather than by the electorate. She was of course prime minister throughout. But that hierarchical position in and of itself guaranteed nothing.

Power—and leadership—in this type of account becomes a self-fulfilling projection. The more leaders are able to support the perception in others that they are in fact power-ful, the more powerful they become. Whether they are successful in that projection relies on the type of authority they are able to generate, and the degree to which they are able to persuade others. Thus we see political executives building up and then spending 'moral capital', an intangible projection of power that lives entirely in the perception of its beholders (see Kane 2001). Nevertheless, leadership is in reality seldom the individual business that powerful leaders like to make out. Leaders share power with a variety of key actors who gather around them.

Which leads to the second observation which is that power is exercised by a 'core executive' or a 'court' with a changeable membership and agenda (see Rhodes 1995; Elgie 2011; Rhodes and Tiernan 2016). In other words, political executives are not set in stone and do not move in and out of office and power in clean breaks. Rather they meander along in overlapping relationships, at times all dominant and at times barely consequential. And this extends far beyond just the leader themselves. Executives are made up of political players, party powerbrokers, key civil servants, and sometimes powerful media voices. For example, no leader in modern democracies can govern effectively without some level of bureaucratic support (see Chapter 26 in this volume). But where this is found varies dramatically. In the UK, some leaders have leant more on the Cabinet Office, whereas others have favoured the Treasury. Sometimes the head of the Civil Service is a powerful figure, whilst at other times the real power lies elsewhere. The continued growth of the power and number of special advisers appointed for their political loyalty to the government of the day complicates that picture still further in many modern parliamentary democracies (see Eichbaum and Shaw 2010).

The same is true in other systems. As President Trump has found out through bitter experience, the US presidency shares power whether it likes it or not. It shares it with congressional leaders in both the House and the Senate. It shares it with Cabinet members who are striving to build their own profile, and with Whitehouse staffers wielding an influence that rises and falls with perceptions of their own influence with the incumbent president. It is a complex picture of executive government. Different approaches have tried to unpack its complexity in different ways. From the formal-legal approach of traditional institutionalism, to modern variations of game theory, there is no shortage of theoretical ideas about how to understand the way that political executives work.

So how have constructivists sought to break into this circle of complexity? Rather than following hierarchy trails, or attempting to quantify interests to predict behaviour, they have generally embraced a range of more inductive approaches. Investigations have focused as much on what actors think and say as on what they do. Methodologically, this has generally favoured qualitative rather than quantitative approaches, but certainly not exclusively so. Semi-structured interviews, content analysis, different forms of discourse analysis, rhetorical assessments, and process tracing have sought to expose the ideas that are driving actors forward in order to analyse the realities they see themselves as constructing. As Chapter 6 (in this volume) by Rod Rhodes and Jack Corbett reveals, this has extended to drawing on political ethnography as part of an explicitly interpretivist agenda.

Alan Finlayson and his co-authors have advocated for a form of 'rhetorical political analysis' that focuses on the power of arguments as the means through which politics is shaped and given effect (Finlayson 2007; Finlayson and Martin 2008; Atkins and Finlayson 2013; Atkins et al. 2014). To put it simply politics *is* argument, so to understand the former we must analyse the latter. Contemporary rhetorical analysis can be usefully juxtaposed against an earlier institutionalist tradition of analysing rhetoric as an extension of the institutional power of the speaker. The seminal work in this area is Jeffrey Tulis's 1987 book *The Rhetorical Presidency* (see Chapter 2 in this volume). Tulis's defining insight was that whilst the US president's freedom of unilateral action is constrained in the separation of powers system—as envisioned by the founding fathers—she or he has a unique pulpit from which to speak. If the other branches of government are proving an obstacle, the president has the rhetorical capacity to reach out over their heads and connect directly with the people themselves. Samuel Kernell explored a similar theme through the concept of 'going public' (2006). In theory, if you sway public opinion with these direct appeals, the Congress in particular will be forced to bend in response. It is the art of Aristotelian persuasion reshaped for modern politics. With his penchant for Twitter, President Trump has demonstrated an institutional capacity to reach out not just over the other branches of government, but also over the media itself (see Chapter 29 in this volume). The age of social media is the age of direct communication, which poses both opportunities and challenges for the next wave of study of political executives. But more on that below.

Tulis's approach has spurred three decades of scholarship on the rhetorical presidency in the United States (Medhurst 2006; Friedman and Friedman 2012), and the study of rhetoric in parliamentary systems is beginning to catch up (Toye 2011; Bennister 2013; Grube 2013; Uhr and Walter 2014, 2015). Whilst much of that work is institutionalist rather than constructivist in orientation, what it has done is help in bringing discourse to the centre of scholarly political attention. And in studying discourse, we find the passionate arguments about *ideas* that are the defining feature of constructivism. Work by scholars like Richard Holtzman, Wes Widmaier, and others has shown how the powers of the rhetorical presidency are used to *construct* pictures of particular events as a crisis—or not—and what effect that has in how governments respond to them (Widmaier 2007; Widmaier et al. 2007; Holtzman 2011). The same constructivist lens can be seen at work in discursive approaches to public policy, where scholars like Frank Fischer have been instrumental in fashioning a critical policy studies approach by privileging what has been described as the 'argumentative turn' (see Fischer and Gottweis 2012).

What the literature in critical policy studies has done is provide new avenues of enquiry for those scholars frustrated with the technocratic focus inherent in 'evidence-based' conceptions of public policy. It seeks to problematize the nature of expertise, and question the extent to which any policy analysis can truly claim to be an objective exercise. To quote Fischer et al., 'Critical policy studies, as such, emphasizes the importance of contextual understanding, ordinary knowledge, narrative storytelling, emotional expression and communicative practices generally' (2015: 6). This has particular implications for the study of political executives, because it de-emphasizes the alleged ontological certainty of data and evidence in favour of understanding how policy is shaped by people. Whether that be politicians, civil servants, political advisers, third sector organizations, or the citizens themselves—constructivist approaches to the study of public policy share the underpinning belief that positivist/rationalist approaches cannot alone account for how policy is actually made.

At its furthest edge, the resurgent use of constructivist approaches to study the workings of political executives has led to the adoption of a specifically interpretivist agenda. The work of Mark Bevir and Rod Rhodes looms large here, both in defining what is distinct about the interpretivist approach and empirically demonstrating how it can be applied (Bevir and Rhodes 2001, 2003, 2010; Rhodes 2011). Interpretivism embraces the core insights of constructivism in the privileging of agency; in the belief that reality is constructed through ideas, words, and traditions that together constitute the 'webs of belief' within which individuals see the world; and that change within organizations occurs when existing structures find themselves under challenge. But interpretivists specifically see such moments as 'dilemmas'—as challenges to embedded traditions that individual agents resolve through their own webs of belief. As such, traditional institutional boundaries provide little in the way of firm structure capable of shaping behavioural responses. Instead, it is tradition which shapes the views of actors and binds them together.

8.3 What Does the Future Hold?

As so many commentators have noted, the tumultuous political events of the last decade have tested the predictive capacity of 'traditional' political science and found it wanting. The Global Financial Crisis and the response to it, the rise of the new nationalism, of Brexit, and of Donald Trump, have demonstrated anew the ways in which politics is a domain not just of competing interests but of competing arguments about those interests that are rooted in a complex mix of ideas, beliefs, and historical understandings. As Hay (2016: 533) suggests, 'The powerful may well be those who get to project what they perceive to be their interest *as if it were* the general interest'.

The future therefore offers a rich research agenda for constructivists seeking to stretch and build upon existing theory through detailed empirical engagement with some big questions. In studying political executives over the course of the next decade, constructivists must engage with the ways in which populism, ideas, and politics are interacting through the prism of language, rhetoric, and discourse. This offers sites of study that embrace both the forums that shape the processes of executive decision-making (like cabinets, parliament itself, political offices) and the way in which those bodies frame ideas for wider consumption. The current climate offers constructivism the chance to engage with the apparent irrationalities of politics in what some commentators have characterized as a 'post-truth' governing environment. If the world is collectively searching for 'meaning' in uncertain times, then what can a perspective which is all about 'meaning' have to offer? The first observation to make of course is that to the constructivist, contemporary perceptions of the 'irrationality' of politics are themselves a construction of what 'normal' politics is believed to be.

With that in mind, opportunities for advancing our theoretical frameworks may well arise from clearer conceptualizations of what 'normal' politics in fact is. There is understandably tremendous focus in the contemporary popular press, and amongst academic commentators, on whether politics is currently experiencing a profound change in its very nature, or whether this is simply a cyclical upswing in particular ideological perspectives that will soon wane. The idea that political changes happen within particular envelopes of 'political time' is well-entrenched within the literature on historical institutionalism (see Skowronek 2008; Widmaier 2016; Chapter 2 in this volume). What the next decade offers constructivists is the chance to reflect further on the relationship between time and ideas, to probe the ways in which 'discursive institutions' interact with the times in which they live. Are the traditions and beliefs from which agents construct their understanding of their world in a constant state of flux, or are there particular moments of stress in which 'dilemmas' are more likely to emerge and demand resolution? To put that as an empirical question, is Trump's rhetorical impact as US president linked to the times in which we live or could the Trump phenomenon have emerged at any time over the past seventy years?

The second area offering real opportunities for further theory building is to apply the constructivist lens vertically as well as horizontally. Our understanding of network governance, of the ways in which political executives work together with each other and with myriad non-government actors, has grown tremendously over the past twenty years. Constructivism has helped us to better understand the horizontal distribution of power. The challenge over the next decade will be to push our theoretical understanding of the two-way interactions between political executives and the mass citizenry that they represent (see Chapter 31 in this volume). The study of political executives should not only be a story about the study of elites and the ideas that drive them, but also how those elites are themselves constructed entities imbued with the characteristics that their followers wish to project upon them. The construction of leaders is a two-way process; they frame a particular picture of themselves for wider consumption, but the citizens in turn reflect back a view of their own. Leaders are taken to heart as 'of the people' or 'out of touch' not as an objective, rational reality but as a constructed perception projected onto them by their democratic audience. The opportunities to theorise that process further—following the work of McDonnell (2016) already alluded to—are extensive.

These opportunities for extending our theoretical reach are matched by the range of empirical opportunities on offer that engage with the nature of contemporary politics. I offer a brief discussion of three potential areas below. The first is the construction of 'truth' by political executives and their critics. In an actor-centric perspective like constructivism, understanding who is arguing about truth and how they are doing so becomes vital. Second, we need to encourage more research on elite perceptions of the world they are governing. In other words, do the populist critiques that traditional political executives are out of touch and out of time actually have a point in terms of how these elites themselves perceive the people they govern? And, third, constructivism can offer unique perspectives when engaging with the challenges of so-called 'populism' by analysing how much the ideas and values of political executives translate into the perceived ideas and values of the people they govern. In other words, how much do citizens believe what they are being told, and how does that shape the discursive boundaries of the polity?

8.3.1 The Construction of Truth

Battles about 'truth' are in reality battles about ideas viewed through competing rhetorical frames. This brings into stark relief the underlying populist debate about what now constitutes political 'truth' and who can be trusted to tell it. Political executives, at least in established Western democracies, have lost little of the established accoutrements of power. Their 'resources' in terms of money and institutional structures remain intact. The parliaments and systems of courts alongside which they govern are little changed. There have been exogenous shocks aplenty in recent years, but few have actually changed fundamental institutional shapes sufficiently to allow for a traditional institutionalist explanation of the current popular disconnect between rulers and ruled. What has changed is perception, shaped by discourse, rhetoric, values, and ideas.

The traditional purveyors of 'truth' in all its forms are finding fewer buyers for their 'facts' in this era of disillusionment. There are climate change scientists staring in disbelief at the number of politicians who are able to assert that their object of study simply is not real—and gain a substantial following in doing so (Dunlap and McCright 2015). There are pro-European British groups bewildered why the seemingly incontrovertible 'truth' about the likely economic impacts of Brexit was not able to sway a majority of voters their way during the referendum. What is abundantly clear is that the problem is not actually about a lack of evidence. There is no shortage of economic data available. What is missing is the leap of understanding that data and evidence do not in fact speak for themselves. They rely on human interpretation to give them meaning.

In 'normal' times, the transactional language of every day expertise in government is sufficient. But we live in a transformational moment, and at such times truth itself re-emerges as a site for empirical study. What that means for a constructivist agenda on political executives is studying the construction of the very categories of 'truth' and 'lies' as understood by political executives. It means looking at the interaction between arguments, ideas, and values—and the new technologies capable of transmitting them with a greater level of targeted sophistication than ever before. Jacques and Knox (2016), for example, undertook an analysis of the discourses motivating individual citizens in their views on climate change following the destructive impacts of Hurricane Sandy in 2012.

8.3.2 How Elites See Themselves

Many different disciplinary perspectives have sought to study elites across the social sciences. We have learned much. As discussed above, structural and traditional institutional perspectives can tell us a great deal about the material resources that political executives have available. They can tell us what those executives see as their interests, and how those interests translate into expressed preferences. But the pressing concern for political scientists in particular at the moment must be to understand the disconnect between the perceived interests of these 'elites' and the perceived interests of citizens. A straightforward economic analysis of rises and falls in inflation, household income, debt, wages, and spending can provide us with useful data. What they cannot do is tell us how those data are interacting with the beliefs and values of politicians and the citizens they serve. To do that we must study more closely how elites actually see themselves, and how they understand what it is that they think they are doing (see Chapters 4 and 14 in this volume). This offers us the chance to interrogate empirically whether politicians from mainstream parties are in fact more out of touch then they once were. It offers the opportunity to triangulate what political executives *say* with what they *do*, and with what they *think* they are doing.

8.3.3 Citizen Constructions of Interests and Identities

Politics is complex. Every political scientist knows it. Yet for years, politicians themselves have been trying to deny it when out on the election stump. Their critiques of opposition parties focus on how easily things could be fixed if people just applied some 'good old common sense'. What we know less about than we perhaps should is what citizens actually make of such political assertions. Thanks to the breadth of polling now available, and the sophistication of much contemporary electoral studies work, we certainly know plenty about how people vote. We increasingly know about how their demographics correlate with particular hot button issues at election time. We can certainly drill down well into what kind of profile typical Brexit and Remain voters were likely to have in the UK, or who is supporting the rise of the new far right parties in Germany.

The challenge here is to peel back a further layer to ask *why* citizens hold the views they do about what they perceive as being in their interests, and how that relates to their sense of identity. The much discussed malaise of 'populism' is surely capable of rendering forth a more sophisticated diagnosis of what ails our body politic. Did American voters who supported Trump, and British voters who supported Brexit, and French voters who supported the Front National support those positions because they felt it was in their economic interest to do so? Do voters really believe the rhetoric of leaders who speak out against immigration as undermining the jobs of people already in the country? Does the rhetoric of leaders about a 'global Britain' and 'American carnage' really resonate in shaping the perceptions of how voters see their nations and their governments?

These are questions that of course extend far beyond political executives. They cross all sorts of sub-disciplinary boundaries within political science. But for our purposes here, they are central for understanding the relationship between the words and actions of political executives and wider perceptions about their authenticity.

It helps us to tease out who is seen as fit to lead in the current political environment, and how we can shape executive structures in ways that are likely to 're-connect' citizens with decision-makers.

8.4 CONCLUSION

Constructivism is no longer the new kid on the block. Its essential characteristics, its boundaries, and its intellectual claims are now well-established. Over the course of the last two decades in particular it has challenged the entrenched ontological certainties of positivist political science, beginning with IR and spreading rapidly throughout the discipline. But critiques remain. Institutionalists of many stripes argue that constructivism, especially in its interpretivist guises, blends into some kind of unrelenting relativism where nothing solid remains. All that is left are ideas and values floating freely through the body politic, waiting to be perceived. Positivists and rational-choice theorists are no less implacable in their view that interests and preferences still offer much surer guides to human understanding. For them, the sureties of the natural sciences remain within grasp.

What I have tried to show in this chapter is that constructivism has demonstrated a remarkable resilience in the face of such critiques. It has shown not only that interests alone do not provide a sufficient understanding of what drives human nature, but that interests are themselves constructed perceptions. If we want to understand political executives as something other than rational actors, we need to position them within this wider constructed world. We need to understand how rhetoric interacts with 'reality', and how much political executives are capable of using ideas and values to restitch together those aspects of democratic trust that are currently under challenge.

REFERENCES

Atkins, J. and Finlayson, A. (2013). '"…A 40-Year-Old Black Man Made the Point to Me": Everyday Knowledge and the Performance of Leadership in Contemporary British Politics,' *Political Studies* 61: 161–77.

Atkins, J., Finlayson, A., Martin, J., and Turnbull, N. (2014) (eds). *Rhetoric in British Politics and Society*. Basingstoke: Palgrave Macmillan.

Bell, S. (2011). 'Do We Really Need a New "Constructivist Institutionalism" to Explain Institutional Change?,' *British Journal of Political Science* 41: 883–906.

Bennister, M. (2013). 'Tony Blair's Oratory,' in R. Hayton and A. Crines (eds) *Labour Party Oratory from Bevan to Brown*. Manchester: Manchester University Press.

Bennister, M., Worthy, B., and 't Hart, P. (2017) (eds). *The Leadership Capital Index: A New Perspective on Political Leadership*. Oxford University Press.

Bevir, M. (2008). *Key Concepts in Governance*. London: Sage.

Bevir, M. and Rhodes, R. A. W. (2001). 'Decentering Tradition: Interpreting British Government,' *Administration and Society* 33: 107–32.

Bevir, M. and Rhodes, R. A. W. (2003). *Interpreting British Governance*. London: Routledge.

Bevir, M. and Rhodes, R. A. W. (2010). *The State as Cultural Practice*. Oxford University Press.

Blyth, M. (2002). *Great Transformations: Economic Ideas and Institutional Change in the Twentieth Century*. Cambridge: Cambridge University Press.

Blyth, M. (2013). 'Paradigms and Paradox: The Politics of Economic Ideas in Two Moments of Crisis,' *Governance: An International Journal of Policy, Administration, and Institutions* 26(2): 197–215.

Craig, D. (2010). '"High Politics" and the "New Political History",' *The Historical Journal* 53: 453–75.

Doyle, D. and Elgie, R. (2014). 'Maximizing the Reliability of Cross-National Measures of Presidential Power,' *British Journal of Political Science* 46: 731–41.

Dunlap, R. E. and McCright, A. M. (2015). 'Challenging Climate Change: The Denial Countermovement,' in R. E. Dunlap and R. J. Brulle (eds) *Climate Change and Society: Sociological Perspectives*. New York: Oxford University Press, 300–32.

Durkheim, E. ([1893] 2014). *The Division of Labor in Society*. New York: Free Press.

Eichbaum, C. and Shaw, R. (2010) (eds). *Partisan Appointees and Public Servants: An International Analysis of the Role of the Political Adviser*. London: Edward Elgar.

Elgie, R. (2011). 'Core Executive Studies Two Decades On,' *Public Administration* 89(1): 64–77.

Elgie, R. (2015). *Studying Political Leadership: Foundations and Contending Accounts*. Basingstoke: Palgrave Macmillan.

Finlayson, A. (2007). 'From Beliefs to Arguments: Interpretive Methodology and Rhetorical Political Analysis,' *British Journal of Politics and International Relations* 9: 545–63.

Finlayson, A. and Martin, J. (2008). '"It Ain't What You Say…": British Political Studies and the Analysis of Speech and Rhetoric,' *British Politics* 3: 445–64.

Fischer, F., Torgerson, D., Durnová, A., and Orsini, M. (2015). 'Introduction to Critical Policy Studies,' in F. Fischer, D. Torgerson, A. Durnová, and M. Orsini, (eds) *Handbook of Critical Policy Studies*. London: Edward Elgar.

Fischer, F. and Gottweis, H. (2012) (eds). *The Argumentative Turn Revisited: Public Policy as Communicative Practice*. Durham, NC: Duke University Press.

Friedman, J. and Friedman, S. (2012). *Rethinking the Rhetorical Presidency*. Abingdon: Routledge.

Gaffney, J. (2014). 'Political Leadership and the Politics of Performance: France, Syria and the Chemical Weapons Crisis of 2013,' *French Politics* 12(3): 218–34.

Gaffney, J. (2017). *Leadership and the Labour Party: Narrative and Performance*. London: Palgrave Macmillan.

Grint, K. (2014). 'Social Constructionist Analysis,' in R. A. W. Rhodes and P. 't Hart (eds) *The Oxford Handbook of Political Leadership*. Oxford: Oxford University Press.

Grube, D. C. (2012). 'Prime Ministers and Political Narratives for Policy Change: Towards a Heuristic,' *Policy and Politics* 40(4): 569–86.

Grube, D. C. (2013). *Prime Ministers and Rhetorical Governance*. Basingstoke: Palgrave Macmillan.

Grube, D. C. (2016). 'Sticky Words? Towards a Theory of Rhetorical Path Dependency,' *Australian Journal of Political Science* 51(3): 530–45.

Grube, D. C. (2017). 'Civil Servants, Political History, and the Interpretation of Traditions,' *The Historical Journal* 60(1): 173–96.

Hall, P. A. and Taylor, C. R. (1996). 'Political Science and the Three New Institutionalisms,' *Political Studies* 44: 936–57.

Hardin, R. (1982). *Collective Action*. Baltimore: Johns Hopkins University Press.

Hajer, M. (2005a). 'Setting the Stage: A Dramaturgy of Policy Deliberation,' *Administration and Society* 36: 624–47.

Hajer, M. (2005b). 'Rebuilding Ground Zero: The Politics of Performance,' *Planning Theory and Practice* 6: 445–64.

Hajer, M. (2006). 'The Living Institutions of the EU: Analysing Governance as Performance,' *Perspectives on European Politics and Society* 7: 41–55.

Hay, C. (2010). 'Ideas and the Construction of Interests,' in D. Beland and R. H. Cox (eds) *Ideas and Politics and Social Science Research*. Oxford: Oxford University Press.

Hay, C. (2016). 'Good in a Crisis: The Ontological Institutionalism of Social Constructivism,' *New Political Economy* 21(6): 520–35.

Helms, L. (2019). 'When Less is More: 'Negative Resources' and the Performance of Presidents and Prime Ministers,' *Politics* 39(3): 269–83 (early view. https://doi.org/10.1177/0263395717738964).

Holtzman, R. (2011). 'What's the Problem Mr. President? Bush's Shifting Definitions of the 2008 Financial Crisis,' *International Social Science Review* 86(3–4): 95–112.

Howarth, D. (2000). *Discourse*. Oxford: Oxford University Press.

Howarth, D., Norval, A. J., and Stavrakakis, Y. (2000) (eds). *Discourse Theory and Political Analysis: Identities, Hegemonies and Social Change*. Manchester: Manchester University Press.

Jacques, P. J. and Knox, C. C. (2016). "Hurricanes and Hegemony: A Qualitative Analysis of Micro-level Climate Change Denial Discourses,' *Environmental Politics* 25(5): 831–52.

Kane, J. (2001). *The Politics of Moral Capital*. Cambridge: Cambridge University Press.

Kane, J. and Patapan, H. (2012). *The Democratic Leader: How Democracy Defines, Empowers and Limits its Leaders*. Oxford: Oxford University Press.

Kernell, S. (2006). *Going Public: New Strategies of Presidential Leadership*. 4th ed. Thousand Oaks, CA: CQ Press.

McDonnell, D. (2016). 'Populist Leaders and Coterie Charisma,' *Political Studies* 64(3): 719–33.

Mackay, F., Monro, S., and Waylen, G. (2009). 'The Feminist Potential of Sociological Institutionalism,' *Politics and Gender* 5: 253–62.

Mahoney, J. and Thelen, K. (2010). *Explaining Institutional Change: Ambiguity, Agency and Power*. Cambridge: Cambridge University Press.

March, J. G. and Olsen, J. P. (1989). *Rediscovering Institutions: The Organizational Basis of Politics*. New York: The Free Press.

Marsh, D. (2009). 'Keeping Ideas in their Place: In Praise of Thin Constructivism,' *Australian Journal of Political Science* 44(4): 679–96.

Medhurst, M. J. (2006) (ed.). *The Rhetorical Presidency of George H.W. Bush*. Texas: A&M University Press.

Panizza, F. and Miorelli, R. (2013). 'Taking Discourse Seriously: Discursive Institutionalism and Post-Structuralist Discourse Theory,' *Political Studies* 61: 301–18.

Parsons, C. (2010). 'Constructivism and Interpretive Theory,' in D. Marsh and G. Stoker (eds) *Theory and Methods in Political Science*. Basingstoke: Palgrave Macmillan.

Pierson, P. (2000). 'Increasing Returns, Path Dependence, and the Study of Politics,' *American Political Science Review* 94: 251–67.

Pierson, P. (2004). *Politics in Time: History, Institutions and Social Analysis*. Princeton: Princeton University Press.

Rhodes, R. A. W. (1995). 'From Prime Ministerial Power to Core Executive,' in R. A. W. Rhodes and P. Dunleavy (eds) *Prime Minister, Cabinet and Core Executive*. London: Macmillan, 11–37.

Rhodes, R. A. W. (2008). 'Old Institutionalisms,' in S. A. Binder, R. A. W. Rhodes, and B. A. Rockman (eds) *The Oxford Handbook of Political Institutions*. Oxford: Oxford University Press.

Rhodes, R. A. W. (2011). *Everyday Life in British Government*. Oxford: Oxford University Press.

Rhodes, R. A. W. and Tiernan, A. (2016). 'Court Politics in a Federal Polity,' *Australian Journal of Political Science* 51(2): 338–54.

Schmidt, V. A. (2010). 'Taking Ideas and Discourse Seriously: Explaining Change Through Discursive Institutionalism as the Fourth 'New Institutionalism',' *European Political Science Review* 2(1): 1–25.

Schmidt, V. A. (2012). 'A Curious Constructivism: A Response to Professor Bell,' *British Journal of Political Science* 42: 705–13.

Shepsle, K. A. (2008). 'Rational Choice Institutionalism,' in S. A. Binder, R. A. W. Rhodes, and B. A. Rockman (eds) *The Oxford Handbook of Political Institutions*. Oxford: Oxford University Press.

Skowronek, S. (2008). *Presidential Leadership in Political Time: Reprise and Reappraisal*. Lawrence, KS: University Press of Kansas.

Stone, D. (2012). *Policy Paradox: The Art of Political Decision Making*. New York: W.W. Norton & Co.

Toye, R. (2011). 'The Rhetorical Premiership: A New Perspective on Prime Ministerial Power since 1945,' *Parliamentary History* 30: 175–92.

Tulis, J. (1987). *The Rhetorical Presidency*. Princeton: Princeton University Press.

Uhr, J. and Walter, R. (2014) (eds). *Studies in Australian Political Rhetoric*. Canberra: ANU Press.

Uhr, J. and Walter, R. (2015). 'The Rhetorical Standards of Public Reason in Australia,' *Australian Journal of Politics and History* 61: 248–62.

Weber, M. ([1930] 2002). *The Protestant Ethic and the Spirit of Capitalism and Other Works*. London: Penguin Books.

Weber, M. (2005). *Readings and Commentary on Modernity*, ed. S. Kalberg. Laden, MA: Balckwell.

Wendt, A. (1999). *Social Theory of International Politics*. Cambridge: Cambridge University Press.

Widmaier, W. (2007). 'Constructing Foreign Policy Crises: Interpretive Leadership in the Cold War and War on Terrorism,' *International Studies Quarterly* 51(4): 779–94.

Widmaier, W. (2016). *Economic Ideas in Political Time: The Rise and Fall of Economic Orders from the Progressive Era to the Global Financial Crisis*. Cambridge: Cambridge University Press.

Widmaier, W., Blyth, M., and Seabrooke, L. (2007). 'Exogenous Shocks or Endogenous Constructions? The Meanings of Wars and Crises,' *International Studies Quarterly* 51(4): 747–59.

CHAPTER 9

ETHICAL APPROACHES TO THE STUDY OF POLITICAL EXECUTIVES

JOHN UHR

9.1 INTRODUCTION

STUDENTS of the political executive acknowledge that there is no common academic journal devoted to this topic of executive ethics. The political executive is the leading institution in almost all contemporary systems of government and there is no shortage of specialist academic journals covering this central branch of government (see, e.g., *Governance*; *Presidential Studies Quarterly*; *Public Administration*). Yet few if any concentrate on executive ethics. While there are quite a few academic journals interested in ethics (see, e.g., *Ethics*; *Philosophy and Public Affairs*; *Journal of Political Philosophy*), only a very few cover this sphere of political and administrative activity (see, e.g., *Ethics and International Affairs*). Others will have noted the many limitations to coverage of gender and leadership ethics for political executives (Eagly and Heilman 2016). The result is that a chapter on 'ethical approaches' to political executives risks wandering far and wide across the scholarly landscape of executive and administrative studies, accumulating handfuls of interesting reports on how differently placed political executives have or have not acted ethically, judged according to whatever standards of ethics are accepted as politically appropriate.

A chapter on 'ethical approaches' inevitably turns the attention away from what political executives have done to what commentators and critics say about the ethical conduct of executives. The usual aim is to run the tape over the leading schools of thought in order to show strengths and potential limitations in the relevant academic literature. This chapter follows this model but in an unusual way. The fact that there are so few academic journals devoted to this quite central theme in government means that contemporary social science has not yet found a convenient language or methodology to represent preferred ways of studying executive ethics in political systems. This tentativeness reflects a more basic defect in contemporary studies of leadership, with three broadly separate research avenues examining the empirical behaviour of leadership roles performed by 'executives' in modern Western society. The first is a psychology research model which tends to treat political executives as one of a number of samples of group leadership where executive ethics is illustrated by choice of styles of organizational leadership (see, e.g., *Leadership Quarterly*). A second research model measures political executives against standards for business ethics where executive ethics is related to conventions of entrepreneurship and corporate productivity found in business or management schools (see, e.g., *Business Ethics*). A third research model relates to civil service bureaucracy where executive ethics deals with the forms of management and interaction by elected political officials over appointed and career civil services (see, e.g., *Public Administration Review*).

None of these three promising research pathways is wholly focused on the executive branch of modern government. Even the third pathway of public administration can often separate politics from administration and so promote detailed studies of civil service professionalism with many studies of the ethics of senior civil service executives—but surprisingly few studies of the ethics of the political executive of ministers, cabinet members, agency heads, and of course heads of government who hold peak offices in the political executive. One result of this academic diversity is that the contemporary study of the ethics of political executives lacks a coherent focus. Of course, there are many important political science journals welcoming studies of political executives. They publish new reports on leadership transitions or changes which can have important ethical issues. But most of these leadership studies say little about the nature of executive ethics—which forces us to attempt to do something different in this chapter.

My aim here is to promote a fresh framework for 'ethical approaches' of political executives by recovering what I think is the first and now sadly neglected foundation story about leadership ethics in Western narratives of the political executive. The purpose is to uncover an historical insider's forgotten but very realistic benchmark in order to help contemporaries assess 'ethical approaches'. My aim is far from conservative: it is to help construct greater intellectual coherence into the developing ethical role or office of Western political executives. My source is a founding member of the political executive who happens to be one of the most significant philosophers of the Enlightenment: English statesman and philosopher Francis Bacon (1561–1626).

Why bother with Bacon? First, he practised many demanding roles in the political executive as those ministerial and judicial roles were being devised and first developed in his many years in the House of Commons (1581–1617) and later years in the House of Lords (1618–21). He knew the political executive from his many years serving at the top in the executive branch of British monarchs, serving finally as Lord Chancellor: effectively, the head of government. Second, he reflected in pioneering ways on the nature of public leadership exercised not only by political executives but also by leaders in civil society who would carry on the social project of the Enlightenment Bacon helped to promote. The famous 'Baconian method' includes detailed analysis of leadership ethics for those 'methodising' modernity—then in Bacon's time and now as we live late in the life of Baconian modernity (Faulkner 1993). Third, his views cut deep, wounding his conservative enemies who brought his political career to an end through a corruption charge now thought to be crassly motivated with few traces of hard evidence (Vickers 2002). Bacon pushed to the limits, knowing that the ethics of political executives has its trials and tribulations, often with disappointing political results. But intellectual results can still emerge, as Bacon knew so well from his great work cultivating the leadership ethics of political executives—his ever-lasting *Essays* (Bacon 1985).

Future studies of executive ethics need a new theory to draw our diverse 'ethical approaches' into greater intellectual coherence. The social sciences of leadership studies have done well enough in dispersing our studies of executive ethics over many disciplines to produce important case studies. Yet at some point, the case studies have to be compared and the competing norms of executive ethics evaluated. My claim is in defence of Bacon's *theory* rather than his own executive *practice*: as befits an intellectual founder, Bacon knew that many centuries after him people would need a foundational story about executive ethics, regardless of how little they knew or cared about his own political story (Briggs 1989: 215–48; Faulkner 1993: 261–82; Vickers 2002).

9.2 Research Themes

9.2.1 Defining the Problem

There are many different scholarly approaches to the study of political executive ethics (Uhr 2015). Most common are highly personalized studies of the character of different leaders whose impact on their organization and on society reflects the personal morality— or the absence of personal morality—of those in charge. These studies can be colourful but they can also be moralistic: judging leaders harshly when they fall below whatever benchmark of public morality is invoked by critics. US President Trump is a good example (Tourish 2017; Miroff 2018). A typical claim would be that 'Trump has no real character we can admire' and so does not deserve to occupy the office of US president. A frequent alternative approach examines the ethics of office associated with specific leadership roles, with the aim of examining individual leadership performance according to formal and cultural ethics of office shaping particular public offices or roles. Not all public offices encourage exactly the same form or substance of personal ethics, with students of leadership ethics noting that liberal-democratic systems of governance are quite plural-ist about the nature of leaders' personal morality—so long as leaders guide their conduct by the expected or acceptable ethics of the specific public office they hold. A typical claim would be that the office of US president expects its occupants to 'carry out the duties of the office according to the Constitution', regardless of their personal morality. US political theorists Galston and Thompson call this 'constitutional character' which is about ethics of role rather than personal morality (Galston 2010; Thompson 2010).

My own preference is for a liberal orientation to leadership which focuses more on *role ethics* than the *personal morality* of those occupying the role (Uhr 2015: 147–67). I concede that few individuals can hold high public office without drawing heavily on their own deeper moral creed which can help them 'fit into' the ethics of their office. Examples like US President Lincoln and UK Prime Minister Churchill expanded the ethics of the offices they occupied through their somewhat circumspect reliance on doctrines of liberal justice not formally enshrined in their historical public offices. Yet a core component of both of these national leaders is that they justified their ethics of office according to constitutional principles closely associated with the roles they occupied and the constitutional regime framing those offices. The public integrity associated with these two outstanding leaders relates more closely to ethics of office than to personal morality: both are models of integrity because of the way they integrated themselves into the office or role, avoiding (at least when performing at their best) personal crusades against threats of immorality. In this way, systems of public integrity effectively regulate official *conduct* and are much less effective in regulating the morality of personal *beliefs*. Hence the prudence of looking 'beyond the great and glorious' to recover a better fit between executive competence and liberal-democratic executive institutions (Helms 2012; see also Chapter 32 in this volume).

Here I want to trace the liberal-democratic *ethos* or spirit back to the seventeenth century when an innovative 'business ethic' of leadership was devised by Bacon—recently studied by Masters and Uhr (2017: 4–14, 139–46). For one who knew only too well that 'There is little friendship in the world', Bacon's intellectual realism differs from conventional preoccupations in leadership ethics (Bacon 1985: 206). There are two extreme positions either side of Bacon's valuable realism: a misguidedly optimistic form of *idealism* and a deeply pessimistic form of *cynicism*. Between these two extremes, we can locate Bacon's more promising 'realistic' position. It is worth noting that Bacon is not alone in these competing frameworks for leadership ethics: all three approaches highlight an intellectual champion from the past whose own philosophy has generated a model of leadership in ethics and politics. My preference for Bacon notes his impressively prudent approach to leadership ethics—over the imprudently pure Immanuel Kant and the imprudently impure Machiavelli.

Kantian philosophy stands out as idealistic because of the 'categorical imperative' of unavoidable duty, and substantively because of norms of autonomy and shared sovereignty promoted by Kant (Uhr 2015: 103–23). The best examples of leadership idealism relate to a demanding personal morality of strict Kantianism where leaders bring to their role a commitment to strict obligation, with minimal deviation according to changing circumstances or self-interested inclinations. A valuable model of this Kantian approach to leadership ethics is Terry Price (Price 2006, 2008b).

Machiavelli is unrivalled as a model for flexible public responsibility promoting almost a duty of 'dirty hands' for those wily enough to circumvent the rules when community interest might require such unconventional leadership strategies (Uhr 2015: 63–82; Grint 2016). The best examples of leadership cynicism relate to appealing versions of Machiavellianism, with leaders tempted to use dishonourable measures justified by appeals to urgency in responding to threats against national security. Attractive models of Machiavellian leadership ethics in contemporary political theory are various examples of contemporary utilitarianism, but there are also outstanding examples of high-minded Machiavellianism, such as that provided by the cautiously apologetic Viroli or by the energetic proponent of democratic populism, McCormick (McCormick 2011; Viroli 2014).

9.2.2 Moral Solutions

In many ways, a major foundation of current thinking about executive leadership ethics was the edited book *The Quest for Moral Leaders: Essays on Leadership Ethics* (Ciulla et al. 2005). Many of the contributors have since developed very influential accounts of this explicit concept of 'leadership ethics', with strong links between leadership and moral theory. My own approach is cautious about the benefits of thinking of leadership in strictly moral terms, in part because, as a political scientist, I see greater value in linking leadership to professional role ethics reflecting debates over appropriate community standards. The domain of public ethics is removed to some degree from deeper theories of morality. For some researchers, 'the quest' is for leadership to be exercised by moral persons; for others like me, leadership has its own ethics of office drawn more from politics than morality (Spector 2017).

Advocates of moral theories of executive ethics have made their case extensively, with Ciulla's research taking prominent place (see, e.g., Ciulla 2003, 2010, 2013, 2014). Philosophical theories of ethics tend to be presented as doctrines of morality with hope that systems of public morality can be shaped closely around favoured philosophical concepts. Price's work also reflects the influential role of the US Jepson School of Leadership Studies, with fascinatingly direct accounts of 'Kant's advice for leaders' (which is that 'no, you aren't special') and quite detailed critiques of teaching and research programmes for 'critical leadership ethics' (Price 2008a).

Of course, my response is not that politics should be divorced from morality. My argument is that political and related forms of public leadership are constructed flexibly around social ethics—and not inflexibly around individual morality. We know that 'ethics' and 'morality' derive from very similar philosophical origins in classical Greek and Roman life; but we can also see that modern liberal democracy tends to regulate public and private belief differently, distancing external norms of public ethics from internal conscientious beliefs of private morality. Ciulla's important 'Introduction' to *The Quest for Moral Leaders* notes that leadership is 'morality and immorality magnified' which certainly makes leaders resemble the very best and the very worst of humanity (Ciulla 2005: 1). Yet liberal constitutionalism paints a different picture of public integrity, constructed around institutional rather than moral relationships where the integrity of public leaders is tested by their role ethics. Leadership ethics thus understood sits more conventionally between 'morality and immorality magnified'. My own research leans away from ideals of morality towards this more realistic liberal model of leadership ethics (Uhr 2005, 2010).

9.2.3 Ethical Solutions

A model of the type of liberal institutional research was pioneered by US theorist of public administration, John Rohr, whose early book on *Ethics for Bureaucrats* had a brief but powerful 'Foreword' on the role of 'regime values' by Herbert J Storing (Rohr 1978: v–vi). The idea was that each polity defines itself by reference to a core set of 'regime values', so that political and institutional 'dialogue' over competing interpretations of these core governance values frames the professional ethics of administrative as well as elected executives. Rohr later published a very substantial account of the 'constitutional governance' of two influential modern republics—France and the United States (Rohr 1995). This work compared the distinctive forms of executive ethics shaped by the three branches of government in both constitutional systems. Rohr's later book on ethics and constitutional practice compared the strategies used by political executives in 'managing the state' in several modern liberal-democracies, noting the differences in political ethics relied on by elected and career executives (Rohr 1998). Rohr's research findings provide strong empirical evidence supporting Storing's more general theories about ethics of 'statesmanship' exercised by elected and career executives in liberal-democratic political systems (Bessette 1995; Uhr 2014).

The 'case for ethics' draws heavily on concepts of leadership ethics used in the history of political philosophy but grounds this analysis in a political and constitutional framework. This framework is that of Western liberal constitutionalism and my aim is to tease out from this liberal intellectual movement a fresh way of examining leadership ethics in modern democracies. I will refer to leadership offices in alternative political regimes but most of the theory and the case material comes from the world of public leadership found in liberal-democracy. An exemplar in historical studies of executive ethics is Mansfield's *Taming the Prince* which examines 'the ambivalence' of modern executive power from Aristotle to the US Federalist Papers (Mansfield 1993). The research of Rohr and Storing tend to follow Mansfield's historical interpretation of 'ambivalence' in the ethics of executive power as articulated by the influential framers of modern executive power: notably Machiavelli, Hobbes, Locke, Montesquieu, and the framers of the US constitution. All three researchers note that liberal constitutionalism promotes an ethic of 'liberal individualism' moderated by the due processes of a system of checks and balances centrally managed by political executives; yet Mansfield draws extensively on his close knowledge of Machiavelli to make the case for 'the Machiavellian origin of the liberal individual' who uses 'necessity' to magnify executive powers as ethical attributes of state power. In Mansfield's cryptic language, Machiavellian necessity can teach contemporary political executives that their ethical virtues are 'indispensable and undependable' (Mansfield 1993: xv–xvii).

The debate between Mansfield and his anti-Machiavellian critic Sheldon Wolin is a very important source document in the argument over executive ethics (Mansfield 1992; Wolin 1992). If the ethics of political executives reflects their public role, what happens when advocates like Mansfield invite us to see that role as a form of rule richly captured by Machiavelli in his notorious concept of *virtu*? This rare debate in US political science is very relevant to scholars of executive ethics because it unpacks the envelope of 'ethics' so that we begin to see it as containing a set of antagonistic contentions about the nature of political virtue. Mansfield turns ethics in the direction of virtuous monarchic responsibility while Wolin defends ethics as a form of democratic accountability against ever-present threats of deceptive misrule. This debate links up with wider discussions of 'bad leadership' which relates to executive power used for either improper official purposes or for inappropriate personal benefit. In the eyes of many analysts of the political executive, 'bad leadership' is what occurs whenever public accountability fails to restrain personal irresponsibility; in these eyes, constitutional systems for the rule of law might lack the power to deliver high ethical responsibility but they certainly do act against low unethical conduct often described as 'bad leadership'.

Harvard University's Center for Public Leadership gave 'bad leadership' the lengthy book portrait it deserves, complete with many case studies of those in high power 'leading badly' (Kellerman 2004). While evil rulers like Pol Pot appear for close study, many conventional holders of political executive office also come into focus in Kellerman's study: such as mayors, legislators, even US presidents such as Bill Clinton. The Clinton case is not about Monica Lewinsky but US relations with Rwanda (Kellerman 2004: 174–90). A related issue is the way 'good governments' overhaul earlier 'bad governments' or 'bad leadership' through formal acts of apology—with competent leaders strengthening their profile through careful management of incompetent predecessors (Cels 2017).

Research by Helms relates 'bad leadership' to norms of 'good democratic leadership' (Helms 2014a). In an edited book examining 'prudence and judgment', Helms' chapter helps us see examples of poorly performing executives lacking the right sort of prudence and judgment. Helms recovers the importance of the liberal-democratic political regime as the playing field for executive conduct: bad leadership resembles bad play, with poor performers failing to use the many roles and responsibilities available to them to engage in that special kind of shared team work encouraged by 'any truly liberal democracy'— decent institutions with supportive 'cultural norms and values' (Helms 2014a: 53, 56; see also Chapter 32 in this volume). The striking example of the wayward George Bush Sr. shows how close case study helps distinguish the many categories of poor performers— reaching all the way beyond Bush or the lacklustre Jimmy Carter to anti-regime types like Italy's Berlusconi (see also Helms 2014b).

9.2.4 Machiavelli without Machiavellism?

The literature on leadership ethics is vast but often difficult to apply to concrete examples of serving leaders. The vastness reflects the huge variety of leadership scenarios or case studies highlighting many ethical challenges facing public leaders in many different types of organizations. Even when confined to leaders of government, the literature tends to remain very extensive, reflecting the many different types of political office leaders occupy. The implication seems to be that what is ethical for leaders holding presidential office will differ substantially from ethical expectations for leaders of parliamentary offices. There is some truth in framing leadership ethics around such institutional differences, because leadership in all its facets is a relationship enterprise: presidential and parliamentary leaders tend to relate to different types of office-holders, including that most important of democratic offices—the electorate, which might stamp public authority on a president but might disperse a mandate across competing political parties in many parliamentary systems (Uhr 2005: 119–57; Uhr 2015: 169–88).

Another reason for the vastness of leadership ethics literature is the huge variety of schools of ethics contributing to leadership ethics. Many of these schools have little regard for conventional variations in types of political regime, with the result that many schools of ethics claim that their own distinctive approach can fit each and every variety of institutional circumstance. This unusual ambition can be seen among optimistic idealists as well as pessimistic cynics, both of which can reduce leadership ethics to a set of convenient simplicities. My alternative approach takes its line on leadership ethics from Bacon, one of the most experienced politicians ever to write about the nature of politics and of political leadership. Frequently, Bacon stands solidly behind Machiavelli who wins the highest praise as the intellectual founder of leadership studies (Faulkner 1993: 59–83).

Sure enough, Bacon does appear to be a pioneering follower of Machiavelli in whose quite realistic steps Bacon seems so assured as a practising politician. Bacon is one of the very first statesmen to praise Machiavelli so that we can better understand self-interested power hiding beneath the rituals of rule. Yet Bacon is quite critical of Machiavelli for allowing the celebration of indecent means to creep ahead of leaders' understanding of worthy ends: Bacon is perhaps the first critic of 'Machiavellianism' precisely because he insists that the choice of remarkably flexible means must serve a just cause larger and more substantial than the security or pride or glory of a powerful leader (Faulkner 1993: 59–83). Machiavelli writes of allies; Bacon writes of friends: thus the two thinkers conceive of different forms of leadership. Both write about ambition and both accept fame as a price worth paying for ambitious national leaders. Both write about greatness as the defining quality of leaders. Bacon's distinctive approach is to distinguish between 'mean men' and 'great men', thereby sorting out the capacity for *virtu* Machiavelli retained in one ambiguous whole (Bacon 1985: 211). Bacon praises Machiavelli but often conditionally, as though his predecessor had failed to make the case for the justice of the ends served by his innovative means. Bacon's account of ambition notes how important it is for rulers to 'handle' ambitious followers 'so as they be still progressive and not retrograde' (Bacon 1985: 173). Machiavelli has a large gallery of notable great leaders; Bacon's gallery is similar yet it includes philosophers like Socrates (twice) and Cicero (eight times) who prefigure the 'progressive' type of leadership favoured in the *Essays*. Unlike Machiavelli,

Bacon explicitly refers to 'the public good' or 'the good of their country' as his ultimate goal, praising those intent 'rather to seek merit than fame' (Bacon 1985: 207, 219, 221).

Machiavelli exercises powerful influence over contemporary studies of leadership which follow his example of evaluating leaders in terms of their use of means to benefit their own ends. In this view, leadership ethics is the right choice of means to promote the goals of the means-manager, whether it be to get to office or to retain office. Even anti-Machiavellian approaches such as those drawn from Kantian ethics do so by praising the choice of means separate from explicit ranking of the leaders' ends (Price 2008b: 173–84). Bacon provides a promising alternative which is quietly daring in its approach to the choice of means but is persistently principled about the nature of the goals being promoted. Students of leadership tend to follow Machiavelli who tolerates unethical means used to defend or promote 'great foundations for future power' to avoid the threat of 'ruin' by a ruler or a state (Mansfield 1993:121–49; Machiavelli 1998: 25–33). Bacon has stricter tests of public benefit. These tests place ethical burdens on leaders who fall short in their integrity by advancing themselves ahead of their community. Bacon shifts the focus from the great leadership of the solitary prince celebrated by Machiavelli and followers to a new model of greatness with many individuals sharing roles in public leadership.

The so-called 'Baconian method' usually refers to new mechanisms of *natural science* devised to unleash the world of modernity. The *Essays* shows that Bacon himself sketched out something of a transformative *social science*, calling on many leading followers to commit to the type of leadership ethics favoured by Bacon. The kind of 'utility' invoked by Bacon is more closely related to beneficial social ends than to the elevation of cleverly powerful leaders (see, e.g., Bacon 1985: 104–7; Briggs 1989: 233–48). Bacon even suggests that praise of leaders who show goodness but use their power for other purposes is 'fit for a satire'; but what is not fit for satire is Bacon's central theme of 'friendship' understood as a kind of public 'fellowship' or even 'union' of those who are *partners* rather than *favourites*. The important contrast is between the flattery which fails to help or improve leaders and that better counsel 'which setteth business straight'. Bacon goes much further, arguing that a chief benefit of friendship is for those, like Bacon himself, who knew that one day soon he would die, before completing the project of intellectual reform outlined in the *Essays*. Hence, the very real importance for Bacon of knowing that 'the care of those things will continue after him'—carried on by those deserving to be called 'his deputy' (Bacon 1985: 136–44).

An important example of role ethics is Bacon's essay on 'judicature' which is a companion to his earlier essay on 'great place', also about role ethics (Bacon 1985: 90–3, 222–5). The 'judicature' essay on that remarkable combination of 'just laws and true policy' examines the professional ethics of judges through close attention to the judicial office or role for leading members of the judicial branch of government. Bacon draws on his own experience as a judicial officer by separating out the two sets of competencies and lowering the claims of individual moral (and indeed political) beliefs of a judge against the higher claims of role ethics relevant for all judges. Leadership ethics for judges is satisfied by their compliance with their integrity to support the professional ethics of the office—and not by their adherence to whatever individual moral beliefs to which they subscribe. For judges, 'integrity is their portion and proper virtue', regardless of whether their individual sense of morality is acknowledged or ignored. Bacon especially notes the power of 'an ancient clerk' helping to manage 'the business of the court' through application of skilful precedents, prudent proceedings and competent understanding of the judicial process (Bacon 1985: 225).

I hope that my recovery of Bacon's leadership ethic will allow contemporary public leaders to see foundational pictures of themselves in the intellectual generation of modernity. Bacon's larger philosophy of leadership is modelled on the science of medicine which innovates even against the traditional comforts of custom (see, e.g., Bacon 1985: 156–7). The new science of medicine offers hope that the world can indeed be made a better place if the world is prepared to allow new leaders to 'try experiments in states'— however unwise that experimentation might normally be, except (as Bacon carefully urges) when 'necessity' makes the search for new medicine 'urgent'—or when 'the utility is evident' (Bacon 1985: 132). The *Essays* themselves are experiments used by Bacon to make evident the public utility of a new style of leadership ethics.

9.3 MAIN RESEARCH AVENUES

The scope of existing research on executive ethics is very wide, with many research avenues frequently disconnected from one another. But we can superimpose a grid of competing perspectives using the two normative concepts of 'responsibility' and 'accountability'. Although this convenient grid lacks much of the detailed complexity found in current research on executive ethics, it can help students and researchers get a better picture of the larger themes informing current research. With apologies for this simplification, we will use these two very frequently discussed concepts to try to provide a fresh guide to some of the main themes in current research of executive ethics.

9.3.1 Competing Norms: Responsibility and Accountability

The academic discipline of ethics examines human conduct: concrete *behaviour* rather than abstract *thought*. I have argued that leadership ethics examines leaders' conduct in office, and not primarily their moral beliefs. The conduct of leaders when managing their official responsibilities is very much part of their personal conduct. Thus it is almost impossible to examine leadership ethics in terms of impersonal conduct: the person of the leader is very much in the picture even when we decide not to examine the inner morality of leaders' personal conscience (see also Chapter 24 in this volume). Our focus then is on what we might call the leaders' public or official conscience as they carry out what they see as the ethics of role open to them. The term 'responsibility' adequately captures this dimension of leadership ethics; we can use the related term 'personal responsibility' to highlight the sense of personal vision which leaders bring to their role or office (Voegtlin 2016). Admittedly, many public institutions already have their own distinctive 'vision statement' but these are more formal and somewhat impersonal. Those leading such organizations are expected to bring their own dynamic vision to illuminate the policy and administrative priorities they intend to champion.

For convenience, leadership ethics in liberal-democratic systems of politics can be measured along two axes: first, the axis measuring the reach of leaders' official responsibility; and second, the axis measuring leaders' obligations of public accountability. Good systems of leadership ethics have high scores on both sets of measures (Uhr 2005: 119–57). What we call 'official' responsibility is often understandably called 'personal' responsibility because it refers to leaders' strong commitment to the role ethics of the office they personally lead. There is no equivalent 'official morality' expected of leaders. The personal morality or creed of leaders sharing power at or near the top is less immediately important than is their integrity in honouring the ethic of specific office they lead. It is all about managing relationships of power (Liu 2015).

Ethical public leadership combines high official responsibility with high commitments to public accountability. The two terms 'official' and 'public' identify in convenient shorthand the potentially contrasting qualities being compared: the official vision of those foreseeing a role in an office of leadership; and the willing participation by leaders in accounting publicly for their official performance. It is not hard to see imbalances between 'dirty hands and clean heels' in leadership ethics, with dominating personalities uncomfortable with what are seen as intrusions of accountability or with impersonal leaders distractedly weighed down by onerous accountability burdens (Grint 2016).

The 'ethics' in leadership ethics means getting the balances right between the two worlds of responsibility and accountability. Importantly, this approach to leadership ethics locates ethics in the context of leadership rather than in the personality of leaders. The study of leadership ethics is about the relationships between leaders and their authorising environments rather than about the search for a 'perfect leader' displaying 'perfect ethics' (Liu 2015). The focus on the social context rather than the 'perfect leader' means that one of the core values associated with leadership ethics is public integrity which requires ethical competence on those giving as well as those receiving formal delegations of leadership. Public leadership is exercised by those holding high offices of public trust delegating power and reviewing performance of those occupying the very highest offices in what we call the political executive. Public integrity in most systems of executive government requires that those holding the highest executive powers live up to their highest official responsibilities as holders of distinctive public trust—while also honouring their obligations to satisfy their accountability communities (e.g. legislatures, courts as well as political parties and voters).

It would be a mistake to think of the two axes of leadership ethics as a blend of *positive* ('high responsibility') and *negative* ('high accountability') qualities. In fact, both elements are positive in modern democracy—activating rather than restraining the work of public leaders. For liberal-democratic regimes, public accountability is very much a positive quality where leaders do what they can to build their public trust through sustained public dialogue with the political community. Leadership ethics begins and ends with relationships between leaders and their supporting political communities—their 'followers' (Ford and Harding 2015; Sy et al. 2018). From one perspective, leaders using their considerable public power not only *to inform* but also to shape and *to give form* to their preferred community of followers. Yet from another perspective, diverse political communities exercise their own civic powers as electors and advocates to shape the kind of public leadership, including its agenda and momentum, desired by the many competing public activists comprising 'the civic community'.

9.3.2 Contrasting Executives

Leadership ethics thus assumes that the institutional culture of the entities being lead can respond positively to the authority of leaders who themselves can respond positively to the forms of accountability required of those holding high offices of public trust. Not every public institution passes this test. Many civil service agencies overrate the importance of 'the minister' and underrate the importance of external accountability. Many regulatory commissions shift their own accountability burdens away from their external stakeholders to the executive decision makers they advise; and many electoral agencies prefer to satisfy participating political parties rather than the voters themselves. Leadership ethics will only be as good as is the balance between responsibility and accountability in the institutional environment (Uhr 2005: 189–211).

Non-democratic regimes will have different measures of ethical leadership. For example, contemporary authoritarian political systems might well measure personal responsibility quite differently, with either highly personalized systems of responsibility like those associated with the autocratic North Korean regime; or more corporatized systems of responsibility like those associated with one-party rule as in China or Vietnam. The 'liberal' qualifier in the term 'liberal-democracy' refers to the core value of individual rights in modern doctrines of liberalism, which implies the presence of an individual rights reading of both core values of responsibility and accountability.

In this liberal-democratic model, leaders like Angela Merkel, Emmanuel Macron, Theresa May, or recent 'heroes' like Nelson Mandela have to pass two ethics tests: first, validating their own individual rights through their agenda of responsibility shaping their leadership project; and second, justifying the accountability rights of those who manage their public mandate. Neither test is easy to confront or negotiate or satisfy. Both tests are heavily procedural, with leaders facing expectations of exceptional public rhetoric as they drive and justify their leadership. Rhetoric might seem like as unusual and unnecessary part of the business of leadership, with readers understandably fearing that pretending or misleading public actors might engage in deceptive public rhetoric more like clever demagogues than competent statesman. Below I will defend the vital role of rhetoric in the leadership art, drawing very much on leadership practice as delivered and surprisingly debated by Bacon—who warned us that reading 'good books of morality is a little flat and dead' (Bacon 1985: 143).

Public rhetoric is one of the most important things that leaders do. Rhetoric features high on the list of responsibility and accountability activities required of leaders. If ethics is about hard choices leaders make when balancing competing objectives, then one of the hardest choices is over the craft of language used in public explanations of their leadership behaviour (Lord 2003: 180–91). It is impossible to imagine a contemporary public leader in modern systems of governance carrying out their leadership functions wordlessly, with no temptation to 'talk up' their plans or achievements. Negotiation is more practical than other leadership activities like speculation or imagination: negotiation excels when leaders enrich their practical reason with effective forms of rhetoric to inform and persuade parties to the negotiation—not only friends who warmly support it but also enemies who can learn to respect it. Praising friendship, Bacon celebrates those who 'may speak as the case requires, and not as it sorteth with' those gathered to listen (Bacon 1985: 144).

9.3.3 Recovering Classical Perspectives

Democratic systems have long prided themselves on elevating representative leaders who carry on with public business as demanded of them by their mandated popular sovereigns. The classical historian Thucydides allows readers to see much of this in ancient Athens as popular interests in that city demand that leaders like Pericles pay close attention to public affairs as framed and formulated by influential public activists. Thucydides's acknowledged 'realism' then reframes this picture of democratic leadership by providing evidence that remarkable leaders like Pericles exercised their own counter-vailing influence—so much that Thucydides suggests that Athens enjoyed the reputation of being a 'democracy' while actually behaving more like a 'monarchy' under the skilful leadership, or indeed rulership, of Pericles (Thucydides 1972: 163–4).

Other classic sources can help. The two-test scheme of responsibility and accountability resembles the practical advice given by the Greek political philosopher Aristotle who summarized the teaching of his *Politics* in terms of 'ruling and being ruled' (Mansfield 1993: 45–71; Lord 2003: 21–32, 42–9). Open democratic polities have their own distinctive form of rule based on changing popular interests. Modern critics of Aristotle's classical orientation to politics, follow Thomas Hobbes who claimed that Aristotle's surprising republicanism reflects the corrosive influence of popular power in Athenian theorizing about politics (Hobbes 1968: 211, 225, 267). Whatever the origins, Aristotle wrote his *Politics* in ways that politically ambitious readers would learn to see and accept that political sense meant taking turns at 'ruling and being ruled'. Those with political wisdom need to know that in any decent political regime they will have to rule at some time and at other times learn to be ruled by others, who are likely to be wise in importantly different ways. The classical view from Aristotle has survived the onslaught from the enlightened despotism of Hobbes: Aristotle's practical wisdom resists the brusque paternalism of Hobbes' leadership ethics and supports the model outlined here with its defence of the twin values of responsibility and accountability (Aristotle 2013, see, e.g., Books 1–3: 7, 21–2, 27, 68–9, 93–6).

The responsibility axis thus measures the level of personal responsibility leaders bring to the leadership task—which can be simplified as either high or low. A high level of personal responsibility matches the model of exemplary leadership sketched early in studies of modern leadership by scholars like Max Weber who praised 'responsibility' to its highest limits (see, e.g., Weber 1994: 309–69; Uhr 2015: 69–75). High responsibility signals one valuable indicator of ethical initiative, understood as Weber suggested in terms of powerful 'ownership' of the leadership project. The ethics of responsibility vary according to the levels of intense commitment activated by leaders. But that activity alone is not strong evidence of leadership ethics: the programme of highly energized leaders requires public support, in terms understood by the public or their chosen representatives. The accountability axis measures a corresponding public value relating to what we might call 'trusteeship', where leaders can be measured in terms of their level of responsiveness to the public to whom leaders are meant to account. High levels of public accountability tend to reinforce authority, with low levels indicating lower or defective levels of authority (Masters and Uhr 2017: 17–30).

Importantly, leadership ethics with high levels of public accountability but low levels of personal responsibility might still measure well on some scales of leadership ethics—even with low scores of responsibility ethics. Some heads of state occupy public offices that are managed along these ultra-safe lines. The leadership ethics expected of the British monarch is one example, where the British political community seems reassured that the monarch displays only very reserved elements of personal responsibility but complies quite strictly with rituals and routines of public accountability. The proof of this head of state model becomes evident when we examine the rare examples where a head of government expels a head of state, as occurred when conservative Australian Prime Minister John Howard forced the resignation of governor-general Hollingworth in 2003 for professional misconduct as an Anglican bishop many years before his 2001 appointment as Australian governor-general.

9.4 FUTURE RESEARCH AGENDA

Ciulla (2014) is right that one important pathway for future research is 'biographical research'. Her case of Nelson Mandela is a good example of how past characters can help generate insights into options for research of use to future executives. Grint (2016) does something similar with his brief studies of Boris Johnson, Tony Blair, Nigel Farage, and Theresa May. My own suggestion goes back further, using Bacon to help clarify future research options. My aim is not to engage in a biographical study of Bacon's own experience as a leading political executive but to mediate between Bacon and our own research community by carrying forward some of the forgotten secrets of Bacon's concept of executive power. Echoing Dennis Tourish, we need to look for ways of 'writing differently about leadership', including fresh studies of unconventional writing on executive power by experts like Bacon (Tourish 2016).

9.4.1 Baconian Methods

As we face the future, several ethical approaches are unlikely to change greatly, so we can expect to see more of those three schools of analysis highlighted earlier. The contributions from the discipline of social psychology will continue to chart pathways between leaders and followers in many spheres, including the types of identify management open to political executives promoting identity communities around ethically valued beliefs about the good community. Contributions from disciplines of business and management will promote many fascinating models of executive effectiveness which are often accepted as 'translatable' to the political world. The degree of relevance really depends on the notions of probity and integrity attached to these models, where effectiveness tends to relate to economic productivity much more closely than to social or political justice (Uhr 2017). Contributions from the disciplines of public policy and administration will reach much closer into the world of governance, and it is here that research on executive ethics can expect to find a wider research base on changing relationships between the two worlds of executive government led by politicians and bureaucrats. Of special importance here is the growth of research interest in federated layers of cooperation involving increasing ambiguities between the contrasting professional ethics of politicians and bureaucrats at local, provincial, national, and trans-national levels.

Coherent disciplines of social science and less coherent systems of government will both drive the research agenda in these three important areas of interest to political executives. But neither driver will necessarily focus on the vision of executive power revealed by that exemplary reflective practitioner, Francis Bacon. The ethics of role required of political executives is an element of liberal-democratic constitutionalism often ignored by value-neutral social sciences and by value-partisan executive governments. As mentioned earlier, researchers like Rohr and Storing understood that political executives draw their ethics of office from 'regime values' often only dimly understood by those leading or managing executive power in contemporary systems of liberal-democratic governance. It is therefore important that our 'ethical approaches' remain informed by Bacon's defence of executive ethics amid the 'regime values' we associate with liberal modernity.

Bacon's leading followers or deputies would learn about 'the power to do good', because 'the end of man's motion' is 'merit and good works'. Their 'conscience' would be judged according to 'whether thou didst not best at first' (Bacon 1985: 91). Evidence that Bacon differed substantially from Machiavelli's self-interested concept of goodness is Bacon's reliance on the two terms *philanthropy* and *charity* to convey the meaning of 'goodness'. In this his first essay mentioning Machiavelli, Bacon contrasts his own view with that of others called '*misanthropi*' who share the 'natural malignity' of those who lack the 'vocation' to do 'much good'—acting as that special minority of public leaders who see themselves in very un-Machiavellian terms pioneered by Bacon explicitly as 'a citizen of the world' (Bacon 1985: 98).

During his parliamentary career, Bacon published three editions of his *Essays* on 'counsel, civil and moral', to cite from the title page (Bacon 1985: 55). Bacon's model or framework of ethics is conveyed by this term 'essays', referring to many formulations attempting to capture the public realm of relationships confronting those with legislative or executive or judicial ambition. The fifty-eight essays in the final, third edition are pathways towards what we can think of as leadership 'power'—the term 'power' being used twenty-five or so times in the *Essays*. Ethics emerges because 'power' has to be negotiated through the help of willing supporters, many of whom can be expected to exercise considerable powers of their own which the ambitious leader does not want to see used against them. The term 'prudence' is used only in one *Essay*—'Of Counsel'— where it is formulated as the 'prudence and power' of a prince properly 'counselled' (Bacon 1985: 121; Lord 2003: 207–14). Bacon's essays demonstrates how a wise counsellor might try to combine these two capacities of 'prudence and power' as skills in one's supporters—or 'followers' in what is becoming a very important research area (Ford and Harding 2015; Krylova et al. 2017; Sy et al. 2018).

The choice of supporters and followers matters as much as the choice of counsellors and advisers: leaders can decide but it takes many others to *implement* decisions, so that students of leadership learn that 'the execution of affairs resteth in the good choice of persons'. Surprisingly, here Bacon refers to the place of books—those written by writers like Bacon himself who 'have been actors upon the stage'—which can 'speak plain when counsellors blanch'. Even more surprisingly, Bacon here speaks very personally, twice using the phrase 'I commend...' when describing forms and procedures generating and implementing counsel (Bacon 1985: 123). The stated theme is that rulers need to know much about the 'greatest trust' between givers and receivers of counsel; but the important unstated theme is that rulers alone can do little without a body of trustworthy counsellors—and an adviser like Bacon who knows more than most about the difference between trusted counsellors and those examined in the essays to follow: the cunning, those wise for themselves, and those of promise who are in fact only 'seeming wise'.

9.5 CONCLUSION

My aim has been to consolidate a view of executive ethics around Bacon's hopeful picture of executive power. My suggestion is that one way forward is through recovery of Bacon's original map of the nature and, importantly, future of executive power. Studies of executive ethics can still be philosophically rich even when they lean deeply into institutional conflicts around executive power. Part of Bacon's project in his *Essays* is to help later generations understand the ethical agenda of executive power.

The term 'leaders' is used only once in Bacon's *Essays*, referring to those 'right hands' who perform as 'great leaders' under the direction of 'princes' (Bacon 1985: 220). Bacon, however, frequently used the term 'followers' to clarify the means required by leaders to perform their important role. The arts of negotiation exercised by leaders include the difficult arts of negotiating a body of 'followers' who can help deliver the programme initiated by the leaders, who alone lack sufficient power to carry through the leadership programme. If the term 'leader' is infrequent in Bacon's *Essays*, we can still note the importance of Bacon's advice on how to 'lead' or 'work any man' through negotiation. This short essay on negotiation illustrates how a leader like Bacon helps readers learn about how 'to lead' subordinates who tend to be useful instruments but unwilling followers: here we see Bacon's oddly calculating ethics at work, advising readers when to summon 'bold men', when to turn to 'fair-spoken men', when to rely on 'crafty men', when to take a chance with 'froward and absurd men' (Bacon 1985: 203–4).

Bacon warns readers about the many self-interested types of 'followers' who emerge as potential 'friends' (Bacon 1985: 205–6). Appearances can be deceptive: Bacon warns readers against 'costly followers' who trespass on one's fortune, 'ordinary followers' who expect too much from you, 'factious followers' who wage war against their hidden enemies, 'glorious followers' who often arouse envy against those they praise. These unworthy followers can be compared to 'the most honourable kind' who try to 'advance virtue and desert in all sorts of persons'—by which Bacon means that this rare type of 'honourable' follower sees their role as cultivating and developing 'all sorts of persons', and not simply the able leader and the busy follower. The task for us, then, is be worthy followers of Bacon's distinctive 'ethical approach' to executive ethics.

References

Aristotle (2013). *The Politics*, ed. C. Lord. 2nd ed. Chicago: University of Chicago Press.

Bacon, F. (1985). *Essays*, ed. J. Pitcher. London: Penguin Books.

Bessette, J. M. (1995) (ed.). *Towards a More Perfect Union: Writings of Herbert J Storing*. Washington, DC: American Enterprise Institute.

Briggs, J. C. (1989). *Francis Bacon and the Rhetoric of Nature*. Cambridge, MA: Harvard University Press.

Cels, S. (2017). "Saying Sorry," *The Leadership Quarterly* 28: 759–79.

Ciulla, J. B. (2003). *The Ethics of Leadership*. Belmont: Wadsworth.

Ciulla, J. B. (2005). "Introduction," in J. B. Ciulla, T. L. Price, and S. E. Murphy (eds) *The Quest for Moral Leaders: Essays on Leadership Ethics*. Northampton: Edward Elgar, 1–9.

Ciulla, J. B. (2010). "Being There," *Presidential Studies Quarterly* 40(1): 38–56.

Ciulla, J. B. (2013) (ed.). *Leadership Ethics*. 3 Vols. Sage.

Ciulla, J. B. (2014). "Searching for Mandela," *Leadership* 12(2): 186–97.

Ciulla, J. B., Price, T. L., and Murphy, S. E. (2005) (eds). *The Quest for Moral Leaders: Essays on Leadership Ethics*. Northampton: Edward Elgar.

Eagly, A. and Heilman, M. (2016). "Gender and Leadership: Introduction to the Special Issue," *The Leadership Quarterly* 27(3): 349–53.

Faulkner, R. K. (1993). *Francis Bacon and the Project of Progress*. Lanham: Rowman and Littlefield.

Ford, J. and Harding, N. (2015). "Followers in Leadership Theory," *Leadership* 14(1): 3–24.

Galston, W. (2010). "Commentary: Ethics and Character in the US Presidency," *Presidential Studies Quarterly* 40(1): 90–101.

Grint, K. (2016). "Dirty Hands and Clean Heels," *Leadership* 12(5): 564–80.

Hobbes, T. (1968). *Leviathan*, ed. C. B. Macpherson. London: Pelican Books.

Helms, L. (2012). "Beyond the Great and Glorious," *Journal of Comparative Government and European Policy* 10: 492–509.

Helms, L. (2014a). "When Leaders Are not Good," in J. Kane and H. Patapan (eds) *Good Democratic Leadership*. Oxford: Oxford University Press: 51–69.

Helms, L. (2014b) (ed.). *Poor Leadership and Bad Governance*. Cheltenham: Edward Elgar.

Kellerman, B. (2004). *Bad Leadership*. Cambridge, MA: Harvard Business School Press.

Krylova, K., Jolly, P., and Phillips, J. (2017). "Followers' Moral Judgments and Leaders' Integrity-Based Transgressions," *The Leadership Quarterly* 28: 195–209.

Liu, H. (2015). "Reimagining Ethical Leadership as a Relational, Contextual and Political Practice," *Leadership* 13(3): 343–67.

Lord, C. (2003). *The Modern Prince: What Leaders Need to Know Now*. New Haven: Yale University Press.

Machiavelli, N. (1998). *The Prince*, ed. H. Mansfield. Chicago: University of Chicago Press.

Mansfield, H. (1992). "Executive Power and the Passion for Virtue," *Studies in American Political Development* 6(1): 217–24.

Mansfield, H. (1993). *Taming the Prince: The Ambivalence of Modern Executive Power*. Baltimore: John Hopkins University Press.

Masters, A. and Uhr, J. (2017). *Leadership Performance and Rhetoric*. London: Palgrave.

McCormick, J. P. (2011). *Machiavellian Democracy*. Cambridge: Cambridge University Press.

Miroff, B. (2018). "Crucible: Trump's First Year," *Presidential Studies Quarterly* 48(3): 631–63.

Price, T. L. (2006). *Understanding Ethical Failures in Leadership*. Cambridge: Cambridge University Press.

Price, T. L. (2008a). "Kant's Advice for Leaders," *Leadership Quarterly* 19: 478–87.

Price, T. L. (2008b). *Leadership Ethics*. Cambridge: Cambridge University Press.

Rohr, J. (1978). *Ethics for Bureaucrats*. New York: Marcel Dekker.

Rohr, J. (1995). *Founding Republics in France and America*. Lawrence, KC: University Press of Kansas.

Rohr, J. (1998). *Public Service, Ethics and Constitutional Practice*. Lawrence, KC: University Press of Kansas.

Spector, B. (2017). "Moral Leadership?," *Leadership* 15(1): 1–9.

Sy, T., Horton, C., and Riggio, R. (2018). "Charismatic Leadership," *The Leadership Quarterly* 29: 58–69.

Thompson, D. F. (2010). "Constitutional Character," *Presidential Studies Quarterly* 40(1): 23–37.

Tourish, D. (2016). "Introduction: Writing Differently about Leadership," *Leadership* 13(1): 3–4.

Tourish, D. (2017). "The Election of Trump," *Leadership* 13(4): 391–2.

Thucydides (1972). *History of the Peloponnesian War*. London: Penguin Books.

Uhr, J. (2005). *Terms of Trust: Arguments over Ethics in Australian Government*. Sydney: UNSW Press.

Uhr, J. (2010). "Be Careful of What You Wish For," in J. Boston, A. Bradstock and D. Eng (eds) *Public Policy: Why Ethics Matters*. Canberra: ANU E Press, 79–97.

Uhr, J. (2014). "John Rohr's Concept of Regime Values," *Administration and Society* 46(2): 141–52.

Uhr, J. (2015). *Prudential Public Leadership*. London: Palgrave.

Uhr, J. (2017). "Leadership Effectiveness," in A. Farazmand (ed.) *Global Encyclopedia of Public Administration, Public Policy, and Governance*. Switzerland: Springer International, 1–10.

Vickers, B. (2002). "Introduction," in B. Vickers (ed.) *Francis Bacon: The Major Works*. Oxford: Oxford University Press, xv–xliv.

Viroli, M. (2014). *Redeeming "The Prince": The Meaning of Machiavelli's Masterpiece*. Princeton: Princeton University Press.

Voegtlin, C. (2016). "What Does It Mean to Be Responsible," *Leadership* 12(5): 581–608.

Weber, M. (1994). *Political Writings*, ed. P. Lassman and R. Speirs. Cambridge: University of Cambridge Press.

Wolin, S. (1992). "Executive Liberation," *Studies in American Political Development* 6(1): 211–16.

CHAPTER 10

....

METHODOLOGY AND THE STUDY OF THE POLITICAL EXECUTIVE

....

†ROBERT ELGIE

THIS chapter examines the issue of methodology and the study of the political executive. Whether or not they make it clear, all scholars adopt a methodology when they engage in research, including research on the political executive. Moreover, whether or not scholars are aware of it, their methodology is based on a particular philosophy of inquiry, including a judgement about what we can know about the world. In these ways, methodological issues raise profound questions about the conduct of social and political research. These issues relate to the questions we wish to ask about the world and the epistemological status of the conclusions we wish to reach about the world. In this broad context, this chapter begins by sketching the intellectual history of the predominant methodologies that have been applied to the study of the political executive. It then points to the material that scholars usually draw upon to engage in the study of the political executive, pointing to the most commonly used qualitative and quantitative methods that are used in this domain. It ends by suggesting some ways in which our understanding of the political executive could be improved by a careful consideration of issues relating to research design and the application of new methodological techniques. The hope is that this chapter will help to improve the validity of the conclusions that scholars wish to draw about the political executive.

10.1 METHODOLOGIES AND THE STUDY OF THE POLITICAL EXECUTIVE

....

Over the years, scholars researching the political executive have called upon a wide range of methodologies. Indeed, many political science methodologies have been applied to the study of the political executive at one time or another. That said, two points should be emphasized. First, over time the methodological focus has shifted, reflecting changing trends in the dominant approaches to the study of political life. Here, we understand an 'approach' to refer to a general way of thinking about a topic, including the objects of inquiry and the questions asked about them, and a 'method' to be how researchers try to arrive at a valid answer to the questions that are asked. Second, the application of particular methodologies is currently uneven, reflecting certain basic methodological problems with studying the political executive. This section begins by identifying the research methods associated with the different approaches that have been taken to the study of politics at least as they have been applied to the political executive. It then identifies some of the general methodological challenges that researchers typically face when studying the political executive whatever approach is taken.

For a long period of time, the study of politics was associated with what has since been labelled the 'old institutionalist' approach (March and Olsen 1984: 738). In relation to the political executive, this work can be traced at least as far back as *The Federalist Papers* (Rossiter 1961) in the late eighteenth century and includes contributions by scholars such as Walter Bagehot ([1867] 1964) and Woodrow Wilson (1885) in the latter part of the nineteenth century. It also includes work in the early part of the twentieth century by scholars such as Leonard Alston (1905), James Bryce (Viscount Bryce) (1921), and Charles E. Martin (1925). Peters (1998: 3) characterizes the 'old institutionalism' as being 'about the formal aspects of government, including law, and its attention was squarely on the machinery of the governing system'. To the extent that the 'old institutionalist' approach employed a methodology at all, then it was primarily descriptive, highly normative, and never quantitative. The task was to describe and analyse constitutions and the institutions of government, including the political executive, typically with a view to defending and even recommending a particular type of institutional arrangement.

The label 'old' institutionalism suggests that this way of approaching the study of the political executive is no longer current. However, its contemporary equivalent can still be identified in countries with a strong public law tradition, such as France, Italy, and Portugal. Here, the study of the political executive continues to be approached from a highly normative, legalistic perspective. In these countries, erudite analysis is still often acknowledged to comprise the description and analysis of constitutional law and institutional features usually combined with a qualitative study of how political practice meshes with these formal arrangements. There is also an ongoing tradition of English-language scholarship that can be located at the interface of public law and the study of politics. This work can be found in journals such the *International Journal of Constitutional Law*. In the US, the presidency is also sometimes interpreted from the perspective of constitutional law (e.g. Corwin 1957; Fisher 2014). These scholars would most likely reject the idea that they should be labelled as 'old institutionalists', but there is a sense in which their approach and methods are in tune with the spirit of a previous generation of scholars to whom this label is typically applied.

In the 1930s and then notably in the period after the Second World War, the study of political life was marked by a shift from the 'old' institutionalist approach to behaviourism. This change marked the beginning of the attempt to study social life, including politics scientifically. In its early form, the behavioural approach required the study of only observable phenomena. In politics, this encouraged research on electoral politics, because votes could be directly observed, and attitudes could be measured by social surveys. Accordingly, behaviourism was also associated with the development of quantitative analysis as the most appropriate method for analysing the correlations between the data that had been collected. In addition, the behavioural revolution was characterized by the application of the experimental method to the social sciences, particularly in the field of psychology and social psychology.

As will be discussed below, the behavioural revolution posed certain problems for the study of the political executive, some of which remain unresolved. Nonetheless, it has left a distinct methodological legacy. For example, Chapter 31 by Pedro Magalhães in this volume demonstrates that studies relying on surveys and opinion polling remain current. In addition, as Margaret Hermann and Juliet Kaarbo note in Chapter 4, political psychology, whose origins are rooted in the experimental methods associated with psychology and social psychology, is also routinely applied to the study of the political executive. Indeed, while some aspects of the behavioural approach have since fallen by the wayside, notably the insistence on the study of only directly observable phenomena, the shift to the study of politics as a science was the precursor to much of the work in the positivist tradition that remains very strong to this day, including an emphasis on quantitative methods and data-driven enquiry (see below).

In response to some of the limitations of the behavioural approach, the 1980s saw the rise of the so-called 'new institutionalism' (March and Olsen 1984). Framed in deliberate counterpoint to the 'old' institutionalism, the aim of this approach was to re-emphasize the centrality of institutions to the study of political life, but also to downplay the normative aspect of institutional enquiry, as well as to stress the importance of the informal aspects of institutional effects. As Klaus Goetz demonstrates in this volume (Chapter 3), the new institutionalist approach continues to shape the study of the political executive. This is unsurprising to the extent that the political executive comprises the institutions of the presidency, the prime ministership, and accompanying executive offices, as well as the incumbents of those institutions and offices. The standard observation about the 'new institutionalism' is that it is not so much one approach, but an overarching label for a number of different approaches. For his part, Peters (1998: 17) states that there are 'at least six versions of the new institutionalism'. Typically, though, scholars tend to identify three types—historical, sociological, and rational choice (Hall and Taylor 1996).

There is a sense in which sociological institutionalism has had less of an impact on the study of the political executive than its main new institutionalist counterparts. Indeed, it is not included for consideration as a separate approach in this Handbook at all. That said, there is a strong tradition of political sociology in France that includes the study of political elites from this perspective, including the executive. In English, Ezra Suleiman (1974) and Mattei Dogan (1989, 2003) were closely associated with this type of executive elite-oriented political sociology. They tried to show how the operation of institutions is shaped by the patterns of elite recruitment to them. To do so, they tended to privilege descriptive statistics, often demonstrating how recruitment to particular high-level offices within the political executive passed disproportionately through certain elite civil service training schools, or universities. In general, though, this work remains underdeveloped in the relation to the current study of the political executive, though there is the potential for it to be applied in new ways (see below).

By contrast, historical and rational choice institutionalism have had a major effect on the study of the executive. As Laing and McCaffrie show (see Chapter 2 in this volume), there is a strong tradition of historical institutionalism in the study of the political executive. Unsurprisingly, this version of the new institutionalist approach privileges methods associated with historical inquiry, including archival work, documentary analysis, and interviewing to the extent that the protagonists in the executive in the period under investigation are still available to be interviewed. They also employ qualitative methods such as analytical narratives (see below) in their work.

For its part, the methodological emphasis associated with rational choice institutionalism has changed somewhat over time. In the 1980s and early 1990s there was an emphasis on comparative statics. This involves modelling and comparing equilibrium outcomes under different institutional conditions all other factors equal. This was sometimes a purely formal model with little or no empirical application, but where the mathematical proof of the model was privileged. Now, though, rational choice institutionalism is typically more empirically focused and relies on quantitative methods. As Indriði Indriðason shows in this volume (see Chapter 5), rational choice institutionalism is invariably a hypothesis-based approach. The resulting propositions are usually tested using regression-analytic methods. It is also worth noting that rational choice institutionalism is still often synonymous with the comparative method, particularly medium and large-n country cross-sectional or time-series cross-sectional (TSCS) regressions.

In recent years, new approaches to political inquiry have been developed. In particular, there has been a reaction against what has often been perceived as the dominance of positivism in the study of politics as exemplified by rational choice institutionalism. This rejection of positivism has led to the development of critical approaches, including the constructivist approach presented by Dennis Grube in this Handbook (see Chapter 8). This approach once again places normative issues at the heart of the analysis of the executive. In a similar vein, Jack Corbett and Rod Rhodes point to the development of ethnographic approaches (see Chapter 6 in this volume). Both of these approaches reject the methods typically associated with positivism, but more so than constructivism ethnographic approaches are firmly rooted in anthropological methods, including participant observation and the total immersion of the researcher in the daily life of the subject.

With the remnants of the 'old institutionalism' still current at the interface of public law and political studies, the legacy of behaviourism strong, the pertinence of the different varieties of the 'new institutionalism' firmly intact, and the development of new approaches ongoing, the study of the political executive is now characterized by more analytical approaches and by extension a greater degree of methodological pluralism than ever before. Indeed, this pluralism is exemplified in feminist approaches. As Karen Beckwith shows in Chapter 7 in this volume, feminist approaches are defined by their subject of inquiry. This leaves them open to adopting whichever form of methodological inquiry best suits the investigation at hand. For that reason, feminist approaches embrace the full range of research methods from in-depth qualitative inquiry to large-n time-series quantitative comparisons.

A word of warning, though, is in order. A long-standing feature of work on the political executive is that some scholars routinely fail to elaborate their methodological choices. The research method is simply taken for granted, being secondary to the study of the particular issue in question. Work on the political executive is not alone in this regard. Nonetheless, the absence of methodological considerations continues to characterize a proportion of the publications in this area. Such work is invariably descriptive; the empirical material is based on the scholar's personal interpretation of events rather than interviews or documentary analysis; the case selection is not properly justified; and so on. Such work is perhaps better thought of as 'current affairs', academic 'think-pieces' or long journalistic-style 'op-eds', rather than the systematic presentation of primary or sometimes even secondary material, never mind the application of rigorous scientific inquiry to the study of the political executive. This is not to discount the potential importance of 'mere description' (Gerring 2012). It can be a source of useful information, especially in the context where access to information about the executive is difficult. It can also help to generate ideas and hypotheses that can then be tested more systematically in other studies. All the same, it is worth keeping an open mind about the basic validity of the arguments made in such work, given the absence of methodological clarity.

A further and more general point should also be made. The study of the political executive may now be characterized by a greater methodological pluralism than ever before, but researchers have always faced and continue to face some important methodological problems when conducting work in this area. These problems limit the applicability of certain methodologies. A number of problems can be identified. They are similar to the ones presented by Helms (2012) in his review of the difficulties involved with the comparative study of political leadership. There is also some overlap with those noted by King (1993) in his discussion of methodology and the study of the US presidency.

There is a basic problem of information availability. For instance, many parliamentary systems are governed by the principles of cabinet confidentiality and collective responsibility. The principle of cabinet confidentiality means that discussions within the cabinet are simply not made public until sometimes decades after the event, or at least the formal communiqué that emerges from such meetings is uninformative. The principle of collective responsibility further increases the lack of information. This principle states that even if a cabinet member disagrees with the decision that the cabinet has made in private, they must either defend the position in public or resign. Needless to say, more often than not ministers prefer the former course of action to the latter and, hence, keep quiet. Taken together, these principles mean that researchers do not know for sure what discussions have taken place in cabinet and who supported or opposed whom in those discussions. This basic point can be generalized to the political executive more widely. In the US, there is a well-developed principle of executive privilege, whereby presidents have claimed the right to refuse subpoenas for information about the executive branch, most notably, though unsuccessfully in the case of *United States v. Nixon, 418 U.S. 683 (1974)*. Generally, bilateral meetings between presidents and prime ministers and other actors are usually held in private. The political advice received by these leaders is usually confidential, and so on. For sure, there can be the selective leaking of information. It is also true that cabinet operations and executive life generally have become a little more transparent in recent years. Moreover, researchers often rely on research material that aims to pull back the veil of secrecy at least a little (see below). Yet, much of the life of the political executive remains confidential. There are perfectly reasonable electoral and party-political interests, concerns relating to the national interest, and even international security considerations to justify such confidentiality. Whatever the reasons, though, this problem affects researchers no matter what methodologies they wish to employ in a way, for example, that does not affect students of voting behaviour in the same way.

A further problem for quantitative-minded researchers is the relatively small number of certain units of observation. For example, there have been only forty-five presidents of the United States. If individual US presidents are the units of observation, then the n is too small for any meaningful quantitative analysis, especially in the context where the 'modern' US presidency is typically considered to have begun with Franklin D. Roosevelt (Greenstein 1995). If the pre- and post-Franklin D. Roosevelt presidencies are incommensurable for that reason, then the n suddenly becomes very small indeed. What is more, often researchers are interested in comparing only a very small number of presidents and prime ministers in a given country or a very limited number of countries. Indeed, they may be concerned with researching only one political leader in one country. Even if the researcher is employing a rigorous qualitative methodology in such cases, this strategy raises the issue of whether the results of such studies are generalizable. Any findings may reflect either the idiosyncratic personalities of the small number of leaders under investigation and/or the specific context in which they are operating. For sure, if presidents and/or prime ministers are the desired units of observation, then a potential solution is to engage in a TSCS quantitative analysis. This strategy can increase the n to a few hundred. If the unit of observation is a cabinet, then it is possible to use data sets such as ParlGov (n.d.) to increase the n somewhat further still. If the unit of observation is a minister, then the n in TSCS studies can indeed be much greater. The chapters in this volume by Müller-Rommel et al. (Chapter 12), Schleiter Chapter 15, and Bäck and Carrol (Chapter 16) illustrate that good comparative and even country-specific work can be undertaken on both cabinets and ministers. If, however, the unit of observation is the president or prime minister in a particular country, then the small-n problem remains.

There is a further basic problem when the executive institution under consideration—a presidency, a prime ministership, the powers given to an actor in a constitution, and so forth—is being studied as the explanatory variable. This is the endogeneity problem. This problem concerns all forms of institutional analysis. Institutions are human creations. Their design reflects the preferences of the political actors who created them in the first instance. Institutional analysis, however, assumes that institutions have an independent effect on some or other outcome. Yet, if institutions reflect the preferences of those who created them, then any outcomes are arguably a reflection of those original human preferences, rather than the institution itself. The endogeneity issue is particularly problematic for rational choice institutionalists who engage in comparative statics. It is also a problem for those engaged in normative institutional inquiry, including debates about whether young democracies should choose a presidential, parliamentary, or semi-presidential form of government to facilitate the survival of democracy. Given the study of political executives is so associated with institutionalism in its different forms, researchers need to be fully aware of the endogeneity problem.

There is a further problem of observational equivalence. Again, this problem is not confined to the study of the political executive, but it can cause particular problems for researchers in this domain. Much of the work on the political executive concerns the behaviour of political actors, including presidents and prime ministers. The researcher may wish to explain why the person behaves in one way at one time and in a different way at another. Yet, sometimes one form of behaviour is equivalent to the other, rendering conclusions about the causes of variation in behaviour potentially problematic. Take, for example, presidential vetoes of legislation. Such vetoes are often consequential. For that reason, identifying the conditions under which presidents either veto legislation or sign it into law is an important research topic. Yet, imagine two scenarios. In the first, the legislature passes a piece of legislation, the president vetoes it, the legislature rewrites the bill in a way that the president wants and passes it again, and the president signs the rewritten bill into law. In the second, the president signals in private to the government what he or she wants from a bill prior to it being passed by the legislature. The government writes the bill in a way that takes account of the president's preferences. The bill passes and the president signs it into law. Here, there is a problem of observational equivalence. Let us assume that the final bill is the same in the two scenarios, yet a veto is observed in the first instance but not the second. Indeed, in the scenario presented here, the president has not even issued a public threat to veto the bill. This is clearly a problem for researchers using quantitative methods who need to code bills that are vetoed on the one hand and those that are not on the other. Yet, it can also be a problem for researchers using qualitative methods. If the president makes his or her preferences known to the government in private, scholars may be unaware that the bill has been written to meet those preferences and the researcher's interpretation of events may be incorrect as a result.

Finally, there is a more basic issue with general methodological consequences. It is important to appreciate that presidents and prime ministers are the most senior constitutional and/or political figures in their respective countries' political systems. Indeed, their actions form an indelible part of their own country's historical record. Inevitably, though, this means that they are a unique subject of inquiry. They are rarely if ever available to the researcher for direct questioning or surveying. This means that researchers who rely on interviews almost invariably receive only second-hand information about the most senior political figure in the system they are studying. Equally, wonderful though it would be if President Trump were to fill out a standard psych test, he is not going to do so. Consequently, as Hermann and Kaarbo note in Chapter 4 of this volume, political psychologists have to engage in research 'at a distance' when senior political leaders are their subject. In other words, while, for example, the votes won by political parties can be counted and the beliefs and values of individuals can be surveyed directly, presidents and prime ministers cannot be directly investigated. More than that, is it really possible even to comprehend what it means to be a president or prime minister? For example, clearly presidents and prime ministers cannot be investigated under laboratory conditions. More pertinently, though, when 'ordinary' people are asked under laboratory conditions to imagine how they would react if they were a president or prime minister, is it really feasible to think that they could possibly know what they would do? In other words, there is something extraordinary about the political executive. For that very reason, though, research into the political executive can be extraordinarily difficult. For sure, presidents and prime ministers are well aware that they are likely to be the subject of historical investigation at some point in the future. This is one reason why they sometimes establish presidential libraries and keep detailed diaries. Generally, though, researchers studying contemporary presidents and prime ministers have to be creative in their methodological efforts. More often than not, they also have to be satisfied with only limited pieces of information about their subjects of inquiry. For that reason, the basic validity of at least some conclusions can be called into question. With that in mind, the next section examines the research material that scholars typically rely upon to study the political executive and the main methods that are used.

10.2 STUDIES OF THE POLITICAL EXECUTIVE AND METHODOLOGY

The aims of this section are to identify the material that researchers typically gather to investigate the political executive and to review the main ways in which they employ this material. Given the extensive amount of work that has been conducted on the political executive, the aim is not to provide an account of all the studies that have ever been written on this topic, but to focus on a small number of studies to identify the methodologies that have typically been used and the implications for the conclusions that can be drawn. We begin with a brief discussion of the types of primary and secondary research material that students of the political executive tend to rely upon. We then outline the main methods that researchers in this area usually employ with this material, drawing on the standard distinction between qualitative and quantitative methods. We leave aside discussion of ethnographic methods, specifically participant observation and ethnographic interviewing, as these are discussed in Chapter 6 of this volume by Rhodes and Corbett. We also leave aside discussion of political psychology as Hermann and Kaarbo have a very helpful discussion of the main methods associated with this approach in Chapter 4.

10.2.1 Primary and Secondary Material

The term 'primary material' refers to research resources that have not been subjected to any after-the-fact interpretation. Primary sources typically take the form of events in the world (the formation of a new government, for example), material that was generated contemporaneously with a certain event (e.g. the policy programme of the new government), or original material that was deliberately generated by the researcher with a view to allowing subsequent interpretation (e.g. a dataset recording government formation and termination). By contrast, the term 'secondary material' refers to research resources that have already been subject to some form of interpretation (e.g. a book explaining the formation and termination of governments). This distinction seems clear, but, as we shall, the boundaries between the two concepts are sometimes porous. All researchers rely upon primary and secondary material for their work. However, the type of material required by them varies from one discipline to the next. Students of the political executive rely upon primary and secondary resources that would be familiar to most students of politics generally. Nonetheless, the study of the political executive has tended to privilege certain types of resources more than others. In part, this is because of some of the limitations inherent in the study of the political executive that were identified in the previous section.

The study of the political executive relies heavily on primary material. This is particularly the case when the aim of the inquiry is simply to gain information about how the political executive operates and how decisions are made within it. To do so, researchers rely on resources that can help to lift the veil of secrecy behind which the political executive operates, albeit sometimes some years after the fact. To this end, scholars often rely on material that was generated independently of the researcher's own efforts. Some of these resources were designed at least in the first instance to be private. They include archival material, such as the records of Cabinet meetings. They also include personal archives, diaries, and private correspondence. In addition, scholars also rely on primary resources that were always designed to be public. They include legal documents, including Court decisions relating to the political executive. They also include speeches by members of the political executive, as well as press conferences, television interviews, interventions in the legislature, Tweets, and so on. Scholars also use publicly available information in contemporary newspaper accounts of the political executive. Here, though, we reach the boundary of primary and secondary material very quickly. Strictly factual reporting is typically included as primary material. We need to be aware, though, that facts often have to be interpreted before they are reported. Can we be sure that *Fox News* or *The Washington Post* report events without any *de facto* interpretation? In other words, even if the media are contemporaneously reporting events relating to the political executive, their reporting has already gone through some process of journalistic or editorial interpretation, meaning that it might best to consider it as secondary material. Aware of this issue, researchers often choose to focus on the reports from a certain news outlet of reference, including news agencies such as Agence France-Presse, Associated Press, or Reuters. In so doing, they are effectively justifying it as a reliable primary source.

Students of the political executive rely on a different type of primary material too. This is original material that has been deliberately generated for the purposes of *ex post facto* interpretation. Most notably in this regard, students of the political executive rely heavily on elite interviews. Indeed, this is the main way in which researchers try to lift the veil of secrecy on the political executive, particularly in relation to the study of relatively recent events. There are well-known limitations to elite interviewing (Tansey 2007). Nonetheless, interviews allow scholars to obtain information that would not otherwise be available. In this category, we can also include datasets. Some datasets are derived from raw facts about the world. Here, the data have not been generated by the scholar him- or herself, but the dataset has been. For example, ParlGov's (n.d.) database records information about the party composition of European governments. Other datasets are derived from original scholarly research. Here, the data comprise primary material and both the data and the dataset are original resources that have been generated by the scholar. For example, O'Malley conducted an expert survey that generated a dataset about the relative power of prime ministers. The results of this survey were simply reported in a journal without any specific interpretation (O'Malley 2007). This was a clear indication that the survey had produced primary research material. In addition, and somewhat paradoxically, some datasets are derived from secondary material. Here, the data comprise material that has already been subject to interpretation, but the dataset is an original resource that has been generated by the scholar. For example, Mayhew's (2005) classic study of presidential/Congressional relations in the US is based on a dataset of so-called 'important laws'. Such laws were identified on the basis of 'the end-of-session reviews by contemporary journalists and historical analyses of policy specialists' (Smith 1992: 341), both of which are examples of secondary material. Whatever the type of material the dataset is based upon and its source, once an original dataset has been made publicly available, it constitutes a primary research resource for all scholars to draw upon.

The study of the political executive also relies heavily on secondary material. To reiterate, secondary material comprises resources that have already been subject to some form of interpretation, analysis, or evaluation. We have treated elite interviews as primary material. This is because they are original, first-hand accounts from protagonists within the political executive. Yet, we should probably treat autobiographies or conference talks by former members of the political executive as secondary material. This is because these formats comprise material that has been deliberately subject to prior interpretation, even if the interpretation has been undertaken by the protagonists themselves. Whether or not we place autobiography in the category of secondary material, biographies should certainly be placed in this category. Autobiographies, confessional talks, and biographies are staple research resources for students of the political executive, again with a view to trying to lift the veil of secrecy behind which the political executive operates. Similarly, even if we consider contemporary newspaper reporting to be primary material, we should definitely think of newspaper editorials and articles in weekly or monthly journalistic reviews, as well as online resources such as blog posts as secondary material. Again, these can be a useful source of information when trying to gain knowledge about how what is going on within the political executive, but they are material that has been subject to reflection and in that sense constitute secondary material. Far and away the most common secondary resource that researchers rely upon, though, are academic studies themselves. Such studies may have been based on some form of primary material in the first instance, but once that material has been interpreted by the researcher, it becomes secondary material when cited by another researcher. Much of the work on the political executive comprises researchers citing the work of other researchers.

Together, primary and secondary material constitute the raw data of researchers. That is to say, we can think of the words spoken by an interviewee or a corpus of legal texts as data just as we can think of numerical information as data, such as the duration in office in days of every government in Europe since 1945. Having gathered data on the political executive in these different forms, researchers have to decide how to use their material to construct an argument. To do so, they employ either qualitative or quantitative methods.

10.2.2 Qualitative Methods

To illustrate the methods that scholars choose to employ with the primary and secondary material at their disposal, we select a small number of studies. We begin with studies that apply qualitative methods. Such methods are typically used when the researcher is privileging inductive rather than deductive reasoning, that is, when the researcher is aiming to form a new argument rather than testing the implications of an existing argument. We have seen that the political executive tends to operate behind a veil of secrecy. The absence of information often nudges the researcher in the direction of inductive reasoning when studying the executive. This is because the aim is often simply to find out and what happened and make sense of it, rather than to see if there is evidence for what we already expected to find. Qualitative methods are also used when the number of observations is too small for statistical analysis. We have also seen that the study of the political executive is typically faced with a small-n problem. Finally, qualitative methods are also used when the researcher rejects the foundational principles of positivist-style scientific inquiry. For a mix of these reasons, the vast majority of the work on the political executive has been conducted using qualitative methods. Here, we focus on two types of qualitative methods that are typically used—we label them 'analytical narratives' and 'textual analysis'.

We can think of analytical narratives as studies that rely primarily on words to present an argument as opposed to inferences drawn from statistical analysis. The object of inquiry is very varied. It can be the study of a particular decision and how it was made within the political executive; the investigation of the actions of a particular officeholder; the analysis of the workings of a specific office, or department; or a study of the political executive as a whole and/or its relationship with other institutions or indeed the wider political system generally. The vast majority of work that uses qualitative methods to study the political executive employs analytical narratives. We highlight two studies.

The first example is one that relies solely on words to make the argument. Hennessy's (2000) book on the British prime minister is a fine example in this regard. Hennessy examines all UK prime ministers in chronological order from Clement Attlee in 1945 to Tony Blair in 1997. He provides an object lesson in how to weave together different types of primary and secondary material using words alone. The book runs to 675 pages, of which no fewer than 117 are notes. The notes include abundant references to archival documents in the Public Records Office, including now declassified notes of Cabinet meetings from decades back; quotations from hundreds of what would appear to be unstructured personal interviews, most of which are directly attributed, though some are unattributed and recorded as 'Private information'; plentiful citations of prime ministerial and ministerial diaries and other primary material; exhaustive use of after-the-fact testimonies by former members of the political executive; mentions of newspaper reports; and multitudinous references to existing studies of the prime minister and the political executive generally. On the basis of this material and using inductive reasoning, Hennessy concludes that the power of the prime minister has increased over time and hopes that ways can be found to keep future officeholders in check. We may or may not agree with Hennessy's conclusions, but he cannot be faulted for the way in which he has marshalled the primary and secondary material at his disposal to deliver a compelling analytical narrative about the political executive that relies solely on words.

The second example is one that relies primarily on words to make the argument, but that also includes consideration of numerical data. Here, Blondel et al.'s (2007) book stands out. They study the functioning of the cabinet system in ten former Communist Central and East European countries. Their book includes many references to existing studies of prime ministers, cabinets, and political executives generally. However, partly because the object of inquiry is more general than Hennessy's in-depth study, they do not include newspaper reports or official documents as their research material. Like Hennessy, though, they do rely heavily on elite interviews for their analysis. We focus on this element of their study. In terms of their interview material, they depart from Hennessy's method in three ways. First, they conducted structured and semi-structured interviews. This was because they wished to gather interview material systematically. Second, they are very transparent about how they gathered such material. For example, they provide an appendix (Blondel et al. 2007: 205–22) that tables the number of elite interviews that were conducted in each country (320 in total); that reproduces the structured questionnaire that was designed to gather standardized information about the conduct of cabinet and cabinet committee meetings in those countries; that reports the semi-structured questionnaire that was the basis of the 320 ministerial interviews; and that details the codebook that was used to capture the responses to the questionnaires as reliably as possible. Third, and most importantly for our purposes, their method generates a dataset that forms the foundation of some of the empirical analysis in the book. For instance, they report the percentage of ministerial interviewees who consider their country's prime minister to be either a strong or weak leader, or neither (Blondel et al. 2007: 185–8). On the basis of all this material and again using inductive reasoning, they conclude that Central and East Europe countries have operated their cabinet systems successfully since the early 1990s (Blondel et al. 2007: 193). Again, we may or may not agree with their conclusions, but their study shows that the use of numerical data per se is not inconsistent with the application of qualitative methods and that it can be used to strengthen an analytical narrative that is nonetheless still based mainly on words.

The other type of qualitative method that we signal here is textual analysis. This is a much more recent method and there are still relatively few examples of work that use this method. Like analytical narratives, textual analysis results in arguments that are usually based solely on words. The defining feature of textual analysis is that it relies almost exclusively on forms of political communication as the principal research material. These can be very wide ranging and can include official documents, all type of public statements, the words of interviewees, as well as other non-verbal forms of communication.

An example of textual analysis that focuses solely on public statements is Grube's (2013) study of rhetorical governance. He examines prime ministerial rhetoric in Australia, Canada, New Zealand, and the UK. He defines rhetoric simply as 'political talk' (Grube 2013: 3). Politicians use rhetoric to try to shape the political debate, including the policy agenda, with a view to persuading voters to support them. They do so by communicating publicly in many different ways, from giving formal speeches in very traditional settings to using Twitter. In his analysis of political rhetoric, Grube does not include material from elite interviews at all. Indeed, he does not systematically include reference to newspaper reports, official documents, or other standard types of research material. Instead, he relies almost entirely on the analysis of official communications made by members of the political executive. For example, he cites no fewer than twenty-five communications by Ken Henry, the former Secretary of the Department of the Treasury in Australia. Some of the citations are also very long. For instance, he cites an exchange between a television interviewer and Bill Shorten, the former Australian Minister for Workplace Relations that runs to over half a page (Grube 2013: 14). The citations are also very frequent. Almost every page has a first-hand quotation from a prime minister or public servant. Using this material, Grube argues that there is a rhythm to the type of rhetorical governance used by prime ministers during the course of their time in office and that this rhythm can be observed cross-nationally. Again, we may or may not agree with his conclusions, but the key point is that in contrast with standard analytical narratives Grube relies almost exclusively on specific forms of political speech to make his argument.

We can extend this point further by looking at examples of textual analysis that move beyond the study of text as talk. Here, Zarefsky's (2004) work of presidential rhetoric is instructive. He argues that presidential rhetoric is 'often understood too narrowly' (Zarefsky 2004: 608). The targets of his criticism are scholars who use speeches for the purposes of quantitative methods, rather than colleagues such as Grube. Nonetheless, Zarefsky still presents the study of rhetoric differently from Grube. He argues that presidents make choices about how to deliver the words they use. Those choices include 'matters as argument selection, framing, phrasing, evidence, organization, and style, as well as about staging, choreography, and other aspects of the presidential performance' (Zarefsky 2004: 609). For Zarefsky, therefore, primary research material includes consideration of the location where the speech was given, the background that was chosen for the speech, the clothes the president was wearing when delivering the speech, and so on. In this regard, Mast's (2013) work is also useful. In his study of President Clinton, he includes photographs of both the former president delivering his infamous 'I did not have sexual relations with that woman' comments and Independent Counsel, Ken Starr, taking out the trash when talking to reporters. For Mast, presidents are actors. Their words are merely part of a broader way of communicating with the public. For that reason, Mast's primary material includes not just the analysis of the president's words, like Grube, or the *mise-en-scène* of those words, like Zarefsky, but also the manner in which the president delivered the speech, the gestures that were used, the tone of voice, the body language, and so on. As with Grube, both Zarefsky and Mast are providing an analysis of the political executive that relies solely or at least almost exclusively on the use of words to make their argument and we may disagree with their arguments, but again by privileging different types of research material they employ a qualitative method that reads differently from a standard analytical narrative.

10.2.3 Quantitative Methods

We have seen that authors associated with qualitative methods sometimes use numerical data. Reporting such data can help to strengthen the analytical narrative, but it does not in itself constitute the application of quantitative methods. Here, we consider quantitative methods to be the use of numerical data in a statistical test or model with a view to generating an inference about the probability of a certain outcome occurring. Accordingly, the use of numerical data is not the defining feature of the method. Instead, quantitative methods are defined by how the data are used and the epistemological status of the conclusions that can be drawn from the data analysis. Quantitative methods can range from inferences derived from simple bivariate correlation coefficients to complex multivariate models. Relative to studies that use qualitative methods, there are relatively few studies of the political executive that employ quantitative methods. To illustrate the difference between the use of qualitative and quantitative methods, we single out one study.

We consider Tavits's (2009) study of presidential activism. In this book, she tries to identify the reasons why presidents in some European countries are more active, or powerful, than others. We focus on the chapter where she uses statistical analysis to draw conclusions about why this is the case (Tavits 2009: chapter 2). To this end, she constructs an original dataset. To capture the level of presidential activism, she focuses on presidents' power to control the composition of their country's cabinet. To capture this feature, she calculates the percentage of non-partisan members in each cabinet.

She assumes that the more powerful the president, the greater the number of non-partisan ministers. She then wishes to estimate the statistical relationship between various factors and the percentage of non-partisan cabinet members. These factors include whether or not the president is directly elected in a country, how many constitutional powers the president enjoys, how many parties are represented in the cabinet, and so on. Again, she needs numerical data that capture each of these variables. So, for example, whether or not the president is directly elected is simply coded as 1 for yes and 0 for no. Using an extended-beta binomial model, she finds a positive correlation between the number of non-partisan cabinet members and presidential power, the absence of the president's party in the cabinet, and the presence of minority government (Tavits 2009: 50). These results are statistically significant at the 1 per cent level, suggesting a strong relationship. The substantive effects are also relatively large. For example, when the president's party is not represented in the cabinet, the odds of having a non-partisan minister in the cabinet are twice as great relative to when the president's party is represented. Overall, the main conclusion she wishes to draw is that directly elected presidents are not necessarily more powerful than indirectly presidents. Instead, other features of the political opportunity structure are more important in this regard.

For the purposes of this chapter, the key point about Tavits's study is not her main conclusion, but the way in which she reaches that conclusion and its epistemological status relative to studies using qualitative methods (Elgie 2015). Tavits's method requires her to assign numerical values to various features of the world. She can capture some of those features only indirectly and perhaps imperfectly, for example the idea that presidential power over cabinet formation can be represented by the percentage of non-partisan ministers in the government. She then employs a statistical model to draw an inference about why some presidents are more powerful than others. In this way, she is using numerical data in a different way from how they are used in a purely qualitative study. Tavits's method is also consequential for the epistemological status of at least some of her conclusions. Here, it is worth considering some of the similarities and differences between the status of her conclusions and those derived from qualitative methods. For example, her conclusions are probabilistic, not deterministic. In this regard, there is essentially no epistemological difference between her study and those based on qualitative methods. When Hennessy makes the argument that British prime ministers have become more powerful over time, he is certainly making the argument with conviction, but he is only making an argument. Like Tavits, he is not elevating the argument to some law of nature. Tavits's conclusions are also based on average effects. Here, again, there is essentially no epistemological difference between her study and those based on qualitative methods. When Blondel, Müller-Rommel, and Malovà argue that Central and East Europe countries have operated their cabinet systems successfully since the early 1990s, they are also drawing a general conclusion. Like Tavits, they are not suggesting that their conclusion applies to every cabinet in every country in the whole period under investigation. There is, though, at least one fundamental difference between the status of the conclusions drawn from Tavits's method and those based on qualitative methods. She can report the results of a test of statistical significance. For us, that is the defining feature of a quantitative study. For example, given how Tavits has chosen to undertake her study and professional conventions about what level of statistical significance we should choose to employ, she can reject the proposition that there is no relationship between the presence of the president's party in the cabinet and the percentage of non-partisan ministers there and, crucially, she can do so knowing that her conclusion is valid. By contrast, when Grube argues that there is a rhythm to the type of rhetorical governance used by prime ministers he is no doubt very confident about the validity of his argument, but he cannot make the same epistemological claim about it as Tavits. This is one of the main reasons why some scholars privilege quantitative methods. Grube can reply by rejecting the validity of arguments derived from the use of quantitative methods. This would require him to adopt a different epistemological foundation to Tavits. This would be a perfectly reasonable philosophical position to adopt. Grube can also accept the validity of Tavits's arguments in principle, but reject her application of them in practice, for example by suggesting that the percentage of non-partisan ministers does not reliably capture presidential power. Again, this would be a perfectly reasonable argument to make and one that could be made by quantitative scholars too.

The key point is that the choice of qualitative vs. quantitative methods is both a choice of research materials and how they are applied and also a choice about the type of conclusions that can be drawn about the operation of the political executive and the epistemological status of the validity of those conclusions.

10.3 Research Design, Research Methods, and the Future Study of the Political Executive

The main aim of this section is to highlight various ways in which methodological considerations might help us to improve our understanding of the political executive. We begin with a general discussion of how to think more carefully about research design. We then identify a number of specific research methods that students of the political executive might fruitfully employ. Again, we leave aside discussion of developments in relation to ethnography and political psychology as these approaches are discussed at length in other chapters. Except where indicated, the issues apply to studies using both qualitative and quantitative methods.

To improve the validity of the conclusions drawn about the political executive, we would encourage scholars to think about their research design. Specifically, we encourage scholars to think systematically in terms of samples and populations. Typically, scholars cannot study the whole population of a given object of inquiry (e.g. every prime minister in every country). Instead, they have to study of sample of the population and infer their findings from that sample to the population as a whole. For a finding to be generalizable to a population, the sample must be representative of that population.

For scholars engaged in cross-national comparative studies of the political executive, this raises the issue of case selection. Here, there is a certain tradition of inquiry that is based on the study of just one country, usually the US or the UK, or on the comparison of a very small number of countries, for example the UK, France, and the US. Even when a larger number of countries is compared, there is a further tendency for those countries to be the 'usual suspects', for example big countries, or West European countries with perhaps a few others sprinkled in. These case selection strategies raise the concern that the sample of countries under consideration is unrepresentative of the population of countries of interest as a whole and indeed that the sample may be systematically skewed, leading to doubts about the validity of the conclusions drawn from them. To address this issue, we would encourage comparativists to think in the first instance about the population of countries to which they want their conclusions to apply and then to investigate a representative sample of that population.

We can extend this point further. We saw that Grube's (2013) study of prime ministerial rhetoric was based on the analysis of a large number of public statements. Leaving aside any issue relating to the representativeness of the four countries that Grube (2013) chose to study and the generalizability of his findings to some broader population of countries, we can question the representativeness of the sample of public statements that he chose to focus on. For example, he draws on seven statements made by Helen Clark, the former prime minister of New Zealand. We are left to assume that this is a representative sample of the population of statements that she made across her premiership, or at least the relevant ones for his purposes, but this may not be the case. If the sample of speeches is systematically skewed, the validity of the claims that Grube wishes to make about the ebbs and flows of prime ministerial rhetoric can be questioned. In response, Grube could reject the underlying reasoning behind the talk of populations and samples on fundamental epistemological grounds. This would be a reasonable philosophical position to adopt. However, if he does not, and there is nothing in that particular book to suggest that he is rejecting it, then we have grounds to be sceptical of the validity of his claims. To address this issue, we would again encourage scholars to think about the population of material that is under investigation and then to select a representative sample of that material.

This point can be extended yet further still. We have seen that students of the political executive rely heavily on elite interviews. A well-known problem with this material is that researchers cannot usually interview all the people they would like. They can interview only those people who are available and willing to be interviewed. This raises the concern that the sample of interviewees is not representative of the population of potential interviewees as a whole. If the sample is systematically skewed towards a certain cohort of interviewees, then the conclusions drawn from the interview material may be invalid. Leaving this concern aside, there is a further issue to consider in these terms. Typically, scholars tend to cherry pick quotes from interviews as evidence to back up their argument. We have to ask, though, whether the sample of quotations provided is representative of the population of interview material that was gathered. Again, this is a well-known problem, yet this practice continues to be prevalent among students of the political executive. To address this issue, we would encourage scholars to use software such as NVivo. This package allows words to be treated as numerical data and for systematic conclusions to be drawn from the material as a whole. More generally, we would encourage all scholars to be transparent about both their population of interest and to justify the representativeness of the sample that they have chosen to study. These practices will help to increase confidence in the validity of the findings that are presented.

In addition to these points about research design, we wish to signal a number of research methods that scholars of the political executive might consider adopting. In terms of qualitative methods, we would encourage the application of prosopography. This is a method that is rooted in the discipline of history (Smythe 2008). In the context of political science, it is related to the long tradition of the study of the sociology of political elites that we signalled earlier in the chapter. Prosopography uses biographical information to reveal connections between members of a certain group. Behr and Michon (2013) have shown the potential for this method to be applied to the study of the political executive. They examined the biographies of French cabinet ministers. On the basis of their biographical data, they argue that although 'the proportion of women and members of the so-called "visible" minorities has increased in cabinets, closer examination of the backgrounds of individuals heralded as symbols of change' reveal strong similarities with the backgrounds of traditional ministers. In other words, what is often presented as change towards a greater diversity of political representation masks continuities in recruitment. We encourage this method because it has the potential to increase the rigour with which researchers apply the study of political biography.

Another method that might usefully be employed is process tracing. There is a tendency to think of process tracing as merely 'thick description', or an in-depth analytical narrative. However, Beach and Pedersen (2013) have shown that process tracing is a discrete method with its own methodological requirements. It is typically suited to small-n studies, indeed n=1 studies, and it requires the same sort of primary and secondary research material that analytical narratives are usually built upon. It is useful, though, because it is explicitly causal. Its aim is not just to provide an account of what happened with the political executive, but to establish a rigorous method for identifying the causes of why something happened. In this way, it allows researchers to move beyond simply making an argument by providing them with the tools to arrive at a systematic explanation of why a particular phenomenon occurred.

A further method that has great potential to be applied to the study of the political executive is Qualitative Comparative Analysis (QCA). This method is becoming very popular in the study of politics (Schneider and Wagemann 2012). However, its application to the political executive remains limited, though Pérez-Liñán's (2007) study of presidential impeachment in Latin America is a notable exception. QCA is used to identify whether there are any necessary and/or sufficient conditions consistent with the presence or absence of an outcome. Thus, like process tracing its aim is explicitly causal rather than merely descriptive. QCA is very useful for studies where the n is too large for the application of standard analytical narratives or process tracing, but too small for quantitative methods. In contrast to statistical analysis, QCA also provides the opportunity for the researcher to drill down into individual cases, examining the context in which outcomes occur as well as the circumstances that can sometimes confound the presence of such outcomes. In other words, it is not inherently susceptible to the ecological fallacy. While QCA has many critics within the political science community, it is worth exploring because like prosopography and process tracing it provides the potential to arrive at more rigorous conclusions about the politics of the political executive.

In terms of quantitative methods, we encourage scholars to embrace the identification revolution. Previously, quantitative studies have generated essentially associational results, that is, the probability that one variable is associated with another variable all else equal. This is how we should interpret the findings of Tavits's study. However, there has recently been a move towards the application of causal statistical analysis, such as Difference in Differences (DiD), and a Regression Discontinuity Design (RDD). These statistical methods mimic an experimental research design, allowing more robust conclusions to be drawn about the direction of the relationship between two variables. It can be challenging to apply DiD, RDD, and equivalent techniques to the study of executive politics, but the rewards from being able to do so in a creative, but reliable way could be great.

We would also encourage scholars to engage in laboratory experiments themselves. Students of political psychology have a long record of employing experimental methods to the study of decision-making in the executive, as Hermann and Kaarbo note in Chapter 4 in this volume. Outside this domain, it can be difficult to construct an experimental research design that relates to the study of executive politics and that has both external and internal validity. However, in principle institutions are well-suited to experimental methods. At the core of institutional analysis is the idea that institutions affect behaviour, that is, they have a psychological effect. If so, then hypothesized institutional effects should be testable under laboratory conditions. Elgie and Doyle have shown that it is possible to apply experimental methods to the study of executive institutions in this way (Elgie 2018—see chapter 3, which is co-written with Doyle).

We also encourage students of the political executive to follow up on innovations in the analysis of big data. For example, we have seen that there is a tradition of textual analysis using qualitative methods. However, there is now also a growing trend towards using words as numerical data and engaging in statistical analysis. For example, Arnold et al (2017) analysed 305 annual 'state of the union' addresses by seventy-three presidents in thirteen Latin American countries to identify the conditions under which presidents are willing to compromise with the legislature. With the growth of social media, the opportunity to generate text as data has grown. For instance, studies are increasingly using the text in Tweets as data. Technological advances have also allowed text to be scraped from websites, again allowing the words there to be studied using statistical methods. There may be limitations to the type of conclusions that can be drawn from this type of analysis—typically they generate a lot of associations and little substantive effects. Again, though, there is great potential for these new methods to be employed to the study of the political executive.

Finally, we wish to encourage the use of mixed-method research (MMR). We have to recognize that some questions relating to the political executive are better suited to qualitative methods, while others best fit quantitative methods. Nonetheless, there are certainly areas where questions can be tackled using a mix of methods. Here, we need to move beyond one standard MMR tactic whereby the findings of a statistical model are illustrated by way of simple qualitative vignettes. In this regard, Seawright's (2016) book is very helpful. He identifies a number of MMR design strategies that allow causal statistical analysis to be complemented by causal qualitative analysis. One lesson from Seawright's book is that an MMR design needs to be constructed at the outset of a research project. This is a useful tip generally.

The take-home message of this chapter is that researchers need to think about their research design and method both deliberately and carefully. They should be explicit about their research design and method and they should be transparent about the material they have used in their research. If scholars were to follow this advice, it is perfectly possible that the conclusions reached may not be very different from the ones they would have arrived at anyway. Even if that were the case, though, we would still have greater confidence in the validity of those conclusions. In a supposed 'post-truth age', that would be an advance in itself.

References

Alston, L. (1905). *Modern Constitutions in Outline: An Introductory Study in Political Science.* London: Longmans, Green and Co.

Arnold, C., Doyle, D., and Wiesehomeier, N. (2017). 'Presidents, Policy Compromise, and Legislative Success', *Journal of Politics* 79(2): 380–95.

Bagehot, W. (1964). *The English Constitution.* London: C. A. Watts and Co. Ltd.

Beach, D. and Pedersen, R. B. (2013). *Process-Tracing Methods: Foundations and Guidelines.* Ann Arbor: The University of Michigan Press.

Behr, V. and Michon, S. (2013). 'The Representativeness of French Cabinet Members in the Fifth Republic: A Smokescreen?', *French Politics* 11(4): 332–55.

Blondel, J., Müller-Rommel, F., and Malovà, D. (2007). *Governing New European Democracies.* London: Palgrave Macmillan.

Bryce, J. (1921). *Modern Democracies*, Vol. 1. New York: The Macmillan Company.

Corwin, E. S. (1957). *The President: Office and Power.* New York: New York University Press.

Dogan, M. (1989) (ed.). *Pathways to Power: Selecting Rulers in Pluralist Democracies.* Boulder, CO: Westview Press.

Dogan, M. (2003) (ed.). *Elite Configurations at the Apex of Power.* Leiden: Brill.

Elgie, R. (2015). *Studying Political Leadership: Foundations and Contending Accounts.* London: Palgrave Macmillan.

Elgie, R. (2018). *Political Leadership: A Pragmatic Institutionalist Approach.* London: Palgrave Macmillan.

Fisher, L. (2014). 'Connecting Presidential Power to Public Law', *Presidential Studies Quarterly* 44(1): 157–72.

Gerring, J. (2012). 'Mere Description', *British Journal of Political Science* 42(4): 721–46.

Greenstein, F. I. (1995) (ed.). *Leadership in the Modern Presidency*. Cambridge, MA: Harvard University Press.

Grube, D. (2013). *Prime Ministers and Rhetorical Governance*. London: Palgrave Macmillan.

Hall, P. A. and Taylor, R. C. R. (1996). 'Political Science and the Three New Institutionalisms', *Political Studies* 44(5): 936–57.

Helms, L. (2012). 'Introduction: The Importance of Studying Political Leadership Comparatively', in L. Helms (ed.) *Comparative Political Leadership*. London: Palgrave Macmillan, 1–24.

Hennessy, P. (2000). *The Prime Minister: The Office and its Officeholders since 1945*. London: Penguin Books.

King, G. (1993). 'The Methodology of Presidential Research', in G. King, G. C. Edwards III, B. A. Rockman, and J. H. Kessel (eds) *Researching the Presidency: Vital Questions, New Approaches*. Pittsburgh: University of Pittsburgh, 387–412.

March, J. G. and Olsen, J. P. (1984). 'The New Institutionalism: Organizational Factors in Political Life', *American Political Science Review* 78(3): 734–49.

Martin, C. E. (1925). 'Growth of Presidential Government in Europe', *American Political Science Review* 17(4): 567–83.

Mast, J. L. (2013). *The Performative Presidency*. Cambridge: Cambridge University Press.

Mayhew, D. R. (2005). *Divided We Govern: Party Control, Lawmaking, and Investigations, 1946-2002*. 2nd ed. New Haven CT: Yale University Press.

O'Malley, E. (2007). 'The Power of Prime Ministers: Results of an Expert Survey', *International Political Science Review* 28(1): 7–27.

ParlGov (n.d.) Database, http://www.parlgov.org

Pérez-Liñán, A. (2007). *Presidential Impeachment and the New Political Instability in Latin America*. Cambridge: Cambridge University Press.

Peters, B. G. (1998). *Institutional Theory in Political Science: The 'New Institutionalism'*. London: Pinter.

Rossiter, C. (1961) (ed.). *The Federalist Papers*. New York: New American Library.

Schneider, C. Q. and Wagemann, C. (2012). *Set-Theoretic Methods for the Social Sciences: A Guide to Qualitative Comparative Analysis*. Cambridge: Cambridge University Press.

Seawright, J. (2016). *Multi-Method Social Science: Combining Qualitative and Quantitative Tools*. Cambridge: Cambridge University Press.

Smith, S. S. (1992). 'Book Review: Divided We Govern: Party Control, Lawmaking, and Investigations, 1946–1990, by David R. Mayhew', *Constitutional Commentary* 9: 339–45.

Smythe, D. (2008). 'Prosopography', in R. Cormack, J. Haldon, and E. Jeffreys (eds) *The Oxford Handbook of Byzantine Studies*. Oxford: Oxford University Press, 176–81.

Suleiman, E. N. (1974). *Politics, Power, and Bureaucracy in France: The Administrative Elite*. Princeton, NJ: Princeton University Press.

Tansey, O. (2007). 'Process Tracing and Elite Interviewing: A Case for Non-probability Sampling', *PS: Political Science and Politics* 40(4): 765–72.

Tavits, M. (2009). *Presidents with Prime Ministers: Do Direct Elections Matter?* Oxford: Oxford University Press.

Wilson, W. (1885). *Congressional Government*. New York: Houghton Mifflin.

Zarefsky, D. (2004). 'Presidential Rhetoric and the Power of Definition', *Presidential Studies Quarterly* 34(3): 607–19.

PART II

COMPOSITION AND LIFE CYCLE OF POLITICAL EXECUTIVES

CHAPTER 11

....

PRESIDENTIAL PATHWAYS AND PROFILES

....

MAGNA INÁCIO AND MARIANA LLANOS

11.1 INTRODUCTION

....

THE United States was the first country to have a chief executive selected through an electoral process distinct from the election of legislators. In the two centuries since the establishment of the US constitution, many more countries adopted systems with separated elections for the two branches of government. In the second half of the nineteenth century and in the early twentieth century, nearly all countries in Latin America established direct presidential elections. Recently, the number of countries with such elections has grown globally. Although not all systems that hold presidential elections are pure presidential systems, such as those in the Americas are, together the semi-presidential and presidential types account for the majority of constitutional types today (Sedelius and Linde 2018). The direct election of the president has become *de rigueur* (Elgie 2012) and, particularly in the case of non-ceremonial presidencies, the presidential election is, undoubtedly, a pivotal political event.

Our substantive concern in this chapter is to build bridges among different theoretical perspectives in order to answer the following questions: What are the procedures and practices to select these representatives in democratic regimes? What are the attributes of those who are elected? What are the factors explaining which candidate types have greater chances to win? In other words, we analyse what the pathways are that candidates follow and what the profile of those who manage to get elected is.

The scholarship production on elected presidents has continuously moved forward with new insights and contributions. From country-case analyses to comparative approaches, studies have shed light on how certain attributes of political executives link to electoral incentives as well as to other constraints present at the selection moment. A vast literature has improved our understanding about the institutional, partisan, and contextual factors that shape the structure of opportunity for those with presidential ambition, including those without a partisan background and political experience. Their findings, which call for further research, have also pointed out several analytical gaps, particularly in linking the micro-motivations with the organizational and institutional aspects that underpin the paths of presidential candidates, winning or not, in different political systems.

Three main sections make up this review chapter. The first researches the state of the literature on the selection of presidential candidates. These studies define the pathways that exist for potential candidates, how open such pathways are, and their potential effects on the candidate profiles. The second section identifies the presidential profiles as they have been researched to date, paying attention to partisan background, political experience, and social attributes. Section three summarizes the contributions, highlights the gaps, and suggests avenues for further research on both presidential pathways and profiles. A short conclusion follows.

11.2 PRESIDENTIAL PATHWAYS: CANDIDATES' SELECTION AND NOMINATION

Running for the presidency means more than surmounting hurdles. However, how candidate selection and nomination processes add hurdles to the presidential contest remains an understudied topic beyond the US. The study of candidate selection matters because it is a fruitful way to uncover the links among intra-party, inter-party, and executive politics, even when outsiderness and patronal networks forge alternative routes to the presidency. The growing scholarly debate on candidate selection contributes to building a broader theoretical framework on presidential pathways, one that embraces a varying combination of stages, constraints, and incentives.

Candidate selection is conventionally seen as an intra-party issue. It is regarded as a game that is primarily controlled by party leaders, with specific dynamics that vary across parties and according to the positions in dispute. However, the selection of candidates for the presidential office, an electorally challenging and politically strategic contest, differs from the selection for partisan and legislative positions. One reason is that the candidates' electability is a critical concern driving their selection by parties (Samuels and Shugart 2010), especially in context of high interparty competition.

Drawing on Juan Linz (1994),[1] Samuels and Shugart (2010) argue that the separation of powers forces parties to make different leadership-selection choices. Parties in pure

---

[1] Juan Linz (1994) was critical of the several implications that a political system in which the people directly elect the president may have for the electoral process. Among them, he pointed out that the presidential system enhanced the risk of a recruitment of 'amateur outsiders,' while parties in parliamentary systems instead tended to select party leaders or 'insiders' when they recruited for the position of a prime minister responsive to the legislature.

presidential systems face a tension over candidate selection because their candidates must have appeal to voters in order to win an electoral contest separate from legislative elections. Therefore, parties may select candidates for characteristics unrelated to their faithfulness to the party, which are appropriate for the broad electoral contest but may later bring about serious political complications, such as a tense relationship with the legislative branch of government. These authors build upon research on political ambition and analyse the career paths of the universe of national executives—every president and every prime minister—around the world between 1945 and 2007, a sample of 852 executives. They define *insiderness* as the nature and extent of a prospective executive's links to a central party organization (Samuels and Shugart 2010: 67) and measure it as a combination of partisan and political experience: the less a potential executive has built up these sorts of ties, the more the party is *presidentialized*. Their research proves that as one moves away from pure parliamentarism, the profile of executive candidates begins to lose the characteristics of the party insider. In semi-presidential regimes, the degree of presidentialization varies, according to whom the cabinet is responsible to and the extent of political cohabitation. The subtype of semi-presidentialism known as premier-presidentialism is the one that shows a behaviour similar to that of parliamentary regimes—that is, its candidate selection tends towards the ideal-type insider. In contrast, in presidentialist and presidential-parliamentary regimes—those semi-presidential regimes where the government can be dismissed by both president and parliament—partisan ties are weaker and political outsiders are more likely to be successful.

As Elgie (2011: 396) has pointed out, a real strength of Samuels and Shugart's book is that it provided for the comparison across presidential, semi-presidential, and parliamentary regimes. Both the terminology as well as the theoretical underpinnings—that the party organization mimics the constitutional structure—are very influential in the literature and have been further developed by other authors. However, in addition to the constraints that the broad constitutional framework poses, the parties' and candidates' moves depend on other rules as well, particularly on whether the selection process occurs in one or several stages, and on the selection method used.

11.2.1 Presidential Selectorates

A promising perspective is provided in the literature focusing on the selectorate of presidential candidates. It posits that candidates' odds to be nominated are directly affected by how inclusive the selectorate is, ranging from the leader, throughout the party elite, party delegates, party members, to all voters (Hazan and Rahat 2010). These clusters of voters might evaluate or rank differently candidates' attributes, affecting their chances to move forward to the next stage.

Leaders and elite party actors are the most traditional selectorate, and party endorsement has long been the more successful route for achieving a presidential nomination in most democracies. This type of selectorate chooses the candidate through formal or informal methods, such as party conventions, party endorsements, or even public endorsements from elected officials, former officeholders, fundraisers, and interest group leaders. As Jones (2017) argues, these methods are still predominant in the selection of the majority of presidential candidates across the world. Between 1978 and 2001, 60 per cent of the relevant Latin American parties still selected their presidential candidates through party conventions controlled by their leaders (Freidenberg 2015). Colombia, Chile, Brazil, Bolivia, Guatemala, Nicaragua, and the Dominican Republic have continued to hold party conventions, which are partially regulated by their internal party rules, even after the diffusion of party primaries in this region.

To what extend party leaders remain as gatekeepers in the presidential nomination vary considerably in terms of how legally binding the selection procedures are and how much intraparty dynamics can constrain closed-door discretionary decisions by party leaders. Besides the US case, empirical evidence shows a predominance of non-regulated and non-standardized party mechanisms, which empower party leaders even where party primaries are hold (Hazan and Rahat 2010; Sandri et al. 2015). This phenomenon has been associated not only to the leaders' capacity to bypass rebels' and mavericks' ambitions, but also as a source of patronal control in the selection of presidential candidates, particularly in contexts of weakly institutionalized party systems or dominant party systems. Studies on the Caucasus and Central Asian semi-presidential systems have shown how patronal presidents and their personalistic networks prevent that challengers and the opposition get access to the presidential ballot by controlling political careers and party nominations (Hale 2014; Baturo 2016). The use of violence at the nomination stage has been strategic for some party leaders and incumbents in some African countries, even in the more democratic ones, which shows that this strategy can be related to party-specific attributes and not only to national politics (Seeberg et al. 2018).

However, the control of candidate recruitment by party elites has been increasingly challenged by different factors. Intra- and inter-party pressures have effectively impelled traditional parties to change their selection procedures for presidential candidates, as is shown by the recent worldwide diffusion of either closed- or open-party primaries in democratic regimes.[2] In addition, the electoral prospects of anti-establishment and anti-politics forces competing at elections has expanded opportunities for the self-recruitment of presidential candidates, either as non-partisan or partisan newcomers.

---

[2] The Americas are the region with the highest number of countries where parties use primaries to select presidential candidates. Open, compulsory, and simultaneous primaries, as well as those organized by national authorities, were introduced in Argentina, Uruguay, and Honduras. Multi-stage, closed, or open primaries are organized at the party level in Panamá, Paraguay, Ecuador, Peru, Costa Rica, and Venezuela. In turn, non-compulsory but legally regulated and state-led primaries can take place in Colombia and Chile (Alcántara 2001; Freidenberg 2015). Only Brazil, Guatemala, Dominican Republic, Bolivia, and Nicaragua have no legal provisions for presidential nomination primaries. In 250 primaries held from 1978 to 2014 in eighteen Latin American democracies, 39 per cent of nominees won the presidential election (Freidenberg 2015).

What types of presidential candidates benefit from the widen scope of the party selectorate? Does this widening mean the lowering of entry barriers for self-recruitment? These questions have been partially answered by the vast, existing literature on US primaries by asking, for example, which candidates will be chosen by these enlarged selectorates (and boosted by which resources), and how those candidates affect the electoral dynamics. In this context, a controversial issue is whether primary dominance triggers a candidate-centred or a party-centred logic of presidential nomination.[3]

11.2.2 Candidate-Centred Nominations

Following Key (1967) and Polsby (1985), a strand of the US literature stresses that the presidential primaries, in the way in which they are institutionalized in that country, have favoured factional candidates or unconnected outsiders (Busch 1997), while raising barriers for party insiders. The increasing participation of hardcore partisans and more ideologically polarized party activists forging manifold pathways to the ballot revealed the negative side of the primary system, that is, the higher likelihood that unappealing or extremist candidates be selected. The causal mechanism leading to these effects consists of an increasing ideological misalignment between the primary electorate and the party/voter medians, which deepens the representational gap in the partisan nomination of presidential candidates (Ranney 1972; Polsby 1983).[4] Further, the divisive effects of the primaries and, therefore, lower levels of turnout may, in turn, reduce a party' electoral and legislative cohesiveness and, thus, raise the risks of the elected president be backed by a disjointed party.

In this context, the party capacity to nominate a high-quality candidate, that is, one characterized by temperamental steadiness, political skills, and electability in general elections tend to decline. Two practices, invisible primaries and front-loading, have been directly associated with this result since they forge a plebiscitary dynamic at this early stage of presidential candidate selection. These practices lead to a premature cleaning of the candidacy field and reduce the chances for candidates fitted for 'presidential greatness' or, at least, seen as capable of getting things done (Aldrich 1980; Norrander 2006). In addition, when the strategic opportunities for outsider and factional candidates widen, interest groups and individuals feel at the same time invited to groom them.

Being a front-runner at the beginning of the presidential race matters. Scholars have shown the increase relevance of the 'invisible primary' for candidates to gain media and money-driven momentum and to show themselves as front-runners (Aldrich 1980, 2009; Bartels 1988). Most candidates' efforts to recruit campaign teams, gather resources,

---

[3] In the United States, the mixed nomination system, inaugurated by Democratic Party's reforms in the 1960s, encompasses different types of primaries (closed, semi-open, and open) and party caucuses, which are sequentially scheduled.

[4] The nomination of unappealing or extremist candidates in party primaries have been also observed in the recent diffusion of presidential primaries in Latin America (Colomer 2002), even when the participation of rank-and-file party members was massive.

obtain party endorsements, and attract media coverage occur at the pre-nomination season (six-twelve months leading up to the early primaries). As Norrander (2006) showed, experienced politicians have shorter candidacies and less successful runs if they do not meet the condition of front-runners, while non-traditional candidates who are risk-takers, remain in the race for longer. While the anticipation of these invisible moves, uncontrolled by voters, extends the length of the presidential campaign, a second practice shortens the period during which voters can scrutinize the candidates. It is known as 'front-loading', a practice propelled by state authorities that consists of scheduling their primaries earlier and earlier to gain national attention and influence the presidential nomination. This practice reduces the nomination season from a three-month 'marathon' to a month-long 'sprint', thus forcing the early selection of nominees and giving an asymmetrical advantage to the front-runners who emerge during the invisible primary (Wattier 2004). To win in early multi-state primaries, known as Super Tuesday or Titanic Tuesday, has become a good predictor of who will be the party nominee.[5]

These debates shed light on how primaries impact on cross-district electoral coordination, which is more relevant in presidential than in legislative elections, and what factors favour a candidate-centred campaign. In the US case, coordination is weakened by the non-concurrent and decentralized primaries, which are led by party leaders and state authorities, preceding the indirect winner-take-all general election (Kamarck 1987; Ansolabehere and King 1990; Wattenberg 1991, Norrander 1993, 2006). The 2016 US presidential election and the failure of party leaders to coordinate the nomination process have revived concerns about the risks stemming from the decentralized and faction-friendly system of presidential selection (Cohen et. al 2016; Mayer 2016).

11.2.3 Party-Centred Nominations

Conversely, party-centred studies argue that an inclusive nomination process only changes the incentives and constraints for selecting elite-endorsed candidates. Thus, a party-centred logic of presidential nomination remains, even if open or closed primaries are used to select the candidates. Analysing the US case, some scholars claim that party leaders have actually learned to manage the risks of the party divide triggered by the nomination process, especially from 1980 to 2004. Cohen et al. (2008) argue that the locus of party decision-making has moved to the invisible primary, since the national nominating conventions became merely ceremonial. Partially disagreeing with this claim, Steger (2016) argues that party insiders engage in the endorsement game only

---

[5] Parties organize the national convention, but they leave the decisions on primaries and caucus business at the state's and the party leaders' discretion. The choice of whether to adopt a closed or an open primary, as well as on which selection methods will be used, has resulted in the use of proportional methods by Democrats and a mix of majority and proportional methods by Republicans.

when the front-runner is backed early by a stable coalition of party stakeholders in the primary and he or she is an appealing candidate.

From this perspective, the presidential election changes the party leaders' leverage in shaping the process of candidate selection. Party leaders do not ignore appealing outsiders or popular newcomers with great chances to win the presidential election, even when candidates belonging to the traditional establishment were preferred. Some scholars have shown that party leaders might avoid losing control of nominations by exploring the primaries' potential in selecting candidates with 'more campaign skills' and by shaping it as an information-revelation process, allowing voters to learn about the candidates (Bartels 1988; Serra 2011). Alcántara (2001) stresses the strategic use of primaries by leaders to solve pre-electoral coordination problems among coalition partners, as observed in Argentina (1988–1989) and Chile (1999). In addition, legitimacy's gains are an asset that leaders pursue through primaries in order to increase the party's vote share at the direct presidential election (Carey and Polga-Hecimovich 2006).

In support of this view of the presidential nomination as a party-centred process, some scholars argue that setbacks in presidential nomination just reflect the deliberate moves of party leaders to strengthen their gatekeeper powers on candidate selection. Party-specific challenges may be a critical factor in explaining why these moves take place in some, but not all, parties in the same party system. Thus, where they are not legally mandatory, the adoption and the rejection of presidential primaries reveal endogenous moves of party leaders to handle internal or external challengers.

The ebbs and flows of candidate selection methods adopted by Taiwan parties since 1990's reinforce this point. The later dominance of 'polling primaries' as the method for selecting the candidates of the main parties (KMT and PDD) points to the endogenous changes led by party leaders seeking to expand voter engagement, without losing control of nomination, and with the purpose of choosing competitive candidates after electoral reforms (Yu et al. 2014).

11.2.4 Self-Recruitment

A different pathway to the presidency refers to the self-recruited candidates, who are favoured by rules lowering barriers to independent candidacies and the entry of new parties favouring these strategies. However, scholars have also highlighted factors that are critical barriers to lower their chances. The ballot access requirements—such as petitions backed by a set number of eligible voters or monetary deposits—and electoral formulas encouraging strategic voting represent the most notable institutional barriers to the nomination of candidates not affiliated with parties (Abramson et al. 1995; Brancati 2008). Since obtaining a nomination does not automatically mean a viable candidacy, some scholars emphasize presidential power as a more decisive barrier to independents, and even non-partisan candidates, in popular elections for the presidency. Strong presidencies make the race more competitive and the victory of someone with a partisan background more likely (Elgie et al. 2014).

Despite these constraints, the recent election of independents, non-partisans and splinter parties' candidates points to variants of this subset of presidential pathways. Yet, how this strategy to 'send myself to the competition' connects to the broad dynamics of the presidential contest, in different stages, is still undertheorized or sparsely supported by empirical analysis beyond the US. Formal models and experiments have been investigating whether outsider or non-partisan candidates decide to run alone when party leaders raise the costs of party nomination (Buisseret and van Weelden 2017). In addition, weak party attachments of a candidate may be compensated by other political assets. Prior experience in government seems to pave alternative routes in getting access to the presidential ballot in several countries. While popular governments may offer additional incentives to boost former ministers or appointed authorities through incumbent endorsement, underperforming governments and those marked by public distrust instead fuel independent candidacies. The remarkable election of the French president Emmanuel Macron illustrates this path. As an independent, leading the movement *En Marche!*, he vigorously linked his image to the spirit for political renewal at the same time he disconnected himself of the unpopular cabinet that he served before. Given the higher number of non-partisan cabinet members in presidential and semi-presidential systems (Samuels and Shugart 2010), it is important to explore whether and to what extend such positions impact de supply-side of independent or outsider candidates.

11.3 Presidential Profiles: The Research Agenda

Presidential races heighten the importance of individual personalities within specific historical and political contexts, loosening the candidates' bonds of loyalty to other persons, parties, or groups. Once James Bryce asked, referring to the US presidency, why this great office, the greatest in the world, was not more frequently filled by great and striking men (Bryce, cited in Nelson 1987: 120). Today this question regarding presidential races extends throughout the world and has been translated into enquiring what sorts of people actually compete for and manage to win the highest executive position. As shown in the previous section, existing studies focus on the interaction of legal and party variables to explain different outcomes in terms of candidate type. Studies focusing particularly on presidential profiles pay attention to three distinctive aspects: the extent to which the presidential candidate is a party-loyal person; what kind of previous political experience he/she has; and what the typical social background of the candidate is, which tackles issues of representation. Empirically, the strategy has mostly concentrated on studying the profiles of past candidates and incumbents through case studies, although a few interesting large-N and medium-N comparative analyses stand out as well.

11.3.1 Partisan Background (Insiders, Adherents, Outsiders)

A first observation is that the profile of candidates with chances of winning the offices of president and prime minister differ, with a wider range of options—extending between the extremes of party insider and outsider—for the presidential candidates. Siavelis and Morgenstern (2008: 25–36) yield four stylized types of presidential profile: party insiders, party adherents, freewheeling independents, and group agents. They explain variations in the prevailing partisan background through the combination of certain constitutional or legal rules (electoral formula, re-election, and geographic organization, among others) and the degree of party institutionalization or the degree to which voters are attached to extant parties. Research shows that when parties are both organized and bureaucratic and seen by voters and candidates as providing the only realistic path to the presidency, candidates rise through existing party ranks, thus mostly producing candidates that are *insiders* or *adherents*.[6] In contrast, *freewheeling independents* have no long-term identification with a party and may create a personal vehicle for the electoral contest. Lastly, *group agents* are recognized leaders of defined societal, functional, or corporate, groups, such as business organizations. Empirically, Siavelis and Morgenstern's book builds upon case studies on the multi-party presidential systems of Latin America. The authors also contribute a typology of legislator-candidates, which shows that the constitutional framework of separation of power not only impacts the level of party *insiderness* of presidential profiles, but also makes them distinguishable from the profiles of legislators.

Party outsiders play a great role in the existing literature. In the US case, party persons are considered outsiders—a concept that resembles the party adherent described above by Siavelis and Morgenstern—if they do not belong to the mainstream of the party and, in fact, reject the dominant party leadership (Busch 1997: 2). Busch (1997) explains that outsiders may sometimes create their own electoral vehicle: these 'unconnected outsiders' are an extreme form of outsider, a person who relies on personal charisma as well as the media, and communicates often through direct popular appeals. As the US primary system exists in combination with other rules, such as the majoritarian electoral system, outsider movements normally emerge within the boundaries of the institutionalized two-party system. From this perspective outsiderness is less an attribute of the leader than a rhetoric of change. If the defining condition of the outsider is that change in some form is the candidate's central promise, an insider leader, such as Barack Obama, may thus be considered an outsider (Hinich et al. 2010).

Recent research on populism stresses that outsiderness is mostly rhetorically defined. According to ideational approaches to populism, all forms of this phenomenon fall under the core idea that populism is a frontal attack to the establishment and an appeal to 'the people' (Mudde and Kaltwasser 2012, 2017). Neither is populism defined by nor

---

[6] The party adherents have strongly partisan profiles, but differ from the insider in that they are not the party's undisputed leaders. They may, for example, jump to the national campaign from subnational positions. In the US literature, such a candidate is usually considered an 'outsider' (Busch 1997: 2).

wedded to a specific type of leader, and populist actors may mobilize in many different ways, from loosely organized movements to tightly structured political parties. Despite their outsider rhetoric, populist leaders do have connections to the elite. Mudde and Kaltwasser (2017: 73–4) classify populist leaders as insiders, insider-outsiders, and outsiders. Interestingly, the real outsiders—both in demographic and political terms— are rare, and most likely to be found in developing democracies with presidential systems and weakly institutionalized political parties. In contrast, the populist outsider is scarce in the European parliamentary democracies where populist party structures instead prevail.

The concept of populist leaders becoming presidents without an attachment to a political party goes back to Juan Linz's seminal contribution on presidentialism. For Linz, the personalized character of the presidential election, particularly in the age of mass media, makes it likely that someone without previous political experience (but with wealth and popularity) could appeal directly to the voters without needing the support of a party (Linz 1994: 26–8). Drawing on this idea, Samuels and Shugart (2010)'s book *Presidents, Parties, and Prime Ministers*, on which we commented before, defined and measured levels of insiderness, which they understood as the nature of the link between the prospective chief executive and the party organization.

Since then, the literature on insiderness/outsiderness has been growing, but the scope of these concepts remains a matter of debate. Referring to Samuels and Shugart (2010), Elgie (2011: 396) points out that it is not entirely clear how the authors operationalized non-partisanship: sometimes non-partisan is merely a front for someone who is clearly partisan, at other times it refers to someone genuinely non-partisan at the election but who receives party endorsement afterwards, and then becomes partisan. In fact, it seems that the outsider type is more subject to change than the insider type, a reason why a procedural or dynamic operationalization would probably fit better, and a systematic enquiry about the sources of such change would need to be undertaken. Siavelis and Morgenstern (2008: 33) have noted, for instance, how the re-election rule may help ensure that a party adherent does not become an outsider by encouraging accountability. Mudde and Kaltwasser (2017: 76) point to the example of Hugo Chávez of Venezuela, a successful populist outsider, and the rise of a new ruling class after his permanence in power for more than a decade. Meanwhile, writing on the Ukraine, Sedelius (2015: 139–40) has warned that party candidates may actually tamper with rules while in office and create barriers for party development that enhance their personal dominance and further personalize future electoral competition. Not only the constitutional structure but also the strength with which this structure is applied in practice may have an impact on defining a candidate's profile and his or her chances of evolution as an insider.

Definitions that point to the candidates' attributes, and exclude emotional or ideological components as well as measures based on external assessments, have allowed the comparative literature to move forward by teasing out those components. One of the steps has been to distinguish the level of partisan identification from the political experience.

11.3.2 Previous Political Experience (from Newcomers to Incumbents)

Carreras (2016) has called attention to *newcomers* running for the presidency, which he distinguishes from outsiders. The author asks whether both independents and candidates from established parties have occupied legislative or executive positions before running for the highest office. Based on a database including biographical information on all the heads of government that arrived in power following parliamentary and presidential elections in all democratic countries for the 1945–2015 period, a total of 870 democratic national elections, Carreras finds that more than 8 per cent of those elections led to the election of a political newcomer as head of government—that is, a candidate that had at most three years of political experience before reaching office, including both executive and legislative experience.

The newcomer discussion features prominently in the comparative literature on presidentialism, where the Latin American cases stand out. Newcomers have competed in almost 20 per cent of all elections in this region (Corrales 2008) and in 10 per cent of the cases they have become presidents (Alcántara et al. 2018). As in the previously discussed literature, these authors find evidence that link the arrival of newcomers not only to the system of separation of powers but also to weak party systems, especially in lower quality and younger democracies where governments are responsible for policy and moral failures. This is confirmed in case studies on established democracies, where political parties tend to control the selection of candidates. The French system of presidential recruitment, for example, ensures that the main contenders will be experienced in the affairs of state at the highest level (Pierce 1995: 224).

Concerning presidential candidates *with* previous political experience, incumbents stand out. In effect, unless re-election is forbidden, incumbents have the advantage that their decision to run again relies more on their own expectations of success than on the opinion of their party (Carey and Polga 2008: 536). Of 13 per cent of incumbents who tried for re-election in Latin America, 57 per cent succeeded. Several studies have found similar evidence of the incumbency relevance for winning candidacies. Incumbents' participation in elections affects the patterns of electoral competition by reducing fragmentation in the presidential field (Jones 2017). These actors have additional, strong advantages in political competitions because of their control over the agenda, greater media coverage, and access to the instruments and resources of power (Ginsburg et al. 2010: 1819–20).[7] Because of the importance of incumbents as winning presidential

---

[7] Przeworski (2015: 104) found that of 2,230 contested presidential elections between 1788 and 2008, 70 per cent were won by incumbents. Even when the historical and regional focus is narrowed, the incumbency advantage remains clear. Cheeseman examined electoral turnovers in non-founding elections (1990–2009) in sub-Saharan Africa and observed that turnovers occurred in only 12 per cent of incumbent elections but in 45 per cent of open-seat elections. Even if countries rated as 'not free' by Freedom House were excluded, ruling parties won higher vote shares in incumbent elections (Cheeseman 2010: 142). Corrales and Penfold (2014) analysed 137 presidential elections in Latin America (1953–2012) and discovered that re-election success depends on the term-limit rule. Incumbents won

candidates, presidential term limit constitutional clauses are said to promote competition and the alternation of power. For this reason, they have been subject to revisions in the real world. First, the term-limit rule spread with the widespread adoption or resumption of presidential and semi-presidential systems of government during the third wave of democratization; subsequently, a corrective amendment fever has led to their relaxation or abolition. A booming literature has accompanied this trend in constitutional engineering (Carey 2009; Baturo 2014; Corrales and Penfold 2014; Jones 2017; see also Chapter 28 in this volume).

In the US case as well, the term limit clause has been regarded as the most notable constitutional feature with an impact on the profile of presidential candidates (Helms 2005: 27). In this country, the career pattern for ascending to the presidency has been that of a party politician who has served in elected public office from an early stage. Recent, prominent governmental experience has defined the pool of the presidentially eligible, which since the 1930s has been limited to senators, governors, vice presidents, and the presidents themselves (Nelson 1987: 133). The party controlling the presidency has turned to the presidency or vice presidency for candidates, while the opposition party has turned primarily to governors and secondarily to senators. Candidates with other political backgrounds have been unsuccessful, as have candidates without experience in public office—until 2016 (Pika et al. 2018: 48). Donald Trump became the first major party nominee in US history to have no record of public service—elected, appointed, or military—before entering the presidency. Even though other outside and extremist figures had not been absent from the political landscape, such candidates had not made it through the parties' gatekeeping checks (Levitsky and Ziblatt 2018: 57). Trump's triumph occurred in spite of the background of a long-term democracy and an institutionalized party system, but could be foreseen after the adoption of the primary system that weakened the party leadership's role in the presidential nomination process. It also confirms the highlighted risks inherent in presidential elections under a system of separation of powers. The mass media role in enhancing the outsider's chances, which had often been pointed out as a potential risk, proved crucial in this election (Levitsky and Ziblatt 2018: 58).

Although the presidential position carries importance in itself, it is so identified with the occupant that his or her name also has consequences for other presidential candidacies. Corrales (2008) calls attention to the fact that at least one ex-president ran in roughly half the Latin American elections in which ex-presidents were constitutionally allowed to compete; and ex-presidents won in almost 40 per cent of those races. To the various ways that ex-presidents impart importance, the author adds the 'ex-presidents

---

90 per cent of consecutive re-elections, 83 per cent of elections when indefinite re-election was permitted, and only 40 per cent of non-consecutive elections (Corrales and Penfold 2014: 163). In electoral authoritarian regimes, they can count on a greater degree of popular support because of their higher visibility and familiarity, because they present themselves as guarantors of stability, and because they have several instruments at their disposal that can impede political competition: they can repress the opposition using the state apparatus, conduct electoral manipulation through the electoral administration, and control the rival factions within the ruling party (Maltz 2007: 132–3).

names'—that is, candidates with a familial relationship with an ex-president. These candidates, who are expected not to deviate much from the programmes associated with the president whose last name they bear, are also considerably more successful in Latin America than in Europe (Corrales 2008: 7). Although a long-term public career path prevails in the majority of the presidential races, the more frequent emergence of the latter, unconventional candidacies in the Latin American region is often connected to some form of party breakdown, within a more general setting of socioeconomic disarray. In critical contexts, ambitious career party leaders are prone to reduce resistance to ex-presidents whose comeback could represent a chance to save the party. However, the return of ex-presidents may in turn lead to more party system fragmentation or polarization and does not necessarily help calm economic anxieties, conditions that may, in turn, lead to the appearance of newcomers. Thus, for Corrales, the rise of both ex-presidents and newcomers is causally interconnected.

11.3.3 Social Background or Personal Characteristics

The study of presidential profiles also refers to the social background of candidates and, thus, tackles issues of representation (Hazan and Rahat 2010). Still, cross-national comparisons on the topic of the personal characteristics of presidents and presidential candidates are scarce, and tend to be highly descriptive. Even on the issue of gender, which is much more developed, studies tend to focus more on legislatures than on elected executives (see Chapter 13 in this volume). From the gender literature on legislative representation we learn that the basic type of electoral system influences the inclusiveness of the elected bodies and, among those types, majoritarian systems are less favourable for the nomination and election of women and minorities (Norris 2006). As presidential elections are majoritarian by nature, this rule is a major factor working against varied representation. If we add the pervasive importance of incumbency in those elections, we have a situation where if incumbents are allowed to run, their replacement by social groups that are underrepresented becomes even more difficult. Primary systems of candidate selection will not necessarily improve social inclusiveness. In fact, they have brought about an ever-increasing role for financial supporters of prospective candidates, which has negatively affected the representation of some social groups (Hazan and Rahat 2010: 112). Instead, in selection systems where party leaders centralize power, the leaders can form agreements on balancing among different profiles and act as gatekeepers for potential candidates.

Formal rules or constitutional requirements exist in all constitutions, but they still leave the competition open to many candidates. It is the informal requirements that may, instead, be more demanding than the formal rules. Referring to the US presidential candidacies, Nelson (1987) wrote that, in effect, women, blacks, other racial minorities, non-Christians, and the never married could be eliminated from the pool of eligible contenders. However, social conventions change over time, often accompanying changes in the electorate. Barack Obama's triumph over Hilary Clinton altered the pattern in the

US presidential election of 2008, with him becoming not only the first African-American president, but also the first non-southern Democratic president in almost half a century (Abramowitz 2010: 594). His triumph has been connected to the rapid growth of the non-white share of the American electorate (Abramowitz 2010, 2014). According to this author, although short-term factors may always bring other candidates to victory, the non-white share of the electorate, and especially the Latino share, will continue to grow and to show its changing power in the party primaries over the long term. This will reinforce the already occurring trend of people with varied backgrounds occupying seats in the Senate as well as governorships, and will increase the chances that they become serious candidates for the presidency (Pika et al. 2018: 53).

The existing comparative studies we reviewed proceed similarly to the previously discussed studies on career backgrounds by looking at those individuals who have actually been presidents and comparing their profiles. Alcántara et al. (2018) focus on the political socialization of Latin American presidents ruling between 1978 and 2015. They find that 94.6 per cent of those presidents were men, and approximately 49 per cent had family members involved in politics; a good proportion of presidents had family ties to other presidents. These political dynasties facilitate the entrance into politics, add to the candidate's political capital, and, as we saw before, carry electoral advantage because 'ex-presidents' names' are highly successful in presidential electoral contests.

11.4 THE FUTURE RESEARCH AGENDA

Despite considerable advances in the study of executive politics, through historical, institutional, and leadership approaches, the need for more theoretically grounded explanatory models on presidential pathways and profile persists, particularly concerning the election of the chief executive under presidentialism and semi-presidentialism.

Only recently has the formal-theoretical literature addressed issues connected to presidential selection, employing principal-agent and veto-player models to explore its implications, such as adverse selection problems, for executive politics. A promising path we see is the use of these models to build testable propositions on whether nomination and election processes reduce or deepen the risks of adverse selection at the level of the presidency, either softening post-electoral coordination or generating problems of accountability.

As we have shown in these pages, the process of presidential recruitment encompasses many stages and actors, which challenges any efforts to build comprehensive theories. Unsurprisingly, recent scholarship has concentrated on candidate selection inside political parties and, primarily, on selection methods. However, more attention should be paid to inter-party competition and how it affects those intra-party decisions. This would allow us to disentangle better the incentives that underpin different paths and produce one winner and several losers. Similarly, the comparative literature has made progress in the study of presidential profiles with definitions of types of profiles that point to candidates' attributes, rather than to emotional or ideological components, and measures that are based on external assessments. A flourishing literature on outsiderness and populism, however, entails the danger of adding more conceptual complexity than clarity.

11.4.1 Comparative Concerns and Data Collection

At present, the most important challenges to this research agenda arise from the issue of comparability. The literature has advanced different avenues for comparing presidentialism and semi-presidentialism, taking the direct election, the feature they both have in common, as a point of departure and exploring candidate selection and presidential profiles across those systems. However, these studies have been growing unevenly, both geographically and thematically, with more attention paid to presidential systems and fewer studies on semi-presidentialism. The number of large-N studies has increased recently, but analyses are limited when we come to case studies and longitudinal data at the country level. Medium-N comparisons have been developing, but cross-regional studies remain rare. A challenging issue in moving multi-country comparisons forward has been the different criteria for classifying systems of government. However, the universe of comparable cases has now widened with more agreement on definitional aspects and a better delimitation of the universe of presidential and semi-presidential cases (Elgie 2015; Sedelius and Linde 2018). Despite these advances, the availability of data remains a critical limit for assessing empirical propositions in different institutional or political settings. More collaborative efforts in this research direction will help boost comparative studies, which can be eased by broader theoretical frameworks (see also Chapter 10 in this volume).

11.4.2 New Topics of Study

In our view, the following topics would help to move this research agenda forward. First, we need to further explore the analytical consequences and properly model how the differences in the institutional format of executive leadership (dual or not) are associated with variants of presidential pathways. How is incumbent advantage shaped in each case? To what extent does the institutional format affect presidential ambitions and careers? Being a prime minister matters not only because of the powers he or she holds vis-à-vis the president, but also because this position may pave the way to the presidential race or may be used to block challengers' moves to get it. Second, we see the need to endogenize the ministers' or appointees' tenures as strategies of the political elites to recruit candidates in presidential and semi-presidential systems. This would help us to understand better how non-partisans or outsiders follow the presidential path, as these systems not only have a higher rate of outsiders running for the presidency but also, more frequently, adopt non-partisan cabinet politics when compared to parliamentarism. Finally, regarding the presidential profiles, there has also been a bias towards studying the problematic profiles (such as the emerging role of the outsider or the recurrent cases of presidential re-election), while more regular candidacies (such as those with long-term party careers) have received less attention. In addition, with the new trend of outsiders and newcomers exceeding the realm of developing democracies and becoming a more global phenomenon, the explanatory power of certain variables, such as collapsing party systems or economic disarray, may lose relevance once those new cases begin to be included in large-N analyses. The impact of the outsider phenomenon on the social backgrounds of chief executives should be observed closely as well.

11.5 CONCLUSION

Despite advances in the third wave of parliamentarism-presidentialism studies (Elgie 2015), which are characterized by a rigorous methodology and a diversified research agenda, the topic of presidential pathways and profiles is still in an initial phase of development.

We can make two further general comments on the way the literature has dealt with the rules that frame presidential selection processes. First, as we pointed out above, the presidential race is shaped not only by the direct character of the election, but also by a complex set of rules operating at different levels, and in several steps and stages, that affect the actors' strategic decisions. Some presidential pathways consist of a very tough process with an erratic outcome for candidates, particularly when the rules tend to fragment and decentralize the arenas of competition. In addition, party nomination rules have evolved in recent years, after party system crises and demands for democratization. The evolution of these rules and their combination with other, existing institutions has brought more uncertainty to the field in which presidential competition is taking place. Outsiders are now able to profit from such changes, due to contexts of disenchantment with the political offering and governing experience of traditional parties and with the responses of these parties to new social challenges, such as the massive waves of immigration in Europe. In critical contexts, the direct election of the presidency represents a major incentive than legislative representation to control the political agenda. Political outsiders sitting at the presidency may engage in institutional warfare with opposing legislatures or, if politically powerful, in institutional engineering. Both make political scenarios connected to the presidentialization and the personalization of parties, and to the wide pathways to the presidential office, difficult.

zero

REFERENCES

Abramowitz, A. (2010). 'Transformation and Polarization: The 2008 Presidential Election and the New American Electorate,' *Electoral Studies* 29: 594–603.

Abramowitz, A. (2014). 'Long-Term Trends and Short-Term Forecasts: The Transformation of the US Presidential Elections in an Age of Polarization,' *PS: Political Science & Politics* 47(2): 289–92.

Abramson, P. R., Aldrich, J. H., Paolino, P., and Rhode, D. W. (1995). 'Third-Party and Independent Candidates in American Politics: Wallace, Anderson and Perot,' *Political Science Quarterly* 110(3): 349–67.

Alcántara, M. (2001). 'Experimentos de democracia interna. Las primarias de partidos en América Latina'. *Documentos de Trabajo Doctorado en Ciencia Política*, 6. México: FLACSO.

Alcántara, M., Blondel, J., and Thiébault, J. (2018) (eds). *Presidents and Democracy in Latin America*. New York: Routledge.

Aldrich, J. (1980). 'A Dynamic Model of Presidential Nomination Campaigns,' *American Political Science Review* 74(3): 651–69.

Aldrich, J. (2009). 'The Invisible Primary and Its Deleterious Effects on Democratic Choice,' *PS: Political Science* 42: 33–8.

Ansolabehere, S. and King, G. (1990). 'Measuring the Consequences of Delegate Selection Rules in Presidential Nominations,' *Journal of Politics* 52: 609–21.

Bartels, L. M. (1988). *Presidential Primaries and the Dynamics of Public Choice*. Princeton: Princeton University Press.

Baturo, A. (2014). *Democracy, Dictatorship, and Term Limits*. Ann Arbor: University of Michigan Press.

Baturo, A. (2016). 'From Patronal First Secretary to Patronal President: Post-Soviet Political Regimes in Context,' in R. Elgie and S. Moestrup (eds) *Semi-Presidentialism in the Caucasus and Central Asia*. London: Palgrave Macmillan, 29–59.

Brancati, D. (2008). 'Winning Alone: The Electoral Fate of Independent Candidates Worldwide,' *The Journal of Politics* 70(3): 648–62.

Buisseret, P. and van Weelden, R. (2017), 'Crashing the Party? Elites, Outsiders, and Elections,' Wallis Conference.

Busch, A. (1997). *Outsiders and Openness in the Presidential Nominating System*. Pittsburgh: University of Pittsburgh Press.

Carey, J. and Polga-Hecimovich, J. (2006). 'Primary Elections and Candidate Strength in Latin America,' *The Journal of Politics* 68(3): 530–43.

Carey, J. and Polga-Hecimovich, J. (2008). 'The Primary Elections "Bonus" in Latin America,' in M. Levi, J. Johnson, J. Knight, and S. Stokes (eds) *Designing Democratic Government. Making Institutions Work*. New York: Russel Sage Foundation.

Carey, J. M. (2009). 'The Reelection Debate in Latin America,' in W. C. Smith (ed.) *Latin American Democratic Transformations*. Oxford: Wiley-Blackwell.

Carreras, M. (2016). 'Institutions, Governmental Performance and the Rise of Political Newcomers,' *European Journal of Political Research* 56: 364–80.

Cohen, M., Karol, D., Noel, H., and Zaller, J. (2008). *The Party Decides: Presidential Nominations Before and After Reform*. Chicago: University of Chicago Press.

Cheeseman, N. (2010). 'African Elections as Vehicles for Change,' *Journal of Democracy* 21(4): 139–53.

Cohen, M., Karol, D., Noel, H., and Zaller, J. (2016). 'Party Versus Faction in the Reformed Presidential Nominating System,' *PS: Political Science & Politics* 49(4): 701–8.

Colomer, J. M. (2002). 'Las elecciones primarias presidenciales en América Latina y sus consecuencias políticas,' in M. Cavarozzi and J. A. Medina (eds) *El asedio a la política. Los partidos latinoamericanos en la era neoliberal.* Rosario: Homo Sapiens Ediciones, 117–34.

Corrales, J. (2008). 'Latin America's Neocaudillismo: Ex-Presidents and Newcomers Running for President... and Winning,' *Latin American Politics and Society* 50(3): 1–35.

Corrales, J. and Penfold, M. (2014). 'Manipulating Term Limits in Latin America,' *Journal of Democracy* 25(4): 157–68.

Cox, G. (1997). *Making Votes Count: Strategic Coordination in the World's Electoral Systems.* New York: Cambridge University Press.

Elgie, R. (2011). 'Presidentialism, Parliamentarism and Semi-Presidentialism: Bringing Parties Back In. Review Article,' *Government and Opposition* 46(3) 392–409.

Elgie, R. (2012). 'The President of Ireland in Comparative Perspective,' *Irish Political Studies* 27: 502–21.

Elgie, R. (2015). 'Three Waves of Semi-Presidential Studies,' *Democratization* 22(7): 1–22.

Elgie, R., Bucur, C., Dolez, B., and Laurent, A. (2014). 'Proximity, Candidates, and Presidential Power: How Directly Elected Presidents Shape the Legislative Party System,' *Political Research Quarterly* 67(3): 467–77.

Freidenberg, F. (2015). 'La reina de las reformas: las elecciones internas a las candidaturas presidenciales en América Latina,' in F. Freidenberg and B. Muñoz-Pogossian (eds) *Las Reformas Políticas a las Organizaciones de Partidos en América Latina.* México: INE, TEPJF, OEA, Instituto de Iberoamérica and SAAP.

Ginsburg, T., Melton, D., and Elkins, Z. (2010). 'On the Evasion of Executive Term Limits,' *William and Mary Law Review* 52: 1807–72.

Hale, H. (2014). 'Patronal Politics and the Great Power of Expectations,' in *Patronal Politics: Eurasian Regime Dynamics in Comparative Perspective.* Cambridge: Cambridge University Press, 19–38.

Hazan, R. and Rahat, G. (2010). *Democracy within Parties. Candidate Selection Methods and Their Political Consequences.* New York: ECPR/OUP.

Helms, L. (2005). *Presidents, Prime Ministers and Chancellors: Executive Leadership in Western Democracies.* New York: Palgrave Macmillan.

Hinich, M., Shaw, D. and Huang, T. (2010). 'Insiders, Outsiders, and Voters in the 2008 Presidential Elections,' *Presidential Studies Quarterly* 40(2): 264–85.

Jones, M. P. (2017). 'Presidential and Legislative Elections,' in E. S. Herron, R. J. Pekkanen, and M. S. Shugart (eds) *The Oxford Handbook of Electoral Systems.* Oxford: Oxford University Press.

Kamarck, E. C. (1987). 'Delegate Allocation Rules in Presidential Nomination Systems: A Comparison Between the Democrats and Republicans,' *Journal of Law and Politics* 4: 275–310.

Key, V. O. (1967). 'The Presidential Primary,' in F. M. Carney and H. Frank Way (eds) *Politics 1968.* Belmont, CA: Wadsworth.

Levitsky, S. and Ziblatt, D. (2018). *How Democracies Die.* New York: Crown.

Linz, J. (1994). 'Presidential or Parliamentary Democracy: Does It Make a Difference?,' in J. Linz and A. Valenzuela (eds) *The Failure of Presidential Democracy.* Baltimore and London: The John Hopkins University Press.

Maltz, G. (2007). 'The Case for Presidential Term Limits,' *Journal of Democracy* 18(1): 128–42.

Maltz, G. (2007). 'The Case for Presidential Term Limits,' *Journal of Democracy* 18(1): 128–42.

Mayer, W. (2016). 'Why Trump—and How Far Can He Go?,' *The Forum* 13(4): 541–58.

Mudde, C. and Kaltwasser, C. R. (2012) (eds). *Populism in Europe and the Americas. Threat or Corrective for Democracy?* New York: Cambridge University Press.

Mudde, C. and Kaltwasser, C. R. (2017). *Populism: A Very Short Introduction.* New York: Oxford University Press.

Nelson, M. (1987). 'Who Vies for President?,' in A. Hear and M. Nelson (eds) *Presidential Selection.* Durham: Duke University Press.

Norrander, B. (1993). 'Nomination Choices: Caucus and Primary Outcomes, 1976–88,' *American Journal of Political Science* 37(2): 343–64.

Norrander, B. (2006). 'The Attrition Game: Initial Resources, Initial Contests and the Exit of Candidates during the US Presidential Primary Season,' *British Journal of Political Science* 36: 487–507.

Norris, P. (2006). 'The Impact of Electoral Reform on Women's Representation,' *Acta Politica* 41: 197–213.

Pierce, R. (1995). *Choosing the Chief. Presidential Elections in France and the United States.* Ann Arbor: The University of Michigan Press.

Pika, J., Maltese, J., and Rudalevige, A. (2018). *The Politics of the Presidency.* Washington, DC: Sage.

Polsby, N. W. (1983). 'The Reform of Presidential Selection and Democratic Theory,' *PS: Political Science & Politics* 16: 695–8.

Polsby, N. W. (1985). 'The Democratic Nomination and the Evolution of the Party System,' in A. Ranney (ed.) *The American Elections of 1984.* Washington, DC: American Enterprise Institute, 36–65.

Przeworski, A. (2015). 'Acquiring the Habit of Changing Governments through Elections,' *Comparative Political Studies* 48(1): 101–29.

Ranney, A. (1972). 'Turnout and Representation in Presidential Primary Elections,' *American Political Science Review* 66: 221–37.

Samuels, D. J. and Shugart, M. S. (2010). *Presidents, Parties, and Prime Ministers: How the Separation of Powers Affects Party Organization.* New York: Cambridge University Press.

Sandri, G., Seddone, A, and Venturino, F. eds. (2015). *Party Primaries in Comparative Perspective.* Farnham: Ashgate.

Sedelius, T. (2015). 'Party Presidentialization in Ukraine,' in G. Passarelli (ed.) *The Presidentialization of Political Parties: Organizations, Institutions and Leaders.* Houndmills: Palgrave Macmillan.

Sedelius, T. and Linde, J. (2018). 'Unravelling Semi-Presidentialism: Democracy and Government Performance in Four Distinct Regime Types,' *Democratization* 25(1): 1–22.

Seeberg, M. B., Wahman, M., and Skaaning, S.-E. (2018). 'Candidate Nomination, Intra-party Democracy, and Election Violence in Africa,' *Democratization* 25(6): 959–77.

Serra, G. (2011). 'Why Primaries? The Party's Tradeoff between Policy and Valence,' *Journal of Theoretical Politics* 23(1): 21–51.

Siavelis, P. and Morgenstern, S. (2008). *Pathways to Power: Political Recruitment and Candidate Selection in Latin America.* Pennsylvania: The Pennsylvania State University Press, University Park.

Steger, W. (2016). 'Conditional Arbiters: The Limits of Political Party Influence in Presidential Nominations,' *PS: Political Science & Politics* 49(4): 709–15.

Wattenberg, M. P. (1991). *The Rise of Candidate-Centered Politics*. Cambridge, MA: Harvard University Press.

Wattier, M. J. (2004). 'Presidential Primaries and Frontloading: An Empirical Polemic,' paper prepared for 'State of the Party: 2004 & Beyond', University of Akron, 5–7 October 2005.

Yu, C., Che-Hua Yu, E., and Shoji, K. (2014). 'Innovations of Candidate Selection Methods: Polling Primary and Kobo under the New Electoral Rules in Taiwan and Japan,' *Japanese Journal of Political Science* 15(4): 635–59.

CHAPTER 12

....

POLITICAL CAREERS OF MINISTERS AND PRIME MINISTERS

....

FERDINAND MÜLLER-ROMMEL, CORINNA KROEBER, AND MICHELANGELO VERCESI

12.1 INTRODUCTION

....

THE concept of career, while ubiquitous in elite research, has hardly received any comprehensive analytical treatment in the study of political executives. In a first empirical analysis of world rulers, Jean Blondel (1985: 8) claimed that 'the study of ministers and of ministerial careers is in its infancy'. Since then, further research on the structures and dynamics of ministers' and prime ministers' pathways to power have been provided but these have surely not yet reached maturity (Berlinski et al. 2012: 3). This chapter will summarize and develop the basic theoretical and methodological approaches as well as empirical findings of studies investigating political careers of cabinet members in mainly democratic parliamentary and semi-presidential systems at the national level.

A political career is defined by a sequence of positions taken over by an individual politician in a certain period of time. These positions are usually ranked hierarchically in relation to their power and prestige. Every political career involves selection to office, duration in office and exit from office. Thus, the period from ministers' and prime ministers' first political appointment to their exit from political office can be regarded as the parameters of their political careers (Bakema 1991: 71). Despite some structural similarities, each political career is distinctly individual. For instance, single ministers and prime ministers usually held different positions for different periods of time on their pathway to cabinet. Consequently, they may have acquired varying political and technical types of experiences in office.

In the early years, most research on political careers has typically concentrated on anecdotal and descriptive biographies about highly visible and influential presidents and prime ministers. However, scholarly interest into those who govern increased with cabinet members growing as drivers of decision-making in the heart of government and their recognition as architects and agenda setters of national politics in the media. Questions about their social origin, their intra-party and parliamentary career paths to power as well as their formal and informal qualifications for governing have raised several theoretical and normative issues about the performance and the legitimacy of democratic governance. To understand popular notions of 'good' leadership as well as the mechanisms of executive-legislative relations in parliamentary democracies, systematic research on political career patterns of top politicians is necessary. Despite its relevance for theory and practice, the number of studies that has examined the political pathways to chief executive positions remains rather limited, especially compared to the extensive literature on legislative careers (MacKenzie and Kousse 2014).

Those scholars concerned with executive careers engage with three distinct albeit related research interests. A first group of scholarly works aims to uncover the individual and contextual factors that explain political careers. In these studies, career paths are treated as dependent variable. Making use of individuals' social and occupational background and arguing for the importance of political experiences of politicians, authors identify similarities and differences between the broad number of eligible people and the smaller group of those who aspire to enter office. Focusing on the step from aspiring office to becoming a ministerial candidate, further studies highlight selection procedures as determinants of successful career trajectories. A second set of scholars is interested in the development of executive careers after selection into office. By studying duration in office and post-ministerial activities, researchers provide nuanced typologies of cabinet careers trajectories. Through descriptive analyses, these works highlight variation by world regions as well as country-specific patterns. Applying again a different logic, the third set of literature is interested in the effects of executive career trajectories, in particular on performance in office. These studies suggest that insiders and outsiders, technocrats and generalists, or more and less experienced cabinet members survive longer in office, set different policy priorities and introduce substantially different policies.

This chapter reviews and discusses this literature in detail. For that purpose, it is divided into three sections. The first one provides a sketch of the basic research questions that have been raised (and discussed) in the field of executive careers studies over the past decades. The second part offers a systematic survey of the current state of the literature concerned with ministers' and prime ministers' political careers. The third section presents some avenues for future research, including the potential for further theoretical and methodological improvement, followed by some concluding remarks.

12.2 KEY RESEARCH QUESTIONS

Three sets of research questions guide scholarly work examining the careers of ministers and prime ministers. The first aims to uncover similarities and differences of ministerial and prime ministerial career trajectories across countries and over time. Focusing on similarities, researchers ask which type of individuals successfully aims for executive careers (Blondel and Thiébault 1991; Dowding and Dumont 2009, 2015). Are there homogenous career patterns that constitute a veritable 'ruling class' in parliamentary democracies? Which individual characteristics make successful executive careers more likely or hamper them? Other empirical studies are more concerned with differences and ask to what extent executive careers vary over time and space (De Winter 1991; Verzichelli 1998; Berlinski et al. 2012; Jalalzai 2013: 81–2; Bright et al. 2015; Martocchia Diodati and Verzichelli 2017; Costa Pinto et al. 2018; Marino et al. 2018). How do individuals enter office? Can the career paths be clustered along certain types? Are some of these trajectories more or less prominent in certain countries or at certain points in time? Similar questions have been asked in relation to those in office (Blondel 1985; Bakema 1991; Fettelschoß and Nikolenyi 2009; Keane 2009; Theakston 2010; Strangio 2011). Are there specific career paths describing the survival and future careers of cabinet members? How long do cabinet members survive? How do careers continue after cabinet office?

A second set of research questions addresses the causes of different trajectories to executive office (Vercesi 2018). What explains the choice of career paths—individual or contextual factors? Focusing on individuals' capacity to design successful executive careers, 'actor-oriented' (Jahr and Edinger 2015: 13–14) approaches ask about the impact of personal characteristics (e.g. Allen 2013; Baturo 2016; Öhberg 2017): How can political ambition, political socialization, and political experience lead individuals to make different career choices? How does gender in particular impact career trajectories? 'Context-oriented' scholarly work (Jahr and Edinger 2015), in turn, asks how macro-level factors explain career choices through their enabling (or disabling) effect on aspirants (e.g. Borchert 2003; Edinger and Jahr 2015; Barnes and Taylor-Robinson 2018: 231). How do political institutions create opportunities for those aiming for executive positions? Which selection mechanisms lead aspirants to choose certain career trajectories? And how do these factors influence women's chances to get to the top?

A final set of research calls the diverse effects of different career trajectories into question (Blondel 1991; Claveria and Verge 2015; Baturo and Mikhaylov 2016). Focusing on the likelihood to reach top executive positions, researchers ask whether different career profiles such as insider or outsider, politician or technician, expert or generalist provide more promising avenues to government offices. Other works expect effects of executive career trajectories on office holders' capacity to fulfil their job. They study how ministers and prime ministers with certain backgrounds perform in office.

12.3 Studies of Career Trajectories to Executive Office

Aiming to understand who gets into office under which conditions, four distinct sets of literature study political careers as a dependent variable. The first one provides inductive analyses of the social and occupational background of cabinet members aiming to show the shared characteristics of those in power. The second set of studies highlights the importance of experience in political offices for successful executive careers and provides evidence for the professionalization of politics. Another set of scholarly work aims to explain why individuals with a certain set of characteristics are selected (and deselected), taking strategic incentives of the party selectorate into account. A last share of the literature highlights political opportunity structures to explain differences in executive career patterns worldwide.

12.3.1 Social and Occupational Background

The social and occupational background of ministers and prime ministers constitutes a first indicator for actor-oriented explanations of executive careers. One of the main assumptions of this research is that people with certain characteristics are more likely to reach executive office than others. Therefore, those who reach cabinet membership do not mirror all societal groups equally but are characterized by exceptional social backgrounds (Blondel and Thiébault 1991; Blondel and Müller-Rommel 2007). Ministers and prime ministers are mostly drawn from a homogenous 'upper class' with an own elite configuration, for instance in terms of occupational composition. Putnam (1976: 37) refers in this context to the 'law of increasing disproportion': as the level of elite status increases, the bias in the social characteristics between the elite and the remaining population expands. Put differently, executives tend to be internally coherent and homogenous with respect to individual profiles and, probably, prime ministers are all the more exceptional because they need specific political experiences to conduct their tasks in office (Bennister et al. 2015, 2017).

The most extensive empirical investigation of the social and occupational composition of executive members has been provided by Blondel and Thiébault (1991). In a comparative research project, they collected individual biographies of more than 2,000 ministers in post-war Western Europe over a period of forty years. Overall, they found that cabinet ministers are not socially representative of the population in their country. Only certain segments of the middle class (i.e. lawyers, civil servants, teachers, business people) have a high potential to become cabinet ministers. Despite the presence of many socialist and social-democratic parties in government, white collar and manual workers were clearly underrepresented in executive offices all over Europe. Cairney (2007) confirmed these initial findings arguing that certain occupations—in sectors such as law, public adminstration, journalism, and education—support the development of the necessary skills, networks, and political capital for an executive career. For instance, lawyers learn to argue for and against certain positions, which enables them to comply with cabinet discipline (Dowding and Lewis 2015: 52). Moreover, a career in bureaucracy and private companies may lead to strong managerial skills. Thiébault (1991: 29–30) highlighted that the openess of executive careers for various professions varies across country and distinguishes between governments 'for the people'—with most cabinet members from very few professions such as Italy, France, or Sweden—and governments 'by the people', with considerably higher numbers of ministers from other occupations, for instance Germany, Austria, or Great Britain. Hallerberg and Wehner (2012) suggested that the degree of corporatism in the political system determines the proportion of ministers whose first occupation was in law, public administration, and education.

Exceptional levels of education constitute another core characteristic of cabinet members, as for instance Bovens and Wille (2017) showed for Western Europe. Similar findings exist for the new democracies in Central and Eastern Europe. According to Fettelschoß and Nikolenyi (2009: 220), university degrees provide politicians in Central and Eastern Europe with the necessary skills to succeed in executive careers, in particular the ability to communicate efficiently with other cabinet members, the parliament, the people, and the media. An equivalent pattern seems to exist for prime ministers, given that chief executives in democracies are about twenty times more likely to be highly educated than leaders of autocracies (Besley and Reynal-Querol 2011).

With regard to gender, men are (even nowadays) more likely than women to start political careers and reach top executive positions. However, entirely male cabinets are rare in modern democracies, while gender-parity is becoming a more frequent occurrence (Davis 1997; Barnes and Taylor-Robinson 2018). Since 1960, when the first woman became prime minister in Sri Lanka, fifty-one female office-holders followed worldwide until 2018 (Jalalzai 2018: 261). Most of them served during the last two decades in Europe, albeit with intra-regional differences. There are more female executive members in Scandinavia than in Southern Europe (Jalalzai 2014). By and large, women prime minister usually have similar education and social background characteristics as their male counterparts. Thus, there are no gendered differences for prime ministers in this respect (Müller-Rommel and Vercesi 2017: 250).

The social and occupational background approach has been criticized in the literature for at least four reasons (e.g. Jahr and Edinger 2015: 17): First, it does not account for the political success of people from mid-lower classes. Second, the approach ignores agency and freedom of choice about career paths. Third, 'it reduces the entry into a political career to a one-step act rather than viewing it as a sequence of decisions taken at different times and in different circumstances' (Jahr and Edinger 2015: 17). Fourth, social characteristics are often treated as 'static', while they can be subject to modifications over time.

12.3.2 Ambition and Professionalization

A second explanation for executive career trajectories builds on the assumption that ambitious individuals acquire a set of useful attributes while following career steps towards executive office strategically. This idea builds on the ambition theory which was prominently introduced by Schlesinger (1966). He argued that politicians aim to reach particular political offices and take career steps accordingly. Ambitions are a consequence of politicians' psychological traits as well as the role they perform in office and shape individuals' career paths (Black 1972). To climb to the top of the executive, politicians require what is called progressive ambition, which describes the feeling to want more from a career. Factors such as minority status, family contexts, or relationships with political parties moderate individuals' levels of ambition (Lawless 2012).

The strategic behaviour of ambitious aspirants for executive office causes a process of professionalization (Baturo 2016). Experience in political office enables individuals to learn the handcraft of politics in the sense of a 'Berufspolitiker' (Weber [1919] 1992). Several empirical studies indicate that ambitious full-time politicians are indeed most likely to become ministers and prime ministers. The vast majority of all prime ministers held ministerial portfolios in the most powerful and prestigious departments prior to entering office (De Winter 1991). Having held a parliamentary seat, a ministerial position, and the party leadership in sequence is part of the standard political career of heads of executives (Blondel 1980: 137–8; Rose 2001: 72). Looking at ministers, Öhberg (2017) shows that most politicians achieving national executive office in Sweden are full-time politicians. Allen (2003) finds that in Great Britain, legislators who lived from politics even before election to parliament enter the cabinet more frequently than 'hobby politicians' serving in local councils, arguing that they are better prepared for executive tasks (for similar findings for Great Britain, see Rose 1987).

The strong relationship between executive office and careers in politics led researchers to distinguish the mainstream of political insiders from the rare occurrence of political outsiders (De Winter 1991; Verzichelli 1998; Indriðason and Kam 2008; Martocchia Diodati and Verzichelli 2017; Costa Pinto et al. 2018). Outsiders reach executive office with lower political expertise and mixed professional background. Insiders, in turn, have a long tenure in politics and, therefore, a higher degree of professionalization. They gather experience in legislative or executive offices at the local or regional level or in the national parliament, before stepping up the ladder to the national executive. Many also hold front-offices in their party. This provides aspirants for executive positions with knowledge about the formal and informal procedures of policy-making and the means to gather support by relevant actors inside and outside the political system. Various empirical works underpin this argument by showing that political experience stemming from occupations in the public sector, parliamentary and ministerial positions, or party leadership is a common denominator of (nearly all) executive office holders worldwide (Dogan 1989; De Winter 1991; Thiébault 1991; Beckman 2006; Curtin 2015). As Rose (1987: 76) puts it, a politician (and in case of Great Britain in particular a member of parliament) 'can learn to think like a minister before gaining office, and thereby advance his [sic!] chances of becoming a minister'.

Another way to describe the degree of professionalization is to distinguish between 'amateurs/generalists' and 'specialists' (Blondel 1985; Bakema and Secker 1988; Martocchia Diodati and Verzichelli 2017). Amateurs are defined as those executive members whose previous occupation (before entering into politics) is not related to their cabinet post. They are also called generalists because they have moved from one political position to the next (including ministerial positions) in a short period of time. These politicians have gained political experiences in different political offices and developed a more general knowledge about political structures and processes. Specialists, in turn, are those ministers who have gained specific qualifications for their ministerial position. They usually spend many years in the same ministry and never occupy any other position in cabinet. Furthermore, they are mostly recruited from outside politics. The finance and defence portfolios are, for instance, often in the hands of non-parliamentarians, such as members of the armed forces, economists, or bankers. According to Blondel (1985: 23), both types of ministers exist in nearly all parliamentary governments. Yet, he also claims that the amateur type is more common than the specialist. The majority of ministers in European cabinets are selected because they belong to a political party (or party faction) and not necessarily because they have been technically prepared for the job.

Contextual factors moderate the demand for technocrats: As Hallerberg and Wehner (2013) have shown the number of technocrats among European cabinet members tends to increase substantially in times of economic crisis, when governments are led by left-wing parties, and during transition to democracy. Recent Italian cabinets provide further support for this argument, given that they include increasing numbers of outsiders with technocratic knowledge. These 'high flyer' professionals reach cabinet office without party ties or legislative experience (Martocchia Diodati and Verzichelli 2017: 1367). Throughout Southern Europe, 'technical experience' outside politics has become an increasingly more important factor for determining 'who governs' as a consequence of the changing context (Bermeo 2003: 224; Cotta 2018).

12.3.3 Selection

A third contribution on career trajectories builds on the argument that party and institutional gatekeepers select individuals with certain social and professional characteristics to occupy cabinet posts. This approach relies on the principal-agent theory. In a nutshell, the theory posits that some political positions are filled by principals who select prospective agents to be placed in other political offices (Miller 2005; see also Chapter 16 in this volume). The main reason for principals to delegate are scarcity of time, transaction costs, problems of competence, and problems of social choice and collective action (Strøm 2003: 56–8). In parliamentary democracies, for instance, voters are the principal of members of parliament, who are the principals of prime ministers.

The prime minister and the collective cabinet are the principal of line ministers, who are the principals of the civil servants in their respective ministry. Thus, in this case, the principal (the cabinet) is made up of its own agents (the ministers) (Andeweg 2000: 377). To ensure that agents follow the principal's will, different accountability mechanisms can be employed (Bergman et al. 2003). Because of conflicting interests as well as a lack of information, principals face the risk to choose agents that either do not pursue the same goals (adverse selection) or take action deviating from their preferences (moral hazard). This leads to what is called agency loss (Lupia 2003). Dowding and Dumont (2015) further introduce the problem of agency rent, that is, that agents might not work efficiently. Principals may screen agents before (*ex-ante*) and after (*ex-post*) the selection to reduce these risks. *Ex-ante* screening is particularly interesting for selection, *ex-post* for de-selection and turnover. While the ultimate decision about who is selected for ministerial or prime ministerial office depends on the preferences of the principal, political parties are crucial mediators of the selection process in party governments (Müller 2000; Strøm 2003; Samuels and Shugart 2010).

The literature on selection highlights, first, the importance of social background characteristics as a factor considered during the screening process. Bovens and Wille (2017: 133) argue, for instance, that in modern-day cartel parties 'the like choose the like. The university-educated cadres in political parties, wittingly or unwittingly, select candidates that resemble themselves'. Second, career trajectories matter for selectors. Parties tend to choose political insiders who have proved to be reliable party agents inside their organization, in parliament, and as ministers (Dowding and Dumont 2009, 2015).

This literature with its strong focus on the qualification of candidates as perceived by selectors has been criticized for neglecting how the political context limits selectors' choices and room for manoeuvre. Fleischer and Seyfried (2015: 503) highlight the importance of intra-party screening in the selection process of ministers. Their longitudinal analysis of the German case reveals that the policy expertise of cabinet members is less relevant than the size of the pool of potential ministers and the day they enter this pool. Furthermore, Amorim Neto and Strøm (2006: 643) have used a game-theoretic model to corroborate the hypothesis that non-partisan ministers have better chances to get selected in semi-presidential countries where the prime minister faces electoral uncertainty and the president is endowed with extensive powers. Addressing the increasing number of ministers from outside politics in Central and Eastern Europe, Semenova (2018: 179) underlined how this trend emerges in particular in policy sectors 'subject to public discontent'. Selecting outsiders for sensitive tasks (often associated with unpopular policies) is one strategy to minimize parties' losses in future elections. For prime ministers, in turn, Samuels and Shugart (2010) find that the appointment of candidates with extra-parliamentary experiences is less likely in parliamentary than in semi-presidential systems, where the parliamentary facet of the system is outplayed by the presidential one. Protsyk (2005) argues that in semi-presidential systems powerful presidents select technocratic prime ministers because they can be closer to their ideal policies than other high-ranking party officials. However, complex parliamentary bargaining environments can increase the likelihood of having the powerful president and the prime minister from the same party (Bucur and Cheibub 2017). Grotz and

Weber (2017) have shown that the selection of prime ministers in Central and Eastern European democracies is further moderated by the timing of government formation processes. After elections, parties tend to select their leaders for prime ministerial offices, but if the office needs to be refilled during a term, parties favour experienced cabinet members to ensure short-term stability before the next election. In addition, several scholarly works highlight the role of the voters as selectors. Although not formally referring to the principal-agent framework, this set of research investigates the linkage between candidates' personal traits, public perceptions, and ability to reach office as prime minister ('t Hart and Tindall 2009; Campus 2010; Garzia 2014).

A major deficit of the selection (and de-selection) approach is that contextual factors are taken in consideration only in terms of expectations about party and institutional roles, without paying the due attention to other relevant structural factors such as the availability and the attractiveness of the political posts. Methodologically, this set of scholarly work mostly applies 'event history' and duration models. A major problem with these models is that they are relatively static and, therefore, only account for the single paths from one position to another (Jäckle and Kerby 2018).

12.3.4 Opportunity Structures

A final set of explanations for careers trajectories highlights the limited opportunities for ambitious politicians within institutions. The political structures—reads the argument—affect pathways while individual decisions about career paths follow. Borchert (2003) claimed that the opportunity structure for political careers is determined by three aspects: the availability of political offices (how many posts exist?), their accessibility (how easy is it to reach these posts?), and their attractiveness (are these posts sources of material and/or non-material benefits and skills?). Borchert, Stolz, and colleagues have provided a comprehensive study of careers in multi-level systems using this framework (Borchert and Stolz 2011). For them, the territorial state organization is a key determinant. With a larger number of available positions, federal and decentralized states provide more opportunities than strictly centralized states (Borchert 2011; Stolz 2001). In Germany, for instance, the regional executives constitute an important direct link to the national executive. A similar effect is brought by the supra-national level in the European Union (Stolz 2015). Decentralization also increases the prestige and the power of subnational political offices. Centrifugal drives in career pathways are thus more likely in decentralized state structures because ambitious politicians will pursue local and regional offices to a greater extent (Stolz 2003; Botella et al. 2010; Stolz and Fischer 2014; Dodeigne 2018; Grimaldi and Vercesi 2018).

While the opportunity structure approach has been widely applied in political career studies of parliamentarians (Edinger and Jahr 2015), the 'politics and gender' literature is the only one that has systematically resorted it to analyse careers of chief executive members (see also Chapter 13 in this volume). Scholars identify the scarcity of available offices as a major obstacle to women's selection for executive positions (Barnes and Taylor-Robinson 2018) and uncover a broad variety of moderating factors. In a comprehensive study on the political careers of female prime ministers and presidents worldwide, Jalalzai (2013) shows that women have higher access to executive positions in dual executives, especially as prime ministers when there is a dominant elected president (i.e. in semi-presidential systems). Institutionalized leadership-selection processes are another factor opening opportunities for women to enter government, just like major political transitions within political regimes. The availability of offices for female aspirants might also increase if parties face internal leadership crises as the examples of Merkel in Germany as well as Thatcher and May in the UK showed (Jensen 2008; Jalalzai 2018). Building on such examples, Beckwith (2015) states that the most beneficial party crises for female prime ministers are either scandals or electoral failures. Moreover, corporatist catch-all parties (like the centre-right Christian Democratic Party in Germany) are favourable for women's executive careers (Wiliarty 2008). Given the broad membership of these parties, they aim to promote different factions by representing female politicians in various committees and offices, thereby allowing minorities to climb the ladder towards the head of executives (Jalalzai 2011).

Aiming to explain women's ministerial careers, studies emphasize how coalition governments reduce the posts available to women by limiting the number of seats per party. Consequently, only the high ranking (usually male) party officials enter executive office (Reynolds 1999; Krook and O'Brien 2012). Women are, in turn, more likely to become ministers when parties adopt gender quotas (Claveria 2014). Moreover, female politicians' chances to become ministers are smaller in ethnically divided states, such as many in sub-Saharan Africa, because incumbents use appointments to build patronage networks with 'big men' (Arriola and Johnson 2014: 497). Barnes and O'Brien (2018) and Goddard (2019) have also observed that the attractiveness of ministerial portfolios may well affect women's selection to office, with the most prestigious and influential positions being least accessible to female aspirants.

12.4 STUDIES OF CAREER DEVELOPMENTS IN AND AFTER EXECUTIVE OFFICE

With the endeavour to understand the proceeding of executive careers after reaching the highest political offices in mind, scholars study cabinet members' career trajectories in and after office. Through descriptive analyses, researches have provided, first, a nuanced picture of patterns of re- and de-selection; and, second, post-ministerial activities.

12.4.1 Duration in Office

How long cabinet members remain in office is a key question for researchers studying career developments of ministers and prime ministers. In his seminal book on ministerial careers, Blondel (1985) developed an index of duration ('attrition rate') that he applied to the comparative analysis of ministers' careers across space and time. The index measures the proportion of ministers (in relation to the total number of ministers) who have left the cabinet during one year. Based on this measure, Blondel shows that ministers around the world remained on average three and a half years in office. Variation of ministerial duration in office is, however, considerable: In the Western world ('Atlantic countries'), he identified remarkable variation on both sides of this average. While Swiss ministers lasted on average for about eight years in office, ministers in Greece lasted a little over two years only. Yet, the duration of ministers in most European countries were fairly stable at around four years in office (Blondel 1985: 90–107). In Communist countries and in sub-Saharan Africa, ministers stayed in office much longer than in Latin America and Asia.

Six years later, Bakema (1991: 73) suggested extending the measure of ministerial careers to three indices: 'the length of ministerial tenure (duration), the participation in successive governments (continuity), and the transfer of ministers to different posts (mobility)'. In her longitudinal and cross-national examination of these measures she provides a typology of three career types: ministerial persistence; ministerial rotation and change, ministerial persistence and change (Bakema 1991: 96). 'Ministerial persistence' is characterized by ministers with long lasting, continuous careers in one job. This type is dominant in Austria, Sweden, Germany, and the Netherlands. These senior ministers have developed wide expertise in cabinet decision-making. They usually provide a predictable and professional behaviour in cabinet as well as towards the public. In a political career with 'ministerial rotation and change' cabinet members stay in office for short periods, come to office more than once and occupy more than one post in succession. Italy, Belgium, France, and Finland constitute typical cases for this executive career path. Most recently, this pattern has also been identified for cabinets in Central and Eastern Europe (Fettelschoß and Nikolenyi 2009). Third, 'ministerial persistence and change' is characterized by ministers who stay in cabinet fairly long, but their careers tend to be interrupted. This ministerial type is mostly observed in Ireland, Britain, and Denmark.

12.4.2 Post-Executive Careers

Recent empirical findings show that for most former ministers there is a professional life after having served in cabinet (Musella 2015: 301–2; see also Chapter 17 in this volume). This is especially true for ministers who leave the executive at a younger age (Keane 2009; Theakston 2010; Strangio 2011). Claveria and Verge (2015) find that a new position in politics is the most common scenario, followed by re-appointment and a new career in business. The authors also state that seniority and party experience increase the likelihood of remaining in politics, while policy expertise favours returns to previous jobs or the attainment of international and advocacy roles. Rewarding private sectors incentivize leading politicians to leave politics and to enter business (Mattozzi and Merlo 2008).

Some recent studies have further shown that post-ministerial jobs in business appear especially attractive for politicians in democratic and economically developed countries (Baturo 2017). Moreover, prime ministers who successfully initiated economic growth and reduced state spending while in office are more likely to start a new career in the economic sector after leaving executive office (Baturo and Mikhaylov 2016: 336–7).

12.5 STUDIES OF THE EFFECTS OF EXECUTIVE CAREERS

The last set of literature studying executive careers takes a different perspective. It makes use of career trajectories as causes of other phenomena. Various individual-level differences in ministerial and prime ministerial performance are explained based on varying career trajectories. Within this subset of the literature, one share of scholarly works aims to explain the de-selection of ministers, thus cabinet members' survival in executive office as a consequence of the qualifications developed earlier in their political career. Others aim to explain policy priorities and policy change induced by office-holders based on their career trajectories.

12.5.1 De-selection

Variation in political careers (before entering the executive) is a key explanatory factor for ministers' and prime ministers' survival in office because it provides them with the necessary skills to fulfil their tasks. In this regard, works again build on principal-agent theory and highlight the role of party selectorates and their perception of aspirants' characteristics. In their comparative study of seven West European countries, Bright et al. (2015) show that ministers with previous executive experience tend to survive longer in office since they are better prepared for the tasks they are expected to fulfil. Furthermore, descriptive analyses suggest that '[m]inisters who ascend through the party or through other political offices might be more durable, having already proved themselves' (Fischer et al. 2012: 515). Berlinski et al. (2012) stress that high levels of education also help ministers to survive. However, additional political factors matter for the de-selection of ministers, such as partisan differences, type of government (majority or coalition), and government term (Berlinski et al. 2012: 76ff.). Quiroz Flores (2017) stresses that ministers are likely to stay longer in office when they provide necessary public goods, under the condition that they are not potential challengers of cabinet leaders. Overall, these studies thus point towards the importance of pre-executive political career patterns as explanations for survival in office, but also carve out more complex, context-dependent explanations.

Huber and Martinez-Gallardo (2008) discussed the problems that party leaders have in identifying which politicians have the necessary qualities to do their ministerial job well. In a nutshell, they argued that certain contextual factors, first, make successful screening of candidates more likely; and, second, hinder the correction of false decisions. For instance, ministers belonging to parties that are ideologically distant from the median of the coalition government should survive longer, since they could potentially damage the coalition's policy agenda and are thus screened particularly carefully. Ministers with considerable independent decision-making powers are also selected more carefully and stay in office for longer periods. In large parties, competition for ministerial posts is higher, decreasing the chances for successful screening and, in this manner, ministerial tenures. Ministers holding important portfolios also last longer because they are usually screened more carefully. Hansen et al. (2013) argue that in times of decreasing government approval rates, prime ministers will be more risk averse and thus less likely to dismiss important ministers than in times of high popularity. However, as Bright et al. (2015) point out, the lacking capacity to remove powerful ministers might lead to the end of coalition governments, thereby relating ministerial and prime ministerial duration to the stability or instability of party governments. With regard to prime ministers, political experience seems to be the key determinant of survival in office. Politically well-trained prime ministers tend to serve longer periods, indicating that they perform more successfully. Related empirical evidence was, for instance, provided by Baylis (2007), who argued that prime ministers in Central and Eastern Europe serve on average shorter terms than their Western counterparts because they lack experience necessary to perform convincingly, usually developed in decades of party membership. Grotz and Weber (2017) also show that prime ministers who served as party leaders are more likely to stay in office than those who were only ministers (again based on a study of Central and Eastern Europe). Furthermore, Byrne et al. (2017) highlight the role of opposition leadership as a career step in the United Kingdom, arguing that this experience shaped Cameron's capacity to adapt his policy positions in office.

12.5.2 Performance of Individual Ministers and Prime Ministers

A final subset of research promotes the argument that certain types of career trajectories relate to specific policy priorities of cabinet members. This literature focuses mostly on prime ministers, in particular given their large agenda-setting power. These studies reveal the impact of political careers on their performance evaluations. On the one hand, Theakston and Gill (2006) find that expert ratings of British prime ministers do not clearly correlate with personal background. On the other hand, Helms (2018) clarifies that, for 'heir' prime ministers (those who get their office from a predecessor between two parliamentary elections), the link between political careers and governmental performance exists, albeit not in the expected direction: best performing 'heir' prime ministers are those with less parliamentary and ministerial experience.

Some scholars have further sought to disentangle the impact of prime ministers' backgrounds on specific types of policy. For example, Horowitz and Stam (2014) studied the relationship between personal military experiences and propensity for war. Their findings indicate that leaders with a military past who have not fought are more likely to pursue a militarized policy than those who have participated in wars. Furthermore, Besley et al. (2009) showed that well educated executive leaders correlate with economic growth (Jones and Olken 2005). Hayo and Neumeir (2016) assessed the impact of social status, finding that prime ministers from poorer background tend to promote public spending.

Career trajectories are also associated with the substantial direction of ministers' policy initiatives: in times of economic crisis, technocrats might be more committed to realize liberal market reforms than politicians. To assess ministerial economic performances in eighteen developed democracies, Alexiadou (2015, 2016) has used career patterns to single out three types of ministers: (1) loyalists (loyal to party leaders and office-seeking), (2) partisans (prominent party leaders who aspire to become party leaders), and (3) ideologues (committed policy-seeking ministers, resistant to policy compromises).

12.6 Prospects for Future Research

Future research on political careers of ministers and prime ministers is needed in at least three areas: (1) impact of regime types on career patterns; (2) contemporary political changes and 'new' pathways to executive posts; (3) theoretically grounded studies explaining different pathways to executive posts and their effects.

A first research deficit consists in the absence of a comprehensive knowledge about differences and similarities in the career patterns between political executives in 'new', 'old', and 'defected' democracies as well as in parliamentary and semi-presidential political regimes. Studies on parliamentary elites indicate that the degree of professionalization within new democracies approximates those of old democracies—even though some country-specific differences persist (Semenova et al. 2014). Overall, it still remains unclear to what extent and how far a similar process of professionalization emerges for political executives in all parliamentary democracies. Future studies, therefore, need to address the question whether different types of democracy demand different career profiles of their political executive. Does the institutional setting in these countries mediate between career experience, personalities, and performance of the political executive? Future studies may also seek to find systematic nexuses between the pathways to executive positions in 'defected' democracies. It would, for instance, be most interesting to analyse the effect of increasing emancipative values in these democracies on the stability of the prime ministers and ministers (Welzel 2013). One lesson from the existing literature is that in all democracies both context and personal ambition matter for a political career. A historical institutionalist approach may help to disentangle the role of path dependent effects as a source for explaining career profiles in different regime types.

Second, scholars who study careers of political executives should develop new theoretical ideas about the effect of political changes, such as mediatization, globalization, and personalization, on the political careers of ministers and prime ministers. Top-level aspirants and office-holders in the twenty-first century require, for instance, new types of competences and personality styles to successfully participate in global summit meetings and to communicate in new social media. Since these skills are not necessarily acquired during 'established' political careers, the door to executive positions opens for political outsiders. To what extent do these new skills outperform established individual characteristics such as political experience and occupational and social background as explanatory factors for political careers? Furthermore, do factors such as gender, age, immigration background, or belonging to national minorities have an increasing effect on a successful political career of ministers and prime ministers? Well-known examples such as the German chancellor Angela Merkel, Austria's exceptionally young chancellor Sebastian Kurz, or a highly diverse Canadian government led by Justin Trudeau indicate increasing access of different societal groups to the chief executive. One might parallel this process with the increasing number of outsiders with professional business experience in several South European countries. New insights into the importance that party gatekeepers assign to 'traditional' and 'new' qualifications of candidates would enhance the ongoing discussion about career pathways of the political executives.

New explanatory topics constitute a final research agenda. To begin with, future studies need to develop comprehensive explanations for variation in career trajectories across and within the various types of democracies. For instance, we need to clarify the political conditions under which ministers and prime ministers with a 'technocratic' background are selected into office. Why and under which circumstances are 'technocrats' preferred over 'professionals'? Researchers, additionally, have to develop a better understanding about the psychological resources that determine individual political careers. Which personality traits support or hinder the pathways to executive office? Moreover, research should attempt to explain why some cabinet members make career comebacks after a period out of office, while others end their political careers after resignation. Which factors explain the duration of career breaks and why ministers and prime ministers come back into office? Finally, future research needs to address the direct and indirect relations between certain career trajectories and successful or unsuccessful government performance in parliamentary democracies. Do different career patterns cause variation in governmental performance and, if so, why is this the case? How do technocratic governments perform? Are there certain individual types of ministers and prime ministers with specific skills and motivations who make a difference in policy-making while others do not?

These are only some of the questions which need empirically grounded answers. In many ways, this research deficit follows from the absence of a comprehensive dataset on ministers' and prime ministers' political careers in parliamentary (and semi-presidential) democracies worldwide. As indicated above, empirical research on political careers of executive members is mostly limited to single countries. Existing cross-national studies have focused on the career patterns of executive members in Western Europe and in Westminster democracies. Yet, a cross-national, longitudinal, publicly available dataset on political careers of ministers and prime ministers around the world does not exist in the political science discipline. This lack of data makes large-scale comparative analysis a difficult endeavour. Further efforts need to be invested into collecting standardized longitudinal data on all ministers' and prime ministers' career trajectories to, in, and after executive office for parliamentary democracies in all world regions. Without a comparative dataset, all theoretical considerations about political careers patterns and their effects in different countries under varying political opportunity structures remain up to speculation.

12.7 CONCLUSION

In parliamentary democracies ministers and prime ministers are the most visible and successful politicians. Being a member of the cabinet government is the summit of a political career, which is only reached by a few who started to climb the ladder. The small numbers of those succeeding constitute the main barrier for the development of knowledge in this research field. After all, every state has only one head of government and about one or two dozen ministers at a time, making any insights strongly context dependent. Nevertheless, over seventy-five years after the beginning of the second wave of democratization, large-scale comparisons over time and space applying advanced statistical methods are possible and can allow for new insights. Future studies can build on a solid set of scholarly work, which identifies the variables that determine the emergence of successful executive careers, such as individuals' social background as well as professional experience or the strategies of party selectorates, and the opportunities provided by the political systems. We also have a good understanding of how political careers proceed in office, that is, the factors that influence survival and different patterns of post-ministerial careers. Scholars should now make use of new innovative research designs to test causal claims about the reasons as to why contemporary political changes matter for career patterns. However, the main pre-condition to move the research field from inductive approaches and untested theoretical arguments towards a set of solidly tested theories is the provision of a worldwide dataset on national ministers and prime ministers, covering all parliamentary systems since their democratization.

REFERENCES

Alexiadou, D. (2015). 'Ideologues, Partisans, and Loyalists: Cabinet Ministers and Social Welfare Reform in Parliamentary Democracies,' *Comparative Political Studies* 48(8), 1051–86.

Alexiadou, D. (2016). *Ideologues, Partisans, and Loyalists. Ministers and Policymaking in Parliamentary Cabinets*. Oxford: Oxford University Press.

Allen, P. (2003). 'Linking Pre-Parliamentary Political Experience and the Career Trajectories of the 1997 General Election Cohort,' *Parliamentary Affairs* 66(4): 685–707.

Allen, P. (2013). 'Gendered Candidate Emergence in Britain: Why are More Women Councillors Not Becoming MPs?', *Politics* 33(3): 147–59.

Amorim Neto, O. and Strøm, K. (2006). 'Breaking the Parliamentary Chain of Delegation: Presidents and Non-Partisan Cabinet Members in European Democracies', *British Journal of Political Science* 36(4): 619–43.

Andeweg, R. B. (2000). 'Ministers as Double Agents? The Delegation Process Between Cabinet and Ministers', 37(3): 377–95.

Arriola, L. R. and Johnson, M. C. (2014). 'Ethnic Politics and Women's Empowerment in Africa: Ministerial Appointments to Executive Cabinets', *American Journal of Political Science* 58(2): 495–510.

Bakema, W. E. (1991). 'The Ministerial Career', in J. Blondel and J.L. Thiébault (eds) *The Profession of Government Minister in Western Europe*. Basingstoke: Macmillan, 70–98.

Bakema, W. E. and Secker, I. P. (1988). 'Ministerial Expertise and the Dutch Case', *European Journal of Political Research* 16(2), 153–70.

Barnes, T. and O'Brien, D. Z. (2018). 'Defending the Realm: The Appointment of Female Defense Ministers Worldwide', *American Journal of Political Science* 62(2): 355–68.

Barnes, T. and Taylor-Robinson, M. M. (2018). 'Women Cabinet Ministers in Highly Visible Posts and Empowerment of Women: Are the Two Related?', in A. C. Alexander, C. Bolzendahl, and F. Jalalzai (eds) *Measuring Women's Political Empowerment across the Globe: Strategies, Challenges and Future Research*. London: Palgrave Macmillan, 229–55.

Baturo, A. (2016). '*Cursus Honorum*: Personal Background, Careers and Experience of Political Leaders in Democracy and Dictatorship—New Data and Analyses', *Politics and Governance* 4(2): 138–57.

Baturo, A. (2017). 'Democracy, Development, and Career Trajectories of Former Political Leaders', *Comparative Political Studies* 50(8): 1023–54.

Baturo, A. and Mikhaylov, S. (2016). 'Blair Disease? Business Careers of the Former Democratic Heads of State and Government', *Public Choice* 166(3–4): 335–354.

Baylis, T. A. (2007). 'Embattled Executives: Prime Ministerial Weakness in East Central Europe', *Communist and Post-Communist Studies* 40(1), 81–106.

Beckman, L. (2006). 'The Competent Cabinet? Ministers in Sweden and the Problem of Competence and Democracy', *Scandinavian Political Studies* 29(2): 111–29.

Beckwith, K. (2015). 'Before Prime Minister: Margaret Thatcher, Angela Merkel, and Gendered Party Leadership Contests', *Politics & Gender* 11(4): 718–45.

Bennister, M., 't Hart, P., and Worthy, B. (2015). 'Assessing the Authority of Political Office-Holders: The Leadership Capital Index', *West European Politics* 38(3): 417–40.

Bennister, M., Worthy, B., and 't Hart, P. (2017) (eds). *The Leadership Capital Index: A New Perspective on Political Leadership*. Oxford: Oxford University Press.

Bergman, T., Müller, W. C., Strøm, K., and Blomgren, M. (2003). 'Democratic Delegation and Accountability: Cross-National Patterns', in K. Strøm, W. C. Müller, and T. Bergman (eds) *Delegation and Accountability in Parliamentary Democracies*. Oxford: Oxford University Press, 109–220.

Berlinski, S., Dewan, T., and Dowding, K. (2012). *Accounting for Ministers. Scandal and Survival in British Government 1945-2007*. Cambridge: Cambridge University Press.

Bermeo, N. (2003). 'Ministerial Elites in Southern Europe: Continuities, Changes and Comparisons', in P. Tavares de Almeida, A. Costa Pinto, and N. Bermeo (eds) *Who Governs Southern Europe? Regime Change and Ministerial Recruitment, 1850–2000*. London: Frank Cass, 205–27.

Besley, T., Montalvo, J. G., and Reynal-Querol, M. (2009). 'Do Educated Leaders Matter?,' *The Economic Journal* 121(554): F205–27.

Besley, T. and Reynal-Querol, M. (2011). 'Do Democracies Select More Educated Leaders?,' *American Political Science Review* 105(3): 552–66.

Black, G. S. (1972). 'A Theory of Political Ambition: Career Choices and the Role of Structural Incentives,' *The American Political Science Review* 66(1): 144–59.

Blondel, J. (1980). *World Leaders: Heads of Government in the Postwar Period.* Beverly Hills: Sage.

Blondel, J. (1985). *Government Ministers in the Contemporary World.* London: Sage.

Blondel, J. (1991). 'The Post-Ministerial Career,' in J. Blondel and J.-L. Thiébault (eds) *The Profession of Government Minister in Western Europe.* Basingstoke: Macmillan, 153–73.

Blondel, J. and Müller-Rommel, F. (2007). 'Political Elites,' in R. J. Dalton and H.-D. Klingemann (eds) *The Oxford Handbook of Political Behavior.* Oxford: Oxford University Press, 818–32.

Blondel, J. and Thiébault, J.-L. (1991) (eds). *The Profession of Government Minister in Western Europe.* Basingstoke: Macmillan.

Borchert, J. (2003). 'Professional Politicians: Towards a Comparative Perspective,' in J. Borchert and J. Zeiss (eds) *The Political Class in Advanced Democracies: A Comparative Handbook.* Oxford: Oxford University Press, 1–25.

Borchert, J. (2011). 'Individual Ambition and Institutional Opportunity: A Conceptual Approach to Political Careers in Multi-level Systems,' *Regional & Federal Studies* 21(2): 117–40.

Borchert, J. and Stolz, K. (2011) (eds). *Moving through the Labyrinth: Political Careers in Multi-level Systems.* Special issue of *Regional & Federal Studies* 21(2).

Botella, J., Rodríguez Teruel, J., Barberà, O., and Barrio, A. (2010). 'A New Political Elite in Western Europe? The Political Careers of Regional Prime Ministers in Newly Decentralised Countries,' *French Politics* 8(1): 42–61.

Bovens, M. and Wille, A. (2017). *Diploma Democracy: The Rise of Political Meritocracy.* Oxford: Oxford University Press.

Bright, J., Döring, D., and Little, C. (2015). 'Ministerial Importance and Survival in Government: Tough at the Top?,' *West European Politics* 38(3): 441–64.

Bucur, C. and Cheibub, J. A. (2017). 'Presidential Partisanship in Government Formation: Do Presidents Favor Their Parties When They Appoint the Prime Minister?,' *Political Research Quarterly* 7(4): 803–17.

Byrne, C., Randall, N., and Theakston, K. (2017). 'Evaluating British Prime Ministerial Performance: David Cameron's Premiership in Political Time,' *The British Journal of Politics and International Relations* 19(1): 202–20.

Cairney, P. (2007). 'The Professionalization of MPs: Refining the 'Politics-Facilitating' Explanation,' *Parliamentary Affairs* 60(2), 212–33.

Campus, D. (2010). 'Mediatization and Personalization of Politics in Italy and France: The Cases of Berlusconi and Sarkozy,' *International Journal of Press/Politics* 15(2): 219–35.

Claveria, S. (2014). 'Still a 'Male Business'? Explaining Women's Presence in Executive Office,' *West European Politics* 37(5), 1156–76.

Claveria, S. and Verge, T. (2015). 'Post-Ministerial Occupation in Advanced Industrial Democracies: Ambition, Individual Resources and Institutional Opportunity Structures,' *West European Politics* 54(4): 819–35.

Costa Pinto, A., Cotta, M., and Tavares de Almeida, P. (2018) (eds). *Technocratic Ministers and Political Leadership in European Democracies*. Basingstoke: Palgrave Macmillan.

Cotta, M. (2018). 'Technocratic Government Versus Party Government? Non-partisan Ministers and the Changing Parameters of Political Leadership in European Democracies,' in A. Costa Pinto, M. Cotta, and P. Tavares de Almeida (eds) *Technocratic Ministers and Political Leadership in European Democracies*. Basingstoke: Palgrave Macmillan, 267–88.

Curtin, J. (2015). 'New Zealand: Stability, Change or Transition?,' in K. Dowding and P. Dumont (eds) *The Selection of Ministers around the World*. London: Routledge, 25–43.

Davis, R. H. (1997). *Women and Power in Parliamentary Democracies: Cabinet Appointments in Western Europe, 1968–1992*. Lincoln: University of Nebraska Press.

Dodeigne, J. (2018). 'Who Governs? The Disputed Effects of Regionalism on Legislative Career Orientation in Multilevel Systems,' *West European Politics* 41(3): 728–53.

De Winter, L. (1991). 'Parliamentary and Party Pathways to the Cabinet,' in J. Blondel and J.-L. Thiébault (eds) *The Profession of Government Minister in Western Europe*. Basingstoke: Macmillan, 44–69.

Dogan, M. (1989) (ed.). *Pathways to Power: Selecting Rulers in Pluralist Democracies*. Boulder, CO: Westview.

Dowding, K. and Dumont, P. (2009) (eds). *The Selection of Ministers in Europe: Hiring and Firing*. Abingdon: Routledge.

Dowding, K. and Dumont, P. (2015) (eds). *The Selection of Ministers around the World*. London and New York: Routledge.

Dowding, K. and Lewis, C. (2015). 'Australia: Ministerial Characteristics in the Australian Federal Government,' in K. Dowding and P. Dumont (eds) *The Selection of Ministers around the World*. Abingdon and New York: Routledge, 44–60.

Edinger, M. and Jahr, S. (2015) (eds). *Political Careers in Europe: Career Patterns in Multi-Level Systems*. Baden-Baden: Nomos.

Fettelschoß, K. and Nikolenyi, C. (2009). 'Learning to Rule: Ministerial Careers in Post-Communist Democracies,' in K. Dowding and P. Dumont (eds) *The Selection of Ministers in Europe: Hiring and Firing*. Abingdon: Routledge, 204–27.

Fischer, J., Dowding, K., and Dumont, P. (2012). 'The Duration and Durability of Cabinet Ministers,' *International Political Science Review* 33(5): 505–19.

Fleischer, J. and Seyfried, M. (2015). 'Drawing from the Bargaining Pool: Determinants of Ministerial Selection in Germany,' *Party Politics* 21(4): 503–14.

Garzia, D. (2014). *Personalization of Politics and Electoral Change*. Basingstoke: Palgrave Macmillan.

Goddard, Dee (2019). 'Entering the Men's Domain? Gender and Portfolio Allocation in European Governments,' *European Journal of Political Research* 58(2): 631–55.

Grimaldi, S. and Vercesi, M. (2018). 'Political Careers in Multi-Level Systems: Regional Chief Executives in Italy, 1970–2015,' *Regional & Federal Studies* 28(2): 125–49.

Grotz, F. and Weber, T. (2017). 'Prime Ministerial Tenure in Central and Eastern Europe: The Role of Party Leadership and Cabinet Experience,' in P. Harfst, I. Kubbe, and T. Poguntke (eds) *Parties, Governments and Elites: The Comparative Study of Democracy*. Wiesbaden: Springer, 229–48.

Hallerberg, M. and Wehner, J. (2012). 'The Educational Competence of Economic Policymakers in the EU,' *Global Policy* 3(1): 9–15.

Hansen, M. E., Klemmensen, R., Hobolt, S. B., and Bäck, H. (2013). 'Portfolio Saliency and Ministerial Turnover: Dynamics in Scandinavian Postwar Cabinets,' *Scandinavian Political Studies* 36(3): 227–48.

Hayo, B. and Neumeir, F. (2016). 'Political Leaders' Socioeconomic Background and Public Budget Deficits: Evidence from OECD Countries,' *Economics & Politics* 28(1): 55–78.

Helms, L. (2018). 'Heir Apparent Prime Ministers in Westminster Democracies: Promise and Performance,' *Government and Opposition* First View, doi: 10.1017/gov.2018.22

Horowitz, M. C. and Stam, A. C. (2014). 'How Prior Military Experience Influences the Future Militarized Behavior of Leaders,' *International Organization* 68(3): 527–59.

Huber, J. D. and Martinez-Gallardo, C. (2008). 'Replacing Cabinet Ministers: Patterns of Ministerial Stability in Parliamentary Democracies,' *American Political Science Review* 102(2): 169–80.

Indriðason, I. H. and Kam, C. (2008). 'Cabinet Reshuffles and Ministerial Drift,' *British Journal of Political Science* 38(4): 621–56.

Jäckle, S. and Kerby, M. (2018). 'Temporal Methods in Political Elite Studies,' in H. Best and J. Higley (eds) *The Palgrave Handbook of Political Elites*. Basingstoke: Palgrave Macmillan, 115–33.

Jahr, S. and Edinger, M. (2015). 'Making Sense of Multi-Level Parliamentary Careers: An Introduction,' in M. Edinger and S. Jahr (eds) *Political Careers in Europe. Career Patterns in Multi-Level Systems*. Baden-Baden: Nomos, 9–26.

Jalalzai, F. (2011). 'A Critical Departure for Women Executives or More of the Same? The Powers of Chancellor Merkel,' *German Politics* 20(3): 428–48.

Jalalzai, F. (2013). *Shattered, Cracked, or Firmly Intact? Women and the Executive Glass Ceiling Worldwide*. Oxford: Oxford University Press.

Jalalzai, F. (2014). 'Gender, Presidencies, and Prime Ministerships in Europe: Are Women Gaining Ground?,' *International Political Science Review* 35(5): 577–94.

Jalalzai, F. (2018). 'Women Heads of State and Government,' in A. C. Alexander, C. Bolzendahl, and F. Jalalzai, (eds) *Measuring Women's Political Empowerment across the Globe: Strategies, Challenges and Future Research*. Basingstoke: Palgrave Macmillan, 257–81.

Jensen, J. S. (2008). *Women Political Leaders: Breaking the Highest Glass Ceiling*. Basingstoke: Palgrave Macmillan.

Jones, B. F. and Olken, B. A. (2005). 'Do Leaders Matter? National Leadership and Growth Since World War II,' *The Quarterly Journal of Economics* 120(3): 835–64.

Keane, J. (2009). 'Life after Political Death: The Fate of Leaders after Leaving High Office,' in J. Keane, H. Patapan, and P. 't Hart (eds) *Dispersed Democratic Leadership. Origins, Dynamics, and Implications*. Oxford: Oxford University Press, 279–98.

Krook, M. L. and O'Brien, D. Z. (2012). 'All the President's Men? The Appointment of Female Cabinet Ministers Worldwide,' *The Journal of Politics* 74(3): 840–55.

Lawless, J. L. (2012). *Becoming a Candidate: Political Ambition and the Decision to Run for Office*. Cambridge: Cambridge University Press.

Lupia, A. (2003). 'Delegation and Its Perils,' in K. Strøm, W. C. Müller, and T. Bergman (eds) *Delegation and Accountability in Parliamentary Democracies*. Oxford: Oxford University Press, 33–54.

MacKenzie, S. A. and Kousse, T. (2014). 'Legislative Careers,' in S. Martin, T. Saalfeld, and K. Strøm (eds) *The Oxford Handbook of Legislative Studies*. Oxford: Oxford University Press, 286–307.

Marino, B., Martocchia Diodati, N., and Verzichelli, L. (2018). 'From the Demolition to the Re-Composition of Parliamentary Elites Novelties and New Modes of Political Recruitment in the 2018 Italian Lower Chamber,' *Italian Political Science* 13(2).

Martocchia Diodati, N. and Verzichelli, L. (2017). 'Changing Patterns of Ministerial Circulation. The Italian Case in a Long-Term Perspective,' *West European Politics* 40(6): 1352–72.

Mattozzi, A. and Merlo, A. (2008). 'Political Careers or Career Politicians?,' *Journal of Public Economics* 92(3–4): 597–608.

Miller, G. J. (2005). 'The Political Evolution of Principal-Agent Models,' *Annual Review of Political Science* 8: 203–25.

Müller, W. C. (2000). 'Political Parties in Parliamentary Democracies: Making Delegation and Accountability Work,' *European Journal of Political Research* 37(3): 309–33.

Müller-Rommel, F. and Vercesi, M. (2017). 'Prime Ministerial Careers in the European Union. Does Gender Make a Difference?,' *European Politics and Society* 18(2): 245–62.

Musella, F. (2015). 'Presidents in Business: Career and Destiny of Democratic Leaders,' *European Political Science Review* 7(2): 293–313.

Öhberg, P. (2017). *Ambitious Politicians: The Implications of Career Ambition in Representative Democracy*. Lawrence, KC: University Press of Kansas.

Quiroz Flores, A. (2017). *Ministerial Survival during Political and Cabinet Change: Foreign Affairs, Diplomacy and War*. Abingdon: Routledge.

Protsyk, O. (2005). 'Prime Ministers' Identity in Semi-Presidential Regimes: Constitutional Norms and Cabinet Formation Outcomes,' *European Journal of Political Research* 44(5): 721–48.

Putnam, R. D. (1976). *The Comparative Study of Political Elites*. Englewood Cliffs: Prentice-Hall.

Reynolds, A. (1999). 'Women in the Legislatures and Executives of the World: Knocking at the Highest Glass Ceiling,' *World Politics* 51(4), 547–72.

Rose, R. (1987). *Ministers and Ministries: A Functional Analysis*. Oxford: Clarendon Press.

Rose, R. (2001). *The Prime Minister in a Shrinking World*. Boston: Polity Press.

Samuels, D. and Shugart. M. S. (2010). *Presidents, Parties, and Prime Ministers: How the Separation of Powers Affects Party Organization and Behavior*. Cambridge: Cambridge University Press.

Schlesinger, J. A. (1966). *Ambition and Politics: Political Careers in the United States*. Chicago: Rand McNally & Co.

Semenova, E. (2018). 'Recruitment and Careers of Ministers in Central Eastern Europe and Baltic Countries,' in A. Costa Pinto, M. Cotta, and P. Tavares de Almeida (eds) *Technocratic Ministers and Political Leadership in European Democracies*. Basingstoke: Palgrave Macmillan, 173–202.

Semenova, Elena, Edinger, Michael, and Best, Heinrich (2013) (eds). *Parliamentary Elites in Central and Eastern Europe: Recruitment and Representation*. London: Routledge.

Stolz, K. (2001). 'The Political Class and Regional Institution-Building: A Conceptual Framework,' *Regional & Federal Studies* 11(1): 80–100.

Stolz, K. (2003). 'Moving Up, Moving Down: Political Careers across Territorial Levels,' *European Journal of Political Research* 42(2): 223–48.

Stolz, K. (2015). 'Legislative Careers in a Multi-Level Europe,' in M. Edinger and S. Jahr (eds) *Political Careers in Europe: Career Patterns in Multi-Level Systems*. Baden-Baden: Nomos, 179–204.

Stolz, K. and Fischer, J. (2014). 'Post-Cabinet Careers of Regional Ministers in Germany, 1990–2011,' *German Politics* 23(3): 157–73.

Strangio, P. (2011). ' "The Tideless Pond that Seemed Waiting for Me": The Afterlife of Australian Prime Ministers,' in P. 't Hart and J. Uhr (eds) *How Power Changes Hands. Transition and Succession in Government*. Basingstoke: Palgrave Macmillan, 208–29.

Strøm, K. (2003). 'Parliamentary Democracy and Delegation,' in K. Strøm, W. C. Müller, and T. Bergman (eds) *Delegation and Accountability in Parliamentary Democracies*. Oxford: Oxford University Press, 55–106.

't Hart, P. and Tindall, K. (2009). 'Leadership by the Famous: Celebrity as Political Capital,' in J. Kane, H. Patapan, and P. 't Hart (eds) *Dispersed Democratic Leadership. Origins, Dynamics, and Implications*. Oxford: Oxford University Press, 255–78.

Theakston, K. (2010). *After Number 10: Former Prime Ministers in British Politics*. Basingstoke: Palgrave Macmillan.

Theakston, Kevin and Gill, Mark (2006). 'Rating 20th-ceuntry British Prime Ministers,' *British Journal of Politics and International Relation* 8: 193–213.

Thiébault, J.-L. (1991). 'Local and Regional Politics and Cabinet Membership,' in J. Blondel and J.-L. Thiébault (eds) *The Profession of Government Minister in Western Europe*. Basingstoke: Macmillan, 31–43.

Vercesi, M. (2018). 'Approaches and Lessons in Political Career Research: Babel or Pieces of Patchwork?,' *Revista Española de Ciencia Política* 48: 183–206.

Verzichelli, L. (1998). 'The Parliamentary Elite in Transition,' *European Journal of Political Research* 34(1): 121–50.

Weber, M. ([1919] 1992). *Politik als Beruf*. Stuttgart: Reclam.

Welzel, C. (2013). *Freedom Rising: Human Empowerment and the Quest for Emancipation*. Cambridge: Cambridge University Press.

Wiliarty, S. E. (2008). 'Angela Merkel's Path to Power: The Role of Internal Party Dynamics and Leadership,' *German Politics* 17(1): 81–96.

CHAPTER 13

WOMEN AND EXECUTIVE POLITICS

DIANA Z. O'BRIEN AND CATHERINE REYES-HOUSHOLDER

WOMEN have made significant inroads in national-level executive politics. These global gains were perhaps most visible in Latin America, which by 2014 was on the vanguard of women's executive power. For a few months that year, female presidents simultaneously led four Latin American countries governing approximately 40 per cent of the region's population. Chile's *presidenta* appointed a gender parity cabinet at the beginning of her first term, naming an equal number of female and male ministers. Other presidents in the region followed suit with parity or near-parity cabinets.

Yet, Latin America also demonstrates the precariousness of these advances. Despite viable female candidacies in most recent elections, men regained their monopoly on presidential power in March 2018. Women's headway in cabinets has likewise shown signs of stagnation or even regression. Brazil, which was once governed by a woman who appointed record numbers of female ministers, now features an all-male cabinet. Policy outcomes for women have also been mixed, and it is unclear how citizens have reacted to women's variable gains in executive politics.

The Latin American experience illustrates how the notable advances in women's entry into the executive branch have also been accompanied by unexpected setbacks. To address these gains and reversals, this chapter poses three related questions. Why do we need women in executive politics? How do women access executive power? What are the consequences of their inclusion?

In answering these questions, we argue that this comparatively young subfield can advance its research agenda in four ways: first, by clarifying the normative imperatives for women's presence in executive politics in modern democracies; second, by borrowing less from women and legislative politics research and integrating more insights from executive politics; third, by developing conditional hypotheses to explain women's mixed impact on policy and public opinion; and, fourth, by exploring new arenas in which women presidents, prime ministers, and cabinet officials may shape politics.

Below we begin by identifying a central paradigm driving this literature—the executive branch is gendered masculine, perpetuating women's exclusion. We next explore normative arguments for women's greater participation that are tailored to executives' distinct positions and roles. We then outline the main methodological challenges to this normatively compelling research for both quantitative and qualitative scholars. Despite these challenges, we find that existing work has produced studies of women's access to power. It shows that cultural variables and mass-level indicators of gender equality do not explain women's inclusion in executive politics as well as they predict women's presence in legislative politics. Instead, candidate supply and the existence of political opportunities are more important factors.

Beyond access, we also consider the consequences of women in the executive branch with respect to policy and audience effects. Initial findings on these fronts are decidedly mixed. Overall, female leaders and ministers appear less likely to prioritize women-friendly reforms than female legislators, possibly due to differences in their roles, constituencies and institutions. Finally, while some studies find that female executives exert different symbolic effects on citizens, others reveal null results. Building on these insights, we outline strategies for advancing research on women in executive politics.

13.1 Motivating Paradigm: The Executive Branch as a Gendered Institution

Gender—often defined as the characteristics and roles associated with biological males and females—creates power inequalities. A central assumption of the literature on women in the executive branch is that this political arena is gendered masculine. Executive branch institutions were designed (or have evolved) to privilege biological males, particularly those with masculinist traits. Qualities linked to the male gender—such as toughness and decisiveness—as well as conventionally masculine leadership styles, are highly valued within these institutions (Sjoberg 2014; see also Chapter 7 in this volume). Indeed, the executive branch is arguably more masculine than other political institutions, including legislatures, which place greater value on deliberation and collaboration (Duerst-Lahti and Kelly 1995). This institutional masculinity is in turn linked to the undervaluing of feminalist leadership and the long-standing, systematic exclusion of women.

Building on this observation, a second underlying assumption is that we cannot wholly understand the executive branch without accounting for gender. Taking gender seriously not only allows us to explain why men are overrepresented, but also how ministries are allocated (with women more likely to serve in the education and health portfolios and men more likely to serve in finance and defence ministries). Considering gender can even illuminate research puzzles that may initially seem unrelated to women and politics. For example, acknowledging that policy remits are gendered (i.e. that they privilege masculine or feminine traits) helps to explain the differential prestige and desirability of cabinet portfolios. Gendered expectations explain why some chief executives can politically capitalize on crises and others fail to do so. Gender likewise shapes how citizens perceive and judge their (fe)male leaders. Any study that does not account for gender thus lacks at least some explanatory power.

A third premise embedded in this literature is that women have been unjustly excluded from executive politics, not only to their own detriment, but also to the detriment of the political system and society. Existing literature, however, has yet to fully justify this fundamental, and highly consequential, assumption. We help rectify this oversight by clarifying the rationale for more female chief executives and cabinet ministers (i.e. a reduction in male dominance and bias in the executive branch). While far from exhaustive, these arguments can help further motivate scholarship on this topic.

13.1.1 Why Democracies Need Women in Executive Politics

Drawing heavily on theories of legislative representation, justifications for increasing women's presence in politics have focused on both the normative and policy implications of their inclusion in (and exclusion from) office. Though often applied to women in executive politics, the different roles and responsibilities of legislators and executives render these arguments more strained.

First, advocates for women's numeric (descriptive) representation rightly argue that women's exclusion from politics is fundamentally unjust. Women make up half the population and should thus hold half of all political posts. This is an especially compelling argument with respect to legislatures, which are explicitly tasked with representing the will of the people. Indeed, parliamentarians provide the only direct link between citizens and the state. It is less clear, however, that these arguments apply to executive branch posts, where the link to the public is often indirect. Citizens vote for members of parliament rather than for their prime minister, for example. Cabinet members in both presidential and parliamentary systems are appointed rather than popularly elected. The executive branch does not have the mandate to mirror the citizenry, but rather can be viewed as a team selected by the winning party or parties to govern the state. The representational burden is thus thought to be lower than in legislatures, which is in part why gender quota laws are much less likely to be applied to these offices.

Second, and again in contrast to legislators, executives are not necessarily expected to give voice to, and act on behalf of, subsets of constituents. To the contrary, chief executives and their cabinets must interpret and pursue the country's broader interests, which can be at odds with those of some legislators' constituencies (Kriner and Reeves 2015). It is thus unclear whether we can claim that women in the executive branch should act specifically on behalf of women. Even if we could normatively justify this demand, in practice the relationship between descriptive and substantive representation in the executive branch is equivocal (see more below).

Based on these arguments, one might conclude that as long as democracies elect enough female legislators, there is little need to increase women's presence in executive politics. This directly contradicts paradigmatic assumptions of the literature on gender and the executive branch, and suggests the need for stronger arguments supporting women's (s)election to these posts. Thus, rather than emphasizing descriptive and substantive representation, scholars should consider other ways in which greater gender balance in executive politics could enhance modern democracies.

An alternative argument for women's inclusion concerns the quality of executive governance. Chief executives and their ministers wield unparalleled formal power (Carey and Shugart 1998; Cox and Morgenstern 2001; Alemán and Tsebelis 2005). The high concentration of authority raises the stakes for (s)electing the most competent executives. Political talent—or the ability to exercise executive power effectively—is randomly distributed between the sexes (Phillips 1995). Women's exclusion reduces countries' pools of potential presidents, prime ministers, and cabinet officials by about half. This likely diminishes the quality of leadership. Put differently, the overwhelming and unwarranted pro-male bias constitutes a failure in meritocracy, or the ideal of governance by 'the best of the best'. The obvious solution is to allow women and men to compete on more even ground for executive offices, thereby broadening the talent pool and enhancing the quality of governance. Indeed, empirical evidence shows that greater competition between men and women at the subnational level enhances competency among elected politicians by weeding out 'mediocre' men (Besley et al. 2017).

Executives' unparalleled symbolic power likewise augments the importance of women's participation. Presidents, prime ministers, and their cabinets are the state's most visible political figures. Many have argued that the exclusion of women in politics signals that governance is primarily a male affair, discourages women citizens' participation, and ultimately erodes the legitimacy of modern democracies (Mansbridge 1999; Burns and Schlozman 2001; Clayton et al. 2019). Executives' unique symbolic roles multiply the importance of women's presence in this arena. Demonstrating that all citizens—women and men—can participate in executive politics may enhance citizens' support for, and trust in, democracies.

Finally, women's inclusion may be a necessary (though likely not sufficient) condition for positively regendering executive branch politics and meeting citizens' evolving demands. Global trends, including the decline of war and citizens' increased reliance on the welfare state, suggest a feminization of executive branch politics (Barnes and O'Brien 2018). Chief executives and their ministers may, in turn, need to demonstrate more gender diverse traits and leadership styles. Although biological males can display stereotypically feminine characteristics (and vice versa), the entry of more women in executive politics may also help address demands for certain types of leaders. This could further enhance the quality and legitimacy of modern democracies, particularly in light of the executive branch's unique policy-making and symbolic powers.

13.2 CHALLENGES TO STUDYING WOMEN AND EXECUTIVE POLITICS

Increasing women's access to national executive posts could improve democracies worldwide. This observation, in turn, motivates research on how women gain and wield executive power. Yet, scholars face significant challenges in pursuing this research due to (1) limited observations and randomization; and (2) difficulty in data acquisition. The first challenge pertains mostly to quantitative scholarship, while the second affects both quantitative and qualitative research.

13.2.1 Limited Observations and Randomization

For many years, there seemed to be too few women in executive office to generate reliable statistical estimates of the causes and consequences of women's access to power. Women first gained executive power via ministerial positions over a hundred years ago. Early examples of female cabinet members include Alexandra Kollontai (People's Commissar for Social Welfare in the Russian Soviet Federative Socialist Republic, 1917–18), Constance Markievicz (Minister for Labour of the Irish Republic, 1919–22), and Margaret Bondfield (British Minister of Labour, 1929–31). The first female head of government in the modern era, Sirimavo Bandaranaike became prime minister of Sri Lanka in 1960, and the first female president, Argentina's Isabel Perón, came to power in 1974. Yet, despite these early inroads, men continue to dominate national executive politics. As of January 2018, women hold approximately 18 per cent of ministerial posts and 7 per cent of chief executive positions worldwide.

Though women remain underrepresented in the executive branch, particularly as heads of government, their numbers are now sufficiently large to support statistical analyses. Beginning in the 1990s, scholars began using quantitative methods to study female cabinet appointees (Davis 1997; Reynolds 1999). A number of more recent works examine female ministers globally (Krook and O'Brien 2012) and in virtually every region of the world, including Latin America (Escobar-Lemmon and Taylor-Robinson 2005, 2016), sub-Saharan Africa (Arriola and Johnson 2014), and Western (Claveria 2014) and Eastern Europe (Bego 2014). While small numbers continue to challenge the study of female chief executives, scholars have found several workarounds. Some increase the number of observations by taking a global, rather than regional, perspective (Jalalzai 2013) or achieve this by studying male and female candidates for executive office, including party leaders (O'Brien 2015). Others use duration models to examine the time until women first enter office (O'Brien 2015; Barnes and O'Brien 2018), or model the election of a female chief executive as a rare event (Thames and Williams 2013).

A more intractable challenge concerns credibly inferring causality via the potential outcomes framework. Here the problem is identifying a random source of variation in the explanatory variables of interest. Countries with female heads of government, and governments that appoint many female cabinet ministers, differ from those that do not on a number of dimensions. Research on the causes and consequences of women's access to executive power thus often suffers from endogeneity issues. Some studies have ameliorated such concerns by leveraging natural (O'Brien and Rickne 2016) or survey (Schwindt-Bayer and Reyes-Housholder 2017) experiments, but this work remain rare.

13.2.2 Difficulty in Data Acquisition

Although relatively few women occupy executive-level positions, this political arena generates a wealth of other data, such as media coverage of executives' activities as well as their (auto)biographies. Executive decision-making nevertheless remains difficult to observe, as it often occurs in closed-door meetings and informal stages and settings. It is particularly challenging for gender scholars to gain insights by interviewing executive officials (an approach widely used in the women in legislative politics literature).

To begin with, executive institutions' masculinist characteristics mean that gender topics are often seen as 'niche' issues, relevant only for small constituencies of women activists, and hence insufficiently important to merit discussion with a researcher. Men may also refuse interview requests because they fear accusations of (presumably unintentional) sexism, or fail to recognize their own privilege as men. Women operating in the executive branch may prefer to discuss topics other than gender because they are concerned that their gender will overshadow their other, more highly valued qualities. In short, gender is often seen as a relatively unimportant, but also highly sensitive issue.

Finally, even when scholars do secure interviews with (former) presidents, prime ministers, and cabinet officials, gender often operates in ways that can be difficult for them—and the researcher—to discern. Respondents may fail to see the ways in which 'politics as usual' is gendered, and because the male-dominated culture is so deeply ingrained in executive institutions, female interviewees may not recognize or acknowledge sexism. Together these issues reduce the availability and reliability of data.

A final challenge concerns media reports on executive politics. Although press coverage of executive activities abounds, it is hardly 'objective' data that researchers can unproblematically employ in historical or statistical analyses (see Chapter 29 in this volume). Issues related to women and gender receive less attention than economic and security issues, and this coverage is often sexist. Researchers must thus account for the potential inaccuracies in these second-hand accounts, which could require triangulating data sources. Gender scholars often critically interpret the coverage of female and male executives, sometimes by explicitly applying a gendered analytical lens (Murray 2010).

13.3 Existing Scholarship on Women and Executive Politics

Despite these limitations, a growing literature explores the causes and consequences of women's inclusion in the executive branch. Scholars to date have paid the most attention to women's entry into office, particularly cabinet posts. A secondary, but rapidly accumulating group of studies considers the policy and audience effects of women's inclusion. Much of this scholarship borrows theories concerning women in legislatures and tests them on executive posts. Together, these studies suggest that the results from scholarship on female parliamentarians do not generalize to female cabinet ministers and heads of government.

13.3.1 Accessing Executive Power

Quantitative and qualitative research has examined many possible predictors of women's variable presence in office, which we categorize into three groups: culture and development, selection criteria, and political opportunities. This line of research suggests that the effects of societal levels of gender equality and economic advancement indirectly operate through increasing the number of female legislators. Formal rules and informal norms, on the other hand, create diverse obstacles to women's entry into the executive branch. Finally, crises can open opportunities for women seeking chief executive posts.

13.3.1.1 *Culture and Development*

Scholars have imported versions of modernization theories from the literature on women in legislatures to establish whether these factors also predict women's entry into executive politics (Norris and Inglehart 2003). However, the notion that more gender egalitarian and economically developed societies include more women in the executive branch does not consistently hold. Indeed these cultural factors sometimes operate in ways that undermine such hypotheses.

Whereas some works find that economic development and women's education levels (Arriola and Johnson 2014; Bego 2014) and religious traditions (Reynolds 1999) are positively correlated with female ministers, others do not (Escobar-Lemmon and Taylor-Robinson 2005; Krook and O'Brien 2012; Stockemer and Sundström 2017). Contradicting cultural theories, research also consistently finds that women's workforce participation is negatively associated with women's inclusion in cabinets (Escobar-Lemmon and Taylor-Robinson 2005; Arriola and Johnson 2014; Barnes and O'Brien 2018). Gender equality at the mass level also fails to explain women's (s)election as chief executives (Jalalzai 2008). Indeed, the first female heads of government emerged in highly gender-segregated developing states, such as the aforementioned Sri Lanka in the 1960s and Argentina in the 1970s.

The role of these mass-level factors thus appears primarily indirect, operating through their effect on the overall supply of women with prior political experience (Blondel 1987; Escobar-Lemmon and Taylor-Robinson 2005; Whitford et al. 2007; Krook and O'Brien 2012). Gender equality and economic development can bolster the number of women in legislatures (Inglehart and Norris 2003), which is the most consistent predictor of women's inclusion in the executive branch. In parliamentary systems, this is because ministers are often drawn directly from the legislature. Female parliamentarians thus act as the 'supply force for the presence of women in ministerial lines' (Whitford et al. 2007: 563). Even in presidential systems, where ministers do not have to come from the national assembly, Escobar-Lemmon and Taylor-Robinson (2005) suggest that the presence of female legislators increases the number of women eligible for cabinet posts. Women's presence is likewise positively correlated with the (s)election of female presidents and prime ministers (Jalalzai 2013).

13.3.1.2 *Selection Rules and Norms*

In contrast to mass-level factors, women's inclusion is more influenced by the rules and norms governing (s)election to executive posts (see also Chapter 16 in this volume). One of the primary factors affecting selection procedures is the distinction between presidential and parliamentary regimes, though regime type operates differently for cabinets and heads of government. Women's presence in ministerial positions tends to be somewhat higher in presidential than parliamentary systems (Bego 2014; Stockemer and Sundstrom 2017), but women are more likely to become prime ministers than presidents (Jalalzai 2013; Thames and Williams 2013). The positive impact of presidential regimes on women's selection as ministers may result from presidents' greater discretion in assembling their cabinets (Blondel 1985). The negative impact on women's likelihood of governing could relate to the fact that direct presidential elections require candidates to finance and mount national campaigns.

Political parties' preferences also shape selection criteria. In Europe and Latin America, left-leaning governments are more likely to place women in cabinets (Goddard 2020; Moon and Fountain 1997; Reynolds 1999; Escobar-Lemmon and Taylor-Robinson 2005; Claveria 2014; Reyes-Housholder 2016) and to nominate women to high prestige portfolios (Studlar and Moncrief 1999; Escobar-Lemmon and Taylor-Robinson 2005). Looking across fifty-three established democracies, Stockemer and Sundström (2017) find that the positive effect of leftist and liberal governments is even more pronounced after 2000. The hypothesis that left parties are more conducive to women's rise to chief executive posts has received more mixed support. On the one hand, a global analysis from 1960 to 2010 suggests that women are more likely to come from left-wing parties than those on the right (Baturo and Gray 2018), and Latin America's recent female presidents mostly subscribed to a leftist ideology. On the other hand, Müller-Rommel and Vercesi (2017) show that in Europe female prime ministers are more likely to come from centre-right parties.

In addition to regime type and party preferences, women's entry is also shaped by informal ways of doing politics and often unstated selection rules. Women initially ascended to chief executive offices in countries governed by family dynasties (Genovese and Steckenrider 2013; Jalalzai 2016). Marital and father-daughter relationships, especially in Asia, seemed to be an important selection factor (Richter 1990; Thompson 2002). Opportunities for women to uphold their family's grip on power tended to emerge when no male relative was available to lead (Richter 1990). Despite an early emphasis on family ties, these connections were never as salient in established parliamentary democracies, and scholars question their applicability to the post-2005 rise of Latin American *presidentas* (Reyes-Housholder and Thomas 2018).

Though family ties are becoming less important as women's participation in politics becomes more normalized (Baturo and Gray 2018), scholars have continued to examine the role of other informal selection norms. Unwritten selection criteria can relate to candidates' qualifications such as background characteristics, credentials, and connections. Escobar-Lemmon and Taylor-Robinson (2016) find that male and female cabinet appointees in five presidential democracies bring similar political capital resources to their positions. Because female ministers have comparable backgrounds to men, and experience equal treatment in their posts, they can be viewed as integrated into male appointment norms. Examining women's ministerial careers in federal, provincial, and territorial cabinets, Tremblay and Stockemer (2013) find that Canadian women holding cabinet portfolios differ from female legislators with no ministerial responsibilities with respect to education, parliamentary experience, and age when first elected. A comparison of twenty-three advanced industrial democracies shows no statistically significant gender differences in subsequent career paths of most departing ministers (Claveria and Verge 2015). This literature therefore suggests that in order to gain executive power, women must (and indeed do) obtain similar qualifications as men. At the same time, these studies help to explain women's relatively reduced ministerial presence, as men are more likely to meet these criteria than women.

Norms about selection criteria extend beyond individual-level characteristics. Annesley et al. (2019) note that ministers are often chosen in accordance with informal rules about which groups must be represented in cabinet. Although frequently contested, such norms concerning women's inclusion in executive office have diffused across countries and regions (Bauer and Okpotor 2013; Jacob et al. 2014), and today some baseline level of women's ministerial presence is expected in many states. At the same time, only a handful of countries have formally established gender quotas for cabinets. And, despite a handful of high-profile gendered-balanced cabinets in countries like Chile, Canada, France, Italy, Spain, and Sweden, male-dominated cabinets remain the informal norm (Franceschet and Thomas 2015). Arguably, no country has established a norm of gender parity, or a fifty-fifty distribution of ministerial posts between women and men.

Finally, the power and remit of a particular post affects the number of women considered viable contenders. Institutional power shapes the desirability of executive positions, meaning that some posts are imbued with more authority and resources, and have more prestigious remits. While no formal rule excludes women from the most prestigious executive posts, these positions are both highly coveted and gendered masculine, and thus more likely to be held by men. Female cabinet ministers are more likely to occupy low-prestige portfolios with feminine remits (Goddard 2019; Reynolds 1999; Studlar and Moncrief 1999; Escobar-Lemmon and Taylor-Robinson 2009). Similarly, to the extent that women have acted as national leaders, they are more likely to serve in dual executives where power is shared between the president and prime minister. The female leader often acts as a ceremonial figurehead with real authority exercised by her male counterpart (Jalalzai 2013).

13.3.1.3 *Political Opportunities*

Finally, scholars have dedicated special attention to the role played by political opportunity structures. In particular, women are sometimes able to leverage political openings resulting from crises in order to access chief executive posts. Early research suggested that women became presidents and prime ministers in unstable or transitioning countries (Jalalzai 2008; Genovese and Steckenrider 2013; Montecinos 2017). Indeed, twentieth century examples from Asia seem to substantiate this explanation (Richter 1990; Thompson 2002), though the rise of female presidents in Latin America appears less related to regime crisis (Reyes-Housholder and Thomas 2018).

Recent explanations for the rise of female prime ministers focus on the role of party-level crises (Wiliarty 2008; Beckwith 2015; O'Brien 2015). Beckwith argues that women are more likely to take over party leadership when scandals or electoral failures oust the male party leader. Such situations create uncertainty about the future success of the party, effectively dissuading some male party elites from competing and clearing the way for female leadership. O'Brien shows that women are more likely to head parties that are losing vote share, which further suggests that these women must reverse their parties' fortunes in order to become prime minister.

Political opportunities appear to operate differently according to regime type. Women in parliamentary regimes are more likely to come to power in weakened parties. In contrast, female presidents in Latin America have gained office by succeeding popular male incumbents from the same party. Research on Latin America further suggests that representational critiques launched against strong parties can motivate them to nominate women as president. Female candidates allow these parties to signal novelty and change, credibly commit to 'feminine' issues such as dealing with corruption, and better mobilize women voters (Reyes-Housholder and Thomas forthcoming). Together, these findings suggest that different modes of leadership selection across regime types create divergent gendered outcomes.

13.3.2 Executive Gender and Policy Effects

Influenced by theories of the descriptive-substantive representation link in legislatures, scholarship on the policy impact of female executives has focused largely on women's issues. A second line of research addresses conventionally masculine policy domains, including conflict and defence. Both sets of studies yield mixed results.

13.3.2.1 *Female-Friendly Policies*

Because of women's unique life experiences, scholars expect female legislators to promote gender equality and female-friendly policies more than their male counterparts. A vast set of empirical studies supports this prediction. Yet, research on executive politics has yielded inconsistent findings. Women's greater presence in cabinets is positively associated with policies facilitating paid employment during motherhood (Atchison and Down 2009; Atchison 2015), as well as status gains in gender-equality issues, like reproduction and gender violence (Annesley et al. 2015). Other studies yield null results (Annesley et al. 2010; Annesley et al. 2015).

Compared to female legislators, female chief executives seem to pursue women-friendly and gender equality legislation far less, and their efforts seem to vary even more widely. Explanations for this variation among heads of government have focused on idiosyncratic differences related to leaders' feminism, individual psychologies and personalities, career trajectories, or country contexts (Bauer and Tremblay 2011; Davidson-Schmich 2011; Von Wahl 2011; Genovese and Steckenrider 2013; Macaulay 2017). Feminist attitudes and actors interact with institutions to shape outcomes (Waylen 2016).

Beyond individual personalities and preferences, the behaviour of women in the executive branch is explained by the incentives these female leaders face. Reyes-Housholder (2019b) argues that female leaders in Latin America possess greater incentives (core constituencies of women) and capacities (access to pro-women policy-making expertise) to promote pro-women reforms. In contrast, Sykes (2009: 38) argues that Anglo systems discourage women from acting on behalf of women, claiming that 'female cabinet ministers have generally needed to put aside feminalist priorities and preferences and embrace the masculinism that Anglo institutions require'. Together, these insights suggest that scholars should not simply ask whether women in the executive branch promote gynocentric policy, but why politicians of both sexes take up (or ignore) these issues. Recognizing the motivations and constraints facing executive branch politicians is also a further reminder that the descriptive-substantive link should not be a central argument for women's inclusion in this branch of government.

13.3.2.2 *Masculine Policies*

Another body of scholarship addresses women's effects on policy areas stereotypically associated with men: military conflict and defence. The fact that these are among the most conventionally masculine policy domains—and that they are central to the functioning of the state and responsibilities of the executive branch—doubly augments interest in this topic. However, as with female-friendly policy, initial work in this area yields mixed findings.

In some instances, women appear to make different, more stereotypically feminine policy decisions. Female foreign policy and defence leaders sometimes promote gender-focused aid and 'pro-feminist [policy] rhetoric' (Bashevkin 2014). Female defence ministers facilitate access to frontline combat positions for women in the military (Barnes and O'Brien 2018). In other cases women conform to—or even strengthen—the masculinist status quo. Female chief executives and defence ministers increase defence spending and conflict behaviour in advanced industrialized democracies (Koch and Fulton 2011). Female foreign ministers likewise decrease foreign aid spending (Lu and Breuning 2014). Female chief executives appear slightly more likely to initiate a military dispute (Horowitz et al. 2015). Female-led states are more likely to have their disputes reciprocated, and consequently escalate disputes more than male-led governments (Post and Sen 2020).

What explains these mixed findings on women's decision-making on these traditionally masculine issues? Existing literature suggests that women may be responding to their diverse political environments. In some cases, the regimes that are most willing to select women for conventionally male-dominated posts (such as defence ministers) are also more conflict averse (Barnes and O'Brien 2018). It is unsurprising that women's presence is associated with dovish policies in these circumstances. In other cases, female politicians find themselves combating gender stereotypes. Female chief executives are thought to escalate disputes because male leaders perceive them to be weaker. Female leaders thus adopt more aggressive foreign policies in order to gain credibility in masculinized leadership positions (Koch and Fulton 2011; Dube and Harish 2020).

Although these initial mixed findings are far from conclusive, they do seem to contradict the expectation that women's entry into executive politics and the spread of democratic peace go hand in hand (see above). The results also may suggest that it is unrealistic to expect the few women who have entered the executive branch to immediately upend centuries-long traditions of masculinist bias and preferences. As we explain below, future work in this area will require scholars to account for the different political contexts that shape incentives and constraints for women and men to challenge the status quo. Significant regendering of executive politics, particularly in highly masculine policy areas, is more likely to occur over the long- rather than the short-term.

13.3.3 Executive Gender and Audience Effects

Does the gender of executive office holders influence citizens' behaviours, attitudes, and beliefs? Symbolic representation theories posit that the mere presence of women in office sends cues that shape political participation, attitudes toward government, and views on gender equality. Yet, the handful of initial studies conducted so far have yielded both positive and null results concerning the impact of women in this arena.

Several projects examine citizens' attitudes and behaviour in cross-national perspective. O'Brien (2019) uses public opinion data on 269 parties in 35 countries between 1976 and 2016, to demonstrate that female-led parties are perceived as more moderate than male-led organizations, even when accounting for voters' prior beliefs about the party and the organization's stated policy positions. Using World Values Survey (WVS) data, Liu and Banaszak (2017) find that female ministers are associated with higher levels of political participation in established democracies. Alexander and Jalalzai (2016) use a broader set of WVS data to suggest that female executives are associated with higher voting rates and greater political interest for both men and women. Female chief executives are also linked to support for female leaders, though only in low democracy states. Focusing on twenty advanced industrial democracies, Beauregard (2018) shows that women's numeric representation in cabinets is linked to protest participation, but has no effect on (or even decreases) other forms of political activity. Finally, Barnes and Taylor-Robinson (2018) find women's presence in high-profile, typically masculinized cabinet portfolios to be positively associated with both women's and men's satisfaction with, and confidence in, government, but uncorrelated with more positive evaluations of women's ability to lead.

A subset of work focuses special attention on Latin America, a site of notable female gains. Morgan and Buice (2013) find that women's presence in Latin American cabinets bolsters men's support for women as political leaders. Barnes and Jones (2018) likewise show that women's appointments to provincial cabinets in Argentina are associated with female (but not male) constituents willingness to contact local-level officials. Concerning chief executives, Reyes-Housholder and Schwindt-Bayer (2016) show that the presence of a female president is correlated with higher levels of women's political activity. Yet, Carreras (2017) finds no immediate impact of viable female presidential candidates on women's political engagement in the region.

In addition to generating mixed results, these observational studies are limited in their ability to infer causality. Because female leaders are not randomly assigned, polities that (s)elect them may also express different attitudes and behaviours, evoking the classic endogeneity problem: these women may not cause, but instead are a consequence of, these other factors. The following section elaborates on ways to overcome these issues with experimental approaches.

13.4 DIRECTIONS FOR FUTURE RESEARCH

Existing research offers an important set of results on how women access power. We know, for example, that women's presence in legislatures opens doors for women seeking executive posts. Informal norms establish baseline expectations about women's inclusion, and variation in selection criteria affects women's numeric representation. Likewise, moments of crisis can create opportunities to deviate from the male-dominated status quo. At the same time, preliminary studies also yield mixed findings, particularly with respect to women's impact. Women's presence does not generate uniform policy changes and citizens do not respond to female chief executives and ministers in predictable ways.

These findings likely reflect both the nuances of political life and the relative youth of this subfield. They also suggest conditional relationships that have yet to be fully theorized. Research on women in executive politics can further develop by more fully integrating both the executive politics and gender and politics literatures, thereby explicating the gendered consequences of the institutional rules and norms regulating executive branch politics. Doing so reveals that women face specific challenges and opportunities in terms of access, governing, and public perceptions.

13.4.1 Rethinking and Broadening Pathways to Power Research

Despite the blossoming scholarship on women's access to executive office, scholars have yet to adequately theorize how pathways to power may be gendered. Existing research generally ignores the fact that entry into the executive branch is a multi-stage process. Work on female chief executives, for example, contrasts states that have been female led to those that have not, and therefore only considers the final step in this process. Consequently, we know little about where and why women are exiting the pipeline to power. More studies should compare cases where women ran in elections and won to those in which they ran and lost, and those in which they failed to emerge as viable candidates.

Questions about the mechanisms driving the negative correlation between presidentialism and female leadership are related to this problem of under theorized pathways to power. Voter or elite biases against women may account for this relationship, but the extent to which such biases harm female candidates are likely influenced by the size of the selectorate, campaign regulations, and the formalization and personalization of the overall selection procedures. Work establishing when, where, and why women are losing out in leadership selection processes can help solve outstanding puzzles in the literature on women in executive politics.

Focusing on pathways to power also raises question about which kinds of women reach executive posts. Future studies can further test Escobar-Lemmon and Taylor-Robinson's (2016) argument concerning the similarities between female and male ministers by examining cabinet appointees in regions outside of Latin America, as well as female presidents and prime ministers. This is crucial not only for identifying the supply pool for executive positions, but also for understanding the consequences of women's access to power. If the women (s)elected have identical backgrounds to their male counterparts, women's inclusion—although still normatively justified by other arguments—may not radically alter executive politics. Indeed, this may explain some of the null findings vis-à-vis policy and audience effects.

13.4.2 Rethinking and Broadening Policy Impact Research

To enrich the study of women's impact on executive politics, researchers should look beyond gendered policy arenas to examine alternative dimensions of policy and also gendered differences in governing styles. At the same time, we counsel caution when asking whether women are transformational leaders. Women in executive politics are sometimes incentivized to innovate in terms of legislative content and leadership style, but also face constraints in doing so. Research should therefore explore the conditions under which women and men legislate and lead both differently and similarly.

Turning to policy impacts, we showed above that scholarship on chief executives' promotion of pro-women legislation has often posited idiosyncratic explanations, such as female leaders' career trajectories and personalities. Yet, individual life experiences may be less determinant for chief executives than for legislators. In part because of the complexity of their role and the daily crises they must manage, executives rely more heavily on bureaucrats and experts to help them prioritize issues and craft long-term policy solutions.

Moving forward, we recommend a more systematic theorization of female and male leaders' motivations and constraints for innovating policy content. Reyes-Housholder (2019b), for example, argues that female presidents are more likely to mobilize women voters, and therefore often face greater incentives to pursue pro-women reforms. Female presidents are also more likely to network with elite feminists who then provide them with greater policy-making expertise, thus enhancing their capacity to legislate on behalf of women. Not all women, however, are incentivized to pursue female-friendly policy. Indeed, Reyes-Housholder concludes that female presidents who do not mobilize women and network with feminists are unlikely to do so. Likewise, female prime ministers dependent on maintaining the confidence of overwhelmingly male legislatures—or female ministers selected by male chief executives—may be less likely to innovate. To the contrary, we would expect these women to behave similarly to their male counterparts.

Beyond feminine and masculine issue areas, researchers should also pursue broader questions surrounding the construction of the policy agenda. For example, Greene and O'Brien (2016) assess whether the presence of a female leader is associated with issue entrepreneurship and greater issue diversity on parties' policy platforms. Future work could likewise examine whether women are more likely to hue to party platforms and honour their campaign promises, particularly if women are especially likely to come to power via institutionalized parties.

New work should also move beyond policy outcomes to examine the ways in which women deploy executive power and fulfil its unique roles. As in policy research, scholarship on governing styles will likely generate competing hypotheses and reveal conditional relationships. On the one hand, we may expect few across-the-board differences. Many sociological and psychological studies show that specific positions or roles determine leadership styles more than gender (Eagly and Johannesen-Schmidt 2001). Men and women, in turn, will fulfil their duties according to their identities as executives, not their gender-role identities. The masculine nature of executive office may also pressure women to act like their male predecessors and/or adopt a conventionally masculine style and discourse (as was famously the case for Britain's first female prime minister, Margaret Thatcher).

On the other hand, we may anticipate at least some differences in the ways women and men govern. Women's traditional exclusion from executive politics clearly affects their access to power, which may in turn encourage different, and perhaps more democratic, ways of governing. If citizens are more likely to select female leaders during crises and scandals, for example, they may also expect women to behave differently from their male counterparts. This could motivate women to prioritize anti-corruption issues, unilaterally oust officials accused of corruption, and/or more carefully monitor their own behaviour in office. Likewise, if women campaign in ways that positively highlight their gender identity (Reyes-Housholder 2018), then the public may be more likely to reward them for cultivating a stereotypically feminine leadership style while in office.

These competing theoretical expectations suggest a series of questions that extend far beyond whether women in the executive promote female-friendly or masculine policies. Under what conditions, for example, do women display more democratic and horizontal governance styles? Shair-Rosenfield and Stoyan (2018) detect differences in the use of unilateral executive power contingent on presidential popularity. When their approval ratings are high, female presidents issue fewer decrees than men in Latin America. Yet, when their ratings are low, female and male presidents behave similarly. Future work in this vein could examine whether women are less likely to act in personalistic ways and if this is a function of the types of parties that select female leaders. Likewise, work should ask whether and when female leaders cooperate more with the legislature and their coalition partners.

Gender likely not only affects governing styles, but is also conditionally salient depending on the broader institutional context. Consider, for example, the delegation of power. O'Brien et al. (2015) and Reyes-Housholder (2016) both show that the sex of the chief executive influences the appointment of female cabinet ministers. Their findings suggest that these differing governing styles are contingent on the incentives facing women in power. Female prime ministers are less likely to appoint female ministers than their left-leaning male counterparts (O'Brien et al. 2015), while female presidents are more likely to do so (Reyes-Housholder 2016). Among other questions, future research can explore the conditional relationships between leaders' gender and cabinet instability, examining whether and when female leaders are more or less likely to replace ministers, for example in times of crisis.

13.4.3 Rethinking and Broadening Audience Effects Research

The empirical evidence on citizens' perceptions of, and reactions to, female leaders is also preliminary and inconclusive, with some (but not all) studies yielding null results. Just as women govern differently than men under some conditions but not others, male and female leaders sometimes send different signals to—and are evaluated differently by—the electorate. We reiterate our call for more nuanced research on this front, particularly scholarship theorizing and testing the conditional relationship between executive gender and citizens' behaviours, attitudes, and opinions.

With respect to audience effects, a foundational and yet understudied question concerns perceptions of the 'success' of women in executive politics, particularly citizens' approval ratings. Higher levels of public approval enable executives to lead more effectively, pursue their legislative agendas, and protect their legacies. Female presidents have lower ratings than their male counterparts, controlling for potential confounders such as the state of the economy (Carlin et al. 2019; Reyes-Housholder 2019a), suggesting that differential citizen evaluations may impede women's successful governance.

Assessments of women's 'successful' performance in executive politics will likely affect both their longevity in office and the subsequent (s)election of women for these posts. Approval ratings are closely related to likelihoods of impeachment or coups in presidential systems (Pérez-Liñán 2007), prime ministers' tenures (Müller-Rommel and Vercesi 2017), as well as re-election rates in virtually all modern democracies. Ministers' popularity likewise helps determine their longevity in their posts. Müller-Rommel and Vercesi (2017) show that female prime ministers have a shorter duration in office, another sign that female leaders possibly face greater challenges in governing. Yet, the exact nature and scope of these gendered challenges to female leadership remain unknown.

One gendered obstacle to achieving high public approval ratings may relate to the often-cited double binds and different—indeed higher—expectations for women in office (Murray 2010; O'Brien 2015). A number of factors may drive gendered divergences in expectations, including media coverage and electoral campaigns. If by virtue of their novelty, for example, female presidents raise expectations for change, then they may be more susceptible to disappointing the public. Similarly, Reyes-Housholder (2019a) shows that Latin American citizens punish female presidents more for corruption scandals. She argues that the public expects these women to be more honest and less corrupt than men, and thus holds them to higher moral standards.

Approval ratings, in turn, likely condition the symbolic consequences of women's presence in office. Most obviously, they can affect perceptions about women's ability to govern and the likelihood of other women accessing executive power in the near future. The mixed results concerning female leaders' effects on citizens' attitudes and behaviour may thus be explained by variation in the popularity and perceived effectiveness of female leaders. The burden on women is particularly great for first female presidents and prime ministers. Highly successful female leaders will likely erode traditional gender stereotypes about women in politics, while failed female leaders will likely reinforce these ideas.

Finally, complementing observational studies, natural and survey experiments can increase the validity of findings concerning audience effects. In addition to minimizing endogeneity problems, experimental research could also help isolate mechanisms that amplify and/or inhibit these outcomes. Evidence from a survey experiment conducted in Brazil, for example, suggests that citizens respond differently to male and female executives at the subnational level. A hypothetical female governor positively affected women's political attitudes, engagement, and anticipated political activity, but had a lesser effect on men's attitudes (Schwindt-Bayer and Reyes-Housholder 2017). This study focused on novelty, but other survey experiments can test whether governing style and approval ratings may also condition the relationship between executives' gender and citizen behaviours and attitudes.

13.5 Conclusions

This chapter surveys the rapidly developing literature on women's variable inclusion in multiple types of national executive offices worldwide. This line of research clearly shares a set of underlying assumptions: the executive branch is a highly masculine institution that has systematically excluded women and cannot be understood without considering gender (i.e. the norms, stereotypes, expectations, and power relations applied to men and women). Empirical work, in turn, has made impressive inroads in explaining women's access to power, but to date has yielded mixed results concerning the consequences of women's inclusion. These mixed findings in turn suggest that a myriad of exciting research avenues lie ahead.

The career of Angela Merkel, Germany's current Chancellor and the *de facto* leader of Europe, exemplifies the importance of this area of study. Gender influenced not only her rise to power in a party weakened by a corruption scandal (Wiliarty 2008; Beckwith 2015), but also her strategies to maintain and enhance that power. Her cabinet appointments, policy goals, and public image have each been shaped by gender, in ways that can be both subtle and more overt. Failing to take gender seriously thus results in an incomplete portrait of executive politics.

The Merkel case illustrates that executive branch scholars must pay greater attention to gendered dynamics, particularly as women's presence grows. Women and politics researchers, in turn, should also incorporate insights from the broader executive politics literature. Doing so will facilitate the development of rigorous, context-dependent theories that account for the unique opportunities and constraints facing female heads of government and ministers. The ascension of women like Merkel, Ellen Johnson Sirleaf, and Jacinda Ardern—coupled with the persistence and re-emergence of male dominance in other countries and posts—suggest that the study of women's uneven gains in this arena, and their contingent impact on policy and governance, are among the most innovative and exciting areas of research in executive politics.

References

Alemán, E. and Tsebelis, G. (2005). 'The Origins of Presidential Conditional Agenda Setting Power in Latin America,' *Latin American Research Review* 9(3): 3–26.

Annesley, C. and Gains, F. (2010). 'The Core Executive: Gender, Power and Change,' *Political Studies* 58(5): 909–29.

Annesley, C., Engeli, I., and Gains, F. (2015). 'The Profile of Gender Equality Issue Attention in Western Europe,' *European Journal of Political Research* 54(3): 525–42.

Annesley, C., Beckwith, K., and Franceschet, S. (2019). *Cabinets, Ministers, and Gender*. New York: Oxford University Press.

Arriola, L. and Johnson, M. C. (2014). 'Ethics Politics and Women's Empowerment in Africa: Ministerial Appointments to Executive Cabinets,' *American Journal of Political Science* 58(2): 495–510.

Atchison, A. (2015). 'The Impact of Female Cabinet Ministers on a Female-Friendly Labor Environment,' *Journal of Women, Politics & Policy* 36(4): 388–414.

Atchison, A. and Down, I. (2009). 'Women Cabinet Ministers and Female-Friendly Social Policy,' *Poverty & Public Policy* 1(2): 1–23.

Barnes, T. D. and Jones, M. P. (2018). 'Women's Representation in the Argentine National and Subnational Governments,' in L. A. Schwindt-Bayer (eds) *Gender and Representation in Latin America*. New York: Oxford University Press, 121–39.

Barnes, T. D. and O'Brien, D. Z. (2018). 'Defending the Realm: The Appointment Works of Female Defense Ministers Worldwide,' *American Journal of Political Science* 62(2): 355–68.

Barnes, T. D. and Taylor-Robinson, M. (2018). 'Women Cabinet Ministers and Empowerment of Women: Are the Two Related?,' in. A. Alexander, C. Bolzendahl, and F. Jalalzai (eds), *Measuring Women's Political Empowerment across the Globe: Strategies, Challenges and Future Research*. Basingstoke: Palgrave Macmillan, 229–55.

Bashevkin, S. (2014). 'Numerical and Policy Representation on the International Stage: Women Foreign Policy Leaders in Western Industrialised Systems,' *International Political Science Review* 35(4): 409–29.

Baturo, A. and Gray, J. (2018). 'When Do Family Ties Matter? The Duration of Female Suffrage and Women's Path to High Political Office,' *Political Research Quarterly* 71(3): 695–709.

Bauer, G. and Okpotor, F. (2013). '"Her Excellency": An Exploratory Overview of Women Cabinet Ministers in Africa,' *Africa Today* 60(1): 76–97.

Bauer, G. and Tremblay, M. (2011) (eds). *Women in Executive Power: A Global Overview*. New York: Taylor & Francis.

Bauer, G. and Okpotor, F. (2013). '"Her Excellency": An Exploratory Overview of Women Cabinet Ministers in Africa,' *Africa Today* 60(1): 76–97.

Beauregard, K. (2018). 'Women's Representation and Gender Gaps in Political Participation: Do Time and Success Matter in a Cross-national Perspective?,' *Politics, Groups, and Identities* 6(2): 237–63.

Beckwith, K. (2015). 'Before Prime Minister: Margaret Thatcher, Angela Merkel, and Gendered Leadership Contests,' *Politics & Gender* 11(4): 718–45.

Bego, I. (2014). 'Accessing Power in New Democracies: Women's Path of Least Resistance in Postcommunist Eurpoe,' *Political Research Quarterly* 67(2): 347–60.

Besley, T., Folk, O., Persson, T., and Rickne, J. (2017). 'Gender Quotas and the Crisis of the Mediocre Man: Theory and Evidence from Sweden,' *American Economic Review* 107(8): 2204–42.

Blondel, J. (1985). *Government Ministers in the Contemporary World*. London: SAGE Publishing.

Blondel, J. (1987). *Political Leadership: Towards a General Analysis*. London: SAGE.

Burns, N., and Schlozman, K. L. (2001). *The Private Roots of Public Action: Gender, Equality, and Political Participation*. Cambridge, MA: Harvard University Press.

Carey, J. M. and Shugart, M. S. (1998). *Executive Decree Authority*. Cambridge: Cambridge University Press.

Carlin, Ryan E., Miguel Carreras, y Gregory J. Love. 'Presidents' Sex and Popularity: Baselines, Dynamics and Policy Performance»' *British Journal of Political Science*, 2019, 1-21. https://doi.org/10.1017/S0007123418000364.

Claveria, S. (2014). 'Still a 'Male Business'? Explaining Women's Presence in Executive Office,' *West European Politics* 37(5): 1156–76

Claveria, S. and Verge, T. (2015). 'Post-ministerial Occupation in Advanced Industrial Democracies: Ambition, Individual Resources and Institutional Opportunity Structures,' *European Journal of Political Research* 54(4): 819–35.

Clayton, A., O'Brien, D. Z., and Piscopo, J. (2019). 'All Male Panels? Representation and Democratic Legitimacy,' *American Journal of Political Science* 63(1): 113–29.

Cox, G. and Morgenstern, S. (2001). 'Latin America's Reactive Assemblies and Proactive Presidents.' *Comparative Politics* 33(2): 171–89.

Davidson-Schmich, L. K. (2011). 'Gender, Intersectionality, and the Executive Branch: The Case of Angela Merkel,' *German Politics* 20(3): 325–41.

Davis, R. H. (1997). *Women and Power in Parliamentary Democracies: Cabinet Appointments in Western Europe. 1968–1992*. Lincoln, NE: University of Nebraska Press.

Dube, O. and Harish, S. P. (2020). 'Queens,' *Journal of Political Economy*. doi: 10.1086/707011

Duerst-Lahti, G. and Kelly, R. M. (1995) (eds). *Gender Power, Leadership, and Government*. Ann Arbor, MI: University of Michigan Press.

Eagly, A. H. and Johannesen-Schmidt, M. C. (2001). 'The Leadership Styles of Women and Men,' *Journal of Social Issues* 57(4): 781–97.

Escobar-Lemmon, M. and Taylor-Robinson, T. M. (2005). 'Women Ministers in Latin American Government: When, Where, and Why?' *American Journal of Political Science* 49(4): 829–44.

Escobar-Lemmon, M. and Taylor-Robinson, M. M. (2009). 'Getting to the Top: Career Paths of Women in Latin American Cabinets,' *Political Research Quarterly* 62(4): 685–99.

Escobar-Lemmon, M. and Taylor-Robinson, M. T. (2016). *Women in Presidential Cabinets: Power Players or Abundant Tokens?* New York: Oxford University Press.

Franceschet, S. and Thomas, G. (2015). 'Resisting Parity Gender and Cabinet Appointments in Chile and Spain,' *Politics & Gender* 11(4): 643–64.

Genovese, M. A. and Steckenrider, J. S. (2013) (eds). *Women as Political Leaders: Studies in Gender and Governing*. New York: Routledge.

Goddard, D. (2019). 'Entering the Men's Domain? Gender and Portfolio Allocation in European Governments,' *European Journal of Political Research* 58(2): 631–55.

Goddard, D. (2020). 'Examining the Appointment of Women to Ministerial Positions across Europe: 1970–2015,' *Party Politics*, doi: 10.1177/1354068819878665

Greene, Z. and O'Brien, D. Z. (2016). 'Diverse Parties, Diverse Agendas? The Parliamentary Party's Role in Platform Formation,' *European Journal of Political Research* 55(3): 435–53.

Horowitz, M. C., Stam, A. C., and Ellis, C. M. (2015). *Why Leaders Fight*. New York: Cambridge University Press.

Inglehart, R. and Norris, P. (2003). *Rising Tide: Gender Equality and Cultural Change around the World*. Cambridge: Cambridge University Press.

Jacob, S., Scherpereel, J. A., and Adams, A. (2014). 'Gender Norms and Women's Political Representation: A Global Analysis of Cabinets, 1979–2009,' *Governance* 27(2): 321–45.

Jalalzai, F. (2008). 'Women Rule-Shattering the Executive Glass Ceiling,' *Politics & Gender* 4(2): 1–27.

Jalalzai, F. (2013). *Shattered, Cracked, or Firmly Intact? Women and the Executive Glass Ceiling Worldwide*. New York: Oxford University Press.

Jalalzai, F. (2016). *Women Presidents of Latin America: Beyond Family Ties?* New York: Routledge.

Koch, M. T. and Fulton, S. A. (2011). 'In the Defense of Women: Gender, Office Holding, and National Security Policy in Established Democracies', *The Journal of Politics* 73(1): 1–16.

Kriner, D. L. and Reeves, A. (2015). 'Presidential Particularism and Divide-the-Dollar Politics', *American Political Science Review* 109(1): 155–71.

Krook, M. L. and O'Brien, D. Z. (2012). 'All the President's Men? The Appointment of Female Cabinet Ministers Worldwide', *The Journal of Politics* 74(3): 840–55.

Liu, S.-J. S. and Banaszak, L. A. (2017). 'Do Government Positions Held by Women Matter? A Cross-national Examination of Female Ministers' Impacts on Women's Political Participation', *Politics and Gender* 13(1): 132–62.

Lu, K. and Breuning, M. (2014). 'Gender and Generosity: Does Women's Representation Affect Development Cooperation?', *Politics, Groups, and Identities* 2(3): 313–30.

Macaulay, F. (2017). 'Dilma Rousseff (2011–2016): A Crisis of Governance and Consensus in Brazi', in Verónica Montecinos (ed.) *Women Presidents and Prime Ministers in Post-Transitional Contexts*. London: Palgrave Macmillan UK, 123–40.

Mansbridge, J. (1999). 'Should Blacks Represent Blacks and Women Represent Women? A Contingent "Yes"', *The Journal of Politics* 61(3): 628–57.

Montecinos, V. (2017). *Women Presidents and Prime Ministers in Post-Transition Democracies*. Basingstoke: Palgrave Macmillan.

Moon, J. and Fountain, I. (1997). 'Keeping the Gates? Women and Ministers in Australia, 1970–1996', *Australian Journal of Political Science* 32: 455–66.

Morgan, J. and Buice, M. (2013). 'Latin American Attitudes toward Women in Politics: The Influence of Elite Cues, Female Advancement, and Individual Characteristics', *American Political Science Review* 107(4): 644–62.

Müller-Rommel, F. and Vercesi, M. (2017). 'Prime Ministerial Careers in the European Union: Does Gender Make a Difference?', *European Politics and Society* 18(2): 245–62.

Murray, R. (2010). *Cracking the Highest Glass Ceiling: A Global Comparison of Women's Campaigns for Executive Office*. Santa Barbara, CA: Praeger.

O'Brien, D. Z. (2015). 'Rising to the Top: Gender, Political Performance, and Party Leadership in Advanced Industrial Democracies', *American Journal of Political Science* 59(4): 1022–39.

O'Brien, D. Z. (2019). 'Female Leaders and Citizens' Perceptions of Political Parties', *Journal of Elections, Public Opinion and Parties* 29(4): 465–89.

O'Brien, D. Z. and Rickne, J. (2016). 'Gender Quotas and Women's Political Leadership', *American Political Science Review* 110(1): 112–26.

O'Brien, D. Z., Mendez, M., Peterson, J. C., and Shin, J. (2015). 'Letting Down the Ladder or Shutting the Door: Female Prime Ministers, Party Leaders, and Cabinet Ministers', *Politics and Gender* 11(4): 689–717.

Pérez-Liñán, A. (2007). *Presidential Impeachment and the New Political Instability in Latin America*. Cambridge: Cambridge University Press.

Phillips, A. (1995). *The Politics of Presence*. Oxford: Clarendon Press.

Post, A. S. and Sen, P. (2020). 'Why Can't a Woman Be More Like a Man? Female Leaders in Crisis Bargaining', *International Interactions* 46(1): 1–27.

Reyes-Housholder, C. (2016). 'Presidentas Rise: Consequences for Women in Cabinets?', *Latin American Politics and Society* 58(3): 3–25.

Reyes-Housholder, C. (2018). 'Women Mobilizing Women: Candidates' Strategies for Accessing the Presidency'. *Journal of Politics in Latin America* 10(1): 69–97.

Reyes-Housholder, C. (2019a). 'A Theory of Gender's Role on Presidential Approval Ratings in Corrupt Times,' *Political Research Quarterly*, https://doi.org/10.1177/1065912919838626

Reyes-Housholder, C. (2019b). 'A Constituency Theory for the Impact of Female Presidents,' *Comparative Politics* 51(3): 429–41.

Reyes-Housholder, C. and Schwindt-Bayer, L. (2016). 'The Impact of *Presidentas* on Women's Political Activity,' in Janet M. Martin and MaryAnne Borrelli (eds) *The Gendered Executive: A Comparative Analysis of Presidents, Prime Ministers and Chief Executives*. Philadelphia: Temple University Press, 103–23.

Reyes-Housholder, C. and Thomas, G. (2018). 'Latin America's Presidentas: Challenging Old Patterns, Forging New Pathways,' in L. A. Schwidt-Bayer (eds) *Gender and Representation in Latin America*. New York: Oxford University Press, 19–38.

Reyes-Housholder, C. and Thomas, G. (forthcoming). "Gendered Incentives, Party Support and Female Presidential Candidates." *Comparative Politics*.

Reynolds, A. (1999). 'Women in the Legislatures and Executives of the World: Knocking at the Highest Glass Ceiling,' *World Politics* 51(4): 547–72.

Richter, L. K. (1990). 'Exploring Theories of Female Leadership in South and Southeast Asia.' *Pacific Affairs* 63(4): 524–40.

Schwindt-Bayer, L. and Reyes-Housholder, C. (2017). 'Citizen Responses to Female Executives: Is It Sex, Novelty, or Both?,' *Politics, Groups and Identities* 5(3): 373–98.

Shair-Rosenfield, S. and Stoyan, A. (2018). 'Gendered Opportunities and Constraints: How Executive Sex and Approval Influence Executive Decree Issuance,' *Political Research Quarterly* 71(3): 586–99.

Sjoberg, L. (2014). *Gender, War, and Conflict*. London: Polity Publisher.

Stockemer, D. and Sundström, A. (2017). 'Women in Cabinets—The Role of Party Ideology and Government Turnover,' *Party Politics* 24(6): 663–73.

Studlar, D. T. and Moncrief, G. F. (1999). 'Women's Work? The Distribution and Prestige of Portfolios in the Canadian Provinces,' *Governance: and International Journal of Policy and Administration* 12(4): 379–95.

Sykes, P. (2009). 'Incomplete Empowerment: Female Cabinet Ministers in Anglo-American Systems,' in John Kane, Haig Patapan, and Paul 't Hart (eds) *Dispersed Democratic Leadership: Origins, Dynamics, & Implications*. Oxford: Oxford University Press, 37–59.

Thames, F. and Williams, M. (2013). *Contagious Representation: Women's Political Representation in Democracies around the World*. New York: New York University Press.

Thompson, M. R. (2002). 'Female Leadership of Democratic Transitions in Asia,' *Pacific Affairs* 75(4): 535–55.

Tremblay, M. and Stockemer, D. (2013). 'Women's Ministerial Careers in Cabinet, 1921–2010: A Look at Socio-Demographic Traits and Career Experiences,' *Canadian Public Administration* 56(4): 523–41.

Von Wahl, A. (2011). 'A "Women's Revolution from Above"? Female Leadership, Intersectionality, and Public Policy under the Merkel Government,' *German Politics* 20(3): 392–409.

Waylen, G. (2016). *Gender, Institutions, and Change in Bachelet's Chile*. New York: Palgrave.

Whitford, A. B., Wilkins, V. M., and Ball, M. G. (2007). 'Descriptive Representation and Policymaking Authority: Evidence from Women in Cabinets and Bureaucracies,' *Governance* 20(4), 559–80.

Wiliarty, S. E. (2008). 'Chancellor Angela Merkel—A Sign of Hope or the Exception that Proves the Rule?,' *Politics & Gender* 4(3): 485–96.

....

CHAPTER 14

PERSONALITIES AND BELIEFS OF POLITICAL EXECUTIVES

....

MARK SCHAFER AND GARY SMITH

14.1 INTRODUCTION
....

THE study of the beliefs and personality of political executives has a rich and important history in the field, and yet there is much room for future work in this area in terms of theory, methods, and empirical findings. Indeed, there is a bit of irony associated with this research programme: when we discuss political executives casually, we almost always intuit that their unique personalities and beliefs matter, and yet the field, in spite of its richness and intuitiveness, remains underresearched. We return to this theme in our concluding section of this chapter, but we begin by discussing the central questions and methods used in the field, and an examination of many of the important findings generated thus far. It is an exciting research area, to be certain, and certainly one that is ripe for many more contributions.

14.2 RESEARCH QUESTIONS IN THE FIELD
....

In this section we identify many of the questions pertaining to political executives that are being asked by researchers in this area. Here we briefly specify and explain some of these questions, leaving for the next section of our chapter the discussion of findings pertaining to them. We focus on three broad sets of question areas that are common in the field: (1) the kinds of beliefs and personality characteristics that researchers think matter; (2) beliefs and personality characteristics as dependent variables, which means the description or comparison of political executives, or the analysis of changes over time for an executive; and, (3) beliefs and personality characteristics as the independent variables, specifically the causal effect of these variables on a wide array of political behaviours and outcomes. Later in this section we also discuss some of the methods that are common in the area, and how the methods have evolved over time. But first we begin with a discussion of why we think the beliefs and personalities of political executives should matter.

We are not interested in differences in beliefs and personalities of political executives per se. While noting how political executives differ may be interesting parlour talk, much more important is the *effect* that these differences have on executive behaviour, for instance why one executive may choose war vs. accommodation, or assistance vs. uninvolvement, or alliance vs. isolation. Given that the behaviour of political executives (policies, preferences, advocacy activities, etc.) is the fundamental topic we care about in our study of them, if beliefs and personalities affect behaviour, then studying these characteristics in executives is essential. Each individual is unique, meaning he or she each has a different array of beliefs and personality characteristics. By extension, this means that who the individual is in the executive position will affect the behaviours of the office. A simple thought experiment makes the point clear: replace Adolf Hitler in history with, say Gandhi or Jimmy Carter or Nelson Mandela, and imagine how history would have been different. Each of these individuals is unique and would bring a different set of beliefs and personalities—and, therefore, behavioural propensities—to each situation, meaning that patterns regarding policies and interactions would certainly have been different.

History, of course, does not let us replay things, and, of course, there are important structural pieces of most historical moments that affect who comes to power and what they do: post-World War I Germany chose Hitler to govern, and did not choose someone like Gandhi. But, virtually no political psychologist argues that situations and structures do not matter. Nonetheless, it most certainly is the case that the individual who occupies the executive office, with his or her unique array of beliefs and personality characteristics, will matter in interaction with the situation. As we write this chapter, US President Donald Trump is finishing his second year in office, a tumultuous two years indeed. Trump was elected by a very narrow, almost random margin (indeed, Hillary Clinton won the popular vote). This means that under the exact same structural conditions Trump came to be president instead of Clinton. And yet, by any stretch of the imagination, it seems clear that, in spite of the same structural antecedent conditions and the near randomness of the electoral outcome, their behaviours in the executive office would be very, very different.

Focusing on the unique beliefs and personality characteristics of an individual is radically different from other approaches, particularly those that are grounded in rational-actor models (see Chapter 5 in this volume). While the former investigates the uniqueness of each individual actor's beliefs and personalities, the latter assumes-away uniqueness and assumes instead that all actors similarly pursue simple cost-calculating, means-ends rationality. Not only is that intuitively unsatisfying (after all, we continuously see the unique, less-than-rational behaviour of individuals every time we go out driving or shopping or having a pint), but it is also well-supported with some excellent experimental work in fields such as political psychology and behavioural economics (Simon 1972; Khaneman and Tversky 1979; Tversky and Khaneman 1986; Berejikian and Early 2013; Linde and Vis 2017): the empirical evidence is clear that individuals are not good rational calculators and their behaviours are deeply affected by their beliefs, personality structures and cognitive limitations. In order to understand the behaviour of political executives, therefore, we must study their beliefs and personalities. The next question to consider is what we mean by beliefs and personalities, and what the various constructs are in these areas that researchers have included in their study of executive psychology.

Conceptually, of course, there are multiple conceptual components of individual-level psychological differences, including such things as traits, motives, affect, behaviour, beliefs, and attitudes (see Chapter 4 in this volume). As Greenstein (1969) points out, psychologists typically consider all of these to be part of the broad concept of *personality*. However, as Greenstein also points out, others, particularly those studying psychology in field of political science (where much of the research on political executives can be found), have found it useful to distinguish these components into two broad categories: *personality* and *cognition*, with the former pertaining to the more unconscious parts of psychological makeup and the latter pertaining to the more conscious parts. Then, building on Winter's (2013) distinctions, we include two sets of constructs in the unconscious category of personality: traits and motives. And, we use the more vernacular term *beliefs* to pertain to those conscious, cognitive components of an individual's psychology, those things that an individual *thinks* about. While we focus more extensively on these different constructs in the next section of the chapter, we provide short overviews here to help frame some of our discussion on important questions in the field. In the following paragraphs we discuss each of these constructs in more detail.

In the field of psychology, traits are the most common psychological construct investigated, though the most prominent personality trait research programme, the Big Five (Goldberg 1990; Gerber et al. 2011) is less common in the analysis of political executives. David Winter describes traits as the 'public, observable element of personality,' and as 'consistencies of style readily noticed by other people,' which tend to 'reflect the language of "first impressions"' (Winter 2013: 427). He argues that traits are the things we see in people in quite casual and impressionistic ways, such as how kind or outgoing or adventurous a person is. The Big Five traits are: warmth/agreeableness, introversion/extraversion, openness to experience, conscientiousness, and neuroticism. However, Winter (2013: 440–1) argues that the utility of the Big Five is limited when it comes to investigating specifically political behaviour; there are not overly obvious directional hypotheses for the effect of things like introversion and conscientiousness on political actions like conflict escalation and bargaining behaviour. Despite Winter's (2013) insights about the difficulty of constructing logical hypotheses for the Big Five traits in the domain for executive behaviour, some scholars have assessed the Big Five traits of key US presidents (Rubenzer et al. 2000). The authors find that almost all US presidents can fit into one or more personality typologies that are built around the Big Five traits.

These categories are: dominators, introverts, good guys, innocents, actors, maintainers, philosophers, and extroverts (Rubenzer et al. 2000: 412).

Motives are unconscious personality characteristics that push an individual in goal-seeking directions. They are often referred to as drives or needs. The most prolific research programme investigating the motives of political executives is David Winter's work on need for power, affiliation, and achievement (1973, 1993; Winter and Stewart 1977). Political hypotheses are easily derived from motives, such as higher need for affiliation is likely to correlate with more diplomatic or peaceful approaches to conflict situations.

Many cognitive characteristics are also fairly easy to hypothesize effects on political phenomena. On the conscious end of the psychological perspective, cognitive characteristics pertain to the thoughts and beliefs held by a political executive. They include such things as schemas, attitudes, stereotypes, and prejudices. It is easy to hypothesize that someone with highly negative prejudice against a political opponent may be more likely to escalate aggressive political behaviour toward that opponent. One prominent research programme in this area is called image theory (Boulding 1959; Holsti 1967; R. Cottham 1977; M. Cottham 1985, 1994; R. K. Herrmann 1985, 1986; Herrmann and Fischerkeller 1995; Hymans 2006), which assesses the object-specific image a political executive holds toward other, with the expectation that such images influence policy choices. Another prominent research programme grounded in cognitive theory is called the operational code (Leites 1953; George 1969). Rather than limiting the analysis to a single object-specific other, operational code analysis looks at an executive's broad political belief *system*. This includes beliefs about human nature and other actors in the political universe, beliefs about self and the utility of self's conflict vs. cooperation strategies and tactics, and beliefs about control and timing of political actions.

One of the most prominent quantitative research programmes in the field includes variables from across these three areas (traits, motives, and cognitions). Margaret Hermann's (1980) Leadership Trait Analysis (LTA) includes seven different variables that she anticipates as potential explanatory variables for political behaviour. The variables are: Distrust, Belief in Ability to Control Events, Need for Power, In-group Bias, Self Confidence, Conceptual Complexity, and Task Orientation. Some of these are more cognitive in nature, such as distrust and in-group bias, others look more like traits, such as self-confidence and task orientation, and, obviously, need for power is a motive. Hermann's work also frequently combines some of these variables to construct broader indicators, such as whether the executive is a constraint challenger or respecter (see Chapter 24 in this volume), or whether she or he is open (or not) to information.

Many research contributions to the study of the beliefs and personality of political executives place these characteristics on the dependent side of the equation. This often shows up in two different kinds of studies. First are descriptive and comparative studies. Researchers describe the beliefs and personalities of a political executive in a psychobiographic manner to paint a full picture of the depth psychology of the executive (George and George 1956; Renshon 2003; Schultz 2005; Walter 2007). Other studies use either qualitative or quantitative methods to compare a small number of political executives, asking if there are key differences or similarities in their personalities and cognitions that might help us better understand broader patterns (Barber 1972; Etheredge 1975; Johnson 1977; Walker and Schafer 2000; Feng 2005; Robison 2006).

The second common use of beliefs and personalities as dependent variables pertains to changes in the executive over time. Some researchers have asked if a major shock to the system (such as a major life experience or an international catastrophe or crisis) can fundamentally change a political executive's beliefs (e.g. Renshon 2008). Others have looked for slower changes over time, or patterns we might call learning effects (e.g. Crichlow 1998; Walker and Schafer 2000).

In our opinion, the most important questions being investigated in the field place the beliefs and personalities of political executives on the independent variable side of the equation, asking if particular characteristics or patterns have an effect on political behaviour. Sometimes the political behaviour pertains to the individual executive, such as a preference for a particular policy or a specific action taken by the individual. Other times the political behaviour of interest pertains to the entity that the political executive is leading, such as a state's escalation in an international conflict, or a significant shift in the bargaining behaviour of state negotiators.

Executive personality and beliefs may be investigated qualitatively or quantitatively (more on methods below), and often includes (but is not limited to) variables from the research programmes noted above. What is different here is the range of dependent variables of interest (i.e. the political behaviour of executives or the entities they lead). Researchers have asked about the effect of an executive's personality traits on subsequent processes by the national legislature (e.g. Crichlow 2002). Others have looked at political behaviours in terms of risk acceptance or aversion (e.g. Khaneman and Tversky 1979; Fuhrmann and Horowitz 2014; Horowitz et al. 2015). Some ask if the beliefs and personality characteristics of a political executive increase or decrease the chance of a state intervening with another state (e.g. Hermann and Kegley 1995; Saunders 2011).

Some puzzling behaviour investigated in the field pertains to bargaining strategies and tactics taken by state actors. Others have wondered if executive beliefs affect international behaviour toward both democracies and non-democracies, or if beliefs can explain different behaviours toward these different regime types (e.g. Schafer and Walker 2006). Researchers have investigated the effect of the beliefs and personalities of political executives on cooperation patterns, such as levels of interdependence.

Perhaps the most common broad category of dependent variables investigated in conjunction with these psychological independent variables is conflict behaviour, which is, of course, a central broad question in the field of international relations. Researchers have investigated if motives, traits, and beliefs matter for inter-state crisis behaviour (Keller 2005; van Esch and Swinkels 2015), militarized interstate disputes (Smith 2014a, 2014b; Schafer et al. 2016; Smith et al. 2016; Schwarz and Smith 2017), game-theoretic escalatory behaviour (Kydd 2005), the efficacy of the use of military force (Driver 1977), and conflict behaviour by specific states, such as the United States (Foster and Keller 2014), United Kingdom (Dyson 2006; Schafer and Walker 2006),

Israel (Crichlow 1998), China (Feng 2005), Turkey (Gorener and Ucal 2011; Kesgin 2013; Cuhadar et al. 2017a, 2017b), and many others.

One prominent research programme has asked whether beliefs and personality characteristics of political executives have an effect on diversionary behaviour by the state. The diversionary theory of war in the field of international relations predicts that some political executives may escalate an international conflict situation when the political executive faces some domestic problems, such as low approval poll numbers or a poorly performing economy. The idea is that the constructed or elevated international crisis will distract constituents away from the domestic problems (Foster and Keller 2010, 2014; Keller and Foster 2012).

Finally, some researchers have asked if beliefs and personality characteristics of political executives have an effect on the decision-making process in an executive's regime. We know from other research in political science and elsewhere that the quality of the decision-making process has a probabilistic effect on the quality of outcomes; in other words, how decision-making is done matters. Researchers in this area have wondered if the executive's own personality characteristics have an effect on such process components as selection of advisors, methodological rigor in the process, openness to information, undue group efficacy or overconfidence, and high levels of bias in the decision-making process (Schafer and Crichlow 2010).

Methods in this area have included both qualitative and quantitative approaches. Much of the early research in the field was marked by thick, qualitative studies about the depth psychology of an individual based upon his or her psychobiographic life histories (Erikson 1975; Post 2004) or the cognitive beliefs of an individual based upon his or her writings and public comments (Holsti 1970; McLellan 1971; Johnson, 1977; Walker 1977).

Beginning in the late 1970s and evolving quickly since then, however, has been a particular type of quantitative research that now is most prominent in the field as it continues to develop as a science. Since researchers do not have easy access to political executives such that they could administer standard psychometric measures, methods were developed to measure beliefs and personality characteristics 'at-a-distance' (Hermann 1980; Walker et al. 1998). Researchers developed systematic content-analysis methods using publicly available verbal material of executives. The idea is that what individuals say and how they say things can provide key insights into their personalities and beliefs. These methods, in combination with modern computing capabilities and today's big-data world, mean we are now able to scientifically and quantitatively assess the beliefs and personality characteristics of a very wide array of political executives, both past and present, and include those measurements in our best statistical models of executive behaviour.

14.3 REVIEW OF EXISTING RESEARCH

The ways in which the beliefs and personalities of individual political executives can affect political outcomes has garnered limited research in the field compared to other areas. However, there has been growing attention in the scholarly literature to the effect that individual political executives, and their idiosyncratic personality characteristics and general beliefs, can affect a variety of political outcomes of interest. This section discusses findings from the literature on beliefs and personalities with a special—though by no means exclusive—emphasis on foreign policy behaviours[1] and preferences. This review of select empirical findings in the literature will explore a number of different approaches in the field that have contributed to our broader understanding of the role of the beliefs and personality characteristics of political executives.

One important question that has received attention in the literature concerns the beliefs and personality characteristics of political executives as the dependent variables. Are these characteristics consistent over time? Are there learning effects? Or are leaders' characteristics sensitive to certain 'shocks'? Walker and Schafer (2000) assessed the operational code of Lyndon Johnson during two key periods in his administration: (1) the period that ended with Johnson ordering Operation Rolling Thunder; and (2) the period between Operation Rolling Thunder and his decision to begin an open-ended ground campaign in South Vietnam (Walker and Schafer 2000: 536). The authors find that Johnson experienced a significant negative shift in his belief about his ability to shape events, and attributed a greater role to chance in politics. Additionally, they find that he became more risk-averse and showed a greater propensity to shift between words and deeds (Walker and Schafer 2000: 537). In the same article, Walker and Schafer (2000) explored how Johnson's operational code differed when he was talking about domestic politics, foreign affairs (excluding Vietnam), and the Vietnam conflict. They find few differences between Johnson's operational code when he spoke about foreign and domestic politics. Importantly, however, they find a significant negative shift in Johnson's operational code when speaking about Vietnam (Schafer and Walker 2000: 538).

Jonathan Renshon (2008) explored the stability of beliefs of George W. Bush over time. He argues that the study of belief stability of individuals has received far less attention in the literature than is warranted (2008: 823). Using operational code analysis, the author looked for shifts in George W. Bush's belief system over key phases of his presidency: (1) the transition from candidate to president, (2) the transition from pre-9/11 to post-9/11, and (3) the transition from post-9/11 political environment to his last year in office (Renshon 2008: 828). He finds that the transition to the presidency reinforced his generally positive belief about the nature of the political universe. Conversely, the trauma of the unexpected attacks on 9/11 resulted in a significant and negative shift in Bush's beliefs (Renshon 2008: 835).[2] Finally, Renshon finds that Bush experienced a

---

[1] Obviously, personalities and beliefs of political executives can affect political behaviour both domestically and internationally. However, the vast majority of the research in these areas has looked at the effect of these characteristics on foreign policy behaviour. This follows the somewhat arbitrary divide of the political psychology field particularly in the United States, where researchers in the subfield of American politics have tended to focus on voting patterns and other mass political phenomenon, whereas researchers in the subfield of international relations focused more on political elites.

[2] This finding mirrors the findings of Walker et al. (1998) that indicate a significant and negative shift in Jimmy Carter's cooperative view of the political universe as a result of international political shocks.

slight decrease in his belief in his ability to control historical events when comparing Bush's final year in office to his post-9/11 period (Renshon 2008: 836–7).

These findings indicate that beliefs can shift over time (e.g. Crichlow 1998) or in response to an executive's political situation, role, or external shocks (e.g. Renshon 2008). Moreover, it is apparent that political executives may hold different beliefs when working in different policy domains, which can be discerned by observing speech material specific to each policy area rather than aggregating material into a single indicator (e.g. Walker and Schafer 2000).

Turning to personality as the independent variable, one of the earliest attempts to link a single political executive's personality to a political outcome is *Woodrow Wilson and Colonel House: A Personality Study* by Alexander George and Juliet George (1956). One of the central puzzles the authors attempted to solve was why Woodrow Wilson refused to make concessions demanded by the Senate during the attempted ratification of the Treaty of Versailles (George and George 1956). Wilson's refusal to negotiate had been observed well before the outbreak of World War I. Wilson spearheaded the passing of several controversial pieces of legislation over the objections of his own party in both houses of Congress[3] (George and George 1956). The Georges argue that such rigidity on Wilson's part stemmed from his relationship with an overbearing and impossible-to-please father. As a result, Wilson perceived every initiative he supported as a reflection of his self-worth and accomplishment (George and George 1956). Inevitably, the heavy-handed tactics used by Wilson to pass various domestic measures soured his relationship with key members of his own party in both houses of Congress and led to the re-assertion of its authority when the time came to ratify the Treaty of Versailles. The Georges' work is still considered one of the most thorough and rigorous psychobiographical studies of a political executive (Post 2013: 466). Despite this exemplary work, the psychobiographical approach has largely fallen out of favour because of the subjective nature of such research and its limited generalizability.

Others have also explored the way in which life experiences can affect an executive's risk behaviour, which, according to recent research, is a type of personality trait (Frey et al. 2017). Horowitz and colleagues examine how certain key life experiences can affect the willingness of political executives to accept greater risks and use more forceful foreign policy tools (2015). Building on theories from social psychology, the authors' key findings indicate that military experience is central to understanding why leaders may be more or less risk-acceptant (Horowitz et al. 2015). They find that executives with a history of military service, but no combat experience, are more likely to believe that military force is useful for resolving foreign policy disputes (Horowitz et al. 2015). They also find that leaders who serve in the military and see frontline combat are more likely to see military force as something that is costly. This is because they have seen first-hand

---

[3] Wilson utilized a technique that would make the bills in question a matter of party policy, thus requiring all Democrats in the House and Senate to vote in favour of them despite personal objections. Failure to vote with the party would result in the withdrawal of party support during re-election and less favourable considerations for committee seats.

the human costs of using the military as a foreign policy tool (Horowitz and Stam 2014; Horowitz et al. 2015). Rather than focusing explicitly on personality, Horowitz and colleagues focus on how life experiences can influence beliefs about the efficacy of the use of force and risk-acceptance more broadly.[4]

Other scholars have opted to investigate the importance of a variety of cognitive constructs. These cognitive constructs include images of the other and the operational codes of political executives. Image theory explores the effect that object-specific beliefs a political executive holds about other actors can influence the executive's foreign policy choices (Boulding 1959). In particular, Boulding emphasized the images of general hostility or friendliness of other actors (1959). Several researchers have applied this theoretical programme to the empirical study of foreign policy behaviours of political executives (Holsti 1967; Cottam 1977; Cottam 1985, 1994; Herrmann 1985, 1986; Herrmann and Fischerkeller 1995). An example of this research is Ole Holsti's (1962) analysis of John Foster Dulles and how his images of the Soviet Union affected his policy recommendations. He finds that Dulles's image of the Soviet Union as an inherently hostile and untrustworthy actor led him to make more aggressive policy recommendations (Holsti 1962).

Other work shifted away from focusing exclusively on the so-called 'enemy image' to include other images political executives hold about other actors. Richard Cottam (1977) argued that the enemy image is not the only way to approach how perceptions of other actors can affect foreign policy preferences. He argued that a combination of three key components of an image have an effect on the relationship with other. These include: perceptions of threat, perceptions of capabilities, and perceptions of social status (Cottam 1977). When an executive perceives another actor as more threatening, with weaker military capabilities, and a lower cultural status, there will be a more antagonistic relationship (Cottam 1977). Later, Richard Herrmann (1985) named this combination of image components the *degenerate* image, and argued that it should be associated with a political executive's willingness to intervene in the affairs of another state and assert its control over those affairs (Herrmann 1985).

Another approach that considers the beliefs of political executives is called the operational code, which focuses on an executive's beliefs about the political universe in which he or she operates. Nathan Leites (1953) initiated the operational code research programme, supported by the RAND corporation to investigate what US foreign policy practitioners saw as the unpredictable bargaining behaviour of the Soviet Union. Leites argued that there was a pattern of broad psychological characteristics that was consistent across members of the Soviet Politburo; further, this operational code could be traced back to the personalities of Stalin and Lenin (1953). Later, Alexander George (1969) sought to make this construct more precise by focusing only on cognitive beliefs rather than on broader psychological patterns as Leites (1953) did. George (1969) argued that a leader's operational code could be determined by answering ten key

---

[4] Their data on military experience is part of a larger data set they constructed called the Leadership Experience and Attributes Dataset (LEAD). For detailed description of their data see Ellis et al. (2015).

questions about the executive's political worldview. These ten questions consisted of five philosophical beliefs (e.g. how a leader perceives the political universe and the actors that occupy it) and five instrumental beliefs (e.g. the beliefs executives hold about the self and self's possible strategies and tactics in the political universe). In the early years of operational code research, there was a heavy reliance on thick, qualitative answers to these questions. In particular, there was an emphasis on investigating the operational codes of key US foreign policy decision-makers (e.g. Holsti 1967, 1970; McLellan 1971; Anderson 1973; Tweraser 1974; Caldwell 1976; Johnson 1977; Walker 1977).

In the last two decades, however, scholars have generated methods that provide quantitative measures of the philosophical and instrumental beliefs of political executives[5] (Walker et al. 1998, 2003). As with earlier studies applying operational code analysis to political executives, the research in this area has focused almost exclusively on foreign policy behaviours and preferences. For example, Walker et al. (1999) examine the conflict management behaviours of George H. W. Bush and Bill Clinton in the Post-Cold War era. The authors find that Clinton's beliefs focused more on cooperative actions, while Bush's beliefs focused more on cooperative promises. They also find that Bush was more flexible in his foreign policy choices than his successor. Taken together, the authors conclude that while Bush was less cooperative than Clinton, he was also more flexible (Walker et al. 1999: 618–19).

Schafer and Walker (2006) use operational code methods to investigate implications for the democratic peace. They explore the operational codes of Bill Clinton and Tony Blair to determine if there are differences in the two executives' beliefs about non-democratic and democratic actors in the international system. The authors demonstrate that both political executives see democratic states as more peaceful and both executives are optimistic about the likelihood of achieving their political goals with democratic states (Schafer and Walker 2006: 578). However, one interesting difference between the two executives is that Clinton has a more cooperative orientation toward non-democracies than Blair (Schafer and Walker 2006: 573).

An additional approach to the study of political executives incorporates both beliefs and personality. The psychoanalytic approach considers how the needs and drives of political leaders and how those factors affect information processing techniques and management structures. For example, Jerrold Post (2003) categorizes leaders into broad personality typologies (i.e. narcissistic personality, obsessive personality, and paranoid personality). Post points out that leaders who are narcissistic or paranoid tend to process information inefficiently because of aversion to appearing ignorant (in the case of the narcissist) or a rigid belief that his or her worldview is the true interpretation of the world around them (in the case of the paranoid leader). These different typologies provide useful insights into management styles. Post argues that the narcissist will create a management structure in which he or she is at the centre, but also one in which group

---

[5] This method is referred to as the Verbs in Context System (VICS). For a thorough explanation of the coding procedures, see Walker et al. (1998 or 2003).

members are exploited. Similarly, paranoid leaders will create management structures that encourages a competitive advisory environment. The leader who fits in the category of the obsessive-compulsive personality tends to be open to information, almost to a fault. At the same time, he or she prefers an advisory structure that is methodical and thorough (Post 2003: 81–100).

Another prominent research paradigm in the study of political executives is the LTA approach (Hermann, 1980). LTA includes seven psychological characteristics as being key for explaining policy behaviour and management style. These seven characteristics are: need for power, belief in ability to control events, conceptual complexity, self-confidence, task-orientation, distrust, and in-group bias[6] (Hermann 1980). Hermann's early study using LTA explored how these characteristics affect an executive's conduct of foreign policy (either unilaterally or multilaterally) and how they relate to overall aggression. She finds that distrust and need for power are negatively correlated with an interdependent foreign policy orientation, while conceptual complexity is positively correlated with an interdependent foreign policy orientation (Hermann 1980: 32).

Margaret Hermann's early quantitative work (1980) stemmed a research agenda that applies LTA to various political outcomes. Some have studied how leadership style can affect the ways in which political executives manage the foreign policy decision-making process (Barber 1972; Johnson 1974; George, 1980; Crabb and Mulcahy 1988; Burke and Greenstein 1991; Hermann and Preston 1994; Kaarbo and Hermann 1998; Dyson and Preston 2006; Schafer and Crichlow 2010). Others have focused on policy preferences, such as the use of force of as a foreign policy tool (Driver 1977; Hermann 1980; Keller; 2005; Dyson 2006, 2007; Foster and Keller 2010, 2014; Keller and Foster 2012; Keller and Yang 2016).

One of the most consistent variables associated with both a preference for military options as well as the willingness to use them is a political executive's level of distrust. Distrust is a belief that other actors should be viewed with suspicion (Tucker 1965; Stuart and Starr 1982). Driver (1977), performing an experimental analysis, finds that individuals with higher scores for distrust tend to believe that military force is a more effective tool for resolving foreign policy uncertainty than less distrustful individuals. This finding has been used to build and test subsequent theories using observational data. Margaret Hermann (1980) finds that distrust is positively correlated with general foreign policy aggression in her sample of forty-five political executives.

A more recent and larger-n example of the application of LTA to questions of foreign policy behaviour is the work of Foster and Keller (2014). These authors combine distrust, conceptual complexity, and the human misery index to create an interaction term that measures the proclivity of American political executives to use force to divert attention from domestic economic woes (Foster and Keller 2014). They find that distrustful and less conceptually complex executives are more likely to use force to divert attention from domestic economic struggles (Foster and Keller 2014). Additionally, higher scores for distrust have been shown to play a role in the generation of foreign policy options

---

[6] In the early days of LTA, in-group bias was referred to as 'nationalism'.

(Keller and Yang 2016). The authors find that distrustful individuals tend to eliminate less aggressive options in the first stage of the decision-making process. Then, in the second stage of decision-making, individuals tend to have fewer non-violent options to choose from (Keller and Yang 2016).[7]

Another personality characteristic that has often been associated with aggressive foreign policy preferences is an executive's need for power (Winter and Stewart 1977; Hermann 1980; Winter 1993). A higher need for power is associated with more competitive, manipulative, and aggressive behaviour in bargaining situations (Keller 2005: 211). Furthermore, scholars have found that a higher power motive is associated with a greater willingness to use violence against domestic and international opposition (McLellan 1971: 314–59; Winter 1973). Winter's (1993) subsequent case study examination of the motive profiles of political elites finds that there was a marked increase in the power motive of leaders leading to the outbreak of World War I. Other quantitative studies have found that a high need for power is correlated with an executive's desire to pursue a more independent approach to foreign policy and to be more aggressive in the conduct of foreign policy (Hermann 1980). In recent years, there has been a move toward aggregating need for power into a measure that captures an executive's willingness to respect or challenge potential constraints. This measure is a combination of need for power and belief in ability to control events (Hermann 2003). Keller (2005) uses this aggregate measure to explore the dynamics of a potential monadic democratic peace. The author finds that democratic executives willing to respect constraints are far less likely to rely on force during a foreign policy crisis than a democratic executive who is a constraint challenger (Keller 2005: 225). This finding has helped scholars identify the possibility of a 'contingent' monadic democratic peace.[8]

Another trait of political executives associated with aggression is in-group bias.[9] This characteristic involves a view of the world in which an executive's group or nation holds centre-stage (Druckman 1968; LeVine and Campbell 1972; Hermann 2003). Furthermore, individuals who score high on this characteristic believe that their group or nation is more virtuous than others. Political executives who are more nationalistic also tend to be hyper-vigilant and wary of threats from outgroups or 'degenerate' others. As a result, these executives tend to prefer more forceful foreign policy options (Crow and Noel 1977). At the most extreme, these individual executives may be motivated to 'purify' their own state or region of foreign influences (Smith 1993; Keller 2005: 211). In recent years, scholars have considered the effect of in-group bias on the willingness of

---

[7] This research emerges out of the poliheuristic theory of decision-making, which argues that individuals make decisions in two stages. In the first, individuals eliminate certain possible decisions using heuristics that stem from their psychological limitations, and in the second stage, individuals rationally choose a decision from the remaining options (Mintz 1993).

[8] This finding is particularly interesting because the vast majority of research finds that democracies are *not* less conflict prone in general, but they are more peaceful in their conduct with other democratic states.

[9] In this section, though nationalism and in-group bias have some key conceptual differences, we use the terms interchangeably following the evolution of the terms in the field.

leaders to scapegoat out-groups and engage in the diversionary use of force (Foster and Keller 2012). The authors find that—contrary to previous expectations—executives who score high on in-group bias are *less* likely to engage in armed-scapegoating and more likely to engage in summits when faced with domestic economic hardship. Further, they find that only leaders who score the lowest for in-group bias are those who are more likely to engage in the use of diversionary force (Foster and Keller 2012: 434).

Finally, another exploration of the correlates of the diversionary use of force using LTA looks at another aggregated measure that is called 'locus of control' (LoC; Keller and Foster 2012). Keller and Foster (2012) argue that an executive's LoC refers to whether or not he or she believes that that his or her own skills or efforts (internal locus) can shape events and subsequent outcomes (Rotter 1966; Davis and Phares 1967). The authors create a measure for LoC using belief in ability to control events and self-confidence. They argue that belief in ability to control events measures LoC in the political arena, and self-confidence captures a belief about one's own skills and experience (Keller and Foster 2012). The authors find support for their hypothesis that leaders with a stronger internal LoC will be more likely to use force to distract the population from economic or political issues (Keller and Foster 2012: 594–5).

A final area of study focuses on how the beliefs and personality characteristics of political executives can affect the quality of decision-making processes. Specifically, there has been some interesting recent research that investigates the effect of the political executive's beliefs and personality characteristics on patterns of faulty group decision-making (Schafer 1999; Schafer and Crichlow 2010; Schafer et al. 2011). But first, let us describe the *locus classicus* in the area of group decision-making. Irving Janis (1971) coined the term *groupthink* to identify a decision-making process that often resulted in poor foreign policy outcomes. Specifically, Janis said the faulty decision-making happened because of a psychological pattern in the group, where members of the group reached premature consensus on a policy as a way to maintain group cohesion. Or, to put it colloquially, members of the group go-along-to-get-along. The result is a poorly processed, poorly vetted decision that significantly increased the probability of a poor outcome. The classic case cited by Janis was US President John Kennedy's decision-making in the case of the Bay of Pigs, where the group never questioned some incredibly questionable assumptions about proceeding with the invasion of Cuba. Relevant to this chapter is the question of whether the executive's own beliefs and personality characteristics might have an effect on subsequent flawed decision-making by his or her group. Is it possible that the political executive's personality and beliefs contribute to patterns of dissent, stereotyping the situation, methodical procedures, and other patterns in group decision-making?

While it is well-documented that groupthink can have a negative effect on the quality of outcomes, far less scholarly attention is paid to the effect that individual political executives have on the decision-making process. The work of Schafer and Crichlow (2010) explores this question. In addition to investigating how groupthink can affect the quality of decision outcomes, the authors explore how the beliefs and personality characteristics of political executives can affect both the quality of the decision-making process and the structure of key advisory groups. Schafer and Crichlow (2010) find that presidents who score higher on self-confidence than conceptual complexity are likely to experience fewer decision-making faults. Additionally, they also find that executives who have higher scores for in-group bias tend to experience fewer instances of decision-making faults (Schafer and Crichlow 2010). Their regression analysis of group-structure faults finds that the psychological characteristics of presidents can affect how they structure foreign policy advisory groups. They find that political executives who are more distrustful are more likely to have higher instances of group-structure faults. Additionally, they find that executives who have a high belief in their ability to control events and a low need for power will experience higher instances of group-structure faults (Schafer and Crichlow 2010).

14.4 THE PERSONALITIES AND BELIEFS OF POLITICAL EXECUTIVES: LOOKING FORWARD

We mentioned in the introduction of this chapter that, even though there is a rich history in the field, the analysis of the beliefs and personalities of political executives is underdeveloped and underresearched. That means, of course, that there is a large amount of room for original research contributions now and into the future. In this concluding section we discuss some of the research areas and projects that form the basis of a possible future agenda.

In our view, the most important immediate need in the field is more empirical testing and analysis. Only in recent years has the field taken on the markings of a young science by moving away from single case studies and simple comparisons to larger statistical models. As discussed earlier, we have seen progress in testing the effects of the beliefs and personality characteristics of political executives on such things as conflict escalation, diversionary-war behaviour, and decision-making processes. Not only is there much more to do in these areas, but there are many additional studies that could be done to test theories and advance our knowledge in the field. Much of this work should have beliefs and personality characteristics on the independent-variable side of the equation, with a variety of new and innovative behavioural dependent variables. We wonder if executive beliefs and personalities affect such domestic political and social matters as interaction patterns with legislatures and the legislative process, media coverage and public approval levels of the executive, economic patterns in a state, domestic attitudes toward race, gender, religion, or other identity-based constructs, or attitudes toward democratic norms and values.

There is perhaps an even larger set of foreign policy dependent variables that could be investigated: alliance behaviour, participation in or adherence to intergovernmental organizations, foreign aid and assistance, standing up for (or not) human rights, involvement in environmental regimes, as well as a very large variety of conflict and conflict-resolution variables that are standard fare in the field of international relations. It is also highly appropriate that these methods and these variables be applied to domestic policy areas as well. What is the effect of political executives' beliefs and personalities on policies pertaining to race, ethnicity, and other identity-based areas, economic policies such as spending and growth, and infrastructure policies such as transportation, energy, and development?

Earlier, we discussed some of the work where executive psychology is on the dependent side of the equation, but here again there is room for much more. How stable are executive beliefs and personalities? What factors can cause it to change, adapt, or adjust? Are some individuals more stable than others, and if so, what factors affect that? Does political experience or time in office coincide with personality or belief stability? What about international travel or living experiences? Are there personal life experiences that produce patterned results in executive personalities and beliefs, such as a generational effect, early traumatic life event, military experience, or coming of age in war-torn society? Do different demographic or identity-based categories of the executive correlate with different psychological patterns in political executives? Feminist international relations theorists (e.g. Bettencourt and Miller 1996; Caprioli and Boyer 2001) argue that gender matters in the conduct of foreign affairs, but little research has been done to support that proposition. We could also investigate differences for other categories, such as partisan identification, race, the age of the executive, or whether the executive leads a democracy or a non-democracy. These and many other questions could also be investigated for temporal effects.

In addition to many more scientific empirical projects, there is also room for the development of new and additional theoretical insights. While all of the empirical ideas discussed above will require their own theoretical development—and subsequently lead to new tests and new theories—here we identify one particular area that we believe is important for theoretical development: conditionality and interaction effects with structural and situational variables. As noted briefly above, political psychologists rarely if ever conceive of personality and beliefs as having effects in isolation. Instead, most researchers discuss the effects that beliefs and personalities have in any given set of structural or situational constraints. While some very good theoretical work in this area has already been done (see the discussion on this in Chapter 4 in this volume), there is much more work to be done. On the theoretical side of things, this seems particularly important to us in the new complexities of the twenty-first century, which includes such things as the post-Cold-War international arena, major, powerful non-state actors such as al Qaeda and ISIS, technological changes happening at exponential rates, and new and quickening international challenges in such areas as the environment and disease. Is this new world, marked by faster rates of change than ever before in history, likely to enhance or diminish the general effect of the personalities and beliefs of political executives? Or are the effects likely to be conditional, with certain types of psychological profiles emerging and gaining more power in the quick moving and challenging new environment?

We also anticipate the development of new constructs pertaining to personality and beliefs, and perhaps the revisiting of old ones that may yet prove useful in today's world. As discussed above, the common constructs in use thus far—traits, cognitions, and motives—have served the field well and are certainly convenient psychological categories. But we must not rest on convenience or past convention to dictate our approaches into the future. Are there parts or pieces of executive personality that are important but underdeveloped or underinvestigated? Are there new concepts to develop, define, and operationalize? In addition, like many fields, the study of personality and beliefs has its fads and its fortunes when it comes to constructs. For example, the 'cognitive revolution' of the 1960s and 1970s caused many other research programmes to be largely disregarded or discounted for many years, but we now know that was a mistake. Similarly, the old 'authoritarian personality' and its subsequent variations, such 'RWA' (Right Wing Authoritarianism), were largely criticized and dismissed in the past for both sociopolitical reasons and methodological reasons. But neither of those sets of reasons is grounded in sound theoretical or empirical bases. And, indeed, the concept of a personality complex that tends toward authoritarianism not only strikes us as having potential for powerful explanatory effects regarding the behaviour of political executives, but it also strikes us as being highly relevant in today's world.

As technology rapidly changes, we anticipate a future with rapidly changing and developing methods as well. Once again, the current ways—particularly the verbal-based content analysis systems—have served us well and created opportunities for the field to become a genuine science. We know enough from the studies conducted thus far that verbal behaviour by political executives can provide many different indicators of their beliefs and personality characteristics. But certainly there is more to the story, and those methods have clear limitations. For instance, no content analysis system based on words and phrases can account for such things as tone, irony, and sarcasm. In addition, it seems very likely that additional dimensions of psychology may be detected using non-verbal indicators, such as body language or eye movement (just ask a good poker player if those things provide meaningful tells!). And while today in political psychology there is little scientific, technological development in these areas, it is the case that we live in a big-data world with significant computing capabilities, and that means we have the potential to develop the scientific capabilities.

Finally, and critically important for each of the previously mentioned areas, it is imperative that the field develop more data including large, publicly available data sets with psychological variables. Virtually all of the studies discussed in this chapter have been one-offs: researchers identify a political executive of interest, or perhaps a sample of executives, gather the data on those specific executives, conduct the hypothesis tests, and report the results. There has been virtually no effort to standardize data collection, or to centralize it, or systematize it, or to expand it extensively for other researchers to use in their own original research designs. While the existing studies form the basis of validity checks, and provide some initial scientific results, the field will not make significant advancements until much more data is systematically gathered and made publicly available to a wide array of researchers. As of today, there is very little cumulative knowledge in the scientific study of the beliefs and personality characteristics of political executives. Until we have much more data, we will be limited in our empirical testing, our development and investigation of new theories, our conceptualization and expansion of psychological constructs, and our development of new methods. Indeed, it seems to us that rapid expansion of available data may be the first and foremost challenge before us.

REFERENCES

Anderson, J. (1973). 'The Operational Code Belief System of Senator Arthur Vandenberg: An Application of the George Construct.' University of Michigan, Unpublished Ph.D. dissertation.

Barber, J. (1972). *The Presidential Character: Predicting Performance in the White House*. Englewood: Prentice-Hall.

Berejikian, J. D. and Early, B. R. (2013). 'Loss Aversion and Foreign Policy Resolve,' *Political Psychology* 34(5): 649–71.

Bettencourt, B. and Miller, N. (1996). 'Gender Differences in Aggression as a Function of Provocation: A Meta-Analysis,' *Psychological Bulletin* 119(3): 205–27.

Boulding, K. E. (1959). 'National Images and International Systems,' *Journal of Conflict Resolution* 3(2): 120–31.

Burke, J. P. and Greenstein, F. I. (1991). *How Presidents Test Reality: Decisions on Vietnam 1954 and 1965*. New York: Russell Sage Foundation.

Caldwell, D. (1976). 'The Operational Code of Senator Mark Hatfield.' Stanford University Mimeo.

Caprioli, M. and Boyer, M. A. (2001). 'Gender, Violence, and International Crisis,' *Journal of Conflict Resolution* 45(4): 503–18.

Cottham, M. L. (1985). 'The Image of Psychological Images on International Bargaining: The Case of Mexican Natural Gas,' *Political Psychology* 6(4): 413–39.

Cottham, M. L. (1994). *Images and Intervention: U.S. Policies in Latin America*. Pittsburgh: Pittsburgh University Press.

Cottham, R. (1977). *Foreign Policy Motivations: A General Theory and a Case Study*. Pittsburgh: Pittsburgh University Press.

Crabb, C. V. and Mulcahy, K. V. (1988). *Presidents and Foreign Policy Making*. Baton Rouge: Louisiana State University.

Crichlow, S. (1998). 'Idealism or Pragmatism? An Operational Code Analysis of Yitzhak Rabin and Shimon Peres,' *Political Psychology* 19(5): 638–706.

Crichlow, Scott (2002). 'Legislators' Personality Traits and Congressional Support for Free Trade,' *Journal of Conflict Resolution* 46(5): 693–711.

Crow, W. and Noel, R. (1977). 'An Experiment in Simulated Historical Decision-Making,' in M. G. Hermann (ed.) *A Psychological Examination of Political Leaders*. New York: The Free Press.

Cuhadar, E., Kaarbo, J., Kesgin, B., and Ozkecec-Taner, B. (2017a). 'Examining Leaders' Orientations to Structural Constraints: Turkey's 1991 and 2003 Iraq War Decisions,' *Journal of International Relations and Development* 20(1): 29–54.

Cuhadar, E., Kaarbo, J., Kesgin, B., and Ozkecec-Taner, B. (2017b). 'Personality or Role? Comparisons of Turkish Leaders Across Different Institutional Positions,' *Political Psychology* 38(1): 39–54.

Davis, W. L. and Phares, E. J. (1967). 'Internal-External Control as a Determinant of Information-Seeking in a Social Influence Situation,' *Journal of Personality* 35(4): 547–61.

Driver, M. J. (1977). 'Individual Differences as Determinants of Aggression in the Inter-Nation Simulation,' in M. G. Hermann (ed.) *A Psychological Examination of Political Leaders.* New York: Free Press.

Druckman, D. (1968). 'Ethnocentrism in the Inter-Nation Simulation,' *Journal of Conflict Resolution* 12(1): 45–68.

Dyson, S. B. (2006). 'Personality and Foreign Policy: Tony Blair's Iraq Decisions,' *Foreign Policy Analysis* 2(2): 289–306.

Dyson, S. B. (2007). 'Alliances, Domestic Politics, and Leader Psychology: Why Did Britain Stay Out of Vietnam and Go into Iraq,' *Political Psychology* 28(6): 647–66.

Dyson, S. B. and Preston, T. (2006). 'Individual Characteristics of Political Leaders and the Use of Analogy in Foreign Policy Decision-Making,' *Political Psychology* 27(2): 265–88.

Ellis, C. M., Horowitz, M., and Stam, A. C. (2015). 'Introducing the LEAD Data Set,' *International Interactions* 41(4): 718–41.

Erikson, E. (1975). *Life History and the Historical Moment.* New York: Norton.

Etheredge, L. S. (1975). *A World of Men: The Private Sources of American Foreign Policy.* Cambridge, MA: The MIT Press.

Feng, H. (2005). 'The Operational Code of Mao Zedong: Defensive or Offensive Realist,' *Security Studies* 14(4): 637–62.

Foster, D. and Keller, J. W. (2010). 'Rallies to the "First Image": Leadership Psychology, Scapegoating Proclivity, and the Diversionary Use of Force,' *Conflict Management and Peace Science* 27(5): 417–41.

Foster, D. and Keller, J. W. (2014). 'Leaders' Cognitive Complexity, Distrust, and the Diversionary Use of Force,' *Foreign Policy Analysis* 10(3): 205–23.

Frey, R., Pedroni, A., Mata, R., Rieskamp, J., and Hertwig, R. (2017). 'Risk Preference Shares the Psychometric Structure of Major Psychological Traits,' *Science Advances* 3(10).

Fuhrmann, M. and Horowitz, M. C. (2014). 'When Leaders Matter: Rebel Experience and Nuclear Proliferation,' *Journal of Politics* 77(1): 72–87.

George, A. (1969). 'The "Operational Code": A Neglected Approach to the Study of Political Leaders and Decision-Making,' *International Studies Quarterly* 13(2): 190–222.

George, A. (1980). *Presidential Decisionmaking in Foreign Policy.* Boulder, CO: Westview Press.

George, A. and George, J. (1956). *Woodrow Wilson and Colonel House: A Personality Study.* Lexington: Plunkett Lake Press.

Gerber, A. S., Huber, G. A., Doherty, D., and Dowling, C. M. (2011). 'The Big Five Personality Traits in the Political Arena,' *American Review of Political Science* 14: 265–87.

Goldberg, L. R. (1990). 'An Alternative "Description of Personality": The Big-Five Factor Structure,' *Journal of Personality and Social Psychology* 59(6): 1216–29.

Gorener, A. S. and Ucal, M. S. (2011). 'The Personality and Leadership Style of Recep Tayyip Erdogan: Implications for Turkish Foreign Policy,' *Turkish Studies* 12(3): 357–81.

Greenstein, F. I. (1969). *Personality and Politics.* Chicago: Marham.

Hermann, M. G. (1980). 'Explaining Foreign Policy Behavior Using the Personal Characteristics of Political Leaders,' *International Studies Quarterly* 24(1): 7–46.

Hermann, M. G. (2003). 'Assessing Leadership Style: Trait Analysis,' in Post, J. M. (ed.) *The Psychological Assessment of Political Leaders*. Ann Arbor, MI: University of Michigan Press, 178–214.

Hermann, M. G. and Kegley Jr, C. W. (1995). 'Rethinking Democracy and International Peace: Perspectives from Political Psychology,' *International Studies Quarterly* 39(4): 511–33.

Hermann, M. G. and Preston, T. (1994). 'Presidents, Advisers, and Foreign Policy: The Effects of Leadership Style on Executive Agreements,' *Political Psychology* 15(1): 75–96.

Herrmann, R. K. (1985). *Perceptions and Behavior in Soviet Foreign Policy*. Pittsburgh, PA: University of Pittsburgh Press.

Herrmann, R. K. (1986). 'The Power of Perceptions in Foreign-Policy Decision Making: Do Views of the Soviet Union Determine Policy Choices of American Leaders,' *American Journal of Political Science* 30(4): 841–75.

Herrmann, R. K. and Fischerkeller, M. (1995). 'Beyond the Enemy Image and Spiral Model: Cognitive-Strategic Research after the Cold War,' *International Organization* 49(3): 415–50.

Holsti, O. (1962). 'The Belief System and National Images: A Case Study,' *Journal of Conflict Resolution* 6(3): 244–52.

Holsti, O. (1967). 'Cognitive Dynamics and Images of the Enemy,' *Journal of International Affairs* 21(2): 16–39.

Holsti, O. (1970). 'The "Operational Code" Approach to the Study of Political Leaders: John Foster Dulles' Philosophical and Instrumental Beliefs,' *Canadian Journal of Political Science* 3(1): 123–57.

Horowitz, M. and Stam, A. C. (2014). 'How Prior Military Experience Influences Future Militarized Behavior of Leaders,' *International Organization* 68(3): 527–99.

Horowitz, M., Stam, A. C., and Ellis, C. M. (2015). *Why Leaders Fight*. Cambridge: Cambridge University Press.

Hymans, J. (2006). *The Psychology of Nuclear Proliferation: Identity, Emotions, and Foreign Policy*. Cambridge: Cambridge University Press.

Janis, I. (1971). 'Groupthink,' *Psychology Today* 5(6): 43–6.

Johnson, L. K. (1977). 'Operational Codes and the Prediction of Leadership Behavior: Senator Frank Church at Midcareer,' in M. G. Hermann (ed.) *A Psychological Examination of Political Leaders*. New York: Free Press.

Johnson, R. T. (1974). *Managing the White House: An Intimate Study of the Presidency*. New York: Harper Row.

Kaarbo, J. and Hermann, M. G. (1998). 'Leadership Styles of Prime Ministers: How Individual Differences Affect the Foreign Policy Decision-Making Process,' *Leadership Quarterly* 9(3): 243–63.

Keller, J. (2005). 'Leadership Style, Regime Type, and Foreign Policy Crisis Behavior: A Contingent Monadic Peace,' *International Studies Quarterly* 49(2): 205–31.

Keller, J. and Foster, D. (2012). 'Presidential Leadership Style and the Political Use of Force,' *Political Psychology* 33(5): 581–98.

Keller, J. and Yang, Y. (2016). 'Problem Representation, Option Generation, and Polyheuristic Theory: An Experimental Analysis,' *Political Psychology* 37(5): 739–52.

Kesgin, B. (2013). 'Leadership Traits of Turkey's Islamist and Secular Prime Ministers,' *Turkish Studies* 14(1): 136–57.

Khaneman, D. and Tversky, A. (1979). 'Prospect Theory: An Analysis of Decision Under Risk,' *Econometrica* 47(2): 263–91.

Kydd, Andrew. (2005). *Trust and Mistrust in International Relations*. Princeton: Princeton University Press.

Leites, N. (1953). *A Study in Bolshevism*. New York: New York Free Press.

LeVine, R. A. and Campbell, D. T. (1972). *Ethnocentrism*. New York: Wiley.

Linde, J. and Vis, B. (2017). 'Do Politicians Take Risks Like the Rest of Us? An Experimental Test of Prospect Theory Under MPs,' *Political Psychology* 38(1): 101–17.

McLellan, D. (1971). 'The Operational Code Approach to the Study of Political Leaders: Dean Acheson's Philosophical and Instrumental Beliefs,' *Canadian Journal of Political Science* 4(1): 52–75.

Mintz, A. (1993). *Integrating Cognitive and Rational Theories of Foreign Policy Decision-Making*. New York: Palgrave Macmillan.

Post, J. M. (2003). 'Assessing Leaders at a Distance: The Political Personality Profile,' in Post, J. M. (ed.) *The Psychological Assessment of Political Leaders*. Ann Arbor, MI: University of Michigan Press, 69–104.

Post, J. M. (2004). *Leaders and Their Followers in a Dangerous World: The Psychology of Political Behavior*. Ithaca, NY: Cornell University Press.

Post, J. M. (2013). 'Psychobiography,' in L. Huddy, D. O. Sears, and J. Levy (eds) *Oxford Handbook of Political Psychology*. Oxford: Oxford University Press.

Renshon, J. (2008). 'Stability and Change in Belief Systems: The Operational Code of George W. Bush,' *Journal of Conflict Resolution* 52(6): 820–49.

Renshon, S. A. (2003). 'Psychoanalytic Assessments of Character and Performance in Presidents and Candidates: Some Observations on Theory and Method,' in J. M. Post (ed.) *The Psychological Assessment of Political Leaders*. Ann Arbor, MI: University of Michigan Press, 105–33.

Robison, S. (2006). 'George W. Bush and the Vulcans: Leader-Advisor Relations and America's Response to the 9/11 Attacks,' in M. Schafer and S. G. Walker (eds) *Rethinking Foreign Policy Analysis: States, Leaders, and the Microfoundations of Behavioral International Relations*. New York: Palgrave-Macmillan.

Rotter, J. B. (1966). 'Generalized Expectancies For Internal Versus External Control of Reinforcement,' *Psychological Monographs: General and Applied* 80(1): 1–28.

Rubenzer, S. J., Faschingbauer, T. R., and Ones, D. S. (2000). 'Assessing U.S. Presidents Using the Revised NEO Personality Inventory,' *Assessment* 7(4): 403–19.

Saunders, E. N. (2011). *Leaders at War: How Presidents Shape Military Interventions*. Ithaca, NY: Cornell University Press.

Schafer, M. (1999). 'Explaining Groupthink: Do the Psychological Characteristics of the Leader Matter,' *International Interactions* 25(2): 1–31.

Schafer, M. and Crichlow, S. (2010). *Groupthink Versus High-Quality Decision Making in International Relations*. New York: Columbia University Press.

Schafer, M. and Walker, S. G. (2006). 'Democratic Leaders and the Democratic Peace: The Operational Codes of Tony Blair and Bill Clinton,' *International Studies Quarterly* 50(3): 561–83.

Schafer, M., Nunley, J., and Crichlow, S. (2011). 'Small Group Dynamics: The Psychological Characteristics of Leaders and the Quality of Group Decision Making,' in S. G. Walker, A. Malici, and M. Schafer (eds) *Rethinking Foreign Policy Analysis: States, Leaders, and the Microfoundations of Behavioral International Relations*. New York: Routledge.

Schafer, M., Walker, S. G., Besaw, C., Gill, P., and Smith, G. (2016). 'Introducing a New Data Set: Psychological Correlates of U.S. Conflict Behavior,' Presented at the Annual Meeting of the International Society of Political Psychology. Warsaw, Poland.

Schultz, W. T. (2005). *Handbook of Psychobiography*. New York: Oxford University Press.

Schwarz, C. and Smith, G. (2017). 'Better Together: A Psychological Bargaining Model of War,' Presented at the Annual Meeting of the International Studies Association. Baltimore, MD.

Simon, H. (1972). 'Theories of Bounded Rationality,' in C. B. McGuire and R. Radner (eds) *Decision and Organization: A Volume in Honor of Jacob Marschak*. Amsterdam: North-Holland Publishing, 161–76.

Smith, A. (1993). 'The Ethnic Sources of Nationalism,' in M. E. Brown (ed.) *Ethnic Conflict and International Security*. Princeton: Princeton University Press, 27–41.

Smith, G. (2014a). 'Distrust and Militarized Interstate Dispute Initiation,' Presented at the Annual Meeting of the Southern Political Science Association. New Orleans, LA.

Smith, G. (2014b). 'Leader Psychology and the Initiation of Militarized Interstate Disputes,' Presented at the Annual Meeting of the International Society of Political Psychology. Rome, Italy.

Smith, G., Schwarz, C., and Brooks, A. (2016). 'At the Nexus of Life Experience and Leadership Psychology: How Leaders Decide to Initiate Conflict,' Presented at the Annual Meeting of the International Society of Political Psychology. Warsaw, Poland.

Stuart, D. and Starr, H. (1982). 'The Inherent Bad Faith Model Revisited: Dulles, Kennedy, and Kissinger,' *Political Psychology* 3(3/4): 1–33.

Tucker, R. C. (1965). 'The Dictator and Totalitarianism,' *World Politics* 17(4): 555–83.

Tversky, A. and Khaneman, D. (1986). 'Rational Choice and Framing of Decisions,' *Journal of Business* 59(4): S251–78.

Tweraser, K. (1974). 'Changing Patterns of Political Beliefs: The Foreign Policy Operational Code of William J. Fulbright.' *Sage Professional Papers in American Politics*, 04–016.

Van Esch, F. and Swinkels, M. (2015). 'How Europe's Political Leaders Made Sense of the Euro's Crisis: The Influence of Pressure and Personality,' *West European Politics* 38(6): 1203–55.

Walker, S. G. (1977). 'The Interface between Beliefs and Behavior: Henry Kissinger's Operational Code and the Vietnam War,' *Journal of Conflict Resolution* 21(1): 129–68.

Walker, S. G. and Schafer, M. (2000). 'The Political Universe of Lyndon B. Johnson and His Advisors: Diagnostic and Strategic Propensities in Their Operational Codes,' *Political Psychology* 21(3): 529–43.

Walker, S. G., Schafer, M., and Young, M. (1998). 'Systematic Procedures for Operational Code Analysis: Measuring and Modeling Jimmy Carter's Operational Code,' *International Studies Quarterly* 42(1): 175–89.

Walker, S. G., Schafer, M., and Young, M. (1999). 'Presidential Operational Codes and Foreign Policy Conflicts in the Post-Cold War World,' *Journal of Conflict Resolution* 43(5): 610–25.

Walker, S. G., Schafer, M., and Young, M. (2003). 'Profiling the Operational Codes of Political Leaders,' in J. M. Post (ed.) *The Psychological Assessment of Political Leaders*. Ann Arbor, MI: University of Michigan Press, 215–45.

Walter, J. (2007). 'Handbook of Psychobiography—Edited by William Todd Schultz,' *Political Psychology* 28(2): 257–9.

Winter, D. G. (1973). *The Power Motive*. New York: Free Press.

Winter, D. G. (1993). 'Power, Affiliation, and War: Three Tests of a Motivational Models,' *Journal of Personality and Social Psychology*. 65(3): 532–45.

Winter, D. G. (2013). 'Personality Profiles of Political Elites,' in L. Huddy, D. O. Sears, and J. Levy (eds) *The Oxford Handbook of Political Psychology*. Oxford: Oxford University Press, 423–58.

Winter, D. G. and Stewart, A. J. (1977). 'Power Motive Reliability as a Function of Retest Instructions,' *Journal of Consulting and Clinical Psychology* 45(3): 436–40.

CHAPTER 15

....

GOVERNMENT FORMATION AND TERMINATION

....

PETRA SCHLEITER

15.1 INTRODUCTION

....

BARGAINING between politicians about government formation and termination counts among the most consequential negotiations in democratic politics. Which parties enter or leave office has far-reaching implications that affect every group in society. It determines which manifesto pledges may be translated into policy, shapes taxation and spending, the scope and quality of public services, regulation of the private sector, and government priorities in areas such as education, inequality, and immigration.

Since cabinets are the nexus through which democracies funnel representation, the constitutionally structured system of democratic representation determines who bargains about cabinets, and what their institutional resources are: Voters in parliamentary democracies are represented by parliament alone, to which government is exclusively responsible. Hence parliamentary governments are negotiated and broken by legislative parties. Semi-presidential democracies complement a government that is responsible to parliament with a popularly elected president, who then generally becomes an additional participant in negotiations about government formation and termination, endowed with greater or lesser constitutional powers. Presidential constitutions, likewise, represent voters via a popularly elected president and assembly, but make the president head of the government, to whom the cabinet is exclusively responsible. Under presidential constitutions, it is the separation of powers that requires presidents, who wish to enact their policies through legislation, to negotiate about their policy programme, and therefore potentially about their cabinet choices, with the legislature. In sum, cabinet formation and termination is negotiated between the popularly elected national representatives of the electorate, that is, legislative parties, and where applicable, the president. The more presidential the constitution, the greater, on average, the institutional resources that presidents bring to the table.

Politicians bargain about government formation and termination, whenever a single political party—or in presidential systems, the presidential party—does not control a legislative majority, as is the case in most democracies, most of the time. Hence, across parliamentary, semi-presidential, and presidential democracies, coalition government is the norm (Müller and Strøm 2000; Amorim Neto 2006: 427; Samuels and Shugart 2010: 57–60). This raises a plethora of questions: What motivates politicians in forming cabinets and which resources enable parties (and presidents) to secure cabinet representation? What are the attributes of cabinets that form? How is power distributed within cabinets? How durable are they? What drives politicians to terminate cabinets and under which conditions do different modes of cabinet termination occur?

While the current understanding of coalition bargaining has its roots predominantly in the literature on *parliamentary* governments, the 1990s marked a turning point in the study of governing coalitions. The confluence of two independent intellectual developments opened up new research agendas that now define the field: First, motivated by the failure of institution-free explanations, to predict which *parliamentary* governments actually from, scholars began to give due attention to the institutional context in which bargaining over governments unfolds (Baron and Ferejohn 1989; Laver and Shepsle 1990; Strøm 1990a; Lupia and Strøm 1995). Indeed, since the 1990s, research in the field has recognized that the explanatory power and accuracy of accounts of government formation and termination depends on the incorporation of the institutional rules that shape who bargains and what resources these actors can bring to bear. Second, the durability of *multiparty presidential* and *semi-presidential* democracies shifted the focus of work on these political systems in the late 1990s from a preoccupation with their presumed propensity to collapse, to the study of multiparty governance with popularly elected presidents in practice (Altman 2000; Elgie 2004; Amorim Neto 2006; Cheibub 2007; Schleiter and Morgan-Jones 2009b; Alemán and Tsebelis 2011; Martínez-Gallardo 2012; Camerlo and Martínez-Gallardo 2017; see also Chapter 21 in this volume). The institutionalist turn in the literature on parliamentary coalition governance struck a chord with these scholars who were working on political systems where the institutional resources of presidents—in addition other factors such as the size and ideology of parties—clearly play a major role in shaping coalition bargaining.

To review these developments, this chapter is structured as follows: the first half focuses on a discussion of the literature on *government formation*; the second half on *government survival and termination*. In both areas of research, work on bargaining about parliamentary governments is foundational, and I begin by reviewing this work along with the institutionalist turn and recent theoretical and methodological advances. I then explore how this new, institutionally grounded understanding of bargaining about parliamentary coalition governance complements—and contrasts with—the literature on coalition formation and termination in semi-presidential and parliamentary systems. The chapter concludes with a discussion of the research agenda and potential synergies between these research streams.

15.2 THE LITERATURE ON
GOVERNMENT FORMATION

In the context of West European parliamentary democracies, the motivations of politicians in coalition bargaining are typically taken to reflect the broader aims of political parties, which include securing office, policy, and votes (Riker 1962; Axelrod 1970; De Swaan 1973; Strøm, 1990b). That is, in forming coalitions, the interest of parties may lie in controlling governmental office and the privileges that flow from it, in shaping policy and deciding distributive conflicts, and in positioning themselves for electoral contests. All of these considerations will normally play some role in parties' decisions to join (or indeed, leave) a coalition, although their relative weight may vary across parties and over time.

With these goals in mind, coalition bargaining centres on a range of *outcomes*. Most fundamentally, parties must negotiate whether to seek office at all by forming and supporting a fully empowered party-based government, or whether a technical or caretaker government is preferable. If a party-based government is to be formed, and no single party has a parliamentary majority, the government's coalition status must be negotiated, the alternative being a single party minority government. Once parties choose to form a coalition, they need to decide its majority status, that is, whether majority status is desired, and if so, how large that majority ought to be. Parties must also consider the composition of the government, for instance, its ideological connectedness, whether to include the median party, and the reputation of potential coalition partners for smooth (or poor) collaboration. Scholars have studied these outcomes using three types of dependent variables: the attributes (or type) of coalition formed, the coalition inclusion probability of individual parties with particular attributes or resources, and the formation probability of a particular coalition that has specific attributes and includes particular parties.

Early accounts of coalition formation made the complexity of these choices tractable by making a series of simplifying assumptions about the motivations of parties and the irrelevance of the institutional environment they bargain in. For instance, seminal work by Gamson (1961) and Riker (1962) assumed that parties are driven exclusively by the motivation to seek office. According to these studies only minimum winning coalitions (which include only the minimal number of parties required to form a legislative majority) are expected to form because they enable governing parties to maximize office benefits. Yet, these expectations were manifestly at variance with the observed distribution of cabinet types (Laver and Schofield 1990): minimal winning coalitions account only for about a third of all cabinets and other types of governments such as minority governments or surplus coalitions (which include more parties than is required to form a legislative majority) remained entirely unexplained from this perspective.

In a next step, scholars therefore incorporated into their models more complex assumptions regarding the motivations of parties by adding policy considerations.

According to Axelrod (1970) and De Swaan (1973), for instance, coalitions of ideologically compatible parties are more likely to form. Laver and Schofield (1990) suggested that governments are likely to include the median party, which provided a rationale for the formation of minority governments in the context of an ideologically divided opposition. This research programme, which relied extensively on formal theory and spatial modelling, made considerable contributions. Most notably, it laid strong theoretical foundations for the field and produced the first hypotheses about the effect of party size and ideology on coalition formation. Yet, its empirical success remained limited. Attention to policy considerations yielded only modest improvements in the ability of coalition theories to predict which coalitions form. Moreover, disturbingly, the findings of studies appeared to be driven more by the countries included than by theoretically relevant explanatory variables (Franklin and Mackie 1984).

Responding to this challenge, scholars began to scrutinize institutions—such as who can propose governments and what level of legislative support is required for a coalition to govern successfully—as a key source of country-level heterogeneity in cabinet bargaining. Research began to introduce institutional context into the study of government coalitions, focussing in particular on political institutions that (i) regulate the government formation process and (ii) affect policy-making once a coalition is in office.

The assumption underpinning the first strand of literature was that the *institutions, which structure the process of coalition negotiation,* confer bargaining power to some actors, making them disproportionately successful in securing their inclusion in government. Foundational for much of this work was Baron and Ferejohn's (1989) sequential bargaining model, which draws attention to the importance of *proposal power* in coalition bargaining. According to Baron and Ferejohn (1989), parties that are empowered to make the first offer in coalition negotiations (also known as *formateurs*), enjoy disproportionate success in securing office and extracting a disproportionate portfolio share. Despite the absence of empirical support for that expectation (Laver et al. 2011), this model proved tremendously influential because it opened the door to the consideration of the institutional resources and constraints that shape actors' strategies in bargaining about government formation.

Subsequent work considered the *recognition rules* employed in different counties (Diermeier and van Roozendaal 1998) that determine which actor is asked to form the government—that is, to assume the role of the *formateur*. Several studies identified the *continuation rule*, which enables the incumbent to act as *formateur* after an election, as central in accounting for the striking advantage of previous incumbent parties in negotiating their return to government (Warwick 1996; Diermeier and van Roozendaal 1998; Martin and Stevenson 2010). However, the attention to *formateur* power per se ultimately yielded limited empirical success. As Bassi (2013) notes, this is not surprising given that *formateurs* are often not chosen on the basis of exogenous rules, but emerge endogenously from the bargaining situation in parliament. Moreover, the disproportionate focus on *formateur* power distracted from other institutions that shape coalition bargaining. This variation has hardly been explored. A rare exception is Strøm's (1990a) work, which notes the importance of *investiture rules* in advantaging coalitions with majority status over minority coalitions in bargaining about government formation. According to Strøm (1990a) the absence of a formal *investiture* vote in parliament raises the odds of minority government formation.

In addition scholars began to pay attention to *institutions that condition a coalition's success once in office*. The insight underpinning this work is that parties care not only about office, but also about achieving policy goals. Hence, their choices in bargaining about coalition formation can be expected to take account of the institutional environment that conditions their ability to pursue those policy goals. Laver and Shepsle (1990) introduced this intuition through the concept of the structurally induced equilibrium, which suggests that parties negotiate coalitions in the light of anticipated government behaviour. They assumed that government behaviour is shaped by the ability of individual ministers to set the legislative agenda in their policy area, which made it possible to account for a range of outcomes, including minority cabinets. While scholars subsequently rejected as unrealistic the assumption that ministers are policy dictators in their area of responsibility (Warwick 1996; Martin and Stevenson 2001), Laver and Shepsle's (1990) work inspired scholars to pay close attention to the institutions that condition a cabinet's legislative success and the opposition's policy influence. Institutional rules that generate incentives to form surplus coalitions, for instance, include bicameralism (Druckman et al. 2005) and super-majority requirements for legislation crucial to the government's programme (e.g. a government may wish to enact constitutional amendments that require a supermajority). Conversely, strong legislative committee systems raise the incidence of minority cabinets by enabling potential minor coalition partners to exercise policy influence from the opposition benches instead of joining a government, when the anticipated electoral costs of doing so are high (Strøm 1990a).

Recent work has contributed to a better understanding of cabinet formation in two further respects. First, scholars have provided a more nuanced account of the *motivations*, beyond the office and policy concerns, which may cause parties to enter, or refrain from joining, coalitions. Work on the importance of pre-electoral pacts and anti-pacts in coalition formation, for instance, draws attention to the influence of parties' *electoral motivations* on their coalition choices (Laver and Budge 1992; Golder 2006). Other research has foregrounded the anticipated *transaction costs* of governing. For instance, Tavits (2008) finds that following a coalition breakup, the conflicting parties are less likely to form another coalition in future, while Martin and Stevenson (2010) show that governments whose members have demonstrated a capacity to rule together without public conflict are likely to remain in office (see also Glasgow et al. 2012). These results are consistent with findings in social psychology that negotiators consider the anticipated transaction costs of working with 'angry' partners, whose demeanour is difficult, and shun such coalitions when they can (van Beest et al. 2008).[1]

Second, scholars made progress in empirically modelling the government formation process in more adequate ways. Thus, Martin and Stevenson (2001) suggested that the

---

[1] This work forms part of a wider literature which draws attention to the impact of psychological factors in coalition bargaining (see van Beest 2011 for a review).

conditional logit model offers an appropriate way of analysing the central problem in coalition formation, that is, the selection of a single coalition from the set of all possible coalitions. This approach models government formation as an 'unordered discrete choice problem where each formation opportunity (not each potential coalition) represents one case and where the set of discrete alternatives is the set of all potential combinations of parties that might form a government' (Martin and Stevenson 2001: 38). Subsequently, Glasgow et al. (2012) proposed the use of a mixed logit model with random coefficients to take account of unobserved heterogeneity in the government formation process and of potential violations of the assumption of the independence of irrelevant alternatives. Both approaches offer more appropriate ways of modelling coalition choice than traditional linear regression models, moreover, in practice, they often yield similar results.

How well, then, does this scholarship account for government formation outcomes? In a recent controversy, Golder et al. (2012) cast radical doubt on the insights gained, and propose a 'zero intelligence' model of government formation, based on two minimal assumptions (an incumbent government always exists and all governments must enjoy majority legislative support). This approach is categorically rejected by Martin and Vanberg (2014), who argue that conclusions about the predictive success of the 'zero intelligence' model are based on inferential errors. Once these are corrected, the 'zero intelligence' model makes no better than random predictions. Moreover, it is based on the implausible behavioural assumption that party leaders have no preferences over alternative viable governments. Hence, Martin and Vanberg (2014) conclude that scholars would be ill-advised to reject the considerable insights generated by existing coalition theories.

15.2.1 Government Formation in Semi-Presidential Regimes

Many of the insights that derive from by the literature on cabinet formation in *parliamentary* democracies generalize to *semi-presidential* regimes, and in fact early studies typically did not differentiate between the two constitutional formats. That changed when the institutional turn in work on parliamentary coalition formation connected with a budding interest among scholars of semi-presidentialism in the performance rather than the survival of these regimes from the 1990s onward. The central insight generated by the confluence of these research streams is that semi-presidential constitutions render the popularly elected president an additional actor with bargaining power in coalition formation. The institutions that condition this bargaining power include the president's prerogatives to affect (i) negotiations about government formation; (ii) the policy process (and hence, the success of coalitions once in office); and (iii) the survival of governments.

Shugart and Carey's (1992) seminal analysis began to map the tremendous institutional variation in presidential powers in each of these areas. In government formation negotiations, for instance, presidents may be veto players, empowered to approve or veto a new government; they may be *formateurs* with discretion to name a prime minister designate, subject to assembly approval; or they may be able to appoint a prime minister and government without assembly investiture. In the legislative process, presidents may have proposal, veto, and executive decree powers. With respect to government termination, they may have prerogatives to dismiss the government and a role in the process of assembly dissolution (Shugart and Carey 1992; Strøm and Swindle 2002; Goplerud and Schleiter 2016).

Several important insights resulted from the literature that explored the implications of these powers for government formation. First, the institutional variation within semi-presidential regimes, like that among parliamentary systems, is consequential when it comes to government formation: Generally, the greater a president's institutional powers in these three areas, the more extensive their influence on cabinet composition, other things equal (Shugart and Carey 1992; Protsyk 2005; Amorim Neto and Strøm 2006; Schleiter and Morgan-Jones 2009a).

Second, presidential influence on the cabinet affects party political participation in government. When semi-presidential regimes grant presidents a role in making and breaking governments and in shaping their legislative success in office, they empower an actor with a separate electoral mandate that may diverge from the mandate of a legislative majority and even from that of the president's legislative party (Samuels and Shugart 2010). This reduces the influence of legislative parties on cabinet formation and may also decrease their utility from participating in cabinet. Hence, compared to parliamentary democracies, semi-presidential regimes feature non-party, president-supported ministers more frequently, and occasionally even fully non-party, technical cabinets (Amorim Neto and Strøm 2006; Schleiter and Morgan-Jones 2009c).

Third, when cabinets are formed with the support of legislative parties, presidential bargaining power affects their coalition and majority status. A president who has the power to block or affect the formation, policy success, and survival of a government has resources to negotiate coalition participation for his or her party. Other things equal, this makes the formation of coalition governments more likely (compared to single party minority governments) and it tends to make coalitions larger. That is, compared to parliamentary regimes, coalitions in semi-presidential systems typically control a *larger* number of legislative seats: they are more likely to have majority (rather than minority) status and to be oversized, that is, to include more parties than is necessary to control a parliamentary majority (Cheibub 2007: 81; Mitchell and Nyblade 2008: 229).

Finally, semi-presidential regimes (unlike parliamentary or presidential systems) have unique flexibility in sourcing political support for cabinets, which may come principally from the assembly, or the president, or both actors, depending on their formal powers, capacity, and willingness to collaborate, and their electoral support (Pasquino 1997; Schleiter and Morgan-Jones 2009b). Thus, over time, most semi-presidential regimes have formed governments supported and directed by the assembly and the president collaboratively, but at other times had governments controlled by the parliamentary opposition to the president (a situation also known as cohabitation), or presidential, technical governments without active party participation. This flexibility can facilitate effective governance when the parliamentary party system is weakly institutionalized or fragmented, but also entails the potential for conflict between president, assembly, and government (Protsyk 2006; Elgie 2011).

15.2.2 Government Formation in Presidential Democracies

Compared to semi-presidential democracies, presidential democracies shift the balance of influence regarding government formation further in favour of the president in three areas: (i) The power to appoint presidential cabinets, and hence the role of the *forma-teur*, always lies with the president, regardless of the size of his or her legislative party. (ii) Presidential cabinets do not depend for their survival on legislative support, but solely on the president. (iii) The legislative powers of presidents tend to be greater in presidential democracies (Shugart and Carey 1992).

Since presidential cabinets do not require legislative support to remain in power, office motivations cannot be the driver of a president's choice to form coalitions under presidential constitutions. For this reason, scholars initially expected coalitions to be an exception in presidential democracies (Mainwaring 1993; Linz 1994). Yet multiple studies document that coalition cabinets frequently form (Altman 2000; Amorim Neto 2006; Alemán and Tsebelis 2011; Martínez-Gallardo 2012), which raises the question why presidents choose to invite legislative parties into the cabinet and what characteristics these coalitions have (see also Chapter 20 in this volume).

The literature on coalitional presidentialism focusses overwhelmingly on policy motivations, arguing that presidents form cabinet coalitions to construct reliable legislative support for their policy agendas. Consistent with that assumption, multiple studies show that coalition participation in presidential democracies is predicted by many of the same characteristics as in parliamentary or semi-presidential democracies, for example party size and ideology (Altman 2000; Amorim Neto 2006; Cheibub 2007; Alemán and Tsebelis 2011; Martínez-Gallardo 2012). Even the policy motivation to form coalitions, however, is weaker than in semi-presidential democracies because, on average, presidential legislative powers tend to be greater in presidential democracies (Shugart and Carey 1992).[2]

As a result, the attributes of presidential cabinets differ significantly from those of parliamentary and semi-presidential cabinets. Since the president is always the *forma-teur*, the presidential party is typically included in cabinet regardless of its legislative size and of its ability to negotiate a legislative majority. Even if a presidential party only commands a minority of assembly seats and fails to enter a coalition, it may rule on its own, precisely because the cabinet does not depend on assembly confidence. Hence, given a minority situation, coalition formation, while significantly more common than originally

---

[2] Recent work by Freudenreich (2016) suggests that electoral motivations and the widespread use of pre-electoral coalitions also play a role in motivating the formation of cabinet coalitions in presidential democracies. This finding is consistent with work that stresses the importance of pre-electoral coalition for government formation choices in parliamentary democracies and opens up a promising new avenue for research on coalitional presidentialism.

anticipated (Mainwaring 1993; Linz 1994), is less likely than in semi-presidential and parliamentary democracies. According to Cheibub (2007: 81), for instance, the share of coalition governments formed in minority situations by presidents is 52 per cent compared to 75 per cent in parliamentary and 86 per cent in semi-presidential democracies. In addition, cabinets that form are less likely to have majority status (Amorim Neto 2006; Cheibub 2007: 81). Portfolio allocation is on average also less proportional than in parliamentary systems because cabinets in presidential systems tend to represent the president's party to a greater extent than is warranted by its legislative size (Amorim Neto and Samuels 2010: 17). Moreover, presidential cabinets include a greater share of non-party ministers—around 21 per cent compared to 2 per cent in parliamentary and 7 per cent in semi-presidential regimes (Amorim Neto and Samuels 2010: 14). This reflects the tensions that the distinct electoral mandates of president and assembly may engender between the president and his or her party, as well as the extensive powers of presidents to determine cabinet composition (Martínez-Gallardo and Schleiter 2015).

In sum, presidents' strategies for using cabinet formation as a tool to construct legislative support can vary from cooperative to unilateral. Moreover, a president's reliance on coalition building is systematically related to his or her need to negotiate with opposition parties in order to achieve his or her policy objectives, which varies with the president's political and institutional powers (Camerlo and Martínez-Gallardo 2017).

15.3 The Literature on Government Survival and Termination

In the study of government termination, as in government formation, research on parliamentary democracies is foundational. It identifies political parties—motivated by office, policy, and electoral concerns—as the central actors and focuses on two types of outcomes: government duration (i.e., how long a government survives) and the nature of government terminations (i.e., how a government terminates).

Early accounts of cabinet survival in parliamentary democracies built directly on the research concerning government formation and sought the causes of government termination in the *structural attributes* of cabinets, their parliamentary and political environment. This work in effect treated the causes of cabinet duration as *fixed* at the point of government formation and found that a cabinet's vulnerability to early termination rises in cabinet fragmentation and the ideological diversity of the cabinet, minority and coalition status. Yet, as critical events theorists argued, cabinets typically terminate in response to unpredictable events such as scandals, sudden shifts in public opinion, crises, deaths, or illness of the prime minister, which makes the determinism of explanations that solely rely on the structural attributes inappropriate (Frendreis et al. 1986). This analysis gave rise to the understanding that government termination is—at least in part—the product of a stochastic process (King et al. 1990). However, as Strøm (1988) notes, the overwhelming majority of government terminations are not the automatic consequence of events, instead they result from the *strategic political choices* of parties inside or outside the government in response to such events.

Lupia and Strøm's (1995) game theoretic model of government termination proved seminal in developing an understanding of these strategic choices. It made clear that politicians may choose several mutually exclusive ways of terminating a government early, that is, early elections, and the non-electoral replacement of a government during a sitting parliament. It also provided a bargaining-theoretic account of how politicians' choices between these options are shaped by the value of the current coalition, transaction costs, and the payoffs promised by their outside options in light of exogenous shocks. This work triggered two major developments in the study of cabinet survival. First, Diermeier and Stevenson (2000) demonstrated that the twin risks of early government termination identified by Lupia and Strøm (1995) are empirically distinguishable and have distinct correlates. This transformed the study of cabinet survival into the study of *competing risks*. Second, the formulation of an explicit bargaining model by Lupia and Strøm (1995) made it easy to see that the literature up to this point had not adequately captured how political *institutions* structure bargaining about cabinet termination.

The first of these developments caused scholars to pay closer attention to the previously unexplored variety of ways in which governments terminate. The differences in the mode of government termination, this research argues, are important because they indicate an underlying diversity in the causal processes, political actors, and motivations that precipitate cabinet terminations. Schleiter and Issar (forthcoming), for instance, shed light on the heterogeneity of early elections. Merging the literatures on cabinet termination and opportunistic election timing, they characterize the difference between opportunistic elections that are used by the prime minister's party to consolidate its position, and failure elections, directed against the prime minister's party when its hold on power slips (see also Schleiter and Tavits 2016). Similarly, Fernandes and Magalhães (2016) contrast non-electoral replacements in which the prime minister's party does and does not change. Both papers show that politicians who terminate governments early choose between a considerably more complex range of outside options than Lupia and Strøm (1995) had originally anticipated. The two papers also offer a first account of the constitutional, economic, and political circumstances that make each type of early termination more likely and show that their predictors are distinct. In short, these contributions reconceptualise the dependent variable in work on government termination and duration (i.e., the competing termination types of which governments are at risk), and change our understanding of the causal processes that precipitate those terminations.

In a second development scholars explored the effect of *institutions* on bargaining about cabinet termination. As in the literature on government formation, the institutionalist turn drew attention to institutions that (i) regulate the government termination process and (ii) affect the value of the cabinet to parties by conditioning its ability to pursue its policy goals. This work highlighted that constitutional powers to influence and manage government termination (e.g. by withholding confidence or invoking confidence motions, dismissing the government, or calling early elections) confer bargaining power on specific actors (Baron 1998; Strøm and Swindle 2002; Schleiter and Morgan-Jones 2009a; Schleiter and Tavits 2016; Evans 2017). Similarly, researchers showed that the value of cabinets to political parties, and hence government survival, is influenced by institutions which structure the life and work of cabinets once in office. These institutions include, for instance, the vote of investiture, opposition influence in parliament, the prime minister's agenda setting powers and bicameralism (King et al. 1990; Druckman and Thies 2002; Tsebelis 2002; Bergman et al. 2003; Saalfeld 2008).

15.3.1 Government Survival and Termination in Semi-Presidential Regimes

As in the literature on government formation, many of the insights generated by the literature on cabinet duration and termination in *parliamentary* democracies generalize to *semi-presidential* regimes. Moreover, the institutionalist turn made it easy to see that a president's constitutional powers were likely to translate into bargaining leverage over cabinet terminations.

Nonetheless, any bargaining theoretic assumptions remained implicit in early work on the durability and termination of semi-presidential governments, which developed instead the general expectation that a popularly elected president, as an additional actor with influence on government survival, renders semi-presidential cabinets less stable than parliamentary governments (Linz 1994). However, this expectation receives no support in systematic controlled comparative studies of government survival in semi-presidential and parliamentary regimes. The majority of this work finds that a popularly elected president per se has no significant effect on cabinet durability (Strøm and Swindle 2002; Cheibub and Chernykh 2008: 279; Somer-Topcu and Williams 2008; Schleiter and Morgan-Jones 2009a: 510; however see Saalfeld 2008 for a divergent conclusion).

Scholars therefore turned to the specific sources of presidential bargaining power and initially privileged presidential powers of cabinet dismissal. According to Shugart and Carey (1992) a president's power to dismiss the cabinet distinguishes two types of semi-presidential constitutions with distinct arrangements regarding authority over the cabinet: premier-presidentialism (which makes the cabinet responsible only to the assembly, not the president), and president-parliamentarism (which enables cabinets to be dismissed by the assembly and the president). President-parliamentarism is generally expected to give rise to less stable cabinets than premier-presidentialism (Shugart and Carey 1992: 118–21). The primary concern is the potential under president-parliamentary constitutions for conflicts between president and assembly over control of the government, which is thought to contribute to unstable patterns of cabinet appointment and dismissal (Shugart and Carey 1992: 121; Elgie 2004, 2011). Although Sedelius and Ekman (2010) find support for this expectation in a sample of Central and East European democracies, it remains unsupported in research that uses a larger sample of democracies (Schleiter and Morgan-Jones 2009a).

Responding to such contradictory findings, recent scholarship has refined its approach in three respects. First, there is, by now, a recognition that presidential bargaining power in relation to cabinet survival is likely to arise from an array of institutional prerogatives—including powers of assembly dissolution, cabinet dismissal, and the popular mandate (Strøm and Swindle 2002; Schleiter and Morgan-Jones 2009a; Fernandes and Magalhães 2016). When studies omit some of these rules, their conclusions regarding the institutional sources of presidential leverage are likely to be characterized by omitted variable bias.[3] Second, attention to the counterfactual, to which the influence of presidents is compared, is essential. In samples that comprise parliamentary and semi-presidential democracies, for instance, presidents with influence on parliamentary dissolution do not raise the risk of early elections compared to the baseline constitution which enables governments to trigger early elections for partisan gain (Strøm and Swindle 2002; Schleiter and Morgan-Jones 2009a). However, in a restricted sample of semi-presidential democracies, where powers of parliamentary dissolution either fall to the president or tend to be heavily constrained, presidential dissolution powers, in fact, raise the risk of early elections (Fernandes and Magalhães 2016). Put differently, there is a growing recognition of the need to distinguish the effect of cross-national and, indeed, cross-temporal confounders from the effect of presidential powers. Third, recent work has begun to pay attention to the heterogeneity of cabinet termination modes. Fernandes and Magalhães (2016), for instance, find that presidential powers of cabinet dismissal make major inter-electoral government replacements more likely in which the prime minister's party loses office, but not those in which a minor coalition partner changes.

15.3.2 Government Survival and Termination in Presidential Regimes

In presidential democracies, the president's fixed term and the independence of cabinet survival from assembly confidence have two implications. First, presidents can replace ministers without having to preserve a supporting majority in the legislature. Second, the inability of coalition partners to bring down the government weakens the bargaining power of legislative parties and hence their ability to extract concessions from the president in return for their continued support of the cabinet. This renders cabinet

---

[3] An interesting and perhaps surprising finding of this literature is that cohabitation, that is, the co-existence of a president with a prime minister and cabinet of a different political persuasion, does not in and of itself raise the risk of early cabinet termination (Strøm and Swindle 2002; Schleiter and Morgan-Jones 2009a; Fernandes and Magalhães 2016). In all probability this null finding suggests that the effect of partisan conflict is mediated by presidential powers and the likelihood of parliamentary override, which is often not explored.

participation less valuable for assembly parties and weakens the incentives for legislative parties to maintain party discipline (Clark et al. 2009: 447). As a result, the commitment of assembly parties and the president to coalition governance is, on average, less reliable than in semi-presidential in parliamentary democracies so that presidential coalition cabinets tend to be less stable.

Moreover, these differences alter the political implications of cabinet stability in presidential democracies (Camerlo and Martínez-Gallardo 2017): Since party discipline tends to be weaker in presidential democracies, it is not always clear to what extent party affiliated ministers in fact act as agents of their party in government. For instance, it is not uncommon for party affiliated ministers to lack political leverage within their party, in which case their departure from the cabinet may have no effect on their party's relationship with the government. This implies that the most common way of determining when a presidential cabinet terminates, which focuses on changes in the party composition of the cabinet (in addition to elections), becomes a less reliable indicator of cabinet change with less obvious political implications.

Despite these caveats, however, there are significant differences in the duration of presidential cabinets. On average, presidential coalition cabinets are more durable when presidents have weak legislative powers (Amorim Neto 2006), and when the legislature is effective (Martínez-Gallardo 2012), so that presidents have incentives to seek stable support from legislative parties in order to advance their policy goals. Conversely, when parties that pursue particularistic goals (rather than programmatic policy) control a larger share of the legislature, presidents are more likely to form flexible coalitions, and to change the party composition of their cabinets more often (Kellam 2015). Finally, legislative parties are less likely to defect from presidential cabinets when the executive is successful and effective, that is, when the government is performing well, the president is popular, the cabinet is less fragmented, and when the government controls a larger share of legislative seats (Martínez-Gallardo 2012; Shin 2013). These findings suggest that coalition stability in presidential systems rises in the policy, office, and electoral benefits for parties of participating in cabinet, which is consistent with work on government stability in semi-presidential and parliamentary democracies.

15.4 FUTURE RESEARCH AGENDA

As this review has demonstrated, extensive progress has been made in understanding cabinet formation and termination, in particular since the 1990s, when the institutionalist turn in the literature on parliamentary governments was complemented by the rising interest in cabinet formation and termination among scholars who study semi-presidential and presidential democracies. These developments lent increasing realism to models of government formation and termination, and yielded significant improvements in the ability of scholars to account for observed outcomes. At the same time, however, the confluence of these different research traditions highlights new challenges and opens up new avenues for research in many areas. In this concluding section, I focus on five particularly urgent challenges.

Traditionally, research on government formation and termination has assumed that politicians are motivated by three concerns in negotiating about cabinets: office, policy, and votes. Of these, office and policy concerns have received by far the greatest attention, ever since foundational models of parliamentary government formation foregrounded these concerns. There is, however, growing evidence that our conception of politicians' motivations remains (i) underdeveloped and (ii) too narrow. First, electoral motivations remain strikingly understudied despite their centrality in Lupia and Strøm's (1995) influential model of coalition termination. Changing electoral expectations can be expected to affect the coalition exit and inclusion probabilities of parties. Yet, to date, no dynamic account of coalition termination and formation exists that measures and probes the effect of these changing expectations.[4] Scholars have also paid relatively little attention to pre-electoral coalitions, which are routinely formed in many democracies, and play a central role in accounting for the coalitions that politicians form after elections in parliamentary as well as presidential democracies (Golder 2006; Freudenreich 2016). In short, the role of electoral motivations in government formation and termination deserves greater attention. Second, policy, office and vote-related motivations fail to capture a range of additional concerns that demonstrably affect coalition politics. Several studies indicate, for instance, that the desire to avoid the transaction costs of coalitions with potential partners who invite conflict is a powerful motivation in cabinet formation (Tavits 2008; van Beest et al. 2008; Martin and Stevenson 2010). Moreover, in new and less developed democracies, completely different motivations may drive the making and breaking of cabinets. For instance, Kellam's (2015) work on presidential cabinets highlights that some parties focus primarily on particularistic benefits rather than policy. Hence, the formation and maintenance of coalitions with such parties may depend critically on president's budgetary authority and ability to channel particularistic benefits to these parties, rather than on the effective pursuit of shared policy goals. One challenge for future work on government formation and termination is therefore to construct accounts that integrate a broader and more accurate range of political motivations.

Equally important is more detailed attention to the institutional environment in which politicians bargain about cabinet formation and termination. Institutions, in particular presidential powers, have been a natural focus in the literatures on presidential and semi-presidential cabinets. However, in work on *parliamentary* governments, the implications of several types of institutional rules for government formation and termination remain, as yet, surprisingly poorly understood despite the institutionalist turn in this literature. These understudied institutions include the formal powers of *indirectly* elected presidents to exercise leverage in negotiating about cabinets (Tavits 2009), and the bargaining power that government and opposition may derive from variation in

---

[4] Note, however, that two recent working papers by Heller (2016) and Kayser et al. (2017) explore this theme.

some of the most consequential institutional rules in parliamentary democracies: confidence and no-confidence vote procedures (Evans 2017).

In the literature on cabinet survival, a distinct challenge remains the need to develop a more nuanced understanding of the dependent variable, that is, the nature of cabinet terminations. For instance, major government replacements, in which the prime minister's party changes, and minor replacements, in which the dominant governing party carries on, are likely to have divergent predictors, not only in semi-presidential democracies (Fernandes and Magalhães 2016), but also in parliamentary regimes. Likewise, early elections in parliamentary and semi-presidential democracies may require further disaggregation. Powers to trigger premature elections may not only lie with the government and its parliamentary majority, but also with the president (Goplerud and Schleiter 2016). Presidents have been shown to use this power for partisan gain (Schleiter and Morgan-Jones 2017), and they are likely to deploy it under conditions that diverge from those under which governments and assembly majorities may seek early elections. This heterogeneity of outcomes presents challenges for work on cabinet termination: Studies that elide these differences in termination outcomes yield results that average across qualitatively distinct outcomes and are unlikely to characterise termination causes accurately.

In addition, formidable inferential challenges arise from the fact that government formation and termination are jointly determined outcomes, which should be, but are not usually, analysed as such. The two outcomes are jointly determined because (i) cabinet formation opportunities are the result of strategic choices (rather than random events), and (ii) politicians select and form coalitions which are likely to be durable.

As strategic models of cabinet termination make clear, the decision to topple a cabinet and form a new one is a political choice (Strøm 1988; Lupia and Strøm 1995). Hence cabinet formation opportunities result from the strategic choices of politicians, such as, for instance, a president's dismissal of the cabinet, a prime minister's decision to schedule an early election, or a minor coalition partner's choice to withdraw and topple the government. In each of these instances, political actors may choose to terminate a government precisely because that choice has implications for their party's electoral prospects, chances of claiming portfolios in the next government and the pursuit of their policy goals. Put differently, the choice to create a government formation opportunity and the formation outcome are likely to be endogenous to a range of variables that jointly predict both. Similarly, politicians do not choose the cabinets that they form at random, but with an eye to their durability (Chiba et al. 2015). As a result, the cabinets that form are on average, significantly more likely to endure than cabinets that do not form. Thus, the choice to form a cabinet and that government's duration are likely to be endogenous to a range of variables that jointly predict both. Unless this endogeneity between cabinet formation and survival is taken account of, inferences regarding the predictors of both outcomes are likely to be biased. However, the task of theorizing and modelling this dependence between government termination and formation is methodologically challenging and, as yet, only in its infancy.

Chiba et al. (2015) make a seminal contribution in addressing this challenge in the study of cabinet survival. Their argument is that the cabinets which politicians choose to form are on average significantly more likely to endure than potential cabinets that do not form. Thus the durability of observed cabinets is biased upwards and unless that selection process is corrected for, inferences about the causes of cabinet duration will be biased, too. Chiba et al. (2015) address this problem by modelling the sample selection bias using a copula framework, and apply this approach to the study of parliamentary coalition governments. Work on the duration of semi-presidential and presidential cabinets, however, has yet to address the challenges of selection bias. Similarly, the literature on government formation is yet to theorize the dependence between government termination and formation. These challenges are likely to require not just econometric solutions (Chiba et al. 2015), but will also benefit from identification strategies anchored in careful research design.

Finally, bargaining between politicians about government formation and termination has attracted such extensive scholarly attention because it is expected to impact on real world outcomes such as elections, government spending, tax regimes, and policy with respect to education, inequality and immigration. Yet, very few studies link cabinet formation and termination to outcomes in the electoral or policy arena. One rare example is a study by Schleiter and Morgan-Jones (2017) which shows that presidents in parliamentary and semi-presidential democracies use their influence on the calling of early elections for partisan benefit and are able to affect the electoral success of incumbents. Likewise, recent work by Heller (2016) begins to explore how the 'exit power' of governing parties affects economic policy. Yet, these are only first steps in the process that requires much greater efforts to map how bargaining over cabinets affects outcomes in the electoral and policy arenas.

REFERENCES

Alemán, E. and Tsebelis, G. (2011). 'Political Parties and Government Coalitions in the Americas,' Journal of Politics in Latin America 3(1): 3–28.

Altman, D. (2000). 'The Politics of Coalition Formation and Survival in Multiparty Presidential Democracies: The Case of Uruguay, 1989–1999,' Party Politics 6(3): 259–83.

Amorim Neto, O. (2006). 'The Presidential Calculus: Executive Policy Making and Cabinet Formation in the Americas,' Comparative Political Studies 39(4): 415–40.

Amorim Neto, O. and Strøm, K. (2006). 'Breaking the Parliamentary Chain of Delegation: Presidents and Non-Partisan Cabinet Members in European Democracies,' British Journal of Political Science 36(4): 619–43.

Amorim Neto, O. and Samuels, D. (2010). 'Democratic Regimes and Cabinet Politics: A Global Perspective,' Revista Ibero-Americana de Estudos Legislativos 1(1): 10–23.

Axelrod, R. (1970). Conflict of Interest. Chicago: Markham.

Baron, D. P. (1998). 'Comparative Dynamics of Parliamentary Governments,' American Political Science Review 92(3): 593–609.

Baron, D. P. and Ferejohn, J. A. (1989). 'Bargaining in Legislatures,' American Political Science Review 83(4): 1181–206.

Bassi, A. (2013). 'A Model of Endogenous Government Formation,' *American Journal of Political Science* 57(4): 777–93.

Bergman, T., Müller, W., Strøm, K., and Blomgren, M. (2003). 'Democratic Delegation and Accountability: Cross-National Patterns,' in K. Strøm, T. Bergman, and W. C. Müller (eds) *Delegation and Accountability in Parliamentary Democracies*. Oxford: Oxford University Press, 109–220.

Camerlo, M. and Martínez-Gallardo, C. (2017) (eds). *Government Formation and Minister Turnover in Presidential Cabinets: Comparative Analysis in the Americas*. London: Routledge.

Cheibub, J. A. (2007). *Presidentialism, Parliamentarism, and Democracy*. Cambridge: Cambridge University Press.

Cheibub, J. A. and Chernykh, S. (2008). 'Constitutions and Democratic Performance in Semi-Presidential Democracies,' *Japanese Journal of Political Science* 9(3): 269–303.

Chiba, D., Martin, L. W., and Stevenson, R. T. (2015). 'A Copula Approach to the Problem of Selection Bias in Models of Government Survival,' *Political Analysis* 23(1): 42–58.

Clark, W. R., Golder, M., and Golder, S. N. (2009). *Principles of Comparative Politics*. Washington, DC: CQ Press.

De Swaan, A. (1973). *Coalition Theories and Cabinet Formations*. Amsterdam: Elsevier.

Diermeier, D. and Stevenson, R. T. (2000). 'Cabinet Terminations and Critical Events,' *American Political Science Review* 94(3): 627–40.

Diermeier, D. and Van Roozendaal, P. (1998). 'The Duration of Cabinet Formation Processes in Western Multi-Party Democracies,' *British Journal of Political Science* 28(4): 609–26.

Druckman, J. N., Martin, L. W., and Thies, M. F. (2005). 'Influence without Confidence: Upper Chambers and Government Formation,' *Legislative Studies Quarterly* 30(4): 529–48.

Druckman, J. N. and Thies, M. F. (2002). 'The Importance of Concurrence: The Impact of Bicameralism on Government Formation and Duration,' *American Journal of Political Science* 46(4): 760–71.

Elgie, R. (2004). 'Semi-Presidentialism: Concepts, Consequences and Contesting Explanations,' *Political Studies Review* 2(3): 314–30.

Elgie, R. (2011). *Semi-Presidentialism: Sub-types and Democratic Performance*. Oxford: Oxford University Press.

Evans, G. (2017). 'Setting the Agenda: Variation in the Vote of Confidence Procedure and Cabinet Survival in Europe.' BA Thesis, University of Oxford.

Fernandes, J. M. and Magalhães, P. C. (2016). 'Government Survival in Semi-Presidential Regimes,' *European Journal of Political Research* 55(1): 61–80.

Franklin, M. N. and Mackie, T. T. (1984). 'Reassessing the Importance of Size and Ideology for the Formation of Governing Coalitions in Parliamentary Democracies,' *American Journal of Political Science* 28(4): 671–92.

Frendreis, J. P., Gleiber, D. W., and Browne, E. C. (1986). 'The Study of Cabinet Dissolutions in Parliamentary Democracies,' *Legislative Studies Quarterly* 11(4): 619–28.

Freudenreich, J. (2016). 'The Formation of Cabinet Coalitions in Presidential Systems,' *Latin American Politics and Society* 58(4): 80–102.

Gamson, W. A. (1961). 'A Theory of Coalition Formation,' *American Sociological Review* 26(3): 373–82.

Glasgow, G., Golder, M., and Golder, S. N. (2012). 'New Empirical Strategies for the Study of Parliamentary Government Formation,' *Political Analysis* 20(2): 248–70.

Golder, S. N. (2006). *The Logic of Pre-Electoral Coalition Formation*. Columbus, OH: Ohio State University Press.

Golder, M., Golder, S. N., and Siegel, D. A. (2012). 'Modeling the Institutional Foundation of Parliamentary Government Formation,' *The Journal of Politics* 74(2): 427–45.

Goplerud, M. and Schleiter, P. (2016). 'An Index of Assembly Dissolution Powers,' *Comparative Political Studies* 49(4): 427–56.

Hansen, M. E., Klemmensen, R., Hobolt, S. B., and Bäck, H. (2013). 'Portfolio Saliency and Ministerial Turnover: Dynamics in Scandinavian Postwar Cabinets,' *Scandinavian Political Studies* 36(3): 227–48.

Heller, M. (2016). 'Keep Me If You Can: Exit Power and Government Spending,' paper presented at MPSA.

Kayser, M., Rehmert, J., and Schleiter, P. (2017). 'Dynamic and Strategic Coalition Termination,' paper presented at APSA.

Kellam, M., (2015). 'Parties for Hire: How Particularistic Parties Influence Presidents' Governing Strategies,' *Party Politics* 21(4): 515–26.

King, G., Alt, J. E., Burns, N. E., and Laver, M. (1990). 'A Unified Model of Cabinet Dissolution in Parliamentary Democracies,' *American Journal of Political Science* 34(3): 846–71.

Laver, M., Budge, I. (1992) (eds). *Party Policy and Coalition Government*. London: Macmillan.

Laver, M. and Schofield, N. (1990). *Multiparty Governments: The Politics of Coalition in Europe*. Oxford: Oxford University Press.

Laver, M. and Shepsle, K. A. (1990). 'Coalitions and Cabinet Government,' *American Political Science Review* 84(3): 873–90.

Laver, M., De Marchi, S., and Mutlu, H. (2011). 'Negotiation in Legislatures over Government Formation,' *Public Choice* 147(3): 285–304.

Linz, J. (1994). 'Presidential or Parliamentary Democracy?,' in J. Linz and A. Valenzuela (eds) *The Failure of Presidential Democracy: The Case of Latin America*. Baltimore: Johns Hopkins University Press.

Lupia, A. and Strøm, K. (1995). 'Coalition Termination and the Strategic Timing of Parliamentary Elections,' *American Political Science Review* 89(3): 648–65.

Mainwaring, S. (1993). 'Presidentialism, Multipartism, and Democracy: The Difficult Combination,' *Comparative Political Studies* 26(2): 198–228.

Martin, L. W. and Stevenson, R. T. (2001). 'Government Formation in Parliamentary Democracies,' *American Journal of Political Science* 45(1): 33–50.

Martin, L. W. and Stevenson, R. T. (2010). 'The Conditional Impact of Incumbency on Government Formation,' *American Political Science Review* 104(3): 503–18.

Martin, L. W. and Vanberg, G. (2014). 'A Step in the Wrong Direction: An Appraisal of the Zero-Intelligence Model of Government Formation,' *Journal of Politics* 76: 873–9.

Martínez-Gallardo, C. (2012). 'Out of the Cabinet: What Drives Defections from the Government in Presidential Systems?,' *Comparative Political Studies* 45(1): 62–90.

Martínez-Gallardo, C. and Schleiter, P. (2015). 'Choosing Whom to Trust: Agency Risks and Cabinet Partisanship in Presidential Democracies,' *Comparative Political Studies* 48(2): 231–64.

Mitchell, P. and Nyblade, B. (2008). 'Government Formation and Cabinet Type in Parliamentary Democracies,' in K. Strøm, W. C. Müller, and T. Bergman (eds) *Cabinets and Coalition Bargaining: The Democratic Life Cycle in Western Europe*. Oxford: Oxford University Press, 201–36.

Müller, W. C. and Strøm, K. (2000) (eds). *Coalition Governments in Western Europe*. Oxford: Oxford University Press.

Pasquino, G. (1997). 'Semi-Presidentialism: A Political Model at Work,' *European Journal of Political Research* 31(1–2): 128–37.

Protsyk, O. (2005). 'Prime Ministers' Identity in Semi-Presidential Regimes: Constitutional Norms and Cabinet Formation Outcomes,' *European Journal of Political Research* 44(5): 721–48.

Protsyk, O. (2006). 'Intra-Executive Competition between President and Prime Minister: Patterns of Institutional Conflict and Cooperation under Semi-Presidentialism,' *Political Studies* 54(2): 219–44.

Riker, W. H. (1962). *The Theory of Political Coalitions*. New York: Yale University Press.

Saalfeld, T. (2008). 'Institutions, Chance and Choices: The Dynamics of Cabinet Survival in the Parliamentary Democracies of Western Europe (1945–99),' in K. Strøm, W. C. Müller, and T. Bergman (eds) *Cabinets and Coalition Bargaining: The Democratic Life Cycle in Western Europe*. Oxford: Oxford University Press, 327–68.

Samuels, D. J. and Shugart, M. S. (2010). *Presidents, Parties, and Prime Ministers: How the Separation of Powers Affects Party Organization and Behavior*. Cambridge: Cambridge University Press.

Schleiter, P. and Issar, S. (forthcoming). 'The Heterogeneity of Early Elections.'

Schleiter, P. and Morgan-Jones, E. (2009a). 'Constitutional Power and Competing Risks: Monarchs, Presidents, Prime Ministers, and the Termination of East and West European Cabinets,' *American Political Science Review* 103(3): 496–512.

Schleiter, P. and Morgan-Jones, E. (2009b). 'Citizens, Presidents and Assemblies: The Study of Semi-Presidentialism beyond Duverger and Linz,' *British Journal of Political Science* 39(4): 871–92.

Schleiter, P. and Morgan-Jones, E. (2009c). 'Party Government in Europe? Parliamentary and Semi-Presidential Democracies Compared,' *European Journal of Political Research* 48(5): 665–93.

Schleiter, P. and Morgan-Jones, E. (2017). 'Presidents, Assembly Dissolution, and the Electoral Performance of Prime Ministers,' *Comparative Political Studies* 51(6): 730–58.

Schleiter, P. and Tavits, M. (2016). 'The Electoral Benefits of Opportunistic Election Timing,' *The Journal of Politics* 78(3): 836–50.

Sedelius, T. and Ekman, J. (2010). 'Intra-Executive Conflict and Cabinet Instability: Effects of Semi-Presidentialism in Central and Eastern Europe,' *Government and Opposition* 45(4): 505–30.

Shin, H. J. (2013). 'Cabinet Duration in Presidential Democracies,' *Political Science Quarterly* 128(2): 317–39.

Shugart, M. S. and Carey, J. M. (1992). *Presidents and Assemblies: Constitutional Design and Electoral Dynamics*. Cambridge: Cambridge University Press.

Somer-Topcu, Z. and Williams, L. K. (2008). 'Survival of the Fittest? Cabinet Duration in Postcommunist Europe,' *Comparative Politics* 40(3): 313–29.

Strøm, K. (1988). 'Contending Models of Cabinet Stability,' *American Political Science Review* 82(3): 923–30.

Strøm, K. (1990a). *Minority Government and Majority Rule*. Cambridge: Cambridge University Press.

Strøm, K. (1990b). 'A Behavioral Theory of Competitive Political Parties,' *American Journal of Political Science* 34(2): 565–98.

Strøm, K. and Swindle, S. M. (2002). 'Strategic Parliamentary Dissolution,' *American Political Science Review* 96(3): 575–91.

Tavits, M. (2008). 'The Role of Parties' Past Behavior in Coalition Formation,' *American Political Science Review* 102(4): 495–507.

Tavits, M. (2009). *Presidents with Prime Ministers: Do Direct Elections Matter?* Oxford: Oxford University Press.

Tsebelis, G. (2002). *Veto Players: How Political Institutions Work.* Princeton: Princeton University Press.

van Beest, I. (2011). 'A Neglected Alternative? Psychological Approaches to Coalition Formation,' in R. B. Andeweg, L. de Winter, and P. Dumont (eds) *Puzzles of Government Formation: Coalition Theory and Deviant Cases.* London: Routledge, 24–43.

van Beest, I., Van Kleef, G. A., and Van Dijk, E. (2008). 'Get Angry, Get Out: The Interpersonal Effects of Anger Communication in Multiparty Negotiation,' *Journal of Experimental Social Psychology* 44(4): 993–1002.

Warwick, P. V. (1996). 'Coalition Government Membership in West European Parliamentary Democracies,' *British Journal of Political Science* 26(4): 471–99.

CHAPTER 16

....

THE DISTRIBUTION OF
MINISTERIAL POSTS IN
PARLIAMENTARY
SYSTEMS

....

HANNA BÄCK AND ROYCE CARROLL

16.1 INTRODUCTION

....

AT the core of government is the division of power among winners. In parliamentary systems, the makeup of the cabinet is the locus of this bargaining, influencing the direction of policy, the potential for policy change, and the stability of government itself. Ministerial portfolios are important payoffs for parties, intra-party factions, and individual politicians entering a government in parliamentary democracies, and portfolio allocation clearly constitutes a crucial intervening link between party policy and government action through the control of relevant ministries in the government. This renders bargaining over portfolios an important phase of the government formation process. In this chapter, we focus on this phase, taking our starting point in previous research on portfolio allocation in parliamentary democracies, and incorporate the literature on ministerial selection and de-selection as extensions of the broader politics of allocating power.

The literature on portfolio allocation can be divided into two strands, where the first focuses on the *quantity* of portfolios allocated, asking how many portfolios each party gets. Comparative analyses of portfolio allocation have produced clear-cut empirical findings: coalition parties receive ministerial posts in close proportion to their parliamentary seats contribution (e.g. Warwick and Druckman 2006). The second strand of the literature, which has recently gained more interest, focuses on the *quality* of ministerial posts, asking in particular 'which party gets what and why?' (e.g. Bäck et al. 2011).

Since the literature on portfolio allocation has focused exclusively on the distribution of ministerial posts between different political parties, it has often ignored intra-party dynamics and the individual characteristics of politicians when predicting the allocation of posts. There is however a growing literature that focuses on ministerial selection and de-selection that has shed light on these phenomena. This literature generally takes the so-called 'chain of delegation' and principal-agent theory as its starting point, typically assuming that the prime minister (PM) can be characterized as a principal delegating power to his or her line ministers as agents (see, e.g., Dowding and Dumont 2009a for an overview).

After reviewing the previous literature, we present a research agenda for studying the distribution of ministerial posts in parliamentary democracies. We suggest that it is important to integrate the key findings in the various fields that we have reviewed, especially to connect the literature on portfolio allocation with the literature on ministerial selection. We argue that the quantity and quality of portfolio allocation between parties should be treated as an integrated process with intra-party ministerial selection. Jointly considering these topics, we propose that there may be an opportunity to understand why in some cases parties may gain control over certain ministerial posts because they have specific individuals among their 'pool of candidates', with certain backgrounds or policy positions that make them central in certain bargaining situations.

16.2 Basic Research Questions

16.2.1 Questions about the Allocation of Portfolios between Parties in Coalitions

A large part of the research on portfolio allocation in parliamentary democracies focuses on the *quantity* of posts allocated, asking the question, *why do some parties get more portfolios than others?* Starting with the early work by Browne and Franklin (1973), a number of studies have presented large-n analyses of portfolio allocation, analysing the statistical relationship between party seat shares and ministerial portfolio shares, producing clear-cut empirical findings: coalition parties receive ministerial posts in close proportion to their parliamentary seat contribution to the government.

One of the main reasons for interest in the proportionality of portfolio distributions is the discrepancy between the empirical record and certain theoretical expectations. A key question raised in this literature is why 'formateur' parties—that is, parties that are given a first chance to form a government—are not able to reap some bargaining advantage from their role as agenda setter (Baron and Ferejohn 1989). Related to this, parties are expected to benefit from their 'bargaining weight', that is, their pivotalness in forming a coalition (Ansolabehere et al. 2005). While many of these answers have been theoretical, many have focused on re-evaluating the empirical measures used in analyses of portfolio allocation. Some scholars have raised the question of whether we should really treat all ministerial portfolios as equal in our analyses, considering that some posts are clearly more important than others. For example, the finance and foreign minister posts are typically seen as highly important in most countries, whereas some other posts, such as the minister of culture, are typically seen as being less important (Warwick and Druckman 2006).

A second strand of the literature on portfolio allocation, which has recently gained more interest, has focused on the *quality* of ministerial posts, asking, *why do parties get specific portfolios?* The idea is that we cannot assume that the importance of specific ministerial posts are the same for all parties, for example, for an agricultural party, the post as minister of agriculture is clearly more important than for other parties. Also, for a Green party, the minister of environment is a post that they should be especially interested in when entering the cabinet, whereas a Social Democratic party may fight less to get this kind of post during the negotiations. Hence, parties are likely to have specific portfolio preferences, and several studies have aimed at analysing such preferences and their impact on portfolio allocation, for example by statistically analysing whether parties that emphasize specific themes in their election manifestos corresponding to specific cabinet portfolios are more likely to obtain control over these portfolios (e.g. Bäck et al. 2011).

The general theoretical approach dominating the field of portfolio allocation is rational choice theory, where the actors, the political parties, are assumed to be driven by office-, policy-, and vote-seeking, just as in the general literature on coalition formation (e.g. Müller and Strøm 1999). Most empirical work has been based on analyses of portfolio allocation in Western European cabinets during the post-war period, using various regression analysis techniques. Since the literature on portfolio allocation has focused exclusively on the distribution of ministerial posts between different parties, it has largely ignored intra-party dynamics and individual characteristics of politicians when predicting the allocation of posts—these topics are addressed in the literature on ministerial selection.

16.2.2 Questions about Ministerial Selection and De-Selection

The hiring and firing of cabinet ministers is a natural part of all parliamentary democracies, where democratic accountability allows the PM and the coalition as a whole to delegate power to individual ministers and to withdraw this power (see, e.g., Strøm 2000). Here we are thus dealing with two processes, the appointment of individuals to the cabinet, and the de-selection of ministers. These two processes have largely been kept separate in the literature, where some scholars focus exclusively on selection and others on reshuffles.

The general question asked in the literature on ministerial selection is, *why are some individuals appointed to the cabinet?* This question has been of interest in the literature on political elites and political careers, and in the literature on representation. In early elite studies, scholars asked, 'who is appointed to the cabinet?', focusing on the various background features of individual ministers, such as their parliamentary background (see, e.g., De Winter 1991). Later work has instead aimed at modelling the entire pool of ministerial candidates and has focused on which ideological positions of individual politicians make them more likely to be appointed to the cabinet. In the literature on representation, scholars have asked why women are more likely to be appointed to the cabinet and hold certain positions in some countries rather than others (e.g. Krook and O'Brien 2012; see also Chapter 13 of this volume).

There is a growing body of work on the resignation of ministers and on cabinet reshuffles. The questions asked in this literature are all related to the general question, *why do some ministers sit longer on their posts than others?* Several explanations have been advanced in the literature for cabinet reshuffles more generally. PMs may use ministerial dismissals for strategic purposes, for example by blaming policy failures or scandals on individual ministers, electoral losses can be avoided, and to increase competence among cabinet members when appointments have not resulted in a 'good' selection of ministers. Hence, some questions asked in this literature are: When are PMs likely to fire individual ministers? Are ministers fired when they have performed badly, or when they are involved in a scandal? Or are they used as 'scapegoats' when the government is doing badly at the polls? Some scholars have also asked whether gender matters, for example, are female ministers removed from their posts due to other reasons than their male colleagues?

A general theoretical approach that has dominated the literature on ministerial selection and de-selection is the rational choice approach (see Chapter 5 of this volume). Here, a specific variant of this approach has been especially influential—principal-agent theory. This approach builds on economic theories of delegation and argues that some principal (e.g. the PM), delegates power to some agents (here, individual line-ministers), who are more or less faithful 'agents' of the principal. The most common methodological approach used in studies of ministerial selection and de-selection is quantitative, applying various statistical techniques (e.g. event history models). Most studies rely on country-specific data on the backgrounds of individual ministers and why they have exited their ministerial post, and few studies are large-n comparative studies (see however Huber and Martínez-Gallardo 2008).

16.3 State of the Art

16.3.1 Research on 'Quantitative' Portfolio Allocation

Most previous work on portfolio allocation has focused on predicting how many portfolios each party gets. In the top part of Table 16.1, we give an overview of important works on this topic. The proportionality prediction was originally derived from

Table 16.1 Overview of important (selected) studies of portfolio allocation

	Authors	Methods and data	Selected Findings
Why do some parties get more portfolios than others?	Browne and Franklin (1973)	A comparative evaluation in Western European, regression with parties as units of analysis	The correlation between party seat share and portfolio share is over 0.90
	Warwick and Druckman (2006)	Expert survey in fourteen Western European countries to measure portfolio salience, regression with parties as units	Proportionality rule is supported even when portfolio payoffs are weighted by saliency
	Carroll and Cox (2007)	Formal model and statistical evaluation in Western European and a broader sample	More 'Gamsonian' portfolio allocation when bargaining is not post-electoral
	Falcó-Gimeno and Indriðason (2013)	Comparative regression analysis of portfolio allocation in Western Europe	Proportionality higher in complex and uncertain cases
Why do parties get specific portfolios?	Browne and Feste (1975)	Preferences of eight party families, comparative analysis Western Europe	Only Agriculture consistently goes to Agrarian parties
	Budge and Keman (1990)	Classification of portfolio preferences for five party families, comparative analysis WE	Socialists get Labour, Health, and Social posts 80 per cent of the time
	Laver and Shepsle (1996)	(Theoretical model)	Parties controlling median positions in the policy area controlled by a portfolio are more likely to obtain posts
	Bäck et al. (2011)	Connects Comparative Manifestos Project data to portfolio allocation in twelve Western European countries, conditional logit analysis	Parties who stress certain policy issues in their manifesto get the post controlling these issues
	Ecker et al. (2015)	Governments in Western and Central Eastern Europe	A sequential logic results in better predictions than assuming mutual independence in portfolio allocation (PA)

Gamson's (1961: 376) idea that coalition partners will expect a share of payoffs that is 'proportional to the amount of resources which they contribute to a coalition'. Drawing on Gamson, Browne and Franklin (1973: 457, 460) argue that the 'share of ministries received by a party participating in a governing coalition and the percentage share of that party's coalition seats will be proportional on a one-to-one basis'. They evaluated this hypothesis on a comparative dataset and demonstrated that the correlation between party seat share and portfolio share is over 0.90, concluding that, the share of ministerial posts a party receives is explained, 'almost on a one-to-one basis' by the seats the party brings to government.

Several empirical tests have confirmed that the proportionality relationship is associated with an extremely high explained variance. Therefore, it has been described as one of the strongest relationships in the social sciences, and has been dubbed 'Gamson's Law'. Warwick and Druckman (2001, 2006), Druckman and Warwick (2005), and Druckman and Roberts (2008) have contributed to this literature by evaluating the idea that all portfolios are not valued equally. Warwick and Druckman (2006: 636) argue that treating ministerial portfolios as equally important 'is clearly a gross mischaracterization of reality in extant parliamentary systems'. Therefore, Warwick and Druckman (2006) measure portfolio salience by performing an expert survey in fourteen European countries, and find that the proportionality rule is supported even when portfolio payoffs are weighted by salience (Bäck et al. 2009; see also Druckman). Bucur (2016) finds, analysing France, that a more precise measure of salience even further improves the finding of a proportional pattern.

Even though the proportionality relationship has been strongly supported, some deviations have been noted. The main deviation from this one-to-one proportionality relationship that was found already by Browne and Franklin (1973: 460) is that small parties seem to be receiving ' "bonus" ministries to be distributed above their proportional shares', suggesting that there is a 'small party bias' in portfolio allocation.

Figure 16.1 illustrates the relationship between parties' seat contributions and their portfolio shares, using Warwick and Druckman's data over the post-war period (1945–9) across fourteen countries. The left-hand figure plots the seat contributions against the

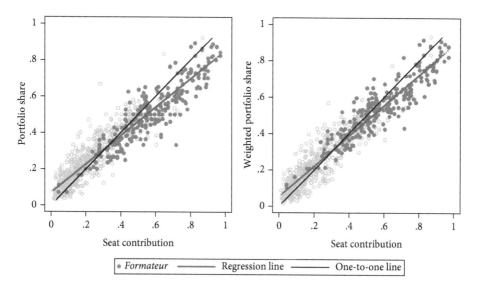

FIGURE 16.1 The relationship between parties' seat contributions and their portfolio shares

Note: Data from Warwick and Druckman (2006), modified for the German cases by Bäck et al. (2009).

unweighted portfolio shares, whereas the right-hand figure plots the seat contributions against the portfolio shares weighted by Warwick and Druckman's (2006) expert survey saliency measure. Both figures also include the regression line and a line representing one-to-one proportionality. As can clearly be seen in both figures, both a party's unweighted and weighted portfolio share is predicted by the party's seat contribution. The fact that the regression slope is somewhat flatter than the one-to-one line illustrates the small-party bias described above, which remains when focusing on weighted portfolio shares.

A question that has been raised in this literature is whether parties' seat share contribution to the government is the best way to conceptualize a party's 'resources'. Some authors have suggested focusing on parties' bargaining power instead of their seat contribution, arguing that parties with a great deal of bargaining power, rather than of significant legislative size, should be able to obtain a large portfolio payoff (see, e.g., Ansolabehere et al. 2005). Warwick and Druckman (2006) find that the proportionality relationship holds even when taking bargaining power into account, and they find no evidence that bargaining power is a better predictor of portfolio payoffs than seat shares.

Another discussion in this literature focuses on the puzzle resulting from the fact that many bargaining models are based on the idea that the *formateur* should have a superior position in coalition bargaining, which is not in line with the empirical record. For example, Baron (1991) models government formation as a sequential game and concludes that the party selected first to form a government should have a considerable bargaining advantage in negotiations. Thus, *formateur* parties should be able to reap more benefits in portfolio allocation than if a proportionality rule is followed (see, e.g., Baron and Ferejohn 1989).

However, as shown by Warwick and Druckman (2006: 639), empirically, *formateur* parties do not seem to be overcompensated, even when controlling for the fact that *formateurs* are likely to obtain some of the most important posts. This fact is also illustrated in Figure 16.1, where it is clear that most of the *formateur* parties (illustrated by darker circles) can be found below the one-to-one line, showing that they typically get fewer posts than would be expected if a proportionality rule is followed.

Hence, most scholars would agree that there is a clear proportional relationship between party seat shares and their portfolio payoffs. However, it has been stressed that we need a better understanding of the mechanism that explains why parties receive a proportional payoff, especially since it goes against the predictions made in most bargaining models. As Warwick and Druckman (2006: 660) argued, Gamson's Law 'is an empirical relationship still deserving of its law-like status—but in acute need of a firm theoretical foundation'.

The general approach to this has been to point out that the portfolio bargaining environment bears little resemblance to that of classical models of distribution such as Baron-Ferejohn (Laver et al. 2011). Carroll and Cox (2007), for example, argue that parties' pivotalness in bargaining is constrained by the potential coalitions competing to become governments. In their model, a proportional allocation provides parties an incentive to gain more votes, thereby increasing the coalition's chances of entering government. Using pre-electoral pacts as cases likely to exhibit these cooperative conditions, they show these cases have highly proportional allocations. Other works that have added other dynamics that lead to equilibria consistent with Gamson's Law include Bassi (2013), who predicts proportional allocations when both government formation and allocation are jointly considered. Recent empirical work in a similar spirit by Cutler et al. (2016) uses a joint model of government membership and portfolio distribution to show that bargaining weight *does* explain government *membership* if portfolios are not allocated by those governments.

A number of other empirical works have also focused various ways in which the reality of portfolio bargaining is more complex than formal models suggest. For example, Golder and Thomas (2014) argue that one such omission is the vote of no confidence, which explains the tendency to overcompensate small partners where present. Falcó-Gimeno (2012) argues that underpayment in portfolios may arise from a willingness to accept concessions on the part of parties with larger amounts of time out of office. Carroll et al. (2004) point out that the ability to pursue a bargaining advantage is limited in cases of high fragmentation, due to the complexity of the bargaining environment. Falcó-Gimeno and Indriðason (2013) similarly argue that in uncertain and complex bargaining situations, parties 'have a difficult time exploiting their bargaining advantage' and find support for this hypothesis when analysing portfolio allocation in Western Europe. The notion that proportionality can serve as a 'focal point' is supported by Bäck et al. (2009), who find, in two case studies, that proportionality is a 'bargaining convention' among the possible distribution rules available. Further work has explored aspects of intraparty dynamics of portfolio allocations (Ono 2012; Ennser-Jedenastik 2013; Ceron 2014).

The empirical literature has also moved into other related allocation topics such as the role of junior ministers, which operates as both a compensating aspect of overall portfolio allocation as well as playing a substantive policy function within coalitions (Mershon 2001; Thies 2001; Manow and Zorn 2004; Lipsmeyer and Pierce 2011). In either case, junior ministers, along with other factors such as committee assignments (Carroll and Cox 2012), further alter the value of holding a given ministry.

16.3.2 Research on 'Qualitative' Portfolio Allocation

Parties may of course have specific portfolio preferences since policy seeking parties will have 'a particular set of policy concerns, seeing control over a specific portfolio as an instrumental means of advancing these' (Laver and Schofield 1990: 183). Given a certain degree of ministerial discretion, control over specific ministries gives the party an advantage in implementing its preferred policies in the relevant sector (Bäck et al. 2011). Hence, it is important to also study which parties get which portfolios, or to analyse what has been dubbed the 'qualitative portfolio allocation'. In the second part of Table 16.1, we give an overview of important studies focusing on this question.

This qualitative aspect of portfolio allocation is critical to Laver and Shepsle's (1996) influential 'portfolio allocation model'. In this model, to solve the 'chaos problem' of indefinite cycling of majority preferences over policy in two or more dimensions, they relied on the assumption that the minister of a department has considerable discretion to act on his or her own. Hence, to be credible, a proposed policy position must correspond to the position of the party assigned to the portfolio that controls this specific dimension. A main implication of this model is that parties controlling the median on a specific dimension that is the jurisdiction of a ministerial post are more likely to obtain the portfolio since median parties have positions that are preferred by a majority (Bäck et al. 2011).

In the first comparative analysis of the role of party ideology in portfolio allocation, Browne and Feste (1975: 533) conjectured that 'some portfolios are viewed by parties as being especially important for the purpose of reinforcing the loyalty of certain extra-parliamentary clientele groups on which they depend for the maintenance of their parliamentary standing'. Classifying the preferences of parties belonging to one of eight party families, however, they did not find strong support for their prediction: only the Ministry of Agriculture consistently appeared to go to Agrarian or Christian parties.

Budge and Keman (1990) later performed a similar analysis, creating a ranking of general party policy interests that was supposed to indicate substantive preferences of parties for specific ministries. Relying on studies on party families, historical studies of party support groups, and programmatic statements, Budge and Keman (1990) distilled a ranking of portfolio types for five party families. Their propositions were evaluated on a comparative data set, showing that, for instance, when in cabinet Socialist parties get the Labour, Health, and Social Welfare posts more than 80 per cent of the time (Bäck et al. 2011).

Bäck et al. (2011) build on this work, presenting a hypothesis based on a policy saliency theory of portfolio allocation. They suggest that the more important a party considers a particular policy area, that is, the more salient this policy area is to the party, the more likely it is that this party will try to get the ministerial post controlling this particular policy field. Using data drawn from the Comparative Manifestos Project (see, e.g., Budge et al. 2001), and studying portfolio allocation in twelve Western European countries Bäck and colleagues (2011) show that parties who stress certain policy issues in their electoral programme are indeed more likely to obtain the portfolio controlling these particular policy areas. Raabe and Linhart (2015), analysing German state governments, also find that parties have advantages is obtaining their most political salient portfolios, while also showing that improvement in quality appears to compensate losses on quantity.

Ecker et al. (2015: 802) argue that the importance of individual preferences means that 'coalition negotiations are sequential choice processes that begin with the allocation of those portfolios most important to the bargaining parties'. Their analysis of coalition governments in Western and Central Eastern Europe shows that this sequential bargaining predicts the allocation of ministerial portfolios better than assumptions of mutual independence.

16.3.3 Research on the Selection of Ministers

While portfolio allocation studies have focused mainly on the role of political parties, research on the ministerial selection has instead focused on individual-level characteristics (also see Chapter 12 of this volume). Table 16.2 gives an overview of important works focusing on the question of which politicians are selected to the cabinet. As noted by Dowding and Dumont (2009b), until recently there has not been much work on the mechanisms behind ministerial selection. There is, however, some early work on the representative role of political elites, specifically examining the backgrounds of ministers (see Blondel and Thiébault 1991; Tavares de Almeida and Costa-Pinto 2002). One the main results in the literature on political elites is that a parliamentary career is the main path for becoming a minister (De Winter 1991; see also Costa-Pinto et al. 2018 for a more recent comparative analysis).

One trait that has received particular attention is that of gender (see Chapter 13 of this volume). Several scholars have studied the selection of women to the cabinet and found that women are less likely to obtain a ministerial post in general, and when they do enter cabinet, they are likely to be found in less prestigious posts (see, e.g., Reynolds 1999; Escobar-Lemmon and Taylor-Robinson 2005; Krook and O'Brien 2012). In addition, this literature has shown that women tend to be appointed to ministerial posts that deal with 'softer' policy issues. For example, Reynolds (1999: 564) finds that 'one sees a worldwide tendency to place women in the softer sociocultural ministerial positions rather than in the harder and politically more prestigious positions'. Aiming to explain such gendered patterns in cabinet appointments across the world, Krook and O'Brien (2012) find that women's appointments are to a large extent explained by the presence of more women among political elites, which they stress can partly be promoted by, for example, gender quotas.

Some scholars studying ministerial selection have also drawn on work that suggest that executive-legislative relations in parliamentary democracies are undergoing important changes, suggesting that there is a trend towards 'presidentialization' of parliamentary politics, in which more power resources are concentrated to PMs (Poguntke and Webb 2005, see Chapter 18 of this volume). Bäck et al. (2009) assess the validity of such claims by studying Swedish post-war ministerial selection. Their findings suggest that there is some evidence in favour of an ongoing shift in executive politics in terms of a decrease in the appointment of political insiders and an increase in expert ministers. Their results also indicate that such changes in ministerial selection can partly be explained by an increase in European integration.

Similar analyses have been performed by scholars focusing on the appointment of 'technocrats'. For example, Amorim Neto and Strøm (2006) discuss how appointments of non-partisan ministers—often associated with skilled technocrats or experts—signal that 'efficiency concerns' trump 'redistributive ambitions'. In a similar fashion, Hallerberg and Wehner (2018) argue that certain backgrounds will be more likely among ministers appointed during times of economic crisis. Governments in an economic crisis need to gain the confidence of both investors and of voters, and the appointment of a technically

Table 16.2 Overview of important (selected) studies on ministerial selection and de-selection

	Authors	Methods	Selected Findings
Why are certain individuals appointed to the cabinet?	Amorim Neto and Strøm (2006)	Formal model, predictions are evaluated in comparative analysis of European governments	Non-partisan appointments are more common when PM's electoral prospects are weak
	Kam et al. (2010)	Study of the 'pool' of candidates through the use of UK MP surveys	Closeness to party backbenchers make MPs more likely to be appointed to the cabinet
	Krook and O'Brien (2012)	Comparative worldwide analysis of ministerial appointments in 2009	Women's appointments are explained by the presence of women among elites
	Hallerberg and Wehner (2018)	Comparative analysis of data for economic policy-makers in EU and OECD countries	More technically competent economic policy-makers appointed during financial crises
	Bäck et al. (2016)	Study of the 'pool' of candidates through the analysis of speeches in Austria, Germany and Sweden	Closeness to coalition matters for selection in Austria, whereas the PM matters more in Germany
Why do some ministers sit longer on their posts?	Dewan and Dowding (2005)	Analysis of opinion polls and ministerial dismissals in the UK	Ministerial resignations affect government popularity positively
	Indriðason and Kam (2008)	Formal model, Australian and British data to evaluate predictions	Cabinet reshuffles can benefit the PM by reducing agency loss
	Huber and Martínez-Gallardo (2008)	Comparative survival analysis across nineteen countries	Ministers holding important posts and in coalitions are less likely to be reshuffled
	Berlinski et al. (2010)	Resignation calls are used as performance indicators, analysis of ministerial tenure in post-war UK	A minister's risk of losing his or her post sharply after the first individual call for resignation

competent minister may help the government gain credibility (Hallerberg and Wehner 2018). Alexiadou and Gunaydin (2018) argue that technocrat ministers are selected to reduce problems of agency within their party and government and to send a signal to markets and voters about pro-reform intentions. They suggest that, as non-elected experts, technocrats have policy expertise and the commitment and willingness to adopt tough economic policies irrespective of their short-term electoral effects.

While the literature above focuses on the background and traits of individual ministers, other work focuses on how the policy positions of individual politicians influence their likelihood of entering cabinet. This work generally relies on principal-agent frameworks in which principals appoint to limit 'agency loss'. Kam et al. (2010: 1) argue principals have to 'work to ensure that their ministers [...] are behaving as faithful agents behind closed doors of the cabinet office'. Focusing on the UK, the key question they ask is who the principal is in the ministerial appointment process: the party leader or party backbenchers, where the latter could function as a 'collective principal'. A challenge for answering this question is measuring the policy positions of the 'pool' of ministerial candidates. As Kam et al. (2010) can define this as MPs in the British case, they analyse policy positions from British MP surveys and show that the ideal points of ministerial appointees for the Labour and Conservative parties are significantly closer to their parties' backbenchers' positions than those of their non-ministerial colleagues. This suggests that the backbenchers act as a collective principal.

Bäck et al. (2016) argue that there are three potentially dominant principals in ministerial selection in coalition governments: the party, the PM, and the coalition as a collective. Which principal becomes dominant, they argue, depends on the institutional setting. Bäck et al. (2016) present an empirical analysis of ministerial selection in six governments, measuring individual politicians' positions through an analysis of speeches. They show that the institutional context matters for which principal is 'dominant' in ministerial selection. In Austria, for example, where the Chancellor's power is limited and coalition governance is strong, ministers tend to be selected in accordance to the policy distance between themselves and the coalition. By contrast, the stronger Chancellor in Germany means that the policy position of the PM is influential in ministerial selection.

16.3.4 Research on the De-Selection of Ministers and Cabinet Reshuffles

Several researchers have stressed that the selection and de-selection of ministers is an important element of control over the core executive since it defines actors' opportunity to mitigate typical delegation problems (cf. Dowding and Dumont 2009b). While extensive 'screening' is the most important *ex ante* measure to avoid agency loss arising from delegation, the most important *ex post* measure is the ability to simply remove the agents. Thus, the opportunity to dismiss ministers deemed incompetent, disloyal or exceeding their range of discretion is typically characterized as an effective sanctioning instrument for the PM, who is typically portrayed as the main principal in this literature (see, e.g., Huber and Martínez-Gallardo 2008).

There is a growing field of research focusing on explaining why certain ministers hold their posts while other ministers are 'reshuffled' or 'fired'. In Table 16.2 we give an overview of important works in this field. Like the principal-agent theories of the ministerial selection literature, this work views reshuffles as a means to limit the 'agency loss' of delegation to ministers (also see Chapter 5 of this volume). First, dismissals mitigate the adverse selection problem by 're-matching' portfolio and talents or weeding out of 'bad' ministers (Huber and Martínez-Gallardo 2008; Indriðason and Kam 2008). Thus, reshuffling ensures the right person at the right post. Second, the PM faces moral hazard problems that can arise from 'ministerial drift' since 'all ministers have motive and opportunity to use their portfolios in a manner that runs against the PM's interests' (Indriðason and Kam 2008: 624).

Some of these moral hazard problems arise from the fact that the PM cannot control the screening and selection procedures for potential cabinet members, particularly in coalition cabinets. Furthermore, ministers face incentives to implement policies different from those favoured by the PM and their political fortunes are at least partly independent of those of the government as a whole (Indriðason and Kam 2008). Ministerial drift can arise from the fact that ministers show a tendency to become too aligned with their particular ministry and the sectoral interests associated with the portfolio (Andeweg 2000). Therefore, 'rematching' of ministers and portfolios can prevent ministers from 'going native'.

Huber and Martínez-Gallardo (2008: 172) argue that ministers who hold 'portfolios that are most central to the government's policy agenda' have the greatest potential to influence policy are more likely to be carefully screened. By implication, such ministers are less likely to be affected by reshuffles due to this more intense screening, which they find in a comparative analysis of cabinet reshuffles in 19 countries (see also Berlinski et al. 2007). Further, ministers in coalition governments are less likely to be 'fired' than in single-party cabinets, suggesting that the PM is more constrained in these contexts.

A related literature has focused on the 'performance' of individual ministers and the notion that the PM monitors to detect 'ministerial drift'. As this is hard to observe directly, scholars have relied on indirect measures such as the relationship between scandals and subsequent resignation calls. Berlinski et al. (2010) use the resignation calls for a minister in the UK as reported in the media as an individual performance indicator and show that a minister's risk of losing his or her post rises sharply after the first individual call for resignation. Using an alternative approach to analysing performance, Bäck et al. (2016) focus on whether foreign ministers are more likely to be fired from their posts after certain events, finding that this is associated with involvement in international conflict (see also Quiroz Flores 2016).

While most work on ministerial de-selection uses the principal-agent framework, some focus on other motivations for reshuffles. For example, PMs may use dismissals as a response to scandals, or public opinion shocks (see, e.g., Berlinski et al. 2012). Dewan and Dowding (2005) argue that the dismissal of a scandal-ridden minister can restore public confidence in the government as a whole by pinning blame on an individual minister. There is little work examining the role of gender in ministerial de-selection in parliamentary regimes, but Escobar-Lemmon and Taylor-Robinson (2015) provide compelling evidence for this line of inquiry using five presidential democracies. They show that gender affects what factors matter for the mode of exit. For example, women with organizational ties are less likely to be fired, whereas no such effect is found for male ministers.

16.4 A Research Agenda

The main challenge facing the literatures on portfolio allocation and ministerial selection is the need to connect the different topics covered in each field, both theoretically and empirically. Here, we describe why we believe that these connections are important. First, we argue for modelling qualitative and quantitative portfolio allocation simultaneously. Second, we suggest that the topics of ministerial selection and de-selection could be more clearly connected by looking at factors that limit agency loss at both the selection and the de-selection stage. Most importantly, we believe that we can greatly improve our understanding of executives by treating portfolio allocation and ministerial selection as an integrated process where party leaders bargain simultaneously over which parties get which post and which individuals should fill this post.

16.4.1 Connecting Quantity and Quality in Portfolio Allocation

The connecting between the quantity and quality of portfolio allocation is a natural one (see Martin 2016). These topics deal with essentially the same outcome of coalition bargaining, the allocation of ministerial portfolios between parties. Thus, it is natural to merge two different literatures that have focused on different aspects of the allocation—*how many* posts or *which* posts parties obtain—and to focus on the general question, *how are portfolios distributed between parties in coalition governments?*

The main reason for keeping these aspects separate in previous work is methodological—until recently, an empirical approach that properly models the quantity and quality aspects of portfolio allocation was lacking. Bäck et al. (2011) focus on predicting the qualitative side of portfolio allocation and present an empirical approach which allows them to include several predictors of portfolio allocation. They use a conditional logit model where each portfolio is seen as the unit of analysis and the different parties in government are the discrete choice alternatives. The main problem is that this empirical approach does not allow for a proper evaluation of the proportionality prediction since the assignment of ministerial parties are treated as 'separate, independent decisions', even though the concept of proportionality relies on dependence in assignments (Martin 2016: 16).

Martin (2016) has recently presented an empirical approach that aims to simultaneously analyze parties' portfolio payoffs in numerical and policy terms. In this approach, the unit of analysis is a bargaining situation, and the dependent variable represents a choice between potential portfolio allocations rather than between parties. A potential portfolio allocation is a 'combination' of coalition parties across the available ministries. Martin (2016: 19) suggests that the key advantage of this design is, that 'because potential port-folio allocations contain information both about how many and which ministries parties receive [...], the allocation choice can be modeled as a function of quantitative and quali-tative characteristics simultaneously'. Applying this approach to portfolio allocation in Western Europe, Martin (2016) finds that parties distribute both the number and the types of portfolios in proportion to the parties' seat contribution. Hence, parties seem to distrib-ute portfolios in a 'fair' manner both in terms of the quantity and quality of the payoffs.

The empirical approach proposed by Martin (2016) marks a way forward for this literature, allowing scholars to more clearly connect the qualitative and quantitative aspects of portfolio allocation and to investigate the impact of various party features on portfolio allocation in parliamentary democracies.

16.4.2 Connecting Ministerial Selection and De-Selection

Another potential for integration lies in connecting questions about ministerial selec-tion to those about de-selection. Certain constraints on the PM as principal may have opposite effects on the potential for agency loss in selection, on the one hand, and the likelihood of reshuffles on the other. Here, we focus on two contextual features that may constrain a PM in selection and de-selection: the institutional power of PMs to appoint and dismiss individual ministers and whether the PM heads a single-party or coalition cabinet. In Figure 16.2, we illustrate the constraints that these two features may have on the PM's ability to control agency loss in his or her cabinet.

The PM's institutional powers are typically assumed to influence selection and de-selection (see, e.g., Bäck et al. 2016). However, the impact of such institutional features has not been investigated systematically in the literature, even though we know that PM power varies substantially across countries. For example, Bergman et al. (2003: 179–80) identify a number of sources of PM influence, where appointment and dismissal powers can be identified as some of the most important powers of the PM. Hence, as Sartori (1994: 102–3) puts it, that the 'head of government may relate to the members of his government as: (i) a first *above unequals*; (ii) a first *among unequals*; (iii) a first *among equals*'.

In a case where the PM does not have strong appointment powers, he or she is not likely to be able to select the 'good' ministers, and thus to limit agency loss *ex ante*. For example, the PM may not be able to select individuals for cabinet that hold policy posi-tions close to his or her own (see, e.g., Bäck et al. 2016). Thus, a PM with weak appointment powers must rely more on *ex post* mechanisms to control agency loss, which may lead to a higher likelihood of reshuffles. The problem is that a PM with weak appointment powers is likely to have weak dismissal powers with which to limit agency loss *ex post*, decreasing the likelihood of cabinet reshuffles. Hence, the impact of PM appointment and dismissal powers on cabinet reshuffles may cancel each other out in many cases—a

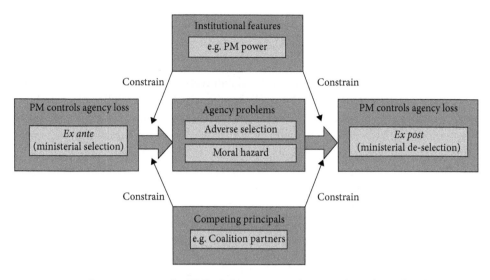

FIGURE 16.2 Constraints on the PM's ability to control agency loss through selection and de-selection of ministers.

weak PM is not likely to be able to select 'good' ministers, which should result in more reshuffles, but a weak PM is also not likely to be able to freely dismiss ministers, which should result in fewer reshuffles. Due to the correlation between PM appointment and dismissal powers, it is thus not certain that we will observe the expected effect of PM powers on reshuffles.

As mentioned above, one important result in Huber and Martínez-Gallardo's (2008) comparative analysis of cabinet reshuffles is that ministers are less likely to be removed in coalition governments. Drawing on Budge (1985), they suggest that this is because the PM is constrained by the coalition partners with regard to deselection. However, coalition status is also likely to influence ministerial *selection*. The PM is not likely to have a 'free hand' in selecting individuals and limiting agency loss *ex ante*, as the coalition partners will want to influence selection. Hence, this aspect of coalitions—constraints on selection—may increase the likelihood of reshuffles even while the decreasing the likelihood of reshuffles due to constraints in de-selection. Huber and Martinez-Gallardo's (2008) result may suggest, then, that coalition partners' constraints on de-selection is the stronger effect. However, ideally, the relationship between coalition status and ministerial de-selection should be integrated with work on ministerial selection, which shows the PM influencing who gets appointments (see Bäck et al. 2016).

An alternative avenue of research relating the constraints on the PM, agency loss and cabinet reshuffles, would be to analyse the so-called 'exit reasons' for departing ministers. It is important to differentiate between ministerial exits that are in fact 'promotions', when a minister is appointed to a higher post inside or outside cabinet, and ministerial exits that are clearly 'demotions', where a minister is fired or moved to a lower ranked post. The latter type of exit may be more likely to be motivated by concerns about agency loss.

16.4.3 Connecting Portfolio Allocation and Ministerial Selection

As with need to integrate of the number and nature of portfolio allocation at the party level, the individual-level and party-level phenomena of portfolio allocation are inextricably linked (Verzichelli 2008). Portfolio allocation and ministerial selection are in practice an integrated process, whereby parties bargain first over which party gets what ministerial portfolios, and, second, over which individual politicians receive particular posts. However, it is important to note that sometimes the process of ministerial selection *within* parties is likely to influence the allocation of posts *between* parties. Jointly considering these topics, we can understand why in some cases parties may gain control over certain posts because they have specific individuals among their 'pool of candidates', with backgrounds or policy positions that make them attractive for cabinet in some situations. Hence, we suggest, as argued by Laver and Shepsle (2000: 114), that 'whether or not a politician is ministrable might be as much an endogenous feature of the government formation process as an exogenous input to it'.

To give an example, after the Swedish 2014 election the Greens and the Social Democrats negotiated for the first time over the formation of a minority coalition government. Several important posts beyond the PM were also allocated to the *formateur* party, the Social Democrats (e.g. finance), whereas the Greens appointed the minister of environment. The latter was clearly expected considering the Green party's emphasis on environmental issues. All in all, a proportionality principle seemed to have guided the distribution of portfolios, even though there was clearly a small-party bias in which the Greens obtained 25 per cent of the posts with 20 per cent of the legislative seat contribution. The most difficult negotiations appeared to be over the Ministry of Education, as both parties had stressed education issues in their electoral campaigns. This post ultimately went to one of the Green party leaders, Gustav Fridolin, who had a strong background in the education field, both for being a folk high school teacher and for having pushed education issues as MP (Bäck and Hellström 2015).

Examples such as this suggest that the party that will obtain specific posts is not only determined by the parties' seat shares, their policy positions, or how much the party emphasizes certain policy areas. Instead, the 'pool' of ministerial candidates within the negotiating parties may also matter. In a case where the negotiating parties place equal emphasis on a policy area (or have overlapping interests), saliency is not likely to predict which party will obtain the post, and here candidate quality may determine the outcome.

In the analysis performed by Bäck et al. (2011) looking at the saliency at the party-level, some posts were easier to predict than others. For example, the posts of minister of agriculture and the minister of environment typically went to the party that stressed those policy issues in their electoral manifesto. The allocation of the Labour ministry was also relatively straightforward when predictions were based on party-level saliency. Other posts, such as the defence minister, justice minister, and the minister of education were more difficult to predict based on party-specific saliency. Defence issues and issues related to justice were scarcely mentioned in any parties' programmes, while education was common across all parties. For such cases, where it is difficult to predict which party gets which post based on party-specific saliency, individual-level features may play a decisive role. That is, accurately predicting the allocation require knowing which parties had particularly suitable candidates (e.g. in terms of experience or profile) for specific ministerial posts. In the Swedish 2014 case, the Greens likely obtained the education post because they had a strong candidate in their leadership.

Following this line of argument, we suggest that future research should theoretically and empirically evaluate how a party's pool of candidates may influence the likelihood that the party is allocated specific posts. This type of research could build on the work by scholars such as Kam et al. (2010), who has modelled ministerial selection as a choice among a pool of candidates by analysing the policy positions of all members of parliament (MPs) in the British parliament. Here, information on MPs' backgrounds, such as their educational, occupational, and political background, should also be taken into account. For example, the saliency of specific policy issues for each individual MP can be captured by the number of speeches made in specific policy areas (see, e.g., Bäck and Debus 2016). Such individual-level information on MPs could be integrated in models of portfolio allocation, such as the approach suggested by Martin (2016), to account for whether party has especially strong candidates for a specific ministry's policy area.

16.5 CONCLUSIONS

We have in this chapter reviewed several different areas of research on the distribution of power within executives, focused on ministerial posts in parliamentary democracies. The questions in these literatures all fall under the general question, 'how are ministerial portfolios distributed between and within political parties?'.

However, despite this general overarching question, few scholars have approached this as a unified topic. Instead four different literatures, which we have reviewed here, ask different questions about portfolio allocation: (1) the literature on quantitative portfolio allocation, which has asked 'why do some parties get more portfolios than others?', (2) the literature on qualitative portfolio allocation, which has asked, 'why do parties get specific portfolios?', (3) the literature on ministerial selection, which has asked 'why do specific individuals get into the cabinet?', and (4) the literature on ministerial de-selection, which has asked, 'why do some ministers sit longer on their posts?'.

We suggest that future research should seek to connect these different literatures into a more unified framework. These literatures already share a grounding in rational choice theory and most studies are based on statistical analyses of various features of political parties or individual politicians. Our main argument for connecting these different fields is that the processes of portfolio allocation and ministerial selection are not separate. Instead, political parties negotiating over portfolio allocation will also consider what 'ministrables' the different parties have in their party leadership, and this could clearly influence which party gets what portfolio.

By doing so, we should gain further insights into portfolio allocation in parliamentary democracies, which is clearly an important step in the democratic process, as the allocation of ministerial posts constitutes a key intervening link between the policies presented by parties and politicians at the polls, and the policies implemented by a government.

REFERENCES

Alexiadou, D. and Gunaydin, H. (2018). 'Commitment or Expertise? Technocratic Appointments as Political Responses to Economic Crises,' *European Journal of Political Research* 58(3): 845–65.

Amorim Neto, O. and Strøm, K. (2006). 'Breaking the Parliamentary Chain of Delegation: Presidents and Non-partisan Cabinet Members in European Democracies,' *British Journal of Political Science* 36(4): 619–43.

Andeweg, R. (2000). 'Ministers as Double Agents? The Delegation Process between Cabinet and Ministers,' *European Journal of Political Research* 37(3): 377–95.

Ansolabehere, S., Snyder, J. M., Strauss, A. B., and Ting, M. M. (2005). 'Voting Weights and Formateur Advantages in the Formation of Coalition Governments,' *American Journal of Political Science* 49(3): 550–63.

Bäck, H. and Debus, M. (2016). *Political Parties, Parliaments and Legislative Speechmaking*. Houndsmills: Palgrave Macmillan.

Bäck, H. and Hellström, J. (2015). 'Efter valet 2014. Regeringsbildningen och det inställda extra valet,' *Statsvetenskaplig tidskrift* 2: 261–78.

Bäck, H., Dumont, P. Meier, H. E., Persson, T., and Vernby, K. (2009). 'Does European Integration Lead to a 'Presidentialisation' of Executive Politics? Ministerial Selection in Swedish Postwar Cabinets,' *European Union Politics* 10(2): 226–52.

Bäck, H., Debus, M., and Dumont, P. (2011). 'Who Gets What in Coalition Governments? Predictors of Portfolio Allocation in Parliamentary Democracies,' *European Journal of Political Research* 50(4): 441–78.

Bäck, H., Debus, M., and Müller, W. C. (2016). 'Intra-party Diversity and Ministerial Selection in Coalition Governments,' *Public Choice* 166(3–4): 355–78.

Baron, D. (1991). 'A Spatial Bargaining Theory of Government Formation in Parliamentary Systems,' *American Political Science Review* 85(1): 137–64.

Baron, D. P. and Ferejohn, J. A. (1989). 'Bargaining in Legislatures,' *American Political Science Review* 83(4): 1181–206.

Bassi, A. (2013). 'A Model of Endogenous Government Formation,' *American Journal of Political Science* 57(4):777–93.

Bergman, T., Müller, W. C., Strøm, K., and Blomgren, M. (2003). 'Democratic Delegation and Accountability: Cross-national Patterns,' in K. Strøm, W. C. Müller, and T. Bergman (eds) *Delegation and Accountability in Parliamentary Democracies*. Oxford: Oxford University Press, 109–220.

Berlinski, S., Dewan, T., and Dowding, K. (2007). 'The Length of Ministerial Tenure in UK 1945–1997,' *British Journal of Political Science* 37(2): 245–62.

Berlinski, S., Dewan, T., and Dowding, K. (2010). 'Individual and Collective Ministerial Performance and the Tenure of Ministers in the UK 1945–1997,' *Journal of Politics* 72(2): 559–71.

Berlinski, S., Dewan, T., and Dowding, K. (2012). *Accounting for Ministers: Scandal and Survival in British Government 1945–2007*. Cambridge: Cambridge University Press.

Blondel, J. and Thiébault, J.-L. (1991) (eds). *The Profession of Government Minister in Western Europe*. Basingstoke: Macmillan.

Browne, E. C. and Feste, K. (1975). 'Qualitative Dimensions of Coalition Payoffs,' *American Behavioral Scientist* 18: 530–56.

Browne, E. C. and Franklin, M. N. (1973). 'Aspects of Coalition Payoffs in European Parliamentary Democracies,' *American Political Science Review* 67(2): 453–69.

Bucur, C. (2016). 'Cabinet Payoffs in Coalition Governments: A Time-Varying Measure of Portfolio Importance,' *Party Politics* 24(2): 154–67.

Budge, I. (1985). 'Party Factions and Government Reshuffles: A General Hypothesis Tested against Data from 20 Post-war Democracies,' *European Journal of Political Research* 13(3): 327–33.

Budge, I. and Keman, H. (1990). *Parties and Democracy: Coalition Formation and Government Functioning in Twenty States*. Oxford: Oxford University Press.

Budge, I., Klingemann, H.-D., Volkens, A., Bara, J., and Tanenbaum, E. (2001) (eds). *Mapping Policy Preferences: Estimates for Parties, Electors and Governments 1945–1998*. Oxford: Oxford University Press.

Carroll, R. and Cox, G. W. (2007). 'The Logic of Gamson's Law: Pre-Electoral Coalitions and Portfolio Allocations,' *American Journal of Political Science* 51(2): 300–13.

Carroll, R. and Cox, G. W. (2012). 'Shadowing Ministers: Monitoring Partners in Coalition Governments,' *Comparative Political Studies* 45(2): 220–36.

Carroll, R., Cox, G. W., and Pachón, M. (2004). 'Gamson's Law: How Coalition Governments Allocate Offices,' Unpublished manuscript.

Ceron, A. (2014). 'Gamson Rule Not for All: Patterns of Portfolio Allocation among Italian Party Factions," *European Journal of Political Research* 53(1): 180–99.

Costa Pinto, A., Cotta, M., Tavares de Almeida, P. (2018) (eds). *Technocratic Ministers and Political Leadership in European Democracies*. Basingstoke: Palgrave.

Cutler, J., De Marchi, S., Gallop, M., Hollenbach, F. M., Laver, M., and Orlowski, M. (2016). 'Cabinet Formation and Portfolio Distribution in European Multiparty Systems,' *British Journal of Political Science* 46(1): 31–43.

Dewan, T. and Dowding, K. (2005). 'The Corrective Effect of Ministerial Resignations on Government Popularity,' *American Journal of Political Science* 49(1): 46–56.

De Winter, L. (1991). 'Parliamentary and Party Pathways to the Cabinet,' in J. Blondel and J.-L. Thiébault (eds) *The Profession of Government Minister in Western Europe*. Basingstoke: Palgrave 44–69.

Dowding, K. and Dumont, P. (2009a) (eds). *The Selection of Ministers in Europe: Hiring and Firing*. London: Routledge.

Dowding, K. and Dumont, P. (2009b). 'Structural and Strategic Factors Affecting the Hiring and Firing of Ministers,' in K. Dowding and P. Dumont (eds) *The Selection of Ministers in Europe: Hiring and Firing*. London: Routledge, 1–20.

Druckman, J. N. and Roberts, J. (2008). 'Measuring Portfolio Salience in Eastern European Parliamentary Democracies,' *European Journal of Political Research* 47(1): 101–34.

Druckman, J. N. and Warwick, P. V. (2005). 'The Missing Piece: Measuring Portfolio Salience in Western European Parliamentary Democracies', *European Journal of Political Research* 44(1): 17–42.

Ecker, A., Meyer, T. M., and Müller, W. C. (2015). 'The Distribution of Individual Cabinet Positions in Coalition Governments: A Sequential Approach', *European Journal of Political Research* 54(4): 802–18.

Ennser-Jedenastik, L. (2013). 'Portfolio Allocation Within Parties: The Role of Regional Party Branches', *The Journal of Legislative Studies* 19(3): 309–27.

Escobar-Lemmon, M. and Taylor-Robinson, M. M. (2005). 'Women Ministers in Latin American Government: When, Where, and Why?', *American Journal of Political Science* 49(4): 829–44.

Escobar-Lemmon, M. and Taylor-Robinson, M. M. (2015). 'Sex, Survival, and Scandal: A Comparison of How Men and Women Exit Presidential Cabinets', *Politics & Gender* 11(4): 665–88.

Falcó-Gimeno, A. (2012). 'Parties Getting Impatient: Time Out of Office and Portfolio Allocation in Coalition Governments', *British Journal of Political Science* 42(2): 393–411.

Falcó-Gimeno, A. and Indriðason, I. H. (2013). 'Uncertainty, Complexity, and Gamson's Law: Comparing Coalition Formation in Western Europe', *West European Politics* 36(1): 221–47.

Gamson, W. (1961). 'A Theory of Coalition Formation', *American Sociological Review* 26: 373–82.

Golder, S. N. and Thomas, J. A. (2014). 'Portfolio Allocation and the Vote of No Confidence', *British Journal of Political Science* 44(1): 29–39.

Hallerberg, M. and Wehner, J. (2018). 'When Do You Get Economists as Policy Makers?', *British Journal of Political Science* 36(4): 619–32.

Huber, J. D. and Martínez-Gallardo, C. (2008). 'Replacing Cabinet Ministers: Patterns of Ministerial Stability in Parliamentary Democracies', *American Political Science Review* 102(2): 169–80.

Indriðason, I. H. and Kam, C. (2008). 'Cabinet Reshuffles and Ministerial Drift', *British Journal of Political Science* 38(4): 621–56.

Kam, C., Bianco, W. T, Sened, I., and Smyth, R. (2010). 'Ministerial Selection and Intraparty Organization in the Contemporary British Parliament', *American Political Science Review* 104(2): 289–306.

Krook, M. L. and O'Brien, D. Z. (2012). 'All the President's Men? The Appointment of Female Cabinet Ministers Worldwide', *The Journal of Politics* 74(3): 840–55.

Laver, M. and Schofield, N. (1990). *Multiparty Government: The Politics of Coalition in Europe.* Ann Arbor, MI: University of Michigan Press.

Laver, M. and Shepsle, K. (1996). *Making and Breaking Governments. Cabinets and Legislatures in Parliamentary Democracies.* Cambridge: Cambridge University Press.

Laver, M. and Shepsle, K. A. (2000). 'Ministrables and Government Formation: Munchkins, Players and Big Beasts of the Jungle', *Journal of Theoretical Politics* 12(1): 113–24.

Laver, M., De Marchi, S., and Mutlu, H. (2011). 'Negotiation in Legislatures Over Government Formation', *Public Choice* 147(3–4): 285–304.

Lipsmeyer, C. S. and Pierce, H. N. (2011). 'The Eyes that Bind: Junior Ministers as Oversight Mechanisms in Coalition Governments', *The Journal of Politics* 73(4): 1152–64.

Manow, P. and Zorn, H. (2004). 'Office Versus Policy Motives in Portfolio Allocation: The Case of Junior Ministers', No. 04/9 MPIfG Discussion Paper.

Martin, L. (2016). 'The Allocation of Ministries in Multiparty Governments,' Unpublished manuscript, Rice University.

Mershon, C. (2001). 'Party Factions and Coalition Government: Portfolio Allocation in Italian Christian Democracy,' *Electoral Studies* 20(4): 555–80.

Müller, W. C. and Strøm, K. (1999) (eds). *Policy, Office or Votes? How Political Parties in Western Europe Make Hard Decisions*. Cambridge: Cambridge University Press.

Ono, Y. (2012). 'Portfolio Allocation as Leadership Strategy: Intraparty Bargaining in Japan,' *American Journal of Political Science* 56(3): 553–67.

Poguntke, T. and Webb, P. (2005) (eds). *The Presidentialization of Politics: A Comparative Study of Modern Democracies*. Oxford: Oxford University Press.

Quiroz Flores, A. (2016). *Ministerial Survival During Political and Cabinet Change: Foreign Affairs, Diplomacy and War*. London: Routledge.

Raabe, J. and Linhart, E. (2015). 'Does Substance Matter? A Model of Qualitative Portfolio Allocation and Application to German State Governments between 1990 and 2010,' Party Politics 21(3): 481–92.

Reynolds, A. (1999). 'Women in the Legislatures and Executives of the World: Knocking at the Highest Glass Ceiling,' *World Politics* 51(4): 547–72.

Sartori, G. (1994). *Comparative Constitutional Engineering*. London: MacMillan.

Strøm, K. (2000). 'Delegation and Accountability in Parliamentary Democracies,' *European Journal of Political Research* 37(3): 261–90.

Tavares de Almeida, P. and Costa Pinto, A. (2002). 'Portuguese Ministers, 1851–1999: Social Background and Paths to Power,' *South European Society and Politics* 7(2): 5–40.

Thies, M. F. (2001). 'Keeping Tabs on Partners: The Logic of Delegation in Coalition Governments,' *American Journal of Political Science* 45(3): 580–98.

Verzichelli, L. (2008). 'Portfolio Allocation. Cabinets and Coalition Bargaining: The Democratic Life Cycle in Western Europe,' in K. Strøm, W. C. Müller, and T. Bergman (eds) *Cabinets and Coalition Bargaining: The Democratic Life Cycle in Western Europe*. Oxford University Press, 237–67.

Warwick, P. V. and Druckman, J. N. (2001). 'Portfolio Salience and the Proportionality of Payoffs in Coalition Governments,' *British Journal of Political Science* 31(4): 627–49.

Warwick, P. V. and Druckman, J. N. (2006). 'The Portfolio Allocation Paradox: An Investigation into the Nature of a Very Strong but Puzzling Relationship,' *European Journal of Political Research* 45(4): 635–65.

CHAPTER 17

....

POST-EXECUTIVE
ACTIVITIES

....

FORTUNATO MUSELLA

17.1 INTRODUCTION

....

ACCORDING to the 'ambition theory' proposed by Joseph A. Schlesinger (1966) in the introduction to one of his more famous books, professional politicians are guided more by where they want to get to than by how they got where they are.[1] Indeed, although ambition is not the only motivating factor for representatives, expectations regarding their post-office activities, within a given structure of opportunity,[2] are a very important influence on their political action and choices (Nicholls 1991: 149). If one starts with this basic assumption, the study of post-executive activities of top politicians appears even more crucial to an understanding of political executives, and as a relevant point of observation for explaining both the inner functioning of the cabinet as well as inter-institutional dynamics. Moreover, additional value to the study of post-executive careers comes from the observation that top political leaders are younger today than in the past, so that they may have more time to move toward other political or not-political positions: indeed when former leaders 'leave office they find they still have many extra-years in their hands' (Keane 2009: 282). Thus, this topic, which has been largely ignored until recently, is now making its way onto the political science research agenda.

---

[1] This theory has been largely applied to legislative studies in United States, yet only recently Schlesinger's approach has been adopted for the study of cabinet members (cf. Mezey 1970; Hibbing 1986; Herrick and Moore 1993).

[2] Indeed, as anticipated by the American author himself and then developed by a rich tradition of study, ambition is also shaped by institutional incentives and constraints (see Sartori 1997). In a contribution devoted to *The New American Party*, Schlesinger (1985: 1154) defines the structure of political opportunities as the offices that parties seek, the rules for attaining them, and the general patterns of behaviour surrounding their attainment.

After reviewing the literature on post-office political careers, this chapter will focus on more recent directions of research in this field: (a) the attempt to extend the number of empirical observations by assuming systematic and large-N comparative research; (b) the move from an empiricist-individualistic conception of career patterns to an institutional one, so that transformations in post-executive paths will be considered a crucial aspect to understanding the relationship between different layers of government; (c) investigation into new politics-market linkages in democratic regimes deriving from the new activism of former leaders, by evidencing that, over the past few years, career paths for the highest-level politicians do not stop with politics but continue through a complex system of relationships and very often go into business. Jointly considering these lines, the final part of the chapter will be devoted to develop a future research agenda concerning post-executive patterns and raise relevant questions on the changes to representative regimes.

17.2 Why Study Post-Executive Activities?

The first reason for investigating post-executive careers derives directly from Schlesinger's research, by basically focusing on the behavioural consequences of office goals. As ambition 'lies at the heart of politics', detailed pictures of type, frequency, and directions of post-office careers help understand how political action and the decisions of cabinet members are influenced by the desire of office-holders to proceed toward other posts. Throughout the last century, the destiny of leaders and cabinet members was assumed to be in the territory of further confirmation or retirement: indeed, since being part of the executive body was the apex of a political career, leaving office was often perceived as a form of decline (Blondel 1991). Yet more recently, with the complicity of a lower average age, top politicians may strive for other relevant positions after a cabinet post, and this is especially true for governmental leaders, who are increasing their political resources with the strengthening of monocratic actors in post-partycratic regimes (Poguntke and Webb 2005; Musella 2018a). Consequently, the field of post-executive activities is becoming much broader compared to the past, and new studies are exploring a great variety of occupations of former executive members in their 'second life'.

Second, the study of the careers of top politicians provides us with relevant insights into political institutions. As political phenomena are not only 'the aggregate consequences of individual behaviour' based on calculated self-interest (March and Olsen 1983: 734), movements of political class are embedded in the set of institutional rules, norms, and procedures of a political system.[3] Indeed, political ambition, rather

---

[3] According to the political science school of New Institutionalism such institutional factors may be also considered as independent variables in the process of political career (see Dogan 1981; Norris 1997).

than being free-floating, depends on concrete institutional settings and modifies along with changing relationships between spheres of authority. For instance, while in the past a political *cursus honorum* followed a linear path from the local through to regional or state level, or opened up the space for rotation at the same level of power, in recent years regional or supra-national positions are becoming a more and more frequent exit for national politicians, and even for executive members.[4] Thus, career research may contribute to an understanding of the relational structure of a polity, by giving information on how 'the relative power of different institutions makes them more or less attractive to serve in' (Borchert 2011: 125).

Finally, the analysis of post-executive careers may also provide relevant information for considering how political systems are changing their nature and confines. What Jean Blondel (1980) has called 'new career' patterns in politics have very much increased: many politicians, after working their way up to the highest political positions, then work in a completely different field. While until recently, becoming president or prime minister was the highest accolade after a long and arduous journey through the institutional ranks, and the last step before retirement or withdrawal to an undemanding seat on the back benches, over the past few years career paths for the highest-level politicians do not stop with politics but continue through a complex system of relationships. Very often a good number of former members of the national executive are involved in international affairs[5] or go into business directly. Their new jobs differ greatly from the government role they held before, but it is believed that the experience of the latter provides the resources and instruments necessary to gain entry to the new positions.

Consequently, the field of post-executive activities has become also the terrain on which to evaluate the autonomy of politics. If, according to Max Weber (1958: 84–7), the process of modernization of politics is strongly tied to the professionalization of a political class who lives off politics[6] (Borchert and Zeiss 2003), as a first step in the large-scale historical process in which the political sphere separated from society at large, the link between economic and political power in advanced democracies ends up influencing the way politicians act during and after their political mandate. One may also doubt whether politics is still as autonomous as in the past, when private interests may condition any component of a political career, and consequently political decisions themselves.

---

[4] Depending on the opportunities available in each national context, two-way careers moving from national to local politics and vice versa are possible. Moreover, this occurs both in consolidated local areas and in democracies where devolution is pushing for change. For a definition of types of career patterns within different levels of government, see Borchert (2001).

[5] It is worth noting that specific think tanks have also been founded to favour the coordination of former heads of government. For instance, Club de Madrid acts as an independent non-profit organization by connecting ninety-five regular members, of whom sixty-four are former presidents and thirty-nine of whom are former prime ministers, in order to increase their role in the international sphere.

[6] According to Max Weber (1958: 85), there are two ways 'of making politics one's vocation: Either one lives "for" politics or one lives "off" [it]'. In modern times the politician must be economically independent in order to be also politically independent: otherwise 'the politician must be wealthy or must have a personal position in life which yields a sufficient income' (Weber 1958: 85).

17.3 RESEARCH FINDINGS

Despite the relevance of the study of post-executive activities for understanding both political behaviour and institutions, and the fact that theoretical bases for studying political careers are 'wonderfully diverse' (Hibbing 1999: 153), this crucial field of analysis has remained quite neglected in political science until a few years ago. Indeed, whereas career patterns of presidents, prime ministers, and other executive members have been widely scrutinized, and a rich literature on the consequences focusing on the inner functioning of cabinets has been developed (Blondel and Müller-Rommel 1993, see also Chapter 22 in this volume), there are very few studies on what top politicians do after leaving office. The lack of empirical analysis is accompanied by the absence of adequate theoretical reflection so that 'the subject of ex-office holders is under-theorized, under-researched, under-appreciated, and—in many cases—under-regulated' (Keane 2009: 192).

Moreover, the political 'second life' that follows a governmental office has been investigated on an empiricist-individualistic biographical basis, focusing particularly on those great men who attracted the admiration of a plethora of historians, political scientists, and commenters. Thus, initial contributions in this field, often not written by political scientists, have concentrated on the profile of single politicians, often opening the way for 'popular biographies of individual prime ministers with varying degrees of lurid detail about their private lives' (Rhodes 2008: 323). Histories of great presidents or ministers have described differences in personal characteristics and political style,[7] along with writings in constitutional analysis describing the evolution of their office (see also Chapter 2 in this volume).

Given the role of the apex of government in the United States, which appears so unique to so many observers, it is no surprise that the literature on former leaders has been largely dominated by studies of former American presidents (Theakston and de Vries 2012). Figures of memorable American presidents, such as Theodore Roosevelt or Harry Truman, have inspired detailed narratives on their presidential and post-presidential life (Norton Smith and Walch 1990; Skidmore 2004; Updegrove 2006). Very often, however, the largeness of their individual characters has been assumed to be the main variable explaining their destiny, with limited attention on how personal traits interact with institutional factors. More rarely has the theme of regulatory measures emerging to discipline the status of former presidents been dealt with. For instance, in his study on US ex-presidents departing the White House, Paul B. Wice (2009) notes that the retirement experiences may vary throughout time depending on the introduction of provisions that gave diverse lifetime benefits such as a pension, office, funding, and a staff to conduct their ongoing activities, as occurred in the late 1950s with the Former Presidents Act.

---

[7] On the use of the biographic method in social sciences, see Miller and Brewer (2003) and Merril and West (2009).

A more systematic classification of former presidents develops when they started to become more active after serving in the nation's highest political office. In the last quarter of a century, detailed explorations have indicated that, while no institutional role has been designated for those who left the White House, former American presidents have increased the number of possible 'exits' as private citizens, from public commitment to commercial activities (Benardo and Weiss 2009; Anderson 2010). Belenky (1999) identified six recurrent models or categories of ex-presidents: the still ambitious; exhausted volcanoes; political dabblers; first citizens; embracers of a cause; and seekers after vindication. Further contributions have been devoted to understanding the reasons for an increasingly marked activism among former presidents. Although personality and health factors have usually been assumed to be key factors explaining the nature and success of post-presidential life, Winger and Jain emphasize that expanded opportunities offered by changes in geopolitics, institutions, and communication technologies lead to increasing post-presidential involvement in foreign affairs. By identifying eight different roles—bystander, elder statesman, private diplomat, government envoy, public supporter, public critic, humanitarian, and official—they reach the conclusion that 'as the office of president continues to evolve, so too will the activities of the individual after leaving office' (Winger and Jain 2016: 26). In their view, the passage from the pinnacle of American institution to positions of worldwide post-presidential influence will be more and more frequent in future.

Post-executive studies have then moved from the United States to other national contexts. For instance, the experience of former British prime ministers has become one of the most privileged cases for studies on post-executive activities (Theakston 2006, 2010), as the 'best known and longest established headships of government in Western Europe' (King 1991: 25). Concentrating on a single country, such research tends not to point out a common pattern within leaders' careers, rather it states that the 'second act' of prime ministers depends on their personal choice and on circumstances, with longevity and good health as essential ingredients for a successful post-premiership (Theakston 2010: 6). Yet, if the modern trend of modern UK premiership is to stand down as party leader immediately after losing a general election, it may underline a common career pattern among British premiers: more and more frequently they have not opted to stay in the House of Lords, despite the fact that former leaders are traditionally awarded a peerage which opens the way for a parliamentary seat, but they 'have taken up well-paid business posts (Major, Blair), set up foundations (Thatcher, Blair), or sought to operate as active and roving figures on the world stage (Blair)' (Theakston and de Vries 2012: 235).

Other countries have also been put under investigation, even evidencing the increasing influence of prime ministers after stepping down from their office. Shifting from the English democracy to non-Western countries, the analysis of post-office activities has been much more limited, as it is more difficult to find pattern of differences across regimes where political leaders stay in office longer since they are not subject to elections. The scarcity of satisfactory analysis is also due to the diffuse phenomenon in not-democratic succession for which rulers have been often executed in recent years outside the developed world. As observed by Egorov and Sonin (2015), available examples of countries that have witnessed at least two killings of fallen leaders during the last fifty years include many countries such as Afghanistan, Bangladesh, Iraq, Nigeria, Comoros, and Liberia, with other examples of rulers who have been killed in Guatemala, Cambodia, or Romania. Moreover, it is worth noting that in other fragile democracies, such as Latin American countries, presidencies may end in political corruption and often be interrupted by a judicial sentence: for instance the Brazilian president Lula has begun serving a twelve-year prison sentence for accepting bribes in exchange for government contracts while in office, while recently the Peruvian president Kuczynski has resigned because of a corruption scandal involving his administration.

Despite the lack of an extensive comparative study on post-office activities of ministers in non-democratic regimes, specific case studies are increasing in number: in countries where the circulation of a political elite has not been the norm in the past few decades, or has been produced by a violent succession or judicial intervention, the number of peaceful presidential transitions has raised important questions about the role and status of former leaders as a consequence of progressive democratization. For instance in *Legacies of Power*, Roger Southall and Henning Melber (2006) consider the recent phenomenon of African former heads of state and presidents by showing how ex-presidents are becoming more active in both domestic and international affairs in the latest decades: if the figure of Nelson Mandela represents one of the highest models for civil commitment after office, the ordinariness of presidential retirement opens a space for a large set of post-office occupations.

A quite different phenomenon has occurred in other geographical areas, with a mix of immobilism at the top of political executives and rapid ministerial and parliamentary turnover (Fisher et al. 2012; see also Chapter 16 in this volume). Indeed, after the collapse of the Soviet Union, and especially with the shift toward super-presidentialism expressed by Vladimir Putin, cabinets have been increasingly composed of bureaucrats, whereas businessmen, party politicians, and celebrities represent a high percentage of the State Duma. In terms of post-office career, the lack of professionalization of political elites has led a good number of ministers not to take a position after their cabinet activities, or to move to other administrative careers. Otherwise members of parliament (MPs) have tended to use the parliamentary service to increase social capital in order to venture into private or state-owned business enterprises (Semenova 2011: 922).

Research in the early eighties set the stage for studying pathways to and from government 'not only from a longitudinal perspective, but also in a comparative framework' (Dogan 1979: 23, see also Chapter 12 in this volume), according to a research agenda on post-office life that has not been followed since.[8] An authoritative example is the well-known Jean Blondel's (1980) *World Leaders*, the first systematic attempt at fully-documented investigation of top politicians' careers, which takes into consideration 138

---

[8] Extensive comparisons of top executive elites have been produced during the 1980s also thanks to the commitment of Mattei Dogan as Chairman of the Research Committee on Political Elites of the International Political Science Association (cf. Dogan 1989; Verzichelli 2018).

post-World War II chief executives. In his classical typology of political leaders' routes, the author identifies three main career patterns: at one end of the spectrum, there is the normal pattern of those who slowly work their way up the political ladder to the higher echelons of government and then retire from active political life once their term as president is over (*linear career*). At the other extreme, he puts the kind of leader who is on hire to politics from another field, and who returns to this profession once their contribution to society has been made (*bell-shaped career*). In the middle we find those politicians who remain 'close to the corridors of power after their downfall from high office, hoping to return to the leadership position later and perhaps succeeding in remaining ministers' (Blondel 1980: 196). In this case, the former leaders become members of an oligarchy, as often happens in continental Europe. For instance, in its first fifty years of republican history, Italy is one of the clearest models of such a tendency, with a restricted government circle and a clear institutional profile in terms of recruitment, specialization, and career, anchored in the Christian Democrat style of government (Calise and Mannheimer 1982). It is worth noting that in Blondel's typology there is no room for those leaders who, after working their way up to the highest political positions, then work in a completely different field, often earning significant amounts of money, as this route represents a more recent phenomenon (see below). Different results have been reached by Theakston and de Vries (2012) in the volume *Former Leaders in Modern democracies*, who have provided a comparative analysis of the post-executive destiny of political leaders in a large set of Western democratic states, from Great Britain and France to Israel and Australia, on the basis of the assumption, also confirmed by their analysis, that 'different countries, political systems and contexts shape the lives of former leaders' (Calca 2013: 889). However, despite the authors' attention to national peculiarities, they evidence a common trend toward increasing opportunities for former leaders in new roles outside the sphere of domestic politics or in money-making activities.

The same global comparative approach has been attempted for the analysis of ministers' careers. In a chapter of the volume edited with Jean-Louis Thiébault, *The Profession of Government Minister in Western Europe*, Jean Blondel (1991) provided one of the first extensive comparative examinations of ministerial post-office activities, and concluded that there are few opportunities after the profession of government minister in Western countries. While cabinet members mostly leave office relatively too young to retire immediately, they experiment a form of pre-retirement in parliament or by returning to their last job: the ministerial position is interpreted as 'the apex of a political career and indeed of a career tout court' (Blondel 1991: 153). Almost concurrently, however, Nicholls (1991) showed the US exceptionalism a quarter of a century ago, when cabinet service seemed to improve career opportunities in the private/business sector. Today this topic appears even more important, because the way in which ministers are recruited and selected, in an increasing number of cases because of personal ties with the head of government, or on the basis of technical knowledge and specialized expertise (Costa Pinto et al. 2018). This means that a greater proportion of ministers comes from outside the realm of politics, and so presents a relevant premise for a closer relationship between political institution and private actors. Yet very few studies have continued to work on Blondel's hypothesis over the last few years, so that, although many contributions regard the ministers' role and pathway,[9] literature on post-ministerial activities remains in its infancy.

17.4 RESEARCH APPROACHES

17.4.1 From an Empiricist-Individualistic to Institutional Analysis

Studying post-office occupation of former cabinet members is not only a way of observing the conduct of single politicians through an empiricist-individualistic approach. Sharing a common reaction against behaviourism, new and old institutionalist scholars—as does the mainstream tradition of political science (Rhodes 2009)—argue that political action does not exist outside the institutional frame that shapes it. This leads to the conclusion that post-executive patterns depend on personal characteristics and contingent choices of former cabinet members, as well as on the political and institutional context in which they develop. Consequently, post-executive careers may say a lot about the structure of opportunity in a given political system and also about what is considered as a privileged position at a certain time: 'in some countries a move from national legislator to the state executive or even the regional legislature or to big city mayor is considered a rational upward move, whereas in others such a move would be regarded as an inconceivable degradation' (Borchert and Zeiss 2003: 17). Thus, individual courses of politicians change along with transformations in the institutional structure of a political system, which determines to what extent political offices are *available*, that is, the formal or informal rules to achieve it; *accessible*, how easily a certain position can be obtained; and *attractive*, with reference to the property of the office in itself, for instance in terms of perceived prestige or income (Borchert 2003).

Since there is large support in the literature for the hypothesis that politicians' career paths are affected by the configuration of institutional authority, as it has been tested for the distinction between presidential and parliamentary regimes (Samuels and Shugart 2010), or for the differentiation between Westminster and consensus democracy (Berlinski et al. 2007), and it was noticed for specific constitutional provisions concerning the hiring and firing of members of the executive (Dowding and Dumont 2009). The same may be stated for the post-office phase of political trajectory. Indeed, all

---

[9] Only a limited number of contributions have worked on Blondel's preliminary generalisations in the last few years, and even those scholars devoted to comparative diachronic study of similarities and differences in the personal characteristics of European representative elites have concentrated their investigation on patterns of recruitment, with rare reference to the post-executive segment of political life (see Best and Cotta 2000; Dowding and Dumont 2009).

aspects concerning the institutional asset are able to influence selection, duration, and post-office opportunities for executive members. For instance, former leaders and ministers in parliamentary regimes are supposed to stay in power longer than their counterparts in presidential regimes. Moreover, population size of countries also represents an important factor when the dimension of states decreases: indeed, microstates seem to demonstrate a strong correlation between smallness and personalistic and patrimonial politics, which results in a not-democratic stability of government (Veenendaal 2014). With regards to post-office career, post-office exits to private activities appears more common in parliamentary systems than in presidential and semi-presidential systems (Musella 2015), yet much more use needs to be made of that data in empirical analysis, as one could suppose that the emergence of the former leaders occupied in business activities particularly seems to concern mature democracies with developed economies.

Furthermore, differences between majoritarian and consensus democracies may be underlined. For instance, Theakston and de Vries (2012) note that most departing British prime ministers tend to fit Blondel's (1980) 'linear' career model, so acting in a minor political position or quietly retiring after being chief executive. Moreover, in Australia, public life for deposed leaders appears as quite limited, and the path that makes former prime ministers stay in parliament and seek further ministerial office is becoming unconventional (Strangio 2012). Instead, in consensus democracies like Belgium, the premiership may result in an unexpected intermezzo in which to build a significant post-prime ministerial career as MPs, ministers, or other roles on the international stage (De Winter and Rezsöhazy 2012). The same occurs in the Netherlands where prime ministers tend to go on to hold public offices of various types, in parliament as well as in the Council of State or central bank.

However, although it is becoming clear that institutional factors, including regime type, constitutional and parliamentary rules, and party systems, affect post-executive activities (Fisher et al. 2012: 505) a general theory and systematic comparison are still missing.

Focusing on careers of ministers, other studies seem to lead to similar conclusions on the effective relationship between institutional variables and political careers. To cite a contribution, in their post-office investigation on former cabinet members, Sílvia Claveria and Tània Verge (2015) take into account twenty-three advanced industrial democracies to show that, instead of proceeding chaotically or being only related to personal traits of single politicians such as ambition or seniority, career paths strongly depend on country-specific institutional factors. For instance, looking at the type of ministerial recruitment, they distinguish generalist systems under which ministers are typically recruited from parliament from specialist systems where cabinets are more populated with political outsiders, and note relevant differences among them in terms of post-tenure orientations and activities: indeed

> under generalist systems, ex-ministers typically have more seniority and usually hold party office, which are stepping stones to other political positions once cabinet service ends, whereas under specialist systems ex-ministers tend to be political outsiders, making them more likely to land in non-political occupations.
>
> (Claveria and Verge 2015: 831)

In their comparison of UK and US post-ministerial careers, Stolz and Kintz (2014: 7) use other relevant institutional factors in order to explain differences between the two countries. First, government structure: parliamentary systems allow former ministers to hold a position in the legislative branch, while in systems of separation of powers, such as American presidentialism, ex-cabinet ministers do not have this opportunity and consequently tend to search for an occupation outside politics, especially in the private sector. Moreover, post-ministerial trajectories are strongly determined by a large set of additional institutional factors such as 'state structure (federal vs. unitary), the politi-cization of the higher administration (neutral or strongly political), the prominence of the political parties in the political process, the prestige of the cabinet post' (Stolz and Kintz 2014: 7). The two authors conclude that the stark contrast that different political regimes may show in pre-cabinet trajectories is even more pronounced when post-cabinet paths are under investigation, and that 'future studies exploring the complex causal nexus between different institutional settings and (post-) ministerial careers would have to include many more country cases' (Stolz and Kintz 2014: 26).

17.4.2 Post-Executive Activities and the Relationship between Different Political Layers

Career patterns also allow for a better understanding of the institutional stability and change with a special focus on the emerging political balance between institutional levels (Borchert 2011; Pilet et al. 2014). Indeed, while cabinet position was considered the top of a ladder conducting from the periphery to the national centre, today career move-ments are becoming less uniform than in the past on the basis of the increasing differen-tiation of polities into multi-level systems. This is particularly true for cabinet members, whose office was at the top of a long *cursus honorum* during the nineteenth century, but nowadays appears more as a springboard to other different roles, with various ways of moving between territorial levels. According to Jens Borchert and Klaus Stoltz (2011: 107) three noteworthy processes of institutional change have to be taken into account to comprehend the distance from the past:

> the professionalization of the state level in federal systems (most notably in Germany and in the USA since the 1970s); the regionalization of formerly unitary states (like the UK, Spain, France and Italy); and the development of supranational institutions (such as the European Parliament).

With regards to the first process, regional positions were considered as 'step stones on the way to federal or national offices' in the past (Stolz 2003). Yet if one sheds light on the more recent phenomenon of differentiation of polities into multi-level systems, several types of multi-level political careers may be noticed for the study of what has been defined the 'labyrinth' of career movements (Borchert and Stolz 2011). For instance, by concentrating on the post-cabinet careers of regional ministers in Germany, a recent study by Stolz and Fisher (2014) shows that regional cabinet office constitutes an important premise for climbing up the German institutions, and, at the same time, ex-cabinet members are more attracted by *Länder* or regional posts, that now offer more power, prestige, and pay than in the past. What seems increasingly clear is that regional ministers, rather than considering intermediate positions as a temporary role that is useful for moving up as soon as possible, spend much more time at the regional level, thus showing a change in the 'structure of the German career ladder' (Stolz and Fisher 2014: 170). Moreover, if bi-directionality appears as a new trait of political routes as well, in a context where regional politics is becoming the apex of their political career and thus an end in itself, also other less traditional career paths are considered: for instance there are also far more examples of 'the cross-over into "political" positions outside representative politics (e.g. consultancy, lobbying, etc.) as well as into the non-political private sphere' (Stolz and Fisher 2014: 171).

Other analyses indicate that meso-government is becoming appealing due to the processes of regionalization of politics that is affecting so many European modern states, first produced by supra-national policies (Sharpe 1993; Keating 2004) and in many cases encouraged by national institutional restructuring (Behnke and Benzy 2009; Musella 2009). For instance, in Italy, especially after the constitutional reform introducing the direct election of regional presidents in 1999, which brought about a large increase in their popularity and consequent evolution of Italian political parties toward a stratarchical model (Wilson 2016), bi-directional movements among different levels of government are becoming more frequent. Thus, while in the period 1990–2000 regional presidents largely came from an institutional position at the regional level (88.8 per cent), in the last fifteen years the number of those heads of regional government coming from the national layer have largely increased: a quarter of presidents have previous experience as an MP or minister (Musella 2018b; Lo Russo and Verzichelli 2016). Thus, on the one hand the fact of being regional president remains a good prerequisite for a political career at the national level, on the other hand 'the regional presidential post has become very attractive due to its political benefits' (Grimaldi and Vercesi 2018: 130).

Finally, new career paths may also prove the strengthening of the European supra-national level. Indeed, the slow and controversial formation of a European political class highlights the emergence of specific patterns of political career toward and from the European Union, so that

> being elected within the EP can provide significant advantages both for those who want to have good results in a more and more important sort of 'political champions league' and for those who are preparing themselves to 'win something important' at the domestic level.   (Verzichelli and Edinger 2005: 255)

Thus member states have shown that the relationship between European Union and domestic institutions has changed over time in terms of politicians' careers: as it has been noticed with regard to the French political class, although the structural looseness and general instability of European institutions remains a fairly clear trait of supra-national democracy, European MPs and commissioners have started being inserted in more, both ascending and descending, stable political trajectories (Kauppi 1996). With reference to post-executive careers, European institutions provide a possible option for a good exit from national politics, so confirming the role of a new multi-level structure of opportunity in shaping individual ambitions and choices.

17.4.3 Presidents and Ministers in 'Business'

Post-cabinet occupations also provide relevant information on the relationship between politics and other spheres of human behaviour such as markets. The professionalization of politics has been a way to protect representatives by giving them—in the well-known Weberian terms—a way of living off politics and not only for politics, allowing them to act independently of certain social or economic constraints, and without worrying about their own subsistence. This has constituted an important pillar of representative democracies throughout the twentieth century, as one of the prerequisites for guaranteeing the supremacy of politics. Yet over the last few years, research has shown the emergence of a new career pattern in politics, where business activities may intervene as a step after political career, thus raising important questions on how the autonomy of politics may be preserved.

First contributions analysing the politics-business nexus in political careers deal with the American presidential cabinet. The seminal article by Keith Nicholls (1991) on 'The Dynamics of National Executive Service', as a fundamental starting point in a field that has remained largely underinvestigated in the latest years, shows that the US political system is an important case study for the fact that 'cabinet service does not currently constitute a step toward still higher public service' (Nicholls 1991: 152). On the contrary the 'peak of the national opportunity structure' (Schlesinger 1966: 23) opens doors to other activities in the private sector, where cabinet members may progress in terms of wealth and capitalize what they have accumulated during their tenure: 'knowledge, experience, reputation, and connections which can facilitate one's entry in to the executive suites and corporate boardrooms of America' (Schlesinger 1966: 170). Consequently, the significant number of moves from cabinet to private law activities let business interests play an increasing role in governmental affairs, and probably also in the recruitment process, of executive members. At the same time, cabinet members' expectations in terms of career may influence their decisions during the ministerial mandate.

More recently, by examining a dataset of 441 leaders in seventy-eight different democratic countries over a period dating from 1989 to 2012, Fortunato Musella (2015) has shown that recent heads of government are enthusiastically seeking alternative ways to capitalize on their prestige and contacts portfolio, often ending up in the world of business or international finance. The fact that leaders are now younger when they retire reinforces this trend (more than 40 per cent of presidents and prime ministers take over the leadership of the national executive before they are 50). They are also much more active after their presidential mandate. However, this raises the clear suspicion that, if former political leaders end up in the world of private affairs, they often prepare for these roles during their term in office, with controversial questions where democracy is concerned (Anderson, 2010).

At the same time, through an empirical study on career paths of German ministers from 1949 until 2014, Nora Dörrenbächer (2016) shows that revolving doors, which attracted scholarly attention on the US landscape especially with reference to congressional careers (Diermeier et al. 2005; Mattozzi and Merlo 2007), may be now largely observed also in Europe in different institutional fields, with high potential, especially in the passage from government to business, 'to violate the conflict of interest principle, enhance interest group clientelism, regulatory capture and undemocratic elite networks' (Dörrenbächer 2016: 473). Indeed, while one may observe a general pattern of post-cabinet careers where, one year after their cabinet position, most former cabinet ministers (60 per cent) still assume party political jobs, the second largest category of post-cabinet career (18 per cent) is occupied by those former ministers who 'switched directly into a typical revolving door position such as in lobby firms, advisory boards of big businesses, consultancies and so on' (Dörrenbächer 2016: 481). On the same line, other studies also investigate post-career earnings of former cabinet members. For instance, González Bailón et al. (2013: 870) confirm the close relationship between politics and business in Great Britain, showing that 'there is a correspondence between certain and highly select high offices of state and business'.

17.4.4 A Faster Passage from the Executive to the Market

A number of factors have led to the development of a new trend in which former leaders obtain enormous amounts of money in the private sector. First, presidents and prime ministers are acquiring more powers and visibility than in the past. At the beginning of the 1990s, two important volumes by Michael Foley (1993, 2000) presented the thesis of the 'rise of the British presidency', suggesting a steady increase of prime ministerial power at the expense of the cabinet. This influenced the debate on the various manifestations of presidentialization in many of the major parliamentary democracies (Helms 2005). As a successful volume by Thomas Poguntke and Paul Webb (2005) has demonstrated, processes of 'presidentialization of politics' in a large group of countries have brought about relevant transformations leading presidents and prime ministers to gain a more central position in those political systems. Leaders often act as the main political actor in electoral processes where success is strongly related to their, more or less charismatic, personalities, and they consequently become more and more autonomous vis-à-vis the party in governmental activities. They also greatly increase their powers on the legislative arena, through the expansion of the use of normative instruments such as decree laws and delegated legislation, as the Italian case clearly shows[10] (Musella 2018a, see also Chapter 18 in this volume). Moreover, the process of the internationalization of

---

[10] Relationship with private actors is one of the three basic ingredients for the spread of personal leaders, besides the increase in legitimacy and governmental power: indeed we can clearly register 'once gained control on institutional structures and resources, the tendency of political leaders to use them for private ends' (Musella 2018a).

politics, while stimulating the active role of leaders in inter-governmental negotiations, offers them the opportunity to develop a significant network beyond national borders. Since combinations of such processes produce the political centrality of political leaders, the shift of power from collegial to monocratic actors gives single politicians a more significant amount of political and relational resources. Subsequently politicians could also use such capital in post-office life and make their engagement more desirable for private actors.

This leads us to consider another relevant factor that can be identified for explaining changes in post-office careers: the closer relationship between politics and corporations, which may lead to various forms of collusion, from pre-packaging the contracting-out of public works to circulation between top administrative posts and corporate boards of directors, to mere 'coziness between ministerial officials and their counterparts in private industry and banking' (Schneider 1991 in Useem 1984; Calise and Lowi 2010: 61). The documented phenomenon of 'revolving doors' refers to the fact that government service can serve as a conduit for joining the ranks of the corporate elite. So, when politicians fail to get re-elected, they can be recycled into government or business positions—a well-noted phenomenon in the Italian republican history (Keane 2009). In Northern America such processes have become so noteworthy that specific legal regulations have been established to close the revolving doors through which public officials sell their expertise and inside knowledge when they leave public office (see, e.g., the Canadian Federal Accountability Act, Government of Canada, 2006). For instance, Baumgartner et al. (2009: 199–200) analysed 1,244 lobbyists working in the United States and confirmed that the average business in their sample has 'about one recent former covered official working on its behalf' (jobs such as members of Congress, congressional staff members, or high-level agency officials during the past two years). Yet studies on the relationship between public administration and private corporations have been continued only in the United States, whereas this topic has been investigated in Europe mainly with reference to European Union 'as a new venue point for private interest articulation' (Dörrenbächer 2016: 473; see also Bouwen 2004, Eising 2004, and Chapter 33 in this volume). In both cases, however, the theme of the direct channel from top political institution to private world, as evidenced in political leaders' careers, although highly relevant for the functioning of democratic regimes, has remained out of analytical focus.

17.5 FUTURE RESEARCH AGENDA

Studies in post-governmental activities are taking their first steps. Indeed, since seminal quantitative investigations on cabinet ministers produced in the eighties, a few contributions have regarded political career patterns, with a particular silence on that segment of politicians' trajectories concerning post-office.

In this chapter, three reasons for focusing attention on this emerging field of study have been considered, that are also very relevant reasons to keep researching in the domain of post-executive activities. First, following the famous Schlesinger's (1966) 'ambition politics', the politicians' office goals act as an important explicatory factor of political behaviour, so that career expectations end up strongly influencing the way in which office is held. With regards to this point, a significant lack of empirical research in post-executive activities may be evidenced, especially in less consolidated democracies. Future research should aim at investigating post-executive activities in a large comparative framework, especially by including geographical zones outside Northern America and Europe that have been underexamined until now. An additional question regards the presence of women leaders in contemporary executives. Since 1990, a significant number of women have served on political executives, and several books and articles have focused on differences between men and women leaders. On the point of post-government activities, it seems that only a few women remain at the top of national politics after leaving the executive office, while several tend to be engaged in international circles with a humanitarian mission, often becoming 'vocal sponsors of women's rights in international arenas' (Montecinos 2017: 4). Yet it appears too soon to make generalizations on the pattern of women presidents and prime ministers, and the gendered nature of executives still remains, with a few exceptions, unexamined (Kellerman and Rhode 2007; Rhode 2016).

Second, the direction and frequency of politician's behaviour offer relevant insights into the relationship between institutional spheres. Indeed, career patterns allow for analysis of institutional stability and change, by suggesting generalization on the relational structure of a polity. Especially after the spread of multi-level politics, research in post-executive activities may lead us to consider the development of new political linkages across local, national, and supra-national levels. Here the need for multivariate analysis on the diverse links between institutional factors and political career may be underlined, starting from the main features of political systems.

Finally post-cabinet activities have also shown new career paths in recent years that have to be put under analysis. On the one hand, former heads of government or ministers may enjoy rising public prominence on an international stage, so experimenting a new way of 'losing political office' (Roberts 2017) by preserving not power but influence (Skidmore 2004: 3). Besides personal traits of politicians, who end their political occupation when they are much younger than in the past, changes in geopolitics, institutions, and communication technologies also condition activities of the contemporary former president, who someone metaphorically calls 'Mr. Worldwide' (Winger and Jain 2016). On the other hand, post-office trajectories may say something very relevant about the relationship between the world of politics and the private sector, also delineating serious challenges for maintaining the autonomy of political activities. Since former presidents have the kind of relevant information and network resources that make them an attractive proposition for corporations, their fate seems to lie more and more in the world of business in posts such as business consultants or directors. So, instead of accepting losing an election, which is a central principle of democratic politics (Anderson 2010), the development of an international web of ties and opportunities will allow top level politicians to continue their activities after stepping down from their office, often by switching to more profitable roles.

17.6 CONCLUSION

This chapter has underlined some directions for future research on post-executive activities, by noting the lack of updated and extensive comparative analysis of former leaders and executive members, the need for a comprehensive theory and generalization on the influence of cultural and institutional factors on political careers, the absence of systematic studies concerning not-democratic countries, the necessity to focus on new links between democratic governments and business that are changing the nature, and the perspectives, of representative regimes.

Moreover, new trends in political careers also invite theoretical reflection on how post-executive career might raise some delicate questions for the future of democracy, so that further studies have to be devoted to the consequences of the rise of 'presidents in business'. A nagging doubt remains that they can establish special links with private companies during their term in office and make decisions that benefit these companies, losing that sense of distinction between public interest and the private interests they are busy protecting[11] (Musella 2015). Indeed, what a politician considers as a future aspiration also influences his or her activities in office, and the way in which he or she acts and interacts with other social actors. The logic of democratic representative systems supposes that the electorate is able to influence those they elect, and representatives tend to respond to citizens with a certain degree of independence from corporate business. Yet the emergence of a career path that leads directly from politics to business, rather than being simply a free personal option for world leaders, strikes at the heart of democracy. Whose continued functioning and survival remain related to the autonomy of the highest-ranking democratic officers of a country.

REFERENCES

Anderson, L. (2010). 'The Ex-Presidents', *Journal of Democracy* 21(2): 64–78.
Baumgartner, F. R., Berry, J. M., Hojnacki, M., Kimball, D. C., and Leech, B. L. (2009). *Lobbying and Policy Change: Who Wins, Who Loses, and Why*. Chicago: University of Chicago Press.

[11] When politics as vocation is strongly undermined as long as a high number of political paths end up in private and money-making activities, this also contradicts, as observed by Keane (2009: 295), the ancient conception emerging from the Middle Age as a basic principle of representative democracy: 'the rule that specified that holding office implied faithful performance of a specific set of tasks'.

Behnke, N. and Benzy, A. (2009). 'The Politics of Constitutional Change between Reform and Evolution,' *Publius: The Journal of Federalism* 39(2): 213–40.

Belenky, I. (1999). 'The Making of the Ex-Presidents, 1797–1993: Six Recurrent Models,' *Presidential Studies Quarterly* 29(1): 150–65.

Benardo, L. and Weiss, J. (2009). *Citizen-in-Chief: The Second Lives of the American Presidents*. New York: William Morrow.

Berlinski, S., Dewan, T., and Dowding, K. (2007). 'The Length of Ministerial Tenure in the United Kingdom, 1945–1997,' *British Journal of Political Science* 37(2): 245–62.

Best, H. and Cotta, M. (2000). *Parliamentary Representatives in Europe 1848–2000*. Oxford: Oxford University Press.

Blondel, J. (1980). *World Leaders: Heads of Government in the Postwar Period*. London: Sage.

Blondel, J. (1991). 'The Post-Ministerial Careers,' in J. Blondel and J.-L. Thiébault (eds) *The Profession of Government Minister in Western Europe*. New York: Palgrave, 153–73.

Blondel, J. and Müller-Rommel, F. (1993) (eds). *Governing Together: The Extent and Limits of Joint Decision-Making in Western European Cabinets*. London: Palgrave Macmillan.

Borchert, J. (2001). 'Movement and Linkage in Political Careers: Individual Ambition and Institutional Repercussions in a Multi-level Setting,' ECPR Joint Sessions of Workshops, Grenoble.

Borchert, J. (2003). 'Professional Politicians: Towards a Comparative Perspective,' in J. Borchert and J. Zeiss (eds) *The Political Class in Advanced Democracies*. Oxford: Oxford University Press, 1–25.

Borchert, J. (2011). 'Individual Ambition and Institutional Opportunity: A Conceptual Approach to Political Careers in Multi-level Systems,' *Regional and Federal Studies* 21(2): 117–40.

Borchert, J. and Stolz, K. (2011). 'Introduction: Political Careers in Multi-Level Systems,' *Regional and Federal Studies* 21(2): 107–15.

Borchert, J. and Zeiss, J. (2003) (eds). *The Political Class in Advanced Democracies: A Comparative Handbook*. Oxford: Oxford University Press.

Bouwen, P. (2004). 'Exchanging Access Goods for Access: A Comparative Study of Business Lobbying in the EU Institutions,' *European Journal of Political Research* 43(3): 337–69.

Calca, P. (2013). 'Former Leaders in Modern Democracies: Political Sunsets,' *West European Politics* 36(4): 889–90.

Calise, M. and Mannheimer, R. (1982). *Governanti in Italia. Un trentennio repubblicano, 1946–1976*. Bologna: Il Mulino.

Calise, M. and Lowi, T. J. (2010). *Hyperpolitics: An Interactive Dictionary of Political Science Concepts*. Chicago: Chicago University Press.

Claveria, S. and Verge, T. (2015). 'Post-Ministerial Occupation in Advanced Industrial Democracies: Ambition, Individual Resources and Institutional Opportunity Structures,' *European Journal of Political Research* 54(4): 819–35.

Costa Pinto, A., Cotta, M., and Tavares de Almeida, P. (2018). 'Beyond Party Government? Technocratic Trends in Society and in the Executive,' in A. Costa Pinto, M. Cotta, and P. Tavares de Almeida (eds) *Technocratic Ministers and Political Leadership in European Democracies*. Cham: Palgrave, 1–26.

De Winter, L. and Rezsöhazy, I. (2012). 'The Afterlives of Belgian Prime Ministers,' in K. Theakston and J. De Vries (eds) *Former Leaders in Modern Democracies*. London: Palgrave Macmillan, 186–211.

Diermeier, D., Keane, M., and Merlo, A. (2005). 'A Political Economy Model of Congressional Careers,' *American Economic Review* 95(1): 347–73.

Dogan, M. (1979). 'How to Become a Cabinet Minister in France: Career Pathways, 1870–1978,' *Comparative Politics* 12(1): 1–25.

Dogan, M. (1981). 'Introduction. La selection des ministres dans diverse regimes politiques,' *International Political Science Review* 2(2): 129–37.

Dogan, M. (1989) (ed.). *Pathways to Power: Selecting Rulers in Pluralist Democracies*. San Francisco: Westview Press.

Dörrenbächer, N. (2016). 'Patterns of Post-cabinet Careers: When One Door Closes Another Door Opens?,' *Acta Politica* 51(4): 472–91.

Dowding, K. and Dumont, P. (2009) (eds). *The Selection of Ministers in Europe: Hiring and Firing*. London: Routledge.

Egorov, G. and Sonin, K. (2015). 'The Killing Game: A Theory of Non-Democratic Succession,' *Research in Economics* 69(3): 398–411.

Eising, R. (2004). 'Multilevel Governance and Business Interests in the European Union,' *Governance* 17(2): 221–46.

Fischer, J., Dowding, K., and Dumont, P. (2012). 'The Duration and Durability of Cabinet Ministers,' *International Political Science Review* 33(5): 505–19.

Foley, M. (1993). *The Rise of the British Presidency*. Manchester: Manchester University Press.

Foley, M. (2000). *The British Presidency*. Manchester: Manchester University Press.

González-Bailón, S., Jennings, W., and Lodge, M. (2013). 'Politics in the Boardroom: Corporate Pay, Networks and Recruitment of Former Parliamentarians, Ministers and Civil Servants in Britain,' *Political Studies* 61(4): 850–73.

Grimaldi, S. and Vercesi, M. (2018). 'Political Careers in Multi-Level Systems: Regional Chief Executives in Italy, 1970–2015,' *Regional and Federal Studies* 29(2): 125–49.

Helms, L. (2005). 'The Presidentialisation of Political Leadership: British Notions and German Observations,' *The Political Quarterly* 76(3): 430–8.

Herrick, R. and Moore, M. K. (1993). 'Political Ambition's Effect on Legislative Behavior: Schlesinger's Typology Reconsidered and Revisited,' *The Journal of Politics* 55(3): 765–76.

Hibbing, J. R. (1986). 'Ambition in the House: Behavioral Consequences of Higher Office Goals among US Representatives,' *American Journal of Political Science* 30(3): 651–65.

Hibbing, J. R. (1999). 'Legislative Careers: Why and How We Should Study Them,' *Legislative Studies Quarterly* 24(2): 149–71.

Kauppi, N. (1996). 'European Union Institutions and French Political Careers,' *Scandinavian Political Studies* 19(1): 1–24.

Keane, J. (2009). 'Life after Political Death: The Fate of Leaders after Leaving High Office,' in J. Kane, H. Patapan and P. 't Hart (eds) *Dispersed Democratic Leadership: Origins, Dynamics and Implications*. Oxford: Oxford University Press, 279–96.

Keating, M. (2004) (ed.). *Regions and Regionalism in Europe*. Cheltenham: Edward Elgar Publishing.

Kellerman, B. and Rhode, D. L. (2007) (eds). *Women and Leadership: The State of Play and Strategies for Change*. San Francisco: Jossey-Bass.

King, A. (1991). 'The British Prime Ministership in the Age of the Career Politician,' *West European Politics* 14(2): 25–47.

Lo Russo, M. and Verzichelli, L. (2016). 'Reshaping Political Careers in Post-Transition Italy A Synchronic Analysis,' in M. Edinger and S. Jahr (eds.) *Political Careers in Europe: Career Patterns in Multi-Level Systems*. Baden-Baden: Nomos, 27–54.

March, J. G. and Olsen, J. P. (1983). 'The New Institutionalism: Organizational Factors in Political Life,' *American Political Science Review* 78(3): 734–49.

Mattozzi, A. and Merlo, A. (2007). 'Political Careers or Career Politicians,' PIER Working Paper 07-009, University of Pennsylvania.

Merril, B. and West, L. (2009). *Using Biographical Methods in Social Science*. London: Sage.

Mezey, M. L. (1970). 'Ambition Theory and the Office of Congressmen,' *The Journal of Politics* 32(3): 563–79.

Miller, R. L. and Brewer, J. D. (2003). 'Biographical Method,' in R. L. Miller and J. D. Brewer (eds) *The A–Z of Social Research: A Dictionary of the Key Social Science Research Concepts*. London: Sage.

Montecinos, V. (2017) (ed.). *Women Presidents and Prime Ministers in Post-Transition Democracies*. Basingstoke: Palgrave Macmillan.

Musella, F. (2009). *Governi monocratici. La svolta presidenziale nelle regioni italiane*. Bologna: Il Mulino.

Musella, F. (2015). 'Presidents in Business: Career and Destiny of Democratic Leaders,' *European Political Science Review* 7(2): 293–313.

Musella, F. (2018a). *Political Leaders beyond Party Politics*. Cham: Palgrave.

Musella, F. (2018b). 'The Italian Governors from the Constitutional Reform to the Crisis of Regionalism,' in F. Tanács-Mandák (ed.) *Identity Crisis in Italy*. Budapest: Dialóg Campus.

Nicholls, K. (1991). 'The Dynamics of National Executive Service: Ambition Theory and the Careers of Presidential Cabinet Members,' *Western Political Quarterly* 44(1): 149–72.

Norris, P. (1997). 'Introduction: Theories of Recruitment,' in P. Norris (ed.) *Passages to Power: Legislative Recruitment in Advanced Democracies*. Cambridge: Cambridge University Press, 1–14.

Norton Smith, R. and Walch, T. (1990). *Farewell to the Chief: Former Presidents in American Public Life*. Worland: High Plains Publishing.

Pilet, J. B., Tronconi, F., Onate, P., and Verzichelli, L. (2014). 'Career Patterns in Multilevel Systems,' in K. Deschouwer and S. Depauw (eds) *Representing the People: A Survey among Members of Statewide and Sub-State Parliaments*. Oxford: Oxford University Press, 209–26.

Poguntke, T. and Webb, P. (2005) (eds). *The Presidentialization of Politics: A Comparative Study of Modern Democracies*. Oxford: Oxford University Press.

Rhode, D. L. (2016). *Women and Leadership*. Oxford: Oxford University Press.

Rhodes, R. A. W. (2008). 'Executives in Parliamentary Government,' in R. A. W Rhodes, S. A. Binder, and B. A. Rockman (eds) *The Oxford Handbook of Political Institutions*. Oxford: Oxford University Press, 324–45.

Rhodes, R. A. W. (2009). 'Old Institutionalisms: An Overview,' in R. E. Goodin (ed.) *The Oxford Handbook of Political Science*. Oxford: Oxford University Press, 141–58.

Roberts, J. (2017). *Losing Political Office*. Basingstoke: Palgrave Macmillan.

Samuels, D. J. and Shugart, M. S. (2010). *Presidents, Parties, and Prime Ministers: How the Separation of Powers Affects Party Organization and Behaviour*. Cambridge: Cambridge University Press.

Sartori, G. (1997). *Comparative Constitutional Engineering: An Inquiry into Structures, Incentives, and Outcomes*. New York: New York University Press.

Schlesinger, J. A. (1966). *Ambition and Politics: Political Careers in the United States*. Chicago: Rand McNally.

Schlesinger, J. A. (1985). 'The New American Political Party,' *The American Political Science Review* 79(4): 1152–69.

Schneider, B. R. (1991). *Politics within the State: Elite Bureaucrats and Industrial Policy in Authoritarian Brazil*. Pittsburgh: University of Pittsburgh.

Semenova, E. (2011). 'Ministerial and Parliamentary Elites in an Executive-Dominated System: Post-Soviet Russia 1991–2009,' *Comparative Sociology* 10(6): 908–27.

Sharpe, L. J. (1993) (ed.). *The Rise of the Meso Government in Europe*. London: Sage.

Skidmore, M. (2004). *After the White House: Former Presidents as Private Citizens*. New York: Palgrave Macmillan.

Southall, R., and Melber, H. (2006). *Legacies of Power: Leadership Change and Former Presidents in African Politics*. Nordiska Afrikainstitutet: HSRC Press.

Stolz, K. (2003). 'Moving Up, Moving Down: Political Careers across Territorial Levels,' *European Journal of Political Research* 42(2): 223–48.

Stolz, K. and Fischer, J. (2014). 'Post-cabinet Careers of Regional Ministers in Germany, 1990–2011,' *German Politics* 23(3): 157–73.

Stolz, K. and Kintz, M. (2014). 'Post-Cabinet Careers in Britain and the US: Theory, Concepts and Empirical Illustrations,' paper prepared for the ECPR General Conference, Glasgow, 3–6 September.

Strangio, P. (2012). 'The Evolution of Prime Ministerial Afterlives in Australia,' in K. Theakston and J. De Vries (eds) *Former Leaders in Modern Democracies*. London: Palgrave Macmillan, 78–102.

Theakston, K. (2006). 'After Number 10: What Do Former Prime Ministers Do?,' *Political Quarterly* 77(4): 448–56.

Theakston, K. (2010). *After Number 10: Former Prime Ministers in British Politics*. Basingstoke: Palgrave Macmillan.

Theakston, K. and De Vries, J. (2012) (eds). *Former Leaders in Modern Democracies*. New York: Palgrave Macmillan.

Updegrove, M. (2006). *Second Acts: Presidential Lives and Legacies After the White House*. Guilford: The Lyons Press.

Useem, M. (1984). *The Inner Circle: Large Corporations and the Rise of Business Political Activity in the US and UK*. Oxford: Oxford University Press.

Veenendaal, W. (2014). *Politics and Democracy in Microstates*. London: Routledge.

Verzichelli, L. (2018). 'Elite Circulation and Stability,' in H. Best and J. Higley (eds) *The Palgrave Handbook of Political Elites*. London: Palgrave, 363–80.

Verzichelli, L. and Edinger, M. (2005). 'A Critical Juncture? The 2004 European Elections and the Making of a Supranational Elite,' *The Journal of Legislative Studies* 11(2): 254–74.

Weber, M. (1958). *From Max Weber: Essays in Sociology*, ed. H. H. Gerth and C. W. Mills. New York: Oxford University Press.

Wice, P. B. (2009). *Presidents in Retirement: Alone and Out of the Office*. Lenham: Lexington Books.

Wilson, A. (2016). 'Regional Presidents, Multi-Level Parties and Organizational Stratarchy: The Case of Italy,' in F. Müller-Rommel and F. Casal Bértoa (eds) *Party Politics and Democracy in Europe: Essays in Honour of Peter Mair*. London: Routledge, 65–79.

Winger, G. H. and Jain, A. (2016). 'Mr. Worldwide: International Affairs and the American Post-Presidency,' *Congress & the Presidency* 43(1): 1–54.

PART III

DYNAMICS AND
DEVELOPMENTS
WITHIN
POLITICAL
EXECUTIVES

CHAPTER 18

··

THE PRESIDENTIALIZATION OF POLITICAL EXECUTIVES

··

†ROBERT ELGIE AND GIANLUCA PASSARELLI

18.1 INTRODUCTION

THE idea that there has been a presidentialization of prime ministerial politics is not new. For example, Allen (2018: 13) quotes a journalist from 1904 who claimed that the British prime ministership was becoming more like the office of an elected president at that time. Blick and Jones (2010: 32) have also pointed to claims in the early 1920s that British Prime Minister David Lloyd George was acting like a president. They also cite work in the 1960s that was making similar comments about British prime ministers then (Blick and Jones: 59–63). In a scholarly context, though, the term 'presidentialization' seems to have originated in Canada in the 1970s among scholars looking at their own political system and comparing its development with that of the US presidency (Smith 1977). This origin is instructive because, as Helms (2015: 2) points out, at this time presidentialization was often equated with the more general concept of 'Americanization'. In Britain, the prime ministership of Margaret Thatcher (1979–90) provoked more general discussion of whether the system there had become presidentialized. This led to Michael Foley's (1993) book about the supposed rise of the British presidency. This was the first full-length work on the presidentialization of a parliamentary system. From this point onwards, the presidentialization thesis was present in the scholarship about Britain (e.g. Pryce 1997). Gradually, this thesis started to gain traction elsewhere too. In 2000, Thomas Poguntke and Paul Webb organized a workshop on 'The Presidentialization of Parliamentary Democracies?' at the European Consortium for Political Research Joint Sessions in Copenhagen. This initiative led eventually to Poguntke and Webb's

(2005a) ground-breaking edited volume. Theirs was the first comparative study of presidentialization. More so than Foley's work or any other, Poguntke and Webb's book constitutes the academic point of reference on this topic. In this sense, it marks the beginning of what we can think of as the contemporary period in the scientific study of presidentialization. Thereafter, Samuels and Shugart (2010) made another important contribution to the study of this topic, but in a way that was markedly different from Poguntke and Webb's approach. Thus, there are now effectively two ways of studying presidentialization. We consider both in this chapter.

There are three parts to this chapter. The first section briefly identifies the four main questions that are asked in the contemporary study of presidentialization. The second section reviews the existing work that has tried to answer those questions. The third section establishes a research agenda for the future study of presidentialization.

18.2 What Do We Want to Know About Presidentialization?

There are four general questions in the study of presidentialization.

First, what is meant by the term and how should it be defined? This question begs a further question. What is the difference, if any, between presidentialization and cognate concepts such as personalization and prime ministerialization? Another question that is asked in this regard is whether the concept of presidentialization can be applied to the study of presidents in presidential and indeed semi-presidential countries, or whether it is applicable only to the study of prime ministers in parliamentary systems? A further question still can be asked. Is the presidentialization of prime ministerial politics the equivalent of what used to be termed 'prime ministerial government'? These conceptual questions are foundational to the contemporary study of presidentialization.

Second, what are the sources of presidentialization? This question treats presidentialization as the dependent variable. Here, there is a debate as to whether presidentialization is the product of institutional features, or a broader process of societal change (Elgie and Passarelli 2019). If its source is institutional as Samuels and Shugart (2010) understand it to be, what is the relationship between institutional variation and different degrees of presidentialization? If it is the result of a process of societal change as Poguntke and Webb (2005a) believe, what are the historical, cultural, sociological, political, and other factors that have caused presidentialization in general and that lead to cross-national variation in the level of presidentialization?

Third, whatever we understand by the term 'presidentialization' and whatever its sources, to what extent has there been a presidentialization of contemporary polities in practice? Clearly, this is an empirical question. Poguntke and Webb's (2005a) volume was extremely influential in this regard. They provided a general template that scholars could apply to study the degree of presidentialization in a country and change over time.

A number of studies have been published applying their framework and usually finding at least some evidence to support the presidentialization thesis.

Finally, what are the consequences of presidentialization? This question treats presidentialization as the explanatory variable. As we shall see, Poguntke and Webb's framework is not very helpful in this regard. By contrast, Samuels and Shugart's (2010) method of analysis offers more potential for systematic research in this regard.

In the next section, we review the existing work on presidentialization, referring back to the four basic research questions that we outlined here.

18.3 What Do We Know About Presidentialization?

18.3.1 What Is Meant by the Term and How Should It Be Defined?

The concept of presidentialization has proven difficult to define. Indeed, rather than trying to provide a rigorous definition of the concept, scholars typically focus on the defining features of presidentialization, often providing a list of such features. Even then, scholars tend to identify those features in relatively general terms. Nonetheless, the basic claim is that certain general features are constitutive of presidentialization.

Foley (1993: 24) identifies the defining feature of the US presidential system to be what he calls 'spatial leadership'. He states: 'This refers to the way that recent presidents have sought to enhance their position in Washington by creating as much distance between it [Washington] and the presidency' (Foley 1993: 24). He argues that US-style spatial leadership was the result of 'deep-seated and long-term changes in the American polity' (Foley 1993: 59). He also argues that similar changes occurred in Britain in the 1980s. In this way, he concludes, spatial leadership became a 'feature of the British political landscape' (Foley 1993: 59), leading to the rise of the British presidency during the Thatcher premiership. This way of thinking supports the idea that presidentialization is often synonymous with Americanization (Helms 2015). That said, Foley (1993: 263) states that he is not implying 'a convergence of the British premiership with the American presidency'. 'The presence of a *de facto* presidency in the British system', he argues, 'has been conditioned by British circumstances and tradition' (Foley 1993: 278). Instead, he argues that there has been the rise of 'an authentically British president' (Foley 1993: 283). Whether or not we agree with his argument, we can see that Foley is not defining presidentialization. He is treating it as an analogy. He argues that there have been analogous developments in Britain and the US, leading to what he believes to be the rise of the British presidency.

Mughan (2000) follows a slightly different but essentially similar thought process. He does provide a definition of presidentialization. He states that it 'implies movement over time away from collective to personalized government, movement away from a pattern of governmental and electoral politics dominated by the political party towards one where the party leader becomes a more autonomous political force' (Mughan 2000: 7). Like Foley, Mughan (2000: 7) makes a direct analogy with the US system. Unlike Foley, though, he believes that there has been a 'convergence on the individualist American model'. For Mughan (2000: 10), presidentialization is a 'straightforward, empirically detectable' phenomenon. For him, presidentialization is

> a personalization of electoral politics that on the one hand occurs within the param-
> eters of an unchanging parliamentary constitution and on the other persists over
> time, albeit that the actual impact of the party leaders on mass political behaviour
> and election outcomes can vary in magnitude from one contest to the next.
>
> (Mughan 2000: 9)

On basis of these features, assessing presidentialization thesis involves 'mapping whether party leaders have indeed become more prominent in election campaigns and determining whether they are more influential electoral forces than they used to be' and 'explaining any presidentialization of impact that has taken place' (Mughan 2000: 12). Thus, Mughan differs from Foley in providing a definition, but engages in essentially the same exercise as Foley, namely identifying the observable features of a presidentialized system.

Both Foley and Mughan make direct reference to the US when thinking about the concept of presidentialization. Poguntke and Webb (2005b) differ in this regard. Like Mughan, they provide a definition of presidentialization. They state that it 'denominates a process by which regimes are becoming more presidential in their actual practice without, in most cases, changing their formal structure, that is, their regime-type' (Poguntke and Webb 2005b: 1). As they immediately note, though, this definition merely begs the question of what it means for a country to become more presidential. Like both Foley and Mughan, they then provide a sketch of what they consider be an ideal-typical presidential system. They do not define the idea in purely constitutional terms (Poguntke and Webb 2005b: 2). Instead, Poguntke and Webb claim that 'the *de facto* presidentialization of politics can be understood as the development of (a) increasing leadership power resources and autonomy within the party and the political executive respectively, and (b) increasingly leadership-centred electoral processes'. Specifically, they argue that these developments affect three 'central arenas of democratic govern-ment'. This leads them to identify what they call the 'three faces of presidentialization, namely *the executive face, the party face,* and *the electoral face*' (Poguntke and Webb 2005b: 5; italics in the original). Thus, like both Foley and Mughan, Poguntke and Webb provide a set of features that can be observed to determine whether or not a country has undergone a process of presidentialization. Unlike Foley and Mughan, though, at no point in their introductory discussion do they refer to the US model as an analogy, or to a process of Americanization.

Samuels and Shugart (2010) provide an alternative way of thinking about the concept of presidentialization. Like both Mughan and Poguntke and Webb, they provide a definition of presidentialization. Unlike all three authors we have considered so far in this subsection, though, Samuels and Shugart define the concept in terms of the institutional features of a regime. They 'define presidentialization as *the way the separation of powers fundamentally shapes parties' organizational and behavioral characteristics, in ways that are distinct from the organization and behavior of parties in parliamentary systems*' (Samuels and Shugart 2010: 6; italics in the original). In terms of the separation powers, they are concerned with, first, electoral origin, meaning whether the executive comes to office with the support of the legislature or separately, usually through the direct election of the president; and, second, electoral survival, referring to whether the continuing existence of the executive in office is independent of the legislature or whether it can be provoked by the legislature through a motion of no confidence. This is a very different way of thinking about presidentialization. We should immediately signal, though, that Samuels and Shugart are primarily concerned with the presidentialization of political parties, whereas Foley, Mughan, and Poguntke and Webb are interested in broader electoral and political features. Nonetheless, Samuels and Shugart argue that variation in the presidentialization of parties causes variation in such features. Therefore, indirectly they are concerned with the broader operation of the political executive.

To sum up, scholars have identified the defining features of presidentialization, but there is no commonly accepted definition of the term. Perhaps, though, there is no need for any such definition. If we can identify the constitutive features of presidentialization, then arguably we have sufficient grounds to go ahead and examine whether or not there is evidence for presidentialization in practice. The defining features of presidentialization vary from one author to the next. However, to the extent that Poguntke and Webb's account has become the standard way of thinking about the concept, then the study of presidentialization is often associated with consideration of one or more of their three faces of presidentialization.

18.3.2 What Is the Difference, If Any, between Presidentialization and Cognate Concepts Such as Personalization and Prime Ministerialization?

Whatever the definition of presidentialization, or the defining features of it, how does the concept of presidentialization relate to similar concepts such as personalization and prime ministerialization?

For some writers, the concepts of presidentialization and personalization are synonymous. For example, we have seen that Mughan (2000: 9) states that presidentialization can be defined as 'a personalization of electoral politics'. Jou and Endo (2015) take this argument to its logical extreme. In their article on the presidentialization of Japanese politics, they state explicitly that 'the terms "personalization" and "presidentialization" are used interchangeably' (Jou and Endo 2000: 358). Thus, the title of their article is the 'Presidentialization of Japanese Politics?', but the first section reviews the existing literature on the '[p]ersonalization of politics in parliamentary systems'. For other writers, though, the two concepts are different. For example, Karvonen's (2010) volume on the personalization of parliamentary democracies does include a brief discussion of the presidentialization thesis. However, Karvonen is rather dismissive of the idea, stating the 'general "gut impressions" of expert authors seem to be more in favour of the presidentialization thesis than the actual evidence presented in the various country studies' (Karvonen 2010: 20). From thereon in, he focuses exclusively on the personalization thesis, for which he believes the evidence is also relatively mixed.

In their work, Samuels and Shugart (2010) have clearly differentiated between the concepts of presidentialization and prime ministerialization. They argue that the 'reliance on an individual leader is more accurately identified as personalization than as presidentialization' (Samuels and Shugart 2010: 249). The 'notion of presidentialization', they state, 'differs fundamentally from the concept of personalization'. For them, the most important point in this respect is that 'parties in parliamentary systems can never become truly presidentialized because the fusion of electoral origin and survival gives parties tools to minimise both adverse selection and moral hazard problems' (Samuels and Shugart 2010: 249). Thus, the crucial issue here is that even though parliamentary parties can fire their leaders after having selected them, presidential parties can neither choose nor dismiss the president. For Samuels and Shugart (2010: 250), what differentiates personalization from presidentialization is the emphasis on candidates 'who enjoy some personal reputation distinct from their party's collective reputation'. For them, personalization as a concept can 'be applied fruitfully to executives and their parties' (Samuels and Shugart 2010: 250), yet presidentialization means something more than personalization. This is because of their institutional perspective. In essence, there is presidentialization when a president is heading a branch of political authority constitutionally separate from the legislature, but this does not automatically mean that there is personalization too. This is because such a president does not necessarily enjoy the high personal reputation that is constitutive of personalization.

There is now a considerable literature on the topic of personalization. The aim here is not to review this literature, but to illustrate how it relates to the concept of presidentialization. For example, Cross et al. (2018) consider personalization to be a general phenomenon affecting politics and polities across the world. They argue that the 'implications of personalized politics are necessarily widespread and can be found across many different aspects of political parties and our democratic politics more generally' (Cross et al. 2018: 10). Specifically, they and most authors argue that personalization influences electoral campaigns, voting behaviour, and indirectly but importantly in the context of this chapter, the functioning of governments, and, therefore, of the political executive. For their part, Rahat and Kenig (2018) examine the cross-national variation in the levels and patterns of party change and political personalization. Reviewing the literature on personalization, Costa Lobo (2017: 159) reports that 'there is no strong trend towards personalization of party organizations, whereas in electoral behaviour the evidence points to the increasing use by voters of leaders as heuristics'. In this way, the personalization of politics is often equated with leader effects on voting behaviour. In this regard, contributors to Aarts et al. (2013) show that voters tend to let themselves be guided by the leaders they like rather than turning away from those they dislike.

There is, thus, a large literature on the personalization of politics. However, very little of this work directly invokes the concept of presidentialization. Instead, it tends to be very focused on the role of political leaders, including presidents and prime ministers, the changing role of political parties, and the impact of leaders and parties on electoral politics. In this context, Poguntke and Webb's idea of the three faces of presidentialization is useful. As we noted above, they identify an 'electoral face' of presidentialization. This idea concerns '*electoral processes*' and the 'shift from partified control to domination by leaders' (Poguntke and Webb 2005b: 10). Specifically, they refer to the '*growing emphasis on leadership appeals in election campaigning*', the fact that '*media coverage of politics focuses more on leaders*', and '*the growing significance of leader effects in voting behaviour*' (Poguntke and Webb 2005b: 11; italics in the original). These are the classic themes of the literature on the personalization of electoral politics. Thus, in contrast to Mughan's definition that conflates the two concepts, we can reasonably conclude that presidentialization is not the same as personalization, but that the two concepts do overlap. In other words, from the perspective of Poguntke and Webb at least, personalization is merely one of the features of the broader concept of presidentialization. Put differently, for them the personalization of electoral politics is part of the electoral face of presidentialization, meaning that it is a necessary but not a sufficient condition of presidentialization.

In contrast to personalization, the concept of prime ministerialization relates more to the role of the head of the executive within the executive branch, or what Poguntke and Webb call the executive face of presidentialization. Scholars have debated whether politics in modern democracies is witnessing a trend towards the increased centralization of political power in the hands of the chief executive, though in practice the study of the concentration of power in this regard dates back to the first decade after World War II. In particular, it has increasingly come to be accepted that prime ministers in parliamentary regimes are accumulating organization resources, including personal staffs and political advisors. In addition, growing attention has been paid to the changing relationship between parliaments and heads of governments in parliamentary democracies. In particular, it has been shown that prime ministers have intervened in parliamentary debates more infrequently over time (Dunleavy et al. 1990), suggesting that parliaments are no longer the main arenas of political debate and communication. This situation seems to resemble the politics of the chief executive in presidential regimes. Here, presidents are usually not allowed even to set foot in the legislative chamber, except for annual set-piece state of the union speeches. Given these developments, there may be a *prima facie* case that prime ministerships are becoming increasingly similar to presidencies in presidential regimes.

Without exception, scholars accept that there have been changes to the role of the head of government in parliamentary systems. The question is whether these changes should be understood as the presidentialization of prime ministerial politics, or the prime ministerialization of parliamentary politics. We will discuss the empirical evidence in favour of the presidentialization thesis below. Suffice to say here, though, that plenty of authors have understood the changes to the role of prime minister through the lens of the concept of presidentialization. For example, we have already seen that Foley (1993) was one of the first authors arguing in favour of a presidentialization of the British executive, a theme to which he returned later (Foley 2008). Heffernan and Webb (2005: 56) also discussed the three faces of presidentialization in the context of the British prime minister, concluding that 'politics in Britain's parliamentary democracy has come to operate according to a logic which more closely echoes presidentialist politics than was hitherto the case'. Kefford (2013) has applied Poguntke and Webb's schema to the Australian case, finding mixed evidence for the presidentialization thesis during the premiership of Kevin Rudd at least.

Other scholars, though, prefer to consider these changes differently. Here, the contributions by Dowding (2013a, 2013b, 2013c) are noteworthy. He explicitly contests the concept of 'presidentialisation' and also the work of Poguntke and Webb (2005a) generally. Instead, he argues that the term 'prime ministerialisation' should be preferred to 'presidentialisation' at least in empirical studies that deal with processes of change in parliamentary systems. Dowding makes his position very clear, stating that the 'presidentialisation of the prime minister thesis should be expunged from political science vocabulary' (Dowding 2013a: 617). Interestingly, he criticizes the concept at least in part because of the recurrent analogy with the US presidency. This Americanization, he states, is 'what commentators seem to have in mind' (Dowding 2013a: 618). Instead, he argues that 'executive behaviour can only be analysed through the institutional form that makes it appropriate' (Dowding 2013a: 617). For Dowding, there are important institutional and behavioural differences between presidents in presidential regimes and prime ministers in parliamentary regimes. This leads him to the claim that even though personalization is occurring in both presidential and parliamentary systems, the increasing power of the prime minister that 'Foley and others identify is not a presidentialization but, gratingly or not, a prime ministerialization of the British prime minister' (Dowding 2013a: 619). For their part, Peters and Helms (2012: 30) have argued that the term presidentialization 'may be something of a misnomer'. This because while 'presidents appear to be extremely powerful, they are in many ways more constrained than are prime ministers'. In other words, if the term 'presidentialization' is being used to refer to the idea that prime ministers are becoming as strong as (US) presidents, then the term is being misused, because many prime ministers are stronger than their (US) presidential counterparts especially in domestic policy.

From this discussion, we can see that the concepts of personalization and presidentialization are sometimes thought of as interchangeable. For scholars following Poguntke and Webb, though, personalization is best considered to be a subset of

THE PRESIDENTIALIZATION OF POLITICAL EXECUTIVES

presidentialization. Dowding thinks of the relationship between personalization and prime ministerialization in the same way. However, we can also clearly see that the concepts of presidentialization and prime ministerialization are mutually exclusive. That said, some scholars reject the concept of presidentialization without necessarily embracing the concept of prime ministerialization (Rhodes et al. 2009: 110–12). Nonetheless, if scholars believe that there have been changes to prime ministerial politics in parliamentary systems that include but are not confined to a process of personalization, then they have to choose between characterizing those changes as either presidentialization or prime ministerialization, or use some other term altogether.

18.3.3 Can There Be Presidentialization in Presidential and Semi-Presidential Countries?

We have seen that the concept of presidentialization has its origins in the discussion of the changing role of prime ministers in parliamentary regimes. This discussion was closely associated with the idea of the Americanization of parliamentary politics. This historiography might suggest that presidentialization is a concept that applies only to prime ministers. Yet, what about presidents? Can the concept of presidentialization be applied to the study of directly elected presidents in presidential and semi-presidential regimes? Here, it is useful to distinguish between the general idea of presidentialization and the application of Poguntke and Webb's more specific version of this concept to presidential and semi-presidential regimes.

The idea that countries with directly elected presidents have become presidentialized without reference to Poguntke and Webb's concept is widespread. In this context, presidentialization simply refers to some general process of increasing presidential power. For example, Cason and Power (2009) discuss the presidentialization of foreign policy making in Brazil without making any reference to any of Poguntke and Webb's three faces of presidentialization. Indeed, while this chapter focuses on scholarly work in English, it is worth noting *en passant* that there is a vast French-language literature on the presidentialization of French politics that goes back to the early 1960s and the de Gaulle presidency. In a sense, this way of thinking about presidentialization is merely the presidential mirror image of Dowding's idea of the prime ministerialization of parliamentary politics. Here, it is worth recalling Dowding's claim (2013a: 618) that 'executive behaviour can only be analysed through the institutional form that makes it appropriate'. Understood this way, presidentialization and prime ministerialization are mutually exclusive but effectively equivalent concepts, capturing the same general process of power concentration but in different institutional contexts.

The more interesting recent development is the application of Poguntke and Webb's (2005a) presidentialization schema to presidential and semi-presidential regimes. For example, their volume included a chapter by Fabbrini (2005) on the US. He argues that

US electoral politics have become personalized over the years (Fabbrini 2005: 313). He also notes that the system of separation of powers entails structural differences between the US president and prime ministers in parliamentary regimes. In particular, he states that 'individual incumbents have to cope with the structural constraints of their position' (Fabbrini 2005: 330). Nonetheless, he also makes the case that 'the American system of separated government has gradually presidentialized in the last three decades' (Fabbrini 2005: 331). He argues that in both the US and parliamentary regimes 'a common transformation of the governmental process seems to have taken place: the legislature and the chief executive have moved apart'. In the US context, this means that the president 'has had to rely on his own personal mandate and resources in order to negotiate his way through the political agenda' (Fabbrini 2005: 331). So, we can see that there are specificities to the application of Poguntke and Webb's version of presidentialization to the US, but we can also see that both they and their contributors believe that presidentialization is not just a phenomenon that applies to parliamentary regimes.

A similar logic underpins Helms' (2015) work. He also applied Poguntke and Webb's version of presidentialization to the US context. That said, he did so on the basis of 'a slightly amended version' (Helms 2005: 1) of the concept. He excludes consideration of the electoral face, arguing that in contrast to prime ministers in parliamentary regimes US presidents do not usually claim a mandate from their electoral victories (Helms 2005: 3). He also wishes to consider what he calls the 'legislative face' of presidentialization, which is one of the ways in which the party face manifests itself in presidential systems. Specifically, and consistent with Fabbrini's analysis, he wishes to see if there has been 'a growing divide between the executive and the legislative branch' (Helms 2005: 3). For the purposes of this section, the key question is not whether Helms finds evidence for presidentialization in the US—though he does—but the mere fact that he believes Poguntke and Webb's concept 'can in fact be meaningfully applied to the study of presidential leadership [there]' (Helms 2005: 11).

Poguntke and Webb (2005a) applied their schema to semi-presidential regimes too. They included chapters on Finland, France, and Portugal. Scholars have subsequently followed up on the logic of this inquiry. For example, Sturzu (2011: 326) has applied Poguntke and Webb's framework to Romania, concluding that 'Western presidentialization and the Romanian way of making politics seem to converge on several points'. Zaznaev (2008) has applied Poguntke and Webb's framework to Russia. That said, and somewhat reminiscent of Helms, he wishes to emphasize two aspects of presidentialization (Zaznaev 2008: 31). These are the president's increased control over resources and the president's autonomy from the legislature. He concludes by arguing that the 'concept of "presidentialization" is useful for providing an understanding of the complicated and contradictory processes currently developing within the framework of the various forms of government in different countries' (Zaznaev 2008: 40). In this way, Zaznaev captures the general consensus among scholars of presidentialization. Those who believe the concept has traction tend also to believe that it can be applied, albeit in a somewhat modified form, not just to prime ministers in parliamentary regimes, but to chief executives in all systems.

18.3.4 Is the Presidentialization of the Premiership the Equivalent of 'Prime Ministerial Government'?

We have seen that Poguntke and Webb identify a so-called 'executive face' of presidentialization. This element of the presidentialization thesis concerns the growth of prime ministerial advisers, the centralization of political communication, the capacity to set the policy agenda, pre-eminence in international negotiations and so forth. These developments are not new. Indeed, there is a sense in which they echo themes associated with debates about prime ministerial government that emerged in the UK in the 1960s and that were paralleled by work on chancellor democracy in Germany and equivalent research elsewhere. So, is the presidentialization thesis merely the 'latest version' of the old prime ministerial government thesis? Indeed, we can extend this line of thinking a little further still. In the early 1900s Dunleavy and Rhodes (1990) challenged the narrow terms of the traditional prime ministerial vs. cabinet government debate by introducing the concept of the 'core executive'. This concept referred to 'all those organizations and structures which primarily serve to pull together and integrate central government policies or act as final arbiters within the executive of conflicts between different elements of the government machine' (Dunleavy and Rhodes 1990: 4). The core executive approach paved the way for a perspective which focuses on dynamic relationships between multiple actors within the executive as a whole, rather than the consideration of essentially static formal structures centred on the prime minister. How does the presidentialization thesis relate to work on the core executive?

We can say that the presidentialization thesis is consistent with a critique of the traditional prime ministerial government debate. The clue is in the suffix. Similar to the core executive approach, the *-ization* suffix suggests the consideration of a dynamic process of change. Indeed, Poguntke and Webb (2005a: 5) discuss the idea of presidentialization 'as a process', stating that the central research question of their volume concerns whether 'there are contingent and structural (as opposed to formal- constitutional) factors at work that push modern democracies towards a more presidential working mode'. Arguably, the presidentialization thesis requires scholars to adopt a diachronic perspective, making comparisons of change over time. Thus, the presidentialization thesis is not merely the repackaging of the old prime ministerial government debate. In this regard, it shares common ground with the literature on core executive politics.

That said, there would appear to be a potentially important difference between the presidentialization debate and the core executive approach. There is a sense in which Poguntke and Webb's version of the presidentialization thesis does indeed emphasize relationships between multiple actors (see below) and a dynamic process of change, but it also perhaps suggests the presence of a long-term, seemingly ineluctable, and general trend towards presidentialization (Elgie and Passarelli 2019). For them, there is something almost inevitable about the development of presidentialization in modern democratic societies. For sure, not all countries may experience the process of presidentialization in the same ways and to the same degree, but the direction of change seems to be clear.

To the extent that there is a process of change, then it is towards presidentialization. This perspective is different from the core executive politics approach. Indeed, the apparently unidirectional nature of the change inherent in the presidentialization thesis has been explicitly criticized by those most closely associated with the core executive approach. For example, Rhodes et al. (2009: 219) state that 'there is nothing as distinct as a "trend" towards greater centralization [...]'. Instead, prime ministerial power is always 'contingent, interdependent, and variable'. Indeed, whereas proponents of the presidentialization thesis wish to present a picture of the trend regarding the executive as a whole, the core executive approach emphasizes the multiple relationships, or 'court politics', that exist within the executive. Thus, Rhodes et al. (2009: 112) conclude that while 'the core executive thesis can encompass the several varieties of court politics, the presidentialization thesis cannot'. Overall, there is a clear sense in which the Poguntke and Webb's version of the presidentialization thesis and the Rhodes et al.'s version of the core executive politics approach are mutually exclusive, even if both challenge the old-style prime ministerial vs. cabinet government debate.

18.3.5 What Are the Sources of Presidentialization?

We have seen that there are now two very different ways of thinking about the concept of presidentialization. Poguntke and Webb identify the three faces of presidentialization, with personalization being effectively subsumed under the electoral face. By contrast, Samuels and Shugart understand presidentialization from the perspective of the electoral origins and survival of chief executives, with personalization being a separate phenomenon. Unsurprisingly, these different interpretations of the concept lead to differences in how the two sets of scholars think about the sources of presidentialization.

Poguntke and Webb adopt a broad sociopolitical approach to explaining presidentialization, or what we have termed a 'grand historical narrative' (Elgie and Passarelli 2019). For them, presidentialization is a general process that is occurring in modern democracies and that is separate from any other process of constitutional change. In this regard, they make it quite clear that there are non-institutional forces driving presidentialization (Poguntke and Webb 2005b: 12–13). For Poguntke and Webb presidentialization is the result of the interaction of many different factors. They identify four 'underlying structural causes' of presidentialization (Poguntke and Webb 2005b: 16). They are the internationalization of politics, the growth and increasing complexity of the state, the changing structure of mass communications, and the erosion of social cleavages. They also identify two 'contingent causes' (Poguntke and Webb 2005b: 16) that intervene to shape the relationship between the structural causes and the three faces of presidentialization. These are the personality of leaders and the political context, meaning the state of the economy and so forth. We have seen that Poguntke and Webb believe there has been a general trend towards presidentialization over time. However, they make it clear that the structural forces shaping presidentialization do not necessarily operate in tandem, stating that it should not be assumed that these triple processes run in perfect simultaneity with each other: since our main causal factors have more immediate effects on some faces of presidentialization than on others, they might progress at different speeds and over different time-spans.   (Poguntke and Webb 2005b: 16)

This is why the degree of presidentialization overall is likely to differ from one country to another, even if there is a basic historical trend towards presidentialization in general. Indeed, it could even vary from one leader to another in the same country, even if there is a general trend towards presidentialization.

Samuels and Shugart (2010) have a very different starting point. They

do not claim that [their] argument supersedes or supplants the importance of social, economic, or cultural forces that drive party formation, evolution, and behaviour [...] but analysis of these differences should begin with the difference in constitutional design.   (Samuels and Shugart 2010: 18)

Specifically, they are concerned with whether or not the origins and survival of the chief executive are separate from the legislature. They state: 'to the extent that the constitutional structure separates executive and legislative origin and/or survival, parties will tend to be presidentialized' (Samuels and Shugart 2010: 37; italics in the original). Separate origin refers to the situation where there is a direct presidential election that is held separately from legislative elections, albeit perhaps simultaneously. Separate survival 'means that a party or legislative majority cannot remove a sitting president' (Samuels and Shugart 2010: 15). This schema allows them to distinguish between four different institutional configurations—presidentialism, two forms of semi-presidentialism—president-parliamentarism and premier-presidentialism—and parliamentarism—with the degree of presidentialization descending ordinally across the four regimes respectively. Samuels and Shugart have a particular focus on what Poguntke and Webb would call the 'party face' of presidentialization. They state,

to the extent that capture of a separately elected presidency is important for control over the distribution of the spoils of office and/or the policy process, party behavior and organization will tend to mimic constitutional structure, giving rise to 'presidentialized' parties.   (Samuels and Shugart 2010: 396; emphasis in the original)

Thus, Samuels and Shugart are not concerned with identifying any broad historical trend towards presidentialization. Instead, they are concerned with the institutional origins of presidentialization, particularly as they shape the organization of political parties.

Scholars have not challenged Poguntke and Webb's origin story. However, Samuels and Shugart's framework has been reconsidered. Here, Passarelli's (2015a) contribution is important. He has shown that the 'genetic origins' of political parties interact with the institutional features of the regime to shape the degree of presidentialization. By 'genetic origins', he means 'the original organizational characteristics of a party' (Passarelli 2015b: 2). Following Panebianco (1988), he identifies three such characteristics: '1) the organization's construction and development; 2) the presence or the absence (at the party's origin) of an external "sponsor"; 3) the role of charisma in the party's formation' (Passarelli 2015b: 11). He states that the

> interaction between constitutional features and the organization of the features of endogenous parties means that the presidentialization of parties is not a monolithic phenomenon. Rather it varies as a function of organizational development, the presence of factions, the role conferred to the leadership, etc.
>
> (Passarelli 2015b: 16)

Indeed, he argues that the genetic origins of political parties 'can (to some extent) counter balance the effects of institutions' (Passarelli 2015b: 15). Having remodelled Samuels and Shugart's framework in this way, Passarelli's (2015b) volume then presents a number of country case studies, showing how constitutional form and party origins interact to shape the presidentialization of party politics.

18.3.6 To What Extent Has There Been a Presidentialization of Contemporary Polities?

The concept of presidentialization may be difficult to define, but as we have seen plenty of scholars have identified what they consider to be the constitutive features of the concept. On that basis, the claim is that if these features can be observed in practice, then there is evidence that presidentialization has occurred. We have also seen that scholars have identified the various sources of presidentialization and argued that the degree of presidentialization is like to vary from one country to another according to differences in these sources. These foundations have led to a number of empirical studies exploring the extent of the presidentialization of executive politics in various countries.

We have seen that the first claims of a presidentialization of parliamentary politics were made in Canada in the 1970s (Smith 1977) and that this idea was then popularized in the UK media during the Thatcher premiership in the 1980s. At this time, scholars were more inclined to go into print to reject the presidential analogy. For example, Wearing (1977) immediately critiqued Smith's claims of the presidentialization of the Canadian prime ministership. For his part, Courtney (1984: 238) reported the claim that Canadian prime ministers had 'fashioned their position and their powers on the example of the American president' and that parliament had been 'transformed into an institution of little value and consequence in the policy-making process'. However, he was sceptical of the presidentialization thesis, arguing that 'while the pendulum of power may have swung too far in the direction of the executive and away from parliament, the charge of "presidentialization" of the office misses the point' (Courtney 1984: 239). In the British context, a similarly sceptical position was taken by G. W. Jones (1991). He stated that even Prime Minister Thatcher was only as strong as her party and parliament 'allowed her to be', concluding that 'Mrs Thatcher was no president' (Jones 1991: 134).

Interestingly, prior to Foley's (1993) book on the topic, scholars typically failed to refer to any specific scholarship on the presidentialization thesis, even when they claimed that it was a 'well-argued over' theme (Jones 1991: 111). Indeed, writing a long time after Foley's work, King (2007: 318–22) also provided an empirical critique of the presidentialization of British politics thesis, but without citing the work of anyone who had actually made such a claim.

The scholarship has now fundamentally changed. Beginning with Poguntke and Webb (2005a) volume, most studies have tended to accept the presidentialization thesis and have also concluded that there is at least some empirical evidence to back it up. Most notably, in the conclusion to their book Poguntke and Webb report the trends towards presidentialization in fourteen countries (Webb and Poguntke 2005: 338–9). Summarizing the findings across the three faces of presidentialization as a whole, they conclude that there was a strong change towards presidentialization in three countries (Germany, Israel, and Italy), a moderate change in nine (Belgium, Denmark, Finland, Netherlands, Portugal, Spain, Sweden, the UK, and the US), and a small change in two countries (Canada and France), both of which had already exhibited a high degree of presidentialization for a considerable time. Overall, this led them to claim that they 'feel confident' that 'it is reasonable to talk of the "presidentialization" of contemporary democracy' (Webb and Poguntke 2005: 347).

With Poguntke and Webb's template in hand, scholars have begun to apply the presidentialization thesis to their country of interest. Typically, scholars have found evidence in favour of the thesis, though it has usually been mixed. For example, Kolltveit (2012: 372) has argued that in Norway the prime minister's office has 'clearly strengthened, suggesting that the prime minister's ability to coordinate cabinet policy has increased'. This is an indicator of presidentialization. However, he finds no clear evidence to support the presidentialization thesis in terms of the background of ministers or cabinet reshuffles. In Sweden, Sundström (2008: 166) states that the 'presidentialisation thesis gains only some support'. He identifies nine indicators of presidentialization, including a weakening of the government's collective deliberations, a more presidential leadership style, and so on. He finds full or partial evidence for seven of those indicators, but no evidence for the other two. Also in Sweden, Bäck et al. (2011: 273) conclude that Prime Minister Persson 'resembled the more presidential figures described in the literature on contemporary parliamentary governments'. However, they also claim that 'our own assessment of two important indicators of presidentialization—the selection of ministers and the reshuffling of ministries—uncovers no convincing evidence of any steady development towards a more president-like prime minister in Sweden'. So, again a mixed picture emerges. In Germany, Helms (2005: 430) concludes that the country 'has witnessed a rather limited amount of what has been conceptualised in the more recent literature on the parliamentary democracies as ' "presidentialism" '. In a follow-up case study, applying Poguntke and Webb's framework to the chancellorship of Angela Merkel, the same author identified manifestations of presidentialization in particular in terms of the party face, but less with regard to the electoral and executive faces of presidentialization (Helms 2014: 108–16). For their part, Chohan and Jacobs (2017) have pointed to developments in Canada that go against the presidentialization thesis. We might also note that there is some very limited work on the presidentialization of presidents in parliamentary regimes, notably Italy (Palladino 2015). Overall, there is good evidence to suggest that Poguntke and Webb have identified a general cross-national trend towards presidentialization, but that many countries still have a long way to go if they are to end up fully presidentialized.

Passarelli's (2015b) volume also includes a number of empirical case studies. His summary reports how constitutional form and parties' genetic origins interact to shape the degree of presidentialization (Passarelli 2015c). For example, he concludes that in Chile the presidential regime and the origins of political parties served to reinforce the high level of party presidentialization there. By contrast, in the US the genetic features of the two main parties 'have "downsized" the presidential effects on parties generated by institutions' (Passarelli 2015c: 257). This conclusion is noteworthy because whereas Samuels and Shugart would assume that the degree of party presidentialization was the same in both Chile and the US, Passarelli's framework allows us to identify variation within the set of presidential regimes. The same point applies to parliamentary regimes too. Here, there is a difference between Japan and Italy on the one hand, and Australia, Germany, and the UK on the other. In the former, the nature of political parties means that the level of presidentialization is much lower than in the latter. Indeed, Passarelli's framework has a further implication. It allows us to consider within-country variation too. That is to say, the genetic origins of political parties vary within countries. This means that the degree of presidentialization can differ across time within the same country and the same institutional structure as one party with one type of genetic origin takes power at the expense of another with a different type. Passarelli's study represents a first step in this type of analysis.

18.3.7 What Are the Consequences of Presidentialization?

In one sense, there has been relatively little work on the consequences of presidentialization. An exception is Sykes' (2009: 235) general claim that 'presidentialisation intensifies the masculinist nature of the top job', referring to prime ministers.

Perhaps one of the reasons why there has been little emphasis on this aspect of the concept can be found in Poguntke and Webb's (2005a) introduction to the concept. We have seen that they believe presidentialization to be the result of a whole range of economic, social, and political developments. They then state that

> [e]qually, however, it is possible that causality flows in the opposite direction since structural changes like the internationalization of politics give more executive power to leaders and this, in turn, may strengthen their electoral appeal and their ability to dominate their party; that is, as executive presidentialization occurs, so the media focus more on leaders and voters then become more susceptible to leadership effects.
>
> (Poguntke and Webb 2005a: 17)

In other words, presidentialization is the result of the structural changes they identify, but at the same time presidentialization is also a further cause of those self-same structural changes. Needless to say, this circularity makes it difficult to treat presidentialization as an explanatory variable at least when it might be used to try to explain variation in anything that relates to the structural and indeed contingent causes they identify as the sources of presidentialization. Given those structural and contingent causes refer to wide-ranging aspects of modern democracy, it becomes very difficult to separate out the independent effect of presidentialization if the aim is to explore its specific consequences. Thus, Poguntke and Webb's framework may be very useful for assessing the extent of the presence of presidentialization in contemporary democracies, but it is not very helpful for identifying the effects of presidentialization.

In another sense, though, the effects of presidentialization have been studied in some detail. Here, though, we have to turn to Samuels and Shugart (2010). They were explicitly concerned with exploring not only the presence of presidentialization, but also its effects on a wide range of outcomes. Given their approach is purely institutional, they can identify its independent effect without falling into the obvious circularity that limits Poguntke and Webb's framework in this regard. For example, Samuels and Shugart show that political outsiders are more likely to hold office as regimes become presidentialized. They also show that in pure parliamentary systems, 'about three in ten changes in prime minister result from purely *intra*party politics' (Samuels and Shugart 2010: 120; italics in the original). A similar finding occurs under semi-presidentialism, but here presidents also have influence over prime ministerial appointments and dismissals, indicating the presidential 'contamination' of intra-party relations under the most presidentialized system. By contrast, under presidentialism parties have almost no direct influence over the removal of presidents. Samuels and Shugart (2010: 221) also show that regime type interacted with party system variables affects the likelihood of policy switching, with greater switching the more presidentialized the system.

Overall, we can see that there is considerable potential for scholars to study the effects of presidentialization. To do so systematically, though, we have to move away from Poguntke and Webb's understanding of the concept, or if we are going to use their idea then we would have to focus on a set of outcomes that are unrelated to the structural and contingent factors that they believe to be the causes of presidentialization.

18.4 What Do We Need to Know About Presidentialization?

Having identified the main research questions relating to the study of presidentialization and having reported the state of the art regarding the answers to those questions, we now turn our attention to the research agenda for the future study of this topic. We focus on three main areas—the concept itself, the application of the concept, and the other factors that need to be considered when applying the concept.

18.4.1 Understanding the Concept of Presidentialization

There is still a need to clarify what scholars mean by the concept of presidentialization and in two respects. First, the same term is currently being used in two very different ways (Elgie and Passarelli 2019). As we have seen, there is a sense in which Poguntke and Webb's use of the concept is incommensurable with Samuels and Shugart's understanding of it. To avoid confusion, we might wish to relabel the term in one of these cases. A suggestion is that we keep the term 'presidentialization' for studies that apply Poguntke and Webb's framework or an equivalent one and use a term such as 'constitutional presidentialization' for studies that use Samuels and Shugart's schema. This move might at least make it clearer that the two sets of scholars are each engaged in a different type of analytical exercise. Second, in relation to work that is concerned with Poguntke and Webb's understanding of the concept, or at least a non-Samuels and Shugart understanding of it, then we might also need to move closer to some consensus about the constitutive elements of the concept of presidentialization. Currently, authors tend to identify their own constitutive features, or they tweak Poguntke and Webb's features for the purposes of studying their chosen country of interest. This means, though, that we are failing to compare like with like. To be clear, we do not necessarily have to agree on a standard definition of presidentialization as such, but it would help to reach agreement on the specific features of political life that we should be focusing on when we wish to observe whether there is evidence for the presidentialization of contemporary polities.

There is also a need to clarify the relationship between the concepts of presidentialization and prime ministerialization and in turn their relationship with the concept of personalization. We have seen that some scholars object to the use of the term 'presidentialization' when applied to the study of parliamentary regimes, preferring the term 'prime ministerialization' instead. In this respect, we need to know whether scholars are talking about the same phenomena but in two different institutional contexts, or whether they are talking about two different phenomena altogether. If the former, then we could use both terms but in the knowledge that they are referring to the same sources of change that Poguntke and Webb identified and that are expressed in the same three faces of presidentialization/prime ministerialization that they identified, and so on. If the concepts are not synonymous, though, what are the differences between them? How are the constitutive features of presidentialization different from those of prime ministerialization? If the features are different, could a parliamentary country be exhibiting some degree of both presidentialization and prime ministerialization? More pertinently perhaps, could a semi-presidential regime be exhibiting both presidentialization and prime ministerialization? Some work is still needed to provide clear answers to these questions. Whatever the answers to them, we would like to suggest that the relationship between these concepts and the concept of personalization has been resolved. We should see personalization as an expression of the electoral face of Poguntke and Webb-style presidentialization/prime ministerialization and as a phenomenon separate from Samuels and Shugart-style constitutional presidentialization.

18.4.2 Applying the Concept of Presidentialization

When undertaking empirical work, we would encourage scholars to think about three issues. The first concerns the observable features of presidentialization. This issue is clearly bound up with the discussion in the previous subsection. Until we have a clear sense of what to look for, then the empirical evidence regarding the extent of presidentialization will remain fundamentally unreliable. Poguntke and Webb have given us some general characteristics to consider with regard to the three faces of presidentialization, but we need more specific indicators. That said, scholars should also aim to find evidence for the presence of presidentialization broadly rather than focusing on a small number of specific indicators. For example, both Bäck et al.'s (2011) study of Sweden and Kolltveit's (2012) study of Norway examine only particular features of their country's political process. Yet, for Poguntke and Webb presidentialization is a process that has an effect on three faces of politics, each of which comprises a number of different aspects of political life. To test whether or not there is evidence for presidentialization in the way that they understand it, we need to have a broader sense of the political system. An alternative strategy is to see whether there is evidence for the idea that there has been a presidentialization of contemporary politics. Arguably, presidentialization changes expectations about politics, including what voters consider to be important in candidates, would-be leaders, and so on. If so, it would be useful to know whether people consider systems to have been presidentialized, whatever they may understand by that term. To what extent is the idea of presidentialization factoring into their perceptions of the political process?

The second issue concerns the geographical application of empirical studies. Thus far, scholars have applied the concept almost exclusively to individual countries. Webb and Poguntke (2005) have provided a summary of the case studies in their volume, but to date there has been no comparative or large-n study. Again, on the basis of work that can clearly identify the observable implications of presidentialization, we would encourage scholars to undertake more comparative and large-n studies. More than that, while relatively few country case studies have been conducted so far, some countries have been examined more than once. In particular, Germany, Sweden, and the UK have already been the subject of a number of inquiries. We encourage scholars to widen the set of countries under investigation. We also encourage scholars to increase the geographical range of the countries under consideration. To date, the thesis has been applied to the 'usual suspects', namely West European countries, Westminster democracies, specifically Australia and Canada, Japan, and the US. There is plenty of opportunity to expand the country selection. Is presidentialization really a general phenomenon or is it limited to only some countries or regions?

The third issue concerns the nature of the empirical studies. While we encourage large-n comparative studies, single country case studies are likely to remain the chosen research design strategy. In this respect, though, we would encourage scholars to engage in diachronic comparisons. We have seen that presidentialization is considered to be a process of change. So, taking a contemporary snapshot of a country does not provide evidence of whether such a process has occurred, only whether there is currently evidence of a presidentialized political system. Diachronic studies would test the idea that there has been a change over time.

18.4.3 Placing the Study of Presidentialization in Context

From the perspective of Samuels and Shugart's (2010) understanding of constitutional presidentialization, two factors could usefully be considered. The first concerns political parties. We have seen that Passarelli (2015a) has introduced the genetic origins of political parties as a factor that conditions the effects of constitutional presidentialization. We need more work on this topic. Specifically, while Passarelli's volume includes a set of case studies showing how these two factors interact to shape the level of party presidentialization, we now need to examine whether the resulting variation in party presidentialization affects the outcomes that Samuels and Shugart considered in their volume. So, Passarelli's study is merely a first step. The second factor concerns the constitutional powers of the chief executive. Samuels and Shugart confined their study to the effect of regime types. Yet, the constitutional power of presidents varies within regime types. How does this variation, potentially in interaction with the genetic origins of parties affect the outcomes that Samuels and Shugart are interested in? This point can be applied to prime ministers too. As Doyle shows elsewhere in this volume, there have been attempts to measure not just presidential but also prime ministerial power (see also Chapters 19 and 28 in this volume). Again, how does the variation in the formal powers of the principal figure within the political executive condition the effect of constitutional presidentialization?

From the perspective of Poguntke and Webb, the power of chief executives is potentially important too. In presidential and semi-presidential regimes, is the degree of presidentialization conditioned by the constitutional powers of the president? Would we expect to see a greater presidentialization of the presidency in countries where the president has some constitutional prerogatives than in those countries where the president is merely a figurehead? In countries where the president has some constitutional prerogatives, would we expect the presidentialization of the prime minister's office to be restricted? In parliamentary regimes, does the power of the prime minister differ conditional upon whether there is a majoritarian or a consensual system? Does presidentialization have a greater impact on consensual systems, making the prime minister a more important political broker among the different forces? These are questions that can reasonably be asked in the context of Poguntke and Webb's presidentialization thesis.

Finally, we would encourage more work to be conducted on the effect of presidentialization on voting behaviour. There has been plenty of work on personalization and voting behaviour as well as work on leader effects on voting behaviour. However, if we consider presidentialization to be a general process and personalization to be merely part of the electoral face of presidentialization, then there is the potential for systemic presidentialization to have an effect on voter expectations, perhaps in terms of attitudes towards what political leaders can be expected to achieve, or the electoral mandate that they are given.

Overall, we see a vibrant research agenda for the study of both presidentialization generally and constitutional presidentialization specifically. We would encourage scholars to follow up on these suggestions for the research agenda and to generate new ideas in this up and coming domain.

References

Aarts, K., Blais, A., and Schmitt, H. (2013) (eds). *Political Leaders and Democratic Elections*. Oxford: Oxford University Press.

Allen, N. (2018). 'Great Expectations: The Job at the Top and the People Who Do It,' *Political Quarterly* 89(1): 9–17.

Bäck, H., Persson, T., Vernby, K., and Westin, L. (2011). 'Presidentialisation from a Historical Perspective: Ministerial Selection and Reshuffling in Swedish Cabinets,' in G.-E. Isaksson and T. Persson (eds) *Parliamentary Government in the Nordic Countries at a Crossroads: Coping with Challenges from Europeanisation and Presidentialisation*. Stockholm: Santérus Förlag, 245–76.

Blick, A., and Jones, G. (2010). *Premiership: The Development, Nature and Power of the Office of the British Prime Minister*. Exeter: Imprint Academic.

Cason, J. W. and Power, T. J. (2009). 'Presidentialization, Pluralization, and the Rollback of Itamaraty: Explaining Change in Brazilian Foreign Policy Making in the Cardoso-Lula Era,' *International Political Science Review* 30(2): 117–40.

Chohan, U. W. and Jacobs, K. (2017). 'The Presidentialisation Thesis and Parliamentary Budget Offices,' *Parliamentary Affairs* 70: 361–76.

Costa Lobo, M. (2017). 'Personality Goes a Long Way,' *Government and Opposition* 53(1): 159–79.

Courtney, J. C. (1984). 'Has the Canadian Prime Minister become "Presidentialized"?,' *Presidential Studies Quarterly* 14(2): 238–41.

Cross, W. P., Katz, R. S., and Pruysers, S. (2018). 'Personalism, Personalization and Party Politics,' in W. P. Cross, R. S. Katz, and S. Pruysers (eds) *The Personalization of Democratic Politics and the Challenge for Political Parties*. London: Rowman & Littlefield International, 1–18.

Dowding, K. (2013a). 'The Prime Ministerialisation of the British Prime Minister,' *Parliamentary Affairs* 66: 617–35.

Dowding, K. (2013b). 'Beneath the Surface: Replies to Three Critics,' *Parliamentary Affairs* 66: 663–72.

Dowding, K. (2013c). 'Presidentialisation Again: A Comment on Kefford,' *Australian Journal of Political Science* 48(2): 147–9.

Dunleavy, P. and Rhodes, R. A. W. (1990). 'Core Executive Studies in Britain,' *Public Administration* 68(1): 3–28.

Dunleavy, P., Jones, G. W., and Leary, B. O. (1990). 'Prime Ministers and the Commons: Patterns of Behaviour, 1868–1987,' *Public Administration* 68(2): 123–40.

Elgie, R. and Passarelli, G. (2019). 'Presidentialisation: One term, Two Uses—Between Deductive Exercise and Grand Historical Narrative,' *Political Studies Review* 17(2): 115–23.

Fabbrini, S. (2005). 'The Semi-Sovereign American Prince: The Dilemma of an Independent President in a Presidential Government,' in T. Poguntke and P. Webb (eds) *The Presidentialization of Politics in Democratic Societies: A Framework for Analysis*. Oxford: Oxford University Press, 313–35.

Foley, M. (1993). *The Rise of the British Presidency*. Manchester: Manchester University Press.

Foley, M. (2008). 'The Presidential Dynamics of Leadership Decline in Contemporary British Politics: The Illustrative Case of Tony Blair,' *Contemporary Politics* 14(1): 53–69.

Heffernan, R. and Webb, P. (2005). 'The British Prime Minister: Much More Than 'First Among Equals',' in T. Poguntke and P. Webb (eds) *The Presidentialization of Politics in Democratic Societies: A Framework for Analysis*. Oxford: Oxford University Press, 26–62.

Helms, L. (2005). 'The Presidentialisation of Political Leadership: British Notions and German Observations,' *Political Quarterly* 76(3): 430–8.

Helms, L. (2014). 'Political Leadership,' in S. Padgett, W. E. Paterson, and R. Zohlnhöfer (eds) *Developments in German Politics 4*. Basingstoke: Palgrave Macmillan, 103–17.

Helms, L. (2015). 'Is There a Presidentialization of US Presidential Leadership? A European perspective on Washington,' *Acta Politica* 50(1): 1–19.

Jou, W. and Endo, M. (2000). '"Presidentialization of Japanese Politics" Examining Political Leader Evaluations and Vote Choice,' *Japanese Journal of Political Science* 16(3): 357–87.

Jones, G. W. (1991). 'Presidentialization in a Parliamentary System?,' in C. Campbell and M. J. Wyszomirski (eds) *Executive Leadership in Anglo-American Systems*. Pittsburgh: University of Pittsburgh Press, 111–37.

Karvonen, L. (2010). *The Personalisation of Politics: A Study of Parliamentary Democracies*. Colchester: ECPR Press.

Kefford, G. (2013). 'The Presidentialisation of Australian Politics? Kevin Rudd's Leadership of the Australian Labor Party,' *Australian Journal of Political Science* 48(2): 135–46.

King, A. (2007). *The British Constitution*. Oxford: Oxford University Press.

Mughan, A. (2000). *Media and the Presidentialization of Parliamentary Elections*. London: Palgrave Macmillan.

Kolltveit, K. (2012). 'Presidentialisation in the Executive Sphere? Evidence from Norwegian Cabinets,' *Scandinavian Political Studies* 35(4): 372–92.

Palladino, N. (2015). '"Presidentialisations' in Italy: The Battle for Leadership between the Prime Minister and the President of the Republic,' *Contemporary Italian Politics* 7(2): 107–26.

Panebianco, A. (1988). *Political Parties: Organization and Power*. Cambridge: Cambridge University Press.

Passarelli, G. (2015a). 'Parties' Genetic Features: The Missing Link in the Presidentialization of Parties,' in G. Passarelli (ed.) *The Presidentialization of Political Parties*. London: Palgrave Macmillan, 1–25.

Passarelli, G. (2015b) (ed.). *The Presidentialization of Political Parties: Organizations, Institutions and Leaders*. London: Palgrave Macmillan.

Passarelli, G. (2015c). 'The Presidentialization of Parties: Why, When, Where?,' in G. Passarelli (ed.) *The Presidentialization of Political Parties*. London: Palgrave Macmillan, 235–63.

Peters, B. G. and Helms, L. (2012). 'Executive Leadership in Comparative Perspective: Politicians, Bureaucrats and Public Governance,' in Helms, L. (ed.) *Comparative Political Leadership*. London: Palgrave Macmillan, 25–55.

Poguntke, T. and Webb, P. (2005a) (eds). *The Presidentialization of Politics in Democratic Societies: A Framework for Analysis*. Oxford: Oxford University Press.

Poguntke, T. and Webb, P. (2005b). 'The Presidentialization of Politics in Democratic Societies: A Framework for Analysis,' in T. Poguntke and P. Webb (eds) *The Presidentialization of Politics in Democratic Societies: A Framework for Analysis*. Oxford: Oxford University Press, 1–25.

Pryce, S. (1997). *Presidentializing the Premiership*. Basingstoke: Macmillan Press.

Rahat, G. and Kenig, O. (2018). *From Party Politics to Personalized Politics?* Oxford: Oxford University Press.

Rhodes, R. A. W., Wanna, J., and Weller, P. (2009). *Comparing Westminster*. Oxford: Oxford University Press.

Samuels, D. and Shugart, M. (2010). *Presidents, Parties and Prime Ministers: How the Separation of Powers Affects Party Organization and Behavior*. Cambridge: Cambridge University Press.

Smith, D. (1977). 'President and Parliament: The Transformation of Parliamentary Government in Canada,' in T. A. Hockin (ed.) *The Apex of Power: The Prime Minister and Political Leadership in Canada*. Scarborough, Ontario: Prentice-Hall, 224–41.

Sturzu, A. (2011). 'The Presidentialization of the Romanian Political System: An Interplay between Structures and Contingencies,' *Studia Politica: Romanian Political Science Review* 11(2): 309–27.

Sundström, G. (2008). 'He Who Decides: Swedish Social Democratic Government from a Presidentialisation Perspective,' *Scandinavian Political Studies* 32(2): 143–70.

Sykes, P. L. (2009). 'The Gendered Nature of Leadership Analysis: Lessons from Women Leaders as Executives in Anglo-American Systems,' in J. Masciulli, M. A. Molchanov, and W. A. Knight (eds) *The Ashgate Research Companion to Political Leadership*. London: Routledge, 219–40.

Wearing, J. (1977). 'President or Prime Minister,' in T. A. Hockin (ed.) *The Apex of Power: The Prime Minister and Political Leadership in Canada*. Scarborough, Ontario: Prentice-Hall, 242–60.

Webb, P. and Poguntke, T. (2005). 'The Presidentialization of Contemporary Democratic Politics: Evidence, Causes and Consequences,' in T. Poguntke and P. Webb (eds) *The Presidentialization of Politics in Democratic Societies: A Framework for Analysis*. Oxford: Oxford University Press, 336–56.

Zaznaev, O. (2008). 'The Presidentialization of a Semi-Presidential Regime: The Case of Russia,' in Stephen White (ed.) *Politics and the Ruling Group in Putin's Russia*. London: Palgrave Macmillan, pp. 27–41.

CHAPTER 19

MEASURING PRESIDENTIAL AND PRIME MINISTERIAL POWER

DAVID DOYLE

19.1 INTRODUCTION

THE study of politics is, in its most basic form, the study of power. It is about the distributional battles that shape society and the relative power of different actors and groups to control and influence political outcomes. Central to such political conflicts is the head of government, or the executive, in the form of a president in presidential systems and a prime minister and his or her cabinet in parliamentary systems. To understand the role and influence of the executive in politics, we must understand the power that he or she wields, but for political scientists, this has not always proven an easy task.

Although the power of the executive, broadly understood as the ability to influence policy, has long been of interest to political theorists (e.g. Montesquieu [1793] 1989), initial work on the role of the executive in comparative politics tended towards the anecdotal or 'descriptive' (King 1975: 173) and did not explicitly operationalize or attempt to measure the power of these offices (although, see Jones 1964). This began to change however with Juan Linz's (1990) now seminal contribution to the initial edition of the *Journal of Democracy*. Linz argued that the separate origin and separate survival of the executive branch in presidential systems creates a psychological incentive for the executive that is not present in parliamentary systems, to adopt a more hostile attitude towards the legislative branch and for Linz, this was the root cause of the apparent democratic fragility of presidential systems. Linz's thesis inspired a whole generation of work on the executive and an early influential study by Shugart and Carey (1992) in this vein, contended that presidential systems are marked by notable heterogeneity in the power of the executive, and that this variable could help explain some of the apparent issues with this system of government. This work, together with the increasing quantification of contemporary comparative politics and the popularity of 'new institutionalism', generated the incentive for scholars to begin developing cross-national empirical measures of executive power.

Today, the measurement of executive power is something of a cottage industry in political science (for discussions of some of these studies, see O'Malley 2007; Fortin 2013; Doyle and Elgie 2016), yet no clear consensus exists as to exactly how we should measure executive power. Part of the issue stems from the different sources of executive power for presidents compared with prime ministers, but there is also disagreement about the nature of power within regime types. If we are to advance as a social science, we must empirically validate or refute our theories and the degree to which such an endeavour will be successful will depend on the quality of our measurements. Of course, if we measure the same thing in lots of different ways, then this can help us overcome measurement error, but it can also produce a lot of random noise. For example, if two studies, interested in how varying levels of presidential power shape the budget process across different countries operationalize presidential power in divergent ways, then they may produce different or even conflicting results. This will make it difficult to robustly defend a particular theoretical argument, which in turn will hamper the advancement of this literature.

The purpose of this chapter is to provide some synthesis to the large amount of work that measures either presidential or prime ministerial power. The chapter is divided into three sections. In section 19.1, I discuss the importance of executive power, before considering the conceptual clarity of such measures. In section 19.2, I consider existing measures of executive power from presidents to prime ministers and discuss the varying methodical approaches and strategies adopted to measure the power of presidents and prime ministers. In the final section, 19.3, I consider the research agenda for work that employs measures of executive power.

19.2 WHAT IS EXECUTIVE POWER?

The power of the executive is central to any understanding of politics. Because of this, executive power, in conceptual, and to a lesser extent in empirical, terms has long been of interest to scholars. With the increasing quantification of political science beginning in the 1980s, and as the discipline began adopting a much more aggressive comparative agenda, a usable cross-national measure of executive power that could be plugged into regression models, either as an independent or dependent variable, became something of an imperative. This coincided with Linz's broadside on presidential systems and Shugart and Carey's (1992) rejoinder, which emphasized that the deficiencies of presidentialism lay not with the constitutional format of the regime, but with varying levels of executive power. To determine whether presidents with strong power were more likely to collapse back into some form of authoritarianism, relative to weaker presidents, a cross-national measure of executive power was needed. And so Shugart and Carey's measure of presidential power was born.

Early initiatives to quantify executive power were largely motivated by the Linzian debate about the relative debility of presidential systems (e.g. Metcalf 2000). Measures of presidential power continue to be used to address this question today. Consider Gretchen Helmke's (2017) recent book on inter-branch crises in Latin America. In Helmke's model of inter-branch bargaining, the level of presidential power remains a crucial determinant of inter-branch conflict. But the drive to employ measures of executive power in quantitative models has gone far beyond work on democratic reversals in presidential regimes. Scholars have been motivated to use measures of presidential power to explain outcomes as diverse as variation in the size of the presidential party (Hicken and Stoll 2008), economic performance (Frye 2002), fiscal profligacy (Cheibub 2006), the speed of economic reform (Hellman 1996), the extent of privatization (Doyle 2010), and turnout in parliamentary elections in semi-presidential countries (Tavits 2009). Other still have been motivated to use measures of executive power to explore why and when presidents might be willing to engage in ideological compromise (Arnold et al. 2017) or to share cabinet portfolios (Neto 2006). Carlin and Singh (2015) needed a cross-national measure of executive power to test their argument that the degree to which voters will either reward or punish an incumbent for economic outcomes will vary according to a president's legislative power.

The list goes on. To consider and test a whole range of questions in comparative politics, measures of executive power have become essential. What becomes important, then, is how we measure executive power and whether there is consensus on this issue. But in nearly all of the studies mentioned above, power has been operationalized in different ways. And this is partly due to different conceptualizations of what executive power actually comprises. Before we can arrive at a universal measure for something, we must firstly agree on a common meaning. Increasingly, an understanding of executive power as *policy-making power*, which is reasonably narrow in focus, has formed the central tenet of executive power for contemporary scholars, both in a theoretical and empirical sense (see, e.g., Elgie 1997; O'Malley 2007; Fortin 2013). Executive power however, has often been understood in much broader terms, while decisions about what actually *comprises* policy-making power, particularly with regards the division between presidents and prime ministers, have proven more contentious.

For early political theorists in the nascent democracies of Europe and the Americas (Montesquieu [1793] 1989; also Madison [1787] in Hamilton et al. 1948; Bagehot [1873] 2000), the power of the executive became integral to debates about constitutionalism, but how they understood and defined executive power varied. Montesquieu ([1793] 1989: 156–7) considered executive power as explicitly related to policy-making, but also concerned with foreign affairs and the defence of the state more generally. Alexander Hamilton ([1788] in Hamilton et al. 1948) adopted a similar holistic understanding of presidential power, rooted in policy-making power, but which also includes control over the army and navy, the power of pardon and the power to make treaties. Importantly,

Hamilton et al.'s understanding of executive power was largely defined, and limited, by the constitution. In early work on parliamentary systems however, executive power was defined less in terms of explicit constitutional provision and more with regard the manner that the executive interacts with other government bodies. The prototypical expression of this is Bagehot's ([1873] 2000: 50) insight that the innate power of the executive office in the British parliamentary system derived not from the ability of the prime minister to craft legislation, but rather to dissolve the legislature. It is the fusion of powers in parliamentary systems that provides the foundation for an interpretation of prime ministerial power as relational to other political actors.

This emphasis on the importance of relational considerations has provided the starting point for work in comparative politics concerned with the policy-making power of prime ministers. For example, for Jones (1964: 173), executive power is a product of the ability of the prime minister to control his or her party, parliament, the cabinet, and the civil service. This broad conceptualization of power begins with the ability of the prime minister to command loyalty from members of parliament, which will be shaped by electoral costs and the threat of dissolution and more nebulous sentiments of party loyalty. If the prime minister can control his or her party, then he or she can control parliament. In turn, his or her ability to exercise influence over the cabinet will be a product of his or her ability to distribute patronage. The implicit assumption here is that power over policy is shaped by the power of the prime minister relative to other actors, notably the parliament and the cabinet.

Consequently, several subsequent works on parliamentary systems understood executive power as the ability of the prime minister to exert power over the cabinet, giving rise to debate, particularly in the UK, about the power of the prime minister relative to the cabinet (e.g. Heclo and Wildavsky 1981; see Dunleavy and Rhodes 1990 for an overview). For those interested in comparisons of 'prime ministerial influence' (King 1994) above and beyond Europe, the importance of single party versus coalition government was noted (e.g. Rose 1991; Blondel and Müller-Rommel 1993; also Laver and Shepsle 1996). In single party governments, the power of the prime minister over the cabinet, relative to a coalition government, would be much greater, given that cabinet posts would not need to be shared among coalition partners. Bergman et al. (2003) reiterate this emphasis on the importance of the party system in shaping the power of the prime minister over his or her cabinets and subsequently his or her ability to shape legislative outcomes. Others, such as King (1994) and echoing Montesquieu, emphasized the importance of executive patronage and the ability to shape legislative careers, together with public visibility, as an important source of prime ministerial power.

Nearly all of these conceptualizations of prime ministerial power sought to explain the influence of the prime minister on the policy-making process, but they were criticized for their explicit focus on executive power as largely a product of party and legislative government (see Dunleavy and Rhodes 1990; also Elgie 1997). The core executive approach, while still primarily concerned with the power of the head of government 'to leave a personal imprint on the decision-making process' (Elgie 1997: 217), proposed that executive power was not just simply about the power of the prime minister relative to the cabinet or the legislature, but must also include the power of departmental ministers and the bureaucracy (Dunleavy and Rhodes 1990). The key point from the core executive approach is that executive power is not fixed, but rather contingent and relational (Elgie 2011a: 5).

As such then, while executive power in parliamentary systems is generally understood as the ability of a prime minister to exert control over policy-making outcomes, this is not necessarily a constitutional or institutional power, but rather a relational power dependent on interaction with other government actors.

In contrast, executive power in presidential systems has proven far easier to conceptualize. With a specific focus on the power of the president in the legislative process, Shugart and Carey (1992: 131–2) in their now seminal contribution, contended that presidential power is a function of the extent of constitutional power, or what they term entrenched power, together with the extent of legislative power delegated to the president by Congress. Shugart and Carey (1992) were particularly concerned with the constitutionally allocated powers of the president, and focused on variation across presidential systems in veto powers (either partial or pocket), rights to exclusively initiate legislation together with control over the budgetary process, and decree rights, that is, the ability of the executive to issue a law or regulation. Such decree power can be constitutionally defined, but it can also, under specific circumstances, be delegated to the executive by congress (Shugart and Carey 1992: 144–6).

Subsequent interpretations of executive power in presidential systems were largely based on Shugart and Carey's conceptualization. Shugart and Mainwaring (1997: 40), when considering presidential power as the 'president's ability to put their own stamp on policy—to get an agenda enacted' made a distinction between the constitutional powers of presidents, and their partisan power, or legislative support. By constitutional powers, Shugart and Mainwaring were referring to the legislative powers of the president as defined by the constitution, and they made a further distinction between *proactive* powers and *reactive* powers. Proactive powers, best encapsulated by decree power and the exclusive right to introduce legislation, are powers that allow the president to establish a new status quo, while reactive powers, in the form of the veto and partial veto, allow the president to defend the status quo against attempts by the legislature to change it (Shugart and Mainwaring 1997: 41; also Haggard and McCubbins 2001).

This is not to say that all conceptualizations of presidential power are purely related to legislative power. In a nod to work on parliamentary systems, both Shugart and Carey (1992) and Shugart and Mainwaring (1997) also consider non-legislative powers. For Shugart and Carey (1992), this largely comprises power over the formation and dismissal of the cabinet, while for Shugart and Mainwaring (1997), this is the degree of support that the president has in congress, shaped by both inter and intra party dynamics. Similarly, Haggard and McCubbins (2001), in the tradition of the core executive agenda, also consider the separation of purpose within the executive, as defined by delegation to cabinet ministers and the role of other consultative bodies. Others such as Siaroff (2003: 303; also Cranenburgh 2009) consider 'actual political practice', or behavioural and relational considerations, as important for any understanding of presidential power.

Nonetheless, as Fortin (2013) notes, when it comes to an understanding of presidential power, there is more consensus among scholars than most other aspects of political science. The clear majority of studies focus on the formal constitutional powers of the president and so therefore, 'most of the unresolved debate in the literature focuses on which powers should be considered as defining features, rather than on a comprehensive approach to capturing the concept of executive strength' (Fortin 2013: 92).

In a general sense then, there is a consensus that executive power, either in presidential or parliamentary democracies, is best conceptualized as the power of the executive to make and influence policy. However, the separation of powers in presidential systems and the fusion of powers in parliamentary systems means that it becomes more difficult to arrive at a unified consensus as to what actually *comprises* this ability to make and influence policy. As Lijphart (1992: 4) has noted, 'the separation of executive from legislative power means the limiting of power and the need for sharing power, but the unipersonal president means the concentration of power *within* the executive—the very opposite of limited and shared power'. In presidential systems, constitutional provisions can most easily identify this unipersonal policy-making power. So, although behavioural practice might be important (Siaroff 2003), as might the partisan power of the president (Mainwaring and Shugart 1997), we can largely understand and conceptualize the power of the president according to his or her specific constitutional powers over policy-making, such as his or her reactive and proactive legislative powers and his or her right to exclusively initiate legislation (e.g. Haggard and McCubbins 2001: 11).

Given the shared nature of power within parliamentary executives however, identifying and conceptualizing the power of prime ministers over policy-making is a more difficult task. As O'Malley (2007: 8) notes,

> in only a few countries do constitutions or legislation give the prime minister the right to make policy directly and even then, only in a few areas. In some countries' constitutions, such as Australia's, the office of the prime minister is not even mentioned.

As such, this undermines the utility of conceptualizing prime ministerial power according to constitutional provisions. We are, in effect, forced to adopt a more relational interpretation of power and to understand prime ministerial power with respect to the cabinet, to individual ministers, to committees, and to the bureaucracy. This means that measuring prime ministerial power becomes a far trickier task than measuring the constitutionally defined powers of the president.

As I will discuss in section 19.3, this divergent conceptualization of executive power has informed the way scholars have operationalized this concept. Measures of presidential power are largely based on constitutional provisions (e.g. Shugart and Carey 1992); in contrast, measures of prime ministerial power are based on more diffuse characteristics, including existing qualitative descriptions or 'personal observations' (King 1994: 152), weighted influence in cabinet committees (e.g. Dunleavy 1995), indices of power based on institutional prerogatives and the party system (Bergman et al. 2003) and expert survey evaluations of prime ministerial control over the policy process (O'Malley 2007). It is to these different measurement strategies that I now turn.

19.3 MEASURING EXECUTIVE POWER

Prior to the now seminal contribution of Shugart and Carey (1992), and outside of the US, very little attention was paid from a comparative perspective to the importance of presidential power (Shugart and Mainwaring 1997) and no systematic effort had been made to measure this variable. The Shugart and Carey (1992) book was inspired by the debate sparked by Juan Linz (1990). Linz had noticed that presidential systems, or at least the Latin American presidential systems that he was interested in, appeared to regress to some form of authoritarianism at a far greater rate than parliamentary democracies. Linz contended that the root cause of this anomaly lay in the separate origin and survival of presidential democracies, which generated a psychological incentive for the president to be less willing to compromise and work with the legislature, relative to prime ministers in parliamentary systems whose very political survival depends on the support of legislators. When presidents face a hostile majority opposition or are highly unpopular, the above dynamic will be exacerbated and often legislative gridlock will ensue. With the fixed-term rigidity of presidential systems, there is no way to release the tension from the system and under the right circumstances, this can lead to some form of democratic breakdown (see Linz 1990; Mainwaring 1993).

Shugart and Carey (1992) set out, not only to examine the validity of the claims made by Linz and others, but also to provide the first systematic comparative exploration of the functioning of presidential systems. One of the major contributions of this work was to highlight the heterogeneity of presidential regimes, particularly with regards the levels of legislative power afforded to the president by the constitution. Their empirical work suggested that the most democratically problematic presidential governments are those where the president has great legislative power: 'Thus, a fundamental conclusion is that the criticisms of presidential regimes should not be put forward as if all presidencies were created equal; rather, these criticisms apply with greatest force to strong presidents' (Shugart and Carey 1992: 165).

To reach this conclusion, Shugart and Carey needed to examine the effect of varying levels of power across countries and for this purpose, they developed what has become the cornerstone for empirical measures of presidential power. They divided presidential power into two main components: presidential legislative power and non-legislative power. Legislative power comprises six constitutional prerogatives. The first of these is the package veto and the veto override, or the ability of the president to veto the legislative initiatives of the assembly. The second power is the partial, or item veto, which gives presidents the right to veto parts of a bill, while the third power is decree power. Shugart and Carey (1992: 151) understood decree power here as the authority to make new laws or suspend old ones without any prior form of legislative delegation. The fourth power is the exclusive introduction of legislation, where the assembly cannot consider legislation in certain areas unless the president first introduces a bill on the topic, while the fifth legislative power concerns the president's right over budget initiatives and the sixth and final legislative power captures the president's power to propose popular referenda. The four non-legislative powers include the president's power over cabinet formation and cabinet dismissal, together with the power to dissolve the assembly and the power of censure. Censure refers to the ability of the assembly to remove cabinet ministers; where the assembly has no such power, then only the president may remove ministers, and executive authority over the cabinet is maximized (Shugart and Carey 1992: 153). Each of these powers, for each country constitution, was placed on a scale (most commonly some form of 0–4 scale), and then added together to provide a composite measure of legislative and non-legislative presidential power for each country.

It is worth outlining the way they constructed this measure of presidential power in some detail, as it has served as the template for a host of subsequent modifications. The Shugart and Carey (1992) book not only set the industry standard for the measurement of presidential power, but this work has also inspired a large amount of studies, from the 1990s to the present day, that have empirically explored presidential power, either as an independent variable or a dependent variable. Some of this work simply used the Shugart and Carey measure, others modified their template to suit their own specific purpose, while others still created a completely new measure of power. Shugart and Carey provide the foundation for nearly all of this work.

Table 19.1 lists the major measures of presidential power that have been developed in comparative politics over the last twenty-five years, together with a small sample of studies that have employed these measures, or slight variations on these measures. Table 19.1 also indicates whether these studies were primarily concerned with institutional or behavioural measures of power. This is not an exhaustive list by any means, but it does include many of the most widely used measures of presidential power.[1]

For example, Hicken and Stoll (2008) simply took the Shugart and Carey measure and extended it to other countries. In their case, they used presidential power as a central explanatory independent variable and explored the size of the presidential party as captured by the effective number of presidential candidates, and found a significant non-linear relationship between presidential power and the size of the party system. Others, such as Frye et al. (2000) slightly modified the Shugart and Carey scale and then expanded the coding schema to a larger cross-national set of countries, which was then used by Frye (2002) as an independent variable in his work on the determinants of economic performance in post-communist countries while Payne (2007) developed a slightly modified version of the Shugart and Carey schema for Latin American countries.

---

[1] This list of studies is heavily based on the list provided by Doyle and Elgie (2016). There are other studies, such as that of Tsebelis and Alemán (2005), which focus on specific aspects of presidential power, such as veto power, which I do not include here.

Table 19.1 Main Measures of Presidential Power

Authors	Type of Measure	Notes	Other Studies	Coverage
Shugart & Carey (1992)	Constitutional powers		For example, Frye, Hellman, and Tucker (2000); Frye (2002); Hicken and Stoll (2008), Payne (2007)	Thirty-five presidential countries; forty-four constitutions beginning with Chile (1891)
Frye, Hellman and Tucker (2000)	Constitutional powers	Slight modification of Shugart and Carey		Sixty-eight countries
Metcalf (2000)	Constitutional powers	Revision of Shugart and Carey	For example, Costa Lobo and Amorim Neto (2009); Tavits (2009); Özsoy (2010)	Nine European countries
Nijzink, Mozaffar and Azevedo (2006)	Constitutional powers	Only the non-legislative powers of Shugart and Carey (1992)		Thirteen African countries
UNDP (2004)	Constitutional powers	Based on Shugart and Carey (1992), but an expanded scale (weighted average)	For example, Doyle (2010)	Eighteen Latin American constitutions as of 2002
Roper (2002)	Constitutional powers	Based on Shugart and Carey, but uses only three each of the legislative and non-legislative powers		Ten semi-presidential countries
Siaroff (2003)	Behavioural and constitutional		For example, Costa Lobo and Amorim Neto (2009); Cranenburgh (2009); Tavits (2009); Elgie (2011)	Ninety-two countries; 132 constitutions
Hellman (1996)	Constitutional powers	Twenty-seven specific appointments and legislative powers, weighted		Twenty-four post-communist countries

Study	Measure	Description	Example studies using measure	Sample
Frye (1997)	Constitutional powers	Twenty-seven constitutional prerogatives as per Hellman, but different weighting	For example, Luong (2002); Ishiyama (2003)	Twenty-four post-communist countries
Armingeon and Careja (2008)	Constitutional powers	Based on Frye (1997)—but with twenty-nine items		Twenty-seven post-communist countries (1990–2002)
Johannsen and Nørgaard (2003)	Constitutional powers	Thirty-seven constitutional prerogatives, political, appointive, and symbolic powers		Ninety-eight presidential and semi-presidential countries
Shugart (1996)	Constitutional powers	Based on part of the original Shugart and Carey (1992) index		
Clark and Wittrock (2005)	Constitutional powers	Modification of Shugart (1996)		Thirteen post-communist countries (1990–2002)
Taghiyev (2006)	Constitutional powers	Twenty-five presidential powers based on Shugart and Carey (1992); Lucky (1994); Frye (1997)		Fifteen post-Soviet countries
Negretto (2013)	Constitutional powers	Legislative power, agenda power, and veto power and non-legislative power		Eighteen Latin American countries, plus the US (1900–2014)
Doyle and Elgie (2016)	Constitutional powers	Based on a large set of existing measures of institutional power		116 countries (181 country time periods)

Others developed new indices of presidential power, but based on subcomponents of the Shugart and Carey schema. For example, Nijzink et al. (2006: 321–2), in their examination of sub-Saharan African parliaments, followed the framework developed by Shugart and Carey, but only that of the non-legislative powers, and coded the relative powers of presidents in thirteen African countries for two dimensions only: power over the appointment and dismissal of ministers and power in cases of censure and dissolution of the assembly. In an examination of the degree of similarity among semi-presidential regimes, Roper (2002: 257–8) considers only three each of Shugart and Carey's legislative and non-legislative powers: veto power, decree power, and the power to propose referenda, together with power over cabinet formation and dismissal and power over the dissolution of parliament. Roper's case is indicative of the way that scholars have adapted the Shugart and Carey measure for their own needs. Roper's modifications to the dimensions and scoring are specific to premier-presidential regimes, as some of the powers included in the original index, such as budgetary power, censure of cabinet ministers, and exclusive authority over legislation, simply do not apply to presidents in premier-presidential regimes. In a similar vein, Negretto (2013), inspired by Shugart and Carey's distinction between legislative and non-legislative power, used a categorical principal component analysis of 132 constitutions to derive measures of institutional power for eighteen Latin American countries between 1900 and 2014.

The UNPD (2004) developed a measure of presidential power for eighteen Latin American countries as of 2002, which is based on the six formal legislative powers from the Shugart and Carey index. The difference with this schema is that the scale for some of the legislative powers has been notably expanded. For example, the scale for the package and partial veto now runs from 0 to 13 (as opposed to 0 to 4) and each score is then normalized, added together and averaged.

Metcalf (2000: 668), in a similar vein to Roper, suggests that the Shugart and Carey scale, 'by treating the president and the assembly as the only relevant actors [...] does not capture well the dual authority structure of semi-presidentialism'. Metcalf also contends that the original index captures notable variation across countries at high levels of presidential power, but struggles to do so at low levels of power. Therefore, Metcalf (2000), in his exploration of presidential power and democratic consolidation, proposes minor revisions and clarifications to the scales developed by Shugart and Carey (1992) across their ten components of presidential power and he also adds an eleventh category: judicial review. Here, Metcalf (2000: 671) understands judicial review as the ability of courts to overrule the assembly or the political executive and is scaled from 4, where the president alone has the right to refer legislation for review, to 0, where the president has no right of referral.

Despite the clear influence of the Shugart and Carey measure in the literature, and here I have only discussed a handful of the very large number of studies that use some variant of this measure, not all empirical work involving measures of formal constitutional presidential power rely on Shugart and Carey. Hellman (1996: 52–3), jointly with

Frye (1997), developed an index of presidential powers based on a list of twenty-seven specific appointment and legislative powers for twenty-four post-communist countries.[2] Hellman then weights these powers depending on whether the system is presidential or semi-presidential; in presidential systems, a score of 1 is given for an exclusive power, 0.5 for a qualified power, and 0 if the power is not granted to the president at all, while in semi-presidential systems, the scores are 0.75, 0.375, and 0, respectively. Hellman finds that formal powers are a significant impediment to economic reform in post-communist countries.

Frye (1997), who developed this list of powers with Hellman (1996), employs a slightly different weighting: exclusive specific powers are counted as 1 and shared powers are weighted by 0.5. Frye (1997: 525–6) also considers both specific powers as granted to the president in the constitution and also residual powers, such as the power to make decisions in circumstances not specified by the constitution, for example, an economic crisis. Other political agents can limit the scope and extent of specific powers and this can affect the resources available to the executive. For his index however, Frye only considers the twenty-seven specific powers and he uses this measure of power as a dependent variable to explore changes in institutional structure.

This list of constitutional prerogatives developed by Hellman (1996) and Frye (1997), just like the Shugart and Carey index, has also inspired new modified indices of presidential power. For example, Armingeon and Careja (2008), and building on Frye's list of powers, developed an index of presidential power coded from country constitutions that included twenty-nine specific formal powers for twenty-seven post-communist countries. Again, these twenty-nine powers are weighted and this index is used as a dependent variable in an exploration of institutional change. Although not directly related, but in a very similar vein, Johannsen and Nørgaard (2003) propose the Index of Presidential Authority (IPA), consisting of thirty-seven different items, covering the political, appointive, and symbolic powers of presidents for ninety-eight different countries.

Shugart (1996), in later work, also proposed an additional measure of presidential power, heavily influenced by his original index with John Carey, with a specific focus on semi-presidential regimes. Clark and Wittrock (2005: 186) use a modified variant of this index for thirteen post-communist countries and examine the effect of presidential strength on the effective number of parties and discover that strong presidents can lead to an increase in the number of electoral and parliamentary parties, an effect independent of the electoral system. And in yet another variant, Taghiyev (2006: 15), develops a measure of presidential power rooted in the formal constitutional powers of the president, but one which is based on the indices developed by Shugart and Carey (1992), Lucky (1993), and Frye (1997). Taghiyev's list of twenty-five presidential powers are grouped into fourteen equally important dimensions, while each indicator, and therefore dimension, is scored from 0 to 4. The scores for the indicators within each dimension are then added together and averaged.

---

[2] Based on original schemas by Lucky (1993) and McGregor (1994).

While the Shugart and Carey (1992) measure and the Frye (1997) and Hellman (1996) measure correlate highly (Krouwel 2003), suggesting a high degree of face validity, the correlation among other measures is rather poor. For example, as Doyle and Elgie (2016) note, the correlation between the Shugart and Carey measure and the Johannsen measure is −0.19. It is perhaps no surprise then that measures of presidential power based on lists of formal constitutional presidential prerogatives are not without their critics. Fortin (2013), by performing an exploratory factor analysis on a dataset that pooled Shugart and Carey's presidential power scores with those of Frye, Hellman, and Tucker has shown that the indicators that make up these measures of power are not actually capturing a single latent construct. They also do not neatly map onto the two-dimensional concept of legislative and non-legislative powers. A similar exercise on Armingeon and Careja's measure of presidential power, consisting of twenty-nine items, produced similar results. In fact, in this instance she found that many of the items included in this list were not closely linked to any underlying factor and she suggests that 'including such items in a composite index would only serve to make the measurement difficult to interpret, since the components do not share a common causal influence' (Fortin 2013: 104). This leaves Fortin (2013: 108) to conclude that for any given measure 'not all items hypothesized to capture the concept of presidential power seem to matter equally in accounting for composite scores' thereby suggesting that existing measures of power have 'limited validity'.

Of course, not all measurements of presidential power are based solely on such institutional considerations. In what is perhaps the most-well known example, Siaroff (2003: 303) develops a measure of presidential power based on constitutional *and* behavioural indicators, or what Siaroff terms 'actual political practice'. This index of power is based on nine items where each item is scored dichotomously depending on whether it is present or not and includes whether 'the president has a central role in foreign policy' (Siaroff 2003: 304). While this behavioural measure has been used widely by other scholars (e.g. Costa Lobo and Amorim Neto 2009; Cranenburgh 2009; Elgie 2011b), and can help address some of the critiques of purely constitutional measures of power, such measures also come with their own problems. For example, Tavits (2009) examines the effect of both Siaroff's behavioural index and Metcalf's institutional index on turnout in parliamentary elections in semi-presidential countries. She finds that while the Siaroff index has a substantial and significant negative effect, Metcalf's index has a positive and non-significant effect. Such behavioural indices are clearly capturing something different from direct presidential power. In fact, they may be tapping into something more related to relational power, or how the president interacts with different actors or agencies within the government, which can prove fluid over time, thus making measurement difficult.

In a bid to address some of these issues, Doyle and Elgie (2016: 732), rather than constructing yet another new measure of power, propose 'drawing upon the comparative and local knowledge embedded in the existing measures of presidential power' to construct two new measures: one which is a simple average of existing standardized scores for each country constitution, and another weighted score for each constitution. By using all existing measures of institutional power, the authors can take advantage of the large volume of studies that operationalize a measure of power, and generate scores across 116 countries and 181 country constitutions.

When it comes to parliamentary systems, however, things have proven more difficult and far fewer studies have operationalized a measure of prime ministerial power. One reason for this is that Linz's argument suggested the democratic deficiency lay with presidents rather than prime ministers, and so there was no rush to explore the effect of variation in power among prime ministers and most theoretical models focused on the executive-parliament relationship, as opposed to the distinct power of the prime minister (e.g. Laver and Shepsle 1996; Woldendorp et al. 2013). The other reason lies with the fact that the power of the prime minister, as discussed in section 19.1, cannot simply be measured from the constitution, but is rather relational and dependent on other political actors. Heffernan (2013: 639) nicely captures the essence of this issue:

> Prime ministerial power, because it is such a moveable feast, is extraordinarily prob-
> lematic to measure, understand or theorize. Prime ministers, being prime ministers,
> not 'presidents', will matter more when they have more power and influence within
> their executive. But when? To what extent? And why?

Nonetheless, there have been some notable efforts to measure prime ministerial power. Table 19.2 lists a selection of the main measures of prime ministerial power developed in the literature over the last thirty years. Again, this list is far from exhaustive. Interest in measuring the power of prime ministers does appear to be increasing. Part of the reason for this must surely lie in the gradual presidentialization of many parliamentary systems, whereby increasing power is centralized in the prime ministerial office (the executive face) relative to the their own parties (the party face), resulting in prime ministers, rather than parties, fronting electoral campaigns (the electoral face) (see Poguntke and Webb 2007). Importantly, this conceptualization of increasing prime ministerial power is still one construed as largely relational (see Chapter 18 in this volume).

In one of the first attempts to quantify prime ministerial power in a comparative perspective, King (1994: 152), 'on the basis of the existing literature (and a certain amount of personal observation and enquiry)' divided the prime ministers of thirteen Western Europe countries, in terms of influence over government, into three broad categories: high, medium, and low. King (1994: 151) does emphasize that he is comparing the office of the prime minister, rather than individual holders of the office, but his categorization is still very much predicated upon relational criteria. For example, when discussing the role of the Irish *Taoiseach*, he highlights the power of patronage and the relationship of the prime minister with other ministers.

Dunleavy (1995: 36–7) provides a ranking of prime ministerial power based on the influence of the prime minister in cabinet committees. He only provides this measure for the UK government under John Major, but there is no reason why it could not be extended to other countries to provide a comparative measure of prime ministerial strength. The measure is based on a two-step process. In the first step, the relative

Table 19.2 Main Measures of Prime Ministerial Power

Authors	Type of Measure	Notes	Coverage
King (1994)	'Capacity to influence events'	Based on subjective assessment from existing literature and personal observation, prime ministers are divided into three categories: high, medium, and low	Thirteen Western European countries
Dunleavy (1995)	Weighted influence in cabinet committees	Calculates the importance of each committee, and then weights by chair	For the UK during the government of John Major
Bergman, Müller, Strøm and Blomgren (2003)	Institutional powers	Consists of two institutional variables, six active prime ministerial powers and the personnel resources at the prime minister's disposal. In a nod to the relational aspect, they also consider the power of the prime minister as derived from the format of the party system and party cohesion	Seventeen Western European countries since 1945.
O'Malley (2007)	'Influence over policy output'	Based on an expert survey, with, on average, fifteen to twenty experts per country	Twenty-two Western European parliamentary countries (139 prime ministerial terms)
Goplerud and Schleiter (2016)	Dissolution power	Part of a larger index on assembly dissolution power, which also includes measures for government, legislature and the president (where applicable)	Thirty-nine OECD and EU parliamentary democracies

importance of each committee is established. In the second step, each minister, including the prime minister, is given a committee influence score and for committee chairs, this score is doubled. Then all committee scores for all ministers are added together to provide their overall influence score. Although a neat quantitative way to measure the influence of the prime minister, this is not a strict institutional measure of power. Committee membership changes, often at the behest of prime ministers, and cabinet committees come and go. Indeed, the prime minister will have an important role in creating or dissolving committees and will often most likely do so for strategic purposes. If this is the case, then this measure of influence might be endogenous to the prime minister's strength (in a more relational sense).

Bergman et al. (2003:183–9) consider the power of the prime minister to be comprised of two dimensions: the party system and the institutional powers of the prime minister. The first dimension is inherently relational and concerns the size of the party system, together with the internal cohesion of parties. For Bergman et al. (2003), power will also be a function of 'institutional choices' including the formal right of the prime minister to appoint and dismiss cabinet ministers, together with the formal decision-making rules of the cabinet, including whether cabinet decisions must be by majority, by unanimity or simply by consensus. They also include the right of the prime minister to determine ministerial jurisdictions, the right to coordination vis-à-vis ministers, the right to set the cabinet agenda, the nature of ministerial accountability (directly to parliament or via the prime minister) and the extent of personal staff of each prime minister. These powers are then weighted and the respective weights added together for each country, to give a maximum score of 15 (Spain) and a possible minimum score of 0 (the lowest score is four in the case of Austria). When this index of powers is considered together with the party dimension, it provides a spatial map of prime ministerial power that incorporates both institutional and relational aspects.

Expert surveys have also been used to try and capture prime ministerial power. O'Malley (2007: 11) sent a survey to, on average, fifteen to twenty experts per country for twenty-two countries to estimate the level of prime ministerial 'influence over the policy output of the government' and the ability of prime ministers to get their 'preferred policies enacted' across 139 prime ministerial terms. Clearly, this is a relational measure as it is not based on constitutional prerogatives (or at least explicitly), and experts probably relate their power score to the relationship of each prime minister to his or her cabinet, his or her party, the parliament, coalition, etc., together with more diffuse characteristics such as his or her leadership quality.

Finally, some measures focus only on specific aspects of what might be considered prime ministerial power to provide a purely institutional measure of power. Recently, Goplerud and Schleiter (2016: 432) proposed a measure of power exclusively concerned with assembly dissolution. They develop a more general index of dissolution for a range of actors, ranging from 0, denoting the absence of any constitutional power to trigger dissolution, to 10, which indicates complete discretion to dissolve the assembly, and part of this index includes a specific measure for prime ministers. They start from the maximum score and penalize each prime minister, according to five different dimensions. This measure is an easily replicable constitutional measure of power, and although it does not explicitly consider the relational aspect of prime ministerial power, by focusing on the power of assembly dissolution, it does hone in on the crucial tenet of power first identified by Bagehot.

19.4 WHAT NEXT FOR EXECUTIVE POWER?

The discussion above naturally raises the question as to what next for work that is interested in measures of executive power. The starting point for any work involving executive power should begin with theory and conceptualization. Scholars should think carefully about what exactly they need to measure. Are they interested in measures of executive power more generally, or does their theory specify a certain aspect of presidential power, such as veto power or decree power? For some studies, a more general measure of presidential or prime ministerial power will be unsuitable. For example, there is work that necessitates a focus on one subcomponent of presidential power; Cheibub (2006) examines the president's power over the budget to investigate electoral identifiably, while Martínez-Gallardo (2012) examines the role of decree authority in driving the duration of cabinets in presidential systems. If the theory specifies an aspect, or subcomponent, of presidential power, then scholars will need to create a measure to suit their theoretical purposes. But scholars also need to think about whether their study requires a purely constitutional and formal measure of executive power, or whether they are interested in a more relational or behavioural dynamic. The institutional measures have the advantage of being relatively objective to code and replicate and tend to be sticky over time, but the behavioural measures may more accurately reflect the actual practice of politics and tend to be more fluid over time and more subjective to measure.

If the study calls for a more general measure of power however, rather than create yet another measure of executive power, scholars should consider drawing upon the wide array of existing measures already out there. There are now behavioural and institutional measures of executive power, for both presidents and prime ministers, covering most democratic countries. It may be easier and completely valid to use one of the existing measures of executive power to test your theory, rather than constructing another measure, which may just add to the empirical noise. At the least, it would certainly be worth testing the robustness of any theories with some of these off-the-shelf measures. Alternatively, scholars could make use of the existing measures and employ a data reduction method that employs existing knowledge and expertise (e.g. Doyle and Elgie 2016) to extract the underlying latent agreement among different measures of power for each country time period. Item response theory models may be particularly suitable for this purpose.

And if a new general measure of power is required, then it would be worth heeding the advice of Fortin (2013). Checklist measures of constitutional power may not be tapping into the same latent construct. Consider what is important for your measure of power and spend some time inductively exploring what your measure is capturing across the countries in your sample. A fine-grained and careful approach to index construction will be empirically and theoretically advantageous.

Finally, it may prove very difficult to measure and compare executive power across prime ministers and presidents. Doing so may be akin to comparing apples and oranges. While relational considerations, such as partisan power, are important for the power of presidents, presidential power is inherently more unidimensional and rooted in constitutions than prime ministerial power, where although constitutions are important, power is inherently more relational and rooted in the interaction of the prime minister with different actors both within and without the executive. This is not to say that a generic measure of executive power across different constitutional formats would be unwanted, but it would require both careful conceptual and empirical considerations.

REFERENCES

Armingeon, K. and Careja, R. (2008). 'Institutional Change and Stability in Postcommunist Countries, 1990–2002,' *European Journal of Political Research* 47(4): 436–66.

Arnold, C., Doyle, D., and Wiesehomeier, N. (2017). 'Presidents, Policy Compromise, and Legislative Success,' *The Journal of Politics* 79(2), 380–95.

Bagehot, W. [1873] (2000). *The English Constitution.*

Bergman, T., Müller, W. C., Strøm, K., and Blomgren, M. (2003). 'Democratic Delegation and Accountability: Cross-National Patterns,' in K. Strøm, W. C. Müller, and T. Bergman (eds) *Delegation and Accountability in Parliamentary Democracies.* Oxford: Oxford University Press, 109–20.

Blondel, J. and Müller-Rommel, F. (1993). *Governing Together: The Extent and Limits of Joint Decision-Making in Western European Cabinets.* New York: St. Martin Press.

Carlin, R. E. and Singh, S. P. (2015). 'Executive Power and Economic Accountability,' *The Journal of Politics* 77(4): 1031–44.

Cheibub, J. A. (2006). 'Presidentialism, Electoral Identifiability, and Budget Balances in Democratic Systems,' *American Political Science Review* 100(3): 353–68.

Clark, T. D. and Wittrock, J. N. (2005). 'Presidentialism and the Effect of Electoral Law in Postcommunist Systems: Regime Type Matters,' *Comparative Political Studies* 38(2): 171–88.

Costa Lobo, M. and Neto, O. A. (2009). 'Um modelo lusófono de semipresidencialismo?,' in M. Costa Lobo and O. Amorim Neto (eds) *Semipresidencialismo nos Países de Língua Portuguesa.* Lisbon: Imprensa de Ciências Sociais, 261–80.

De Montesquieu, C. [1793] (1989). *Montesquieu: The Spirit of the Laws.* Cambridge: Cambridge University Press.

Doyle, D. (2010). 'Politics and Privatization: Exogenous Pressures, Domestic Incentives and State Divestiture in Latin America,' *Journal of Public Policy* 30(3): 291–320.

Doyle, D. and Elgie, R. (2016). 'Maximizing the Reliability of Cross-National Measures of Presidential Power,' *British Journal of Political Science* 46(4): 731–41.

Dunleavy, P. (1995). 'Estimating the Distribution of Positional Influence in Cabinet Committees under Major,' in *Prime Minister, Cabinet and Core Executive.* London: Macmillan Education UK, 298–321.

Dunleavy, P. and Rhodes, R. A. W. (1990). 'Core Executive Studies in Britain,' *Public Administration* 68(1): 3–28.

Elgie, R. (1997). 'Models of Executive Politics: A Framework for the Study of Executive Power Relations in Parliamentary and Semi-presidential Regimes,' *Political Studies* 45(2): 217–31.

Elgie, R. (2011a). 'Core Executive Studies Two Decades On,' *Public Administration* 89(1): 64–77.

Elgie, R. (2011b). 'Semi-Presidentialism: An Increasingly Common Constitutional Choice,' in R. Elgie, S. Moestrup, and Y.-S. Wu (eds) *Semi-Presidentialism and Democracy.* London: Palgrave, 1–20.

Fortin, J. (2013). 'Measuring Presidential Powers: Some Pitfalls of Aggregate Measurement,' *International Political Science Review* 34(1): 91–112.

Frye, T. (1997). 'A Politics of Institutional Choice: Post-Communist Presidencies,' *Comparative Political Studies* 30(5): 523–52.

Frye, T. (2002). 'The Perils of Polarization: Economic Performance in the Postcommunist World,' *World Politics* 54(3): 308–37.

Frye, T., Hellman, J., and Tucker, J. (2000). 'Data Base on Political Institutions in the Post-Communist World,' Unpublished Data Set. Ohio State University, Columbus.

Goplerud, M. and Schleiter, P. (2016). 'An Index of Assembly Dissolution Powers,' *Comparative Political Studies* 49(4): 427–56.

Haggard, S. and McCubbins, M. D. (2001) (eds). *Presidents, Parliaments, and Policy*. Cambridge: Cambridge University Press.

Hamilton, A., Madison, J., and Jay, J. (1948). *The Federalist: Or, The New Constitution*, ed. Max Beloff. Oxford: Basil Blackwell.

Heclo, H. and Wildavsky, A. (1981). *The Private Government of Public Money: Community and Policy Inside British Politics*. Springer.

Heffernan, R. (2013). 'There's No Need for the "-isation": The Prime Minister Is Merely Prime Ministerial,' *Parliamentary Affairs* 66(3): 636–45.

Hellman, J. (1996). 'Constitutions and Economic Reform in the Postcommunist Transitions,' *East European Constitutional Review* 5: 46–56.

Helmke, G. (2017). *Institutions on the Edge: The Origins and Consequences of Inter-Branch Crises in Latin America*. Cambridge: Cambridge University Press.

Hicken, A. and Stoll, H. (2008). 'Electoral Rules and the Size of the Prize: How Political Institutions Shape Presidential Party Systems,' *Journal of Politics* 70(4): 1109–27.

Ishiyama, J. T., (2003). 'Women's Parties in Post-Communist Politics,' *East European Politics and Societies* 17(2): 266–304.

Johannsen, L. and Nørgaard, O. (2003). 'IPA: The Index of Presidential Authority. Explorations into the Measurement of Impact of a Political Institution,' paper prepared for the ECPR Joint Sessions of Workshops, Edinburgh, 28 March–4 April 2003.

Jones, G. W. (1964). 'The Prime Minister's Power,' *Parliamentary Affairs* 18(2): 167–85.

King, A. (1975). 'Executives,' in N. W. Polsby and F. I. Greenstein (eds) *Handbook of Political Science*. Reading: Addison Wesley.

King, A. (1994). 'Chief Executives in Western Europe,' in I. Budge and D. H. McKay (eds) *Developing Democracy: Comparative Research in Honour of JFP Blondel*. London: Sage Publications Ltd, 150–63.

Krouwel, A. (2003). 'Measuring Presidentialism and Parliamentarism: An Application to Central and East European Countries,' *Acta Politica* 38: 333–64.

Laver, M. and Shepsle, K. A. (1996). *Making and Breaking Governments: Cabinets and Legislatures in Parliamentary Democracies*. Cambridge: Cambridge University Press.

Lijphart, A. (1992) (ed.). *Parliamentary Versus Presidential Government*. Oxford: Oxford University Press.

Linz, J. J. (1990). 'The Perils of Presidentialism,' *Journal of Democracy* 1(1): 51–69.

Lucky, Christian (1993). 'A Comparative Chart of Presidential Powers in Eastern Europe,' *East European Constitutional Review* 2(4): 81–94.

Lucky, C. (1994). 'Table of Presidential Powers in Eastern Europe,' *East European Constitution Review* 3: 81.

Luong, P. J. (2002). *Institutional Change and Political Continuity in Post-Soviet Central Asia: Power, Perceptions, and Pacts*. Cambridge: Cambridge University Press.

Mainwaring, S. (1993). 'Presidentialism, Multipartism, and Democracy: The Difficult Combination,' *Comparative Political Studies* 26(2): 198–228.

Mainwaring, S. and Shugart, M. S. (1997) (eds). *Presidentialism and Democracy in Latin America*. Cambridge: Cambridge University Press.

Martínez-Gallardo, C. (2012). 'Out of the Cabinet: What Drives Defections from the Government in Presidential Systems?,' *Comparative Political Studies* 45(1): 62–90.

McGregor, J. (1994). 'The Presidency in East Central Europe,' *RFE/RL Research Report* 3(2): 23–31.

Metcalf, L. K. (2000). 'Measuring Presidential Power,' *Comparative Political Studies* 33(5): 660–85.

Negretto, G. L. (2013). *Making Constitutions: Presidents, Parties, and Institutional Choice in Latin America*. Cambridge: Cambridge University Press.

Neto, O. A. (2006). 'The Presidential Calculus: Executive Policy Making and Cabinet Formation in the Americas,' *Comparative Political Studies* 39(4): 415–40.

Nijzink, L., Mozaffar, S., and Azevedo, E. (2006). 'Parliaments and the Enhancement of Democracy on the African Continent: An Analysis of Institutional Capacity and Public Perceptions,' *Journal of Legislative Studies* 12(3–4): 311–35.

O'Malley, E. (2007). 'The Power of Prime Ministers: Results of an Expert Survey,' *International Political Science Review* 28(1): 7–27.

Özsoy, Ş. (2010). 'What Does Turkey's Choice of Popular Presidential Elections Mean?,' *European Public Law* 16(1): 139–60.

Payne, J. Mark (2007). 'Balancing Executive and Legislative Prerogatives: The Role of Constitutional and Party-based Factors,' in J. Mark Payne, Daniel G. Zovatto, and Mercedes Mateo Díaz (eds) *Democracies in Development: Politics and Reform in Latin America*. Washington, DC: Inter-American Development Bank, 81–116.

Poguntke, T. and Webb, P. (2007). 'The Presidentialization of Politics in Democratic Societies: A Framework for Analysis,' in T. Poguntke and P. Webb (eds) *The Presidentialization of Politics: A Comparative Study of Modern Democracies*. Oxford: Oxford University Press.

Roper, S. D. (2002). 'Are All Semipresidential Regimes the Same? A Comparison of Premier-Presidential Comparison Regimes,' *Comparative Politics* 34(3): 253–72.

Rose, R. (1991). 'Prime Ministers in Parliamentary Democracies,' *West European Politics* 14(2): 9–24.

Shugart, M. S. (1996). 'Executive-Legislative Relations in Post-Communist Europe,' *Transition* 13 December: 6–11.

Shugart, M. S. and Carey, J. M. (1992). *Presidents and Assemblies: Constitutional Design and Electoral Dynamics*. Cambridge: Cambridge University Press.

Siaroff, A. (2003). 'Comparative Presidencies: The Inadequacy of the Presidential, Semi-Presidential and Parliamentary Distinction,' *European Journal of Political Research* 42: 287–312.

Taghiyev, E. A. (2006). 'Measuring Presidential Power in Post-Soviet Countries,' *CEU Political Science Journal* 3: 11–21.

Tavits, M. (2009). 'Direct Presidential Elections and Turnout in Parliamentary Contests,' *Political Research Quarterly* 62(1): 42–54.

Tsebelis, G. and Alemán, E. (2005). 'Presidential Conditional Agenda Setting in Latin America,' *World Politics* 57(3): 396–420.

UNDP (2004). *La Democracia en América Latina. Hacia una democracia de ciudadanas y ciudadanos*. New York: Programa de las Naciones Unidas para el Desarrollo.

Van Cranenburgh, O. (2009). 'Restraining Executive Power in Africa: Horizontal Accountability in Africa's Hybrid Regimes,' *South African Journal of International Affairs* 16(1): 49–68.

Woldendorp, J. J., Keman, H., and Budge, I. (2013). *Party Government in 48 Democracies (1945–1998): Composition-Duration-Personnel*. New York: Springer Science & Business Media.

CHAPTER 20

....

PRESIDENTS AND
CABINETS

....

†ROBERT ELGIE

20.1 INTRODUCTION

THIS chapter examines the study of president/cabinet relations. For Samuels (2007: 714), *'the power to influence the cabinet is more fundamental to the policy process than any of the unilateral powers that many presidents possess'* (emphasis in the original). Certainly, the organization of president/cabinet relations raises fundamental questions of good governance. Paradoxically, though, the study of president/cabinet relations remains relatively underdeveloped, certainly in comparison with the study of prime minister/cabinet relations. There are signs, though, that this situation is changing. In part, this is due to the increasing propensity for students of Latin American presidents to apply work originally designed for the study of parliamentary regimes to the set of presidential systems there. In part, it is due to a realization that the study of president/ cabinet relations is not merely confined to the study of presidential regimes but concerns the study of semi-presidential and even parliamentary regimes too. It is also in part due to the development of principal-agent theory as a way of conceptualizing the organization of president/cabinet relations in very clear terms. To discuss the study of president/cabinet relations, the first part of the chapter presents the way in which relationship between the president and the cabinet is now typically captured in theoretical and conceptual terms, emphasizing the development of the principal-agent approach. The second part presents an overview of the study of the relationship between the president and cabinet in practice, showing that work in this area has tended to focus on variation in the president's power over the cabinet and in the level of president/cabinet conflict. The third section aims to move the study of president/cabinet relations forward, arguing for a more fine-grained approach to work in this area.

20.2 THINKING ABOUT PRESIDENT/ CABINET RELATIONS

Typically, we now approach the study of president/cabinet relations from a principal-agent perspective. Using this approach, we can capture the basic organization of president/ cabinet relations under the four standard constitutional regime types—presidentialism, parliamentarism, and the two forms of semi-presidentialism, premier-presidentialism, and president-parliamentarism (Strøm 2000; Schleiter and Morgan-Jones 2009; Samuels and Shugart 2010). Under presidentialism, the directly elected president is the agent of the voters and, in turn, the cabinet is the agent of the president. Crucially, though, the cabinet is not the agent of the directly elected legislature. That is to say, the origin (or appointment) and survival (or dismissal) of the cabinet is completely separate from the legislature. Under president-parliamentarism, by contrast, the president is again the agent of the voters and the cabinet is again the agent of the president. Here, though, the cabinet is also the agent of the legislature. In other words, the cabinet has two principals. Thus, the origin and survival of the cabinet is connected to both the president and the legislature. Under both premier-presidentialism and parliamentarism (at least in parliamentary republics), the legislature is the agent of the voters and the cabinet is the agent of the legislature and is not the agent of the president. The origin and survival of the cabinet is totally separate from the president. However, under premier-presidentialism the president remains an agent of the voters, being directly elected. This means that the president's relationship with the people is different under premier-presidentialism relative to parliamentarism and in ways that can have consequences for president/cabinet relations.

This way of thinking about president/cabinet relations allows us to distinguish between the organization of president/cabinet relations under different regime types. These distinctions are important because they raise fundamental issues of good governance. In the design and functioning of political systems, there is generally a trade-off between, on the one hand, efficiency or effectiveness and, on the other, representativeness or togetherness (Blondel et al. 2007: 5). This trade-off expresses itself in terms of the general organization of the executive. Some believe there is a need for strong, single-person leadership. Such leadership, they believe, provides coherence to systems in which there are multiple interests, demands, and concerns. As Alexander Hamilton put it in *The Federalist* (Hamilton et al. 1948: no. 70) papers, '[e]nergy in the executive is a leading character in the definition of good government'. From this perspective collective governance can lead to stalemate. By contrast, others prefer a more collegial style of executive leadership in which decisions are the result of a more collective decision-making process (Baylis 1989). Such leadership, it can be argued, helps to reconcile the conflicting interests, demands, and concerns that are present in any society. Conversely, some believe that single-person leadership can be ineffective and even dangerous (Brown 2014). In terms of the trade-off between efficiency and togetherness, what is the best way of organizing the relationship between presidents and cabinets to maximize the potential for good governance?

Thinking about president/cabinet relations from a principal-agent perspective is useful because it crystallizes the basic problem of good governance in this context. In principal-agent terms, this problem has been characterized as Madison's Dilemma (Kiewiet and McCubbins 1991: 25). As Samuels and Shugart (2010: 25–6) put it,

> Just as [James] Madison feared politicians could use delegated power to oppress citizens, leaders of any organization can use the resources or authority they have been delegated to further their own private interests, which may be at odds with their principal's collective, organizational interests.

Put differently, presidents, especially directly elected presidents with significant constitutional powers, may have both the incentive and, crucially, the opportunity to behave in ways that benefit their own personal interest and/or the interests of their most loyal cohort of supporters, rather than the collective, or national interest. Typically, Madison's Dilemma is discussed in terms of the organization of executive/legislative relations. Yet, principal-agent theory shows that it applies to president/cabinet relations too. If the cabinet is an agent of the president, then Madison's Dilemma potentially extends to the executive branch as a whole, creating the opportunity for presidents to dominate the executive for their own purposes. By contrast, if the cabinet is an agent of the legislature, then perhaps it can as a check on the president, helping to mitigate the problems associated with Madison's Dilemma. If, though, the cabinet is an agent of both the president and the legislature, then president/cabinet relations are perhaps complicated, creating the conditions for conflict and incoherence within the executive. From this perspective, what is the best way of organizing president/cabinet relations to offset the problems associated with Madison's Dilemma?

We can see, therefore, that the study of president/cabinet relations raises important political questions. It is perhaps surprising, then, that there has been relatively little scholarly work in this area. For example, in their volume on cabinets in Central and Eastern Europe, Blondel et al. (2007: 62–4) devote only two pages to president/cabinet relations, despite the presence of a number of significant presidential actors in that region. Elsewhere, Bonvecchi and Scartascini (2014: 155) state that there 'is practically no research on the relationship between presidents and cabinet ministers in Latin America'. Indeed, Samuels (2007: 714) states that cabinets are the 'missing link' in the study of the separation of powers, reflecting the emphasis that has traditionally been placed on executive/legislative relations in the study of presidencies rather than president/cabinet relations. For sure, plenty of work has focused issues that are more or less related to president/cabinet relations, some of which is reviewed in contributions elsewhere in this volume. For example, the chapters by Schleiter and Bäck and Carroll review the work on government formation and dismissal and ministerial portfolio allocation. In addition, many of the issues raised in Chapter 22 by Vercesi on cabinet decision making in parliamentary democracies are also relevant to the work on president/cabinet relations. In this chapter, though we review the scholarly work in two specific areas that relate directly to the issues of good governance that we have outlined here. They are, first, the study of presidential control over the cabinet; and, second, the study of president/cabinet conflict.

20.3 Studying President/Cabinet Relations

20.3.1 The Power of the President Over the Cabinet

The issue of the president's power over the cabinet relates directly to the question of whether there is single-person or collective government within the executive branch. In parliamentary systems, where the prime minister is typically portrayed as the 'first among equals', this is a 'live' issue and has been the subject of considerable study. In countries with presidencies, though, the topic has been debated much less extensively. This is at least partly because in presidential systems presidents are clearly more than just first among equals in the cabinet context, while in parliamentary republics presidents may not even attend cabinet meetings. However, we have already hinted at the fact that not all presidential regimes are the same. Moreover, there is considerable variation among presidents in semi-presidential countries and even presidents in parliamentary systems too (Tavits 2008). To illustrate these points and provide a sense of the work in this area, we distinguish between three types of studies: those that try to quantify the variation in the president's power over the cabinet; those that describe the president's power in this domain; and those that aim to explain the variation in the president's power over the cabinet.

20.3.2 Quantifying Variation in Presidential Power over the Cabinet

Scholars have tried to quantify the extent to which presidents control the cabinet (see also Chapter 19 in this volume.) Typically, this work is cross-sectional, with the relative power of the president being measured on a cross-national basis. The focus is usually on the constitutional powers of the president. This is because these powers are easily identifiable, facilitating cross-national comparisons. For example, in their widely used index of presidential power, Shugart and Carey (1992) include the president's power over the formation and dismissal of the cabinet in their set of indicators. For each, they give selected countries a score in a range from 0 to 4. They find that most presidential regimes score a maximum of 4 for both indicators. Nonetheless, there is some variation within presidential countries. For instance, South Korea after 1987 scores 1 and 4 respectively, while both the Philippines and the US score 3 and 4. The Shugart and Carey scores for semi-presidential countries are much lower. For example, Portugal after 1982 scores 1 for cabinet formation and 2 for dismissal. There is, though, variation within the set of semi-presidential countries, with Bulgaria scoring 0 and 0, and both France and Romania scoring 1 and 0. Shugart and Carey's indicators are only one way of capturing the president's formal power over the cabinet. Moreover, they do not include parliamentary countries in their study. Siaroff (2003) has provided another widely used scale that does include parliamentary presidents. He identifies nine indicators of presidential power and codes them in a simple binary manner. One of these indicators is whether the president chairs the cabinet and another is whether the president plays a role in foreign policy, capturing the extent to which the president controls at least one policy area where a cabinet minister is also likely to have some responsibility. Siaroff finds no variation among presidential regimes. The president always chairs the cabinet and plays a major role in foreign policy. He also finds that only rarely do parliamentary presidents chair the cabinet and fewer still have ever played a role in foreign policy. However, he finds considerable variation across semi-presidentialism. Presidents in about half of the semi-presidential countries in Siaroff's study chair the cabinet and in nearly two-thirds they have a role to play in foreign policy. What this suggests is that the standard regime classification of presidentialism vs. parliamentarism serves as a reliable proxy for the relative power of the president over the cabinet. Under presidentialism, presidents do indeed control the cabinet relative to their counterparts under parliamentarism. However, the same is not true for semi-presidentialism. Within this regime type, there is much more cross-national variation in president/cabinet relations. Overall, in their survey of ninety-eight presidencies across all types of regimes, Johanssen and Nørgaard (2003: 8) found that just under 50 per cent of presidencies worldwide had the power to summon a cabinet meeting, while just over 50 per cent participated in cabinet meetings.

Both Shugart and Carey's study and Siaroff's suggest that there are basic differences between presidential and parliamentary countries, but they also suggest that the president's control over the cabinet in presidential regimes is relatively similar across the board. However, when we consider more fine-grained constitutional features, we find variation across presidential countries too. For example, Araújo et al. (2016: 10) explicitly set out to 'measure the dominance of the president vis-à-vis the other members of the executive cabinet'. They proposed five indicators of presidential power over the cabinet: the rules governing the selection and dismissal of the cabinet; whether there are restrictions as to who can be appointed a minister; whether the minister's countersignature is required for executive decisions; and the legislative powers of ministers (Araújo et al. 2016: 8–10). They confine their index to presidential countries and they apply their scale solely to Latin America. They show that the country scores range from 0 in Bolivia to 1 in Argentina; 2 in a set of countries including Peru and Uruguay; 3 in the largest number of countries, including Chile and Ecuador; and a high of 4 in five countries, including Brazil and Mexico. They believe that these figures capture 'the variation of the power sharing within the executive cabinet' (Araújo et al. 2016: 11). They also show the variation within presidentialism.

So far, we have focused on cross-sectional measures of the president's power over the cabinet. However, presidential power can also vary over time within countries. In addition, we have reported work that has tried to measure the president's control over the cabinet by focusing on constitutional features. In this context, Octavio Amorim Neto's is highly innovative. He is associated with two indicators that aim to capture time-series cross-sectional variation based on the behavioural features of president/cabinet relations. In his study of cabinet appointments in presidential countries in Latin America, he proposes a measure of cabinet coalescence (Amorim Neto 2006). Indirectly, this allows us to see whether the president's party is overrepresented at the cabinet table compared with the relative strength of the other cabinet parties in the legislature. The calculation can be made for each cabinet, providing time-series cross-sectional figures for the skewed nature of cabinet representation. In his own work (Amorim Neto 2006) and together with Kaare Strøm (Amorim Neto and Strøm 2006), Amorim Neto has also proposed the application of the percentage of non-partisan ministers in the government as a proxy for presidential power generally, including the president's control over the cabinet. The assumption is that party shares in the legislature tend to shape the basic composition of the cabinet, even under presidential systems. However, strong presidents can skew the composition of the cabinet in their favour by appointing non-partisan ministers. Typically, such ministers are loyal to the president. Again, the number of partisan ministers can be calculated for each cabinet, provided time-series, cross-sectional variation in presidential power over the cabinet. This measure of presidential power has subsequently been taken up by many authors. For example, Schleiter and Morgan-Jones (2010) employed it specifically to investigate who was in charge of semi-presidential cabinets in Europe.

20.3.3 Describing the Power of the President Over the Cabinet

There is, then, a body of work that has tried to measure variation in presidential power over the cabinet. This work has tended to focus on the constitutional powers of presidents, mainly because these powers are easy to identify and to count. In parliamentary systems, though, the power of the prime minister is often not very well specified in the constitution. What is more, precisely because the cabinet is an agent of the legislature, the prime minister's power over the cabinet often depends on the vagaries of party politics in ways that cannot be captured in a constitution. Partly for this reason, studies of prime ministers and cabinets have often tended to be qualitative, describing how prime minister/cabinet relations are organized. The difference with the study of president/cabinet relations is notable in this regard. There have been scarcely any qualitative studies of president/cabinet relations. There has, though, been some work on the US, even if it pales into insignificance relative to the work on, say, prime minister/cabinet relations in the UK.

In his work, Valadés (2005) has tried to describe some of the basic features of president/cabinet relations in Latin America, identifying appointment and dismissal procedures, as well as the functions of cabinets. He also shows how countries approach the work of coordinating the cabinet's business in different ways (Valadés 2005: 6–8). He shows that in some countries presidents have appointed coordinators to manage the cabinet's business. In Argentina, the cabinet chief is a constitutionally designated positon. In Peru, too, there is a chair of the Council of Ministers. In Venezuela the vice-president has a formal role to play in managing the cabinet. In Chile, the constitution allows the president to appoint a minister to coordinate the cabinet's work (Valadés 2005). Valadés (2005: 8) makes the crucial point that being the cabinet coordinator in a presidential regime is not the same as being the head of government in a parliamentary system. In the latter, the prime minister is solely the agent of the legislature. In the former, though, the cabinet coordinator 'is a presidential delegate' (Valadés 2005: 8). In other words, the president retains the sole power to appoint and dismiss the cabinet coordinator. That said, in Argentina the cabinet chief is individually responsible to the legislature and in Peru the legislature can also dismiss the chair of the Council of Ministers. This means that in these countries the cabinet coordinator has two principals. Indeed, in Peru the dismissal of the chair of the Council of Ministers by the legislature also entails the collective dismissal of the cabinet as a whole, meaning that constitutionally Peru has a president-parliamentary regime rather than a pure presidential regime. Overall, Valadés (2005: 13) concludes that 'Latin American neopresidentialism rests to an ever-increasing extent on a cabinet government, more than on a personal exercise of power'. This conclusion is consistent with the recent interest in the study of coalitional presidentialism in Latin America, including the work on the presidential 'toolkit' as presented by the Chapter 21 by Chaisty, Cheeseman, and Power in this volume, perhaps suggesting that there will be an increase in the study of president/cabinet relations in Latin America in the future.

Outside Latin America, qualitative studies of president/cabinet relations are few and far between. In an overview of the role of presidents in Central and Eastern Europe, Hloušek (2013: 21) states that the Czech Republic, Hungary, Poland, Slovakia, and Slovenia 'approach a form of cabinet governance in which the real executive power is concentrated in the hands of the government and not the president'. While this statement is couched in the terms of the classic UK-style prime ministerial vs. cabinet government debate, no attempt is subsequently made to apply the existing literature on this topic to these countries, never mind integrate the presidency into such literature. Instead, we have to turn to studies of individual countries to gain some insight into president/cabinet relations in Europe. For example, Blondel and Müller-Rommel (1988) include chapters on Finland and France, discussing the role of the president in relation to the cabinet. These chapters do provide some specific information in this regard, but only in the context of a wider discussion of the two countries as a whole. Indeed, this is typical of the qualitative work on president/cabinet relations. Scholars have to rely on scraps of information from broader studies of either presidents or governments generally. One of the very few studies that explicitly focuses on executive coordination is Sedelius and Raunio's (2018) study of Lithuania. They are interested in how coordination works between the president and prime minister and how institutional design influences the relationship between the two parts of the executive (Sedelius and Raunio 2018: 3). They note that intra-executive cooperation 'takes many forms, but almost none of it is based on written rules' (Sedelius and Raunio 2018: 10). This is consistent with the earlier point about how president/cabinet relations are difficult to quantify over and above a census of basic constitutional powers. They also state that coordination is greater in foreign and security policy (Sedelius and Raunio 2018: 12), which is consistent with the greater influence that presidents typically have in this area. They also assert that the personality of the president shapes president/cabinet relations (Sedelius and Raunio 2018: 12). Sedelius and Raunio's study shows that president/cabinet relations can be approached in the same way as standard studies of prime minister/cabinet relations. There is, though, room for much more work of this sort in this area.

Perhaps unsurprisingly, the only country where there is a pronounced literature on president/cabinet relations is the US. Even here, though, the amount of work on this topic relative to the work on almost all other aspects of the presidency remains very small. For example, it is noteworthy that the prestigious *Oxford Handbook of the American Presidency* does not include a discrete chapter on president/cabinet relations and that references to the cabinet in the text are relatively few and far between. Nonetheless, there is a long history of work on the US cabinet (e.g. Hinsdale 1911). For example, Richard Fenno (1958) questions the hierarchical nature of president/cabinet relations in the US, likening them instead to pluralist political relationships with a heavy dose of departmentalism. Similarly, in his history of president/cabinet relations up to the mid-1980s, Hoxie (1984: 227) refers to the 'constant pull between the individual policy view of a particular department and the overview that the Cabinet as a whole should help provide.' He also emphasizes the extent to which Cabinet ministers look to Congress at least as much as the president. Citing Hamilton (in Hamilton et al. 1948), he concludes (Hoxie 1984: 228) that a revitalized cabinet is needed to provide much needed 'energy in the executive'. Bennett (1996) frames his study of president/cabinet relations from Kennedy to G. H. W. Bush with reference to this perspective and Fenno's classic study in particular. Bennett (1996: 216–17) concludes that 'Fenno and the conventional wisdom was, and is, correct'. Without a comparative perspective to this work, it is difficult to know whether the US experience is unique or whether it is representative of presidential systems generally. If the latter, then it challenges the standard principal-agent perspective that the cabinet is merely the agent of the president. In this sense, if no other, the work on the US cabinet suggest that there is plenty to be gained from in-depth studies of cabinets in other presidential ad semi-presidential countries.

20.3.4 Explaining the Variation in the President's Power over the Cabinet

We have identified a small amount of qualitative work that describes president/cabinet relations in certain countries. Needless to say, some of this work spills over into an explanation of why president/cabinet relations operate in the way that they do. For example, we noted that Sedelius and Raunio privilege institutions and personality as factors that explain why president/cabinet relations vary in Lithuania. There are, though, some studies that explicitly aim to identify the sources of presidential control. This work is quantitative, relying on the measures of presidential power that we outlined previously and using these measures as the dependent variable in the study.

Using his measure of cabinet coalescence and the proportion of non-partisan ministers as a proxy for the president's control over the cabinet and, indeed, the legislative process more generally, Amorim Neto (2006: 435) reported two main findings in his study of presidential cabinets in Latin America. First, when presidents are backed by large parties, they tend to appoint cabinets that enjoy majority support in the legislature. They calculate that this is the best strategy to pass the policies they wish to propose. By contrast, when presidents are not supported by a large party and when there is an economic downturn, they tend to appoint cabinets with only minority support in the legislature. This is partly because the constitution tends to give them decree-making power, which allows them to bypass the legislature and still pass policy. Second, when presidents lack support in the legislature, when they have decree-making powers, and when they have the power to veto bills passed by a hostile legislature, then they tend to appoint a higher share of non-partisan or technocratic ministers too. Overall, we can see that party organization, party politics in the legislature, and the president's constitutional powers combine to shape the composition of cabinet, which in turn will affect the president's relationship with cabinet members.

In their study of European semi-presidential and parliamentary democracies, Amorim Neto and Strøm (2006) examined why the share of non-partisan ministers and, by extension, presidential control over the cabinet varies across time. Even though the top-level institutional context is different from Amorim Neto's (2006) own study of Latin America, the results are relatively consistent. Amorim Neto and Strøm (2006: 643) find that the proportion of non-partisan ministers is positively correlated with electoral volatility and with the presence of minority governments. The share is also higher in countries with a directly elected president, that is, in semi-presidential countries, and when the president has greater constitutional powers over the legislative process. By contrast, they find, somewhat surprisingly, that the presence of an economic crisis tends to reduce the proportion of non-partisan ministers. Thus, we can see once again that the president's control over the cabinet is shaped by constitutional features, partisan factors, and contextual reasons.

Finally, we consider Schleiter and Morgan-Jones' (2010) study of presidential control over semi-presidential cabinets in Europe, once again as measured by the percentage of non-partisan ministers in the cabinet. Consistent with previous studies, they find that the president's constitutional powers are correlated with greater presidential control. They also find that higher legislative fragmentation, that is, more parties in parliament, increases the president's control. These findings are consistent with those presented by Amorim Neto and Strøm (2006). In effect, when the legislature is divided a president with certain constitutional powers has more opportunity to shape the composition of cabinet and thereby exercise control over it. Conversely, Schleiter and Morgan-Jones

(2010: 1431) find that the president's control over the cabinet is reduced when cabinets are formed immediately after a legislative election. In principal-agent terms, legislative elections emphasize the fact that under semi-presidentialism cabinets are an agent of the legislature. They also find that caretaker cabinets and economic crises increase the share of non-partisan ministers and that party presidents decrease it. The share is also higher in weaker democracies. Finally, country-specific factors can also be important. In Bulgaria, Poland, and Portugal, there tends to be a generally high level of non-partisan ministers, whereas in Ireland and Macedonia it is relatively low (Schleiter and Morgan-Jones 2010: 1430).

Together, these studies show that, all else equal, constitutional, party political, and contextual factors shape the president's control over the cabinet. Importantly, they allow us to move beyond very basic conclusions about differences between regime types. For sure, the president's control over the cabinet is greater in presidential regimes than in parliamentary regimes, but such a finding is little more than banal. These studies also allow us to move beyond conclusions about the basic differences between countries. Of course, countries have their own specificities that shape president/cabinet relations. Yet, sometimes we wish to go beyond such an uncontroversial statement. Overall, these studies show that the president's control over the cabinet is shaped by many different factors and in ways that can be studied systematically on a time-series, cross-sectional basis.

20.3.5 President/Cabinet Conflict

We have noted that the study of president/cabinet relations is often indirectly related to broader research topics, including the large body of work on cabinet formation and dismissal. However, work on president/cabinet conflict is discrete to the study of president/cabinet relations. This is an important research area. We can reasonably assume that president/cabinet conflict leads to sub-optimal outcomes. It can cause policy gridlock and can lead to inefficient compromise deals. For these reasons and others, it can also have party political repercussions. Thus, we want to know the circumstances in which conflict occurs. In this section, we outline the circumstances in which president/cabinet conflict is likely to occur, examine work on cohabitation under premier-presidentialism, identify how conflict has been measured in comparative studies of this topic, and report the general factors that are associated with such conflict.

There has been 'practically no research on the relationship between presidents and cabinet ministers in Latin America' (Bonvecchi and Scartascini 2014: 155). This point can be extended to presidential regimes generally. From a principal-agent perspective, this is unsurprising. With the cabinet solely the agent of the president and with the president having the unilateral power to dismiss cabinet members, ongoing conflict between the president and individual members or the cabinet as a whole is unlikely. Instead, research on president/cabinet conflict has to date been confined primarily to work on semi-presidential regimes, particularly premier-presidential regimes. Again, principal-agent theory indicates why (Samuels and Shugart 2010). In president-parliamentary regimes, the cabinet is the agent of two principals—the president and the legislature—both of whom have a claim over the control of the cabinet. The fact that the legislature has some say over the selection of the cabinet, perhaps leading to the appointment of ministers who are not necessarily loyal to the president, means that there is likely to be a greater degree of president/cabinet conflict under president-parliamentarism than under presidentialism. Nonetheless, the president still has the power to dismiss the prime minister and cabinet under president-parliamentarism. Therefore, if conflict occurs, it is unlikely to last very long. In premier-presidential regimes, by contrast, the cabinet is the agent of only one principal—the legislature. This means that the selection of the cabinet is separate from the president, increasing the likelihood that ministers will be appointed whom the president opposes. At the same time, the directly elected president remains the agent of the people, providing the office with a popular legitimacy that can lead the president to want to assert some control over the cabinet. In this context, president/cabinet conflict is likely to occur. To sum up, the level of president/cabinet conflict is likely to be greater under president-parliamentarism than under presidentialism, but greater still under premier-presidentialism. We should also note that the level of conflict is likely to be greater under both of these regimes than under parliamentarism where the cabinet is solely the agent of the legislature and where the indirectly elected president is not an agent of the people.

In this context, it is unsurprising that the majority of work on president/cabinet conflict has focused on premier-presidential regimes, particularly during periods of cohabitation. Cohabitation occurs when the majority in the legislature is opposed to the president. Given the cabinet is an agent of the legislature, the opposition will want the prime minister and cabinet to reflect the majority there. This leads to the appointment of a prime minister and cabinet who are also opposed to the president, leaving the president alone in the executive, facing a hostile government, and creating the ideal conditions for president/cabinet conflict. The first period of cohabitation that came to public attention occurred in France from 1986–8. This led to numerous studies of this experience, which was indeed marked by sharp president/cabinet conflict (e.g. Pierce 1991), as well as studies of subsequent periods from 1993–5 and 1997–2002 (Elgie 2002; Lazardeux 2015). Yet, France was not the only country to experience cohabitation. There were particularly conflictual episodes in Romania, which also led to studies of president/cabinet conflict there (Marian and King 2011; Gherghina and Miscoiu 2013). Indeed, there are plenty of single-country studies that address the issue of president/cabinet conflict, usually in the context of a larger study of the executive or executive/legislative relations and particularly in European premier-presidential countries, for example Amorim Neto and Costa Lobo (2009) on Portugal; Krok-Paszkowska (2001) on Poland. Moestrup's (1999) study of the effect of president/cabinet conflict on the collapse of democracy in premier-presidential Niger is a rare example of a study outside Europe, though Beuman (2013) also finds greater conflict during cohabitation in premier-presidential Timor-Leste than during periods of unified government there.

Rather like the qualitative studies of president/cabinet relations reviewed previously, single-country studies of president/cabinet conflict during cohabitation tend to focus on the country-specific reasons why cohabitation occurred, reporting the institutional features of the country, the reasons why the president's party lost the legislative election, and so forth. This work also often describes the conflict between the president and the prime minister/cabinet, reporting presidential vetoes of legislation, public disagreements between the president and the government, and often noting difficulties in foreign policy-making, which is an area where, as we have already noted, presidents often feel they have the legitimacy to intervene even during cohabitation. This work also often studies the effect of cohabitation on outcomes. At this point, president/cabinet conflict goes from being the *de facto* dependent variable to the explanatory variable. We have noted Moestrup's study of cohabitation in Niger and the problems it caused for democratization there. The effect of cohabitation on democratization has also been studied generally (Elgie 2010). However, scholars have been interested in more than just the study of cohabitation and democratization. In this context, the work of Sébastien Lazardeux (2015) is noteworthy. He focuses solely on France, but he leverages the fact that France has had three periods of cohabitation to engage in a more systematic comparison of the effects of cohabitation. Hs study is a mix of descriptive and quantitative methods. He finds that when cohabitation was combined with a small legislative majority, the number of government bills increased. By contrast, when the cohabitation government had a large majority, the figure declined. This study is particularly interesting because it challenges the simple idea that cohabitation entails a shift from presidential to prime ministerial government. Instead, Lazardeux shows that the nature of prime ministerial government varies under cohabitation contingent on other factors, including the nature of the legislative majority.

There is, then a body of mainly single-country work on president/cabinet conflict during periods of cohabitation. There is also a separate body of comparative work. These studies aim to study the causes of president/cabinet conflict generally. This work is often quantitative, manipulating the increased number of observations from comparative analysis to propose general reasons for the presence of conflict. One of the challenges with this work has been how to capture variation in president/cabinet conflict comparatively. Essentially, there have been two strategies. The first is to rely on reports of conflict in newspapers or other publications. This strategy is employed by Protsyk (2005, 2006), who relies on mentions of intra-executive conflict in the *East European Constitutional Review* and Radio Free Europe/Radio Liberty reports. Sedelius and Ekman (2010) and Sedelius and Mashtaler (2013) also use these sources as well Freedom House's *Nations in Transit* reports, *The Political Data Yearbook* of the *European Journal of Political Research*, and online sources to capture such conflict. The second strategy is a survey of country experts. Sedelius and Ekman (2010) and Sedelius and Mashtaler (2013) surveyed fifty 'country experts on constitutional and political issues', asking them to estimate the degree of conflict between the president and prime minister/cabinet for each cabinet in a number of countries. Elgie (2018) also adopts this method, preferring to survey only academics and returning more than a hundred replies. Both strategies create the potential to identify the level of president/cabinet conflict on a time-series, cross-sectional basis. They can be used separately or together.

Using the data from these strategies as the dependent variable, these studies have tried to explain variation in president/cabinet conflict. Why is there more conflict in some cabinets than others? This work has tested the intuition that conflict is likely to be higher under premier-presidentialism than under president-parliamentarism and has found support for it. For example, Protsyk (2006) compared three president-parliamentary countries (Armenia, Russia, and Ukraine) with five premier-presidential countries (Bulgaria, Lithuania, Moldova, Poland, and Romania) from 1991–2002, finding that conflict was much higher in the latter. Sedelius and Mashtaler (2013) also found that the level of conflict was somewhat greater in the six premier-presidential regimes in their study (Bulgaria, Croatia after 2000, Lithuania, Moldova, Poland, and Romania) relative to the president-parliamentary regimes (Croatia before 2000, Ukraine, and Russia). It is worth noting, though, that both studies did find examples of president/cabinet conflict under president-parliamentarism. Again, this supports the general intuition from principal-agent theory that such conflict is likely to be present in these countries, but that it is likely to be less prevalent than under premier-presidentialism.

This work has also tried to identify the factors associated with president/cabinet conflict over and above the regime type. This work takes us beyond the importance of top-level constitutional features, focusing on other institutional, party political, and wider contextual factors. For example, Protsyk (2006) finds that president/cabinet conflict increases when presidents have had a different political orientation to the cabinet, that is, under cohabitation, and when cabinets have enjoyed only minority support in the legislature. He argues that fragmented legislatures reduce the cost of potentially conflictual presidential intervention (Protsyk 2006: 153). By contrast, he also finds that the level of conflict was low when there was a technocratic government in office (Protsyk 2006: 153). Using a mix of standard regression analysis and Qualitative Comparative Analysis, Elgie (2018) compares levels of president/cabinet conflict in premier-presidential and parliamentary countries in Europe. His survey finds that president/cabinet conflict has been found in parliamentary regimes, though, as expected, at lower levels than under premier-presidentialism. That said, he finds that president/cabinet conflict is conditional upon the presence of a strong president, cohabitation, and the formation of a government after a legislative election rather than a presidential election. He finds no difference in the likelihood of conflict during periods of minority government. Finally, Sedelius and Mashtaler (2013) investigate not only the causes of president/cabinet conflict in Central and Eastern Europe, but also the variation in conflict across specific aspects of president/cabinet relations. For example, they found that conflict was particularly prevalent on questions of whether the president or the prime minister/cabinet was responsible for a particular problem as well as on policy issues, though there was also conflict over responsibility for public sector appointments too.

Overall, there is a discrete body of work on the issue of president/cabinet conflict. This work has generated specific debates, such as whether conflict is more likely under premier-presidentialism than under president-parliamentarism. To date, though, such work has been conducted almost exclusively on semi-presidential systems, sometimes in comparison with parliamentary regimes. However, if the conclusion from the work on the president's control over the cabinet is correct and there has been a 'parliamentarization' of presidential regimes in recent times, then the door is almost certainly open for the study of president/cabinet conflict in these regimes too. Work on these countries would be a welcome complement to the existing studies of president/cabinet conflict.

20.4 MOVING THE STUDY OF PRESIDENT/ CABINET RELATIONS FORWARDS

We have seen that while there is a body of scholarly work on the president's control over the cabinet and president/cabinet conflict, many issues have not yet been considered and as many questions remain unanswered. In this section, we identify a research agenda for the future study of president/cabinet relations in these two areas.

The clearest message that comes across from this review of president/cabinet relations is that more work needs to be conducted on presidential regimes, particularly in Latin America. Principal-agent theory allows us to understand why attention has not focused on this topic in this area. Nonetheless, work in cognate areas of the discipline as well as reviews by scholars such as Valadés (2005) indicate that we have missed a potentially important aspect of presidential politics by ignoring this area almost completely. After all, Latin American presidents have to work with ministers from different parties in coalition governments. In some countries, they also delegate authority to agents within the cabinet, even if there is a single-party government. In this context, we need basic, descriptive information about president/cabinet relations. How often does the cabinet meet? What are its decision-making rules? Are any votes taken? What are the informal decision-making arenas outside the cabinet? Are there cabinet committees? If so, who chairs them and how do they report to the president and the full cabinet? And so on. In short, these are the sorts of questions that we would ask in the study of prime minister/cabinet relations in any parliamentary system. There is no reason why we should not ask them in presidential systems. In fact, as we have seen, there is also no reason why we should not ask them in many semi-presidential systems too. Here, too, basic information is very scarce. So, the first item on the research agenda is simply more information about the organization and operation of president/cabinet relations, particularly in presidential countries, but in semi-presidential regimes too.

While we need more descriptive information, fundamentally we want to be able to explain the differences in president/cabinet relations that we observe. Again, this review of the existing literature suggests that we already know quite a lot about the effect of regime-level differences. As before, this is partly because principal-agent theory has provided us with the conceptual tools to generate informed hypotheses about the likely effects of such top-level constitutional differences. Yet, regime-level differences only take us so far. For example, we have seen that there are both constitutional and broader institutional differences within the set of presidential countries, relating to whether ministerial nominations have to be approved by the legislature and whether ministers can be individually dismissed by the legislature. How does this variation within presidentialism play out with regard to president/cabinet relations? Other differences are likely to be consequential too. There may be variation in the extent to which cabinet ministers can themselves issue decrees. There will be variation in the extent to which presidents can appoint figures to public sector office in domains nominally under the control of ministers. How do these differences affect president/cabinet relations? Again, we can ask these questions of presidential regimes, but we can ask similar questions of semi-presidential countries. Here, we already know that there is considerable constitutional and institutional variation. What is the effect of other forms of institutional variation in this context? To answer these questions, we need research that goes beyond the hypothesized effect of regime-level differences. One strategy is to estimate the effect of variation in a bundle of presidential powers, usually captured by a measure of some or other set of the president's constitutional prerogatives. This strategy can be very useful. In particular, it allows us to estimate the effect of variation within semi-presidentialism, demonstrating the effect of stronger vs. weaker presidents. However, as we have seen, this strategy does not necessarily help us when it comes to presidentialism. For some measures of presidential power, there is very little variation within presidentialism, taking us back, in effect, to an estimate of regime-level effects. So, estimating the general effect of variation in overall presidential power can help, especially if we are interested only in the set of semi-presidential cases. Yet, if we want to move beyond consideration of regime-level differences we need to estimate the effect of variation in individual presidential powers. We also need theories that generate expectations about what the likely effects of such variation will be.

We have discussed studies that have measured variation in both cabinet coalescence and the percentage of non-partisan ministers in a cabinet as ways of capturing the power of the president over the cabinet. These measures are innovative and seem reliable. However, we can question whether they are the best way of capturing what we wish to measure. Are non-partisan ministers really always *de facto* presidential nominees? Given there are rarely very many non-partisan ministers in any government, even if we are mistaken about the president's relationship with such ministers in some cases, our empirical results may be affected by simply assuming that they are presidential loyalists. There is also the possibility of systematic error in this regard. Maybe non-partisan finance ministers are less likely to be *de facto* presidential appointees than other ministers. Perhaps the business community or the international financial community insists on certain types of non-partisan ministers. So, while these measures are very helpful, we need to think about other ways of capturing the president's power over the cabinet in a reliable manner. The same point applies to measure of president/cabinet conflict. We noted that there are two strategies for identifying variation in the level of such conflict. Yet, both are potentially problematic. Relying on secondary material to identify conflict does not necessarily capture the level of conflict reliably. It is also a strategy that is potentially difficult to replicate. Often, scholars have to interpret secondary material on an ad hoc basis, making it problematic for other scholars to replicate their methodology. There are also problems with expert surveys. Elgie (2018) reports the inter-coder reliability scores for country experts in his survey of president/cabinet conflict. He finds that often there is very little agreement among experts about the level of conflict. This reduces confidence in the reliability of the reported conflict scores. So, while we need measures of presidential power over the cabinet and president/cabinet conflict in order to engage in systematic empirical analysis, we can question the reliability of the measures that are currently being used. In short, we need better data.

Finally, we need to think about the general relationship between scholarship on president/cabinet relations and scholarship on related questions in the discipline. We have noted that work on prime minister/cabinet relations under parliamentarism has the potential to inform the study of president/cabinet relations under both presidentialism and semi-presidentialism. We need to apply that work in the same way that scholars of coalitional presidentialism have applied work on coalition-building under parliamentarism to the study of presidential politics in Latin America. Yet, we should not think of the relationship as being purely one way. Chapter 18 of this volume discusses the presidentialization of prime ministerial politics. In short, prime ministers in parliamentary regimes are behaving more like presidents in parliamentary and some semi-presidential regimes. In this context, the study of president/cabinet relations is likely to be increasingly relevant to the study of prime ministerial politics. Indeed, this point only reinforces the need for more scholarly work on president/cabinet relations generally.

References

Amorim Neto, O. (2006). 'The Presidential Calculus: Executive Policy Making and Cabinet Formation in the Americas,' *Comparative Political Studies* 39(4): 415–40.

Amorim Neto, O. and Costa Lobo, M. (2009). 'Portugal's Semi-Presidentialism (Re)considered: An Assessment of the President's Role in the Policy Process, 1976–2006,' *European Journal of Political Research* 48: 234–55.

Amorim Neto, O. and Strøm, K. (2006). 'Breaking the Parliamentary Chain of Delegation: Presidents and Non-partisan Cabinet Members in European Democracies,' *British Journal of Political Science* 36: 619–43.

Araújo, V., Silva, T., and Vieira, M. (2016). 'Measuring Presidential Dominance over Cabinets in Presidential Systems: Constitutional Design and Power Sharing,' *Brazilian Political Science Review* 10: 1–23.

Baylis, T. A. (1989). *Governing by Committee: Collegial Leadership in Advanced Societies*. Albany, NY: SUNY Press.

Bennett, A. J. (1996). *The American President's Cabinet from Kennedy to Bush*. London: Palgrave Macmillan.

Beuman, L. M. (2013). 'Cohabitation in New Post-Conflict Democracies: The Case of Timor-Leste,' *Parliamentary Affairs* 68(3): 453–75.

Blondel, J. and Müller-Rommel, F. (1988) (eds). *Cabinets in Western Europe*. London: Macmillan.

Blondel, J., Müller-Rommel, F., and Malovà, D. (2007). *Governing New European Democracies*. New York: Palgrave Macmillan.

Bonvecchi, A. and Scartascini, C. (2014). 'The Organization of the Executive Branch in Latin America: What We Know and What We Need to Know,' *Latin American Politics and Society* 56(1): 144–65.

Brown, A. (2014). *The Myth of the Strong Leader: Political Leadership in the Modern Age.* New York: Basic Books.

Elgie, R. (2002). 'La Cohabitation de Longue Durée: Studying the 1997–2002 Experience,' *Modern and Contemporary France* 10(3): 297–311.

Elgie, R. (2010). 'Semi-presidentialism, Cohabitation and the Collapse of Electoral Democracies 1990–2008,' *Government and Opposition* 45(1): 29–49.

Elgie, R. (2018). *Political Leadership: A Pragmatic Institutionalist Approach.* London: Palgrave Macmillan.

Fenno, R. F. (1958). 'President-Cabinet Relations: A Pattern and a Case Study,' *American Political Science Review* 52(2): 388–405.

Gherghina, S. and Miscoiu, S. (2013). 'The Failure of Cohabitation: Explaining the 2007 and 2012 Institutional Crises in Romania,' *East European Politics and Societies and Cultures* 27(4): 668–84.

Hamilton, A., Madison, J., and Jay, J. (1948). *The Federalist: Or, The New Constitution*, ed. Max Beloff. Oxford: Basil Blackwell.

Hinsdale, M. L. (1911). *A History of the President's Cabinet.* Ann Arbor, MI: George Wahr.

Hloušek, V. (2013). 'Heads of State in Parliamentary Democracies: The Temptation to Accrue Power,' in V. Hlousek (ed.) *Presidents Above Parties? Presidents in Central and Eastern Europe, Their Formal Competencies and Informal Power.* Brno: Masaryk University, Faculty of Social Studies, Internal Institute of Political Science, 19–29.

Hoxie, R. G. (1984), 'The Cabinet in the American Presidency, 1789-1984,' *Presidential Studies Quarterly* 14(2): 209–30.

Johannsen, L. and Nørgaard, O. (2003). 'IPA: The Index of Presidential Authority. Explorations into the Measurement and Impact of a Political Institution,' paper prepared for the ECPR Joint Sessions of Workshops, Edinburgh, 28 March–4 April 2003.

Kiewiet, D. R. and McCubbins, M. D. (1991). *The Logic of Delegation. Congressional Parties and the Appropriations Process.* Chicago: The University of Chicago Press.

Krok-Paszkowska, A. (2001). 'Divided Government in Poland,' in R. Elgie (ed.) *Divided Government in Comparative Perspective.* Oxford: Oxford University Press, 127–45.

Lazardeux, S. (2015). *Cohabitation and Conflicting Politics in French Policymaking.* London: Palgrave Macmillan.

Marian, C. G. and King, R. F. (2011). 'A War of Two Palaces: Semi-Presidential Government and Strategic Conflict,' in R. F. King and P. E. Sum (eds) *Romania under Basescu: Aspirations, Achievements, and Frustrations during His First Presidential Term.* New York: Lexington Books, 107–34.

Moestrup, S. (1999). 'The Role of Actors and Institutions: The Difficulties of Democratic Survival in Mali and Niger,' *Democratization* 6: 171–86.

Pierce, R. (1991). 'The Executive Divided Against Itself: Cohabitation in France, 1986–1988,' *Governance* 4(3): 270–94.

Protsyk, O. (2005). 'Politics of Intraexecutive Conflict in Semipresidential Regimes in Eastern Europe,' *East European Politics and Societies* 19(2): 135–60.

Protsyk, O. (2006). 'Intra-Executive Competition between President and Prime Minister: Patterns of Institutional Conflict and Cooperation under Semi-Presidentialism,' *Political Studies* 54: 219–44.

Samuels, D. (2007). 'Separation of Powers,' in C. Boix and S. C. Stokes (eds) *The Oxford Handbook of Comparative Politics*. Oxford: Oxford University Press, 703–26.

Samuels, D. J., and Shugart, M. S. (2010). *Presidents, Parties and Prime Ministers: How the Separation of Powers Affects Party Organization and Behavior*. Cambridge: Cambridge University Press.

Schleiter, P. and Morgan Jones, E. (2009). 'Review Article: Citizens, Presidents and Assemblies: The Study of Semi-Presidentialism beyond Duverger and Linz,' *British Journal of Political Science* 39: 871–92.

Schleiter, P. and Morgan-Jones, E. (2010). 'Who's in Charge? Presidents, Assemblies, and the Political Control of Semi-Presidential Cabinets,' *Comparative Political Studies* 43(11): 1415–41.

Sedelius, T. and Ekman, J. (2010). 'Intra-executive Conflict and Cabinet Instability: Effects of Semi-presidentialism in Central and Eastern Europe,' *Government and Opposition* 45(4): 505–30.

Sedelius, T. and Mashtaler, O. (2013). 'Two Decades of Semi-Presidentialism: Issues of Intra-Executive Conflict in Central and Eastern Europe 1991–2011,' *East European Politics* 29(2): 109–34.

Sedelius, T. and Raunio, T. (2018). 'Shifting Power-Centres of Semi-Presidentialism: Exploring Executive Coordination in Lithuania,' *Government and Opposition* 54(4): 637–60. doi: 10.1017/gov.2017.31

Shugart, M. S., and Carey, J. M. (1992). *Presidents and Assemblies: Constitutional Design and Electoral Dynamics*. Cambridge: Cambridge University Press.

Siaroff, A. (2003). 'Comparative Presidencies: The Inadequacy of the Presidential, Semi-Presidential and Parliamentary Distinction,' *European Journal of Political Research* 42: 287–312.

Strøm, K. (2000). 'Delegation and Accountability in Parliamentary Democracies,' *European Journal of Political Research* 37: 261–89.

Tavits, M. (2008). *Presidents with Prime Ministers. Do Direct Elections Matter?* Oxford: Oxford University Press.

Valadés, D. (2005). 'Cabinet Government and Latin American Neopresidentialism,' *Mexican Law Review* 4: 1–14.

CHAPTER 21

....

INSIDE THE COORDINATION PARADIGM

*New perspectives on minority presidents
and coalition management*

....

PAUL CHAISTY, NIC CHEESEMAN,
AND TIMOTHY J. POWER

21.1 INTRODUCTION

....

THE comparative literature on executive-legislative relations has recently undergone
something of an analytical convergence. As Maria Escobar-Lemmon and Michelle
Taylor-Robinson note in their contribution to this *Handbook* (see Chapter 21). Rather
than overemphasizing institutional differences between presidential and parliamentary
formats, scholars increasingly see both presidents and prime ministers as executives
driven by a common purpose: 'managing the legislative branch to advance their policy
goals' (see Chapter 21). This convergence has improved comparative analysis by encouraging scholars to 'work backwards' from executive goals, thus illuminating strategies
and tactics that are common to executives everywhere, while at the same time factoring
in the hard-wired constraints of constitutional formats. For many colleagues working in
this field, presidentialism and parliamentarism have been downgraded from fetishes to
control variables.

As Escobar-Lemmon and Taylor-Robinson demonstrate, the empirical and theoretical
payoffs of this convergence have been high. At the same time, the search for a unified
theory of executive-legislative relations has re-oriented the literature in an asymmetric
way: it has affected the way we understand presidentialism far more than the way we

understand parliamentarism. This is because while research on parliamentarism has traditionally focused on prime ministers' struggle to *coordinate* executive-legislative relations, the early 'Third Wave' (Huntington 1991) literature on presidentialism emphasized the potential for *conflict* instead (Cheibub and Limongi 2010). A belated discovery of coordination mechanisms available to presidents, particularly those governing in multi-party contexts, has created a conceptual vocabulary that is now common to students of both presidentialism and parliamentarism. This convergence is something like a minor 'paradigm shift' (Kuhn 1962)—clearly not of Copernican significance, but with Juan Linz (1990) playing a role akin to Ptolemy. Linzian understandings of the 'perils' of presidentialism, inspired by what Cheibub (2007) called the 'intrinsic features' of the separation of powers, have largely given way to a focus on inter-branch *coordination*.

In this chapter, we review the best example to date of this mini-paradigm shift: the literature on coalitional presidentialism. Moving from the general to the specific, we first briefly review the Linzian hypotheses that inspired a new subfield of comparative presidentialism. We then show how a simultaneous empirical trend—rising party fragmentation around the globe—has created a 'world of minority presidents' in which the formation and maintenance of inter-party coalitions is paramount. The tools and skills of coordination are more important than ever before, and political scientists have benefited greatly from tracking these trends; without the increasing minority status of directly elected executives, it is unlikely that students of presidentialism and parliamentarism would have discovered their kinship. In the subsequent section, we then make a case for why coalitional presidentialism 'matters' for both empirical and theoretical reasons. We then go on to review the state of the literature on coalitional presidentialism, which is now completing roughly two decades of existence. In the final section of the chapter, we sketch an agenda for future research on coalition management: both its causes and its consequences. Thus, while the chapter begins by revisiting the familiar 'conflict' paradigm in presidential studies, it invests heavily in fleshing out some of the assumptions and early findings of the 'coordination' paradigm that has taken shape in the twenty-first century.

21.2 THE MAJOR DEBATES IN RESEARCH

21.2.1 Revisiting Linz: The Early Third Wave

Political science research on presidentialism has evolved substantially since Juan Linz first posed a link between presidentialism and democratic instability in the 1980s (Linz 1990). Linz gave special attention to the challenges faced by minority presidents under the separation of powers. The arguments are familiar to two generations of graduate students. Linz assumed that minority executives would be debilitated by policy gridlock, thus aggravating inter-branch conflict, incentivizing praetorian politics, and possibly even leading to democratic breakdown. The Linzian conflict hypothesis was endorsed by authors such as Mainwaring (1993), Stepan and Skach (1993), and Jones (1995). Jones echoed the Linzian view that coalition government was rare under presidentialism and that the minority status of the executive was far more viable under parliamentarism than under the separation of powers. As Jones (1995: 38) put it bluntly:

> When an executive lacks a majority in parliamentary systems, the norm tends to be what Lijphart terms 'consensual government' (i.e. government by coalition). In presidential systems, when the executive lacks a majority (or close to it) in the legislature, the norm is conflictual government.

In the decade after these somewhat alarmist hypotheses debuted, a new wave of studies—overwhelmingly on Latin America—suggested that not only was coalitional government fairly common under the separation of powers, but that party fragmentation did not doom presidentialism to breakdown. Moreover, with regard to policy, minority presidents could achieve reasonable legislative throughput by fostering inter-party alliances on the assembly floor. These findings were confirmed on a cross-national basis in a landmark large-N analysis by Cheibub et al (2004). In demonstrating that presidential democracies did not collapse due to 'intrinsic' characteristics (i.e. the minority status of the executive due to the separation of powers), that study severed the theoretical link between Linzian conflict and regime survival, effectively ending the 'breakdown debate' that had pervaded the first two decades of scholarly debate on Third Wave democratization (see also Cheibub 2007). By that point, many empirical studies of executive-legislative relations in presidential regimes had already begun to highlight the role of (a) inter-party coalitions as a mechanism of inducing cooperation between the *formateur* and the assembly; and, (b) the role of institutional design in facilitating or impeding these horizontal political alignments. Two perceptive review essays by Elgie (2005) and Cheibub and Limongi (2010) showed that the comparative literature on presidentialism was shifting rapidly from the study of 'conflict' to the study of 'coordination'.

Linz had depicted multi-party presidentialism as an arena unusually ripe for conflict, with immobilism leading to temptations of unilateral action by both the executive and a hostile legislature. But, as Cheibub and Limongi (2010: 49) put it, under the separation of powers 'policies cannot be enacted unilaterally by one of the branches, [thus] it is only through the continuous existence of a majority that controls both the executive and the legislature that the policies preferred by both will become reality'. The new objective of the 'coordination paradigm' was the identification of those mechanisms that would lead to the cultivation of such a majority.

21.2.2   A World of Minority Presidents

In the early literature on Third Wave democracy, it was commonly noted that presidential systems are often characterized by powerful executives who deploy important agenda-setting powers. As a result, the comparative politics literature initially focused on forms of presidential dominance: from 'neo-patrimonialism' in Africa (Erdmann and Engel 2007; Cheeseman 2015) to 'superpresidentialism' in the former Soviet Union (Fish 1997). This focus on how the directly elected executive 'gets its way' discouraged scholars from asking about the constraints facing presidents and the types of bargains they need to make in order to govern. Although the public image of presidents is of leaders who operate with few checks and balances (Prempeh 2008), the reality is often much more complex. The reason is that today, most directly elected presidents lack a parliamentary majority. In 1974, usually taken as the onset of the global Third Wave of democratization (Huntington 1991), the average effective number of parties in a competitively elected legislature was 2.94, but by 1995 this had risen to 3.54, and then spiked again to 3.83 in 2005 (Chaisty et al. 2018: 2). Put differently, the probability that two randomly selected legislators would not belong to the same party had risen by more than 27 per cent during the first three decades of liberalization and democratization.

As a result, the odds that executives will enjoy a majority of co-partisans in the legislature have fallen dramatically. In situations of party-system fractionalization, questions about how presidents approve their legislative proposals, and how they avoid the formation of counter-majorities that might prevent them from finishing their terms in office, have become especially pertinent.

In response to these questions, a new literature has emerged that seeks to understand what has come to be known as *coalitional presidentialism*—'a strategy of directly elected minority presidents to build stable majority support in fragmented legislatures' (Chaisty et al. 2018: 14). The way in which presidents deal with their minority status by building coalitions—and the impact of this strategy on the wider political system—tackles one of the most important debates in the comparative executive politics literature: why have presidential systems proved to be more durable than was initially predicted? As we show below, the myriad answers that have been put forth have been largely responsible for the paradigm shift of conflict to coordination.

21.2.3 Why Coalitional Presidentialism Matters

The literature on coalitional presidentialism has changed the way we think about institutional design and democratic consolidation in two important ways. First, as our introduction has already hinted, it has rehabilitated the reputation of multi-party presidentialism—once viewed as unviable—as a sustainable political matrix. Second, it has called into question how different the strategies employed by presidents and prime ministers really are in practice (see also Chapter 20 in this volume).

The Linzian 'perils of presidentialism' argument was a useful foil. Yet as empirical evidence began to cast doubt on Linz's argument in the late 1980s, a number of scholars sought to reformulate it (see Elgie 2005; Cheibub 2007). Most influentially, both Mainwaring (1993) and Stepan and Skach (1993) proposed that it was not simply presidentialism that was the problem, but mainly those countries that featured the 'difficult combination' of presidentialism and multi-party politics. According to this argument, it was the greater coordination challenge of having to deal with complex constellations of parties that undermined the ability of presidents to establish stable governments.

However, this argument also came under fire, as some presidents not only survived their minority status but also implemented their policy agendas in decisive ways. In response, a number of young Latin American scholars completing their doctorates in the late 1990s and early 2000s sought to explain this reality by demonstrating that presidentialism could work like parliamentarism (Chaisty et al. 2014: 75). By forming cross-party coalitions, presidents could build effective and durable legislative alliances in a manner similar to prime ministers. Doing this not only enabled them to deflect challenges to their authority, but also increased the success rate of executive-sponsored bills in the legislature (Saiegh 2011).

While never denying the formal distinction between presidentialism and parliamentarism—that is, the fact that presidents are separately elected and have a fixed term in office—coalitional presidentialism suggests that presidents are not necessarily doomed by rising pluralism in the partisan and factional organization of contemporary legislatures. Minority presidents look for coping strategies, often involving power-sharing arrangements.

The analytical breakthroughs of recent Latin American literature provided a compelling answer to the puzzle of why multi-party presidential political systems have been more durable than was initially predicted. Minority presidentialism need not undermine democratic consolidation if the executive is reasonably adept at coalitional politics. Moreover, a broader lesson for the present *Handbook* is that if minority presidents engage with fragmented assemblies through goal-oriented behaviour, then the respective roles of presidents and prime ministers may be more similar than previously believed.

However, saying that 'coalitions matter' is not enough. There remains considerable controversy over the question of exactly *how* minority presidents seek to construct and manage their coalitions, and which tools at their disposal are the most effective. Is the distribution of cabinet positions more effective than the use of legislative powers? Does the distribution of pork trump a president's partisan influence (i.e. his or her control over his or her own party)? To what extent are different tools 'substitutable', in the sense that more of one can be used to compensate for less of another? And to what extent is legislative alliance formation undermined by practices of patronage and clientelism? The answers to these questions are important for understanding both how coalitional presidentialism works and—if we assume that presidents will consistently adopt the most effective strategies available to them, other things being equal—the kinds of political practices that it encourages.

There is also an emerging debate over macropolitical externalities generated by coalitional presidentialism. Does the co-optation of opposition parties weaken their development and so undermine the evolution of the party system? Does the continual need to convert a minority of seats into a majority of votes lead to dubious exchanges of favours, perhaps shading into political corruption? Do minority presidents who resort disproportionately to their own agenda-setting powers undermine parliamentary scrutiny and hence political accountability? In other words, does coalitional presidentialism involve a 'tradeoff between governability and accountability' (Chaisty et al. 2014), that is, generating stability while undermining the quality of democracy?

Finally, there are questions about how far the concept of coalitional presidentialism can travel. Given that this literature was developed in Latin American scholarly circles, with a heavy reliance on the case of Brazil (Power 2010), it is not always clear how far its findings can be generalized. The scope conditions of coalitional presidentialism are particularly significant, because if presidents in other parts of the world are managing their minority status in alternative ways—or failing to manage it at all—this would cast doubt on the centrality of coalitional politics to the stability of democratic presidential political systems.

In responding to this question, we can draw some clues both from variation across time—that is, within Latin America itself—and across region. Historical case studies of minority presidential breakdowns in the Second Wave of democratization, as in Brazil in 1964 (Stepan 1978) or Chile in 1973 (Valenzuela 1978), suggest that coalition formation is easier said than done when inter-party polarization is extreme and/or when domestic political cleavages are embedded in regional or global conflicts (i.e. the Cold War). Moreover, newer work on Africa and Asia suggests that traditional theories of coalition formation are less relevant when presidents either aim to form oversized coalitions to project an air of legitimacy (Opalo 2011) or persuade parliament to act by consensus (Kawamura 2013). In the traditional Eurocentric concept of coalitional politics, coalitions are intended both to include and to exclude, but the omnidirectional co-optative practices observed in cases such as Indonesia may thwart the emergence of effective opposition (Slater and Simmons 2013; Mietzner 2016; Slater 2018).

21.3 THE PRESIDENTIAL TOOLBOX: THE STATE OF THE LITERATURE

The extant research on coalitional presidentialism has focused largely on the discrete tools or strategies that minority presidents deploy to manage legislative coalitions. Scholars of Latin America have centred on familiar instruments such as cabinet portfolio allocation or budgetary payoffs. This research has helped to identify the different individual coalition management strategies that are available to presidents, and it has deduced and tested a range of hypotheses that seek to explain the conditions under which presidents deploy such tools. More recently, researchers have sought to take this analysis one stage further by integrating the distinct strategies of coalition management into a holistic basket of executive options. This work has begun to delineate the entire 'toolbox' (Raile et al. 2011; Chaisty et al. 2018) of strategies available to presidents, and it seeks to understand the factors shaping why and how presidents choose particular tools or combinations of tools at certain moments in time. It contends that coalition management is a multivariate decision-making process, and that presidents enjoy a high degree of discretion when making their choices.

The earliest work in this vein, influenced heavily by Shugart and Carey's (1992) institutionalist approach, placed particular emphasis on the 'agenda-setting powers' that minority presidents use to achieve legislative throughput. The ability of Third Wave presidents to wield significant legislative power, it was argued, creates strong incentives for parties to ally with the president (Amorim Neto and Santos 2011). The agenda-setting powers that received most attention include proactive legislative powers like constitutional decree authority, the right to initiate statute law, urgency and fast-track provisions, rules that give priority consideration to executive bills over private members' legislation, as well as reactive powers like amendment rights, package and partial vetoes, and so on. As with all research on minority presidentialism, most of this early work took its empirical evidence from Latin America. Later analysis included countries from other regions, particularly in the former Soviet Union (Remington et al. 1998; Protsyk 2004). The analysis of post-Soviet cases added further agenda-setting powers to the toolbox. In their study of presidential agenda setting in the post-communist world, Tsebelis and Rizova (2007) highlight the importance of the presidential power of 'amendatory observations', that is, the power of presidents to suggest revisions to the bills that they have vetoed. Beliaev (2006) also shows how the power of Russian presidents to arbitrate in inter-branch conflicts augments their agenda control.

This research on agenda-setting powers illustrates the variety of legislative options that presidents have at their disposal. On their own, agenda-setting powers comprise a range of legislative instruments that presidents can deploy when governing through legislatures. In effect, these instruments constitute a toolbox in miniature. Yet, scholarship has also uncovered alternative strategies of coalition management, which suggests that in practice the toolbox of resources available to presidents is likely to be substantially larger in most cases. After research on agenda-setting powers, perhaps the second most commonly explored avenue of research is the 'cabinet powers' that presidents use in coalition management. Drawing on the mechanisms of coalition management used by prime ministers in parliamentary systems, scholars have studied how presidents seek to secure coalition support by trading cabinet portfolios with their allies (e.g. Amorim Neto 2002, 2006). This line of inquiry is associated with a subtly different portrayal of executives: presidents are now seen as sharing executive power with their coalition partners rather than dominating the assembly though agenda control. They do this in a number of ways. Research has focused on how presidents manipulate the size of their cabinets (Altman 2000; Arriola 2009; Meireles 2016), their proportional representativeness (Amorim 2002; Pereira et al. 2005), and their level of partisanship and ideological polarization (Alemán and Tsebelis 2011; Camerlo and Pérez-Liñán 2015; Gaylord and Rennó 2015). Again, this research has focused largely on Latin America, albeit with more recent application to other countries and regions (e.g. Chaisty and Chernykh's 2017 research on Ukraine).

Other tools of coalition management that feature in univariate studies of presidentialism include 'partisan powers', 'budgetary powers', and 'informal powers'. Partisan powers of coalition management refer to the ability of presidents to discipline their coalitions through the dominance of their own parties (Mainwaring and Shugart 1997; Samuels and Shugart 2010). Put simply, minority presidents who lead large and disciplined parties that dominate their coalitions are less reliant on other coalition parties, while leaders of potential allied parties are unlikely to invest heavily in a coalition when the *formateur* cannot extract support from his or her own party.

The literature also highlights the budgetary authority of presidents as a resource to maintain inter-party alliances. Drawing on the distributivist understanding of executive-legislative relations in the United States, scholars have adapted the logic of 'pork-barrel' politics to explore the strategies that presidents use to manage their coalition partners. This analysis has been especially fruitful in countries like Brazil that have strong regional interests and a legacy of uneven development. The deployment of discretionary budgetary payments to the districts of legislative supporters is an effective strategy used by many presidents in Latin America (Ames 2001; Pereira and Mueller 2004; Alston and Mueller 2006; Araya 2015).

Finally, univariate studies of presidential systems apply the notion of 'informal institutions' (Helmke and Levitsky 2006) in their analysis of coalition management. Given the significance of clientelistic authority networks in many Third Wave democracies and hybrid regimes, the informal mechanisms of exchange between presidents and their coalition allies (referred to here as the 'exchange of favours') are a common feature of coalitional politics. Several studies have identified paraconstitutional practices emerging to resolve the coordination problems posed by minority presidents and fragmented assemblies (Mejía Acosta 2006; Siavelis 2006).

Taken together this univariate research presents a picture of presidents deploying a wide variety of tools in coalition management. This summary is organized around five main management strategies—legislative or agenda setting tools, cabinet authority, partisan powers, budgetary authority, and informal institutions—but this classification is far from exhaustive. It is certain to expand as we learn more about coalitional presidentialism, especially in the less-researched cases of Asia and Africa. Moreover, while this research is largely univariate in focus, it has taken the first steps toward examining the relationships between different presidential strategies. Scholars recognize that cabinet portfolio payoffs, for instance, do not exist in isolation from other tools of coalition management. In research on Latin America, an inverse relationship has been shown to exist between the magnitude of presidential agenda tools such as decree and veto powers, and the propensity of presidents to share cabinet portfolios (Amorim Neto 2006; Martínez-Gallardo 2012). This interaction between different strategies implies that presidents do have strategic *choices* to make when dealing with their coalitional partners. Thus, this literature provides the empirical basis for a more holistic understanding of coalition management, one that considers the multivariate and dynamic nature of presidential decision-making. Subsequent research on the presidential toolbox has sought to unpack the factors that shape this decision-making process.

Raile et al. (2011) provide one attempt to develop the idea of a presidential toolbox. Their analysis focuses on how Brazilian presidents have used a combination of cabinet and budgetary authority to manage multi-party coalitional support. In this work, portfolio payoffs establish the baseline of coalition deals, while budgetary payments manage the ongoing operational costs of binding cross-party alliances. Central to the analysis is the idea that different tools of coalition management are imperfectly substitutable and interrelated: their deployment can achieve the same outcome but with different levels of efficiency, and as presidents invest more heavily in one high-value tool, their deployment of other tools falls. This approach emphasizes a highly dynamic relationship between coalitional strategies. For example, Raile et al. (2011: 329) find that, as presidents form broader and more proportionally representative cabinets, they tend to spend less on budgetary pork.

In our own work, we extended this analysis by exploring the dynamic relationships between the full panoply of the aforementioned tools that comprise the presidential toolbox (Chaisty et al. 2018). Analysing these strategies across three regions—Africa, Latin America, and the former Soviet Union—we identify the contextual and temporal conditions under which presidents opt for one instrument of coalition discipline over another, or choose to deploy one or more tools. This analysis depicts the toolbox in terms of coalition *management*, not necessarily coalition *formation*, a distinction that we insist is of paramount importance to the emerging literature. Although tools of coalition formation (such as cabinet posts) constitute part of the presidential toolbox, and the 'Day One coalition' affects the subsequent choices made by the presidents, we understand the tools used in coalition management to be far more complex, given the ongoing operational challenges that affect minority presidents over the course of their terms in office. In making choices about the deployment of different tools, we assume that presidents are cost minimizers: 'they will choose the tool (or tools) which *seem* least costly to them at a given moment in time' (Chaisty et al. 2018: 88). The factors affecting the costs of each tool are analysed in terms of three broad categories: system-level (institutional factors like the type of the electoral system or the nature of the party system); coalition-level (the characteristics of the supporting parties and legislators that make up the presidential coalition), and conjunctural factors such as presidential popularity and external shocks.

What does this research on the presidential toolbox tell us about the strategies of coalition management that minority presidents deploy? First, that minority presidents maintain inter-party alliances with a broad range of problem-solving instruments. Cross-regional research finds that professional legislators around the world (and not just political scientists) identify a multiplicity of tools of coalition management. Of all the tools presidents deploy, cabinet authority is the preferred tool of choice in most cases, but it is not omnipotent.

Second, presidents choose coalitional strategies in a dynamic environment shaped by different structural, coalitional, and conjunctural factors. Our research finds, for example, that agenda-setting tools are far more important in Latin America and the former Soviet Union where the constitutional powers of presidents are highly concentrated, than in African presidential systems (Cheeseman 2015). Toolbox research also finds *inter alia* that the budgetary prerogatives of presidents are sensitive to economic conditions; that the costs of deploying the informal exchange of favours between presidents and their coalition partners appear to fall when regimes display lower transparency and weaker commitment to the rule of law; and that the institutionalization of party systems raises the value of partisan powers.

Third, this research shows that presidents appear to consider the trade-offs between different tools when dealing with management issues. Trade-offs exist between cabinet powers and budgetary authority; between partisan powers and cabinet powers; between legislative powers and cabinet powers; and between the deployment of cabinet powers and use of the informal exchange of favours.

Fourth and finally, our cross-regional research shows that tools commonly fail. As anyone who owns a real toolbox knows, one often has to reach for a second or third tool in order to fix what the first could not achieve. When faced with defections or wholescale breakdowns of their coalitions—most likely to happen in the face of controversial economic or constitutional reforms—presidents may resort to certain tools in order to contain their losses or 'clean up' after coalitional failure. Executive-legislative relations under minority presidents is characterized by high levels of contingency and improvization, and thus we argue that coalition management should be seen as a goal, not a stable outcome.

In sum, the toolbox approach seeks to situate minority presidents in a highly dynamic environment, and it emphasizes the high degree of discretion that they enjoy under the separation of powers. This high level of discretion combined with a dynamic environment means that coalitional management generates a lot of noise in presidential systems. To date, the research on coalitional presidentialism has only just begun to clarify the general parameters of this phenomenon. In the next section, we will discuss the likely future directions of research on the use of the presidential toolbox in coalition management.

21.4 A New Research Agenda for the Study of Coalitional Presidentialism

Minority presidents abound; they tend to form coalitions; and coalitional presidentialism is viable even in emerging democracies. As minority presidents have become the modal outcome in direct elections for political executives around the world, we have greatly improved our understanding of the tools they used to govern in concert with fragmented legislatures. In searching for these tools, the literature began with the 'usual suspects' of agenda control and portfolio allocation, and has since gone on to list other instruments available to minority presidents. Nonetheless, despite the advances made in outlining a 'presidential toolbox', there are a number of unanswered questions with which the emerging literature needs to engage.

First, in a perfect world we would be able to say more about the *precise* conditions under which minority presidents are likely to reach for specific instruments of governance in multi-party settings. Why does one president deal with coalitional dissatisfaction by undertaking a cabinet reshuffle, while another president prefers to use pork-barrel spending instead? Why do some presidents push their constitutional agenda-setting powers (e.g. decree authority) to the very limits of legality, while others willingly abstain from draconian instruments available to them? While we have some ideas about how systemic, coalitional, and conjunctural factors may shape the broad probabilities of these outcomes, we are far from being in a position to be able to predict bounded and concrete presidential choices (i.e. the choice of tool *a*, *b*, or *c*, under conditions *x*, *y*, and *z*, at time *t*). This is admittedly an ambitious goal for theory development in the future. We suspect that the tremendous personal discretion available to presidents—not to mention the infinite combinations of presidential tools, environmental conditions, and demand-side factors within legislatures—will complicate our ability to generalize. Nevertheless, further case study research, operating with a common set of concepts and indicators pertaining to coalitional presidentialism, can begin to make some headway on this task.

Second, future research should continue to explore the extent to which the tools in the presidential toolbox are effectively interchangeable. The degree to which tools are fungible for the same purposes—and the prevailing 'exchange rates' among them in different contexts—is central to the way that the toolbox is deployed and the extent to which tools constrain or empower presidents to solve the challenges of inter-party coordination. In order to estimate how much of one tool is needed to compensate for the absence of an alternative, we would need a series of case studies, conducted in data-rich contexts, and with appropriate within-case variation over time. Scholars will require careful longitudinal analysis of cases in which fine-grained legislative data is simultaneously available not only for key tools—notably cabinet posts, budget allocations, the use of presidential decrees and vetoes, etc.—but for key outcome variables, such as legislative success rates and coalition discipline. These outcome variables can be surprisingly asymmetric across cases: legislative success rates can only be measured in cases with recorded voting, and coalition discipline can only be measured where it is possible to define, *ex ante*, the contours of the pro-presidential coalition on the assembly floor (without using observed voting patterns to arrive at this same definition). Future studies of tool substitutability, therefore, are most likely to take the form of time-series analysis of president-coalition relations in those legislatures with high levels of transparency and consistent production of individual-level voting data.

Third, future research should interrogate the impact of coalitional presidentialism on various public policy outputs. Most promising among these is a focus on what has been termed the 'cost of governing'. This research agenda has its origins not only in bargaining models and decision-making models such as Tsebelis' (2002) veto players theory (how do numbers of actors and decision points affect the probability of changing the status quo?) but also institutionalist approaches to political economy such as Persson and Tabellini's (2003) work on 'the economic effects of constitutions' (how does the design of political institutions affect economic management, public policy, and fiscal policy outcomes?). Adapting the broad insights of these literatures, we can ask to what extent coalitional presidentialism inflates the budgetary costs of day-to-day governance. For example, exploiting diachronic analysis of a data-rich case of consistent minority presidentialism, Bertholini and Pereira (2017) explore how expensive it is for Brazilian executives to share power with other parties. This study features an excellent innovation of the kind of outcome variables we need to test theory: the authors create an 'Index of Governing Costs' comprising the number of ministries created, the total expenditures by ministries, and pork allocation to individual deputies. They find that the size, heterogeneity, and portfolio disproportionality of coalitions are all associated with a higher financial cost of governing. The implication of this study, echoing Persson and Tabellini on parliamentary systems, is that coalitional choices matter for fiscal outcomes. But expenditure is not the only outcome variable that scholars of coalitional presidentialism should explore: others might include political corruption, regional policies, or human development. If the power-sharing elements of coalitional presidentialism approximate what Lijphart (2012) called the 'consensus' model of democracy, then logically coalitional presidentialism should generate superior welfare outcomes to majoritarian presidentialism, and variation in power-sharing patterns should be reflected in variation in human development.

The high discretion of *formateurs* over power-sharing arrangements is matched by their ability to reshape the very office they occupy. This brings us to a fourth element of a promising research agenda: the beginnings of new work on the 'core executive'. Until the 2000s, political science work on the institutional presidency—that is, presidential organization and staffing, the presidential advisory system, and the agencies and units that directly support the work of the presidency—was basically restricted to one case, the United States (for a review, see Dickinson and Lebo 2007). However, scholars such as Bonvecchi and Scartascini (2014) and Inácio and Llanos (2015) have successfully introduced the concept of the core executive to the literature on comparative presidentialism as well. A key finding of this nascent research programme is how much the interior design of the presidency reflects the coalitional or majoritarian bent of the wider political system: 'presidents adjust the format and mandate of the different agencies under their authority so as to better manage their relations with the political environment' (Inácio and Llanos 2015: 39). Majoritarian presidents with unipartisan cabinets build a unipartisan core executive, the goal of which is largely administrative; in contrast, coalitional *formateurs* redesign the institutional presidency to mirror the multi-party composition of their cabinets, while at the same time using executive staffing and agencies to strengthen the monitoring ('watchdog') function of the core executive in order to minimize agency loss (Pereira et al. 2015). Although the core executive is sometimes opaque, the literature on coalitional presidentialism needs to take seriously this broad and influential arena of executive discretion over institutional design.

Fifth, given that the literature on presidentialism has been overwhelmingly dominated by institutionalists, we continue to know very little about how presidential leadership and styles affect the management of inter-party coalitions by minority presidents.

We have little to say on this matter, because this is uncharted territory, and we see this lacuna as unlikely to be filled anytime soon. Outside the United States and perhaps France, there is virtually no tradition of conducting longitudinal within-case study of how different executives lead, govern, and otherwise shape the historical development of the presidential office; moreover, contemporary institutionalists will not touch the concept of leadership even with a 10-foot pole. There is, as yet, no comparative equivalent of Richard Neustadt's classic study ([1960] last edition 1990), which claimed that US presidential power is essentially the 'power to persuade', and that the development of this power is contingent on the president's standing with both the public (i.e. popularity) and with the political class (i.e. professional prestige). Yet our own comparative work on coalitional presidentialism in which we interviewed 357 members of parliament across nine countries in three world regions, uncovered significant evidence that parties and legislators take seriously the qualitative differences among presidents in their capacity to engage in dialogue, to share power, and to cultivate inter-party coalitions (Chaisty et al. 2018). While our findings need broader confirmation, our first reaction was that Neustadt's insights seem to travel: the power to manage coalitions is in part the power to 'persuade' current and potential partners, and this ability is contingent upon professional prestige within the political class. This first impression can be translated into more empirical research questions for the future: to what extent does the prior political experience (e.g. a more legislative or executive profile) of the *formateur* matter? Are presidents who were subnational *formateurs* (mayors, governors) better at being national *formateurs*? What sorts of political skills are required of *formateurs* in environments where party politics tends toward the clientelistic rather than toward the programmatic?

The sixth and final point on a future research agenda is the most macropolitically important: does coalitional presidentialism undermine democratic consolidation? In our cross-national work, many of the members of parliament that we talked to seemed to believe that this is the case. In every country bar Chile, a majority of legislators believe that the practice of coalition making has blurred the boundaries between opposition and ruling parties, encouraging 'opportunistic support for the government of the day' and undermining the development of coherent and distinctive party identities (Chaisty et al. 2015: 9). Along with the way in which coalitions can empower minority presidents to secure viable majorities and force through their legislative agenda, this helps to explain why a majority of parliamentarians in every country view coalitional presidentialism as a governing strategy that has 'encouraged the legislature to transfer policy-making authority to the president' (Chaisty et al. 2018: 118), undermining accountability and—according to legislators in seven of our nine cases—leading to 'a form of governance based on the exchange of favours' (Chaisty et al. 2018: 208). It is therefore unsurprising that legislators in Brazil (71 per cent) Ukraine (70 per cent), Russia (70 per cent), and Malawi (55 per cent) believe that the practice of coalitional presidentialism in their country has failed to enhance the quality of democracy. Only in Chile do we see a strong majority (87 per cent) who view coalitional presidentialism as a boon to democratic consolidation (Chaisty et al. 2015: 9).

However, while fascinating, the attitudes of members of parliament towards coalitional politics raise as many questions as they answer. One question is whether our informants are correct to believe that coalitional presidentialism reduces accountability. It could be that our legislators, all of whom operate in coalitional contexts, exaggerate the impact of coalition formation and maintenance, blaming it for a range of ills that may actually have other drivers. To rule this out, it will be necessary to collect objective indicators of legislative scrutiny and presidential ease of governance to compare our cases with similar political systems in which minority presidents seek to govern without a coalition, and those in which the president enjoys an absolute majority and so does not need to form coalitions at all. Another question is whether the negative consequences of coalitional presidentialism outweigh the positive. After all, the literature on coalitional presidentialism emerged in the first place partly to explain why multi-party presidential systems in new democracies had not collapsed into deadlock and backsliding. In other words, there is something of a tension between the academic literature, which emphasizes the way in which coalitional presidentialism resolves the 'difficult combination' of multi-party politics under the separation of powers, and the negative perception of the some of many political practitioners around the world, who argue that coalitional politics erodes checks and balances.

Of course, these two views can be reconciled if the net effect of coalitional presidentialism is to generate political regimes that last longer but at a lower quality of democracy. However, this has yet to be systematically demonstrated. Moreover, even if this does prove to be an accurate depiction of the long-term effects of coalitional presidentialism, it would leave open two possible 'end states': first, that over time the erosion of checks and balances renders these regimes particularly vulnerable to democratic reversal, undermining earlier gains from political stability; and, second, that the short-term stability generated through coalition formation facilitates long-term processes of democratic consolidation in which early teething problems are eventually overcome. Our own research suggests that both of these outcomes are feasible, and that the net effect of coalitional presidentialism varies according to the initial quality of democracy, the particular combination of the tools used by presidents, the party system, and a number of other factors such as the degree of institutionalization of political parties (on this last point, see Kellam 2015, 2017). Developing a stronger understanding the relationship between coalitional presidentialism, stability, accountability, and democratization is critical if we are to better understand the political prospects for the increasing number of countries that feature minority presidents.

21.5 Conclusion: The Coordination Paradigm as 'Grand Unification?'

The emerging literature on coalitional politics is but one example of the post-Linzian revolution in comparative presidentialism. As Escobar-Lemmon and Taylor-Robinson

(Chapter 27 in this volume) note, this is part and parcel of a growing convergence between scholars of presidentialism and scholars of parliamentarism: both groups now tend to understand executives as motivated by a common goal of extracting support from legislatures. The convergence has affected the presidential literature far more than the parliamentary literature: the former has drawn closer to the latter. In our review, we extended the intellectual history traced by Elgie (2005) and extended by Cheibub and Limongi (2010), who claim that the presidentialism literature has undergone a shift from a preoccupation with *conflict* to a preoccupation with *coordination*. These outlooks approximate mini-paradigms: they shape the questions we ask.

Why did this shift occur? Partly it was due to effective theoretical critiques of the original Linzian hypotheses, and partly it was due to an exogenous empirical trend: the rise of party fragmentation around the globe. The advent of a 'world of minority presidents' has allowed scholars to see directly elected executives in a different light, and has revealed more clearly than ever before the travails of building legislative support. In attempting to understand these travails, scholars began to view 'presidents as prime ministers' (Colomer and Negretto 2005). Scholars of presidentialism invested heavily in longstanding research programmes associated with parliamentary democracy, such as cabinet formation and termination, portfolio allocation, and coalitional politics. The literature on coalitional presidentialism, which we have reviewed and expanded in this chapter, is the best manifestation of this trend to date. Much like this *Handbook* as a whole, the coalitional presidentialism literature is a step forward toward a potential 'grand unification' of previously disparate literatures on parliamentary and presidential politics. Thanks in part to the challenges of party system fragmentation in democracies everywhere, we are closer than ever before to a single, coherent, integrated literature on comparative executive politics.

References

Alemán, E. and Tsebelis, G. (2011). 'Political Parties and Government Coalitions in the Americas,' *Journal of Politics in Latin America* 3(1): 3–28.

Alston, L. J. and Mueller, B. (2006). 'Pork for Policy: Executive and Legislative Exchange in Brazil,' *Journal of Law, Economics and Organisation* 22(1): 87–114.

Altman, D. (2000). 'The Politics of Coalition Formation and Survival in Multiparty Presidential Democracies: The Case of Uruguay, 1989–1999,' *Party Politics* 6(3): 259–83.

Ames, B. (2001). *The Deadlock of Democracy in Brazil.* Ann Arbor, MI: University of Michigan Press.

Amorim Neto, O. (2002). 'Presidential Cabinets, Electoral Cycles, and Coalition Discipline in Brazil,' in S. Morgenstern and B. Nacif (eds) *Legislative Politics in Latin America.* Cambridge: Cambridge University Press, 48–78.

Amorim Neto, O. (2006). 'The Presidential Calculus: Executive Policy Making and Cabinet Formation in the Americas,' *Comparative Political Studies* 39(4): 415–40.

Amorim Neto, O. and Santos, F. (2011). 'The Executive Connection: Presidentially Defined Factions and Party Discipline in Brazil,' *Dados* 44(2): 291–321, http://www.scielo.br/scielo.php?pid=S0011-52582001000200003&script=sci_arttext

Arana Araya, Ignacio. (2015). 'Budgetary Negotiations: How the Chilean Congress Overcomes its Constitutional Limits,' *Journal of Legislative Studies* 21(2): 213–31.

Arriola, L. (2009). 'Patronage and Political Stability in Africa,' *Comparative Political Studies* 42(10): 1339–62.

Beliaev, M. V. (2006). 'Presidential Powers and Consolidation of New Postcommunist Democracies,' *Comparative Political Studies* 39(3): 375–98.

Bertholini, F. and Pereira, C. (2017). 'Pagando o preço de governar. Custos de gerência de coalizão no presidencialismo brasileiro,' *Revista de Administração Pública* 51(4): 528–50.

Bonvecchi, A. and Scartascini, C. (2014). 'The Presidency and the Executive Branch in Latin America: What We Know and What We Need to Know,' *Latin American Politics and Society* 56(1): 144–65.

Camerlo, M. and Pérez-Liñán, A. (2015). 'The Politics of Minister Retention in Presidential Systems: Technocrats, Partisans, and Government Approval,' *Comparative Politics* 47(3): 315–33.

Chaisty, P. and Chernykh, S. (2017). 'How Do Minority Presidents Manage Multiparty Coalitions? Identifying and Analyzing the Payoffs to Coalition Parties in Presidential System,' *Political Research Quarterly* 70(4): 762–77.

Chaisty, P., Cheeseman, N., and Power, T. J. (2014). 'Rethinking the "Presidentialism Debate": Coalitional Politics in Cross-Regional Perspective,' *Democratization* 21(1): 72–94.

Chaisty, P., Cheeseman, N., and Power, T. J. (2015). 'The Coalitional Presidentialism Project Research Report: How MPs Understand Coalitional Politics in Presidential Systems,' Available from: https://www.politics.ox.ac.uk/materials/publications/15239/ccp-research-report.pdf (accessed on 8 September 2018).

Chaisty, P., Cheeseman, N., and Power, T. J (2018). *Coalitional Presidentialism in Comparative Perspective: Minority Presidents in Multiparty Systems*. Oxford: Oxford University Press.

Cheeseman, N. (2015). *Democracy in Africa: Successes, Failures, and the Struggle for Political Reform*. New York: Cambridge University Press.

Cheibub, J. A. (2007). *Presidentialism, Parliamentarism, and Democracy*. New York: Cambridge University Press.

Cheibub, J. A. and Limongi, F. (2010). 'From Conflict to Coordination: Perspectives on the Study of Executive-Legislative Relations,' *Revista Iberoamericana de Estudos Legislativos* (RIEL) 1(1): 38–53.

Cheibub, J. A., Przeworski, A., and Saiegh, S. M. (2004). 'Government Coalitions and Legislative Success under Presidentialism and Parliamentarism,' *British Journal of Political Science* 34(4): 565–87.

Colomer, J. and Negretto, G. (2005). 'Can Presidentialism Work Like Parliamentarism?,' *Government and Opposition* 40: 60–89.

Dickinson, M. J. and Lebo, M. J. (2007). 'Reexamining the Growth of the Institutional Presidency, 1940–2000,' *Journal of Politics* 69: 206–19.

Elgie, R. (2005). 'From Linz to Tsebelis: Three Waves of Presidential/Parliamentary Studies?,' *Democratization* 12(1): 106–22.

Erdmann, G. and Engel, U. (2007). 'Neopatrimonialism Reconsidered: Critical Review and Elaboration of an Elusive Concept,' *Commonwealth & Comparative Politics* 45(1): 95–119.

Fish, M. S. (1997). 'The Pitfalls of Russian Superpresidentialism,' *Current History* 96: 326.

Gaylord, S. and Rennó, L. (2015). 'Opening the Black Box: Cabinet Authorship of Legislative Proposals in a Multiparty Presidential System,' *Presidential Studies Quarterly* 45(2): 247–69.

Helmke, G. and Levitsky, S. (2006) (eds). *Informal Institutions and Democracy: Lessons from Latin America*. Baltimore: Johns Hopkins University Press.

Huntington, S. P. (1991). *The Third Wave: Democratization in the Late Twentieth Century*. Oklahoma: University of Oklahoma Press.

Inácio, M. and Llanos, M. (2015). 'The Institutional Presidency from a Comparative Perspective: Argentina and Brazil since the 1980s', *Brazilian Political Science Review* 9(1): 39–64.

Jones, M.P. (1995) (ed.). *Electoral Laws and the Survival of Presidential Democracies*. Michigan: University of Michigan.

Kawamura, K. (2013). 'President Restrained: Effects of Parliamentary Rule and Coalition Government on Indonesia's Presidentialism', in Y. Kasuya (ed) *Presidents, Assemblies, and Policy Making in Asia*. New York: Palgrave, 156–93.

Kellam, M. (2015). 'Parties for Hire: How Particularistic Parties Influence Presidents' Governing Strategies', *Party Politics* 21(4): 515–26.

Kellam, M. (2017). 'Why Pre-electoral Coalitions in Presidential Systems?', *British Journal of Political Science* 47(2): 391–411.

Kuhn, T. S. (1962). *The Structure of Scientific Revolutions*. Chicago: University of Chicago Press.

Linz, J. J. (1990). 'The Perils of Presidentialism', *Journal of Democracy* 1(1): 51–69.

Lijphart, A. (2012). *Patterns of Democracy: Government Forms and Performance in Thirty-Six Countries*. 2nd ed. New Haven, Yale University Press.

Mainwaring, S. (1993). 'Presidentialism, Multipartism, and Democracy: The Difficult Combination', *Comparative Political Studies* 26(2): 198–228.

Mainwaring, S., and Shugart, M. S. (1997). 'Conclusion: Presidentialism and the Party System', in Scott Mainwaring and Matthew Soberg Shugart (eds) *Presidentialism and Democracy in Latin America*. Cambridge: Cambridge University Press, 394–437.

Martínez-Gallardo, C. (2012). 'Out of the Cabinet: What Drives Defections from the Government in Presidential Systems?', *Comparative Political Studies* 45(1): 62–90.

Meireles, F. (2016). 'Oversized Government Coalitions in Latin America', *Brazilian Political Science Review* 10(3).

Mejía Acosta, A. (2006). 'Crafting Legislative Ghost Coalitions in Ecuador: Informal Institutions and Economic Reform in an Unlikely Case', in G. Helmke and S. Levitsky (eds) *Informal Institutions and Democracy: Lessons from Latin America*. Baltimore: Johns Hopkins University Press, 69–84.

Mietzner, M. (2016). 'Coercing Loyalty: Coalitional Presidentialism and Party Politics in Jokowi's Indonesia', *Contemporary Southeast Asia: A Journal of International and Strategic Affairs* 38(2): 209–32.

Neustadt, R. E. ([1960] 1990). *Presidential Power and the Modern Presidents: The Politics of Leadership from Roosevelt to Reagan*. New York: The Free Press.

Opalo, K. O. (2011). 'Ethnicity and Elite Coalitions: The Origins of 'Big Man' Presidentialism in Africa', Working Paper: http://ssrn.com/abstract=1853744.

Pereira, C. and Mueller, B. (2004). 'The Cost of Governing: Strategic Behavior of the President and Legislators in Brazil's Budgetary Process', *Comparative Political Studies* 37(7): 781–815.

Pereira, C., Power, T. J., and Rennó, L. (2005). 'Under What Conditions Do Presidents Resort to Decree Power? Theory and Evidence from the Brazilian Case', *Journal of Politics* 67(1): 178–200.

Pereira, C., Praça, S., Batista, M. and Lopez, F. (2015). 'A nomeação de secretários-exeuctivos e o monitoramento da coalizão no presidencialismo brasileiro', in F. Lopez Garcia (ed) *Cargos de Confiança no Presidencialismo de Coalizão Brasileiro*. Brasilia: IPEA, 139–66.

Persson, T. and Tabellini, G. (2003). *The Economic Effects of Constitutions*. Cambridge, MA: MIT Press.

Power, T. J. (2010). 'Optimism, Pessimism, and Coalitional Presidentialism: Debating the Institutional Design of Brazilian Democracy,' *Bulletin of Latin American Research* 29(1): 18–33.

Prempeh, H. K. (2008). 'Presidents Untamed,' *Journal of Democracy* 19(2): 109–23.

Protsyk, O. (2004). 'Ruling With Decrees: Presidential Decree Making in Russia and Ukraine,' *Europe-Asia Studies* 56(5): 637–60.

Raile, E., Pereira, C., and Power, T. J. (2011). 'The Executive Toolbox: Building Legislative Support in a Multiparty Presidential Regime,' *Political Research Quarterly* 64(2): 323–34.

Remington, T. F., Smith, S. S. and Haspel, M. (1998). 'Decrees, Laws, and Inter-branch Relations in the Russian Federation,' *Post-Soviet Affairs* 14(4): 287–322.

Saiegh, S. M. (2011). *Ruling by Statute: How Uncertainty and Vote Buying Shape Lawmaking*. New York: Cambridge University Press.

Samuels, D. and Shugart, M. S. (2010). *Presidents, Parties, and Prime Ministers: How the Separation of Powers Affects Party Organization and Behavior*. New York: Cambridge University Press.

Shugart, M. S., and Carey, J. M. (1992). *Presidents and Assemblies: Constitutional Design and Electoral Dynamics*. Cambridge: Cambridge University Press.

Siavelis, P. (2006). 'Accommodating Informal Institutions and Chilean Democracy,' in G. Helmke and S. Levitsky (eds) *Informal Institutions and Democracy: Lessons from Latin America*. Baltimore: Johns Hopkins University Press, 33–55.

Slater, D. (2018). 'Party Cartelization, Indonesian-Style: Presidential Powersharing and the Contingency of Democratic Opposition,' *Journal of East Asian Studies* 18(1): 23–46.

Slater, D. and Simmons, E. (2013). 'Coping by Colluding: Political Uncertainty and Promiscuous Power-sharing in Bolivia and Indonesia,' *Comparative Political Studies* 46(11): 1366–93.

Stepan, A. (1978). 'Political Leadership and Regime Breakdown: Brazil,' in J. Linz and A. Stepan (eds) *The Breakdown of Democratic Regimes: Latin America*. Baltimore: Johns Hopkins University Press, 110–37.

Stepan, A. and Skach, C. (1993). 'Constitutional Frameworks and Democratic Consolidation: Parliamentarianism versus Presidentialism,' *World Politics* 46(1): 1–22.

Tsebelis, G. (2002). *Veto Players: How Political Institutions Work*. Princeton: Princeton University Press.

Tsebelis, G. and Rizova, T. (2007). 'Presidential Conditional Agenda Setting in the Former Communist Countries,' *Comparative Political Studies* 40(10): 1155–82.

Valenzuela, A. (1978). *The Breakdown of Democratic Regimes: Chile*. Baltimore: Johns Hopkins University Press.

CHAPTER 22

CABINET DECISION-MAKING IN PARLIAMENTARY SYSTEMS

MICHELANGELO VERCESI

22.1 Introduction: The Research Field

THIS chapter focuses on the internal decision-making process of *national* cabinet governments. In particular, three aspects will be analysed: (1) how cabinets and cabinet decision-making have been conceptualized; (2) how cabinet decision-making can take shape and its possible variations; (3) the main factors affecting cabinet decision-making procedures. Henceforth, cabinet decision-making means the process through which executive cabinets reach their final governmental outputs. What happens after an executive has taken a decision—for example, in the parliament—is not taken into account.

Cabinet decision-making is a worthy research topic in a twofold sense. On the one hand, political outputs are crucial for the smooth functioning of any political system. Although trends such privatization, decentralization, and globalization have 'hollowed out' governments' prerogatives, executives remain the most central institutions with the power to take authoritative decisions valid for all citizens (Andeweg 2003: 39–40). In this regard, cabinets stand out, since governmental final decisions eventually pass through it. The need for joint ratification—and not the assumption that all decisions are taken together—is the typical feature of cabinet government (Blondel and Manning 2002: 468). The second reason to investigate cabinet decision-making refers in particular to democratic theory. In terms of accountability, understanding how governmental decisions are taken and who is actually in charge provides heuristic shortcuts to evaluate elected politicians. These clues are especially valuable in case of coalition governments, when inter-party bargaining and compromises make the identification of political responsibilities harder (Martin and Vanberg 2008, 2014; Müller and Meyer 2010).

One of the most tackled issues in cabinet decision-making literature is the extent to which prime ministers or other actors are prominent and able to lead the process. Building on this and looking at the ways power is exerted, cabinets have been clustered into a few models or types. While several theoretical and empirical researches have been made in this respect, there has been a relative paucity of systematic and multi-factorial explanations, although recent rational-choice analyses have partially filled the gap (see also Chapter 5 in this volume). As it will be argued in the following pages, several suggestions can be however found in the literature, with potential for more comprehensive explanatory studies.

For this chapter's purposes, the analysis is limited to parliamentary democracies (Samuels and Shugart 2010: 26–7). Here, democracy is understood as a political regime where rulers obtain political power through free and competitive elections *and* constitutional provisions (either written or unwritten) constrain the power of the same rulers (Dahl 1971).

In parliamentary systems of government, the cabinet is a collective political body, which comprises a prime minister and only a few apical ministers, usually called senior ministers. However, other figures are often involved in the cabinet decision-making process; Rhodes et al. (2009: 108) have for example suggested seeing cabinet decision-making 'as a set of expanding circles', where 'the prime minister is the core' and the borders extend beyond the full cabinet. For this reason, this analysis embraces the broader notion of cabinet system. As pointed out by Blondel (2001: 12), in this system the actions of the prime minister and senior ministers are intertwined with those of executive (either political or administrative) figures that are out of the cabinet—such as junior ministers and top civil servants—as well as of party prominents outside the government and personal advisers.

In the next section, the main concepts, questions, and debates that have characterized the scholarship on cabinet decision-making are presented. A review of how the literature has responded and of provided explanations follows. Before entering conclusions, section 22.4 stresses the existing deficits and proposes outlooks for future research.

22.2 Concepts and Debates

22.2.1 Definitions of Cabinet Government and Research Questions

One major issue scholars have focused on is the conceptualization of cabinet government. In this regard, the perhaps most detailed account remains Weller (2003), where the author identifies five approaches in the literature, each based on 'a different set of assumptions about the significant features of cabinet' (Weller 2003: 704). Legal traditions treats the cabinet as a focus where constitutional principles of ministerial responsibility and political accountability are (or should be) fulfilled. Public administration and public policy approaches see instead cabinets, respectively, as regulated administrative institutions and forums to take policy decisions. A more political science-oriented approach conceives of the cabinet as an arena for power struggles between political actors. Finally, cabinet can be considered as a system of government; in this case, the focus is not on cabinet proper, rather on the executive institutional web the cabinet is placed in (Weller 2003: 704–8). Moreover, a sixth interpretation presents cabinet government as a forum for the representation of different societal interests. In this regard, Rhodes et al. (2009: 109) have pointed out that these interests can be strictly political or territorial too, especially in ethnically and linguistically fragmented countries such as Canada (see also Chapter 6 in this volume).

Putting the contributions of these conceptual perspectives together, the cabinet results to be a set of institutional actors (political science approach), a set of structures performing given functions (legal, policy, and representational approaches) or a set of governmental procedures and arrangements (public administration and systemic approaches). Actor-centred perspectives differentiate between government members, based on held departmental and/or other political resources, and see the cabinet as a narrow political 'club' (Blondel 1999; Barbieri and Vercesi 2013). To some extent, this definition is reminiscent of Bagehot's (1968: 9, 11) idea of cabinet as 'a committee' or 'a board of control' of prominent political personalities. In functional terms, the cabinet would be instead defined by the functions it performs: typically, implementation of rules (Almond 1960) and policy-making coordination (e.g. Rhodes and Dunleavy 1995). Andeweg (1997: 59, 2003: 40) has criticized such definition, by stressing its vagueness and the *a priori* choice of what is the main defining function. Moreover, one can argue that this way of proceeding does not provide a proper definition; rather it posits a research question, because only empirical investigation can tell who fulfils a given function (Barbieri and Vercesi 2013: 527–8). Finally, the third definition assumes that cabinets are different from other institutional branches because of their own specific working procedures. In this regard, it has however been observed that governmental institutions are 'multiprocedural' and that thus the concept is hard to be clarified in this way (King 1975: 179).

A further conceptual issue discussed by the empirical literature is concerned with the question of when cabinets' life starts and when it terminates. In this regard, Laver (2003: 27) has observed that scholars often adopt definitions which are 'influenced by the availability of convenient datasets'. A widely accepted definition is that a cabinet terminates when: a general election occurs, the prime minister changes, and/or the cabinet party composition changes. An alternative common definition adds government (accepted) resignations as a fourth criterion (Laver and Schofield 1990: 145–7; Woldendorp et al. 2000: 10–11; Damgaard 2008: 302–3). In both cases the assumption is that cabinets end when there is a change in their bargaining environment. However, definitions of cabinet are 'not given; [they depend…] on […] choices made by the researcher that may well have a significant effect on results. And these choices will inevitably be conditioned by the theoretical concerns of the analyst' (Laver 2003: 26).

Over the years the aforementioned conceptualizations of cabinet have led scholars to ask a few main recurring questions: (1) 'who decides?'; (2) 'how are decisions taken?'; (3) 'what does decision-making process depend on?'.

22.2.2 Prime Ministerial Government and Core Executive

Usually, investigations of cabinet decision-making have been based on a certain idea of power distribution and/or resource allocation within the governmental institution at issue (however defined). A straightforward distinction is that between cabinets where the prime minister is prominent and cabinets where all ministers, prime minister included, are on an equal footing with respect to their say in the process. The foundations of the 'prime ministerial vs. cabinet government' debate were set in the 1960s by Mackintosh (1962) and Crossman (1963, 1972) for framing British politics. Their argument was that the cabinet as the materialization of the principle of collective government was not fitting anymore with the reality of modern executives. In contrast, a new form of prime ministerial government would have taken place, due to trends such as mediatization and political personalization: prime ministers would be the actors who actually set the agenda and steer cabinet decisions. By looking at several indicators of strength and political constraints, Jones (1964) scaled down the prime ministerial impact. Other scholars, such as Gordon Walker (1970), followed in his steps. As stated by Weller (2014: 491), 'the problem with the debate was that it often seemed to contrast prime-ministerial government with cabinet government, as though the two were polar opposites. They never were'. Prime ministers are embedded into cabinets and their 'tactics change to suit circumstance and personality' (Weller 2003: 712).

Between the 1990s and 2000s, the discussion about the increasing importance of prime ministers over cabinets was revitalized by the advocates of the presidentialization thesis (see Chapter 18 in this volume). Prime ministers—this is the core argument—are becoming more similar to presidents in presidential systems in their freedom of action, although the institutional settings remain parliamentary. Prime ministers—in fact—would have acquired a greater control over ministerial careers and policy guidelines, backed by influential centralized staff. Moreover, they would be more prominent as leaders within their own parties and dominate electoral campaigns (Foley 1993, 2000; Poguntke and Webb 2005). As was with the former juxtaposition, this argumentation has stimulated harsh criticisms. Focusing on American, British, and German heads of government, Helms (2005: 259) has reached the conclusion that 'there is rather limited evidence of presidentialization', an empirical finding later recognized by Rhodes (2008: 328–9) in his account of parliamentary executives. Dowding (2013: 632) has put into question the very viability of the concept of presidentialization. 'There has been a growing centralisation of policy and a growing personalisation of politics. These processes have been occurring in all countries [...]. We should not mistake these institutional and social forces for presidentialisation'.

At least in its first phase, the debate whether prime ministers are (becoming) more important or not has been a domain of traditional—or 'old'—institutionalism. The focus has been on how governmental structures affect the role of prime ministers in parliamentary systems; analyses have been poorly theoretical and methodologically unsound. More recent contributions have extended the focus to the role of agency and incorporated lessons from 'new institutionalism', such as the broader notion of institutions comprising informal rules (Helms 2014: 198–9; see also Chapter 3 in this volume). For example, one can mention the attempts of modelling the connections between prime ministerial authority and cabinet's functioning of rational choice scholars (Dewan and Hortala-Vallve 2011; Dewan et al. 2015).

Dissatisfied with the rigidity of the 'prime ministerial vs. cabinet' framework and its incapability to promote advancements in the knowledge of cabinet governance, Dunleavy and Rhodes (1990) sought to provide a new conceptual framework for comparative studies in an article of 1990. Here, the two authors introduced the concept of 'core executive': 'all those organizations and structures which primarily serve to pull together and integrate central government policies, or act as final arbiters within the executive of conflicts between different elements of the government machine' (Dunleavy and Rhodes 1990: 4). As a result, the attention shifted from the core ministerial group to a larger set of actors, whose borders can change contingently and depending on who performs given tasks, including civil servants and personal advisors. The conceptual boundaries were later even more blurred by Rhodes' (2013) concept of 'court politics',[1] which prompts to disentangle the everyday life of governmental networks by observing traditions, beliefs, and practices. Perhaps because older or because more able to travel across countries, the core executive notion has proved more successful than the court politics', at least in terms of number of applications for empirical analyses (e.g. Smith 1999; Wright and Hayward 2000; Marsh et al. 2001; Hayward and Wright 2002). In core executive studies, power relations are not understood as part of a static zero-sum game: power is relational and contingent and 'actors within the centre are dependent on each other' (Smith 2000: 25). Within the core executive strand of literature, different sub-approaches developed (Elgie 2011). Some scholars have argued that specific institutional and party roles provide specific locational power resources (Heffernan 2003; Barbieri and Vercesi 2013). Finally, Helms (2017) has proposed keeping in the analysis of prime ministerial influence the concept of 'negative resource', that is, 'a constraint successfully transformed into a positive source that may benefit the status and performance of a leader' (Helms 2017: 6).

Although subject to different uses, core executive has become a *passe-partout* term for the study of government decision-making. The other side of the coin of this development

---

[1] However, the label can be found also in earlier works. Hayward and Wright (2002: 61) had employed it to depict the inner executive circle of French politics.

has been that '[t]he debate about prime ministerial vs. cabinet government [...] has been relegated to academic history' (Elgie 2011: 64).

22.3 RESPONSES AND EXPLANATIONS

Empirical analyses have provided evidence of significant variations of cabinet decision-making procedures and styles in time and space. Scholarship offers either extensive historical reconstructions of single-country tendencies (e.g. Jennings 1959; James 1999; Weller 2007; Woodall 2014) or comparative (mostly single-chapter) studies (e.g. Blondel and Müller-Rommel 1993, 1997, 2001; Laver and Shepsle 1994a; Müller and Strøm 2000; Strøm et al. 2003; Blondel et al. 2007).

Information about empirical variabilities has been ordered by scholars through interpretative taxonomies and typologies of cabinet decision-making. While the former simply systemize—based on given criteria—the reality into models (Sartori 1975), the latter logically derive types from the intersection of analytical dimensions.

22.3.1 Forms of Cabinet Decision-Making and Conflict Management

The literature has mostly resorted to three classificatory criteria for isolating models of cabinet decision-making: the role of cabinet members; the *locus* of the process; and the presence of external political constraints.[2] The broadest academic consensus is perhaps on the possible existence of ministerial and bureaucratic governments, in addition to the classic prime ministerial and cabinet government models[3] (e.g. O'Leary 1991; Laver and Shepsle 1994b; Rhodes 1995; Elgie 1997; Keman 2006). The distinctive traits of ministerial government are that ministers are autonomous when they take decisions into their departmental jurisdiction and only limited interministerial coordination occurs. The extreme version of this model is Laver and Shepsle's (1990: 888, 1996) well-known idea of ministers as 'policy dictators' within their own policy field. On the other hand, the bureaucratic model provides for a decision-making process that develops peculiarly in civil servants' offices. Both Rhodes (1995) and Elgie (1997) have argued that the cabinet system may be organized around models of segmented government—when in the cabinet there is a functional division of labour according to policy areas—and models of shared power between a couple of prominent figures, being the prime minister usually part of. Laver and Shepsle (1994b) have also suggested that legislative governments are those constrained by the legislature, whereas party governments 'are

---

[2] A fourth criteria used is the decision-making style. Müller-Rommel (1988: 187–9) has related it to the type of decision; Campbell (1980: 85–6) and Weller (2003: 712–13) to the tactics of prime ministers.

[3] Sometimes different authors use different labels for the same models.

subject to the discipline of well-organized political parties' (Laver and Shepsle 1994b: 7). Finally, Hallerberg (2004) has used the phrase commitment government for those situations in which written government programmes are the source of constraint. It is interesting noting that, some time before these classifications were put forward, other scholars had already distinguished between arenas of cabinet decision-making, thus focusing in particular on the second classificatory criterion (Mackie and Hogwood 1985; Baylis 1989: 145).

The first attempt to employ proper dimensions for the analysis dates earlier than these models. In a working paper of 1988, Blondel (1988) tried to isolate types of decision-making, based on possible combinations between the degree of (external) party control, the role of the prime minister, and the participation of ministers. Some scholars (Elgie 1997; Barbieri 2003; Vercesi 2012a) have criticized the inclusion of the first dimension, claiming that it is external to cabinets and that internal dynamics should be studied irrespective of institutional autonomy. One can see in the other two dimensions the embryos of those around which all the main subsequent typologies have been built: the *internal distribution of power* and the *centralization of the decision-making process*. Unlike taxonomies of decision-making, typologies keep these aspects analytically separated and conceive of them as continua (Andeweg 1997: 61).

A seminal systematization of these dimensions has been made by Andeweg (1993). The author has stressed that collegiality (i.e. equal say in the process) and collectivity (i.e. joint decision-making) are conceptually different and that different combinations lead to different types of decision-making. In particular, Andeweg (1993) has claimed that—based on who actually decides—a cabinet can be prime ministerial (or mono-cratic), oligarchical, or truly collegial; in this regard, an inner cabinet would be '[t]he indicator par excellence of an oligarchical cabinet system' (Andeweg 1993: 28). Second, he has argued that the decision-making process may be fragmented when decisions are taken within ministries; segmented if the process is carried on by smaller groups, such as cabinet committees; and collective, especially when decisions are taken in the full cabinet meeting. According to Andeweg (1993: 29–30), segmentation can be moreover distinguished in partisan and sectoral, based on the nature of the lines of divisions between groups. Twelve types ensue from this framework.

Direct or indirect references to the two dimensions may be found in several later theoretical and empirical works (e.g. James 1994; Burch and Holliday 1996; Andeweg 1997, 2003; Aucoin 1999; Helms 2005). It has also been observed that, by distinguishing between strong prime ministers, weak prime ministers, and heads of government with a medium degree of influence within the cabinet (King 1994; O'Malley 2007), oligarchies may be with prime minister or acephalous. Only in the former case, the prime minister is strong enough to be included in the leading circle, but not so strong to exercise a monocratic leadership (Vercesi 2012a).

Comparative evidence has highlighted that the full cabinet is only seldom a true decision-making arena. Rather, it operates as a 'rubber stamp' of decisions taken elsewhere or as a 'court of appeal' for unsatisfied ministers. Often, both formal and informal interministerial meetings are the main arenas for the decisive talks. In these venues, strong prime ministers can lead more collective discussions. In contrast, when the process is fragmented, monocratic leadership is exerted through bilateral meetings. Cabinets characterized by fragmented decision-making processes and dispersal of power, on their turn, approach the ministerial model. It should be observed that cabinets where the prime minister is a fully-fledged *primus inter pares*, the power distribution is collegial, and the process is strongly inclusive are the exception, rather than the norm. Finally, it is not uncommon that civil servants and personal advisers impact directly on the process, especially during phases of preparation and technical definition of the governmental outputs (Blondel and Müller-Rommel 1993; Blondel and Manning 2002: 458).

These typologies are tailored to purely parliamentary systems. However, they prove to be flexible enough to be extended to situations of presidential dominance in semi-presidential countries (e.g. Helms 2005). Overall, typologies of cabinet decision-making are heuristic devices for framing processes' variations and understanding why some practices are more common in some cabinets, rather than others. Nonetheless, a disadvantage is that, while these frameworks provide pictures of the structural conditions that shape decision-making, they do not account for the dynamic aspect of the process' unfolding (Andeweg 2003: 48). Political conditions and decision-making mechanisms of coordination define the game-field for the settlement of policy disagreements and the accommodation of divergent preferences (Goetz 2003: 79). Deviations from smooth decision-making and the respective impact on cabinet dynamics have been the focus of the literature on intra-executive conflict management.

Presenting his typology of cabinets, Andeweg (1993: 39) underlined the importance of the internal level of conflict as a third dimension to understand cabinet decision-making processes. In this context, Marangoni and Vercesi (2015) have suggested distinguishing between four categories of conflicts, from the least to the most detrimental ones for smooth decision-making and cabinet stability (all else equal): intra-party conflicts; inter-departmental conflicts; conflicts between party and governments; and inter-party conflicts. The dangerousness of inter-party conflicts would be due to the fact that parties are what constitutes the coalition.

In particular from the 2000s, scholars have sought to pinpoint the structural mechanisms used to manage intra-executive conflicts in parliamentary systems. A framework for coalition governments has been put forward by Andeweg and Timmermans (2008). These authors look at the arenas for conflict resolution and group them into three main classes (1) internal arenas, if only senior and junior ministers (and possibly their personal advisers) attend meetings; (2) mixed arenas, when both government and non-government members gather; (3) external arenas in case that only actors who are outside the government—for example, external party leaders and civil servants—meet to manage the conflict. More than during times of uncontroversial decision-making, non-government actors enter the process (e.g. Müller and Strøm 2000; Miller and Müller 2010). Andeweg and Timmermans (2008) have argued that six arenas are at stake (inner cabinets; cabinet committees; coalition committees; committees of ministers and parliamentary leaders; meetings of parliamentary leaders; party summits). Further detected arenas have been the full cabinet and bilateral contacts, which can fall in all categories, depending on who is involved. In this respect, actors with a major role in the process are the prime minister; ministers; party leaders; leaders of party factions; parliamentary leaders. Overall, empirical data on Western Europe tells that usually conflict management occurs in more internal arenas and prime ministers have a significant impact on the process (Vercesi 2016).

22.3.2 Explanations of Cabinet Decision-Making and Conflict Management

The literature on cabinet decision-making has provided explanations of three broad related aspects: the structural and agential conditions of the process; the potential for conflict of the process; the mechanisms and dynamics of conflict resolution.[4]

With regard to the first aspect, it is possible to find two clusters of explaining factors. One the one hand, scholars have focused on resources and styles of single actors; on the other hand, attention has been payed to idiosyncratic traditions and administrative 'cultures' of political systems (Müller-Rommel 1988, 2001: 198–201). The resource-oriented approach is especially used to explain the internal distribution of power within cabinets. As pointed out by Helms (2017: 2), the term resource can mean political-institutional resource or personal resource, being the latter some particular attributed or acquired trait. A prime minister is assumed to be stronger when he or she is also party leader, when only one party is in government, and when the cabinet can muster a disciplined party majority in parliament. Moreover, a prominent position in the largest party of the government coalition is a further possible source of strength (Vercesi 2012b: 273; Martocchia Diodati et al. 2018). It is also worth noting that a prime minister (or a head of state) can benefit from the resources associated to his or her office, such as consequential supporting staff (e.g. Peters et al. 2000). Symmetrically, political actors may face power constraints. For example, a high level of party factionalization may undermine the ability of party leaders to set the guidelines in the party (Baylis 1989: 86). Alongside party constraints, Jones (1991) has argued that the dispersal of power between institutional levels of government limits the influence of prime ministers. Moreover, some personalities can hinder chances of prime ministerial impact over policy (Brummer 2016). Gender may be another variable. In this regard, empirical comparisons between male and female prime ministers have shown that being women can lead to higher instability in office (Müller-Rommel and Vercesi 2017, see also Chapter 13 in this volume). Some authors have suggested that prime ministerial power is the result of interplay between institutional resources and personal attitude towards the exploitation of these resources (Theakston 2002; Heffernan 2003; Kaarbo 2008; Bennister 2012; Strangio et al. 2013). In this sense, agency mediates structures' effect. These resource-oriented arguments

---

[4] Explanations of outputs are here excluded.

mostly refer to prime ministers. However, they present logical implications about other executive members. Like in a system of communicating vessels, cabinet ministers will be stronger vis-à-vis the prime minister when the resources of the head of government are scarce. Power in cabinet system would be positional *and* relational, since prime minister's own actual clout ultimately depends on the contrasting clout of other members (Helms 2017: 3–5). Thus, collegial cabinets limit the individual room for manoeuvre (Blondel and Manning 2002); one can think of coalition governments where party leaders counterbalance each other and oligarchical distributions of power are likely to form (Barbieri and Vercesi 2013: 533–4). Coalitions are motivated to encourage ministerial autonomy, as far as departmental decisions fall within the bounds set by coalition partners. This 'constrained ministerial government' is expected to help compromise over unanticipated issues (Dragu and Laver 2019). However, coalition agreements can constrain ministers and increase prime ministerial oversight over cabinets' works (Moury 2013).

Party factors may foster or restrain the recourse to collective decision-making venues. Based on a cross-country survey of Western Europe, Frognier (1993: 70–1) has concluded that coalitions provide more opportunities for inclusive processes and that large coalitions are more prone to using formal arenas, rather than informal meetings. Thiébault (1993: 89) has stated that both intra- and inter-party fragmentation leads to decentralized decision-making. However, the impact of the distinction between single-party and coalition cabinets is overall circumscribed (Blondel and Müller-Rommel 1993). It has been noticed that ministerial autonomy may ensue from administrative traditions and/or intra-executive hierarchical interactions; at the same time, constitutional emphasis on the principle of collective ministerial responsibility is conducive to centralization (Thiébault 1993: 88–9). Comparing some Westminster and European continental systems, Andeweg (1997: 77–82) has found moreover that neo-corporatism and tight ministerial connections to interest groups facilitate cabinet decision-making departmentalization; symmetrically, the claim for representation of interests other than those of ministerial portfolios boosts centralized practices. This holds, for example, for territorial, ethnic, and/or linguistic interests. A similar effect is played by the generalist character of ministers' competences. Finally, the search for policy coherence may call for collective decision-making as well (Rhodes et al. 2009: 102).

The so far reviewed explanatory argumentations refer to situations of 'normal' decision-making. The research strand on conflict management has provided specific explanations of cabinet strain and conflict resolution procedures. The focus is primarily on conflicts between coalition parties. The reason appears twofold: first, inter-party conflicts are posited to be the most serious for cabinet survival; second, it is possible to extend—*mutatis mutandis*—findings' logic from coalitions to single-party cabinets. Indeed, intra-party politics can be understood as a 'coalitional game' between party factions (Laver and Shepsle 1999).

The emergence of conflicts in cabinets can modify the way in which cabinet members reach their joint decisions. A first finding is that coalition agreements do not prevent conflicts, but they restrict the area of the discussed issues (e.g. Timmermans and

Moury 2006). Second, conflicts are supposed to emerge less over routine issues, which are usually handled autonomously by ministers within their own department (Blondel and Manning 2002: 467; Vercesi 2016: 180). From a broader perspective, Tsebelis (2002) has also argued that ideologically heterogeneous coalitions are more likely to be conducive to decision-making gridlocks. In a multidimensional political space of competition, indeed, coalition partners are veto players within the government, whose decisions needs unanimity. Policy change will be possible only if the status quo is external to the governmental Pareto set (the area circumscribed by the boundary that connects each party's ideal policy points) and if the change takes the status quo closer to the Pareto set itself. Policy stalemate can derive from the fact that intra-coalition polarization makes the Pareto set larger and thus increases the likelihood that the status quo is placed inside it. As a matter of fact, empirical research has found that, when the number of coalitional veto players increases, even larger coalition partners lose decision-making influence (Green-Pedersen et al. 2018).

With regard to the salience of conflicts, Andeweg and Timmermans (2008: 276) have assumed that more serious conflicts are likely to occur when coalition partners have divergent preferences on the content of valued decisions. More specifically, it has been argued that this kind of disputes fosters rigid party behaviours, undermining the expected cooperation of joint decision-making. Radicalization, moreover, would be more pursued by those parties with a higher strategic strength within the coalition (Vercesi 2016). A study of Italian coalitions has shown that inter-departmental conflicts concern policy issues invariably. Conflicts involving parties are instead more likely to be related to cabinet structure and coalitional equilibria when the cabinet does not form in the aftermath of a general election. Moreover, this study has found that prime ministers with a programmatic electoral mandate play a more active role in the policy making than those who enter office after inter-term cabinet crises and new inter-party negotiations (Marangoni and Vercesi 2015: 26–7).

With regard to the analysis of conflict management processes in cabinets, an empirical inquiry of the determinants of resolution mechanisms is in the already cited Andeweg and Timmermans (2008). In their longitudinal comparison of Western European countries, the authors have resorted to both general statistical analyses and deeper case studies of Dutch and Irish governments. Overall, they have found that comprehensive coalition agreements, party fragmentation, parliamentary polarization, and negative parliamentarism increase the likelihood of the use of internal arenas. However, the externalization of the decision-making process has proved to be especially fostered by the high dangerousness of conflicts and—first and foremost—by the absence of party leaders in the cabinet. Party leaders seem to be the major players of conflict management and, thus, even the most serious conflicts will be taken to internal cabinet arenas when party prominents are ministers (see also Marangoni and Vercesi 2015). These results echo those of a pilot comparative research on Western Europe of the early 1990s: first, that prime ministers tend to be involved in more sensitive disputes; second, that coalition cabinets suffer more from the management of intra-executive conflicts than single-party cabinets; finally, that single-party cabinets internalize conflict management to a greater extent. The same study has shown also that inter-party conflicts last longer than intra-party disputes (Nousiainen 1993). More generally, it has been claimed that the adoption of procedures for conflict management correlates with heterogeneous coalitions and shorter policy contracts (Bowler et al. 2016).

Based on in-depth qualitative examinations of inter-party conflicts in Italian coalitions, attempts to account for dynamic variations during the process of conflict management have also suggested that (1) coalitions first seek to internalize the process and move to more external arenas if conflict radicalization increases; (2) stronger prime ministers[5] centralize the process as long as the dispute is not too radical, while weaker prime ministers tend to use collective arenas since the very beginning; overall (3) conflict radicalization leads to a more inclusive process; (4) weaker heads of government follow a more arbitrating approach, letting party leaders have more influence while in contrast, a strong prime minister is more activist; and finally (5), it has been observed that when intra-party divisions in the prime minister's party overlap inter-party conflicts, even stronger prime ministers tend to be arbitrators (Vercesi 2013, 2016: 205). This evidence matches the previous observation of Blondel and Nousiainen (2000) that cabinets are more active in the first phases of the process and supporting parties enter especially at a later stage.

To wrap up, the scholarship on conflict management and resolution in cabinet government tells that also the nature of the decision that is discussed concurs to define the form of the decision-making process. This is due to the fact that controversial issues modify the political climate of cabinets.

22.4 WHERE ARE WE AND WHERE DO WE GO NOW?

22.4.1 Conceptual, Theoretical, and Empirical Challenges

The systematic study of cabinet decision-making is challenging because it refers to a process, which involves women and men, who coordinate themselves in non-public meetings. Not surprisingly, the relevant literature is affected by three consequent deficits: disagreements about concepts; lack of an integrated theory of the role of agency within changing contexts; lack of systematic and parsimonious empirical comparisons based on precise theoretical expectations.

With regard to the first point, the research field has been delimited by the denotative confines of the concept of cabinet government. In this regard, the scope of the dominant notion of core executive has been broadened, to the detriment of its connotative precision

---

[5] Prime ministerial strength is operationalized as being coalition leader, leader of the largest coalition party, and benefiting from 'direct' electoral legitimation (Vercesi 2013).

(Sartori 1984). However, the enlargement of the focus beyond the apical ministerial group can lead to definitional problems, when it comes to observing *cabinet* decision-making. A potential pitfall is conceptual stretching and this can jeopardize the clear-cut identification of the conceptual space of interest for the analysis.

Explanations, on their turn, have swung between structure and agency, without tending clearly to one side or the other. Structural factors are ultimately attributable to power resources as well as to institutional and cultural environments. It has been said that power is positional, but also relational because it refers to relationships between actors (e.g. Dowding 2008). However, the effective use of resources depends also on individual abilities and inclinations. As long as structures define incentives and limits of decision-making and an 'all else equal' condition[6] applies, then process' variations will be subsumable under agential effects. To use Elgie's (2012: 289) words, 'the impact of human agency [...is] the error term of a statistical equation, whereas the impact of [...structures] can be estimated directly'. Scholarship is still vague in this respect.

22.4.2 Proposals for a Research Agenda

From a conceptual viewpoint, the acknowledgement of the role of third parts in the making of governmental outputs does not imply that the cabinet as the main conceptual referent must not be isolated. Cabinet decision-making may be understood as a process typical of a restricted group of apical executive members. It will be then an issue for empirical research to see how much this process is permeable towards external actors (e.g. bureaucratic, party, legislative actors, and/or interest groups). Thus, a stricter notion of core executive could be a steadier compass for the analysis. Moreover, any definition of cabinets' life time should take into account the conditions for the decision-making. As mentioned above, to decide when a cabinet forms and when it ends implies substantive theoretical considerations about the bargaining environment of cabinet actors. For this reason, it seems reasonable to see reshuffles of key cabinet portfolios as an additional (sufficient) condition for counting new cabinets. This approach has already been followed for example by Laver and Shepsle's (1996) model of portfolio allocation, which has been proposed to study the making and breaking of parliamentary governments.

With regard to theory development, the path to follow may be twofold. On the one hand, the overall picture of the explanatory factors needs to be better delineated, paying the due attention to both macro and micro aspects. On the other hand, the focus can be on the dynamic variations of the process and on how they relate to the channelling drives produced by the opportunity structure.

Several factors seem to have an impact on cabinet decision-making. However, it is not fully clear what matters more and when: impressionistic and scattered qualitative

---

[6] Also historical moments and events can be a further element to take into consideration (Strangio et al. 2013).

assessments and correlational analyses have shown that combinational effects and cross-country differences apply. For this reason, a theoretical configurational approach could help systematize this knowledge. This approach leaves behind the notions of causal homogeneity and variables' net effects, while, at the same time, allows the extension of the explanatory logic of case studies for larger-N comparisons (Ragin, 2008). The structural explaining factors would be treated as conditions—not variables—for the emergence of different types of decision-making. These outcomes (i.e. the types) would be explained by combinations (or by the absence) of given necessary and/or sufficient conditions, across and within countries; case selection should be made based on already known outcomes, not on conditions. The integration of agency in the emerging picture would then follow. If all other conditions are equal, agency's impact will be assumed to be located—as said—within variations between outcomes. In-depth case studies could be used to assess better this 'added' effect of personal traits; if differences of personalities occur, they would work as reciprocal counterfactual analyses. The explanation of process' dynamic changes requires instead more fine-grained qualitative studies, guided by theory; cabinet minutes, newspapers, expert surveys, and elite interviews remain rich sources of information in this regard. Process tracing (Bennett and Checkel 2014) could prove to be a fruitful methodological choice for the modulation of theories and data.

To achieve these goals, systematic data collection is necessary. Information should refer to both conditions and forms of cabinet decision-making, so that broad comparative pictures can flank in-depth case studies' findings. Some information about the reviewed potential explaining factors is already available in databanks. One can think of those on cabinet party compositions (e.g. Woldendorp et al. 2000; Döring and Manow 2018) and personnel changes, such as the monthly *Chiefs of State and Cabinet Members of Foreign Governments Reports*, issued by the US Central Intelligence Agency. Individual data on prime ministerial backgrounds and resources (e.g. Goemans et al. 2009; Baturo 2016; Müller-Rommel and Vercesi 2017; Vercesi 2019) also exist for comparative analysis. Even basic information on leaders' psychological traits can be found in large-N datasets (Ellis et al. 2015); this could be an aspect to insist on, in order to have comparable data for the study of deviant cases. On the other hand, gathering systematic data on decision-making types in different countries across-time can prove to be a very demanding and time-consuming challenge. However, some promising studies already exist. For example, Häge's (2011) European Union Policy-Making (EUPOL) dataset shows how information about decision-making practices and process duration can be used as proxies for understanding actors' role and decision-making complexity. Unfortunately, the 'hidden' character of many interactions within cabinets does not allow collecting data on every single decision. However, criteria to select the most significant decision-making episodes can be proposed. If this is done, participants of collective research enterprises could analyse them, relying on public records and various journalistic sources.

A final remark concerns countries and areas that future research could focus on. For obvious reasons, most studies focus on European and Anglo-Saxon countries. In the former case, attention has been payed to the impact of party-coalitional features on cabinet decision-making and ministerial autonomy. In the latter, scholars have variously stressed how favourable constitutional and party conditions affect the prominent role of prime ministers in Westminster systems as well as differences in rarer multi-party circumstances (Weller 1985, 2018; Bakvis 2001; Mulgan 2004; Strangio et al. 2013). Beyond these geographical areas, extensive analyses of government decision-making in parliamentary systems are hardly detectable, with some noticeable exceptions concerning Japan[7] and—to a lesser extent—other countries such as India (e.g. Jain 2003) and Israel (e.g. Kaarbo 1996; Arian et al. 2002). Future research could indeed try to fill this gap. Only by doing this, scholars will be able to assess more precisely to what extent our knowledge about European and Westminster systems can be generalized. Finally, it is worth mentioning that there is a relation between smaller population sizes and typical dynamics of party government (Veenendaal 2015). It would thus be interesting to investigate how cabinet government works in small polities, compared to larger and more studied countries.

In a nutshell, more research beyond traditional focuses is needed. As a matter of fact, the coverage of a larger number of countries and the collection of new data on cabinet decision-making would provide information about deviant cases, which can be similar in their structural features but differ in their functioning. This, in turn, can provide important insights about agency's impact against general theoretical expectations in different contexts.

22.5 CONCLUSION

Over the years, cabinet decision-making has been a central topic of executive studies. Initially, it mostly pertained to British politics. However, the number of covered countries soon increased, up to the inclusion of extra-European parliamentarism and Central-Eastern European democracies. In 2003, Andeweg (2003) claimed that—after a phase of maturation—the research on governments was coming to its age. This opinion can be shared, when it comes to assess the achievements in the study of cabinet decision-making. A wealth of material has been provided and especially the studies on conflict management have heralded a welcome trend towards systematic empirical comparisons.

However, open questions remain. Building on what has been already done, new research strategies can bring fresh air in the field. A first benefit could be a genuine scientific accumulation of knowledge. Second, the re-organization of debates and discussions about cabinet decision-making could be the basis for further dialogues with

---

[7] Japan is a non-European parliamentary system, which has relatively been investigated extensively by the international literature. In particular, scholars' attention has been attracted by the role of the prime minister. Overall, the Japanese prime minister has suffered from a weak position within the cabinet, in the context of severe intra-party competition. However, it has been also observed that the prime ministerial figure has become more central in the policy-making over the years (e.g. Hayao 1993; Elgie 1995; Shinoda 2000; Krauss and Nyblade 2005).

close research areas. For example, both macro and micro elements concur shaping the process. One can seek to disentangle (if any) the impact of personal experiences, careers, and reputational capitals on the agential side of the coin. In fact, the topic has to some extent already been introduced by the literature on intra-cabinet principal-agent relationships (e.g. Berlinski et al. 2012). The issue appears particularly relevant if one considers the changing nature of elite structures in modern democracies (Vogel et al. 2019). It may well be that the modification of elite profiles and pathways to power are conducive to the change of cabinet decision-making modes. Findings from a few explorative studies are encouraging in this sense (e.g. Worthy 2016; Helms 2018). However, from this viewpoint the literature is still poor and new investigations would be welcome contributions. On the other hand, the existing literature could be completed by the examination of the link between decision-making styles, personal performances, and governmental outputs. Cabinet decision-making is crucial for governments' activity. Further theoretical, methodological, and empirical contributions will help the advancements of executive studies altogether.

REFERENCES

Almond, G. A. (1960). 'Introduction: A Functional Approach to Comparative Politics,' in G. A. Almond and J. S. Coleman (eds) *The Politics of Developing Areas*. Princeton: Princeton University Press, 3–64.

Andeweg, R. B. (1993). 'A Model of the Cabinet System: The Dimensions of Cabinet Decision-Making Processes,' in J. Blondel and F. Müller-Rommel (eds), *Governing Together: The Extent and Limits of Joint Decision-Making in Western European Cabinets*. New York: St. Martin's Press, 23–42.

Andeweg, R. B. (1997). 'Collegiality and Collectivity: Cabinets, Cabinet Committees, and Cabinet Ministers,' in P. Weller, H. Bakvis, and R. A. W. Rhodes (eds) *The Hollow Crown. Countervailing Trends in Core Executive*. Basingstoke: Macmillan, 58–83.

Andeweg, R. B. (2003). 'On Studying Governments,' in J. Hayward and A. Menon (eds) *Governing Europe*. Oxford: Oxford University Press, 39–60.

Andeweg, R. B. and Timmermans, A. (2008). 'Conflict Management in Coalition Government,' in K. Strøm, W. C. Müller, and T. Bergman (eds) *Cabinets and Coalition Bargaining: The Democratic Life Cycle in Western Europe*. Oxford: Oxford University Press, 269–300.

Arian, A., Nachmias, D., and Amir, R. (2002). *Executive Governance in Israel*. Basingstoke: Palgrave.

Aucoin, P. (1999). 'Prime Minister and Cabinet. Power at the Apex,' in J. Bickerton and A. G. Gagnon (eds) *Canadian Politics*. 3rd ed. Peterborough: Broadview Press, 109–28.

Bagehot, W. (1968). *The English Constitution*. London: Oxford University Press.

Bakvis, H. (2001). 'Prime Minister and Cabinet in Canada: An Autocracy in Need of Reform?,' *Journal of Canadian Studies* 35(4): 60–79.

Barbieri, C. (2003). 'Dentro il cabinet. Novità istituzionali nei rapporti tra ministri,' in C. Barbieri and L. Verzichelli (eds) *Il governo e i suoi apparati. L'evoluzione del caso italiano in prospettiva comparata*. Genova: Name, 103–52.

Barbieri, C. and Vercesi, M. (2013). 'The Cabinet: A Viable Definition in View of a Comparative Analysis,' *Government and Opposition* 48(4): 526–47.

Baturo, A. (2016). 'Cursus Honorum: Personal Background, Careers and Experiences of Political Leaders in Democracy and Dictatorship—New Data and Analyses,' *Politics and Governance* 4(2): 138–57.

Baylis, T. A. (1989). *Governing by Committee: Collegial Leadership in Advanced Societies.* Albany, NY: Sate University of New York Press.

Bennett, A. and Checkel, J. T. (2014) (eds). *Process Tracing: From Metaphor to Analytic Tool.* Cambridge: Cambridge University Press.

Bennister, M. (2012). *Prime Ministers in Power: Political Leadership in Britain and Australia.* Basingstoke: Palgrave Macmillan.

Berlinski, S., Dewan, T., and Dowding, K. (2012). *Accounting for Ministers: Scandal and Survival in British Government 1945–2007.* Cambridge: Cambridge University Press.

Blondel, J. (1988). 'Decision-Making Processes, Conflicts and Cabinet Government,' EUI Working Papers 88/327.

Blondel, J. (1999). 'Processi decisionali, conflitti e governo di cabinet,' *Quaderni di scienza politica* 6(2): 187–210.

Blondel, J. (2001). 'Cabinets in Post-Communist East-Central Europe and in the Balkans: Introduction,' in J. Blondel and F. Müller-Rommel (eds) *Cabinets in Eastern Europe.* Basingstoke: Palgrave, 1–14.

Blondel, J. and Manning, N. (2002). 'Do Ministers Do What They Say? Ministerial Unreliability, Collegial and Hierarchical Governments,' *Political Studies* 50(3): 455–76.

Blondel, J. and Müller-Rommel, F. (1993) (eds) *Governing Together: The Extent and Limits of Joint Decision-Making in Western European Cabinets.* New York: St. Martin's Press.

Blondel, J. and Müller-Rommel, F. (1997) (eds). *Cabinets in Western Europe.* 2nd ed. Basingstoke: Macmillan.

Blondel, J. and Müller-Rommel, F. (2001) (eds). *Cabinets in Eastern Europe* Basingstoke: Palgrave.

Blondel, J. and Nousiainen, J. (2000). 'Governments, Supporting Parties and Policy-Making,' in J. Blondel and M. Cotta (eds) *The Nature of Party Government: A Comparative European Perspective.* Basingstoke: Palgrave Macmillan, 161–95.

Blondel, J., Müller-Rommel, F., and Dalová, M. (2007). *Governing New Democracies.* Basingstoke: Palgrave Macmillan.

Bowler, S., Bräuninger, T., Debus, M., and Indriðason, I. H. (2016). 'Let's Just Agree to Disagree: Dispute Resolution Mechanisms in Coalition Agreements,' *The Journal of Politics* 78(4): 1264–78.

Brummer, K. (2016). ' "Fiasco Prime Ministers": Leaders' Beliefs and Personality Traits as Possible Causes for Policy Fiascos,' *Journal of European Public Policy* 23(5): 702–17.

Burch, M. and Holliday, I. (1996). *The British Cabinet System.* Hemel Hempstead: Prentice Hall/Harvester Wheatsheaf.

Campbell, C. (1980). 'Political Leadership in Canada: Pierre Elliott Trudeau and the Ottawa Model;' in R. Rose and E. N. Suleiman (eds) *Presidents and Prime Ministers.* Washington, DC: AEI, 50–93.

Crossman, R. H. S. (1963). 'Introduction,' in Bagehot, W. *The English Constitution.* London: Fontana, 1–57.

Crossman, R. H. S. (1972). *The Myths of Cabinet Government.* Cambridge, MA: Harvard University Press.

Dahl, R. A. (1971). *Polyarchy: Participation and Opposition.* New Haven: Yale University Press.

Damgaard, E. (2008). 'Cabinet Termination,' in K. Strøm, W. C. Müller, and T. Bergman (eds) *Cabinets and Coalition Bargaining: The Democratic Life Cycle in Western Europe.* Oxford: Oxford University Press, 301–26.

Dewan, T. and Hortala-Vallve, R. (2011). 'The Three As of Government Formation: Appointment, Allocation, and Assignment,' *American Journal of Political Science* 55(3): 610–27.

Dewan, T., Galeotti, A., Ghiglino, C., and Squintani, F. (2015). 'Information Aggregation and Optimal Structure of the Executive,' *American Journal of Political Science* 59(2): 475–94.

Döring, H. and Manow, P. (2018). 'Parliaments and Governments Database (ParlGov): Information on Parties, Elections and Cabinets in Modern Democracies.' Development version.

Dowding, K. (2008). 'Agency and Structure. Interpreting Power Relationships,' *Journal of Power* 1(1): 21–36.

Dowding, K. (2013). 'The Prime Ministerialisation of the British Prime Minister,' *Parliamentary Affairs* 66(3): 617–35.

Dragu, T. and Laver, M. (2019). 'Coalition Governance with Incomplete Information,' *Journal of Politics* 81(3): 923–36.

Dunleavy, P. and Rhodes, R. A. W. (1990). 'Core Executive Studies in Britain,' *Public Administration* 68(1): 3–28.

Elgie, R. (1995). *Political Leadership in Liberal Democracies.* Basingstoke: Palgrave Macmillan.

Elgie, R. (1997). 'Models of Executive Politics: A Framework for the Study of Executive Power Relations in Parliamentary and Semi-presidential Regimes,' *Political Studies* 45(2): 217–31.

Elgie, R. (2011). 'Core Executive Studies Two Decades On,' *Public Administration* 89(1): 64–77.

Elgie, R. (2012). 'Political Leadership in Old and New Democracies,' in L. Helms (ed.) *Comparative Political Leadership.* Basingstoke: Palgrave Macmillan, 272–91.

Ellis, C. M., Horowitz, M. C., and Stam, A. C. (2015). 'Introducing the LEAD Data Set,' *International Interactions* 41(4): 718–41.

Foley, M. (1993). *The Rise of the British Presidency.* Manchester: Manchester University Press.

Foley, M. (2000). *The British Presidency: Tony Blair and the Politics of Public Leadership.* Manchester: Manchester University Press.

Frognier, A.-P. (1993). 'The Single-Party/Coalition Distinction and Cabinet Decision-Making,' in J. Blondel and F. Müller-Rommel (eds) *Governing Together: The Extent and Limits of Joint Decision-Making in Western European Cabinets.* New York: St. Martin's Press, 43–73.

Goemans, H., Gleditsch, K., and Chiozza, G. (2009). 'Introducing *Archigos*: A Data Set of Political Leaders,' *Journal of Peace Research* 46(2): 269–83.

Goetz, K. H. (2003). 'Executives in Comparative Context,' in J. Hayward and A. Menon (eds) *Governing Europe.* Oxford: Oxford University Press, 74–91.

Gordon Walker, P. (1970). *The Cabinet.* London: Jonathan Cape.

Green-Pedersen, C., Mortensen, P. B., and So, F. (2018). 'The Agenda-Setting Power of the Prime Minister Party in Coalition Governments,' *Political Research Quarterly* Online First, doi: 10.1177/1065912918761007

Häge, F. M. (2011). 'The European Union Policy-Making Dataset,' *European Union Politics* 12(3): 455–77.

Hallerberg, M. (2004). 'Electoral Laws, Government, and Parliament,' in H. Döring and M. Hallerberg (eds) *Patterns of Parliamentary Behavior: Passage of Legislation across Western Europe.* Aldershot: Ashgate, 11–33.

Hayao, K. (1993). *The Japanese Prime Minister and Public Policy.* Pittsburgh: Pittsburgh University Press.

Hayward, J. and Wright, V. (2002). *Governing from the Centre: Core Executive Coordination in France*. Oxford: Oxford University Press.

Heffernan, R. (2003). 'Prime Ministerial Predominance? Core Executive Politics in the UK,' *British Journal of Politics and International Relations* 5(3): 347–72.

Helms, L. (2005). *Presidents, Prime Ministers and Chancellors: Executive Leadership in Western Democracies*. Basingstoke: Palgrave.

Helms, L. (2014). 'Institutional Analysis,' in R. A. W. Rhodes and P. 't Hart (eds) *The Oxford Handbook of Political Leadership*. Oxford: Oxford University Press, 195–209.

Helms, L. (2017). 'When Less Is More: 'Negative Resources' and the Performance of Presidents and Prime Ministers,' *Politics* First Published online, doi: 10.1177/0263395717738964

Helms, L. (2018). 'Heir Apparent Prime Ministers in Westminster Democracies: Promise and Performance,' *Government and Opposition* First View, doi: 10.1017/gov.2018.22

Jain, H. M. (2003). *Indian Cabinet and Politics*. New Delhi: Gyan.

James, S. (1994). 'The Cabinet System Since 1945: Fragmentation and Integration,' *Parliamentary Affairs* 47(4): 613–29.

James, S. (1999). *British Cabinet Government*. 2nd ed. London: Routledge.

Jennings, I. (1959). *Cabinet Government*. 3rd ed. Cambridge: Cambridge University Press.

Jones, G. W. (1964). 'The Prime Minister's Power,' *Parliamentary Affairs* 18: 167–85.

Jones, G. W. (1991) (ed.). *West European Prime Ministers*. London: Frank Cass.

Kaarbo, J. (1996). 'Power and Influence in Foreign Policy Decision Making: The Role of Junior Coalition Partners in German and Israeli Foreign Policy,' *International Studies Quarterly* 40(4): 501–30.

Kaarbo, J. (2008). 'Coalition Cabinet Decision Making: Institutional and Psychological Factors,' *International Studies Review* 10(1): 57–86.

Keman, H. (2006). 'Parties and Government: Features of Governing in Representative Democracies,' in R. S. Katz and W. Crotty (eds) *Handbook of Party Politics*. London: Sage, 160–74.

King, A. (1975). 'Executives,' in F. I. Greenstein and N. Polsby (eds) *Handbook of Political Science: Governmental Institutions and Processes*. Vol. 5. Reading: Addison-Wesley, 173–255.

King, A. (1994). ''Chief Executives' in Western Europe,' in I. Budge and D. McKay (eds) *Developing Democracy. Comparative Research in Honour of J.F.P. Blondel*. London: Sage, 150–63.

Krauss, E. S. and Nyblade, B. (2005). '"Presidentialization" in Japan? The Prime Minister, Media and Elections in Japan,' *British Journal of Political Science* 35(2): 357–68.

Laver, M. (2003). 'Government Termination,' *Annual Review of Political Science* 6: 23–40.

Laver, M. and Schofield, N. (1990). *Multiparty Government. The Politics of Coalition in Europe*. Oxford: Oxford University Press.

Laver, M. and Shepsle, K. A. (1990). 'Coalitions and Cabinet Government,' *American Political Science Review* 84(3): 873–90.

Laver, M. and Shepsle, K. A. (1994a) (eds). *Cabinet Ministers and Parliamentary Government*. Cambridge: Cambridge University Press.

Laver, M. and Shepsle, K. A. (1994b). 'Cabinet Ministers and Government Formation in Parliamentary Democracies,' in M. Laver and K. A. Shepsle (eds) *Cabinet Ministers and Parliamentary Government*. Cambridge: Cambridge University Press, 3–12.

Laver, M. and Shepsle, K. A. (1996). *Making and Breaking Governments: Cabinets and Legislatures in Parliamentary Democracies*. Cambridge: Cambridge University Press.

Laver, M. and Shepsle, K. A. (1999). 'How Political Parties Emerged from the Primeval Slime: Party Cohesion, Party Discipline, and the Formation of Governments,' in S. Bowler, D. M. Farrell, and R. S. Katz (eds) *Party Discipline and Parliamentary Government*. Columbus, OH: Ohio State University Press, 23–48.

Mackie, T. T. and Hogwood, B. W. (1985). 'Decision-Making in Cabinet Government,' in T. T. Mackie and B. W. Hogwood (eds) *Unlocking the Cabinet. Cabinet Structures in Comparative Perspective*. London: Sage, 1–15.

Mackintosh, J. P. (1962). *The British Cabinet*. London: Stevens & Sons.

Marangoni, F. and Vercesi, M. (2015). 'The Government and Its Hard Decisions: How Conflict Is Managed within the Coalition,' in N. Conti and F. Marangoni (eds) *The Challenges of Coalition Government: The Italian Case*. Abingdon: Routledge, 17–35.

Marsh, D., Richards, D., and Smith, M. (2001). *Changing Patterns of Government in the United Kingdom: Reinventing Whitehall?* Basingstoke: Palgrave Macmillan.

Martin, L. W. and Vanberg, G. (2008). 'Coalition Government and Political Communication,' *Political Research Quarterly* 61(3): 502–16.

Martin, L. W. and Vanberg, G. (2014). 'Parties and Policymaking in Multiparty Governments: The Legislative Median, Ministerial Autonomy, and the Coalition Compromise,' *American Journal of Political Science* 58(4): 979–96.

Martocchia Diodati, N., Marino, B., and Carlotti, B. (2018). 'Prime Ministers Unchained? Explaining Prime Minister Policy Autonomy in Coalition Governments,' *European Political Science Review* First View, doi: 10.1017/S1755773918000085

Miller, B. and Müller, W. C. (2010). 'Managing Grand Coalitions: Germany 2005–9,' *German Politics* 19(3–4): 332–52.

Moury, C. (2013). *Coalition Government and Party Mandate: How Coalition Agreements Constrain Ministerial Action*. Abingdon: Routledge.

Mulgan, R. (2004). *Politics in New Zealand*. 3rd ed. (updated by P. Aimer). Auckland: Auckland University Press.

Müller, W. C. and Meyer, T. M. (2010). 'Meeting the Challenges of Representation and Accountability in Multi-party Governments,' *West European Politics* 33(5): 1065–92.

Müller, W. C. and Strøm, K. (2000) (eds). *Coalition Governments in Western Europe*. Oxford: Oxford University Press.

Müller-Rommel, F. (1988). 'The Centre of Government in West Germany: Changing Patterns under 14 Legislatures (1949–1987),' *European Journal of Political Research* 16(2): 171–90.

Müller-Rommel, F. (2001). 'Cabinets in Post-Communist East-Central Europe and the Balkans: Empirical Findings and Research Agenda,' in J. Blondel and F. Müller-Rommel (eds) *Cabinets in Eastern Europe*. Basingstoke, Palgrave Macmillan, 193–201.

Müller-Rommel, F. and Vercesi, M. (2017). 'Prime Ministerial Careers in the European Union: Does Gender Make a Difference?,' *European Politics and Society* 18(2): 245–62.

Nousiainen, J. (1993). 'Decision-Making, Policy Content and Conflict Resolution in Western European Cabinets,' in J. Blondel and F. Müller-Rommel (eds) *Governing Together: The Extent and Limits of Joint Decision-Making in Western European Cabinets*. New York: St. Martin's Press, 259–82.

O'Leary, P. (1991). 'An Taoiseach: The Irish Prime Minister,' in G. W. Jones (ed.) *West European Prime Ministers*. London: Frank Cass, 133–62.

O'Malley, E. (2007). 'The Power of Prime Ministers: Results of an Expert Survey,' *International Political Science Review* 28(1): 7–27.

Peters, B. G., Rhodes, R. A. W., and Wright, V. (2000) (eds). *Administering the Summit: Administration of the Core Executive in Developed Countries*. Basingstoke: Macmillan.

Poguntke, T. and Webb, P. (2005) (eds). *The Presidentialization of Politics: A Comparative Study of Modern Democracies*. Oxford: Oxford University Press.

Ragin, C. C. (2008). *Redesigning Social Inquiry: Fuzzy Sets and Beyond*. Chicago: University of Chicago Press.

Rhodes, R.A.W. (1995), 'From Prime Ministerial Power to Core Executive,' in R. A. W. Rhodes and P. Dunleavy (eds) *Prime Ministers, Cabinet and Core Executive*. New York: St. Martin's Press, 11–37.

Rhodes, R. A. W. (2008). 'Executives in Parliamentary Government,' in R. A. W. Rhodes, S. A. Binder, and B. A. Rockman (eds) *The Oxford Handbook of Political Institutions*. Oxford: Oxford University Press, 323–42.

Rhodes, R. A. W. (2013). 'From Prime-Ministerial Leadership to Court Politics,' in P. Strangio, P. 't Hart, and J. Walter (eds) *Understanding Prime-Ministerial Performance: Comparative Perspectives*. Oxford: Oxford University Press, 318–33.

Rhodes, R. A. W. and Dunleavy, P. (1995) (eds). *Prime Ministers, Cabinet and Core Executive*. New York: St. Martin's Press.

Rhodes, R. A. W., Wanna, J., and Weller, P. (2009). *Comparing Westminster*. Oxford: Oxford University Press.

Samuels, D. J. and Shugart, M. S. (2010). *Presidents, Parties, and Prime Ministers: How the Separation of Powers Affects Party Organization and Behavior*. Cambridge: Cambridge University Press.

Sartori, G. (1975). 'The Tower of Babel,' in G. Sartori, F. W. Riggs, and H. Teune (eds) *Tower of Babel: On the Definition and Analysis of Concepts in the Social Sciences*. Pittsburgh: University of Pittsburgh Press, 7–37.

Sartori, G. (1984). 'Guidelines for Concept Analysis,' in G. Sartori (ed.) *Social Science Concepts: A Systematic Analysis*. London: Sage, 15–85.

Shinoda, T. (2000). *Leading Japan: The Role of the Prime Minister*. Westport: Praeger.

Smith, M. J. (1999). *The Core Executive in Britain*. London: Palgrave Macmillan.

Smith, M. J. (2000). 'Prime Ministers, Ministers and Civil Servants in the Core Executive,' in R. A. W. Rhodes (ed.) *Transforming British Government*. Volume 1: *Changing Institutions*. Basingstoke: Palgrave Macmillan, 25–45.

Strangio, P., 't Hart, P., and Walter, J. (2013) (eds). *Understanding Prime-Ministerial Performance: Comparative Perspectives*. Oxford: Oxford University Press.

Strøm, K., Müller, W. C., and Bergman, T. (2003) (eds). *Delegation and Accountability in Parliamentary Democracies*. Oxford: Oxford University Press.

Theakston, K. (2002). 'Political Skills and Context in Prime Ministerial Leadership in Britain,' *Politics & Policy* 30(2): 283–323.

Thiébault, J.-L. (1993). 'The Organisational Structure of Western European Cabinets and its Impact on Decision-Makings,' in J. Blondel and F. Müller-Rommel (eds) *Governing Together: The Extent and Limits of Joint Decision-Making in Western European Cabinets*. New York: St. Martin's Press, 77–98.

Timmermans, A. and Moury, C. (2006). 'Coalition Governance in Belgium and the Netherlands: Rising Government Stability against All Electoral Odds,' *Acta Politica* 41(4): 389–407.

Tsebelis, G. (2002). *Veto Players: How Political Institutions Work*. Princeton: Princeton University Press.

Veenendaal, W. (2015). *Politics and Democracy in Microstates*. London: Routledge.

Vercesi, M. (2012a). 'Cabinets and Decision-Making Processes: Re-Assessing the Literature,' *Journal of Comparative Politics* 5(2): 4–27.

Vercesi, M. (2012b). 'Le coalizioni di governo e le fasi della politica di coalizione. Teorie e riscontri empirici,' *Quaderni di scienza politica* 19(2): 233–99.

Vercesi, M. (2013). 'Party, Coalition, Premiership: The Role of Silvio Berlusconi in Coalition Dynamics and Its Determinants,' *Contemporary Italian Politics* 5(3): 292–308.

Vercesi, M. (2016). 'Coalition Politics and Inter-Party Conflict Management: A Theoretical Framework,' *Politics & Policy* 44(2): 168–219.

Vercesi, M. (2019). 'Il "decision making" dell'esecutivo,' in F. Musella (ed.) *Il Governo in Italia. Profili costituzionali e dinamiche politiche*. Bologna: Il Mulino, 219–41.

Vogel, L., Gebauer, R., and Salheiser, A. (2019) (eds). *The Contested Status of Political Elites: At the Crossroads*. Abingdon: Routledge.

Weller, P. (1985). *First Among Equals: Prime Ministers in Westminster Systems*. Sidney: Allen & Unwin.

Weller, P. (2003). 'Cabinet Government: An Elusive Ideal?,' *Public Administration* 81(4): 701–22.

Weller, P. (2007). *Cabinet Government in Australia, 1901–2006: Practice, Principles, Performance*. Sidney: UNSW Press.

Weller, P. (2014). 'The Variability of Prime Ministers,' in R. A. W. Rhodes and P. 't Hart (eds) *The Oxford Handbook of Political Leadership*. Oxford: Oxford University Press, 489–502.

Weller, P. (2018). *The Prime Ministers' Craft: Why Some Succeed and Others Fail in Westminster Systems*. Oxford: Oxford University Press.

Woldendorp, J., Keman, H. and Budge, I. (2000). *Party Government in 48 Democracies: Composition—Duration—Personnel*. Dordrecht: Kluwer Academic Publishers.

Woodall, B. (2014). *Growing Democracy in Japan: The Parliamentary Cabinet System since 1868*. Lexington: University Press of Kentucky.

Worthy, B. (2016). 'Ending in Failure? The Performance of "Takeover" Prime Ministers 1916–2016,' *The Political Quarterly* 87(4): 509–17.

Wright, V. and Hayward, J. (2000). 'Governing from the Centre: Policy Co-ordination in Six European Core Executives,' in R. A. W. Rhodes (ed.) *Transforming British Government*. Volume 2: *Changing Roles and Relationships*. Basingstoke: Macmillan, 27–46.

CHAPTER 23

PARTIES AND EXECUTIVES IN PARLIAMENTARY SYSTEMS

from party government to party governance

RUDY B. ANDEWEG

23.1 ORIGINS: POLITICAL PARTIES, EXECUTIVES, AND LEGITIMACY

THE study of the relationship between political parties and political executives is inspired, explicitly or implicitly, by normative questions about the democratic legitimacy of government (e.g. Frognier 2000). Collectively, political parties constitute a linkage mechanism between society and the state, and by entrusting the party or parties with a majority or at least a plurality of the votes with the responsibility to give direction to the government, that government and its policies are deemed to be legitimate. Theoretically, and to some extent historically, other legitimizing linkage mechanisms may be distinguished, such as 'Parliamentarism' (Manin 1997) or 'Pluralist Democracy' (Katz 1987; Strøm 2000) in which individual representatives are elected by and held accountable to territorial constituencies and in which parties play no role; neo-corporatist arrangements, in which public policy results from negotiations between affected interests in society rather than parties (Katz 1987; Strøm 2000); 'Audience democracy' (Manin 1997) in which the competition for government is personal rather than partisan, and based on performance rather than policy proposals. Reflecting more recent debates, Caramani (2017) discusses populism and technocracy as new rivals to party democracy.

We shall return to some of these alternatives after having reviewed the state of the discipline, but for the moment it suffices to note a widespread agreement that political parties are best placed to provide democratic legitimacy to the executive by monopolizing both the electoral and the governmental arena, and by linking these two. From this normative point of departure, the study of the relationship between parties and political executives has been dominated by questions about the conditions necessary for parties to optimally perform their legitimizing function, and about the degree to which parties do control the political executive. In addition, there is a growing realization that treating both 'party' and 'government' as singular and unitary actors is an oversimplification, and a growing concern over the consequences of the weakening role of parties in society for their legitimizing function.

23.2 Overview: The Empirical Study of a Normative Question

23.2.1 'Responsible Party Government'

23.2.1.1 Conditions and Requirements

Although this chapter focuses primarily on parties in parliamentary systems of government, the study of parties in government started in the United States, where political parties are considered to be relatively weak. That paradox is easily explained by the very normative concerns that have inspired this strand of research: they were felt most acutely where they were least fulfilled. In 1950, for example, a Committee on Political Parties, set up by the American Political Science Association (APSA) issued its report *Towards a More Responsible Two-Party System*, with as the main thesis that:

> Historical and other factors have caused the American two-party system to operate as two loose associations of state and local organizations with very little national machinery and very little national cohesion. As a result, either major party, when in power, is ill-equipped to organize its members in the legislative and the executive branches into a government held together and guided by the party program. Party responsibility at the polls thus tends to vanish.

Although many of the report's findings and recommendations were not new, it is generally seen as the starting point of 'the doctrine of responsible party government' (Ranney 1954), which has found both advocates and students outside the US as well. The 'doctrine' was intended to have practical impact, but in this chapter we focus on its impact on the study of parties in government.

462 RUDY B. ANDEWEG

The first step has been a theoretical exercise, the identification of the conditions that need to be fulfilled for responsible party government to come into existence, but there is no consensus in the literature on what these conditions are. Scholars have differed, for example, on the relative emphasis on personnel or programme. Katz (1986) emphasizes that policy and other major governmental decisions must be taken by individuals who are recruited by the governing party. 'It is not necessary that parties compete on the basis of alternative policy proposals, but whatever policies are made must be made by individuals who owe their authority directly or indirectly to the electoral success of their parties' (Katz 1986: 43). Rose (1974: 380–3) shares Katz's emphasis on recruitment: the governing party must nominate sufficient partisans, and partisans of sufficient skill, to important positions in the government to enable the party to control the government bureaucracy. However, Rose also requires the parties to formulate policy intentions for enactment once in office. After all: 'Where the life of party politics does not affect government policy, the accession of a new party to office is little more significant than the accession of a new monarch: the party reigns but does not rule' (Rose 1974: 379). But Rose does not stipulate that the parties should make their policy proposals known before the elections. In fact, Rose does not mention elections at all, calling vaguely for 'some form of contest' to determine which party is to govern.

For other authors the choice between different policy programmes in elections is crucial. Thomassen (1994: 251–2), for example, is largely silent about the recruitment of partisans to government offices, etc., but he does require that two or more parties must present different policy alternatives to the voters, and that voters must vote for the party with the programme that is closest to their own exogenous preferences. Other authors implicitly allow for voters to develop their preferences in reaction to the different policy proposals presented to them in the election campaign. Moreover, Thomassen also adds a further condition, if the voters' choice is to provide the winning party with a mandate for its policy programme. After all, voters may like most, but not all of the policies proposed by the party of their choice, and collectively the result may be that there is a majority for a particular party, but not for each individual policy proposal of that party—a situation known as the Ostrogorski paradox (cf. Rae and Daudt 1976). The only way to mitigate that risk is if both the policy programmes of the parties and the policy preferences of the voters are constrained by the same single ideological dimension. Rose (1974: 380–3) also attaches conditions to the policy programmes formulated by the parties: they must not be empty promises, but should be accompanied by statements of realistic means.

The introduction of a mandate for a governing party's policy proposals adds conditions for the behaviour of the party's nominees to government office. Rose stipulates that partisans in office must give priority to the implementation of the party's policies, and Thomassen requires political parties to be sufficiently cohesive to enable them to implement their policy programme. The requirement of party cohesion is a direct echo of the APSA committee's reason for developing the doctrine of responsible party government.

Following Mair (2008: 568–9) I attempt to synthesize the most important conditions:

1. More than one party offers voters distinct and realistic policy programmes, preferably constrained by a single ideological dimension.
2. Voters vote for the party with the policy programme they prefer most.
3. The party that wins the elections recruits partisans to occupy sufficient key positions in the political executive to control policy-making.
4. The party is cohesive, so that all partisans in policy-making positions give priority to implementing the party's policy programme.
5. Partisans in policy-making positions are accountable to the party.
6. The party is held accountable to the voters for the performance of its partisans in policy-making positions.

The use of terms such as 'conditions' or 'requirements' might give the impression that party government either exists or it does not, but this is not what these authors are arguing. Thomassen concedes that 'According to a less rigid view, representatives and political parties should not necessarily reflect the will of the electorate on each and every single issue, but should at least be responsive, that is to say, should take the opinions and interests of the people into account' (Thomassen 1994: 258), and such responsiveness is a matter of degree. According to Rose, 'Party government is a variable, rather than a pervasive and constant force; one can have more or less of it' (Rose 1974: 379). Katz distinguished two dimensions along which party government may vary: *partyness of government*, referring to a narrow institutional sense of party government as party control of the formal government apparatus, and *party governmentness*, referring to a broader sense of party government as a general social characteristic '([...], i.e. the proportion of all social power exercised by parties within the framework of the party government model'). These two dimensions are not correlated, that is, higher party governmentness does not necessarily go hand in hand with higher partyness of government (Helms 1993; Andeweg 2000a). Mostly, however, the discussion has focused on the 'partyness of government'.

23.2.1.2 *Consequences*

So far, this review is confined to theorizing the relationship between party and government, and the resulting degree of partyness of government, although many have buttressed their arguments with anecdotal evidence from memoirs by or interviews with government ministers.

The more systematic empirical evidence that is available comes mainly from studies that compare governing parties' programmes to government policy. This is not the place for a full review of that literature, but we can discern two main strands in the literature (one on 'do parties matter?' and one on the 'party mandate', the latter in two varieties) and highlight some of the main findings. The differences between these literatures are primarily in the degree of specificity. The 'Do parties matter?' literature typically makes a crude distinction between Left and Right parties, and the hypothesis is that the size of the state or the volume of welfare spending is higher when Leftwing parties are in government than when Rightwing parties are in government (e.g. Blais et al. 1993; Imbeau et al. 2001; Potrafke 2017). Depending on how long a party is in office, or on the degree of party polarization over welfare spending, some impact of the ideological composition of government was found, but there was at best modest support for the hypothesis, especially since the 1990s. To some extent this may be due to the fact that institutional constraints on party government (e.g. federalism) were not always taken into account. When they were included in the analysis it was clear that fewer such constraints resulted in a stronger policy impact of the governing party (Schmidt 1996, 2002). Dalton et al. (2011: 205–8) took this approach a step further by specifically looking at the effects on social spending of *changes* in government composition (from Left to Right or vice versa). They found that, on average, such changes had the predicted effect: higher spending when the government's composition shifted to the Left, and lower spending after a shift in the opposite direction.

In the 'Party Mandate' literature, parties in government are not just classified as Left or Right, but the actual content of their election manifestos is compared to government policy. In one variant, 'the saliency approach', studies compare the relative emphases on various policy areas in the election manifesto of parties that entered government with the relative emphases on these policy areas in government spending. Studies using this approach report substantial correlations between manifesto emphases and spending priorities in countries such as the US (e.g. Budge and Hofferbert 1990) and the UK (Hofferbert and Budge 1992), King et al. have pointed out that these studies fail to control for spending patterns in previous years, and that controlling for past spending substantially weakens the correlation. However, the effect does not disappear completely, and the correlation between governing parties' manifestos and government spending remains stronger than that between opposition parties' manifestos and government spending (King et al. 1993).

In another, even more detailed, variant of the 'Party Mandate' literature, 'the pledge approach', studies seek to ascertain how many of a party's individual election pledges are turned into government policy when that party takes office. Here several studies report quite substantial percentages of pledges fulfilled by governing parties in the UK and, usually to a lesser extent, the US (e.g. Pomper and Lederman 1980; Rallings 1987; Royed 1996). One of the most encompassing studies (Thomson et al. 2017) estimates the probability that pledges are at least partially fulfilled at around .8 for single party governments. Note, however, that these percentages or probabilities look at the fulfilment of pledges in the manifesto, not at the proportion of all government policies that can be traced back to the manifesto. In 1997, the UK Labour Party famously published a list of only five pledges, distributed on little cards the size of a credit card, which summed up Tony Blair's key targets for his first term of office. It is possible that a party strategically limits its number of pledges, so that even when it fulfils them all, it still keeps ample room to implement policies unfettered by election promises (Louwerse 2011: 24–5). Studies taking into account how much of a government's policy is based on the party mandate are rare. Rose (1980), for example, estimated that the 1970–4 Heath Government in the UK fulfilled at least 80 per cent of the pledges in the Conservative Party's election manifesto (65), but that only 8 per cent of that government's bills originated from that manifesto (72)!

If we look at these studies in combination, a cautious conclusion would be that the responsible party model finds moderate support: when in government parties do seek to implement policies that are consistent with their ideology or election promises, but this is not to say that parties in government only pursue policies for which they have a popular mandate.

23.2.2 Inter-Party Dynamics and Government

23.2.2.1 *Mechanisms for Conflict Resolution and Monitoring in Coalition Government*

Even though some of the publications cited above also refer to coalition or even minority government, so far our discussion has been confined to two-party systems, or to be more precise: to single-party government. That is what the 1950 APSA report explicitly called for, and that is how the logic of a party mandate in government works best: two parties with different policy proposals compete for the people's vote, and the winner is mandated to form a government to implement its policy proposals. However, empirically, single-party majority government is quite exceptional: depending on the selection of (European) countries and period, studies find that only between 6 (Laver and Schofield 1990, 70) and 13 per cent (Gallagher et al. 2006: 401; Mitchell and Nyblade 2008: 206) of governments fall into that category. Government by a coalition of parties is much more common.

Originally, the study of parties in coalition government focused primarily on the formation and termination (or duration) of such governments (see Chapter 15 of this volume), treating the period in between as a temporary equilibrium that held no interest for political scientists. This long neglect of the actual period in office was legitimized by the portfolio allocation approach of Laver and Shepsle (e.g. 1990; also see Chapters 5 and 16 of this volume). This theory argues that during the coalition formation parties primarily negotiate which party gets to appoint the minister in which portfolio. Once agreement is reached, through the selection of likeminded ministers a party gets full control over 'its' departments, at the price of letting the other coalition parties exercise complete control over the other departments. From this perspective, there is no inter-party dynamics within coalition governments that needs to be studied. The prime minister, lacking a portfolio of his or her own, would serve primarily ceremonial functions and the weekly cabinet meetings might as well be abandoned. The assumption of ministerial autonomy has been heavily contested (e.g. Warwick 1999; Andeweg 2000b; Dunleavy and Bastow 2001). In fact, recent decades have shown increasing attention to cabinet decision-making in between government formation and termination (see Chapter 22), and inter-party dynamics play a large part in that.

This starts with the writing of a coalition agreement by the prospective governing parties. The use of a written coalition agreement has gradually increased from one-third of all coalition governments in the 1940s to 81 per cent in the 1990s (Müller and Strøm 2008: 172). In single-party cabinets the pledges in the ruling party's election manifesto give direction to government policy, and the coalition agreement—although lacking the direct legitimacy conferred by the voters—is the functional equivalent for coalition government. Coalition agreements considerably vary in size and comprehensiveness (Müller and Strøm 2008: 176). It stands to reason that the coalition agreement is most detailed in coalitions that contain many parties and that are ideologically heterogeneous (Indriðason and Kristinsson 2013)—the coalition agreement as 'a codification of mistrust' in the words of a former Dutch prime minister. A minority of coalition agreements also include procedural rules. A study of regional governments' coalition agreements in Germany suggests that the inclusion of dispute resolution mechanisms in coalition agreements to some extent is an alternative to policy detail (smaller size agreements), but that this also correlates with ideological heterogeneity (Bowler et al. 2016).

However, it should be noted that the coalition agreement is not a legally binding contract. During the lifetime of a government conflicts are bound to occur over the interpretation of the policy compromises in the agreement, in addition to conflicts over policies on which the coalition agreement is silent. Such conflicts may be resolved in the weekly cabinet meeting. Although a tacit rule of mutual non-intervention usually prevents a departmental minister from interfering in a colleague's portfolio, in a coalition cabinet it is generally accepted for ministers, especially a party's most senior ministers, to speak out if party interests are concerned (Andeweg 1997: 81–3). However, it is more likely that an attempt is made to defuse an interparty conflict before it comes to the full cabinet because of the risk that the party that is outvoted leaves the coalition and brings down the government. All of the governments in fifteen West European countries studied by Andeweg and Timmermans (2008) had some form of committee for this purpose, either composed exclusively of ministers (an 'inner cabinet'), or of the coalition parties' leaders outside the government (a 'party summit'), or some combination (a 'coalition committee'). The most common conflicts (between government departments) tend to be dealt with by an internal committee, but the most serious conflicts (between the coalition parties) are often referred to a party summit, less so when there is a coalition agreement or when all coalition parties' leaders are themselves members of the cabinet (also see Vercesi 2016; and Chapter 22 of this volume).

Dispute resolution by such a committee can only work if a conflict between the coalition parties becomes manifest. Without additional mechanisms, there is a risk that information asymmetry between ministers prevents deviation from the coalition agreement from becoming known (also see Chapter 5 of this volume). One way for coalition parties to monitor each other's ministers would be to ensure that all coalition parties are represented by a minister in all cabinet committees, or at least in each policy area broadly defined (i.e. foreign affairs (Foreign Affairs, Defence, European Affairs, Development Aid, etc.); or socio-economic affairs (Finance, Economic Affairs, Social Affairs, Agriculture, Trade, etc.)). Although the overall proportional distribution of cabinet positions across coalition parties is such a general finding that it has been accorded law-like status ('Gamson's Law'; see, e.g., Gamson 1961; Browne and Franklin 1973), we know very little about the extent to which this applies to individual policy areas. More is known about another mechanism for this purpose: the appointment of junior ministers of one coalition party to a department led by another coalition party's cabinet minister.

Verzichelli (2008: 259–64) found that 134 out of 264 coalition cabinets (51 per cent) in fifteen West European countries studied, had at least one junior minister serving with a senior minister from a different party, and that this practice has become more widespread in recent decades. It is telling that such appointments are more frequent in the most important portfolios (Thies 2001), as the ideological distance between the coalition parties is larger (Lipsmeyer and Pierce 2011), and as the coalition agreement is more detailed (Verzichelli 2008; Indriðason and Kristinsson 2013), but it is not yet empirically established that such junior ministers actually behave as party watchdogs rather than as *postillons d'amour* between the two coalition parties involved.

Intra-coalition monitoring mechanisms need not be confined to the government. A coalition party's members of parliament may also function to keep tabs on a coalition partner's ministers. Martin and Vanberg (2011) show that strong parliamentary committees may serve to facilitate control of one coalition party over another coalition party's ministers, in particular if that party has no junior minister appointed to that senior minister: the more the coalition parties have different positions on the issue, the longer the parliamentary review of the proposal takes, and the more likely it is that amendments to the bill will be proposed. Also looking at parliamentary committees, Carroll and Cox (2012) suggest that a coalition party may seek to appoint the chair of the parliamentary committee shadowing the portfolio controlled by a minister from another coalition party; again, ideological diversity plays a role: the more divergent the political parties, the more likely such appointments are. However, Fortunato et all (2017), studying the fate of over a thousand bills in three countries, found no evidence that control of a committee chair by one coalition party actually results in greater scrutiny of bills proposed by a minister of another coalition party.

23.2.2.2 *Consequences*

Given these inter-party dynamics, we should expect that the consequences of party government in coalitions differ from those in single-party government. Kaarbo (2012) makes such a comparison in the field of foreign policy and draws some counterintuitive conclusions: for example that the foreign policy decisions of coalitions are more extreme, that is, either more radically cooperative or more radically conflictual, and that where a junior party is located ideologically to the right of the largest party in the coalition more cooperative foreign policy choices tend to be adopted. The latter finding gives rise to the more general question of the relationship between party ideology or programme, coalition agreement, and government policy. Moury (2013) found a strong impact of the coalition agreement on the policies adopted: on average 70 per cent of the testable policy proposals in the coalition agreements were adopted. Even in the country where the coalition agreement was taken least seriously (Italy), 58 per cent of the proposals were transformed into government decisions. But this says little about the fulfilment by individual coalition parties of pledges in their own election manifesto.

In coalition government, pledge fulfilment is a two stage process: a party must first seek to secure inclusion of its manifesto proposals into the coalition agreement, and then work to get the coalition agreement implemented. Coalition parties in Ireland and in the Netherlands were able to get only between a quarter and a third of their election pledges adopted in the coalition agreement (Mansergh and Thomson 2007). It should not come as a surprise that parties are less successful in fulfilling their election pledges when they enter a coalition government compared to when they can govern alone. Above, we referred to Thomson et al.'s (2017) finding that the probability of at least partial pledge fulfilment was about .8 for parties governing alone. Their study included parties in coalitions, and here the probability of at least partial pledge fulfilment is significantly lower: about .6 for the senior party in a coalition, and .5 for a junior coalition partner.

However, there is another side to the coin of the party mandate in coalition government. When discussing the party mandate in single party governments, we discussed that even in situations of perfect pledge fulfilment, many of the policies pursued by the government cannot be traced back to an election pledge. Weller (1997) suggests that coalition government requires greater party involvement in policy development, and that coalition agreements provide more detailed partisan input than is the case in single-party government. Indeed, Moury (2013) found that, in the coalition governments of Germany, Italy, Belgium, and the Netherlands, on average 60 per cent (with very little variation across countries) of important cabinet decisions originate in the coalition agreement. Although this percentage cannot be directly compared with Rose's 8 per cent for a British single party government reported above, it would seem that parties in a single-party government can fulfil more of their election pledges than parties in a coalition government, but that of all government policies fewer originate in a ruling party's manifesto in a single party government than in a coalition government.

23.2.3 Towards Party Governance

The shift from normative theorizing to the empirical study of party government has not stopped at the realization that party government is usually coalition government, with all the inter-party dynamics that come with it. It has also questioned whether both parties and governments are indeed the unitary actors they should be if party government is to work best.

23.2.3.1 *Unpacking Parties in Government as Unitary Actors*

The literature on parties in government tends to assume that political parties are unitary actors. It is well-known that they are not, but the consequences of intra-party differentiation are ignored in normative accounts of party government, and only rarely addressed in empirical studies of parties in government. However, even if the prime minister is often his or her party's leader, and even if most ministers are part of their party's leadership, this does not imply that there will not be opposition to the government from within the party. The party congress is the most likely place where such internal opposition will become manifest. Some parties require that a party congress formally approves government participation, thus binding the congress. Studies of speeches at party congresses also indicate that criticism tends to be muted once a party is in government (e.g. Greene and Haber 2014). Critical party congress resolutions may not be binding formally—as a Dutch minister of defence once dismissed such a resolution: 'party congresses do not buy jet fighters', but they do signal a weakening of the government's position. This is not the place for an extensive discussion of intra-party divisions, but we can briefly relate two types of internal differentiation to the role of parties in government.

Factionalism is the clearest example of intra-party divisions (e.g. Boucek 2009). Where a single but factionalized political party forms the government, the situation may closely resemble that of coalition government as described in the previous section: what were called inter-party dynamics there are now intra-party dynamics, but otherwise most of the discussion would apply. Party government gets considerably more complicated, however, if the government is made up of a coalition of parties that are each highly factionalized. Before entering the coalition government, a leader of such a party must first form a coalition within his or her own party that is sufficiently cohesive for the party to be a reliable partner in the governing coalition. Moreover, entering into a governing coalition in itself may exacerbate pre-existing divisions: being only one of several coalition parties reduces the number of ministerial positions to offer to leading party politicians, and increases the number of disappointed heavy-weights on the backbenches. In addition, the price for entering the governing coalition is having to make policy concessions, and members of parliament may be loathe to support government policies that are at odds with the party's own manifesto, in particular when the party's rank and file are grumbling. That 'Such situations create ample potential for intra-party conflict' (Strøm and Müller 2009: 41) may be an understatement.

The study of the impact of party factionalism on government is still in its infancy, but several contributions to Gianetti and Benoit (2009) provide evidence that factionalism may affect for example the composition of the governing coalition (Bäck 2009), the appointment of ministers (Debus and Bräuninger 2009), and the stability of the government (Saalfeld 2009). Through such factors, it is likely that factionalism also has an impact on the link between citizens and outcomes in terms of policy and patronage, but we lack studies that actually show that this is the case, and to what extent.

A second type of intra-party division is linked directly to the constitutional chain of delegation from electorate to parliament and, at least in parliamentary systems, from parliament to government. In order to be effective, political parties seek to control every link in this chain and this has created a parallel chain of delegation within the party: from the extra-parliamentary party organization to the parliamentary party group to the party in government (Müller 2000a). Political parties are often attributed a role in minimizing agency loss in the constitutional chain of delegation, but this has merely transferred to problem of agency loss to within the party. The external party organization may monopolize access to the electoral arena and effectively control the parliamentary party group, but when it comes to the party in government (let alone civil servants) the situation is very different. Müller (2000a: 330) suggests that 'The fact that the role of political parties deteriorates the more the delegation chain develops, reflects increasing information asymmetries and the relevance of normative constraints (i.e. what party influence is considered legitimate or at least tolerable)'. With the latter factor he points to the fact that, while it is generally considered appropriate for party representatives in parliament to pursue the party's ideological goals, ministers are generally expected to rise above party interests. In addition, ministers may also be affected by a more psychological mechanism. As a government minister they spend most of their time within their department, and are continuously surrounded by their departmental officials. In Rhodes' political ethnography of British ministers, the minister's 'political role' is not defined as going to bat for his party, but as 'winning resources for the department in cabinet' (Rhodes 2011: 53). This phenomenon is not confined to the UK: ministers are prone to 'go native', to become the bridgehead of the department in the cabinet rather than the cabinet's—and the party's—bridgehead in the department. Thus, ministers may turn into 'double agents' (Andeweg 2000b), reversing the direction of delegation at the very point where it matters most: the transformation of the party's proposals into government policy.

23.2.3.2 *Multi-Level Governance*

If parties cannot be considered unitary actors, the same can be said of many governments. Federalism and decentralization have always been recognized as obstacles to party government (Katz 1986; Weller 1997), but territorial differentiation has increased in recent decades. A long-term trend of decentralization has made the regional and local levels of government more important, and transnational institutions have added a layer of government for some countries—with the European Union as the most prominent case. The concept of 'multi-level governance' has been introduced to capture this trend, but also the fact that the relations between the levels of government are now often negotiated rather than hierarchical (cf. Marks and Hooghe 2003; Piattoni 2009). Apart from making it more difficult for parties to control 'government', there are at least three additional consequences.

First, multi-level governance affects party unity. The national party organization and the regional and local branches of the same party may well develop different goals and strategies in the face of the different contexts in which they operate. It is not self-evident that parties are always sufficiently hierarchical for the national party organization to impose its preferences on its subnational counterparts, and concepts such as 'party stratarchy' (Eldersveld 1964) or 'party franchise systems' (Carty 2004) have been developed to capture the relations between a party's organizations at different levels. The trend towards multi-level governance heightens the intra-party tensions between the branches of political parties at the various levels mentioned above, even more so because this trend roughly coincided with the erosion of social cleavages, weakening the traditional social and ideological cohesion that used to keep the party at different levels together (e.g. Deschouwer 2006; various contributions to Swenden and Maddens 2009; Detterbeck 2012).

Second, multi-level governance may complicate party government when the composition of governments at the various levels is incongruent (e.g. Stefuriuc 2009). In Belgium, for example, federalization has caused nearly all political parties to split in a

Flemish party and a francophone party, with only one truly national party remaining. As a result, the same party leaders square off against each other in elections at different levels, most importantly in the federal and regional elections. After the elections, coalition governments have to be formed at all levels. As long as it was possible to form a coalition of parties from the same party families in both Flanders and Wallonia, and a coalition of all these regional governing parties at the federal level (symmetrical and congruent coalitions), there was still no problem. However, since the electoral cycles have been decoupled in 2003, such congruence has proved more difficult to achieve, and a party may now find itself in one coalition at the regional level and in a differently composed coalition at the federal level, or in government at one level and in opposition at another level (Swenden 2002; Deschouwer 2009). Whenever some form of cooperation or coordination is required between levels of government, inevitably tensions arise. A different variety can be observed in Germany, where the party composition of the governments of the *Länder* often varies from the composition of the federal government. As the federal upper house, the *Bundesrat*, consists of the governments of the *Länder*, its majority therefore may be different from the majority in the directly elected lower house, the *Bundestag*, and the federal government may need the consent of opposition parties in the *Bundesrat*. Governing and opposition parties have to form an 'informal grand coalition' (Sturm 2001: 181) to avoid paralysis. Thus, multi-level governance can be a cause of 'divided government', although it is not the only cause (see Elgie 2001).

Third, and specific for EU member-states, the emergence of a European level of government has a far more radical impact on party government. Delors' prediction that 80 per cent of national economic regulation would originate in Brussels has yet to come true, but there is no gainsaying the significant influence of the EU on public policy in the member states. However, the formulation of these policies has been effectively removed from the reach of political parties. To the extent that there is a government of the European Union, it is composed of representatives of the member states' governments (the Council), or it consists of individuals appointed by the member states' governments (the Commission) (see Chapter 33). Individual members of both Council and Commission may be party members, but political parties as such are absent at that level. Parties must influence European 'government' indirectly. As the national governments are involved in the Council, the domestic party government chain of delegation and accountability also applies to ministers' activities in Brussels, but in particular for Council decisions taken by (qualified) majority rather than unanimity, parties are not fully in control. The European Parliament's powers have been extended, which gives parties in the European Parliament an important role in European legislation, and even some influence over the composition of the Commission, but the parties in the European parliament are not elected as such. Instead European elections are contested by national political parties in their respective countries, campaigning primarily on domestic political issues, and these national parties form coalitions in the European Parliament (called Euro parties) with ideologically like-minded parties from other member states. The Euro parties may have become increasingly cohesive (at least in roll-call votes) and compete with each other along familiar Left v. Right lines (and recently pro-EU v. EU-sceptic lines) (e.g. Hix et al. 2005, 2018), but the absence of both a direct electoral link and party penetration of the executive makes it impossible to speak of party government at the EU level.

23.2.3.3 *Reversing the Direction of Influence?*

As we discussed at the start of this chapter, normatively, party government is a means to link the preferences of the citizens to the actions of the government. In the terminology of agency theory citizens are the principals, delegating to the parties, which are the agents, and which in turn delegate to the government. This one-directional view of parties in government has been challenged (Blondel 1995; Blondel and Cotta 1996, 2000). The core of the problem is that 'it may be impossible to reconcile the purpose of parties—to ensure representation and majority rule—with the purpose of government—to provide leadership in the "general interest" of the nation' (Blondel 2000: 10.). Government is located at the interface between politics and administration, and given the thrust of the literature on relations between government ministers and civil servants, it seems unlikely that governments are completely controlled by the parties in government.

> Given what government is, given also what parties are, given the complex questions posed by the contrasts between representation and leadership, between the 'party side' and the 'administrative side' of government and between majority (party) rule and the search for the 'general interest', it is surely right to question the notion that supporting parties are the 'principal' and governments the 'agents'. The answer cannot be so simple.   (Blondel 2000: 16)

Blondel c.s. studied the relations between governing parties and governments in several West European countries and in three domains: appointments (both to government and party positions), policy-making (in several areas), and patronage. It remains inherently difficult to disentangle party and government (e.g. in the case of a prime minister also being his or her party's leader). However, with that caveat in mind, the project tentatively concluded that when it comes to appointments, the government is not just a passive recipient, but there is more evidence of the government being influenced by the parties than the other way around; with regard to policy-making, however, in line with the deterioration of intra-party delegation at this level mentioned above, the government tends to dominate the initiation phase, with the governing parties reacting to those initiatives in the elaboration phase; the pattern for patronage varies widely across countries: in countries such as Belgium and Italy, the parties control patronage that is materially handed out by the government, but in France the government is much more in charge itself (Cotta 2000: 196–222).

It may well be that the direction of influence will become more frequently from the government to the parties rather than the other way around. This, at least, would be a likely consequence of the emergence of 'the cartel party' as reported by Katz and Mair (1995, 2018). In their view, the roots of political parties in society have atrophied (e.g. declining membership) and they have taken up a position closer to other parties and to the state (e.g. state financing of political parties). Political parties increasingly represent the government in society rather than society in government. In later publications, Mair (2008: 570–4) identified developments that reinforce this 'waning of party government' such as the selection of party leaders not by party organs but through direct election by party members, or the formulation of policy by non-majoritarian institutions such as the European Union. In his last publications, Mair (e.g. 2009) has argued that political parties must be both responsive (or representative) to electoral opinion and responsible in the sense of adhering to accepted procedural norms and abiding by agreements that previous governments have made with other governments and international organizations. It has always been difficult for parties in government to balance responsiveness and responsibility (e.g. Keman 2017), but the tension between these two demands has grown: it is more difficult for parties to be in touch with a society from which parties have increasingly withdrawn, and even if they still can read electoral opinion, the international constraints make it increasingly difficult to act responsively. As a consequence we may witness a bifurcation of party systems into established parties that act responsibly but are no longer responsive, and new populist challengers that are responsive, but have no desire to act responsibly. If realized this would mean the end of the normative ideal of party democracy: parties that govern do no longer represent, and parties that represent do not govern.

23.3 AGENDA: TOWARDS A DOCTRINE OF PARTY GOVERNANCE?

The normative ideal that political parties form a linkage between citizens and the state, thereby giving democratic legitimacy to the political executive and its policies, has given rise to a large and still growing body of literature on the relations between political parties and political executives. The development of that literature can be summarized as a journey from 'party government' to 'party governance'. After the initial conceptualization of party government as a single party having obtained a popular mandate taking control of government and transforming its election manifesto into public policy came first the realization that single party government is quite exceptional, and the study of the inter-party dynamics within coalition government, and subsequently the unpacking of both political parties and political executives as unitary actors: depending on the context parties may have fewer or more factions, territorial branches, and organizations of its representatives outside and inside public office. The resulting intra-party dynamics interacts with political executives in what is increasingly multi-level government. The state of the discipline does not present a picture of party *government*, but of party *governance*, in which parts of parties seek to influence parts of government, and in which parties, weakened by the erosion of their roots in society, are also influenced by government themselves.

The question arises what this implies for the doctrine of responsible party government—for the question whether parties still convey democratic legitimacy to government, or whether alternatives to party government would fit the current situation better. At the beginning of this chapter, several alternatives were briefly identified. One of these, neo-corporatism, is an unlikely contender. Interest groups have been affected by many of the same social developments (such as individualization and globalization) that have weakened political parties, and the expansion of institutions for tripartite governance has stopped, and in many countries reversed. Several of the other alternatives have in common that the main actors in democratic politics are not party organizations, but individual political leaders (parliamentary government, pluralist democracy, audience democracy), and personalization is definitely to be considered as a challenge to party government, along with the two most recently added challenges of populism and technocracy.

The common starting point of all three alternatives or challenges—personalization, populism, and technocracy—is that political parties are outdated: they have lost their social and ideological identity, are desperately trying to identify new issues with which to attract new voters, but fail because they have taken up a position too close to the state to enable them to strike base with the voters. The three alternatives are not mutually exclusive, but they emphasize different aspects of the problem and offer different solutions.

Populism argues that parties have lost touch with the people and offers an alternative in which leaders, unhindered by intermediary organizations such as political parties, identify with the people and divine what is in the people's interest. Technocracy argues that parties, faced with an increasingly volatile electorate, try to be responsive to every short-term hype, thus ignoring the long-term interests of the people; it is the task of technocratic leaders to use scientific means to objectively determine what the main problems and the best solutions for these problems are. Both alternatives are as of yet rather underspecified in terms of how they would actually work. But more importantly, as Caramani (2017) points out, both alternatives to party government have in common that they are monolithic: there is only one people, and therefore only one popular will, or there is only one correct definition of a problem facing society, with only one scientifically proven best solution. This is in direct contrast to the (growing) heterogeneity and complexity of both society and the state that resulted in the trend away from party government and towards party governance.

Populism and technocracy also emphasize the role of political leaders, but personalization need not be associated with the abolition of pluralism and competition. In Manin's 'audience democracy' the person of the leader becomes the vehicle of representation, campaigning is through the media rather than through party channels, and elections serve to hold leaders accountable for their performance rather than to provide a mandate for a policy programme (Manin 1997: 218–24). Poguntke and Webb (2005) likewise see a trend towards a 'presidentialization' of parliamentary systems of government in which elections are increasingly personalized and individual political leaders are becoming more powerful and autonomous both within their parties and within political executives (see Chapter 18). Interestingly, among the putative causes of presidentialization are internationalization and the growing complexity of the state, but the question whether a single strong leader may be able to control these centrifugal forces is not addressed (but see Brown 2014). In that sense personalization, populism, and technocracy have in common a romantic quest for control, a nostalgically harking back to the less complicated world of the past—if such a world ever existed. None of these potential challenges therefore really provides an alternative doctrine for conveying legitimacy to governing in today's complex societal and statal reality.

But perhaps the search for an alternative normative theory is premature. First, we should note that the programme-to-policy link has but weakened marginally since the 1970s for parties governing alone and that it has even strengthened for coalition parties (Thomson et al. 2017: table 3). Moreover, studies on intra-party divisions, multi-level government, and the reversal of influence have not (yet) reached the level of empirical depth and detail that is offered by, for example, studies of parties in coalition government. Studying the actual consequences for the making and substance of government decisions of these developments will take up a large part of any agenda for the future study of parties in political executives. Second, the literature on both party government and its challenges, is focused on established Western democracies, and on established West European democracies in particular. While party government in those countries may show signs of weakening, the post-Cold War wave of democratization has expanded the scope of party government to a range of countries, and another part of the agenda will be to study the role of political parties in the political executives of such countries in comparison with the situation in the established democracies (following Keman and Müller-Rommel 2012). In addition, the heritage of the work on parties by Duverger, Sartori, and other European political scientists has given the study of parties a distinctly European flavour. Despite its American origin, this is even true for party government. Elsewhere, the focus on ideology and policy, developed in the context of European party government, may be less appropriate and other ways in which parties may link citizens to the state, such as patronage and clientelism should be added to the agenda. Parties in government can use the state's resources to provide supporters with positions, subsidies, and other particularized benefits (e.g. Müller 2000b), even in coalition governments (Ensser-Jedenastik 2014). It might well be that by focusing on Western established democracies the literature underestimates the importance of particularized benefits in party government, but even on the European continent there are developments that might give more emphasis to patronage at the expense of policy: the shift from mass party to cartel party, and the decline of ideology in party competition (Kopecký and Mair 2012: 10–12).

Rather than a return to the drawing table for an alternative to the normative ideal of party government, the current state of the discipline concerning the role of parties in political executives requires a more realistic reconsideration of the doctrine of responsible party government, recognizing that parties and governments operate in complex networks in which they hold no monopoly positions, but also recognizing that parties occupy a privileged position in those networks by offering to all citizens a regular opportunity to choose between them.

ACKNOWLEDGEMENT

This chapter's subtitle is after the title of Helms (2014).

REFERENCES

Andeweg, R. B. (1997). 'Collegiality and Collectivity: Cabinets, Cabinet Committees and Cabinet Ministers,' in P. Weller, H. Bakvis, and R. A. W. Rhodes (eds) *The Hollow Crown: Countervailing Trends in Core Executives*. London: Macmillan, 58–83.

Andeweg, R. B. (2000a). 'Party Government, State and Society: Mapping Boundaries and Interrelations,' in J. Blondel and M. Cotta (eds) *The Nature of Party Government: A Comparative European Perspective*. Houndmills: Palgrave, 38–55.

Andeweg, R. B. (2000b). 'Ministers as Double Agents? The Delegation Process between Government and Ministers,' *European Journal of Political Research* 37: 377–95.

Andeweg, R. B. and Timmermans, A. (2008). 'Conflict Management in Coalition Government,' in K. Strøm, W. C. Müller, and T. Bergman (eds) *Cabinets and Coalition Bargaining. The Democratic Life Cycle in Western Europe*. Oxford: Oxford University Press, 269–300.

Bäck, H. (2009). 'Intra-Party Politics and Local Coalition Formation,' in D. Gianetti and K. Benoit (eds) *Intra-Party Politics and Coalition Governments*. London: Routledge, 53–68.

Blondel, J. (1995). 'Toward a Systematic Analysis of Government-Party Relationships,' *International Political Science Review* 16: 127–43.

Blondel, J. (2000). 'Introduction,' in J. Blondel and M. Cotta (eds) *The Nature of Party Government: A Comparative European Perspective*. Houndmills: Palgrave, 1–17.

Blondel, J. and Cotta, M. (1996) (eds). *Party and Government: An Inquiry into the Relationship between Governments and Supporting Parties in Liberal Democracies*. Houndmills: Macmillan.

Blondel, J. and Cotta, M. (2000) (eds). *The Nature of Party Government: A Comparative European Perspective*. Houndmills: Palgrave.

Boucek, F. (2009). 'Rethinking Factionalism: Typologies, Intra-Party Dynamics and Three Faces of Factionalism,' *Party Politics* 15: 455–85.

Bowler, S., Bräuninger, T., Debus, M., and Indriðason, I. H. (2016). 'Let's Just Agree to Disagree: Dispute Resolution Mechanisms in Coalition Agreements,' *The Journal of Politics* 78: 1264–78.

Brown, A. (2014). *The Myth of the Strong Leader: Political Leadership in the Modern Age*. London: Vintage.

Browne, E. C. and Franklin, M. N. (1973). 'Aspects of Coalition Payoffs in European Parliamentary Democracies,' *American Political Science Review* 67: 453–69.

Budge, I. and Hofferbert, R. I. (1990). 'Mandates and Policy Outputs: US Party Platforms and Federal Expenditures,' *American Political Science Review* 84: 111–32.

Caramani, D. (2017). 'Will vs. Reason: The Populist and Technocratic Forms of Political Representation and Their Critique to Party Government,' *American Political Science Review* 111: 44–67.

Carrol, R. and Cox, G. W. (2012). 'Shadowing Ministers: Monitoring Partners in Coalition Governments,' *Comparative Political Studies* 45: 220–36.

Carty, R. K. (2004), 'Parties as Franchise Systems: The Stratarchical Organizational Imperative,' *Party Politics* 10: 5–24.

Cotta, M. (2000). 'From the Simple World of Party Government to a More Complex View of Party-Government Relationships,' in J. Blondel and M. Cotta (eds) *The Nature of Party Government: A Comparative European Perspective*. Houndmills: Palgrave, 196–222.

Dalton, R. J., Farrell, D. M., and McAllister, I. (2011). *Political Parties and Democratic Linkage: How Parties Organize Democracy*. Oxford: Oxford University Press.

Debus, M. and Bräuninger, T. (2009). 'Intra-Party Factions and Coalition Bargaining in Germany,' in D. Gianetti and K. Benoit (eds) *Intra-Party Politics and Coalition Governments*. London: Routledge, 121–45.

Deschouwer, K. (2006). 'Political Parties as Multi-Level Organizations,' in R. S. Katz and W. Crotty (eds) *The Handbook of Party Politics*. London: Sage, 291–300.

Deschouwer, K. (2009). 'Coalition Formation and Congruence in a Multi-Layered Setting: Belgium 1995–2008,' *Regional and Federal Studies* 19: 13–35.

Detterbeck, K. (2012). *Multilevel Party Politics in Western Europe*. Houndmills: Palgrave: Macmillan.

Dunleavy, P. and Bastow, S. (2001). 'Modelling Coalitions That Cannot Coalesce; A Critique of the Laver-Shepsle Approach,' *West European Politics* 24: 1–26.

Eldersveld, S. (1964). *Political Parties: a Behavioral Analysis*. Chicago: Rand McNally.

Elgie, R. (2001) (ed.). *Divided Government in Comparative Perspective*. Oxford: Oxford University Press.

Ennser-Jedenastik, L. (2014). 'The Politics of Patronage and Coalition: How Parties Allocate Managerial Positions in State-Owned Enterprises,' *Journal of Politics* 62: 398–417.

Fortunato, D., Martin, L. W., and Vanberg, G. (2017). 'Committee Chairs and Legislative Review in Parliamentary Democracies,' *British Journal of Political Science*, doi 10.1017/S0007123416000673

Frognier, A.-P. (2000). 'The Normative Foundations of Party Government,' in J. Blondel and M. Cotta (eds) *The Nature of Party Government: A Comparative European Perspective*. Houndmills: Palgrave, 21–37.

Gallagher, M., Laver, M., and Mair, P. (2006). *Representative Government in Europe*, Boston: McGraw-Hill.

Gamson, W. A. (1961). 'A Theory of Coalition Formation,' *American Sociological Review* 26: 373–82.

Gianetti, D. and Benoit, K. (2009) (eds). *Intra-Party Politics and Coalition Government*. Abingdon: Routledge.

Greene, Z. and Haber, M. (2014). 'Leadership Competition and Disagreement at Party National Congresses,' *British Journal of Political Science* 46: 611–32.

Helms, L. (1993). 'Parteienregierung im Parteienstaat. Strukturelle Voraussetzungen und Charakteristike der Parteienregierung in der Bundesrepublik Deutschland und in Österreich (1949 bis 1992),' *Zeitschrift für Parlamentsfragen* 24: 635–54.

Helms, L. (2014). 'From Party Government to Party Governance,' *Government and Opposition* 49: 120–38.

Hix, S., Noury, A., and Roland, G. (2018). *Changing Political Cleavages in Advanced Democracies: Evidence from the European Parliament*. Mimeo, July 4 2018.

Hix, S., Noury, A., and Roland, G. (2005). 'Power to the Parties: Cohesion and Competition in the European Parliament 1979–2001,' *British Journal of Political Science* 35: 209–34.

Hofferbert, R. I. and Budge, I. (1992). 'The Party Mandate and the Westminster Model: Election Programmes and Government Spending in Britain 1948–85,' *British Journal of Political Science* 22: 151–82.

Imbeau, L. M., Pétry, F., and Lamari, M. (2001). 'Left-Right Party Ideology and Government Policies: A Meta-Analysis,' *European Journal of Political Research* 40: 1–29.

Indriðason, I. H. and Kristinsson, G. H. (2013). 'Making Words Count: Coalition Agreements and Cabinet Management,' *European Journal of Political Research* 52: 822–46.

Kaarbo, J. (2012). *Coalition Politics and Cabinet Decision Making: A Comparative Analysis of Foreign Policy Choices*. Ann Arbor, MI: University of Michigan Press.

Katz, R. S. (1986). 'Party Government: A Rationalistic Conception,' in F. Castles and R. Wildenmann (eds) *The Future of Party Government. Volume 1: Visions and Realities of Party Government*. Berlin: De Gruyter, 31–71.

Katz, R. S. (1987). 'Party Government and its Alternatives,' in R. S. Katz (ed.) *The Future of Party Government. Volume 2: Party Governments, European and American Experiences*. Berlin: De Gruyter, 1–26.

Katz, R. S. and Mair, P. (1995). 'Changing Models of Party Organization and Party Democracy: the Emergence of the Cartel Party,' *Party Politics* 1: 5–28.

Katz, R. S. and Mair, P. (2018). *Democracy and the Cartelization of Political Parties*. Oxford: Oxford University Press.

Keman, H. (2017). 'Responsible Responsiveness of Parties in and out of Government,' in P. Harfst, I. Kubbe, and T. Poguntke (eds) *Parties, Governments and Elites: The Comparative Study of Democracy*. Wiesbaden: Springer, 25–52.

Keman, H. and Müller-Rommel, F. (2012) (eds). *Party Government in the New Europe*. Abingdon: Routledge.

King, G., Laver, M., Hofferbert, R. I., Budge, I., and McDonald, M. (1993). 'Party Platforms, Mandates, and Government Spending,' *American Political Science Review* 87: 744–50.

Kopecký, P. and Mair, P. (2012). 'Party Patronage as an Organizational Resource,' in P. Kopecký, P. Mair, and M. Spirova (eds) *Party Patronage and Party Government in European Democracies*. Oxford: Oxford University Press, 3–16.

Laver, M. and Schofield, N. (1990). *Multiparty Government: The Politics of Coalition in Europe*. Oxford: Oxford University Press.

Laver, M. and Shepsle, K. A. (1990). 'Coalitions and Cabinet Government,' *American Political Science Review* 87: 873–90.

Lipsmeyer, C. S. and Pierce, H. N. (2011). 'The Eyes that Bind: Junior Ministers as Oversight Mechanisms in Coalition Government,' *Journal of Politics* 73: 1152–64.

Louwerse, T. (2011). 'Political Parties and the Democratic Mandate: Comparing Collective Mandate Fulfilment in the United Kingdom and the Netherlands.' Doctoral dissertation, Leiden University.

Mair, P. (2008). 'The Challenge to Party Government,' *West European Politics* 31: 211–34.

Mair, P. (2009). 'Representative versus Responsible Government.' MPIFG Working Paper 8. (Reprinted in I. Van Biezen (2014) (ed.). *On Parties, Party Systems and Democracy: Selected Writings of Peter Mair*. Colchester: ECPR Press, 581–93.)

Manin, B. (1997). *The Principles of Representative Government*. Cambridge: Cambridge University Press.

Marks, G. and Hooghe, L. (2003). 'Unravelling the Central State, But How? Types of Multi-Level Governance,' *American Political Science Review* 97: 233–43.

Mansergh, L. and Thomson, R. (2007). 'Election Pledges, Party Competition, and Policymaking,' *Comparative Politics* 39: 311–29.

Martin, L. and Vanberg, G. (2011). *Parliaments and Coalitions: The Role of Legislative Institutions in Multiparty Governance*. Oxford: Oxford University Press.

Mitchell, P. and Nyblade, B. (2008). 'Government Formation and Cabinet Type,' in K. Strøm, W. C. Müller, and T. Bergman (eds) *Cabinets and Coalition Bargaining. The Democratic Life Cycle in Western Europe*. Oxford: Oxford University Press, 201–35.

Moury, C. (2013). *Coalition Government and Party Mandate. How Coalition Agreements Constrain Ministerial Action*. London: Routledge.

Müller, W. C. (2000a). 'Political Parties in Parliamentary Democracies: Making Delegation and Accountability Work,' *European Journal of Political Research* 37: 309–33.

Müller, W. C. (2000b). 'Patronage by National Governments,' in J. Blondel and M. Cotta (eds) *The Nature of Party Government: A Comparative European Perspective*. Houndmills: Palgrave.

Müller, W. C. and Strøm, K. (2008). 'Coalition Agreements and Cabinet Governance,' in K. Strøm, W.C. Müller, and T. Bergman (eds) *Cabinets and Coalition Bargaining: The Democratic Life Cycle in Western Europe*. Oxford: Oxford University Press, 159–99.

Piattoni, S. (2009). 'Multi-Level Governance: A Historical and Conceptual Analysis,' *Journal of European Public Policy* 31: 163–80.

Poguntke, T. and Webb, P. (2005). 'The Presidentialization of Politics in Democratic Societies: A Framework for Analysis,' in T. Poguntke and P. Webb (eds) *The Presidentialization of Politics: A Comparative Study of Modern Democracies*. Oxford: Oxford University Press.

Pomper, G. M. and Lederman, S. S. (1980). *Elections in America: Control and Influence in American Politics*. New York: Longman.

Potrafke, N. (2017). 'Partisan Politics: The Empirical Evidence from OECD Panel Studies,' *Journal of Comparative Economics* 45: 712–50.

Rae, D. W. and Daudt, H. (1976). 'The Ostrogorski Paradox: A Peculiarity of Compound Majority Decision,' *European Journal of Politcal Research* 4: 391–8.

Rallings, C. S. (1987). 'The Influence of Election Programmes: Britain and Canada 1945–1979,' in I. Budge, D. Robertson, and D. Hearl (eds), *Ideology, Strategy and Party Change*. Cambridge: Cambridge University Press, 1–14.

Ranney, A. (1954). *The Doctrine of Responsible Party Government*. Urbana, IL: University of Illinois Press (repr. 1962).

Rhodes, R. A. W. (2011). *Everyday Life in British Government*. Oxford: Oxford University Press.

Rose, R. (1974). *The Problem of Party Government*. London: Macmillan.

Rose, R. (1980). *Do Parties Make a Difference?* Chatham, NJ: Chatham House.

Royed, T. J. (1996). 'Testing the Mandate Model in Britain and the United States: Evidence from the Reagan and Thatcher Eras,' *British Journal of Political Science* 26: 45–80.

Saalfeld, T. (2009). 'Intra-Party Conflict and Cabinet Survival in 17 West European Democracies, 1945–1999,' in D. Gianetti and K. Benoit (eds) *Intra-Party Politics and Coalition Governments*. London: Routledge, 169–86.

Schmidt, M. G. (1996). 'When Parties Matter: A Review of the Possibilities and Limits of Partisan Influence on Public Policy,' *European Journal of Political Research* 30: 155–83.

Schmidt, M. G. (2002). 'The Impact of Political Parties, Constitutional Structures and Veto Players on Public Policy,' in H. Keman (ed.) *Comparative Democratic Politics*. London: Sage, 166–84.

Stefuriuc, I. (2009). 'Governing Strategies in Multilevel Settings: Coordination, Innovation or Territorialization,' in W. Swenden and B. Maddens (eds) *Territorial Party Politics in Western Europe*. Houndmills: Palgrave Macmillan, 183–203.

Strøm, K. (2000). 'Parties at the Core of Government,' in R. J. Dalton and M. P. Wattenberg (eds) *Parties without Partisans: Political Change in Advanced Industrial Democracies*. Oxford: Oxford University Press, 180–207.

Strøm, K. and Müller, W. C. (2009). 'Parliamentary Democracy, Agency Problems and Party Politics,' in D. Gianetti and K. Benoit (eds) *Intra-Party Politics and Coalition Governments*. London: Routledge, 25–49.

Sturm, R. (2001). 'Divided Government in Germany: The Case of the Bundesrat,' in R. Elgie (ed.) *Divided Government in Comparative Perspective*. Oxford: Oxford University Press, 167–81.

Swenden, W. (2002). 'Asymmetric Federalism and Coalition Making in Belgium,' *Publius* 32: 67–88.

Swenden, W. and Maddens, B. (2009) (eds). *Territorial Party Politics in Western Europe*. Houndmills: Palgrave Macmillan.

Thies, M. (2001). 'Keeping Tabs on Partners: The Logic of Delegation in Coalition Governments,' *American Journal of Political Science* 45: 590–8.

Thomassen, J. (1994). 'Empirical Research into Political Representation: Failing Democracy or Failing Models?,' in M. K. Jennings and T. Mann (eds) *Elections at Home and Abroad*. Ann Arbor, MI: University of Michigan Press, 237–65.

Thomson, R., Royed, T., Naurin, E., Artés, J., Costello, R., Ennser-Jedenastik, L., Ferguson, M., Kostadinova, P., Moury, C., Pétry, F., and Praprotnik, K. (2017). 'The Fulfillment of Parties' Election Pledges: A Comparative Study of the Impact of Power Sharing,' *American Journal of Political Science* 61: 527–42.

Vercesi, M. (2016). 'Coalition Politics and Inter-Party Conflict Management: A Theoretical Framework,' *Politics & Policy* 44: 168–219.

Verzichelli, L. (2008). 'Portfolio Allocation,' in K. Strøm, W. C. Müller, and T. Bergman (eds) *Cabinets and Coalition Bargaining: The Democratic Life Cycle in Western Europe*. Oxford: Oxford University Press, 237–68.

Warwick, P. (1999). 'Ministerial Autonomy or Ministerial Accommodation? Contested Bases of Government Survival in Parliamentary Democracies,' *British Journal of Political Science* 29: 369–94.

Weller, P. (1997). 'Political Parties and the Core Executive,' in P. Weller, H. Bakvis, and R. A. W. Rhodes (eds) *The Hollow Crown: Countervailing Trends in Core Executives*. London: Macmillan, 37–57.

CHAPTER 24

LEADERSHIP STYLES OF POLITICAL EXECUTIVES

JONATHAN W. KELLER

24.1 INTRODUCTION

THIS chapter focuses on the leadership styles of political executives. Leadership style refers to an executive's general approach or orientation toward the tasks of leadership; it is therefore a broader concept than individual personality traits or beliefs (see Chapter 14 in this volume), although such characteristics certainly shape one's leadership style. Leadership style can be defined as 'the ways in which leaders relate to those around them—whether constituents, advisers, or other leaders—and how they structure interactions and the norms, rules, and principles they use to guide such interactions' (Hermann 2003: 181).

Leadership style is an important topic of inquiry for several reasons. First, given the pivotal roles played by political executives, such research can shed light on the causal drivers of processes and outcomes in the political realm. Specifically, an executive's leadership style influences how they perform a range of vital tasks such as defining problems, generating and evaluating options, choosing policies, and overseeing the implementation of these decisions. This research aids theory building and hypothesis testing regarding the links between leadership style and political outcomes, and may even permit conditional forecasts with profound policy relevance. Second, the comparative study of leadership styles and their consequences is of great practical importance to those who seek to improve the quality of policy-making processes and generate insights for leadership training (e.g. Boin et al. 2017). Third, from a normative standpoint, studying the implications of various political leadership styles can help to promote democracy and good governance by revealing the consequences of different leadership approaches for accountability, transparency, efficiency, development, and the rule of law (Helms 2012).

There is a substantial and growing body of literature on executive leadership styles, spanning the fields of political science, psychology, management science, and public administration. Much of this work, as shown below, focuses on the domain of foreign policy. This chapter highlights the major questions addressed by this work, reviews what we have learned so far, identifies gaps and unanswered questions, and suggests important pathways for future research.

24.2 Leadership Style: Key Questions

The most fundamental question posed by scholars about executive leadership is whether leaders' characteristics or styles matter at all. As discussed in the next section, scholarship focusing on institutions, structural conditions (e.g. economic interdependence), cultural norms, and rational choice explanations has at times cast doubt on whether individual leaders exercise any autonomous influence over political outcomes. If one accepts that leaders matter at least some of the time—as most scholars do—then a crucial question becomes: under what circumstances do leaders and their styles make a difference? That is, what institutional structures, political conditions, cultural attitudes, leadership traits, and situational pressures (e.g. crises) are conductive to leaders mattering more or less? Must there be a fit between an executive's leadership style and key features of the political context in order to produce impactful or high quality outcomes? A related set of questions involves the relative importance of leadership style and situational variables—the perennial agency versus structure question—in shaping policy processes and outcomes. Does leadership style only matter at the margins, or is it potentially the decisive influence over such matters as war and peace, democratization, and economic development?

Moving from the general to the specific, scholars have explored which dimensions of leadership style are particularly important in the political realm, and how these aspects of leadership style shape the content and quality of political processes and outcomes. For example, what are the different approaches a political executive might take to managing advisory systems, and what are the implications of these styles for timeliness of response, information distortion, bureaucratic conflict, and the political viability of solutions? (Johnson 1974). Or, what alternative styles do leaders exhibit with regard to responsiveness to political constraints, and what are the consequences for the roles of public opinion, the legislative branch, and international actors in the policy-making process? (Keller 2005b). A key question that looms over all such studies is whether certain leadership styles are more effective than others, at least in certain contexts. Considerable attention has been paid to answering the effectiveness question, particularly in the management science literature (e.g. Blake and Mouton 1964; Fiedler 1967; Barber 1977; Burns 1978).

A final set of questions treats leadership style as a dependent variable and seeks to explain variation in leadership styles exhibited by different leaders or by the same leader in different contexts. Political psychologists have explored the origins of different leadership styles, with particular reference to trait-based building blocks and developmental influences (e.g. George and George 1956; Hermann 2003; Renshon 2008). Other studies have examined whether styles are largely static or vary based on the context and perceived demands of the situation (e.g. Keller 2009; Boin et al. 2017).

These questions have generated a remarkably rich and diverse body of literature that includes a myriad disciplinary frames, methodological approaches, and theoretical perspectives. The next section reviews major contributions to the literature on executive leadership styles and evaluates the scope, methods, persuasiveness, and coherence of these findings.

24.3 LEADERSHIP STYLE: WHAT HAVE WE LEARNED?

24.3.1 Agency vs. Structure

As noted above, the most fundamental question addressed by research on political leadership is whether leadership style even matters, and if so, when. That is, does agency or structure predominate? Or do agents and structures interact as coequal forces in predictable ways to shape outcomes? ('t Hart 2014).

Thomas Carlyle's (1927) 'great man' thesis makes the case for agency: powerful individuals such as Muhammad, Luther, and Napoleon drive the course of history. Hook's (1943) contemplation of *The Hero in History* likewise shines a spotlight on momentous, 'event-making' leaders. Early studies of political leadership emphasized the ways in which leaders' psychological makeup shaped their leadership styles and, in many cases, altered the course of world affairs. Lasswell's (1930) classic *Psychopathology and Politics*, Leites' (1951) study of Soviet leaders' operational codes, George and George's (1956) analysis of Woodrow Wilson, and Weber's (1958) notion of charismatic leadership emphasized the ways in which leaders' personal characteristics had important political consequences at the local, national, and global levels. These studies, and work in this tradition to this day, have marshalled compelling evidence to support the notion that leaders' traits and styles are important causal drivers of political processes and outcomes. While such studies have sometimes included nuanced consideration of the interplay between structure and agency, these insights are often neglected when scholars distil the essence of this work—and the core takeaway argument becomes that a variety of leadership traits and styles shape political outcomes in important ways. This emphasis on traits as drivers has contributed to a tendency—particularly within political psychology—to discount the importance of structural constraints in favour of agency-based explanations.

In contrast, structural explanations have gained increased prominence in the broader political science literature since the 1970s. Rhodes and 't Hart (2014) note that the field of political leadership studies 'lost its way with the rise of structuralism, neo-institutionalism, and rational choice approaches to the study of politics, government, and governance' (see Chapters 3 and 5 in this volume). Disturbingly, studies of political phenomena that by all accounts should have included a sizeable role for political leaders often completely ignored leadership. Bueno de Mesquita's (1981) *The War Trap* claimed to be explaining war decisions and calculations, but predicted conflict using objective structural conditions married to the assumption that decision-makers are rational utility maximizers. Democratic peace theory (e.g. Russett 1993) often paid lip service to leaders as decision-makers, but in practice assumed that all democratic leaders simply recognize and submit to domestic institutional and normative constraints. Work on the diversionary use of force similarly conceded that leaders' calculations were at the centre of the theory, but then proceeded to assume that all leaders respond similarly and automatically to the political and economic difficulties in their environments (e.g. Ostrom and Job 1986). Traditional work on political executives, which highlights institutional constraints, role requirements, path-dependency and political and cultural drivers of change, has also tended to discount the role of agency in favour of contextual explanations (e.g. Rose 1991; Lijphart 1992; Edwards 2003).

Leadership studies that take agency seriously have seen something of a renaissance in the last couple of decades (Rhodes and 't Hart 2014). While such work continues to undervalue structural drivers, there appears to be increasing acceptance of the importance of contingent explanations and the need for attention to the scope conditions under which leadership style makes a difference (e.g. Keller 2005a; Skowronek 2008; Kettell 2009; see also Chapter 4 in this volume). Indeed, a careful reading of the literature on leadership—from its inception—provides a clear answer to the agent-structure question posed above: leadership style does matter, but it is powerfully conditioned by the context. We now turn to a review of these findings.

24.3.2 Context is Critical

Leaders do not exist in a vacuum; they can exercise agency but structural factors are usually influential and sometimes decisive. The very nature of leadership is relational, and political executives must contend with an array of powerful institutional, cultural, and political forces that provide both constraints and opportunities for action. These contextual factors shape both *when leadership style matters* and *how effective various approaches will be*. In short, agents and structures are inseparably linked.

Research in political science has shown that executives' leadership styles are more likely to influence political outcomes during crisis situations, when problems are ambiguous, when bureaucracies and institutional constraints are less developed, and when leaders have more interest in the issue at hand. During crises—characterized by short decision time, high threat to basic values, and surprise—decision authority contracts to a small group of elite decision-makers given the high stakes and the need for a quick response by accountable authorities (Boin et al. 2017). Not only are leaders more central during crises—they also tend to fall back on their pre-existing world views and habitual behaviours, further amplifying the importance of leaders' styles (e.g. Larson 1994; Boin et al. 2012). When situations are ill-defined, leaders are called upon to frame the problem and the viable responses, which maximizes the influence of their beliefs and decision-making styles (Jervis 1976; Sylvan and Voss 1998). Clearly, leaders in institutional contexts that provide greater decision latitude and fewer veto points or sources of legitimate opposition—for example, autocratic regimes—will have greater opportunity to shape decision processes and policies in line with their own preferences. Among democracies, the distinction between presidential and parliamentary systems is an oft-studied institutional difference that conditions whether leaders confront a separation of powers or a fusion of powers (Lijphart 1992; Helms 2005). Paradoxically, political leaders in democracies can be either greatly empowered or severely constrained, depending on whether they enjoy the trust and authority of the people (Kane and Patapan 2012). Furthermore, any political system with highly developed bureaucratic structures will make it difficult for leaders to steer the 'ship of state' in a new direction— or frequently even to effectively monitor and implement policies that are not particularly novel or controversial. In his classic treatise on *Presidential Power* (1960), Neustadt revealed the striking inability of US presidents to obtain their goals through mere command, and the need for bargaining and persuasion to influence even executive branch officials who theoretically should be carrying out the president's wishes without resistance. Similarly, Allison's influential *Essence of Decision* (1971) highlighted the ways in which political executives in the US government were frequently hamstrung by bureaucratic conflict and organizational routines, even during the existential threat of the Cuban Missile Crisis. At the international level, growing economic interdependence, supranational governance, and issue complexity in the era of globalization has made it more difficult for leaders to act decisively, forge independent paths for their countries, and control (or even predict) the second- and third-order effects of policy decisions (Rose 1991, 2001).

Lest one assume, however, that leaders are hopelessly constrained by these situational obstacles, research indicates that leaders can also act upon their contexts—an important example of the dynamic interplay between agents and structures. For example, as a rejoinder to Neustadt and Allison, Krasner (1972) noted that bureaucratic politics and organizational standard operating procedures are more likely to determine outcomes on routine issues or in policy areas that are not presidential priorities, but when the president is engaged and committed to a particular outcome, he or she will bring the full power of the office to bear and his or her own values and decision style will drive policy-making. Similarly, Greenstein's (1969) classic formulation of when actor-centred explanations are appropriate notes that the actor must have both the power and the motivation to shape outcomes in a particular arena. Rose (2001), Theakston (2002), and Hargrove (2002) have shown that political skill and knowledge can allow leaders to shape outcomes even when contextual obstacles are present. And, as discussed below, leaders' responsiveness to political constraints will affect whether they respect, or seek to challenge, the institutional and political obstacles that they confront (e.g. Keller 2005b; Dyson 2007).

The context also influences how effective various leadership styles will be. In the management science literature, Fiedler's (1967) contingency model is premised on the notion that there is no ideal leadership style. Rather, the fit between the manager's style and features of the situation will determine success or failure. For example, when team members have a high level of trust in the leader, the task at hand is structured, and the leader has the authority to dispense rewards and punishments, executives with a task-oriented style will be most effective. In contrast, when the leader has authority to reward and punish but trust is low in the leader and the task is unstructured, a relations-oriented style is most effective. Similarly, Johnson's (1974) study of how presidents manage their advisory systems finds that different styles (formalistic, competitive, and collegial) are better suited to accomplishing different types of goals. The formalistic approach (Eisenhower and Nixon) implies a hierarchical staff system that allows thorough ana-lysis but may distort information and obscure political realities. The competitive approach (Franklin Roosevelt) encourages conflict among subordinates with overlap-ping jurisdictions and stimulates creative thinking but may harm morale and produce incomplete information. Finally, the collegial approach (Kennedy) encourages staff to build consensus; while this approach can produce options that are both politically feasible and substantively optimal, it requires the leader to invest considerable effort in mediating differences and maintaining collegiality. The formalistic style works best for managing the bureaucracy but the competitive style is most effective in dealing with a politically fractured Congress. Finally, Burns' (1978) famous dichotomy between transformational and transactional leadership styles (discussed in more detail below) suggests that the former style is preferable; but even here, each style may be better suited to different conditions. Transformational leadership appears best suited to majoritarian political systems or those undergoing economic development or other major transformations (Manning 2001), whereas the transactional style is more effective in consensual political systems (Peters and Helms 2012) and in business contexts where the goal is short-term productivity on straightforward tasks.

There is also intriguing evidence that political executives' electoral success and performance in office is determined by the fit between their leadership styles and the situations in which they find themselves. Winter (1987) finds that US presidents whose motive profiles—based on needs for power, achievement, and affiliation—fit the motive profiles of their contemporary societies have greater electoral success. Skowronek (2008) finds that leaders' success in office is greatly influenced by the match between their leadership style and the challenges presented by the viability of the current regime. For example, if the regime is declining or low in viability, leaders can either seek to reconstruct the regime ('preservation') or to replace the regime ('innovation'). In turn, if the regime is ascending or high in viability, leaders can either attempt to further institu-tionalize the regime ('articulation') or to destroy the regime ('pre-emption'). Some of these challenges—such as destroying a viable and highly popular regime or preserving a declining regime—are more difficult than others. If a leader's beliefs, skills, and man-agerial style incline him or her toward disruption, creative destruction, and mobilizing followers for dramatic change, he or she will do much better in an era of regime decline than of high regime viability. Some work on birth order and political leadership also suggests that certain leadership styles are better suited than others to the political circumstances of the times. Stewart (1977) presents evidence that first-born children become more assertive leaders, middle children take on a mediator/integrator role, and last-born children develop a revolutionary outlook. He finds that in times of imperialistic expansion and confrontation, first-born children come to power, in periods of retrenchment and re-alignment middle children take the stage, and in eras of rebellion and revolt, last-born children assume power. More recent research on birth order casts doubt on some of these conclusions, however (Hudson 1990). While the above work provides some evidence that leaders' characteristics may affect their electoral fortunes, King's (2002) edited volume examining the electoral politics of six countries finds that *voters' perceptions of leaders' personalities* rarely determined election outcomes.

In general, careful comparative studies of leaders—particularly those that seek to rate leaders in terms of their performance and impact—have understood the necessity of taking the historical context into account. Even if they possess the requisite leadership skills, not all leaders have an opportunity to become a great wartime leader, an innovator driving his or her country's economic development, or a mediator healing divisions in a newly independent state. In their analysis of presidential leadership styles, Genovese, Belt, and Lammers (2014) divide US presidents into high-opportunity presidents such as Franklin D. Roosevelt and Ronald Reagan, moderate-opportunity presidents like Dwight Eisenhower and Barack Obama, and low-opportunity presidents such as Jimmy Carter and George H. W. Bush. A study of the gap between President Obama's sweeping policy ambitions and his more modest achievements concludes that one cannot understand these outcomes without considering both Obama's leadership style and the political, economic, and institutional constraints that he faced—an approach termed 'structured agency' (Jacobs and King 2010). Work by Theakston (2002), Hargrove (2002), and Hargrove and Owens (2003) examines political leadership 'in context' across a variety of political systems and time periods, and reaches compelling conclusions about the interplay between leaders and their environments. These scholars conclude not only that the combination of political skill and a favourable context (e.g. a political and cultural climate reinforcing leaders' policy goals) can produce great successes, but that skilled leaders can achieve some success even in unfavourable contexts and that personal weaknesses can spell disaster despite favourable climates. In contrast with Neustadt's president-centred model, these frameworks explicitly consider the interaction between contextual variables and presidential skill in determining leaders' effectiveness. Even James Barber's (1977) classic work on *The Presidential Character*, which might be criticized for equating leadership style with destiny, reached conclusions similar to those described above. That is, 'active-positive' presidents such as Franklin Roosevelt and John F. Kennedy succeeded by pragmatically identifying contextual opportunities while 'active-negatives' such as Lyndon Johnson and Richard Nixon found their weaknesses triggered and amplified by the conditions inherent in the Vietnam War and the Watergate crisis.

In sum, we may conclude that leaders' characteristics and styles matter, under certain circumstances and in ways conditioned by the context. For a comprehensive recent review of the ways in which contextual factors shape leadership and outcomes, see Oc (2018). The next section turns to specific leadership styles and considers what has been learned about the impact of certain styles on processes and outcomes in the political realm.

24.3.3 Key Dimensions of Leadership Style: Concern for People or Production?

The cross-disciplinary literature on leadership style is replete with typologies, frameworks, and labels for different approaches to leadership in the public and private domains. In fact, many studies focus on a single leader, deal with a very specific type of leadership, or employ unique leadership categories that are not developed elsewhere in the literature. This diversity can be useful for exploring leadership in specific contexts, or examining the impact of narrow aspects of leadership style, but it presents a challenge for efforts to accumulate knowledge and reach general conclusions about leadership style across issue areas, regime types, geographical regions, and time periods. Still, there are striking areas of unity amid this diversity. Two such areas will be examined in the following pages, involving the importance of the task versus interpersonal orientation and leaders' responsiveness to contextual constraints. First, many studies of leadership in the political and business domains have converged on the finding that the most important dimension of leadership style is a leader's emphasis on meeting people's needs versus achieving task-related goals.

In an influential early study, social psychologist Kurt Lewin and his colleagues (1939) identified three leadership styles and their consequences through experimental analysis: the autocratic, democratic, and laissez-faire leadership styles. Autocratic leaders make all of the decisions themselves, assign roles to subordinates, and issue orders in a hierarchical manner. Democratic leaders allow group members to participate meaningfully in decision-making, although the leader may have the final say. Laissez-faire leaders allow the group members to do whatever they want with very little supervision. Lewin found that the democratic leadership style was most effective; it fostered creativity, friendship, and hard work, even when the leader was not watching. Autocratic leadership produced hard work when the leader was present, but generated little 'ownership' or creativity among group members and actually generated scapegoating, anger, and various forms of aggression. Laissez-faire leadership was associated with laziness and a lack of productivity among group members.

Blake and Mouton's (1964) managerial grid overlaps to some degree with Lewin's framework but yields some additional insights. This grid identifies two underlying dimensions that together determine one's leadership style: a manager's degree of concern for people and their degree of concern for accomplishing tasks. Leaders who are very low in concern for both people and production exhibit an 'impoverished' management style that is similar to Lewin's laissez-faire approach and produces little in the way of results. Leaders with a maximum concern for people and a minimum concern for production exhibit a 'country club' management style, in which maintaining relationships and good feelings takes precedence over production. This style yields an enjoyable work environment but is inferior in terms of task accomplishment. In contrast, managers with a minimum concern for people and a maximum concern for production have an autocratic, or 'produce-or-perish' management style. Such leaders view their subordinates as means to an end, and can generate high production in the short term, but this cannot be sustained as morale problems and resistance accumulate. Managers with a medium degree of concern for both people and results are 'middle-of-the-road' managers, who can maintain the status quo but generally fail to inspire more than mediocre performance. Finally, those with a maximum concern for both people and production are 'team managers' who motivate their workers to achieve outstanding results by meeting their needs and inspiring them to 'buy in' to the mission of the organization by identifying this mission with their personal goals. As a result, Blake and Mouton contend that team management is the most effective leadership style. As discussed below, this leadership style has much in common with the transformational approach described by Burns (1978).

A similar framework—but oriented toward the political realm—was developed by Byars (1972, 1973). Byars built on Bales's (1950) study of leadership in small groups, and undertook an analysis of political leadership styles at the societal level. Byars proposed that developing societies require leaders who balance the 'task' and 'affective' leadership orientations in order most effectively to achieve their economic development goals. Task-oriented leaders are those who focus intensively on economic development, while affect-oriented leaders seek to perform socioemotional or expressive-integrative functions to overcome the hostilities and antagonisms produced by development activities. Occasionally one leader can serve both functions by simultaneously having high task and affect orientations; more often, different leaders must fulfill the task-related and affect-based needs of society.

Like the frameworks advanced by Byars and by Blake and Mouton, Fiedler's (1967) contingency model of leadership views a manager's leadership style as a reflection of their relative concern for task accomplishment versus relationship building. Fiedler's Least Preferred Co-Worker (LPC) scale measures a person's relative task or relationship orientation by asking the person to rate his or her LPC favourably or unfavourably on a number of non-task related dimensions such as friendliness, loyalty, and trustworthiness. Those who rate the LPC unfavourably on these non-task dimensions are assumed to be task-motivated, since their inability to work with that person colours their evaluation of the person in other areas. In contrast, those who rate the LPC highly in the non-task areas are relationship-motivated, since they can see value in the LPC outside of the work environment. In contrast to the conclusions of Lewin (who favours the democratic leadership style) and Blake and Mouton (who favour the team manager style), Fiedler contends that there is no ideal leadership style; rather, key features of the situation determine whether task-oriented or relations-oriented leadership will be more effective. These situational factors are (1) leader-member relations (how much trust team members have in the leader); (2) task structure (either structured or unstructured); and (3) the leader's position power (strong or weak, as determined by the leader's ability to provide rewards and punishments and direct the group). Not all permutations will be considered here, but as noted in the previous section, in situations where team members have a high level of trust in the leader, the task at hand is structured, and the leader has the authority to dispense rewards and punishments, executives with a task-oriented style will be most effective. In contrast, when the leader has authority to reward and punish but trust is low in the leader and the task is unstructured, building relationships takes precedence and a relations-oriented style is called for.

Perhaps the best known leadership framework is the dichotomy between transformational and transactional leadership, as developed by James McGregor Burns (1978, 2003) and elaborated by Bernard Bass (1985). Transactional leadership involves motivating people through rewards and punishments, closely monitoring compliance with expectations, and providing clear direction. The central transaction between leaders and followers in the political realm may be 'jobs for votes, or subsidies for campaign contributions' (Burns 1978: 4), or in the business world, production in exchange for pay and other tangible benefits. While this approach has much in common with the more hierarchical and compliance-based autocratic and produce-or-perish management styles, it overcomes some of the downsides of this approach by focusing on meeting the needs of team members through attractive rewards (often allowing workers some choice in their rewards) and providing some autonomy due to the short-term and straightforward nature of the tasks. Transformational leadership, on other hand, involves creating a compelling vision, motivating team members to 'buy in' to that vision, and inspiring them toward higher levels of performance and morality. Transformational leaders, like Blake and Mouton's team managers, do not view people and production as a zero-sum game, but devise methods of meeting both people's needs and organizational needs simultaneously by redefining people's perceptions of their interests. More recent research confirms the enduring utility of the transformational leadership model for explaining productivity, employee creativity, and organizational innovation across a variety of organizational, cultural, and national contexts (e.g. Bass 1997; Jung and Avolio 2000; Jung et al. 2003; Gumusluoglu and Ilsev 2009; Wang et al. 2011; Moynihan et al. 2012; Shin and Zhou 2017; Ng 2017). Interestingly, the transactional versus transformational leadership distinction closely parallels Joseph Nye's (2005) conception of hard versus soft power. Transactional leadership relies on hard power because it utilizes rewards and punishments to influence followers to take actions they otherwise would not take. Transformational leadership, however, shapes followers' perceptions so that they now want to take actions consistent with the leader's preferences, even in the absence of explicit rewards and punishments. This is the essence of soft power.

The degree to which these various frameworks spanning the fields of political science, psychology, and management science have converged on the task versus relations dimension as the crucial determinant of leadership style is striking but perhaps not surprising. Since leadership in business and politics is about managing people to achieve task-related results, it matters greatly whether one sees these people as cogs in the organizational (or societal) machine who are instrumentally valuable as producers, or whether one sees them as intrinsically valuable team members whose needs and preferences must be part of the decision process. From the theoretical arguments and empirical evidence reviewed here, we can draw several conclusions. First, a lopsided preference for production over people will generate an autocratic leadership style that may generate compliance and high productivity in the short term (particularly if the leader carefully monitors behaviour) but is not conducive to creativity, healthy relations among group members, or sustainable morale and motivation. But if followers have great trust in the leader, tasks require little creativity, the leader enjoys considerable position power, and/or the followers are motivated by short-term transactional interests, then this style may have some benefit. Second, an equally lopsided emphasis on relationships over production will yield an easy-going management style that strengthens relationships and maximizes team members' participation and enjoyment, but at the cost of greatly reduced productivity. This seemingly flawed leadership style may in fact be desirable in the short term in a country or organization plagued by divisions, distrust, and conflict. Third, a lack of concern for both people and production will result in a laissez-faire leadership style that is by some measures the worst of all approaches as production suffers and people's needs are simultaneously neglected. Fourth, the most effective leadership style for most situations combines a concern for people with a concern for production—but if one merely balances these concerns and does not maximize each, mediocrity may result (Blake and Mouton 1964). Both Burns' transformational leadership and Blake and Mouton's team management style are premised on a high degree of concern both for people and for task-related results. Perhaps the only way to square the circle of maximizing people's needs while maximizing organizational (or state) goals is to align people's perceived interests with the interests of the organization or the state. Such a leadership style requires at least an intuitive understanding of soft power, which is notoriously difficult to wield reliably (Nye 2005). Therefore, executives must be aware that transformational leadership is more easily described than achieved.

24.3.4 Key Dimensions of Leadership Style: Sensitivity to the Political Context

A second area of consensus in the diverse literature on leadership style concerns the importance of leaders' responsiveness to the political context. Many studies have identified a fundamental distinction between leaders who are more ideologically driven or task-motivated on the one hand, and those who are more contextually sensitive or situationally responsive on the other. That is, some leaders are internally motivated by an ideology, a task, or a problem, and thus less responsive to opposition, institutional constraints, or disconfirming information in the environment, while other leaders are more externally validated or 'other-directed' and seek to establish and maintain the approval of key constituencies. This difference is related to the task versus interpersonal distinction highlighted above, but it is broader in scope and concerns how leaders deal with the full range of constraints in the political environment—not merely the management of followers and subordinates. Key typologies here include 'crusaders' versus 'pragmatists' (Stoessinger 1979), 'ideologues' versus 'opportunists' (Ziller et al. 1977), 'directive' versus 'consultative' leaders (Bass and Valenzi 1974), and 'constraint challengers' versus 'constraint respecters' (Keller 2005b).

Understanding a leader's orientation toward the political environment is of paramount importance if one wishes to explain and forecast policy-making processes and outcomes. Political scientists have identified a broad range of contextual variables— political, economic, and social factors at the governmental, societal, and international system level—that may shape decisions, but whether these variables will enter into the decision process in a given case depends greatly on how leaders perceive and respond to these potential influences. A leader who is ideologically or task-driven and faces a decision on a matter related to this motivating ideology or task will typically move decisively to implement policies consistent with his or her views, even in the face of considerable opposition. Unless the leader's political survival is directly threatened, he or she will generally not make it a priority to seek out the preferences of key political actors and to incorporate these views into the policy-making process. Thus, the roles of public opinion, legislative leaders' views, bureaucratic interests, and allies' preferences will be minimized in the decision-making process. In contrast, leaders who are sensitive to the political context and motivated by a desire to build consensus and maintain others' approval will perceive that they cannot take actions without considerable support from such actors as the public, legislative blocs, cabinet officials, or even allied countries.

Case studies support these process-related propositions. The uncompromising behaviour of Woodrow Wilson with regard to the League of Nations is an oft-cited case of the 'crusading' leader in action (George and George 1956; Stoessinger 1979). An analysis of the decision-making processes employed by President Reagan (a 'constraint challenger') and President Kennedy (a 'constraint respecter') during international crises found that Reagan generally ignored or sought to circumvent public opinion and Congressional opposition—perceiving such opposition to be illegitimate and harmful to the national interest—while Kennedy perceived himself to be constrained, for normative and practical reasons, to behave in accordance with public and Congressional preferences (Keller 2005b). Similarly, Dyson (2007) found that Great Britain's willingness to commit troops to the 2003 Iraq War while staying out of Vietnam—both domestically unpopular wars fought by an important ally, the United States—can be traced to the contrasting leadership styles of Prime Ministers Harold Wilson (a constraint respecter) and Tony Blair (a constraint challenger). In a more in-depth study of Tony Blair's leadership style, Dyson (2009) shows that across multiple foreign policy crises, including Kosovo, Sierra Leone, the War on Terror, and Iraq, Blair consistently exhibited a tendency to view situations in black-and-white terms, had confidence in his ability to shape events, and was willing to persevere in policies driven by his convictions despite considerable political opposition and setbacks. Research on the nexus between leadership style and advisory systems (Preston and 't Hart 1999; Preston 2001) has found that leaders who are less sensitive to the political context and have a greater need for control over the policy process develop more centralized and closed advisory systems. In this same vein, Mitchell (2005) finds that leaders' management styles with regard to willingness to delegate and involve a range of voices in the policy-making process shape how centralized and formalized the advisory system is, with important implications for how susceptible policy-making is to factors in the broader political environment. Beyond case studies, the importance of decision-makers' sensitivity to the political context has also been established through experimental studies (e.g. Keller and Yang 2008) and statistical analyses of a larger sample of cases (e.g. Hermann and Hermann 1989; Keller 2005a).

Leaders' varying responsiveness to political constraints is particularly important for explaining policy-making in democratic countries—where potential opposition is more varied, legitimate, and institutionalized—but these insights also apply to non-democratic systems. In autocratic states, political leaders cannot entirely dismiss the views of the masses and must deal with elite constituencies such as the military, the secret police, party officials, or corporate interests. Whether they seek to accommodate or challenge these political constraints will shape policy outcomes and at times determine their own political survival.

As for the relative effectiveness of the constraint challenging versus constraint respecting leadership styles, the literature suggests some interesting conclusions. Constraint challengers may perform better during crises, when decisive leadership is expected and there is not time for consensus-building or drawn-out deliberation over policy alternatives. Such leaders are also capable of bold, transformative initiatives since they do not perceive themselves to be constrained by convention, political opposition, or perhaps even contemporary institutional structures. They often have a visionary quality and display remarkable persistence in pursuing their goals despite political opposition and setbacks. Of course, the downside of this leadership style flows from these same qualities. Such leaders may unnecessarily provoke political opposition and imperil their future success as they seek to circumvent or frustrate the ambitions of key domestic political actors. They may persist in failing policies, refusing to change course as a more pragmatic leader would, and thus bringing upon themselves and their country heavier costs than would otherwise be borne. In extreme cases, their willingness to challenge norms and even longstanding constitutional structures may undermine political systems and imperil democratic governance.

The constraint respecting leadership style likewise exhibits both strengths and weaknesses. Constraint respecters are more open to information and advice, and will generally consider a wider array of options, perspectives, and risks when making decisions. This minimizes the chances of getting locked into failed policies or pursuing politically unpopular initiatives. Their participatory decision style ensures a diverse set of voices are heard and can help to heal societal divisions and build trust. Their adherence to established norms and institutional processes provides stability and predictability. However, such leaders generally take a long time making decisions (particularly in a polarized climate) and may become paralysed by indecision. Their choices, while politically palatable to a wide array of actors, may be diluted to 'lowest common denominator' solutions that are ineffective in addressing the targeted policy problems. Their risk aversion may prevent them from taking advantage of windows of opportunity to make changes that are beneficial or necessary but not widely popular. As with leaders' emphasis on people versus production, extremes in leaders' orientations toward the political context are best avoided. That is, both ideology devoid of political sensitivity and pragmatism that lacks vision are unlikely to be successful leadership approaches. While they may lean toward the crusading or the pragmatic end of the spectrum, the most effective leaders possess both a well-defined policy vision and a keen sensitivity to political realities.

24.3.5 Integrating Insights on Leadership Style

The most ambitious effort to integrate existing insights on leadership style into a comprehensive framework comes from Hermann (2003). This framework identifies eight different leadership styles based on different combinations of three variables: responsiveness to constraints, openness to information, and motivation (problem or relationship focus). Notice that two of these three underlying variables—sensitivity to context and task vs. relationship focus—are the ones that the literature has converged upon as the most important predictors of leadership behaviour. A strength of this framework is that it goes beyond single-dimension explanations and specifies how, for example, a 'constraint challenger' may actually exhibit quite different leadership styles depending on whether or not that leader is open or closed to information and has a problem or relationship focus. A constraint challenger who is closed to information and has a task (problem) focus will take on the 'expansionist' leadership style, which emphasizes expanding the leader's, government's, or state's area of control. For example, in a study of ten executives of intergovernmental organizations (six UN secretaries-general and four EU Commission presidents), Kille and Scully (2003) found that executives whose traits more closely approximated the expansionist leadership style expended more effort on raising the profile, influence, and independence of their organizations. However, a constraint challenger who is closed to information and has a relationship focus will exhibit the 'evangelistic' leadership style, which emphasizes persuading others to join the leader's mission and mobilizing others around that message. To take but one other example, a constraint respecter who is open to information and has a relationship focus will exhibit the 'collegial' leadership style, which emphasizes reconciling differences and building consensus by empowering others and sharing accountability. This nuanced framework is a noteworthy example of an attempt to unify the various streams of research on leadership style and show how these pieces fit together. It lacks the parsimony of a single-factor model (e.g. crusaders vs. pragmatists) but this very complexity may make such frameworks more useful for explaining and predicting leadership behaviour.

24.4 An Agenda for Future Research

Thanks to the work of scholars from fields including psychology, sociology, political science, and management science over the last century, we now know quite a bit about when leadership style matters and how specific aspects of leadership style shape processes and outcomes in the political realm. But there is much more work to be done.

One striking feature of the current literature—particularly the classic and most influential work—is its emphasis on Western leaders (especially American presidents and British prime ministers) in democratic and free-market contexts. Exceptions (e.g. King 2002; Kille and Scully 2003) have yielded great insights but are all too rare. Some of this emphasis can be justified by the outsized influence of the United States and its political and business leaders since the mid-twentieth century, but this narrow focus hampers our ability to develop generalizable propositions about leadership across various institutional and geographical contexts and to determine what features of leadership in the US context are unique or are broadly shared with other systems. Part of the challenge is that scholars focusing on leadership often lack the comparative, linguistic, or cultural knowledge that would allow in-depth investigation of leadership in non-Western contexts. This is where cross-disciplinary collaboration can be particularly fruitful. For example, collaboration between political psychologists and comparative politics specialists can allow nuanced analysis of the ways in which political leaders' styles shape, and are shaped by, a variety of institutional and cultural contexts.

A related problem is that, while comparative analysis is crucial for theory building and hypothesis testing, there is a dearth of rigorous, systematic comparative work on political leadership (Helms 2012). Many studies continue to focus on a single leader or leaders within a single country, time period, or institutional context. There are substantial methodological challenges that confront comparative research on leadership, related to source availability, substantive expertise, and the difficulty of designing comparative studies that hold constant, and allow variation in, key variables related to leadership style and the context. For example, even efforts to compare US presidents' styles and performance will be deeply flawed unless the researcher finds a way to take into account variation in constraints and opportunities based on the historical and political context (Genovese et al. 2014). Nevertheless, rigorous comparative work is indispensable for theoretical and empirical advances in our understanding of political leadership.

Continued methodological advances and refinement are also necessary to expand the reach and persuasiveness of leadership analysis beyond subfields such as political psychology. Among mainstream political scientists, leaders' traits and styles are often seen as idiosyncratic, conceptually vague, and difficult to measure. As noted earlier, this has contributed to a reliance on structural explanations and to research that seeks to correlate political outcomes with economic conditions, institutional structures, power capabilities, and other variables that are perceived as more objective and easier to measure. This trend coincided with the rise of modern political science in the 1960s and its emphasis on rigorous measurement and valid research designs. (It is not surprising that some of the most insightful leadership studies came from the era of traditional political science (roughly 1930–60) that valued historical, philosophical, and psychobiographical studies). There have indeed been important methodological advances over the last few decades in the measurement of leaders' traits and styles 'at a distance' through the development of rigorous assessment schemes and the automation of these systems (e.g. Walker et al. 1998; Hermann 2003). However, more work can be done to refine our understanding of precisely what these coding schemes are measuring—particularly when there is variation in scores across different topics, time periods, audiences, and types of material (e.g. scripted versus spontaneous remarks). Scholars employing qualitative methods can also benefit from efforts to enhance the rigour and objectivity of their leadership categories and measures.

Moreover, greater methodological rigour is only part of the solution—a larger obstacle may be the balkanization of political science scholarship and the associated ignorance and scepticism by many regarding the role of political leadership. It is not uncommon to hear leadership style or psychological explanations dismissed as too idiosyncratic or merely the province of Freudian psychoanalysis—an oversimplification that betrays a lack of understanding of the myriad ways in which leaders' beliefs and styles have been measured and shown to affect outcomes. Therefore, part of the solution is for scholars of political leadership to more actively seek to bridge this divide by bringing leadership 'into the territory' of commonly recognized structural explanations and demonstrating empirically how leadership style interacts with structural factors. Research that 'brings leaders back in' to established research programmes such as the democratic peace (e.g. Hermann and Kegley 1995), diversionary war (e.g. Keller and Foster 2012), and the study of international norms (e.g. Shannon and Keller 2007), and demonstrates how taking leadership seriously can enhance existing models' explanatory power can help to achieve this objective. Interactive, bridge-building scholarship that takes seriously both agency and structure can also help to ensure that leadership studies do not discount the importance of structural factors.

There is also much more to learn about leadership style as a dependent variable. That is, what dispositional and contextual factors cause political executives to embrace different leadership styles? Some good work in this vein has been done in political psychology but more is needed. In particular, there is ample research on the links between specific traits and political behaviour, but how these traits are aggregated into broader styles whose explanatory power might be greater than the sum of their parts needs to be better clarified. Equally important, what explains variation in the same leader's style over time? The effects of contextual factors such as crises (e.g. Boin et al. 2012; Boin et al. 2017) can be decisive and deserve further examination. More generally, static leadership categories such as crusader and pragmatist do not fully capture what we observe in the tenure of real-world leaders. For example, as president Ronald Reagan exhibited periods of rigidity and flexibility, of great interest and extraordinary disengagement, of visionary leadership and aloofness. These fluctuations were not random but were driven in predictable ways by the interaction between Reagan's traits and key features of the situation

(Keller 2009). Leadership categories and typologies are very useful, but their explanatory power is enhanced when we can specify when each style will become operative.

Finally, more work is needed to unify existing theoretical and empirical knowledge on leadership style. The literature boasts an impressive collection of theories, models, and case studies from diverse methodological and theoretical perspectives, but without much systematic effort to pull these insights together. One path toward developing these links is to specify the conditions under which one model versus another can be expected to explain behaviour. Another approach is to discern areas of functional agreement among apparent diversity. There are areas of unity, particularly surrounding the dual importance of context and political skill and the central roles played by leaders' task versus relations emphasis and their responsiveness to political constraints. A careful reading of this work indicates that frequently scholars are tapping into the same essential insights but using different terminology, methods, or contexts which obscures this common ground and impedes cumulation of knowledge. These links between existing studies must be better articulated and explored.

References

Allison, G. (1971). *Essence of Decision*. Boston, MA: Little, Brown, and Company.

Bales, R. (1950). *Interaction Process Analysis*. Cambridge, MA: Harvard University Press.

Barber, J. D. (1977). *The Presidential Character: Predicting Performance in the White House*. Englewood Cliffs, NJ: Prentice-Hall.

Bass, B. M. (1985). *Leadership and Performance Beyond Expectations*. New York: Free Press.

Bass, B. M. (1997). 'Does the Transactional-Transformational Leadership Paradigm Transcend Organizational and National Boundaries?', *American Psychologist* 52(2): 130–9.

Bass, B. M. and Valenzi, E. (1974). 'Contingent Aspects of Effective Management Styles,' in J. G. Hunt and L. L. Larson (eds) *Contingency Approaches to Leadership*. Carbondale, IL: Southern Illinois University Press, 130–52.

Blake, R. and Mouton, J. S. (1964). *The Managerial Grid: Key Orientations for Achieving Production Through People*. Houston: Gulf Publishing Company.

Boin, A., 't Hart, P., and Van Esch, F. A. W. J. (2012). 'Political Leadership in Times of Crisis: Comparing Leader Responses to Financial Turbulence,' in L. Helms (ed.) *Comparative Political Leadership*. Basingstoke: Palgrave Macmillan, 119–41.

Boin, A., 't Hart, P., Stern, E., and Sundelius, B. (2017). *The Politics of Crisis Management: Public Leadership Under Pressure*. Cambridge: Cambridge University Press.

Bueno de Mesquita, B. (1981). *The War Trap*. New Haven: Yale University Press.

Burns, J. M. (1978). *Leadership*. New York: Harper and Row.

Burns, J. M. (2003). *Transformational Leadership*. Oxford: Oxford University Press.

Byars, R. (1972). 'The Task/Affect Quotient: A Technique for Measuring Orientations of Political Leaders,' *Comparative Political Studies* 5(1): 109–20.

Byars, R. (1973). 'Small-Group Theory and Shifting Styles of Political Leadership,' *Comparative Political Studies* 5(4): 443–69.

Carlyle, T. (1927). *On Heroes, Hero-Worship and the Heroic in History*. London: Macmillan.

Dyson, S. B. (2007). 'Alliances, Domestic Politics, and Leader Psychology: Why Did Britain Stay Out of Vietnam and Go into Iraq?' *Political Psychology* 28(6): 647–66.

Dyson, S. B. (2009). *The Blair Identity: Leadership and Foreign Policy*. Oxford: Oxford University Press.

Edwards, G. C., III (2003). *On Deaf Ears: The Limits of the Bully Pulpit*. New Haven, CT: Yale University Press.

Fiedler, F. E. (1967). *A Theory of Leadership Effectiveness*. Maidenhead: McGraw Hill.

Genovese, M. A., Belt, T. L., and Lammers, W. W. (2014). *The Presidency and Domestic Policy: Comparing Leadership Styles, FDR to Obama*. New York: Routledge.

George, A. L. and George, J. (1956). *Woodrow Wilson and Colonel House: A Personality Study* New York: John Day.

Greenstein, F. I. (1969). *Personality and Politics: Problems of Evidence, Inference, and Conceptualization*. Chicago: Markham.

Gumusluoglu, L. and Ilsev, A. (2009). 'Transformational Leadership, Creativity, and Organizational Innovation,' *Journal of Business Research* 62(4): 461–73.

Hargrove, E. C. (2002). 'Presidential Leadership: Skill in Context,' *Politics & Policy* 30(2): 211–35.

Hargrove, E. C. and Owens, J. E. (2003) (eds). *Leadership in Context*. Lanham, MD: Rowman and Littlefield.

Helms, L. (2005). *Presidents, Prime Ministers and Chancellors: Executive Leadership in Western Democracies*. London: Palgrave Macmillan.

Helms, L. (2012). 'Introduction: The Importance of Studying Political Leadership Comparatively,' in L. Helms (ed.) *Comparative Political Leadership*. London: Palgrave Macmillan, 1–24.

Hermann, M. G. (2003). 'Assessing Leadership Style: Trait Analysis,' in J. M. Post (ed.) *The Psychological Assessment of Political Leaders: With Profiles of Saddam Hussein and Bill Clinton*. Ann Arbor, MI: University of Michigan Press, 178–212.

Hermann, M. G. and Hermann, C. F. (1989). 'Who Makes Foreign Policy Decisions and How: An Empirical Inquiry,' *International Studies Quarterly* 33(4): 361–87.

Hermann, M. G. and Kegley, C. W. (1995). 'Rethinking Democracy and International Peace: Perspectives from Political Psychology,' *International Studies Quarterly* 39(4): 511–33.

Hook, S. (1943). *The Hero in History*. New York: John Day.

Hudson, V. M. (1990). 'Birth Order of World Leaders: An Exploratory Analysis of Effects on Personality and Behavior,' *Political Psychology* 11(3): 583–601.

Jacobs, L. R. and King, D. (2010). 'Varieties of Obamaism: Structure, Agency, and the Obama Presidency,' *Perspectives on Politics* 8: 793–802.

Jervis, R. (1976). *Perception and Misperception in International Politics*. Princeton, NJ: Princeton University Press.

Johnson, R. T. (1974). *Managing the White House: An Intimate Study of the Presidency*. New York: Harper and Row.

Jung, D. I. and Avolio, B. J. (2000). 'Opening the Black Box: An Experimental Investigation of the Mediating Effects of Trust and Value Congruence on Transformational and Transactional Leadership,' *Journal of Organizational Behavior* 21(8): 949–64.

Jung, D. I., Chow, C., and Wu, A. (2003). 'The Role of Transformational Leadership in Enhancing Organizational Innovation: Hypotheses and Some Preliminary Findings,' *The Leadership Quarterly* 14(4/5): 525–44.

Kane, J. and Patapan, H. (2012). *The Democratic Leader: How Democracy Defines, Empowers and Limits Its Leaders*. Oxford: Oxford University Press.

Keller, J. W. (2005a). 'Leadership Style, Regime Type, and Foreign Policy Crisis Behavior: A Contingent Monadic Peace?' *International Studies Quarterly* 49(2): 205–31.

Keller, J. W. (2005b). 'Constraint Respecters, Constraint Challengers, and Crisis Decision Making in Democracies: A Case Study Analysis of Kennedy vs. Reagan,' *Political Psychology* 26(6): 835–67.

Keller, J. W. (2009). 'Explaining Rigidity and Pragmatism in Political Leaders: A General Theory and a Plausibility Test from the Reagan Presidency,' *Political Psychology* 30(3): 465–98.

Keller, J. W. and Foster, D. M. (2012). 'Presidential Leadership Style and the Political Use of Force,' *Political Psychology* 33(5): 581–98.

Keller, J. W. and Yang, Y. (2008). 'Leadership Style, Decision Context, and the Poliheuristic Theory of Decision Making: An Experimental Analysis,' *Journal of Conflict Resolution* 52(5): 687–712.

Kettell, S. (2009). 'The Curious Incident of the Dog that Didn't Bark in the Night-Time: Structure and Agency in Britain's War with Iraq,' *Politics & Policy* 37(2): 415–39.

Kille, K. J. and Scully, R. M. (2003). 'Executive Heads and the Role of Intergovernmental Organizations: Expansionist Leadership in the United Nations and the European Union,' *Political Psychology* 24(1): 175–98.

King, A. (2002). *Leaders' Personalities and the Outcome of Democratic Elections*. Oxford: Oxford University Press.

Krasner, S. D. (1972). 'Are Bureaucracies Important? (Or Allison Wonderland),' *Foreign Policy* 7: 159–79.

Larson, D. W. (1994). 'The Role of Belief Systems and Schemas in Foreign Policy Decision-making,' *Political Psychology* 15(S1): 17–33.

Lasswell, H. D. (1930). *Psychopathology and Politics*. Chicago: The University of Chicago Press.

Leites, N. (1951). *The Operational Code of the Politburo*. New York: McGraw-Hill.

Lewin, K., Lippett, R., and White, R. (1939). 'Patterns of Aggressive Behavior in Experimentally Created 'Social Climates',' *Journal of Social Psychology* 10: 271–99.

Lijphart, A. (1992). *Parliamentary versus Presidential Government*. Oxford: Oxford University Press.

Manning, N. (2001). 'The Legacy of the New Public Management in Developing Countries,' *International Review of Administrative Sciences* 67(2): 297–312.

Mitchell, D. (2005). 'Centralizing Advisory Systems: Presidential Influence and the U.S. Foreign Policy Process,' *Foreign Policy Analysis* 2(2): 181–206.

Moynihan, D. P., Pandey, S. K., and Wright, B. E. (2012). 'Setting the Table: How Transformational Leadership Fosters Performance Information Use,' *Journal of Public Administration Research and Theory* 22(1): 143–64.

Neustadt, R. E. (1960). *Presidential Power: The Politics of Leadership*. New York: John Wiley & Sons.

Ng, T. W. H. (2017). 'Transformational Leadership and Performance Outcomes: Analyses of Multiple Mediation Pathways,' *The Leadership Quarterly* 28(3): 385–417.

Nye, J. S. (2005). *Soft Power: The Means to Success in World Politics*. New York: Public Affairs.

Oc, B. (2018). 'Contextual Leadership: A Systematic Review of How Contextual Factors Shape Leadership and Its Outcomes,' *The Leadership Quarterly* 29(1): 218–35.

Ostrom, C. and Job, B. (1986). 'The President and the Political Use of Force,' *American Political Science Review* 80(2): 541–66.

Peters, B. G. and Helms, L. (2012). 'Executive Leadership in Comparative Perspective: Politicians, Bureaucrats and Public Governance,' in L. Helms (ed.) *Comparative Political Leadership*. London: Palgrave Macmillan, 25–55.

Preston, T. (2001). *The President and his Inner Circle: Leadership Style and the Advisory Process in Foreign Affairs*. New York: Columbia University Press.

Preston, T. and 't Hart, P. (1999). 'Understanding and Evaluating Bureaucratic Politics: The Nexus Between Political Leaders and Advisory Systems,' *Political Psychology* 20(1): 49–98.

Renshon, S. (2008). *High Hopes: The Clinton Presidency and the Politics of Ambition*. New York: Routledge.

Rhodes, R. A. W. and t' Hart, P. (2014) (eds). *The Oxford Handbook of Political Leadership*. Oxford: Oxford University Press.

Rose, R. (1991). *The Post Modern President: George Bush Meets the World*. New York: Chatham House.

Rose, R. (2001). *The Prime Minister in a Shrinking World*. Cambridge: Polity Press.

Russett, B. (1993). *Grasping the Democratic Peace*. Princeton, NJ: Princeton University Press.

Shannon, V. P. and Keller, J. W. (2007). 'Leadership Style and International Norm Violation: The Case of the Iraq War,' *Foreign Policy Analysis* 3(1): 79–104.

Shin, S. J. and Zhou, J. (2017). 'Transformational Leadership, Conservation, and Creativity: Evidence from Korea,' *Academy of Management Journal* 46(6): 703–14.

Skowronek, S. (2008). *Presidential Leadership in Political Time: Reprise and Reappraisal*. Lawrence, KS: University Press of Kansas.

Stewart, L. H. (1977). 'Birth Order and Political Leadership,' in M. G. Hermann (ed.) *A Psychological Examination of Political Leaders*. New York: Free Press, 206–36.

Stoessinger, J. (1979). *Crusaders and Pragmatists: Movers of Modern American Foreign Policy*. New York: W.W. Norton.

Sylvan, D. A. and Voss, J. F. (1998). *Problem Representation in Foreign Policy Decision Making*. Cambridge: Cambridge University Press.

't Hart, P. (2014). *Understanding Public Leadership*. New York: Palgrave.

Theakston, K. (2002). 'Political Skills and Context in Prime Ministerial Leadership in Britain,' *Politics & Policy* 30(2): 283–323.

Walker, S. G., Schafer, M., and Young, M. D. (1998). 'Systematic Procedures for Operational Code Analysis: Measuring and Modeling Jimmy Carter's Operational Code,' *International Studies Quarterly* 42(1): 175–90.

Wang, G., Oh, I., Courtright, S. H., and Colbert, A. E. (2011). 'Transformational Leadership and Performance Across Criteria and Levels: A Meta-Analytic Review of 25 Years of Research,' *Group & Organization Management* 36(2): 223–70.

Weber, M. (1958). *From Max Weber: Essays in Sociology*. Oxford: Oxford University Press.

Winter, D. G. (1987). 'Leader Appeal, Leader Performance, and the Motive Profiles of Leaders and Followers: A Study of American Presidents and Elections,' *Journal of Personality and Social Psychology* 52(1): 196–202.

Ziller, R., Stone, W., Jackson, R., and Terbovic, N. (1977). 'Self-Other Orientations and Political Behavior,' in M. G. Hermann (ed.) *A Psychological Examination of Political Leaders*. New York: Free Press, 174–204.

....

CHAPTER 25

POLITICAL ADVISERS IN THE EXECUTIVE BRANCH

....

YEE-FUI NG

25.1 INTRODUCTION

....

THE elected representatives in a democracy are faced with numerous multi-directional pressures: hierarchically via the chief executive, other ministers (in parliamentary systems), the civil service, and oversight bodies; as well as through the wider network of governance via the factions within their political party, the political opposition, interest groups, and the media. The need to maintain and manage multiple multi-faceted relationships creates an impetus for coordinating policy, media and administrative functions within the minister's office. The immediacy, ubiquitousness, and continuous nature of the twenty-four-hour media cycle dramatically increase the pressure on governments to respond to issues almost instantaneously, without much time for reflection. The sheer volume and complexity of tasks and responsibilities that chief executives and ministers have to shoulder have created a need for trusted advisers. This chapter situates political advisers within the executive branch of government, focusing primarily on the political executive (presidents, prime ministers, cabinet, and junior ministers) and the bureaucracy.

Although the civil service is the traditional source of advice for chief executives and ministers, the large, complex, and powerful Weberian bureaucracies that have developed in modern democracies do not necessarily enjoy their trust. Conservative governments suspected that the bureaucracy was secretly biased against them and were progressive at heart, while progressive governments chafed against the passivity of the civil service and doubted that a sluggish bureaucracy could implement innovative and ambitious reform agendas (Rourke 1992: 541). This meant that chief executives and ministers started to clamour for their advisory system to shift from the 'neutral competence' of the impartial civil service towards one of loyalty or 'responsive competence' (Aberbach and Rockman 1994: 461), to better serve the needs of the elected politicians.

The struggle by the political executive to exert power and control over a large, expert and impassive bureaucracy has led to the rise of partisan political advisers, personal advisers to chief executives and ministers that are appointed on the basis of patronage rather than merit.

Political advisers have become significant and entrenched actors within the executive of various administrative traditions, including in Westminster jurisdictions, Europe, the United States, and beyond. Their role is explicitly partisan and political, attuned to media reaction, and calibrated to maximize their principal's electoral success. Political advisers occupy the intermediate position between the elected political executive and the bureaucracy. Alongside the entrenchment of political advisers has been rather unflattering assessments of their roles and performance, including derogatory monikers such as 'spin doctors', 'junk yard attack dogs' (Weller 2002: 72), 'kids in short pants' (Canada, Senate 2013: 56), and a 'mob of interlopers, freeloaders, ratbags and carpetbaggers' (Freudenberg 2006: 147).

This chapter will outline the major research questions regarding political advisers. It will then consider how the contemporary literature addresses these issues in terms of the roles and influence of political advisers, their interaction with the political executive and the bureaucracy, and their regulation and accountability. Finally, the chapter will propose a future research agenda in the area of political advisers.

25.2 Political Advisers: Major Issues and Research Questions

Modern democracies have established constitutional systems of diffused power between the arms of government, where the power of the executive is checked by that of the judiciary and legislature. The power of the executive is commonly constitutionally vested in a head of state, whether a president or monarch, which sometimes conceals rather than reveals the true head of government exercising power (Daintith and Ng 2018). Within the executive branch lies the president or the elected representatives in parliamentary systems, alongside their political advisers, departments, and agencies. The multiplicity of functions exercised by the executive and the variety of bodies subsumed within it leads to the major overarching normative research question in this area: how to ensure the accountability of the executive within a constitutional system, particularly that of the triumvirate of the political executive, political advisers, and the bureaucracy.

Another normative research question that forms a counterweight to accountability relates to governmental effectiveness, that is, what structure and organization of the executive leads to the most effective operation of government. The organization of the political executive and its apolitical (civil service) counterparts is a primary determinant of the effectiveness of governmental operation and function. Thus, several subsidiary research questions arise as to how elected representatives can control the bureaucracy through institutional structures of political advice, the appropriate roles of political advisers in a system of governance, and their interrelationship with other political actors (see also Chapter 26 in this volume).

A central preoccupation of elected representatives is how to control the vast bureaucracy under their command. The public choice principal-agent literature suggests that civil servants will 'shirk' from their duties and sabotage their ministers in a self-serving way (Niskanen 1971). The basic problem of the political executive as principal is how to harness the agent's experience while reining in programmatic bias (Saunders 2017: 227). A major tension in modern democracies is thus how to delineate the relationship between elected representatives and the bureaucracy through the use of institutional structures of political advice. The question of how to bridge the politics/administration divide has resulted in the coalescing of three major systems of political advice: the Westminster model, the United States model, and the *cabinet* model evident in several European countries, although other variants can be observed across the world.

The Westminster model cleaves the strongest separation between politics and the bureaucracy, where civil servants are expected to be neutral, apolitical, tenured, and recruited and promoted on the basis of merit. This model, originating in the United Kingdom (Blick 2004; Yong and Hazell 2014), is also apparent in countries inheriting that tradition, such as Australia (Ng 2016), New Zealand (Shaw and Eichbaum 2018), and Canada (Craft 2016). These advisers undertake a wide range of functions, including advising on public policy, media, political, parliamentary management, and party management matters. The number of policy advisers varies widely between countries, from eighty-seven advisers in the United Kingdom to 544 in Canada in 2015 (Ng 2018: 50).[1]

The traditional Westminster advisory system is predicated on a binary relationship between ministers and civil servants. However, over the last forty years, partisan ministerial advisers have become major institutional actors within the executive, interposed between ministers and civil servants. Ministerial advisers in the Westminster system are personally appointed by ministers and work out of their private offices. Their partisan nature poses a significant challenge to the Westminster civil service, which was constructed as a bulwark against patronage.

Presidents in the United States have always had large numbers of political staff at a scale, depth, and breadth that vastly exceeds the Westminster political advisory system due to the concentration of executive power in one person, rather than a ministry, as well as the complete separation between the legislature and executive. These institutional arrangements justify stronger support for the executive in order to pass legislation.

The US advisory system involves the president appointing numerous advisers within his or her office, as well as the top layer of the civil service. In addition to the president's own personal appointees in the White House Executive Office of the president, which

---

[1] The figures are limited to advisers to ministers/assistant ministers and parliamentary secretaries, and exclude non-ministerial roles such as whips and leaders of the House. The political staff figures also exclude non-advisory staff where possible, such as administrative staff, support staff, and drivers.

numbers about 1,500 employees (Peters 2015: 790–1), the president can appoint over 3,000 employees at the top of federal public service organizations (Dickinson 2017: 201). The Civil Service Reform Act 1978 allows up to 10 per cent of the Senior Executive Service to be political appointees; a legacy of the nineteenth-century 'spoils system', where high and low official positions were used to reward friends, cronies, and supporters (Page 1992: 27). Although this is a small fraction of the 2.1 million civilian career employees, the political appointees are concentrated at the top ranks of the civil service (Dickinson 2017: 193). A major difference between the United States and traditional Westminster system is that, with the former, partisan political appointments are pervasive and incorporate the top layer of each department in the bureaucracy, where civil servants find themselves at a ceiling for promotions within a department unless they take a political appointment (Heclo 1977: 116–20, 133–4). In short, the US system involves politics permeating bureaucratic structures, creating a politicized bureaucracy.

The other main model is the long-standing 'cabinet ministériel' or ministerial *cabinet* of nations such as France and Belgium that dates from the 1840s, the more recent ministerial cabinets in Greece, Portugal, and Spain, and even a supra-national *cabinet* in the European Commission (Gouglas 2015; Gouglas et al. 2017: 359). The size and function of *cabinets* range from the smaller, more politicized Belgian *cabinet* of thirty-three staff (Portail Belgium 2014) to the substantial French *cabinet* system staffed mostly by civil servants, with thirty-nine cabinets containing 2,983 advisers (Republique Française 2017). It should be noted for the sake of completeness that the *cabinet* system is not a pan-European phenomenon. There are other European countries that employ political staff or their functional equivalents without a *cabinet* model, including those from the Germanic administrative tradition (such as Germany and the Netherlands) (Hustedt 2018; Van den Berg 2018), as well as the Scandinavian administrative tradition (such as Denmark, Sweden, Norway, and Iceland) (Dahlström 2009; Christiansen et al. 2016; Kristinsson 2016).

The ministerial *cabinet* system consists of informal groups of personal advisers attached to each minister that comprise a mix of civil servants and political advisers. The *cabinets* are interposed between the minister and the civil service. The institution of the *cabinet* system has tended to follow a critical political-historical event: the break from monarchical rule (France and Belgium), the democratization after fascism (Italy), the end of military dictatorships (Greece, Portugal, and Spain), or the creation of a European economic community (European Commission) (Gouglas 2015; Brans et al. 2017). The ministerial *cabinet* structure has proven to be remarkably resilient. Although in the 1990s Belgium underwent the Copernicus reforms which sought to abolish the old ministerial *cabinets*, and Italy sought to modernize ministerial *cabinets* based on managerialist reforms, researchers have found a path dependency where the patterns of the previous patronage-based *cabinet* structures were simply replicated in new forms (Brans et al. 2006; Di Mascio and Natalini 2013, 2016).

These three models of political advice demonstrate the structural and institutional mechanisms by which the political executive has sought to bolster the responsiveness of the bureaucracy to their demands. Delving deeper into these models, further questions arise as to the appropriate role of political advisers within the Westminster, European *cabinet*, and US systems, and their interactions with other actors within the system of governance, such as ministers, the civil service, interest groups, and the media, which will be addressed in the next section.

25.3 CONTEMPORARY RESEARCH PERSPECTIVES ON POLITICAL ADVISERS

To address the large, looming questions on the appropriate roles of political advisers within the Westminster, European *cabinet*, and United States models, and how to hold them to account, the literature on political advisers has proceeded along three main dimensions: empirically in fleshing out the roles, power, and influence of political advisers; relationally in analysing the interaction between political advisers and ministers and the bureaucracy; and legally, in assessing the control, regulation, and accountability of political advisers.

25.3.1 The Empirical: The Roles, Power and Influence of Political Advisers

The bulk of the scholarship on political advisers has been on empirically mapping their roles and influence in various Westminster and European countries. This is a substantial contribution, as the work of political advisers is often conducted covertly behind closed doors, without public scrutiny. There is increasingly sophisticated scholarship that seeks to create a typology of the work of political advisers by categorizing the functions that they undertake. For instance, Connaughton (2010) identified a model that differentiated between four main roles of political advisers: expert, partisan, coordinator, and minder. The expert is a highly qualified political outsider who initiates and contests policies and ideas, while the coordinator's role is procedural and includes monitoring and liaising with various groups to facilitate oversight and delivery of the minister's agenda. On the political dimension, the partisan is appointed predominantly on the basis of political affiliation rather than specific expertise, and undertakes work of a politically partisan nature. Another political role, the minder, protects the minister by looking out for issues that may harm the minister politically and in terms of reputation. In other typologies, academics have focused particularly on the policy roles of advisers, illustrating the expansion of the roles of policy advisers across the policy spectrum. These range from policy formation to substantive policy advice, as well as procedurally coordinating policy though networking both horizontally and vertically across and beyond government (Maley 2000, 2015; Craft 2016). These typologies provide a useful framework to analyse the distinctive work carried out by political advisers.

In the Westminster context, although advisers were initially limited to procedural administrative roles, as time went on, they started adopting more substantive policy roles (Ng 2018). As governments struggled to adapt to media demands following the 24/7 news cycle, media advisers became extremely important figures. In addition, the range of stakeholders that advisers interacted with increased over time, from merely dealing with their own minister and department, to coordinating through horizontal networks across other ministerial offices, the Prime Minister's Office, and external stakeholders (Maley 2011; Ng 2018).

Ministerial advisers in the Westminster system are undoubtedly powerful and influential. As Maley (2002: 64, 106) argued, ministerial advisers are influential *functionally* in the roles they perform, *structurally* from the institutional arrangements in which they work, and *implicitly* from the relationship they have with their minister. As the most proximate advisers to ministers, they have unprecedented access to their ministers and are the final port of call for ministers seeking advice. Further, some of the more recently developed roles—namely gate-keeping, filtering departmental advice, and brokering positions between departments—provide advisers with power and hierarchical superiority over the civil service. Further, the functions of speaking on behalf of the minister and filtering the advice that reaches the minister effectively give advisers political power and allow them to influence the minister's policy decisions. More intangibly, political advisers are influential because of the relationship of trust and confidence they have with their minister. In a hot-house, high pressure environment where the minister feels besieged on all fronts by enemies in the form of political factions, the opposition, the hungry media, or perhaps a cold, inscrutable bureaucracy, they turn to their trusted partisan advisers for advice and emotional support (Ng 2018).

By contrast, in the United States, ironically the large number of political appointees did not initially translate to them exerting a great influence on government. Heclo's seminal work on political appointees in the 1960s painted a picture of transient outsiders to government with short tenures who were isolated from policy communities and other political appointees. This, combined with their lack of a relationship with the president, led to a situation that Heclo evocatively described as a 'government of strangers' (Heclo 1977: 100–12). Without the necessary relational networks to advance their agendas, the political appointees in agencies were vulnerable to being captured by the policy communities of the bureaucracy, Congress, and lobby groups, who had 'dense, multiple, and enduring' networks (Heclo 1977: 112).

Since Heclo's assessment, the tenure and skill levels of political appointees increased over subsequent administrations in the 1970s and 1980s, which increased their ability to shape policy (Maranto 2005; Peters 2010). Over the years, the politicization of the US federal bureaucracy solidified or 'thickened', as Congress and presidents added layer upon layer of political and career management to the hierarchy under various titles (secretary, deputy secretary, under secretary, assistant secretary, and administrator), each title subsuming many other layers of hierarchy. Light's significant work demonstrated this gradual accretion over the last half century, a phenomenon that shows no sign of abating, with research updated to the Bush administration (Light 1995, 2004).

The roles of political appointees in the Washington bureaucracy are as managers (managing programmes), political enforcers (monitoring bureaucratic agencies and ensuring that they are following the programmes of the principal), political advisers, and perhaps policy advisers (Peters 2010: 182–3). The use of political appointees has been moving away from policy advice towards more political roles, such as enforcing the agenda of the party and president (Peters 2010: 194). This reflects the most recent trend from the 1990s of a deep polarization of politics, such that the quality of political appointees has diminished over time as partisan loyalty has come to outweigh competence in making political appointments (Edwards 2001; Moynihan and Roberts 2010).

Finally, there is the 'cabinet ministériel' or ministerial *cabinet* system adopted in several European nations, commonly of the Napoleonic administrative tradition. The deeply-entrenched French and Belgian *cabinet* systems are extremely powerful and eclipse the influence of the bureaucracy. The French ministerial *cabinets* have roles encompassing public policy, media, and coordination. *Cabinet* members supervise the activity of the ministry's central administration, intervene (sometimes decisively) in strategic choices and the development of public policy, participate in the drafting of bills, conceive of and implement the media plan, and engage in inter-ministerial coordination (Krynen 2015). *Cabinet* members have a broader remit than Westminster political advisers as they also have the power to direct officials and speak on behalf of the minister.

Belgian advisers have been characterised as 'fixers who steer and mend policy' and minders, who protect the minister from harmful issues (Brans et al. 2017: 74). Belgian ministerial *cabinets* undertake political functions, including party control and smoothing the relationship between coalition governments of between four to six parties, and are able to issue instructions in the minister's name and sign documents on the minister's behalf (Brans et al. 2006: 62; de Visscher and Salomonsen 2013: 83). In addition, Belgian *cabinets* dominate all elements of the policy process: they produce policy advice and interfere with bureaucratic functions as a 'shadow administration', including taking on secondary legislation and executive tasks (Brans et al. 2006: 62). In the Napoleonic system of powerful ministerial *cabinets*, the bureaucracy is consistently undermined (Brans et al. 2006: 62; de Visscher and Salomonsen 2013: 86).

Nevertheless, not all *cabinet* systems share this deep power and influence. A study in 2015 found that Greek ministerial advisers have tended to play the role of the coordinator, with a main focus on management of the government programme, and do not perform policy or partisan functions (Gouglas 2015: 25). However, following a change in government in 2012, the advisers have adopted more political and partisan roles (Gouglas 2018: 98). Despite this, their main function remained that of the political coordinator, to mobilize line departments and facilitate the coordination of the government programme across the core executive. One main differentiator between the European nations and other jurisdictions is the greater need for political coordinators in countries with multi-party consociational systems, such as Norway, Denmark, Sweden, and Greece; a situation that is also replicated in New Zealand with its mixed-member proportional voting system.

Further, in an era of multi-level governance, political advisers now operate at the supra-national level at the European Commission (see also Chapter 33 in this volume). Since 1958, the European Commission established private offices for the commissioners based on the French ministerial *cabinets* (Ritchie 1992: 98). Gouglas et al. (2017) found that these advisers played the role of 'coordinating minders': both coordinating and process-managing policy, but also protecting their commissioner from political harm. By contrast to political advisers operating in a national context, supra-national political advisers were not partisan in an electoral or political party sense as the European commissioners are not elected; rather the adviser sought to advance causes based on the commissioners national affiliation. These supra-national advisers actively liaised with the department, other European Commission *cabinets*, and external stakeholders. Gouglas et al. (2017: 370) concluded that ultimately the political advisers to the European Commission *cabinets* represented a variant of the European *cabinet* tradition, rather than a *sui generis* model.

From this broad sweep of political advisory systems across the nations, it is apparent that the roles of political advisers vary over time, even within the same jurisdiction, depending on the needs of the government of the day. At a more granular level, the roles, power, and influence of an individual adviser are also contextual. Askim et al. (2017) have developed an explanatory framework for the roles that political advisers play, based on three context-dependent characteristics: *supply*, that is, the role a political appointee has depends on his or her personal skills, background, and experience; *demand*, that is, what is required of the adviser depends on what ministers lack in their own experience; and, third, *formal structure*, that is, power is asymmetrically distributed based on structural arrangements such as the type of ministry and the appointee's formal position. This contextualism was exhibited in a study by Müller-Rommel (2008), which found that the roles of prime ministerial staff in ten post-communist Central and Eastern European countries differed based on the leadership style of the individual prime minister, with staff of 'weak' prime ministers being more influential and adopting predominantly political roles, while 'strong' prime ministers had staff that played largely administrative roles. Likewise, studies in Germany (Müller-Rommel 2000) and France (Elgie 2000) have found that the influence of the staff of the chief executive varied according to both structural and contingent factors, such as the number of staff, inter-ministerial communication processes, political circumstance, and the personality of the chief executive.

Another trend in policy advisory systems is that of centralization by the chief executive. In the United States, public attention is centralized upon the lone figure of the president, who in contemporary times operates a 'muscular presidency' through the use of regulatory review and presidential directives to agencies, combined with the strategic placement and increases in the numbers of political appointees (Aberbach and Peterson 2005: 541; Kagan 2001). This has led commentators to conclude that presidents such as Nixon created an 'administrative presidency', by using administrative means to overcome opposition from Congress and the career bureaucracy (Nathan 1984), a charge that remained relevant in the following decades (Rudalevige 2009). In addition, US presidents have sought to centralize functions within the Office of the Executive

President, instead of the wider executive branch (Rudalevige 2009). Likewise, the Westminster advisory systems, particularly Australia and Canada, have also displayed elements of centralization to the prime minister, in terms of centralized appointments processes for ministerial advisers, media vetting by the Prime Minister's Office, and larger numbers and influence of advisers at the centre of government (Marland 2016; Ng 2016, 2018). In the European context, Askim et al. (2017) found that power within the Norwegian executive was dispersed unevenly, with some ministers at the centre of power, such as the prime minister and finance minister, being more powerful than others (see also Chapter 18 in this volume).

The steady accumulation of research demonstrating the concentration of staff within the office of the chief executive supports the 'presidentialization of politics' thesis. The presidentialization argument is that many democratic political systems, including Westminster and European ones, have moved towards a growing 'leader centredness' of electoral, executive, and party politics that have brought these countries closer to the presidential model; the main features of which include a greater accretion of resources within the office of the chief executive, trends towards an integrated communication strategy controlled by the chief executive, and centralized coordination of policy-making (Poguntke and Webb 2005; see also Chapter 18 in this volume). An overt goal of the increased politicization at the centre of government is to strengthen political control by chief executives, thus enabling them to 'steer from the centre' (Dahlström et al. 2011).

25.3.2 The Relational: The Politics/Administration Interface

Another strand of research examines the politics/administration interface, and how political advisers mediate between the political executive and appointed bureaucracy. Zussman (2009) conceived of three main models of how political advisers interact with ministers and the civil service: collaborative, gatekeeper, and triangulated. The collaborative model involves a cooperative relationship between civil servants and political advisers, with advice being jointly tendered to the minister in a collaborative fashion. The triangulated model involves civil servants and political advisers independently and separately providing advice to the minister. These two models are the most conducive to harmonious relationships. On the other hand, the gatekeeper envisages political advisers as funnels or filters who interpose themselves between the minister and the civil service and potentially block officials from accessing ministers. This model might cause friction within the ranks of the civil service and may negatively affect the quality of advice. As Walter (2006: 26) argued, where advice is funnelled, this may result in 'narrowing the options only to those predetermined by an ideological agenda rather than seriously "testing reality"'.

In a parallel development in the US context, scholars have advanced three political models: capture, conquest, or comity (Lorentzen 1985; Heclo 1987; Maranto 1991). Capture happens where the political appointees become captured by their agency and take their viewpoint over that of the White House, while conquest is where the White

House looks to dominate the bureaucracy and subvert its work through strategic political appointments. Comity represents the most harmonious position where political appointees and careerists eventually learn to trust or at least work together, which may lead to 'conditional cooperation' of mutual benefits between political appointees and career civil servants (Heclo 1987).

Another major element of the literature examines whether the civil service has become politicized (Peters and Pierre 2004), with a distinction between *functional politicization*, where the civil service engages in tasks that go beyond bringing neutral expertise to the political and administrative processes (Hustedt and Salomonsen 2014), and *administrative politicization*, where political advisers seek to interfere in the policy activities of the civil service such that the bureaucracy's ability to provide frank and fearless advice is compromised; for example, by limiting civil servants' access to ministers or politicizing the content of policy advice from the civil service (Eichbaum and Shaw 2008: 342). In this respect, several studies in the Westminster and European contexts have shown that political advisers in fact insulated the bureaucracy from being politicized (Eichbaum and Shaw 2007, 2008; Christiansen et al. 2016), although other research has found that a more politicized top layer of the bureaucracy led to decreased access to ministers by civil servants, meaning that there was administrative politicization (Öhberg et al. 2017).

In the explicitly politicized bureaucracy in the United States, there is a great abundance of literature on bureaucratic politicization, with a depth and breadth of descriptive, empirical, and normative scholarship focusing on how the president is able to control the bureaucracy and avoid bureaucratic sabotage. Before the 1980s, the perception was that presidents lacked the resources to monitor and control the bureaucracy effectively (Koenig 1975; Cronin 1980). However, the dominant paradigm then shifted to a contention that presidents were able to shape bureaucratic behaviour, with political appointees seen to be a successful method of bureaucratic control (Moe 1985; Wood and Waterman 1991, 1994). Proponents of the appointment of loyalists who have asserted that it increases the responsiveness of the bureaucracy and the president's ability to deliver his or her policy agenda (Moe 1985; Maranto 2005) have been matched by detractors who have argued that there is a deleterious effect of excessive patronage appointments on the performance of agencies, with empirical analysis showing that political appointees systematically performed worse than career civil servants in managing programmes (Lewis 2007, 2008).

Literature in the United States has also empirically and descriptively examined patterns of political appointment by the president based on the loyalty/competence nexus (Lewis and Waterman 2013; Ouyang et al. 2017). Presidents have utilized appointments as a political tool to be traded in exchange for electoral or political support (Weko 1995; Tolchin and Tolchin 2010), including to help unite party factions and align members of Congress (Bearfield 2009; Rottinghaus and Bergan 2011), meaning that presidents are not at liberty to select all personnel on the basis of both loyalty and competence. Due to these constraints, presidents have to be selective in choosing the types of agencies they target for increased political control (Hollibaugh et al. 2014). Lewis argued that presidents aggressively politicized departments whose policy preferences are furthest from their own, and placed fewer political appointees in agencies that demand technical and professional knowledge (Lewis 2008).

Political advisers are but one actor in the broader policy process. To this end, a strand of literature on policy advisory systems has developed that examined various internal and external sources of policy advice beyond ministers and civil servants, and explicitly seeks to incorporate the position of political advisers into the system (Halligan 1995; Craft and Howlett 2012). In contemporary times, the civil service no longer holds the monopoly on advice to ministers. Rather, a range of stakeholders now provide policy advice to ministers, including internal governmental advisers, such as partisan political advisers, as well as external advisers such as non-governmental organizations, think tanks, universities, and political parties. Proponents of the literature on policy advisory systems have argued that political advisers have become one element of an overarching policy advisory system to ministers, that is, an interlocking set of actors who provide information, knowledge, and recommendations to policy-makers (Halligan 1995; Craft and Howlett 2012).

The policy advisory systems literature sits alongside a long tradition of American scholarship from the 1960s and 1970s that explored the dense and influential policy networks that existed in the United States in the form of the 'iron triangles' of interest groups, Congress, and government agencies (Cater 1954; McCornell 1966), contending that these 'iron triangles' controlled policy-making across many sectors and under-mined the ability of political appointees and the president to successfully pursue their policy agenda. Dickinson argued, however, that the iron triangle phenomenon has weakened in the last three decades due to increased policy complexity and congestion, accompanied by an increase in transparency in government operations and a diffusion in political control (Dickinson 2017).

25.3.3 The Legal: The Control, Regulation and Accountability of Political Advisers

The rise of political advisers as a major source of advice has given rise to a number of scandals and controversies in various jurisdictions where advisers have overstepped the boundaries of their roles, leaked confidential information to the media, or interfered in bureaucratic decision-making (Ng 2018). Accordingly, scholars have focused on the accountability deficits that arise from the insertion of political advisers into the governance system (Walter 2006; Tiernan 2007), where ministers have been able to escape accountability for various controversies by utilizing their advisers as scapegoats. In addition, literature has examined the legal, political, and parliamentary regulation of political advisers (Gay and Fawcett 2005; Ng 2016, 2018), as well as their constitutional position in the Westminster tradition (Ng 2016).

There are a few regulatory methods that have been adopted by the Westminster and European jurisdictions to target political advisers (OECD 2007; Ng 2018). The first is government-wide restrictions on the employment of advisers, either in terms of numbers of advisers or budget limits on advisers' salaries (Ng 2018). The second is regulation targeted at the advisers themselves, including positive requirements set out in legislation or codes of conduct, such as the requirement to act ethically, to avoid conflicts of interest, and to make financial disclosures. Negative stipulations on advisers can also be observed, such as prohibitions on advisers exercising executive power, expending public funds, or directing civil servants (Ng 2018).

In terms of the effectiveness of Westminster accountability mechanisms, Ng's research (2018: 166–72) showed that parliamentary accountability is a weak method of ensuring the accountability of advisers, as ministers tended to block advisers from appearing before parliamentary committees (Ng 2016a; 2018). Parliamentary accountability represents a vertical form of accountability based on a chain of hierarchy dependent on the answerability of civil servants to their minister, and the ministers' accountability to parliament. This embodies the traditional Westminster concept of ministerial responsibility, which is highly variable in theory, practice, political, and media interpretation. As a result, horizontal accountability mechanisms have become important to provide a framework of accountability for political advisers, including arms-lengths scrutineers such as ombudsmen and commissioners, as well as the media (Ng 2018).

Unlike the weakened parliamentary accountability in Westminster jurisdictions, the institutionally separate US Congress plays a strong and vociferous role in the oversight of political appointees, in addition to confirming the appointments of about one-quarter of the most senior political appointees (Weingast 2005; Lewis 2011). Political appointees in the United States face the scrutiny of Congress in relation to agency process and decision-making, which appointees have described as 'micromanagement' (Aberbach and Rockman 2000: 120–1). Intense congressional oversight both in terms of periodic audit-like oversight and 'fire alarm' responses to political problems creates an incentive for political appointees, with their short tenures and desire to seek promotion following their appointment, to avoid actions that might trigger the close scrutiny of 'fire alarm' oversight (Weingast 2005: 329–30). Even so, there are reports of executive intransigence to congressional oversight in the American context, as well as diminished congressional oversight in periods of united government (where one party controls both Houses of Congress as well as the presidency) (Levinson and Pildes 2006; Metzger 2009: 437–8).

Other commentators have focused on the roles of political actors outside the tripartite separation of powers in maintaining accountability. Michaels (2015) posited a theory of administrative checks and balances that triangulated regulatory power among political appointees who led agencies, an independent civil service, and a vibrant and pluralistic civil society. Michaels argued that the emergence of the modern administrative state concentrated too much state power in the hands of political appointees running government agencies, which led to the gradual development of subconstitutional rivalrous counterweights that constrained the political appointees, in the form of the tenured civil service and civil society. Michaels contended that this development was consistent with the intention of the framers of the US constitution, who envisaged a system of 'encumbered, rivalrous government' as a normative ideal.

Despite these accountability mechanisms, the US appointee system suffers from institutional pathologies. As Light (1995: 64) argued, the large numbers of political appointees compounded by many layers of hierarchy results in the 'diffusion of account-ability that comes in nearly infinite numbers of decision points throughout government', meaning that no one can be held accountable for any decision. Moreover, the consistent pattern of appointing unqualified partisans to run agencies has led to catastrophic staff misjudgement, where political appointees have botched the management of major crises or programmes such as the Hurricane Katrina response and the US post-war reconstruction project in Iraq (Chandrasekaran 2006; Cooper and Block 2006), lead-ing to deaths that marked the ultimate cost of excessive politicization at the expense of competence.

25.4 Future Research Agenda

As the discussion in the previous section shows, there is clearly a depth of empirical scholarship on political advisers that has shed light on an element of the executive that was previously hidden in the shadows of public administration. Significant progress has been made in ascertaining the roles of political advisers within the Westminster, European, and US systems, as well as their interactions with ministers and the bureau-cracy. Yet there is a veritable smorgasbord of research questions that remain to be explored; jurisdictionally, comparatively, institutionally, theoretically, and normatively.

First of all, in terms of jurisdictions, the literature on political advisers has been largely Westminster-focused, with European researchers more recently joining the fray in conducting empirical research about advisers in their respective countries. The US literature has taken a separate trajectory, with a rich vein of literature on the politiciza-tion and control of the bureaucracy. Outside of the liberal democratic tradition, there is scant research on political advisers. For instance, literature on advisers in authoritarian countries or non-Anglo countries (e.g. Asia, the Middle East, the Pacific Islands, or the Caribbean) is limited apart from discrete exceptions, such as Neary's (2000) contribu-tion on the staff of the Japanese prime minister. Further, Jones (2019) examined Arab Gulf monarchies where expert advisers from top universities and global consulting firms have been flown in to contribute to state-building. Jones found that expert advis-ers in these authoritarian countries did bring knowledge, data, and experience, but over time there was a disincentive to speak truth to power and consequently these experts failed to check their rulers' unrealistic expectations. More research along this vein might focus on how political advisers operate in illiberal political contexts, and the tension between political, bureaucratic, and expert advice.

Another avenue for research is a broader comparative multi-jurisdictional question: how have the political advisory systems in the various countries diverged and converged over time from a historical and comparative perspective? Although there is a growing comparative literature on political advisers on the Westminster and European systems (Fleischer 2008; Müller-Rommel 2008; Maley 2017, 2018; Ng 2018), the great preponderance of research on political advisers remains country-specific. There remains scope for a large-scale, international empirical project that examines the convergences and divergences between the Westminster, European, and US political advisory systems over a large span of time. Such a research design would need to be carefully constructed to account for political, institutional, social, and cultural differences across jurisdictions. One possibility could be to draw on Lijphart's seminal contribution with its archetypes of consociational and majoritarian democracies (Lijphart 1999).

In terms of institutional research, although there is much empirical research on the politics/administration dichotomy in the form of interactions between ministers, political advisers and the bureaucracy, there is less focus on other dimensions of interaction such as the media/politics, factions/opposition, and core executive/external actor interfaces for the various jurisdictions. Ng has found that the media/politics interface poses great problems in modern Westminster democracies and leads to issues relating to information management, including political advisers 'leaking' negative stories against factional or political opponents or fabricating negative stories against their opponents to publish on blogs (Ng 2018). Yet the roles of media advisers remain relatively understudied compared to their policy-based counterparts, with limited exceptions (Marland 2016).

Another element that has become increasingly prominent in the Westminster system is the factions/opposition interface, where political advisers have a primary loyalty to a particular person or group, which might be their minister alone, at the expense of the government as a whole; or their faction within their political party, at the expense of their minister (Ng 2018). The opposition can be factional opponents within their own party or the political opposition. These tensions and dynamics could be further investigated through empirical analysis. Further, moving beyond the core executive relationship of ministers, civil servants, and political advisers, there could be efforts in the Westminster and European contexts paralleling the US 'iron triangle' literature that empirically examine the relative influence of political advisers compared to other actors in the policy space, such as civil servants, parliamentarians, and interest groups.

The empirical examination of these interfaces that move beyond the traditional politics/administration dichotomy could potentially be combined with a theoretical framework utilizing the literature on public service bargains. According to this theory, bargaining relationships between ministers, civil servants, and political advisers involve parties that either deliver or cheat (Hood 2001; Hood and Lodge 2006). Political advisers have a personal agency bargain of loyalty to their minister as their appointment is tied to a particular Minister, but may cheat by demonstrating disloyal behaviour to the minister, such as leaking sensitive material to the media to undermine their minister (de Visscher and Salomonsen 2013: 76). Ministers in turn might cheat by blaming political advisers for their own failures. A combination of empirical, descriptive, and theoretical analysis of the media/politics, factions/opposition, and core executive/external actor interfaces will be invaluable to illuminate areas that have been steadily increasing in importance with the intensification of the media cycle, the unregulated nature of social media, and the factionalization of political parties.

Another element of theoretical development could be to apply a behavioural methodology to analyse the relationship between ministers and their advisers. For example, to assess two presidents' approaches to wars and the impact of their advisers, Saunders (2017) combined individual-level approaches in the principal-agent literature with behavioural economics, incorporating aspects of individual level bias. Utilizing this framework, Saunders found that the balance of experience between chief executives and their advisers shaped their behaviour, as experience influenced a leader's ability to monitor his or her advisers, the credibility of his or her delegation, and his or her ability to diversify advice. Ultimately Saunders (2017) concluded that a leader's experience is non-fungible and that experienced advisers cannot compensate for a lack of experience at the top. Further research in Westminster and European jurisdictions along this line in various policy areas would illuminate both individual-level and group-level effects of the behaviour and expertise of ministers and their advisers, as well as the consequential impact on policy-making and decision-making.

Finally, research on political advisers could develop normatively. A core concern across all jurisdictions is how the political executive is able to control the bureaucracy through the use of political advisers. Yet there is little theoretical work on what composition of political advisers and civil servants is optimal for performance (Lewis 2011), which provides a crucial anchor for administrative reform. In this context, more empirical work can also be done in examining the effect of political advisers on agency performance. Apart from the US context, there is scarce literature on the influence of political advisers on agency performance and outputs in terms of the 'number of lawsuits, enforcement actions, evaluations and certificates issued, as well as budgets and other agency outputs' (Lewis 2011: 58; see also Wood and Waterman 1991, 1994). A major research question could be: what are the most effective mechanisms of political control of the bureaucracy to enhance performance? As Wood and Waterman (1991: 823) ask, does bureaucratic responsiveness depend on 'bureaucratic structure, personnel attributes, mission complexity, or administrative constraints? How do constituency effects relate to political-bureaucratic equilibria?' How important is the salience of the issue?

Further illumination of these empirical, jurisdictional, comparative, institutional, theoretical, and normative issues will enhance and deepen our understanding of partisan political advisers, including their roles, performance, and interactions with other political actors in a modern democracy, and sets an agenda for future scholarship in this vibrant area.

25.5 CONCLUSION

Whether political advisers have been entrenched for more than a century, as in the United States model and the Napoleonic French and Belgian *cabinet* systems, or represent a more recent phenomenon that has evolved over the last few decades, such as the Westminster model, it is clear that these partisan advisers are now an entrenched part of the system of governance. This chapter has shown the rich diversity in the models of political advice that have been utilized in the developed world, and the increasing scholarly focus on the roles and influence of political advisers. A theme that recurs throughout the literature is how chief executives can control the policy agenda through a process of centralization in their private offices, as well as the politicization of advice through the strategic appointment and deployment of political advisers. This has been accompanied by cautionary tales of the costs of excessive politicization in terms of short-termism, loss of expertise, and zealous factional misbehaviour.

Ministers are now served by increasingly well-honed and sophisticated political advisory systems that support their policy, media, stakeholder liaison, and administrative functions. In the increasingly frenetic media and policy environments of modern democracies, political advisers now operate in a complex web of heterogeneous relationships between ministers, civil servants, the media, parliamentarians, and interest groups, who all jostle for power and influence over the policy process. We have moved well beyond the traditional politics/administration dichotomy into a new world of polycentric networks of governance.

Even with this multiplicity of political actors, it is undeniable that in many democratic systems, political advisers have become the gatekeepers to power, the guardians, the trusted allies, and the final port of call for the political executive; it is clear that they wield immense power and are now a permanent and enduring feature of executive government. Thus, it is time to face the pressing normative challenges of balancing between political and bureaucratic advice, balancing political influence with accountability and, more broadly, balancing the power of the executive within the wider system of governance.

References

Aberbach, J. D. and Peterson, M. A. (2005). 'Control and Accountability: Dilemmas of the Executive Branch,' in J. Aberbach and M. Peterson (eds) *The Executive Branch*. Oxford: Oxford University Press, 525–53.

Aberbach, J. D. and Rockman, B. A. (1994). 'Civil Servants and Policymakers: Neutral or Responsive Competence?,' *Governance* 7(4): 461–9.

Aberbach, J. D. and Rockman, B. A. (2000). *In the Web of Politics: Three Decades of the US Federal Executive*. Washington, DC: Brookings Institution.

Askim, J., Karlsen, R., and Kolltveit, K. (2017). 'Political Appointees in Executive Government: Exploring and Explaining Roles Using a Large-N Survey in Norway,' *Public Administration* 95(3): 342–58.

Bearfield, D. A. (2009). 'What is Patronage? A Critical Reexamination,' Public Administration Review 69: 44-76.

Blick, A. 2004. *People Who Live in the Dark*. London: Politico.

Brans, M., de Visscher, C., Gouglas, A., and Jaspers, S. (2017). 'Political Control and Bureaucratic Expertise: Policy Analysis by Ministerial Cabinet Members,' in M. Brans and D. Aubin (eds) *Policy Analysis in Belgium*. Bristol: Policy Press, 57–77.

Brans, M., Pelgrims, C., and Hoet, D. (2006). 'Comparative Observations on Tensions between Professional Policy Advice and Political Control in the Low Countries,' *International Review of Administrative Sciences* 72(1): 57–71.

Canada, Senate (2013). *Debates*. 22 October.

Cater, D. (1954). *Power in Washington*. New York: Vintage.

Chandrasekaran, R. (2006). *Imperial Life in the Emerald City: Inside Iraq's Green Zone*. New York: Knopf.

Christiansen, P. M., Niklasson, B., and Öhberg, P. (2016). 'Does Politics Crowd Out Professional Competence? The Organisation of Ministerial Advice in Denmark and Sweden,' *West European Politics* 39(6): 1230–50.

Cooper, C. and Block, R. (2006). *Disaster: Hurricane Katrina and the Failure of Homeland Security*. New York: Times Books.

Craft, J. (2016). *Backrooms and Beyond: Partisan Advisers and the Politics of Policy Work in Canada*. Toronto: University of Toronto Press.

Craft, J. and Howlett, M. (2012). 'Policy Formulation, Governance Shifts and Policy Influence: Location and Content in Policy Advisory Systems,' *Journal of Public Policy* 32(2): 79–98.

Cronin, T. E. (1980). *The State of the Presidency*. Boston, MA: Little Brown.

Connaughton, B. (2010). 'Glorified Gofers, Policy Experts or Good Generalists: A Classification of the Roles of the Irish Ministerial Adviser,' *Irish Political Studies* 25(3): 347–69.

Dahlström, C. (2009). 'Political Appointments in 18 Democracies, 1975–2007,' WoG Working Paper Series 2009, Göteborg University, https://www.gu.se/digitalAssets/1314/1314625_political-app.pdf

Dahlstrom, C., Peters, B. G., and Pierre, J. (2011) (eds). *Steering from the Centre: Strengthening Political Control in Western Democracies*. Toronto: University of Toronto Press.

Daintith, T. and Ng, Y. F. (2018). 'Executives,' in C. Saunders and A. Stone (eds) *The Oxford Handbook of the Australian Constitution*. New York: Oxford University Press.

De Visscher, C. and Salomonsen, H. H. (2013). 'Explaining Differences in Ministerial Ménages à Trois: Multiple Bargains in Belgium and Denmark,' *International Review of Administrative Sciences* 79(1): 71–90.

Di Mascio, F. and Natalini, A. (2013). 'Analysing the Role of Ministerial Cabinets in Italy: Legacy and Temporality in the Study of Administrative Reforms,' *International Review of Administrative Sciences* 79(2): 328–46.

Di Mascio, F. and Natalini, A. (2016). 'Ministerial Advisers between Political Change and Institutional Legacy: The Case of Italy,' *Acta Politica* 51(4): 517–38.

Dickinson, M. J. (2017). 'Presidents, the White House and the Executive Branch,' in L. C. Han (ed.) *New Directions in the American Presidency*. New York: Routledge, 173–209.

Edwards, G. C. (2001). *Why Not the Best? The Loyalty—Competence Trade-off in Presidential Appointments*. Washington, DC: Brookings Institution.

Eichbaum, C. and Shaw, R. (2007). 'Ministerial Advisers, Politicization and the Retreat from Westminster: The Case of New Zealand,' *Public Administration* 85(3): 609–40.

Eichbaum, C. and Shaw, R. (2008). 'Revisiting Politicization: Political Advisers and Public Servants in Westminster Systems,' *Governance* 21(3): 337–63.

Elgie, R. (2000). 'Staffing the Summit: France,' in B. G. Peters, R. A. W. Rhodes, and V. Wright (eds) *Administering the Summit: Administration of the Core Executive in Developed Countries*. Basingstoke: Macmillan, 225–44.

Fleischer, J. (2008). 'Power Resources of Parliamentary Executives: Policy Advice in the UK and Germany,' *West European Politics* 32(1): 196–214.

Freudenberg, G. (2006). *Figure of Speech: A Political Memoir*. Brisbane: Wiley.

Gay, O. and Fawcett, P. (2005). 'Special Advisers.' United Kingdom, Parliament and Constitution Centre, House of Commons Library, Standard Note SN/PC/3813.

Gouglas, A. (2015). 'Greek Ministerial Advisers: Policy Managers, Not Experts?,' *International Journal of Public Administration* 38(1): 15–27.

Gouglas, A. (2018). 'Greece: Political Advisers and Circles of Trust in Greek Ministerial Cabinets: Cardinals of the Conclave, Managers and the Children of Favouritism,' in R. Shaw and C. Eichbaum (eds) *Ministers, Minders and Mandarins: An International Study of Relationships at the Executive Summit of Parliamentary Democracies*. Cheltenham: Edward Elgar, 91–109.

Gouglas, A., Brans, M. and Jaspers, S. (2017). 'European Commissioner Cabinet Advisers: Policy Managers, Bodyguards, Stakeholder Mobilizers,' *Public Administration* 95(2): 357–97.

Halligan, J. (1995). 'Policy Advice and the Public Sector,' in B. G. Peters and D. T. Savoie (eds) *Governance in a Changing Environment*. Montreal: McGill-Queen's University Press, 138–72.

Heclo, H. (1977). *A Government of Strangers: Executive Politics in Washington*. Washington, DC: Brookings Institution.

Heclo, H. (1987). 'The In and Outer System: A Critical Assessment,' in G. C. Mackenzie (ed.) *The In-and-Outers: Presidential Appointees and Transient Government in Washington*. Baltimore: John Hopkins University Press, 195–218.

Hollibaugh, G. E., Horton, G. and Lewis, D. E. (2014). 'Presidents and Patronage,' *American Journal of Political Science* 58(4): 1024–42.

Hood, C. (2001). 'Public Service Bargains and Public Service Reform,' in B.G. Peters and J. Pierre (eds) *Politicians, Bureaucrats and Administrative Reform*. London: Routledge, 13–23.

Hood, C. and Lodge, M. (2006). *The Politics of Public Service Bargains: Reward, Competency, Loyalty—and Blame*. Oxford: Oxford University Press.

Hustedt, T. (2018). 'Germany: The Smooth and Silent Emergence of Advisory Roles,' in R. Shaw and C. Eichbaum (eds) *Ministers, Minders and Mandarins: An International Study of Relationships at the Executive Summit of Parliamentary Democracies*. Cheltenham: Edward Elgar, 145–62.

Hustedt, T. and Salomonsen, H. (2014). 'Ensuring Political Responsiveness: Politicization Mechanisms in Ministerial Bureaucracies,' *International Review of Administrative Sciences* 80(4): 746–65.

Jones, C. W. (2019). 'Adviser to the King: Experts, Rationalization, and Legitimacy,' *World Politics* 71(1): 1–43.

Kagan, E. (2001). 'Presidential Administration,' *Harvard Law Review* 114(8): 2245–385.

Koenig, L. W. (1975). *The Chief Executive*. 3rd ed. New York: Harcourt, Brace, Jovanovich.

Kristinsson, G. (2016). 'Specialists, Spinners and Networkers: Political Appointments in Iceland,' *Acta Politica* 54(4): 413–32.

Krynen, J. (2015). 'Le conseil du roi, siège de la prudence royale,' in J. Eymeri-Douzans, X. Bioy and S. Mouton (eds) *Le règne des entourages. Cabinets et conseillers de l'exécutif*. Paris: Presses de Sciences Po, 113–40.

Levinson, D. J. and Pildes, R. H. (2006). 'Separation of Parties, Not Powers,' *Harvard Law Review* 119(8): 2311–86.

Lewis, D. E. (2007). 'Testing Pendleton's Premise: Do Political Appointees make Worse Bureaucrats?', *Journal of Politics* 69(4): 1073–88.

Lewis, D. E. (2008). *The Politics of Presidential Appointments: Political Control and Bureaucratic Performance*. Princeton: Princeton University Press.

Lewis, D. E. (2011). 'Presidential Appointments and Personnel', *Annual Review of Political Science* 14: 47–66.

Lewis, D. E. and Waterman, R. W. (2013). 'The Invisible Presidential Appointments: An Examination of Appointments to the Department of Labor, 2001–11', *Presidential Studies Quarterly* 43(1): 35–57.

Light, P. C. (1995). *Thickening Government: Federal Hierarchy and the Diffusion of Accountability*. Washington, DC: The Brookings Institution.

Light, P. C. (2004). 'Fact Sheet on the Continuing Thickening of Government', 23 July, Washington, DC, Brookings Institution, https://www.brookings.edu/research/fact-sheet-on-the-continued-thickening-of-government

Lijphart, A. (1999). *Patterns of Democracy: Government Forms and Performance in Thirty-Six Countries*. 2nd ed. Yale: Yale University Press.

Lorentzen, P. (1985). 'Stress in Political-Career Executive Relations', *Public Administration Review* 45(3): 411–14.

Maley, M. (2000). 'Conceptualising Advisers' Policy Work: The Distinctive Policy Roles of Ministerial Advisers in the Keating Government, 1991–96', *Australian Journal of Political Science* 35(3): 449–70.

Maley, M. (2002). 'Partisans at the Centre of Government: The Role of Ministerial Advisers in the Keating Government 1991–96.' PhD Thesis, Australian National University, Canberra.

Maley, M. (2011). 'Strategic Links in a Cut-Throat World: Rethinking the Role and Relationships of Australian Ministerial Staff', *Public Administration* 89(4): 1469–88.

Maley, M. (2015). 'The Policy Work of Australian Political Staff', *International Journal of Public Administration* 38(1): 46–55.

Maley, M. (2017). 'Temporary Partisans, Tagged Officers or Impartial Professionals: Moving between Ministerial Offices and Departments', *Public Administration* 95(2): 407–22.

Maley, M. (2018). 'Understanding the Divergent Development of the Ministerial Office in Australia and the UK', *Australian Journal of Political Science* 53(3): 320–35.

Maranto, R. (1991). 'Does Familiarity Breed Acceptance? Trends in Career-Noncareer Relations in the Reagan Administration', *Administration and Society* 23(2): 247–66.

Maranto, R. (2005). *Beyond a Government of Strangers: How Career Executives and Political Appointees Can Turn Conflict into Cooperation*. Lanham: Lexington.

Marland, A. (2016). *Brand Command: Canadian Politics and Democracy in the Age of Message Control*. British Columbia: University of British Columbia Press.

McCornell, G. (1966). *Private Power and American Democracy*. New York: Alfred Knopf.

Metzger, G. E. (2009). 'The Interdependent Relationship between Internal and External Separation of Powers', *Emory Law Journal* 59(2): 423–57.

Michaels, J. D. (2015). 'An Enduring, Evolving Separation of Powers', *Columbia Law Review* 115(3): 515–98.

Moe, T. M. (1985). 'The Politicized Presidency', in J. E. Chubb and P. E. Peterson (eds) *The New Direction in American Politics*. Washington, DC: Brookings Institution, 235–71.

Moynihan, D. P. and Roberts, A. S. (2010). 'The Triumph of Loyalty over Competence: The Bush Administration and the Exhaustion of the Politicized Presidency', *Public Administration Review* 70(4): 572–81.

Müller-Rommel, F. (2000). 'The German Chancellor's Office,' in B. G. Peters, R. A. W. Rhodes, and V. Wright (eds) *Administering the Summit: Administration of the Core Executive in Developed Countries*. Basingstoke: Macmillan, 81–100.

Müller-Rommel, F. (2008). 'Prime Ministerial Staff in Post-Communist Central and Eastern Europe: A Role Assessment by Cabinet Ministers,' *East European Politics* 24(2): 256–71.

Nathan, R. (1984). *The Administrative Presidency*. New York: MacMillan.

Neary, I. (2000). 'Serving the Japanese Prime Minister,' in B. G. Peters, R. A. W. Rhodes, and V. Wright (eds) *Administering the Summit: Administration of the Core Executive in Developed Countries*. Basingstoke: Macmillan.

Ng, Y. F. (2016). *Ministerial Advisers in Australia: The Modern Legal Context*. Sydney: Federation Press.

Ng, Y. F. (2016a). 'Dispelling Myths about Conventions: Ministerial Advisers and Parliamentary Committees,' *Australian Journal of Political Science* 51(3): 512–29.

Ng, Y. F. (2018). *The Rise of Political Advisors in the Westminster System*. London: Routledge.

Niskanen, W. (1971). *Bureaucracy and Representative Government*. Chicago: Aldine-Atherton.

OECD (2007). 'Political Advisors and Civil Servants in European Countries,' SIGMA Papers, No. 38, OECD Publishing, Paris.

Öhberg, P., Christiansen, P. M., and Niklasson, B. (2017). 'Administrative Politicization or Contestability? How Political Advisers affect Neutral Competence in Policy Processes,' *Public Administration* 95(1): 269–85.

Ouyang, Y., Haglund, E. T., and Waterman, R. W. (2017). 'The Missing Element: Examining the Loyalty-Competence Nexus in Presidential Appointments,' *Presidential Studies Quarterly* 47(1): 62–91.

Page, E. C. (1992). *Political Authority and Bureaucratic Power: A Comparative Analysis*. 2nd ed. Hertfordshire: Harvester Wheatsheaf.

Peters, B. G. (2010). 'The United States,' in C. Eichbaum and R. Shaw (eds) *Partisan Appointees and Public Servants*. Cheltenham: Edward Elgar Publishing, 180–97.

Peters, B. G. (2015). 'Les hommes du president,' in J. Eymeri-Douzans, X. Bioy, and S. Mouton (eds) *Le règne des entourages. Cabinets et conseillers de l'exécutif*. Paris: Presses de Sciences Po, 787–98.

Peters, B. G. and Pierre, J. (2004) (eds). *The Politicization of the Civil Service in Comparative Perspective: A Quest for Control*. London: Routledge.

Poguntke, T. and Webb, P. (2005) (eds). *The Presidentialisation of Politics: A Comparative Study of Modern Democracies*. Oxford: Oxford University Press.

Portail Belgium (2014). *Adresses et cellules strategiques du gouvernement fédéral*. Brussels: Portail Belgium.

Republique Française (2017). *Personnels affectés dans les cabinets ministériels*. Paris: Republique Française.

Ritchie, E. 1992. 'The Model of French Ministerial Cabinets in the Early European Commission,' in E. V. Heyen (ed.) *Yearbook of European History*. Volume 4: *Early European Community Administration*. Baden-Baden: Nomos, 95–106.

Rottinghaus, B. and Bergan, D. E. (2011). 'The Politics of Requesting Appointments: Congressional Requests in the Appointment and Nomination Process,' *Political Research Quarterly* 64(1): 31–44.

Rourke, F. E. (1992). 'Responsiveness and Neutral Competence in American Bureaucracy,' *Public Administration Review* 52(6): 539–46.

Rudalevige, A. (2009). 'The Administrative Presidency and Bureaucratic Control: Implementing a Research Agenda,' *Presidential Studies Quarterly* 39(1): 10–24.

Saunders, E. N. (2017). 'No Substitute for Experience: Presidents, Advisers, and Information in Group Decision Making,' *International Organization* 71: S219–47.

Shaw, R. and Eichbaum, C. (2018). 'New Zealand: Bargains, Compacts and Covenants in the Core Executive,' in R. Shaw and C. Eichbaum (eds) *Ministers, Minders and Mandarins: An International Study of Relationships at the Executive Summit of Parliamentary Democracies.* Cheltenham: Edward Elgar, 145–62.

Tiernan, A. (2007). *Power Without Responsibility: Ministerial Staffers in Australian Governments from Whitlam to Howard.* Sydney: UNSW Press.

Tolchin, M. and Tolchin, S. (2010). *Pinstripe Patronage: Political Favoritism from the Clubhouse to the White House and Beyond.* Boulder, CO: Paradigm.

Van den Berg, C. (2018). 'The Netherlands: The Emergence and Encapsulation of Ministerial Advisers,' in R. Shaw and C. Eichbaum (eds) *Ministers, Minders and Mandarins: An International Study of Relationships at the Executive Summit of Parliamentary Democracies.* Cheltenham: Edward Elgar, 129–44.

Walter, J. (2006). 'Ministers, Minders and Public Servants: Changing Parameters of Responsibility in Australia,' *Australian Journal of Public Administration* 65(3): 22–7.

Weingast, B. R. (2005). 'Caught in the Middle: The President, Congress, and the Political-Bureaucratic System,' in J. D. Aberbach and M. A. Peterson (eds) *The Executive Branch.* Oxford: Oxford University Press, 312–43.

Weko, T. J. (1995). *The Politicizing Presidency: The White House Personnel Office.* Lawrence: University Press of Kansas.

Weller, P. (2002). *Don't Tell the Prime Minister.* Melbourne: Scribe Publications.

Wood, B. D. and Waterman, R. W. (1991). 'The Dynamics of Political Control of the Bureaucracy,' *American Political Science Review* 85(3): 801–28.

Wood, B. D. and Waterman, R. W. (1994). *Bureaucratic Dynamics: The Role of Bureaucracy in a Democracy.* Boulder, CO: Westview Press.

Yong, B. and Hazell, R. (2014). *Special Advisers: Who They Are, What They Do and Why They Matter.* Oxford: Hart Publishing.

Zussman, D. (2009). *Political Advisers.* Paris: OECD.

DYNAMICS AND DEVELOPMENTS BETWEEN POLITICAL EXECUTIVES AND THE BROADER POLITICAL CONTEXT

PART IV

DYNAMICS AND
DEVELOPMENTS
BETWEEN
POLITICAL
EXECUTIVES
AND THE
BROADER
POLITICAL
CONTEXT

CHAPTER 26

··

POLITICIANS AND BUREAUCRATS IN EXECUTIVE GOVERNMENT

··

TOBIAS BACH AND KAI WEGRICH

26.1 INTRODUCTION

WITHOUT a permanent administrative apparatus that prepares and implements public policy, political executives are unable to exercise political authority. They depend on the analytical, regulatory, coordination, and delivery capacities of public organizations to effectively and legitimately address pressing societal challenges and to pursue their political agendas (Lodge and Wegrich 2014). This chapter focuses on the relationship between political executives (presidents, prime ministers, cabinet, and junior ministers) on the one hand and policy bureaucracies on the other hand. We use the term policy bureaucracies for those organizations variously labelled departments, ministries, or central agencies primarily tasked with developing and maintaining public policy (Page and Jenkins 2005).

In constitutional terms, the relationship between political executives and policy bureaucrats—public officials working in policy bureaucracies—is hierarchical in nature, and there is usually no doubt about who should be calling the shots. The fact that political executives are either democratically elected into office or selected by the head of government authorizes them to set the policy agenda within their sphere of responsibility and to direct the administrative apparatus to pursue this agenda. At the same time, political executives crucially depend on policy bureaucracies, which have both substantial policy expertise and in-depth knowledge about the policy-making process. Moreover, political executives' information processing and conflict resolution capacities are limited, which means they can only concentrate on a few flagship policies and handle the most pressing problems (Scharpf 1994). This combination of information asymmetries and capacity limitations potentially turns actual power relationships between political executives and policy bureaucracies upside down. In consequence, political executives face a permanent challenge to ensure that bureaucrats are responsive to their policy preferences.

This chapter provides a review of the literature on the relations between political executives and policy bureaucrats, highlighting theoretical perspectives and empirical findings on how the tension between political control and bureaucratic power is addressed in different contexts. To this end, the next section elaborates on three major research topics that have been asked addressed by political scientists about the relationship between political executives and policy bureaucracies, providing an overview of substantial findings and research designs. This is followed by an overview of key theoretical perspectives in the literature. The chapter then moves on to discuss emerging topics in the contemporary literature. The chapter's final section sketches directions for future research on politicians and bureaucrats in executive government around the world.

26.2 POLITICIANS AND BUREAUCRATS IN EXECUTIVE GOVERNMENT: MAJOR RESEARCH TOPICS AND THEORETICAL PERSPECTIVES

This section discusses three interrelated, but analytically distinct topics that constitute the core of political science research on political executives' relations to policy bureaucracies. The first two topics—the recruitment and replacement of top officials, and the organization and power of policy bureaucracies—share an analytical focus on how political executives deal with the fundamental problem of ensuring the permanent bureaucracy's responsiveness to their policy preferences, but emphasize different means (politicization, centralization) employed to achieve this objective (Rudalevige 2009; Dahlström et al. 2011). The third topic, in contrast, is more concerned with understanding and explaining what happens in the 'machine room' of executive government, asking how political and administrative policy-makers interact, and what those processes tell us about the relative power of political executives and policy bureaucrats (Aberbach et al. 1981; 't Hart and Wille 2006; Page 2012; Christensen and Opstrup 2018).

26.2.1 The Recruitment and Replacement of Top Officials

A first major topic in the study of political executives and bureaucrats addresses the balance of political control and bureaucratic power, yet focuses on a specific instrument of political control, namely the authority (or its absence) of political executives to appoint and replace top officials. The influence of politicians on personnel decisions in the public sector is a long-standing topic in the study of public administration as evidenced by a comprehensive literature on 'politicization' and 'patronage' (Derlien 1996; Peters and Pierre 2004; Hollibaugh et al. 2014; Hustedt and Salomonsen 2014; Kopecký et al. 2016). The starting point of much of this literature is the well-known politics-administration dichotomy, which goes back to the writings of Max Weber and Woodrow Wilson (Sager and Rosser 2009). Although addressing different problems, both Weber and Wilson concluded that politics and administration, or more precisely the careers of politicians and bureaucrats, should be separated. Although often mistaken as an advocate of bureaucratic organization, Weber argued that politicians are needed to curb a potentially all-too-powerful permanent bureaucracy. In contrast, Wilson was concerned with the detrimental effects of the spoils system the United States in which administrative positions were filled according to political rather than competency criteria, which resulted in an inefficient and corrupt bureaucracy. There is now good empirical evidence that a close connection between administrative and political careers has detrimental effects on good government (Dahlström and Lapuente 2017). However, this literature primarily focuses on bureaucrats outside policy bureaucracies.

The most obvious manifestation of politicization of the bureaucracy is the existence of positions within policy bureaucracies for which political executives have some degree of formal powers to appoint or remove individuals (see also Chapter 19 in this volume). A widely used definition of formal politicization is 'the substitution of political criteria for merit-based criteria in the selection, retention, promotion, rewards and disciplining of members of the public service' (Peters and Pierre 2004: 2). An important question in comparative research—both over time and between countries—is the degree to which such formally politicized positions exist in policy bureaucracies (Page and Wright 1999). In studies of parliamentary systems where top-level positions are formally politicized, scholars usually consider partisan loyalty as the core political criterion for appointing and replacing top officials, and seek to describe and explain the occurrence of party political backgrounds among top officials, based on biographical information (Derlien 2003; Dahlström and Niklasson 2013; Ennser-Jedenastik 2016b; Veit and Scholz 2016). Another strand of research investigates the politicization of top officials by studying how political change such as cabinet or minister turnover affects top officials' turnover (Derlien 2003; Meyer-Sahling 2008; Boyne et al. 2010; Meyer-Sahling and Veen 2012; Christensen et al. 2014; Dahlström and Holmgren 2019), using various methods such as event-history-analysis or descriptive analyses of the degree of replacement of top officials.

The literature on political influence on personnel decisions often takes the delegation problem in a principal-agent relationship as a starting point, arguing that politicians face a delegation problem, as they cannot be sure that bureaucrats share their policy preferences (Huber and Shipan 2006; see also Chapter 3 in this volume). Not only do they have limited expertise, but they also face important capacity constrains to oversee the bureaucracy. To avoid a 'runaway bureaucracy' (McCubbins et al. 1987), politicians can staff key positions with individuals that have policy priorities similar to their own (Lewis 2008). By selecting individuals with a known loyalty to their own political party, politicians can minimize the problem of adverse selection—choosing a person without knowing for sure that she will act as intended. Those 'allies' will make sure that decisions are biased in favour of politicians' preferences (Bach and Veit 2018; Dahlström and Holmgren 2019). The appointment and replacement of top officials are potentially powerful instruments of political control. Knowledge about whether and how politicians use those instruments is fundamental for understanding the nature of democratic governance, as politicians may also use their formal powers as a patronage tool to reward loyalists with doubtful qualifications for the job at hand (Grindle 2012; Kopecký et al. 2016).

More recently, scholars have started to investigate that political executives may select (or replace) top officials based on other criteria than partisan loyalty, including political and public management skills (Fleischer 2016; Bach and Veit 2018). Another typology of political appointees' qualifications distinguishes professionalism, political allegiance, and personal loyalty as selection criteria (Kopecký et al. 2016). The question why political executives appoint political appointees, and more specifically what qualifications they look for, has been studied most intensely in the US, where scholars have studied how presidents balance loyalty and competence when selecting top officials (Lewis 2008; Lewis and Waterman 2013; Hollibaugh et al. 2014; Ouyang et al. 2017). A key argument in this literature is that political executives (in this case the US president) will consider different kinds of qualifications depending on the kind of post to be filled. They may be able to compromise on professional competence for positions in organizations which are at the margins of the president's agenda, yet they have strong incentives to fill positions with loyal and competent candidates in organizations ranking high on their agenda to ensure the achievement of policy objectives. In studies of other contexts, only few studies explicitly address differential patterns of politicization within the executive (Christensen et al. 2014; Ennser-Jedenastik 2016b; Kopecký et al. 2016; Bach et al. 2020). We will address this emerging research theme more thoroughly in this chapter's final section.

26.2.2 The Organization and Power of Policy Bureaucracies

The study of the relationship between political executives and policy bureaucrats is invariably connected to the structure and organization of government, and more specifically to the balancing of political control and bureaucratic power. A key question in the literature is therefore how policy bureaucracies are organized, and how this affects power relations between politics and administration. Here, we can broadly distinguish power relationships between political executives and bureaucrats on the one hand, and power relationships inside the executive, for example between a prime minister's office and line departments, on the other hand. These relationships will also differ between parliamentary and presidential systems of government, but also between countries with similar systems of government because of variation in organizational structures and processes.

The notion that organization affects power relations goes back at least to Max Weber's works on bureaucratic organization, who suggested that politicians will always remain 'dilettantes' in comparison to expert bureaucracies. As mentioned above, this line of reasoning is concerned with how much power permanent bureaucracies actually have, and how political executives can make them responsive to their policy preferences. In Weber's view, the existence of a political leadership with a power base outside the bureaucracy, usually through an electoral mandate, is an important condition for the exercise of political control over the bureaucracy. Although political leaders differ in terms of their authority across countries (Page 1992), the basic condition for the exercise of political control over policy bureaucracies, that is, having a political rather than an administrative leadership, is usually fulfilled in modern democratic states. What this perspective highlights, though, is the usefulness of looking at the power and resources of political executives to understand power relations with bureaucracies.

More specifically, scholars working in this tradition have studied organizational and procedural mechanisms for avoiding different kinds of 'drift' away from the wishes of elected politicians, using the analytical toolbox of principal-agent models (Huber and Shipan 2006). There is a large body of literature on the political control of the federal bureaucracy in the United States, yet this literature primarily addresses questions regarding congressional control over bureaucracy and the relative influence of the president and congress over bureaucratic decision-making (see Moe 2012 for an overview). Hence, in terms of political control over bureaucracy, presidential systems are characterized by a situation in which both the legislative and the executive branch are potentially facing problems of political responsiveness among bureaucrats (Weingast 2005). This is different in parliamentary systems of government, where political executives have been delegated authority to govern by parliament. Having said that, one of the main areas of research related to the political control of the bureaucracy by the US-president are political appointments in the federal bureaucracy (see below) and the centralization of resources within the Executive Office of the President (Rudalevige 2009). The different approaches of US presidents to increase the political responsiveness of the US federal bureaucracy, which for instance also include the appointment of 'policy czars', are discussed under the label of 'administrative presidency' and continuously attract the attention of executive politics scholars (see Helms 2017 for an overview of this literature).

In the context of parliamentary systems of government, questions about the organization of the executive apparatus and political control of the bureaucracy have centred on the capacity of the political leadership relative to the permanent civil service. This debate is related to issues of size in terms of relative numbers of political executives in a department, such as cabinet and junior ministers or staff units such as 'cabinets ministériels' in Austria, France, Belgium, or the European Commission (Schnapp 2004). A key topic in debates of the 1970s was the use of planning units, based on the idea to increase capacities for long-term and comprehensive, cross-sectoral policies (Fleischer 2009). A related, more contemporary phenomenon is the increasing use of special advisers who directly support the political executive but who (at least formally) do not have any managerial authority within a department (Eichbaum and Shaw 2008). This is an emerging area of research, which we address in more detail below. The common denominator of those topics is a focus on increasing the leadership capacity of political executives vis-à-vis permanent bureaucracies as a means of improving political control.

Another key aspect of political control over bureaucracy is related to questions of coordination within the government apparatus, more precisely related to the ability of presidents, prime ministers, as well as finance ministers, to control and coordinate other departments and the public sector at large (Dahlström et al. 2011). The starting point of this perspective is a 'natural' tendency of public organizations such as line ministries to pursue distinct and (necessarily) selective policy objectives. In other words, the basic problem or challenge is that governments are characterized by a division of labour, which requires some degree of coordination (Wegrich and Štimac 2014). This challenge arguably has increased over time, especially in the wake of administrative reforms resulting in a higher fragmentation of public bureaucracies around the world (Bouckaert et al. 2010). Hence, questions of organization and political control are not simply about the relation between politicians and bureaucrats, but also about power relations between the 'core executive' (i.e. those organizations set up to 'pull the strings' in government in order to achieve some coherence and to solve conflicts) and other governmental bodies. In a broader perspective, issues of control over bureaucracy also touch upon the relation with other administrative organizations, in particular executive and regulatory agencies (see below).

26.2.3 The Interaction of Political Executives and Policy Bureaucrats in Policy-making

The third field where the power relation between elected politicians and the policy bureaucracy plays out is the actual interaction in policy-making. Who is really calling the shots when it comes to setting the agenda, formulating policy lines and designing individual policies? Max Weber's model of bureaucratic rule has long been interpreted as a normative model that calls for a strict separation of roles in policy-making, with politicians setting the objectives and allocating values and bureaucrats merely implementing the directions by filling in the details (Aberbach et al. 1981). And while this myth prevails as a normative model also within the bureaucracy, it has been repeatedly debunked by empirical research since the late 1960s and early 1970s.

Mayntz and Scharpf's (1975) study was among the first that debunked the myth of a strong hierarchical relation between executive politicians and policy bureaucrats. Their in-depth empirical studies of policy-making in the German federal bureaucracy revealed two key findings. One is the central role of the smallest organizational units in the German ministries—the *Referate* (sections)—in the policy formulation process. Not only was policy knowledge concentrated in these units, they also maintained relations with external stakeholders, such as interest organizations. Much of the policy knowledge was generated through these interactions. Mayntz and Scharpf (1975) showed that these units where not only critical in formulating a first draft of a policy, but also in initiating policies. The second key finding was that the relation between the lower levels and the political leadership was characterized by a (silent) dialogue. In this dialogue model, the policy bureaucracy was taking into account signals from the higher echelons in their rather independent policy work, while the political level values the subject matter related expertise of policy bureaucrats. While the dialogue model is suggestive of a relatively harmonious relation between the two antipodes, Mayntz and Scharpf (1975) pointed at the limited capacities of the political level to actually lead the policy-making process, given their limited resources for policy analysis and development work.

And while this study was limited to Germany, and is by now four decades old, its core empirical findings have displayed remarkable longevity. Aberbach et al. (1981) have confirmed in the comparative study of the policy bureaucracy that bureaucrats are indeed involved in all dimensions of policy-making (including aggregation of interests). The integration of political aspects of policy-making by civil servants, such as anticipating potential opposition and support for policy alternatives, has subsequently been labelled 'functional politicization' denoting distinct role perceptions as well as decision-making behaviour (Derlien 1996; Hustedt and Salomonsen 2014). Peters (1988) has outlined five different ideal-type models of politics-administration interaction that mainly point at cross-national variation in relational distance between politicians and bureaucrats— with the 'village life' model being at one end and the 'adversarial model' at the other. Peters builds his typology on seminal studies of individual countries, such as Heclo and Wildavsky's (1974) work on the UK civil service that indeed stresses the informal character of the club like caste of higher civil servants in this country. Heclo's (1977) study highlights the contrasting model of the US, which he characterizes as a 'government of strangers' given the high fluctuation of public officials in the US 'spoils system'.

But despite these cross-national differences, the hybridisation of roles, the significance of policy bureaucrats in policy development and the limited role of hierarchy in politics-administration relations within a policy-making context has been confirmed by the many studies that have been published in the 1970s and 1980s. More recent follow-up studies, however, indicate shifting tectonics in this relation. For example, Goetz (2007) in a review of the key claims of Mayntz and Scharpf (1975) points at politicization, outsourcing of policy advice and Europeanization as key trends undermining the central role of the bureaucratic policy-makers in Germany. For other countries the shifting relation have been characterized as more disruptive, that is, as the 'breaking of the bargain' (Savoie 2003). The rise of the New Public Management (NPM) since the 1980s can be seen as a driver and manifestation of such disruption. With tailwind from a general rise of 'bureaucracy bashing', politicians demand more managerial skills and 'delivery competencies' (Hood and Lodge 2006) and also more direct accountability of bureaucrats for results—and in particular failure. The trend of politicization, discussed above, is linked to the increasingly widespread perception of growing estrangement between executive politicians and policy bureaucrats, with the former trying to strengthen loyalty and thinking in political terms within the bureaucracy and the latter perceiving a decline of influence in policy-making.

Such a claim can however not be generalized. While there is a growing number of studies that suggest that tensions between politicians and policy bureaucrats have resulted in more strained interactions or the side-lining of the permanent bureaucracy in policy-making (e.g. 't Hart and Wille 2006 studying interactions of ministers and officials in the Netherlands), we lack systematic and cross-national comparative research that would allow to generalize such a claim. At the same time, there is sufficient empirical ground to suggest that the rapidly changing context of policy-making—mediatization, austerity, political polarization—has had its toll in terms of challenging if not disrupting the 'dialogue model' of politics-bureaucracy interactions in policy-making. We should just be aware of a potentially wide range of variation cross nationally with regard to the strength and impact of these disruptive trends.

26.2.4 Theoretical Perspectives on Political Executives and Bureaucrats

Empirical research on the three big questions discussed above has been shaped by a variety of theoretical approaches. Max Weber's model of bureaucratic rule is an enduring reference point, mainly used as a yardstick for assessing the empirical reality in contrast to normative ideals of politics-bureaucracy relations. Weber's thinking has also been very influential in studying how different national systems deal with the challenges of controlling bureaucracy (Page 1992). But research on the politics-bureaucracy relation has also been influenced by the dominant general theoretical frameworks in political science, namely the rational choice (or public choice; also political economy) approach and the family of institutional approaches (see Chapter 5 in this volume). The political economy perspective is particularly significant, not primarily because of its explanatory power of behaviour. Its significance lies also in its practical relevance in shaping or justifying sentiments about the politics-bureaucracy relation being mainly a problem of controlling a bureaucracy that is always trying to shirk and drift (Pierre and Peters 2017).

Niskanen's (1971) model of the budget-maximizing bureaucrat was the first influential rational-choice/political economy approach dedicated to the behaviour of bureaucrats. Wilson (1989) and Dunleavy (1991) have debunked its simple claim—that bureaucrats seek expanding budgets because this comes with opportunities for increasing salary and power. Wilson argued that an increasing budget might undermine the coherence of an agency's mission; taking on tasks that do not fit into the existing portfolio might also undermine the reputation of the agency or create divided constituencies. Dunleavy (1991) remained within the bounds of the rational choice logic, but argued that bureaucratic leaders are more interested in maximizing interesting policy work and engagement with the political leaders, rather than cumbersome administrative (i.e. implementation) work that comes with risks of conflict and blame. The creation of a number of executive agencies that relieved UK central government departments from implementation tasks was used as an example to develop that theory and later on tested empirically (James 2003).

Despite these challenges, the rational choice perspective remained the central parsimonious theoretical framework for the analysis of the politics-bureaucracy relation. In particular the principal-agent framework (see Bendor et al. 2001 for a review) took centre stage in the theoretical debates. Not so different from Weber's take, it highlighted the 'information asymmetry' between the political principals and the bureaucratic agents—and assumed that the bureaucrats would use this asymmetry for their private gain by way of shirking and drifting. The model became the reference point and justification for performance contracts and incentive systems that aimed at minimizing risks of bureaucratic shirking and agency drift and provided a key academic justification of the NPM revolution sweeping across many governments in the OECD world and beyond (Boston et al. 1996). For executive politicians, the NPM approach promised a solution to the problem of the 'shirking bureaucrat' (Pierre and Peters 2017), also in light of doubts about the loyalty of bureaucrats having already served for previous governments.

It took two decades of NPM reform practices with a range of unintended effects, such as pervasive 'gaming' of target regimes, crowding out of intrinsic motivation (or public service motivation), before challenges of the principal-agent-perspective received more voice in the debate and competing approaches emerged. The Public Service Bargain (PSB) theory of Hood and Lodge (2006) is one exhibit of this new line of theorizing. The PSB perspective conceives the relation between executive politicians and policy bureaucrats as a bargain where both parties gain something but also have to give up something. Loyalty, reward, and competencies are the three main dimensions of this bargain, and Hood and Lodge (2006) can demonstrate that the managerial agency bargain that is part of the NPM reform toolkit is but one of many different bargains that have developed since the departure from the classic PSB. This classic bargain, originally formulated by Bernard Schaffer, consists of politicians giving up the right to hire and fire bureaucrats at their will but gain a certain set of competences and loyalty to the government of the day; bureaucrats give up their right to criticize the government in public and gain an accepted position in the policy-making system and a set of rewards, of which job security and predictable career patterns are the most important ones. Hood and Lodge (2006) draw on various country contexts (the United Kingdom and Germany, in particular) to show how this classic bargain varied between these two countries early on (with a more 'agency' type in the United Kingdom and a more independent 'trustee' bargain in Germany) and how administrative reforms and contextual changes have changed the bargains. The PSB perspective in particular allows to explore how changes in one dimension, for example the reward dimension, can have (unintended) downstream effects on other dimensions. For example, the idea to buy-in more 'delivery' skills with a more managerial ('turkey race') reward structure can—and did—undermine the loyalty of bureaucrats to support executive politicians in critical situations.

The PSB perspective is an important departure from the unidirectional perspective of the principal-agent framework that is limited to exploring ways to control the runaway agent—an assumption that has been challenged on empirical and theoretical grounds (see Pierre and Peters 2017 for a summary). It stresses the exchange relation between the two parties and the significance of informal expectations and understandings, with some form of capricious equilibrium as an underlying criterion for a 'good' relation between politicians and bureaucrats (although Hood and Lodge would not state that so bluntly). Further scholarship of the current decade has added to the challenges of the principal-agent perspective by pointing at the often problematic behaviour of the political principal. In these accounts, the key problem is not the bureaucrat, but the cheating, shirking, and drifting principal who does not hold his or her end of the bargain, undermining policy effectiveness, bureaucratic professionalism, and democratic accountability (Schillemans and Busuioc 2015; Miller and Whitford 2016).

Further tailwind for the more critical take on the role of politicians in the relation with bureaucrats comes with the recent wave of research following the 'behavioural' turn in economics and beyond. Mainly being interested in the prevalence of biases among actor groups, including but not limited to politicians and bureaucrats, experimental designs have explored the prevalence of, in particular, confirmation bias, that is, the tendency to pay greater attention to information supporting existing causal understandings and worldviews. These studies show that politicians indeed display a strong confirmation bias when confronted with new information (such as information of performance about schools)—and providing more evidence that challenges prior attitudes actually results in stronger confirmation biases and motivated reasoning (Baekgaard et al. 2019). These studies, and the 'behavioural' theorizing on which they are based, have as yet not contributed to the exploration of the politics-bureaucracy relation—mainly because they are focusing on individual behaviour and have trouble conceptualising interaction between actors and how organizational context shapes individual biases (or adds new ones). However, the mechanisms uncovered, such as the biases and uses of heuristics, have already played an important role in the development of theories of administrative behaviour (Simon 1947), and indeed build on Simon. Today, these approaches have the potential to uncover dynamics in the politics-administrative relation that could be integrated into or combined with other approaches that seek to develop the classic principal-agent perspective. And new challenges of political polarization, hyper-politicization, and weaponizing public administration for political approaches call for such integration of perspectives (see final section).

26.3 POLITICIANS AND BUREAUCRATS IN EXECUTIVE GOVERNMENT: CONTEMPORARY RESEARCH PERSPECTIVES

26.3.1 Comparative Perspectives on Political Control and Bureaucratic Power

The comparative study of political executives and policy bureaucracies is certainly one of the most fruitful areas of research within the literature discussed in this chapter.

The most influential comparative study to date was published in the early 1980s, focusing on the interaction of (executive and legislative) politicians and policy bureaucrats (Aberbach et al. 1981). This study showed significant cross-country differences in the respective roles and interactions of politicians and bureaucrats. Most subsequent comparative analyses are edited volumes with country chapters often using somewhat different theoretical and empirical approaches, rather than being the result of tightly integrated comparative projects (Page and Wright 1999; Peters and Pierre 2004; Dahlström et al. 2011).

Yet despite being mostly comparable rather than comparative, those studies have moved the research frontier and have paved the ground for later research. To engage in meaningful comparative research on a larger scale requires conceptual development based on thick contextual analysis. In particular, this literature highlights different institutional arrangements for addressing the delegation problem faced by political executives. Those arrangements can be thought of as a continuum, where some countries are characterized by politically neutral, purely merit bureaucracies without formal politicization of top official positions (e.g. United Kingdom, Denmark, the Netherlands), whereas others have politicized positions at the 'commanding heights' of policy bureaucracies (e.g. Germany, Sweden, USA, France), and still others apply political criteria for political appointments also below the very top level of policy bureaucracies (e.g. Austria, Belgium, Spain, Greece) (Derlien 1996; Page and Wright 1999).

Moreover, scholars have also proposed other typologies of political and administrative relationships for comparative research. Meyer-Sahling (2008) differentiates four types politicization according to two criteria: (1) is bureaucratic turnover systematically taking place after change in government; and (2) what is the recruitment pool for top officials? The resulting typology includes non-politicization (no replacement, internal recruitment pool, e.g. UK, Denmark), bounded politicization (replacement, internal recruitment pool, e.g. Germany), open politicization (replacement, external recruitment from outside political settings, e.g. United States), and partisan politicization (replacement, external recruitment from political settings, e.g. Hungary). However, even within non-politicized settings, political executives may replace top officials after political changes, such as in Denmark, with incoming top officials being selected on meritocratic, rather than party political grounds (Christensen et al. 2014).

In particular, contemporary scholars have engaged in comparative studies covering smaller numbers of countries, addressing topics such as functions and interactions of politicians, special advisers, and career officials (de Visscher and Salomonsen 2013; Christiansen et al. 2016), interactions of politicians and bureaucrats in rule-making (Page 2012), the politicization of the civil service (Meyer-Sahling and Veen 2012), and the organization of executive bureaucracy (Fleischer 2009). Having said that, there are several noteworthy comparative studies covering more than a handful of countries, including a study on 'party patronage' (Kopecký et al. 2012; Kopecký et al. 2016) based on face-to-face expert interviews. This research not only looks at the prevalence of politicization of (different parts of) the state apparatus but also at the kind of qualifications of political appointees sought by politicians, and politicians' motives for politicization. A key finding is that politicians' motives for politicization are primarily about exercising political control, although often in combination with the desire to reward loyal followers.

Another approach is to collect survey data among senior officials to assess cross-country variation in politicized appointments. Bach et al. (2020) show that patterns of politicization in Europe fit squarely with established administrative traditions, such as low levels of politicization in Anglo-Saxon and Scandinavian countries and high levels of politicization in Napoleonic countries, but also shows how countries considered being part of the same tradition vary substantially in terms of politicized appointments, such as the post-communist countries (Meyer-Sahling and Veen 2012). A third approach is to gauge politicization by mapping party political backgrounds of top officials. There are to date no examples of comparative studies of top officials in policy bureaucracies using this approach, but there are several single country studies, which provide useful starting points for international comparisons (Christensen 2006; Meyer-Sahling 2008; Ennser-Jedenastik 2016a; Bach and Veit 2018).

26.3.2 Leadership Capacity and Political Control: The Growth, Function, and Effects of Ministerial Advisers

The increasing use of ministerial advisers who enter and leave their position together with their political superiors and are appointed on political rather than meritocratic grounds is another key topic in contemporary research on politico-administrative relations (Shaw and Eichbaum 2015; Hustedt et al. 2017; see also Chapter 25 in this volume). This body of scholarship focuses on the expansion, roles, and effects of ministerial advisers (Eichbaum and Shaw 2008; Yong and Hazell 2014; Christiansen et al. 2016; Askim et al. 2017; Hustedt and Salomonsen 2017). The main reasons for the growth of ministerial advisers (who are also known as 'special advisers' or 'political advisers') include a need to increase the political leadership's capacity to control the policy bureaucracy, the emergence of more complex policy problems (see also the final section on 'stress factors'), and permanent attention by the news media on political executives. All these developments create the need for political executives to surround themselves with 'personal loyalists' (Hood and Lodge 2006), who help politicians to navigate through rougher political waters.

The literature suggests that the numbers of special advisers have in particular grown in systems with a politically neutral, meritocratic civil service (Dahlström et al. 2011). The potential threat these special advisers pose to civil service neutrality and impartiality are a cross-cutting theme in this body of scholarship (Shaw and Eichbaum 2015). Many studies on special advisers aim at gaining a better understanding of 'the nature of the beast', including growth patterns (Dahlström 2009), career backgrounds (Yong and Hazell 2014), and the functions and role understandings of special advisers (Askim et al. 2017). The latter body of research has produced several typologies of ministerial advisers, functional roles (see Hustedt et al. 2017 for an overview). For instance, Askim et al.

(2017) find that ministerial advisers in Norway encompass 'stand ins' for their minister, 'media advisers' (also known as 'spin doctors'), and political coordinators. In other contexts, ministerial advisers also perform genuine policy advisory functions or oversee policy implementation.

Moving from the description of backgrounds and roles, this body of research has increasingly focused on investigating special advisers in the broader context of executive politics and their impacts on intra-executive relationships between career bureaucrats, political executives, and special advisers. A key question in this regard is whether special advisers insulate policy bureaucrats from political executives or otherwise control the flow of information from policy bureaucrats to political executives. However, empirical evidence about these implications is mixed. To illustrate, whereas Eichbaum and Shaw (2008) suggest that this kind of 'administrative politicization', is not practiced on a routine basis in New Zealand, comparative research on Denmark and Sweden by Öhberg et al. (2017) shows that a higher number of special advisers decreases policy bureaucrats' access to political executives. There is evidence that special advisers have an impact on career bureaucrats, in the sense that the latter are less functionally politicized (and hence coming closer to the Weberian ideal type) in systems with special advisers compared to their peers in systems without any substantial numbers of special advisers (Christiansen et al. 2016). In contexts with few special advisers and a highly meritocratic career civil service, such as Denmark, the latter effectively perform genuinely political functions which otherwise would be performed by ministerial advisers. However, this functional politicization seems to come at the price of a lower proportion of genuine policy-making functions performed by policy bureaucrats. In that sense, ministerial advisers may contribute to a more clear-cut separation of political and administrative functions, rather than politicizing policy bureaucracies.

Another theme related to ministerial advisers relates to their role in executive coordination, which effectively means whether special advisers effectively are 'delivering' increased levels of political control of permanent bureaucrats. Here, research indicates that special advisers may indeed increase political control over policy coordination, although their authority is shaped by the institutional context, such as systems with high degrees of prime ministerial authority (and hence powerful special advisers) as opposed to systems with strong line ministers (Hustedt and Salomonsen 2017). Taken together, recent scholarship on interactions and functions of special advisers and policy bureaucrats not only highlights implications of political leadership capacity on political control over the bureaucracy, but also sheds new light on the roles and functions of career officials and their responsiveness to political preferences.

26.3.3 Governing Executive and Regulatory Agencies

Although this chapter primarily focuses on political executives and policy bureaucracies, any contemporary analysis of the relation between politicians and bureaucrats in executive government would remain incomplete without considering executive and regulatory agencies which have become an integral component of governments around the world (Levi-Faur and Jordana 2004; Verhoest et al. 2012). The delivery of public services and the exercise of regulatory functions by agencies with an appointed leadership have become a cornerstone of public sector organizations in the wake of managerial reforms and liberalization and privatization policies throughout the world. Having said that, the provision of public services by organizations operating at arm's length from executive politicians is far from new and has a long tradition, for example in Scandinavia. From the perspective of political executives, agencies pose a potential problem of political control over policy implementation, but they may also provide advantages to politicians by serving as 'lightning rods' for problems of policy implementation (Hood 2011). There is a growing body of literature addressing different aspects of political control, party patronage, and bureaucratic autonomy in relation to arm's length government.

First, executive politicians may consider agencies and other arm's length bodies as job machines providing employment opportunities for loyal supporters. Likewise, boards of public corporations can fulfil a similar function of generating 'jobs for the boys'. The key rationale for politicians motivated by rewarding supporters is that senior appointments in organizations outside the policy bureaucracy will provoke less public attention and are attractive due to the large number of positions available. Moreover, senior positions in agencies may not be subject to the same civil service regulations regarding selection and tenure. Alternatively, political executives may seek to exercise control over arm's length agencies by appointing political allies in order to compensate for limited means of direct control over those bodies (Ennser-Jedenastik 2016b; Bach et al. 2020).

The empirical literature indicates generally lower levels of politicization for appointments in agencies (and other arm's length bodies) compared to ministerial departments (Kopecký et al. 2016; Bach et al. 2020). At the same time, in particular in developing contexts, the creation of agencies has been linked to the idea of 'islands of excellence' in otherwise highly politicized and unprofessional bureaucracies. Hence, the idea would be to deliberately create organizations protected from politicians' (ab)use of appointment powers (Roberts 2010). This notion of credible commitment is also at the core of the discussion about regulatory agencies. Assuming time-inconsistent preferences among politicians, regulators are created as formally independent, protected from political interference by various tools of institutional design (Roberts 2010). Again, the idea is one of de-politicization, creating effective government by delegating discretion to professional civil servants. However, this type of delegation does not mean that politicians completely abstain from exercising political control, but compensate their lack of influence over substantial agency decisions (i.e. formal agency independence) by appointing partisan loyalists to leadership positions (Ennser-Jedenastik 2016b). This research shows that higher levels of formal agency independence are positively associated with the level of party politicization.

Finally, whereas scholars of politicization in Europe have shown that patterns of (de) selection of top officials are not the same for all ministries or agencies (Kopecký et al. 2016), they are only gradually beginning to understand the reasons for the differential politicization of the government apparatus (Ennser-Jedenastik 2016b; Bach et al. 2020). The public sector has witnessed increasing levels of delegation to executive and regulatory agencies operating at a distance from ministerial departments. Agencies perform important societal functions, which may prompt ministers to politicize agency heads. To date, only a handful of studies have examined the politicization of agency heads, providing mixed results (Dahlström and Niklasson 2013; Ennser-Jedenastik 2016b; Petrovsky et al. 2017; Dahlström and Holmgren 2019). This is different in the US, where scholars have extensively studied political appointments across the entire government apparatus. Importantly, this literature shows how differences between organizations' political relevance and complexity affect patterns of top official (de)selection (Lewis 2008; Lewis and Waterman 2013; Hollibaugh et al. 2014). As of now, the European literature has largely ignored within-country variation of politicized appointments (with few exceptions, see Kopecký et al. 2016).

26.4 A RESEARCH AGENDA FOR THE STUDY OF POLITICAL EXECUTIVES AND POLICY BUREAUCRACIES

The three fundamental topics discussed in the second section of this chapter will still feature prominently in future research on the relation between executive politicians and policy bureaucrats. What has changed since the first wave of research on these topics is, however, the social, political, technological, and economic context in which the 'natural' tensions between politicians and bureaucrats play out. These changes call for a development, if not reconsideration (or overhaul) not only of the empirical focus of research and the respective theoretical lenses, but also of the normative orientation marks to make sense of shifting patterns and responses to new challenges.

26.4.1 The New 'Stress Factors' in Executive Politics

How the politics-bureaucracy nexus responds to new 'stress factors' that are putting pressure on both parties, has been a key research topic, as we discussed above. The rise of 'bureaucracy bashing' and belief in the superiority of private sector management techniques and market incentives have challenged the classic PSB (although in more diverse ways than the NPM folk story has it). But while these developments are very much on the radar of public administration research, new 'stress factors' and pressure points call for a further development of this line of research. The rise of wicked and unruly problems—such as climate change, migration, terrorism, and digitization—is combined with the changing media landscape, and in particular the rise of social media that not only puts politicians and also increasingly public agencies under constant scrutiny, but also fuels political polarization and 'truth decay' (Kavanagh and Rich 2018).

These trends translate into the politics-administration relation by further distancing the two parties: under tighter media scrutiny and more rapid communication cycles, and the increasing risk of malicious critique, the significance of purely political thinking and strategic communication increases—something that the traditional policy bureaucrat might not be able or dispositioned to deliver. One the one hand, this development calls for a further exploration of the dynamics of politicization. In addition to studying personnel decisions and their effects (see below), such a research agenda should focus on (changes in) role understandings and interaction patterns between political executives, special advisers, and policy bureaucrats.

One the other hand, a key question is how this development sits together with the increasing technical and analytical demands placed on policy bureaucrats. The rise of complex policy challenges calls for a major update of the competency profile and the attraction of 'nerd type of competencies' (Lodge and Wegrich 2012). Ironically political polarization and 'truth decay' come together—with stronger calls for more technocracy and analytical skills—be that in the form of 'experimental policy-making' or impact assessment procedures. One can both argue for these to be counter-trends to politicization and that there is an overlap between technocracy and anti-politics pursued by populist parties and public moods. In other words, the policy bureaucracy is pushed to fulfil contradictory demands: being more political responsive and savvy in supporting tactical communication but also to keep up with the increasing demands for state of the art analytical policy work (Veit et al. 2017). While the PSB perspective is well placed to capture the changing patterns in terms of mutual expectations for competency, reward and loyalty, future studies should re-orient towards one of the field's core topics by investigating what is happening inside the 'machine room' of government. Such studies could investigate politico-administrative interactions in policy-making processes with different degrees of political contestation or degrees of analytical requirements.

26.4.2 Politicization: Appointments, Replacements, Effects

Although being an established field of research, many puzzles in the study of politicization of senior level appointments remain unsolved. A key argument in the contemporary literature is that the delicate balance between safeguarding the bureaucracy's professional autonomy and ensuring its responsiveness to elected politicians preferences has tipped towards the latter as a result of increasing levels of political influence on the (de)selection of top officials (Suleiman 2003; Peters and Pierre 2004; Dahlström et al. 2011; Aucoin 2012). Yet this claim of an increase in civil service politicization stands on shaky empirical ground. Most politicization research is primarily cross-sectional or retrospective in nature, rather than truly longitudinal. For instance, Dahlström (2009) uses country experts' estimates of the numbers of political appointees over time, whereas others rely on survey data, expert interviews, or mixed methods to track politicization dynamics (Hustedt and Salomonsen 2014; Kopecký et al. 2016; Bach et al. 2020). Those studies face obvious methodological limitations in grasping long-term trends, and we clearly need better data, for instance based on document or biographical analysis to track changes over time and to compare developments over time.

More substantially, we know little about the actual motivations and criteria for (de) selecting top officials used by political executives. There is some evidence about control versus reward as motivations (Kopecký et al. 2016), but analyses of top officials' partisan loyalty or of political change as driver of bureaucratic turnover represent cases of observational equivalence—they are compatible with both reward and control types of motivations (Dahlström and Holmgren 2019). Moreover, we know little about substantial criteria for appointing and replacing top officials beyond measures of partisan loyalty, including politicized contexts but also countries with meritocratic personnel systems where politicians have more limited influence on personnel decisions regarding top officials. The literature on the loyalty-competence nexus in political appointments in the US could potentially serve as a way forward for research outside the US context (Lewis and Waterman 2013; Hollibaugh et al. 2014; Ouyang et al. 2017).

Another important future challenge is that almost all studies of politicization concentrate on incumbent office holders, which substantially limits the possibility for drawing inferences on politicians' reasons for selecting top officials in the first place. For instance, partisan loyalty might be widespread among senior officials below the level of top officials as well; yet we simply do not know whether this characteristic makes a difference for individual career success. Bach and Veit (2018) address those problems and demonstrate the analytical purchase of studying the promotion of top officials in Germany among a pool of candidates based on multiple selection criteria. A comparison of potential and actual office holders is considered the ideal research design for studying politicians' selection criteria (Ouyang et al. 2017). However, in contrast to research on the selection of ministers among members of parliament (Bäck et al. 2016), this approach has until recently not been used in politicization research.

Finally, the politicization of civil service appointments raises important questions about the desirability and effects of politicization. There is a growing body evidence that politicization has detrimental effects on government performance and increases risks of corruption (Lewis 2007; Moynihan and Roberts 2010; Dahlström and Lapuente 2017). Again, the US-literature offers the most comprehensive analyses, indicating lower levels of administrative performance for public agencies managed by political appointees as opposed to career officials (Lewis 2007; Moynihan and Roberts 2010). Moreover, there is empirical evidence about the negative effects of politicization of the public sector on various aspects of good government (Dahlström and Lapuente 2017). However, we know little about the effects of politicization of policy bureaucracies (which may not necessarily coincide with the politicization of the public sector in general) on some measure of 'government performance'.

26.5 CONCLUSION

The starting point of this chapter was the observation that political executives inevitably face problems of delegation vis-à-vis policy bureaucracies. In consequence, the study of the relationship between political executives and policy bureaucrats is concerned with the problem of ensuring political control over the bureaucracy, and the assessment of bureaucrats' influence on policy-making. Whereas the principal-agent framework and other political economy approaches have generated important insights into politico-administrative relations, there is growing evidence that several of these theories' core assumptions are empirically standing on shaky grounds (Pierre and Peters 2017), and that one of the big theoretical challenges is to understand the conditions under which bureaucratic autonomy, rather than political control, should be a guiding principle for organizational design (Miller and Whitford 2016; Dahlström and Lapuente 2017).

In order to answer questions such as how much bureaucratic autonomy is required for good governance, we need a sound knowledge base about the antecedents and effects of politico-administrative relations in executive politics. Future research on the relation between political executives and policy bureaucrats should not only develop causal models explaining the dynamics of this relation in increasingly turbulent times; it should also contribute with normative theories about appropriate degrees of bureaucratic autonomy on the one hand and (the boundaries of) legitimate political control on the other hand. The implicit normative underpinnings of principal-agent approaches has too long shaped our debates about what happens and what should happen in the relationship between politicians and bureaucrats.

REFERENCES

Aberbach, J. D., Putnam, R. D., and Rockman, B. A. (1981). *Bureaucrats and Politicians in Western Democracies*. Cambridge, MA: Harvard University Press.
Askim, J., Karlsen, R., and Kolltveit, K. (2017). 'Political Appointees in Executive Government: Exploring and Explaining Roles Using a Large-N Survey in Norway,' *Public Administration* 95(2): 342–58.
Aucoin, P. (2012). 'New Political Governance in Westminster Systems: Impartial Public Administration and Management Performance at Risk,' *Governance* 25(2): 177–99.
Bäck, H., Debus, M., and Müller, W. C. (2016). Intra-Party Diversity and Ministerial Selection in Coalition Governments,' *Public Choice* 166(3): 355–78.
Bach, T. and Veit, S. (2018). 'The Determinants of Promotion to High Public Office in Germany: Partisan Loyalty, Political Craft, or Managerial Competencies?,' *Journal of Public Administration Research and Theory* 28(2): 254–69.
Bach, T., Hammerschmid, G., and Löffler, L. (2020). 'More Delegation, More Political Control? Politicization of Senior Level Appointments in 18 European Countries,' *Public Policy and Administration* 35(1): 3–23.

Baekgaard, M., Christensen, J., Dahlmann, C. M., Mathiasen, A., and Petersen, N. B. G. (2019). 'The Role of Evidence in Politics: Motivated Reasoning and Persuasion among Politicians,' *British Journal of Political Science* 49(3): 1117–40.

Bendor, J., Glazer, A., and Hammond, T. (2001). 'Theories of Delegation,' *Annual Review of Political Science* 4(1), 235–69.

Boston, J., Martin, J., Pallot, J., and Walsh, P. (1996). *Public Management: The New Zealand Model*. Auckland: Oxford University Press.

Bouckaert, G., Peters, B. G., and Verhoest, K. (2010). *The Coordination of Public Sector Organizations: Shifting Patterns of Public Management*. Basingstoke, NY: Palgrave Macmillan.

Boyne, G. A., James, O., John, P., and Petrovsky, N. (2010). 'Does Political Change Affect Senior Management Turnover? An Empirical Analysis of Top-Tier Local Authorities in England,' *Public Administration* 88(1): 136–53.

Christensen, J. G. (2006). 'Ministers and Mandarins under Danish Parliamentarism,' International Journal of Public Administration 29(12): 997–1019.

Christensen, J. G. and Opstrup, N. (2018). 'Bureaucratic Dilemmas: Civil Servants Between Political Responsiveness and Normative Constraints,' *Governance* 31(3): 481–98.

Christensen, J. G., Klemmensen, R., and Opstrup, N. (2014). 'Politicization and the Replacement of Top Civil Servants in Denmark,' *Governance* 27(2), 215–41.

Christiansen, P. M., Niklasson, B., and Öhberg, P. (2016). 'Does Politics Crowd Out Professional Competence? The Organisation of Ministerial Advice in Denmark and Sweden,' *West European Politics* 39(6), 1230–50.

Dahlström, C. (2009). 'Political Appointments in 18 Democracies, 1975–2007.' QoG Working Paper 18, Gothenburg.

Dahlström, C. and Holmgren, M. (2019). 'The Political Dynamics of Bureaucratic Turnover,' *British Journal of Political Science* 49(3): 823–36.

Dahlström, C. and Lapuente, V. (2017). *Organizing Leviathan: Politicians, Bureaucrats and the Making of Good Government*. Cambridge: Cambridge University Press.

Dahlström, C. and Niklasson, B. (2013). 'The Politics of Politicization in Sweden,' *Public Administration* 91(4): 891–907.

Dahlström, C., Peters, B. G., and Pierre, J. (2011) (eds). *Steering from the Center: Strengthening Political Control in Western Democracies*. Toronto: Toronto University Press.

Derlien, H.-U. (1996). 'The Politicization of Bureaucracies in Historical and Comparative Perspective,' in B. G. Peters and B. A. Rockman (eds) *Agenda for Excellence 2. Administering the State*. Chatham: Chatham House Publishers, 149–62.

Derlien, H.-U. (2003). 'Mandarins or Managers? The Bureaucratic Elite in Bonn, 1970 to 1987 and Beyond,' *Governance* 16: 401–28.

de Visscher, C. and Salomonsen, H. H. (2013). 'Explaining Differences in Ministerial "Ménage à Trois": Multiple Bargains in Belgium and Denmark,' *International Review of Administrative Sciences* 79(1): 71–90.

Dunleavy, P. (1991). *Democracy, Bureaucracy and Public Choice: Economic Explanations in Political Science*. New York: Harvester Wheatsheaf.

Eichbaum, C. and Shaw, R. (2008). 'Revisiting Politicization: Political Advisers and Public Servants in Westminster Systems,' *Governance* 21(3): 337–63.

Ennser-Jedenastik, L. (2016a). 'The Party Politicization of Administrative Elites in the Netherlands,' *Acta Politica* 51(4): 451–71.

Ennser-Jedenastik, L. (2016b). 'The Politicization of Regulatory Agencies: Between Partisan Influence and Formal Independence', *Journal of Public Administration Research and Theory* 26(3), 507–18.

Fleischer, J. (2009). 'Power Resources of Parliamentary Executives: Policy Advice in the UK and Germany', *West European Politics* 32(1), 196–214.

Fleischer, J. (2016). 'Partisan and Professional Control: Predictors of Bureaucratic Tenure in Germany', *Acta Politica* 51(4), 433–50.

Goetz, K. H. (2007). 'German Officials and the Federal Policy Process: The Decline of Sectional Leadership', in E. C. Page and V. Wright (eds) *From the Active to the Enabling State: The Changing Role of Top Officials in European Nations*. Basingstoke: Palgrave Macmillan, 164–88.

Grindle, M. S. (2012). *Jobs for the Boys: Patronage and the State in Comparative Perspective*. Cambridge, MA: Harvard University Press.

Heclo, H. (1977). *A Government of Strangers: Executive Politics in Washington*. Washington, DC: Brookings Institution.

Heclo, H. and Wildavsky, A. B. (1974). *The Private Government of Public Money: Community and Policy Inside British Politics*. Berkeley, CA: University of California Press.

Helms, L. (2017). 'Leadership and Public Administration', in W. R. Thompson (ed.) *Oxford Research Encyclopedia of Politics*. Oxford: Oxford University Press.

Hollibaugh, G. E., Horton, G., and Lewis, D. E. (2014). 'Presidents and Patronage', *American Journal of Political Science* 58(4): 1024–42.

Hood, C. (2011). *The Blame Game: Spin, Bureaucracy, and Self-Preservation in Government*. Princeton: Princeton University Press.

Hood, C. and Lodge, M. (2006). *The Politics of Public Service Bargains: Reward, Competency, Loyality and Blame*. Oxford: Oxford University Press.

Huber, J. D. and Shipan, C. R. (2006). 'Politics, Delegation, and Bureaucracy', in B. R. Weingast and D. A. Wittman (eds) *The Oxford Handbook of Political Economy*. Oxford: Oxford University Press, 256–72.

Hustedt, T. and Salomonsen, H. H. (2014). 'Ensuring Political Responsiveness: Politicization Mechanisms in Ministerial Bureaucracies', *International Review of Administrative Sciences* 80(4): 746–65.

Hustedt, T. and Salomonsen, H. H. (2017). 'Political Control of Coordination? The Roles of Ministerial Advisers in Government Coordination in Denmark and Sweden', *Public Administration* 95(2): 393–406.

Hustedt, T., Kolltveit, K., and Salomonsen, H. H. (2017). 'Ministerial Advisers in Executive Government: Out from the Dark and into the Limelight', *Public Administration* 95(2): 299–311.

James, O. (2003). *The Executive Agency Revolution in Whitehall: Public Interest versus Bureau-Shaping Perspectives*. Basingstoke: Palgrave Macmillan.

Kavanagh, J. and Rich, M. D. (2018). *Truth Decay: An Initial Exploration of the Diminishing Role of Facts and Analysis in American Public Life*. Santa Monica: RAND Corporation.

Kopecký, P., Mair, P., and Spirova, M. (2012) (eds). *Party Patronage and Party Government in European Democracies*. Oxford: Oxford University Press.

Kopecký, P., Meyer Sahling, J.-H., Panizza, F., Scherlis, G., Schuster, C., and Spirova, M. (2016). 'Party Patronage in Contemporary Democracies: Results from an Expert Survey in 22 Countries from Five Regions', *European Journal of Political Research* 55(2), 416–31.

Levi-Faur, D. and Jordana, J. (2004). *The Politics of Regulation: Institutions and Regulatory Reforms for the Age of Governance*. Cheltenham: Edward Elgar.

Lewis, D. E. (2007). Testing Pendleton's Premise: Do Political Appointees Make Worse Bureaucrats?, *Journal of Politics* 69(4): 1073–88.

Lewis, D. E. (2008). *The Politics of Presidential Appointments: Political Control and Bureaucratic Performance*. Princeton, NJ: Princeton University Press.

Lewis, D. E. and Waterman, R. W. (2013). 'The Invisible Presidential Appointments: An Examination of Appointments to the Department of Labor, 2001–11', *Presidential Studies Quarterly* 43(1): 35–57.

Lodge, M. and Wegrich, K. (2012). 'Executive Politics and Policy Instruments', in M. Lodge and K. Wegrich (eds) *Executive Politics in Times of Crisis*. Basingstoke: Palgrave Macmillan, 118–35.

Lodge, M. and Wegrich, K. (2014) (eds). *The Problem-Solving Capacity of the Modern State*. Oxford: Oxford University Press.

Mayntz, R. and Scharpf, F. W. (1975). *Policy-Making in the German Federal Bureaucracy*. Amsterdam; New York: Elsevier.

McCubbins, M. D., Noll, R. G., and Weingast, B. R. (1987). 'Administrative Procedures as Instruments of Political Control', *Journal of Law, Economics, & Organization* 3(2): 243–77.

Meyer-Sahling, J.-H. (2008). 'The Changing Colours of the Post-Communist State: The Politicisation of the Senior Civil Service in Hungary', *European Journal of Political Research* 47(1): 1–33.

Meyer-Sahling, J.-H. and Veen, T. (2012). 'Governing the Post-Communist State: Government Alternation and Senior Civil Service Politicisation in Central and Eastern Europe', *East European Politics* 28: 4–22.

Miller, G. J. and Whitford, A. B. (2016). *Above Politics: Bureaucratic Discretion and Credible Commitment*. New York: Cambridge University Press.

Moe, T. M. (2012). 'Delegation, Control, and the Study of Public Bureaucracy', *The Forum* 10(2).

Moynihan, D. P. and Roberts, A. S. (2010). 'The Triumph of Loyalty Over Competence: The Bush Administration and the Exhaustion of the Politicized Presidency', *Public Administration Review* 70: 572–81.

Niskanen, W. A. (1971). *Bureaucracy and Representative Government*. Chicago: Aldine, Atherton.

Öhberg, P., Munk Christiansen, P., and Niklasson, B. (2017). 'Administrative Politicization or Contestability? How Political Advisers Affect Neutral Competence in Policy Processes', *Public Administration* 95(1): 269–85.

Ouyang, Y., Haglund, E. T., and Waterman, R. W. (2017). 'The Missing Element: Examining the Loyalty-Competence Nexus in Presidential Appointments', *Presidential Studies Quarterly* 47(1): 62–91.

Page, E. C. (1992). *Political Authority and Bureaucratic Power: A Comparative Analysis*. 2 ed. New York: Harvester Wheatsheaf.

Page, E. C. (2012). *Policy Without Politicians*. Oxford: Oxford University Press.

Page, E. C. and Jenkins, B. (2005). *Policy Bureaucracy: Government with a Cast of Thousands*. Oxford: Oxford University Press.

Page, E. C. and Wright, V. (1999). 'Conclusion: Senior Officials in Western Europe', in E. C. Page and V. Wright (eds) *Bureaucratic Elites in Western European States*. Oxford: Oxford University Press, 266–79.

Peters, B. G. (1988). *Comparing Public Bureaucracies: Problems of Theory and Method*. Tuscaloosa: University of Alabama Press.

Peters, B. G. and Pierre, J. (2004). 'Politicization of the Civil Service. Concepts, Causes, Consequences', in B. G. Peters and J. Pierre (eds) *Politicization of the Civil Service in Comparative Perspective*. London: Routledge, 1–13.

Petrovsky, N., James, O., Moseley, A., and Boyne, G. A. (2017). 'What Explains Agency Heads' Length of Tenure? Testing Managerial Background, Performance, and Political Environment Effects,' *Public Administration Review* 77(4), 591–602.

Pierre, J. and Peters, B. G. (2017). 'The Shirking Bureaucrat: A Theory in Search of Evidence?,' *Policy & Politics* 45(2), 157–72.

Roberts, A. (2010). *The Logic of Discipline: Global Capitalism and the Architecture of Government*. New York: Oxford University Press.

Rudalevige, A. (2009). 'The Administrative Presidency and Bureaucratic Control: Implementing a Research Agenda,' *Presidential Studies Quarterly* 39(1): 10–24.

Sager, F. and Rosser, C. (2009). 'Weber, Wilson, and Hegel: Theories of Modern Bureaucracy,' *Public Administration Review* 69(6): 1136–47.

Savoie, D. J. (2003). *Breaking the Bargain: Public Servants, Ministers, and Parliament*. Toronto: Toronto University Press.

Scharpf, F. W. (1994). 'Games Real Actors Could Play: Positive and Negative Coordination in Embedded Negotiations,' *Journal of Theoretical Politics* 6(1): 27–53.

Schillemans, T. and Busuioc, M. (2015). 'Predicting Public Sector Accountability: From Agency Drift to Forum Drift,' *Journal of Public Administration Research and Theory* 25(1): 191–215.

Schnapp, K.-U. (2004). *Ministerialbürokratien in westlichen Demokratien. Eine vergleichende Analyse*. Opladen: Leske+Budrich.

Shaw, R. and Eichbaum, C. (2015). 'Following the Yellow Brick Road: Theorizing the Third Element in Executive Government,' *International Journal of Public Administration* 38(1): 66–74.

Simon, H. A. (1947). *Administrative Behavior: A Study of Decision-Making Processes in Administrative Organizations*. New York: Macmillan.

Suleiman, E. N. (2003). *Dismantling Democratic States*. Princeton, NJ: Princeton University Press.

't Hart, P. and Wille, A. (2006). 'Ministers and Top Officials in the Dutch Core Executive: Living Together, Growing Apart?,' *Public Administration* 84(1): 121–46.

Veit, S. and Scholz, S. (2016). 'Linking Administrative Career Patterns and Politicization: Signalling Effects in the Careers of Top Civil Servants in Germany,' *International Review of Administrative Sciences* 82(3): 516–35.

Veit, S., Hustedt, T., and Bach, T. (2017). 'Dynamics of Change in Internal Policy Advisory Systems: The Hybridization of Advisory Capacities in Germany,' *Policy Sciences* 50(1): 85–103.

Verhoest, K., van Thiel, S., Bouckaert, G., and Lægreid, P. (2012) (eds). *Government Agencies: Practices and Lessons from 30 Countries*. Basingstoke: Palgrave Macmillan.

Wegrich, K. and Štimac, V. (2014). 'Coordination Capacity,' in M. Lodge and K. Wegrich (eds) *The Problem-Solving Capacity of the Modern State*. Oxford: Oxford University Press, 41–62.

Weingast, B. R. (2005). 'Caught in the Middle: The President, Congress, and the Political-Bureaucratic System,' in J. D. Aberbach and M. A. Peterson (eds) *The Executive Branch*. New York: Oxford University Press, 312–43.

Wilson, J. Q. (1989). *Bureaucracy: What Government Agencies Do and Why They Do It*. New York: Basic Books.

Yong, B. and Hazell, R. (2014). *Special Advisers: Who They Are, What They Do and Why They Matter*. London: Bloomsbury Publishing.

CHAPTER 27

EXECUTIVE-LEGISLATIVE RELATIONS IN DEMOCRATIC REGIMES

managing the legislative process

MARIA C. ESCOBAR-LEMMON AND
MICHELLE M. TAYLOR-ROBINSON

27.1 INTRODUCTION

CAN we compare how executives negotiate with or try to manage the legislative process in parliamentary, presidential, and semi-presidential systems? Mechanisms of accountability differ across the regimes, yet executives want to manage the legislative process to ensure success of their policy agenda, and how they attempt to do so can be compared across the three.

In the past the answer might have been that a comparison was ill advised. Scholars often argued that presidential and parliamentary systems were too different due to the mode of selection of the executive, and the rules that determined the executive's survival. In addition, the perceived instability of presidential systems, which were prone to gridlock and over-reach by presidents often prompting the military to intervene in politics (see Linz 1993; Mainwaring 1993), made presidential systems appear quite distinct from parliamentary systems, while semi-presidential systems remained an uncertain hybrid.

However, scholars have come to see more similarities across democratic regimes, and many of those similarities result from the need of both presidents and prime ministers to work with, or attempt to manage, the legislative branch to achieve their policy goals (see Cox and Morgenstern 2002; Cheibub and Limongi 2011). Older work often viewed the parliament as an unimportant actor after it voted confidence in the government, unless it brought down the government with a vote of no confidence. The real action in policy-making was viewed as taking place within the cabinet. But, more recent research argues that the parliament often plays a more important role in policy as evidence shows that 'government bills typically undergo a substantial amount of change in the course of legislative review' (Martin and Vanberg 2005: 97). In presidential systems, the relationship between the president and congress was often viewed as antagonistic, with the president frequently imposing policy through decrees circumventing the legislature. But again, more recent research argues that presidents often work with the congress to make policy (see Siavelis 2002; Cheibub and Limongi 2011). Consequently, the questions of what tools executives use to work with legislatures, and when the executive obtains policy that it desires have become vibrant research topics. While formation and dissolution mechanisms for presidential and parliamentary systems remain distinct, there is now much fruitful work being done in the area of executive-legislative relations where scholars can speak to one another 'across the institutional ocean' and we see even more areas where overlap will be beneficial for theory development and empirical testing. Tsebelis (1995: 292) argues, 'the logic of decision making in presidential systems is quite similar to the logic of decision making in multi-party parliamentary systems.' He shows how the number of veto-players, their congruence, and internal cohesion matter for policy stability. Shugart (2006: 359–60) also emphasizes comparability by focusing on whether executive-legislative relations encourage bargaining. He argues that,

> policy-output variables are related to interactions between the executive-legislative structure and the party system [...] patterns of party competition are crucial to the extent to which the formal hierarchy of parliamentary inter-branch relations is tempered with interparty transactions. Similarly, the formal inter-branch transactions of presidentialism may give way to elements of informal hierarchy if the president is the head of a majority party or a coalition that controls the congressional agenda.

Thus, the mix of institutions chosen might produce more similar outcomes in terms of relations between the branches than would be expected simply based on system type.

In this chapter we review ways executives interact with legislatures in presidential, parliamentary, and semi-presidential systems that could loosely be described as fitting under headings of trying to control the legislature (from bargaining through cabinet coalitions to threatening an end-run around the legislature via decree) versus negotiating deals and then trying to make the deal stick. We then offer suggestions for how the study of executive-legislative relations should be expanded, to build broader linkages across institutional designs, and to incorporate some of the ways that democratic regimes are changing—and in particular becoming more broadly representative—in the twenty-first century, and how those changes may impact executive-legislative relations.

27.2 Controlling the Legislature or Trying to Negotiate Policy?

How do executives try to form working relationships with the legislative branch, or how can executives try to achieve control so that they obtain their preferred policy outcomes? Scholars have pursued these questions from several angles such as coalitions and how to police behaviour by partners, use of constitutional or chamber rules to control debate and bill amendment, and use of committees in the legislature to negotiate policy deals.

27.2.1 Managing Coalitions during the Legislative Process

Formation of a coalition cabinet to obtain a vote of confidence in parliament is the subject of a large literature that is important in its own right beyond just how it affects executive-legislative relations.[1] However, once installed a coalition continues to influence policy-making in ways that can play out within the cabinet or legislature. By managing the coalition and utilizing institutional structures it is possible for the government to take the risk of submitting bills that are contentious, which is essential if the government wants to make new policy and not just defend the status quo (Huber 1996; Döring 2003; Hindmoor et al. 2009).

In presidential systems, the president is not compelled to form a coalition cabinet if his or her party lacks majority support in congress (see Chapter 21 in this volume). Nonetheless, coalitions are common, and are an important tool presidents use to enhance their working relationship with the congress (Amorim Neto 2002; Cheibub et al. 2004; Camerlo and Martínez-Gallardo 2018). Amorim Neto (2002: 60) argues that presidents 'with strong party support tend to make policy mostly through statute. Thus, they build more coalitional cabinets to solidify support in the legislature.' Alemán and Tsebelis (2011: 25) show that presidents are more likely to form a coalition when the congress is strong, that is, 'composed of professional legislators capable of meaningful oversight' to help them to work with the legislature because the president has 'greater concerns about how their proposals will fare in congress'. A strong congress, not just an institutionally weak executive, prompt the president and congress to work together (Alemán and Tsebelis 2011). Cheibub et al. (2004) argue that presidents often form

---

[1] Tools governments use to police coalition partners, such as assigning a junior minister from another coalition party are important, but are beyond the scope of this chapter. We do note, however, that use of junior ministers as a monitoring device is more common in parliaments that lack a strong committee system (Lipsmeyer and Pierce 2011). Evidence from thirty-one advanced industrial democracies also indicates that 'where multiparty government is the norm, governing parties [...] tend to develop strong committee structures allowing parties to effectively curtail ministerial drift' (André et al. 2016: 109).

coalitions via their cabinet, but many presidents have minority cabinets, yet successfully form legislative coalitions to pass bills. When there are other parties in the legislature whose policy preferences are close to the president, they find a president will often forgo the cost of 'buying' support with cabinet portfolios and instead negotiate a legislative coalition. As Cox and Morgenstern (2002: 446) explain, 'The optimal strategy for even the most autocratically minded president is not to pretend that the legislature does not exist and propose whatever policies he likes, then react spasmodically when the legislature refuses to assent.' However, coalitions can be difficult to manage, as demonstrated by lack of backbench support in the congress, if cabinet posts are not allocated proportionally to parties (see Amorim Neto 2002; Hiroi and Rennó 2017 for evidence from Brazil).

By design, semi-presidential systems have a deliberate coalition building element which some argue helps to secure democratic stability (Moestrup 2007; see also Chapter 20 in this volume). This system can be adopted to force coalition building among dissenting players while deliberately weakening the power of the president. Moestrup (2007: 108) argues that the adoption of semi-presidentialist regimes in Francophone Africa occurred, in part, because of 'a desire to avoid the autocratic excesses of variously "reinforced" presidential regimes'. If one defines executives along constitutional lines a semi-presidential regime is one in which 'there is a directly elected, or popularly elected, president who serves for a fixed term; there is a separate position of prime minister; and the prime minister and cabinet are collectively responsible to the legislature' (Elgie 2011: 2). Because the prime minister is responsible to the legislature, it is the ability, or inability, of the prime minister and the president to work together that characterizes executive-legislative relations in these systems. On the one hand, coalitions should be encouraged in semi-presidential systems because of the dual executive. On the other hand, not all semi-presidential systems distribute power the same way between presidents and prime ministers. This division matters because, 'highly presidentialized semi-presidentialism appears to be more vulnerable to democratic breakdown than semi-presidentialism of the premier-presidential kind, in the event of divided government' (Elgie and Moestrup 2007: 246; also Elgie and Moestrup 2008). Highly personalized semi-presidential systems, which tip the balance of power toward the president, can also produce intra-executive conflict if presidents and prime ministers, even from the same party, have different goals and ambitions. Roper (2002: 265) notes that there is great cabinet instability in semi-presidential regimes which lean toward presidentialism compared to those that lean toward parliamentarism. The failure of the executive and legislative branches in semi-presidential systems to work together can, in extreme cases, result in serious crisis and ultimately the collapse of democracy.

> Niger exemplifies the classical case of gridlock within the dual executive resulting in the breakdown of democracy, on which critics of semi-presidentialism base their worries with regards to the impact of this regime type on the survival of young democracies.   (Moestrup 2007: 105)

Yet coalition partners, and opposition parties, have policy and electoral incentives to draw policy away from the coalition agreement (Huber 1996; Döring 2003). Martin and Vanberg (2005: 102) find that parties that are part of the governing coalition will be more likely to amend government bills when the coalition has bigger differences on policy. Franchino and Høyland (2009), studying implementation of EU directives in fifteen member states find that the parliament is more involved in amending government bills when the responsible minister is more distant from the coalition preference. However, parliament is strategic about the use of its time, as this involvement is conditional on the strength of executive tools to control legislative proceedings. Pedrazzani and Zucchini (2013: 705), in an analysis of government bill amendments in the Italian parliament, conclude that

> the size of the changes that inflate and disfigure the initial [bill's] shape depends, first, directly or indirectly (i.e. through the conflict), on the position-taking utility enjoyed by the government actors [...] Parliament appears to be an arena at the coalition partners' disposal, where a second, decisive round of the cabinet decision-making process is played.

A study of the Scottish Parliament by Shephard and Cairney (2005) found that many successful, substantive amendments to government bills were made by members of the Scottish parliament or were minister responses to backbencher concerns (p. 313 and table 4). Fortunato (n.d.: 20) finds that the more voters see parties in the government coalition as close, the more those parties will amend government bills to try to differentiate their party for voters. He also finds that 'cabinet parties use legislative amendments to police the coalition bargain, rather than to pull the legislative proposals of their partners toward their own ideal point' (p. 21).

Committees in the legislature (discussed further below) are a common venue for shaping legislation in both presidential and parliamentary systems. Recent work has begun to explore whether chairs of strong committees can change the content of government bills. Examining the cases of Denmark, Germany, and the Netherlands, Fortunato et al. (2017: 11) find that 'if opposition parties are able to secure the chairs of relevant committees, they are able to have an impact in the legislative process.' Though interestingly for parties in the government coalition holding the committee chair does not enhance their ability to effectively scrutinize bills. Studying committees in Chile's Congress, Magar et al. (2017) find that committees chaired by a member of the president's party or from the governing coalition negotiate policy deals with the president, and that the president then helps to ensure the deal sticks by declaring the bill 'urgent' which gives it a closed rule for plenary debate. In Colombia, Avellaneda et al. (2012) find executive bills are more likely to become law than legislative bills, but that not all executive bills become law. Pachón and Johnson (2016) confirm this finding in Colombia and offer an explanation for it. In the absence of rules allowing a formal discharge petition, committees have significant control over legislation. Committee chairs use this power by strategically assigning responsibility for writing the committee's report to advantage coalition allies and the executive. Yet not all executive bills are assigned to coalition members and in those cases they find a significant negative effect, signifying chairs were looking for a negative report and thus suggesting some legislative control over the executive.

27.2.2 Legislative Tools that Can Impact the Approval of Executive Bills, and How Much the Executive Likes the Final Product

One advantageous tool for the executive is getting to offer amendments late in the bill debate process. Heller (2001), studying Western European parliaments, explores how the power of last offer amendments enables the government to beat 'the reversion [so a bill will] emerge recognizable from the muck of opposition attacks and amendments on the floor' (p. 782).[2] The ability to make a 'last offer' empowers the government because it is a way to force the parliament to make a choice without having to invoke a vote of confidence. However, further research calls into question whether it is opposition from parties outside of government—the official opposition—that the government needs to guard against, or opposition from within the governing coalition. Martin and Vanberg (2005), examining amendments of government bills in Germany and the Netherlands, find that it is primarily policy distance within the coalition that predicts quantity of changes to government bills, rather than distance between the opposition and the government. Yet the government does not want such proposals to lead to a showdown that could bring down the government. The power to make a 'last offer amendment' is a tool that enables a government to accept policy debate, and even amendments, while still being able to bring the policy back in the direction of the government's policy ideal point (Heller 2001). In some presidential systems the executive can use veto powers in a somewhat analogous fashion. Some presidents have constitutional powers to, in essence, amend bills as part of the veto process. Presidents' veto powers are generally categorized by the size of the vote needed in congress to override (e.g. simple majority, two-thirds vote, two-thirds vote in both chambers). However, when the president can veto certain parts of the bill while enacting the rest of the bill, this creates another stage in the policy negotiating process. As Mustapic (2002: 31–2) explains for the case of Argentina, presidents have used their item veto when they opposed how their own bills were modified in Congress. 'The item veto is a most useful means to further the executive's goals when the president lacks a majority in the legislature and is therefore forced to negotiate with other parties'. Some presidents can even submit new language to congress for the part(s)

---

[2] Alemán and Tsebelis (2016: 18) discuss the power of committee managers to make a last counter-proposal in presidential systems in Latin America.

of the bill they want changed, thus allowing the executive to propose an amendment to the bill after the congress has passed the bill (for examples of this tool being used, see Ponce 2016 for Peru; Chasquetti 2016 for Uruguay). Tsebelis and Alemán (2005: 396–7) argue this is a 'conditional agenda-setting power' that 'enables the president to introduce a last proposal that can mitigate unwanted features of the congressional bill' (see also Alemán and Pachón 2008; Alemán and Tsebelis 2016).

Another tool is the ability to exclude floor amendments. Closed rules are a possibility in some congresses (e.g. the US House of Representatives, Chile's Congress) and parliaments (e.g. the package vote in France; Huber 1996). Where such rules exist the 'government may posit the final up-or-down proposal at the "borderline" of the intersection of MPs' preferences' selecting 'among all the points contained in the "winset" the one that he prefers' (Döring 2003: 150). In Chile this tool is used by the executive, working in concert with allies in the relevant committee, to make a carefully crafted deal on a bill stick, and not allow it to be unravelled via plenary debate (Magar et al. 2017). Because in Chile it is the president, through assignment of an 'act now' or a 'two week' urgency 'who decides whether a bill proceeds to the floor with a close rule [...] committee members negotiate with the president to receive that label' (Magar et al. 2017: 3).

A third tool is restricting the timetable of debate. This power is particularly important if a bill dies if it is not voted on by the end of the legislative period, thus making time a scarce resource for committees and the plenary, as well as for an executive facing upcoming elections. Restricting the timetable for debate is a way for the government to protect their bills against delaying attempts. Döring (2003: 148) gives the example of the 'British guillotine' where the government can compel a vote be taken on a bill on a pre-set date, regardless of how much of the bill has been discussed. Döring (2003: 147) expects that both limits on amendments and limits on the timetable will be used by the government 'where it expects discipline to fail.' Presidents, in countries where the constitution grants them urgency powers, also use their ability to restrict the timetable for their bills. This has been studied extensively in Chile, where the designation of a bill as urgent is viewed as a device to signal that the president cares about a bill (see Siavelis 2002; Alemán and Navia 2009), and as a way 'to speed along the final touches on proposals that have already been negotiated with leading opposition parties' (Alemán and Navia 2009: 404). However, Chilean presidents have been flexible once urgency is assigned to a bill, granting extensions 'in order to be assured of the overall coherence and passage of the ruling Concertación coalition's legislative package' (Siavelis 2002: 95). An urgency provision for discharging a bill from committee also exists in Brazil, and limits how and by whom the bill can be amended. Interestingly, while in Brazil most bills that are designated urgent are executive bills, the urgency is normally requested by congress (Pereira and Muller 2004b: 15–16). Mustapic (2002) identifies a different bill delay tactic frequently used by the Argentine Congress, both by opposition parties and by members of the president's party—breaking quorum, though using this tool incurs the cost of negative public opinion because the public views it as obstructionist (note 31, p. 40). In Brazil, Amorim Neto (2002: 62) explains that the use of roll-call votes is an obstructionist, time consuming tactic of the opposition. Hiroi and Rennó (2017: 25), also studying Brazil, show that procedural votes are common tactics for the Congress to delay executive bills, but more proportional cabinets face fewer procedural votes on their bills.

A different tool that can be utilized by the government to help it get policy closer to its ideal point is found in bicameral legislatures. Where both chambers are powerful and have different preferences over a policy, agenda-setting by the government is expected to be more difficult, especially if the composition of one of the chambers could change during the time between bill proposal and approval. However, the government may be able to make use of formal policy conciliation procedures to obtain policy closer to its ideal point. If there is no formal institution where different versions of policy can be negotiated after a bill has passed both chambers but in different forms, the government has to anticipate what type of policy will pass both chambers and make a policy proposal that may be quite different from its ideal point. However, Fortunato et al. (2013) show, using data from the German parliament, that where a formal conciliation institution exists the government can propose a policy closer to its ideal and then work within the conciliation body to make the minimal amount of policy concession at the final stage in the legislature's multi-stage approval process. Alemán and Pachón (2008) examine conference committee powers in Colombia and Chile. They show how conference committee members have strategic power to move policy toward their preference because their proposal is voted with a closed-rule. However, the conference committee must consider the president's ability to veto specific clauses of the final bill, and the nature of the reversion point if the congress does not override the veto.

A fourth tool used by presidents is the budget. According to Pereira and Muller (2004a: 783), 'one of the most important mechanisms that the [Brazilian] executive uses to negotiate with his or her coalition in Congress [is] the appropriation of congresspersons' amendments to the annual budget.' They argue that presidential power combines with incentives induced by electoral rules to determine how backbenchers vote. Deputies, even those elected under personal vote seeking systems, have an incentive to follow their party leaders, and the president when their party is in the governing coalition, because the president can offer (budget) incentives to loyal legislators 'that will increase their individual chances of surviving politically' (p. 786). What makes the tool so powerful is the Brazilian president's discretion about which items in the budget to appropriate.

The committee system can also be part of how executive-legislative relations play out. Important aspects of the committee system include whether the jurisdictions of standing committees parallel cabinet portfolios, whether parties are proportionally represented on committees, how committee leaders are chosen, and how committee assignments for bills are made. Bill assignment to multiple committees is a common delaying tactic (Alemán and Navia 2009: 409 and 414; Alemán and Calvo 2010: 517). 'The party government model (Cox and McCubbins 1993, 2005) maintains that committees are tools of the majority, used to prevent the passage of policies that may be harmful to the majority's brand' (Fortunato 2013: 938). Strong standing committees—that have clear policy jurisdictions, the power to subpoena witnesses and amend bills—help members to develop policy expertise and engage in oversight of the executive or amend government bills. This forces the government or president to take the parliament or congress seriously as a player in the legislative process (see Alemán and Tsebelis 2011; Barkan 2009 about legislatures in African democracies; Helms 2004 about Germany). In Brazil the executive has several tools that facilitate control of committees. For example, working through party leaders in congress, deputies who oppose an executive bill have been removed from a committee before a key vote. More generally, the executive can 'stack certain committees with loyal members' (Pereira and Muller 2004b: 17). In Colombia, conference committees are found to be stacked when they address important bills (Alemán and Pachón 2008: 22). In Uruguay, special committees that are set up to study a specific important bill are commonly stacked with loyalist legislators (Chasquetti 2016: 204–5). Taylor-Robinson and Ross (2011), studying Costa Rica during the time when formal rules granted strong majoritarian powers to the largest party, found that opposition parties were still able to be full participants in committee decisions, including helping to kill executive bills. Calvo (2014: 147) found in Argentina that committees are less likely to report out executive bills when the president has low public support. Even in the British parliament, which is typically viewed as ceding legislative power to a single party in government, select committees have been found to engage in 'pre-legislative scrutiny' that can prompt the minister to edit a bill (Hindmoor et al. 2009: 72).[3] It is notable, however, that an analysis of committee systems and committee powers in thirty-one advanced industrial parliamentary democracies finds that 'strong committees emerge to serve the needs of the parties in government rather than the parties in opposition' (André et al. 2016: 117; but see Garritzmann 2017 for a counter-argument).

Parliamentary questions (PQs) enable parliament to hold the government accountable in a way that lacks a parallel in presidential systems. 'PQs solicit information from the government on issues of policy development and implementation, and therefore have the potential to be an important *ex post* control mechanism' (Martin 2011: 265). However, the utility of PQs as an oversight tool varies, for example with which actors determine who gets to ask questions, and on what topics (see Hayward 2004 about France).

Parliaments and congresses have directing boards that set the chamber's agenda. In some countries the members of the directing board are selected by 'winner-take-all' rules, in others the membership includes multiple parties, and in some it is proportional. Directing boards have agenda setting powers that can keep bills from being brought up for debate (Baldez and Carey 1999; Alemán 2006; Calvo 2014: 152). This tool can be used to maintain the government coalition, and Alemán (2006: 144) found

[3] In Chile, as well, pre-proposal scrutiny of the president's budget is important. The demands of legislators from the president's party and coalition and from the opposition 'are often incorporated into the president's proposal' (Siavelis 2002: 97). Such consultation also occurs with the secretary of the presidency (SEGPRES) for other items on the legislative agenda of the president (Siavelis 2002: 103). Additionally, the strategy of cooperation is used to make the budget, rather than relying on constitutional powers to impose the budget if it is not approved by Congress within sixty days, because the president must continue to work with the Congress after the budget is adopted (Siavelis 2002: 99).

evidence in Argentina and Chile that 'the scheduling process filters bills in such a way that policy changes carry the support of the majority party' though that study did not look specifically at the impact of this agenda control for executive bills (also see Chasquetti 2016 regarding Uruguay). Calvo (2014), also studying Argentina, shows that gate-keeping powers do not guarantee success for the president's bills.

> Gatekeeping prerogatives allow the plurality [president's] party to restrict the set of amendments, however, exposing the plurality party to a vanishing quorum and reducing overall success [...] the loss of majority support by the president's party and the strategic use of quorum rules by the minority fosters more intense bargaining and more consensual legislative strategies.   (p. 150; also see Mustapic 2002)

In sum, there are multiple tools that executives can use to try to control policy outcomes. Several aspects of the design of legislatures can also empower the opposition. Garritzmann (2017) examines the committee system, question time, rules for written and oral questions, and influence over the agenda, creating an 'Opposition Power Index' for twenty-one parliamentary democracies, showing that some legislatures create much stronger opportunities than others for the opposition to control the government or to present alternatives to voters.

27.2.3 Context and Political Variables that Can Change the Weight of the President Relative to the Congress

In parliamentary systems if the government loses support it runs the risk of being brought down by a vote of no confidence (see Chapter 16 in this volume for review of that literature). Presidents, however, have fixed terms in office regardless of their popularity, with the exception of rare cases of impeachment or resignation.[4] Barkan (2009: 17–18) argues in African countries after democratic regimes are installed and several competitive elections occur, a 'coalition for change' in the legislature is key. This coalition is led by reformers who want to strengthen the legislature so that it can be a genuine source of accountability of the executive. As was noted previously in some places this built support for the adoption of semi-presidential regimes.

While institutional structures might not change, the political situation can change in ways that weaken or strengthen the executive's hand during their term. Some presidential systems have mid-term elections that change the partisan composition of congress. Because of the fixed length of presidential terms, the electoral calendar is often viewed as an important factor in the tenor of executive-legislative relations. Thus, a

---

[4] Forcing presidents to resign through street protest or ousting presidents by a military coup represent extra-constitutional means of executive removal, but they may have consequences for regime, as well as government survival.

changing legislative context has been another focus of research about executive-legislative relations, particularly in presidential systems.

One aspect of context is the extent of the president's partisan support in congress, determining whether government is divided or unified. This topic has received extensive research in the US, due to its two-party system (see Edwards and Howell 2009). While we might expect the president to be the leader in policy-making under unified government, Alemán and Calvo (2010: 512) 'expect the president's relative weight to increase in the absence of unified government.' They theorize that 'individual legislators are more sensitive than presidents to changes in the partisan control of Congress'. Testing their theory with data from Argentina, they show that the president still retains a strong agenda-setting ability because party leaders in the chamber control the legislative agenda. The party leaders bargain about what bills to bring to a vote based on whether their party supports the bill, with the intent to derail bills their party opposes, and party leadership posts in the legislature are often 'either assigned by or negotiated with the executive' (p. 514). In contrast, with regard to Chile and the strong legislative powers given to the president by the constitution, Siavelis (2002: 82) argues that 'the degree of legislative influence varies according to the distribution of government-opposition seats in the legislature and appears to have been maximized by a less than unified, though not intransigent Congress.' Saiegh (2011: chapter 8) conducts a multi-country test and finds that if the executive lacks a majority whether members of other parties face strong control by party leaders, or are relatively free from party sanctions and thus can support the executive is also crucial for the executive's legislative success. Weak opposition parties can help a minority executive pass legislation by trading their support on elements of the president's agenda or particularistic resources (Kellam 2015). Cox and Morgenstern (2002: 453) also conclude that

> a president's level of support in the assembly will have a larger impact on his or her overall policy-making strategy—whether to seek a mostly statutory implementation of goals (governing through the assembly) or to seek a mostly non-statutory implementation (governing around the assembly).

Another, potentially volatile aspect of context is the president's popularity. Presidents can 'go public'[5] with a campaign to obtain passage of key legislation, but their ability to put pressure on the congress to pass a bill depends on the president's popularity. The impact of presidential popularity has been studied in Argentina, with the finding that positive public opinion of the president helps the president's legislative success (Calvo 2007; Alemán and Calvo 2010: 526). By contrast, in Chile public opinion has not been found to be a significant factor in predicting the legislative success rate of presidents (Alemán and Navia 2009: 415). In Uruguay, low presidential approval is associated with increased chances that a party will leave the cabinet (Altman 2000), and that standing committees will block or amend executive bills (Chasquetti 2016: 205). By definition,

---

[5] See Mustapic (2002: 41) for examples of this being done in Argentina.

parliamentary systems avoid the problem of divided government, although multi-party systems can complicate government formation leading in some cases to strategic delays (Golder et al. 2012). But, this does not mean that the partisan composition of the legislature is unimportant in these systems. Quite the contrary, the large literature on cabinet formation (see Müller-Rommel et al. (Chapter 12) or Schleiter (Chapter 15) this volume) has identified the ability of smaller coalition parties to be over-represented (e.g. Gamson's law). Golder and Thomas (2014) argue that in parliamentary systems with a vote of no confidence smaller parties are offered more portfolios in an effort to increase stability because it is more costly for them to defect (see also Volden and Carrubba 2004).

The electoral calendar has been shown to matter, with increased defections from the president's coalition late in the term (see Altman 2000, Morgenstern 2001, Chasquetti 2016 for Uruguay; Amorim Neto 2002: 69, 74 for Brazil; Molinas et al. 2004 for Paraguay). Parties are also less likely to enter the president's cabinet late in the term (Alemán and Tsebelis 2011: 22). In Costa Rica, where neither the president nor members of congress can be immediately re-elected, presidents have greater difficulty working even with members of their own party after their party has selected its candidate for the next election. The new party leader, if successful at winning office, is the person who can help members of congress to continue their political careers, so deputies no longer have an incentive to work with the lame duck president (Carey 1997). Ponce (2016: 191) also found the electoral cycle is relevant for the ability of Peru's presidents to pass their bills, as they are more successful in the first year honeymoon period.

27.3 Ways to Move the Literature on Executive-Legislative Relations Forward

Clearly there is growing scholarly recognition, that the legislature is a player to be considered by a government that wants to pass its legislative agenda. The legislature has to be managed to get policy made in a timely fashion and obtain policy close to the executive's ideal point. Even where the constitution endows the executive with extensive legislative powers, the president often chooses to work with the congress to pass bills into law rather than working via executive decrees. Yet the literatures on parliamentary systems, presidential systems, or semi-presidential systems do not directly speak to each other often enough about the ways that executives successfully obtain their policy preferences from the legislature. Who are the actors that pose the biggest challenges to the executive: a recalcitrant opposition or parties (factions) within the executive's coalition (party) that have their own, sometimes quite different policy preferences, and that need to differentiate themselves for the next election? This question is similar to the one Anthony King outlined in his seminal 1976 paper about modes of executive-legislative relations. Are committees in the legislature the most important venue for designing a mutually beneficial compromise on policy and then using chamber rules to limit changes in the deal when it comes to the plenary? Is it the ability to control the chamber's order of business that is key to keeping disliked bills from coming to a vote and moving up bills the executive favours? When can the president or cabinet effectively use such agenda control to get its preferred policy enacted? Most research looks at the ability of the executive branch to pass their bills,[6] but rarely do we know how much an executive bill was changed by the legislature during the approval process.[7] Executives obviously care about whether their bills get amended in unacceptable ways, as seen with their use of vetoes and 'last offer' amendments. But future research needs to explore when, where, and which actors in the legislature are able to successfully amend policy bills. There is much room for further research that determines when different actors and different types of rules give the executive the ability to obtain its preferred policy even when working with a strong legislature, and for determining which actors can prevent the executive from getting the policy it wants. That research will tell us much more about how presidential, parliamentary, and semi-presidential systems are similar or different, going beyond the formation of coalitions to govern.

There are also new topics that should be pursued. Much of the extant research looks at the overall ability of the executive to get legislation passed, focusing on characteristics of the executive, but it does not often consider characteristics of the bill. For example, is the executive's ability to pass its bills different for policy proposals which are a radical versus incremental departure from the status quo? Do characteristics of the executive interact with characteristics of the bill such that if a new party with a new platform comes to power, having campaigned that it will make major policy changes, can it do so? Or will elements in the legislature 'dig in their heels' and defend the status quo? This could be a particularly important research topic as both populist executives and parties without prior governing experience continue to win office. But, it could also be an important attribute, constraining the legislative ability of the executive if it wants to push policy further than it has gone in the past. For example, when Michelle Bachelet was elected president in Chile in 2006, her Concertación coalition had governed since the beginning of the democratic regime in 1990. Yet she had a new policy agenda, including more feminist policies that were not popular with some opposition parties, or with the Christian Democratic Party within her coalition (see Waylen 2016). Most of her successes on these policies had to be implemented through the executive branch, working outside of the Congress. This prompts the question of when does an executive with new policy ideas get those through the labyrinth of executive-legislative negotiations.

---

[6] There is a lack of consensus on how to measure the legislative success rate of executives (see Saiegh 2011: chapter 4 for a useful discussion). Saiegh (2011: chapter 6) shows, using sabermetric analysis of forty-two countries with data from 1946–2006, that in addition to aspects of institutional context and partisan support, other factors—good years or bad, regime transitions, economic crisis—can, along with the skill of the chief executive, effect their success at passing legislation, making some executives more (or less) successful than the average in their country.

[7] See Martin and Vanberg (2005), Bonvecchi and Zelaznik (2010), Pedrazzani and Zucchini (2013), Calvo (2014: chapter 8), Chasquetti (2016), Ponce (2016) for studies of changes made to executive bills.

Another new topic that should be examined is the impact of more diverse cabinets and legislatures; diverse in the sense of increasing representation of historically under-represented groups, such as women and racial/ethnic minorities (see also Chapter 13 in this volume). Cabinets are becoming more diverse (e.g. Escobar-Lemmon and Taylor-Robinson 2005; Krook and O'Brien 2012; Jacob et al. 2014), but are legislatures equally willing to work with ministers who are outside of the mould of traditional party leaders? Ministers are often called upon to explain their policies to standing committees, and sometimes even have to work to win the support of backbenchers within their own parties (see Hindmoor et al. 2009; Chasquetti 2016; Magar et al. 2017). Are backbenchers equally willing to grant a hearing to a non-traditional minister, and to stand by a policy deal they negotiated? Ministers who come from different backgrounds than traditional party leaders may work to promote different types of policies. Will their efforts be supported by the legislature, especially if that policy means traditionally privileged groups lose some of their privilege? Relatedly, does the inclusion of a party that represents the interests of a racial/ethnic/regional minority in a governing coalition change how the executive strategically cooperates with the legislature to pass legislation (e.g. an indigenous party in a Latin American presidential system, or a regional party in a European parliamentary system)? Even if non-traditional cabinet ministers and executives are 'equally' successful in working with the legislature (which Escobar-Lemmon and Taylor-Robinson 2016 question), is greater political capital required or must they employ different strategies and tactics?

There are also fruitful opportunities for more extensive work on how the legislature is organized and how its organization impacts the executive's ability to achieve its legislative agenda, especially in semi-presidential systems. For example, what makes a committee system powerful, and for which parties? When (and how) are committees *de facto* controlled by the chamber leadership or the executive? How does that strengthen or weaken the legislature as it negotiates policy with the executive? When opposition parties hold the leadership posts in committees are they side-lined, or do they obtain a real venue for amending the executive's bills and play a role in policy negotiations?

What is the impact of a new party rising to top leadership posts, or of a big change in a country's party system, on the executive's ability to work with the legislature? (see Chapter 23 in this volume) If a new party wins power how long does it take the newcomer to learn how to use the institutional machinery to its advantage so that it can implement the policies that presumably played an important role in winning the party the support that got it elected? This line of research could identify how much of the executive's ability to utilize institutional rules to pursue its preferred policy is due to experience, such as learning how to make use of a 'last offer amendment' or conciliation institutions, and how much is due to partisan forces? What happens to executive-legislative relations when a country that historically was governed by a party that could single-handedly form a (near) majority government experiences an increase in the effective number of parties such that (near) majority government is no longer possible? Do leaders of traditional parties quickly figure out how to govern through minority governments, or how to form coalition governments or functioning legislative coalitions to get legislation passed, thereby avoiding popular frustration with government gridlock? These are questions of similar magnitude to the old question of how (or if) cohabitation would work in a semi-presidential system, but they remain relevant in parliamentary and presidential systems as well. Actors in democratic systems may change while the formal rules of the institutions stay the same. Will those institutional rules, which often worked quite well for making policy, still work for the new actors or in a changed party system? Or, will this lead to a revision in the rules? Relatedly, are executive-legislative relations changed when a 'far left' or 'far right' party enters government? Is it experience or ideological position that drives outcomes?

We also need to study how executive-legislative relations work in a broader range of countries. Studying more countries would enhance our understanding of how different kinds of systems, with differences in institutional rules, function. This means paying more attention to parts of the world that have been largely ignored to date, and also likely doing fieldwork to collect archival data and to interview key players to ensure understanding of how the legislature and executive work, and identify how the resources the executive and legislative have to do their jobs might affect executive-legislative relations. Additionally, little research exists on the nature of executive-legislative relations outside of parliamentary and presidential systems, yet semi-presidential systems are increasingly common. These systems constitutionally mandate power sharing between executives and legislatures, yet their rules vary. While some scholars have addressed the relationship between semi-presidentialism and democracy (e.g. Elgie and Moestrup 2007, 2008; Elgie et al. 2011), further work could seek to examine this growing number of countries systematically. Understanding how these systems work could have important implications for regime stability. Additionally, as many new democracies or semi-democracies adopt this structure, examining executive-legislative relations in these contexts might breathe new life into debates on the importance of presidential and parliamentary government for the endurance of democracy.

References

Alemán, E. (2006). 'Policy Gatekeepers in Latin American Legislatures,' *Latin American Politics and Society* 48(3): 125–55.

Alemán, E. and Calvo, E. (2010). 'Unified Government, Bill Approval, and the Legislative Weight of the President,' *Comparative Political Studies* 43(4): 511–34.

Alemán, E. and Navia, P. (2009). 'Institutions and the Legislative Success of "Strong" Presidents: An Analysis of Government Bills in Chile,' *Journal of Legislative Studies* 15(4): 401–19.

Alemán, E. and Pachón, M. (2008). 'Las comisiones de conciliación en los procesos legislativos de Chile y Colombia,' *Política y Gobierno* 15(1): 3–34.

Alemán, E. and Tsebelis, G. (2011). 'Political Parties and Government Coalitions in the Americas,' *Journal of Politics in Latin America* 1: 3–28.

Alemán, E. and Tsebelis, G. (2016). 'Introduction: Legislative Institutions and Agenda Setting,' in E. Alemán, and G. Tsebelis (eds) *Legislative Institutions and Lawmaking in Latin America*. Oxford: Oxford University Press, 1–31.

Altman, D. (2000). 'The Politics of Coalition Formation and Survival in Multi-Party Presidential Democracies: The Case of Uruguay, 1989–1999,' *Party Politics* 6(3): 259–83.

Amorim Neto, O. (2002). 'Presidential Cabinets, Electoral Cycles, and Coalition Discipline in Brazil,' in S. Morgenstern and B. Nacif (eds) *Legislative Politics in Latin America*. New York: Cambridge University Press, 48–78.

André, A, Depauw, S., and Martin, S. (2016). "Trust is Good, Control Is Better': Multiparty Government and Legislative Organization,' *Political Research Quarterly* 69(1): 108–20.

Avellaneda, C. N., Botero, F. J., and Escobar-Lemmon, M. C. (2012). 'Policymaking in Parochial Legislatures: What Laws Pass the Colombian Legislature?,' *The Latin Americanist* 56(2): 7–33.

Baldez, L. and Carey, J. (1999). 'Presidential Agenda Control and Spending Policy: Lessons from General Pinochet's Constitution,' *American Journal of Political Science* 43(1): 29–55.

Barkan, J. D. (2009). 'African Legislatures and the 'Third Wave' of Democratization,' in J. D. Barkan (ed.) *Legislative Power in Emerging African Democracies*. Boulder, CO: Lynne Reinner, 1–32.

Bonvecchi, A. and Zelaznik, Jr. (2010). 'Measuring Legislative Input on Presidential Agendas (Argentina, 1999–2007),' in *Congress of the Latin American Studies Association* Toronto, Canada.

Calvo, E. (2007). 'The Responsive Legislature: Public Opinion and Policymaking in a Highly Disciplined Legislature,' *British Journal of Political Science* 37: 263–80.

Calvo, E. (2014). *Legislator Success in Fragmented Congress in Argentina: Plurality Cartels, Minority Presidents, and Lawmaking*. Cambridge: Cambridge University Press.

Camerlo, M. and Martínez-Gallardo, C. (2018) (eds). *Government Formation and Minister Turnover in Presidential Cabinets: Comparative Analysis in the Americas*. New York: Routledge.

Carey, J. M. (1997). 'Strong Candidates for a Limited Office: Presidentialism and Political Parties in Costa Rica,' in S. Mainwaring and M. S. Shugart (eds) *Presidentialism and Democracy in Latin America*. Cambridge: Cambridge University Press, 199–224.

Chasquetti, D. (2016). 'Agenda Setting and Lawmaking in Uruguay,' in E. Alemán and G. Tsebelis (eds) *Legislative Institutions and Lawmaking in Latin America*. Oxford: Oxford University Press, 199–224.

Cheibub, J. A., Przeworski, A., and Saiegh, S. M. (2004). 'Government Coalitions and Legislative Success under Presidentialism and Parliamentarism,' *British Journal of Political Science* 34(4): 565–87.

Cheibub, J. A. and Limongi, F. (2011). 'Legislative-Executive Relations,' in T. Ginsburg and R. Dixon (eds) *Comparative Constitutional Law*. Cheltenham: Edward Elgar, 211–33.

Cox, G. W. and McCubbins, M. D. (1993). *Legislative Leviathan: Party Government in the House*. New York: Cambridge University Press.

Cox, G. W. and Morgenstern, S. (2002). 'Epilogue: Latin America's Reactive Assemblies and Proactive Presidents,' in S. Morgenstern and B. Nacif (eds) *Legislative Politics in Latin America*. New York: Cambridge University Press, 446–68.

Döring, H. (2003). 'Party Discipline and Government Imposition of Restrictive Rules,' *Journal of Legislative Studies* 9(4): 147–63.

Edwards III, G. C. and Howell, W. G. (2009) (eds). *The Oxford Handbook of the American Presidency*. Oxford: Oxford University Press.

Elgie, R. (2011). 'Semi-Presidentialism: An Increasingly Common Constitutional Choice,' in R. Elgie, S. Moestrup, and Y.-S. Wu (eds) *Semi-Presidentialism and Democracy* New York: Palgrave Macmillan, 1–18.

Elgie, R. and Moestrup, S. (2007). 'The Choice of Semi-Presidentialism and Its Consequences,' in R. Elgie and S. Moestrup (eds) *Semi-Presidentialism Outside Europe: A Comparative Study.* New York: Routledge Research in Comparative Politics, 237–48.

Elgie, R. and Moestrup, S. (2008). 'The Impact of Semi-Presidentialism on the Performance of Democracy in Central and Eastern Europe,' in R. Elgie and S. Moestrup (eds) *Semi-Presidentialism in Central and Eastern Europe.* Manchester: Manchester University Press, 239–57.

Elgie, R., Moestrup, S., and Wu, Y.-S. (2011) (eds). *Semi-Presidentialism and Democracy* New York: Palgrave Macmillan.

Escobar-Lemmon, M. C. and Taylor-Robinson, M. M. (2005). 'Women Ministers in Latin American Government: When, Where, and Why?,' *American Journal of Political Science* 49(4): 829–44.

Escobar-Lemmon, M. C. and Taylor-Robinson, M. M. (2016). *Women in Presidential Cabinets: Power Players or Abundant Tokens?* New York: Oxford University Press.

Fortunato, D. (2013). 'Majority Status and Variation in Informational Organization,' *Journal of Politics* 75(4): 937–52.

Fortunato, D. (n.d.), 'Legislative Review and Party Differentiation in Coalition Governments,' Working Paper. (Reprinted in 2019 in *Political Science Review* 113(1): 242–7.)

Fortunato, D., König, T., and Proksch, S.-O. (2013). 'Government Agenda-Setting and Bicameral Conflict Resolution,' *Political Research Quarterly* 66(4): 938–51.

Fortunato, D., Martin, L. W., and Vanberg, G. (2017). 'Committee Chairs and Legislative Review in Parliamentary Democracies,' *British Journal of Political Science* doi:10.1017/S000712346000673

Franchino, F. and Høyland, B. (2009). 'Legislative Involvement in Parliamentary Systems: Opportunities, Conflict, and Institutional Constraints,' *American Political Science Review* 103(4): 607–21.

Garritzmann, J. L. (2017). 'How Much Power Do Oppositions Have? Comparing the Opportunity Structures of Parliamentary Oppositions in 21 Democracies,' *Journal of Legislative Studies* 23(1): 1–30.

Golder, M., Golder, S. N., and Siegel, D. A. (2012). 'Modeling the Institutional Foundation of Parliamentary Government Formation,' *Journal of Politics* 74(2): 427–45.

Golder, S. N. and Thomas, J. A. (2014). 'Portfolio Allocation and the Vote of No Confidence,' *British Journal of Political Science* 44(1): 29–39.

Hayward, J. (2004). 'Parliament and the French Government's Domination of the Legislative Process,' *Journal of Legislative Studies* 10(2/3): 79–97.

Heller, W. B. (2001). 'Making Policy Stick: Why the Government Gets What It Wants in Multiparty Parliaments,' *American Journal of Political Science* 45(4): 780–98.

Helms, L. (2004). 'Germany: Chancellors and the Bundestag,' *Journal of Legislative Studies* 19(2/3): 98–108.

Hindmoor, A., Larkin, P., and Kennon, A. (2009). 'Assessing the Influence of Select Committees in the UK: The Education and Skills Committee, 1997–2005,' *Journal of Legislative Studies* 15(1): 71–89.

Hiroi, T. and Rennó, L. (2017). 'Origins of Legislative Delay and Activism in Coalitional Presidential Systems: The Case of Brazil,' Paper presented at the American Political Science Association meeting, San Francisco, CA, 1 September.

Huber, J. D. (1996). 'The Vote of Confidence in Parliamentary Democracies,' *American Political Science Review* 90(2): 269–82.

Jacob, S., Scherpereel, J. A., and Adams, M. (2014). 'Gender Norms and Women's Political Representation: A Global Analysis of Cabinets, 1979–2009,' *Governance* 27(2): 321–45.

Kellam, M. (2015). 'Parties for Hire: How Particularistic Parties Influence Presidents' Governing Strategies,' *Party Politics* 21(4): 515–26.

King, A. (1976). 'Modes of Executive-Legislative Relations: Great Britain, France, and West Germany,' *Legislative Studies Quarterly* 1(1): 11–36.

Krook, M. L. and O'Brien, D. Z. (2012). 'All the President's Men? The Appointment of Female Cabinet Ministers Worldwide,' *Journal of Politics* 74(3): 840–55.

Linz, J. J. (1993). 'The Perils of Presidentialism,' in L. Diamond and M. F. Plattner (eds) *The Global Resurgence of Democracy*. Baltimore, BD: Johns Hopkins University Press, 108–26.

Lipsmeyer, C. S. and Pierce, H. N. (2011). 'The Eyes that Bind: Junior Ministers as Oversight Mechanisms in Coalition Governments,' *Journal of Politics* 73(4): 1152–64.

Magar, E., Palanza, V., and Sin, G. (2017). 'Restrictive Rules in the Chilean Cámara: Fighting Floor Amendments with the Urgency Authority,' Paper presented at the American Political Science Association meeting, San Francisco, CA, 1 September.

Mainwaring, S. (1993). 'Presidentialism, Multipartism, and Democracy: The Difficult Combination,' *Comparative Political Studies* 26(2): 198–228.

Martin, L. W. and Vanberg, G. (2005). 'Coalition Policymaking and Legislative Review,' *American Political Science Review* 99(1): 93–106.

Martin, S. (2011). 'Parliamentary Questions, the Behaviour of Legislators, and the Function of Legislatures: An Introduction,' *Journal of Legislative Studies* 17(3): 259–70.

Moestrup, S. (2007). 'Semi-presidentialism in Niger: Gridlock and Democratic Breakdown-Learning from Past Mistakes,' in R. Elgie and S. Moestrup (eds) *Semi-presidentialism Outside Europe: A Comparative Study*. New York: Routledge Research in Comparative Politics, 105–20.

Molinas, J., Pérez-Liñán, A., and Saiegh, S. (2004). 'Political Institutions, Policymaking Processes, and Policy Outcomes in Paraguay, 1954–2003,' *Revista de Ciencia Política* 24(2): 67–93.

Morgenstern, S. (2001). 'Organized Factions and Disorganized Parties: Electoral Incentives in Uruguay,' *Party Politics* 7(2): 235–56.

Mustapic, A. M. (2002). 'Oscillating Relations: President and Congress in Argentina,' in S. Morgenstern and B. Nacif (eds) *Legislative Politics in Latin America*. New York: Cambridge University Press, 23–47.

Pachón, M. and Johnson, G. B. (2016). 'When's the Party (or Coalition)? Agenda-Setting in a Highly Fragmented, Decentralized Legislature,' *Journal of Politics in Latin America* 8(2): 71–100.

Pedrazzani, A. and Zucchini, F. (2013). 'Horses and Hippos: Why Italian Government Bills Change in the Legislative Arena, 1987–2006,' *European Journal of Political Research* 52: 687–714.

Pereira, C. and Muller, B. (2004a). 'The Cost of Governing: Strategic Behavior of the President and Legislators in Brazil's Budgetary Process,' *Comparative Political Studies* 37(7): 781–815.

Pereira, C. and Muller, B. (2004b). 'A Theory of Executive Dominance of Congressional Politics: The Committee System in the Brazilian Chamber of Deputies', *Journal of Legislative Studies* 19(1): 9–49.

Ponce, A. F. (2016). 'Strong Presidents, Weak Parties, and Agenda Setting: Lawmaking in Democratic Peru', in E. Alemán and G. Tsebelis (eds) *Legislative Institutions and Lawmaking in Latin America*. Oxford: Oxford University Press, 175–98.

Roper, S. D. (2002). 'Are All Semipresidential Regimes the Same? A Comparison of Premier-Presidential Regimes', *Comparative Politics* 34(3): 253–72.

Saiegh, S. M. (2011). *Ruling by Statute: How Uncertainty and Vote Buying Shape Lawmaking*. New York: Cambridge University Press.

Shephard, M. and Cairney, P. (2005). 'The Impact of the Scottish Parliament in Amending Executive Legislation', *Political Studies* 53: 303–19.

Shugart, M. S. (2006). 'Comparative Executive-Legislative Relations', in R. A. W. Rhodes, S. A. Binder, and B. A. Rockman (eds) *The Oxford Handbook of Political Institutions*. New York: Oxford University Press, 344–65.

Siavelis, P. M. (2002). 'Exaggerated Presidentialism and Moderate Presidents: Executive-Legislative Relations in Chile', in S. Morgenstern and B. Nacif (eds) *Legislative Politics in Latin America*. New York: Cambridge University Press, 79–113.

Taylor-Robinson, M. M. and Ross, A. D. (2011). 'Can Formal Rules of Order be Used as an Accurate Proxy for Behaviour Internal to a Legislature? Evidence from Costa Rica', *The Journal of Legislative Studies* 17(4): 479–500.

Tsebelis, G. (1995). 'Decision Making in Political Systems: Veto Players in Presidentialism, Parliamentarism, Multicameralism and Multipartyism', *British Journal of Political Science* 25(3): 289–325.

Tsebelis, G. and Alemán, E. (2005). 'Presidential Conditional Agenda Setting in Latin America', *World Politics* 57(3): 396–420.

Volden, C. and Carrubba, C. J. (2004). 'The Formation of Oversized Coalitions in Parliamentary Democracies', *American Journal of Political Science* 48(3): 521–37.

Waylen, G. (2016) (ed.). *Gender, Institutions and Change in Bachelet's Chile*. Houndsmills: Palgrave Macmillan.

CHAPTER 28

....

JUDICIALIZATION AND THE POLITICAL EXECUTIVE

....

GEORG VANBERG

28.1 INTRODUCTION

A notable feature of contemporary politics in most democratic regimes is an increasingly prominent and significant role for courts—particularly constitutional courts—in the political process. At first glance, this 'global expansion of judicial power,' to use Tate and Vallinder's (1995) phrase, appears to have emerged at the expense of legislatures and executives. Policy-making by these branches is increasingly subject to judicial scrutiny in ways that can derail governments' signature initiatives and force elected politicians to 'govern with judges' (Stone Sweet 2000). To name but a few examples, consider the quick action of American federal courts in blocking President Trump's executive orders restricting immigration, the *Conseil Constitutionnel*'s limitations on the French socialist government's efforts to nationalize the financial sector in the early 1980's, or the constraints imposed by the German *Bundesverfassungsgericht* on the ability of German governments to transfer competencies to the European Union. Moreover, courts not only engage in review of substantive policy decisions by deciding *what* those in office can do. They also play an increasingly central role in regulating the political process itself by shaping *who* holds office. Examples include the US Supreme Court's decision in *Bush v. Gore*, on-going litigation over 'gerrymandering' of American electoral districts, or the Austrian *Verfassungsgerichtshof*'s decision to annul the results of the 2016 presidential election and order a revote. Finally, as a number of scholars have pointed out, the influence of courts extends beyond those instances in which judges actively intervene in the political process. Anticipation of a judicial veto can lead other policy-makers to trim their legislative and executive sails by engaging in 'autolimitation'—crafting policies in ways that they believe will pass judicial muster, thus forestalling a judicial veto (Landfried 1984; Stone Sweet 1992; Vanberg 1998).[1]

In short, contemporary democratic governance is, to a significant degree, 'judicialized'.[2] This chapter offers an overview of the scholarly literature that has attempted to explain this phenomenon, and sketches an account of judicial-executive relations that qualifies the popular perception that executives have lost power to courts. While contemporary scholarship suggests the conclusion that courts can (and do) impose restrictions on executives (and legislatures) that are genuinely unwanted by these policy-makers, it is also true that the growth of judicial power has been encouraged by executives that stand to gain politically by shifting responsibilities for difficult political choices to the judiciary.

The chapter is organized as follows. The next section (28.2) provides a sketch of the key research questions surrounding judicialization and the relationship between executives and courts. I then provide an overview of the prevailing approaches and methods employed. In section 28.3, I survey the literature that has emerged in response to these research questions. A final section (28.4) offers thoughts on productive future avenues of inquiry. Before turning to these tasks, it is useful to clarify the chapter's focus: I am primarily concerned with the relations between *executives* and courts, putting aside the interactions between courts and legislatures. That said, it is worth keeping in mind that the theoretical concerns that characterize considerations of executive-judicial relations largely apply to legislative-judicial interactions in the same manner. Second—and perhaps more importantly—the very distinction between executive and legislative powers is itself a function of constitutional design. Presidential systems, which separate control of legislative and executive power, make it more meaningful to focus on courts' interactions with executives as a separate matter than would be appropriate in parliamentary systems. In such systems, the fusion of executive and legislative office in the cabinet, and the requirement that the cabinet maintain the confidence of a legislative majority, largely undercut a clear separation of executive and legislative powers.

---

[1] The willingness of policy-makers to engage in autolimitation turns primarily on the costs of a judicial veto, which include the opportunity costs of having spent resources (such as legislative time) on a policy that is ultimately struck down and the potential reputational costs of a negative judicial decision for policy-makers (see Vanberg 1998). At the same time, these costs may often be outweighed by the benefits of adopting a particular policy, even if policy-makers anticipate a judicial veto. Below, I detail some of these, including the desire to 'pass the buck' for unpopular policy choices to the judiciary.

[2] This is not to suggest that courts cannot, or do not, play an important role in non-democratic politics. However, as Helmke and Rosenbluth (2009) explain, the politics surrounding courts and their impact under authoritarian regimes raise issues that are theoretically distinct, and beyond the scope of the current essay.

28.2 THE RESEARCH TERRAIN: RESEARCH QUESTIONS AND APPROACHES

The scholarly literature that has examined the apparent encroachment of judiciaries on executive and legislative branches—the 'judicialization of politics'—can be usefully grouped into two (related) lines of inquiry. The first—and foundational—of these is the question of judicial independence and power. Judicial involvement in the political process is of interest primarily if courts are not merely extensions of legislative or executive office-holders (i.e. act as perfect agents of these branches) but are able to exercise *independent* influence over the decisions of other policy-makers. Put differently, judicial independence and power are a precondition for meaningful judicialization. But such independent influence immediately raises a puzzle. As Alexander Hamilton famously observed in *Federalist 78*, courts have 'no influence over either the sword or the purse [...] but merely judgment'. Given this weak institutional position, what are the conditions that give rise to, and sustain, an independent and influential judiciary?

A second line of inquiry focuses on the dynamics of judicialization. Judicial involvement in the political process is, of course, not new. The US Supreme Court, for example, has been a significant force in the political system for the better part of two centuries. At the same time, as a number of scholars have noted (e.g. Ferejohn 2002; Hirschl 2008), the last twenty to thirty years have witnessed a substantial expansion of judicial 'intrusion' into the political process. What factors explain the increasingly active role played by courts, at least in some polities? What conditions allow or induce courts to become more assertive in exercising their powers? In short, the scholarly literature on judicialization revolves largely around two broad themes:

1. What conditions give rise to, and sustain, an independent judiciary that can effectively curb executive (and legislative) action?
2. What factors explain the increasingly assertive role of courts in the political process?[3]

Traditionally, scholarship in judicial politics, broadly conceived, has been methodologically and theoretically diverse. (Soft) rational choice accounts (e.g. Murphy 1964; Epstein and Knight 1998) have existed side-by-side with theoretical approaches

---

[3] While the social science literature on judicialization takes a largely positive approach to these research questions, the expansion of judicial influence has also generated a substantial normative literature. The primary emphasis of this literature has been to wrestle with the apparent tension between judicial review and democracy—encapsulated in Alexander Bickel's (1962) famous formulation of the 'countermajoritarian difficulty': How can the exercise of judicial review by judges—who are typically far less accountable to citizens than elected policy-makers—be reconciled with an underlying commitment to democratic values? This normative literature is beyond the scope of this essay, but Friedman (2002) and Vanberg (2018) provide useful reviews.

rooted in behavioural and psychological models, including those focused on judicial role-orientations (e.g. Gibson 1978), or judges' attitudes (e.g. Segal and Spaeth 2002). Empirically, too, the literature encompasses a broad array of methods, ranging from qualitative and historical work to large-N, quantitative approaches. More recently, a desire for robust causal inference has also begun to introduce more careful research designs into this literature (e.g. Kastellec 2013; Budziak and Lempert 2018). This diversity of approaches is a direct consequence of the highly interdisciplinary nature of the field, which sits squarely at the intersection of law, political science, sociology and (to some extent) economics.

While judicial politics scholarship reflects significant diversity, the contributions that focus on judicialization and executive-judicial relations have been heavily influenced by rational choice models. In part, this may be a result of the nature of the puzzles that are of central concern in this research area. These puzzles revolve around the interactions between judges and executive branch officials (including elected policy-makers and bureaucrats). The fact that the interactions between distinct actors with separate preferences are central naturally suggests an approach that considers under what conditions executives (and other policy-makers) tolerate independent courts, or the benefits that such courts can provide to other actors in a strategic environment. Rational choice approaches are well-suited to such analysis.

28.3 THE STATE OF THE LITERATURE

The literature reviewed in this section focuses on the relationship between executives and domestic courts, though many of the issues touched on apply equally to the interactions between executives and supranational courts.[4] I begin with the foundational issue that is the *sine qua non* of judicialization: The conditions that can give rise to, and sustain, a judiciary that has a substantial degree of independence from the executive, and is sufficiently influential to constrain executive action.

28.3.1 Judicial Independence and Influence

The ideal of judicial independence rests on the notion that judges ought to be free from influences that are considered inappropriate. This immediately implies that the concept requires a normative foundation that allows us to identify those influences from which the judicial process should be insulated, as well as those that are unproblematic or perhaps even desirable. Put differently, the concept of judicial independence is intimately

---

[4] The literature on supranational courts is numerous and highly developed. For an excellent overview, see Carrubba and Gabel (2015).

tied to the issue of judicial accountability (see Vanberg 2008 for a more detailed discussion). I sidestep this broader discussion. Instead, I begin with definitions of judicial independence and judicial influence that are relevant to the topic of executive-judicial relations. For current purposes, I understand courts to be *independent* if they are (reasonably) free from effective pressure to bend them to the will of executive branch officials. Courts are *influential* if executive branch officials cannot easily evade decisions or refuse to comply with them. Independence and influence are logically separate properties, and neither can be taken for granted: As scholars have long recognized, while there are prominent examples of powerful courts that constrain executives and legislative majorities, many courts around the world—both historically and in the contemporary context—are neither independent of, nor have influence over, the elected branches.

There is a simple reason why judicial independence and influence pose a challenge: To the extent that powerful, independent courts can interfere with executive action, executives face clear incentives to undermine judicial independence. Moreover, they often have means at their disposal to do precisely this. Executives (in concert with legislative majorities) typically control the size and structure of the judiciary, as well as its jurisdiction and budget. Moreover, the implementation of judicial decisions often requires the cooperation of executive agencies. Historically, examples abound of executives using these tools in attempts to constrain or limit judicial influence. Given that executives possess institutional resources to resist unwelcome judicial decisions, or to retaliate against an unfriendly judiciary, what explains why, and under what conditions, courts can be independent and powerful entities vis-à-vis the executive branch? Answers to this question can be usefully grouped into two types: *Exogenous* explanations focus on constraints beyond the control of executives that place courts in a powerful position. In contrast, *endogenous* explanations highlight the internal incentives executives may face to respect an independent judiciary because doing so serves their interests.

28.3.1.1 *Exogenous Explanations*

Judicial independence poses a puzzle because executives often have access to resources to resist unfriendly courts, including refusing to comply with decisions, or retaliating against the judiciary through its control over budgets, jurisdictions, or other resources of significance to the judiciary (e.g. Ramseyer 1994 documents that Japanese governments have used control over the assignment of judges to different courts and locations as a vehicle for punishing and rewarding judges; see also Vanberg 2000; Whittington 2003; Clark 2011). Exogenous explanations for judicial independence focus on the *ability* of executives to confront a judiciary by employing these tools, and the *costs* they may face for doing so.

One prominent strand of this literature examines the extent to which judicial independence and influence are affected by constitutional design. The key insight is that political structures that require coordinated action by several political actors to resist or attack the judiciary increase the power of courts compared to settings in which executives can act unilaterally. A simple spatial model (based loosely on Ferejohn and

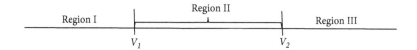

FIGURE 28.1 Illustration of judicial discretion interval

Shipan 1990) can illustrate the point. Suppose that moving against the judiciary (by passing legislation to restrict the court's jurisdiction, or engaging in other forms of court-curbing, or to override a decision) requires the agreement of two veto players (e.g. an executive and an independently elected legislature). In Figure 28.1, the preferences of each veto player are represented by ideal points at v_1 and v_2, respectively, and each veto player prefers policy outcomes closer to her ideal point over outcomes that are more distant.

Consider the ability of a court to 'set policy' this space through its decisions. A decision that attempts to move policy into regions I or III may give rise to resistance or retaliation by the veto players, since both agree on the direction in which they prefer to move policy in response to the court's decision. But the same is not true in region II. Inside the Pareto set of the veto players, the court is in a strong position to set policy in accordance with its own preferences because the veto players—who must agree on any response—have divergent views over how to react to a judicial decision. Thus, the Pareto set of the veto players defines a 'judicial discretion interval' within which the court enjoys wide latitude.

This simple illustration highlights several key points. First, the presence of multiple veto players whose agreement is required to undermine judicial independence strengthens courts (Ferejohn 2002). Second, the 'judicial discretion interval' that courts enjoy as a result of such political fragmentation increases as the preferences of veto players diverge (the Pareto set grows in size). Finally, the influence that courts can acquire as a result of political fragmentation is *conditional* and *limited*: Courts must remain within the boundaries of those decisions that will not provoke a unified response, that is, within the judicial discretion interval (see also Epstein et al. 2001).

The insights of this approach have been applied by a number of scholars to understand the (lack of) influence of courts in a variety of contexts. These applications focus on the number of veto players, and their relative preferences. For example, the approach suggests that presidential 'separation of powers' systems, which provide for independently elected executives and legislatures, will generally strengthen the position of courts compared to parliamentary 'fusion of powers' systems in which executives are supported by a cohesive legislative majority (see Shapiro 1981; Whittington 2003; Friedman 2004).

Within each of these systems, the approach further distinguishes conditions that will enhance or limit judicial influence. Thus, Whittington (2003) shows that court-curbing in the American presidential system has been most successful in periods when a dominant political coalition controls Congress and the presidency, effectively negating the protections offered by a separation of powers (see also Rosenberg 1992; Clark 2011).

In contrast, Chavez et al. (2011) argue that the US Supreme Court has historically been more aggressive in asserting its powers when the other branches have not been controlled by a unified coalition, thereby enlarging the judicial discretion interval. In parliamentary systems, coalition governments in which separate government parties can exercise veto powers as 'partisan veto players' (Tsebelis 2002) will be more conducive to judicial influence than single party governments. Of course, other features of a political system that provide for additional veto points have a similar effect. For example, federal systems that separate powers across levels of government, and provide veto player status (at least in some areas) to lower level governments can strengthen courts (Bednar 2005). Thus, Vanberg (2000) shows that the German *Bundesverfassungsgericht* was able to take advantage of representation by state governments in the upper house of the legislature to assert its independence vis-à-vis the federal executive.

As just argued, political fragmentation (induced by the presence of veto players) can enhance judicial independence by restricting the *ability* of executives to move against an assertive judiciary. A separate exogenous mechanism that scholars have focused on as a potential source of judicial independence is the cost that executives may incur for undermining judicial independence and influence in the presence of strong public support for the judiciary. If courts possess sufficient public support, executive interference with judicial independence, or resistance to decisions, is likely to result in a significant public backlash. Elected officials—who are dependent on public support for their continued hold on office—may conclude that the costs of such a backlash are prohibitive. A number of studies, some US-focused and some comparative, have argued that public support constitutes a critical resource for courts in asserting their authority (Vanberg 2001; Stephenson 2004; Carrubba 2009; Carrubba and Zorn 2010; Staton 2010). Elite interviews with members of the German parliament, conducted for Vanberg's (2005) study of the *Bundesverfassungsgericht*, illustrate the logic: 'No other institutions has as much trust in the population. [...] Anyone who would try to brush aside the court or to limit its competencies would have enormous problems' (cited in Vanberg 2005: 121).

Like political fragmentation, public support provides *conditional* support for judicial independence and influence. As scholars have emphasized, there are several dimensions to this conditionality. One is that if public support constitutes a key resource for courts, judges must be sensitive to the need to build and sustain public confidence and trust in the judiciary. A broad literature has investigated the sources of public support for courts, and the general conclusion that has emerged from this scholarship is that two aspects are particularly important: Support for courts depends in part on the perception of courts as impartial institutions (see Shapiro 1981; Gibson 1989, 1991; Tyler and Rasinski 1991). At the same time, experimental and observational research has demonstrated that support for courts is shaped by individual's policy agreement with specific decisions (Mondak 1991, 1992; Gibson et al. 1998; Durr et al. 2000). The implication of these findings is that to build and sustain support, judges must be attentive *both* to maintaining public perceptions of courts as non-partisan actors and, at the same time, be sensitive to not frustrate clear trends in public opinion. Of course, these two aims can, at least on occasion, come into conflict (see Vanberg 2005: 52f.).

A second feature is that public support for courts—if it is sufficiently widespread to deter attacks on the judiciary—can only act as a shield if citizens (i.e. a sufficient number of them) become aware and convinced that executives are attempting to undermine particular decisions or the judiciary as an institution. This, in turn, depends on the broader political context surrounding judicial decisions and executive reactions to them. The greater the salience of a decision, and the less complex the issues involved, the more difficult it is for executives to resist because non-compliance is easier to observe (Vanberg 2005; Carrubba and Zorn 2010). Similarly, in his seminal study of the impact of interest groups on judicialization, Charles Epp has shown that the presence of numerous, well-organized interest groups increases pressure for compliance substantially— primarily because these groups can bring renewed legal challenges and raise public awareness of judicial decisions and executive responses (Epp 1998).

Finally, compliance pressure also depends on features of judicial opinions—most importantly the clarity with which decisions spell out the implications of rulings for executive actions. As several empirical studies (focused on the US Supreme Court) have demonstrated, the greater the clarity of judicial decisions, the more likely rulings are to be implemented (Baum 1981; Spriggs 1997). This fact opens up an intriguing possibility: As a number of scholars have argued, judges can strategically manipulate some of these factors, thus increasing (or decreasing) pressure for compliance. In a careful study of the Mexican Supreme Court, for example, Staton shows that the court uses sophisticated media strategies to affect public awareness of its decisions through the selective use of press releases (Staton 2006, 2010). Judges may also strategically choose how clearly to articulate judicial demands in decisions, either increasing pressure for compliance or providing cover for evasion (Staton and Vanberg 2008).[5]

28.3.1.2 *Endogenous Explanations*

In contrast to exogenous explanations, endogenous explanations for judicial independence and influence point to the fact that the presence of powerful courts can (often indirectly) serve the interests of executives. In other words, endogenous explanations suggest that while powerful courts may, at first glance, appear to impose unwelcome constraints on executives, a closer look reveals that such institutions can be useful for executive office holders. The dominant endogenous explanation—made prominent by Ramseyer's (1994) seminal work and further developed by a number of scholars (most notably Hirschl 2000; Ginsburg 2003; Stephenson 2003)—is the aptly named 'insurance theory'. The lynchpin for this argument is a distinction between an *office* (in our case, the executive) and *office-holders* (in our case, elected politicians and parties). The distinction is critical because in a competitive political setting, the interests of office-holders

---

[5] One critical question in this context concerns the sources of public support for courts. This is a broad topic beyond the scope of this essay. However, Gibson et al. (1998) and Vanberg (2005: chapter 2) provide useful introductions.

can extend beyond their terms in office to periods in which they find themselves in opposition. If parties and politicians expect to move in and out of power over time, the familiar logic of cooperation in a repeated Prisoner's Dilemma (Taylor 1979) opens up the possibility of executive respect for judicial independence and influence. Parties in office may be willing to accept judicial constraints on their power if they expect that doing so will preserve an independent, influential judiciary that can constrain the executive and protect their interests should they lose power and find themselves in opposition.

Stephenson (2003) formalizes the logic of the insurance theory in a game-theoretic model of two parties that alternate probabilistically in power. The party in power chooses policies subject to review by a court with no direct enforcement powers: In each period, the executive must choose whether to respect or ignore the court's ruling. Stephenson shows that it is possible to sustain an equilibrium in which each party respects the court's authority as long as the other party does so as well. This formalization highlights three key aspects of the insurance argument that define its scope conditions.

1. The insurance logic requires that office-holders have sufficiently long time horizons so that the benefits of judicial protection when out of office in the future outweigh the costs of respecting judicial decisions in the present.
2. The political environment must be competitive. It is only when parties believe that they are sufficiently likely to find themselves in opposition in the future that they are willing to preserve the judiciary as an institution by respecting its authority in the present. Because this must be true of *all* parties, no party can be electorally dominant.
3. The judiciary must be attuned to the interests of current office-holders. The logic of the insurance argument is that the benefits of maintaining judicial authority for the future must outweigh the costs of compliance in the present. This immediately implies that there is a limit to the costs that a court can impose on executives before provoking an attack. The court must remain within the 'tolerance limit' of the executive. Critically, this tolerance level varies with a party's political competitiveness. For parties that are electorally more competitive, and expect to hold office more frequently, the benefits of judicial protection decrease and as a result, their tolerance threshold is lower. To preserve their institutional integrity, judges must be more accommodating to the preferences of such parties.

The insurance argument highlights that executive respect for a powerful judiciary can reflect an inter-temporal trade-off in which parties or politicians in power accept limits on their authority in expectation of judicial protection when in opposition. Under this account, the benefits of judicial independence to executive office-holders are thus *indirect*: Judicial oversight is an unwelcome constraint that is tolerated because its acceptance offers future benefits. A second line of scholarship on endogenous explanations for judicial independence argues that strong courts can also offer *direct* benefits to executives. This literature points to a number of potential advantages.

One derives from the temporal place of judicial decision-making in most (though not all) political systems. Because courts typically review policies after implementation, they are able to evaluate them in light of the actual results that flow from them. As a result, as Rogers (2001) has argued, courts can serve to weed out (or adapt) policies that have unintended negative consequences—a potential benefit from the perspective of executive and legislative policy-makers who cannot perfectly anticipate how policy choices translate into political outcomes (see also Whittington 2003).[6] Another benefit that a strong judiciary can offer to executives (and other policy-makers) is particularly relevant in political systems that fragment decision-making, and require the cooperation of multiple institutions to adopt policy. In such settings, policy-makers may be able to turn to strong courts to 'overcome gridlock' through judicial imposition of policies that are difficult to advance through regular channels (Whittington 2005).

But perhaps the most prominent of direct benefit of strong courts for executives is the opportunity to use courts to shift blame for unpopular policy choices from elected officials to the judiciary. Of course, such a strategy requires that the judiciary is perceived to be (reasonably) independent of the executive and legislature—a dependent and compliant judiciary cannot be credibly saddled with responsibility for controversial policy choices. The desire to play such a 'blame shift' game not only explains why executives may support a powerful judiciary. It can also help to explain the increasing trend towards judicial involvement in the political process. As parties and politicians have discovered the benefits of deflecting difficult decisions to the courts, courts have increasingly been called upon to settle controversial policy disputes. As Mark Graber (1993: 37) has observed, elected officials 'encourage or tacitly support judicial policy-making both as a means of avoiding responsibility for making tough decisions and as a means of pursuing controversial policy goals that they cannot publicly advance through open legislative and electoral politics' (see also Salzberger 1993; Hirschl 2004; Whittington 2005, 2007).[7]

As this review has demonstrated, the contemporary literature on the conditions that give rise to and sustain an independent, powerful judiciary is rich and multi-faceted. It encompasses endogenous explanations that root executive respect for judicial authority in the (long-run) interests of elected office-holders, and exogenous explanations that highlight that structural conditions beyond the control of particular office-holders may force them to accept judicial oversight even if it constitutes an unwelcome constraint.

---

[6] Two points are worth highlighting. First, this argument obviously does not apply to a priori judicial review in which policies are subject to judicial scrutiny before implementation—a widely practice form of judicial review in Europe (see Rogers and Vanberg 2002). Second, it is not obvious that reaping the benefits of informational judicial review requires an *independent* judiciary; a dependent judiciary that serves as an agent of the executive or legislature can also serve this purpose.

[7] Incentives for policy-makers to employ an independent judiciary to shift blame for unpopular policy choices, will limit the phenomenon of 'autolimitation', in which policy-makers preemptively craft policy to pass judicial muster (see Landfried 1984).

The fundamental conclusion common to all of these approaches is that ultimately, judicial independence and influence are *conditional*. In the final analysis, courts are institutionally weak, and dependent on the cooperation of other branches for the implementation of their rulings and their institutional integrity. Thus, judges must be sensitive to the political environment in which they act. They must remain within the tolerance thresholds of other policy-makers, and they must be attuned to maintaining public support. How significant these limitations are will depend, of course, on the particular context within which a court is situated.

28.3.2 Judicialization and Judicial Activism

The presence of a judiciary that is sufficiently strong to assert itself in the political process is a *necessary* but not a *sufficient* condition for judicialization. Courts are, with very few exceptions, reactive institutions. Executive and legislative policy-makers possess agenda setting powers that allow them to take on an issue and initiate policy action. In contrast, courts are typically restricted to addressing 'cases and controversies' that are brought to them by other actors, be they private litigators or government officials. Moreover, for many courts, the resolution of disputes properly before the court is not a matter of choice: Many courts are required to issue a decision, some even within strict time limits.[8] The fact that courts act largely in reaction to disputes brought to them by other actors already suggests an important caveat for any discussion of judicialization. Judicialization is not a phenomenon that is driven exclusively—perhaps not even primarily—by unilateral judicial action. Judicialization can only proceed when outside, non-judicial actors bring issues to the courts. In this sense, judicialization can be as much the product of judges being 'dragged' into the political realm as the result of judicial enthusiasm for injecting courts into politics.

Viewed from this perspective, it is useful to distinguish—as the scholarly literature has done—between activation of courts 'from below' (i.e. by private litigants, including civil society groups) and 'from above' (i.e. by political elites, including office-holders in other branches).

28.3.2.1 *Judicialization from Below*

'Activation from below' refers to the role played by private actors—principally organized groups—in bringing issues to courts that allow (or induce) judges to expand their reach into the political process. The literature that addresses this phenomenon largely derives from Charles Epp's (1998) seminal comparative work. The extent to which organized groups serve as catalysts for judicialization by bringing cases to the judiciary depends on

---

[8] This is not true, of course, of all courts: Some courts (the US Supreme Court being the most obvious example) enjoy a discretionary docket, and the ability to pick and choose among cases provides these courts with limited agenda powers. Nevertheless, even these courts are restricted to those cases that other actors place before them.

a number of factors, three of which have received particular attention: (1) The number and organizational structure of groups, (2) the fragmentation of the political system, and (3) the nature of the legal (especially constitutional) framework.

The central argument of Epp's *Rights Revolution* is that policy change through judicial action requires effective legal campaigns before the courts, including sustained long-term litigation strategies that build on incremental victories, monitor compliance, and bring renewed challenges when other policy-makers resist. Individual litigants are unlikely agents for such campaigns. They typically have narrow interests in a particular dispute, and limited resources. Organized groups, in contrast, can bring organizational capacity, greater resources, and a long-term strategy to bear. Of course, these efforts typically work through individual litigants—but the key point is that individual cases now receive backing by an organized group and become part of a broader litigation effort. As a result, the number and organizational capacity of interest groups is a critical factor in driving 'judicialization from below'. As Epp puts it, the emergence of multiple, well-organized groups that acted as rights advocates (what he calls a rights 'support structure') 'propelled rights issues into the higher courts, encouraged the courts to render favorable decisions and, at least to some extent, provided the judiciary with active partners in the fight against implementation of the new rights' (Epp 1998: 22).

The other two factors that have received scholarly attention focus on the ability of groups to bring challenges, and the incentives they have to do so. The first concerns the nature of the surrounding legal framework. Unlike legislative and executive policy-makers, judges must justify their decisions with reference to a legal framework, and fit their decisions into the existing legal structure. Where constitutional provisions or precedent provide opportunities for groups to more easily advance rights claims through the courts, the opportunities for judicialization from below therefore expand.

While the legal context affects the ability of groups to turn to the courts in order to advance particular rights claims, another critical factor concerns the incentives of groups to pursue these avenues. In the previous section, I argued that fragmentation of the political system is conducive to judicial independence because it raises hurdles to the ability of other policy-makers to resist or retaliate against unwelcome judicial decisions. That is, because fragmentation makes policy-making in the ordinary political process more difficult, it expands the 'judicial discretion interval' within which judges can act independently. But this is not the only way in which political fragmentation is relevant to judicialization from below. Because fragmentation makes it more difficult to pursue policy goals through legislative or executive action, it not only expands the opportunity for courts to act independently. It also increases the incentives for organized groups to turn to courts, especially if the legal environment is favourable. As Ferejohn (2002: 55) observes, '(w)hen the political branches cannot act, people seeking resolution to conflicts will tend to gravitate to institutions from which they can get solutions; courts (and associated legal processes) often offer such venues'. The recent movements for marriage equality provide an instructive example. In European parliamentary systems that typically ensure that executives are backed by a cohesive legislative majority, the push for recognition of same-sex marriage focused primarily on legislative action. In contrast, in the highly fragmented American political system, which made the prospects for legislative establishment of same-sex marriage highly uncertain, marriage equality was achieved primarily through cumulative victories in the courts.

In short, a critical driver of judicialization is the presence of organized groups in a context that favours and encourages these groups to turn to courts to advance their claims. As courts are increasingly besieged by demands for rights protections, judges who are sympathetic to expanding the role of courts have more opportunities to do so—and judges who are reluctant will often have no choice but to wade into waters that might ordinarily have been left as the exclusive domain of elected policy-makers.

28.3.2.2 *Judicialization from Above*

The logic of endogenous explanations for judicial independence laid out in section 28.3.1.2 is that the presence of influential courts can provide benefits to executive and legislative policy-makers that make these actors willing to tolerate an independent judiciary. These benefits not only explain support for the judiciary as an institution, they also contribute to 'judicialization from above' by encouraging political elites not only to tolerate independent courts, but actively to turn to these institutions in pursuit of their political agendas. Corresponding to the distinction between indirect and direct benefits, such judicialization from above occurs through two channels.

The first—corresponding to the indirect benefit of judicial independence captured by the insurance logic—revolves around the incentives for parties and politicians *in opposition* to take advantage of judicial processes to challenge the actions of incumbent executives and legislative majorities. While opposition parties across a large variety of political systems take advantage of opportunities to continue political disagreements through judicial means, this avenue to judicialization is particularly prominent in (largely European) systems of concentrated judicial review. These systems, which derive from Hans Kelsen's draft of the Austrian constitution of 1920, rely on a constitutional tribunal that is separate from the ordinary judicial hierarchy, and has the exclusive right to exercise constitutional review (see Cappelletti 1989). In addition to an individual right to bring complaints, these systems typically also allow specific political actors to initiate constitutional review proceedings by challenging executive and legislative action before the constitutional court immediately after adoption of a policy. For example, in Germany, the federal government, any state government, or one-quarter of the members of the federal parliament can directly challenge legislative and executive action before the constitutional court. In France, the president, the presiding officers of the national assembly and senate, or sixty members of the national assembly or senate can initiate abstract review proceedings. In practice, as one might imagine, such pro-ceedings are most often initiated by parties or politicians that challenge contentious policy initiatives by the government of the day—essentially turning the constitutional court into a 'third legislative chamber' (see Stone Sweet 1992, 2000; Ishiyama Smithey and Ishiyama 2002; Dotan and Hofnung 2005; Vanberg 2005). Constitutional courts are thus drawn directly into some of the most contentious political issues of the day. To take only one recent example, German participation in the European Union's Outright

Monetary Transactions (OMT) programme, designed to stabilize the financial situation of the EU member states in the aftermath of the financial crisis (particularly Greece), was challenged in front of the German constitutional court by a German member of parliament, directly drawing the court into one of the most salient and significant policy questions in European politics of the last decades (see Gulati and Vanberg 2019).[9]

But opposition forces are not the only elite actors with incentives to turn to courts for the resolution of political disputes. For political executives, the direct benefits—outlined above—that effective courts can provide generate additional momentum for judicialization from above. As Whittington (2005) argues—and illustrates with several close case studies of decisions by the US Supreme Court—courts can provide powerful allies for executives who are frustrated in the pursuit of political goals in the ordinary political process. Perhaps more significantly, executives often face strong incentives to turn over controversial political decisions that may disappoint or antagonize key constituencies to the judiciary, thus avoiding responsibility for tough choices. In the American context, for example,

> presidents and legislative leaders must similarly sometimes manage deeply divided or cross-pressured coalitions. When faced with such issues, elected officials may actively seek to turn over controversial political questions to the courts so as to [...] avoid the political fallout that would come with taking direct action themselves.
> (Whittington 2005: 591–2)

The response of many European countries to the recent financial crisis provides a powerful example. Faced with the need for significant austerity measures and budgetary reforms that were likely to be highly unpopular, EU member states imposed—through EU treaties (including the Fiscal Compact)—legal requirements that would turn enforcement of austerity measures over to the courts. As Kelemen (2019: 13) concludes,

> Lacking the political courage to face their electorates and to take responsibility for their fiscal policy choices, they established a system that would enable them to claim that they had no choice when imposing austerity. Henceforth, they could claim that they were forced to impose painful cuts by EU legal requirements and by the national and European courts that enforced these. They hoped this approach would deflect blame for the pain of austerity measures away from governments and redirect it at the EU and the courts.

---

[9] Of course, this is not to suggest that courts in decentralized systems of judicial review that do not follow the Kelsen model are not used by political elites in opposition to challenge governmental policy. In the United States, for example, courts have been drawn into the contentious issue of drawing legislative boundaries by parties and politicians who challenge the way in which legislative majorities have designated electoral districts. However, in such systems, the more restrictive requirements on standing make such action more difficult than the relatively open systems of abstract review that explicitly empower certain actors, including opposition parties, to bring cases.

In short, judicialization has occurred not only 'from below' as organized interests advance rights claims through the courts when doing so through the ordinary political process proves difficult. It has also occurred 'from above' as political elites—including executive policy-makers—have actively brought issues to the courts in the pursuit of their political goals, or have willingly turned over controversial political decisions to judges in an effort to avoid accountability for potentially unpopular policy choices.

The key implication of these findings is clear. Far from a process in which judges encroach on the domain of executives and legislatures *against* the interests of these actors, the rise of more active and prominent courts with an increasingly large footprint in the political realm is encouraged and accelerated by political elites who benefit from the ability to overcome political opposition through judicial action, or to deflect blame for difficult policy choices onto judges. As Hirschl (2008: 113) concludes,

> [it] is naïve to assume that core political questions [...] could have been transferred to courts without at least the implicit support of influential political stakeholders [...] the portrayal of constitutional courts and judges as the major culprits in the all-encompassing judicialization of politics worldwide is simplistic. Strategically motivated political stakeholders are at least as responsible.

Judicialization is not simply a judge-imposed phenomenon—it is a phenomenon driven in significant part by political actors outside the courts, including executive policy-makers.

28.3.3 Judicial Appointments

Before concluding, I briefly take up a final element of direct relevance to the relations between executives and constitutional courts: the process of judicial appointment. Whether courts—assuming they are independent and influential—shape the outcomes of the policy process, and whether the various actors who have access to the judiciary have incentives to bring cases, depends critically on judicial 'preferences'. Do the considerations judges regard as relevant, and on the basis of which they will decide, place them at odds with the preferences of executive (and legislative) policy-makers? Judicial preferences (which should be understood broadly to encompass the various considerations that judges bring to the table, including their jurisprudential and legal philosophy, as well as their political views), in turn, are shaped significantly by the appointment process that governs judicial selection.

Surprisingly, the academic literature on judicial appointments is sparse. Most studies focus on a single country, with particular attention being showered on appointments to the US Supreme Court and the changing nature of Supreme Court appointments (e.g. see Shipan and Shannon 2003; Epstein et al. 2006; Cameron et al. 2013; Cameron and Kastellec 2016). Far fewer studies examine the appointment process in countries other than the US (e.g. Hoennige 2007; Elgie et al. 2018), and rarer still are studies that employ a comparative approach to judicial appointment processes and their conse-quences (for notable exceptions, see Hoennige 2008 and Brouard and Hoennige 2017).

Broadly speaking, appointment processes for high courts vary along three dimensions that impact the relationship between courts and other policy-makers (see Stone Sweet 2002; Ginsburg 2003):

1. The identity of the actors involved in the appointment process.
2. The decision rules by which appointments are made.
3. The length of judicial terms.[10]

The most significant difference with respect to the last item is the contrast between systems that provide for lifetime appointments (such as the United States) and those that feature terms of a defined (typically non-renewable) duration (e.g. nine years in France, and twelve years in Germany). The consequences of limited, staggered terms are intuitive: By increasing turnover on the court, limited terms provide governments with regular and predictable opportunities to appoint new justices. This serves to reduce the political significance of any particular opening compared to systems with lifetime appointments (witness the increasingly partisan battles over Supreme Court nominations in the United States). It also limits the potential for the preferences of high court justices to lag behind significant and consistent shifts in public opinion.

A second key dimension along which appointment processes differ concerns the identity of the appointing actors, and the level of agreement that is required for a successful appointment. In virtually all polities, appointments to high courts involve executive and legislative actors. But there exist significant differences with respect to the level of agreement among actors that is required.[11] France, for example, employs a process that directly empowers individual executive and legislative actors: One-third of the judges of the *Conseil Constitutionnel* are unilaterally appointed by the French president, one-third by the president of the National Assembly, and one-third by the president of the Senate. Because these are unilateral appointments, no need for cross-party compromise exists, and judges typically reflect the partisan position of the appointing actor (Stone Sweet 1992). In contrast, other systems are designed to require some level of partisan compromise. In Germany, for example, one-half of the justices of the *Bundesverfassungsgericht* are appointed by each of the two chambers of parliament (the *Bundestag* and the *Bundesrat*), with an appointment requiring a two-thirds majority, requiring cross-party agreement on acceptable candidates (see Vanberg 2005). In the United States, the requirement for agreement is inter-institutional: presidential nominations require Senate approval.

---

[10] There are also variations in the qualifications required of judges, with legal training required in some cases (e.g. Germany), and no legal qualifications required in others (e.g. the United States, France). *De facto*, even in countries that have no formal requirement of legal training, high court judges typically have a legal background (this is true, most obviously, in the United States). A notable exception is France, where judges of the *Conseil Constitutionnel* are often former politicians.

[11] See Brouard and Hoennige (2017: 20–1) for a detailed table of appointment procedures across European Constitutional Courts.

The consequences of such variation in appointment systems has, to date, received limited scholarly attention. In the most systematic cross-national study, Brouard and Hoennige (2017) have shown that differences in appointment systems have significant consequences for the expected divergence between judicial and executive (and legislative) preferences, especially in the presence of systematic turnover in government. More systematic analysis of judicial appointment systems, and the impact of these systems on judicial behaviour as well as the relations among courts and other policy-makers, represents an obvious and important area for future research.

28.4 Looking Ahead

In most democratic regimes, courts play an increasingly prominent and influential role in the political realm. This development, commonly referred to as judicialization, is often decried as inappropriate judicial activism by those who find themselves on the losing side of judicial decisions and praised as a courageous display of judicial oversight by those who prevail. In contrast to popular perceptions that activist judges are encroaching on realms traditionally reserved for elected policy-makers, the central conclusion of the scholarly literature that has focused on this phenomenon is that judicialization is *not* primarily driven by the actions of judges. Instead, judicialization must be understood as the result of political processes in which the interactions of multiple actors, including organized interests, political elites, and judges, have expanded the scope for judicial decision-making. Because courts are reactive institutions that can only take up issues brought to them by litigants, judicialization requires 'activation' of courts by other actors. Such activation has occurred 'from below' as organized interests have sought to press rights claims through courts, and it has occurred 'from above' as political elites—including executives and legislative majorities—have used courts to advance political agendas in the face of opposition by other policy-makers, or to shift blame for unpopular political choices onto judges. This literature points to a number of systematic factors that favour judicialization:

1. Fragmentation of the political system. By requiring coordinated action of separate policy-makers to resist judicial decisions, political fragmentation creates a 'judicial discretion interval' that provides judges with scope for independent action. In addition, by making the pursuit of policy change through the ordinary political process more difficult, political fragmentation encourages political actors to turn to the courts in the pursuit of their goals.
2. The presence of well-organized interests that can sustain strategic litigation. Such groups are instrumental in bringing rights-claims to courts, thus expanding the reach of the judiciary. Judicialization from below is particularly likely where the legal environment is favourable to advancing rights claims, and where political fragmentation encourages groups to pursue such claims outside of the ordinary political process, that is, through the courts.

3. Conditions that generate incentives for political elites—including executives—to cede political authority to the courts. These include the need to 'break gridlock' in the political process, or the desire to shift blame for politically unpalatable or controversial decisions away from elected officials.

While this literature has generated significant insights into judicialization, clear avenues for future scholarly work remain. Theoretically, several areas of inquiry require more elaboration. One concerns the dynamics of judicialization. The central factors that have been offered as explanations for judicialization—fragmented political systems, the presence of well-organized interests, incentives for political elites to shift political decisions to the courts—are not themselves *dynamic* factors; often, they are constant over long periods of time (particularly the constitutional structure of a polity). As a result, taken on their own, these factors cannot explain the dynamics of the expansion of judicial influence. More work is needed to uncover why, and under what conditions, judicialization accelerates in some contexts, but not in others. Another critical area that has received only limited attention to date concerns the impact of different appointment systems on judicial behaviour and judicialization. While some work, focused on the US context, has explored the politics of judicial appointments (e.g. Shipan and Shannon 2003; Cameron and Kastellec 2016), only a handful of studies have systematically explored how different systems of judicial appointment shape the willingness of judges to play an activist role (e.g. Tiede 2018).

Empirically, too, there are opportunities for pushing ahead. Perhaps most importantly, significant data limitations have hampered contributions to date. Systematic, large-N work on judicialization requires measures of judicial impact that can be collected across a large number of decisions and courts. For practical reasons, researchers have typically been forced to focus on simple measures that can be readily coded (such as the decision to uphold or strike down a law), but to neglect more nuanced—but theoretically relevant—features of judicial decisions that are fundamental to judicialization. Most obviously, quantitative research has typically not been in a position to examine the *content* of the legal rules that judges create, and the degree to which these rules constrain executive and legislative action. As a result, some critics have bemoaned a failure to 'take law seriously' (Friedman 2006). By focusing on a small number of decisions that can be closely examined, qualitative studies have, to some degree, filled this gap. But while these contributions have painted a rich and nuanced picture of the impact of particular decisions, it is difficult to assess to what extent these decisions reflect general trends. Recent methodological developments may provide an opportunity to move beyond this divide. The emergence of automated content analysis tools holds out the possibility that scholars may be able to develop measures that go beyond simple 'output' indicators to data that captures (some of) the legal nuance of judicial decisions (see Todd and Vanberg forthcoming). If so, a new frontier in judicial scholarship will open up as scholars can systematically examine the primary materials that define the interactions between judges and executive policy-makers: legal texts.

References

Baum, L. (1981). 'Comparing the Implementation of Legislative and Judicial Policies,' in Daniel Mazmanian and Paul Sabatier (eds) *Effective Policy Implementation*. Lexington: Lexington Books.

Bednar, J. (2005). 'Federalism as a Public Good,' *Constitutional Political Economy* 16: 189–205.

Bickel, A. (1962). *The Least Dangerous Branch*. New Haven: Yale University Press.

Brouard, S. and Hoennige, C. (2017). 'Constitutional Courts as Veto Players: Lessons from the United States, France, and Germany,' *European Journal of Political Research* 56: 529–52.

Budziak, J. and Lempert, D. (2018). 'Assessing Threats to Inference with Simultaneous Sensitivity Analysis: The Case of US Supreme Court Oral Arguments,' *Political Science Research and Methods* 6: 33–56.

Cameron, C., Kastellec, J., and Park, J. K. (2013). 'Voting for Justices: Change and Continuity in Confirmation Voting 1937–2010,' *Journal of Politics* 75: 283–99.

Cameron, C. and Kastellec, J. (2016). 'Are Supreme Court Nominations a Move the Median Game?,' *American Political Science Review* 110: 778–97.

Cappelletti, M. (1989). *The Judicial Process in Comparative Perspective*. Oxford: Oxford University Press.

Carrubba, Clifford J. (2009). 'A Model of the Endogenous Development of Judicial Institutions in Federal and International Systems,' *Journal of Politics* 71: 55–69.

Carrubba, C. and Gabel, M. (2015). *International Courts and the Performance of International Agreements*. Cambridge: Cambridge University Press.

Carrubba, C. and Zorn, C. (2010). 'Executive Discretion, Judicial Decision-Making, and Separation of Powers in the United States,' *Journal of Politics* 72: 812–24.

Chavez, R, Ferejohn, J., and Weingast, B. (2011). 'A Theory of the Politically Independent Judiciary,' in G. Helmke and R. Rios-Figueroa (eds) *Courts in Latin America*. Cambridge: Cambridge University Press.

Clark, T. (2011). *The Limits of Judicial Independence*. Cambridge: Cambridge University Press.

Dotan, Y. and Hofnung, M. (2005). 'Legal Defeats-Political Wins: Why Do Elected Representatives Go to Court?,' *Comparative Political Studies* 38: 75–103.

Durr, Robert H., Martin, Andrew D., and Wolbrecht, Christina (2000). 'Ideological Divergence and Public Support for the Supreme Court,' *American Journal of Political Science* 44: 768–76.

Elgie, R., McAuley, A., and O'Malley, E. (2018). 'The (Not-So-Surprising) Non-Partisanship of the Irish Supreme Court,' *Irish Political Studies* 33: 88–111.

Epp, C. (1998). *The Rights Revolution: Lawyers, Activists, and Supreme Courts in Comparative Perspective*. Chicago: University of Chicago Press.

Epstein, L. and Knight, J. (1998). *The Choices Justices Make*. Washington, DC: CQ Press.

Epstein, L., Knight, J., and Shvestova, O. (2001). 'The Role of Constitutional Courts in the Establishment and Maintenance of Democratic Systems of Government,' *Law and Society Review* 35: 117–64.

Epstein, L., Lindstädt, R., Segal, J. A., and Westerland, C. (2006). 'The Changing Dynamics of Senate Voting on Supreme Court Nominees,' *Journal of Politics* 68: 296–307.

Ferejohn, John (2002). 'Judicializing Politics, Politicizing Law,' *Law and Contemporary Problems* 65: 41–68.

Ferejohn, J. and Shipan, C. (1990.) 'Congressional Influence on Bureaucracy,' *Journal of Law, Economics, and Organization* 6: 1–20.

Friedman, B. (2002). 'The Birth of an Academic Obsession: The History of the Countermajoritarian Difficulty, Part Five,' *The Yale Law Journal* 112: 153–259.

Friedman, B. (2004). 'History, Politics, and Judicial Independence,' in A. Sajo (ed.) *Judicial Integrity*. Amsterdam: Koninklijke Brill NV.

Friedman, B. (2006). 'Taking Law Seriously,' *Perspectives on Politics* 4: 261–76.

Gibson, J. (1978). 'Judges' Role Orientations, Attitudes, and Decisions: An Interactive Model,' *American Political Science Review* 72: 911–24.

Gibson, James L. (1989). 'Understandings of Justice: Institutional Legitimacy, Procedural Justice, and Political Tolerance,' *Law and Society Review* 23: 469–96.

Gibson, James L. (1991). 'Institutional Legitimacy, Procedural Justice, and Compliance with Supreme Court Decisions: A Question of Causality,' *Law & Society Review* 25: 631–5.

Gibson, J., Caldeira, G., and Baird, V. (1998). 'On the Legitimacy of National High Courts,' *American Political Science Review* 92: 343–58.

Ginsburg, T. (2003). *Judicial Review in New Democracies: Constitutional Courts in Asian Cases*. Cambridge: Cambridge University Press.

Graber, M. (1993). 'The Nonmajoritarian Difficulty: Legislative Deference to the Judiciary,' *Studies in American Political Development* 7: 35–73.

Gulati, M. and Vanberg, G. (2019). 'Financial Crisis and Constitutional Compromise,' in T. Ginsburg, M. Rosen, and G. Vanberg (eds) *Constitutionalism in Times of Financial Crisis*. Cambridge University Press.

Helmke, G. and Rosenbluth, F. (2009). 'Regimes and the Rule of Law: Judicial Independence in Comparative Perspective,' *Annual Review of Political Science* 12: 345–66.

Hirschl, R. (2000). 'The Political Origins of Judicial Empowerment through Constitutionalization: Lessons from Four Constitutional Revolutions,' *Law and Social Inquiry* 25: 91–149.

Hirschl, R. (2004). *Toward Juristocracy*. Cambridge, MA: Harvard University Press.

Hirschl, R. (2008). 'The Judicialization of Mega-Politics and the Rise of Political Courts,' *Annual Review of Political Science* 11: 93–118.

Hoennige, C. (2007). *Verfassungsgericht, Regierung und Opposition. Die vergleichende Analyse eines Spannungsdreiecks*. Wiesbaden: VS Verlag.

Hoennige, C. (2008). 'Verfassungsgerichte in den EU-Staaten. Wahlverfahren, Kompetenzen und Organisationsprinzipien,' *Zeitschrift fuer Staats- und Europawissenschaften* 6: 524–53.

Ishiyama Smithey, S. and Ishiyama, J. (2002). 'Judicial Activism in Post-Communist Politics,' *Law and Society Review* 36: 719–42.

Kastellec, J. (2013). 'Racial Diversity and Judicial Influence on Appellate Courts,' *American Journal of Political Science* 57: 167–83.

Kelemen, D. (2019). 'Commitment for Cowards: Why the Judicialization of Austerity is Bad Policy and Even Worse Politics,' in T. Ginsburg, M. Rosen, and G. Vanberg (eds) *Constitutions in Times of Crisis*. Cambridge: Cambridge University Press.

Landfried, C. (1984). *Bundesverfassungsgericht und Gesetzgeber*. Baden-Baden: Nomos.

Mondak, Jeffery J. (1991). 'Substantive and Procedural Aspects of Supreme Court Decisions as Determinants of Institutional Approval,' *American Politics Quarterly* 19: 174–88.

Mondak, Jeffery J. (1992). 'Institutional Legitimacy, Policy Legitimacy, and the Supreme Court,' *American Politics Quarterly* 20: 457–77.

Murphy, W. (1964). *The Elements of Judicial Strategy*. Chicago: University of Chicago Press.

Ramseyer, J. M. (1994). 'The Puzzling (In)dependence of Courts: A Comparative Approach,' *Journal of Legal Studies* 23: 721–47.

Rogers, J. (2001). 'Information and Judicial Review: A Signaling Game of Legislative-Judicial Interaction,' *American Journal of Political Science* 45: 84–99.

Rogers, J. and G. Vanberg. (2002). 'Judicial Advisory Opinions and Legislative Outcomes in Comparative Perspective,' *American Journal of Political Science* 46: 379–97.

Rosenberg, G. (1992). 'Judicial Independence and the Reality of Political Power,' *The Review of Politics* 54: 369–98.

Salzberger, E. (1993). 'A Positive Analysis of the Doctrine of Separation of Powers, or: Why Do We Have an Independent Judiciary?,' *International Review of Law and Economics* 13: 349–79.

Segal, J. and Spaeth, H. (2002). *The Supreme Court and the Attitudinal Model Revisited.* Cambridge: Cambridge University Press.

Shapiro, M. (1981). *Courts: A Comparative and Political Analysis.* Chicago: University of Chicago Press.

Shipan, C. and Shannon, M. (2003). 'Delaying Justice(s): A Duration Analysis of Supreme Court Confirmations,' *American Journal of Political Science* 47: 654–88.

Spriggs, J. (1997). 'Explaining Federal Bureaucratic Compliance with Supreme Court Opinions,' *Political Research Quarterly* 50: 567–93.

Staton, J. (2006). 'Constitutional Review and the Selective Promotion of Case Results,' *American Journal of Political Science* 50: 98–112.

Staton, J. (2010). *Judicial Power and Strategic Communication in Mexico.* Cambridge: Cambridge University Press.

Staton, J. and Vanberg, G. (2008). 'The Value of Vagueness: Delegation, Defiance, and Judicial Opinions,' *American Journal of Political Science* 58: 504–19.

Stephenson, M. (2003). '"When the Devil Turns..." The Political Foundations of Independent Judicial Review,' *The Journal of Legal Studies* 32: 59–89.

Stephenson, M. (2004). 'Court of Public Opinion: Government Accountability and Judicial Independence,' *Journal of Law, Economics, and Organization* 20(2): 379–99.

Stone Sweet, A. (1992). *The Birth of Judicial Politics in France.* Oxford: Oxford University Press.

Stone Sweet, A. (2000). *Governing with Judges: Constitutional Politics in Europe.* Oxford: Oxford University Press.

Stone Sweet, A. (2002). 'Constitutional Courts and Parliamentary Democracy,' *West European Politics* 25: 77–100.

Tate, N. and Vallinder, T. (1995). *The Global Expansion of Judicial Power.* New York: New York University Press.

Taylor, M. (1979). *The Possibility of Cooperation.* Cambridge: Cambridge University Press.

Tiede, L. (2018). 'Mixed Appointments and Political Co-option on the Chilean and Colombian Constitutional Courts,' Typescript. University of Houston.

Todd, J. and Vanberg, G. (forthcoming). 'Automated Text Analysis in Judicial Politics,' in D. Kapiszewski and M. Ingram (eds) *Concepts, Data, and Methods in Comparative Law and Politics.* Cambridge: Cambridge University Press.

Tsebelis, G. (2002). *Veto Players: How Political Institutions Work.* Princeton: Princeton University Press.

Tyler, Tom R. and Kenneth Rasinski. (1991). 'Procedural Justice, Institutional Legitimacy, and the Acceptance of Unpopular US Supreme Court Decisions: A Reply to Gibson,' *Law and Society Review* 25: 621–30.

Vanberg, G. (1998). 'Abstract Judicial Review, Legislative Bargaining, and Policy Comprise,' *Journal of Theoretical Politics* 10: 299–326.

Vanberg, G. (2000). 'Establishing Judicial Independence in West Germany: The Impact of Opinion Leadership and the Separation of Powers,' *Comparative Politics* 32: 333–53.

Vanberg, G. (2001). 'Legislative-Judicial Relations: A Game-Theoretic Approach to Constitutional Review,' *American Journal of Political Science* 45: 346–61.

Vanberg, G. (2005). *The Politics of Constitutional Review in Germany*. Cambridge: Cambridge University Press.

Vanberg, G. (2008). 'Establishing and Maintaining Judicial Independence,' in G. Caldeira, D. Kelemen, and K. Whittington (eds) *Oxford Handbook of Law and Politics*. Oxford: Oxford University Press.

Vanberg, G. (2018). 'Constitutional Political Economy, Democratic Theory, and Institutional Design,' *Public Choice* 177: 199–216.

Whittington, K. E. (2003). 'Legislative Sanctions and the Strategic Environment of Judicial Review,' *International Journal of Constitutional Law* 1: 446–74.

Whittington, K. E. (2005). ' "Interpose Your Friendly Hand": Political Supports for the Exercise of Judicial Review by the United States Supreme Court,' *American Political Science Review* 99: 583–96.

Whittington, K. E. (2007). *Political Foundations of Judicial Supremacy*. Princeton: Princeton University Press.

....

CHAPTER 29

POLITICAL EXECUTIVES AND THE MEDIATIZATION OF POLITICS

....

DONATELLA CAMPUS

IN contemporary democracies no political executive can govern without gaining access to the media. As Strömbäck and Esser (2009: 214) write,

> Politics is about both power and policies. More importantly, politics is also about communication, and media communication is an integral part of all the dimensions that form what politics is about. Political actors, located within political institutions, consequently need to take the media into consideration, and the media might independently intervene, in all the processes and along all the dimensions that form politics.

This chapter discusses how the media logic influences the sphere of the political executive. Drawing from the research perspective of the mediatization of politics, the chapter focuses on two aspects: how the press portrays governments and governmental leaders and how political executives adapt to the media logic through a proactive process of self-mediatization. I review theoretical and empirical contributions that address these dominant questions in research on political executives and media, highlight the characteristics and the scope of the mediatization process, and address issues that might lead to future research developments, including the impact of the internet and the increasing role of entertainment media in the political field.

29.1 MEDIA LOGIC AND POLITICS

....

How can we characterize the relationship between political executives and the media? How can we evaluate the influence of media systems on the communication of government and chief executive leaders? In a seminal article Mazzoleni and Schulz (1999) applied the concept of mediatization to the political sphere. They defined mediatized politics as 'politics that has lost its autonomy, has become dependent in its central functions on mass media, and is continuously shaped by interactions with mass media' (p. 250). The concept of mediatization has, of course, been extensively elaborated and operationalized in many fields of media and communication research.[1] Given the special focus of this *Handbook*, this chapter only discusses its application to politics, and particularly to political executives.

Although there are some differences in interpretation,[2] most scholarship on mediatization of politics assumes that political actors, either as individuals or political organizations and institutions, have been increasingly guided by elements of the so-called media logic. Following from the groundbreaking book by Altheide and Snow (1979), Mazzoleni and Schulz (1999: 251) describe media logic as 'the frame of reference within which the media construct the meaning of events and personalities they report'. The media logic presupposes that media adopt specific formats consisting of how they produce their content: that is, how they select and organize the material they present. Formats are also frameworks to understand media: 'For a major medium such as television, audiences have become so familiar with different formats that they automatically know when something on television is news, comedy, or fictional drama' (Altheide and Snow 1979: 10). According to Esser (2013: 166 and ff.), the media logic originates from three constituents: *professional aspects*, that is, journalists adopt common norms regarding standards of newsworthiness and have shared beliefs about their mission; *commercial aspects*, that is, media are subjected to commercial influences that push them to enlarge their audience as much as possible; and *technological aspects*, that is, media technology conditions the production and presentation of news. Landerer (2013: 243) argues that the dimension of commercialization should be especially emphasized as it is 'the dominant logic behind the *logics* encompassed by the term "media logic"'. Whichever way we define media logic, the central point is how to assess its impact on political processes. Strömbäck (2008) and Strömbäck and Esser (2009) have provided a four-dimensional conceptualization and developed a theoretical framework of the mediatization of politics. They argue that the degree of influence of media logic on politics and political communication depends on the extent to which 'the requirements of the media take center stage and shape the means by which political communication and governing is played out by political actors, covered by the media, and understood by the people' (Strömbäck and Esser 2009: 214). However, they have also stressed that even if 'the

---

[1] On the mediatizaton of culture and society, see Hjarvard (2013). Lundby (2009) provides a review and a discussion of the concept in various fields and spheres of action. Couldry and Hepp (2013) make a useful distinction between the institutionalist and the social-constructivist traditions of research. The first assumes that media are independent institutions with their own rules and the mediatization concerns the adaptation of politics to those institutionalized rules. The second focuses on the role of various media in the process of constructing social and cultural realities. The two traditions are different, but Couldry and Hepp (2013) argue that they 'have come closer to each other in recent years' (p. 196).

[2] See Landerer (2013) for a discussion of the different definitions of mediatization of politics.

media have increased their status significantly at the expense of political actors and institutions', 'media influence is not unconditional' and is greater with respect to that component of the political logic which relates to strategies for winning public support[3] (Strömbäck and Esser 2014: 21) (see also Chapter 31 in this volume). Moreover, they argue, 'the impact of media logic on political actors, located within political institutions, varies both within and across countries and across time and circumstances' (Strömbäck and Esser 2009: 216).

Although media can be seen as primary agents of mediatization, politicians have adapted to the challenge through a sort of 'accommodation' process (Schulz 2004: 89–90). Indeed, 'often it is that political actors use the mass media for their own ends: they may anticipate media logic by staging events whose sole purpose it is to generate news coverage for their own interests; they may have an interest in playing down others in an effort to hurt the opposition; or they may substitute political activities by mediated activities if the latter allow them to mobilize their base more effectively than via party channels' (Esser and Matthes 2013: 178).

Instead of looking at the interplay between media and political media logics, Landerer (2013: 251) proposes a different conceptualization of mediatization by focusing on the 'audience-oriented market' logic, which should be regarded as the guiding principle for both politicians and the media. In his account, mediatization takes place 'when commercial logic dominates in media coverage and electoral logic dominates the day-to-day decision-making process'. As a result, on both sides, the market logic prevails over other normative ideals and concerns. It is worth noting, however, that 'the audience-oriented market logic in politics is facilitated by the commercialized mass media: the more commercial news companies are concerned with their sales volumes, viewing figures, and shareholders values, the easier it becomes for political actors to anticipate and to produce exactly what these companies are looking for' (Landerer 2013: 253).

Following from these conceptualizations of the relationship between media and politics, a comprehensive understanding of the consequences of mediatization for political executives implies two basic research questions. The first is how media have been agents of change in terms of the public representation of executive leaders, ministers and, in general, governments. The second is how media logic has influenced the communicative practices of the political executives. The next section of this chapter will analyse a number of studies that address these questions through the exploration of specific aspects and dimensions of governments-media relations. Some contributions are more theoretical, others more empirical. They cover a wide range of research topics, including media coverage, government communication strategies and activities, interactions between politicians and journalists, and effects of communication on public opinion.

---

[3] Esser (2013) adopts the triad—politics, policy, polity—originally developed in political science, to distinguish the different constituents of the political logic. News media are expected to report about all three aspects. Media logic is likely to affect more the front-stage dimension (politics) that concerns activities like gaining votes and building support.

Some of the studies reviewed in this chapter have been developed within the research perspective of mediatization and explicitly address the question of whether the media logic prevails or at least has any effects on political processes. Other research does not address directly the question of mediatization but nonetheless focuses on how changes in media technologies have influenced political practices. Some other contributions are relevant because they investigate phenomena that can be considered closely related to the mediatization process, like the personalization of politics or the professionalization of political communication. Not all of the research in this area accepts the proposition of the prevalence of the media logic. Indeed, some scholarship argues that the adaptation of politics to media demands should be seen as 'a function' of trends like professionalization or modernization and 'may obey just as much a "political" as a "media" logic' (Sanders et al. 2011: 525). Some findings seem to support the thesis of a remarkable presence of indicators of mediatization while other studies offer contrasting evidence. In sum, this review highlights several viewpoints concerning mass media influence on governance and leadership.

29.2 Key Research Questions

As Cook (1998) observes in a seminal book about the role of news media in American politics, presidents have a 'near-automatic news value' (134), being 'recognizable protagonists whose tribulations and triumphs can be a continuing saga in and of itself' (118). Not all chief executives are in the position to receive the world-scale attention given to US presidents; nevertheless, at least national news media focus on their governments and governmental leaders extensively, albeit with some variations across countries.[4] News visibility may, however depend on political internal power distribution (Hopmann et al. 2011). Such a privileged presence in the news supposedly originates from an 'incumbency bonus' that the press awards to leaders and parties in government (Hopmann et al. 2011; Green-Pedersen, Mortensen and Thesen 2017). During electoral times the fact that the presidential candidates, the top candidates for the position of prime minister, and the main candidates of each party are especially under the spotlight has encouraged some scholars to distinguish this 'concentrated visibility' (Van Aelst et al. 2012) or 'centralized personalization' (Balmas et al. 2014) as a separate dimension of the more general phenomenon of the personalization of politics. This section presents research on media representation of political executives before then returning to communicative practices of political executives.

---

[4] See Vos (2014) for a review of contributions on the news coverage of individual politicians. Vos and Van Aelst (2018) analyse the variation in media visibility of different types of politicians (including heads of government and cabinet members) across 16 Western democracies.

29.2.1 How Does Media Portray Political Executives?

Before discussing the details of media portrayal of governments and governmental leaders (including candidates for presidents or prime ministers), it is important to identify what characteristics of news coverage have been considered as indicators of the general degree of mediatization of news stories. In their review of the literature on the mediatization of news-media content, Esser and Matthes (2013: 181) emphasize that 'the dominance of media logic is often theorized to result in a simplification, dramatization, or negative representation of politics favoring conflict, scandals, and episodic over schematics frames'. Quite a similar list of items is presented by Maurer and Pfetsch (2014: 341), who carried out a cross national survey of high-ranking politicians and journalists to explore their perceptions about the phenomenon of mediatization. Their research suggests that 'political news coverage that is characterized by media logic typically oversimplifies complex issues, focuses on trivial aspects of politics, frames politics negatively, emphasizes political strategy over substance, stresses conflict rather compromise among actors, and mixes up political news and entertainment'.

Among the aforementioned indicators, one of the most extensively analysed is the media framing of politics as strategy and game.[5] According to Strömbäck and Dimitrova (2011: 36), research has shown that 'this kind of framing is driven by the media rather than by political actors', who would rather prefer to focus on issues. They conclude that 'the degree to which politics is framed as a strategic game or a horse race may be another indicator of the degree media content is mediatized'. To what extent is this relevant to the coverage of political executives? As observed by Aalberg et al. (2012: 165) 'most studies have documented the predominance of the game frame in elections news'. It can also be expected that the competition for top executive offices is represented as a horse race that is a central component of the 'game schema' (Patterson 1993: 97). However, the impact of such an approach goes beyond electoral times: it can be argued that 'the strategy frame is being generalized by journalists from campaigns to governance and discussions of public policy issues' (Cappella and Jamieson 1997: 33).[6] Based on her study of the framing of 1996 U.S. welfare reform, Lawrence (2000: 108) concludes that the game framing is applied to non-electoral contexts as well, albeit with different nuances depending on what stage of policy-making is concerned: 'What is significant is how the framing as well as the content of stories shifted in response to developments in Washington, again indicating that reporters typically apply certain frames to certain news contexts: when bills are being debated, news stories emphasize the strategy and progress of the political game; when bills become law, the substantive issues at stake are more fully explored'.

Frequently game framing 'embodies' a conflict dimension (Patterson 2000: 254). A focus on conflict often elicits a negative view of politicians since 'those cast as combatants are then portrayed as self-interested Machiavellians unconcerned with the public good' (Cappella and Jamieson 1997: 32). 'For reporters, controversy and conflict are the

---

[5] For a review see Aalberg et al. (2012).   [6] Quoted also by Lawrence (2000: 94).

real issues of politics. (...). It is not simply that the press neglects issues in favor of the strategic game: issues, even when covered, are subordinated to the drama of the conflict generated by the opposite sides' (Patterson 2000: 255). In such a perspective, governments are supposed to be leading actors due to their predominant positions in the decision-making process. However, as Van Dalen (2012) found, in those countries where journalists assign to conflict an intrinsic newsworthiness, oppositional politicians may get a voice in the news stories about government exactly because of their disagreement. In light of this, it could be argued that the well-grounded belief that a confrontational style is advantageous may condition the strategic choice of all political actors (Van Dalen 2012: 49). This research also highlights that evaluation of media power should include national differences in political systems and journalistic cultures. Although governments are presumed to receive more media attention in those contexts where the political executives are more powerful, Van Dalen shows that this tendency is affected and moderated by differences in national journalistic cultures. This conclusion is consistent with other studies that have stressed that news practices (including conflict-oriented reporting) are 'representations of institutionally developed pathways of journalism' (Esser and Umbricht 2013: 1003).

Another related feature of mediatization is the negative characterization of politics. Although it may be argued that negativity may also be triggered by politicians themselves, for instance as a consequence of their adversarial style or the adoption of anti-politics as a rhetorical register, negativity can be seen as largely media driven. As Lengauer et al. (2011: 181–3) point out, this phenomenon supposedly results from a number of factors: firstly, the rise of critical journalism; secondly, the journalists' reaction to politicians' news management (to protect their professional autonomy from attempts of manipulation); and thirdly, due to the commercialization of the news business, negativity can be regarded as a way of increasing audiences.

Several authors have expressed concern about potential consequences of negative reporting for how citizens view political executives. Cappella and Jamieson (1997) include negative coverage among the elements that may encourage public cynicism about politics and governments. Nye (1997: 17) argues that 'the way we get our information has had an effect in the political process which is likely to reduce confidence on government'. In sum, a media negative representation of politics presumably deteriorates relationships between government and citizens.

Finally, strategic news coverage tends 'to draw the audience's attention to the motivations of the people depicted' (Cappella and Jamieson 1997: 85). This can be seen as an aspect of a more general process of personalization of news coverage. To what extent the news coverage is focused more on politicians than on issues and political organizations? Are political leaders, in particular presidents and prime ministers (or in electoral time those running for the office), more visible than other political actors like parties? Are their personalities discussed by the press more than issues and ideologies? According to Esser and Matthes (2013: 182), the personalization thesis has intuitive appeal, but only limited empirical support. In an extended and accurate review, Van Aelst et al. (2012: 203) underline that 'the general belief is that the focus of news coverage has shifted from parties and organizations to candidates and leaders. However, evidence is far from conclusive. This is due in no small part to a lack of conceptual clarity and an absence of a common operationalization'. In order to arrive at a systematization of the subject they propose to distinguish between two forms of personalization: the *individualization*— 'individual politicians have become more central in media coverage, while parties and government institutions are less relevant'—and the *privatization*—' the politician is portrayed as private individual' with a special attention to the personal sphere and private life (Van Aelst et al. 2012: 206).

As for the shift of media focus on leaders, studies on US presidential elections offer evidence in favor of the existence of a personalization trend (Dalton et al. 2000), but findings concerning other countries are more mixed. On the basis of his literature review, Ohr (2011: 31) reaches the conclusion that 'for some countries and some indicators, there are slight indications that election campaigns and politics in the mass media have become more candidate-centred, even in the parliamentary democracies where political parties still maintain a strong position. Yet the gap between the presidential system of the United States and the parliamentary democracies is still quite large'. For instance, focusing on national election campaigns in six European countries, Kriesi (2012) argues there is no general trend 'to increasing concentration of the media coverage on a limited set of particularly visible personalities' (825). Rather, he found evidence of the 'incumbent bonus' as 'the members of government are more likely to be visible in public as individual actors than the members of the opposition' (836). According to Kriesi, however, this appears mainly due to 'an increasing relative neglect of the personalities of opposition parties' (841).

As for the privatization aspect, the main question is why the personal sphere of politicians is supposed to have a news value. A vast literature has discussed the role of media technological developments, in particular of television, in creating intimacy between politicians and citizens and removing the dividing line between the public and the private spheres (Meyrowitz 1985; Pels 2003). The increasing mix of different genres underlying the rise of infotainment formats and the popularization of politics (Van Zoonen 2005, Mazzoleni and Sfardini 2009) has paved the way for the rise of 'celebrity politicians' (Street 2004; Wheeler 2013), who can be seen as 'a manifestation of traditional institutional politics coming to terms with the media age and consumer culture' ('t Hart and Tindall 2009: 269). In light of all this, privatization can be considered as a part of a general process of mediatization.

But to what extent do news stories pay growing attention to the personal sphere and the private life of political leaders? Langer (2007), for example, found an increase of references to British Prime ministers' private life over time. In his book on intimate politics James Stanyer (2013) distinguishes three domains that belong to the personal sphere and can be the object of public scrutiny: the *individual domain*, that is, the inner life, life-style choices etc.; the *domain of relationships*, that is, family life, romance and friendships; the *spatial domain*, that is, holidays, off-duty locations etc. Stanyer shows that national differences persist for what concerns either the focus on the personal sphere or the level of media intrusion into politicians' intimacy (e.g. media covering sexual scandals). Holtz-Bacha et al. (2014) have explored two dimensions of personalization-visibility of top candidates/leaders and attention paid to personal characteristics and private life in Germany and the UK. Their results show a high visibility of the leaders of the main parties (but with variations across candidates in the same election) and the existence of an incumbent 'visibility bonus' in the case of the chancellor Merkel. Another finding is that political qualities are discussed in both countries while the discussion of personal qualities is more frequent in British coverage. In conclusion, Holtz-Bacha and colleagues argue that features of personalization vary depending on structural characteristics of the political system and the media market, as well as on individual factors, including the personal style of leaders.

29.2.2 How Do Political Executives Adapt to the Media Logic?

The key concept in describing the process of adaptation of political executives to the media logic is 'self-mediatization'. As argued by Esser and Matthes (2013: 192) 'political actors and organizations are under pressure to engage in self-mediatization because they causally attribute power to the media and their operating logic. The subjective perception of media power is sufficient to prompt changes in political behavior'. Along this line of reasoning it is assumed that democratic governments cannot avoid undertaking a process of self-mediatization. In order to gain citizens' support and approval, they need to communicate to the public. This can be accomplished through a wide range of activities,[7] the majority of which relies on media coverage. This gives rise to a sort of dependency since the media stage has become the primary place where political executives receive legitimacy for their actions (Esser and Strömbäck 2014: 230).

Cook (1998: 119) argues that political actors use media strategies as part of their governing strategies and observes that 'nowadays it is increasingly tough to envision government operating without the news media's communicative abilities or political actors whose functions do not include a sizable amount of mass-mediated communication'. Following Landerer's conceptualization of the mediatization of members of parliament (Landerer 2014: 305–306), it could be argued that political executives also can be tempted to adopt an 'audience-orientation' that consists of the combination of two elements: anticipation of voters' preferences as expressed in opinion polls and adaptation to commercial media's selection criteria.

The concept of self-mediatization implies that 'modern-day politicians have internalized the media's attention rules, production routines and selection criteria and try to exploit this knowledge for attaining political goals' (Esser 2013: 162). As far as political executives are concerned, this development has prompted governments to strengthen their media and public relations staff. Presidents, prime ministers, and other top

---

[7] For a general overview and references see Canel and Sanders (2012, 2013).

executives in government rely on public relations experts who are in charge of 'a process of self-initiated stage-management and media-friendly packaging' (Esser 2013: 162). Through efforts to master the media rules, politicians aim at 'regaining some of their lost autonomy' (Meyer 2002: 52). In this sense the self-mediatization process can be regarded as the result of a proactive attitude, since political actors are not 'objects of media influence and manipulation' but through 'anticipative and adaptive responses', they can 'take advantage of media functions and services and capitalize on media performance' (Schulz 2015: 61). Other scholars, however, are more pessimistic: Meyer (2002: 57) describes the self-mediatization as a part of a process of 'colonization' by which 'the logic of the media system does not simply restructure the way the political is portrayed in relation to other systems; it affects the political process at the "production" level, that is, where the political sphere emerges as a unique form of life'.[8] In sum, a number of scholars seem to believe that the process of self-mediatization has taken place, but the interpretation of its scope and limitations is not unanimous.

Nevertheless, since the process of internalizing media rules requires specific competence and skills, one may assume that the concept of professionalization lies at the core of the discussion of self-mediatization. Generally speaking, it has been suggested to regard professionalization 'as a general descriptor of a whole series of changes that have taken place over time that lead to what is perceived to be a more efficient and more sophisticated use of personnel and facilities for organization and communication' (Negrine 2007: 34). As far as political executives are concerned, 'improving practices may enable governments to deal more adequately with the process of governing in a global, media-saturated world' (Negrine 2007: 29). Sanders et al. (2011) presents a seminal and articulated attempt at developing a model of professionalization that can be specifically employed to analyse government communication. By taking into consideration both communication structures and processes, such as formal rules, human resources, and several communication practices, the authors found evidence of professionalization, albeit at varying speeds, in the three countries under analysis: Germany, Spain, and the UK. Such an analytical framework has been subsequently applied in a more extended exploration of government communication in 15 countries with the aim of identifying common cross-national trends (Sanders and Canel 2013).

I will now illustrate what communication practices can be directly related to the self-mediatization of political executives. First of all, contemporary governments engage in an activity of *news management*, a practice that 'sits at centre of the discussion of mediatization' (Brown 2011: 59). In Barbara Pfetsch's words, 'news management appears as one of the practical solutions for governments and other political actors to communicate strategically and use the media to further their political and policy goals' (Pfetsch 1998: 70). Accordingly, 'the approach of governments to public information has changed from a rather traditional press release policy—based on interpersonal exchanges between politicians and journalists—to a professionalized and specialized process of strategic communication controlling the flow of news' (71). As Davis (2001: 157) points out, it

---

[8] On the divergent viewpoints on self-mediatization see Esser and Strömbäck (2014, 230).

should be kept in mind that 'politicians cannot control the news'. Nonetheless, they can hope to influence it by employing several techniques such as assuring the availability of news for the press, staging events that can be attractive because of their being timely, dramatic, having good visuals, etc. (Davis 2001: 153–7).

In her analysis of government news management in three countries—the United States, the UK, and Germany—Pfetsch (1998: 73) distinguishes between two types of news management strategies: media centred vs. political. 'Media centered news management focuses directly and only on creating positive news coverage [...] the substance of the message is secondary'. By contrast,

> in political news management the strategic political objective are in the center of the strategy [...] the practical task of such news management would be to shape the message according to the political objectives of the executive vis à vis the other political parties and to maximize the political aspects in message production while minimizing the adaptation to the media.

In earlier work (1998: 89) Pfetsch stressed that factors such as the environmental context of the political system, the media system, and the media culture fostered different strategies of news managements. In the updated 2008 edition, she observes that, since the late 1990s, 'differences have become smaller' (2008: 91) so that 'the environment of government news management is becoming more and more conducive to the media-centered styles of communication' (p. 92). On the other hand, the importance of characteristics of national political-media systems have been demonstrated in a number of cases. According to Robin Brown (2011), for example, in Britain the conjunction of a competitive party system with a flexibly partisan media has encouraged an intensive news management whereas in the Netherlands the pillarization has limited the importance of government communication activities. As far as France is concerned, Raymond Kuhn (2005: 318) claims that 'there exists a French variant to news management at the executive level'.

In their efforts to influence news coverage, governments may be motivated by the desire to avoid blame (Weaver 1986). As discussed in the previous section, since the press tends to emphasize failures and liabilities of politics (Hood 2011: 9 and ff.), one may expect that office-holders employ 'strategic communications, and especially news management, as a defense against a more hostile "media-driven" "name, blame, and shame" environment'[9] (Garland 2017: 172). Hood (2011: chapter 3) offers a detailed catalogue of 'presentational strategies' that may be adopted to limit or avoid blame (e.g. offering justificatory arguments or denying problems, changing the subject and diverting attention, coming out with pre-emptive apology, restricting information, engaging only with media outlets likely to be friendly, and keeping a low profile). Another strategy is the use of blame shifting rhetoric or 'finding the scapegoat' (Weaver 1986) that attempts to pass the blame for controversial policies to someone else (such as past governments or supranational institutions like the EU).

---

[9] Lindquist and Rasmussen (2012: 188), quoted by Garland (2017: 172).

In principle, such communication strategies may be effective, but this is not necessarily the case. Helms (2008: 48) observes that

> the more recent history of presidential and prime ministerial communication sug-
> gests that the too-ready adoption of media styles and strategies by governmental
> leaders may do little to increase their leverage. This appears to apply in particular to
> defensive strategies of public leadership.

Helms takes Tony Blair as a paradigmatic example: Blair received so many criticisms for his spin-doctoring[10] that this strategy ended up diminishing his authority (see also Helms 2019: 274). Indeed, at a certain point, Blair felt that the public perception of the government's spin was so damaging that he announced a change in his government's communication approach (Franklin 2004). In general, as Brants and Voltmer (2011: 6) observe, 'professional news management has eventually undermined the foundation of cooperation between journalists and politicians. As political actors become more sophisticated at playing the media game journalists feel increasingly instrumentalized and threatened in their independence'.

This last development is related to the concept of *metacoverage*, as Esser et al. (2001: 39) define as 'the news media self-referential reflections on the nature of the interplay between political public relations and political journalism'. Metacoverage can be seen as 'a journalistic response to the mediatization of politics' (de Vreese and Elenbaas 2011: 77) insofar as news media react to the increasing efforts of politicians to set the agenda with the adoption of a sort of 'counterstrategy to prove their independence' (Esser et al. 2001: 41). Metacoverage may take the form of a description of politicians as 'strategy-oriented actors purposively seeking or eschewing media attention, or granting or blocking access to media, in order to achieve particular political objectives' (de Vreese and Elenbaas 2011: 78). To sum up, as Hood (2011: 64) observes in his discussion of the limits of the presentational approach to blame avoidance, 'investment in spin, rebuttal, and agenda management [...] is another of the many kinds of intervention in social affairs that turn out to have the reverse of their intended effect, at least some of the time'.

Existing analyses on how governments deal with the transformations of political communication have mostly concerned political chief executives—the activities of presidents and prime ministers (see also Chapter 32 in this volume). The national con-texts that have attracted the most significant attention are the US presidency and the British premiership. In the US, there is a vast and well-known literature that centres on the idea that communication is a key presidential resource (Tulis 1987; Campbell and Jamieson 2008).[11] With reference to government action, a seminal concept is that of 'going public' (Kernell 2007). It refers to the presidents' practice of direct public appeals to promote their policies. The emergence of this practice as a proper routine can be

---

[10] The term 'spin doctor' was coined in the 1980s (Garland 2017: note 1). As Esser et al. (2001: 26) illustrate, this neologism may be regarded as an example of metacommunication as it has been used by journalists not in a neutral way but often to discredit the activities of political public relations experts.

[11] For a review and discussion, see Stuckey (2010).

regarded as a consequence of a number of factors, including mass communication developments. As Kernell (2007: 2) writes, 'going public should be appreciated as a strategic adaptation to the information age'.[12]

Another concept developed in the US context as a useful analytical tool is that of 'permanent campaign' (Blumenthal 1980; Ornstein and Mann 2000). Here too there is an evident connection between the evolution of the media system and changes in government practices:

> The techniques of election campaigns—gathering intelligence, targeting audiences, promoting messages, rapid rebuttal—become part of the machinery of government as the ubiquity, speed and quantity of contemporary media result in governments making substantial institutional and personal investments in communication, employing communication specialists to advise on strategy and carry out communication functions. (Canel and Sanders 2012: 87)

An extended literature has analysed the transformations of the rhetoric strategies and communication practices of British prime ministers (Seymour-Ure 2003; Grube 2013: chapter 2). Especially Tony Blair is regarded as the prime minister who boosted all those communication activities that are supposed to reinforce the centrality of the executive leadership (Foley 2000; Heffernan 2006). Another case that has received scholarly attention is the French presidency. Raymond Kuhn (2005) examined presidential news management with a special focus on Chirac. He also analysed the cases of Nicolas Sarkozy and François Hollande and found differences in their degree of mediatization (Kuhn 2017).

Finally, an emerging literature deals with how a plurality of political and administrative actors in government settings responds to the media logic. Especially in parliamentary systems, the media relations of cabinet ministers and ministries appear to be a particularly interesting issue. Figenschou et al. (2017) examined ministerial communication in Norway and found evidence of a personalization that is determined by a number of factors, including developments and demands of the media (e.g. journalists prefer to interview and speak with ministers).

Garland (2017) has analysed the role of Whitehall press officers. Garland, Tambini, and Couldry (2017) have addressed the issue of the mediatization of the UK government by taking into consideration central governing bureaucracies. Other scholars have directed their attention to how government agencies internalize media logic into their activities (Friedriksson et al. 2015), how bureaucracies deal with the news media (Thorbjørnsrud et al. 2014), and how the media exert an influence on governance (Schillemans and Pierre 2016). The focus of this body of literature is, in Friedriksson and coauthors' words, 'not on the mediatization of "politics", but on "policies"' (Friedriksson et al. 2015: 1050). Therefore, even if we can suppose that the media logic primarily affects elected officers that need to invest in self-presentation efforts for electoral purposes, there is evidence that the media environment has an impact on the policy process at all levels.

---

[12] On the phenomenon of 'going public' in parliamentary democracies, see Helms (2008: 53–4).

29.3 Future Research Directions

Most of the theoretical and empirical studies reviewed in the previous sections are focused on the role of traditional media. First and foremost, television and its formats have been considered the driving force of mediatization. In recent years, however, digital media have been increasingly changing the media system. In such an evolving environment it is therefore reasonable to ask if the concepts of mediatization and media logic should not be revised (Mazzoleni 2017). Many scholars have advanced the thesis that the Internet offers new channels of interaction between politicians and citizens. Political actors now have more opportunities of providing news and information, bypassing the mediation of the press (Bentivegna 2015). As Schulz (2014: 67) observes, 'new media compete with the conventional mass media in defining the relevance of political issues and actors; even creating a new breed of celebrities. As a consequence, established power holders may benefit from the public visibility online'. On the other hand, 'political leaders and candidates, besides being challenged by the traditional media, face a new player in the political fray, that is the free flow of opinions expressed by citizens, followers and/or adversaries on social media' (Mazzoleni 2017: 141). Moreover, technology firms (i.e. Twitter, Facebook, and Google) are emerging new actors and active agents in political processes (Kreiss and MacGregor 2018).

A consequence of the arrival of digital media is the expansion of the boundaries of the space of political communication, where the traditional news media have now incorporated digital formats and coexist with a completely new offer of political information. Andrew Chadwick has developed the concept of 'hybrid media system' to describe the effects of digital communication on the relationship between political actors, media and publics. The hybrid media system lays the foundation for an integrated style of communication. The challenge of political actors and institutions is that of dealing with 'older and newer media logics' and traversing and combining these logics to exercise power (Chadwick 2013: 21). Therefore, the interactive dimension between online and offline may well reconfigure the dynamics between political and media logics. Not only is social media management a precious tool to complement traditional news management, but this can also prove to be crucial on many occasions. As Kreiss (2016) has pointed out in his analysis of the 2012 US presidential campaign on Twitter, what matters is 'seizing the moment' in the sense that well-timed and effective tweets may succeed in shaping the perception of the professional press at extraordinary moments. Such dynamics have been observed during elections, yet, in principle, journalists' interpretations could be influenced in non-electoral times as well. The potential of the use of social media as a part of the everyday news management should not be underestimated and deserves further exploration, although in most cases political leaders still appear to employ platforms like Facebook more extensively for campaigning than for governing, as shown by Ceccobelli (2018) in his comparative analysis of eighteen democracies.

To sum up, the abundance of platforms and outlets can be surely regarded as a resource, however it may also pose challenges to leaders and political executives. In this light, it is key that the research on the mediatization directs its attention to the impact of digital media in order to understand how internet has changed the relationship between governments and governmental leaders and the traditional news media, if governments are really less dependent on the traditional media, and the extent to which the vast opportunities are counterbalanced by new pressures and constraints.

Another open question about the effect of the mediatization on the political executive leadership concerns the topic of personalization. As already pointed out, this is one of the most discussed phenomena. Since the available research has not yet provided us with a coherent and conclusive set of findings, the nature, the extent and the impact of personalization requires further efforts. Following Van Aelst et al. (2012), the operationalization of the concept needs to take into consideration two sub-dimensions: individualization and privatization. Especially for privatization, it should be noted that details and disclosures about the personal sphere of politicians are channelled through many different types of media outlets, including popular press and entertaining television. Some studies have highlighted the role that photo-news magazines and even gossip magazines play in the presentation of political leaders as human beings—vastly portrayed on holidays, together with their family, etc. (Ciaglia and Mazzoni 2014; Mazzoni and Ciaglia 2014). In the French case, the *peopolisation* that has transformed presidents and presidential candidates into leading actors of the popular press is a very interesting phenomenon (Dakhlia 2008). Generally speaking, 'entertainment media offer resources (and pose challenges) for political action in addition to those presented by traditional media' (Lawrence and Boydstun 2017: 44). Geoffrey Craig (2016) underlines that the public performance of leaders occurs in multiple sites and a notable role is also played by interviews on soft media and entertainment-based talk shows. Therefore, a more comprehensive understanding of the personalization of politics should include more research analysing the vast and multifaceted world of entertainment formats.

Both the advent of digital technology and the trespassing of the boundaries between political and popular cultures point to a broadening of the media arena,[13] which can be regarded as a distinctive mark of contemporary times. Following Van Aelst and Walgrave (2017), the media arena can be characterized as a virtual place where politicians enter and perform (and where a good performance requires learning the media rules). The first aspect to be stressed is that contemporary chief executives need to be present almost everywhere: from the quality newspapers to the entertainment outlets, from the TV news to the social media. This implies acquiring different skills and adapting to different format rules. Yet one obstacle to the accomplishment of a well-integrated communication strategy is that not all leaders are able to be equally effective in each segment of the media arena. Variations may be due to personal attributes. Langer (2010), for example, stressed the notable differences between the public image of Tony Blair and Gordon Brown, suggesting that the politicization of private persona depends also on the characteristics and predispositions of individual leaders (see Chapters 14 and 24 in this

---

[13] On the need of broadening the media arena by including entertainment media, see Lawrence and Boydstun (2017) and Van Aelst and Walgrave (2017).

volume). Moreover, systemic and institutional features also create more or less favourable conditions for the successful use of a tool, a format or a platform. Several studies cited in the previous sections highlighted variations across countries that depend on characteristics of national political-media system. Quoting Baumgartner (2017: viii), there are 'so many moving parts'—differences in media outlets interact with systemic variations and multiple strategies by politicians and journalists. Besides, media diversification can encourage what Helms, following Kuhn (2005: 309), defined as 'a pick and mix approach designed to reach different target groups through different channels' (Helms 2008: 44). In conclusion, the investigation of the interplay between the personal attributes of leaders, their targetization strategies and the systemic factors should certainly be intensified.

Acknowledgements

The author is grateful to Gianpietro Mazzoleni for having read and commented an early version of the chapter.

References

Aalberg, T., Strömbäck, J., and de Vreese, C. (2012). 'The Framing of Politics as Strategy and Game: A Review of Concepts, Operationalizations and Key Findings,' *Journalism* 13(2): 162–78.

Altheide, D. and Snow, R. (1979). *Media Logic*. Beverly Hills: Sage.

Balmas, M., Rahat, G., Sheafer, T., and Shenhav, S. (2014). 'Two Routes to Personalized Politics: Centralized and Decentralized Personalization,' *Party Politics* 20(1): 37–51.

Baumgartner, F. (2017). 'Foreword: Political Actors and the Media,' in P. Van Aelst and S. Walgrave (eds) *How Political Actors Use the Media*. Houndmills: Palgrave Macmillan, v–viii.

Bentivegna, S. (2015). *A colpi di #Tweet. La politica in prima persona*. Bologna: Il Mulino.

Blumenthal, S. (1980). *The Permanent Campaign*. New York: Simon & Schuster.

Brants, K. and Voltmer, K. (2011) 'Introduction: Mediatization and De-centralization of Political Communication,' in K. Brants and K. Voltmer (eds) *Political Communication in Postmodern Democracy*. Houndmills: Palgrave Macmillan, 1–16.

Brown, R. (2011). 'Mediatization and News Management in Comparative Institutional Perspective,' in K. Brants and K. Voltmer (eds) *Political Communication in Postmodern Democracy*. Houndmills: Palgrave Macmillan, 59–74.

Campbell, K. K. and Jamieson, K. H. (2008). *Presidents Creating the Presidency: Deeds Done in Words*. 2nd ed. Chicago: University of Chicago Press.

Canel, M. and Sanders, K. (2012). 'Government Communication: An Emerging Field in Political Communication Research,' in H. Semetko and M. Scammell (eds) *The Sage Handbook of Political Communication*. London: Sage, 85–96.

Cappella, J. A. and Jamieson, K. H. (1997). *Spiral of Cynicism: The Press and the Public Good*. New York: Oxford University Press.

Ceccobelli, D. (2018). 'Not Every Day is Election Day:A Comparative Analysis of Eighteen Election Campaigns on Facebook,' *Journal of Information Technology & Politics* 15(2): 122–41.

Chadwick, A. (2013). *The Hybrid Media System*. Oxford: Oxford University Press.

Ciaglia, A. and Mazzoni, M. (2014). 'Pop-politics in Times of Crisis: The Italian Tabloid Press during Mario Monti's Government,' *European Journal of Communication* 29(4): 449–64.

Cook, T. (1998). *Governing with the News: The News Media as a Political Institution*. Chicago: University of Chicago Press.

Couldry, N. and Hepp, A. (2013). 'Conceptualizing Mediatization: Context, Tradition, Arguments,' *Communication Theory* 23(3): 191–201.

Craig, G. (2016). *Performing Politics: Media Interviews, Debates and Press Conferences*. Cambridge: Polity Press.

Dakhlia, J. (2008). 'La représentation politique à l'épreuve du people. Élus, médias et peopolisation en France dans les années 2000,' *Le Temps des Médias* 1(10): 66–81.

Dalton, R., McAllister, I., and Wattenberg, M. (2000). 'The Consequences of Partisan Dealignment,' in R. Dalton and M. Wattenberg (eds) *Parties without Partisans. Political Change in Advanced Industrial Democracies*. Oxford: Oxford University Press, 37–63.

Davis, R. (2001). *The Press and American Politics: The New Mediator*. 3rd ed. Upper Sadle River: Prentice Hall.

De Vreese, C. and Elenbaas, M. (2011). 'Spin and Political Publicity: Effects on News Coverage and Public Opinion,' in K. Brants and K. Voltmer (eds) *Political Communication in Postmodern Democracy*. Houndmills: Palgrave Macmillan, 75–91.

Esser, F. (2013). 'Mediatization as Challenge: Media Logic vs Political Logic,' in H. Kriesi, S. Lavenex, F. Esser, J. Matthes, M. Buhlmann, and D. Bochsler (eds) *Democracy in the Age of Globalization and Mediatization*. Houndmills: Palgrave Macmillan, 155–76.

Esser, F. and Matthes, J. (2013). 'Mediatization Effects on Political News, Political Actors, Political Decisions, and Political Audiences,' in H. Kriesi, S. Lavenex, F. Esser, J. Matthes, M. Buhlmann, and D. Bochsler (eds) *Democracy in the Age of Globalization and Mediatization*. Houndmills: Palgrave Macmillan, 177–201.

Esser, F. and Strömbäck, J. (2014). 'A Paradigm in the Making. Lessons for the Future of Mediatization Research,' in F. Esser and J. Strömbäck (eds) *Mediatization of Politics: Understanding the Transformation of Western Democracies*. Houndmills: Palgrave Macmillan, 223–42.

Esser, F. and Umbricht, A. (2013). 'Competing Models of Journalism? Political Affairs Coverage in US, British, German, Swiss, French and Italian Newspapers,' *Journalism* 14(8): 989–1007.

Esser, F., Reinemann, C., and Fan, D. (2001). 'Spin Doctors in the United States, Great Britain, and Germany,' *The International Journal of Press/Politics* 6(1): 16–45.

Figenschou, T., Karlsen, R., Kolltveit, K., and Thorbjørnsrud, K. (2017). 'Serving the Media Ministers: A Mixed Methods Study on the Personalization of Ministerial Communication,' *The International Journal of Press/Politics* 22(4): 411–30.

Foley, M. (2000). *The British Presidency*. Manchester: Manchester University Press.

Franklin, B. (2004). 'A Damascene Conversion? New Labour and Media Relations,' in S. Ludlam and M. Smith (eds) *Governing as New Labour. Policy and Politics under Blair*. Houndmills: Palgrave Macmillan, 88–105.

Friedriksson, M., Schillemans, T., and Pallas, J. (2015). 'Determinants of Organizational Mediatization: An Analysis of the Adaption of Swedish Government Agencies to News Media,' *Public Administration* 93(4): 1049–67.

Garland, R. (2017). 'Between Mediatisation and Politicisation: Can Whitehall Press Officers "Hold the Line"?' *Public Relations Inquiry* 6(2): 171–89.

Garland, R., Tambini, D., and Couldry, N. (2017). 'Has Government been Mediatized? A UK Perspective,' *Media, Culture & Society* 40(4): 496–513.

Green-Pedersen, C., Mortensen, P., and Thesen, G. (2017). 'News Tone and the Government in the News: When and Why Do Government Actors Appear in the News?,' in P. Van Aelst and S. Walgrave (eds) *How Political Actors Use the Media*. Houndmills: Palgrave Macmillan, 207–23.

Grube, D. (2013). *Prime Ministers and Rhetorical Governance*. Houndmills: Palgrave.

Heffernan, R. (2006). 'The Prime Minister and the News Media: Political Communication as a Leadership Resource,' *Parliamentary Affairs* 59(4): 582–98.

Helms, L. (2008). 'Governing in the Media Age: The Impact of the Mass Media on Executive Leadership in Contemporary Democracies,' *Government and Opposition* 45(1): 26–54.

Helms, L. (2019). 'When Less is More: "Negative Resources" and the Performance of Presidents and Prime Ministers,' *Politics* 39(3): 269–83.

Hjarvard, S. (2013). *The Mediatization of Culture and Society*. Abingdon: Routledge.

Holtz-Bacha, C., Langer, A., and Merkle, S. (2014). 'The Personalization of Politics in Comparative Perspective: Campaign Coverage in Germany and the United Kingdom,' *European Journal of Communication* 29(2): 153–70.

Hood, C. (2011). *The Blame Game: Spin, Bureaucracy, and Self-Preservation in Government*. Princeton: Princeton University Press.

Hopmann, D., De Vreese, C., and Albaek, E. (2011). 'Incumbency Bonus in Election News Coverage Explained: The Logics of Political Power and the Media Market,' *Journal of Communication* 61(2): 264–82.

Kernell, S. (2007). *Going Public: New Strategies of Presidential Leadership*. 4th ed. Washington, DC: CQPress.

Kreiss, D. (2016). 'Seizing the Moment: The Presidential Campaigns' Use of Twitter during the 2012 Electoral Cycle,' *New Media & Society* 18(8): 1473–90.

Kreiss, D. and McGregor, S. (2018). 'Technology Firms Shape Political Communication: The Work of Microsoft, Facebook, Twitter, and Google with Campaigns during the 2016 U.S. Presidential Cycle,' *Political Communication* 35(2): 155–77.

Kriesi, H. (2012). 'Personalization of National Election Campaigns,' *Party Politics* 18(6): 825–44.

Kuhn, R. (2005). 'Where's the Spin? The Executive and News Management in France,' *Modern & Contemporary France* 13(3): 307–22.

Kuhn, R. (2017). 'The Mediatization of Presidential Leadership in France: The Contrasting Cases of Nicolas Sarkozy and Francois Hollande,' *French Politics* 15(1): 57–84.

Landerer, N. (2013). 'Rethinking the Logics: A Conceptual Framework for the Mediatization of Politics,' *Communication Theory* 23(3): 239–58.

Landerer, N. (2014). 'Opposing the Government but Governing the Audience? Exploring the Differential Mediatization of Parliamentary Actors in Switzerland,' *Journalism Studies* 15(3): 304–20.

Langer, A. (2007). 'A Historical Exploration of the Personalisation of Politics in the Print Media: The British Prime Ministers (1945–1999),' *Parliamentary Affairs* 60(3): 371–87.

Langer, A. (2010). 'The Politicization of Private Persona: Exceptional Leaders or the New Rule? The Case of UK and the Blair Effect,' *The International Journal of Press/Politics* 15(1): 60–76.

Lawrence, R. (2000). 'Game-Framing the Issues: Tracking the Strategy Frame in Public Policy News,' *Political Communication* 17(2): 93–114.

Lawrence, R. and Boydstun, A. (2017). 'Celebrities as Political Actors and Entertainment as Political Media,' in P. Van Aelst and S. Walgrave (eds) *How Political Actors Use the Media*. Houndmills: Palgrave Macmillan, 39–61.

Lengauer, G., Esser, F., and Berganza, R. (2011). 'Negativity in Political News: A Review of Concepts, Operationalizations and Key Findings,' *Journalism* 13(2): 179–202.

Lindquist, E. and Rasmussen, K. (2012). 'Deputy Ministers and New Political Governance: From Neutral Competence to Promiscuous Partisans to a New Balance,' in H. Bakvis and M. Jarvis (eds) *From New Public Management to New Political Governance: Essays in Honour of Peter C. Aucoin*. Kingston: McGill/Queen's University Press, 179–203.

Lundby, K. (2009). 'Introduction: "Mediatization" as Key,' in K. Lundby (ed.) *Mediatization. Concept, Changes, Consequences*. New York: Peter Lang, 1–18.

Maurer, P. and Pfetsch, B. (2014). 'News Coverage of Politics and Conflict Levels,' *Journalism Studies* 15(3): 339–55.

Mazzoleni, G. (2017). 'Changes in Contemporary Communication Ecosystems Ask for a "New Look" at the Concept of Mediatisation,' *Javnost-The Public* 24(2): 136–45.

Mazzoleni, G. and Schulz, W. (1999). 'Mediatization of Politics: A Challenge for Democracy?,' *Political Communication* 16(3): 247–61.

Mazzoleni, G. and Sfardini, A. (2009). *Politica Pop*. Bologna: Il Mulino.

Mazzoni, M. and Ciaglia, A. (2014). 'An Incomplete Transition? How Italian Politicians Manage the Celebritisation of Politics,' *Celebrity Studies* 5(1–2): 93–106.

Meyer, T. (2002). *Media Democracy*. Oxford: Blackwell.

Meyrowitz, J. (1985). *No Sense of Place: The Impact of Electronic Media on Social Behavior*. Oxford: Oxford University Press.

Negrine, R. (2007). 'The Professionalisation of Political Communication in Europe,' in R. Negrine, P. Mancini, C. Holtz-Bacha, and S. Papathanassopoulos (eds) *The Professionalisation of Political Communication*. Bristol: Intellect, 27–45.

Nye, J. (1997). 'Introduction: The Decline of Confidence in Government,' in J. Nye, P. Zelikov, and D. King (eds) *Why People Don't Trust Government*. Cambridge, MA: Harvard University Press, 1–18.

Ohr, D. (2011). 'Changing Patterns in Political Communication,' in K. Aarts, A. Blais, and H. Schmitt (eds) *Political Leaders and Democratic Elections*. Oxford: Oxford University Press, 11–34.

Ornstein, N. and Mann, T. (2000) (eds). *The Permanent Campaign and Its Future*. Washington, DC: American Enterprise Institute.

Patterson, T. E. (1993). *Out of Order*. New York: A. Knopf.

Patterson, T. E. (2000). 'The United States: News in a Free-market Society,' in R. Gunther and A. Mughan (eds) *Democracy and the Media: A Comparative Perspective*. New York: Cambridge University Press, 241–65.

Pels, D. (2003). 'Aesthetic Representation and Political Style: Rebalancing Identity and Difference in Media Democracy,' in J. Corner and D. Pels (eds) *Media and the Restyling of Politics*. London: Sage, 41–66.

Pfetsch, B. (1998). 'Government News Management,' in D. Graber, D. McQuail, and P. Norris (eds) *The Politics of News: The News of Politics*. Washington, DC: Congressional Quarterly Press, 70–93.

Pfetsch, B. (2008). 'Government News Management: Institutional Approaches and Strategies in Three Western Democracies,' in D. Graber, D. McQuail, and P. Norris (eds) *The Politics of News. The News of Politics*. 2nd ed. Washington, DC: Congressional Quarterly Press, 71–97.

Sanders, K. and Canel, M. (2013) (eds). *Government Communication: Cases and Challenges*. London: Bloomsbury.

Sanders, K., Canel, M., and Holtz-Bacha, C. (2011). 'Communicating Governments: A Three-Country Comparison of How Governments Communicate with Citizens', *International Journal of Press/Politics* 16(4): 523–47.

Schillemans, T. and Pierre, J. (2016). 'Entangling and Disentangling Governance and the Media', *Party & Politics* 44(1): 1–8.

Schulz, W. (2004). 'Reconstructing Mediatization as an Analytical Concept', *European Journal of Communication* 19(1): 87–101.

Schulz, W. (2014). 'Mediatization and New Media', in F. Esser and J. Strömbäck (eds) *Mediatization of Politics: Understanding the Transformation of Western Democracies*. Houndmills: Palgrave Macmillan, 57–73.

Schulz, W. (2015). 'Mediatization of the Publicity Process', in S. Coleman, G. Moss, and K. Parry (eds) *Can the Media Serve Democracy?* Houndmills: Palgrave Macmillan, 53–62.

Seymour-Ure, C. (2003). *Prime Ministers and the Media: Issues on Power and Control*. Oxford: Blackwell.

Stanyer, J. (2013). *Intimate Politics: Publicity, Privacy and the Personal Lives of Politicians in Media Saturated Democracies*. Cambridge: Polity Press.

Street, J. (2004). 'Celebrity Politicians. Popular Culture and Political Representation', *The British Journal of Politics and International Relations* 6(4): 435–52.

Strömbäck, J. (2008). 'Four Phases of Mediatization: An Analysis of the Mediatization of Politics', *The International Journal of Press/Politics* 13(3): 228–46.

Strömbäck, J. and Dimitrova, D. V. (2011). 'Mediatization and Media Interventionism: A Comparative Analysis of Sweden and the United States', *The International Journal of Press/Politics* 16(1): 30–49.

Strömbäck, J. and Esser, F. (2009). 'Shaping Politics: Mediatization and Media Interventionism', in K. Lundby (ed.) *Mediatization. Concept, Changes, Consequences*. New York: Peter Lang, 205–23.

Strömbäck, J. and Esser, F. (2014). 'Mediatization of Politics: Towards a Theoretical Framework', in F. Esser and J. Strömbäck (eds) *Mediatization of Politics. Understanding the Trasformation of Western Democracies*. Houndmills: Palgrave Macmillan, 3–28.

Stuckey, M. (2010). 'Rethinking the Rhetorical Presidency and Presidential Rhetoric', *Review of Communication* 10(1): 38–52.

't Hart, P. and Tindall, K. (2009). 'Leadership by the Famous: Celebrity as Political Capital', in J. Kane, H. Papatan, and P. 't Hart (eds) *Dispersed Democratic Leadership: Origins, Dynamics, and Implications*. Oxford: Oxford University Press, 255–78.

Thorbjørnsrud, K., Figenschou, T., and Ihlen, Ø. (2014). 'Mediatization in Public Bureaucracies: A Typology', *Communications* 39(1): 3–22.

Tulis, J. (1987). *The Rhetorical Presidency*. Princeton: Princeton University Press.

Van Aelst, P. and Walgrave, S. (2017). 'Information and Arena: The Dual Function of News Media for Political Elites', in P. Van Aelst and S. Walgrave (eds) *How Political Actors Use the Media*. Houndmills: Palgrave, Macmillan, 1–17.

Van Aelst, P., Sheafer, T., and Stanyer, J. (2012). 'The Personalization of Mediated Political Communication: A Review of Concepts, Operationalizations and Key Findings', *Journalism* 13(2): 203–20.

Van Dalen, A. (2012). 'Structural Bias in Cross-national Perspective: How Political System and Journalism Cultures Influence Government Dominance in the News', *The International Journal of Press/Politics* 17(1): 32–55.

Van Zoonen, L. (2005). *Entertaining the Citizen: When Politics and Popular Culture Converge*. Lanham: Rowman & Littlefield.

Vos, D. (2014). 'Which Politicians Pass the News Gates and Why? Explaining Inconsistencies in Research on News Coverage of Individual Politicians,' *International Journal of Communication* 8: 2438–61.

Vos, D., and Van Aelst, P. (2018). 'Does the Political System Determine Media Visibility of Politicians? A Comparative Analysis of Political Functions in the News in Sixteen Countries,' *Political Communication* 35(3): 371–92.

Weaver, R. K. (1986). 'The Politics of Blame Avoidance,' *Journal of Public Policy* 6(4): 371–98.

Wheeler, M. (2013). *Celebrity Politics: Image and Identity in Contemporary Political Communication*. Cambridge: Polity Press.

CHAPTER 30

INTEREST GROUPS AND LOBBYING IN POLITICAL EXECUTIVES

DİRENÇ KANOL

30.1 INTRODUCTION: WHAT IS IT THAT WE WANT TO KNOW?

INTEREST groups have close interactions with political executives in democratic, hybrid, as well as authoritarian regimes. In democracies, lobbying occurs naturally as people have the basic freedoms of association, free speech, and political participation. In more authoritarian regimes, the state may co-opt interests. However, this does not mean that interest groups do not have influence on authoritarian governments' decisions. Without studying the connections between interest groups and political executives, one cannot paint a complete picture of how any political executive works. Political executives and interest groups need each other to accomplish their political and policy goals. Important actions taken by top-level bureaucrats, ministers, and heads of states might be influenced by interest groups. These actions are not just confined to domestic politics but are related to international politics too (Milner 1987). Interest groups, in return, might serve as soldiers for executives, gathering information for them or helping them implement policies.

The question of who gets access to and have influence on political executives can have significant normative consequences which experts of political executives should put to debate. This debate goes beyond the study of election outcomes and may show who really governs and how they govern. Normative implications of interest groups' policy work have caught attention of interest group scholars since decades subsequently leading to denouncement of the pluralist theory in its purest form by many scholars. The most renowned work which triggered this denouncement among the scholarly community is arguably *The Semisovereign People: A Realist's View of Democracy in America* authored by Elmer Eric Schattschneider in 1960. This book has helped surface the disparagement of the naïve assumption that creating an opportunity for all types of interests in a society to form groups would lead to an actual equal opportunity for influencing policy. If wealth creates capacity for certain interests to mobilize, carry out daily activities, and transform their effort into actual policy influence, which it does, then the pluralist assumption in notable studies by David Truman (1951) and Robert E. Dahl (1961) was flawed. Schattschneider's (1960) argument about upper-class accent in the American pluralist interest mediation system has fared well in recent empirical research. Policies in the US seem to be tilted towards wealthy business interests (Gilens and Page 2014). This raises concern that one man, one vote strategy does not lead to political equality and it contributes to the argument that we are living in a post-democracy (Crouch 2000).

Researchers have asked multiple interesting questions about interest groups and lobbying in political executives: Do presidencies establish contact with outside interests? What are some different strategies presidencies can follow to communicate with interest groups? When do interest groups lobby the executive? Is the nature of relationship between interest groups and the presidency different than that of other branches of government? What types of groups have access to and influence on the executive branch? How has the level of corporatism changed over time? What are the effects of corporatism on policy outputs? How does party complexion of the government affect interest group behaviour? Do ministers and bureaucrats become lobbyists after employment in the public sector? If so, how does this benefit the company or group they work for? Does this cause policy capture? How can lobbying regulation curb the negative effects of lobbying? Some scholars also examined how political executive types (e.g. presidentialism, semi-presidentialism, parliamentarism, political executives in federal states vs. unitary states, single party vs. coalition governments, political executives in democratic, authoritarian, and hybrid regimes) affect lobbying behaviour and success. They asked questions like: How does divided government affect lobbying behaviour? How does decentralization of the executive power affect lobbying strategies and group influence?

There are succinct book chapters and even book length studies on lobbying the American presidency (e.g. Pika 1983; Furlong 2005; Loomis 2009; Brown 2012). These studies contribute to the development of theoretical perspectives on lobbying the executive branch. Here, an attempt will be made to complement these studies by making a comparative review of interest groups and lobbying in political executives. The next section starts with a review of the working definitions of the interest group and lobbying concepts. It then continues with a discussion of the state of revolving-door activities and lobbying regulation. After reviewing the limited research on how political executive types affect interest groups and lobbying, the chapter then devolves into delivering some examples of lobbying the executive branch. Next, the effects of interest group mediation systems (corporatism vs. pluralism), which define how political executives deal with non-state actors, is discussed. Afterwards, interest groups' decision to target political executives, the peculiarities of lobbying the executive branch, and the executive strategies for dealing with interest groups is discussed. The author, then, reviews the literature on how party complexion of the government influences interest group strategies. In the third and final section, avenues for future research about the relationship between interest groups and different political executive types, and interest groups' impact on policy outcomes are discussed.

30.2 What Do We Already Know?

The simplest way to describe the interest group concept would be to rely on Truman's (1951) understanding of how interest groups are formed in pluralist societies. Interest groups are composed of a set of individuals who have a common interest which can only be achieved by collective action. Interest groups use different strategies to pursue these interests which primarily include lobbying. Not all scholars use this definition, however, as there are three distinct ways of conceptualizing the interest group concept which includes or excludes certain types of organizations as interest groups.

According to the behaviouralist understanding, interest groups are organizations which use lobbying strategies to influence public policies. These organizations do not need to have individuals or organizations as members to be called interest groups, however, they must lobby to shape public policies. Thus, these organizations can be privately owned companies without members but shareholders if they lobby. It is their political behaviour which makes them interest groups. Organizational definition of interest groups, on the contrary, do not define interest groups based on how they behave but their organizational structure. According to the organizational approach, interest groups are organizations which have members. It is having members, not lobbying, which makes an organization an interest group (Jordan et al. 2004). A third way of con-ceptualization is considering both the behavioural and organizational characteristics. To be called an interest group, an organization must have members and engage in activities which aim to influence public policies. These are both necessary conditions for an organization to be considered an interest group (Baroni et al. 2014).

Lobbying is the act of political influence seeking by organized interests. Lobbyists can be interest groups which lobby directly or via their 'hired guns', public affairs companies which are employed by companies and other organized interests. In the literature, there are two main types of lobbying. Inside lobbying creates a direct mechanism of infor-mation flow from the interest group to the governmental actors. Lobbyists can arrange face-to-face meetings or on-the-phone discussions with the prime minister or the president (depending on the political executive type), ministers, or top-level bureaucrats to provide 'input' to specific policies. Outside lobbying, on the other hand, would be con-tacting reporters, organizing demonstrations, petitions, or boycotts (Binderkrantz 2005).

Legislators, ministers, and bureaucrats landing a job in the private sector (e.g. public affairs or consultancy companies, board membership or CEO position in big companies, advisor of big business, etc.) have raised public concern in different countries. Recently, we have witnessed a burgeoning literature on this phenomenon which is known as revolving door. Most of these studies have studied the career patterns of members of Congress or parliamentarians, however, research about ministers and top-level bureaucrats moving to the private sector is also available (see Vaubel et al. 2012; Claveria and Verge 2015; Baturo and Mikhaylov 2016; Dörrenbächer 2016). In some countries like Ireland, revolving door is more common among ministers and top-level civil servants than parliamentarians (Baturo and Arlow 2018). Moreover, Thomas and LaPira (2017) argued that the number of lobbyists who are not registered as such—'shadow lobbyists'—in the US is higher among ex-politicians and civil servants in the executive branch compared to the legislative branch.

In Germany, of all the ministers and chancellors who took office between 1949 and 2014, 18 per cent took jobs in revolving door positions. In a cross-national study of twenty-three countries, mostly covering European countries, Claveria and Verge (2015) found that the percentage of ministers employed in business after their public career was 10.2 per cent. Similarly, Baturo and Mikhaylov (2016) found that 14 per cent of heads of states and governments have turned to a business career in democratic countries between 1960 and 2016. In the European Union, 39 per cent of former European commissioners who served between 1981 and 2009 then took up a public affairs position (Vaubel et al. 2012; see also Chapter 17 in this volume).

Revolving door has critical normative implications for political equality and government effectiveness. Heads of states, ministers, and civil servants might be influenced by financially sound employment opportunities in the private sector after they leave office. Therefore, they might be inclined to formulate, or implement policies that are biased towards certain companies and groups. This, of course, disrupts the political equality concept which is a cornerstone of any healthy democracy. Moreover, ex-ministers or bureaucrats can use their connections whom they have made during public office to influence policy processes when they lobby. For example, one study found that a private South Korean university which employed an ex-vice minister of education received significantly more funding from the Ministry of Education (Hong and Lim 2016). Such a scenario which involves policy capture by ex-public-sector officials can also result in sub-optimal policies. The military-industrial complex theory, for example, argues that the revolving door between ex-military professionals and arms industry which lobby the government have contributed to the growth of military spending and the arms race (Dunne and Sköns 2010; Duncan and Coyne 2015).

Governments can regulate the lobbying process by defining rules for lobbyists who want to contact governmental actors. These rules can oblige any organized interest with the aim of influencing public policy to register on a publicly available list before contacting any policy official. Depending on the regulation, these interests may have to report whom they want to contact, the issues they want to discuss, and money spent on lobbying within a specific period. Lobbying regulation can also ban gift giving to public actors. Revolving door regulation, that is, introducing 'cooling-off' periods which ban civil servants and politicians from taking a public affairs post for a certain period after employment in the public sector is also a form of lobbying regulation. The number of countries which have lobbying regulation has increased drastically in the twenty-first century. However, content, implementation, and effectiveness of regulation have been criticized by policy analysts (Chari et al. 2010; Vargovčíková 2017; Bunea 2018; Năstase and Muurmans 2018). Nevertheless, experimental research shows that if implemented correctly, lobbying regulation can alleviate the anti-politics sentiment among people (Kanol 2018). Moreover, 'cooling-off' periods which regulate politicians' and other public-sector workers' post-employment practices can alleviate the negative consequences of revolving door by limiting the number of politicians turning lobbyists (Cain and Drutman 2014). Therefore, regulating lobbying and revolving door activities is of utmost importance for the ideal of good governance.

Although we don't know exactly to what extent, we know that political institutions can shape lobbying behaviour and success (Kanol 2015a; Hanegraaf et al. 2017). The degree of difficulty in passing legislation or democratic accountability can affect lobbying behaviour and success (Mahoney 2008). Interest groups' decision to lobby politicians or bureaucrats can be influenced by electoral system type (Naoi and Krauss 2009). Institutions of direct democracy can increase the access of citizen groups to policy process (Weiler and Brändli 2015). Lobbying behaviour can also be shaped by the degree of power of political parties in controlling the policy process (Yadav 2011).

The type of political executive also shapes interest group activity. Both the horizontal and vertical distribution of political power affects lobbying. For example, the higher the number of veto players, the harder it is to change policies, especially when there are opposing views among veto players (Tsebelis 1995). The lobbying process is also expected to be complicated when there are multiple veto-players with different policy preferences. Divided government, which is a characteristic of presidential systems, compels groups to lobby at multiple levels to fight potential obstacles which could emerge as a result of the increased number of veto players (Constantelos 2018). Lobbying does not only change based on the horizontal distribution of power. Since regions are stronger in decentralized countries, interest groups are more likely to target the regional governments than in centralized countries (Constantelos 2007). This vertical power-sharing might make lobbying more burdensome as interest groups might have to lobby at multiple levels. However, decentralization can provide more entry points for organized interests, thus, potentially increasing their influence on policies (Choi and Lu 2015; see also Chapter 33 in this volume).

Although research about interest groups and lobbying in the executive branch is not new (see Pika 1983; Wolman and Teitelbaum 1984; Lucco 1992), there are fewer studies and relatively limited knowledge compared to research on interest groups and lobbying in the legislative branch (Loomis 2009). Political executives have both legislative and executive functions. Avenues of influence are available during agenda-setting (Piotrowski and Rosenbloom 2005), grant-making (Lowry and Potoski 2004; Leech 2006), appointment process (Sorge 2015), presidential transition (Brown 2011), and rule-making (Yackee 2006; McKay and Yackee 2007). Studies about lobbying the White House demonstrate unequivocal interest by interest groups (Heinz et al. 1993;

Boehmke et al. 2013). Richard M. Nixon assigned formal tasks to his staff during his presidency with respect to finding ways to communicate with interest groups. The title 'public liaison' was invented under the Ford administration. The Office of Public Liaison has been sort of a public relations unit of the presidents for attending to their relationships with organized interests (Pika 2009). However, each president might have his own way of interacting with lobbyists. Barack Obama, for example, was highly critical of policy capture and tried to restrict access to the White House, although with limited success (Thurber 2011; Brown 2012; Straus et al. 2015).

Rule-making agencies working under the ministers are responsible for making rules. Even though the statutes passed through the Congress form the main framework for laws, rules created by rule-making agencies transform such broader statutes into specific rules which are implementable with specificity about the content and clarity about the procedures to be followed. These rules are not only more specific than legislations, but also of greater number and once they are issued, they come into effect much sooner (Furlong and Kerwin 2005). Interest groups perceive these agencies as of utmost importance for exerting influence on government policies (Furlong 1997; Furlong and Kerwin 2005; Boehmke et al. 2013).

A significant number of lobbying activities take place after the Congress votes on legislation (You 2017). One might expect a considerable amount of these *ex post* lobbying activities to be directed at rule-making processes. Interest groups in the US can also lobby the President's Office of Management and Budget during its review of the rule-making processes (Haeder and Yackee 2015). Research shows that citizen interests are less likely to be active and influential in rule-making procedures and President's Office of Management and Budget's review of rule-making. Business interests are argued to be the dominant non-state actors in administrative lobbying (Golden 1998; Yackee and Yackee 2006; Boehmke et al. 2013; Haeder and Yackee 2015).

Interest mediation systems have implications for the methods the executive branch uses to establish contacts with interest groups and which interest groups they talk to. Tenpas (2005) differentiated between two types of communication between the presidency in the US and interest groups. The first form, which is intuitive for most scholars familiar with the lobbying literature is named 'outside-in'. Here, interest groups use different inside and outside lobbying strategies to gain access and exert influence on the presidency. Not all groups can have the privilege of being an 'insider', and groups which have no access to the presidency can use the media or mobilize the public to influence the presidency. The second, and more unusual, type of communication is named 'inside-out'. Here, it is the presidency which initiates action and lobby the interest groups, not the other way around. Presidents do this because, first, they have the capacity to do so; second, to steer the society to achieve their policy objectives; and, third, to increase re-election prospects by gaining popular support. Interest groups are important for presidents as they can affect presidential approval (Cohen 2012).

Schmitter (1974) used the term corporatism which exists in some of the European countries like Austria and Sweden for differentiating it from the Anglo-Saxon style laissez-faire interest mediation system. Corporatism, as opposed to the pluralist system like that of the US or the UK, gives a more active role to the government in deciding which interest groups should participate in policy processes. In corporatism, interest groups are authorized to carry out certain functions by the state and their access to and influence on the policy processes can be shaped by the governments. In pluralist systems, however, governments are expected to hear as wide a community of groups as possible, although they might still decide whose voice they should take into account. Traits of corporatist governance process can be observed more often in parliamentary systems with proportional representation which pave way for coalition governments with participation of social democrat parties and politicians. Corporatist interest mediation system is more compatible with Lijphart's consensus types of democracy, whereas pluralist interest mediation system is more compatible with majoritarian types of democracy (Lijphart and Crepaz 1991).

An exemplar of corporatist elements in the way political executives deal with interest groups is the wage bargaining process. Peak business associations and labour unions are regularly invited to participate in meetings to set the minimum wage and thus, shape the national economy. By doing this, executives deliberately choose to grant access and offer the chance of meaningful influence for certain groups, while depriving others of this privilege. It is interesting to observe that corporatism combines both 'outside-in' and 'inside-out' communication by political executives to use Tenpas' (2005) terminology. Ministers, business associations, and labour unions sit around a table together and actors try to persuade each other. In line with governance models, the role of the government is to mediate between these two opposing groups and steer the society. The ministers are influenced by what these groups have to say, and they also aim to influence the groups to get their support. One should mention that it is not only business associations and labour unions which are granted institutionalized access in corporatist systems. Christiansen et al. (2018) have observed greater participation by citizen groups in corporatist settings over the years.

Some studies found a decline in corporatism over time (Christiansen and Rommetvedt 1999; Öberg et al. 2011; Rommetvedt et al. 2013) whereas others have found a cyclical change where there can be decline in corporatism in some countries, but at the same time, rise in other countries (Schmitter 1989; Jahn 2014). Studies usually found a positive impact of corporatism on important outputs like economic performance (Bruno and Sachs 1985; Wilensky 2002), social policy (Huber and Stephens 2001; Iversen 2005) and environmental performance (Jahn 1998; Scruggs 2001).

Venue-shopping means organized interests choosing different political arenas to advocate for their interests (Holyoke et al. 2012). Interest groups can switch their lobbying activities to a different venue based on the political opportunity structures available at a certain time. If a group faces barriers in accessing the legislative branch, for example, the group might shift its target towards the executive branch. Or, if a group has limited access at the regional level, it might try to get access at the national level. There are, of course, groups which lobby at multiple arenas at the same time to increase their chances of exerting influence on policies. However, not all groups are able to do this as lobbying at multiple arenas is a resource intensive activity (Holyoke et al. 2012).

Scholars have observed the use of venue-shopping strategies both in the US and the EU (Greene and Heberlig 2002; Beyers and Kerremans 2012). Choosing which venue to pursue one's interests depends on various factors exogenous to the characteristics of the institution one aims to lobby (Holyoke 2003; Kanol 2016a; Jourdain et al. 2017). Still, it might be a fallacy to accept lobbying one branch of government to be the same thing as lobbying another (McKay 2011). Holyoke (2004) understands the process of lobbying the executive branch to be unique. The author contends that the exchange model of lobbying which applies to lobbying the Congress does not apply to lobbying the White House. Holyoke (2004) cites three reasons for this. First, the presidency has access to more resources which provide it with the much-needed information that the Congress does not possess. Second, presidents face constant scrutiny by the media and Civil Society Organisations (CSOs) and should be more careful not to be associated with lobbyists. Finally, interest groups have fewer incentives to establish contact with the presidency since the number of staff in the White House is lower than that of the Congress and the White House has higher rate of turnover. Presidents are more dependent on good relations with interest groups than the members of Congress, and it is usually the presidents who initiate contact, not the other way around (Holyoke 2004).

According to Peterson (1992), presidents need to decide the *breadth* of their relationship with outside interests. They can choose to follow an *exclusive* strategy by establishing contacts with their ideological friends, or an *inclusive* strategy, by granting access to as wide a body of interest groups as possible. With respect to their *substantive focus*, presidents can have either a *programmatic focus* or a *representational focus*. Presidencies with a *programmatic focus* concentrate on their relationship with key interest groups which can influence the decision-making and implementation processes. Their priority is to pass and implement their policies smoothly, and they need the support of powerful groups to do this. Presidencies with a *representational focus*, however, are more politically oriented than policy-oriented. Their aim is to get the support of key interest groups which can then create support of their members for the president in key constituencies.

If presidencies combine an inclusive strategy with a representational focus, they follow an interest group liaison as *legitimisation*. If they combine an inclusive strategy with a programmatic focus, they follow an interest group liaison as *consensus building*. Interest group liaison as *outreach* combine a representational focus with an exclusive set of interest groups. Finally, interest group liaison as *governing party* follows a programmatic approach with an exclusive set of groups. It should be noted that presidents can shift from one type of strategy towards another (and back) during their time in office. The type of strategy to be followed by the presidency depends on various complex institutional, economic, social, and political factors (Peterson 1992).

Peculiarities of the government branches result in different groups targeting and/ or gaining access to different arenas (Salisbury 1984; Bouwen 2004; Schuler and Rehbein 2011; Halpin et al. 2012). Group type, resources, institutions, and policy goals can determine if a group will pursue policy influence in the legislative or administrative branch (Binderkrantz and Krøyer 2012; Pedersen et al. 2014; Binderkrantz et al. 2015). Getting access to and chances of being successful at the administrative arena is more common for insider groups which possess critical information and have expertise in multiple issues (Pedersen et al. 2014; Binderkrantz and Pedersen 2019). Research in Europe shows that administrative actors need technical expertise more than political support, so they grant access to groups which possess such expertise. Sectional groups, and especially business groups, possess such expertise more than public interest groups. Therefore, public interest groups like Non-governmental organizations (NGOs) seek and find access routes in the parliamentary arena more, whereas sectional groups like business associations, labour unions, and professional associations put more effort into lobbying and are relatively more successful at the administrative arena (Beyers 2004; Binderkrantz et al. 2015; Dür and Mateo 2016). Trying to sway policies in favour of special interests and technical goals, as opposed to swaying them in favour of general interests and simple goals are more common at the administrative battleground (Binderkrantz and Krøyer 2012).

The change in party complexion of the government within or between countries is one of the determinants of who lobbies the executive branch of the government. Like political parties, interest groups are associations of people who believe in a certain type of society. Socialist parties would like to see workers obtaining more rights, similarly, labour unions desire a society with stronger workers' rights. Green parties want to protect the environment, so do environmental NGOs. Socially conservative parties oppose, for example, the right to abortion, so do socially conservative groups. Economically liberal parties believe in the free market with limited regulation and redistribution. This is a belief shared by most business groups.

There are two contradicting theories of how party complexion of the government influences interest group behaviour. One theory understands lobbying as transfer of information from interest groups to the government (Bauer et al. 1963; Milbrath 1963). Interest groups, then, lobby only those who are political allies. It is, however, naïve to believe that interest groups do not get anything out of lobbying as it is a costly activity. When interest groups lobby their friends, they use the power of governmental actors to shape public policies in line with what they believe in (Hall and Deardorff 2006). Therefore, there is a clear element of exchange between these actors, each getting something out of lobbying. In persuasion model of lobbying, however, lobbying friendly actors in the government makes sense only when opposing interests lobby them. Most lobbying is targeted towards unfriendly politicians as the aim is persuading them to shift policies closer to their own preference (Austen-Smith and Wright 1994).

30.3 A Research Agenda for Interest Groups and Lobbying in Political Executives

It might be expected (and desired) for future research to conduct comparative research which focuses on the impact of political executive types on interest group strategies, access, and influence. It can be confidently argued that there is limited knowledge about this topic. Some of the possible topics to be surveyed could be the following: How does lobbying behaviour vary between presidential, semi-presidential and parliamentary regimes? Other than the logic of divided government (see Constantelos 2018), are there any other causal mechanisms which affect possible differences in lobbying behaviour across these executive types?

Also, it might be interesting to investigate how lobbying behaviour changes between single party and coalition governments. As there are more veto players in coalition governments, the rate and complexity of lobbying activity might be higher. Interest groups would have to lobby ministers belonging to multiple parties and try to convince actors who might have opposing views. Thus, they might have to lobby friends and foes at the same time. This would require groups to spend more time on a viable strategy and have more resources to be able to be active at different battlegrounds.

When a minority government is formed in parliamentary regimes, interest groups might have to put more attention on lobbying the legislative, not the executive. This is because lobbying is a strategic decision and interest groups choose to lobby at the arena where power resides. Minority governments are much weaker than majority governments, thus, when there is a minority government, it might be more appropriate to concentrate one's activities on the legislature.

Scholars should also move beyond studying a limited number of countries (the EU and the US) to have a truly comparative knowledge of interest groups and lobbying in political executives. There is already some interesting research on interest groups in hybrid and authoritarian regimes. For example, multiple studies appeared on interest group politics in authoritarian China (Kennedy 2008; Yu et al. 2014; Zhang 2015; Popović 2017; Weil 2017). Thomas and Klimovich (2014) examine the peculiarities of interest group politics in Latin America offering avenues of comparative research for causes and consequences of interest group system institutionalization. If information is conveyed by a diverse set of interest groups, one can argue that the interest groups system in that context is institutionalized. Established democracies have a diverse interest group system where groups within have relatively more equal access and chance of influencing public policies than in authoritarian or hybrid regimes or new democracies (Thomas and Hrebenar 2008; Klimovich and Thomas 2014; Thomas and Klimovich 2014; Kanol 2016b).

Nevertheless, there is still an important research gap because of limited number of studies comparing different regime types. Comparing multiple regime types can expand comparative knowledge of interest groups and political executives under democracies, hybrid regimes, and authoritarian regimes. Because the executive is stronger in authoritarian regimes, it might be plausible to expect to observe more lobbying at the executive branch than the legislative branch compared to democratic regimes. However, even such intuitive assumptions can be challenged as their ease of communication with interest groups and their fear of losing grip on political power might, counterintuitevly, make authoritarian leaders susceptible to outside influence (McEachern 2008; Steinberg and Shih 2012). Future research, then, should consider comparing multiple countries with different political institutions.

Power imbalances among different societal actors have created public outcry in almost every country. This issue has also attracted attention of scholars and there is a copious amount of research which investigate bias in interest group systems (e.g. Yackee and Yackee 2006; McKay 2012; Rasmussen and Carroll 2014; Rasmussen and Gross 2015; Schlozmann et al. 2015). Surprisingly, however, there has been limited mobilized effort to measure the effect of interest groups on policy outcomes which is another important normative issue. There is comparative research on how pluralist vs. corporatist interest mediation systems produce different policy outcomes. Public administrators should be informed by this literature and make decisions about increasing the corporatist or pluralist arrangements whenever necessary. It can be said that most research expects better societal outcomes from corporatist interest mediation processes (Kanol 2015b). However, the effect of interest groups on policy outcomes, generally, is understudied. How interest groups influence governance has implications for political executives not only in democratic regimes, but also in authoritarian and hybrid ones. This is not to say that the scholarly community is not aware of the relationship between these two concepts. Policy networks theory acknowledges the important role non-governmental actors play in good policy-making (Daugbjerg et al. 2018). But for some reason, much less effort has been made to demonstrate how exactly interest groups influence policy outcomes.

Many researchers understand the lobbying process between interest groups and policy-makers/implementers as a process of exchange. Interest groups rely on policy-makers/implementers to pass and implement policies that are in harmony with their ideology and interest. Policy officials, on the other hand, require information from non-state actors to pursue their goals. That is why they offer access to actors like interest groups. Organizations like executives and actors therein need resources, and they rely on organizations in their environment to fulfil this need (Levine and White 1961; Jacobs 1974; Pfeffer and Salancik 2003). Interest groups can develop 'policy goods' like technical information which can directly influence policy capacity (Daugbjerg et al. 2018). Political executives are aware of their need for information for formulating and implementing sound policies. Consequently, the profession of policy analysts and public affairs experts has been growing in most developed countries. These analysts and experts deal with complex technical and political problems. Expertise can be used as a depoliticization strategy, transferring intrinsically political issues under the management of experts or international technocratic institutions as a way of shying away from taking responsibility for thorny issues or implementing neo-liberal policies smoothly (Buller et al. 2019). Expertise in politics, then, can turn into politics of expertise (Pfister and Horvath 2014). Nevertheless, the need for outside technical information in today's societies cannot be refuted.

Interest group scholars demonstrated this need of information by showing how groups which have better information capabilities are granted more access points to public institutions, legislatives, as well as political executives (Potters and Van Winden 1992; Pappi and Henning 1999; Bouwen 2002, 2004; Broscheid and Coen 2003; Eising 2007; Reenock and Gerber 2008; Richardson and John 2012). In fact, the lobbying process itself, can be conceptualized as a process where policies are made possible by 'friendly' interest groups putting their labour into offering technical and political information (Hall and Deardoff 2006). Political executives face multiple complex challenges in today's world. As their task is steering the society for dealing with problems, including 'wicked' ones, technical expertise provided by different types of interest groups makes governance better.

Political executives consist of both politicians and bureaucrats taking part in policy initiation, policy formulation, and policy implementation. Ministers and heads of states in democracies, like politicians in legislatures, seek to take as many views into consideration as possible, as they are accountable to the public. Even in undemocratic regimes, politicians, as well as, bureaucrats seek public endorsement and legitimacy, thus, they take citizen support seriously (Poppelaars 2009). Interest groups function as representatives of the citizens and contacts with them can be expected to increase the social acceptance of policies. Moreover, interest groups might act as accountability mechanisms checking executives when implementing policies (Börzel 2010; Schrama and Zhelyazkova 2018). Political executives which establish a healthy information-exchange process with interest groups can be expected to deliver better policy outcomes as they can implement policies more smoothly.

One may argue that interest groups' informative and representative function can positively influence policy outputs as well-informed and inclusive policy-processes will result in more policy expertise and legitimacy. This effect on policy outcomes, however, depends on the rate and quality of information conveyed to political executives by a diverse set of interest groups. If high quality information by a diverse set of organized interests is available, one may expect a positive effect of interest groups on policy outcomes. On the other hand, bias towards certain interest groups can negatively affect policy outcomes as it may result in policy capture. If access is skewed towards few interests which advocate policies against the public interest, policies' capacity to deliver outcomes in line with the public interest might be affected negatively. Therefore, institutionalization of an interest group system largely decides the direction of the effect of interest groups on policy outcomes. These theoretical arguments, however, should be put to test against empirical data in future research.

Because of the accumulation of knowledge about lobbying the political executives, it might not suffice anymore to conduct research by simply stating that there is a lack of understanding of interactions between interest groups and political executives. This, however, is not to say that we have full knowledge of the topic and that future research is not necessary. On the contrary, we have seen that there is need for research aiming to answer important questions like: How do political executive types affect interest group behaviour, access, and influence? There is limited knowledge about this topic and the existing studies imply that different types of executives might have different implications for interest groups and interest group systems. Another important question which begs further investigation is: What is the impact of interest groups on policy outcomes? We know surprisingly little about this topic and it is imperative that researchers put effort into answering this question. These are not merely theoretical questions. They have implications for institutional and policy design and are of utmost importance for practitioners.

References

Austen-Smith, D. and Wright, J. R. (1994). 'Counteractive Lobbying,' *American Journal of Political Science* 38(1): 25–44.

Baroni, L., Carroll, B. J., Chalmers, A. W., Marquez, L. M. M., and Rasmussen, A. (2014). 'Defining and Classifying Interest Groups,' *Interest Groups & Advocacy* 3(2): 141–59.

Baturo, A. and Arlow, J. (2018). 'Is there a "Revolving Door" to the Private Sector in Irish Politics?,' *Irish Political Studies* 33(3): 381–406.

Baturo, A. and Mikhaylov, S. (2016). 'Blair Disease? Business Careers of the Former Democratic Heads of State and Government,' *Public Choice* 166(3–4): 335–54.

Bauer, R. A., Pool, I. D. S., and Dexter, L. A. (1963). *American Business and Public Policy: The Politics of Foreign Trade*. New York: Atherton Press.

Beyers, J. (2004). 'Voice and Access: Political Practices of European Interest Associations,' *European Union Politics* 5(2): 211–40.

Beyers, J. and Kerremans, B. (2012). 'Domestic Embeddedness and the Dynamics of Multilevel Venue Shopping in four EU Member States,' *Governance* 25(2): 263–90.

Binderkrantz, A. (2005). 'Interest Group Strategies: Navigating between Privileged Access and Strategies of Pressure,' *Political Studies* 53(4): 694–715.

Binderkrantz, A. S. and Krøyer, S. (2012). 'Customizing Strategy: Policy Goals and Interest Group Strategies,' *Interest Groups & Advocacy* 1(1): 115–38.

Binderkrantz, A. S. and Pedersen, H. H. (2019). 'The Lobbying Success of Citizen and Economic Groups in Denmark and the UK,' *Acta Politica* 54(1): 75–103.

Binderkrantz, A. S., Christiansen, P. M., and Pedersen, H. H. (2015). 'Interest Group Access to the Bureaucracy, Parliament, and the Media,' *Governance* 28(1): 95–112.

Boehmke, F. J., Gailmard, S., and Patty, J. W. (2013). 'Business as Usual: Interest Group Access and Representation across Policy-making Venues,' *Journal of Public Policy* 33(1): 3–33.

Bouwen, P. (2002). 'Corporate Lobbying in the European Union: The Logic of Access,' *Journal of European Public Policy* 9(3): 365–90.

Bouwen, P. (2004). 'Exchanging Access Goods for Access: A Comparative Study of Business Lobbying in the European Union Institutions,' *European Journal of Political Research* 43(3): 337–69.

Börzel, T. A. (2010). 'Why You Don't Always Get What You Want: EU Enlargement and Civil Society in Central and Eastern Europe,' *Acta Politica* 45(1–2): 1–10.

Broscheid, A. and Coen, D. (2003). 'Insider and Outsider Lobbying of the European Commission: An Informational Model of Forum Politics,' *European Union Politics* 4(2): 165–89.

Brown, H. (2011). 'Interest Groups and Presidential Transitions,' *Congress & the Presidency* 4(2): 152–70.

Brown, H. (2012). *Lobbying the New President: Interests in Transition*. New York: Routledge.

Bruno, M. and Sachs, J. (1985). *Economics of Worldwide Stagflation*. Oxford: Blackwell.

Buller, J., Dönmez, P. E., Standring, A., and Wood, M. (2019). 'Depoliticisation, Post-politics and the Problem of Change,' in J. Buller, P. Dönmez, A. Standring and M. Wood (eds) *Comparing Strategies of (De)Politicisation in Europe*. Palgrave Macmillan, Cham, 1–24.

Bunea, A. (2018). 'Legitimacy through Targeted Transparency? Regulatory Effectiveness and Sustainability of Lobbying Regulation in the European Union,' *European Journal of Political Research* 57(2): 378–403.

Cain, B. E. and Drutman, L. (2014). 'Congressional Staff and the Revolving Door: The Impact of Regulatory Change,' *Election Law Journal* 13(1): 27–44.

Chari, R., Hogan, J., and Murphy, G. (2010). *Regulating Lobbying: A Global Comparison.* Manchester: Manchester University Press.

Christiansen, P. M. and Rommetvedt, H. (1999). 'From Corporatism to Lobbyism?—Parliaments, Executives, and Organized Interests in Denmark and Norway', *Scandinavian Political Studies* 22(3): 195–220.

Choi, S. J., Jia, N., and Lu, J. (2015). 'The Structure of Political Institutions and Effectiveness of Corporate Political Lobbying', *Organization Science* 26(1): 158–79.

Christiansen, P. M., Mach, A., and Varone, F. (2018). 'How Corporatist Institutions Shape the Access of Citizen Groups to Policy-makers: Evidence from Denmark and Switzerland', *Journal of European Public Policy* 25(4): 526–45.

Claveria, S. and Verge, T. (2015). 'Post-ministerial Occupation in Advanced Industrial Democracies', *European Journal of Political Research* 54(4): 819–35.

Cohen, J. E. (2012). 'Interest Groups and Presidential Approval', *Presidential Studies Quarterly* 42(3): 431–54.

Constantelos, J. (2007). 'Interest Group Strategies in Multi-level Europe', *Journal of Public Affairs* 7(1): 39–53.

Constantelos, J. (2018). 'Lobbying across the USA: From State Vetoes to Federal Venues', *Interest Groups & Advocacy* 7(1): 19–40.

Crouch, C. (2000). *Coping with Post-democracy.* London: Fabian Society.

Dahl, R. (1961). *Who Governs? Democracy and Power in an American City.* London: Yale University Press.

Daugbjerg, C., Fraussen, B., and Halpin, D. (2018). 'Interest Groups and Policy Capacity: Modes of Engagement, Policy Goods and Networks', in X. Wu, M. Howlett, and M. Ramesh (eds) *Policy Capacity and Governance: Assessing Governmental Competences and Capabilities in Theory and Practice.* Cham: Palgrave Macmillan, 243–61.

Dörrenbächer, N. (2016). 'Patterns of Post-Cabinet Careers: When one Door Closes another Door Opens?', *Acta Politica* 51(4): 472–91.

Duncan, T. K. and Coyne, C. J. (2015). 'The Revolving Door and the Entrenchment of the Permanent War Economy', *Peace Economics, Peace Science and Public Policy* 21(3): 391–413.

Dunne, J. P. and Sköns, E. (2010). 'The Military Industrial Complex' in A. T. H. Tan (ed.) *The Global Arms Trade: A Handbook.* London: Routledge, 281–92.

Dür, A. and Mateo, G. (2016). *Insiders versus Outsiders: Interest Group Politics in Multilevel Europe.* Oxford: Oxford University Press.

Eising, R. (2007). 'Institutional Context, Organizational Resources and Strategic Choices Explaining Interest Group Access in the European Union', *European Union Politics* 8(3): 329–62.

Furlong, S. R. (1997). 'Interest Group Influence on Rule Making', *Administration & Society* 29(3), 325–47.

Furlong, S. R. (2005). 'Exploring Interest Group Participation in Executive Policymaking', in P. S. Herrnson, R. G. Shaiko, and C. Wilcox (eds) *The Interest Group Connection: Electioneering, Lobbying, and Policy-making in Washington.* Washinton, DC: CQ Press, 282–97.

Furlong, S. R. and Kerwin, C. M. (2005). 'Interest Group Participation in Rule Making: A Decade of Change', *Journal of Public Administration Research and Theory* 15(3): 353–70.

Gilens, M. and Page, B. I. (2014). 'Testing Theories of American Politics: Elites, Interest Groups, and Average Citizens', *Perspectives on Politics* 12(3): 564–81.

Golden, M. M. (1998). 'Interest Groups in the Rule-making Process: Who Participates? Whose Voices Get Heard?', *Journal of Public Administration Research and Theory* 8(2): 245–70.

Greene, S. and Heberlig, E. S. (2002). 'Finding the Weak Link: The Choice of Institutional Venues by Interest Groups,' *The American Review of Politics* 23: 19–38.

Haeder, S. F. and Yackee, S. W. (2015). 'Influence and the Administrative Process: Lobbying the US President's Office of Management and Budget,' *American Political Science Review* 109(3): 507–22.

Hall, R. L. and Deardorff, A. V. (2006). 'Lobbying as Legislative Subsidy,' *American Political Science Review* 100(1): 69–84.

Halpin, D., Baxter, G., and MacLeod, I. (2012). 'Multiple Arenas, Multiple Populations: Counting Organized Interests in Scottish Public Policy,' in D. Halpin and G. Jordan (eds) *The Scale of Interest Organization in Democratic Politics*. London: Palgrave Macmillan, 118–40.

Hanegraaff, M., Poletti, A., and Beyers, J. (2017). 'Explaining Varying Lobbying Styles across the Atlantic: An Empirical Test of the Cultural and Institutional Explanations,' *Journal of Public Policy* 37(4): 459–86.

Heinz, J. P., Laumann, E. O., Nelson, R. L., and Salisbury, R. H. (1993). *The Hollow Core: Private Interests in National Policy Making*. Cambridge, MA: Harvard University Press.

Holyoke, T. T. (2003). 'Choosing Battlegrounds: Interest Group Lobbying across Multiple Venues,' *Political Research Quarterly* 56(3): 325–36.

Holyoke, T. (2004). 'By Invitation Only: Controlling Interest Group Access to the Oval Office,' *American Review of Politics* 25: 221–40.

Holyoke, T. T., Brown, H., and Henig, J. R. (2012). 'Shopping in the Political Arena: Strategic State and Local Venue Selection by Advocates,' *State and Local Government Review* 44(1): 9–20.

Hong, S. and Lim, J. (2016). 'Capture and the Bureaucratic Mafia: Does the Revolving Door Erode Bureaucratic Integrity?,' *Public Choice* 166(1–2): 69–86.

Huber, E. and Stephens, J. D. (2001). *Development and Crisis of the Welfare State: Parties and Policies in Global Markets*. Chicago: University of Chicago Press.

Iversen, T. (2005). *Capitalism, Democracy, and Welfare*. Cambridge: Cambridge University Press.

Jacobs, D. (1974). 'Dependency and Vulnerability: An Exchange Approach to the Control of Organizations,' *Administrative Science Quarterly* 19(1): 45–59.

Jahn, D. (1998). 'Environmental Performance and Policy Regimes: Explaining Variations in 18 OECD-countries,' *Policy Sciences* 31(2): 107–31.

Jahn, D. (2014). 'Changing of the Guard: Trends in Corporatist Arrangements in 42 Highly Industrialized Societies from 1960 to 2010,' *Socio-Economic Review* 14(1): 47–71.

Jordan, G., Halpin, D., and Maloney, W. (2004). 'Defining Interests: Disambiguation and the Need for New Distinctions?,' *The British Journal of Politics & International Relations* 6(2): 195–212.

Jourdain, C., Hug, S., and Varone, F. (2017). 'Lobbying Across Venues: An Issue-Tracing Approach,' *State Politics & Policy Quarterly* 17(2): 127–53.

Kanol, D. (2015a). 'Comparative Lobbying Research: Advances, Shortcomings and Recommendations,' *Journal of Public Affairs* 15(1): 110–15.

Kanol, D. (2015b). 'Pluralism, Corporatism and Perception of Corruption,' *Journal of Public Affairs* 15(3): 243–51.

Kanol, D. (2016a). 'Europeanization of Domestic Interest Groups,' *Interest Groups & Advocacy* 5(2): 165–71.

Kanol, D. (2016b). 'The Impact of Democracy on Interest Group System Institutionalization,' *Journal of Public Affairs* 16(4): 341–9.

Kanol, D. (2018). 'Knowledge of Lobbying Regulations and Attitudes toward Politics: Findings from a Survey Experiment in Cyprus,' *Public Integrity* 20(2): 163–78.

Kennedy, S. (2008). *The Business of Lobbying in China.* Cambridge, MA: Harvard University Press.

Klimovich, K. and Thomas, C. S. (2014). 'Power Groups, Interests and Interest Groups in Consolidated and Transitional Democracies: Comparing Uruguay and Costa Rica with Paraguay and Haiti,' *Journal of Public Affairs* 14(3–4): 183–211.

Leech, B. L. (2006). 'Funding Faction or Buying Silence? Grants, Contracts, and Interest Group Lobbying Behavior,' *Policy Studies Journal* 34(1): 17–35.

Levine, S. and White, P. E. (1961). 'Exchange as a Conceptual Framework for the Study of Interorganizational Relationships,' *Administrative Science Quarterly* 5(4): 583–601.

Lijphart, A., and Crepaz, M. M. (1991). 'Corporatism and Consensus Democracy in Eighteen Countries: Conceptual and Empirical Linkages,' *British Journal of Political Science* 21(2): 235–46.

Loomis, B. A. (2009). 'Connecting Interest Groups to the Presidency,' in G. Edwards III and W. G. Howell (eds) *The Oxford Handbook of American Presidency.* Oxford: Oxford University Press, 403–26.

Lowry, R. C. and Potoski, M. (2004). 'Organized Interests and the Politics of Federal Discretionary Grants,' *Journal of Politics* 66(2): 513–33.

Lucco, J. (1992). 'Representing the Public Interest: Consumer Groups and the Presidency,' in M. P. Petracca (ed.) *The Politics of Interests: Interest Groups Transformed.* Boulder, CO: Westview Press.

Mahoney, C. (2008). *Brussels versus the Beltway: Advocacy in the United States and the European Union.* Washington, DC: Georgetown University Press.

McEachern, P. (2008). 'Interest Groups in North Korean Politics,' *Journal of East Asian Studies* 8(2): 235–58.

McKay, A. M. (2011). 'The Decision to Lobby Bureaucrats,' *Public Choice* 147(1–2): 123–38.

McKay, A. (2012). 'Buying Policy? The Effects of Lobbyists' Resources on Their Policy Success,' *Political Research Quarterly* 65(4): 908–23.

McKay, A. and Yackee, S. W. (2007). 'Interest Group Competition on Federal Agency Rules,' *American Politics Research* 35(3): 336–57.

Milbrath, L. (1963). *The Washington Lobbyists.* Chicago: Rand McNally.

Milner, H. (1987). 'Resisting the Protectionist Temptation: Industry and the Making of Trade Policy in France and the United States during the 1970s,' *International Organization* 41(4): 639–65.

Naoi, M. and Krauss, E. (2009). 'Who Lobbies Whom? Special Interest Politics under Alternative Electoral Systems,' *American Journal of Political Science* 53(4): 874–92.

Năstase, A. and Muurmans, C. (2018). 'Regulating Lobbying Activities in the European Union: A Voluntary Club Perspective,' *Regulation & Governance.* Early View, 1–18, https://www.onlinelibrary.wiley.com/toc/17485991/0/0

Öberg, P., Svensson, T., Christiansen, P. M., Nørgaard, A. S., Rommetvedt, H., and Thesen, G. (2011). 'Disrupted Exchange and Declining Corporatism: Government Authority and Interest Group Capability in Scandinavia,' *Government and Opposition* 46(3): 365–91.

Pappi, F. U. and Henning, C. H. (1999). 'The Organization of Influence on the EC's Common Agricultural Policy: A Network Approach,' *European Journal of Political Research* 36(2): 257–81.

Pedersen, H. H., Binderkrantz, A. S., and Christiansen, P. M. (2014). 'Lobbying across Arenas: Interest Group Involvement in the Legislative Process in Denmark,' *Legislative Studies Quarterly* 39(2), 199–225.

Peterson, M. A. (1992). 'The Presidency and Organized Interests: White House Patterns of Interest Group Liaison,' *American Political Science Review* 86(3), 612–25.

Pfeffer, J. and Salancik, G. (2003). *The External Control of Organizations: A Resource Dependence Perspective*. Stanford: Stanford University Press.

Pfister, T. and Horvath, A. (2014). 'Reassessing Expert Knowledge and the Politics of Expertise,' *Innovation: The European Journal of Social Science Research* 27(4): 311–16.

Pika, J. A. (1983). 'Interest Groups and the Executive: Presidential Intervention,' in A. J. Cigler and B. Loomis (eds) *Interest Group Politics*. Washington, DC: Congressional Quarterly Press, 298–323.

Pika, J. A. (2009). 'The White House Office of Public Liaison,' *Presidential Studies Quarterly* 39(3): 549–73.

Piotrowski, S. J and Rosenbloom, D. H. (2005). 'The Legal-Institutional Framework for Interest Group Participation in Federal Administrative Policymaking,' in P. S. Herrnson, R. G. Shaiko, and C. Wilcox (eds) *The Interest Group Connection: Electioneering, Lobbying, and Policy-making in Washington*. Washington, DC: CQ Press, 258–81.

Popović, E. (2017). 'Lobbying Practices of Citizens' Groups in China,' *Sage Open* April–June, 1–9, doi/10.1177/2158244017713554

Poppelaars, C. (2009). *Steering a Course between Friends and Foes: Why Bureaucrats Interest with Interest Groups*. Delft: Eburon.

Potters, J. and Van Winden, F. (1992). 'Lobbying and Asymmetric Information,' *Public Choice* 74(3): 269–92.

Rasmussen, A. and Carroll, B. J. (2014). 'Determinants of Upper-class Dominance in the Heavenly Chorus: Lessons from European Union Online Consultations,' *British Journal of Political Science* 44(2): 445–59.

Rasmussen, A. and Gross, V. (2015). 'Biased Access? Exploring Selection to Advisory Committees,' *European Political Science Review* 7(3): 343–72.

Reenock, C. M. and Gerber, B. J. (2008). 'Political Insulation, Information Exchange, and Interest Group Access to the Bureaucracy,' *Journal of Public Administration Research and Theory* 18(3): 415–40.

Richardson, L. and John, P. (2012). 'Who Listens to the Grass Roots? A Field Experiment on Informational Lobbying in the UK,' *The British Journal of Politics and International Relations* 14(4): 595–612.

Rommetvedt, H., Thesen, G., Christiansen, P. M., and Nørgaard, A. S. (2013). 'Coping with Corporatism in Decline and the Revival of Parliament: Interest Group Lobbyism in Denmark and Norway, 1980–2005,' *Comparative Political Studies* 46(4): 457–85.

Salisbury, R. H. (1984). 'Interest Representation: The Dominance of Institutions,' *American Political Science Review* 78(1): 64–76.

Schattschneider, E. E. (1960). *The Semisovereign People: A Realist's View of Democracy in America*. New York: Holt, Rinehart and Winston.

Schlozman, K. L., Jones, P. E., You, H. Y., Burch, T., Verba, S., and Brady, H. E. (2015). 'Louder Chorus—Same Accent: The Representation of Interests in Pressure Politics, 1981–2011,' in D. Lowery, D. Halpin and V. Gray (eds) *The Organization Ecology of Interest Communities: Assessment and Agenda*. Basingstoke: Palgrave Macmillan, 157–81.

Schmitter, P. C. (1974). 'Still the Century of Corporatism?,' *The Review of Politics* 36(1): 85–131.

Schmitter, P. C. (1989). 'Corporatism is Dead! Long Live Corporatism!', *Government and Opposition* 24(1): 54–73.

Schrama, R. and Zhelyazkova, A. (2018). '"You Can't Have One without the Other": The Differential Impact of Civil Society Strength on the Implementation of EU Policy', *Journal of European Public Policy* 25(7): 1029–48.

Schuler, D. A. and Rehbein, K. (2011). 'Determinants of Access to Legislative and Executive Branch Officials: Business Firms and Trade Policymaking in the US', *Business and Politics* 13(3): 1–30.

Scruggs, L. (2001). 'Is There Really a Link between Neo-Corporatism and Environmental Performance? Updated Evidence and New Data for the 1980s and 1990s', *British Journal of Political Science* 31(4): 686–92.

Sorge, M. M. (2015). 'Lobbying (Strategically Appointed) Bureaucrats', *Constitutional Political Economy* 26(2): 171–89.

Steinberg, D. A. and Shih, V. C. (2012). 'Interest Group Influence in Authoritarian States: The Political Determinants of Chinese Exchange Rate Policy', *Comparative Political Studies* 45(11): 1405–34.

Straus, J. R., Ginsberg, W. R., Mullan, A. K., and Petruzzelli, J. D. (2015). 'Restricting Membership: Assessing Agency Compliance and the Effects of Banning Federal Lobbyists from Executive Branch Advisory Committee Service', *Presidential Studies Quarterly* 45(2): 310–34.

Tenpas, K. D. (2005). 'Lobbying the Executive Branch: Outside-In and Inside-Out', in P. S. Herrnson, R. G. Shaiko and C. Wilcox (eds) *The Interest Group Connection: Electioneering, Lobbying, and Policy-making in Washington*. Washinton, DC: CQ Press, 249–57.

Thomas, C. S. and Hrebenar, R. J. (2008). 'Understanding Interest Groups, Lobbying and Lobbyists in Developing Democracies', *Journal of Public Affairs* 8(1–2): 1–14.

Thomas, C. S. and Klimovich, K. (2014). 'Power Groups, Interests and Interest Groups in Latin America: A New Era or More of the Same?', *Journal of Public Affairs* 14(3–4): 392–422.

Thomas, H. F. and LaPira, T. M. (2017). 'How Many Lobbyists Are in Washington? Shadow Lobbying and the Gray Market for Policy Advocacy', *Interest Groups & Advocacy* 6(3): 199–214.

Thurber, J. A. (2011). 'The Contemporary Presidency: Changing the way Washington Works? Assessing President Obama's Battle with Lobbyists', *Presidential Studies Quarterly* 41(2): 358–74.

Truman, D. B. (1951). *The Governmental Process: Political Interests and Public Opinion*. New York: Knopf.

Tsebelis, G. (1995). 'Decision Making in Political Systems: Veto Players in Presidentialism, Parliamentarism, Multicameralism and Multipartyism', *British Journal of Political Science* 25(3): 289–325.

Vargovčíková, J. (2017). 'Inside Lobbying Regulation in Poland and the Czech Republic: Negotiating Public and Private Actors' Roles in Governance', *Interest Groups & Advocacy* 6(3): 253–71.

Vaubel, R., Klingen, B., and Müller, D. (2012). 'There is Life after the Commission: An Empirical Analysis of Private Interest Representation by Former EU-Commissioners, 1981–2009', *The Review of International Organizations* 7(1): 59–80.

Weil, S. (2017). *Lobbying and Foreign Interests in Chinese Politics*. New York: Palgrave Macmillan.

Weiler, F. and Brändli, M. (2015). 'Inside versus Outside Lobbying: How the Institutional Framework Shapes the Lobbying Behaviour of Interest Groups', *European Journal of Political Research* 54(4): 745–66.

Wilensky, H. L. (2002). *Rich Democracies: Political Economy, Public Policy, and Performance.* Berkeley, CA: University of California Press.

Wolman, H. and Teitelbaum, F. (1984). 'Interest Groups and the Reagan Presidency,' in L. M. Salamon and M. S. Lund (eds) *The Reagan Presidency and the Governing of America.* Washington, DC. Urban Institute Press.

Yackee, S. W. (2006). 'Sweet-Talking the Fourth Branch: The Influence of Interest Group Comments on Federal Agency Rulemaking,' *Journal of Public Administration Research and Theory* 16(1): 103–24.

Yackee, J. W. and Yackee, S. W. (2006). 'A Bias towards Business? Assessing Interest Group Influence on the US Bureaucracy,' *The Journal of Politics* 68(1): 128–39.

Yadav, V. (2011). *Political Parties, Business Groups, and Corruption in Developing Countries.* Oxford: Oxford University Press.

You, H. Y. (2017). 'Ex Post Lobbying,' *The Journal of Politics* 79(4): 1162–76.

Yu, J., Yashima, K., and Shen, Y. (2014). 'Autonomy or Privilege? Lobbying Intensity of Local Business Associations in China,' *Journal of Chinese Political Science* 19(3): 315–33.

Zhang, C. (2015). 'Non-Governmental Organisations' Policy Advocacy in China: Resources, Government Intention and Network,' *China: An International Journal* 13(1), 181–99.

CHAPTER 31

PUBLIC OPINION AND EXECUTIVE APPROVAL

PEDRO C. MAGALHÃES

31.1 WHY DOES IT MATTER?

WHY should those interested in political executives care about what drives public opinion? Although perhaps obvious, the answers to this question deserve at least a brief restatement. The first is that public opinion should affect who governs and for how long. It is not only the fact that, in democracies, public opinion, by being reflected in election results, determines with more or less institutional mediations who gets to be the president or the composition of legislatures that will support a particular cabinet. It is also the fact that public opinion is supposed to cast a permanent shadow over political executives. Changes in public support for the executive and the parties that compose it disturb existing equilibriums (Laver and Shepsle 1998). Prime ministers with legislative dissolution powers and enjoying a rise in public approval may call elections to reap electoral benefits (Strøm and Swindle 2002; Kayser 2005; Schleiter and Tavits 2016). Coalition partners, depending on the signals they receive from public opinion, the moment in the term they receive them, and the expected net benefits of different possible reactions, may even choose to abandon those coalitions (Grofman and van Roozendaal 1997). Conversely, they may threaten to do so in order to extract more favourable deals in terms of portfolios or policies (Lupia and Strøm 1995; also see Chapter 15).

The second answer is that public opinion affects not only who governs but also what governments do. The policies we expect executives to pursue in a democracy depend, to a great extent, on how we think public opinion works. If the members of the public are myopic and naïve, mostly driven by what governments have delivered lately, and unable to consider either the more distant past or the near future, we can form clear expectations about how re-election-minded incumbents are likely to govern. They will have incentives to stimulate growth and reduce unemployment through expansionary fiscal or monetary policies as elections approach, something for which they are likely to be rewarded, regardless of the price to pay later (Nordhaus 1975; Tufte 1978). However, if voters are seen as more forward-thinking and simply lacking information about government competence (Rogoff and Sibert 1988; Rogoff 1990), or if they are thought to care about the distributive consequences of policies instead of (or in addition to) 'competence' (Drazen and Eslava 2010), re-election-minded governments might pursue different policies under different conditions. The connection between public opinion and the political incentives of executives may even help explaining decisions as momentous and consequential as waging wars. An entire theoretical body of work about why states engage in military conflicts—the 'diversionary theory' of war (Levy 1989)—suggests that governments are more likely to respond to threats with the use of military force when their domestic support is declining. However, this idea is largely predicated on the assumption that the public standing of executives can be boosted by 'rally 'round the flag' effects. Is this the case?

In light of the very broad scope of this volume, this chapter focuses primarily on what the existing research tells us about what drives public opinion. Attitudes of public approval and support for executives and incumbent parties, measured and analysed using quantitative social-scientific methods, will be the central concern here. When available and judged relevant for the important theoretical debates, the literature examining how such attitudes are converted into supportive behaviour, that is, voting for the incumbent parties or candidates, will also be discussed.

Section 31.2 is devoted to some basic generalizations that came out of the initial 'waves' of public approval studies (Gronke and Newman 2003) and the extent to which they were thought to extend to contexts other than the ones from where most of the relevant literature originated (the United States and, to a lesser extent, the United Kingdom). Section 31.3 then raises several of the caveats and complications that emerged from the following wave of research, namely, that which began taking more seriously the heterogeneity of effects, contexts, and publics. As a result, the relatively comfortable safety to be found in the previous conventional wisdom has partially been replaced today by several uncertainties and new avenues of inquiry. The last section (31.4) identifies three possible items of a future research agenda addressing those questions that, so far, have received the least attention from the literature.

31.2 WHAT DRIVES EXECUTIVE APPROVAL?

31.2.1 Outcomes

In people's interactions with all kinds of authorities, as in any other social exchange (Homans 1961), outcomes people perceive as favourable increase support and satisfaction. In what concerns support for executives, 'Bread' and 'Peace' (Hibbs 2000) have from very early on played a prominent role as the main outcomes that governments should be seen as delivering, and thus as main drivers of executive approval.

Governments enjoy resources with which to affect the economy, incumbents and challengers claim to be able to do it, and many people still seem to believe that to be the case. Conveniently for researchers, good data on the macro-economy are also available. Economic outcomes thus took centre stage in the two modern seminal references on executive approval: Mueller's *Presidential Popularity from Truman to Johnson* (1970) and Goodhart and Bhansali's *Political Economy* (1970). The latter found that higher levels of unemployment and higher rates of inflation (both measured at the time of the survey or with a short lag) drove down executive approval in the United Kingdom, as captured through polls. Mueller (1970) showed that presidential approval in the United States was hurt when unemployment became higher than at the beginning of the presidential term. Inflation was soon shown to be also relevant for the US (Monroe 1978).

In the first major survey of the literature, covering research conducted not only in these two countries and also in a small set of European democracies, Nannestad and Paldam (1994) still identified unemployment and inflation as 'the big two' macro-economic variables driving approval. Almost twenty years later, having surmised more than twice as many studies in many more countries, Lewis-Beck and Stegmeier (2013) slightly revised the diagnostic: together with unemployment, gross domestic product (GDP) or income growth took centre stage, an unsurprising development given the global disinflation experienced since the 1980s (Rogoff 2003). Studies of less established democracies—in Southern Europe (Lewis-Beck and Nadeau 2012), Central and Eastern Europe (Roberts 2008), or Latin America (Cuzán and Bundrick 1997; Nadeau et al. 2017)—have not changed these assessments. Peace is arguably the other main outcome upon which a government is likely to be judged. Mueller (1970) was on this as well. He noted how the correlation between presidential popularity and the presence of war was negative, and later expanded on this by showing the negative effect of war casualties on approval (Mueller 1973: 60). Several subsequent studies have confirmed these results (Larson 1996; Hibbs 2000).

31.2.2 Processes

A long tradition in socio-psychological studies suggests that people do not care exclusively about outcomes. 'Citizens [...] care deeply about the process by which conflicts are resolved and decisions are made, even when outcomes are unfavourable' (MacCoun 2005: 171–2). In particular, people care about the fairness of decision-making procedures, including people's ability to have an input in political decisions, impartial and unbiased governance, transparency in decision-making, and dignified treatment by those making the decisions (Murphy 2017).

Indeed, the research shows that the perception that government works under fair process rules increases support for political leaders (Tyler and Caine 1981), that transparency in governance increases executive approval (Alt et al. 2002), and that such procedural aspects may be even more important than distributive ones in determining support for politicians, candidates (Rasinski and Tyler 1988), or sitting presidents

(Kershaw and Alexander 2003). This is also a useful lens with which to interpret the fact that executive support, in most contexts (but not all, more on this later), is negatively affected by the perception that corruption prevails in government affairs (Fackler and Lin 1995; Davis et al. 2004; Krause and Méndez 2009).

31.2.3 Rally Events and the Use of Force

Public support for the executive can also be affected by particular events. Mueller focused on 'boosts', especially those that occurred as reactions to 'international crises and similar phenomena [...] confronting the nation as a whole' (1970: 20–1). He showed that the further away in time from such events (military interventions and developments, diplomatic crises, and the like) one measured presidential approval, the lower approval was likely to be. Hibbs et al. (1982) and others soon confirmed the positive boost that such 'rally' events gave to government approval. The conventional wisdom became that 'the use of force by an American president, under nearly any circumstances, generates a "rally 'round the flag" effect that boosts his popularity among the electorate, if only temporarily' (Levy and Thompson 2010: 100). More recently, the rises in approval that executives and prime ministers' parties received in the aftermath of the Covid-19 pandemic are yet another illustration of the phenomenon.

Why do these boosts occur? Baker and O'Neal (2001) proposed two mechanisms. The first is related to patriotism, and particularly the way international crises lead citizens to support incumbents as symbols of national unity (Lee 1977). The second, 'opinion leadership', suggests that rally events generate public support in response to leaders' handling of events and to elite consensus in contexts of international crises, a consensus that citizens take as a positive cue about executive performance (Brody 1991). These two arguments are not mutually exclusive. Hetherington and Nelson's (2003), in their analysis of the 'rally 'round the flag' effect that followed 9/11 in the US, argue that while an attachment to symbols of national unity under crisis account for why particular events become rally points, presidential responses and elite opinion account for how long the boosts endure (Hetherington and Nelson 2003).

31.2.4 The Cost of Ruling

Executives also seem fated to lose support with time. Mueller (1970) found that, *ceteris paribus*, the time elapsed since an American president's inauguration was negatively related with presidential approval. Coupled with this is the notion of a 'honeymoon' period, during which, at the very beginning of the term, executives benefit from broader public goodwill and support, which subsequently erodes. Goodhart and Bhansali (1970: 61) similarly observed a decline in public support for the UK governments throughout the term, which in their case was found to be parabolic: approval peaks at the beginning of the term and then declines, eventually bottoming out and recovering slightly at the end, but never to return to the original level (see also Stimson 1976 for the US).

More evidence about the costs of ruling elsewhere soon followed. First indirectly through the study of the European parliament 'second-order' elections: the results obtained by government parties in those elections varied according to when they took place after the main first-order election, good if soon after but declining if later in the cycle (Reif and Schmitt 1980 and many others). Later studies in many different contexts, whether looking at approval itself, voting intentions, or election returns, support the notion that support erodes with time (Chappell and Veiga 2000; Nannestad and Paldam 2002). The broadest and most recent confirmatory evidence comes from Green and Jennings (2017), looking at voting intention for the incumbent parties in thirty-one countries between 1942 and 2013. Although there is considerably heterogeneity between countries, the most general pattern is the one first identified by Goodhart and Bhansali (1970): following an initial honeymoon period, there is a general decline through time, with a modest backswing at the end of the term.

31.3 CAVEATS AND COMPLICATIONS

Providing 'bread' and 'peace', employing 'good governance', be "blessed" with (or fabricate) rallies of support, and all this while enduring an almost inevitable decline in support, would already be a tall order for any incumbent. However, there are many caveats and complications that make the case for what is needed to preserve public support even more difficult to articulate unambiguously.

One symptom of this is the typical average effect sizes of the kind of phenomena we have discussed so far. For example, Kayser (2014), discussing the estimated impact of economic growth on incumbent party vote shares across twenty-three OECD countries since 1995, finds that a very large drop from 3 per cent to −2 per cent in GDP growth is expected to result in a small drop of 2.5 percentage points in electoral support, with a similar shift requiring an increase of no less than five percentage points in the unemployment rate. These are small and statistically uncertain effects. Similarly, the conventional wisdom that 'rally 'round the flag' events boost executive approval needs to be squared with the findings that such boosts are relatively small in magnitude, when they can be found at all (Baker and Oneal 2001), and their impact seems to dissipate relatively quickly with time (Erikson et al. 2002: 51–7). Why are effects so small on average, uncertain, and contingent?

31.3.1 Asymmetry

Most of the literature that immediately followed Mueller questioned the notion that 'an economy in slump harms a President's popularity, but an economy in boom does not help his rating' (Mueller 1970: 34). In their 1994 review article, Nannestad and Paldam (1994) saw 'no signs' of asymmetry in the relation between the economy and public support

632   PEDRO C. MAGALHÃES

for incumbents. However, twenty years later, Lewis-Beck and Stegmeier were already assessing the evidence as 'mixed' (2013: 371). Lewis-Beck himself, with Dassonneville (Dassonneville and Lewis-Beck 2014), covering more than thirty countries, showed that, under bad economic times, the (negative) impact of the economy (GDP growth) in incumbent support was about twice as large as the (positive) impact under good times.

Why this asymmetry? One possible mechanism is simply that bad news generate more information and attention than good ones. Soroka (2006) found that the mass media (and the public) tend to respond more to negative economic developments. Similarly, Singer (2011), in a broad cross-national study, showed that a deteriorating economic climate raises the salience of economic issues, in turn increasing the relevance of economic performance for government approval. A second possible mechanism is loss aversion. Nannestad and Paldam (1997) had advanced a griev-ance-asymmetry argument, through which loss-averse voters should react more negatively to bad economic outcomes than they would react positively to good ones. Support for this notion also comes from studies attempting to explain why executive support seems to inexorably decline with time. Using data from five established democracies (US, UK, Canada, Australia, and Germany), Green and Jennings (2017) show that unfavourable perceptions of government competence have a stronger impact on executive support than favourable ones, with the *accumulation* of negative evaluations bringing down support even further. In other words, even if positive and negative governance outcomes (economic or others) cancel out, public reactions do not, resulting in a net loss of support for the executive that tends to cumulate with time.

31.3.2 Myopia

Goodhart and Bhansali (1970) saw popularity as affected by contemporary or very temporally close measures of the economy. Mueller (1970), instead, assumed that what mattered for voters in the assessment of the executive was how unemployment evolved in relation to the beginning of the term. Of course, these empirics are still compatible with different assumptions. Are voters 'myopic', caring just about what 'governments have done for me lately'? Or do they keep in mind and use information about what governments have done throughout an entire term of office?

For most of the immediately subsequent scholarship, the dominant notion was that citizens' time horizon when using economic outcomes to evaluate incumbents is indeed rather short. When support is measured in terms of its behavioural consequences in elections, what happens very soon before such elections—one year or even less—has been argued to matter much more than what happens earlier the term (Nannestad and Paldam 1994; Lewis-Beck and Stegmeier 2013: 378). The public is assumed, and often found to be, structurally 'myopic'.

However, several recent studies have questioned aspects of this assumption. Wlezien (2015) found that US voters give equal importance to developments occurring in the last two years before the election. Healy et al. (2017) show that citizens, when focusing in their personal economic conditions—information which by definition is accessible to them—seem not to suffer from any short-sightedness, considering events and developments that occurred throughout an entire term. It may the case that voters' tendency to use a short-term lens about the national economy is therefore just a consequence of low information. Addressing that question experimentally, Healy and Lenz (2014) find that voters do seek longer-term information about economic outcomes and indeed use it whenever it is made available to them. Thus, lack of information is potentially correctable, and its availability varies in the real world.

These findings have interesting counterparts in the study of the impact of election-year deficit spending on the vote. Brender (2003) shows how an increase in the availability of fiscal information in Israel shifted the sign of the effect of budget deficits on the probability of incumbent re-election, from positive to negative, while Arvate et al. (2009) show that fiscal surpluses are more electorally rewarded in states where voters enjoy greater levels of information. Correspondingly, governments do not seem to invariably engage in a political manipulation of the economy in the run-up to elections, inducing economic expansions through deficit spending, as the assumption of myopic voters would lead us to hypothesize. Instead, political budget cycles are less prevalent when fiscal policy is more transparent (Alt and Lassen 2006) or when the share of informed voters and media freedom or penetration are larger (Shi and Svensson 2006; Shelton 2014; Veiga et al. 2017). In other words, it's possible that 'myopia' is, so to speak, more of a bug than a feature, with implications both for approval and the policies of election-minded governments.

31.3.3 Heterogeneous Contexts

As systematic empirical research on government support expanded beyond the US and the UK, it did not take long to realize that some of its generalizations did not apply everywhere. One guiding principle in the literature to address this instability has been to explore variations in 'clarity of responsibility', that is, the extent to which, across contexts, there is a 'perceived unified control of policymaking by the incumbent government' (Powell and Whitten 1993: 398). When such perceived control is lacking, political support should be less driven by economic outcomes, either because it is more difficult for citizens to assign responsibility for them in order to exact punishments or rewards or because, in such contexts, citizens correctly discount performance as a signal of government competence (Duch and Stevenson 2008).

Thus, the extent to which policy-making institutions disperse power—including bicameralism, power-sharing legislative arrangements, minority or coalition cabinets, divided government in presidential systems, and so on—has been shown to moderate the effects of the economy on support (see Anderson 2000; Nadeau et al. 2002; Van der Brug et al. 2007). When we shift the focus from how voters behave to what election-minded governments do, clarity also seems relevant: fiscal policy manipulation is less common when policy-making is more pervaded by veto-points, that is, when it is more difficult to change policies and when responsibility is more diffuse and, thus, the gains from electoral opportunism less likely (Persson and Tabellini 2003; Chang 2008). A related logic can be extended to other factors that limit 'unified control of policymaking', such as, for example, greater power and fiscal autonomy for subnational levels of governance (Anderson 2006) or greater exposure to international trade and capital markets (Duch and Stevenson 2008). 'Clarity of responsibility' has also been used as the operative concept accounting, for example, for the varying strength in the relationship between the perceived prevalence of corruption and public support for the executive (Tavits 2007).

Another line of research about heterogeneity has been to note how economic conditions themselves can moderate relationships between other variables and public support. Thus, for example, corruption and political scandals only seem to significantly undermine support for the executive when economic conditions are bad (Manzetti and Wilson 2006; Carlin et al. 2015). Whether that occurs because voters explicitly trade-off honesty with economic prosperity (see Winters and Weitz-Shapiro 2013 and Muñoz et al. 2016 for contrasting experimental evidence), because economic performance serves as a perceptual screen of the government's performance (Choi and Woo 2010), or because of any other mechanism is less clear.

Similarly, unfavourable economic conditions also seem to amplify either the negative effects of engagement in interstate military conflicts (Williams et al. 2010) or the positive effects of rally events (Baum 2002). Other conditionalities include the fact that the effects of mounting casualties on government approval depends on perceptions about the 'rightness of conflicts' and the probability of success (Gelpi et al. 2006) or that involvement in conflicts produces different consequences depending on they receive multilateral backing, who initiates them, and what is the target (Chapman and Reiter 2004; Tir and Singh 2013; Singh and Tir 2018). Finally, the ability to generate significant popularity rallies depends on media amplification (Oneal and Bryan 1995) and credible elite and media support (Groeling and Baum 2008). In light of all these contingencies, it is not surprising that the literature about 'diversionary wars' has reached remarkably contradictory results, not only about the empirical regularity itself (Tarar 2006; Chiozza and Goemans 2003) but also about the potential underlying mechanisms (Haynes 2017).

31.3.4 Heterogeneous Publics

Some of earlier arguments in the literature about how the outcomes of governance drive support for the executive are predicated upon the notion that most members of the public are likely to agree upon what are 'good' or 'bad' outcomes. However, electorates are heterogeneous, aggregate national circumstances translate differently in terms of circumstances for different groups of voters, those groups may want different things from government, and parties have different constituencies and reputations they have incentives to preserve.

A first implication of this is captured by the notion of *partisan effects* of the economy (Carlsen 2000): the possibility that different kinds of incumbents may be supported or shunned by voters as a result of developments in different economic variables. Hibbs (1977) had noted early on that unemployment and inflation were targeted differently by left- and right-wing parties, through economic policies that accorded to the different interests and preferences of their electoral constituencies. Kiewiet (1981) then showed that, accordingly, voters concerned with unemployment were more likely to vote for the party that had the reputation of addressing that problem (in the US, the Democrats). In other words, the relationship between economic developments and the vote should not be understood solely in 'incumbency-oriented' terms (who to punish or reward for what), but also in 'policy-oriented' terms (who to support in order to promote which policies). Similar 'policy-oriented' arguments about the economy and approval include the notion that support for left-wing parties—with their taxation, spending, and redistribution 'luxury' agendas—increases with an expanding economy but decreases with downturns (Durr 1993; Stevenson 2001; Kayser 2009).

One possible—only apparently paradoxical—manifestation of this is that negative 'valence' outcomes could actually leave support for some types of government unscathed or even increase it, if their partisan-ideological make up is associated with a policy reputation for dealing with such problems (Rattinger 1991). Recent studies show how combinations of incumbency- and policy-oriented effects emerge. Wright (2012), in the American context, shows how higher unemployment benefits the Democrats, but less so when they are the incumbents, while Lindvall (2014) shows that major economic crises caused incumbents to lose support all over Europe, but less so if they were right-wing (Lindvall 2014). And Van der Brug et al. (2007) suggest that the main role of 'clarity of responsibility' is precisely to affect whether voters tend to hold government parties accountable for performance or, instead (in low clarity situations), tend to focus prospectively in terms of the policies they want to be delivered.

A second implication of the notion of heterogeneous publics is that national economic developments should not translate into changes in concrete economic circumstances in the same way for all people. The notion that 'economic voting is sociotropic' (Lewis-Beck and Stegmaier 2013: 380)—that it is the national rather than the 'personal' economy that matters for support—was sometimes interpreted as a consequence of 'altruistic' voters caring mostly about the competence of governments in promoting the 'public interest' (Lewin 1991: 45). However, this is unlikely to exhaust the issue. On the one hand, people's perceptions of national conditions are coloured by their own personal economic circumstances and by the information they collect in their environment (Reeves and Gimpel 2012; Ansolabehere et al. 2014). On the other hand, the reason why people use 'information about the national economic condition as a superior indicator of the government's ability to promote (eventually) their own economic welfare' (Kinder and Kiewiet 1981: 132) may simply be that it is so difficult to sort out which part of their personal well-being is due to political decisions. However, when they *can* indeed sort that out, they do not seem to ignore that information. An increasing number of studies has shown that government transfers and programmes improving the economic circumstances of specific types of households are indeed rewarded with increased support by the targeted voters (Manacorda et al. 2011; Pop-Eleches and Pop-Eleches 2012). Politicians seem to know this: election-year effects in fiscal policy have been detected not so much at the level of expenditures but rather on their composition, that is, the way they target particular kinds of voters with benefits (Katsimi and Sarantides 2012; Brender and Drazen 2013). More generally, changes in personal economic conditions do seem to affect support for the government whenever such changes can be attributed to government action (Tilley et al. 2018). And the need to focus on personal or socially/spatially close circumstances has also been stressed, for example, in the relationship between war casualties and public support at the *local* level (Gartner and Segura 2000; Karol and Miguel 2007; Althaus et al. 2012).

Finally, if people have preferences over policies, it might be important to look at how they respond to policy. Erikson et al. (2002) provided a broad, dynamic, and integrative way of thinking about this policy-public opinion linkage. They show that unemployment and inflation, rather than being treated solely as 'valence' issues affecting perceptions of government competence, should also be seen as affecting public demands for policy, captured through a generic left-right measure of public opinion (Public Policy Mood). While rises in unemployment increase citizens' demand for more liberal (in the American sense) social and economic policies, inflation pushes demands in the opposite, conservative, direction.

These approaches demonstrate not only that public demands lead to predictable responses by election-motivated incumbents—in the form of policy outputs—but also that those responses produce, in turn, new 'thermostatic' (Wlezien 1995) reactions on the part of the public: the public shifts in a conservative direction when the policy supply is perceived as having become too liberal, and shifts in a liberal direction when the supply is perceived as having become too conservative. Covering a wide variety of policy domains in different countries, Soroka and Wlezien have shown that 'thermostatic public responsiveness' is a rather broad phenomenon, across population sub-groups and even across political systems, with variations accounted, for example, by the salience of policy domains for citizens or the extent to which control over policy is perceived as being concentrated (Soroka and Wlezien 2010; Wlezien and Soroka 2011, 2012). The notion that the public reacts 'thermostatically' to policy outputs when they overshoot public preferences—which they usually end up doing, given the demands of party bases (Stimson 2007)—even provides another cogent explanation for the 'cost of ruling' phenomenon. Building on Stevenson's (2002) extension of Paldam and Skott's (1995) 'median gap' model, Wlezien (2017) shows that the increase of the incumbent disadvantage through time results from the fact that the length of party tenure leads to an accumulation of policies away from mean public preferences, to which the public reacts in a predictable 'thermostatic'—negative—way.

31.4 Contributions for a Research Agenda

The first waves of modern social scientific quantitative research on executive approval seemed to settle on a broad conventional wisdom: the public was mostly composed by myopic and naïve agents, whose opinions and behaviours vis-à-vis incumbents are basically expressed through rewards or punishments on the basis of recent changes in outcomes, rallying events, and elite cues. However, as Solow (1970: 2) famously quipped about other 'stylized facts', 'there is no doubt that they are stylized, though it is possible to question whether they are facts.' Subsequent research has shown that positive economic developments may matter less than negative ones. Rather than being myopic and naïve, voters may simply lack information. What they do with that information may depend on how contextual variables and policy-specific features lead them to connect government actions with actual outcomes. Rather than just caring about recent changes in national circumstances, voters may trade-off between outcomes or between processes and outcomes, and care more about policies and how they are personally affect them.

Looking at the present situation, what might a future research agenda in this field look like? We propose three items for that agenda. First, as we saw, much of unravelling of the early conventional wisdom resulted simply from asking in different contexts the same questions that were asked originally in the US and the UK. This will certainly continue to be important. One priority in this regard concerns the study of the effects of 'rally 'round the flag' events and involvement in military conflicts. These are questions where, with very a few notable exceptions, research seems to remain mostly locked to the context where it was originally studied. The ability to go beyond the United States in this regard seems particularly relevant, considering the singularity of American underlying conditions: the combination between a leader of the executive who is also the head of state, plus an unmatched ability to project force abroad, plus a much higher latent public support for the use of decisive 'hard power' action in international crises than what is known to exist mostly anywhere else (Everts and Isernia 2015). It is enough to move to the UK to see that, with the exception of the Falklands War (Clarke et al. 1993), evidence for similar crises and events producing 'rally 'round the flag effects' is extremely scarce (Lai and Reiter 2005). On both conflicts and causalities, there is great necessity of pursuing further research along the lines of pioneering comparative studies like Williams et al. (2010) and Koch (2011).

A second desirable item in this research agenda concerns the answers that have been found by challenging the original conventional wisdom: some of those answers seem themselves ripe for questioning. 'Clarity of responsibility' is the case in point. There is no shortage of studies showing that 'clarity' has no relevant role as a moderator (Chappell and Veiga 2000; Ecker et al. 2016) or even the opposite role to one that was hypothesized (Royed at al. 2000; Samuels and Hellwig 2010). Results for Latin America are particularly telling of the difficulties in this regard, ranging from incumbent punishment for bad performance being larger under divided than under unified government (Johnson and Schwindt-Bayer 2009) to voters completely failing to discount exogenous economic effects when evaluating the government (Campelo and Zucco 2016). Furthermore, studies using individual-level data suggest that voters' actual assignments of responsibility for outcomes are pervaded by partisan biases and framing effects (Hellwig and Coffey 2011; Bisgaard 2015).

This could be a matter of 'clarity' needing to be captured in different types of systems by different political and institutional variables (Valdini and Lewis-Beck 2018). But it could also be a matter of having to look for other sources of contextual heterogeneity in the relationship between outcomes and support. Brender and Drazen (2008) show how voters in older and more developed democracies are more intolerant of expanding budget deficits and less rewarding of economic growth than in younger democracies (see also Hellwig 2010). This result close matches the fact that political deficit cycles are phenomena that mostly characterize the early years after a country's transition to democracy and disappear with time (Brender and Drazen 2005). Why should this be the case? Is this linked to the previously discussed greater levels of 'information' that conceivably characterize older democracies and more developed nations? To greater levels of quality of governance directing voters' concerns towards less tangible or instrumental outcomes of government action (Magalhães 2017)? To greater prosperity decreasing the salience of economic outcomes (Rohrschneider and Loveless 2010)? To greater party system institutionalization, higher levels of partisanship, and lower electoral volatility (Shelton 2014)? We really do not know.

Finally, a major gap in the literature concerns the question with which we started this chapter: why should students of political executives care about public opinion? Public opinion and the life and internal dynamics and survival of cabinets should be interconnected, particularly in systems where the executive does not enjoy a fixed term of office. 'Public opinion shocks' have long been argued to play a central role in theories about executive stability, as critical events affecting expectations about possible election results and disturbing the bargain that keeps cabinets in place (Laver and Shepsle 1998). However, given the difficulty in obtaining public opinion data over the necessary length of time to examine its effects on cabinet survival, most research, in order to capture such phenomena, has had to do with observable variables thought to affect public opinion, such as, for example, the economy (Somer-Topcu and Williams 2008; Saalfeld 2013; Hellström and Walther 2019).

However, we saw how the relationship between the economy and public approval is complex and contingent. In a study of prime ministerial replacement in Japan, Burden (2015) shows that economic changes produce significant but small effects on prime ministerial popularity, and no effects at all on the approval of the Liberal Democratic Party (LDP). He then shows that LDP's ability to shield itself completely from downturns results from the ability to strategically remove prime ministers before they contaminate the party's standing. In other words, the imperviousness of LDP support to the economy does not prevent—indeed it is allowed by—changes in executive leadership (see also

Matsumoto and Laver 2015, who show that rising support for opposition parties increases the risk of early elections in Japan). Other studies along these lines include Kam and Indriðason (2005), revealing how cabinet reshuffles are linked with declining approval; Becher and Christiansen (2015), showing that increasing support for the prime minister increases the probability of the use of dissolution threats to extract policy concessions; or Walther and Hellström's comparative work (2019), showing that, for single-party cabinets, the risks of dissolution and replacement rise when public support for the government is, respectively above and below average. As public opinion data availability for a variety of democracies increases (Jennings and Wlezien 2016), it is to be expected that these pioneering works find much needed continuity.

References

Alt, J. E. and Lassen, D. D. (2006). 'Transparency, Political Polarization, and Political Budget Cycles in OECD Countries,' *American Journal of Political Science* 50(3): 530–50.

Alt, J. E., Lassen, D. D., and Skilling, D. (2002). 'Fiscal Transparency, Gubernatorial Approval, and the Scale of Government: Evidence from the States,' *State Politics & Policy Quarterly* 2(3): 230–50.

Althaus, S. L., Bramlett, B. H., and Gimpel, J. G. (2012). 'When War Hits Home: The Geography of Military Losses and Support for War in Time and Space,' *Journal of Conflict Resolution* 56(3): 382–412.

Anderson, C. D. (2006). 'Economic Voting and Multilevel Governance: A Comparative Individual-Level Analysis,' *American Journal of Political Science* 50(2): 449–63.

Anderson, C. J. (2000). 'Economic Voting and Political Context: A Comparative Perspective,' *Electoral Studies* 19(2): 151–70.

Ansolabehere, S., Meredith, M., and Snowberg, E. (2014). 'Mecro-Economic Voting: Local Information and Micro-Perceptions of the Macro-Economy,' *Economics & Politics* 26(3): 380–410.

Arvate, P. R., Avelino, G., and Tavares, J. (2009). 'Fiscal Conservatism in a New Democracy: "Sophisticated" Versus "Naïve" Voters,' *Economics Letters* 102(2): 125–7.

Baker, W. D. and Oneal, J. R. (2001). 'Patriotism or Opinion Leadership? The Nature and Origins of the "Rally 'Round the Flag" Effect,' *Journal of Conflict Resolution* 45(5): 661–87.

Baum, M. A. (2002). 'The Constituent Foundations of the Rally-Round-The-Flag Phenomenon,' *International Studies Quarterly* 46(2): 263–98.

Becher, M. and Christiansen, F. J. (2015). 'Dissolution Threats and Legislative Bargaining,' *American Journal of Political Science* 59(3): 641–55.

Bisgaard, M. (2015). 'Bias Will Find a Way: Economic Perceptions, Attributions of Blame, and Partisan-Motivated Reasoning during Crisis,' *The Journal of Politics* 77(3): 849–60.

Brender, A. (2003). 'The Effect of Fiscal Performance on Local Government Election Results in Israel: 1989–1998,' *Journal of Public Economics* 87(9–10): 2187–205.

Brender, A. and Drazen, A. (2005). 'Political Budget Cycles in New Versus Established Democracies,' *Journal of Monetary Economics* 52(7): 1271–95.

Brender, A. and Drazen, A. (2008). 'How Do Budget Deficits and Economic Growth Affect Reelection Prospects? Evidence from a Large Panel of Countries,' *American Economic Review* 98(5): 2203–20.

Brender, A. and Drazen, A. (2013). 'Elections, Leaders, and the Composition of Government Spending,' *Journal of Public Economics* 97: 18–31.

Brody, R. (1991). *Assessing the President: The Media, Elite Opinion, and Public Support.* Stanford: Stanford University Press.

Burden, B. C. (2015). 'Economic Accountability and Strategic Calibration: The Case of Japan's Liberal Democratic Party,' *Party Politics* 21(3): 346–56.

Campello, D. and Zucco Jr, C. (2016). 'Presidential Success and the World Economy,' *The Journal of Politics* 78(2): 589–602.

Carlin, R. E., Love, G. J., and Martínez-Gallardo, C. (2015). 'Cushioning the Fall: Scandals, Economic Conditions, and Executive Approval,' *Political Behavior* 37(1): 109–30.

Carlsen, F. (2000). 'Unemployment, Inflation and Government Popularity—Are There Partisan Effects?,' *Electoral Studies* 19(2–3): 141–50.

Chang, E. C. (2008). 'Electoral Incentives and Budgetary Spending: Rethinking the Role of Political Institutions,' *The Journal of Politics* 70(4): 1086–97.

Chapman, T. L. and Reiter, D. (2004). 'The United Nations Security Council and the Rally 'Round the Flag Effect,' *Journal of Conflict Resolution* 48(6): 886–909.

Chappell Jr., H. W. and Veiga, L. G. (2000). 'Economics and Elections in Western Europe: 1960–1997,' *Electoral Studies* 19(2–3): 183–97.

Chiozza, G. and Goemans, H. E. (2003). 'Peace Through Insecurity: Tenure and International Conflict,' *Journal of Conflict Resolution* 47(4): 443–67.

Choi, E. and Woo, J. (2010). 'Political Corruption, Economic Performance, and Electoral Outcomes: A Cross-National Analysis,' *Contemporary Politics* 16(3): 249–62.

Clarke, H. D., Dutt, N., and Kornberg, A. (1993). 'The Political Economy of Attitudes Toward Polity and Society in Western European Democracies,' *The Journal of Politics* 55(4): 998–1021.

Cuzan, A. G. and Bundrick, C. M. (1997). 'Presidential Popularity in Central America: Parallels with the United States,' *Political Research Quarterly* 50(4): 833–49.

Dassonneville, R. and Lewis-Beck, M. S. (2014). 'Macroeconomics, Economic Crisis and Electoral Outcomes: A National European Pool,' *Acta Politica* 49(4): 372–94.

Davis, C. L., Camp, R. A., and Coleman, K. M. (2004). 'The Influence of Party Systems on Citizens' Perceptions of Corruption and Electoral Response in Latin America,' *Comparative Political Studies* 37(6): 677–703.

Drazen, A. and Eslava, M. (2010). 'Electoral Manipulation Via Voter-Friendly Spending: Theory and Evidence,' *Journal of Development Economics* 92(1): 39–52.

Duch, R. M. and Stevenson, R. T. (2008). *The Economic Vote: How Political and Economic Institutions Condition Election Results.* Cambridge: Cambridge University Press.

Durr, R. H. (1993). 'What Moves Policy Sentiment?' *American Political Science Review* 87(1): 158–70.

Ecker, A., Glinitzer, K., and Meyer, T. M. (2016). 'Corruption Performance Voting and the Electoral Context,' *European Political Science Review* 8(3): 333–54.

Erikson, R. S., Mackuen, M. B., and Stimson, J. A. (2002). *The Macro Polity.* Cambridge: Cambridge University Press.

Everts, P. and Isernia, P. (2015). *Public Opinion, Transatlantic Relations and the Use of Force.* New York: Palgrave Macmillan.

Fackler, T. and Lin, T. M. (1995). 'Political Corruption and Presidential Elections, 1929–1992,' *The Journal of Politics* 57(4): 971–93.

Gartner, S. S. and Segura, G. M. (2000). 'Race, Casualties, and Opinion in the Vietnam War,' *Journal of Politics* 62(1): 115–46.

Gelpi, C., Feaver, P. D., and Reifler, J. (2006). 'Success Matters: Casualty Sensitivity and the War in Iraq,' *International Security* 30(3): 7–46.

Goodhart, C. A. E. and Bhansali, R. J. (1970). 'Political Economy,' *Political Studies* 18: 43–106.

Green, J. and Jennings, W. (2017). *The Politics of Competence: Parties, Public Opinion and Voters.* Cambridge: Cambridge University Press.

Groeling, T. and Baum, M. A. (2008). 'Crossing the Water's Edge: Elite Rhetoric, Media Coverage, and the Rally-Round-The-Flag Phenomenon,' *The Journal of Politics* 70(4): 1065–85.

Grofman, B. and Van Roozendaal, P. (1997). 'Modelling Cabinet Durability and Termination,' *British Journal of Political Science* 27(3): 419–51.

Gronke, P. and Newman, B. (2003). 'FDR To Clinton, Mueller To? A Field Essay on Presidential Approval,' *Political Research Quarterly* 56(4): 501–12.

Haynes, K. (2017). 'Diversionary Conflict: Demonizing Enemies or Demonstrating Competence?,' *Conflict Management and Peace Science* 34(4): 337–58.

Healy, A. and Lenz, G. S. (2014). 'Substituting the End for the Whole: Why Voters Respond Primarily To the Election-Year Economy,' *American Journal of Political Science* 58(1): 31–47.

Healy, A. J., Persson, M., and Snowberg, E. (2017). 'Digging into the Pocketbook: Evidence on Economic Voting from Income Registry Data Matched to a Voter Survey,' *American Political Science Review* 111(4): 771–85.

Hellwig, T. (2010). 'Elections and the Economy,' in L. Leduc, R. G. Niemi, and P. Norris (eds) *Comparing Democracies 3: Elections and Voting in the 21st Century.* Thousand Oaks: Sage.

Hellström, J. and Walther, D. (2019). 'How Is Government Stability Affected by the State of the Economy? Payoff Structures, Government Type and Economic State,' *Government and Opposition* 54(2): 280–308.

Hellwig, T. and Coffey, E. (2011). 'Public Opinion, Party Messages, and Responsibility for the Financial Crisis in Britain,' *Electoral Studies* 30(3): 417–26.

Hetherington, M. J. and Nelson, M. (2003). 'Anatomy of a Rally Effect: George W. Bush and the War on Terrorism,' *PS: Political Science & Politics* 36(1): 37–42.

Hibbs, D. A. (1977). 'Political Parties and Macroeconomic Policy,' *American Political Science Review* 71(4): 1467–87.

Hibbs, D. A. (2000). 'Bread and Peace Voting in US Presidential Elections,' *Public Choice* 104(1–2): 149–80.

Hibbs Jr, D. A. Rivers, R. D., and Vasilatos, N. (1982). 'On the Demand for Economic Outcomes: Macroeconomic Performance and Mass Political Support in the United States, Great Britain, and Germany,' *The Journal of Politics* 44(2): 426–62.

Homans, G. C. (1961). *Human Behavior: Its Elementary Forms.* New York: Harcourt, Brace and World, Inc.

Jennings, W. and Wlezien, C. (2016). 'Replication Data for: The Timeline of Elections: A Comparative Perspective.' Harvard Dataverse, doi.org/10.7910/DVN/28856

Johnson, G. B. and Schwindt-Bayer, L. A. (2009). 'Economic Accountability in Central America,' *Journal of Politics in Latin America* 1(3): 33–56.

Kam, C. and Indriðason, I. (2005). 'The Timing of Cabinet Reshuffles in Five Westminster Parliamentary Systems,' *Legislative Studies Quarterly* 30(3): 327–63.

Karol, D. and Miguel, E. (2007). 'The Electoral Cost of War: Iraq Casualties and the 2004 US Presidential Election,' *Journal of Politics* 69(3): 633–48.

Katsimi, M. and Sarantides, V. (2012). 'Do Elections Affect the Composition of Fiscal Policy in Developed, Established Democracies?,' *Public Choice* 151(1–2): 325–62.

Kayser, M. A. (2005). 'Who Surfs, Who Manipulates? The Determinants of Opportunistic Election Timing and Electorally Motivated Economic Intervention', *American Political Science Review* 99(1): 17–27.

Kayser, M. A. (2009). 'Partisan Waves: International Business Cycles and Electoral Choice', *American Journal of Political Science* 53(4): 950–70.

Kayser, Mark. A. (2014). 'The Elusive Economic Vote', in L. Leduc, R. G. Niemi, and P. Norris (eds) *Comparing Democracies 4: Elections and Voting in a Changing World*. Thousand Oaks: Sage, 112–32.

Kershaw, T. S. and Alexander, S. (2003). 'Procedural Fairness, Blame Attributions, and Presidential Leadership', *Social Justice Research* 16(1): 79–93.

Kiewiet, D. R. (1981). 'Policy-Oriented Voting in Response to Economic Issues', *American Political Science Review* 75(2): 448–59.

Kinder, D. R. and Kiewiet, D. R. (1981). 'Sociotropic Politics: The American Case', *British Journal of Political Science* 11(2): 129–61.

Koch, M. T. (2011). 'Casualties and Incumbents: Do the Casualties from Interstate Conflicts Affect Incumbent Party Vote Share?', *British Journal of Political Science* 41(4): 795–817.

Krause, S. and Méndez, F. (2009). 'Corruption and Elections: An Empirical Study of a Cross-Section of Countries', *Economics & Politics* 21(2): 179–200.

Lai, B. and Reiter, D. (2005). 'Rally 'Round the Union Jack? Public Opinion and the Use of Force in the United Kingdom, 1948–2001', *International Studies Quarterly* 49(2): 255–72.

Larson, E. V. (1996). *Casualties and Consensus: The Historical Role of Casualties in Domestic Support for US Military Operations*. Cambridge: Rand Corporation.

Laver, M. and Shepsle, K. A. (1998). 'Events, Equilibria, and Government Survival', *American Journal of Political Science* 42(1): 28–54.

Lee, J. R. (1977). 'Rallying Around the Flag: Foreign Policy Events and Presidential Popularity', *Presidential Studies Quarterly* 7(4): 252–6.

Levy, J. S. (1989). 'The Diversionary Theory of War: A Critique', in M. I. Midlarsky (ed.) *Handbook of War Studies*. Ann Arbor, MI: University of Michigan Press, 259–88.

Levy, J. S. and Thompson, W. R. (2010). *Causes of War*. Chichester: John Wiley & Sons.

Lewin, L. (1991). *Self-Interest and Public Interest in Western Politics*. Oxford: Oxford University Press.

Lewis-Beck, M. S. and Nadeau, R. (2012). 'PIGS or Not? Economic Voting in Southern Europe', *Electoral Studies* 31(3): 472–7.

Lewis-Beck, M. S. and Stegmaier, M. (2013). 'The VP-Function Revisited: A Survey of the Literature on Vote and Popularity Functions After Over 40 Years', *Public Choice* 157(3–4): 367–85.

Lindvall, J. (2014). 'The Electoral Consequences of Two Great Crises', *European Journal of Political Research* 53(4): 747–65.

Lupia, A. and Strøm, K. (1995). 'Coalition Termination and the Strategic Timing of Parliamentary Elections', *American Political Science Review* 89(3): 648–65.

MacCoun, R. J. (2005). 'Voice, Control, and Belonging: The Double-Edged Sword of Procedural Fairness', *Annual Review Law and Social Sciences* 1: 171–201.

Magalhães, P. C. (2017). 'Economic Outcomes, Quality of Governance, and Satisfaction with Democracy', in C. Van Ham, J. Thomassen, K. Aarts, and R. Andeweg (eds) *Myth and Reality of the Legitimacy Crisis: Explaining Trends and Cross-National Differences in Established Democracies*. Oxford: Oxford University Press, 156–71.

Manacorda, M., Miguel, E., and Vigorito, A. (2011). 'Government Transfers and Political Support,' *American Economic Journal: Applied Economics* 3(3): 1–28.

Manzetti, L. and Wilson, C. J. (2006). 'Corruption, Economic Satisfaction, and Confidence in Government Evidence from Argentina,' *The Latin Americanist* 49(2): 131–9.

Matsumoto, T. and Laver, M. (2015). 'Public Opinion Feedback between Elections, and Stability of Single-Party Majority Governments,' *Electoral Studies* 40: 308–14.

Monroe, K. R. (1978). 'Economic Influences on Presidential Popularity,' *Public Opinion Quarterly* 42(3): 360–9.

Mueller, J. E. (1970). 'Presidential Popularity from Truman to Johnson,' *American Political Science Review* 64(1): 18–34.

Mueller, J. E. (1973). *War, Presidents, and Public Opinion*. New York: John Wiley & Sons.

Muñoz, J., Anduiza, E., and Gallego, A. (2016). 'Why Do Voters Forgive Corrupt Mayors? Implicit Exchange, Credibility of Information and Clean Alternatives,' *Local Government Studies* 42(4): 598–615.

Murphy, K. (2017). 'Procedural Justice and Its Role in Promoting Voluntary Compliance,' in P. Drahos (ed.) *Regulatory Theory: Foundations and Applications*. Acton: Australia National University Press.

Nadeau, R., Bélanger, É., Lewis-Beck, M. S., Turgeon, M., and Gélineau, F. (2017). *Latin American Elections: Choice and Change*. Ann Arbor, MI: University of Michigan Press.

Nadeau, R., Niemi, R. G., and Yoshinaka, A. (2002). 'A Cross-National Analysis of Economic Voting: Taking Account of the Political Context across Time and Nations,' *Electoral Studies* 21(3): 403–23.

Nannestad, P. and Paldam, M. (1994). 'The VP-Function: A Survey of the Literature on Vote and Popularity Functions after 25 Years,' *Public Choice* 79(3–4): 213–45.

Nannestad, P. and Paldam, M. (1997). 'The Grievance Asymmetry Revisited: A Micro Study of Economic Voting in Denmark, 1986–1992,' *European Journal of Political Economy* 13(1): 81–99.

Nannestad, P. and Paldam, M. (2002). 'The Cost of Ruling: A Foundation Stone for Two Theories,' in H. Dorussen and M. Taylor (eds) *Economic Voting*. Didcot: Taylor & Francis, 17–44.

Nordhaus, W. D. (1975). 'The Political Business Cycle,' *The Review of Economic Studies* 42(2): 169–90.

Oneal, J. R. and Bryan, A. L. (1995). 'The Rally 'Round the Flag Effect in US Foreign Policy Crises, 1950–1985,' *Political Behavior* 17(4): 379–401.

Paldam, M. and Skott, P. (1995). 'A Rational-Voter Explanation of the Cost of Ruling,' *Public Choice* 83(1–2): 159–172.

Persson, T. and Tabellini, G. E. (2003). *The Economic Effects of Constitutions*. Cambridge, MA: MIT Press.

Pop-Eleches, C. and Pop-Eleches, G. (2012). 'Targeted Government Spending and Political Preferences,' *Quarterly Journal of Political Science* 7(3): 285–320.

Powell Jr., G. B. and Whitten, G. D. (1993). 'A Cross-National Analysis of Economic Voting: Taking Account of the Political Context,' *American Journal of Political Science* 37(2): 391–414.

Rasinski, K. A. and Tyler, T. R. (1988). 'Fairness and Vote Choice in the 1984 Presidential Election,' *American Politics Quarterly* 16(1): 5–24.

Rattinger, H. (1991). 'Unemployment and Elections in West Germany,' in H. Norpoth, M. Lewis-Beck, and J. Lafay (eds) *Economics and Politics: The Calculus of Support*. Ann Arbor, MI: University of Michigan Press, 49–62.

644   PEDRO C. MAGALHÃES

Reeves, A. and Gimpel, J. G. (2012). 'Ecologies of Unease: Geographic Context and National Economic Evaluations,' *Political Behavior* 34(3): 507–34.

Reif, K. and Schmitt, H. (1980). 'Nine Second-Order National Elections—A Conceptual Framework for the Analysis of European Election Results,' *European Journal of Political Research* 8(1): 3–44.

Roberts, A. (2008). 'Hyperaccountability: Economic Voting in Central and Eastern Europe,' *Electoral Studies* 27(3): 533–46.

Rogoff, K. (1990). 'Equilibrium Political Budget Cycles,' *The American Economic Review* 80(1): 21–36.

Rogoff, K. (2003). 'Globalization and Global Disinflation,' *Economic Review-Federal Reserve Bank of Kansas City* 88(4): 45–78.

Rogoff, K. and Sibert, A. (1988). 'Elections and Macroeconomic Policy Cycles,' *The Review of Economic Studies* 55(1): 1–16.

Rohrschneider, R. and Loveless, M. (2010). 'Macro Salience: How Economic and Political Contexts Mediate Popular Evaluations of the Democracy Deficit in the European Union,' *The Journal of Politics* 72(4): 1029–45.

Royed, T. J., Leyden, K. M., and Borrelli, S. A. (2000). 'Is "Clarity of Responsibility" Important for Economic Voting? Revisiting Powell and Whitten's Hypothesis,' *British Journal of Political Science* 30(4): 669–98.

Saalfeld, T. (2013), 'Economic Performance, Political Institutions and Cabinet Durability in 28 European Parliamentary Democracies, 1945–2011,' in W. C. Müller and H.-M. Narud (eds) *Party Governance and Party Democracy*. New York: Springer, 51–80.

Samuels, D. and Hellwig, T. (2010). 'Elections and Accountability for the Economy: A Conceptual and Empirical Reassessment,' *Journal of Elections, Public Opinion and Parties* 20(4): 393–419.

Schleiter, P. and Tavits, M. (2016). 'The Electoral Benefits of Opportunistic Election Timing,' *The Journal of Politics* 78(3): 836–50.

Shelton, C. A. (2014). 'Legislative Budget Cycles,' *Public Choice* 159(1–2): 251–75.

Shi, M. and Svensson, J. (2006). 'Political Budget Cycles: Do They Differ Across Countries and Why?,' *Journal of Public Economics* 90(8–9): 1367–89.

Singer, M. M. (2011). 'Who Says "It's the Economy"? Cross-National and Cross-Individual Variation in the Salience of Economic Performance,' *Comparative Political Studies* 44(3): 284–312.

Singh, S. P. and Tir, J. (2018). 'Partisanship, Militarized International Conflict, and Electoral Support for the Incumbent,' *Political Research Quarterly* 71(1): 172–83.

Solow, R. M. (1970). *Growth Theory: An Exposition*. Oxford: Clarendon Press.

Somer-Topcu, Z. and Williams, L. K. (2008). 'Survival of the Fittest? Cabinet Duration in Postcommunist Europe,' *Comparative Politics* 40(3): 313–29.

Soroka, S. N. (2006). 'Good News and Bad News: Asymmetric Responses to Economic Information,' *Journal of Politics* 68(2): 372–85.

Soroka, S. N. and Wlezien, C. (2010). *Degrees of Democracy: Politics, Public Opinion, and Policy*. Cambridge: Cambridge University Press.

Stevenson, R. T. (2001). 'The Economy and Policy Mood: A Fundamental Dynamic of Democratic Politics?,' *American Journal of Political Science* 45(3): 620–33.

Stevenson, R. T. (2002). 'The Cost of Ruling, Cabinet Duration, and the 'Median-Gap' Model,' *Public Choice* 113(1–2): 157–78.

Stimson, J. (2007). 'Perspectives on Representation: Asking the Right Questions and Getting the Right Answers,' in R. J. Dalton and H. D. Klingemann (eds) *The Oxford Handbook of Political Behavior*. Oxford: Oxford University Press.

Stimson, J. A. (1976). 'Public Support for American Presidents: A Cyclical Model,' *Public Opinion Quarterly* 40(1): 1–21.

Strøm, K. and Swindle, S. M. (2002). 'Strategic Parliamentary Dissolution,' *American Political Science Review* 96(3): 575–91.

Tarar, A. (2006). 'Diversionary Incentives and the Bargaining Approach to War,' *International Studies Quarterly* 50(1): 169–88.

Tavits, M. (2007). 'Clarity of Responsibility and Corruption,' *American Journal of Political Science* 51(1): 218–29.

Tilley, J., Neundorf, A., and Hobolt, S. B. (2018). 'When the Pound in People's Pocket Matters: How Changes to Personal Financial Circumstances Affect Party Choice,' *The Journal of Politics* 80(2): 555–69.

Tir, J. and Singh, S. P. (2013). 'Is It the Economy or Foreign Policy, Stupid? The Impact of Foreign Crises on Leader Support,' *Comparative Politics* 46(1): 83–101.

Tufte, E. R. (1978). *Political Control of the Economy*. Princeton: Princeton University Press.

Tyler, T. R. and Caine, A. (1981). 'The Influence of Outcomes and Procedures on Satisfaction with Formal Leaders,' *Journal of Personality and Social Psychology* 41(4): 642–55.

Valdini, M. E. and Lewis-Beck, M. S. (2018). 'Economic Voting in Latin America: Rules and Responsibility,' *American Journal of Political Science* 62(2): 410–23.

Van der Brug, W., Van der Eijk, C., and Franklin, M. (2007). *The Economy and the Vote: Economic Conditions and Elections in Fifteen Countries*. Cambridge: Cambridge University Press.

Veiga, F. J., Veiga, L. G., and Morozumi, A. (2017). 'Political Budget Cycles and Media Freedom,' *Electoral Studies* 45: 88–99.

Vergne, C. (2009). 'Democracy, Elections and Allocation of Public Expenditures in Developing Countries,' *European Journal of Political Economy* 25(1): 63–77.

Walther, D. and Hellström, J. (2019). 'The Verdict in the Polls: How Government Stability is Affected by Popular Support,' *West European Politics* 42(3): 593–617.

Williams, L. K., Brule, D. J., and Koch, M. (2010). 'War Voting: Interstate Disputes, the Economy, and Electoral Outcomes,' *Conflict Management and Peace Science* 27(5): 442–60.

Winters, M. S. and Weitz-Shapiro, R. (2013). 'Lacking Information or Condoning Corruption: When Do Voters Support Corrupt Politicians?' *Comparative Politics* 45(4): 418–36.

Wlezien, C. (1995). 'The Public As Thermostat: Dynamics of Preferences for Spending,' *American Journal of Political Science* 39(4): 981–1000.

Wlezien, C. (2015). 'The Myopic Voter? The Economy and Us Presidential Elections,' *Electoral Studies* 39: 195–204.

Wlezien, C. (2017). 'Policy (Mis) Representation and the Cost of Ruling: US Presidential Elections in Comparative Perspective,' *Comparative Political Studies* 50(6): 711–38.

Wlezien, C. and Soroka, S. N. (2011). 'Federalism and Public Responsiveness to Policy,' *Publius: The Journal of Federalism* 41(1): 31–52.

Wlezien, C. and Soroka, S. N. (2012). 'Political Institutions and the Opinion-Policy Link,' *West European Politics* 35(6): 1407–32.

Wright, J. R. (2012). 'Unemployment and the Democratic Electoral Advantage,' *American Political Science Review* 106(4): 685–702.

CHAPTER 32

···

PERFORMANCE AND EVALUATION OF POLITICAL EXECUTIVES

···

LUDGER HELMS

32.1 INTRODUCTION

···

TODAY, few scholars deny that issues of performance and evaluation are at the very heart of notions of democratic governance, and the wider subject of political legitimacy. As Heazle et al. (2016: 3) contend, even under the conditions of full-blown democracy, 'an electoral mandate is merely the bedrock of democratic legitimacy upon which a structure of performance-based legitimacy must be built'. For all the fundamental differences separating democratic and non-democratic regimes, performance marks a key source of legitimacy in authoritarian regimes as well. Performance-related claims have been found to be of great importance to all authoritarian regimes (von Soest and Grauvogel 2017), and there is growing acknowledgment that the performance of autocracies and their very persistence are related (see Croissant et al. 2015).

The exact role of the executive branch in this complex process has remained ambiguous, though. For one thing, in the age of network governance the overall number of actors shaping the public policy-making process has multiplied and effectively circumscribed the status of the executive branch, which marks a key component of the wider notion of a 'depleted state' (Lodge 2013). At the same time, political executives have been considered to be the winner of the turn towards internationalized and 'informal' governance (see, e.g., Raunio 2009; Sassen 2009; Czada 2015). In non-democratic regimes, given their power-concentrating nature, political executives tend to matter even more, rather than less, in terms of their impact on a regime's political and policy performance (see Brooker 2014), though in some types of autocracy, such as one-party dictatorships, the executive typically operates in the shadow of the real power centre (the 'politbureau').

Despite the apparent centrality of issues of performance, and evaluation, to the study of political executives, performance is not a classic subject of executive politics (or at least not in the more narrow sense of the term, which characterizes the agenda of this volume). There are at least three areas in which issues of performance have long figured more prominently than in executive politics research. The first one is electoral studies, or more specifically studies on retrospective voting. Recent empirical research suggests that both governing and opposition parties should expect credit and blame for their respective conduct (see, e.g., Plescia and Kritzinger 2016; Stiers 2018); however, the established focus in this field has clearly been on governments rather than on oppositions. The discipline of legislative studies stands out as a second major field in which 'performance' has traditionally received much attention. Early studies focused on the US (see, e.g., Grumm 1971; Olson and Nonidez 1972; Rosenthal 1974) but there is now a growing comparative literature that involves different parliamentary democracies (see, e.g., Arter 2006) and occasionally extends to authoritarian regimes (see, e.g., Bonvecchi and Simison 2017).

Last not least, the study of performance-related issues has been at the very heart of public administration, which for many scholars marks the natural complement to comparative government as the second core discipline constituting the wider field of executive politics broadly defined (see Lodge and Wegrich 2012: 3–4). In contrast to the different traditions of studying performance in the electoral and legislative arenas, performance at the level of public bureaucracies has not only featured as an abstract scientific concept, but been closely linked to the evolution of the public sector itself. As Bouckaert and Peters (2002: 359) contend, performance measurement and management mark 'an indispensable element in modernizing the public sector', and the more recent literature in this area testifies to the authority of this contention (see, e.g., Olvera and Avellaneda 2017).

Despite, or perhaps because of, the impressive and multi-disciplinary nature of international research on the performance of political executives, it has remained difficult to identify a body of established truths in this field. The sources of perceived good performance of political executives and the concrete effects of those perceptions on the life and death of governments have very much remained a mystery. In stark contrast to measuring presidential or prime ministerial power (see also Chapter 19 in this volume), there are no universally accepted standards for measuring the performance of political executives, only proxy indicators, such as and in particular 'longevity' (see Rhodes and 't Hart 2014: 13; Grotz and Müller-Rommel 2015). This is why looking into those issues can claim to be of major importance for any deeper understanding of executive governance and the wider political process in different types of regime.

The next sections discuss the key questions concerning the performance and evaluation of political executives as a subject of comparative executive research—taking into account the contributions from the neighbouring disciplines—and review the key findings that have been offered when addressing these questions and issues. The final section eventually outlines an agenda for future research in the field.

32.2 KEY QUESTIONS AND FINDINGS

32.2.1 Individual and Collective Actors

Perhaps the most basic question is about who, exactly, is at the centre of attention when publics and scholars look at the performance of political executives. The focus may either be on 'chief executives' (i.e. presidents or prime ministers), on individual senior ministers, or on collective actors, such as in particular cabinets. In many parliamentary democracies, the more natural focus at the level of collective actors within the executive territory is on coalitions (which shape the cabinet system and the more informal arenas of party-based executive decision-making) rather than on the cabinet itself.

Most questions relating to the status of individual and collective actors within the executive branch can be answered meaningfully only when taking into account the different forms of democratic government. Presidential democracies, in addition to the institutional features of a direct election of the president and strict a separation-of-powers between the different branches of government, are marked by 'a broadly shared public perception that places the president at the center of the nation's politics' (Mezey 2013: 8–9)—a structural feature that starkly contrasts with the 'fusion-of-powers' nature characterizing parliamentary democracies. The latter are not only marked by an effective fusion of the legislative branch with the political executive (with the latter requiring the constant support of parliamentary majority in order to survive in office); rather the political executive itself has a structure with strong collective and collegial dimensions (Andeweg 1997). Semi-presidential democracies fall in between these two archetypes of representative government; they know both the structurally elevated position of a directly elected president and the parliamentary responsibility of the prime minister and the cabinet (see Elgie 2011).

While 'cabinet government' has been widely used as a near synonym of parliamentary government, the constitutional practice in different regimes defies the established terminology to some considerable extent. For one thing, in coalitional presidentialism Latin-American style cabinets have been considerably more important than in the US archetype of presidentialism (see Inácio and Llanos 2016). On the other hand, even in parliamentary democracies the role of the full cabinet tends to be more limited than traditional accounts of cabinet government would have it. To some extent, 'governing together' (Blondel and Müller-Rommel 1993) has always been a myth, though evidence from some of the younger democracies suggests that the idea of collegial and collective cabinet government as such is alive and well (see Blondel et al. 2007). The limited realization of cabinet government in the constitutional practice of most parliamentary democracies has been reflected in the scarcity, or in fact near-absence, of more particular research on the performance of cabinets. There is some occasional research on the impact of cabinet stability on the political performance of democratic regimes (see, e.g., Huber 1998), but barely any on the causes and effects of the (perceived) performance of cabinets. The relative neglect of more particular research on cabinet performance may seem justified by the low importance that cabinets apparently tend to play in the public mind. Indeed, recent research on 'performance voting' suggests that voters' knowledge of the cabinet composition tends to be strikingly limited (see Fortunato and Stevenson 2013; Rapeli 2016). There is some notable work on the performance of individual ministers, but most research in this area has centred on the issue of duration and durability. For example, Berlinski et al. (2010) studied the effects of individual and collective ministerial performance on the length of time a minister serves in British government, and found that 'a minister's hazard rate increases sharply after the first individual call for resignation and is decreasing in the cumulative number of resignation calls' (Berlinski et al. 2010: 559). Another study suggests that 'public calls for resignation might be a viable performance indicator', and prime ministers 'are far less likely to fire popular and well-performing cabinet members than underperformers' (Fischer et al. 2012: 514). The latter marks an interesting difference to the politics of hiring and firing in non-democratic regimes. As Flores and Smith have argued, 'since non-democratic leaders face relatively little threat from the masses, their concern is to reduce internal party risk. Therefore, they remove high performing ministers and retain mediocre and poor performers' (Flores and Smith 2011: 345). Other research on cabinet ministers in parliamentary democracies has revealed that the 'type of minister' ('ideologues', 'partisans', or 'loyalists') may have a significant impact on the policy performance of governments which at least equals the effect that different patterns of party control of individual departments tend to have on the policies that governments make (Alexiadou 2016). Individual ministers have also been identified as important independent actors in government communication and the complex game of 'personalized politics' (see Figenschou et al. 2017), which have come to constitute key elements of the politics of executive performance.

However, the ongoing personalization, or 'presidentialization', of politics (see also Chapter 18 in this volume) has moved in particular prime ministers, rather than individual ministers, into the limelight of executive politics, and executive politics research. Personalization is no longer a feature only of presidential and semi-presidential democracies, in which competitors for the top leadership position are directly elected, but has long come to characterize political campaigns, and more generally the media coverage of politics, in parliamentary democracies. Today, both presidents and prime ministers (and contenders for these two offices) tend to be more 'personal candidates' (see Musella 2018). This trend has been particularly prominent in some of the newer democracies, such as those of Central Eastern Europe (Hloušek 2015; Cabada and Tomšič 2016). However, it would not seem to be too much of an exaggeration to speak of a truly 'global rise of personalized politics', involving both democratic leaders and dictators (see Kendall-Taylor et al. 2017).

Obviously, a focus on the personality of leaders, and personality-related leadership skills, is much older than the relatively recent debate on personalization. Such approaches have long been particularly prominent in the study of US presidents and presidential leadership. The works by Greenstein (1975) and Barber (1977) stand out as modern classics in this field which has strong ties to political psychology. In particular Greenstein's more recent study on 'presidential difference' (2001), in which the author develops different skill-related categories for evaluating presidential performance, has had a major impact also beyond the study of US presidential leadership, especially in the study of British prime ministers. The 'leadership style/skills model' by Theakston focuses on prime ministerial performance in relation to public communication, organisational capacity, political skills, policy vision, cognitive style as well as emotional intelligence (see Theakston 2007, 2011, 2012). By contrast, the 'statecraft model' is more specifically interested in how leaders secure office and power, for example through a successful electoral strategy, party management and demonstrating 'governing competence' (see Bulpitt 1986; Buller and James 2012, 2015; Clarke et al., 2015). A more sophisticated tool for evaluating political leaders' performance and style, understood to be essentially reflections of their personality, is leadership trait analysis (see in particular Hermann 2005). There is a specialized Leadership Trait Analysis software, an assessment-at-a-distance tool, which has been used widely in the recent literature on the performance and style of key decision-makers in the executive branch (see, e.g., Rohrer 2014; Dyson 2018; see also Chapter 4 in this volume).

Finally, scholars of parliamentary democracy have long been concerned with assessing the performance of different types of government formats, and more specifically coalitions as a party-related type of collective actor in the executive territory. Although there have been more detailed categorizations of different types of coalition, much work has continued to focus on comparing single-party and coalition governments, conceptualizing performance in terms of cabinet and coalition stability. That said, in particular the study of 'deviant' government formats has inspired the development of more complex sets of performance-related indicators. For example, in a seminal paper Strøm assessed the performance of minority governments applying four indicators: duration, mode of resignation, subsequent alternation, and electoral success (Strøm 1985). Similarly, so-called 'grand coalitions' (involving the two largest parties of a given system) have prompted scholars to inquire if, or to what extent, other 'deviant' coalition formats may have special effects in terms of policy performance (see, e.g., Schniewind et al. 2009), but overall research in this area has remained notably scarce.

32.2.2 Election Pledges and Performance-Focused Strategies of Political Executives

All governments are, virtually by definition, expected to generate solutions to collective problems that create public satisfaction with the state of public affairs. In democratic systems, there is the more particular expectation that the solutions pursued reflect the central campaign promises and manifesto pledges of the parties or candidates that eventually win governmental office. While this applies essentially to all types of democratic government, comparative research has managed to identify certain patterns: Overall, while 'many parties that enter government executives are highly likely to fulfill their pledges [...]',

> parties in single-party executives, both with and without legislative majorities, have the highest fulfillment rates. Within coalition governments, the likelihood of pledge fulfillment is highest when the party receives the chief executive post and when another governing party made a similar pledge.   (Thomson et al. 2017: 527)

Related research has demonstrated that the strength of legislative institutions significantly shapes the relative policy influence of coalition parties in terms of turning electoral commitments into government policy (Martin and Vanberg 2019). Other recent research has pointed to the importance of time in the study of pledge fulfilment. Zubek and Klüver (2015: 603) investigated how coalition governments deal with post-electoral legislative agendas and found that 'pledges dealing with less divisive and more salient issues are likely to be fulfilled with less delay than those dealing with more divisive and less important issues'. A more sweeping judgment comes from Duval and Pétry, who studied a sample of Canadian governments between 1997–2015 (including both majority and minority governments) and six governments in the province of Quebec (1994–2014). They contend that 'if the government does not enact pledges within the first half of its mandate, the probability of these pledges ever being fulfilled drops drastically' (Duval and Pétry 2019: 207).

However, rather than simply seeking to maintain a reasonable connection between promise and performance, political executives tend to develop more specific strategies designed to generate favourable perceptions of their political and policy performance. Governments have long been suspected to operate on a distinct time schedule, with more popular measures being systematically concentrated in election years. There is some empirical evidence justifying this assumption, though most work has focused on economic policies (see, e.g., Rogoff and Sibert 1988). Recent research has looked more specifically into the political calculus of governments. As Bertelli and John have demonstrated in the British context, governments tend to behave like investment managers, 'making choices that yield return through the public valuation of policies' (Bertelli and John 2013: 741), which means, in particular, returns in terms of electoral support. There is also recent evidence from comparative research on public investments in education, research, and infrastructure, which suggests that such investments are 'attractive for parties with high office and vote aspirations, because they anticipate government responsibility in the future and can use investments' dispersed growth effects to appeal broadly to a large, heterogeneous pool of voters' (Kraft 2018: 128). Other comparative research on the making and implementation of retrenchment policies further suggests that there is also a very tangible element of 'strategic timing' at work (see König and Wenzelburger 2017). Such strategic choices become more difficult to make for the government, the more complex the internal structures of the government are. Other things being equal, coalition governments will find it considerably more difficult to agree on 'safe' investments, as different governing parties tend to have different core clienteles they seek to serve and satisfy. Further, parties and governments have distinct political communication strategies that are apparently related to the electoral cycle. While compromise is most likely to prevail during the middle of the term, differentiation dominates towards the end (as well as the beginning) of the legislative term (Sagarzazu and Klüver 2017), and there is good reason to believe that these strategic choices by individual parties tend to be reflected at the level of public policies. Strategic choices designed to develop favourable effects on the perceived performance of the government are not limited to public policies, though. Both presidents and prime ministers have used cabinet reshuffles, and other personnel changes, as well-tested cures against decreasing popularity of their administrations (see Kam and Indriðason 2005; Martínez-Gallardo 2014; Miwa 2018). In many parliamentary democracies the parties, rather than the prime minister, are the key driving force behind major changes to the ministerial team. Reshuffles have histories of their own, and their exact effects on the popularity of the government are difficult to forecast. Some reshuffles may be costly in political terms (see Indriðason and Kam 2008), but there is both impressionistic and hard empirical evidence suggesting that personnel changes—not least changes in the office of prime minister—may give governments a welcome, if temporary, popularity boost (see Green and Jennings 2017: 194).

Government communication, as already mentioned above, deserves to be seen as an independent factor shaping the perceived performance of a government. Among the rising figures of political advisers to political executives that have been observed across countries (see also Chapter 25 in this volume), media advisers have figured particularly prominently. While the accumulation of resources does not always translate neatly into enhanced leverage, more power and control (see Helms 2019), the intake of expert advisers on political communication and media affairs has clearly tended to professionalize government communication. Effective government communication is widely seen as an indispensable resource for effective leadership and governance, and the public perception of effectiveness (see Kane and Patapan 2010; Helms 2012; Grube 2013; McMasters and Uhr 2017; see also Chapter 29 in this volume). Related policy-focused research suggests that the importance of effective communication is indeed difficult to overestimate. In their case study on police performance in Missouri, USA, Ho and Cho found that, 'the perceived effectiveness of public communication has a more substantial impact on public satisfaction with police protection and crime prevention than neighborhood crime rates and broken windows factors' (Ho and Cho 2017: 228).

However, government communication does not necessarily centre on policy issues and the public policies that governments make. As recent research on American presidents suggests, political leaders may seek to distract voters from controversial policies by leading them to focus on image and personality whenever deemed expedient (Druckman and Jacobs 2016). The essence of this observation is neither entirely new nor confined to the United States: In fact, the possible intentions and goals of personalizing strategies have always included the systematic distraction of public attention from both policy and political issues (Kriesi 2004: 199; see also Farwell 2012). Other recent research suggests that even a purposefully created focus on personality, rather than policy, does not make governmental leaders immune to substantive assessments of their political conduct and performance (see Birch and Allen 2015; Allen et al. 2018).

32.2.3 Performance, Popularity and Performance-Voting

Whatever governments do, what matters ultimately is how their respective performance is perceived by others, and how this shapes the public support for the government. That said, there are two key features concerning the status of political executives in the elect-oral arena, which seem to exist to some extent independent of the particular perform-ance of the incumbent government. The first one is an 'incumbency advantage', which has been particularly pronounced in many non-democratic regimes with dictators will-ing and able to use any available means to keep would-be challengers at bay (see Egorov and Sonin 2014). In democratic contexts, a strong incumbency advantage is typical especially of many presidential systems; presidents are difficult to oust by challengers and tend to increase their electoral support when being re-elected. There are signs, though, that the 'incumbency advantage' as we knew it, has begun to wither. The rise of celebrity politicians, who enjoy a 'quasi-incumbency advantage' thanks to their public standing even on entering the race as challenger is changing the established patterns of presidential authority and accountability (see Risoleo 2018). The second feature, which has been observed in most parliamentary democracies, is the existence of particular electoral costs of governing. These do not preclude an 'incumbency advantage', in par-ticular of the prime minister in direct comparison with challengers from the opposition, but many, in fact most, re-elected or takeover prime ministers tend to chair parties or coalitions that see their electoral support base shrink over time (see Ieraci 2012; Green and Jennings 2017: chapters 5 and 6).

While some authors have questioned voters' ability to actually hold governing coalitions accountable, as the power of the parties to influence many of the objective performance metrics (such as the performance of the economy or schools) is often rather limited (Dynes and Holbein 2020), most scholars agree that performance, or perceived performance, does make a difference in terms of government support (see, e.g., Narud and Valen 2008; Giger 2010; Ghergina 2011; Shabad and Slomczynski 2011; Murillo and Visconti 2017). Specifically, election pledges matter for retrospective vot-ing (Matthieß forthcoming) and, overall, governments tend to be penalized for unful-filled pledges more than they are rewarded for fulfilled pledges (Naurin et al. 2019). In any case, voters' ability to hold governing coalitions accountable depends strongly on the cohesion of the government (Hobolt et al. 2013). However, governments obviously do not operate in a political vacuum. The perceived performance of governments tends to be shaped in particular by the opposition's public criticism of governmental performance (Seeberg 2018). Other important work, whose implications remain uncertain, suggests that voters only distinguish between low and at least mediocre performance, but 'there is no reward for high performance' (Boyne et al. 2009: 1273), and that there is a 'sophistication gap in performance voting', so that effectively 'holding governments to account for past performance is mainly the prerogative of the highly sophisticated' (de Vries and Giger 2014: 345). If there is one major element of consensus binding together these different strains of research, it relates to the finding that, other things being equal, economic prosperity is the best assurance an incumbent government can have when it comes to being seen as effective, and to securing re-election.

Some more particular features of performance voting are apparently related to the maturity of a given regime. As Bochsler and Hänni suggest (2019: 30), democratic regimes develop with regard to their operational mode of performance voting:

> In a first stage after the transition to democracy, reform governments suffer from a general anti-incumbency effect, unrelated to economic performance. In a second step, citizens in young democracies relate the legitimacy of democratic actors to their economic performance rather than to procedural rules, and connect economic outcomes closely to incumbent support. As democracies mature, actors profit from a reservoir of legitimacy, and retrospective voting declines.

There has also been some recent research on how misconduct in office and incumbent opportunism impact on perceived performance and electoral support. Ecker et al. found that, other things being equal, corruption performance voting is most likely to be observed with non-partisans and voters who believe that government turnover will bring about change, and in systems where corruption is a salient issue. Yet, perhaps most importantly, corruption performance voting seems not to correlate with the clarity of political responsibility of a given regime (see Ecker et al. 2016). As Cordero and Blais (2017: 645) contend, corrupt governments are not always punished by voters: 'Voters judge corruption in relative terms; what matters is not how corrupt the incumbent party is perceived to be but whether it is deemed to be more corrupt than the other parties'. In their research on voter reaction to incumbent opportunism, Schleiter and Tavits identified another fascinating pattern. They found that opportunistic incumbent behaviour to gain electoral advantage 'negatively affects support for the incumbent because it engenders voter concern about the incumbent's future performance and raises significant concerns about procedural fairness' (Schleiter and Tavits 2018). This would seem to suggest that hyper-strategic activities of governments designed to maintain public support at any cost is doomed to fail, at least if such governments face reasonably sophisticated voters. 'However', as the authors manage to demonstrate, 'under good economic performance, which often triggers electoral opportunism, voters are still more likely to support than oppose the incumbent despite their negative reaction to opportunism' (Schleiter and Tavits 2018: 327).

While related research suggests that the agency of political executives does matter also for explaining more particular phenomena, such as blunders and policy disasters, and more so than any structural features of the executive branch or the wider political system (see Jennings et al. 2018), performance, and the evaluation thereof, continues to be marked by political contingency. Indeed, the perceived performance of governments has been demonstrated to be shaped by 'irrelevant events', such as sport events. For example, Healy et al. found that, in the US, a win in the ten days before an upcoming election caused the incumbent in Senate, gubernatorial, and presidential elections an additional 1.6 percentage points of the Senate (Healy et al. 2010). Other 'irregular events'—from natural disasters to international crises—may also impact on the perceived performance of governments, with a potentially major effect on the government's electoral fortunes (see Heersink et al. 2017; Bovan et al. 2018). While crises are widely seen as a special opportunity for executives to demonstrate their capacity to act, exceptional events do not always, or necessarily, benefit the incumbent government. Rather, such occasions tend to become a testing ground for political leaders who may either boost or undermine their popularity and electoral chances. That said, differences can be found not only with regard to crisis management and leadership performance, but also at the level of crises themselves. Other things being equal, major economic crises stand out for having far more often severely negative electoral consequences for incumbent governments than other types of crisis (see, e.g., LeDuc and Pammett 2013).

Perhaps curiously, given the burgeoning literature on personalization, we still know very little about the relationship between the job approval of the chief executive and the electoral fortunes of those leaders and their governments. There is a conspicuous correlation between the job approval of US presidents and re-elections odds (see Silver 2011). However, the observed patterns do not seem to transcend into the world of parliamentary democracies. Evidence from a recent case study on Italy suggests that the prime minister's party tends to be held responsible for the government's performance to a larger extent than any other coalition partner (see Plescia 2017), yet this is not the same as to say that the prime minister himself or herself is chiefly (being held) responsible for this. Other work, on the UK, specifically points to the obvious limits of calculating, or predicting, the electoral performance of governing parties on the basis of leader approval ratings (see Blumenau 2014). Indeed, it is not even clear that leaders who have won office after a strongly personalized election campaign are held responsible for their government's perceived performance. For example, in 'Angela Merkel's Germany' it was for the Christian Democratic Union (CDU) / Christian Social Union's (CSU) junior partners to take the heat for voters' frustrations with some of the policies of the Merkel government. While most popular decisions were attributed to the chancellor's party, or the chancellor personally, the bulk of more contested decisions were conspicuously blamed on the Social Democratic Party (SPD) and the Free Democratic Party (FDP) which experienced disastrous electoral defeats in 2009, 2013, and 2017 respectively, after having governed alongside the Christian Democrats (see Helms and van Esch 2017).

32.2.4 The Rating and Ranking of Presidents and Prime Ministers

The rating and ranking of political chief executives by experts marks yet another way of assessing the performance of different office-holders. Such expert surveys, not to be confused with popular opinion surveys which are more widespread, have long been a feature of presidential studies in the US, with no real equivalent in any other major country. This can be seen as a result of both the unique resource-richness of American political science and the institutional architecture of the American political system itself, in which the president marks the unchallenged focal point of the political process. The scholarly ranking of US presidents was once launched by Arthur Schlesinger Sr and Jr (in 1948 and 1962, respectively), and has been continued ever since (for a recent example, see Rottinghaus and Vaughn 2018). Such rankings have occasionally been dismissed as arbitrary and shallow, with methodological criticisms relating to the limited expertise and obvious political leanings of evaluators, the proneness to 'presentism', and the systematic disregard of contextual factors (see, e.g., Skidmore 2004). Yet, overall, the possible methodological limitations of such rankings would not appear to be more serious than with any other method. As Nichols has concluded after a careful revision of the field, 'ratings are not, as some critics charge, helplessly subjective. This is demonstrated by the large amount of variance accounted for in every poll, and the many statistically significant determinants of each' (Nichols 2012: 292; see also Theakston 2013: 238).

To date, the only group of countries for which similar surveys have been conducted on a more than occasional basis, and with a reasonable degree of sophistication, are the Westminster democracies (Australia, Canada, New Zealand, and the UK). Many earlier efforts in this vein have been merged and advanced in a recent major volume by Strangio et al. (2013). This work has had several follow-up studies by individual contributors, including one on the perceived performance of Dutch prime ministers ('t Hart and Schelfhout 2016), whose valuable findings suggest that looking at political chief executives from this particular perspective has to be no less illuminating in consociational (or post-consociational) democracies than in Westminster democracies.

Most surveys are rich in empirical detail but weak in terms of explaining the observed patterns. That said, some features and patterns have been identified: A core finding to be corroborated in different surveys is that longevity correlates with high performance scores of individual presidents and prime ministers (see, e.g., Nichols 2012: 290; Theakston 2013: 230–1; Azzi and Hillmer 2016; Helms 2020), if with certain exceptions (see 't Hart and Shelfhout 2016: 169). This may of course, to some extent at least, be owed to the fact that long-term prime ministers are relatively best-known by their jurors, especially if they belong to a more distant historical period. Moreover, longevity is not necessarily causally related to good performance in office. Re-election to office may indicate particular campaign skills rather than governing performance; yet, even in the age of the 'permanent campaign' campaigning and governing have remained fundamentally different activities. Finally, in particular prime ministers at the head of coalition governments can be relatively immune to the electoral costs of governing. For all these caveats, longevity is arguably the single most important determinant of a high ranking-score. Longevity also matters in terms of the burden that departing prime ministers leave for their successors: Successors to long-term prime ministers usually struggle considerably more than other successors to step out of their predecessors' shadow (see Helms 2020: 267).

There are several other patterns that have been observed across different contexts. For example, 'takeover prime ministers' (following an incumbent from their own party between elections), and particularly 'heirs apparent' (widely considered as the 'natural successor' to a prime minister) tend to receive conspicuously low scores (see Worthy 2016; Helms 2020). Time-related aspects also seem to matter within a single government's term. While assessing the government's 'first one-hundred days' has become a popular fashion in many contemporary democracies, which lacks any particular justification, empirical evidence suggests that there is indeed a honeymoon period during which government popularity seems to be largely immune to major setbacks (see König and Wenzelburger 2017). However, notwithstanding the much-referred-to 'power of the beginning', it is worth noting that the first terms of some long-term prime ministers have not unequivocally been considered their most successful ones by scholarly evaluators (see Theakston 2013: 235).

Several factors, including some that have been widely acknowledged as powerful determinants of performance, and performance ratings for that matter, are noteworthy for their conspicuously limited impact: Perhaps most intriguingly, popularity (as measured by approval scores of office-holders) does not correspond closely with 'greatness' at the level of scholarly assessments and ratings of leaders' performance (Simonton 2013: 329–30). Further, there seems to be no particular relationship between the party affiliation of incumbents and his or her perceived performance, even within a single country. Prominent outperformers and underperformers in the office of president or prime minister have come from different parties, with no one party being able to claim to be a 'factory of excellence'. Gender also does not seem to be of any major independent explanatory power. What is striking, though, is that female prime ministers or presidents conspicuously either seem to lead the field (such as Margaret Thatcher, Angela Merkel, or Helen Clark) or to trail far behind (such as Kim Campbell, Édith Cresson, or Julia Gillard). Finally, and perhaps most importantly, there seems to be no clearly established strong correlation between the legislative output, or the amount of major reform bills, of a government and the public evaluation of the political chief executive. Occasional research suggests that a top score for a government in terms of legislative output is not necessarily reflected in a high rating of the prime minister. Indeed, as in the case of Australian Prime Minister Julia Gillard, both scores can be worlds apart (see Evershed 2013). The exact impact of the 'presidential success rate in Congress', as measured by *Congressional Studies Quarterly*, on US presidents' ranking is similarly uncertain, which also points to the inherent weaknesses of this well-established measure of presidential performance (for a critique and a modified focus on key statutes see Barrett and Eshbaugh-Soha 2007).

An important phenomenon observed across different countries and types of government concerns the historical evolution of perceptions: the perceived performance of individual office-holders, and their governments, tends to change over time, and often significantly so. This might reflect new information on a leader, or the long-term effects of his or her leadership, which may prompt observers and evaluators to revise their assessments. However, it may also reflect changing criteria for judging leaders.

As Pfiffner (2003) has contended, the opportunity to reflect about why actually some presidents are being ranked higher than others should in fact be considered as the ultimate value of presidential rankings. These questions become more complex to the extent that such inquiries seek to take into account both expert and popular opinion surveys of past political leaders, and their poorly understood relationship (see Cohen 2018: 11).

32.3 An Agenda for Future Research

As the previous sections suggest, there is an impressive body of research-based knowledge about different notions and manifestations of performance, and different ways of evaluating the performance of political executives in different types of political regime. This notwithstanding, those agendas obviously can be expanded and refined, and this final section seeks to highlight some avenues for future research.

To begin with, it would seem rewarding to expand the established focus of inquiry to include *additional factors that possibly shape the performance* of political executives, and their evaluation. For example, scholars have systematically studied the impact of 'beauty' on the electoral fortunes of parliamentary/legislative candidates, taking into account important institutional differences between democratic regimes (see, e.g., Stockemer and Praino 2017), but not on incumbent holders of executive office seeking re-election. It would be fascinating to see if physical attractiveness also systematically correlates with the electoral vulnerability of different incumbent executive leaders. There is also room for including other qualification-related issues. A recent study on prime ministers in four Westminster democracies found that—contrary to popular assumptions about the indispensable value of experience—top-ranked prime ministers had a conspicuously limited body of ministerial experience (both in terms of length and the number of offices held) before advancing to the job at the top (Helms 2020: 276). It would seem important to learn if, or to what extent, this holds true for executive leaders in other types of parliamentary democracies as well. This research could be meaningfully related with the emerging debate about a new brand of political leaders and would-be leaders—outsiders, and self-proclaimed outsiders, many of whom are conspicuously young—in senior executive office that have entered the scene more recently (see Wood et al. 2016).

While the 'technocratization' of political executives has been on the agenda of international executive research for a while, most published work focuses on conceptual issues (such as the distinction of different types of technocratic government; see McDonnell and Valbruzzi 2014; Brunclík 2015) or the evolution of empirical patterns at the level of ministers (see, e.g., Costa Pinto et al. 2018). Some valuable case studies notwithstanding, (see, e.g., Pasquino and Valbruzzi 2012 on Italian non-party governments), we still know very little about the difference that technocrat ministers and technocratic governments make in terms of performance, and perceived performance.

The same is true for gender-related research into political executives. Despite the impressive international activities in this field, research has overwhelmingly centred on issues of selection and recruitment (see, e.g., Jalalzai 2016; Annesley et al. 2019), complemented by a whole series of descriptive portraits of women presidents and prime ministers (see, e.g., Genovese and Steckenrider 2013). There is some scattered research on the difference that women political leaders may make in terms of performance and style (see, e.g., Campus 2013; Carlin et al. forthcoming); yet the performance, and the perceptions, of female ministers, prime ministers, and presidents has rarely been studied with reasonable rigour.

Future research also needs to take into account the *context* in which political executives operate more carefully, in particular when it comes to making meaningful comparative assessments of performance. We know that patterns of unified or divided government can make much of a difference for executive performance in different types of political regime. Expanding research in this direction can only be the beginning of developing more ambitious research agendas, though. Some authors have sought to develop reasonably fair and substantive categorizations of different administrations. For example, in their study on the US presidents of the post-war period, Genovese et al. distinguish between 'high opportunity' and 'low opportunity presidents', which allows them to provide more context-sensitive, and thus 'fairer', comparative assessments of presidential performance (see Genovese et al. 2014). Other scholars from beyond the family of presidential scholars have readily acknowledged the meaningfulness of carefully constructing 'relevant pair-wise or cohort comparison' ('t Hart 2014: 161). However, (too) many comparative studies follow established conceptual categories, and compare immediate successors in office or different presidents and prime ministers from the same party (or party family), which invites descriptive accounts rather than substantive comparative analysis and assessment.

There are other, more sophisticated concepts designed to study political leaders and their performance in context, with a particular focus on 'time'. The well-known work by Skowronek (1993, 2011), in which the author draws important distinctions between secular and political time, merits first mention in this regard. 'Political time' is conceived of as 'a powerful determinant of leadership authority, of the range of options, of the prospects for success, and of the practical impact of the exercise of presidential leadership on the political system at large' (Skowronek 2011: 78). Skowronek's ideas have more recently been introduced to the study of prime ministerial performance in parliamentary democracies (see, e.g., Laing and McCaffrie 2013; Byrne et al. 2017) and leadership research in transnational multi-level contexts (Goetz 2017). However, to date, those concepts have not really become an established part of research on executive leaders in different institutional and political contexts.

Context-focused research on the performance of political executives should also care more about the legacies that governments and leaders inherit from their predecessors. Legacies that may impact on a leader or government's perceived performance are typically located at the level of public policies (from spectacular policy accomplishments that set high standards and raise public expectations, to policy disasters, such as soaring inflation or a high unemployment rate; see Rockman 2008: 325–30). Yet they may include other aspects, such as political communication and media management, as well (see Langer 2010; Helms 2016). That said, legacies are not by definition a burden for newly incoming governments. Recent research suggests that particularly early in its term new governments may receive certain credits that do not have to be 'earned' by any particular performance: As Green and Jennings have pointed out,

> a new government benefits from a competence boost due to the relative loss of competence of its predecessor. During this period, the previous government is blamed for its failings, and this out-party attribution effect is an important factor for incoming government competence.   (Green and Jennings 2017: 181)

Overall, the focus of research in this vein has been largely on if and how administrations manage to leave a legacy and go down in history. For a fuller understanding of 'performance in context and time' we would need to know more about what particular legacies may mean for their successors in government, and how those legacies are being dealt with. The important recent work by Fong et al. (2019) marks a most promising starting point in this regard.

The effects of governmental performance on other executive-related variables mark another key subject on the larger agenda. There is some recent research on how a bad economic performance of the government and high-level corruption involving the government may shape the rise of 'political newcomers', defined as heads of government with just three years (or less) of total political experience in the executive or legislative branch (Carreras 2017). Yet, while we have a much better understanding of the opportunities, constraints, and strategies of chief executives in the selection and de-selection of ministers than just a few years ago (see, e.g., Dowding and Dumont 2009, 2015), we still know comparatively little about how different dimensions of government performance shape the fate of different actors within the executive territory. Further, if political careers in the executive branch are increasingly followed by post-executive careers (see also Chapter 17 in this volume), with some observers implying that political office-holders use their spell at the top to systematically prepare their professional afterlives, it would be important to gain a deeper understanding of how exactly performance in the executive branch shapes post-executive careers and activities.

New agendas should also emerge from *conceptual and methodological innovations, and a change of perspective on established objects of research*. Recent research on political office-holders, including presidents, prime ministers and party leaders, has demonstrated the considerable potential of linking novel conceptualizations of performance with a particular set of hard and soft indicators that may facilitate the conduct of complex empirical evaluations and assessments (see Bennister et al. 2015, 2017). Another recent study underscores the great potential of crossing established barriers of politics and policy in studying performance (see Brummer 2016), and sets the stage for more such work. Conceptual and methodological innovation is also, and no less importantly, needed to overcome the established divide in studying executive leadership and performance in democratic and autocratic regimes. Recent research on the perceived performance of democratic and authoritarian governments which, curiously, finds authoritarian institutions to be 'more apt to produce the perception of responsive government' (Zhou and Ou-Yang 2017: 297), testifies to the major importance of cross-regime comparative inquiry. There have been passionate 'wake-up calls' recently (see Müller 2017), yet for the time being research on political executives in democratic and autocratic regimes largely tends to co-exist in isolation from each other, not only but also because of a striking lack of suitable concepts (see Helms forthcoming). More generally, as the observations presented in the previous sections suggest, continuous conceptual adaptation is needed to bring out the potential of concepts originally devised in particular contexts in other contexts too. While there is a notable commitment of European, Oceanian, and Asian scholars to adopt concepts from the US and adapt them to the different political contexts of their respective countries and regions, such efforts have not been reciprocal. Many concepts and frameworks for analysis developed by non-American scholars have conspicuously failed to be seriously considered and applied in the US, which puts a major limit to truly international research in an increasingly interdependent world.

Finally, important new input should also, and not least, come from considering *the whole range of semantic dimensions of the key term under study*—'performance'—more systematically and linking them with each other. Politics, and in particular the political agency by holders of senior executive office, has long been considered in analogy to the stage performance of actors (see, e.g., Cronin 2008). However, scholars have only recently begun to engage in recovering the grammar of politics in relation to performance in more detail (see, e.g., Rai 2015; Rai and Reinelt 2015). In this discourse, presidents and prime ministers have, curiously, taken a backseat to many other actors. The bulk of published research centres on parliament and civil society actors, including celebrities. To be sure, as always, exceptions prove the rule (see, e.g., Alexander 2010), yet the full spectrum of fruitful research opportunities relating the 'performing arts' to political executives and executive politics is still to be discovered.

The various ways to expand and deepen our understanding of issues of performance and evaluation highlighted above could be meaningfully complemented by efforts to enhance our ability *to predict the performance of political executives*, and the evaluation thereof. Predicting the performance of political leaders in the executive branch has a long and proud tradition especially in US presidential studies (see, e.g., Barber 1977; Simonton 1981; Simon and Uscinsky 2012). Scholars have combined pre-election biographical data with a wealth of contextual variables in order to predict presidential performance, and with reasonable success, but no equivalent effort has been made for political executives in other democratic and non-democratic regimes. Importantly, predicting presidential, or for that matter prime ministerial, performance does not have to remain a purely scholarly exercise. To the extent that these agendas can be linked with the more recent debate about poor leadership and performance in presidential and prime ministerial office, and the possible safeguards against bad performance (see, e.g., Kellerman 2004; Abbott 2013; Helms 2014), the wisdom flowing from that research could well make a difference for the future study—and politics—of performance.

References

Abbott, P. (2013). *Bad Presidents: Failure in the White House*. New York: Palgrave Macmillan.

Alexander, J. C. (2010). *The Performance of Politics: Obama's Victory and the Struggle for Power*. Oxford: Oxford University Press.

Alexiadou, D. (2016). 'Ideologues, Partisans, and Loyalists: Cabinet Ministers and Social Welfare Reform in Parliamentary Democracies', *Comparative Political Studies* 48(8): 1051–86.

Allen, N., Birch, S., and Sarmiento-Mirwaldt, K. (2018). 'Honesty Above All Else? Expectations and Perceptions of Political Conduct in Three Established Democracies', *Comparative European Politics* 16(3): 511–34.

Andeweg, R. (1997). 'Collegiality and Collectivity: Cabinets, Cabinet Committees, and Cabinet Ministers', in P. Weller, H. Bakvis and R. A. W. Rhodes (eds) *The Hollow Crown*. London: Macmillan, 58–83.

Annesley, C., Beckwith, K., and Franceschet, S. (2019). *Cabinets, Ministers, and Gender*. Oxford: Oxford University Press.

Arter, D. (2006). 'Introduction: Comparing the Legislative Performance of Legislatures', *The Journal of Legislative Studies* 12(3–4): 245–57.

Azzi, S. and Hillmer, N. (2016). 'Ranking Canada's Best and Worst Prime Ministers', *Maclean's*, 7 October, www.macleans.ca/politics/ottawa/ranking-canadas-best-and-worst-prime-ministers

Barber, J. D. (1977). *The Presidential Character: Predicting Performance in the White House*. Englewood Cliffs, NJ: Prentice-Hall.

Barrett, A. W. and Eshbaugh-Soha, M. (2007). 'Presidential Success on the Substance of Legislation', *Political Research Quarterly* 60(1): 100–12.

Bennister, M., 't Hart, P., and Worthy, B. (2015). 'Assessing the Authority of Political Office-Holders: The Leadership Capital Index', *West European Politics* 38(3): 417–40.

Bennister, M., 't Hart, P., and Worthy, B. (2017) (eds). *The Leadership Capital Index: A New Perspective on Political Leadership*. Oxford: Oxford University Press.

Berlinski, S., Dewan, T., and Dowding, K. (2010). 'The Impact of Individual and Collective Performance on Ministerial Tenure', *The Journal of Politics* 72(2): 559–71.

Bertelli, A. M. and John, P. (2013). 'Public Policy Investment: Risk and Return in British Politics', *British Journal of Political Science* 43: 741–73.

Birch, S. and Allen, N. (2015). 'Judging Politicians: The Role of Political Attentiveness in Shaping How People Evaluate the Ethical Behaviour of Their Leaders', *European Journal of Political Research* 54: 43–60.

Blondel, J. and Müller-Rommel, F. (1993) (eds). *Governing Together: The Extent and Limits of Joint Decision-Making in Western European Cabinets*. Basingstoke: Palgrave.

Blondel, J., Müller-Rommel, F., and Malová, D. (2007). *Governing New European Democracies*. Basingstoke: Palgrave.

Blumenau, J. (2014). 'Do Party Leader Approval Ratings Predict Election Outcomes?', http://blogs.lse.ac.uk/politicsandpolicy/party-leader-approval-ratings-and-election-outcomes/

Bochsler, D. and Hänni, M. (2019). 'The Three Stages of the Anti-Incumbency Vote: Retrospective Economic Voting in Young and Established Democracies', *European Journal of Political Research* 58(1): 30–55.

Bonvecchi, A. and Simison, E. (2017). 'Legislative Institutions and Performance in Authoritarian Regimes', *Comparative Politics* 49(4): 521–44.

Bouckaert, G. and Peters, B. G. (2002). 'Performance Measurement and Management: The Achilles' Heel in Administrative Modernization,' *Public Performance & Management Review* 25(4): 359–62.

Bovan, K., Banai, B., and Pavela Banai, I. (2018). 'Do Natural Disasters Affect Voting Behavior? Evidence from Croatian Floods,' PLOS Currents Disasters, 6 April, doi: 10.1371/currents.dis. cbf57c8ac3b239ba51ccc801d3362c07

Boyne, G. A., James, O., John, P., and Petrovsky, N. (2009). 'Democracy and Government Performance: Holding Incumbents Accountable in English Local Governments,' *The Journal of Politics* 71(4): 1273–84.

Brooker, P. (2014). *Non-Democratic Regimes.* 3rd ed. Basingstoke: Palgrave.

Brummer, K. (2016). 'Fiasco Prime Ministers': Leaders' Beliefs and Personality Traits as Possible Causes for Policy Fiascos,' *Journal of European Public Policy* 23(5): 702–17.

Brunclík, M. (2015). 'The Rise of Technocratic Cabinets: What We Know, and What We Should Like to Know,' *Austrian Journal of Political Science* 44(3): 57–67.

Buller, J. and James, T. S. (2012). 'Statecraft and the Assessment of National Political Leaders: The Case of New Labour and Tony Blair,' *The British Journal of Politics and International Relations* 14(4): 534–55.

Buller, J. and James, T. S. (2015). 'Integrating Structural Context into the Assessment of Political Leadership: Philosophical Realism, Gordon Brown and the Great Financial Crisis,' *Parliamentary Affairs* 68(1): 77–96.

Bulpitt, J. (1986). 'The Discipline of the New Democracy: Mrs Thatcher's Domestic Statecraft,' *Political Studies* 34(1): 19–39.

Byrne, C., Randall, N., and Theakston, K. (2017). 'Evaluating British Prime Ministerial Performance: David Cameron in Political Time,' *British Journal of Politics and International Relations* 19(1): 202–20.

Cabada, L. and Tomšič, M. (2016). 'The Rise of Person-Based Politics in the New Democracies: The Czech Republic and Slovenia,' *Politics in Central Europe* 12(2): 29–50.

Campus, D. (2013). Women Political Leaders and the Media. Basingstoke: Palgrave.

Carlin, R., Carreras, M., and Love, G. (forthcoming). 'Presidents' Sex and Popularity: Baselines, Dynamics and Policy Performance,' *British Journal of Political Science*, published online ahead of print, 30 January 2019, doi: 10.1017/S0007123418000364, 1–21.

Carreras, M. (2017). 'Institutions, Governmental Performance and the Rise of Political Newcomers,' *European Journal of Political Research* 56(2): 364–80.

Clarke, C., James, T. S., Bale, T., and Diamond, P. (2015). *British Conservative Leaders.* London: Biteback.

Cohen, J. E. (2018). 'The Historical Memory of American Presidents in the Mass Public,' *Social Sciences* 7(36): 1–14.

Cordero, G. and Blais, A. (2017). 'Is a Corrupt Government Totally Unacceptable?,' *West European Politics* 40(4): 645–62.

Costa Pinto, A., Cotta, M., and Tavares de Alemeida, P. (2018) (eds). *Technocratic Ministers and Political Leadership in European Democracies.* Basingstoke: Palgrave.

Croissant, A., Kailitz, S., Köllner, P., and Wurster, S. (2015) (eds). *Comparing Autocracies in the Early Twenty-first Century.* Volume 2: *The Performance and Persistence of Autocracies.* London: Routledge.

Cronin, T. E. (2008). ' "All the World's a Stage..." Acting and the Art of Political Leadership,' *The Leadership Quarterly* 19(4): 459–68.

Czada, R. (2015). '"Post-Democracy" and the Public Sphere: Informality and Transparency in Negotiated Decision-Making,' in V. Schneider and B. Eberlein (eds) *Complex Democracy*. Cham: Springer, 231–46.

Dynes, A. M. and Holbein, J. (2020). 'Noisy Retrospection: The Effect of Party Control on Policy Outcomes,' *American Political Science Review* 114(1): 237–57.

De Vries, C. E. and Giger, N. (2014). 'Holding Governments Accountable? Individual Heterogeneity in Performance Voting,' *European Journal of Political Research* 53(2): 345–62.

Dowding, K. and Dumont, P. (2009) (eds). *The Selection of Ministers in Europe: Hiring and Firing*, London: Routledge.

Dowding, K. and Dumont, P. (2015) (eds). *The Selection of Ministers around the World*. London: Routledge.

Druckman, J. N. and Jacobs, L. R. (2016). *Who Governs? Presidents, Public Opinion, and Manipulation*. Chicago: Chicago University Press.

Duval, D. and Pétry, F. (2019). 'Time and the Fulfillment of Election Pledges,' *Political Studies* 67(1): 207–23.

Dyson, S. B. (2018). 'Gordon Brown, Alistair Darling, and the Great Financial Crisis: Leadership Traits and Policy Responses,' *British Politics* 13(2): 121–45.

Ecker, A., Glinitzer, K., and Meyer, T. (2016). 'Corruption Performance Voting and the Electoral Context,' *European Political Science Review* 8(3): 333–54.

Egorov, G. and Sonin, K. (2014). 'Incumbency Advantage in Non-Democracies,' National Bureau of Economic Research (NBER), http://www.nber.org/papers/w20519.pdf

Elgie, R. (2011). *Semi-Presidentialism: Sub-Types and Democratic Performance*. Oxford: Oxford University Press.

Evershed, N. (2013). 'Was Julia Gillard the Most Productive Prime Minister in Australia's History?' https://www.theguardian.com/news/datablog/2013/jun/28/australia-productive-prime-minister

Farwell, J. P. (2012). *Persuasion and Power: The Art of Strategic Communication*. Washington, DC: Georgetown University Press.

Figenschou, T. U., Karlsen, R., Kolltveit, K., and Thorbjørnsrud, K. (2017). 'Serving the Media Ministers: A Mixed Methods Study on the Personalization of Ministerial Communication,' *The International Journal of Press/Politics* 22(4): 411–30.

Fischer, J., Dowding, K., and Dumont, P. (2012). 'The Duration and Durability of Cabinet Ministers,' *International Political Science Review* 33: 505–19.

Flores, A. Q. and Smith, A. (2011). 'Leader Survival and Cabinet Change,' *Economics & Politics* 23(3): 345–66.

Fong, C., Malhotra, N., and Margalit, Y. (2019). 'Political Legacies: Understanding Their Significance to Contemporary Political Debates,' *PS: Political Science & Politics* 52(3): 451–6.

Fortunato, D. and Stevenson, R. T. (2013). 'Performance Voting and Knowledge of Cabinet Composition,' *Electoral Studies* 32: 517–23.

Genovese, M. and Steckenrider, J. S. (2013). *Women as Political Leaders*. London: Routledge.

Genovese, M. A, Belt, T. L., and Lammers, W. W. (2014). *The Presidency and Domestic Policy: Comparing Leadership Styles, FDR to Obama*. 2nd ed. New York: Routledge.

Ghergina, S. (2011). 'Does Government Performance Matter? Electoral Support for Incumbents in Six Post-Communist Countries,' *Contemporary Politics* 17(3): 257–77.

Giger, N. (2010). 'Do Voters Punish the Government for Welfare State Retrenchment? A Comparative Study of Electoral Costs Associated with Social Policy,' *Comparative European Politics* 8(4): 415–43.

Goetz, K. H. (2017). 'Political Leadership in the European Union: A Time-Centred View,' *European Political Science* 16(1): 48–59.

Green, J. and Jennings, W. (2017). *The Politics of Competence: Parties, Public Opinion and Voters*. Cambridge: Cambridge University Press.

Greenstein, F. I. (1975). *Personality & Politics: Problems of Evidence and Conceptualization*. New York: W.W. Norton.

Greenstein, F. I. (2001). *The Presidential Difference: Leadership Style from FDR to Clinton*. New York: The Free Press.

Grotz, F. and Müller-Rommel, F. (2015). 'Schwache Regierungschefs? Politische Erfahrung und Amtsdauer von Premierministern in Mittel- und Osteuropa,' *Zeitschrift für Parlamentsfragen* 46(2): 310–27.

Grube, D. C. (2013). *Prime Ministers and Rhetorical Governance*. Basingstoke: Palgrave.

Grumm, J. G. (1971). *State and Urban Politics*. Boston, MA: Little, Brown.

Healy, A. J., Malhotra, N., and Hyunjung Mo, C. (2010). 'Irrelevant Events Affect Voter's Evaluations of Government Performance,' *Proceedings of the National Academic of Science of the United States of America* 107(29): 12804–9.

Heazle, M., Kane, J., and Patapan, H. (2016). 'Good Public Policy: On the Interaction of Political and Expert Authority,' in M. Heazle and J. Kane (eds) *Policy Legitimacy, Science and Political Authority: Knowledge and Action in Liberal Democracies*. London: Routledge, 1–16.

Heersink, B., Peterson, B. D., and Jenkins, J. A. (2017). 'Disasters and Elections: Estimating the Net Effect of Damage and Relief in Historical Perspective,' *Political Analysis* 25(2): 260–8.

Helms, L. (2012). 'Democratic Political Leadership in the New Media Age: A Farewell to Excellence?,' *The British Journal of Politics and International Relations* 14: 651–70.

Helms, L. (2014). 'When Leaders Are Not Good: Exploring Bad Leadership in Liberal Democracies across Time and Space,' in J. Kane and H. Patapan (eds) *Good Democratic Leadership: On Prudence and Judgment in Contemporary Democracies*. Oxford: Oxford University Press, 51–69.

Helms, L. (2016). 'The Politics of Leadership Capital in Compound Democracies: Inferences from the German Case,' *European Political Science Review* 8: 285–310.

Helms, L. (2019).'When Less Is More: "Negative Resources" and the Performance of Presidents and Prime Ministers,' *Politics* 39(3): 269–83.

Helms, L. (2020). 'Heir Apparent Prime Ministers in Westminster Democracies: Promise and Performance,' Government and Opposition 55: 260–282.

Helms, L. (forthcoming). 'Leadership Succession in Politics: The Democracy/Autocracy Divide Revisited,' British Journal of Politics and International Relations, published online ahead of print on 11 March 2020, https://doi.org/10.1177/1369148120908528

Helms, L. and van Esch, F. (2017). 'Turning Structural Weakness into Personal Strength: Angela Merkel and the Politics of Leadership Capital in Germany,' in M. Bennister, P. 't Hart, and B. Worthy (eds) *The Leadership Capital Index: A New Perspective on Political Leadership*. Oxford: Oxford University Press, 27–44.

Hermann, M. G. (2005). 'Assessing Leadership Style: A Traits Analysis,' in J. M. Post (ed.) *The Psychological Assessment of Political Leaders: With Profiles of Saddam Hussein and Bill Clinton*. Ann Arbor, MI: The University of Michigan Press, 178–215.

Hloušek, V. (2015). 'Two Types of Presidentialization in the Party Politics of Central Eastern Europe,' *Italian Political Science Review/Rivista Italiana di Scienza Politica* 45(3): 277–99.

Ho, A. T.-K. and Cho, W. (2017). 'Government Communication Effectiveness and Satisfaction with Police Performance: A Large-Scale Survey Study,' *Public Administration Review* 77(2): 228–39.

Hobolt, S., Tilley, J., and Banducci, S. (2013). 'Clarity of Responsibility: How Government Cohesion Conditions Performance Voting,' *European Journal of Political Research* 52(2): 164–87.

Huber, J. D. (1998). 'How Does Cabinet Instability Affect Political Performance? Portfolio Volatility and Health Care Cost Containment in Parliamentary Democracies,' *American Political Science Review* 92(3): 577–91.

Ieraci, G. (2012). 'Government Alternation and Patterns of Competition in Europe: Comparative Data in Search of Explanations,' *West European Politics* 35(3): 530–50.

Inácio, M. and Llanos, M. (2016). 'The Institutional Presidency in Latin America: A Comparative Analysis,' *Presidential Studies Quarterly* 46(3): 531–49.

Indriðason, I. H. and Kam, C. (2008). 'Cabinet Reshuffles and Ministerial Drift,' *British Journal of Political Science* 38: 621–56.

Jalalzai, F. (2016). *Shattered, Cracked, or Firmly Intact? Women and the Executive Glass Ceiling Worldwide*. New York: Oxford University Press.

Jennings, W., Lodge, M., and Ryan, M. (2018). 'Comparing Blunders in Government,' *European Journal of Political Research* 57(1): 238–58.

Kam, C. and Indriðason, I. (2005). 'The Timing of Cabinet Reshuffles in Five Westminster Parliamentary Systems,' *Legislative Studies Quarterly* 30(3): 327–63.

Kane, J. and Patapan, H. (2010). 'The Artless Art: Leadership and the Limits of Democratic Rhetoric,' *Australian Journal of Political Science* 45: 371–89.

Kraft, J. (2018). 'Political Parties and Public Investments: A Comparative Analysis of 22 Western Democracies,' *West European Politics* 41(1): 128–46.

Kellerman, B. (2004). *Bad Leadership: What It Is, How It Happens, Why It Matters*. Boston, MA: Harvard Business School Press.

Kendall-Taylor, A., Frantz, E., and Wright, J. (2017). 'The Global Rise of Personalized Politics: It's Not Just Dictators Anymore,' *The Washington Quarterly* 40(1): 7–19.

König, P. and Wenzelburger, G. (2017). 'Honeymoon in the Crisis: A Comparative Analysis of the Strategic Timing of Austerity Policies and Their Effect on Government Popularity in Three Countries,' *Comparative European Politics* 15(6): 991–1015.

Kriesi, H. P. (2004). 'Strategic Political Communication: Mobilizing Public Opinion in 'Audience Democracies',' in F. Esser and B. Pfetsch (eds) *Comparative Political Communication: Theories, Cases, and Challenges*. Cambridge: Cambridge University Press, 184–212.

Laing, M. and McCaffrie, B. (2013). 'The Politics Prime Ministers Make: Political Time and Executive Leadership in Westminster Systems,' in P. Strangio, P. 't Hart, and J. Walter (eds) *Understanding Prime-Ministerial Performance*. Oxford: Oxford University Press, 79–101.

Langer, A. I. (2010). 'The Politicization of Private Persona: Exceptional Leaders or the New Rule? The Case of the United Kingdom and the Blair Effect,' *The International Journal of Press/Politics* 15(1): 60–75.

LeDuc, L. and Pammett, J. H. (2013). 'The Fate of Governing Parties in Times of Economic Crisis,' *Electoral Studies* 32(3): 494–9.

Lodge, M. (2013). 'Crisis, Resources and the State: Executive Politics in the Age of the Depleted State,' *Political Studies Review* 11: 378–90.

Lodge, M. and Wegrich, K. (2012). 'Introduction: Executive Politics in Times of Crisis', in M. Lodge and K. Wegrich (eds) *Executive Politics in Times of Crisis*. Basingstoke: Palgrave, 1–15.

Martin, L. W. and Vanberg, G. (2019). 'Coalition Government, Legislative Institutions, and Public Policy in Parliamentary Democracies', *American Journal of Political Science*, published online ahead of print on 23 August, https://doi.org/10.1111/ajps.12453

Martínez-Gallardo, C. (2014). 'Designing Cabinets: Presidential Politics and Ministerial Instability', *Journal of Politics in Latin America* 6(2): 3–38.

Matthieß, T. (forthcoming). 'Retrospective Pledge Voting: A Comparative Study of the Electoral Consequences of Government Parties' Pledge Fulfilment', *European Journal of Political Research*, https://ejpr.onlinelibrary.wiley.com/doi/abs/10.1111/1475-6765.12377

McDonnell, D. and Valbruzzi, M. (2014). 'Defining and Classifying Technocrat-Led and Technocratic Governments,' *European Journal of Political Research* 53: 654–71.

McMasters, A. and Uhr, J. (2017). *Leadership Performance and Rhetoric*. Basingstoke: Palgrave.

Mezey, M. L. (2013). *Presidentialism: Power in Comparative Perspective*. Boulder, CO: Lynne Rienner.

Miwa, H. (2018). 'Can Reshuffles Improve Government Popularity? Evidence from a "Pooling the Polls" Analysis', *Public Opinion Quarterly* 82(2): 322–42.

Müller, H. (2017). 'Unexplored Parallels: Political Leadership and Economic Policy Across Regime Types', paper prepared for presentation at the DVPW Conference/Section Comparative Politics, 'Unlike Twins?! Comparing Autocracies and Democracies', University of Tübingen, 15 March.

Murillo, M. V. and Visconti, G. (2017). 'Economic Performance and Incumbents' Support in Latin America', *Electoral Studies* 45: 180–90.

Musella, F. (2018). *Political Leaders Beyond Party Politics*. Basingstoke: Palgrave.

Narud, H. M. and Valen, H. (2008). 'Coalition Membership and Electoral Performance', in K. Strøm, W. C. Müller, and T. Bergman (eds) *Cabinets and Coalition Bargaining: The Democratic Life Cycle in Western Europe*. Oxford: Oxford University Press, 369–402.

Naurin, E., Soroka, S., and Markwat, N. (2019). 'Asymmetric Accountability: An Experimental Investigation of Biases in Evaluations of Governments' Election Pledges', *Comparative Political Studies*, published online ahead of print on 14 March, https://doi.org/10.1177/0010414019830740

Nichols, C. (2012). 'The Presidential Ranking Game: Critical Review and Some New Discoveries', *Presidential Studies Quarterly* 42(2): 275–99.

Olson, D. M. and Nonidez, C. T. (1972). 'Measures of Legislative Performance in the U.S. House of Representatives', *Midwest Journal of Political Science* 16(2): 269–77.

Olvera, J. G. and Avellaneda, C. N. (2017). 'Performance Management in Public Administration', *Oxford Research Encyclopedia of Politics*, published online April 2017, doi: 10.1093/acrefore/9780190228637.013.263

Pasquino, G. and Valbruzzi, M. (2012). Non-Partisan Government Italian-Style: Decisionmaking and Accountability', *Journal of Modern Italian Studies* 17(5): 612–29.

Pfiffner, J. P. (2003). 'Ranking the Presidents: Continuity and Volatility', in M. Bose and M. Landis (eds) *The Uses and Abuses of Presidential Ratings*. New York: Nova Science Publishers, 27–42.

Plescia, C. (2017). 'Portfolio-Specific Accountability and Retrospective Voting: The Case of Italy', *Italian Political Science Review / Rivista Italiana di Scienza Politica* 47(3): 313–36.

Plescia, C. and Kritzinger, S. (2017). 'Retrospective Voting and Party Support at Elections: Credit and Blame for Government and Opposition,' *Journal of Elections, Public Opinion and Parties* 27(2): 156–71.

Rai, S. M. (2015). 'Political Performance: A Framework for Analysing Democratic Politics,' *Political Studies* 63: 1179–97.

Rai, S. M. and Reinelt, J. (2015) (eds). *The Grammar of Politics and Performance*. London: Routledge.

Rapeli, L. (2016). 'Who to Punish? Retrospective Voting and Knowledge of Government Composition in a Multiparty System,' *International Political Science Review* 37(4): 407–21.

Raunio, T. (2009). 'National Parliaments and European Integration: What We Know and Agenda for Future Research,' *The Journal of Legislative Studies* 15(4): 317–34.

Rhodes, R. A. W. and 't Hart, P. (2014). 'Puzzles of Political Leadership,' in R. A. W. Rhodes and P. 't Hart (eds) *Oxford Handbook of Political Leadership*. Oxford: Oxford University Press, 1–21.

Risoleo, R. (2018). 'Entertainer Politicians: Popular Icons and "Incumbency Advantage",' *Items: Insights from the Social Sciences*, 21 August, https://items.ssrc.org/entertainer-politicians-popular-icons-and-an-incumbency-advantage/

Rockman, B. A. (2008). 'The Legacy of the George W. Bush Presidency—A Revolutionary Presidency;' in C. Campbell, B. A. Rockman, and A. Rudalevige (eds) *The George W. Bush Legacy*. Washington, DC: Congressional Quarterly Press, 325–48.

Rogoff, K. and Sibert, A. (1988). 'Elections and Macroeconomic Policy Cycles,' *The Review of Economic Studies* 55(1): 1–16.

Rohrer, S. (2014). 'What Makes a Prime Minister Great? The Impact of LTA Psychological Characteristics and the Perceived Effectiveness of British Prime Ministers (1902–2004),' *Journal of Research and Politics* October-December: 1–8.

Rosenthal, A. (1974). *Legislative Performance in the States: Explorations of Committee Behaviour*. New York: Free Press.

Rottinghaus, B. and Vaughn, J. (2018). 'Official Results of the 2018 Presidents & Executive Politics Presidential Greatness Survey,' https://sps.boisestate.edu/politicalscience/files/2018/02/Greatness.pdf

Sagarzazu, I. and Klüver, H. (2017). 'Coalition Governments and Party Competition: Political Communication Strategies of Coalition Parties,' *Political Science Research and Methods* 5(2): 333–49.

Sassen, S. (2009). 'The New Executive Politics: A Democratic Challenge,' https://www.open-democracy.net/article/the-new-executive-politics-a-democratic-challenge

Schleiter, P. and Tavits, M. (2018). 'Voter Reactions to Incumbent Opportunism,' *The Journal of Politics* 80(4): 1183–96.

Schniewind, A., Freitag, M., and Vatter, A. (2009). 'Big Cabinets, Big Governments? Grand Coalitions and Public Policy in the German Laender,' *Journal of Public Policy* 29(3): 327–45.

Seeberg, H. B. (2018). 'The Impact of Opposition Criticism on the Public's Evaluation of Government Competence,' *Party Politics*, published online ahead of print 7 August, https://doi.org/10.1177/1354068818792578

Shabad, G. and Slomczynski, K. M. (2011). 'Voters' Perceptions of Government Performance and Attributions of Responsibility: Electoral Control in Poland,' *Electoral Studies* 30(2): 309–20.

Silver, N. (2011). 'Approval Ratings and Re-Election Odds,' 28 January, https://fivethirtyeight. blogs.nytimes.com/2011/01/28/approval-ratings-and-re-election-odds/

Simon, A. M. and Uscinsky, J. E. (2012). 'Prior Experience Predicts Presidential Performance,' *Presidential Studies Quarterly* 42(3): 514–48.

Simonton, D. K. (1981). 'Presidential Greatness and Performance: Can We Predict Leadership in the White House?,' *Journal of Personality* 49: 306–22.

Simonton, D. K. (2013). 'Presidential Leadership: Performance Criteria and Their Predictors,' in M. G. Rumsey (ed.) *The Oxford Handbook of Leadership*. New York: Oxford University Press, 327–42.

Skidmore, M. J. (2004). *Presidential Performance: A Comprehensive Review*. Jefferson, NC: McFarland & Co.

Skowronek, S. (1993). *The Politics Presidents Make: Leadership from John Adams to George Bush*. Cambridge, MA: Belknap.

Skowronek, S. (2011). *Presidential Leadership in Political Time: Reprise and Reappraisal*. 2nd ed. Lawrence, KS: University Press of Kansas.

von Soest, C. and Grauvogel, J. (2017). 'Identity, Procedures and Performance: How Authoritarian Regimes Legitimize Their Rule,' *Contemporary Politics* 23(3): 287–305.

Stiers, D. (2018). 'Beyond the Distinction Incumbent-Opposition: Retrospective Voting on the Level of Political Parties,' *Party Politics*, published online ahead of print on 15 January, https://doi.org/10.1177/1354068817744201

Stockemer, D. and Praino, R. (2017). 'Physical Attractiveness, Voter Heuristics and Electoral Systems: The Role of Candidate Attractiveness under Different Institutional Design,' *British Journal of Politics and International Relations* 19(2): 336–52.

Strangio, P., 't Hart, P., and Walter, J. (2013) (eds). *Understanding Prime-Ministerial Performance: Comparative Perspectives*. Oxford: Oxford University Press.

Strøm, K. (1985). 'Party Goals and Government Performance in Parliamentary Democracies,' *American Political Science Review* 79(3): 738–54.

't Hart P. (2014). *Understanding Public Leadership*. Basingstoke: Palgrave.

't Hart, P. and Schelfhout, D. (2016). 'Assessing Prime-Ministerial Performance in a Multiparty Democracy: The Dutch Case,' *Acta Politica* 51(2): 153–72.

Theakston, K. (2007). 'What Makes for an Effective British Prime Minister?,' *Quaderni di Scienza Politica* 14(2): 39–61.

Theakston, K. (2011). 'Gordon Brown as Prime Minister: Political Skills and Leadership Style,' *British Politics* 6(1): 78–100.

Theakston, K. (2012). 'David Cameron as Prime Minister,' in T. Heppell and D. Seawright (eds) *Cameron and the Conservatives: The Transition to Coalition Government*. Houndmills: Palgrave Macmillan, 194–208.

Theakston, K. (2013). 'Evaluating Prime-Ministerial Performance: The British Experience,' in P. Strangio, P. 't Hart, and J. Walter (eds) *Understanding Prime-Ministerial Performance: Comparative Perspectives*. Oxford: Oxford University Press, 221–41.

Thomson, R., Royed, T., Naurin, E., Artés, J., Costello, R., Ennser-Jedenastik, L., Ferguson, M., Kostadinova, P., Moury, C., Pétry, F., and Praprotnik, K. (2017). 'The Fulfillment of Parties' Election Pledges: A Comparative Study on the Impact of Power Sharing,' *American Journal of Political Science* 61(3): 527–42.

Wood, M., Corbett, J., and Flinders, M. (2016). 'Just Like Us: Everyday Celebrity Politicians and the Pursuit of Popularity in an Age of Anti-Politics,' *The British Journal of Politics and International Relations* 18(3): 581–98.

Worthy, B. (2016). 'Ending in Failure? The Performance of 'Takeover' Prime Ministers 1916–2016,' *Political Quarterly* 87(4): 509–17.

Zhou, Y. J. and Ou-Yang, R. (2017). 'Explaining High External Efficacy in Authoritarian Countries: A Comparison of China and Taiwan,' *Democratization* 24(2): 283–304.

Zubek, R. and Klüver, H. (2015). 'Legislative Pledges and Coalition Government,' *Party Politics* 21(4): 603–14.

PART V

POLITICAL
EXECUTIVES
BEYOND THE
DEMOCRATIC
NATION-STATE

CHAPTER 33

EXECUTIVE POLITICS OF MULTI-LEVEL SYSTEMS

The European Union

INGEBORG TÖMMEL

33.1 INTRODUCTION

THE post-war political order is increasingly characterized by multi-level systems. Of course, such systems have a longer tradition, particularly in the form of federations or federal states. Yet they recently proliferated through both the creation of additional regimes at the international or global level as well as processes of differentiation and devolution within states. All these forms of political order have in common that authority is dispersed among multiple jurisdictions and, accordingly, multiple executives (Hooghe and Marks 2003). Yet the recently created executives in multi-level systems, particularly those in the international realm, are often comparatively weak in terms of powers, resources, and administrative capacity.

Among these multi-level systems, the European Union (EU) constitutes a distinctive case (Hooghe and Marks 2001). In contrast to international organizations or regimes, usually dealing with specific sectors or issue areas, it disposes of a broad set of powers, functions, and other resources which cover almost all policy areas. In contrast to states, the Union is not sovereign but always dependent on competence transfers from the member states. Nevertheless, the EU is the most advanced non-state multi-level system; this makes it a particularly interesting case for the study of executive politics.

Comparing the EU to international organizations and states brings additional anomalies to the fore. Thus the EU's executive is far more developed and sophisticated than those of international organizations. The Union holds extensive powers, commands ample financial and administrative resources and, most importantly, enjoys a far-reaching degree of autonomy vis-à-vis both the legislatures at the European and national level and the governments of the member states. In comparison to states, the EU's most outstanding characteristic is the lack of a government. Governmental functions are shared between, on the one hand, the European Commission and, on the other hand, the Council and the European Council. Consequently, a separation of powers between legislature and executive could never evolve. Instead, executive politics is divided horizontally between the institutions of the EU and vertically between the European level and the governments and administrations of the member states. In sum, the Union displays a highly compound and at the same time fragmented executive order.

The Union's system of executive politics has posed many intricate questions to scholars of European integration. These questions revolve around four basic themes: (1) what is the institutional structure of the EU executive and how are powers divided within and between government levels? (2) How do EU executive institutions perform and in which way do they interact? (3) To what extent and in which way do European executives exercise political leadership? (4) To what extent and in which way are EU executives democratically legitimized and held accountable? According to this broad spectrum of research questions, answers widely vary, and many puzzles remain unresolved, as this chapter will reveal.

The chapter is organized as follows. Section 33.2 presents a detailed set of questions which have structured and framed research on EU executive politics. Section 33.3 elaborates on the research findings regarding the four basic themes: the institutional structure and powers of the EU executive, its performance and interactions, its political leadership and, finally, its democratic legitimacy and accountability. The concluding section (33.4) provides a brief summary of the state of the art and proposes selected issues for future research.

33.2 THE MAIN RESEARCH QUESTIONS

The multifaceted and compound nature of the EU's executive has evoked a host of research questions and intense scholarly debates. However, even though much of academic writing in effect has been dealing with the Union's executive, an explicit reflection on the issue has hardly taken place. This applies particularly to the earlier years of integration until the mid-1980s. Since then, the theme has gradually attracted attention and figures now more prominently on the research agenda. In terms of methodology, most studies focusing on the EU's executive use qualitative research methods with a strong emphasis on semi-structured expert interviews. Only specific case studies apply quantitative methods, for example content analysis of official documents or speeches.

1. A first set of questions focuses on the *institutional structure and the powers* of the Union's executive(s). Early observers of European integration, departing from international relations theories, paid little attention to these issues. From the mid-1980s onwards, when European integration gained momentum, more focused

questions arose mostly inspired by comparative politics. Where is the locus of executive power in the European Communities (EC)/EU? How are these powers divided between EU institutions and between the European and the national government level? Which additional institutions perform executive tasks? In what respect does the EU's executive resemble or, else, differ from national executives? Most recently, scholars question whether significant power shifts between executive institutions are taking place; furthermore, they reflect on how to assess the compound nature of the EU executive.

2. A second set of questions revolves around the *performance* of and the *interactions* between EU executives (on executive performance, see Chapter 32 in this volume). In this context, the three variants of neo-institutionalism and particularly principal-agent theory (see Chapters 3 and 5 in this volume) as well as organizational theory provide important analytical tools. How does the Commission perform executive tasks; does it act as agent of the intergovernmental bodies or rather as a policy entrepreneur? How do the Council and the European Council perform as executives, how can they overcome collective action problems? To which extent are national executives transformed by functioning as parts of the EU executive? What characterizes the interactions between various executive institutions: cooperation or competition and conflict? To which extent can individual institutions act autonomously within the EU's executive?

3. A third set of questions refers to *political leadership* of the European executive(s). Research on this issue has only recently evolved; it mainly draws on leadership theory in domestic arenas and adapts it to the context of the EU. Initially, such research focused on the Commission presidents; at present, it includes the intergovernmental bodies, national leaders, and, more broadly, cases of shared or collaborative leadership. Salient questions are: What are the resources and constraints of European leaders for exercising political leadership? To what extent is the Union characterized by a system of shared or collaborative leadership and, if so, does this result in effective performance? How are the relationships between European leaders structured; in which way do they interact? To what extent and under which conditions can European leaders successfully perform; when do they fail?

4. Finally, a fourth set of questions revolves around the *democratic legitimacy and accountability* of the European executive. Such studies, drawing on a broad set of democracy theories in national and partly also international contexts, have accompanied European integration since its inception; yet recently they proliferated. To what extent and why does the Union suffer from a democratic deficit? Is the EU characterized by a mismatch between legislature and executive in favour of the latter? To what extent and in which way are the European Commission, the Council and the European Council as executives democratically legitimized? How can EU executives being held accountable? Can holding the Union's executives accountable compensate for the democratic deficits of the multi-level system?

33.3 THE MAIN FINDINGS—FROM AN INCOMPLETE EXECUTIVE TO AN EMERGENT EUROPEAN EXECUTIVE ORDER

In response to the variegated set of questions presented above, findings widely vary, according to the focus of empirical interest and the theoretical approaches applied. Furthermore, research results vary with the progress of European integration. Indeed, the Union is marked by continuous processes of system-building, posing to analysts a moving target. Consequently, concepts of the EU's executive increasingly diversified together with the evolving multi-level system and its institutional differentiation.

33.3.1 The EU Executive: Institutional Structure and Powers

The first set of questions has led to a wide variety of approaches to grasp the *multi-level institutional structure* of the EU's executive. Most scholars agree that the Commission acts as the Union's core executive, even though it lacks key characteristics of national executives, particularly a government. Furthermore, scholars attribute to the Council and, recently, the European Council significant executive powers and, of course, to national executives within EU governance. However, the distribution of powers across these institutions and the power shifts between them has often been an issue of heated debates.

During the early years of European integration, the then dominating views of scholars adhering to either intergovernmentalism or neo-functionalism revolved around the question whether the Commission was an executive actor in its own right. The intergovernmentalists clearly denied this, as they perceived the EC as exclusively governed by the member states (e.g. Hoffmann 1966). By contrast the neo-functionalists conceptualized the EC as an emergent political system and the Commission as its potential executive branch. Thus Haas (1958: 58–9) noted an 'unprecedented' power transfer from the national to the European level, but also the limited scope of these powers and the lack of means for enforcement. Lindberg and Scheingold (1970: 86–7) pointed to the anomalies of the emerging 'would-be polity' and its 'Janus-like' institutions; yet they concluded that the Commission acts 'autonomously in terms of its own view of the "interest" of the Community as a whole'.

From the mid-1980s onwards, the exceptional integration dynamics, fuelled by an entrepreneurial Commission, triggered a more explicit reflection on the EC executive. At first, the dichotomy between intergovernmentalists and neo-functionalists re-emerged, albeit in more sophisticated form. On the one hand, Moravcsik (1991, 1998) under the term liberal intergovernmentalism, launched a theory that conceptualized the member states as the decisive actors in European decision-making. On the other hand, Sandholtz and Zysman (1989), drawing on neo-functionalism, attributed to the Commission the most prominent role in forwarding integration and a key executive function. Yet this debate soon faded away and scholars increasingly perceived the EU as a political system, with comparative politics approaches and particularly neo-institutionalism gaining dominance.

Hix (2005), referring to rational choice institutionalism and principal-agent theory, conceptualized the EU as a political system characterized by a *dual executive*, with government by both the Commission and the Council. While member states delegated far-reaching executive powers to the Commission, they retained also significant powers and control mechanisms for themselves. The Councils set the long- and medium-term policy goals and the member states care for policy implementation (Hix 2005: 27–73). Similarly Bartolini, theorizing system-building in the EU, emphasized the executive functions of both the Commission and the Council. Yet he pointed to the atypical mix of legislative and executive functions characterizing both institutions (Bartolini 2005: 153–4). Thus despite similar concepts of the power structure of the EU executive, authors diverge in their assessment. While Bartolini stresses the anomalies, Hix emphasizes the similarities with 'normal' government. These convergent and at the same time opposite positions continue to characterize the academic debate.

Impressed by an apparently powerful Commission, particularly under the Delors presidency, scholars widely applied principal-agent theory for explaining *that* and *why* the member states, acting as multiple principals, delegated far-reaching executive powers to an agent, the Commission (Franchino 2007). They explained the delegation of powers to the Commission mainly with the need to reduce transaction costs and secure credible commitments (Majone 1996; Pollack 2003). Furthermore, principal-agent theory served to explain why national governments are constrained in exerting control on the Commission, and under which conditions the latter is able to expand its powers beyond the intentions of its principals (e.g. Pollack 2003).

In the 1990s, Marks, Hooghe, and Blank directed attention to the vertical executive relationships in the EU by launching the multi-level governance approach (Marks et al. 1996; Hooghe and Marks 2001). They emphasized the discretionary executive powers of the Commission, attributing to it 'independent influence in policy-making', but also the sharing of such powers in the vertical direction 'by actors at different levels' (Marks et al. 1996: 396). Furthermore, they noted that national governments were no longer in state to monopolize the relationships with regional governments, and thus pointed to the disintegrating impacts of multi-level governance on the member states.

The increasingly differentiated perception of the EU's executive highlighted also the delegation of executive powers to independent agencies. Majone (1996), comparing the EU with the US, was the first to point to these processes. He explained the delegation of executive functions to agencies with credible commitments of national governments to the policy or issue area at stake. Later, scholars identified three waves of 'agencification' and largely confirmed Majone's explanation (e.g. Groenleer 2009). Independent agencies are assumed to act at the interface between the Commission, the Council and national administrations, and to enhance the EU's executive functions (Curtin and

Egeberg 2008). They even might 'indicate a centralization of executive power at EU-level' (Egeberg et al. 2014: 16). Whether the agencies serve to enhance the power position of the Commission or the Councils is an issue of ongoing debate (e.g. Egeberg and Trondal 2011).

Most recently, under the impression of a much more proactive role of the Council and particularly the European Council, researchers observed a major power shift to these bodies. The Maastricht Treaty, by establishing new policy areas under nearly exclusive intergovernmental control,[1] marks the turning point; the financial and sovereign debt crisis exacerbated this development (Fabbrini 2013; Puetter 2014). Speaking of 'new' or 'deliberative intergovernmentalism' (Puetter 2012, 2014), scholars explained this shift with 'transformations in Europe's political economy, changes in preference formation, and the decline of the "permissive consensus"' (Bickerton et al. 2015a: 703; see also 2015b). National executives choose for coordinated policy-making at European level in order to bind themselves to external rules and to 'excise political disagreement' in the domestic arena (Bickerton 2012: 33). Unsurprisingly, other scholars contradict these assumptions, either arguing that no significant power shift has taken place (e.g. Schimmelfennig 2015), or referring to certain increased powers of the Commission and the ECB (Dehousse 2013; Bauer and Becker 2014). Yet the perception of an immensely improved power position of the intergovernmental bodies prevails. Curtin (2009: 71) for example conceptualizes these bodies, alongside the Commission, as core executives, and the European Council as 'the alpha and omega of executive power in the EU political system'. Carammia et al. (2016: 809) even claim that this body 'is developing into the EU's de facto government'.

Independently from this debate, other scholars, mostly drawing on administrative sciences and organization theory, have analysed the executive role of the Commission. For example Wille (2013) conceptualizes the Commission as the Union's core executive and claims its 'normalization', as compared to national executives. She identified an increasing dichotomy in the Commission between a political and an administrative level and a much more professionalized performance of both these levels. Others launch a broader concept of an emergent accumulated or compound executive order in the EU, encompassing the Commission, the independent agencies as well as national executives, and sometimes also the Council and European Council (Curtin 2009; Curtin and Egeberg 2009; Trondal 2010). The Commission in this context figures as a distinctive executive centre that cooperates with executive actors and agencies across government levels.

Drawing conclusions on the institutional structure and powers of the EU's executive, it is apparent that despite certain notions of 'normalization', most observers agree on the distinctive nature of the EU multi-level system. First, legislative and executive powers are not clearly separated in corresponding branches of government, but exerted simultaneously by the core institutions of the EU. Second, executive powers are horizontally

---

[1] These policy areas are: Economic and Monetary Union (EMU), Common Foreign and Security Policy (CFSP), and Justice and Home Affairs (JHA).

fragmented between the core institutions at European level and vertically between the EU and the governments and administrations of the member states. Third, this fragmentation is further exacerbated by an unprecedented 'agencification' of the Union, involving both the European level and, increasingly, the member states.

Other aspects of the EU's executive are more contested. Some scholars emphasize the expanded and enhanced executive powers of the Council and particularly the European Council, at the expense of the executive role of the Commission. Others express reservations to this claim and emphasize the enormous discretionary powers of the Commission. Concepts of the EU's executive as a whole, for example as an emergent, compound, composite, accumulated, or simply variegated order or a multilevel mix of overlapping orders, remain a subject of debate.

33.3.2 European Union Executives: Performance and Interactions

A myriad empirical studies has explored the performance of the EU's executives and the multifaceted interactions among them. Regarding the *performance*, scholars assessed the variety of executive actors and institutions from different perspectives. The Commission was predominantly analysed in its political or rather technocratic orientation and its activism in forwarding European integration. Research on the Council and the European Council primarily focused on the quality and procedures of decision-making and the chances of achieving consensus. National executives were questioned in their behaviour in the framework of EU norms, objectives, and regulations. Yet, all executive institutions of the EU multi-level system were analysed in their capacity to act and, except for the Councils, their scope of autonomy.

Regarding the *Commission*, the early observers already perceived it as an administrative body with 'political skills par excellence' (Lindberg and Scheingold 1970: 94; italics in the original). Later, researchers conceptualized the Commission's performance as both typical bureaucratic, characterized by a low-profile administrative style, *and* political, albeit clearly differing from politics at national level (e.g. Cini 1996; Nugent and Rhinard 2015). The bureaucratic performance of the Commission is generally attributed to its independent position, largely detached from politics in and of the member states, while its political performance is seen as resulting from its agency. Recent studies on the preference formation inside the Commission confirmed the specific mixture of bureaucratic and political motives of Commissioners and officials (Hartlapp et al. 2014).

Particularly during the years of heightened activism, many scholars conceptualized the Commission as a policy entrepreneur, striving to expand and deepen integration. This entrepreneurialism concerned individual policy areas as well as the integration process as a whole. Authors ascribed the successful entrepreneurial performance of the Commission to its formal rights of initiative *and* its skilful use of other, partly informal political tools, such as persuasion of relevant actors, mobilisation of external support, creation of precedents through experimental actions, and frequent appeals to the Court of Justice (e.g. Pollack 1994; Tömmel 1998; Héritier 1999; Schmidt 2004).

In recent years, scholars observed a decline in the Commission's activism, mainly as a consequence of constraints set by the Council and the European Council (Hooghe and Rauh 2017). More specifically, Kreppel and Oztas (2017) revealed that the Commission's role as an agenda-setter has been transformed into a more technical one. Ellinas and Suleiman (2012) report an increasing bureaucratization of the Commission after the Kinnock reforms. By contrast Wille (2013), as a consequence of these reforms noted a more explicit political performance of the Commission, due to a clearer separation of functions between the College of Commissioners and the administration. Other authors conclude that the increased politicization of EU issues and the introduction of the *Spitzenkandidaten*-procedure[2] contributed to the Commission adopting a more political stance (e.g. Christiansen 2016).

In general, scholars attest the Commission a high degree of autonomy and discretion, due to its independent position, its nearly exclusive right of initiative, its supervisory powers, and the close intertwining of legislative and executive powers (e.g. Majone 2005, 2009; Ellinas and Suleiman 2012). Majone even suggests that the Commission enjoys too much discretion. Adherents of principal-agent theory conclude that the Commission has room for bureaucratic drift; yet they also emphasize that the intergovernmental bodies dispose of effective control mechanisms (Pollack 2003).

The performance of the *Council and the European Council* as executives has attracted less scholarly attention. The executive functions of these institutions are less tangible, as they refer to a variety of tasks of differing quality, ranging from constitutional issues via nomination of high level office holders to day-to-day policy-making, particularly in the new areas. Furthermore, in issues of policy-making, the intergovernmental bodies take only the major decisions, while detailed regulations, operational tasks and policy implementation are delegated to their substructure: various committees, the Council secretariat and, most importantly, national governments and administrations. Hence, the salient issue is whether and how the Council and the European Council achieve consensus in decision-making. Regarding the new policy areas, Puetter (2014) observed a significantly improved performance of consensus-building, based on various new procedures and practices. This ranges from simple measures, such as more frequent, more special and more informal meetings, to continuous processes of 'institutional engineering', as for example the establishment of permanent presidencies for the most important Council formations.[3] Bickerton explains this intensified consensus-seeking in the Councils without explicit negotiations as attempts to shield the EU 'as much as possible from the main source of conflict, namely the unpredictability of public debate

---

[2] The EP 'invented' this procedure with the 2014 elections. The party groups of the EP nominated lead candidates; the candidate of the party winning most seats would then be elected Commission president.

[3] The European Council, the Foreign Affairs Council and the Euro-group of the ECOFIN-Council have permanent presidencies.

and of public expectations' (Bickerton 2012: 33). Yet other researchers pointed to the difficulties of the intergovernmental bodies in achieving consensus, particularly when the issues at stake are highly controversial and politicized, as it is increasingly the case (e.g. Fabbrini 2013).

The performance of *independent agencies* depends on their mandate as well as their activism. Even though the mandate is often quite restricted, most agencies enjoy a far-reaching degree of discretion and proactively make use of it (Trondal 2010; Wonka and Rittberger 2010). Thus many observers report that agencies at European level, even those mandated only with tasks of data collection across the Union, increasingly engage in regulatory functions or in monitoring policy implementation (Egeberg and Trondal 2011). Whether such a performance is desired or even promoted by either the Commission or the Councils, is an issue of debate.

The performance of *national executives* in European affairs has many dimensions and is by definition a consequence of direct and indirect interactions with the Union (see below). In general, national executives are involved into all aspects of EU policy-making; this implies they adapt and improve their performance in many ways, so as to cope with the new tasks. Scholars conceptualized these adaptation processes under the term Europeanization (e.g. Bulmer and Lequesne 2013). Processes of Europeanization affect not only the performance of national executives, but also their institutional dimension (Ladrech 2010). This may include re-organizing ministries and the civil service, creating specialized institutions for policy formulation and implementation, introducing new methods of policy coordination and, finally, initiating more fundamental reforms, such as the creation or empowerment of lower level governments and administrations. Some authors even observed a redistribution of powers among national executives. Thus Poguntke and Webb (2005) see Europeanization as one of the causes for the trend towards presidentialization of chief executives in the member states, while Johannsson and Tallberg (2010) assume that EU-summitry has strengthened the power position of prime ministers vis-à-vis their cabinets.

Despite such adaptations, national executives have ample room for discretion to pursue their own preferences and priorities within European affairs, and they make extensively use of it. A vast body of literature on (non-)compliance in the transposition of European legal acts into national legislation as well as on the (sluggish) implementation of EU policies confirms that (e.g. Falkner et al. 2005; Piattoni and Polverari 2016). Olsen views the abundant implementation deficits in EU governance as a necessary 'safety valve' and concludes: 'The challenge is to construct balances between uniform and differentiated implementation which mediate between unity and diversity' (Olsen 2007: 250).

Turning to the *interactions* between European executives, scholars distinguish between horizontal interactions at European level and vertical interactions between EU institutions and national executives. In a certain sense, the apparently horizontal interactions between the Commission and the Councils are also vertical ones, as the two intergovernmental bodies do not just constitute the EU's highest authorities, but as much represent the member states. Furthermore, recent studies point to transversal interactions between the Commission and executive agencies of the member states and horizontal interactions among national executives.

Regarding the *horizontal Commission-Council interaction*, scholars diagnosed a tension between cooperation and competition or conflict (Bartolini 2005; Hayes-Renshaw and Wallace 2006). Cooperation refers to the complementary roles of the intergovernmental Councils and the supranational Commission in decision-making and to their mutually interdependent position. Competitive or conflicting relationships result from both sides striving for a maximum of influence on EU decisions and, more broadly, on European integration. Depending on the period in question, but also the theoretical viewpoint, scholars saw either the Commission or the Councils in a dominant or more influential position (Tömmel 2014). Researchers also pointed to the severe, yet differing constraints to which both sides underlie in their ambiguous relationship: the intergovernmental bodies to collective action problems, often resulting in failures to reach decisions; the Commission to a limited scope of formal powers and situational constraints to its agency.

The competitive relationship between the Commission and the Councils permeates also other interactions within the EU's compound executive. Regarding the *independent agencies*, scholars questioned whether they enhance the position of the Commission or 'act primarily as tools of national governments' (Egeberg and Trondal 2011). In day-to-day politics, the agencies mainly cooperate with the Commission, which deliberately involves them into its work (Egeberg et al. 2014); they thus enhance the Commission's executive functions (Groenleer 2009; Trondal 2010). The Councils are less important as direct interlocutors of the agencies; yet they shape their activities by defining their mandate and, partially, controlling their performance (Trondal 2010; Wonka and Rittberger 2010). The Commission also engages in involving independent agencies of the national level into EU executive politics; by establishing corresponding networks under its guidance, it tends to sideline member states' executives (Egeberg 2008).

The *vertical interactions* between *the European level and national executives* are as well characterized by cooperation and conflict. These interactions are structured by a host of committees, staffed with national diplomats or civil servants who act as advisors, negotiators or even decision-makers at European level. At the top of the pyramid stand COREPER (Committee of Permanent Representatives) and other high level committees for preparing and sometimes adopting Council decisions. Underneath, scholars distinguish three types of committees: advisory committees to the Commission for elaborating on legislative proposals; Council working groups for preparing the adoption of these proposals; and, finally, comitology committees for supervising the Commission at the implementation stage (Trondal 2010: 167–246). Researchers questioned whether the members of these committees primarily pursue the European common good or rather defend national interests or, else, act as neutral experts. For the advisory committees to the Commission, scholars found a predominantly cooperative style oriented on the common good; for the Council working groups, they discovered an astonishing degree of 'esprit de corps' and European perspectives on the issues at stake; regarding the comitology committees, findings vary between a predominantly deliberative style and more conflicting relationships fuelled by national interests (Joerges and Neyer 1997; Alfé et al. 2008; Trondal 2010).

Most recently, scholars pointed to forms of horizontal administrative cooperation between national executives in the framework of EU politics, as a response to manifold unintended consequences of European integration. According to Hartlapp and Heidbreder (2018: 40), 'horizontal administrative cooperation [...] buffers unintended effects of market integration on formally independent but increasingly interdependent member state executive bodies'.

Drawing conclusions on the performance of EU executives and the complex inter-actions among them, scholars agree that executive institutions partly perform in a cooperative manner, according to their complementary functions. Yet partly they also perform in a competitive or conflicting manner, as they pursue different objectives and represent contradictory interests. On the one hand, all European executives, including the agencies, cooperate in order to manage, expand, and advance European governance and policy-making, as well as the integration process as a whole. Yet they also struggle for influence, dominance, and a maximum of autonomy, in order to shape these processes according to their norms, insights, perceptions, preferences, and priorities. Depending on the issue at stake, their manifold direct and indirect interactions are either characterized by deliberations, tough negotiations, or cooperation, or even by ongoing dissent. These multifaceted performances and interactions mirror the contradicting structure of the EU multi-level system that has to balance European and national interests or, simply, unity and diversity.

33.3.3 Political Leadership

The issue of EU executive leadership reached the research agenda comparatively late. The Commission president was the first to figure as object of analysis; the (rotating) presidencies of the Council and the European Council drew also scholarly attention, as well as national leaders, either forwarding or hampering European integration. With progress in analysing the performance of individual leaders, the EU was increasingly perceived as a system of shared or collective leadership. Consequently, attention turned to the interactions among different leaders of executive institutions. At present, the literature on EU executive leadership is proliferating, covering a broad range of themes and debating the specifics of leadership in a multi-level system (e.g. Beach and Mazzucelli 2008; Hayward 2008; Helms 2017; Tömmel and Verdun 2017).

Unsurprisingly, the first studies of EU leadership emerged following the renewed integration dynamic during the second half of the 1980s. Some scholars focused on the leadership of the Commission as an institution (Cini 1996; Nugent 2001), others on the leadership of its president, Jacques Delors. The latter resulted in a series of dense descriptions of Delors' activities, skills, strategies and tactics, as well as his successes and failures (Ross 1995; Drake 2000). Endo (1999) was the first to analyse Delors' leadership within a complex theoretical and analytical framework, derived from theories of leadership in national political systems. He concluded that Delors performed as an extraordinary leader, yet faced also severe constraints, particularly in the last years of his presidency. This study set the scene for further comparative research on the leadership performance of Commission presidents, acting in the framework of institutional, situational, and personal resources and constraints. Such studies revealed enormous differences between Commission presidents, ranging from transactional to transforming leadership; furthermore, they highlighted the constraints of the office and the significance of personal skills, commitment, and strategic behaviour of individual incumbents for transcending them (Cini 2008; Kassim et al. 2013; Tömmel 2013, 2019; Müller 2020).

With perceiving the Commission constrained by the intergovernmental bodies, the leadership of the latter drew increasing attention. Studies on the rotating presidencies of the Councils focused on whether these temporary leaders 'matter' in reaching decisions and whether they use this position to pursue their own preferences (e.g. Tallberg 2006; Bunse 2009; Alexandrova and Timmermans 2013). These studies revealed that the presidencies do matter, that some presidencies are more effective than others in brokering deals, and that the office can, under certain circumstances, be exploited in favour of partisan goals of the chair. Most recently, scholars explored the role of the permanent presidency of the European Council (Dinan 2017; Tömmel 2017). They noticed a significant improvement in the functioning of this body and in achieving compromises, yet often in favour of the preferences of the large and powerful member states and at the expense of the mediation function of the Commission. Scholars also explored the leadership performance of individual heads of state or government or groups of them in European affairs. The leading role of the German-French tandem was of major interest (Schild 2010), as well as the dominant or even hegemonic role of Germany in the recent crisis of the EU (Bulmer and Paterson 2013). Furthermore, research focused on the contradictions which national leaders face, when acting in the European arena (Van Esch 2017).

At present, leadership research in the EU is proliferating, resulting in a broader set of studies on more specific issues, such as leadership in specific situations of the integration process or in crises, leadership of other executive institutions, for example the ECB or the independent agencies, or leadership of the EU in external affairs (e.g. Beach and Mazzucelli 2008; Tömmel and Verdun 2017). Furthermore, increasing attention is given to the exercise of cooperative or collaborative leadership in the EU and patterns of interactions between leaders of different executives (Müller and Van Esch 2019; Beach and Smeets 2020).

Drawing conclusions on political leadership in EU executive politics, the research in this realm so far mirrors the institutional heterogeneity of the multi-level system, as well as the ambiguous relationships between various executive institutions. Scholars have widely elaborated on the challenges that the multi-level structure of the EU poses to committed leaders in various institutional positions. They pointed to varying leadership performances, depending on the institutional context, the favouring or constraining situational factors and the personal skills of the incumbents, resulting in transactional or transforming leadership and sometimes also in failure. Most recently, in view of the compound nature of the EU executive, scholarly attention shifted to the EU as a system of collective or collaborative leadership; this research promises to constitute the future growth area and to provide deeper insights into the opportunities and constraints for providing leadership within a compound executive order.

33.3.4 Democratic Legitimacy and Accountability

Scientific reflection and debate on the democratic legitimacy and accountability of the executive(s) accompanied European system-building since its inception. Yet also in this case, research on these issues slowly evolved from initially occasional observations to carefully elaborated, theoretically informed analyses, drawing primarily on democracy theories in national political systems. Salient issues of debate were: the dominance of the EU's executive(s) vis-à-vis legislatures, the lack of transparency of their operations, and the lack of suited institutions, procedures, and mechanisms to hold the executive(s) accountable. Most of these studies took a comparative perspective, with democratic systems of states explicitly or implicitly figuring as standard model. This resulted in a rich literature on a wide range of legitimacy problems and accountability gaps and also in proposals for possible solutions or alternatives.

Lindberg and Scheingold (1970: 267) already noted that

> the Commission [...] operates without the check of a really effective Parliament. The Commission is controlled by a Council of national cabinet ministers, but these ministers are themselves essentially executive officers, and in any case control over the Commission is twice removed from any control by elected bodies.

Since the 1970s, successive Treaty changes provided the European Parliament (EP) with powers of oversight and control vis-à-vis the Commission; in addition, they empowered national parliaments in European affairs. However, the problem of the executives' lack in democratic legitimacy and accountability did not change; on the contrary, according to many observers the situation has even worsened in recent years.

During the heydays of European integration, and more so after the turning point marked by the Treaty of Maastricht, a vivid debate emerged on the so-called 'democratic deficit' of the EU. The arguments put forward in this debate centred on the following 'deficits': the dominance of executives in EU governance, the limited powers and capacities of both the EP and national legislatures to control the executives, the lack of European elections, the non-transparent decision-making mechanisms, and, finally, policy drift (e.g. Hix 2005: 177; Follesdal and Hix 2006). Of course, there were also scholars who denied a problem at all. Thus Moravcsik (2002: 605) claimed that 'Constitutional checks and balances, indirect democratic control via national governments, and the increasing powers of the European Parliament' were sufficient to render the Union's decisions legitimate. Follesdal and Hix (2006: 552) vehemently objected, by particularly emphasizing the 'lack of electoral contest for [...] the basic direction of the EU policy agenda'.

Other researchers debated possible alternatives for providing legitimacy to the multi-level system. Scharpf (1999), distinguishing between input- and output-legitimacy, argued that input legitimacy is difficult to provide in the Union; yet the effectiveness of its output might compensate for this lack. Some scholars even posed that it is impossible to democratically legitimize the EU multi-level system. Majone (2005: 46–51, 2009: 156) attributed this to the EU's inherent structure of a 'mixed government', representing corporate, not individual interests. Bartolini (2005: 174) concluded that 'the national standards of political legitimacy are too high and inappropriate for the EU'. Neyer (2012) claimed that instead of democracy, justice should be the normative standard for assessing the EU.

Despite this rich literature, recent institutional and procedural changes induced by the multiple crises have triggered a renewed debate on the democratic legitimacy and accountability of the EU. Thus Curtin (2014) noted an increasing executive dominance in the EU and a hollowing out of democracy. More in detail, she argued that neither the EP nor national parliaments can hold the core executives accountable, as the legislatures are 'structurally outsiders' (Curtin 2014: 16). National parliaments lack the necessary information; the EP is being 'sucked into the executive mode of diplomatic and secret negotiations and discussions' (Curtin 2014: 17). Furthermore, she denounces 'novel working methods' in the intergovernmental bodies, such as 'low level executive secrecy' (Council) and 'high-level executive informality' (European Council) (Curtin 2014: 18, 20). Though with less drastic words, both Habermas (2014) and Scharpf (2015) express similar concerns regarding the transformation of the EU in the wake of the financial and sovereign debt crisis. While Habermas (2014: 6) notes that 'national governments [...] have extended their scope of action', Scharpf (2015: 393) referring to the Six-Pack, observes the emergence of an 'entirely discretionary regime' at European level. As a remedy, Habermas (2014: abstract) proposes a transnational democracy, 'constituted by a "doubled" sovereign—the European citizens and the European peoples (the states)'. Scharpf, excluding any majority rule in the EU as normatively unacceptable, promotes a set of 'ground rules for a multilevel European democracy', in fact, smaller incremental steps to ease the most pressing shortcomings (Scharpf 2015: 400–4).

In view of the structural barriers to a full-fledged democratic system at European level, the debate recently shifted to the issue of accountability. According to Majone (2009: 175), 'In the EU the real problem [...] is not the democratic deficit, but the accountability deficit: a good accountability framework, rather than imperfect imitations of national parliamentary institutions, should be the goal'. Indeed, scholars increasingly search for new forms of accountability in the EU by analysing a broad set of institutions, actors, procedures, and mechanisms which together might effectively hold the executive(s) accountable (e.g. Bovens et al. 2010; Curtin at al. 2012). Bovens (2007) analysed administrative accountability forums and social forms of accountability (e.g. civil society organizations or investigative journalism). Yet he admits that these forms alone do not solve the problems; therefore, he pleads for a combination of traditional and new forms of accountability.

Drawing conclusions on the democratic legitimacy and accountability of the EU executive(s), a clear picture, let alone a consensus on these issues, has not emerged. Comprehensive theoretical approaches to grasp the problems as well as scientific reflection on possible solutions have not resulted in broadly accepted views. Scholars basically agree that the nature of the EU multi-level system, with its multiple, yet fragmented and at the same time highly entrenched executives, sets enormous hurdles to establish normatively acceptable procedures and mechanisms of democratic legitimacy and accountability. How to overcome these hurdles, and whether and to which extent the existing systemic structures, institutions and actors, procedures and mechanisms might provide starting points for this purpose, remains an issue of ongoing debate.

33.4 CONCLUSIONS AND FUTURE RESEARCH AGENDA

Summarizing executive politics of the EU multi-level system reveals the emergence of a complex executive order, spanning a broad set of institutions and agencies at both the European and the national government level and integrating them into a multifaceted web of interactions. While the executive at European level is divided between two powerful institutional actors—the supranational Commission and the intergovernmental Council and European Council—the executives of the member states are increasingly involved into their politics and, consequently, transformed. Furthermore, a myriad executive agencies charged with specific tasks act at the interface of these institutions. Altogether, this results in an emergent executive order, which however is less ordered than what this term suggests.

Thus the interactions among executive institutions are not only characterized by cooperation and collaboration, but also by competition and conflict. These interactions reflect the basic contradiction underlying European integration: the contradiction between the common European interest and the divergent national interests of the member states or, simply, between unity and diversity (Olsen 2007: 4–7). Through their interactions, executive institutions attempt to mediate these contradictions. This does not mean that there is always a balance between the institutions representing contradicting interests, and that the core executive institutions at European level clearly represent either of these interests. On the contrary, at present the intergovernmental bodies dominate and attempt to define and pursue the common European interest. However, this imbalance, as well as the overall imbalance between a highly diversified and powerful executive and weak, fragmented legislatures, affects the stability of the multi-level system. The depoliticized, technocratic manner characterizing decision-making of the intergovernmental bodies, but also the executive(s) in general, evokes increased politicization of EU issues and hence conflicts within national political arenas. Nevertheless, the EU displays the most sophisticated multi-level executive order, and its achievements and pitfalls might provide a template for other, evolving multi-level systems, particularly those in the international realm.

In spite of abundant scientific findings on the EU's executive, many aspects of its structure and functioning are under-researched, remain contentious, or evoke new questions. Therefore, a future research agenda on the EU executive(s) should cover the following themes: (1) The power structure of the EU executives and possible imbalances among and within them; (2) the (mal)functioning of the multi-level executive order; (3) the opportunities and constraints for the exercise of individual or collective leadership; (4) the problematic dominance of the executive(s) vis-à-vis the legislatures and the deficiencies in holding the executives accountable.

Regarding theme (1), future research should focus on the power structure within the intergovernmental bodies, the dominance or even hegemony of individual member states or groups of them, and the pursuit of partisan interests by them. Further salient issues are the strategies of the Commission to regain an influential position in European affairs, the empowerment or disempowerment of national executives within the multi-level executive order, and the position of the agencies within the evolving executive power structure. Future research on theme (2) should particularly question the (in) capacities of the intergovernmental bodies to reach consensual decisions, the (in)capacity of the Commission to pursue the common European good, the role of national executives and independent agencies in strengthening or weakening the EU's executive, and the frictions and deadlocks in the interactions between these institutions. Relevant issues in theme (3) are: the scope of executive leadership of various actors and institutions, the opportunities and constraints for the effective exercise of collective or collaborative leadership, and the role of cooperation or conflict and rivalries for the success or failure of collective leadership. In the context of theme (4), essential questions are those which have already been raised: the extent to which EU executives are democratically legitimized, how they can be held accountable, how the system's responsiveness to public demands can be improved, and how these demands can be channelled into functioning political processes.

Finally, the most salient open question overarching all four themes is how to assess the EU's emergent multi-level executive order as a whole. Is the EU's executive developing into a coherent order, or is it full of contradictions? Is it a mix of new and old orders and, if so, what is the interplay between them? When and why do member states choose to delegate powers to existing or new executive institutions; when and why do they prefer to retain powers for themselves? What lessons can be learned from the EU's executive order for other multi-level systems?

In sum, despite a rich literature on the unusual structure of the EU's executive order, salient questions remain open. The Union is a highly dynamic political system, marked by continuous adaptations and transformations of its institutional structure and the power balance between actors and institutions. Furthermore at present, fundamental crises might induce additional changes in unexpected directions. This situation poses enormous challenges for research on the EU's multifaceted executive order; yet it also provides a unique opportunity to observe institution-building in *statu nascendi*.

REFERENCES

Alexandrova, P. and Timmermans, A. (2013). 'National Interest Versus the Common Good: The Presidency in European Council Agenda Setting,' *European Journal of Political Research* 52(3): 316–38.

Alfé, M., Christiansen, T., and Piedrafita, S. (2008). 'Implementing Committees in the Enlarged European Union: Business as Usual for Comitology?,' in E. Best, T. Christiansen, and P. P. Settembri (eds) *The Institutions of the Enlarged European Union: Continuity and Change*. Cheltenham: Edward Elgar, 205–21.

Bartolini, S. (2005). *Restructuring Europe: Centre Formation, System Building, and Political Structuring between the Nation State and the European Union*. Oxford: Oxford University Press.

Bauer, M. W. and Becker, S. (2014). 'The Unexpected Winner of the Crisis: The European Commission's Strengthened Role in Economic Governance,' *Journal of European Integration* 36(3): 213–29.

Beach, D. and Mazzucelli, C. (2008) (eds). *Leadership in the Big Bangs of European Integration*. Basingstoke: Palgrave Macmillan.

Bickerton, C. (2012). *European Integration: From Nation States to Member States*. Oxford: Oxford University Press.

Bickerton, C., Hodson, D., and Puetter, U. (2015a). 'The New Intergovernmentalism: European Integration in the Post-Maastricht Era,' *Journal of Common Market Studies* 53(4): 703–22.

Bickerton, C., Hodson, D., and Puetter, U. (2015b). *The New Intergovernmentalism: States and Supranational Actors in the Post-Maastricht Era*. Oxford: Oxford University Press.

Bovens, M. (2007). 'New Forms of Accountability and EU-Governance,' *Comparative European Politics* 5(1), 104–20.

Bovens, M., Curtin, D., and 't Hart, P. (2010). *The Real World of EU Accountability. What Deficit?* Oxford: Oxford University Press.

Bulmer, S. and Lequesne, C. (2013) (eds). *The Member States of the European Union*. 2nd ed. Oxford: Oxford University Press.

Bulmer, S. and Paterson, W. (2013). 'Germany as the EU's Reluctant Hegemon: Of Economic Strength and Political Constraints,' *Journal of European Public Policy* 20(10): 1387–405.

Bunse, S. (2009). *Small States and EU Governance: Leadership through the Council Presidency*. Houndmills: Palgrave Macmillan.

Carammia, M., Princen, S., and Timmermans, A. (2016). 'From Summitry to EU Government: An Agenda Formation Perspective on the European Council,' *Journal of Common Market Studies* 54(4): 809–24.

Christiansen, T. (2016). 'After the *Spitzenkandidaten*: Fundamental Change in the EU's Political System?,' *West European Politics* 39(5): 992–1010.

Cini, M. (1996). *The European Commission: Leadership, Organisation and Culture in the EU Administration*. Manchester: Manchester University Press.

Cini, M. (2008). 'Political Leadership in the European Commission: The Santer and Prodi Commissions, 1995–2005,' in J. Hayward (ed.) *Leaderless Europe*. Oxford: Oxford University Press, 113–30.

Curtin, D. (2009). *Executive Power of the European Union: Law, Practices and the Living Constitution*. Oxford: Oxford University Press.

Curtin, D. (2014). 'Challenging Executive Dominance in European Democracy', *The Modern Law Review* 77(1): 1–32.

Curtin, D. and Egeberg, M. (2008). 'Tradition and Innovation: Europe's Accumulated Executive Order', *West European Politics* 31(4): 639–61.

Curtin, D. and Egeberg, M. (2009) (eds). *Towards a New Executive Order in Europe?* London: Routledge.

Curtin, D., Mair, P., and Papadopoulos, Y. (2012) (eds). *Accountability and European Governance*. London: Routledge.

Dehousse, R. (2013). 'The Politics of Delegation in the European Union', *Les Cahiers Européens de Sciences Po* 4: 1–27.

Dinan, D. (2017). 'Leadership in the European Council: An Assessment of Herman Van Rompuy's Presidency', *Journal of European Integration* 39(2): 157–73.

Drake, H. (2000). *Jacques Delors: Perspectives on a European Leader*. London: Routledge.

Egeberg, M. (2008). 'European Government(s): Executive Politics in Transition', *West European Politics* 31(1–2): 235–57.

Egeberg, M. and Trondal, J. (2011). 'EU Level Agencies: New Executive Centre Formation or Vehicles for National Control?', *Journal of European Public Policy* 18(6): 868–87.

Egeberg, M., Trondal, J., and Vestlund, N. M. (2014). 'Situating EU Agencies in the Political-Administrative Space'. Arena Working Paper 6.

Ellinas, A. A. and Suleiman, E. (2012). *The European Commission and Bureaucratic Autonomy: Europe's Custodians*. Cambridge: Cambridge University Press.

Endo, K. (1999). *The Presidency of the European Commission under Jacques Delors: The Politics of Shared Leadership*. Houndmills: Macmillan.

Fabbrini, S. (2013). 'Intergovernmentalism and Its Limits: Assessing the European Union's Answer to the Euro Crisis', *Comparative Political Studies* 20(10): 1–27.

Falkner, G., Treib, O., Hartlapp, M., and Leiber, S. (2005). *Complying with Europe: EU Harmonisation and Soft Law in the Member States*. Cambridge: Cambridge University Press.

Follesdal, A. and Hix, S. (2006). 'Why There Is a Democratic Deficit in the EU: A Response to Majone and Moravcsik', *Journal of Common Market Studies* 44(3): 533–62.

Franchino, F. (2007). *The Powers of the Union: Delegation in the EU*. Cambridge: Cambridge University Press.

Groenleer, M. (2009). *The Autonomy of European Union Agencies: A Comparative Study of Institutional Development*. Delft: Eburon.

Haas, E. B. (1958). *The Uniting of Europe: Political, Social and Economic Forces 1950–1957*. London: Stevens & Sons.

Habermas, J. (2014). 'Democracy in Europe: Why the Development of the European Union into a Transnational Democracy is Necessary and How it is Possible.' Arena Working Paper 13.

Hartlapp, M. and Heidbreder, E. G. (2018). 'Mending the Hole in Multilevel Implementation: Administrative Cooperation Related to Worker Mobility', *Governance* 31(1): 27–43.

Hartlapp, M., Metz, J., and Rauh, C. (2014). *Which Policy for Europe: Power and Conflict inside the European Commission*. Oxford: Oxford University Press.

Hayes-Renshaw, F. and Wallace, H. (2006). *The Council of Ministers*. 2nd ed. Basingstoke: Palgrave Macmillan.

Hayward, J. (2008). *Leaderless Europe*. Oxford: Oxford University Press.

Helms, L. (2017) (ed.). 'Leadership Questions in Transnational European Governance', Special Issue, *European Political Science* 16(1).

Héritier, A. (1999). *Policy-Making and Diversity in Europe: Escaping Deadlock*. Cambridge: Cambridge University Press.

Hix, S. (2005). *The Political System of the European Union*. 2nd ed. Houndmills: Palgrave Macmillan.

Hoffmann, S. (1966). 'Obstinate or Obsolete: The Fate of the Nation State and the Case of Western Europe', *Daedalus* 95(3): 862–915.

Hooghe, L. and Marks, G. (2001). *Multi-Level Governance and European Integration*. Lanham: Rowman and Littlefield.

Hooghe, L. and Marks, G. (2003). 'Unraveling the Central State, But How? Types of Multi-Level Governance', *American Political Science Review* 97(2): 233–43.

Hooghe, L. and Rauh, C. (2017). 'The Commission's Services: A Powerful Permanent Bureaucracy', in D. Hodson and J. Peterson (eds) *The Institutions of the European Union*. 4th ed. Oxford: Oxford University Press, 187–212.

Joerges, C. and Neyer, J. (1997). 'From Intergovernmental Bargaining to Deliberative Political Processes: The Constitutionalisation of Comitology', *European Law Journal* 3(3): 273–99.

Johannsson, K. M. and Tallberg, J. (2010). 'Explaining Chief Executive Empowerment: EU Summitry and Domestic Institutional Change', *West European Politics* 33(2): 208–36.

Kassim, H., Peterson, J., Bauer, M., Connolly, S., Dehousse, R., Hooghe, L., and Thomson, A. (2013). *The European Commission of the Twenty-first Century*. Oxford: Oxford University Press.

Kreppel, A. and Oztas, B. (2017). 'Leading the Band or Just Playing The Tune: Reassessing the Agenda-Setting Powers of the European Commission', *Comparative Political Studies* 50(8): 1118–50.

Ladrech, R. (2010). *Europeanization and National Politics*. Houndmills: Palgrave Macmillan.

Lindberg, L. and Scheingold, S. A. (1970). *Europe's Would-Be Polity: Patterns of Change in the European Community*. Englewood Cliffs, NJ: Prentice Hall.

Majone, G. (1996) (ed.). *Regulating Europe*. London: Routledge.

Majone, G. (2005). *Dilemmas of European Integration: The Ambiguities and Pitfalls of Integration by Stealth*. Oxford: Oxford University Press.

Majone, G. (2009). *Europe as the Would-Be World Power: The EU at Fifty*. Cambridge: Cambridge University Press.

Marks, G., Hooghe, L., and Blank, K. (1996). 'European Integration from the 1980s: State-Centric versus Multi-level Governance', *Journal of Common Market Studies* 34(3): 341–78.

Moravcsik, A. (1991). 'Negotiating the Single European Act: National Interests and Conventional Statecraft in the European Community', *International Organization* 45(1): 19–56.

Moravcsik, A. (1998). *The Choice for Europe: Social Purpose and State Power from Messina to Maastricht*. Ithaca, NY: Cornell University Press.

Moravcsik, A. (2002). 'In Defence of the 'Democratic Deficit': Reassessing Legitimacy in the European Union', *Journal of Common Market Studies* 40(4): 603–24.

Müller, H. (2020). *Political Leadership and the European Commission Presidency*. Oxford: Oxford University Press.

Müller, H. and Van Esch, F. (2019). 'Collaborative Leadership in EMU Governance: A Matter of Cognitive Proximity', *West European Politics*, DOI:10.1080/01402382.2019.1678950

Neyer, J. (2012). *The Justification of Europe: A Political Theory of Supranational Integration*. Oxford: Oxford University Press.

Nugent, N. (2001). *The European Commission*. Houndmills: Palgrave Macmillan.

Nugent, N. and Rhinard, M. (2015). *The European Commission*. 2nd ed. Basingstoke: Palgrave Macmillan.

Olsen, J. P. (2007). *Europe in Search of Political Order*. Oxford: Oxford University Press.

Piattoni, S. and Polverari, L. (2016) (eds). *Handbook on Cohesion Policy in the EU*. Cheltenham: Edward Elgar.

Poguntke, T. and Webb, P. (2005). 'The Presidentialization of Contemporary Democratic Politics: Evidences, Causes and Consequences,' in T. Poguntke and P. Webb (eds) *The Presidentialization of Politics: A Comparative Study of Modern Democracies*. Oxford: Oxford University Press.

Pollack, M. A. (1994). 'Creeping Competence: The Expanding Agenda of the European Community,' *Journal of Public Policy* 14(2): 95–145.

Pollack, M. A. (2003). *The Engines of European Integration: Delegation, Agency and Agenda Setting in the EU*. Oxford: Oxford University Press.

Puetter, U. (2012). 'Europe's deliberative Intergovernmentalism: The Role of the Council and European Council in EU Economic Governance,' *Journal of European Public Policy* 19(2): 161–78.

Puetter, U. (2014). *The European Council and the Council: New Intergovernmentalism and Institutional Change*. Oxford: Oxford University Press.

Ross, G. (1995). *Jacques Delors and European Integration*. Cambridge: Polity Press.

Sandholtz, W. and Zysman, J. (1989). '1992: Recasting the European Bargain,' *World Politics* 41(1): 95–128.

Scharpf, F. W. (1999). *Governing in Europe: Effective and Democratic?* Oxford: Oxford Universityty Press.

Scharpf, F. W. (2015). 'After the Crash: A Perspective on Multilevel European Democracy,' *European Law Journal* 21(3): 384–405.

Schild, J. (2010). 'Mission Impossible? The Potential for Franco-German Leadership in the Enlarged EU,' *Journal of Common Market Studies* 48(5): 1367–90.

Schimmelfennig, F. (2015). 'What's the News in 'New Intergovernmentalism'? A Critique of Bickerton, Hodson and Puetter,' *Journal of Common Market Studies* 53(4): 723–30.

Schmidt, S. K. (2004). 'The European Commission's Powers in Shaping European Policies,' in D. G. Dimitrakopoulos (ed.) *The Changing European Commission*. Manchester: Manchester University Press, 105–20.

Smeets, S. and Beach, D. (2020). 'Political and Instrumental Leadership in Major EU Reforms: The Role and Influence of the EU Institutions in Setting-up the Fiscal Compact,' *Journal of European Public Policy* 27(1): 63–81.

Tallberg, J. (2006). *Leadership and Negotiations in the European Union*, Cambridge: Cambridge University Press.

Tömmel, I. (1998). 'Transformation of Governance: The European Commission's Strategy for Creating a 'Europe of the Regions',' *Regional and Federal Studies* 8(2): 52–80.

Tömmel, I. (2013). 'The Presidents of the European Commission: Transactional or Transforming Leaders?,' *Journal of Common Market Studies* 51(4): 789–805.

Tömmel, I. (2014). *The European Union: What It Is and How It Works*. Basingstoke: Palgrave Macmillan.

Tömmel, I. (2017). 'The Standing President of the European Council: Intergovernmental or Supranational Leadership?', *Journal of European Integration* 39(2): 175–89.

Tömmel, I. (2019). 'Political Leaderhip in Times of Crisis: The Commission Presidency of Jean-Claude Juncker', *West European Politics* DOI:10.1080/01402382.2019.1646507

Tömmel, I. and Verdun, A. (2017) (eds). 'Political Leadership in the European Union', Special Issue, *Journal of European Integration* 39(2).

Trondal, J. (2010). *An Emergent European Executive Order*. Oxford: Oxford University Press.

Van Esch, F. (2017). 'The Paradoxes of Legitimate EU Leadership. An Analysis of the Multi-Level Leadership of Angela Merkel and Alexis Tsipras during the Euro Crisis', *Journal of European Integration* 39(2): 223–37.

Wille, A. (2013). *The Normalization of the European Commission: Politics and Bureaucracy in the EU Executive*. Oxford: Oxford Universityty Press.

Wonka, A. and Rittberger, B. (2010). 'Credibility, Complexity and Uncertainty: Explaining the Institutional Independence of 29 EU Agencies', *West European Politics* 33(4): 70–752.

CHAPTER 34

POLITICAL EXECUTIVES IN AUTOCRACIES AND HYBRID REGIMES

JODY LAPORTE

34.1 INTRODUCTION

WITHIN the study of democratic regimes, the analysis of political executives has been a key focus of study for generations of scholars. A central point of inquiry has concerned the analytic value of distinguishing among parliamentary, presidential, and semi-presidential systems. Recent decades have seen further investigations into the effects of executive format on policy-making, the nature of policy outputs, and prospects for democratization. A parallel research agenda examines how other factors, such as leadership style, party and electoral systems, and popular support affects executive dynamics. As a result, we know a considerable amount about the structures, workings, and sources of variation across democratic executives.

In comparison, we know less about executives in non-democratic regimes.[1] Although the study of formal institutions has been an important component of the comparative authoritarianism research agenda over the past decade, this work has largely focused on the role of legislatures, elections, and political parties. Some studies have investigated the relationship between executives and other institutions, but there has been less work done on authoritarian executives themselves. Yet, the executive sits at the heart of politics in non-democratic regimes. It is both a key actor in driving political decisions, as well as an important forum for negotiating between different political interests. Unpacking the way that authoritarian executives work is critical for analysing politics, explaining policy outcomes, and predicting regime durability.

---

[1] Following the definition of authoritarianism provided below, and following standard practices in recent literature, I use the terms non-democratic regime, authoritarian regime, autocracy, and dictatorship interchangeably.

This chapter assesses the state of knowledge about executives in non-democratic regimes. In doing so, it seeks to bring together the findings from two disparate literatures— scholarship on political executives, which largely studies how they work in democratic regimes, and theories of authoritarian rule, which often tends to conceive of the executive as a single ruler. These literatures invoke different concepts, methods, and cases. The goal of this chapter is to translate across the conceptual and theoretical divide in order to highlight points of intersection between them.

The chapter starts by defining authoritarian executives and identifying how they differ from those in democracies. In non-democracies, rulers are not selected through free and fair elections. Section 34.2 assesses how this affects the institutions and behaviour of the executive in non-democracies versus democracies. It also considers how executives in non-democratic regimes vary from one another other. Section 34.3 then turns to key questions and important findings in the study of executives in non-democratic regimes, focusing on competing perspectives on how authoritarian governments maintain power, ensure regime stability, and formulate political decisions. Section 34.4 of this chapter lays out some avenues for future research, including the potential for further investigation into the formal organization of authoritarian executives and the nature of intra-executive politics.

34.2 Executives in Authoritarian Regimes

34.2.1 Distinguishing Democratic versus Non-Democratic Executives

The first task is to define what we mean by the executive in a non-democratic context. Political regimes are understood procedurally, as 'the rules and procedures that determine how national, executive leaders are chosen' (Howard and Roessler 2006: 366 Within this overarching category, democracies are those regimes in which rulers are selected through free and fair elections. Or, as Schumpeter (1950: 269) specifies, democracy refers to 'that institutional arrangement for arriving at political decisions in which individuals acquire the power to decide by means of a competitive struggle for the people's vote'. It follows from this definition that non-democracies are those regimes one in which national-level leaders are selected by any means *other than* free and fair elections (Gandhi 2008: 7). For example, leaders may come to power by fraudulent election, a *coup d'état*, a palace *putsch*, or a revolution. This is a broad definition of autocracy that, as we will see below, includes a range of institutional configurations and political practices.

Across political regimes, the executive refers to the head of government and the cabinet, whose collective job it is to make, enforce, and execute the law (Cheibub et al. 2010).

Executives are readily identifiable in a democracy, where the head of government is elected directly (in a presidential system) or indirectly (in a parliamentary system) to a formal office and constitutionally empowered alongside the cabinet to undertake decisions about the direction of government policy. Pinpointing the executive in a non-democratic regime can be more difficult, because the means by which rulers obtain executive office can vary significantly and there is less clear congruence between formal offices and the *de facto* sources of authority. Executive office-holders also may have different job titles than in democratic regimes. While the head of government is often a president, the title may be one of prime minister (e.g. in Singapore and Malaysia), king, emir, or something more colourful. For example, Maummar Al-Qaddafi's official designation was the 'Brotherly Leader and Guide of the Revolution of Libya'. These differences can make it difficult to observe which individual or groups of individuals hold effective decision-making power.

Scholars have developed a number of different ways to identify the effective head of government in these contexts. One possibility is to associate executive power with those individuals who have *de facto* political decision-making power, irrespective of their formal position (see also Chapter 19 in this volume). Geddes, Wright, and Frantz (2014: 315) call this the 'leadership group', that is, 'the small group that actually makes the most important decisions'. Bueno de Mesquita, Smith, Siverson, and Morrow (2003: 38) further specify that executive power rests in those 'one or more central individuals with the authority to raise revenue and allocate resources'. Another possibility is to start with the institutions normally associated with the executive and assume that they function as the bodies of effective decision-making. To this end, Gandhi (2008: 18) identifies the head of government as the following: (1) the general-secretary of the communist party in a communist dictatorship; (2) the king, president, or in certain cases prime minister in a non-communist dictatorship; (3) another individual or the military if evidence suggests that the nominal office-holder does not hold actual decision-making authority.

How does the non-democratic context affect the composition and operation of the government? For one, the format of the executive varies more widely than in democratic regimes. Democratic executives routinely are led by a team of officials—including president and/or prime minister and a cabinet of ministers—who work together and in tandem with other branches of government, including an elected assembly and judiciary. This is not necessarily the case in non-democratic regimes. In extreme scenarios—for example, the Soviet Union during Stalin or North Korea under the Kim dynasty—executive power might be centralized into the figure of a single individual who effectively governs alone. More often, the head of government rules in conjunction with others with whom they share power. These might be trusted allies who form a council of advisors, organized either informally into an advisory board or institutionalized more formally as a cabinet or Politburo. In other cases, these power-sharing relationships are institutionalized into a legislative body. This format prevails in most cases: between 1946 and 2008, legislative assemblies operated in more than 80 per cent of authoritarian regimes, as measured by country-years (Svolik 2012: 38).

The non-democratic context also affects the functioning of political executives. In the absence of democratic elections, the executive tends to take on the powers afforded to the executive in both presidential and parliamentary systems. As in presidential democracies, the origin and survival of an authoritarian executive is rarely tied to the support of the legislature. Democratic presidents are popularly elected to a fixed term of office, rather than originating in the legislature, and cannot be recalled through a vote of no confidence. In non-democratic regimes, executives are similarly unaccountable to the legislature. In many cases, this can be traced to the formal organization of the executive; many non-democratic executives are set up as presidential systems or a variant thereof (Roberts 2015). But even in parliament-based autocracies, the legislature is unlikely to press for a no confidence vote or otherwise exercise significant oversight over the executive because of the executive's informal sources of authority and *de facto* control over politics. For example, in electoral autocracies it is usually the executive that oversees manipulation of election results and decides which candidates receive seats in parliament. As a result, individual legislators may decline to spearhead a recall of the executive for fear of endangering their own re-election, their career advancement, or in extreme cases their personal safety.[2]

At the same time, as in parliamentary systems, authoritarian executives often have significant control over legislation, and tend to set the direction of policy. In this sense, the policy-making powers of non-democratic executives resemble those of a parliamentary system. In parliamentary democracies, it is the executive that proposes policy and sets the policy agenda. The legislature serves in a reactionary role, responding to the executive's proposals and providing an arena for debate. This accurately describes the relationship in authoritarian regimes. The executive may have formal prerogative to introduce legislation; if not, he or she will rely on loyal allies in the legislature to do so. Regardless, there are fewer constraints on the executive's ability to enact policy. In the absence of free and fair elections, it is less likely that opposition parties will have seats in the legislature. Further, there is a smaller chance of internal opposition to the executive's agenda from within his or her ruling party or affiliated supporters. Thus, unlike in a presidential democracy—where the direct election of both the executive and legislature creates 'two independent agents of the electorate that must cooperate in order to accomplish any legislative change' (Shugart 2008: 350)—the authoritarian executive is more likely to see his preferred policies enacted.

Because they are not subject to the checks and balances built into democratic institutions, it follows that authoritarian executives tend to be more powerful than executives in democratic regimes. But this is not to say that they are invincible. Non-democratic executives still function within the context of certain constitutional constraints, even if those constraints may operate for different reasons or through different mechanisms compared with democracies (Albertus and Menaldo 2012b; Ginsburg and Simpser 2013). There can be considerable variation in the formal prerogatives allocated to the executive

---

[2] See also Simpser (2013). Gehlbach and Simpser (2015) make a similar argument regarding the mechanisms of executive control over lower-level bureaucrats.

(Ginsburg et al. 2013), as well as the contextual circumstances that augment or restrain their power. Additionally, compared with democratic governments, non-democratic executives face a higher chance of losing power through extra-constitutional means (Svolik 2012). And given that violence is an ever-present possibility in these settings, there is much more stake. Rulers who lose power can conceivably face jail, exile, or death (Escribà-Folch 2013a). These factors combine to produce not just institutional restrictions, but also *de facto* constraints against the exercise of despotic power by the executive.

34.2.2 Variation across Non-Democratic Executives

Despite these general commonalities, authoritarian executives vary widely in their form and functioning. As Geddes (1999: 121) notes, 'different kinds of authoritarianism differ from each other as much as they differ from democracy'. Scholars take competing approaches to distinguishing among non-democratic regimes. One perspective emphasizes the means by which rulers come to power and differences in the levels of competition and contestation for executive office. How much input do citizens have in the selection of candidates for executive office? This question is of particular interest to scholars of hybrid regimes, in which the formal institutions of democracy coexist with autocratic practices (Collier and Levitsky 1997; Schedler 2002; Gilbert and Mohseni, 2011). Most countries in the world today hold national-level elections, even if those elections fall far short of the democratic standards. Across the range of 'electoral authoritarian' regimes, there is still significant variation in the degree to which there is meaningful competition between the candidates and the extent of uncertainty about the electoral outcome (Levitsky and Way 2002; Schedler 2006; Handlin 2017).

We can thus differentiate among the types of non-democratic regimes according to the procedures and electoral practices by which national leaders are chosen (Diamond 2002; Howard and Roessler 2006). Among non-democracies, competition is highest in *competitive authoritarian regimes*. These regimes are hybrid in the truest sense. In them, 'formal democratic institutions are widely viewed as the principal means of obtaining and exercising political authority. Incumbents violate those rules so often and to such an extent, however, that the regime fails to meet conventional minimal standards for democracy' (Levitsky and Way 2002: 53). In such regimes, elections are competitive in the sense that opposition groups are allowed to compete, and incumbent's re-election is not guaranteed, as much as it might seem likely. Both sides engage in active campaigning, even if the mechanisms of fraud, coercion, and patronage tip the political playing field to the incumbent's very real advantage. As a result, rulers need to take elections seriously.

Competitive authoritarian regimes stand in contrast to *hegemonic authoritarian regimes* in which regular elections are not competitive contests. Opposition candidates may be banned from registering to compete on technical grounds, or systematically denied access to media coverage, spaces for public rallies, and campaign funding

(LaPorte 2015). In these regimes, the political playing field is tipped so strongly in favour of the incumbent—even outside of electoral campaigns—that it generates few doubts about who will be declared the victor and overwhelming victories for the incumbent. Concretely, scholars usually specify a 70 per cent electoral victory as the threshold between competitive versus uncompetitive elections. Competition for office is lowest in *fully closed regimes*, which do not hold elections for national office at all. Instead, the selection of rulers might be determined by hereditary succession, such as in monarchical rule; the use of threat of violence or military force, such as in military coups or social revolutions; or through negotiations within the ruling party, as sometimes occurs in one-party regimes.

These distinctions influence the functioning of the executive. Higher levels of political competition generally signal a more dispersed distribution of political resources; as a result, they are also associated with a more constrained executive. Levitsky and Way (2002: 56) note that in competitive authoritarian regimes legislatures are often 'relatively weak, but they occasionally become focal points of opposition activity'. They may at times push back against the expansion of executive power, as occurred in Ukraine in 2000–1 when parliament blocked then-President Leonid Kuchma's attempts to call a referendum on reducing the legislature's authority. The government is also unlikely to exercise complete control over the judiciary in these regimes, and so is subject to the possibility of rogue judges who refuse to uphold the government's agenda. In contrast, such developments would be almost unfathomable in hegemonic or closed regimes.

A competing approach to typologizing non-democratic regimes focuses on variation across the set of individuals who are empowered to make executive-level decisions. Rather than observing the formal institutions of executive power, this perspective considers the shape and size of the *de facto* 'ruling coalition'—that is, the number of people involved in decision-making, as well as whose interests are represented. Geddes, Wright, and Frantz (2014: 318) differentiate among military, monarchy, dominant-party, and personalist regimes according to 'whether control over policy, leadership selection, and the security apparatus is in the hands of a ruling party (dominant-party dictatorships), a royal family (monarchies), the military (rule by the military institution), or a narrower group centred around an individual dictator (personalist dictatorships)'. They hypothesize that these differing executive compositions shape the dynamics of executive politics, because they create different chances of internal conflicts among the ruling elite. Military regimes are the most prone to internal conflicts, because they contain a larger range of competing interests and unresolved rivalries among the governing elite (see Chapter 37 in this volume). In personalist regimes, by dint of the fact that one individual has managed to consolidate power, factions in personalist regimes have already resolved the struggle for power. Consequently, they are not subject to the same centripetal political forces. Elites also have incentive to cooperate in single-party regimes, because of the unifying power of the party. This typology thus generates different incentives and payoffs to cooperation versus competition among rival actors within the *de facto* executive branch, and in turn explains the chances of rebellion or compromise on political issues.

While Geddes and her co-authors focus on the composition of the ruling coalition, others highlight the political consequences of variation in the ruling coalition's size. Working from a definition of ruling coalition as the set of individuals who 'support the government and, jointly with the dictator, hold enough power to be both necessary and sufficient for the survival of government' (Svolik 2009: 479), Bueno de Mesquita et al.'s (2003) selectorate theory argues that the size of this coalition shapes decisions about the allocation of resources across society. Their reasoning is as follows. Leaders must satisfy their ruling coalition to stay in office; to do so, they can distribute either private goods to coalition members, or public goods to the population. But as the size of the coalition grows, the value of the private goods going to each member shrinks. At some point, it becomes more efficient to provide public goods to the population, rather than private goods to the entire coalition. Thus, the size of the coalition influences the distribution of resources and, in turn, regime dynamics.

A third dimension of variation concerns the mechanisms and patterns of succession across these types of authoritarianism. The transfer of power from one ruler to another can be problematic for such regimes, as it is a moment when power distributions are renegotiated, elite conflict may come to the fore, and disgruntled outsiders may try to seize the opportunity to bring down the regime. Regimes that can orchestrate an orderly transition of office-holders can effectively extend the time horizon and the longevity of the regime. However, the appointment of a designated successor creates its own challenges, as it raises the possibility that the chosen nominee will overthrow the incumbent and usurp power prematurely (Herz 1952).

Different types of non-democracies institute varying mechanisms to negotiate this problem. Monarchies, in which power is based within a ruling family, are defined by the presence of hereditary succession rules (see also Chapter 35 in this volume). Kokkonen and Sundell (2014: 438) argue that primogeniture offers the ideal solution because it 'provides the autocrat with an heir who, because of his or her young age, can afford to wait to inherit power peacefully, and it provides the elite with assurance that the regime will live on and continue to reward their loyalty after the incumbent autocrat has passed away'. Drawing on this logic, they show that primogeniture facilitated the creation of strong states across Europe through the middle ages and early modern period. These findings bear relevance beyond historical cases: Herb (1999) similarly attributes the stability of Arab monarchies to their dynastic political structures. And, as Brownlee (2007b) shows, it is not just formal monarchies that follow hereditary succession; contemporary republic-style autocracies as diverse as Syria, Azerbaijan, Singapore, and Togo recently have as well.

In other cases, succession decisions are negotiated among a designated group of governing elites, often a subset of the ruling party. A wide range of empirical investigations have shown that the institutionalized opportunities for career advancement within single-party regimes create incentives for cooperation, and in doing so contribute to long-term stability (Geddes 1999; Brownlee 2007a; Magaloni 2008). As Magaloni and Kricheli (2010: 127) point out in their review of party-based autocracies:

the party controls succession and access-to-power positions. [...] Hence, instead of counteracting threats by groups within society, in this approach the party serves to neutralize threats from within the ruling elite by guaranteeing them a share of power over the long run.

Such transfers of power often operate at the intersection of legally codified procedures, informal institutions, and behind-the-scenes political struggles amongst competing elites. For example, in the Soviet Union the Communist Party of the Soviet Union (CPSU) Central Committee was empowered to select a successor; in reality, they served to confirm a selection that had already been made by the Politburo. Although these decisions often involved some degree of last-minute manoeuvring by competing elites, particularly after the deaths of Lenin and Stalin, regularities also emerged. Mitchell (1990: 9) points out that

> in all successions in Soviet history, the top post has gone to the ranking member of the party Secretariat [... which] suggests that the identity of the successor is determined well in advance, and that succession is a lengthier process than commonly understood, with the real contest for the top post preceding the rights of transition.

The importance of formal succession rules is underscored by Frantz and Stein (2017), who argue that such institutions protect dictators from coups. Through statistical analysis, they demonstrate that codified procedures for transferring power within authoritarian regimes reduces insiders' incentives to conspire against the ruler and hampers the coordination efforts of potential coup plotters. Meng (2017) adds that the nature of the constitutional rules also matter. Drawing on a dataset of African countries from 1960–2010, she shows that peaceful transitions are more likely within dictatorships when there is both a constitutional procedure for transferring power, as well as constitutional rules that identify a clear line of succession—and thus, designate a specific individual to come to power.

Yet, some autocracies lack agreed-upon procedures for transferring power. This is most often the case in personalist regimes. Geddes, Wright, and Frantz (2014: 320) find that 'the rates of leader ouster and regime failure are similar for personalist dictatorship', suggesting that few personalist regimes manage to negotiate an intra-regime leadership succession. Kendall-Taylor and Frantz (2016) similarly demonstrate that personalist regimes have a significantly higher rate of collapse following leadership turnovers compared with other authoritarian subtypes.

In sum, authoritarian governments take a variety of different formats and function across a wide range of political settings. Authoritarian executives tend to be more powerful vis-à-vis other branches of government than in democratic regimes, but because the threat of violence and the possibility of extra-constitutional removal from office are ever-present, authoritarian executives also tend to be less secure. Not surprisingly, then, the core research agenda in the study of non-democratic regimes has focused on how rulers work to avoid the prospect of rebellion or revolution. Section 34.3 outlines the main findings in this area.

34.3 KEY FINDINGS IN THE STUDY OF AUTHORITARIAN EXECUTIVES

The central question in the study of authoritarian executives is a simple one: how do rulers maintain power and ensure regime stability? Most explanations conceive of the executive as an individual autocrat who faces two sources of threat to his or her survival in office. One potential danger comes from political elites, especially his or her own allies. Of central concern to an authoritarian leader is the fact that members of his or her ruling coalition—who have insider information about the inner workings of government, not to mention access to the economic and coercive resources necessary to overthrow the regime—might stage a palace coup. The difficulty, then, is to maintain elite cohesion and to secure the ongoing support and loyalty of ruling elites. At the same time, the ruler must stave off challenges from society at large. Average citizens hold the threat of popular mobilization and revolution, which becomes likely when large numbers of people are discontented with their economic, social, or political circumstances. In order to ensure the survival of the regime, rulers must either offer citizens sufficient benefits to gain their (at least tacit) support, or to minimize their ability and opportunity to rebel. Two broad approaches have emerged to explain how rulers navigate these dilemmas.

34.3.1 Agency-Based Explanations of Regime Stability

One set of theories views authoritarian executives as political actors with agency to shape their political environment. This perspective investigates the strategies that incumbents pursue to maintain their hold on power, and the tools available at their disposal to do so.

First, rulers can take steps to manipulate the electoral process. In the post-Cold War era, incumbents have sought ways to create the appearance of public input into the process of leadership selection, while also forestalling the possibility of losing power. To resolve this dilemma, rulers turn to what Schedler (2002) calls the 'menu of manipulation'—that is, the ways of controlling the electoral process to forestall the chances of losing. Rulers can stage-manage the conduct of elections and strategically control the parties and candidates that are, and are not, allowed to participate. Selectively including certain opposition groups in electoral exercises, but not others, increases the coordination problems facing the opposition, making it more difficult for them to mount an effective campaign (Lust-Okar 2005; Beaulieu 2014). Rulers also systematically abuse their power to divert state resources for political purposes, deploying administrative and coercive agencies in order to skew results in favour of the incumbent. For example, Birch (2011: 719) notes in the post-Soviet autocracies, this 'takes many forms, from state financing of incumbent candidates to selective enforcement of the law, bias in state media and harassment of independent media, harassment of opposition politicians and outright fraud'. Electoral misconduct at times may escalate to outright violence and legal coercion. When these efforts fail to ensure victory, some incumbents are not above stuffing ballot boxes on election day and manipulating vote totals (Lehoucq 2003; Schedler 2006).

Second, even outside of electoral campaigns, rulers can make longer-term efforts to co-opt their real and potential opponents. Competing political elites only pose a threat if they believe that they have more to gain by staging a coup than by supporting the existing regime (Bueno de Mesquita et al. 2003). Consequently, autocrats can give challengers a stake in the continued survival of the political system through the allocation of political offices, policy concessions, and economic rents. Often such co-optation occurs via the appointment of ruling elites to political office, particularly legislative seats, which in turn, offers the opportunity to influence policy, to access lucrative revenue streams, and to control state resources (Gandhi 2008; Reuter and Turovsky 2014; Reuter and Robertson 2015). In a study of African leaders, Arriola (2009) finds that appointment to ministerial posts is an especially effective means of buying loyalty, because cabinet position offer opportunities for rent generation and the discretionary allocation of public resources to support their own patronage networks.

Rulers can expand their co-optation efforts to society at large by targeting economic rents and other forms of patronage to average citizens. This is a common strategy in resource-rich countries, where incumbent leaders have access to resource rents that they can use to purchase popular acquiescence. Resource wealth may allow dictators to increase social spending and the provision of public goods (Jensen and Wantchekon 2004; Mahdavi 2015). They also may placate citizens by reducing their tax burden, which—especially if accompanied by a fairly high level of state spending—can reduce the chances of popular revolt (Fails and DuBuis 2015). Recent work indicates that these mechanisms extend beyond the so-called resource curse (Ross 2001, 2015). Morrison (2009: demonstrates that any sort of non-tax revenue, including foreign aid, 'stabilizes autocracies by providing additional resources for social spending and patronage projects'.

A third strategy available to rulers is repression—that is, the state's use of coercive actions against political opponents undertaken for the purpose of 'imposing a cost on the target as well as deterring specific activities and/or beliefs perceived to be challenging to government personnel, practices or institutions' (Davenport 2007: 2). Repression forms a core part of many autocrats' survival strategy. Evidence suggests that coercive capacity and repressive measures are a strong predictor of authoritarian stability (Bellin 2004, 2012; Albertus and Menaldo 2012a; Escribà-Folch 2013b). The mechanisms of repression vary across a number of dimensions, including the identity of the coercive agency, the victim or target, the type of action, and the visibility of these measures (della Porta 1996; Earl 2003). In the non-democratic context, Way and Levitsky (2006: 388) productively differentiate between highly visible acts of high-intensity coercion versus less visible and lower-risk low-intensity coercion. In a similar vein, other scholars focus on efforts to suppress the media, and the specific effects of censorship (Egorov et al. 2009; Guriev and Treisman 2015).

Fourth, rulers also seek ways to legitimate their rule. We can think of legitimation as a process by which rulers secure popular support for the regime, particularly through means other than the targeted distribution of selective benefits. This may include constructing and promoting political ideologies (Linz 1975; March 2003), cults of personality (Wedeen 1999), or tightly controlled national identities (Adams 2010). In other cases, legitimacy may rest on a ruler's tangible policy successes, such as restoring public order (Epstein 1984; Rose 2007), or achieving strong economic performance (Nathan 2003). Legitimation is often attributed as a motivating factor in foreign policy decisions, including the initiation of military conflicts abroad (Lai and Slater 2005). Crucially, rulers can frame their claims to legitimacy and, in doing so actively manipulate the lens through which citizens evaluate political dynamics (Schatz 2006; Grauvogel and von Soest 2014). The mechanisms of legitimation have been comparatively understudied in the recent literature on authoritarian regimes and offer a potentially fruitful avenue for further investigation.

None of these strategies of authoritarian survival are foolproof; each comes with its own drawbacks. Rulers seeking to co-opt their rivals may find it difficult to establish the optimal level of patronage goods to ensure their loyalty. Moreover, there is a real risk to allowing potential adversaries access to the regime institutions. Co-optation potentially 'opens the door for rivals to cultivate their own bases of support' and thus give them 'the capacity to establish an organizational network sufficient to spur the leader's overthrow' (Frantz and Kendall-Taylor 2014: 335). Repression generates a its own difficulties. Reliance on repression as a strategy of authoritarian rule creates a moral hazard problem, because 'the very resources that enable the regime's repressive agents to suppress its opposition also empower them to act against the regime itself' (Svolik 2012: 124; see also Greitens 2016). And as both empirical cases and theoretical models have shown, electoral manipulation can go very wrong (Rundlett and Svolik 2016). Vote fraud and stolen elections can themselves be triggers for popular revolution (Tucker 2007; Kuntz and Thompson 2009; Donno 2013).

In addition, these strategies do not operate independently of each other. For example, rulers inherently draw on aspects of both co-optation and repression when they manipulate the electoral process. More research needs to be done into the ways that these various strategies interact. Scholars commonly assume that co-optation and repression function independently, or that they serve as substitutes for each other. But recent research suggests these assumptions are overly simplistic. Frantz and Kendall-Taylor (2014) find that co-optation changes the types of coercion that is observed; the use of co-optation reduces censorship, but increases physical repression. Furthermore, how do rulers choose among these different strategies? Guriev and Treisman (2015) argue that these decisions are contingent upon economic conditions. We also might expect this decision to vary based on the type of opposition that rulers face and the resources available to them, but further investigation is needed.

34.3.2 Institutionalist Explanations of Regime Stability

An alternate approach starts from the empirical finding that non-democratic regimes that have legislatures and parties are more durable than regimes that lack these institutions (Geddes 1999; Gandhi and Przeworski 2007; Boix and Svolik 2013). In seeking to explain how these institutions contribute to authoritarian stability, scholars have used the tools of formal modelling and quantitative analysis to investigate the working relationships and balance of power between the executive and other formal institutions. Much of this work focuses on the ways that legislatures and parties constrain the executive, and in doing so lead to more effective patterns of co-optation, better policy outcomes, and higher greater regime stability.

These models work from a stylized set of assumptions. The executive is conceptualized as a single ruler who seeks to appropriate power and expropriate society's resources, subject to the constraints of staying in office. If circumstances allow, he or she will move to centralize power—that is, increase his or her capacity to make and implement political decisions. Taken to the extreme, this will culminate in a personalist, extractive autocracy (Bueno de Mesquita et al. 2003; Svolik 2009). It is further assumed that other actors, including members of his or her own ruling coalition, want to prevent this from happening. They too are seeking to maximize their own power, and will rebel against the ruler if doing so offers them a better payoff. This insight sets up a fundamental conflict between the ruler and his or her ruling coalition, which if left unmanaged is likely to undermine the stability and longevity of the autocratic regime.

In view of this conflict, one hypothesis is that legislatures and political parties provide an arena for the ruler and other political actors to forge power-sharing bargains. Although the ruler would prefer not to share the spoils of office, it is sometimes unavoidable, especially if the ruler lacks the resources to govern alone or faces a rebellion from rival elites (Wright 2008). In those cases, he or she will need to offer concessions in order to avoid being ousted. Parties and assemblies serve as a forum for doing so, because they offer a space for rulers and opponents to announce their policy preferences, distribute rents, and negotiate power-sharing agreements (Gandhi and Przeworski 2006; Gandhi 2008; Magaloni and Kricheli 2010).

Others point out that agreements to share power and distribute the spoils of office can only work if the bargains that are forged are credible—that is, binding and self-reinforcing into the future. Non-democratic executives function in the context of a weak rule of law. Whereas executive officers in a democracy are subject to the same laws as other citizens—as enforced by the judiciary (see Chapter 28 in this volume)—this is not inherently true in non-democratic regimes. In the absence of reliable enforcement mechanisms, the ruler can conceivably decide tomorrow to overturn any agreement he has agreed to today. As a result, it can be especially difficult to reach an agreement because the ruling elites can't trust that the ruler will hold to the deal, and he or she can't promise to do so (Acemoglu and Robinson 2005; Magaloni 2008; Gehlbach et al. 2016).

Authoritarian legislatures and political parties solve this problem by offering an effective and credible means of constraining the executive. Legislatures in particular manage to do this by, first, reducing the barriers to collective action amongst real and potential rivals. Having a forum to get together makes it easier for them to coordinate a rebellion. Thus, by allowing a legislature to exist, the ruler is reliably allowing rivals to conspire against him or her if he or she deviates from their agreement. Legislatures also offer a means of reducing informational asymmetries between the ruler and elites and provide a mechanism for intra-elite monitoring. In an environment in which the ruler and his or her allies are pursuing competing objectives, misunderstandings about each other's intentions and capacity are likely to occur. Legislative assemblies reduce this problem by allowing competing elites to observe the ruler's compliance with the bargain, and gives the ruler a way to gather information about the credibility of elites' threats to rebel (Svolik 2012; Boix and Svolik 2013). The overall result is an extended time in office for the ruler and a higher survival rate for the regime.

Related arguments concern the role of ruling parties in non-democratic regimes. Scholars suggest that ruling parties help the ruler make enforceable bargains with potential rivals. But rather than paying through policy concessions, the party offers opportunities for career advancement and access to powerful positions within the government. In doing so, it ties the fate of party *apparatchiks* with their continued support for the regime (Brownlee 2007a; Magaloni 2008; Gehlbach and Keefer 2011).

The overall claim in this literature is that legislatures and other formal institutions extend the lifespan of non-democratic regimes by constraining the executive—specifically, by giving real and potential rival elites a means of punishing the ruler if he reneges on a deal. By reducing the costs to elite rebellion, legislatures and parties incentivize the ruler to uphold his or her end of the power-sharing bargain, and to continue sharing the spoils of office, giving voice to opposition views, and/or accommodating his or her rivals' preferences in the policy-making process.

While much of this work focuses on the impact on intra-elite bargaining, related findings show that these commitment mechanisms have further benefits. By offering a constraint on the executive, these institutions help to attract higher levels of private investment (Gehlbach and Keefer 2011), stronger corporate governance (Jensen et al. 2014), and generate higher levels of economic growth (Gandhi 2008). New research further suggests that, by co-opting opposition elites, legislatures serve to quell demands from average citizens as well (Reuter and Robertson 2015).

34.3.3 Authoritarian Executives and Policy Decisions

Finally, a promising line of inquiry moves beyond regime longevity to ask how the structure and composition of non-democratic executives affects the policies that result. Some work has investigated the implications for economic outcomes. For example, Escribà-Folch (2012) demonstrates that personalist regimes spend less on public goods and services than other types of autocracy, particularly when faced with international sanctions. Eibl et al. (2017) similarly find significant variation in welfare expenditures across these regime types, which they attribute to systematic differences in the coalitional configurations. In a different vein, Steinberg and Malhotra (2014) shows that monarchies are associated with more prudent macroeconomic policies; as a result, they experience fewer currency crises than either democracies or other types of authoritarianism.[3]

There is also some evidence that the composition of the executive may condition the use of state coercion. Many have hypothesized that military governments and personalist regimes are more likely to use force against their populations than civilian leaders (Davenport 2007; Ezrow and Frantz 2011; Svolik 2013). Empirical support for these claims is inconclusive, however, perhaps owing to competing approaches to conceptualizing repression as well as the challenges of data collection in these settings (Geddes, Frantz, and Wright 2014). A related area of research suggests that approaches to conflict management differ across these regime types, with military governments experiencing a higher rate of civil war than other authoritarian executives (Nordlinger 1977; Fjelde 2010).

Weeks (2012, 2014) extends these ideas into the realm of foreign policy and the initiation of military disputes. Drawing on the work of Geddes (2003) and Lai and Slater (2005), she distinguishes among authoritarian executives according to whether rulers are constrained by a domestic audience—that is, regime insiders and ruling elites who will hold leaders accountable for their actions—and whether those domestic audiences are composed of civilian versus military elites. She finds that non-personalist rulers who face an audience composed of civilian advisors are less bellicose. Weeks (2014) adds that these civilian non-personalist regimes are also more likely win wars, but are also more likely to lose power after military defeat.

These topics offer a rich set of questions that scholars have only begun to study. Future research might turn the focus to a larger range of policy areas and unpack in more detail the decision-making processes associated with executive format and intra-executive dynamics.

34.4 New Avenues for Research

This chapter has drawn on two separate literatures—the study of democratic executives and theories of authoritarian rule—to outline the key concepts, questions, and findings in the study of executives in non-democratic regimes. There is much to be learned from further cross-pollination between these theories. In what follows, I lay out some broad avenues for future research and illustrate the productive research agendas that could come out of bringing these literatures into closer dialogue.

One area of inquiry concerns variation in the formal institutions, including the format and powers of the executive across non-democratic regimes. Theories of

---

[3] See Croissant and Wurster (2013) for an overview of this literature.

non-democratic rule often make the simplifying assumption that authoritarian executives function within a presidential system and have considerable authority vis-à-vis other branches of government. But empirically this is not always the case. While many are presidential systems, in others the executive originates from and requires the support of the legislature.[4] This raises a variety of questions for researchers to pursue. For example, how do parliamentary-based autocracies work? How and why do they come about? Is there any practical difference in the operation of presidential versus parliamentary autocracies?

There is also empirical variation in the formal prerogatives allocated to the executive across non-democratic regimes (Davenport 2007; Ezrow and Frantz 2011; Svolik 2013). Scholars of democratic institutions have long debated the importance of constitutionally granted powers of the executive for shaping political outcomes (Shugart and Carey 1992; Siaroff 2003; see also Chapter 19 in this volume). One area for further research would bring these debates to bear on the dynamics of non-democratic executives. When do rulers follow the rules? How does variation in the parchment powers of the executive map onto their activities in reality? How often, and under what conditions, do autocrats overstep beyond their constitutionally granted authority?

This discussion of executive format also points to the importance of understanding informal sources of power and how they relate to the formal institutions in authoritarian regimes (e.g. Hale 2011). Some of the questions raised here are conceptual. For example, how closely does the concept of a 'ruling coalition' relate to the structures of the executive? Amongst the *de facto* leadership group, to what extent do members of this group hold positions in the cabinet, the legislature, or other formal bodies? When do informal sources of authority reinforce versus undermine the formal offices and prerogatives of the executive? There is also need to better understand the way formal and informal institutions interact to produce political outcomes. Henry Hale's (2015, 2005) analysis of patronal politics offers a good example. He argues that the formal institution of presidential term limits interacts with informal patron-client relationships to produce 'regime cycles' centred around lame duck activity. Political elites rally around the president as long as he or she can provide patronage goods into the future, but they fragment in search of a new patron in the face of upcoming elections. There is significant room for further research in this vein.

Another important area for research concerns intra-executive dynamics. In most theories of authoritarian rule, the executive is assumed to be a unitary actor, even perhaps synonymous with the autocrat himself or herself. But there is reason to question how coherent authoritarian executives truly are. Most rulers have a cabinet of ministers or an advisory council that weighs in on foreign and domestic policy and manages the day-to-day operation of various branches of the state. Within these groups, it is inevitable that some cabinet ministers are more powerful than others and that the president maintains

---

[4] It is worth emphasizing that this is different point from the more general finding noted above that non-democratic regimes in which legislative bodies exist have longer survival rates than those that do not.

a distinctive relationship with each member of the committee. This observation raises a rich set of research questions concerning the relationship between different actors within the executive that scholars have only begun to unpack (e.g. Buehler and Ayari 2018). Who gets appointed to the cabinet and why? How do non-democratic presidents manage the power imbalances and conflicts that arise within in the executive? How, if at all, do the dynamics of non-democratic cabinets differ from those in democracies?

It is also not guaranteed that the president is the single most powerful member of the executive. In some cases, the president may be a figurehead or compromise candidate installed to maintain external legitimacy or to present an outward image of continuity amidst a succession crisis. Driscoll (2015) argues that the former occurred during the 1990s in post-Soviet Georgia and Tajikistan. In both cases, the victors of civil war sought to appoint a nominal president who would serve as the external face of power, in order to attract foreign aid and other external rents. Azerbaijan in the early 2000s offers a case of the latter. After the death of President Heydar Aliyev in 2003, the ruling elite agreed to support his son's inheritance of the presidency, even as evidence suggests that they retained significant authority behind the scenes (Radnitz 2012). These are important issues for further investigation. When and how are authoritarian presidents constrained by their own cabinet? How do these different power relations shape policy-making and regime stability?

Authoritarian executives offer an exciting area for future research, and one that would advance our understanding of executive institutions and non-democratic regimes. This chapter has sought to lay out some of the emerging points of debate on this topic, but as this concluding section has shown, there is significant room for further study.

References

Acemoglu, D. and Robinson, J. A. (2005). *Economic Origins of Dictatorship and Democracy: Economic and Political Origins*. New York: Cambridge University Press.

Adams, L. (2010). *The Spectacular State: Culture and National Identity in Uzbekistan*. Durham, NC: Duke University Press Books.

Albertus, M. and Menaldo, V. (2012a). 'Coercive Capacity and the Prospects for Democratization,' *Comparative Politics* 44(2): 151–69.

Albertus, M. and Menaldo, V. (2012b). 'Dictators as Founding Fathers? The Role of Constitutions Under Autocracy,' *Economics & Politics* 24(3): 279–306.

Arriola, L. R. (2009). 'Patronage and Political Stability in Africa,' *Comparative Political Studies* 42(10): 1339–62.

Beaulieu, E. (2014). *Electoral Protest and Democracy in the Developing World*. New York: Cambridge University Press.

Bellin, E. (2004). 'The Robustness of Authoritarianism in the Middle East: Exceptionalism in Comparative Perspective,' *Comparative Politics* 36(2): 139.

Bellin, E. (2012). 'Reconsidering the Robustness of Authoritarianism in the Middle East: Lessons from the Arab Spring,' *Comparative Politics* 44(2): 127–49.

Birch, S. (2011). 'Post-Soviet Electoral Practices in Comparative Perspective,' *Europe-Asia Studies* 63(4): 703–25.

Boix, C. and Svolik, M. W. (2013). 'The Foundations of Limited Authoritarian Government: Institutions, Commitment, and Power-Sharing in Dictatorships,' *The Journal of Politics* 75(2): 300–16.

Brownlee, J. (2007a). *Authoritarianism in an Age of Democratization*. New York: Cambridge University Press.

Brownlee, J. (2007b). 'Hereditary Succession in Modern Autocracies,' *World Politics* 59(04): 595–628.

Buehler, M. and Ayari, M. (2018). 'The Autocrat's Advisors: Opening the Black Box of Ruling Coalitions in Tunisia's Authoritarian Regime,' *Political Research Quarterly* 71(2): 330–46.

Bueno de Mesquita, B., Smith, A., Siverson, R., and Morrow, J. (2003). *The Logic of Political Survival*. Cambridge, MA: MIT Press.

Cheibub, J. A., Gandhi, J., and Vreeland, J. R. (2010). 'Democracy and Dictatorship Revisited,' *Public Choice* 143(1–2): 67–101.

Collier, D. and Levitsky, S. (1997). 'Democracy with Adjectives: Conceptual Innovation in Comparative Research,' *World Politics* 49(3): 430–51.

Croissant, A. and Wurster, S. (2013). 'Performance and Persistence of Autocracies in Comparison: Introducing Issues and Perspectives,' *Contemporary Politics* 19(1), 1–18.

Davenport, C. (2007). 'State Repression and Political Order,' *Annual Review of Political Science* 10(1): 1–23.

della Porta, D. (1996). 'Social Movements and the State: Thoughts on the Policing of Protest,' in J. D. McCarthy and M. N. Zald (eds) *Comparative Perspectives on Social Movements: Political Opportunities, Mobilizing Structures, and Cultural Framings*. New York: Cambridge University Press, 62–92.

Diamond, L. J. (2002). 'Thinking About Hybrid Regimes,' *Journal of Democracy* 13(2): 21–35.

Donno, D. (2013). 'Elections and Democratization in Authoritarian Regimes,' *American Journal of Political Science* 57(3): 703–16.

Driscoll, J. (2015). *Warlords and Coalition Politics in Post-Soviet States*. New York: Cambridge University Press.

Earl, J. (2003). 'Tanks, Tear Gas, and Taxes: Toward a Theory of Movement Repression,' *Sociological Theory* 21(1): 44–68.

Egorov, G., Guriev, S., and Sonin, K. (2009). 'Why Resource-poor Dictators Allow Freer Media: A Theory and Evidence from Panel Data,' *American Political Science Review* 103(04): 645–68.

Eibl, F., Richter, T., and Lucas, V. (2017). 'Do Different Autocracies Spend Differently?,' Presented at the Annual Meeting of the American Political Science Association.

Epstein, E. C. (1984). 'Legitimacy, Institutionalization, and Opposition in Exclusionary Bureaucratic-Authoritarian Regimes: The Situation of the 1980s,' *Comparative Politics* 17(1): 37–54.

Escribà-Folch, A. (2012). 'Authoritarian Responses to Foreign Pressure: Spending, Repression, and Sanctions,' *Comparative Political Studies* 45(6): 683–713.

Escribà-Folch, A. (2013a). 'Accountable for What? Regime Types, Performance, and the Fate of Outgoing Dictators, 1946–2004,' *Democratization* 20(1): 160–85.

Escribà-Folch, A. (2013b). 'Repression, Political Threats, and Survival under Autocracy,' *International Political Science Review* 34(5): 543–60.

Ezrow, N. M. and Frantz, E. (2011). *Dictators and Dictatorships: Understanding Authoritarian Regimes and Their Leaders*. New York: Continuum Books.

Fails, M. D. and DuBuis, M. C. (2015). 'Resources, Rent Diversification, and the Collapse of Autocratic Regimes,' *Political Research Quarterly* 68(4): 703–15.

Fjelde, H. (2010). 'Generals, Dictators, and Kings: Authoritarian Regimes and Civil Conflict, 1973–2004,' *Conflict Management and Peace Science* 27(3): 195–218.

Frantz, E. and Kendall-Taylor, A. (2014). 'A Dictator's Toolkit: Understanding How Co-optation Affects Repression in Autocracies,' *Journal of Peace Research* 51(3): 332–46.

Frantz, E. and Stein, E. A. (2017). 'Countering Coups: Leadership Succession Rules in Dictatorships,' *Comparative Political Studies* 50(7): 935–62.

Gandhi, J. (2008). *Political Institutions under Dictatorship*. New York: Cambridge University Press.

Gandhi, J. and Przeworski, A. (2006). 'Cooperation, Cooptation, and Rebellion under Dictatorships,' *Economics & Politics* 18(1): 1–26.

Gandhi, J. and Przeworski, A. (2007). 'Authoritarian Institutions and the Survival of Autocrats,' *Comparative Political Studies* 40(11): 1279–301.

Geddes, B. (1999). 'What Do We Know About Democratization After Twenty Years?,' *Annual Review of Political Science* 2(1): 115–44.

Geddes, B. (2003). *Paradigms and Sand Castles: Theory Building and Research Design in Comparative Politics*. Ann Arbor, MI: University of Michigan Press.

Geddes, B., Frantz, E., and Wright, J. G. (2014). 'Military Rule,' *Annual Review of Political Science* 17(1): 147–62.

Geddes, B., Wright, J., and Frantz, E. (2014). 'Autocratic Breakdown and Regime Transitions: A New Data Set,' *Perspectives on Politics* 12(2): 313–31.

Gehlbach, S. and Keefer, P. (2011). 'Investment Without Democracy: Ruling-Party Institutionalization and Credible Commitment in Autocracies,' *Journal of Comparative Economics* 39(2): 123–39.

Gehlbach, S. and Simpser, A. (2015). 'Electoral Manipulation as Bureaucratic Control,' *American Journal of Political Science* 59(1): 212–24.

Gehlbach, S., Sonin, K., and Svolik, M. W. (2016). 'Formal Models of Nondemocratic Politics,' *Annual Review of Political Science* 19(1): 565–84.

Gilbert, L. and Mohseni, P. (2011). 'Beyond Authoritarianism: The Conceptualization of Hybrid Regimes,' *Studies in Comparative International Development* 46(3): 270–97.

Ginsburg, T. and Simpser, A. (2013) (eds). *Constitutions in Authoritarian Regimes*. New York: Cambridge University Press.

Ginsburg, T., Elkins, Z., and Melton, J. (2013). 'The Content of Authoritarian Constitutions,' in T. Ginsburg and A. Simpser (eds) *Constitutions in Authoritarian Regimes*. New York: Cambridge University Press.

Grauvogel, J. and von Soest, C. (2014). 'Claims to Legitimacy Count: Why Sanctions Fail to Instigate Democratisation in Authoritarian Regimes,' *European Journal of Political Research* 53(4): 635–53.

Greitens, S. C. (2016). *Dictators and their Secret Police: Coercive Institutions and State Violence*. New York: Cambridge University Press.

Guriev, S. M. and Treisman, D. (2015). 'How Modern Dictators Survive: Cooptation, Censorship, Propaganda, and Repression,' *SSRN Electronic Journal*. https://doi.org/10.2139/ssrn.2571905

Hale, H. E. (2011). 'Formal Constitutions in Informal Politics: Institutions and Democratization in Post-Soviet Eurasia,' *World Politics* 63(4): 581–617.

Hale, H. E. (2015). *Patronal Politics: Eurasian Regime Dynamics in Comparative Perspective.* New York: Cambridge University Press.

Handlin, S. (2017). 'Observing Incumbent Abuses: Improving Measures of Electoral and Competitive Authoritarianism with New Data,' *Democratization* 24(1): 41–60.

Herb, M. (1999). *All in the Family: Absolutism, Revolution, and Democracy in Middle Eastern Monarchies.* Albany, NY: SUNY Press.

Herz, J. H. (1952). 'The Problem of Successorship in Dictatorial Régimes: A Study in Comparative Law and Institutions,' *The Journal of Politics* 14(1): 19–40.

Howard, M. M. and Roessler, P. G. (2006). 'Liberalizing Electoral Outcomes in Competitive Authoritarian Regimes,' *American Journal of Political Science* 50(2): 365–81.

Jensen, N., Malesky, E., and Weymouth, S. (2014). 'Unbundling the Relationship between Authoritarian Legislatures and Political Risk,' *British Journal of Political Science* 44(03): 655–84.

Jensen, N. and Wantchekon, L. (2004). 'Resource Wealth and Political Regimes in Africa,' *Comparative Political Studies* 37(7): 816–41.

Kendall-Taylor, A. and Frantz, E. (2016). 'When Dictators Die,' *Journal of Democracy* 27(4): 159–71.

Kokkonen, A. and Sundell, A. (2014). 'Delivering Stability—Primogeniture and Autocratic Survival in European Monarchies 1000–1800,' *American Political Science Review* 108(02): 438–53.

Kuntz, P. and Thompson, M. R. (2009). 'More than Just the Final Straw: Stolen Elections as Revolutionary Triggers,' *Comparative Politics* 41(3): 253–72.

Lai, B. and Slater, D. (2005). 'Institutions of the Offensive: Domestic Sources of Dispute Initiation in Authoritarian Regimes, 1950–1992,' *American Journal of Political Science* 50(1): 113–26.

LaPorte, J. (2015). 'Hidden in Plain Sight: Political Opposition and Hegemonic Authoritarianism in Azerbaijan,' *Post-Soviet Affairs* 31(4): 339–66.

Lehoucq, F. (2003). 'Electoral Fraud: Causes, Types, and Consequences,' *Annual Review of Political Science* 6(1): 233–56.

Levitsky, S. and Way, L. (2002). 'The Rise of Competitive Authoritarianism,' *Journal of Democracy* 13(2): 51–65.

Linz, J. (1975). 'Totalitarian and Authoritarian Regimes,' in N. Polsby and F. Greenstein (eds) *Handbook of Political Science*, Vol. 3. Reading, MA: Addison-Wesley.

Lust-Okar, E. (2005). *Structuring Conflict in the Arab World: Incumbents, Opponents, and Institutions.* Cambridge: Cambridge University Press.

Magaloni, B. (2008). 'Credible Power-Sharing and the Longevity of Authoritarian Rule,' *Comparative Political Studies* 41(4–5): 715–41.

Magaloni, B. and Kricheli, R. (2010). 'Political Order and One-Party Rule,' *Annual Review of Political Science* 13(1): 123–43.

Mahdavi, P. (2015). 'Explaining the Oil Advantage: Effects of Natural Resource Wealth on Incumbent Reelection in Iran,' *World Politics* 67(02): 226–67.

March, A. F. (2003). 'State Ideology and the Legitimation of Authoritarianism: The Case of Post-Soviet Uzbekistan,' *Journal of Political Ideologies* 8(2): 209–32.

Meng, A. (2017). 'Autocratic Constitutions and Leadership Succession: Evidence from Africa.' Unpublished Manuscript. University of Virginia, Charlottesville, VA.

Mitchell, R. J. (1990). *Getting to the Top in the USSR: Cyclical Patterns in the Leadership Succession Process.* Stanford, CA: Hoover Press.

Morrison, K. M. (2009). 'Oil, Nontax Revenue, and the Redistributional Foundations of Regime Stability,' *International Organization* 63(01): 107.

Nathan, A. J. (2003). 'Authoritarian Resilience,' *Journal of Democracy* 14(1): 6–17.

Nordlinger, E. A. (1977). *Soldiers in Politics: Military Coups and Governments*. Upper Saddle River, NJ: Prentice-Hall.

Radnitz, S. (2012). 'Oil in the Family: Managing Presidential Succession in Azerbaijan,' *Democratization* 19(1): 60–77.

Reuter, O. J. and Robertson, G. B. (2015). 'Legislatures, Cooptation, and Social Protest in Contemporary Authoritarian Regimes,' *The Journal of Politics* 77(1): 235–48.

Reuter, O. J. and Turovsky, R. (2014). 'Dominant Party Rule and Legislative Leadership in Authoritarian Regimes,' *Party Politics* 20(5): 663–74.

Roberts, T. L. (2015). 'The Durability of Presidential and Parliament-Based Dictatorships,' *Comparative Political Studies* 48(7): 915–48.

Rose, R. (2007). 'The Impact of President Putin on Popular Support for Russia's Regime,' *Post-Soviet Affairs* 23(2): 97–117.

Ross, M. (2001). 'Does Oil Hinder Democracy?,' *World Politics* 53(3): 325–61.

Ross, M. (2015). 'What Have We Learned about the Resource Curse?,' *Annual Review of Political Science* 18(1): 239–59.

Rundlett, A. and Svolik, M. W. (2016). 'Deliver the Vote! Micromotives and Macrobehavior in Electoral Fraud,' *American Political Science Review* 110(1): 180–97.

Schatz, E. (2006). 'Access by Accident: Legitimacy Claims and Democracy Promotion in Authoritarian Central Asia,' *International Political Science Review* 27(3): 263–84.

Schedler, A. (2002). 'The Menu of Manipulation,' *Journal of Democracy* 13(2): 36–50.

Schedler, A. (2006). *Electoral Authoritarianism: The Dynamics of Unfree Competition*. Boulder, CO: Lynne Rienner Publishers.

Schumpeter, J. A. (1950). *Capitalism, Socialism, and Democracy*. New York: Harper.

Shugart, M. S. (2008). 'Comparative Executive-Legislative Relations,' in Sarah A. Binder, R. A. W. Rhodes, and Bert A. Rockman (eds) *The Oxford Handbook of Political Institutions*. Oxford: Oxford University Press.

Shugart, M. S. and Carey, J. M. (1992). *Presidents and Assemblies: Constitutional Design and Electoral Dynamics*. New York: Cambridge University Press.

Siaroff, A. (2003). 'Comparative Presidencies: The Inadequacy of the Presidential, Semi-Presidential and Parliamentary Distinction,' *European Journal of Political Research* 42(3): 287–312.

Simpser, A. (2013). *Why Governments and Parties Manipulate Elections*. New York: Cambridge University Press.

Steinberg, D. A. and Malhotra, K. (2014). 'The Effect of Authoritarian Regime Type on Exchange Rate Policy,' *World Politics* 66(3): 491–529.

Svolik, M. W. (2009). 'Power Sharing and Leadership Dynamics in Authoritarian Regimes,' *American Journal of Political Science* 53(2): 477–94.

Svolik, M. W. (2012). *The Politics of Authoritarian Rule*. New York: Cambridge University Press.

Svolik, M. W. (2013). 'Contracting on Violence: The Moral Hazard in Authoritarian Repression and Military Intervention in Politics,' *Journal of Conflict Resolution* 57(5): 765–94.

Tucker, J. A. (2007). 0061Enough! Electoral Fraud, Collective Action Problems, and Post-Communist Colored Revolutions,' *Perspectives on Politics* 5(03): 535–51.

Way, L. A. and Levitsky, S. (2006). 'The Dynamics of Autocratic Coercion after the Cold War,' *Communist and Post-Communist Studies* 39(3): 387–410.

Wedeen, L. (1999). *Ambiguities of Domination: Politics, Rhetoric, and Symbols in Contemporary Syria*. Chicago: University of Chicago Press.

Weeks, J. L. (2012). 'Strongmen and Straw Men: Authoritarian Regimes and the Initiation of International Conflict,' *American Political Science Review* 106(02): 326–47.

Weeks, J. L. P. (2014). *Dictators at War and Peace*. Ithaca, NY: Cornell University Press.

Wright, J. (2008). 'Do Authoritarian Institutions Constrain? How Legislatures Affect Economic Growth and Investment,' *American Journal of Political Science* 52(2): 322–43.

CHAPTER 35

POLITICAL EXECUTIVES IN AUTHORITARIAN MONARCHIES

ANNA SUNIK

35.1 INTRODUCTION

MODERN (authoritarian) monarchies, here understood as political systems with a hereditary head of state with life tenure and wide-ranging powers, have historically been the dominant political system for centuries and possibly millennia. Now, they have become a rarity and research on them has also become rare as a consequence.

Forty-three of the current 193 UN member states and thus almost a fourth are formal monarchies (Friske 2007: 6f), including the sixteen Commonwealth monarchies, most of the remaining European kingdoms, principalities, and grand duchies, and other states whose hereditary head performs merely ceremonial functions, such as Japan. However, the number of authoritarian monarchies, in which the monarch rules and reigns, is far smaller. It ranges between ten and eighteen countries, depending on the definition of either 'authoritarian' or 'monarchy', with most concentrated in the Middle East.[1] Authoritarian monarchies formed about 10–20 per cent of all states since World War II (Geddes et al. 2011: 12–14), but are less studied than other subtypes of political systems that are just as isolated. There are less theocracies, totalitarian states or members of ASEAN and yet, research on them is active and ongoing.

This chapter will show that there are many insights to be gained by looking at monarchies more closely from a political science point of view. To do so, it first takes a look at

---

[1] Bahrain, Jordan, Kuwait, Morocco, Oman, Qatar, Saudi Arabia and the United Arab Emirates in the Middle East; Lesotho and Swaziland in Africa; Bhutan, Brunei Darussalam, Cambodia, Malaysia, Thailand and Tonga in Asia and the Pacific; Liechtenstein, Monaco, and the Holy See are the only remaining European monarchies with significant prerogatives of the monarch (cf. Riescher and Thumfart 2008).

the different kinds of monarchies and presents possible ways to typologize and classify them. Second, the chapter identifies challenges that have provided obstacles to monarchy research and introduces the main topical research questions relating to authoritarian monarchies, before finally setting the future research agenda in the field.

35.1.1 Subtypes of Authoritarian Monarchies

In an authoritarian monarchy, the monarch is the main political executive.[2] Some authoritarian monarchies, however, also feature a prime minister as a separate head of government and a cabinet of ministers who at times hold some (albeit limited) executive powers. The candidate or candidates in line of succession can also have prescribed or traditional executive roles. These systems and their executives will form the focus of this chapter.

As mentioned above, the number of authoritarian monarchies varies depending on the definition of 'authoritarianism' and 'monarchy': While the Middle East monarchies Bahrain, Jordan, Kuwait, Morocco, Oman, Qatar, Saudi Arabia, and the United Arab Emirates as well as Asian Brunei and African Swaziland are unequivocally authoritarian monarchies, others are more controversial: In Tonga, Bhutan, Lesotho, Monaco, and Liechtenstein, the king or prince retains some (significant) prerogatives (Riescher and Thumfart 2008), but the political system overall is either on its way to or already an electoral democracy. While Cambodia, Thailand, and Malaysia are authoritarian, the main executive and centres of political power are alternative political institutions, not the largely ceremonial monarch. The Vatican is a case *sui generis*.

Although monarchy is often described as a regime type, in fact the monarchy-republic binary runs across the distinction between regime types, which are usually divided in democracy and autocracy.[3] Various combinations of the two dimensions, for example of democratic monarchies and autocratic republics, are therefore possible. Therefore, in this chapter, 'political system' is the preferred term instead of regime type as it can be used to encompass both dimensions simultaneously.

Just like there are various kinds of republics, there are also very different kinds of monarchies, which can be divided into subtypes in manifold ways. The divisions are not merely academic, for they illuminate differences among monarchies and enable a nuanced approach instead of lumping them all together.

---

[2] That definition is not unproblematic: it formally excludes elective monarchies and monarchs with a shorter tenure (e.g. the *Yang di-Pertuan Agong* in Malaysia who is only elected for five years). However, elective monarchies are included indirectly, as in most cases, the electorate consists of subnational hereditary executives. Also, the definition implicitly acknowledges more than a single head of state and thus encompasses diarchies like Andorra (headed by two co-princes, the president of France and the bishop of Urgell) and Swaziland (the Swazi king, the *Ngwenyama*, is formally accompanied by the female head of state, the *Ndlovukati*, usually the king's mother).

[3] Immanuel Kant already uses the distinction between state form (*forma imperii*) that defines the position of the head of state, and regime type (*forma regiminis*) to define the shape of power execution (Kant 1796: 1. Definitivartikel).

The most common typology is that of the triad of the absolute, constitutional, and parliamentary monarchies, that is, between states where monarchs have absolute power, or whose power is constrained by the constitution or by the parliament. However, it is also the most problematic regarding how accurately it represents contemporary divisions in monarchies and is least suitable to study authoritarian monarchies as it was shaped in the historic context of European monarchies which underwent periods of constitutionalization and parliamentarization until they reached their current democratic form.

Applying this typology to authoritarian monarchies means dividing them into either 'absolute' or 'constitutional' monarchies—although many of them also have a parliament. Constitutions in autocracies, while not necessarily mere window-dressing, have usually less binding power and different functions than in democracies or semi-democracies (Ginsburg 2015). Far from constraining the monarch, they are often another pillar of regime security. If we are interested in the actual executive powers of their rulers, we might be misled by this formal typology: For instance, we might put Saudi Arabia and Qatar in different categories (see, e.g., Riescher and Thumfart 2008: 334) although the monarch and his extended family have very similar powers, merely because Qatar has a constitution since 2004 while Saudi Arabia only has a 'Basic Law', although both are very similar documents. Following this logic, Qatar, a highly autocratic monarchy, finds itself in the same category as Liechtenstein, a European electoral democracy. Having a constitution that formally circumscribes the powers of the monarch might thus not be a meaningful distinction between authoritarian monarchies. Similar caveats apply to authoritarian monarchies with a parliament like Jordan, Kuwait, or Swaziland, where the legislative's powers are largely symbolic while those of the monarchs are vast.

Another criticism of this typology relates to the term 'absolute' monarchy which implies the king (or—very rarely—queen) wielding exclusive power with no other veto players to challenge him (or her), which is an inaccurate description of most modern monarchs' real powers and limitations. Despite being autocrats, monarchs cannot rule as single absolute sovereigns. Instead, for instance, in Middle Eastern dynastic monarchies like Saudi Arabia or Bahrain, the family is the ruling institution. Consequently, these states are strongly constrained not only by their population which may revolt, but by the balance of power within the royal family and other political elites. This includes the military which might stage a coup, but in particular the royal family itself and the old Arab principles of *shura* and *ijma'* (consultation and consensus) which demand a certain amount of accountability of the monarch (Herb 1999; Lewis 2000). Monarchies with a parliament and a constitution, such as Morocco, Jordan, and Kuwait, also have important veto players in the form of societal, tribal or socioeconomic groups that must be considered. Failure to do so might (and did) result in the toppling of the monarchy like, for example, in Egypt in 1952 or Iraq in 1958. Thus, while the monarch's powers are extensive, they are also by no means 'absolute' in the European understanding shaped by seventeenth-eighteenth-century Louis Quatorzian absolutism.

A more suitable classification by executive monarchic powers is the differentiation of authoritarian 'active' monarchies (to borrow a term from Ben-Dor 2000: 73) from authoritarian formal monarchies (autocracies with a ceremonial monarch and distinct centre of power like the military like Thailand or *shogun*-era Japan) and democratic formal monarchies.

Other classifications differ by other features such as the title of the monarch: Empire (Japan), Kingdom (e.g. Saudi-Arabia, Bhutan), Sultanate (Oman, Brunei), Emirate (Kuwait, Qatar), Grand Duchy (Luxemburg), or Principality (Liechtenstein, Monaco). Alternatively, there are classifications such as elective monarchies (the only remaining are the United Arab Emirates, Malaysia, Cambodia, and the Vatican, while the Holy Roman Empire is a prominent historic example) or hereditary monarchies (most modern monarchies). The distinction between state and substate or regional monarchies which are mostly found in Africa (e.g. in Ghana, Namibia, Togo, and Uganda) is the basis of another monarchy classification (Friske 2008: 17f.).

A useful distinction of the Middle East monarchies, which form the bulk of all remaining authoritarian active monarchies, is between dynastic monarchies where the family is the ruling institution (Herb 1999) (as is the case in all Gulf monarchies except Oman) and linchpin monarchies, where the monarch is the linchpin of the state with the family confined to a smaller or no political role at all (e.g. Jordan, Morocco) (Lucas 2004). A similar but separate distinction is based on their survival strategies, dividing them into 'dynastic rentier' monarchies who cling on to power through the institutionalization of the ruling family, 'linchpin' monarchies based on legitimacy strategies and co-optation of important societal groups and a hybrid 'linchtier' category (Bank et al. 2014).

35.2 Challenges to Monarchy Research: Too Little, Too Old, Too Similar?

Despite the long history of authoritarian monarchy, the phenomenon is understudied—for two main reasons. First, the small and declining number of monarchies led to the academic consensus 'that monarchy is passé' (Anderson 2009: 1). Second, historic and current regional bias resulted in a narrowing of the research focus: Historically, most research on monarchies focused on European (or Western) monarchs who were then still a vital part of global politics. After the disappearance of active authoritarian monarchy in the West, the research focus shifted to the only region where monarchic decline seemed to halt—the Middle East, which is still home to the absolute majority of all authoritarian active monarchies. This means that the Eurocentric bias in monarchy research was replaced by an Arabocentric one, piling on to additional problems of generalizability.

The double regional bias—first Eurocentric, than Middle East-centric—led to a number of misconceptions of extra-European monarchies as well as obstacles to the generalizability of insights. A major consequence of the Eurocentric bias in monarchy research is that classic European monarchic notions which only inadequately portray other monarchies, are at times seen as representative of monarchy per se. Although the legacy of monarchism worldwide is as old as it is in Europe, non-European monarchies have always differed in terms of their institutional set-up and their deployment of religious legitimization. Misleading notions of 'absolutism' (see section 35.1.1 above), and the emphasis on primogeniture and aristocracy as the main ally of the monarch are remnants of that (see Kailitz 2013: 49).

Second, there is a certain Orientalist bias towards non-Western authoritarian monarchies which are, one the one hand, often seen as embodying the image of 'sultanism' (Chehabi and Linz 1998) and 'oriental despotism' (Linz 2000)—of political systems that are characterized by patronage and major wealth gaps, but most of all by principles of capricious and despotic power. Taken from a traditional 'oriental' hereditary title of a political leader in Islamic tradition (*sultan*) it stands for despotism without checks and balances—although as portrayed above, both traditionally and currently, the powers of hereditary heads of states in Muslim-majority countries are heavily curtailed, often much more so than in most periods of European absolutism. Such notions thus often exoticize non-Western states and especially monarchies as imagined locales reminiscent of '1001 nights' fairy tales instead of the products of modernity that they actually constitute.

In addition, many culturalist approaches to Middle East monarchies emphasize religion or patriarchy although their role is often more peripheral to the dynamics of monarchism. The identification of monarchs as patriarchs (Ben-Dor 1983) ignores the same patriarchal element in republics where 'presidents for life' have taken on a very similar role (Owen 2012; Bank et al. 2015).

In contrast to the European medieval principle of rule by divine right and of rare historic examples from other world regions such as the deified *Gurkha* king of Nepal and the Japanese *Tennō*, extant monarchies mostly have a looser relation to religion. A unique exception is the Vatican which could be considered a theocracy. Apart from that, only Saudi Arabia can be said to combine religious and profane authority at the core of the state and regime. However, even there, the royal Al Saud are dependent on the *ulama'*, the Islamic scholars, as well as on the Al Shaikh, the descendants of Mohammad ibn Abd al-Wahhab, to legitimize their rule in religious terms. In other words, the dynasty does not claim to derive its right to rule directly from God although the monarch is a representative of the particular brand of Islam in the country and the custodian of the two holy sites (*khadim al-haramain*), Mecca and Medina (Rasheed 1998; Vassiliev 2013). In other cases, religious legitimacy is based on Sharifian descent (descent from the Prophet), as for the Moroccan, Jordanian, Bruneian and formerly Libyan, Yemeni and Iraqi royal families, but again not on divine right. Most other monarchs do not claim any religious legitimacy at all although they also serve as protectors of the faith and religious role models in terms of public piety (Ben-Dor 2000; Maddy-Weizmann 2000; Krämer 2000). Approaches that intrinsically link Islamic-Arabic culture and monarchy see a 'natural' link between monarchs and religious legitimacy (see, e.g., Sharabi 1988). This is often misleading and simplify the contradictory elements of religious legitimation in different systems. Even monarchs with explicit religious ideologies need to create and adapt religious concepts anew like the state-sponsored Wahhabism in Saudi Arabia or the *Melayu Islam Beraja* (Malay Islamic Monarchy) concept the Bruneian sultan introduced in 1990 (Talib 2002) while other Muslim-majority monarchs to not have any explicit religious legitimation at all like in most small Gulf states.

However, it is essential to remember that the concentration of monarchies and therefore monarchy research on the Middle East has come with its own number of biases that pose problems for the generalizability of concepts related to monarchy. While the distinction between dynastic rentier and linchpin monarchies is a significant one for the Middle East, others are more influential and have more explanatory power in other time periods and regions. Also, certain pillars of stability for the Middle East, such as external superpower support might not be as crucial for other monarchs.

Another bias characterizing today's monarchy research is the overwhelming focus on qualitative studies. Quantitative treatises exist, but are rare (Menaldo 2012). This skewed focus is due to the current rarity of authoritarian monarchy, but also exacerbated by the difficulty to obtain quantifiable data of high quality (see also Chapter 10 in this volume): First, because authoritarian states are opaque and often censure and do not publish statistics and data on a level comparable to democracies (Ahram and Goode 2016). Two other primary reasons can be traced to the problems regarding the regional clustering of monarchies. Quantifiable data is notoriously hard to find for the Middle East where the combination of opaque political systems and limited research and archival funding impede the collection of reliable and comparable data. Also, the regional focus calls for in-depth regional expertise and language skills which are more often found in scholars of area studies where qualitative approaches dominate. The rare cases of quantitative studies either have a scope beyond the examination of monarchies so that the reliability of the data does not hinge upon data obtained from Middle East monarchies (Conrad and Souva 2011), are typological rather than theory-generating or -testing (Hadenius and Teorell 2007) or employ controversial data sources and proxy variables (Menaldo 2012).[4] This bias towards regionalism and qualitative work restricts monarchy research because some questions—especially concerning overarching and global topics—cannot be appropriately addressed.

35.3 The Main Research Questions

However obsolete the study of monarchy can appear at present, the topic is one of the oldest in the field of study of the political. Most of the old classics and philosophic

---

[4] For example, Menaldo uses who the Banks Conflict Index that is less reliable for non-Western states for the independent variable of political turmoil and control variables with a tenuous connection to the theoretical framework such as tribal legacy measured in time since the Neolithic revolution (Menaldo 2012: 716).

treatises of antiquity have juxtaposed monarchy and aristocracy to other forms of rule, notably democracy. Before democratization made the distinction between democracies and autocracies (or rather, non-democracies) dominant, the main and most salient differentiation between different states was the state form—the distinction between monarchies and republics (Friske 2007: 5). Machiavelli emphasized the relevance of this difference when he wrote that 'All states, all powers, that have held and hold rule over men have been and are either republics or principalities' (Machiavelli 2006: xx).

In antiquity and for much of history, while almost every political entity worldwide was ruled by a monarch, the main epistemic interest was what constituted a 'good ruler' and a 'good political system'. Plato and Aristotle (Aristotle 1912: III) developed classifications based on the number of the rulers (one, few, many) and whether the rule was aimed at the good for all of for just a part of society. If it was good for all and only one ruled, it was a monarchy (tyranny was the 'bad' form of government). If it was good only for the ruling and many ruled, it was a democracy. The old traditions were revived in the literature genre of 'Mirrors for princes' (*principum specula*), handbooks on ruling for monarchs in the Middle Ages to the Renaissance, epitomized by (the fairly atypical) *Il Principe* by Niccolò Machiavelli. Throughout the centuries, it was a topic almost all important philosophers took up, including Cicero, Montesquieu, Machiavelli, Thomas Aquinas, Thomas Hobbes, John Locke, Jean-Jacques Rousseau, and Immanuel Kant (Friske 2008: 18f.).

The two World Wars constitute the threshold when the monarchy-republic division lost its importance, while the democracy-autocracy division increasingly gained meaning. As monarchies continued to collapse and new states were increasingly established as republics, monarchy slowly disappeared as the main category, becoming increasingly 'synonymous with irrelevance, ossification, and obsolescence' (Ben-Dor 2000: 71). The republic, on the other hand, went from forming one part of a triad (monarchy-aristocracy-republic) to becoming the opposite of monarchy (Friske 2007: 12ff.). Monarchy theory, once part and parcel of every theory of constitutions and a main field of political philosophy since at least Aristotle, has declined in the same degree as the phenomenon of monarchy declined with the triumphal procession of republicanism.

At the same time, democratization meant that studying monarchs as possible normative examples of 'enlightened autocrats' went out of fashion and the question of the 'good ruler' shifted towards that of 'good governance' and democracy and further disconnected from monarchism. The research shifted to explanations for the continued existence of the remaining monarchies and the discernment of the main differences of monarchies vis-à-vis republics. How such an 'obsolete' form of government has survived into modernity has been a persistent research topic since the last century and possibly the paramount question in monarchy research.

Modernization theorists like Huntington and Halpern were the first to systematically address this seeming anomaly in the 1950s and 1960s (Halpern 1963; Huntington 1968). The focus of these approaches was mostly the dichotomy of tradition and modernity. And what could be more traditional than monarchies? They seemed to lack adaptability to topical demands for liberalization and political and societal modernization, especially regarding the newly important urbanized middle classes. It was therefore expected that monarchies would soon collapse violently and transition to democratic republics: 'The future of the existing traditional monarchies is bleak. [...] They key questions concern simply the scope of the violence of their demise and who wields the violence' (Huntington 1968: 191). The most important notion of that literature was therefore the 'King's Dilemma', coined by Huntington, that formulated the trap monarchs faced: The pressures of modernization create necessity of reform that strips the monarch of his or her powers whereas resistance to these reforms creates the basis for popular unrest that might result in the toppling of the monarchy (Huntington 1968: 177). The monarch's choice seems thus between increasing repression and increasing irrelevance.

However, while the dilemma had explanatory power for 'modernizing' monarchies like Egypt and Iraq that were toppled in revolutions in 1952 and 1958, more conservative and traditional monarchies survived (Ayalon 2000; Ben-Dor 2000). Indeed, apart from some doomsday scenarios predicting the imminent collapse of monarchical rule in the Middle East (Davidson 2012), most recent studies on the durability of authoritarian regimes agree that (modern) monarchies are the most durable and enduring type of political system, even compared to democracies (Hadenius and Teorell 2007; Kailitz 2013; Köllner and Kailitz 2013: 5). Even if monarchs lose their rule, they are in lesser danger to lose their lives along with it (Escribà-Folch 2013). It is all the more surprising that some regime typologies did not even include monarchies until recently (e.g. until the revised edition of the dataset of Geddes et al. 2011) or explicitly excluded such forms of 'traditional or semi-traditional authority' completely (Linz and Stepan 1996).

The question of stability or durability of political executives in monarchies has been revitalized with the 'Arab Uprisings' since 2011, when monarchies fared much better than republics as a group. Newer answers therefore looked to other factors and can be sub-divided into five different clusters: (1) geostrategic, (2) political-economic rentier, (3) institutionalist family-based, (4) legitimacy-based, (5) repression-based, and (6) co-optation-based explanations (Bank et al. 2015).

The first cluster of explanations relate to the fact that especially monarchies in the Middle East are of strategic importance and can therefore generate support by external powers, including superpowers. Military support by the United States or United Kingdom as well as regional powers such as Iran helped quell uprisings historically, examples being the Dhufar rebellion in Oman in the 1970s or the liberation of Kuwait from the Iraqi invasion in 1991. But even with lesser engagement, external support is crucial: for instance, via the provision of military aid and arms deals like in the US relations with the Gulf monarchies (Gause, III 1994: 127). In addition, unconditional foreign aid helps finance repression and co-optation—Jordan being a prime example (Brand 1995: 81ff; Yom 2009:163).

Second, most remaining monarchs have access to large rents that they can distribute among the regime and their immediate allies to buy loyalty. This applies especially to the so-called 'oil monarchies' (Luciani 1987: 81ff; Gause, III 1994), that is, all Gulf monarchies and Brunei who have large oil and gas reserves. Other monarchies, while lacking in oil and gas, have other sources of rent. The Coca Cola factory in Swaziland that provides up to 40 per cent of the country's GDP might have a similar effect in the African kingdom (Mcleod 2013). The European micro-monarchies are among the wealthiest states. Even the poorer monarchies Jordan and Morocco are sometimes described as 'semi-rentiers' because of the large sums of external aid they generate via support from their Western and regional allies (Luciani 2009). Both approaches are complementary rather than exclusive (Yom and Al-Momani 2008: 39–60; Yom and Gause 2012).

Third, an influential explanation particularly for Arab monarchies is dynasticism, especially in combination with the rentier state model. In his seminal work 'All in the family', Michael Herb argues that the inclusion (or exclusion) of family members in key decision-making institutions bolstered monarchic survival (Herb 1999). With the help of massive oil income, the family becomes a 'ruling institution' and monopolizes the central positions in both the administration and the security apparatus. In the Middle East's non-dynastic monarchies Jordan and Morocco, as well as the collapsed monarchies of Egypt (1952), Iraq (1958), Libya (1969), and Iran (1979), where there is no large family to base monarchic power on, co-optation of additional elite institutions like the army or the parliament is necessary for survival. Herb also points out that other crucial factors can account for the fate of monarchs like the support of the military which helps explain why the older and more entrenched Egyptian monarchy collapsed while 'artificial' newer monarchies survived (Herb 1999: 211).

Fourth, while the majority could not rely on a divine right of kings—as depicted above—monarchs have successfully employed traditional, religious, and procedural legitimacy claims that are accepted by large parts of the population (Hudson 1979; Schlumberger 2010). Religious legitimacy claims can be used to weaken the Islamist opposition in Muslim-majority countries (Krämer 2000). Other monarchies rely on traditional legitimation and tribal and kinship networks (Schlumberger 2010: 239–46), even in new monarchies where traditions have to be 'reinvented' (Anderson 2009; Demmelhuber 2011). Legitimacy can also be based on material co-optation via distribution and allocation of resources, for example from oil rents, as noted above.

Contrary to Huntington's argument, (liberalized) monarchies can also call upon procedural legitimation to stabilize their rule. Controlled parliamentarism and gradual top-down reforms ranging from constitutions, laws concerning parties, media freedom, or the introduction of elite-led reform committees bolstered the monarchs in Morocco and Jordan in the 1980s and following the 'Arab Spring' (Albrecht and Schlumberger 2004; Bank 2004; Lust-Okar 2005). Even the 'traditionalist' Gulf monarchies employ participatory elements like the assemblies known as *majalis* or *diwaniyyat*, by following agreed-upon procedures (Demmelhuber 2011). In addition, elections play an increasingly important role for the political executives in many Gulf monarchies (Zaccara 2013).

Fifth, researchers have repeatedly found that that authoritarian monarchies seem to use less or 'softer' (i.e. non-violent) repression than republics, at least in the Middle East. This holds for the 'Arab Spring' period (Yom, 2014) and previously (between 1980 and 2005; see Spinks et al. 2008). However, the small number of monarchies (and the exception of Bahrain) indicates that generalization on this issue is difficult (Josua and Edel 2015).

Sixth, the ability of monarchs to co-opt important factions in society that can help them stay in power. For example, Brumberg (2011) argues that structural differences between monarchies and presidential, party-machine systems lead to a greater success of monarchies in running a state 'protection racket system'. While in many Middle Eastern republics, presidents were perceived as despots with little or no moral bond with the wider population and steeped in a corrupt system or party, most monarchs have operated at some institutional and symbolic distance from the political arena, and thus had a crucial advantage over their presidential comrades: they could drape themselves in the flag of national monarchical patriotism and thus be perceived more widely as legitimate (and effective) arbiters of competing social, economic, religious, and ideological interests. This applies better to linchpin monarchies like Jordan and Morocco than dynastic systems where different family factions compete (Brumberg 2011). Menaldo claims that a specific monarchical political culture makes monarchs resilient by providing a basis for credible commitment that is rare in autocracies. His focus is, however, on political turmoil in general rather than regime survival more specifically (Menaldo 2012).

All explanations when taken on their own, have shortcomings. External support is a double-edged sword as overreliance on it can delegitimize and therefore destabilize a regime as was the case in Saudi Arabia which invited US troops that later had to withdraw and move their air force base from the Prince Sultan Air Base to al-Udeid in Qatar in 2003 following the Gulf War in 1991 due to massive domestic pressure and criticism (Rasheed 2007: 83ff.; Blanchard 2011). The Iranian monarchy broke down in 1979 at the height of rent income and rising state spending, similar to Libya in 1969 and Iraq in 1958. Some authors have therefore attempted to combine several factors to provide a more comprehensive explanation. Yom and Gause (2012) identified rentierism, foreign patronage and cross-cutting coalitions of popular support as three central aspects of monarchic durability. Bank et al. (2015) stress different combinations of rents, external support, legitimacy claims, and repression for different types of monarchies. A more recent answer was provided by Corbett, Veenendaal, and Ugyel (2017) who argued that the inherent resilience and personalization in small states explain the distribution of the remaining monarchies.

It is important to note that while some factors seem monarchy-specific like the specific role of the monarch and particular kinds of legitimacy, others only happen to cluster in monarchies (e.g. oil wealth and small-stateness). Therefore, these explanations do not necessarily address overall monarchic resilience, but rather the specific resilience of the extant modern monarchies.

A related, but not identical research agenda centred on the question of liberalization and democratization of monarchies and by monarchs. Despite the ancientness of the system, monarchs and the aristocracy have at times played a modernizing role, for example in the Meiji era in Japan (McNelly 1969). However, the connection between monarchy and liberalization or even democratization is ambivalent. In its recent form, it harks back to the 'king's dilemma' introduced in the previous section. Despite this dilemma, the monarchies that persisted also resisted democratization. Although the number of transitions from authoritarian monarchy is too small to draw substantial conclusion, of eight transitions since World War II, only one, in Nepal (in 1991 and again in 2006), resulted in democratization. In contrast, many monarchic breakdowns resulted in prolonged violence like in Yemen, Afghanistan, or Ethiopia (Geddes et al. 2014: 326f.).

Scholars tended to focus on what might make democratization more likely in monarchies, but there is no consensus on every issue. Herb (2004) claimed that its likelihood increased with incremental parliamentarization, while Lucas (2004) argued the opposite, that incremental constitutionalization forms an obstacle to democratization. Weiffen (2008) took a general approach towards autocracies in general and stated that democratization was boosted by a high education, the lack of a colonial past and Protestantism, conditions mostly lacking in monarchies whereas some of their distinguishing features like their Muslim identity and oil rents (as well as war or threat of war), impeded democratization. In contrast, Herb (2005) disputed the common notion that oil rents influenced democratization. A dissenting opinion was introduced by Kirby (2000) who formulated the provocative statement 'Want democracy? Get a king'.

However, there is an important difference between liberalization, that is, the easing of authoritarian control of the state, and democratization, that is, the transition from an autocracy to a democracy. The actual progress towards democracy in monarchies which launched reforms is questionable (Bank 2012). To the contrary, the monarch even gained powers in some cases as in Liechtenstein through constitutional reforms in 2003 (Corbett et al. 2017). However, reforms initiated by monarchs have sometimes led to liberalization (Brumberg 2002: 65f.), especially if preceded by incremental reforms (Lucas 2004).

Another important branch of research focused on the difference between monarchs and presidents. Two main aspects can be identified: the process of hereditary succession and the difference between the positions of the heads of state. Although it has become a periphery phenomenon today, there is good reason for the longevity and wide distribution of the process of hereditary succession. Its advantage is the clarity of the succession process, one of the major sources of regime instability. As there is usually an established and institutionalized rule to the monarchic succession, the death of a monarch—no matter how sudden, will not destabilize the regime or the state because of uncertainty (the old adage 'The King is dead, long live the King' embodies that idea of regime continuity) and might be an additional explanation for the durability of modern monarchies (Hadenius and Teorell 2007). Surviving monarchies also mostly ceased to rely on problematic aspects of hereditary succession like strict and inflexible rules of male primogeniture, the prime form of hereditary succession in European monarchies before the advent of democratization. In that case, uncertainty and instability could still ensue if the eldest son is too young, unfit to rule or there is none. In modern monarchies, primogeniture is not used at all (e.g. in Saudi Arabia, Malaysia, Kuwait) or at least not exclusively or officially (Jordan, Qatar, Swaziland), combining clarity with flexibility.

The other major distinction of monarchies is the role of the monarch itself. As already mentioned above, monarchs seem to have a special mechanisms to legitimize their rule and co-opt opposition and rivals. On a broader note, their relation to the state and society in general is distinct from those of presidents which has implications for the institutional and ideological framework of their regimes. Since a monarch is the head of state, but not the head of government (like a prime minister) or head of a definite political movement (like the president by etymologic definition), he or she is perceived to be 'above politics' (Waterbury 1970; Anderson 2000; Lucas 2004). The president 'presides' over a political faction or party and even if he or she manages to overcome these limitations, always remains part of politics. The monarch can remain above the fray: 'Thus, monarchs can stand above tribal, religious, ethnic, and regional divisions by acting as the linchpin of the political system' (Lucas 2004: 106). Friske (2007: 79) calls that the ability to act as a *pouvoir neutre*. They are not the leader of a particular party, but rather 'mediators' between different societal groups (Waterbury 1970: 267–74; Frisch 2011).

This might make monarchs more prone to political pragmatism and mediation position, which restricts ideological dead-ends and brinkmanship. These royal advantages might make state-building easier for monarchs than for presidents (Anderson 1991, 2000). Ideology is also a greater restriction for republican presidents. Especially in the era of decolonization, republics mainly came into being from social revolutionary regime changes and, at least in the first decades of their existence, based their legitimation on ideology and revolutionary values, especially in the Middle East (Hinnebusch and Ehteshami 2002: 335f.). Nonetheless, the ideological underpinnings of republican rule as well as their core institutional differences could not be shed. To the contrary, the transformation from socialist republics into hereditary autocracies ultimately undermined their rule as it went counter to their foundation (Owen 2012). This does not mean that monarchies are inherently averse to ideology or that republics cannot follow pragmatic politics. Saudi Arabia, with its theocratic elements, is an obvious example of an ideologized monarchy.

The institutional role of the monarch provides further legitimation advantages. Many monarchies allow for parliaments occupied with the concrete design of laws while monarchs issue mere directives or royal decrees. Thus, they can employ *divide-et-impera* policies among their political rivals much more easily (Byman and Green 1999; Frisch 2011) and can delegate responsibility for unpopular or failed decisions to the legislative. Because of the comparatively broad basis of their legitimacy, they are less bound to certain allied elites and can choose among different groups more freely (Byman and Green 1999; Anderson 2000; Ben-Dor 2000).

Moreover, monarchies are less vulnerable to open contradictions than republics. Etymologically and historically, as *res publicae*, the latter's legitimacy is officially derived from popular sovereignty forcing their elites to at least nominally fight against nepotism, closed elites and lack of transparency and participation in the political system. But given their authoritarian set-up, they tolerate or even foster these phenomena *de facto* to cement their rule. Monarchs do not rely on the same principles of popular sovereignty, and nepotism is an ingrained or at the very least tolerated part of dynastic systems and thus no jarring open contradiction arises (Owen 2004: 41ff.). Since decision-making processes do usually not have to be justified or openly displayed, monarchies are more independent from the populace in their decisions. They have thus less veto players that must be included in the decision-making process, putting them on another level of political accountability (see Chapter 3 in this volume).

35.4 SETTING THE FUTURE RESEARCH AGENDA

The restricted focus of much of monarchy research calls for the expansion of the research agenda. So far, it has been mainly clustered along three main thematical blocks: the question of how monarchs relate to the quality of rule and governance, how to account for their continued existence and their resistance to transition and what exactly constitutes the distinguishing features of monarchism in contrast to republicanism. This means that in the area of political science, monarchy research was mostly constricted to the sub-disciplines of political philosophy and comparative politics. That leaves much room for future research endeavours and new questions.

A sub-discipline that has only just begun to address monarchism and its links to their outcomes of interest is international relations. The implication that non-personalized non-militarized monarchies are especially unlikely to initiate war (Weeks 2012) has recently been explicitly addressed. The study found a separate zone of 'monarchic peace' among monarchs who recognize each other as part of the same royal club which is not necessarily confined to the Middle East nor even to authoritarian monarchies (Sunik 2015, 2017). While this work was concerned mainly with the aspects of 'political system similarity' among authoritarian monarchies, other studies might look into whether there are indeed specifically monarchic sources that tend to prevent military conflict— analogous to the strand of research on the effect of democratic institutions on the 'Democratic Peace'. This can also be taken as a starting point to look into other characteristics of monarchic foreign policy behaviour like alliance formation, military efficacy, and rivalries, employing qualitative, but especially quantitative, methods.

A related conception by Sean Yom of an 'epistemic community' of monarchs attempts to explain the difference in the level of repression during the 'Arab Spring' and in extension, monarchic resilience. In his study, he shows that 'regularized social interaction' is more prevalent between the monarchic elites which allowed the sharing and diffusion of ideas (Yom 2014: 59). This can be further explored by case studies examining particularly close as well as particularly contentious relationships between monarchs.

Given the dominance of Middle East-centred perspectives, the shift of focus to other areas or interregional comparisons should be encouraged. An example for this approach is the study by Corbett et al. (2017) that compared authoritarian monarchies from three different regions to uncover why these systems mostly cluster in small and micro-states. Interregional comparative studies would especially benefit from more quantitative approaches. To enlarge the universe of cases and counter regional bias while still retaining sufficiently similar context, future studies could focus on historical cases non-Middle Eastern monarchies which have existed since World War II, but have since collapsed into republics or democratized or liberalized respectively, like Laos or Ethiopia prior to the 1970s.

Other relevant questions remain unanswered: Why and how do some republican leaders 'monarchize' their rule? Under what circumstances can such strategies succeed and why do they fail in republics while serving monarchies well? The amalgamation of monarchic elements into republican regimes has been particularly notable in Middle East states and gave rise to the portmanteau *jumlukiyya* that hybridized the Arabic words *jumhuriyya* (republic) and *mamlaka* or *malakiya* (monarchy) (Ibrahim 2000). Non-royal autocrats have always tried to transform their rule from temporary to permanent and (quasi-)hereditary (Owen 2012). Some have succeeded to establish hereditary succession of their sons after their demise like Hafez al-Assad in Syria and Kim Il-sung whose descendants rule North Korea in the third generation and where the bloodline of the Kim family is even cemented in the founding principles of the state since 2013 (*BBC News* 2017). Many others have failed and even thereby destabilized their regime like Hosni Mubarak or Muammar Gaddafi. In addition to hereditary succession, republics have also attempted to re-incorporate traditional legitimacy claims and patriarchic structure which also blurred the lines between the political systems (Billingsley 2009: 62). Insights could also be gained on the reverse process—can 'republicanization' or 'presidentialization' processes in monarchies be identified? Might Saudi Arabia under the influence of Crown Prince Mohammad bin Salman be a case study for *malhariya*, the opposite of *jumlukiyya* (Sunik 2019)? Studies looking at the introduction, abolishment, or reform of the process of hereditary succession and the reform processes of political hierarchies can help address these questions.

While this chapter focused on active authoritarian monarchies, further research should look at formal authoritarian monarchies and political systems, where there is an interplay or rivalry with non-royal executives like in Thailand or where the process towards parliamentarization has already weakened the role of the monarch. How can the dynamics in monarchies with different or shifting centres of power be described and explained? At what point do they stop to be 'authoritarian monarchies' and are better described as a distinct regime type? These and related questions should be addressed in future research on political executives in monarchies.

Monarchs are resilient, and they provide many more aspects to study than the baffling fact of their continued existence in face of modernity and democratization. The issues presented in this chapter provide stepping stones for the revitalization of the study of one of the oldest phenomena in the political realm.

REFERENCES

Ahram, A. I. and Goode, J. P. (2016). 'Researching Authoritarianism in the Discipline of Democracy: Authoritarianism in the Discipline of Democracy,' *Social Science Quarterly* 97(4): 834–49.

Albrecht, H. and Schlumberger, O. (2004). 'Waiting for Godot: Regime Change without Democratization in the Middle East,' *International Political Science Review* 25(4): 371–92.

Anderson, L. (1991). 'Absolutism and Resilience of Monarchy in the Middle East,' *Political Science Quarterly* 106(1): 1–15.

Anderson, L. (2000). 'Dynasts and Nationalists: Why Monarchies Survive,' in J. Kostiner (ed.) *Middle East Monarchies: The Challenge of Modernity*. Boulder, CO: Lynne Rienner, 53–70.

Anderson, L. (2009). 'Absolutism and the Resilience of Monarchy in the Middle East,' in L. Khalili (ed.) *Politics of the Modern Arab World. Critical Issues in Modern Politics*. Volume I: *State, Power and Political Economy*. London: Routledge.

Aristotle (1912). *Politics: A Treatise on Government*, http://www.gutenberg.org/ebooks/6762

Ayalon, A. (2000). 'Post-Ottoman Arab Monarchies: Old Bottles, New Labels?,' in J. Kostiner (ed.) *Middle East Monarchies. The Challenge of Modernity*. Boulder, CO: Lynne Rienner, 23–36.

Bank, A. (2004). 'Rents, Cooptation, and Economized Discourse: Three Dimensions of Political Rule in Jordan, Morocco and Syria,' *Journal of Mediterranean Studies* 14(1–2): 155–79.

Bank, A. (2012). 'Jordan and Morocco: Pacification through Constitutional Reform?,' in M. Asseburg (ed.) *Protest, Revolt and Regime Change in the Arab World: Actors, Challenges, Implications and Policy Options*. Berlin: Stiftung Wissenschaft und Politik, 31–3.

Bank, A. et al. (2014). 'Durable, Yet Different: Monarchies in the Arab Spring,' *Journal of Arabian Studies* 4(2): 163–79.

Bank, A., Richter, T., and Sunik, A. (2015). 'Long-Term Monarchical Survival in the Middle East: A Configurational Comparison, 1945–2012,' *Democratization* 22(1): 179–200.

BBC News (2017). 'Keeping Up with the Kims: North Korea's Elusive First Family,' 29 August, http://www.bbc.com/news/world-asia-41081356

Ben-Dor, G. (1983). *State and Conflict in the Middle East*. Milton Park: Praeger.

Ben-Dor, G. (2000). 'Patterns of Monarchy in the Middle East,' in J. Kostiner (ed.) *Middle East Monarchies—The Challenge of Modernity*. Boulder, CO: Lynne Rienner Publishers, 71–84.

Billingsley, A. (2009). *Political Succession in the Arab World: Constitutions, Family Loyalties and Islam*. London: Routledge.

Blanchard, C. M. (2011). *Saudi Arabia: Background and U.S. Relations*. Washington, DC: Congressional Research Service.

Brand, L. (1995). *Jordan's Inter-Arab Relations: The Political Economy of Alliance Making*. New York: Columbia University Press.

Brumberg, D. (2002). 'Democratization in the Arab world? The Trap of Liberalized Autocracy,' *Journal of Democracy* 13(4): 57–68.

Brumberg, D. (2011). 'Sustaining Mechanics of Arab Autocracies,' http://mideast.foreignpolicy.com/posts/2011/12/19/sustaining_mechanics_of_arab_autocracies

Byman, D. L. and Green, J. D. (1999). 'The Enigma of Political Stability in the Persian Gulf Monarchies,' *Middle East Review of International Affairs* 3(3): 20–37.

Chehabi, H. E. and Linz, J. J. (1998). *Sultanistic Regimes*. Baltimore: JHU Press.

Conrad, J. and Souva, M. (2011). 'Regime Similarity and Rivalry,' *International Interactions* 37(1): 1–28.

Corbett, J. et al. (2017). 'Why Monarchy Persists in Small States: The Cases of Tonga, Bhutan and Liechtenstein,' *Democratization* 24(4): 689–706.

Davidson, C. M. (2012). *After the Sheikhs: The Coming Collapse of the Gulf Monarchies*. London: Hurst.

Demmelhuber, T. (2011). 'Political Reform in the Gulf Monarchies: Making Family Dynasties Ready for the 21st Century,' *Orient* 52(1): 6–10.

Escribà-Folch, A. (2013). 'Accountable for What? Regime Types, Performance, and the Fate of Outgoing Dictators, 1946–2004,' *Democratization* 20(1): 160–85.

Frisch, H. (2011). 'Why Monarchies Persist: Balancing between Internal and External Vulnerability,' *Review of International Studies* 37(1): 167–84.

Friske, T. (2007). 'Staatsform Monarchie. Was unterscheidet eine Monarchie heute noch von einer Republik?,' http://www.freidok.uni-freiburg.de/volltexte/3325/

Friske, T. (2008). 'Monarchien—Überblick und Systematik,' in G. Riescher and A. Thumfart (eds) *Monarchien.* Baden-Baden: Nomos, 14–23.

Gause, III, F. G. (1994). *Oil Monarchies: Domestic and Security Challenges in the Arab Gulf States.* New York: Council on Foreign Relations Press.

Geddes, B. et al. (2011). 'Authoritarian Regimes: A New Data Set.' Unpublished manuscript.

Geddes, B. et al. (2014). 'Autocratic Breakdown and Regime Transitions: A New Data Set,' *Perspectives on Politics* 12(02): 313–31.

Ginsburg, T. (2015). 'Constitutions as Political Institutions,' in J. Gandhi and R. Ruiz-Rufino (eds) *Routledge Handbook of Comparative Political Institutions.* London: Routledge, 101–12.

Hadenius, A. and Teorell, J. (2007). 'Pathways from Authoritarianism,' *Journal of Democracy* 18(1): 143–56.

Halpern, M. (1963). *The Politics of Social Change in the Middle East and North Africa.* Princeton: Princeton University Press.

Herb, M. (1999). *All in the Family: Absolutism, Revolution, and Democracy in the Middle Eastern Monarchies.* Albany, NY: State University of New York Press.

Herb, M. (2004). 'Princes and Parliaments in the Arab World,' *The Middle East Journal* 85(3): 367–84.

Herb, M. (2005). 'No Representation Without Taxation? Rents, Development, and Democracy,' *Comparative Politics* 37(3): 297–316.

Hinnebusch, R. A. and Ehteshami, A. (2002). *The Foreign Policies of Middle East States.* Boulder, CO: Lynne Rienner Publishers.

Hudson, M. C. (1979). *Arab Politics: the Search for Legitimacy.* 2nd print. New Haven: Yale University Press.

Huntington, S. P. (1968). *Political Order in Changing Societies.* New Haven: Yale University Press.

Ibrahim, S. E. (2000). 'Iqtirah bi-insha' malakiyyat dusturiyya fi l-jumhuriyyat al-'arabiyya 'ala l-umma an tudhif mustalah 'jumlukiyya' ila qamusiha l-siyasi,' *al-Majalla* 2 June, www.eicds.org/arabic/publicationsAR/saadarticles/03/nov-dec/gomlokeya.htm

Josua, M. and Edel, M. (2015). 'To Repress or Not to Repress—Regime Survival Strategies in the Arab Spring,' *Terrorism and Political Violence* 27(2): 289–309.

Kailitz, S. (2013). 'Classifying Political Regimes Revisited: Legitimation and Durability,' *Democratization* 20(1), 39–60.

Kant, I. (1796). *Zum ewigen Frieden. Ein philosophischer Entwurf,* http://www.textlog.de/kant_frieden.html

Kirby, O. H. (2000). 'Want Democracy? Get a King,' *Middle East Quarterly,* http://www.mefo-rum.org/52/want-democracy-get-a-king

Köllner, P. and Kailitz, S. (2013). 'Comparing Autocracies: Theoretical Issues and Empirical Analyses,' *Democratization* 20(1): 1–12.

Krämer, G. (2000). 'Good Counsel to the King: The Islamist Opposition in Saudi Arabia, Jordan, and Morocco,' in J. Kostiner (ed.) *Middle East Monarchies: The Challenge of Modernity*. Boulder, CO: Lynne Rienner, 257–88.

Lewis, B. (2000). 'Monarchy in the Middle East,' in J. Kostiner (ed.) *Middle East Monarchies: The Challenge of Modernity*. Boulder, CO: Lynne Rienner, 15–22.

Linz, J. J. (2000). *Totalitarian and Authoritarian Regimes*. Boulder, CO: Lynne Rienner Publishers.

Linz, J. J. and Stepan, A. (1996). *Problems of Democratic Transition and Consolidation: Southern Europe, South America, and Post-Communist Europe*. Baltimore: JHU Press.

Lucas, R. E. (2004). 'Monarchical Authoritarianism: Survival and Political Liberalization in a Middle Eastern Regime Type,' *International Journal of Middle East Studies* 36(1): 103–19.

Luciani, G. (1987). 'Allocation vs. Production State,' in H. Beblawi and G. Luciani (eds) *The Rentier State*. London: Croom Helm, 63–84.

Luciani, G. (2009). 'Oil and Political Economy in International Relations of the Middle East,' in L. Fawcett (ed.) *International Relations of the Middle East*. Oxford: Oxford University Press, 81–103.

Lust-Okar, E. (2005). *Structuring Conflict in the Arab World: Incumbents, Opponents, and Institutions*. New York: Cambridge University Press.

Machiavelli, N. (2006). *The Prince*. Gutenberg Project Ebook, http://gutenberg.org/files/1232/1232-h/1232-h.htm

Maddy-Weizmann, B. (2000). 'Why Did Arab Monarchies Fall? An Analysis of Old and New Explanations,' in J. Kostiner (ed.) *Middle East Monarchies: The Challenge of Modernity*. Boulder, CO: Lynne Rienner Publishers, 37–52.

Mcleod, M. (2013). 'In Swaziland, Coca-Cola Has the Power to Make Democracy the Real Thing,' *The Guardian* 21 November, http://www.theguardian.com/commentisfree/2013/nov/21/swaziland-coca-cola-democracy-king-mswati

McNelly, T. (1969). 'The Role of Monarchy in the Political Modernization of Japan,' *Comparative Politics* 1(3): 366–81.

Menaldo, V. A. (2012). 'The Middle East and North Africa's Resilient Monarchs,' *The Journal of Politics* 74(3): 707–22.

Owen, R. (2004). *State, Power and Politics in the Making of the Modern Middle East*. London: Routledge.

Owen, R. (2012). *The Rise and Fall of Arab Presidents for Life*. Cambridge, MA: Harvard University Press.

Rasheed, M. al- (1998). 'Political Legitimacy and the Production of History: The Case of Saudi Arabia,' in G. M. Lenore (ed.) *New Frontiers in Middle East Security*. Houndmills: Macmillan, 25–46.

Rasheed, M. al- (2007). *Contesting the Saudi State: Islamic Voices from a New Generation*. Cambridge: Cambridge University Press.

Riescher, G. and Thumfart, A. (2008). *Monarchien. Eine Einführung*. Baden-Baden: Nomos.

Schlumberger, O. (2010). 'Opening Old Bottles in Search of New Wine: On Nondemocratic Legitimacy in the Middle East,' *Middle East Critique* 19(3): 233–50.

Sharabi, H. (1988). *Neopatriarchy. A History of Distorted Change in Arab Society*. Oxford: Oxford University Press.

Spinks, B. T. et al. (2008). 'The Status of Democracy and Human Rights in the Middle East: Does Regime Type Make a Difference?,' *Democratization* 15(2): 321–41.

Sunik, A. (2015). 'The Royal Special Relationship. Großbritannien und die arabischen Monarchien,' in S. Harnisch et al. (eds) *Sonderbeziehungen als Nexus zwischen Außenpolitik und internationalen Beziehungen. Außenpolitik und Internationale Ordnung*. Baden-Baden: Nomos, 55–80.

Sunik, A. (2017). *Monarchic Peace? Foreign Policy and Ingroup Identity of Middle East monarchies*. Heidelberg: University of Heidelberg.

Sunik, A. (2019). *Reform ohne Liberalisierung. Die Präsidentialisierung Saudi-Arabiens. [Reform without Liberalization: The Presidentialization of Saudi Arabia]*. Hamburg: GIGA Focus Middle East.

Talib, N. S. (2002). 'A Resilient Monarchy: The Sultanate of Brunei and Regime Legitimacy in an Era of Democratic Nation-States,' *New Zealand Journal of Asian Studies* 4(2): 134–47.

Vassiliev, A. (2013). *The History of Saudi Arabia*. London: Saqi Books.

Waterbury, J. (1970). *The Commander of the Faithful: The Moroccan Political Elite—A Study in Segmented Politics*. New York: Columbia University Press.

Weeks, J. L. (2012). 'Strongmen and Straw Men: Authoritarian Regimes and the Initiation of International Conflict,' *American Political Science Review* 106(02): 326–47.

Weiffen, B. (2008). 'Liberalizing Autocracies in the Gulf Region? Reform Strategies in the Face of a Cultural-Economic Syndrome,' *World Development* 36(12): 2586–604.

Yom, S. L. (2009). 'Jordan: Ten More Years of Autocracy,' *Journal of Democracy* 20(4): 151–66.

Yom, S. L. (2014). 'Authoritarian Monarchies as an Epistemic Community,' *Taiwan Journal of Democracy* 10(1): 43–62.

Yom, S. L. and Al-Momani, M. H. (2008). 'The International Dimensions of Authoritarian Regime Stability: Jordan in the Post-Cold War Era,' *Arab Studies Quarterly* 30(1): 39–60.

Yom, S. L. and Gause, F. G., III (2012). 'Resilient Royals: How Arab Monarchies Hang On,' *Journal of Democracy* 23(4): 74–88.

Zaccara, L. (2013). 'Comparing Elections in Gulf Cooperation Council Countries after the Arab Spring: The United Arab Emirates, Oman, and Kuwait,' *Journal of Arabian Studies* 3(1): 80–101.

CHAPTER 36

....

POLITICAL EXECUTIVES IN PARTY-BASED DICTATORSHIPS

....

ALEXANDER BATURO

36.1 INTRODUCTION

....

THE longest serving contemporary dictatorships in the world were, and remain, party-based: the Communist Party of the Soviet Union (CPSU) has ruled for seventy-seven years, the PRI (Institutional Revolutionary Party) of Mexico ruled for seventy-one years, while the Communist Party of China has been the ruling party since 1949—seventy-one years as of 2020. In terms of regime longevity party-based dictatorships far outlast personal or military-based dictatorships (see Chapters 34 and 37 in this volume) and can only be rivalled by a small number of surviving monarchies. Scholars argue that the longevity of party-based dictatorships is due to their durable institutional framework which provides for intra-elite bargaining, co-optation, and mass mobilization (Geddes 1999; Gandhi 2008; Svolik 2012). Such a framework is primarily based on the institution of a ruling political party (Smith 2005; Magaloni, 2006).

In party-based dictatorships the constitution may stipulate the formal powers of the executive, legislative, and judiciary branches with little or no reference to the real role of a governing party in politics. The ruling party, however, operates as a parallel and informal structure of governance with the *de facto* control of the state. Because of the overarching role of the party, what the political executive *functionally* includes goes beyond the cabinet of ministers and incorporates important institutions of the party executive regardless of whether their role is prescribed as such in the constitution.

Scholars of single-party dictatorships, particularly prior to the advent of comparative large-n studies, clearly distinguished the executive from the institution of the party itself (Ploss 1970; Rigby 1970; Daniels 1976; Davies 1981; Harasymiw 1984). In contrast, more recent, second-generation research on dictatorships that took a comparative and, therefore, more abstract approach to authoritarian institutions, have largely ignored the question of the political executive as such (Geddes 1999; Gandhi 2008; Svolik 2012; Escriba-Folch and Wright 2015). The distinction between the party and the political executive in a party-based dictatorship is important. It allows us to understand the distribution of policy responsibilities between party and state executive institutions, the mechanisms of intra-elite bargaining, and where it occurs within the executive, elite factions and intra-elite policy differences, the mechanisms of collective leadership, and other important questions.

The chapter consists of three related sections. In section 36.2, I define and discuss the political executive in party-based dictatorships, what it does, and what research questions need to be addressed to understand the logic of how the executive operates. In section 36.3, I review how scholars have addressed questions related to the political executive in party-based dictatorships. Primarily, I draw on research on regimes of the Soviet Union, China, Vietnam, and Mexico. In final section (36.4), I outline a possible research agenda and methodological approaches that may assist in addressing difficult questions.

36.2 Basic Research Questions

36.2.1 Party-Based Dictatorships

Before turning to the question of the executive in party-based dictatorships, a few words are in order about what kind of regimes will be discussed. In brief, the chapter examines party-based dictatorships where one party dominates policy and politics (Geddes 1999). Such regimes may be referred to in the literature as party, one-party, single-party, dominant-party, or hegemonic party regimes (Brooker 2000). Henceforth, they will be referred to collectively as party-based. The term 'party-based' is preferred because even the *de facto* single-party regimes typically permit a few minor allied parties to appear in their legislative institutions, however, formally (Linz [1975] 2000: 79). Even in North Korea—one-party regime par excellence—alongside the ruling Workers' Party of Korea, there formally exist two admittedly politically irrelevant parties. Second, in contrast to an (almost) one party regime of North Korea or that of the People's Republic of Poland which permitted several minor *allied* parties, non-democratic regimes also exist that allow *opposition* parties to participate in multiparty elections and to be present in legislatures, such as those of pre-2000 Mexico or contemporary Uganda. Such regimes are often referred to as the dominant (or hegemonic) party autocracies (Magaloni and Kricheli 2010). Throughout the chapter, be they one-party or dominant party regimes, they will all be referred to collectively as party-based dictatorships. In turn, democratic regimes with dominant governing parties, such as that of the African National Congress in South Africa, are excluded as the focus of this chapter is *authoritarian* party-based dictatorships.

36.2.2 Political Executive in Party-Based Dictatorships

Somewhat paradoxically perhaps, the nature of the executive in a party-based dictatorship may not be always clear-cut. To understand what the executive is, it is more advantageous to set aside the conventional division into executive, legislative and judiciary branches. Instead it is important to recognize that primary division is between state and party institutions that in turn may consist of their own executive and legislative institutions. It is also more advantageous to put aside formal constitutional powers and instead focus on whether particular institutions perform 'executive' functions in practice.

Consider Leninist party-based dictatorships. While many such regimes became extinct following the end of the Cold war, several very important regimes in China, Cuba, Laos, and Vietnam continued to exist. In contrast to parliamentary democracies where the cabinet of ministers is a national political executive, in Soviet-style party-based dictatorships the cabinet (the Council of Ministers or the State Council) is better understood to belong not to the executive as such but to the executive-administrative (and apolitical) branch of government, largely responsible for the administration of the economy. In such regimes, the party executive instead manages political affairs and overall national policy. The logic of unity that denies the need for multiparty competition—in the absence of class struggle, it is assumed that there is no need for more than one party which already represents every citizen—applies to the overall government structure as well.

To aggravate likely confusion about governmental branches, the legislature is not only formally vested with the supreme state authority and placed above other branches, it also combines legislative and executive functions. For example, by the logic of the 1977 Soviet constitution the head of state is neither the party leader nor the head of government but the chairperson of the collective Presidium of the Supreme Soviet—national legislature—that in turn exercises 'the functions of the highest body of state authority of the USSR' (art. 119), also has decree-making authority, and can relieve and appoint ministers (art. 122).

In practice, it is the governing party however that 'holds in its hands all the levers of policy in the state' (Kolkowicz 1968: 75). Therefore, the party's Central Committee, the Secretariat (the executive) of the Committee, and particularly its Political Bureau (Politburo), are 'the de facto government of the country, making the key policy decisions and giving instructions to the constitutionally recognized government' (Brooker 2000: 125). The highest party executive organ, the Politburo, consists of full voting members and candidates; non-voting members (loosely resembling cabinet ministers and secretaries of state) may also be known as the Presidium, Politburo Standing Committee (PSC), or National (Central) Executive Committee, *inter alia* (Lowenhardt et al. 1992). The executive organ of the Central Committee, the Secretariat, is also very important: because in practice top secretaries of the Secretariat are also members of the Politburo, the latter can be referred to as 'party executive' overall. In turn, the title of the head of the political executive may also vary. The leader may hold the titles of president, prime minister, *premier*, chairperson, or general-secretary (or first secretary or chairperson of the Central Committee). Almost always, however, it is within the post of the party leader that the political power resides and it is this person who is the *de facto* national political leader. Such a leader, general-secretary (in the USSR or PRC) or *jefe maximo* (Mexico in the 1920s) may or may not occupy other executive posts, such as those of prime minister or president. Even in PRI's Mexico, a party-based dictatorship organized very differently from Leninist dictatorships, it was the party leadership position that was the most important *de facto*: 'Formally, the Mexican president was not a very powerful player. The president dominated the other branches of government only because he was the leader of the PRI' (Magaloni 2006: 101).

In summary, *the political executive in a party-based dictatorship consists of the* de facto *national political leader who is (almost always) the party leader as well as of institutions of party and state executive.* In practice, party and state executives are often fused. This is because many high-ranking party officials will typically also hold high-ranking state positions, while governmental ministries will include party committees responsible to the party directly (Ploss 1970; Shirk 1993; McGregor 2010).

36.2.3 Research Questions about the Political Executive

36.2.3.1 *How Is the Executive Selected or Elected, and How Is It Deselected?*

In Leninist party-based dictatorships, the ruling party selects the national executive. In the People's Republic of China, the party political executive is selected when the National Party's Congress (party legislature, not to be confused with the state legislature) convenes every five years to elect members of the Central Committee, which in turn elects members of the Politburo from which the top executive institution, that of the PSC, is formed (Shirk 1993; McGregor 2010). Scholars understand formal rules (if such rules exist—in the early years of party-based dictatorships, rules may not even be articulated) governing the process of selection and deselection. The challenge for empirically oriented scholars, however, is the extreme opacity of the process and the informal aspects that underpin it. What determines that some individuals are promoted to the highest institutions of the political executive? Is the selection driven by informal and patronage politics, individual policy performance, or something else? In 2017, even well-informed China observers from the Brookings Institution had to qualify their forecasts of the likely outcome of the eighteenth Party Congress in October of that year by emphasizing the fact that China had up to then 'conducted peaceful, orderly, and institutionalized transfers of power' in the past, yet they could not 'meaningfully forecast how many six-generation leaders will enter the PSC and the Politburo' (Li 2017). It therefore remains a challenge as to how to move beyond qualitative assessments toward more systematic analyses of executive leadership selection when so little is revealed to outside observers.

36.2.3.2 *What Determines the Likelihood of Political Cooperation and Conflict between State and Party Institutions?*

Other important questions exist that relate to the relationship of the party executive with other branches of government. Does the duplication of party and state institutions increase the number of policy veto players? What determines dissent? How does intra-elite policy bargaining occur? Do national legislatures in fact provide such a forum for bargaining, as argued in the literature (Gandhi 2008; Wright 2008), even in single-party regimes that do not co-opt opposition parties in their parliaments? If not, then an important question arises as to what institutions within the political executive provide such forums for policy bargaining, how the process occurs, and whether it can be observed and studied. There is a related question as to how policy is made within the executive, and what determines intra-institutional rivalry in the executive. Do we know if revealed policy disagreements are ideological or merely driven by disagreements over power and control over personnel appointments? Is rivalry primarily institutional, as in Politburo versus the Council of Ministers, or does such rivalry crosscut different institutions and is determined by informal politics, policy differences, clans, generations, or different leaders?

36.2.3.3 *What Makes Collective Leadership Work?*

While the questions above about executive selection, policy-making or institutional rivalry are important, one of the most interesting questions for scholars of authoritarian politics relates to what determines whether a party-based dictatorship is able to maintain its collective leadership. Formally, the executive in party-based dictatorships is often a collective institution, the party's Politburo or Central Committee, with the power to dismiss the leader (Shirk 1993; McGregor 2010; London 2014). The key distinction between personalist and party-based dictatorships is in the degree of relative autonomy of institutions versus the leader. In a path-setting study of non-democratic regimes, Geddes (1999: 124) argues that in party regimes it is not the leader but the party that 'controls the career paths of officials, organizes the distribution of benefits of supporters'. In other words, party-based dictatorships practice collective leadership, even though they may have a leader who is constrained by the party. In contrast, in personalist regimes the party does not exercise 'independent decision-making power insulated from the whims of the ruler' (Geddes 1999: 121–2). What determines the breakdown of collective leadership and transition to personalism? The process mainly occurs at the level of political executive, within the highest party and state institutions. The question of power distribution within the executive also entails the study of formal and informal powers and norms (Manion 1993; Dittmer 1995; Shih et al. 2012). What are the formal and informal powers of the political executive? What within the executive determines the norms that govern the range of the accepted leader's authority versus others? For example, the constitutional removal of presidential term limits in China in early 2018 is an important regime development that formally dismantled the principle of leadership turnover at the top. However, an arguably much more crucial change was accomplished earlier, at a party congress in October 2017 when the party's General-Secretary Xi Jinping chose to ignore an important norm of designating successors midway, prior to the second and last term of an incumbent leader (Manion 1993; Wang and Vangeli 2016). The query about collective leadership is therefore related to those on regime institutionalization, elite compliance with norms, and succession.

In summary, the first and most basic question to ask is what to include in the political executive within a party-based dictatorship. This is because of the paramount role of the ruling party as well as the fusion of party and state executive bodies. Important questions exist around the selection and deselection of the executive and the rivalry and cooperation within it, particularly between party and state institutions. Questions also exist that are related to the mechanisms of collective leadership. Other enquiries are methodological and relate to the problem of studying the executive politics in non-democratic regimes that are often opaque in the Churchillian 'bulldogs under the carpet' sense (see Chapter 34 in this volume). These questions require not only a deep understanding of how real-life politics 'really' works but also a theoretical understanding of institutions, leadership theories, coalition politics, and game theory. How do scholars address these questions?

36.3 The State of Research on the Executive in Party-Based Dictatorships

36.3.1 Selection of the Political Executive

The dictator, the effective political leader is usually the leader of a ruling political party, selected indirectly by the party's collective decision-making body such as Central Committee. The Central Committee selects the party's 'cabinet', the highest party executive body, the Politburo (Lowenhardt et al. 1992). In practice, the party leader is selected from the ranks of the Politburo, by members of the Politburo, and later ratified by a larger Central Committee (Strong 1971; Brown 1980; Teiwes 2001). Almost always, little is revealed about what happens at the meeting to select the leader and scholars are only able to reconstruct after the fact, drawing from subsequent appointments or participant memoirs (e.g. Ploss 1982; Ligachev 1993; Brown 1996). While there may be formal rules on the process of selection, in practice the selection of leaders of party-based dictatorships is determined by underlying power relations and informal norms on eligibility as understood (and contested) by the top leadership (Brown 1982). The institution that formally selects top leadership, Central Committee, itself is elected at periodic party congresses (Daniels 1976). However the party executive controls who is selected for such congresses. In a sense, the Central Committee composition is determined by the individual's place in the overall hierarchy, the 'nomenklatura' system, so that the highest officials such as regional party secretaries, top generals, or cabinet ministers assume the Central Committee slots as determined by their posts (Daniels 1976). Roeder (1993), who studied executive politics and recruitment in the USSR, referred to the process of executive selection as *reciprocal accountability*, where individuals who select leaders 'can be appointed and removed by the very leaders whom they appoint and remove' (Roeder 1993: 51). Meyer et al. (2016), who studied China, argue that the process resembles Pareto's circulation of the elite, with individuals alternating between Central Committee, Politburo, and PSC.

More generally, the party carefully selects individuals for party and state leadership positions through the so-called 'nomenklatura' system (Harasymiw 1984; Shambaugh 2009). Scholars have long studied the background and individual characteristics of political actors selected for party leadership (e.g. Ploss 1982; Harasymiw 1984; Burns 2006). Scholars generally find that loyalty and patronage ties are key factors for selection into the ranks of the party executive (Rigby and Harasymiw 1983; Shih 2008; Shih et al. 2012), however, policy performance may also be an important factor behind selection to Politburo and top government posts, in China (Li and Zhou 2005; Jia et al. 2015). In party-based dictatorships, lower-ranked officials first perform a lengthy and costly service for the party while climbing the career ladder, later capitalizing on their prior career when they reach the higher levels of party hierarchy (Svolik 2012: 168–9). As a result of a rigid system of promotion for executive posts, leaders of party-based dictatorships also have on average lengthier experience in politics than those of other dictatorships (Baturo 2016: 154).

With regard to the selection of state executive, the government is within the remit of the 'nomenklatura' system and is determined by the party's secretariat or organization bureau, as instructed by the Politburo, even if it must formally be approved by the national legislature—not to be confused with a party congress. Malesky and Schuler (2013) find that in Vietnam, vote shares for National Assembly seats were irrelevant for subsequent ministerial selection and instead party loyalty was the main determining factor. Other scholars of party regimes have studied the composition, patronage politics, and factions within the cabinet, generally finding stronger support for loyalty or patronage as factors behind political selection, as opposed to competence (Ploss 1970, 1982; Gorlizki 2002; Gorlizki and Khlevniuk 2004; Gregory 2004; Shih 2008; Arriola 2009). In general, party and state executive selection is largely determined by the patronage system and informal agreements within the collective leadership (Rigby and Harasymiw 1983). Because the benefits of such a patron-client relationship are mutual, in turn the strength and reach of clientelistic networks influences the power of patrons within the collective leadership of a party-based dictatorship, as discussed below.

The widely, and not unreasonably, held view is that party election is a sham and lower-level institutions are dominated by the party executive they are supposed to elect. Scholars find that on occasion, however, institutions may be instrumental in leadership selection or deselection. In 2001 in Vietnam, even though the majority in the Politburo voted to keep an unpopular party's secretary-general in his post, the Central Committee overturned the decision and the party leader was obliged to depart (Thayer 2002). As a result, with a larger number of policy veto players, that is, the growing role for Central Committee alongside the Politburo, the power in the party's political executive has arguably become more diffused.

Whether the party leader is elected indirectly by the Central Committee or directly by the electorate as national president (following the party nomination for the presidency), the party political executive determines its leadership selection (Bunce 1986; Manion 1993). In another party-based dictatorship of Mexico under PRI, the national president and ruling party leader, albeit constrained by the elite agreed upon norm of a single six-year term in office (Magaloni 2006), had significant powers to determine the composition of the political executive and to select members of his or her cabinet and successor (Knight 1992). Because the party was central, the president, as head of the party, was preeminent and served as the central mediator of intra-elite disputes (Weldon 1997: 227).

Questions of deselection and, thus, succession of national leaders has also been the subject of multiple publications (Hodnett 1975; Bunce 1986; Manion 1993; Brownlee 2007; Baturo 2014; Ma 2016; Wang and Vangeli 2016; Frantz and Stein 2017). Executive deselection and leadership turnover are also fundamental to the principle of collective leadership.

36.3.2 Collective Leadership Stability and Breakdown

One of the central research questions in authoritarian politics is what determines the relative power of individual leaders versus collective leadership. The power of leaders of party-based dictatorships, where by definition one party dominates national politics, varies. Brooker (2000) proposed considering the degree of the ruler's power as a range from a setting where a leader 'is allowed a deal of autonomy by his party'—such as the Mexican presidency under PRI, to a setting wherein a dictator is able to relegate the party to 'being only an instrument of his personal rule'—such as Stalin's USSR (Brooker 2000: 131). In the former, the ruler remains the agent of the party, while in the latter the ruler becomes the principal who employs the party and the executive as private tools (Brooker 2000: 57–8). Svolik (2012: 53–63) argues that dictators try to accumulate more power at the expense of their allies and when they are successful, collective leadership that previously featured institutional autonomy, is broken. In turn, the goal of collective leadership is to constrain the ruler and remove him or her, if necessary. Thus, the Soviet leadership, threatened by the increasing authority of Khrushchev, in 1964 had him removed. Collective leadership may be particularly sensitive to the leader's attempts to unite party and state offices. 'There is little question that an erosion of the collective principle occurred during the latter part of his tenure—that is, after 1958, when he combined in himself the posts of Premier and party First Secretary' (Ploss 1970: 6).

Indeed, one of the pillars of collective leadership was an implicit understanding to keep party and government leadership posts in different hands, alongside the division of policy authority across the party executive (Rigby 1970).

Collective leadership may also engage in 'dictator-proofing' to prevent the ascent of popular politicians perceived as a threat. Gueorguiev and Schuler (2016) find that the collective leadership may strategically choose not to promote prominent and popular actors (Gueorguiev and Schuler 2016: 89). They give evidence that in China and Vietnam during party congresses in 2012 and 2011, two expected candidates for promotion were sidelined precisely because they had too many followers, as evidenced by the media coverage and online search queries. Another important institution of 'dictator-proofing' practiced by collective leadership is mandatory leadership turnover whether through formal or informal term or age limits (Manion 1993; Wang and Vangeli 2016). However, in the absence of third-party enforcement, turnover norm can only be enforced while the leader has not acquired sufficient power to break it (Svolik 2012: 198–9). What determines the balance of power within the political executive? Formal work exists in which scholars model the power dynamics. Acemoglu et al. (2008) find that the ruling coalition in non-democratic settings is self-enforcing when it does not include a sufficiently powerful and self-enforcing subcoalition, and that the elimination of one or two powerful members may change the balance dramatically, leading to the demise of a collective leadership (Acemoglu et al. 2008: 1003). Acemoglu et al. (2008) further illustrate how observable changes in Stalin's Politburo validate their results. Svolik (2012) models the interaction between the ruler and inner circle where the balance of power is difficult to observe, and the main observable implication is that the threat of elite rebellion diminishes the longer the dictator is in office (Svolik 2012: 75–8).

In practice, that is, in real-life politics, the consolidation of the leader's power occurs at the level of party and state executive (Ploss 1970; Dittmer 1978; Khlevniuk 1996, 2010; Teiwes 2001; Gorlizki and Khlevniuk 2004; Shih et al. 2012). The leader gathers power through strategic appointments and dismissals in the process that can be described as 'authority building' (Breslauer 1982). For example, Ploss (1970: 13) documents that Brezhnev's acquisition of authority over the state executive at some stage was evidenced by his ability to appoint two party officials to key posts designated for the state bureaucracy. Drawing from Soviet archives, Khlevniuk (2010) has traced the breakdown of Soviet collective leadership under Stalin. Stalin became the *de facto* first among equals as early as 1922 due to his unique position to influence appointments as the only full member of three highest party executive institutions. Due to several factors including institutional inertia, Khlevniuk (2010) points out that the breakdown of collective leadership can be dated only from 1934 when Stalin split the post of the second secretary—his second-in-command—between several individuals, and when he began ignoring formal rules and norms of the Politburo's decision-making. In the end, both the party and state executive alike became merely consultative institutions for the ruler. In China, Mao used a permanent, self-inflicted crisis to destroy not only the principles of collective leadership, but also overall party function (Teiwes 2001).

While there exists important formal work on dictators' emergence (e.g. Svolik 2012), and there are detailed accounts of how it occurs on the ground (Khlevniuk 1996, 2010; Gorlizki and Khlevniuk 2004), there is a lack of good understanding about institutions and norms of collective leadership that constrain dictators. Do such rules as those on retirement and promotion, or an oversight over enforcement agencies have systematic effects on the behaviour within the collective leadership? Likewise, while reciprocal benefits exist that accrue from informal ties to both leaders and their followers (e.g. Rigby and Harasymiw 1983; Shih et al. 2012), there is a lack of systematic analyses that explain how informal and formal aspects relate, how leaders 'capitalize' on the powers of office to promote clients, how they 'capitalize' on client networks to change formal rules, and how members of the Politburo monitor and police compliance with informal norms. One rare exception is an excellent re-examination of elite politics in the USSR by Graeme Gill (2018) who combines the rigor of political science with detailed knowledge of Soviet leadership and institutions. Gill demonstrated that contrary to many assumptions in the comparative literature on dictatorships, not all members of the ruling coalition have incentives to resist the ruler, and in fact may have different loyalties and priorities at different points in time; that certain norms of elite behaviour can be close to self-enforcing without resort to violence, and that within-elite rivalry is driven as much by policy as power considerations, among other things.

36.3.3 'Authoritarian Cohabitation'? What Determines Rivalry within the Political Executive?

Generally speaking, party-based dictatorships have a higher number of policy veto players than other dictatorships (Frantz and Ezrow 2011). As a result, elites do not always agree on national policy, which in turn may cause policy inertia or even gridlock (Bunce 1986; Koh 2001). Above, using the example of Vietnam, I discussed how the growing power of the Central Committee could have arguably been understood as the introduction of a new veto player that influenced policy. It is an open question as to the circumstances under which the Central Committee and Politburo can be regarded as independent veto players within the party executive. What can be accepted, however, is that the main institutional division in party-based dictatorships is that between party and state institutions. In general, scholars find that rivalry between party and state leadership is common, particularly when the executive is divided between the posts of party leader and the leader of government, as in Mexico from 1917 to 1936 when the executive power was intermittently divided between the president and the party leader, *jefe maximo* (Weldon 1997: 248–50).

Scholars find that rivalry between party and state executives was endemic in the Soviet regime (Breslauer 1982; Ploss 1982, 1970; Roeder 1993; Brown 1996). In general, the party executive sought to maintain overall control over economic decision-making and executive appointments. In turn, a more technocratic state executive had incentives to ignore party dogmas in running the economy and it prioritized efficiency as a goal (Ploss 1970: 12). Institutional tensions tended to diminish, however, when there was a single leader occupying both party and state offices at the same time, as in 1941–53 and 1958–64 (Ploss 1970). Likewise, in Mexico, only when President Cardenas prevailed over *jefe maximo* in 1936 and added the office of party leader to his presidential duties, the unity of the executive was restored.

It is an open research question as to whether models developed to study the dual executive in democracy, such as those of cohabitation (Duverger 1996) or semi-presidentialism more generally (Elgie 2011; see also Chapter 20 in this volume), have the potential to explain policy-making in dictatorships. Although party leaders and heads of government are from the same party, some kind of 'authoritarian cohabitation' may arise due to informal politics, or leadership rivalry. In Vietnam, for instance, a party-based dictatorship more pluralistic than those of China or Cuba, the collective leadership is based on four institutional pillars, those of the party general-secretary, the state president, the president of the National Assembly, and prime-minister (London 2014). To maintain the principles of collective leadership, distinct individuals occupy four pillars. From 2006 to 2016, Prime Minister Dung arguably cultivated his own power base so that ministers and governors gravitated towards the government and away from the party. Alarmed by the possibility that Dung would follow the steps of Xi Jinping of China who was able to diminish the power of collective leadership, the party leadership blocked Dung's bid to become the next general-secretary in 2016 and had him retired (London 2016). Scholars of Soviet politics have also documented how the party executive restored the balance of power away from state institutions, time and again (Ploss 1970; Breslauer 1982; Khlevniuk 2010).

Rivalry is also common between different departments, often crosscutting party and state divide, whether due to informal factions based on patronage and shared background (Huang 2000; Shih et al. 2012) or institutional rivalry (Khlevniuk 2010). Various executive departments rival each other for resources, personnel appointments, and leader's favours, among other things. Ploss (1970: 6–7) documents intense rivalry within the Soviet Politburo in the late 1960s over investment allocation between heavy, light, and defence industries. The debate over investment priorities was championed by the heads of respective departments posed to benefit from resource redistribution. More generally, policy conflicts within the executive may be triggered by disagreements over allocation of budgetary resources, personnel changes, and criticism from the control institutions (Gorlizki and Khlevniuk 2004; Khlevniuk 2010) In the USSR, such interdepartmental rivalry helped Stalin to play the role of arbiter and consolidate his authority even further (Khlevniuk 2010).

Rivalry can also be caused by genuine ideological differences, such as the disagreements about Mao's legacy between the General Secretary and Premier of China, Hua Guofeng, on the one hand and the ascendant Deng Xiaoping, on the other, in the late 1970s (Shambaugh 2009). It can take the form of intra-elite struggle over Stalin's criticism, as in the USSR (Ploss 1970: 12).

36.3.4 Political Executive as a Bargaining Forum

Many scholars of authoritarian institutions have argued that parties and legislatures provide autocrats with institutional forums to bargain with the elites (see discussion in Magaloni and Kricheli 2010: 125). However, national legislatures in Leninist party dictatorships are largely ceremonial institutions that serve to rubber stamp the decisions of the executive (for the example of a more activist parliament, see Malesky and Schuler 2010). Individuals may hold legislative seats as a ladder toward higher positions in the 'nomenklatura' system within the executive (Rigby and Harasymiw 1983; Harasymiw 1984). As discussed above, in party-based dictatorships it is also more likely that the executive at the party or state institutional side, or both, provides the forum for elite policy negotiations.

Arriola (2009) argues that in both personalist and dominant party regimes in sub-Saharan Africa, it is the cabinet that provides the forum for elite compromise and the autocrats use ministerial positions to leverage concessions to the elites. In Cuba, Dominguez (1989) argues that factional and institutional conflicts within the Integrated Revolutionary Organizations (ORI) national directorate, and then within its successor, the Central Committee of the Communist party, and state institutions, helped to improve policy debate and economic performance in the 1960s. Because factional and institutional cleavages were crosscutting, they did not threaten the party's hold on power. From the end of the 1960s, however, as Fidel Castro dismantled collective leadership, although patronage cliques remained they were no longer able to debate Castro's policies, with disastrous results for the economy (Dominguez 1989: 153). In fact, Cuban party-based dictatorship had no legislature in the first place to provide an institutional intra-elite forum until as late as 1976; policy differences were discussed and negotiated within the political executive structures. Similarly, in the USSR until 1989 the Supreme Soviet played no role in intra-elite policy debates. Instead, Politburo meetings as well as those of the Presidium of the Council of Ministers, or the joint sessions of both executive organs, provided platforms for policy bargaining (Ploss 1970; Ross 1980).

36.3.5 How to Study Political Executive in Party-Based Dictatorship?

Methodological questions, 'how to study' are no less important than 'what to study'. Admittedly, it is difficult to analyse politics within Politburo or Central Committee, in opaque authoritarian settings. The range of approaches varies from highly subjective interpretations that may be difficult to validate to more replicable approaches, such as those based on quantitative biographical data. The examples of qualitative expert reconstructions are numerous. For example, Ploss (1982) interpreted the relative standing of Soviet Politburo members from the coverage and tone of their speeches. In turn, Li (2012) infers the relative power of top politicians from their position during media events or the ordering of names during important events. Scholars have also long paid attention to the informal ties between top leaders and other officials at executive level (Dittmer 1978; Huang 2000; Choi 2012; Shih et al. 2012). For example, Shih et al. (2012) relied on biographical data to explain selection into the Central Committee of the Chinese Communist Party. Khlevniuk (2010), in order to understand changes in the power and status of members of the executive, relies on the appointment book to tally how often and for how many hours Stalin met particular individuals, as well as personal correspondence and the official transcripts from various meetings. Similarly, Gregory (2004: 92–101) draws from frequency of official meetings and appointments to understand changes in the collective leadership of the USSR. In China, Ma (2016) relies on the ability to promote close associates as a proxy for personal influence. In turn, Keller (2016) combines qualitative assessments of informal politics with publicly available data to infer party factions using social network analysis.

36.4 Open Issues and Research Agenda

36.4.1 Toward a Third-Generation Approach to the Study of Authoritarian Politics

During the Cold war, scholars of authoritarian politics focused on many issues and questions of relevance to the study of the political executive in party-based dictatorships: selection and deselection of elites into the executive, factions, and policy-making, succession and elite rivalry, and the mechanisms of collective leadership, *inter alia* (Ploss 1970, 1982; Hodnett 1975; Stern 1978; Brown 1984). The majority of such studies relied on expert reconstructions, internal leaks, telegrams, diaries, interpretations of daily editorials, and even individuals' proximity to leaders during public events. Despite the problem of opacity of politics in dictatorships, this first-generation research on authoritarian politics has illuminated how the political executive operates in Soviet, Chinese, and other party-based dictatorships.

The next, more recent wave of research on dictatorships, largely driven by new statistical methods that revolutionized the study of comparative politics, has arguably taken a different approach. The majority of such second-generation studies have prioritized the rigor of large-n statistical comparisons (Geddes 1999; Wright 2008; Geddes et al. 2014; Escriba-Folch and Wright 2015). As a result of such a bird's-eye approach, scholars largely ignored the study of the political executive *within* dictatorships and instead focused on the identification of effects of parties and legislatures on various outcomes across different non-democratic regime types.

Given the gap between earlier, detailed, 'high-resolution' studies of politics within non-democratic regimes, and technically savvier but 'low-resolution' comparative studies of institutions, a new research programme that will combine the best of both worlds begs to be proposed. As argued in the recent review, despite impressive advances in cross-national studies of institutions in dictatorships, methodologically sound, based on detailed knowledge and data analyses, studies of politics *within* authoritarian regimes are still rare (Pepinsky 2013). Given recent advances in applying rigorous research methods to authoritarian regimes, the next, third generation, research agenda is likely to be about revisiting older research questions and applying novel methods to the study of single-country cases, as they have already been applied *en masse* to the studies across regimes. Below, I outline possible methodological approaches, 'how' to study, and then briefly discuss some important questions that remain to be addressed.

36.4.2 Text Analytics and the Study of Politics within Dictatorships

The study of the executive in party-based dictatorships is difficult because so little is known about internal politics within such an executive. Opacity is probably a given but questions of how policy is made within the collective leadership, how political leaders acquire personal power diminishing the autonomy of institutions in the process, how formal and informal institutions interact are very important subjects of enquiry that can arguably be addressed not only through qualitative assessments and meticulous archival research.

The next research frontier may be driven by applications of novel statistical methods including text analytics and data science, among others. Consider the following example. The politics in Vietnam prior to the 2016 party congress was characterized by rivalry between Prime Minister Dung and the incumbent party leader, Trong. The rivalry was not only personal, over expected succession to the post of the general-secretary, but also institutional. The expert reconstruction by London (2016) indicates that a popular head of government was apparently able to acquire influence over the Council of Ministers at the expense of the party executive. While it alarmed and attracted strong opposition from the Politburo, for a time Dung was able to maintain his authority largely due to the support from Central Committee which was to a large extent composed of cabinet ministers and regional officials, dependent on the head of government for resources. In 2016, however, the head of the party executive, Trong, was able to dismiss Dung by successfully utilizing the procedural and informal powers of his office (London 2016).

Now that the technical limitations related to analysing large quantities of text have been overcome (Grimmer and Stewart 2013), to study intra-elite rivalry scholars can resort not only to biographical data but also text analytics tools. To see this, consider that many important actors in dictatorships make public speeches including the above mentioned Prime Minister Dung and Secretary Trong. Revealed policy differences from texts, whether sincere or strategic, could inform us about policy priorities and even the existence of factions within the executive. For instance, Baturo and Mikhaylov (2014), treating Russian regional governors as a quasi-expert panel, scaled positions revealed in their regional legislative addresses in relation to the positions of President Medvedev and Prime Minister Putin from 2008 to 2012. The analyses revealed that governors moved from an initially neutral position in relation to both leaders to a clearly pro-Putin position in 2011, which arguably indicates how elites perceived the distribution of power at the federal centre over time. Even though politics in Russia at the time was more open than that in party-based dictatorships, the Vietnamese regime has also revealed the existence of competitive factions and a significant degree of pluralism (Malesky and Schuler 2010).

Nguyen Tan Dung, as Prime Minister from 2006 to 2016, made formal reports to the National Assembly; he also made frequent appearances in the media where he advocated for market reform and even human rights and democracy (London 2014). His rival, Trong, in his position as party leader, delivered formal political reports to party's congresses and plena. It is conceivable that their public speeches may provide us with important sources of information to better understand policy and politics within the executive. Text analytic tools may also assist in understanding whether the political executive is unified or split between several power centres. For example, scholars may attempt to compare the likelihood of 'technocratic' topics as opposed to party ideological and dogmatic topics or sentiments over the economy, in various speeches or official media coverage. One recent example of the approach is by Gueorguiev and Schuler (2016) who relied on text data to infer potential challenges to collective leadership in China and Vietnam.

Admittedly, the text-as-data approach is probably more practical in 'presidential' party-based dictatorships such as those of Botswana or PRI's Mexico where political leaders deliver legislative reports as national presidents in the 'state-of-the-union' format. Still, even in more opaque party-based dictatorships such as that of the Soviet Union, intra-elite rivalry was often voiced in printed media or even party plenums. Ploss (1970: 7–8) demonstrated how top-level disagreements could be inferred from very distinct policy priorities voiced in the party media organs of *Pravda* and *Kommunist*, the government organ, *Izvestiya*, and the defence ministry organ, *Krasnaya Zvezda*, in the late 1960s. Given the increased availability of various text data through the digitization of historical newspaper archives, Central Committee plenum records, and transcripts, text analytics methods have the potential to revolutionize the study of authoritarian politics, particularly in more 'talkative' party-based dictatorships that tend to produce considerable amounts of text data.

36.4.3 Remaining Research Questions

The political executive in party-based dictatorships is under theorized and under researched. In particular, future scholarship needs to develop a better understanding of collective leadership and how it relates to regime institutionalization, and of the relative power and mutual dependency of party and state institutions. There are many open issues regarding politics within the executive of party-based dictatorships. Arguably, one of the most important is that which relates to the need for better and multidimensional measures of regime institutionalization. Given that the majority of comparativists rely on categorical definitions of non-democratic regimes (Geddes 1999; Wright 2008; Geddes et al. 2014; Escriba-Folch and Wright 2015), our understanding of authoritarian politics will improve significantly if we are able to utilize additional regime dimensions in research.

Consider the concepts of regime institutionalization, collective leadership, and the turnover of leaders. In regimes with dominant parties, 'leadership turnover is actually a consequence of a prior factor (institutionalization) which causes both frequent turnover of leaders and the relative longevity of the regime itself' (Escriba-Folch and Wright 2015: 41). 'Once the regime is fully institutionalized, there is little opportunity for leaders to consolidate power in their own hands' (Escriba-Folch an Wright 2015: 40). If party regimes are assumed institutionalized by virtue of having a party, then such a definition is certainly useful when comparing party regimes with other dictatorships. If regime institutionalization is inferred from the existence of collective leadership, 'institutionalization-as-collective-leadership', then it is problematic to rely on collective leadership to predict the turnover of leaders. Arguably, the concept of collective leadership rests on the principles of collective decision-making, of the division of policy responsibilities and that of leadership turnover. But if institutionalization is a consequence of (complied with) leadership turnover, then it cannot in turn be the cause of leadership turnover.

It is more advantageous to recognize institutionalization as a multifaceted concept. Institutionalization may vary over time and across different party-based dictatorships. Ambitious leaders such as Josef Stalin or Xi Jinping may subvert the norms of leadership turnover and collective leadership from within highly institutionalized party-based dictatorships. The rigid and formal party rules on decision-making, appointments, promotions, and demotions—the features of a party regime—can remain firmly in place while the relative power within the previously collective leadership may change dramatically. For example, Meyer et al. (2016) have constructed measures of regime institutionalization in China, assuming that a more institutionalized regime features 'more measured ascent through the ranks' in contrast to a less institutionalized one that experiences 'larger and relatively unanticipated promotions and demotions' (Meyer et al. 2016: 153). By this metric, the Chinese regime in 2018 that prioritises formal rules over informal influence is more institutionalized than it was in 1980s. Deng Xiaoping, the undisputed leader of China from 1978 to 1989, was able to exercise power through his exceptional personal standing in the party without occupying the posts of the party's general-secretary or the head of government (Manion 1993). Although his regime was arguably less institutionalized overall, Deng adhered to collective leadership norms within the political executive. In contrast, Xi Jinping, who broke with the regularized succession principle in 2018, operates in a more institutionalized regime overall. His decision to formally extend term limits for the presidential office—the lesser of three offices he occupied as the leader of China—may even be interpreted as a paradoxical reflection of regime institutionalization, the impetus to formalize the *de facto* power relations and avoid exerting influence informally, Deng-like.

Furthermore, as Gill (2018: 21–2) points out, collective leadership itself may be better understood as a multidimensional concept, so that it is not only about the power of a leader versus the elite collective but also about the means of exercising power. It is therefore imperative to develop new tools to account for distinct dimensions of authoritarian politics. One possibility is to rely on detailed archival research to better understand elite politics. Due to decreasing costs and the proliferation of free or cheap online platforms, however, scholars may also turn to expert surveys to gauge the strength of collective leadership and changes thereof over time to understand: 'authoritarian cohabitation' and under what conditions distinct veto players emerge and how they operate within the executive, and measure individual policy influence of various members of the executive, *inter alia*. In general, expert surveys are deployed by researchers in settings where the relevant data is not readily available, and in situations where there is a need to quantify variables that are difficult or impossible to measure (Meyer and Booker 2001; Benoit and Wiesehomeier 2008).

36.5 Conclusions

As Huntington (1968) underlined, party-based dictatorships are very effective at constructing political order. The remarkable durability of party-based dictatorships is oftentimes attributed to their ability to co-opt politically ambitious individuals, ensure public participation in politics, and maintain a regularized succession of the leaders which in turn permit these regimes to survive beyond the departures of such leaders (e.g. Smith 2005; Magaloni 2006; Gandhi 2008; Svolik 2012; Escriba-Folch and Wright 2015). The politics within the executive of party-based dictatorships is central for our understanding of how they function. It is here that it can be determined whether party regime is governed by the principles of collective leadership and how national policy is made.

While there is a well-developed literature on party-based dictatorships in general, and on their differences with other non-democratic regimes, the literature on the *executive* in party-based dictatorships is much more sparse (for an exception, see Gill 2018). Therefore, due to the relative scarcity of existing studies about the political executive in party-based dictatorships, an important step forward for scholars of politics is to follow the lead of historians (e.g. Khlevniuk 1996, 2010; Gorlizki and Khlevniuk 2004; Zubok 2009) and to enlarge the knowledge base by studying executives in opaque settings. In this chapter, I have reviewed how scholars have addressed various questions pertaining to the study of the political executive. While I separated the questions related to executive selection and deselection, relations between party and state executive bodies, intra-elite bargaining, rivalry within the executive and whether it amounts to 'authoritarian cohabitation', these important questions are all connected to the overarching query about collective leadership within the political executive, arguably the most important question. This and related questions are difficult to address for empirically oriented scholars due to the underlying opacity of non-democratic politics. Such opacity, however, is a feature of elite politics in dictatorships; it will not go away and it should not be used as an excuse to avoid researching the political executive.

My review of a first-generation scholarship and scholars—who oftentimes can be collectively referred to as Kremlinologists—is by no means critical. Despite significant limitations of access and data availability, our predecessors were able to provide detailed and insightful descriptions of institutional arrangements and power dynamics within the political executive, based on available data and methods at the time. Newly opened research archives, as well as the growing availability of digitized texts may permit a more rigorous research that relies on text-as-data methodological approaches in addition to broader usage of expert surveys that will address important questions about the politics within the Politburo and similar institutions of political executive in party-based dictatorships.

References

Acemoglu, D., Egorov, G., and Sonin, K. (2008). 'Coalition Formation in Non-democracies,' *Review of Economic Studies* 75: 987–1009.

Arriola, L. (2009). 'Patronage and Political Stability in Africa,' *Comparative Political Studies* 42(10): 1339–62.

Baturo, A. (2014). *Democracy, Dictatorship, and Term Limits*. Ann Arbor, MI: Michigan University Press.

Baturo, A. (2016). '*Cursus Honorum*: Personal Background, Careers and Experience of Political Leaders in Democracy and Dictatorship—New Data and Analyses,' *Politics and Governance* 4(2): 138–57.

Baturo, A. and Mikhaylov, S. (2014). 'Reading the Tea Leaves: Medvedev's Presidency Through Political Rhetoric of Federal and Sub-National Actors,' *Europe-Asia Studies* 66(6): 969–92.

Benoit, K. and Wiesehomeier, N. (2008). 'Expert Judgements,' in S. Pickel, G. Pickel, H. J. Lauth and D. Jahn (eds) *Neuere Entwicklungen und Anwendungen auf dem Gebiet der Methoden der vergleichenden Politik- und Sozialwissenschaft*. Wiesbaden: VS Verlag, 497–515.

Breslauer, G. (1982). *Khrushchev and Brezhnev as Leaders: Building Authority in Soviet Politics*. New York: Harper Collins.

Brooker, P. (2000). *Non-Democratic Regimes: Theory, Government, and Politics*. New York: St. Martin's Press.

Brown, A. (1980). 'The Power of the General Secretary of the CPSU,' in T. Rigby, A. Brown and P. Reddaway (eds) *Authority, Power and Policy in the USSR*. London: Macmillan, 135–57.

Brown, A. (1982). 'Leadership Succession and Policy Innovation,' in A. Brown and M. Kaser (eds) *Soviet Policy for the 1980s*. London: Macmillan.

Brown, A. (1984). 'The Soviet Succession: From Andropov to Chernenko,' *The World Today* 40(4): 134–41.

Brown, A. (1996). *The Gorbachev Factor*. Oxford: Oxford University Press.

Brownlee, J. (2007). 'Hereditary Succession in Modern Autocracies,' *World Politics* 59: 595–628.

Bunce, V. (1986). 'The Effects of Leadership Succession in the Soviet Union,' *American Political Science Review* 80: 215–25.

Burns, J. (2006). 'The Chinese Communist Party's Nomenklatura System as a Leadership Selection Mechanism: An Evaluation,' in K. E. Brødsgaard and Z. Yongnian (eds) *The Chinese Communist Party in Reform*. London: Routledge, 33–58.

Choi, E. K. (2012). 'Patronage and Performance: Factors in the Political Mobility of Provincial Leaders in Post-Deng China,' *The China Quarterly* 212: 965–81.

Daniels, R. (1976). 'Office Holding and Elite Status: The Central Committee of the CPSU,' in P. Cocks, R. Daniels and N. Heer (eds) *The Dynamics of Soviet Politics*. Cambridge, MA: Harvard University Press, 77–95.

Davies, R. W. (1981). 'The Syrtsov-Lominadze Affairs,' *Soviet Studies* 33(1): 29–50.

Dittmer, L. (1978). 'Bases of Power in Chinese Politics: A Theory and an Analysis of the Fall of the "Gang of Four",' *World Politics* 31(1): 26–60.

Dittmer, L. (1995). 'Chinese Informal Politics,' *The China Journal* 34: 1–34.

Dominguez, J. (1989). 'Leadership Changes, Factionalism, and Organizational Politics in Cuba since 1960,' in R. Taras (ed.) *Leadership Change in Communist States*. Boston: Unwin Hyman, 129–55.

Duverger, M. (1996). *Le système politique français*. 21st ed. Paris: PUF.

Elgie, R. (2011). *Semi-presidentialism: Sub-Types and Democratic Performance*. Oxford: Oxford University Press.

Escriba-Folch, A. and Wright, J. (2015). 'Human Rights Prosecutions and Autocratic Survival,' *International Organization* 69: 343–73.

Frantz, E. and Ezrow, N. (2011). *The Politics of Dictatorship: Institutions and Outcomes in Authoritarian Regimes*. London: Lynne Rienner.

Frantz, E. and Stein, E. (2017). 'Countering Coups: Leadership Succession Rules in Dictatorships,' *Comparative Political Studies* 50(7): 935–62.

Gandhi, J. (2008). *Political Institutions under Dictatorship*. Cambridge: Cambridge University Press.

Geddes, B. (1999). 'What Do We Know about Democratization after Twenty Years?,' *Annual Review of Political Science* 2(1): 115–44.

Geddes, B, Wright, J., and Frantz, E. (2014). 'Autocratic Breakdown and Regime Transitions: A New Data Set,' *Perspectives on Politics* 12: 313–31.

Gill, G. (2018). *Collective Leadership in Soviet Politics*. London: Palgrave Macmillan.

Gorlizki, Y. (2002). 'Ordinary Stalinism: The Council of Ministers and the Soviet Neopatrimonial State, 1946–1953,' *The Journal of Modern History* 74(4): 699–736.

Gorlizki, Y. and Khlevniuk, O. (2004). *Cold Peace: Stalin and the Soviet Ruling Circle, 1945–1953*. Oxford: Oxford University Press.

Gregory, P. (2004). *The Political Economy of Stalinism: Evidence from the Soviet Secret Archives*. Cambridge: Cambridge University Press.

Grimmer, J. and Stewart, B. (2013). 'Text as Data: The Promise and Pitfalls of Automatic Content Analysis Methods for Political Texts,' *Political Analysis* 21(3): 267–97.

Gueorguiev, D. and Schuler, P. (2016). 'Keeping Your Head Down: Public Profiles and Promotion under Autocracy,' *Journal of East Asian Studies* 16(1): 87–116.

Harasymiw, B. (1984). *Political Elite Recruitment in the Soviet Union*. London: Macmillan.

Hodnett, G. (1975). 'Succession Contingencies in the Soviet Union,' *Problems of Communism* 24: 1–21.

Huang, J. (2000). *Factionalism in Chinese Communist Politics*. Cambridge University Press.

Huntington, S. (1968). *Political Order in Changing Societies*. New Haven: Yale University Press.

Jia, R., Kudamatsu, M., and Seim, D. (2015). 'Political Selection in China: The Complementary Roles of Connections and Performance,' *Journal of the European Economics Association* 13(4): 631–68.

Keller, F. (2016). 'Moving Beyond Factions: Using Social Network Analysis to Uncover Patronage Networks Among Chinese Elites,' *Journal of East Asian Studies* 16: 17–41.

Khlevniuk, O. (1996). *Politbiuro. Mekhanizmy Politicheskoi Vlasti v 1930-e gody* [*Politburo: The Mechanisms of Political Power in 1930s*]. Moscow: Rosspen.

Khlevniuk, O. (2010). *Khozyain. Stalin i utverzhdenie stalinskoi diktatury* [*The Master: Stalin and the Establishment of Stalin's Dictatorship*]. Moscow: Rosspen.

Knight, A. (1992). 'Mexico's Elite Settlement: Conjuncture and Consequences,' in J. Higley and R. Gunther (eds) *Elites and Democratic Consolidation in Latin America and Southern Europe*. New York: Cambridge University Press.

Koh, D. (2001). 'The Politics of a Divided Party and Parkinson's State in Vietnam,' *Contemporary Southeast Asia* 23(3): 533–51.

Kolkowicz, R. (1968). 'General and Politicians: Uneasy Truce,' *Problems of Communism* XVII(May): 71–6.

Li, C. (2012). 'The Battle for China's Top Nine Leadership Posts,' *The Washington Quarterly* 35(1): 131–45.

Li, C. (2017). 'The Coming-of-Age of China's Sixth Generation: A New Majority in the Party Leadership,' *The Brookings Institution*, 24 August, https://www.brookings.edu/opinions/the-coming-of-age-of-chinas-sixth-generation-a-new-majority-in-the-party-leadership/

Li, H. and Zhou, L.-A. (2005). 'Political Turnover and Economic Performance: The Incentive Role of Personnel Control in China,' *Journal of Public Economics* 89(9–10): 1743–62.

Ligachev, Y. (1993). *Inside Gorbachev's Kremlin*. London: Routledge.

Linz, J. ([1975] 2000). *Totalitarian and Authoritarian Regimes*. London: Lynne Rienner Publishers.

London, J. (2014). *Politics in Contemporary Vietnam: Party, State, and Authority*. London: Palgrave Macmillan.

London, J. (2016). 'Vietnam Leadership Succession Struggle,' *The Diplomat*, 14 January, https://thediplomat.com/2016/01/vietnams-leadership-succession-struggle/

Lowenhardt, J., Ozinga, J., and van Ree, E. (1992). *The Rise and Fall of the Soviet Politburo*. New York: St. Martin's Press.

Ma, X. (2016). 'Term Limits and Authoritarian Power Sharing: Theory and Evidence from China,' *Journal of East Asian Studies* 16: 61–85.

Magaloni, B. (2006). *Voting for Autocracy: Hegemonic Party Survival and Its Demise in Mexico*. New York: Cambridge University Press.

Magaloni, B. and Kricheli, R. (2010). 'Political Order and One-party Rule,' *Annual Review of Political Science* 13: 123–43.

Malesky, E. and Schuler, P. (2010). 'Nodding or Needling: Analyzing Delegate Responsiveness in an Authoritarian Parliament,' *American Political Science Review* 104(3): 482–502.

Malesky, E. and Schuler, P. (2013). 'Star Search: Do Elections Help Nondemocratic Regimes Identify New Leaders?,' *Journal of East Asian Studies* 13(1): 35–68.

Manion, M. (1993). *Retirement of Revolutionaries in China: Public Policies, Social Norms, Private Interests*. Princeton, NJ: Princeton University Press.

McGregor, R. (2010). *The Party: The Secret World of China's Communist Rulers*. London: HarperCollins.

Meyer, D., Ram, M., and Wilke, L. (2016). 'Circulation of the Elite in the Chinese Communist Party,' *Journal of East Asian Studies* 16: 147–84.

Meyer, M. and Booker, J. (2001). *Eliciting and Analyzing Expert Judgment: A Practical Guide*. Philadelphia: Society for Industrial and Applied Mathematics and American Statistical Association.

Pepinsky, T. (2013). 'The Institutional Turn in Comparative Authoritarianism,' *British Journal of Political Science* 44(3): 631–53.

Ploss, S. (1970). 'Politics in the Kremlin,' *Problems of Communism* May: 1–14.

Ploss, S. (1982). 'Signs of Struggle,' *Problems of Communism* September: 41–52.

Rigby, T. (1970). 'The Soviet Leadership: Toward a Self-Stabilizing Oligarchy,' *Soviet Studies* 22(2): 167–91.

Rigby, T. and Harasymiw, B. (1983). *Leadership Selection and Patron-Client Relations in the USSR and Yugoslavia*. London: George Allen and Unwin.

Roeder, P. (1993). *Red Sunset: The Failure of Soviet Politics*. Princeton: Princeton University Press.

Ross, D. (1980). 'Coalition Maintenance in the Soviet Union,' *World Politics* 32(2): 258–80.

Shambaugh, D. (2009). *China's Communist Party: Atrophy and Adaptation*. Oakland, CA: University of California Press.

Shih, V. (2008). ' "Nauseating" Displays of Loyalty: Monitoring the Factional Bargain through Ideological Campaigns in China,' *The Journal of Politics* 70(4): 1177–92.

Shih, V., Adolph, C., and Liu, M. (2012). 'Getting Ahead in the Communist Party: Explaining the Advancement of Central Committee Members in China,' *American Political Science Review* 106(1): 166–87.

Shirk, Susan. (1993). *The Political Logic of Economic Reform in China*. Oakland, CA: University of California Press.

Smith, B. (2005). 'Life of the Party: The Origins of Regime Breakdown and Persistence under Single Party Rule,' *World Politics* 57: 421–51.

Stern, G. (1978). 'Brezhnev and the Future: Leadership and the Problems of Succession in the Soviet Union,' *The Round Table—The Commonwealth Journal of International Affairs* 68(272): 340–7.

Strong, J. (1971). *The Soviet Union under Brezhnev and Kosygin: The Transition Years*. New York: Van Nostrand.

Svolik, M. (2012). *The Politics of Authoritarian Rule*. Cambridge: Cambridge University Press.

Teiwes, F. (2001). "Normal Politics with Chinese Characteristics," *China Journal* 45: 69–82.

Thayer, C. (2002). 'Vietnam in 2001: The Ninth Party Congress and After,' *Asian Survey* 42(1): 81–9.

Wang, Z. and Vangeli, A. (2016). "The Rules and Norms of Leadership Succession in China: From Deng Xiaoping to Xi Jinping and Beyond," *The China Journal* 76: 24–40.

Weldon, J. (1997). 'The Political Sources of Presidencialismo in Mexico,' in S. Mainwaring and M. Shugart (eds) *Presidentialism and Democracy in Latin America*. Cambridge: Cambridge University Press, 225–58.

Wright, J. (2008). 'Do Authoritarian Institutions Constrain? How Legislatures Affect Economic Growth and Investment,' *American Journal of Political Science* 52(2): 322–43.

Zheng, Y. (2015). 'The Institutionalization of the Communist Party and the Party System in China,' in A. Hicken and E. Martinez Kuhonta (eds) *Party System Institutionalization in Asia: Democracies, Autocracies, and the Shadows of the Past*. Cambridge: Cambridge University Press, 162–88.

Zubok, V. (2009). *A Failed Empire: The Soviet Union in the Cold War from Stalin to Gorbachev*. The University of North Carolina Press.

CHAPTER 37

POLITICAL EXECUTIVES IN MILITARY REGIMES

NATASHA LINDSTAEDT

37.1 INTRODUCTION

IN November of 2017 the Zimbabwean military seized control, ousting long-time dictator Robert Mugabe out of power. The elections that eventually took place in July of 2018 were challenged for numerous irregularities. In spite of the electoral victory of civilian Emmerson Mnangagwa from the ruling party, observers claim that Zimbabwe remains under military rule. But in contrast to strongmen who love to boast of their grip on power, when the military holds power it prefers to go under the radar (Geddes 1999).

This is just one distinction of many between military and civilian rule. This chapter explains why we should study military executives as a discrete subset. To do so, we explain what we mean by military regimes and what methods have been used to study military executives. We then provide an overview of the literature on military executives. Much of the early literature focused on the distinctions *between* the military and civilian leadership, civil military relations, the duration of military rule, and why the military seizes power in the first place. The chapter explains the methods that have been used to study military power and how this has changed over time.

The chapter also examines the distinctions *within* military rule. Early works looked at the level of professionalism and the different motivations within the armed forces. Later works distinguished between military regimes run by a junta and those run by a strongman. This led to revelations about how succession is handled, how policy output takes place, and how the legislature is dealt with.

Finally, the chapter closes with a brief examination of the more recent works on military executives and the impact of military rule. What happens *after* the military executive has been in power? Some studies have argued that military rule has a detrimental effect on democratic consolidation. Other studies have demonstrated that this is the case because the military never truly leaves power and continues to rule indirectly. But survey research has revealed an interesting contradiction. While many citizens are nostalgic about past military regimes, citizens that endured military rule still have positive assessments of democracy. Future research may need to continue to look at the impact of military executives.

37.2 Key Research Questions and Dominant Paradigms

37.2.1 What Is a Military Regime?

The distinguishing feature of military regimes is that the individuals working in the executive branch are members of the military. Military officers exercise political power and control over policy either directly or indirectly. Indirect forms of military rule are very common, in both democracies and autocracies. This chapter mostly focuses on military executives in autocracies and competitive authoritarian regimes.

Thus, military regimes are not regimes where someone from a military background has won an open election. There are many democracies around the world where a military leader has been democratically elected. Instead, the executives of military regimes have been installed as a result of a military coup (Finer 1962). Military regimes are also not regimes that are simply ruled by a man in uniform who has coup-proofed the military. Colonel Gamal Abdel Nasser had a military background and ruled Egypt in the early 1950s alongside a military. Colonel Muammar Gaddafi seized power of Libya in 1969 but Libya was not a military regime. Military regimes may have a chief executive that is a civilian (as in the case of Uruguay in 1976), but true power lies in the hands of the military.

Overall, the conceptualization of military regimes has changed over time. In the past definitions of military rule were very expansive. Some definitions of military rule have included any rule that is led by one military officer, regardless of the influence of the rest of the military officers. Thus power could be concentrated in the hands of one single officer. Works of the 1950s and 1960s made the assumption that when someone in uniform is in charge, this constituted a military regime. In contrast to earlier work, new definitions of military rule have distinguished between military regimes that are run by one man and those that were led by a junta (Stepan and Stepan 1971).[1] Others limit

---

[1] Karen Remmer (1989) categorized military regimes by how explained that the duration of military rule varied by how power was concentrated. Military governments that have high concentration of power and high levels of fusion are referred to as sultanistic regimes which tend to last a long time (25.1 years). Those with low concentration or power and high fusion are referred to as feudal regimes which do not last long (6.5 years). Military regimes with a high concentration of power and low levels of fusion are referred to as monarchic regimes (lasting 6.9 years). Finally military governments with low levels of power and fusion are referred to as oligarchic (lasting 16.3 years). According to Remmer military regimes that are more united are better able to weather storms.

military rule to military regimes that are led by collegial bodies such as a junta (Remmer 1989). In this case, the military president is constrained by the other members of the junta.

For the purpose of this chapter, it is also important to distinguish between military executives and civilian executives. Political executives, (which are responsible for managing and leading the government), are usually filled by civilians, who are not members of the military or the police force. Civilian executives work with a professionalized military that is subservient to the civilians (Huntington 1957). However, this chapter is concerned with military executives, where active military officers actually hold positions in the political executive and are responsible for making decisions in the government. Military rule is often associated with the restriction of civil liberties, curfews, and checkpoints to enforce the military's control over the population.

37.2.2 Why Study Military Rule/Executives?

Some studies believe that there is an important distinction to be made between civilian and military rule. While this is true, studies have demonstrated that instead of having a positive effect on development, military executives have a negative impact on the countries they lead. Some scholars have noted that military rulers are more likely than civilian dictators to abuse their citizens (Debs and Goemans 2010; Svolik 2012; Geddes, Wright, and Frantz 2014). Others note that leaders of military regimes are more likely to rely on violence because this is normal behaviour for the military when in power (Brecher 2013). They achieve and sustain power through domestic violence and tend to use this technique in situations of internal stress. They also see violence as both legitimate and effective ways of dealing with the public. Others concur that military rule increases human rights violations compared to civilian governments (Poe et al. 1999). Nevertheless, the military officers themselves are unlikely to execute the repression. They will turn this over to the internal security services instead. Internal security services have been used in military regimes to do a regime's dirty work. Officers generally do not want to directly fire on civilians but they may believe that disciplined obedience requires the use of force (Janowitz 1977).

Military regimes are also more likely than civilian regimes to be involved in civil wars (Fjelde 2010). Past scholars have noted that officers are more likely to engage in violence in response to challenges to national integrity (Nordlinger 1977). Military regimes are less adept at avoiding the escalation of a conflict into a civil war than other regimes. Scholars provide examples of this taking place in Nigeria during the Biafran War (1966–70), which took place when Nigeria was under military rule (Oluḷẹyẹ 1985).

Military executives are also more likely to embroil their countries in inter-state wars as well (Weeks 2011). There are several reasons why this may be the case. Some have argued that military regimes initiate civil war because it prolongs their rule in the case of territorial disputes with neighbours (Buraczynska 2016). Others argue that military regimes are likely to initiate conflicts because military executives are more vulnerable than civilian leadership. Military executives inherently have weak levels of legitimacy because they almost always take power through a coup. Military executives may be conscious of this illegitimacy and may engage in conflict in order to deal with this insecurity. Furthermore, military executives are likely to initiate a dispute because they fear if they make a foreign policy concession, they will appear weak to the public and will be ousted from power (Debs and Goemans 2010). Other scholars note that military executives initiate disputes because they hope that this will distract from poor governance. Due to their vulnerability to being ousted, military executives start conflicts to gain support from their domestic audience (Lai and Slater 2006).

A more recent argument claims that military regimes engage in international conflicts because they are by nature more violent (Weeks 2011). Military executives are more likely than civilians to believe that other states pose a national security threat; their worldview prioritizes the use of military force (Sechser 2004). Military executives are more likely to be sceptical of diplomatic measures for resolving disputes. They may also prefer a larger budget and favour an offensive doctrine in order to justify this. Furthermore, military executives may prefer to initiate a conflict in order to give the military as an institution, more prestige (Posen 1984; Snyder 1984). Military executives may also want to engage in conflict because as scholars have pointed out, military unity is adversely affected when the military is not engaged in coordinated action (King 2006). The military may feel that it cannot successfully govern unless it is engaged in some type of mission (Janowitz 1964).

Military regimes are also unique in that they tend to collapse more peacefully than other regimes, because military officers often negotiate their exits. This is often followed by democratization compared to other types of dictatorships, which are more likely to be overthrown by force, followed by a relapse to authoritarianism. Military leaders are willing to use repression but once a major threat to their rule takes place such as a huge protest or economic crisis, military regimes are likely to want to return to the barracks (Nordlinger 1977). The military realizes that if it negotiates its exit, it will be better able to retain its own autonomy and longevity, albeit outside the ruling regime. In these instances, militaries become more interested in securing autonomy and distancing themselves from the 'meddling of politicians'.

37.2.3 What Methods Have Been Used?

Early studies of military rule were not methodologically rigorous. These studies were qualitative works that mostly used secondary sources to describe the civil military relationship and the overall role of the military in governing. Based on secondary observations a typology of civil-military relationships were constructed which were used as a model for future researchers to learn from. Most studies offered examples, but not a clear methodology. This was one of the major critiques of Huntington's seminal work, *The Soldier and the State: The Theory and Politics of Civil-Military Relations*. Samuel Huntington's study was mostly theoretical in nature arguing that the optimal way for the government to exercise control over the military was to professionalize them rather than place legal and institutional restrictions on the military's autonomy. Samuel Finer's seminal book, *The Man on Horseback* (1962), analysed and classified an exhaustive list of military take-overs that had occurred during the past century. Nevertheless, the book did not offer any in-depth case studies, though the book was strewn with many examples to illustrate. Amos Perlmutter (1969) also researched many different countries to create a taxonomy of civil military relations in developing polities while Eric Nordlinger (1977) also provides a theory for why the military intervenes in politics. But in these earlier works the case studies were given more lax treatment. The examples given are interesting, but were still lacking in more detailed understanding. Earlier works in general made broad theoretical claims without providing extensive supporting evidence or rigorous methods.

Later publications moved away from the question of how the military rule, and focused on why it takes over. Some of these studies introduced statistical analysis. In particular, clear definitions and objective measurements were used to understand why coups were taking place. Though some of the work was regional in nature, focusing on Africa, theories were tested for why military coups take place that generated conclusions to be applied elsewhere. Overall the sample size was very large and the research questions were clearly defined. Later studies of military rule categorized military regimes compared to other types of authoritarian rule, as part of a large dataset that covered both temporal and spatial observations. These studies have been quantitative, testing military regimes' records on governing, why military executives exited and the chances that democratization would take place afterwards. Most of the later works used data that came in the form of statistics, not anecdotes or case studies, that aimed to predict future results and examine causal relationships.

More recent work has tried to use statistical analysis to draw conclusions about military rule and how it differs from other forms of civilian rule. To do so, recent scholarship has attempted to be more rigorous in terms of how to define military rule. While early works used expansive definitions that included anyone in a uniform, later works pared this down to juntas. More recent studies have returned to a more expansive definition of a military regime, to include both juntas (such as Uruguay, 1973–84) and regimes ruled by military strongman (such as Augusto Pinochet, who alongside the military ruled Chile from 1973 to 1990). However, in contrast to the past, these distinctions have been tested to ascertain the different outcomes associated with rule by a junta or a military strongman. Distinguishing between juntas and strongmen has different implications for longevity of military regimes, foreign policy stability, and democratization.

37.3 Contemporary Research

Scholars began to analyse military rule when independent governments were taken over by military regimes in the 1960s onwards. This was especially the case in the Southern cone countries in Latin America. Early studies focused on *why* the military seized power and *what impact* the military had on the state and development once it did take power. Many early studies had argued that military regimes are best suited to fostering a national identity, though later studies noted that they were not likely to stay in power long. The early literature on military rule made the argument that the military is able to govern better than civilian regimes, and was capable of playing a constructive part in the development of a modern democracy (Huntington 1957; Johnson 2015). Initially scholars were optimistic about the military as an institution because the military was perceived to be a strong and organized force.

Early studies also noted that military coups were likely to be a common occurrence in developing countries. Finer expressed that the level of political culture in a society explains a regime's vulnerability to military intervention (Finer 1962). The military is also always the strongest coercive institution if a country has enough fire power to displace a civilian regime. The professional traits of the military are conducive to taking over power quickly. The structure is usually hierarchical and centralized.

Given that military intervention was becoming commonplace in the developing world, Huntington's work developed a theoretical framework to account for when military intervention was likely to take place (Huntington 1957). According to Huntington, when there were low levels of political institutionalization in relation to socioeconomic development, there became a problem of un-governability. This then necessitates the need of a strong military to be the central agent of institutionalization. The military is more likely to emphasize professionalism, discipline, hierarchy, which would make it immune from politicization. Perlmutter (1986) challenged these views and argued that the military was not impartial. He also argued that because the military does not derive its power from elections, the military was more disposed to using brutal force.

37.3.1 Civil Military Relations

In addition to studies that theorized on why militaries should and/or could seize power, other studies examined in the relationships between civilians and the military and how the military was likely to rule. Foundational studies of military rule focused on categorizing military rule into different subtypes. Early work by Finer argued that military regimes could be disaggregated according to *their relations with civilian leadership* (Finer 1962). Finer claimed that there were several structural forms of military rule, which included rule that was both direct and indirect.[2] These civil military relationships

---

[2] Finer claimed there were five types of military rule: indirect limited, indirect complete, dual, direct, and quasi-civilized. Indirect limited rule occurs when the military exerts control over the government intermittently, and only as a means of securing limited objectives. Under indirect complete rule, the military rules continuously and calls the shots of a nominally civilian government. With dual military rule, the leader of the regime develops a political party or organized civilian group to act as a civilian counterweight to the views and the influence of the military. As the name suggests, with direct rule the military overtly determines the policy agenda, and members of a military junta hold key government posts. Lastly, quasi-civilized rule occurs when the military incorporates some civilian elements into the regime, in order to appear more legitimate.

and configurations would be become important in later works that examined the impact of military executives on democratic consolidation.

Later studies focused more on what the *objectives* were of military rulers. According to Eric Nordlinger (1977) there were three types of military rule: moderator, guardian, and ruler. The moderator type seeks to rule the country behind the scenes. The military in this case rules indirectly and privately exercises veto power over policies. The main goal of the military in this model is to maintain political order and stability. The guardian type directly controls the government, in the name of order, stability, and the status quo. The ruler type is the most ambitious of all. The ruler type seeks to implement significant political and economic changes to the system and rule indefinitely. While both moderator and guardian types rule short term, the ruler type makes no promises to step down. The most commonly studied type of military rule is where a military junta is directly in control, but future studies may need to investigate cases where the military is actually ruling the country unofficially (Welch and Smith 1974; Perlmutter 1977; Brooker 2013).

37.3.2 Military Professionalism

Earlier works also examined how military regimes differed by their *level of professionalism*. These works delineated between military regimes that were professionalized or praetorian (Huntington 1957; Perlmutter 1969; Finer 1962). In professional military dictatorships, the military is experienced, well-organized, cohesive, and concerned with maintaining corporate unity. Later studies defined professionalization by how disciplined the military was and how autonomous it was from the leader (Geddes 2009). Professionalization further determines the military council's collective action capacities.

In praetorian military dictatorships, by contrast, the military is poorly funded, with soldiers lacking in experience and education. Because soldiers are poorly trained, the praetorian military dictatorships are ill-prepared for dealing with external enemies (Perlmutter 1969). Praetorian military regimes are characterized by high levels of corruption, little respect for hierarchy, and rampant factionalism. A praetorian military has an incoherent command structure and non-meritocratic promotions (Geddes 2009). The praetorian military's motivation for seizing power is typically to gain access to the spoils of office. Because of this, they frequently intervene in politics, as they see doing so as a means to increase their riches. Praetorian military dictatorships are highly unstable and short-lived, as they usually lack the organizational strength necessary to govern and maintain power.

Factionalized less professionalized militaries may also be more prone to coup plots (Welch and Smith 1974). They may not be as cohesive enough to execute a plot. Strong and unified professionalized militaries may be more likely to intervene because they have greater confidence in their abilities to rule (Jenkins and Kposowa 1992). When professionalized militaries take over they are more ambitious and may want to stay in power indefinitely (Lowenthal 1974).

37.3.3 Why Do Military Executives Seize Power?

With most of Latin America and Africa regularly facing military *coup d'états*, contemporary research turned its attention to why this was the case. There have been many explanations set forth for why coups take place (see Belkin and Schofer 2003). Early work paid attention to historical and regional factors. Countries that have had a history of coups face a coup-trap, whereby one coup leads to others, such as what has happened in Thailand (Londegran and Poole 1990). Countries that have neighbouring countries experiencing coups may also face a higher likelihood of a coup taking place (Pitcher et al. 1978). Moreover, countries that have been colonized are also more likely to experience coups (McGowan and Johnson 1984).

Early studies also noted that coups are likely to take place because the military has become the strongest institution in society, and stronger than civil society as well (Zolberg 1968). In some African countries, scholars have noted that military centrality is the most important cause of military coups (Johnson et al. 1983; Kposowa and Jenkins 1992). Militaries that are unified and powerful will be more likely to step in. However, studies also argued that coups are more likely to take place when the military is *not* professionalized and cohesive. Fractionalized militaries are more likely to stage a coup, because a disgruntled faction may decide to take control against the established hierarchy (Welch and Smith 1974).

Other studies noted that the military is likely to intervene when there is a crisis coupled with the perception that the civilian government is not up to the task of dealing with it. Research on Turkey, suggested that the military will stage a coup when it believes the security of the nation is at stake. The Turkish military is most likely to become involved in Turkish politics when there are coalition governments that are fragmented and disorganized, leading to fears that the government is unstable and ill-equipped to handle external threats (Robins 2003).

Economic crises may also cause a military intervention. Economic downturns can lead to social dislocation, labour unrest, strikes, instability, and violence (Welch and Smith 1974: 67; Johnson et al. 1983). Thus, because the environment has become chaotic, the military may intervene in order to restore order. Studies on Latin America have shown how the failures of civilian governments have created incentives for intervening (Nordlinger 1977). Economic setbacks, such as in the case of Juan Perón's fall in Argentina, helped to solidify the opposition to his rule and provided an opening for the military to take over. The military also sees economic upheaval as a sign of incompetence of the civilian governments and see itself as better equipped to handle the economy. The motivation of the military increases—depending on the type of indoctrination or training it has had—as many militaries develop confidence that they could do a better job than the civilian leadership. Thailand's military has intervened repeatedly, citing civilian incompetence and corruption. Economic inequality is another reason cited for why coups take place. Bigger gaps between rich and poor create more instability, which necessitates the military to step in and restore order (Acemoglu et al. 2010).

However, other works noted that in Latin America, not all military coups took place because of regime performance (Dix 1994). Economic decline may have played a role in creating an environment that was riper for a coup, but it was not always a direct cause. The military may stage a coup because it has ideological support from civilian allies. The Turkish military has plenty of civilian allies that are happy to support the military, including the judiciary, political parties, the media, and segments of civil society. These forces regarded the military's oversight of politics important to maintaining secularism and stability. Civil military cooperation has led to the emergence of military rule in many countries in Latin America as well. Civil actors are often keen to support the military as a way to deal effectively with perceived threats to national security (Heper 2005). Thailand's military has an important ally: the monarchy. The military uses projects to honour the monarchy, and to boost its own image and alliance with the monarchy in the process. In these studies, civil-military relations are harmonious and coups take place due to civilian support.

But there are also studies that see civil-military relations as more hostile, with the military guarding its interests closely against civilian leadership. These studies argued that the military is likely to seize power when it feels that its corporate interests have been threatened. Nordlinger, for instance, states that the defence of military's corporate interests 'easily the most important interventionist motive' (Nordlinger 1977: 65; see also Welch and Smith 1972; Bienen 1974). When military corporate interests are threatened, such as budgetary support, its status with other government entities, tampering with its integrity, prestige, hierarchy of command, and autonomy, the military will feel compelled to intervene (Needler 1975). Thus maintaining autonomy over promotions, demotions, and the budget is of high importance. When military budgets are cut this can serve as a motivation for staging a coup. Low pay for military officers led to a coup in Ghana in 1966 (Austin and Luckham 1966).

Other authors have noted that military coups are the result of personal ambitions of a military strongman or revenge (Decalo 1973; see also Finer 1962). This may help explain how military regimes that are run by one man emerge. These regimes emerge after a military officer has been threatened to be purged or demoted by the leader. Thus system variables are ignored in favour of focusing on the personal ambitions of the military strongman. Anecdotal evidence was used to support this. In Uganda, Idi Amin staged a coup against Milton Obote in 1971 because he knew he was about to be ousted in his position as Chief of the Army. Similar scenarios took place the Central African Republic, Togo, and the Republic of the Congo. There are also more recent examples as well, however. In Pakistan, Pervez Musharraf staged a coup against Nawaz Sharif after he tried to diminish Musharraf's power and reputation.

37.3.4 Duration of Military Rule

Much of the literature on military regimes also focused on the *duration of military dictatorships* or why military regimes were so short-lived. In comparison to other regimes, most military regimes do not rule for long periods of time. Military regimes are incredibly fragile for several reasons. In contrast to elites from other types of dictatorships, military leaders don't always want to hold onto office (Geddes 1999). This view has been echoed by other scholars of military executives who all argue that the most the important goal of the military is to ensure that its own corporate interests are not threatened, placing a high value on its effectiveness and legitimacy above anything else (see Finer 1962; Nordlinger 1977). The interests of the military are to maintain itself as a coherent, disciplined, and hierarchical unit that is not prone to disunity and schisms. The need for corporate unity stems from the importance of achieving goals of security, national order, and territorial integrity. These ideals are indoctrinated into the military during training and remain key components of how the military achieves its objectives.

Military regimes also fall apart because they become more easily factionalized once entering the political arena. Though military regimes have high levels of trust, this trust can diminish when the military is placed in more public settings and when team build-ing efforts, such as collective drills, are not practiced (Siebold 2007). Scholars have noted that once the military enters politics, it becomes more difficult to insulate itself from societal forces and to protect itself from factionalism (Nordlinger 1977). Thus, as Geddes (1999: 12) notes military regimes 'carry with them the seeds of their own disintegration' because it has divergent interests when it is involved in politics. She also claims that transitions from military rule usually begin with splits within the ruling military elite.

Though military rule is usually short-lived, military rule can extend itself when the military acquires civilian allies who are willing to accept subordination to military leadership in exchange for some share in running the state and some share in the benefits (Clapham and Philip 1985). Military executives who have a civilian support base last longer. This is especially true in cases where the regime created a political party. These regimes last three times as long as those who do not have a civilian party (Geddes, Frantz, and Wright 2014).

37.3.5 How Do Military Executives Make Decisions?

Military executive decision-making may not be entirely different from civilian executive decision-making. This is especially the case if the military is professionalized. As stated previously, professionalized military regimes are usually structured in ways that have a clear and respected hierarchy (Jenkins and Kposowa 1992). Professionalized military regimes also have a centralized command with a pyramid style of authority that is highly stratified. Generally speaking military regimes want to be cohesive and tightly organized. Military regimes are also supposed to have high levels of trust and capacity for teamwork as a result of their shared experiences in the military (Siebold 2007).

More recent research has also argued that executive decision-making is affected by whether or not the military executive consists of a strongman or a junta, and less fre-quently a junta and a political party (Geddes 1999). In some instances the military rules as a junta and decision-making is mostly taking place jointly, with some veto powers of members of a cabinet. A leader is selected to take on the role of president, but power is not concentrated entirely in the hands of one person. An example of this type of rule would be the military junta that ruled Argentina from 1975 to 1983. In rare cases, the military rules in conjunction with a ruling party, such as was the case in El Salvador in the 1970s and 1980s. In other cases the military takes over in a coup, but one leader becomes increasingly powerful. This was the case in Chile under Augusto Pinochet (1973–90). Pinochet initially faced more veto power from the other branches of the armed forces, but eventually he was able to consolidate great levels of power.

Military executives ruled by a strongman make decisions in a similar manner to personalist dictators. There could be some consultation with the junta members but the military strongman is fully in charge. There is no succession, there is little power-sharing, there is little consensus, and the military strongman rules by decree. Military executives that are ruled by a junta want to ensure that no one military leader becomes too power-ful. They respect established military hierarchy but aim to make rational decisions about which among the set of top active or retired officers should head the government. They sometimes even require the person selected to retire from active service in order to pre-vent him from controlling promotions and postings, which would enable the leader to eliminate anyone who challenges him. This was certainly the intention when the Chilean junta selected Augusto Pinochet to be the leader (Barros 2002). Though Pinochet held onto power for a long time, he was originally selected because he was perceived to be non-charismatic, legalistic, and unlikely to possess a concentration of power. As history has shown, this assessment proved to be flawed.

By distinguishing between military regimes that are run by a collegial military and a strongman, there are important implications that can be uncovered. Military executives that are run by a junta are better able to increase mobilization of ordinary citizens. However, collegial forms of military rule are less likely to survive a crisis (Geddes 2003; Brownlee 2009; Wright and Escriba-Folch 2012).

37.3.6 Succession

As stated before, juntas and strongman rule very differently. These differences also translate into how succession is handled. Strongmen are less likely to schedule some form of succession since they want to rule indefinitely while juntas want to ensure egali-tarian principles to leadership turnover within the junta are applied.

Whether or not a military is professionalized or not also affects the process of succes-sion. In general, juntas are more likely than military regimes ruled by a strongman to be professionalized. However, not all juntas are professionalized. We explain how profes-sionalized militaries handle the issue of succession.

Professionalized military regimes make rules about how leadership should be rotated and what the rules of succession should be. These regimes are usually legalistic and rule bound. They may even negotiate the details of succession and the institutionalized for-mulas for rotation in power *before* staging a coup (Geddes 1999). For instance, in the Argentine junta in 1976, General Jorge Videla, chief of the army, became president while agreeing on the termination date for his term. The presidential succession was sched-uled for, and took place in March 1981.

The Brazilian military junta offers a case of professionalized collegial rule and the institutionalization of turnover in power. Though the Congress was purged; political parties were dissolved, and presidential elections and gubernatorial elections were made indirect, the notion that no single person had seized power remained entrenched. The military reached consensus on General Arthur Costa e Silva, chosen President in October 1966, who would follow the Brazilian junta's first leader, Humberto de Alencar Castelo Branco. The Brazilian authoritarian regime thus completed a very successful installation featuring institutionalized succession within the authoritarian regime. There would be a total of four peaceful transitions of presidential power during the authoritarian regime (and thus five military presidents) before its end in 1985. The difficulty in executing the coup and consolidating the regime at the start led the Brazilian military to install more collegial and eventually more effective procedures of rule.

37.3.7 Power Sharing and Consensus

In professionalized military regimes, the military executives, the president and the junta share executive power. The junta could have the power to declare a state of emergency, to declare war and to promote military officers for example. Both may appoint Supreme Court justices and provincial governors. The executive may not have the power to decide military promotions or demotions. In the case of Chile under Augusto Pinochet, the military executive was denied the traditional presidential power of naming and retiring commanders in chief of the different services. The aim is also to avoid the emergence of a strongman that could exclude others from decision-making. Military executives want to avoid unilateral decision-making and divvy up executive power to force presidents to form coalitions in the Junta to make decisions.

Professionalized military regimes usually make decisions by some form of consensus. To make decisions, the military junta often operates under rules of full attendance of its membership and some form of majority voting or unanimous voting. For example, in the case of the Argentine military junta of 1976, the junta could not meet outside the presence of any member. The regime wanted decisions to be made unanimously for appointing or removing a president and most other decisions required a majority. In the case of Chile, the junta ruled by unanimity which conferred an absolute veto to each member in the group (Mueller 1989).

37.3.8 Law-Making

When the military first takes over there are no binding rules or institutions about power sharing. Military executives may often use a constitution to use as a base from which to define their powers and the powers of other institutions.

Military executives most often want to ensure that they are constitutionally required to participate in law making. However, over time some military regimes have enabled their legislatures to work in a reviser role. In this case, the legislature may revise the military executive's legislative initiatives, approve the majority but also reject and amend some legislative initiatives. The nature of a military regime's executive and/or power sharing arrangements may change over time. In the case of the Brazilian Congress, during the later years the legislature exercised somewhat autonomous policy-making power (Bonvecchi and Simpson 2017). In the case of South Korea under Park Chung Hee, Park relied on a legislative assembly that had consultative procedures. Some military executives may use the assistance of an advisory commission. In the case of the Argentine junta, the Legal Advisory Commission (CAL) was created to identify legislation that was important, though it never deliberated on this legislation.

37.3.9 Policy Choices

In military juntas, policy is directed and implemented by a military junta (Bratton and van de Walle 1994). The consequences of a military turnover for policy-making varies considerably. Overall, the economic record of military executives has mostly been poor. Once officers take power, they have the opportunity to become very rich, and power tends to corrupt. In Pakistan, the military is known as 'Military Inc.' because of its tremendous financial strength and access to lucrative business opportunities. Military executives tend to ensure that the military has access to profitable business opportunities. The military junta in Thailand ousted democratically leader Thaksin and quickly moved to oversee Thailand's fifty-six state-owned companies (Watts and Chaichalearmmongkol 2014). Egypt's military has control over 50 per cent of manufacturing.

   Most publications have emphasized that the military has a difficult time governing or maintaining a stable government (Finer 1962; Janowitz 1977). In the case of Pakistan, there were thousands of military officers inducted to civilian posts in different ministries and divisions which caused the bureaucracy to decay and become corrupted (Zaidi 2005). However, professionalized militaries that hire a talented civilian workforce have performed better (Janowitz 1977). In South Korea, President Park relied on highly talented and admirably trained civilian economic policy officials, privileging the role of the Economic Policy Bureau. In the case of Brazil, experienced individuals were tasked with key ministries such as finance. Chile's military regime relied on the Chicago Boys or a group of economic policy officials that had studied at the University of Chicago. Thus military regimes have performed best when they have delegated policy-making to civilians in an area of competence and employ some consultation for policy-making. The military executive may focus mostly on national security and consult with civilians in other areas.

   There were also questions as to whether or not the military was usually conservative and represented the interests of elites. Studies of Latin American coups argued that the military staged coups at the behest of the middle and upper classes (Needler 1966). Early studies looked at the class and educational background of officers to understand if that affected their policy choices. Studies showed that most officers came from the lower to middle classes and usually from rural areas (Janowitz 1977; Nordlinger 1977). Officers rarely came from the upper classes. Some military executives have attempted to destroy the power of traditional elites and nationalize large parts of the economy, while other military executives have appeared to be allies of the wealthy. For the most part, military executives have been interested in serving the needs of the military itself. Yet apart from that, there is not consensus over *whose* interests the military serves and what types of policies follow.

37.4 FUTURE RESEARCH AGENDA

As there are far fewer military coups there are also far fewer military executives to study. In spite of this, there are still different areas of military rule to investigate. More recent research has examined the legacy of years of military rule and impact and power of segments of military rule on decision-making and outcomes. Future research will be able to use improved datasets that distinguish military rule by type and make use of new survey data that helps us better understand how citizens were impacted by military rule.

37.4.1 Legacies of Military Rule

Though the military may not rule for very long, it often never truly leaves power. It negotiates its exit with stipulations that it retains important leverage over its own budget, internal promotions and demotions, and ensure that it has amnesty for the abuses it committed in the past. Militaries may not always rule the executive directly, but continue to rule indirectly. Milan Svolik (2008, 2015) finds that a military past has a large, negative, and independent effect on a democracy's susceptibility to reversals. In other words, military regimes have an impact on a democracy's chances of being consolidate. Other scholars also note that a military legacy is particularly bad for democracy (Cheibub 2007).

A history of military rule is likely to have a different impact on democratization than on democratic consolidation. Though the transition is often smooth (because as the chapter earlier noted, the military steps down willingly), the process to democratic consolidation is not. Because the military often negotiates its own exit, it holds a lot of bargaining power. The military uses this power to ensure that safeguards are in place to protect its financial interests, its autonomy, and immunity from prosecution. The military also often wants to be able to dictate who can run for office, who holds important cabinet positions, and the types of policies that are implemented. In Latin America, the transition to democracy from military rule, the military retained too many privileges. The outgoing elites may try to construct a protected version of democracy that hampers the chances of democratic consolidation. This is certainly the case in Brazil where the military negotiated its own amnesty, guaranteed which politicians could participate, and continues to influence economic and social policy. Even today, the military is the most powerful interest group in Brazil (Stepan 2015).

Recent research has also argued that the military has a negative impact on crime rates in new democracies. Democracies emerging from military rule have higher homicide rates because they typically inherit militarized police forces (Frantz 2019). An alternative explanation for this phenomenon is that military rule tends to emerge in countries that have high pre-existing levels of inequality, such as in Latin America.

37.4.2 How Can New Methodological Innovations Help Us Answer These Questions?

In the past, the research agenda on military executives looked at the institutions themselves, and their impact. More recent studies also looked at the effects of military rule on the propensity for democratization. Future research is better advised to look at the legacies of military rule and the chances for democratic consolidation.

Improved datasets that provide a history of military rule offer scholars the opportunity to study the impact of military rule on democratic consolidation. Some recent studies have argued that military rule has a particularly negative effect on democratic consolidation. However, very little attention has been paid to what impact military executives have had on citizens, due to the lack of survey data on individuals living under military rule. Due to growing instability, there has been a rise in nostalgia for military regimes. Military regimes in Egypt and Pakistan in the past enjoy a great deal of genuine public support. According to a poll in 2014, 51 per cent of Brazilians think the streets were safer during the military regime (Barbara 2016). Political rallies in support of military rule have taken place in major cities in Brazil in response to high levels of frustration with civilian rule. Many citizens that have lived through military dictatorships have nostalgia for this period that brought with it order, certainty, and safety. There is also a widespread perception that corruption was less rampant under military rule than today. Though this is not the case, there may be romanticized perceptions of military rule. What is it about military regimes that make them reasonably popular, in spite of the fact that they are incredibly repressive?

New survey data that looks at the legacies of military rule finds a different conclusion to work by Cheibub (2007) and Svolik (2015). Both Cheibub and Svolik argue that military rule is detrimental to democracy, as the military never truly leaves power and is more likely to intervene. However, survey data that examines cohorts of citizens that endured military rule can help us better understand the citizens' reactions to military rule. Recent preliminary studies have found that though there is some nostalgia, periods of military rule do not have a negative effect on citizens' satisfaction with democracy, for example. Furthermore, compared to other types of authoritarian rule, the political trust of citizens who lived in military regimes is also not affected (Neundorff et al. 2017). Further work needs to be done to better understand these dynamics.

Future research will also look at the variation within military rule. There has been no consensus for how to conceptualize military regimes. The beginning of the chapter proposed that military executives are usually defined as regimes that are run by a junta, but more recent research has disagreed with how to classify military rule. Harkening back to earlier writings, Jose Antionio Cheibub et al. (2010) categorize military regimes as any regime which is led by a man who wears or has worn a uniform (with the exception of participation in World War II). Axel Hadenius and Jan Teorell (2006) classify military regimes when they military controls the executive and the legislative is weak or non-existent. Barbara Geddes, Joseph Wright, and Erica Frantz distinguish between military regimes that are run by a collegial military and those that are run by a strongman, compiling a sophisticated dataset that covers all types of military rule from 1945 to 2010 (Geddes 2003; Geddes, Wright, and Frantz 2014). Based on this distinction, more recent work has determined that it is only communal military executives that are fragile and likely to face irregular exits from power. Definitions and operationalizations of military rule need to continue to be more rigorous. Future research will need to make this distinction in order to test theories about the patterns of survival (Kim and Kroeger 2018). It will also be helpful to take note of cases of indirect forms of military rule and code and test these cases appropriately.

Future research also needs to account for segments of militaries that hold power unofficially. In 1979, Iran created a national guard, the Islamic Revolutionary Guards (Sepah) in Iran, which was constructed in order to counterbalance the country's conventional military. Though political elites have tried to keep it in check by offering it modern equipment, a class ranking system, and clear procedures for recruitment and training, it is now the dominant force in power politics. Sepah also has a huge role in the Iranian economy, such as ventures in gas and oil products along with other industries and financial sectors. The volatile environment that Iran faces has given Sepah an enormous influence in foreign policy to sustain Iran's regional influence (Kandil 2016). The Inter Service Intelligence (ISI) in Pakistan also wielded tremendous executive power, making foreign policy decisions that impacted the country. Conceptions of military executives need to account for the political power of segments of the military that may operate unopposed. While datasets have accounted for the variations within military rule, new datasets need to account for both cases of indirect military rule and the power of segments of the military, such as the intelligence services and special guards.

37.5 CONCLUSION

This chapter has highlighted the theoretical developments in the study of military rule, military coups and most specifically military executives. Early works argued that military rule should be studied as a distinct subset of civilian rule, but these early works did not distinguish between authoritarian regimes run by military juntas from those run by a strongman. Instead these studies considered why the military seizes power, inquired whether or not the military was suited to govern and offered explanations as to why they were more likely to step down from power. Later studies examined the effect of the military executive while in power, looking at the propensity for conflict, economic growth and democracy. More recent work that was careful to distinguish juntas from strong-man, was able to identify more valuable information about how military executives function, such as how policy output takes place and how succession is managed.

Although the number of military coups, and therefore military executives in power has dissipated, the study of military executives continues to be important. The military still exercises a great deal of power behind the scenes and has proven to be an obstacle to democracy in cases where it still retains too much power and autonomy. Furthermore, surveys reveal that there is some nostalgia for military rule in democracies, though this research cautions that this does not impact political trust and attitudes towards democracy. The legacies of military rule are important to investigate and new survey research can help us to better understand the implications for these legacies. The exact impact of military executives is important for future research to examine.

References

Acemoglu, D., Ticchi, D., and Vindigni, A. (2010). 'A Theory of Military Dictatorships,' *American Economic Journal: Macroeconomics* 2(1): 1–42.

Austin, D. and Luckham, R. (2014). *Politicians and Soldiers in Ghana 1966–1972*. London: Routledge.

Barbara, V. (2016). 'In Brazil, a New Nostalgia for Military Dictatorship,' *New York Times*, 1 May, https://www.nytimes.com/2016/05/03/opinion/in-brazil-a-new-nostalgia-for-military-dictatorship.html

Barros, R. (2002). *Constitutionalism and Dictatorship: Pinochet, the Junta, and the 1980 Constitution*, Vol. 4. Cambridge: Cambridge University Press.

Belkin, A. and Schofer, E. (2003). 'Toward a Structural Understanding of Coup Risk,' *Journal of Conflict Resolution* 47(5): 594–620.

Bienen, H. (1974). 'Military and Society in East Africa: Thinking Again about Praetorianism,' *Comparative Politics* 6(4): 489–517.

Bonvecchi, A. and Simpson, E. (2017). 'Legislative Institutions and Performance in Authoritarian Regimes,' *Comparative Politics* 49(4): 521–44.

Bratton, M. and Van de Walle, N. (1994). 'Neo-Patrimonial Regimes and Political Transitions in Africa,' *World Politics* 46(4): 453–89.

Brecher, M. (2013). *Crises in World Politics: Theory and Reality*. Oxford: Pergamon Press.

Brooker, P. (2013). *Non-democratic Regimes*. New York: Palgrave Macmillan.

Brownlee, J. (2009). 'Portents of Pluralism: How Hybrid Regimes Affect Democratic Transitions,' *American Journal of Political Science* 53(3): 515–32.

Buraczynska, B. (2016). 'Regional Security and Democratic Transitions: An Alternative Perspective,' in S. N. Romaniuk and M. Marlin (eds) *Democracy and Civil Society in a Global Era*. London: Routledge, 129–44.

Cheibub, J. A. (2007). *Presidentialism, Parliamentarism, and Democracy*. Cambridge: Cambridge University Press.

Cheibub, J. A., Gandhi, J., Vreeland, J. R. (2010). *Democracy and Dictatorship Data Set*, https://netfiles.uiuc.edu/cheibub/www/DDpage.html

Clapham, C. S. and Philip, G. D. (1985) (eds). *The Political Dilemmas of Military Regimes*. London: Taylor & Francis.

Debs, A. and Goemans, H. E. (2010). 'Regime Type, the Fate of Leaders, and War,' *American Political Science Review* 104(3): 430–45.

Decalo, S. (1973). 'Military Coups and Military Regimes in Africa,' *The Journal of Modern African Studies* 11(1): 105–27.

Dix, R. H. (1994). 'Military Coups and Military Rule in Latin America,' *Armed Forces & Society* 20(3): 439–56.

Finer, S. E. (1962). *The Man on Horseback: The Role of the Military in Politics*. London: Routledge.

Fjelde, H. (2010). 'Generals, Dictators, and Kings Authoritarian Regimes and Civil Conflict, 1973–2004,' *Conflict Management and Peace Science* 27(3): 195–218.

Frantz, E. (2019). 'The Legacy of Military Dictatorship: Explaining Violent Crime in Democracies,' *International Political Science Review* 40(3): 404–18.

Geddes, B. (1999). 'What Do We Know About Democratization After Twenty Years?,' *Annual Review of Political Science* 2(1): 115–44.

Geddes, B. (2003). *Paradigms and Sand Castles: Theory Building and Research Design in Comparative Politics*. Ann Arbor, MI: University of Michigan Press.

Geddes, B. (2009). 'How Autocrats Defend Themselves Against Armed Rivals,' paper prepared for presentation at the American Political Science Association Annual Meeting, Toronto, CA, 1–50.

Geddes, B., Wright, J., and Frantz, E. (2014). 'Autocratic Breakdown and Regime Transitions: A New Data Set,' *Perspectives on Politics* 12(2): 313–31.

Geddes, B., Frantz, E. and Wright, J. G. (2014). Military rule. *Annual Review of Political Science*, 17: 147–162.

Hadenius, A. and Teorell, J. (2006). *Authoritarian Regimes: Stability, Change, and Pathways to Democracy, 1972–2003*. Notre Dame, IN: Helen Kellogg Institute for International Studies.

Heper, M. (2005). 'The Justice and Development Party Government and the Military in Turkey,' *Turkish Studies* 6(2): 215–31.

Janowitz, M. (1964). 'The Military in the Political Development of New Nations,' *Bulletin of the Atomic Scientists* 20(8): 6–10.

Janowitz, M. (1977). 'From Institutional to Occupational: The Need for Conceptual Continuity,' *Armed Forces & Society* 4(1): 51–4.

Jenkins, J. C. and Kposowa, A. J. (1992). 'The Political Origins of African Military Coups: Ethnic Competition, Military Centrality, and the Struggle over the Post-Colonial State,' *International Studies Quarterly* 36(3): 271–91.

Johnson, J. A. (2015). *Role of the Military in Underdeveloped Countries*. Princeton, NJ: Princeton University Press.

Johnson, T. H., Slater, R. O., and McGowan, P. (1983). 'Explaining African Military Coups d'Etat, 1960–1982,' *American Political Science Review* 78(3): 622–40.

Kandil, H. (2016). *The Power Triangle: Military, Security, and Politics in Regime Change*. Oxford: Oxford University Press.

Kim, N. K. and Kroeger, A. M. (2018). 'Regime and Leader Instability under Two Forms of Military Rule,' *Comparative Political Studies* 51(1): 3–37.

King, A. (2006). 'The Word of Command: Communication and Cohesion in the Military,' *Armed Forces & Society* 32(4): 493–512.

Lai, B. and Slater, D. (2006). 'Institutions of the Offensive: Domestic Sources of Dispute Initiation in Authoritarian Regimes, 1950–1992,' *American Journal of Political Science* 50(1): 113–26.

Londregan, J. B. and Poole, K. T. (1990). 'Poverty, the Coup Trap, and the Seizure of Executive Power,' *World Politics* 42(2): 151–83.

Lowenthal, A. F. (1974). 'Armies and Politics in Latin America,' *World Politics* 27(1): 107–30.

McGowan, P. and Johnson, T. H. (1984). 'African Military Coups d'État and Underdevelopment: A Quantitative Historical Analysis,' *The Journal of Modern African Studies* 22(4): 633–66.

Mueller, D. C. (1989). *Public Choice II: A Revised Edition of Public Choice*. Cambridge: Cambridge University Press.

Needler, M. C. (1966). 'Political Development and Military Intervention in Latin America,' *American Political Science Review* 60(3): 616–26.

Needler, M. C. (1975). 'Military Motivations in the Seizure of Power,' *Latin American Research Review* 10(3): 63–79.

Neundorf, A., Ezrow, N., Gerschewski, J., Olar, R. G., and Shorrocks, R. (2017). 'The Legacy of Authoritarian Regimes on Democratic Citizenship,' paper presented at the 2017 ECPR Joint Sessions in the workshop 'Legacies of Authoritarian Regimes', University of Nottingham, 26–29 April.

Nordlinger, E. A. (1977). *Soldiers in Politics: Military Coups and Governments*. Englewood Cliffs: Prentice Hall.

Olulẹyẹ, J. J. (1985). *Military Leadership in Nigeria: 1966–1979*. University Press Limited.

Perlmutter, A. (1969). *Military and Politics in Israel: Nation-Building and Role Expansion*. London: Routledge.

Perlmutter, A. (1977). *The Military and Politics in Modern Times: On Professionals, Praetorians, and Revolutionary Soldiers*. New Haven, CT: Yale University Press.

Perlmutter, A. (1986). 'The Military and Politics in Modern Times: A Decade Later,' *The Journal of Strategic Studies* 9(1): 5–15.

Pitcher, B. L., Hamblin, R. L., and Miller, J. L. (1978). 'The Diffusion of Collective Violence,' *American Sociological Review* 43: 23–35.

Poe, S. C., Tate, C. N., and Keith, L. C. (1999). 'Repression of the Human Right to Personal Integrity Revisited: A Global Cross-National Study Covering the Years 1976–1993,' *International Studies Quarterly* 43(2): 291–313.

Posen, B. (1984). *The Sources of Military Doctrine: France, Britain, and Germany between the World Wars*. Ithaca: Cornell University Press.

Remmer, K. L. (1989). *Military Rule in Latin America*. London: Routledge.

Robins, P. (2003). *Suits and Uniforms: Turkish Foreign Policy since the Cold War*. London: Hurst & Company.

Sechser, T. S. (2004). 'Are Soldiers Less War-Prone than Statesmen?,' *Journal of Conflict Resolution* 48(5): 746–74.

Siebold, G. L. (2007). 'The Essence of Military Group Cohesion,' *Armed Forces & Society* 33(2): 286–95.

Snyder, J. L. (1984). *The Ideology of the Offensive: Military Decision Making and the Disasters of 1914*. Ithaca, NY: Cornell University Press.

Stepan, A. C. (2015). *The Military in Politics: Changing Patterns in Brazil*. Princeton, NJ: Princeton University Press.

Stepan, A. and Stepan, A. (1971). *Brasil. Los militares y la política*. Buenos Aires: Amorrortu.

Svolik, M. W. (2008). 'Authoritarian Reversals and Democratic Consolidation,' *American Political Science Review* 102(2): 153–68.

Svolik, M. W. (2012). *The Politics of Authoritarian Rule*. Cambridge: Cambridge University Press.

Svolik, M. W. (2015). 'Which Democracies Will Last? Coups, Incumbent Takeovers, and the Dynamic of Democratic Consolidation,' *British Journal of Political Science* 45(4): 715–38.

Wang, S. (1996). 'Estimating China's Defence Expenditure: Some Evidence from Chinese Sources,' *The China Quarterly* 147: 889–911.

Watts, J. M. and Chaichalearmmongkol, N. (2014). 'In Thailand a Struggle for Control of State Firms,' *Wall Street Journal*, 17 June, https://www.wsj.com/articles/in-thailand-a-struggle-for-control-of-state-firms-1402930180

Way, C. and Weeks, J. L. (2014). 'Making It Personal: Regime Type and Nuclear Proliferation,' *American Journal of Political Science* 58(3): 705–19.

Weeks, J. L. (2011). 'Military Dictatorships and the Initiation of International Conflict,' Working Papers. Department of Political Science, Cornell University.

Welch, C. E. and Smith, A. K. (1974). *Military Role and Rule: Perspectives on Civil-Military Relations*. North Scituate, MA: Brooks/Cole.

Wright, J. and Escribà-Folch, A. (2012). 'Authoritarian Institutions and Regime Survival: Transitions to Democracy and Subsequent Autocracy,' *British Journal of Political Science* 42(2): 283–309.

Zaidi, S. A. (2005). 'State, Military and Social Transition: Improbable Future of Democracy in Pakistan,' *Economic and Political Weekly* 3 December: 5173–81.

Zolberg, A. (1969). 'Military Rule and Political Development in Tropical Africa: A Preliminary Report,' in J. Van Doorn (ed.) *The Military Profession and Military Regimes: Commitments and Conflicts*. The Hague: Mouton.

Index of Names

Subject Index

Note: Tables and figures, are indicated by an italic "*t*" and "*f*" respectively, following the page number.